SCRIBNER DESK DICTIONARY
OF
AMERICAN HISTORY

SCRIBNER DESK
DICTIONARY
OF
AMERICAN
HISTORY

CHARLES SCRIBNER'S SONS / *New York*

Library of Congress Cataloging in Publication Data

Main entry under title:

Scribner desk dictionary of American history.

   1. United States—History—Dictionaries. I. Charles
Scribner's Sons. II. Title: Desk dictionary of American
history.
E174.S36 1984   973'.03'21   84-14019
ISBN 0-684-18154-1

1 3 5 7 9 11 13 15 17 19 F/C 20 18 16 14 12 10 8 6 4 2

PRINTED IN THE UNITED STATES OF AMERICA.

CONTENTS

EDITORIAL NOTE

The *Scribner Desk Dictionary of American History* is a one-volume desk-edition reference work designed to answer all questions about American history, from pre-history to the present day. Based on the eight-volume Bicentennial Edition of the *Dictionary of American History,* the *Scribner Desk Dictionary* contains all the essential information from the more than 6,000 entries in the parent work in concise, readily available form.

This new work also contains many articles specially written to cover events since 1976 and includes the latest US census figures. Numerous cross-references (in small capitals) further facilitate the use of this desk edition. Complete texts of the Declaration of Independence and the Constitution are provided in an Appendix.

The *Scribner Desk Dictionary of American History* has been edited for students, history buffs, business persons, as well as for scholars. It is thus the perfect ready reference for school, home, or office.

SCRIBNER DESK DICTIONARY
OF
AMERICAN HISTORY

AACHEN. First major German city to fall to American troops in World War II (Oct. 21, 1944).

ABILENE. City in Kansas. Settled in 1858, selected as depot to which Texas cattle might be driven for shipment by rail to Kansas City. Pop.: 6,572 (1980).

ABILENE TRAIL. A cattle trail from Texas to Abilene, Kansas. First herds were driven over it in 1866.

AB-INITIO MOVEMENT. Texas Reconstruction controversy (1866): Was secession null and void from the beginning (*ab initio*) or as a result of the Civil War? The anti-Ab-Initios emerged victorious.

ABNAKI. Algonkin-speaking Indians of Maine. A population of 3,000 is estimated for 1600. Hunting was the primary basis of subsistence, and social units were made up of kindred people identified with a particular hunting region. Allied with the French in the 18th c., the Abnaki were unsuccessful in hindering British expansion. Forced to move to Quebec. Best known through a dictionary compiled by the missionary Sebastian Rasles.

ABOLITION. See ANTISLAVERY.

ABOMINATIONS, TARIFF OF. See ANTISLAVERY.

ABORTION. The termination of pregnancy by artificial means. An ancient method of birth control, it has been long opposed by religious groups, especially the Roman Catholic church. It was illegal in all states until 1973, when the Supreme Court (especially in *Wade v. Roe*) ruled such state laws an invasion of the right of privacy. Since then, various religious and political groups, such as the Right to Life movement and the Moral Ma-

jority, have called for a constitutional amendment reversing the court's decisions. Women's groups and civil rights organizations continue to support legal abortion.

A.B. PLOT (1823). William H. Crawford, secretary of the treasury, employed western banks to collect public land revenues in fluctuating banknote currencies, a justifiable but unsuccessful policy. The Washington *Republican*, in articles signed "A.B.," attacked Crawford for malfeasance. These articles were written by Sen. Ninian Edwards of Illinois, who brought charges against Crawford, perhaps to damage him in the 1824 presidential campaign. Crawford was exonerated.

ABRAHAM, PLAINS OF. West of the city of Quebec; scene of the 1759 battle (see QUEBEC, CAPTURE OF) that ended the French empire in North America.

ABRAHAM LINCOLN, FORT. Built in North Dakota by Gen. George A. Custer (1873) on the Missouri R. Abandoned in 1895. Included Fort McKean, a nearby infantry post.

ABSTRACT EXPRESSIONISM. Art movement of the 1940s and 1950s, the first American art style to achieve world stature. The style is characterized by texture, color, and materials in mainly nonrepresentational subjects. Leading artists included Jackson Pollock and William de Kooning.

ACADEMIC FREEDOM. Rights claimed by teachers to study, to communicate ideas, and to publish the results of reflection and research without external restraints. The US Supreme Court ruled (1957) that academic freedom is protected by the due process clauses of the Constitution.

ACADEMIES. A type of secondary school popular 1750–1850. Largely displaced by

1

the public high school. Most were denominational or private, although some states sponsored them. Tuition fees were usually charged, but some scholarships were provided.

ACADIA. Former French colony in Canada in what is now Nova Scotia. Its boundaries overlapped considerably the land claimed by England, which resulted in 150 years of warfare. The Treaty of Utrecht (1713) ceded "all Nova Scotia with its ancient boundaries" to England. The French tacitly narrowed the indefinite limits of Nova Scotia to what is now the peninsula bearing that name. England came to view the French inhabitants of the peninsula, the ACADIANS, with suspicion.

ACADIANS. Acadians came in directly from Nova Scotia to Louisiana (1755–76) and settled in what is now St. James parish, upriver as far as Pointe Coupée, and W seventy to one hundred miles from New Orleans. They founded the town of St. Martinville, which has remained the center of Acadian life in Louisiana, and spread W into the parish named for them, Acadia, and the surrounding territory. They and their descendants are the Cajuns.

ACKIA, BATTLE OF (May 26, 1735). See CHICKASAW-FRENCH WAR.

ACOMA. One of seven Keresan-speaking towns in the center of the present-day Pueblo area of New Mexico; located on a 357-ft. rock mesa. Visited by Spanish explorers and subjected to Franciscan missionization. In 1599 nearly 1,500 Acoma were killed in retaliation for the killing of 15 Spaniards. The Acoma participated in the PUEBLO REVOLT of 1680.

ACRE RIGHT. See CABIN RIGHTS.

ACTION. Principal federal agency for administering volunteer service programs. Created in 1971, it originally included the PEACE CORPS. By 1983 ACTION included the following programs: Foster Grandparent Program, Retired Senior Volunteer Program (RSVP), Senior Companion Program, National Center for Service Learning, Urban Crime Prevention Program, Vietnam Veterans Leadership Program, and Volunteers in Service to America (VISTA).

ACTIVE CASE (*Olmstead et al. v. Rittenhouse's Executives*). Gideon Olmstead of Connecticut and others seized the British sloop *Active* (1777), which was later captured by the Pennsylvania armed brig *Convention*. Award of prize money to the *Convention* crew by state courts of Pennsylvania was set aside by the Supreme Court (1809) after a bitter dispute.

ACTS OF TRADE. See NAVIGATION ACTS.

ADAIR V. UNITED STATES, 208 US 161 (1908). In violation of a federal law, William Adair, acting for the Louisville & Nashville RR, dismissed O. B. Coppage because he was a member of a labor union. The Supreme Court declared the law unconstitutional because it violated the due process clause of the Fifth Amendment.

ADAMS, FORT. Built in Missouri in 1798–99 eight miles above the 31st parallel on the E bank of the Mississippi R for boundary defense against the Spanish. It was the US port of entry on the Mississippi. Abandoned after acquisition of Louisiana and Florida.

ADAMS EXPRESS COMPANY. Founded 1839 by Alvin Adams for transporting mail and small parcels between Boston and Worcester. After several mergers, it became (1918) part of the American Railway Express Company.

ADAMSON ACT (Sept. 2, 1916). It established an eight-hour day in place of a ten-hour day for trainmen. The railroads contested it, but the law was upheld in 1917.

ADAMS-ONÍS TREATY (1819; ratified 1821). Signed by John Quincy Adams, US secretary of state, and Luis de Onís, Spanish minister. It provided for the cession of East Florida, the abandonment of the controversy over West Florida, and a boundary delineation to the Pacific Ocean.

ADDRESS TO THE SOUTHERN DELEGATES. Southern delegates in Congress, aroused by hostile resolutions on slavery, called a caucus for Dec. 23, 1848. John C. Calhoun submitted an address calculated to unite the South. It was adopted, but fewer than half the southern delegates signed it. (See also TARPLEY LETTER.)

ADENA. First of a series of Early and Middle Woodland cultures in E North America. Dating from about 1000 BC to AD 200, mainly in the C Ohio Valley. It is characterized by ceremonial centers with conical earthen burial mounds and large earthworks. The Adena people lived in hamlets nearby. Among the more unusual artifacts are bowls made from human crania, rectangular stone tablets engraved with zoomorphic figures, stone chest ornaments in a variety of geometric shapes, shell beads, tubular pipes, and stone atlatl weights. The Middle Woodland Hopewell cultures were in part a later elaboration of classic Adena.

ADKINS V. CHILDREN'S HOSPITAL, 261 US 525 (1923). Supreme Court decision holding invalid an act of Congress that created a minimum wage board for women employees in the District of Columbia. (See also WEST COAST HOTEL COMPANY V. PARRISH.)

ADMINISTRATIVE DISCRETION, DELEGATION OF. The Constitution was a deliberate attempt to limit the use and abuse of executive discretion in government by a formal differentiation and separation of governmental functions. Delegations of discretionary powers to the president or subordinate executive officers have occurred so frequently as to be commonplace. The hallmark of delegation of administrative powers, particularly in the regulatory agencies, has been the merging of governmental functions ostensibly separated constitutionally. Thus, discretion is conferred not only in executive powers (investigation, supervision, prosecution), but also in the legislative (rulemaking) and judicial spheres. Criticism of this merger led Congress in the Administrative Procedure Act of 1946 to require separate performance of adjudicatory functions by special personnel. Substantial constitutional limitations on discretion exist and are subject to judicial review.

ADMINISTRATIVE JUSTICE. Exercise by an administrative agency of judicial powers delegated to the agency by a legislative body. Agencies that have these judicial powers are often termed "administrative tribunals"; this usage derives from the separation of powers in the Constitution. Administrative tribunals ordinarily deal with individuals in relation to government, in terms of benefits sought or disabilities incurred from government action. Most are empowered to assess various penalties, such as forfeiture of licenses. The jurisdiction of an agency is normally a single economic activity, a set of closely related economic activities, or specific benefits conferred by government. The concern of the National Labor Relations Board with labor relations is an example of the first; the jurisdiction of the Federal Communications Commission over radio, television, and telephone, of the second; and adjudication of the validity of claims to benefits by such agencies as the Veterans Administration, of the third. Administrative regulation and adjudication has become widespread in the states and municipalities, embracing such subjects as public utilities, natural resources, banking, securities, workmen's compensation, insurance, employment discrimination, rents, automobile operation and inspection, corporations, elections, welfare, land use, and environmental and consumer protection.

ADMINISTRATIVE PROCEDURE ACT OF 1946. Imposes uniform procedural requirements on applicable US administrative agencies and requires the judicial function to be separated from the legislative and executive aspects. Provides for a broad right of review of agency adjudication by the courts.

ADMIRALS AND COMMODORES. Prior to the Civil War the highest naval rank was that of captain, equal to an army colonel. In 1862 Congress established the ranks of rear admiral (two stars) and commodore (one star). In 1864 David Farragut was made the first vice admiral (three stars), and in 1865 the first full admiral (four stars). The commodore rank was abolished in 1912, and rear admirals became the one-star rank. World War II saw the revival of the commodore rank and the creation of the lifetime five-star rank of fleet admiral for Ernest King, Chester W. Nimitz, William D. Leahy, and William F. Halsey. The last of these, Leahy, died in 1973. Both ranks now in abeyance, with full admiral (four stars) the highest rank.

ADMIRALTY LAW AND COURTS. Admiralty law governs traffic by water. Most American

3

colonial admiralty tribunals enjoyed a jurisdiction less restricted than in England. Under the Articles of Confederation, most admiralty concerns were under state authority. Under the Constitution, federal authority "extends to all cases of admiralty and maritime jurisdiction" (including inland waterways), and the district courts have original jurisdiction by law. Admiralty jurisdiction includes insurance, bills of lading, charters, general average, seamen's rights, collision, salvage, maritime liens, ships' mortgages, liability limitations, piracy, and the laws of sea warfare.

ADMISSION OF STATES. See STATE-MAKING PROCESS.

ADOBE. A type of construction introduced by the Spanish into the Southwest in the 16th c. Wet clay and chopped hay or other fibrous material are mixed and molded into bricks and sun-dried or molded directly into the wall.

ADOBE WALLS, BATTLE OF. (June 27, 1874). In retaliation against hunters who were killing buffalo, Comanche, Cheyenne, and Kiowa Indians attacked Adobe Walls, a trading post on the Canadian R in the Texas Panhandle.

ADVENTIST CHURCHES. After the failure of the prophecies of William Miller that the Second Coming of Christ would occur in 1843, his disciples, known also as Millerites, became divided. The Advent Christian Church, organized 1860, holds that the soul sleeps until the end of the age, when it is reunited with the body for the Last Judgment. Membership: 31,324 (1980). The Seventh-Day Adventists were organized in 1863. They adoped Saturday as the Sabbath. They believe that the Scriptures are an infallible guide to faith, and they abstain from tobacco, liquor, and sometimes tea and coffee. Each member is expected to contribute a full tithe to the work of the church. Membership: 556,567 (1980).

ADVENTURE. First American sailing vessel built on the Pacific coast (British Columbia, 1791–92).

ADVERTISING. The Boston *News-Letter* contained in its third issue (1704) the first ad-vertisements: an ad for real estate and two notices of lost articles. Benjamin Franklin's Pennsylvania *Gazette* (1728) introduced separation of ads with space and (after 1750) small woodcut illustrations. Amusement notices and "wanted" ads were featured first in separate sections in the 1830s by the New York *Sun*, which also first printed marriage and death announcements for revenue. Single-column agate ads remained standard until the 1860s, when large display ads began to appear. P.T. Barnum's promotional successes led to large increases in outdoor advertising in the form of posters and handbills. The mail-order catalog was introduced in 1870. In the 1830s the New York *Herald* initiated the modern line rate, establishing minimum advertising units and rates. N.W. Ayer and Son of Philadelphia, about 1880, began to offer advertisers an "open contract," in which the advertiser contracted to allow the agent to handle the entire advertisement budget for an unspecified period of time. The cost-plus-15-percent-commission basis for agency payment was accepted industrywide in 1919. Agencies began to perform services that had previously been the responsibility of the advertiser, such as devising slogans and brand names. The Food and Drug Act of 1906 aided "truth in advertising." Several states acted to make false advertising a misdemeanor; and the Better Business Bureau, the Post Office, the Department of Agriculture, and the Federal Trade Commission all sought to prevent fraudulent and deceptive advertising. Radio became a major advertising medium after 1922, and television after 1946. It quickly became the fastest-growing advertising medium and eventually caused the demise of long-established mass-market magazines. With the computerization of mailing lists, direct mail advertising increased substantially after 1955. Circulation of newspapers and periodicals, as well as their advertising revenues, mounted, even though the number of publications declined. Network radio advertising fell, but local radio stations thrived. Consumer surveys became common in the 1930s. After 1950, increased costs of advertising led to the expansion of consumer research organizations. Government action in 1965 severely limited outdoor billboards. The Federal Trade Commission in 1965 ordered all cigarette packages to carry health warnings and in 1971 cigarette advertising was banned on television. In the 1980s cable TV and home video units opened new avenues for the advertiser.

AEF. See AMERICAN EXPEDITIONARY FORCES.

AEOLUS. A yachtlike railroad car designed to sail before the wind. It was tried out on the Baltimore and Ohio RR in 1830.

AERONAUTICS AND SPACE ADMINISTRATION, NATIONAL. See NATIONAL AERONAUTICS AND SPACE ADMINISTRATION.

AFL. See AMERICAN FEDERATION OF LABOR—CONGRESS OF INDUSTRIAL ORGANIZATIONS.

AFRICAN-AMERICAN RELATIONS. The American Colonization Society (1817) and the founding of Liberia (1822) were the beginning of US interest in Africa. Major US impact on Africa came through missionaries. Most important commercial development was the grant (1926) by the Liberian government of a million acres to the Firestone Co. to grow rubber. Politically, Marcus Garvey's American-based Universal Negro Improvement Association (UNIA), founded 1914, with its cry of "Africa for the Africans," served to stimulate African nationalism, particularly in the urban areas of W and S Africa. Italy's conquest of Ethiopia in 1935–36 called forth widespread expressions of pan-African solidarity and served to stimulate US interest in Africa. US involvement in Africa grew enormously after World War II, because of its strategic importance and as a source of raw materials. US bases were established in Morocco and Ethiopia; numerous educational and cultural agencies, including the Peace Corps, operated in newly independent nations. By the 1970s there was considerable US investment in the white-dominated territories of southern Africa (South Africa, Rhodesia, and Angola). US charged with supporting minority white ruling elements against the majority black Africans. However, US government quickly recognized new regimes. The 1970s saw a relative diminution of US governmental and public interest in Africa; but growing US investments, the concern of American blacks, and the potential explosive struggle in S Africa ensure a continuing major American concern with Africa.

AFRICAN COMPANY, ROYAL. English trading company with a monopoly on the African slave trade 1672–97. Formally dissolved in 1750.

AFRICAN METHODIST EPISCOPAL CHURCH. Oldest and largest denomination of black Methodists. Organized in 1816. Doctrinally similar to Methodist Episcopal Church. Membership: 2,000,000 (1980).

AFRO-AMERICAN CHURCHES: See BLACK CHURCHES.

AFRO-AMERICANS. See BLACKS.

AGAMENTICUS. Town in Maine, settled ca. 1624 and successively known as Bristol (1632), Agamenticus (1641), Gorgeana (1642), and York (1652). The first municipal corporation (1642) was created by Sir Ferdinando Gorges.

AGENCY SHOP. Arrangement whereby a nonunion worker may be represented by a labor union for collective bargaining. The worker pays the union a fee equal to what union dues would be. (Compare CLOSED SHOP; OPEN SHOP.)

AGRARIAN MOVEMENT. Mixture of philosophic idealism, rooted in the Enlightenment, and the hard, practical demands of colonial farmers. Became a tradition of independence, self-reliance, progress, and scientific improvement, tinged with a sentimental romanticism. Closely involved with politics and a major force in the national expansionist movement. The expanding frontier was regarded as a natural right, and the image of the farmer-settler became the national ideal.

AGRICULTURAL ADJUSTMENT ADMINISTRATION (AAA). Created in 1933 to stabilize farm prices by restricting production. An important component of the NEW DEAL, it was declared unconstitutional by the Supreme Court in 1936. New law passed in 1938, which was ruled constitutional. The AAA ended as a separate agency in 1942; functions taken over by Department of Agriculture.

AGRICULTURAL EDUCATION. Land Grant College Act (1862) marked beginning of agricultural education in US (See LAND GRANTS FOR EDUCATION). Between 1880–1900, farmers' institutes attempted to bring new discoveries directly to farmers by cooperating with agricultural colleges; these grew into the federal agricultural extension movement. The teaching of agriculture at the secondary school level was given federal support by Smith-Hughes Act (1917). Vocational Education Acts (1946, 1963) considerably broadened the program.

AGRICULTURAL MACHINERY. The cotton gin, patented 1794, brought a boom in cotton farming and a revival of the dying institution of slavery. Exploitation of the rich American prairie was made possible by the invention of the steel plow, the two-wheeled sulky plow, the disk plow, the harrow, and the lister (a double moldboard plow that made it possible to plant row crops in furrows). The horse hoe, designed to be drawn between rows by a single horse, was developed ca. 1820. A second hoe blade was added ca. 1850 and a two-horse, straddle-row cultivator, which doubled productivity, was patented in 1856. Cyrus McCormick developed the reaper in 1831, and it cut harvest time in half. The horse-drawn combine was introduced in 1836. By 1900 combines drawn by mule teams were harvesting two-thirds of the California wheat crop. The basic hay harvesting tool is a mower with a serrated, reciprocating knife. By 1865 nearly all haymowing was done mechanically. A baling press was developed in 1853. Cotton resisted mechanical harvesting. The modern cotton picker is based on the use of a rotating spindle, patented in 1895. It was not until the 1880s that steam traction engines attained widespread success. The first true gasoline traction engine appeared in 1892. The first commercially successful machine (1906) was the Hart-Parr "Old No. 1," for which the name "tractor" was coined. The tractor remained chiefly a pulling vehicle until the development of the power takeoff device, which made it possible to power by the tractor's engine many implements that had formerly been ground-propelled. A tricycle-type all-purpose tractor (1924) made it possible to use the tractor in cultivation. In 1936 the three-point hitch made it possible to tractor-mount other implements. After World War II advances in the use of hydrostatics and hy-draulics broadened the tractor's versatility and many self-propelled machines were developed.

AGRICULTURAL POLICIES, FEDERAL. Homestead Act (1862) provided free title to 160 acres of land to any settler who maintained residence for five years. After 1900 modified to grant larger tracts in arid western regions. Modern land policies stress efforts to conserve and reconstruct soils and to control forest lands, waters, and mineral resources. During World War I, US agriculture was severely depressed. Farm relief was actively discussed and promoted in the next decade. "Orderly marketing" of farm products was encouraged by Cooperative Marketing Act (1922). Other laws provided special credit facilities. Agricultural Marketing Act (1929) created the Federal Farm Board, designed to stabilize prices of commodities; its failure led to more successful efforts in the 1930s, particularly the AGRICULTURAL ADJUSTMENT ADMINISTRATION. The 1956 Soil Bank program was eventually replaced by the 1965 Food and Agriculture Act, which established land-retirement policy and four-year price-adjustment program. Legislation in the 1960s and 1970s indicated a shift away from price supports and to government subsidies for producing food for export, chiefly the Commodity Credit Corporation (CCC), founded in 1933. To increase exports, Congress passed the Agricultural Trade Development Act (1954), authorizing acceptance of foreign currencies as payment for commodities shipped abroad to friendly nations. In 1972 more than 400 million bushels of wheat sold to the Soviet Union. Surplus stocks of American grains were depleted for the first time in a generation but grew again during the remainder of the 1970s and in the early 1980s, despite continuing sales to the Soviet Union. The Agriculture Department is charged with promoting scientific experiments in agriculture, such as chemical analyses of soils and plants, entomological research, and studies of animal and plant diseases. Hatch Act (1887) provided for experiment stations in connection with land-grant colleges. In the 1930s a national experimental station was established at Beltsville, Maryland, along with several regional laboratories and field stations. By the 1980s the extensive application of chemicals had brought about a great increase in agricultural production; but their effects on the environment created such public concern that controls became necessary. Agriculture also adopted ultrasonics for research on plants, livestock, and insects; hormones to increase both the number of multiple births and the size of livestock; brain stimulation devices to increase milk production; infrared photography for identification of crops, forests, and soils; and earth satellites to monitor disease, infestations, and drought.

AGRICULTURAL SOCIETIES AND FARM ORGANIZATIONS. By 1850 agricultural societies had spread to every section of the country and were largely responsible for the creation of the US Department of Agriculture. In 1867 the National Grange was founded; within ten years it had attracted a membership of nearly a million and gave its name to the the Granger movement of the 1870s. Temporarily lost much of its membership to the more radical Farmers' Alliance of the late 1880s. The Grange outlasted the Alliance, however; in the early 1980s the Grange had a membership of more than 500,000. The National Farmers Union, formed in 1902, and also more radical than the Grange, had a membership of 250,000 in 1974. The National Farmers Organization, founded in 1955 to protest low farm prices, had about 70,000 members. Largest and politically most influential of all was the American Farm Bureau Federation, organized 1920. It has more than 2 million members and is active in maintaining a strong farm lobby in Washington and in the state capitals.

AGRICULTURE. Early Indian culture depended on maize, pineapples, tomatoes, bananas, guavas, peanuts, chile peppers, cacao, and potatoes. In Northeast, maize, beans, squash, and tobacco constituted entire farming array. Farming depended entirely on human labor. Irrigation was limited to the Southwest. Principal agricultural tool was the digging stick. General practice was to grow corn in conjunction with bean and squash vines trained against the stalk.

Pioneer farmers adopted the Indian digging stick, flint or bone hoe, and winnowing basket. They learned the Indian art of maple sugaring, the use of dye plants, and the making of pemmican.The New England soil became exhausted and soon the colonists were moving into the interior, resorting to primitive slash-and-burn methods to clear forests. During the 17th and 18th c. labor shortages brought thousands of indentured servants and redemptioners into the middle colonies as farm laborers. Most of these soon gained their independence and acquired farms of their own, and the labor shortage persisted. Eventually slave labor drove out most of the free labor in the South, although only one-fourth of the population there owned slaves. By end of the 18th c. the best farm land E of the Alleghenies was under cultivation. As colonists moved inland, corn was usually the first crop; wheat and rye followed when the ground had been worked sufficiently. In the North, wheat, flax, and livestock began to be grown for export, and the South was exporting great quantities of tobacco, sugar, rice, and indigo before the Revolution. Cotton, grown for home use from early times, did not become a commercial crop until after the Revolution.

Between 1840 and 1860,the beef cattle industry flourished in Ohio and Kentucky, the cattle being trailed overland to markets in the East. Sheep and swine production also shifted westward; dairying remained concentrated in the East. By the 1850s Texans were driving cattle to the Midwest for fattening. At the outbreak of the Civil War, the center of agriculture was shifting to prairies, and invention of steel plow opened this richest grain-growing region in the world. In the South, cotton production was exploding westward. The South produced more than half the nation's corn, almost all of the tobacco, and all of the rice and sugar. Civil War had little effect on agricultural labor supply in the South; the major change was a switch from cotton to food crops. In the North, however, the army drew men from the farms, causing high prices. Homestead Act (1862) was accelerating force in farm frontier moving across the western plains, where wheat became principal crop. Crop failures, overextended debt, and falling prices ended the postwar boom. The late 19th c. saw a major shift of livestock production from East to West, the corn-hog pattern of farming developing in the Middle West; the cattle kingdoms in the Southwest and the Great Plains. The open range was closed; and in the mountain states sheep outnumbered cattle.

After 1900 demand for commodities caught up with supply, and prices rose. The first half of the 20th c. brought an agricultural revolution comparable in scope to the Industrial Revolution. In 1860, 60 percent of the population was engaged in agriculture; in 1900, 37 percent; by 1930 it was 24.9 percent; and in 1981 it was 4.6 percent. Total farm acreage increased, although the number of farms declined from 6.4 million in 1910 to 2.4 million in 1981. Production soared. Federal prices and income supports and soil conservation programs acted as stabilizing forces. In a half century farm assets rose from $40 billion to more than $300 billion. Corporation farming (agribusiness) was on the increase and fear was expressed for the future of the traditional family farm. Orbiting satellites monitored crops, estimating yields, detecting insect and disease outbreaks, observing soil nutrient and moisture conditions, and warning of pollution patterns.

AGRICULTURE, DEPARTMENT OF. Established 1862 and a cabinet-level department since 1889. Major responsibility is the nation's agricultural industry but oversees various consumer projects, including the food stamp program and nutritional services, the Forest Service, Soil Conservation Service, Rural Electrification Administration, Farmers Home Administration, and the Commodity Credit Corporation. Also standardizes farm products and regulates packers and stockyards. Conducts scientific research in all areas of agriculture and disseminates its findings through the state extension services. Gathers and publishes agricultural statistics, administers price-support programs, and promotes exports.

AGUAYO EXPEDITION (1720-22). Marquis San Miguel de Aguayo, governor of Coahuila and Texas, reestablished abandoned Spanish missions and presidios in East Texas, effectively ending French claims in Texas.

AIRCRAFT, COMMERCIAL. See AIR TRANSPORTATION.

AIRCRAFT, MILITARY. World War I aircraft carried either single drum-fed Lewis gun or twin belt-fed machine guns. Between the world wars, US fighters carried either two Browning air-cooled .30-caliber machine guns, or a .30- or .50-caliber machine gun. Enclosed turrets first appeared in 1930 on the B-10 bomber, followed by American adoption of the British power turret, usually mounting twin .50-caliber guns. Remote-controlled turrets came in 1942 and were standard after World War II, as in the retractable twin turrets with 20mm cannon on the B-36 bomber. The B-52 bomber was equipped with radar-aimed 20mm cannon, while fighters carried radar-equipped and computer-fired air-to-air rockets. Rockets are now primary fighter weapon, although most fighters carry at least one gun. The F-14 carries only the Phoenix missile. Other air-to-air ordnance includes the infrared-homing Sparrow III; the Falcon GAR-3 or GAR-4 heat-seeking missiles; and the MB-1 Genie with a nuclear warhead. Gunnery developments include the 20mm T-171 Vulcan multibarreled cannon.

The first US bomber, the Martin MB-1, was developed late in World War I, followed by twin-engine Keystone biplane, which was standard until 1932, and a few Curtiss B-2 Condors. Boeing Y1B-9 twin-engine monoplane replaced the Keystone but was eclipsed by the Martin B-10. Its replacements were the Douglas twin-engine, 218-mph, B-18 and the Boeing four-engine B-17 Flying Fortress. In World War II the main strategic bombers were the B-17 and the Consolidated B-24 Liberator. The Boeing B-29 Superfortress was the war's largest bomber. Medium bombers were the North American B-25 Mitchell and the Martin B-26 Marauder. Attack bombers operated at low altitudes and were noted for speed and maneuverability. The Douglas A-20 Havoc was a twin-engine monoplane. The Douglas A-26 Invader, appearing in 1944, was the war's most advanced attack bomber. The first intercontinental bomber (1946) was the Consolidated-Vultee B-36. The first jet bomber (1948) was the North American B-45 Tornado. The second fully jet-powered bomber was the Boeing B-47 Stratojet. The B-47 replaced the B-29 and B-50 as a medium bomber until the 1960s. The Korean War had demonstrated the need for an attack jet to replace the B-26; the Martin B-57 and the Douglas B-66 Destroyer were chosen. In 1954 the B-52 Stratofortress began replacing the B-36 as the mainstay of the Strategic Air Command. The General Dynamics B-58 Hustler also served the Strategic Air Command until it was retired in 1970. It carried four nuclear weapons underwing. In the 1980s the bomber force comprised the B-52D, B-52H, B-52G, and a few FB-111As.

The first American-built fighter was the Thomas-Morse MB-1 Scout (1919). Army relied on the Curtiss Hawk series until 1930 when faster monoplanes became standard: Boeing P-26, Republic P-35, and Curtiss F-36 (Hawk 75). The standard fighters, the Curtiss P-40 Warhawk (1940) and the Bell P-39 Airacobra (1941), were obsolete at the beginning of World War II. The first advanced US fighter (ordered 1939) was the Lockheed P-38 Lightning. The Republic P-47 Thunderbolt (1943), the air corps's only radial-engine fighter, was widely used for ground support. Perhaps the war's best fighter, the North American P-51 Mustang (1943) was the air force's fastest operational plane. The Northrop P-61 Black Widow (1943) was first US plane specifically designed as a night fighter. First US jet, the Bell XP-59 Airacomet (1943), copied a British engine and was capable of 418 mph. Both it and the Lockheed P-80 Shooting Star (553 mph) arrived too late for combat in World War II. The first postwar fighter was the Republic F-84 Thunderjet (1947). Evolved into 693-mph F-84F Thunderstreak. It remained in service for more than a decade. The North American F-86 Sabre was the first American-built jet with swept wings and tail surfaces; it participated in first jet-versus-jet battles over Korea. The first jet night fighter and the first fighter with an afterburner was the Lockheed F-94. The Northrop F-89 Scorpion was the first successful all-weather jet. The Soviet nuclear tests of 1949 spurred interceptor development. The first automatic inteceptor was the YF-86; its twenty-four 2.75-inch rockets were fired by ground command. Next was the Lockheed F-94C Starfire with forty-eight rockets, followed by the Scorpion with 104. The air force's first supersonic aircraft, in the early 1950s, included the North American F-100 Super Sabre, McDonnell Douglas F-101A Voodoo, Convair F-102 Delta Dagger, and Lockheed F-104 Starfighter. The Republic F-105 Thunderchief (1956) was the first fighter with a bomb bay. The Convair Delta Dart (1956) was an almost fully automatic fighter. In the 1960s, new aircraft included the McDonnell Douglas F-4 Phantom II series, a twin-engine jet carrying a 20mm rapid-fire cannon and performing as both interceptor

and attack plane. In the 1980s, new fighters included the Grumman F-14 Tomcat; the McDonnell Douglas F-15 Eagle; the General Dynamics F-16 Fighting Falcon; and the McDonnell Douglas-Northrop F-18 Hornet.

AIRCRAFT CARRIERS AND NAVAL AIRCRAFT. The first airplane launched from a ship flew from the light cruiser *Birmingham* in 1910; the first shipboard landing was in 1911. The first US carrier, the *Langley*, 1922, was a converted collier. The two first classic attack carriers, the *Lexington* and the *Saratoga* permitted strategies that could project air power across oceans. The *Essex* (1942–46) defined a class of twenty-four 27,000-ton vessels, almost all of which saw service in the Pacific. None was ever sunk. Wartime conversions were effected from light cruisers and merchant hulls into light carriers and escort carriers. Three larger classes of carrier evolved after World War II: *Midway* (53,000 tons, 1945); *Forrestal* (80,000 tons, 1955); the nuclear-powered *Enterprise* (91,000 tons, 1961); *Kitty Hawk* (85,000 tons); and the world's largest warship, the nuclear-powered *Nimitz* (95,000 tons). With them have come jet aircraft with nuclear-bomb capability under all-weather conditions and automatic landing systems. After the 1950s carrier attack planes were available for nuclear missions; the carriers could cover Europe, including the Ukraine and Caucasus; most of China; and eastern Siberia. Since the 1960s much of that responsibility has been taken over by the Polaris submarines and the ICBMs.

Carrier aircraft before World War II were of three basic types: fighter, scout bomber, and torpedo plane. The typical carrier complement included all three types. During World War II fighters evolved from the prewar F2A Brewster Buffalo and the F4F Grumman Wildcat to the F6F Grumman Hellcat and the F4U Chance Vought Corsair. Scout bombers progressed from the fabric-coated SB2U Vought Vindicator, through the SBD Douglas Dauntless, to the SB2C Curtiss Helldiver. Torpedo planes entered the war with the inadequate TBD Douglas Devastator; its replacement was the TBF Grumman Avenger. These basic attack planes were backed up by various types of patrol and scout observation planes, including the famous Consolidated Black Cats and Privateers. Naval aircraft after World War

II was predominantly jet-powered, but the single-engine propeller dive-bomber AD Douglas Skyraider persisted as the world's best attack airplane until the 1970s. During the 1950s, three attack planes and two outstanding fighters emerged. The A4 McDonnell Douglas Skyhawk, designed originally as an atomic-delivery vehicle, was modified for conventional weapons. The twin-engine A-6 Grumman Intruder was introduced in 1963. The A-7 Vought Corsair II, a single-engine jet designed to carry either nuclear or conventional weapons, first saw combat in 1967 in the Tonkin Gulf. The F8U-1 Vought Crusader, a day fighter with missile capability, became operational in 1957. The F4 McDonnell Douglas Phantom II, an all-weather fighter, was first produced in 1961.

AIR DEFENSE. By Dec. 7, 1941, air defense systems, including radar, fighters, antiaircraft artillery, ground observers, and control centers, had been established along both coasts and in Panama and Hawaii. After Pearl Harbor, these defenses were greatly expanded, resulting in a total of more than one hundred radar stations, about a million volunteer civilian ground observers and control center operators, and substantial numbers of fighters and antiaircraft batteries. The Air Defense Command (renamed the Aerospace Defense Command in 1968) assumed responsibility in 1946. Until an electronic network came into operation, about a half million civilian volunteers constituted a Ground Observer Corps, providing backup warning capability. The Distant Early Warning (DEW) radars along the Arctic Circle were completed in 1957. The combined North American Air Defense Command (NORAD) was also created in 1957. Antiaircraft batteries were replaced by surface-to-air missiles; and about twenty Semi-Automatic Ground Environment (SAGE) combat operations centers were created, which integrated all air defense operations. The space age created the need for the Ballistic Missile Early Warning System, erected with special radar systems in Alaska, Greenland, and the United Kingdom. In 1974 the United States constructed a Safeguard missile site, aimed at protecting its ICBM complex, in a cavern in Colorado. The number and location of such complexes as the Safeguard constituted an important point of discussion with

the Soviet Union in the ongoing Strategic Arms Limitation Talks (SALT).

AIR FORCE, UNITED STATES. In 1907 army created aeronautical division within the signal corps; purchased first airplane from the Wright brothers in 1909. At beginning of World War aviation arm had thirty-five pilots and fifty-five mechanics. Congress voted large sums for aviation, but fewer than 200 of the 740 planes in use by American squadrons were American-built. In August 1918 all American frontline air units were placed under a single commander, Brig. Gen. William (Billy) Mitchell. In 1920 the air arm became the air service, and in 1926 it became the air corps. The army air force (AAF) was created in 1941. Its basic tactical unit was the squadron, consisting of air and ground crews for twelve to twenty-four aircraft. Tactical squadrons were combined into groups; later they were placed under a wing headquarters. Several wings were either organized into an air division or placed directly under the next echelon, the numbered air force. The National Security Act (1947) established an air force independent of the army. Reorganization also brought into being the major air commands: the Strategic Air Command (SAC), the Air Defense Command, and the Tactical Air Command. The air force has focused much effort toward future air weaponry. Air force space activities have included unmanned research, weather, detection, and communications satellite projects, as well as systematic tracking of space objects. Since cancellation of air force manned projects, the USAF has supported the activities of the National Aeronautics and Space Administration (NASA), contributing technical personnel and astronauts for its various projects. The air national guard and the air force reserve constitute the US air reserve forces. During the Korean War, all twenty-five reserve troop carrier and light bomber wings were recalled; four squadrons were recalled during the Berlin crisis in 1961; and eight during the Cuban missile crisis of 1962. In 1984 the air reserve numbered thirty-eight squadrons and eighteen associate squadrons, which were affiliated with active units of the military airlift command.

AIR FORCE ACADEMY, UNITED STATES. A four-year undergraduate institute at Colorado

Springs, Colorado, leading to the BS degree and regular air force commission. Established in 1955 in Denver; moved to its permanent site in 1958. In 1964 the enrollment was set at 4,417. Each member of Congress is authorized five appointments each year. The academy provides advanced and accelerated studies beyond the prescribed curriculum. Maintains an all-military faculty.

AIR MAIL. In 1918, the army and the Post Office Department set up an experimental line between New York and Washington, D.C., using army pilots. In three months, the Post Office assumed control of the line and employed civilian aviators. This route was too short to give planes much advantage over trains. Other routes were tried, but all were too short to attract mail at high rates. In 1920 the Post Office began service between New York and San Francisco; the planes flew only by day, the mail being transferred at dusk to trains. Continuous day-and-night service was instituted in 1924. The Kelly Air Mail Act (1925) turned over the handling of airmail to private contractors; branch lines and north-and-south lines were rapidly added. In 1935 regular service began between San Francisco and Manila, and in 1939 between New York and London. After World War II, air mail service quickly spread worldwide.

AIR TRANSPORTATION. The real beginning of air transport began on Dec. 17, 1903, when Orville and Wilbur Wright flew a biplane that achieved sustained, powered, controlled flight. Later in that decade Glen Curtiss conceived the seaplane. James McCurdy demonstrated the feasibility of two-way radio contact between air and ground in 1911. America's principal technological accomplishment of World War I was the liquid-cooled, mass-produced Liberty engine. The 1930s saw the brief days of glory of lighter-than-air craft (see DIRIGIBLES). The most striking achievement of the 1930s was the all-metal, monocoque, low-wing monoplane, with retractable landing gear, variable pitch propeller, wing flaps, and wing slots; it became the virtually universal design for military and commercial transport planes. The first planes to incorporate these features were the Martin B-10 and Boeing B-9 bombers and the Boeing 247 transport. Rivalry between airlines and manufacturers gave the American industry a commanding lead in development and production. The desire for a competitor to the 247 led to the Douglas DC series, with the result that by 1939 the DC-3, introduced in 1935, dominated the world's airways. The introduction of long-range flying boats, the famous clippers, made possible regular transoceanic service. By 1940, Boeing, Douglas, and Lockheed were all working on four-engine land planes with pressurized cabins for high-altitude flight. Simultaneously, the American aviation industry became the leading producer of large bombers, beginning with the Boeing B-17 Flying Fortress in 1935. In World War II the aircraft carrier replaced the battleship as the basis of seapower. The first practical helicopter appeared during the war but too late to see much service. German data on jet propulsion became available to American engineers after the war. In the postwar advance of aviation technology, several experimental craft were trailblazers, such as the rocket-powered Bell X-1, which exceeded the speed of sound in 1947. Most famous was the North American X-15 rocket plane, which exceeded 4,000 mph and climbed above 300,000 feet. American transports continued to dominate the world's commerical airlines. Boeing built a prototype jet transport in 1954; it became the phenomenally successful 707. Almost two decades later Boeing's wide-bodied jumbo, the 747, was to prove equally successful. The McDonnell Douglas DC-10 and the Lockheed L-10ll TriStar were other entrants into the jumbo market. Only in the development of a supersonic transport (SST) did US manufacturers defer to their European counterparts. For economic and environmental reasons the federal government decided against supporting development. Britain and France jointly developed the Concorde, which went into service in 1976.

In 1909 the Wright brothers formed a company to build airplanes and conduct flying schools. They were followed by, among others, Glenn Curtiss (1909), Glenn L. Martin (1912), and William E. Boeing (1915). Growth was slow until World War I, during which time 14,000 planes were manufactured. Armistice brought a virtual collapse of the industry. The principal survivors were the Wright Aeronautical Company, Curtis Aeroplane and Motor, Boeing, and Martin. Important new companies in the 1920s were Douglas, Consolidated, Lockheed, Fairchild, Sikorsky, and Fokker. In 1924 the Ford Motor Co. began producing the famous Trimotor. In 1934 federal legislation ordered the separation of manufacturing and transport companies. By 1939 about 6,000 planes per year were being built, and aviation ranked forty-first among American industries. World War II brought drastic changes. Total output between 1939 and 1945 was approximately 300,000 aircraft. When the war ended, the aviation industry faced major readjustments. A substantial growth in helicopter manufacture took place. Jet airplanes developed much faster than had been anticipated. Airplane manufacturers became the prime producers of missiles and of space vehicles. The industry continued to be acutely dependent on the government, to which it made about 80 percent of its sales. Research and development became the largest single item of cost, and there were more managerial and technical personnel than production workers.

Passenger service was first launched in 1914 between St. Petersburg and Tampa. From 1919 to 1923 both passengers and mail were carried between Miami and the Bahamas and between Key West and Havana during the winter; the same company carried passengers between New York and Cleveland during the summer. In the late 1920s Pan American, United, American, Eastern, and Transcontinental Air Transport (later TWA) were all formed; numerous smaller feeder lines were also established. In 1938 all were placed under the Civil Aeronautics Board. After World War II, PanAm and TWA expanded round-the-world carriers. Northwest Orient acquired a route across the northern Pacific; American flew into the southern Pacific and Braniff into South America. Numerous lines were permitted to fly into the Caribbean, including the largest of the newer lines, Delta. Competition increased with the introduction of large jet fleets, which became a serious capital drain. The fuel crisis of the early 1970s and the resultant higher prices led to a long period of financial difficulties, dramatically illustrated by the bankruptcy of Braniff in 1982, Capital in 1983, and the reorganization of Continental under bankruptcy laws in 1983. The Airline Deregulation Act (1978) provided for dissolution of the CAB by 1985 and, in effect, removed the government from all its regulatory functions (except for safety requirements). The recession in the early 1980s led to price wars and other efforts to attract customers and compete with "no frills" low-fare airlines such as New York Air and People Express.

AISNE DEFENSIVE (May 27–June 5, 1918). The Germans reached the Marne R near Château-Thierry, forty mi. from Paris. They then vainly attempted to establish a bridgehead on the Marne and to push W toward Paris.

AISNE-MARNE OPERATION (July 18–Aug. 6, 1918). Franco-American counteroffensive following the German offensive of July 15 in the Marne salient. From July 21 on, the armies farther E joined in the advance along both faces of the salient. The Germans made an especially strong stand on the Ourcq R on July 28; but early in August they were back behind the Vesle R. Germans were never able again to undertake a serious offensive.

AIX-LA-CHAPELLE, TREATY OF (1748). Ended the war of the Austrian Succession (see KING GEORGE'S WAR). The restoration of Louisburg, Nova Scotia, to France irritated the New Englanders, who had been active in its capture. The peace was merely an intermission in the protracted struggle for control of the Saint Lawrence and Mississippi basins.

AKRON. City in Ohio, founded 1825 as a stopping point on the Ohio and Erie Canal. A rubber-processing center since the early 20th c. after B.F. Goodrich located his factory there. Other industries include salt-processing and chemical plants and earth-moving equipment and tools. Pop.: 237,177 (1980).

ALABAMA. First sighted by Spanish explorers in 1519; first permanent settlement established by Le Moyne at Mobile Bay (1702), which was then part of French Louisiana. In 1763 France ceded the territory to Great Britain, and in 1783 the southern portion was ceded to Spain and the remainder to the US. Mobile, the seat of Spanish power, was taken by the US in 1813. In 1817 the Alabama Territory was organized out of the Mississippi Territory, of which it had been a part since 1798, and was admitted to the Union on Dec. 14, 1819. Cotton farming and the plantation system prevailed. That predominance expressed itself in Jeffersonian, states' rights, and proslavery politics before 1860. On Jan. 11, 1861, Alabama seceded. The Confederate government was organized at Montgomery in 1861, its first capital. Estimates of Alabama's property losses during the Civil War run as high as $500 million; losses among the white male population, which was heavily enrolled in the Confederate army, were one in ten. The state attempted to reenter the Union under President Andrew Johnson's plan for reconstruction; but its provisional government was repudiated by Congress. Reconstruction brought the state under federal military control in 1867. A new constitution was drafted in November 1867, and the state was readmitted to the Union in June 1868. After the Civil War Alabama was torn by party dissension, its government characterized by extravagance and dishonesty. From 1876 through 1944 Alabama was controlled politically by Democrats. In 1948 the state joined other southern states in embracing the States' Rights, or Dixicrat, party. In 1968 it again supported a states' rights, anti-integration party, this time the American Independent party, organized and led by George C. Wallace, several times governor of Alabama. Disturbances in Alabama's allegiance to the Democratic party reflect the controversy over civil rights. In 1956 the state was a focus of national attention as black residents of Birmingham, under the leadership of Martin Luther King, Jr., carried through a successful boycott of local buses, prompted by discriminatory practices. In 1961 a confrontation between civil rights activists and local people necessitated the imposition of martial law. In 1963 Alabama was forced under federal court order to admit blacks to the state university and various public schools. Race relations were much calmer during the 1970s; when George Wallace was elected governor once more in 1982, he won with the support of large numbers of blacks. Cotton has remained the chief money crop of Alabama, but since World War II more farmland has been turned over to the raising of livestock, especially chickens. Two-thirds of the state's land area has come to be devoted to timber, leading to the development of related industries. Iron and steel manufacture have expanded rapidly, especially in Birmingham; but more than 50 percent of the state's mineral production is in bituminous coal. Mobile has remained a leading port. A major aerospace industry has developed around Huntsville. Alabama has followed the national trend toward urbanization: in 1900 the state had an urban population of only 12 percent; by 1975 it was 58 percent. Pop.: 3,900,000 (1980).

ALABAMA CLAIMS. The British-built Confederate cruiser *Alabama* became the terror of Union vessels. Before its destruction in 1864 (see KEARSARGE AND ALABAMA ENCOUNTER), it sank, burned, or captured more than sixty ships. US grievances against Great Britain during and just after the Civil War became known as the Alabama Claims. The Confederate cruisers, built by Britain in the face of its stated neutrality, led the US to lay before the British government a demand for redress. Ultimately, the US entered claims totaling more than $19 million. The claims met with no success until 1868, when the two sides decided that a joint commission should settle a wide range of Anglo-American disputes: Canadian fisheries, northwestern boundary, and the Alabama Claims. In 1871 the commission provided for the submission of the Alabama Claims to a five-nation board of arbitrators. That tribunal decided, in 1872, that Great Britain had failed in its duties as a neutral and awarded the US $15.5 million. (See WASHINGTON, TREATY OF.)

ALABAMA PLATFORM. Adopted by the Democratic state convention in 1848 and approved by other southern groups, it demanded congressional protection of slavery in the Mexican cession. Rejected by the Democrats in 1848, the principle was adopted by a majority of the Democratic convention at Charleston in 1860.

ALAMANCE, BATTLE OF (May 16, 1771). Between the REGULATORS OF NORTH CAROLINA and the provincial government. The two sides met at the Alamance R, near Hillsboro. The battle ended in disaster for the Regulators.

ALAMO, SIEGE OF THE (Feb. 23–Mar. 6, 1836). A battle during the Texas Revolution. William B. Travis was in joint command with James Bowie of about 145 men at San Antonio when attacked by a Mexican force of between 3,000 and 4,000. Travis and Bowie moved into the Alamo mission, refused to surrender, and sent couriers for reinforcements. On the eighth day, 32 recruits crept through the Mexican lines, bringing the strength of the garrison to 187. On the thirteenth day of battle, the Mexicans breached the walls and the defenders fought throughout the mission compound, the last defensive position being the church, where David Crockett fell. All 187 defenders were killed, though the Mexicans spared about 30 noncombatants. Mexican losses were about 1,500. "Remember the Alamo" became the rallying cry of the Texas revolutionaries.

ALASKA. The northwestern extension of the North American continent. Acquired by purchase from Russia in 1867. Became forty-ninth state in 1958. Russians, under Vitus Bering, explored Alaska in early 18th c. Established Russian-American Co. in Alaska and extended the czar's dominions far eastward. Military-trading post named New Archangel, later Sitka, became capital of Russian America. A rival British concessionaire, the Hudson's Bay Co., was advancing westward. Clashes between the two were averted by a convention signed by Britain and Russia in 1828. US purchased territory for $7.2 million, less than two cents per acre. Action denounced as "Seward's Folly," after the US secretary of state who arranged the purchase. The Organic Act of 1884 gave Alaska its first civil government, by providing it with a governor, a federal district judge, and five commissioners. Successive governors voiced concern over the inadequacies of the Organic Act but nothing was done until gold was discovered in the Klondike in the 1890s, resulting in a rush of prospectors. A new Organic Act was passed in 1912. It permitted Alaska to have a legislature, but denied it the control and management of its fisheries and wildlife; forbade the enacting of any basic land laws; kept the judiciary in federal control; and forbade the creation of counties without prior consent of Congress. Successive legislatures pleaded unsuccessfully with Congress to revise the land laws to promote homesteading; to transfer to Alaska the management of the fisheries, which were inadequately protected against depletion under federal management; to make appropriations for highway construction; and to pay the federal lower court judges a salary. A land-grant college (later the University of Alaska) was established; a railroad was built; and a system of roads was established. In Congress, Democrats generally favored statehood for Alaska (expecting it to send Democratic members to the US Congress), while Republicans generally favored statehood for Hawaii (because that territory was expected to send Republicans to Washington). A compromise was finally worked out and legislation admitting both was passed in 1958. The conflict between developers and conservationists has been a recurring one. The discovery of large oil deposits in Prudhoe Bay in the 1960s intensified the war. To get the oil to market, a pipeline to Alaska's gulf coast was planned, but conservationists opposed its construction. Efforts to block the pipeline were eventually defeated and the pipeline was laid. Conservationists were more successful later in the decade: Federal legislation set aside 104 million acres of Alaska as national park. President Carter signed it into law on Dec. 2, 1980. Pop.: 400,581 (1980).

ALBANY. Since 1797 the capital of New York. In 1624 eighteen Walloon families built Fort Orange on the Hudson R on the site of the present capitol building. In 1652 the village became known as Beverwyck and became a center for the fur trade. On Sept. 24, 1664, Fort Orange surrendered to the English and Beverwyck became Albany. During the colonial wars many conferences, including the ALBANY CONGRESS of 1754, were held there. In 1777 Gen. John Burgoyne and Col. Barry St. Leger advanced toward the city (see BRITISH CAMPAIGN OF 1777), but the former surrendered at Saratoga and the latter retreated from Fort Stanwix. The completion in 1825 of the Erie Canal made Albany the junction of the water route from the East to the Great Lakes, and also a point of departure for the Albany-Schenectady RR (1831), which began the city's role as a rail center. Pop.: 101,727 (1980).

ALBANY CONGRESS (1754). Called by the British in order to secure the support of the Iroquois for the war against France. In June commissioners from New York, Massachusetts, Rhode Island, Connecticut, Pennsylvania, New Hampshire, and Maryland met with the chiefs of the Six Nations. Although the alliance was renewed, the Iroquois went away only half satisfied. However, the congress evolved into a discussion of closer union among the colonies. The Albany Plan, proposed by Benjamin Franklin, provided for a voluntary union of the colonies with "one general government," each colony to retain its own separate existence and government. The plan was rejected by the crown and the colonial legislatures.

ALBANY CONVENTION (1689–90). A temporary government, set up at Albany, N.Y., until the intentions of William and Mary were made known. Badly frightened by a French attack on Schenectady, the convention sought aid from New England; later they yielded control to Jacob Leisler, who had seized control of southern New York.

ALBANY REGENCY. The first American political machine. Organized by New York Democrats in 1820 under Martin Van Buren, whose aides in Albany managed the machine during his absence in the US Senate. The spoils system was the core of its philosophy. The regency split following Van Buren's unsuccessful bid for the presidency in 1848.

ALBEMARLE. Confederate ram, built in 1853. In April 1864 sank the gunboat *Southfield*, put the *Miami* to flight, and captured Plymouth, N.C. It was sunk on Oct. 27.

ALBEMARLE AND CHESAPEAKE CANAL. Built in 1856–60 to afford inland navigation between Chesapeake Bay and Albemarle Sound. Consists of two canals, one connecting the Elizabeth R with North Landing R in Virginia, and the other connecting Currituck Sound with the North R in North Carolina.

ALBEMARLE SETTLEMENTS. First permanent settlements in North Carolina, made by Virginians in 1655. The county of Albemarle was instituted in 1664, and an assembly met in 1665. In 1689 county of Albemarle abolished as a unit of government.

ALBUQUERQUE. City in New Mexico. Originated in 1706 as the Spanish villa San Felipe de Albuquerque. It was on the Chihuahua Trail and dominated the Rio Abajo (downriver) part of the province. Exposed to Apache and Navajo inroads, the settlers were "reduced" in 1779 to the plaza arrangement that survives in Old Town. New Albuquerque started a century later (1880) a mile to the

east, as a railroad center. Pop.: 331,767 (1980).

ALCALDES. Mayors of Mexican towns. Recognized by US authorities in California until 1850.

ALDERS GULCH. Site in Montana where gold was discovered in 1863. Virginia City sprang up nearby. Richest gold placer deposits ever discovered; in three years $30 million recovered.

ALDRICH-VREELAND ACT. Emergency currency law enacted 1908 as a result of the panic of 1907. It permitted national banks to issue additional currency and created the National Monetary Commission.

ALEUT. Together with the Eskimo, the Aleut, native inhabitants of SW Alaska, the Shumagin Islands, and the long Aleutian archipelago, form the single language family of Eskaleut. The population was estimated at 16,000 in 1740. Living in sod houses, the Aleut were hunters and fishers. Kinship relationships rather than political organization were the rule. Est. Pop.: 1,800 (1980).

ALEUTIAN ISLANDS. Lying off the Alaska Peninsula, they are largely volcanic and unsuitable for agriculture. Before the Russian exploration in 1741, the islands were peopled exclusively by Aleut. The Russian-American Fur Co. exploited the region and massacred or enslaved the Aleut. Added to the Russian incursions were British and American slaughtering of seals. After the US purchase of Alaska in 1867, controversies over sealing rights in the Bering Sea proliferated; a settlement by a court of arbitration in Paris in 1893 left the sea open (see PELAGIC SEALING DISPUTE). In 1942 the Japanese destroyed military bases at Dutch Harbor and occupied the undefended islands of Attu and Kiska. US forces reclaimed them in 1943. US coast guard fleet at Unalaska Island monitors the international seal protection agreement. Also on the Aleutians are weather and radar stations.

ALEXANDRIA. Located in Virginia on the Potomac R, a suburb of Washington, D.C. First settled in 1695, it was established as a town in 1749. The Fairfax Resolves were signed there on July 18, 1774. From 1791 to 1847 Alexandria was part of the District of Columbia. Pop.: 103,217 (1980).

ALEXANDRIA CONFERENCE (March 28, 1785). Dealing with navigation and commerce in Virginia, Maryland, and Delaware waters, actually took place at Mount Vernon. It called for a meeting of all states to adopt uniform commercial regulations, which in turn resulted in the CONSTITUTIONAL CONVENTION of 1787.

ALGECIRAS CONFERENCE (1906). Met under the good offices of US President Theodore Roosevelt to settle Franco-German dispute over Morocco. England and Spain were also members. German intransigence led Roosevelt to support France, which in the end obtained a privileged position in Morocco. The US Senate ratified the resulting treaty.

ALGIERS, WAR WITH. See BARBARY WARS.

ALGONQUIN. The Algonquin tribe, located in SW Quebec, is to be contrasted with the extensive North American speech family, Algonkin, to which it has lent its name. The tribe was small (perhaps 6,000 in 1660) and consisted of nonagricultural hunters. Extensive use of birch bark for housing, canoes, and containers characterized their culture. The Algonquin, along with the neighboring Ottawa, appear to have been remnants of various Ojibwa bands. The language phylum to which the Algonquin lent their name is one of the most widely spread of the Native Americans, extending to the Arapaho, Cheyenne, and Blackfoot in the Plains and the Yurok and Wiyout in California. Certain Gulf languages and some languages of Central America may also have remote connections with the major Algonkin grouping.

ALGONQUIN ROUND TABLE. An informal literary-luncheon group that gathered in the Algonquin Hotel in New York City during the 1920s and 1930s. Its members, noted for their wit, included Alexander Woollcott, Dorothy Parker, George S. Kaufman, F.P. Adams, Robert Benchley, and Harold Ross.

ALIEN AND SEDITION LAWS. In 1798, the Federalists, fearful of war with France, introduced four bills designed to impede the political opposition of the Republicans, led by Thomas Jefferson. The Naturalization Act made it difficult for aliens to become citizens (repealed 1802). The Alien Friends Act gave the president the power to deport aliens "dangerous to the peace and safety of the United States"; its terms were sweeping, but it was limited to two years and was never enforced. The Alien Enemies Act, a clearly defensive measure in time of declared war, gave the president the power to restrain, arrest, and deport male citizens of a hostile nation (never repealed). The Act for the Punishment of Certain Crimes was the nation's first sedition act. It made it unlawful to write or publish "any false, scandalous and malicious writing" with intent to bring the government, Congress, or the president "into contempt or disrepute." A number of people were convicted under the act before it expired in 1810. Opposition to the Alien and Sedition Laws received its most significant formulation in the KENTUCKY AND VIRGINIA RESOLUTIONS.

ALIEN CONTRACT LABOR LAW. See CONTRACT LABOR, FOREIGN.

ALIEN LANDHOLDING. The common-law disability of aliens to inherit lands in the United States has always been removable by statute and by treaty. JAY'S TREATY guaranteed existing titles wherever held and treated British subjects as equal to citizens. The Convention of 1800 removed the disability for French citizens in all the states. In the absence of specific treaties, state laws apply.

ALIENS. See NATURALIZATION.

ALIENS, RIGHTS OF. The status of aliens residing in the United States in regard to judicial proceedings is virtually the same as that of US citizens. The protection of the Fifth and Fourteenth amendments relate to "persons"; therefore, in 1973 the Supreme Court declared unconstitutional state laws that sought to limit the employment opportunities available to aliens. *Graham* v. *Richardson* nullified various state laws denying welfare benefits to resident aliens.

ALLATOONA PASS, BATTLE AT (Oct. 5, 1864). After the fall of Atlanta, Confederate commander J.B. Hood moved his army N to cut Gen. W.T. Sherman's communications. Sherman followed. Hood detached S.G. French's division to destroy a railroad bridge; on his march French destroyed stores at Allatoona and attacked Union troops stationed there.

ALLEGHENY MOUNTAINS, ROUTES ACROSS. The steep E escarpment of the Alleghenies was an impediment to western migration. The West Branch of the Susquehanna R furnished a route used by the Indians. The branches of the Juniata R provided the Frankstown Path, much used by fur traders, and the Traders Path, followed by the Pennsylvania Road and Forbes's Road. The route used by Christopher Gist, George Washington, and Edward Braddock ran from the Potomac R at Wills Creek. From the headwaters of the Potomac also ran the Northwestern Pike. The headwaters of the James R determined a route to branches of the Great Kanawha R; one branch, the New R, also provided a route from the headwaters of the Roanoke R. Farthest south, Cumberland Gap offered easy passage from E Tennessee to central Kentucky, making possible the WILDERNESS ROAD.

ALLEGHENY PORTAGE RAILWAY. A 36-mi. span between Hollidaysburg and Johnstown that linked the E and W canals of the Pennsylvania System. Constructed 1831–35, when the ascent of 1,400 feet within 10.1 miles seemed a prohibitive gradient for a continuous roadbed, the railway consisted of eleven level stretches and ten inclined planes. Locomotives quickly replaced horses as motive power. In 1856 the planes were superseded by a continuous railway. Line abandoned shortly thereafter.

ALLEGHENY RIVER. Rising in Potter County, Pennsylvania, it flows in an arc through New York and back into Pennsylvania, where it unites at Pittsburgh with the Monongahela R to form the Ohio R.

ALLENTOWN. Industrial city in Pennsylvania on the Lehigh R. Laid out in 1762, the town was settled largely by German immigrants. Pop.: 103,758 (1980).

ALLIANCE. Continental frigate built in 1778. Its first captain, Pierre Landais, showed doubtful loyalty in 1779 and was relieved of command. Defiant, he sailed the *Alliance* from France to America; the crew mutinied twice during the voyage. Capt. John Barry cruised in the *Alliance* from 1780 through the last sea fight of the war with the *Sybil*, Mar. 10, 1783.

ALLIANCE FOR PROGRESS. Latin American policy proposed by President Kennedy in 1961. A ten-year, cooperative plan, it called for economic and social planning, land and tax reform, education and health services, economic integration, and hemispheric defense arrangements. Basically a continuation of the GOOD NEIGHBOR POLICY.

ALMANACS. The first almanac printed in America was the *Almanacke for New England for the Year 1639*, printed in Cambridge; later in the century almanacs were published in Boston, Philadelphia, and New York. The most famous of the early almanacs were the *Astronomical Diary and Almanack* published in Boston (1726–75); and *Poor Richard's Almanac* by Benjamin Franklin in Philadelphia (1732–57). The former included tide charts, solar table calculations and eclipses, and changes of the moon. The most enduring of American almanacs is *The Farmer's Almanac*, begun in 1793 and still being published.

ALPHADELPHIA ASSOCIATION (1844–48). A short-lived Fourierist community established in Kalamazoo County, Michigan, by a German, Dr. H.R. Schetterly.

ALTA CALIFORNIA. Under Spain (1533–1822), California embraced the whole Pacific coast of North America from Cape San Lucas to Oregon. The S portion came to be called Baja (lower) California and the rest Alta (upper) California.

ALTA VELA CLAIM. A claim against the Dominican government by American adventurers ejected in 1861 from the guano island of Alta Vela, located fifteen miles south of the Dominican Republic. President Andrew Johnson in 1868 refused to honor the claim.

ALTON PETROGLYPHS. An imaginary bird painted on a rocky bluff over the Mississippi R, near the present town of Alton, Illinois.

The figure was discovered in 1673 and was destroyed in 1856.

ALUMINUM INDUSTRY. Aluminum, extensively employed in construction, automobile production, and in the packaging industry, was first isolated in metallic form in 1825 in Denmark. In 1886 an American, Charles Martin Hall, and a Frenchman, Paul Heroult, independently discovered the electrolytic process for producing aluminum from the ore bauxite. It remains the sole commercial method, used throughout the world. Hall's invention led to the formation (1888) of what is now the Aluminum Company of America (ALCOA), the world's largest producer. With the advent of the airplane in World War I, the demand for aluminum skyrocketed. In 1918 the primary capacity in the United States had grown to 62,500 short tons; world production amounted to 143,900 tons. Today the United States produces almost 5 million tons, or about 30 percent of the world production.

AMANA COMMUNITY. Founded in Germany in 1714 in protest against the arbitrary rule of church and state. Members crossed the Atlantic in the 1840s and settled near Buffalo, N.Y., where they founded a settlement called Ebenezer and formally adopted communism as a way of life. In 1865 they moved to Iowa and incorporated as the Amana Society, consisting of seven villages and 26,000 acres. In 1932, the community reorganized as a joint stock company where stockholders are both owners and employees.

AMARILLO. City in the Texas Panhandle. A leading center for the production of helium gas, which is found with other natural gases and oils in the vicinity. Founded 1887, it became a resort for cowboys, with shops, hotels, and saloons. Farmers moved into the area, and the city was well established before the first oil and gas discoveries provided it with a major local industry. Beef, cotton, and cotton seed are also produced. Pop.: 149,230 (1980).

AMBASSADORS. Until well into the 19th c., only great powers exchanged ambassadors, traditionally the highest diplomatic grade. Smaller nations exchanged ministers plenipotentiary. The first US ambassador was sent to Great Britain in 1893. By 1939 the United States was exchanging ambassadors with twenty nations. The number increased sharply after World War II; by 1980 the United States was exchanging ambassadors with 146 nations, sending ministers to none. Also, nine ambassadors were accredited to such international organizations as the United Nations and the North Atlantic Treaty Organization.

AMBRISTER. See ARBUTHNOT AND AMBRISTER, CASE OF.

AMELIA ISLAND AFFAIR (1817). The Embargo Act (1807) and the abolition of the American slave trade (1808) made Amelia Island, off the coast of Spanish Florida, a resort for smugglers. One of these, Luis Aury, assumed control of Amelia and urged all Florida to revolt against Spain. The US navy put an end to the miniature republic and returned the island to Spain.

AMENDMENT. Amendments to the US Constitution are discussed in individual articles listed under the number of the amendment. For example, see FOURTEENTH AMENDMENT. See also CONSTITUTION OF THE UNITED STATES.

"AMERICA." See "MY COUNTRY 'TIS OF THEE."

AMERICA. The American yacht that in 1851 won the trophy presented by the Royal Yacht Squadron; since 1857 the trophy has been known as the *America*'s Cup. The *America* later served as a Confederate dispatch boat, was captured, and served as a practice ship at the Naval Academy. Broken up in 1946.

AMERICA, EARLY EXPLORATION OF.
Norse Exploration. Norsemen reached North America ca. 1000, from Greenland and reaching as far S as perhaps Chesapeake Bay. The legends of the voyages of Leif Ericson (who called the new land Vinland) and Thorfinn Karlsefni depend on three manuscripts of sagas.
Spanish Exploration. On Aug. 3, 1492 the Genoese Christopher Columbus sailed from Palos, Spain, under the authority of the Spanish king and queen. On Oct. 12, 1492, Columbus set foot on an island in the Bahamas, which he named San Salvador (probably Watling Island). Columbus made three other

voyages to the New World (1493, 1498, 1502), and touched the coast of South and Central America. In 1499, Alonso de Ojeda and Juan de la Cosa visited South America, and with them went Amerigo Vespucci, whose popular accounts of his own deeds led German geographers to name the new lands America. (See AMERICA, NAMING OF.)

In 1513 Vasco Núñez de Balboa crossed the Isthmus of Panama and discovered the Pacific Ocean. The E coast of the mainland of North America had been mapped by 1502. In 1513 Juan Ponce de Léon had visited the site of St. Augustine, Fla., and by 1526 Spanish explorers had conducted expeditions as far N as Virginia. Meanwhile Hernando Cortés had conquered (1519) Mexico. Pánfilo de Narvaez explored W Florida and possibly Georgia (1528), while Álvar Núñez Cabeza de Vaca walked overland to the Gulf of California. In 1539 Hernando de Soto took an expedition from Tampa Bay, marched N to the Savannah R, and then proceeded W to the Mississippi R in 1541. By this time Franciscan friars were pushing up into what is now the Southwest of the United States. Fray Marcos de Niza (1539) brought back such reports of wealth that Franciso Vásquez de Coronado started out in April 1540 on an expedition that took him as far N as C Kansas (1541).

French Exploration. Giovanni Verrazano, acting under the favor of Francis I, came to North America in 1524 and possibly saw the Lower Bay of New York. Jacques Cartier coasted Labrador in 1534 and in the next year explored the St. Lawrence R to the Lachine Rapids above Quebec. Samuel de Champlain found Maine ca. 1603, Cape Cod in 1605, and got as far as C New York state in 1615.

English Exploration. In May 1497 John Cabot sailed under a patent from Henry VII and probably discovered the continent of North America. The Hawkinses (William, John, and James) explored the West Indies in the late 16th c. Sir Francis Drake rounded Cape Horn and reached the coast of California in June 1579. In 1602 Bartholomew Gosnold reached the coast of Maine, skirted Cape Cod (which he named), and found Narragansett Bay. George Weymouth in 1605 sighted Nantucket. Henry Hudson made two voyages to America in 1609 and 1610–1611. The bay, river, and strait named for him were known from earlier explorers.

Other Exploration. Swedes and Norwegians allegedly discovered America from Greenland in the 13th c., through Hudson Bay and into the present state of Minnesota. This theory rests on an inscribed stone and certain artifacts (see KENSINGTON STONE). There are also legends of pre-Columbian discoveries of America by the Chinese, Egyptians, Welsh, Irish, and Phoenicians.

AMERICA, NAMING OF. The earliest explorers and historians designated America as the Indies, the West Indies, or the New World. Scholars at Saint Dié, in Lorraine, printed Amerigo Vespucci's accounts of his voyages in *Cosmographiae Introductio* (1507). Two names were suggested for the new "fourth part" of the world: Amerige (the *-ge* from the Greek, meaning "earth") and America, which paralleled Europa and Asia.

AMERICA FIRST COMMITTEE. Isolationist group founded in 1940 to oppose US participation in World War II. By October 1941 it had begun to disintegrate.

AMERICAN ACADEMY AND INSTITUTE OF ARTS AND LETTERS. An organization composed of artists from all creative fields. The National Institute was founded in 1898 and incorporated by Congress in 1913. The Academy of Arts and Letters was founded in 1904. The organization disperses funds, grants, and endowment from its headquarters in New York City.

AMERICAN ACADEMY OF ARTS AND SCIENCES. Learned society, the plans of which were conceived by John Adams in 1779. Publications of the academy have included *Memoirs* (twenty-three volumes from 1785 to 1946) and *Proceedings* (1848 to present). In 1955 the academy initiated the quarterly *Daedalus*. The academy gives three prizes: the Rumford for science, the Emerson-Thoreau Medal for humanities, and the Social Science Prize. In 1980 the academy had 2,300 members.

AMERICAN ASSOCIATION FOR THE ADVANCEMENT OF SCIENCE (AAAS). Founded 1847. Quickly became the preeminent scientific organization in the United States. Nearly all practicing scientists became members and attended the annual meetings.

19

After the Civil War, it faced competition from the new National Academy of Sciences and from a movement toward scientific societies organized in specialized fields. In 1873, however, the AAAS adopted a revised constitution that established new possibilities for more diversified sections. Today, it has more than 130,000 members and more than 300 affiliated groups. In addition to its annual volumes of *Proceedings*, it sponsors the magazine *Science*.

AMERICAN AUTOMOBILE ASSOCIATION (AAA). Federation of state and local automobile clubs, the principal service organization and spokesman for American motorists since its formation in 1902. Emergency road service inaugurated in 1915. The AAA issues tour books and road maps and rates tourist accommodations. The AAA has lobbied for toll-free improved highways and bridges, for highway beautification programs, and against the diversion of motor vehicle use taxes into non-highway expenditures. In 1980 the association had 975 clubs and branches throughout the United States and Canada, and membership was 21 million.

AMERICAN BAR ASSOCIATION (ABA). With approximately 270,000 members in 1980, the largest and most influential association of lawyers in the United States. It sponsors some 150 periodicals, including its *Journal*. Founded in 1878, the ABA judges the qualifications of prospective nominees to the federal bench and has had enough influence to prevent some appointments.

AMERICAN BATTLE MONUMENTS COMMISSION. See FEDERAL AGENCIES.

AMERICAN BIBLE SOCIETY. Organized 1816 to promote the worldwide distribution of the Holy Scriptures without doctrinaire comment and without profit. Through its auspices, the Bible has been translated and published in 255 languages, the New Testament in 359 more. The Scriptures have been reproduced on tapes, records, and cassettes, as well as in braille. Total number of Bibles distributed by the society is about 3.2 billion.

AMERICAN CIVIL LIBERTIES UNION (ACLU). Founded 1920 to defend constitutional freedoms. Its main activity consists of court litigation of test cases selected on the basis of constitutional principles involved. Counsel is provided without charge by volunteer lawyers, with expenses paid by contributions from the organization's 200,000 (1980) members. The ACLU defended the right to teach evolution in public schools and the rights of labor unions to organize; was defense counsel in the Sacco-Vanzetti case; and won major Supreme Court cases in the 1930s protecting the right of public protest. More recently it has focused on amnesty for Vietnam War resisters, abortion and birth control, equal rights for women and children, humane treatment of mental patients, and prison reform. (See CIVIL RIGHTS AND LIBERTIES.)

AMERICAN COLONIZATION SOCIETY. Formed 1817 by clergymen to alleviate the plight of free blacks by removing them from the United States to Africa. The society also worked to aid the manumission of slaves and to suppress the African slave trade. In 1822 it established Liberia and aided it both financially and by sponsoring migrants to it. After the Civil War, Republicans reviled the society and most blacks rejected it. By 1900 had all but ceased to exist.

AMERICAN EXPEDITIONARY FORCES (AEF). American troops serving in Europe in World War I, commanded by Gen. John J. Pershing. At first placed under the Allied high command. First independent operation of the war was the capture of Cantigny in May 1918. In June, two divisions stopped the German advance on Paris. In July two US divisions, with one Moroccan division, formed the spearhead of the counterattack against the Château-Thierry salient, the turning point of the war. In September the US First Army reduced the Saint-Mihiel salient. More than 1.2 million US soldiers participated in the Meuse-Argonne offensive, beginning in late September. Smaller units were dispatched to the Italian front. By armistice, approximately 2 million Americans had served in Europe.

AMERICAN EXPRESS COMPANY. In 1850 two express companies merged to form a joint stock association to operate in New England, the Midwest, the Northwest, and parts of Canada. In 1852 Wells, Fargo was organized for the W half of the country. Another subsidiary, the United States Express Company was organized in 1854. In 1918 all the subsidiaries merged their shipping interests in the American Railway Express Agency, which was taken over in 1929 by the Railway Express Agency. The American Express Co., which had begun selling money orders in 1882 and traveler's checks in 1891, continued in banking and tourism. In 1958 it introduced the American Express credit card, and by the 1980s it was a worldwide operation encompassing a wide variety of travel, banking, and investment services. In 1981 merged with Shearson, a brokerage firm, and in 1984 with Lehman Bros.

AMERICAN FEDERATION OF LABOR-CONGRESS OF INDUSTRIAL ORGANIZATIONS (AFL-CIO). The AFL and CIO were united in 1955 after almost twenty years of rivalry. (For a history of the labor organizations and for a list of member unions, see LABOR.) The merger did not change the decentralized nature of the labor movement. The AFL-CIO does not itself engage in collective bargaining nor issue strike calls; this power resides with the autonomous affiliates. The AFL-CIO does have the power to expel affiliates for corruption or for communist domination. It has also adopted a vigorous antidiscrimination vow and created a single political action committee (the Committee on Political Education, or COPE), through which campaign funds are disbursed to candidates supportive of labor. Although the AFL-CIO has traditionally maintained its nonpartisan position, it is in reality in close alliance with the national Democratic party. In 1980 the organization had a total of about 13.6 million members.

AMERICAN FUR COMPANY. Founded by John Jacob Astor in 1808 to compete with the great Canadian fur-trading companies, which were gathering a large percentage of their furs within US territory. The company first went into partnership with its Canadian rivals but soon overwhelmed them. In 1816 Congress excluded foreigners from the fur trade, probably at the instigation of the company. In 1827 it merged with its greatest rival, the Columbia Fur Co., and thereafter had a virtual monopoly. In the 1830s Astor began selling off parts of the company, and by the 1840s it had effectively ended its operations. (See ASTORIA; PACIFIC FUR COMPANY.)

AMERICAN HISTORICAL ASSOCIATION (AHA). Founded 1884 as an offshoot of the American Social Science Association. In 1889 it received a congressional charter and made its headquarters in Washingon, D.C. In 1895 the AHA established the Historical Manuscripts Commission to edit, index, and collect unprinted documents relating to American history. In 1899 it formed the Public Archives Commission, which stimulated twenty-four states to establish archives and led the movement to establish the National Archives and Records Service. The AHA publishes *Papers of the American Historical Association, The American Historical Review,* reports and guides, an annual report, and various bibliographies.

AMERICAN INDEPENDENT PARTY. Organized 1968 by George C. Wallace, governor of Alabama, to support his presidential candidacy that year. Wallace opposed forced racial integration and was a strong states' rights advocate. The party won 13.5 percent of the popular vote and 46 electoral votes, all save one from the Deep South. The party's importance waned after the election.

AMERICAN INDIAN DEFENSE ASSOCIATION. Organized 1923, it emphasized the rights of Indians to religious freedom and opposed bills proposing to take Indian lands. It prompted passage of the Curtis Act (1924), which granted US citizenship to all Indians. Its leader, John Collier, was US Commissioner of Indian Affairs from 1933 to 1946.

AMERICAN INDIAN MOVEMENT (AIM). Organized in 1968 to protest alleged police brutality toward Indians, it became in the 1970s the leading militant Indian rights organization. In 1980 it had about 5,000 members.

AMERICAN JOINT COMMISSION TO FRANCE. See FRANCE, AMERICAN JOINT COMMISSION TO.

AMERICAN LABOR PARTY (ALP). Formed in 1936 in New York state, largely because of a conservative Democratic machine unsympathetic to the New Deal policies of President Franklin D. Roosevelt. The successful campaigns of Fiorello H. La Guardia for mayor of New York City in 1937 and Herbert H. Lehman for governor in 1938 demonstrated that the ALP held the balance of power between the two major parties. Factional disputes and communist influence in the ALP caused it to break up in 1944, with its right wing becoming the Liberal party. The ALP recorded its highest vote in the 1948 presidential election (with its support of Henry A. Wallace), but influence quickly waned afterward.

AMERICAN LAND COMPANY. One of the large speculative land companies, it purchased some 322,000 acres of public land in Mississippi, Arkansas, Michigan, Wisconsin, and Illinois in the 1830s. Fell into financial difficulty following the panic of 1837. Criticized as a monopoly that was corrupting public officials, cheating Indians, preventing competitive bidding at public land sales, and charging exorbitant prices for land it had bought for practically nothing.

AMERICAN LEGION. Largest US veterans' organization, with membership open to any man or woman who has served in the armed forces in wartime. Founded in 1919, it soon became the spokesman for all veterans, although its 1920 membership represented only about 18.5 percent of the veterans. By the late 1930s was one of the nation's most effective interest groups. Its promotion of the GI Bill of Rights for World War II veterans, achieved in 1944, testified to its dedication to all veterans, not just its members. Its membership fluctuated from a low of 610,000 in 1925 to a high of 3,325,000 in 1946, leveling off to about 2,630,000 in 1980. There are about 16,000 local posts throughout the world. Has also become known for its conservative political goals and advocacy of military preparedness.

AMERICAN LIBERTY LEAGUE. Organized 1934 to fight radicalism and protect property rights and the Constitution. Among its organizers were many wealthy, conservative Democrats who opposed the New Deal and Franklin D. Roosevelt. Dissolved in 1940.

AMERICAN MATHEMATICAL SOCIETY. Organized in 1888 by members of the Columbia College faculty as the New York Mathematical Society; name changed to American Mathematical Society in 1894. Publications include the *Bulletin, Colloquium Publica-* *tions, Transactions, Proceedings, Memoirs, Mathematical Review* (a monthly abstracting journal), and *Mathematics of Computing.* It has also initiated a series of translations, including *Soviet Mathematics* and *Chinese Mathematics.* An offshoot organization is the Mathematical Association of America, which meets the interests of teachers and students on the college level. It publishes the *American Mathematical Monthly.*

AMERICAN MEDICAL ASSOCIATION (AMA). National organization of physicians and surgeons, established 1847. Publishes *Journal* to bring medical developments to the attention of doctors and acts as a lobbying organization representing the interest of medical professionals.

AMERICAN-MEXICAN MIXED CLAIMS COMMISSIONS. Established in 1839, it had awarded about $2 million to Americans by 1842 for losses attributed to the actions of the Mexican government. Mexico's failure to honor the adjudication contributed to President Polk's decision to ask Congress for a declaration of war in 1846. In the years after the Mexican War, other claims commissions became necessary, the last resulting from the expropriation of US oil holdings in 1938.

AMERICAN PARTY. See KNOW-NOTHING PARTY.

AMERICAN PHILOSOPHICAL SOCIETY. Oldest learned society in the United States, founded by Benjamin Franklin in 1743 but moribund after 1746. Revived in 1769 by a merger with a rival learned society, again with Franklin as its president. It began publishing *Transactions* in 1771. After the American Revolution, the society became Jeffersonian, deistic, republican, and pro-French. Thomas Jefferson was president of the society and the United States at the same time. The explorers Merriwether Lewis and William Clark deposited their specimens in the society's museum and library, as did many later explorers, natural historians, and archaeologists. During the 19th c. both *Transactions* and *Proceedings* carried many descriptions of the natural and physical sciences. Today, the society sponsors numerous research grants to individuals. Membership: 500 US citizens, 100 foreign.

AMERICAN PROTECTIVE ASSOCIATION. Secret anti-Catholic society, founded at Clinton, Iowa, in 1887. It attracted a million members by 1896. The association gained control of local Republican organizations and carried elections throughout the Midwest. Split over the question of supporting William McKinley in 1896. Lingered until 1911.

AMERICAN RAILWAY ASSOCIATION. Originated as the Time Table Conventions in 1872, its major achievement was the decision to establish the four zones of standard time in the US. In 1889 it became the American Railway Association and eventually (1934) became part of the Association of American Railroads.

AMERICAN RAILWAY UNION. Started by Eugene V. Debs in 1893. In June 1894 it ordered its members not to handle Pullman cars, in sympathy with the Pullman shop strikers. President Grover Cleveland broke the strike with troops, union officers were jailed under the Sherman Antitrust Act, and the union collapsed.

AMERICAN REPUBLICAN PARTY. A nativistic, anti-immigrant political organization, launched in New York in 1843. In 1844 it won city elections in New York City and Philadelphia; in July 1845 its national convention changed the name to the Native American party and drafted a program of sweeping naturalization reforms. Failure to force congressional action on the proposals led to the party's rapid decline.

AMERICAN REVOLUTION. See REVOLUTION, AMERICAN.

AMERICAN SAMOA. See SAMOA, AMERICAN.

AMERICAN STUDIES. University courses that seek to approach American culture in a comprehensive fashion, primarily through its history, literature, religion, fine arts, and philosophy. Also includes anthropology, sociology, historical archaeology, industrial archaeology, folk culture, material culture, museum studies, and popular culture, as well as urban, minority, and women's studies.

AMERICAN SYSTEM. Tariff plan proposed by Henry Clay in 1824. His object was to cre-ate a home market and to check the decline of American industry, primarily by increasing revenues for internal improvements (e.g., roads and canals). The label was soon applied to collateral measures for which Clay stood, such as distributing among the states the proceeds of the sale of public lands.

AMERICA'S CUP RACES. See AMERICA; YACHT RACING.

AMISH MENNONITES. See MENNONITES.

AMISTAD CASE. In 1839 fifty-four slaves on the Spanish schooner *Amistad* mutinied near Cuba, murdered part of the crew, and attempted to cause the remainder to sail to Africa. They landed in Connecticut, and salvage claims were denied by the Supreme Court (1841) and the Africans were freed and returned to Africa. The organized support on their behalf played a part in the founding of the American Missionary Society.

AMNESTY. Decision of a government not to punish certain offenses, typically of a political nature and applying to certain groups of people. The US Constitution gives the president the authority to grant pardons and, by interpretation, amnesty. Presidents have historically granted amnesty to deserters at the end of a war. After World War II, President Truman established an amnesty board, which made individual recommendations for each request. Out of 15,000 requests, only 1,523 pardons were given. No amnesty was granted to draft evaders or deserters after the Korean War. During the Vietnam War over 500,000 men deserted the armed forces; another 8,000 were convicted of draft violations. In 1974 President Ford proclaimed a conditional clemency, and in 1977 President Carter pardoned most Vietnam War evaders. A particularly controversial pardon was that granted former President Nixon by President Ford in 1974.

AMY WARWICK ADMIRALTY CASE, 2 Black 635 (1863). One of the prize cases in which the Supreme Court upheld the power of the president to recognize the existence of a civil war and thereupon to establish a blockade, without awaiting congressional action.

ANACONDA COPPER MINING COMPANY. One of the largest copper mining producers of the Butte district of Montana. Organized in 1881, a smelter was erected in 1884, and 3,000 tons of copper were being treated daily by 1889.

ANAHUAC, ATTACK ON (June 1832). Anahuac was a Mexican military post on the shore of Galveston Bay. To effect the release of William B. Travis and other Americans held there, a group of Texans attacked the post. The resulting negotiations led the Texans to declare for the Santa Anna party in Mexico. The incident was an important preliminary to the Texas Revolution.

ANARCHISTS. Anarchist views in America were expressed very early. The statement "That government is best which governs least," associated with Thomas Jefferson, while not anarchist, moves strongly in that direction. American anarchism between the Civil War and World War I developed into two schools. Some anarchists, like Benjamin E. Tucker (1854–1939), were so-called individualists; while others, like Emma Goldman (1854–1936), were communist. Goldman did much to advance the cause of freedom of expression through her journal *Mother Earth* (1906–17). The so-called anarchists of the deed thought physical violence was permissible, but others stressed the importance of nonviolence. Leon Czolgosz, for example, was the assassin of President McKinley and an anarchist of the deed. Alexander Berkman, who tried to kill the steel magnate Henry Clay Frick in 1892, seemed to espouse the same position. Tucker argued that the state must be abolished by education and nonviolent resistance. American anarchist followers of Leo Tolstoy were known as radical pacifists. The Industrial Workers of the World, founded 1905, was said to be anarchosyndicalist in its outlook; it hoped to reorganize society along syndicalist (industrial union) lines. Anarchist influence declined after World War I. However, many in the New Left movement of the 1960s developed an outlook that resembled anarchist positions.

ANASAZI. Prehistoric culture developed near the juncture of Arizona, New Mexico, Utah, and Colorado, the cliff-dwelling ruins of which have made this the best-known prehistoric culture in the Southwest. A distinctive way of life began to emerge during the Basketmaker II period, which extended from the first to the sixth century AD. It was characterized by pithouses and the raising of corn and squash. Domesticated plant foods became the staple of the economy in later periods as large settlements of contiguous rooms began to replace the pithouses. During the Classic period (AD 1100–1300) most of the population lived in towns. Pueblo Bonito in Chaco Canyon, N.M., the largest of these, was a D-shaped building with about 800 rooms. Advanced agricultural techniques, including irrigation canals, were known, along with high-quality ceramics and textiles and turquoise jewelry. After AD 1300 climatic and social factors resulted in the abandonment of these flourishing towns.

ANCHORAGE. The largest city in Alaska, founded in 1915 in a protected portion of Cook Inlet with easy access to the sea. During World War II, Anchorage became an important headquarters for US ground, sea, and air forces. It is the center for the farming region of the Matanuska Valley and a major shipping and air center. Pop.: 173,017 (1980).

ANDERSONVILLE PRISON. Notorious Confederate prison in Georgia, established 1864. Bad sanitary conditions, poor food, crowding, and exposure resulted in more than 12,000 deaths out of a total prison population of about 31,000. Late in 1864 the prisoners were moved to Charleston, S.C. The commandant of the prison, Capt. Henry Wirtz, was tried and hanged.

ANDRÉ, CAPTURE OF. Major John André, was the intermediary (1779–80) between the British and the American traitor Benedict Arnold. André met Arnold on the Hudson R to complete arrangements for the betrayal of West Point. He was captured trying to escape and was hanged on Oct. 2, 1780, at Tappan, New York.

ANDROS REGIME. See NEW ENGLAND, DOMINION OF.

ANESTHESIA, DISCOVERY OF. William E. Clarke is said to have administered ether successfully for a tooth extraction in 1842. That same year, Crawford W. Long began to perform dental operations with ether anesthesia. Horace Well, a dentist, had nitrous oxide administered to himself and had a tooth extracted while under its influence. Wells's former student and partner, William T.G. Morton, began experimenting with sulfuric ether. After succeeding with a dental patient, Morton received permission to demonstrate his procedure at Massachusetts General Hospital. On Oct. 16, 1846, Dr. John C. Warren operated on a patient after Morton had anesthetized him.

ANGLICAN CHURCH. See CHURCH OF ENGLAND IN THE COLONIES.

ANGLO-AMERICAN RELATIONS. Although the American Revolution snapped the political ties with Great Britain, the United States found it impossible to lessen its economic dependence on Britain immediately. During the peace negotiations following the Revolution, the British refused to send a diplomatic representative to the United States in response to the sending of John Adams to London. The British closed Canada and the West Indies to American ships and most American products; they also refused to turn over the military posts that the treaty of 1783 had placed on the US side of the Canadian border. War between England and France in 1793 brought the United States and Britain to the brink of war; but relations improved greatly in 1794 when JAY'S TREATY addressed the more serious issues between the two nations. By 1805 relations had deteriorated, and President Jefferson embargoed all US exports in retaliation to the capturing of US merchant ships by the British. When this embargo failed, the United States declared war. (See WAR OF 1812.) The Treaty of Ghent (1815), which ended that war, also ushered in a new era of calm relations with Britain. Differences were settled amicably: Britain opened the West Indies; border disputes were settled; and Britain gave up its idea of establishing buffer states in Texas and California as those two areas became part of the United States. The Civil War imposed new strains. The British textile industry depended greatly on southern cotton. Despite this, however, the British never recognized the Confederate government, nor did it make any efforts to break the Union blockade of southern ports. Points of difference that arose during the war were settled (see ALABAMA CLAIMS), as were postwar differences in Latin America. When World War I broke out

in Europe, Americans were overwhelmingly behind the British, largely because of German submarine attacks on US shipping. Thus the 1917 decision to enter the war on the side of Britain was enthusiastically accepted by the public. World War I marked a turning point in Anglo-American economic relationships. England became the debtor and America the creditor; and the British debts proved to be onerous, forcing Britain to demand full reparations from Germany. Anglo-American relations remained good, however, and as World War II approached, again US public opinion was firmly with the British. The LEND-LEASE agreements helped Britain stay in the war and paved the way for further economic aid after the United States entered the war. Relations between the two allies during the war were exceptionally good, despite some quarreling over battle strategy. After the war, mutual fear and distrust of their former ally, the Soviet Union, helped forge what came to be known as the special relationship between Britain and America. England and the United States jointly developed atomic weaponry, the British allowed US bases on British soil, and in 1948 the two nations joined with other Western European nations to form the North Atlantic Treaty Organizaton. The two nations were not in total agreement: Britain recognized (1950) the Communist government of China over the protests of the United States; and the United States opposed Britain's seizure of the Suez Canal (1956). Nevertheless, relations remained good throughout the 1960s and 1970s, and the United States was a firm supporter of the British during its defense of the Falkland Islands in 1982.

ANIÁN, STRAIT OF. Mythical passage, supposed to connect the Atlantic and Pacific, sought by the Spaniards in the 16th and 17th c.

ANIMAL PROTECTIVE SOCIETIES. Incorporated as humane societies, they operate animal shelters, often in conjunction with local city governments. They work to secure and enforce laws that prevent cruelty to animals. The oldest, the American Society for the Prevention of Cruelty to Animals, was organized in 1866. In 1877 the American Humane Association was organized as a federation of animal protective societies. Its headquarters are in Denver and service more than 1,000 local groups.

ANNAPOLIS. Capital city of Maryland, located on the S shore of the Severn R, near Chesapeake Bay. Settled 1694 by Puritan refugees from Virginia, it was originally named Providence. St. John's College and the US Naval Academy are located there. Pop.: 31,740 (1980).

ANNAPOLIS CONVENTION (1786). Precursor of the CONSTITUTIONAL CONVENTION of 1787. On Sept. 11, 1786, commissioners from New York, New Jersey, Pennsylvania, Delaware, and Virginia met at Annapolis to discuss interstate commerce. They took no action except to recommend that a larger convention be held in Philadelphia the following May.

ANNAPOLIS ROYAL. See ROYAL.

ANN ARBOR City in Michigan, home of the University of Michigan and marketing center for the Michigan fruit-raising district. Pop.: 107,316 (1980).

ANNEXATION OF TERRITORY. No specific provision was made in the Constitution for adding territory to the United States. In 1803 President Jefferson purchased by treaty the vast territory of Louisiana. In 1818 England made a boundary treaty that accepted US claims to the Northwest. Spain gave up Florida (1819) in a treaty that established a frontier line from Texas to California. Texas was annexed in 1845 and California and the Southwest were gained as a result of the Mexican War. The modern continental boundaries were set by the OREGON TREATY OF 1846 and the GADSDEN PURCHASE. Alaska was bought from Russia in 1867 and the Philippines, Puerto Rico, and Guam from Spain in 1898. Hawaii was annexed by joint resolution of Congress and the Danish West Indies were purchased in 1917. A number of small islands in both the Atlantic and Pacific were annexed by presidential proclamation.

ANTARCTIC EXPLORATION. See BYRD'S POLAR FLIGHTS; POLAR EXPLORATION; WILKES EXPLORING EXPEDITION.

ANTHRACITE-TIDEWATER CANALS. Anthracite was discovered in NE Pennsylvania in the late 18th c., but could be got to market only by floating it down turbulent streams. Josiah White in 1818 built the Lehigh Canal, completing it to the Delaware R in 1829. During the same period, others built the Morris, Schuykill, and Delaware and Hudson canals. The last great system, known as the Pennsylvania State Canals, was completed in 1838. By mid-century, the importance of the canals had diminished because of the railroad.

ANTHROPOLOGY AND ETHNOLOGY. The distinctive character of American anthropological inquiry was determined by the presence of the Indians on the continent. Systematic inquiry can be traced to the founding of the Standing Committee on Antiquities, formed by the American Anthropological Society in 1797. In 1805 a precedent-setting questionnaire went with the LEWIS AND CLARK EXPEDITION. In 1842 Albert Gallatin founded the American Ethnological Society; and in 1879 a federal agency, the Bureau of Ethnology, was created. Throughout the 19th c. impressive Indian mounds were being systematically examined and anthropometric data were being collected. The American Anthropological Association was founded in 1902. Franz Boas, of the American Museum of Natural History and Columbia University, laid the groundwork for much of modern American anthropology. Among his students and disciples were Ruth Benedict, Edward Sapir, Melville Herskovits, and Margaret Mead. Today, while studies of the American Indian continue, the interests of American anthropologists encompass the whole world.

ANTIBANK MOVEMENT OF THE WEST. Opposition to banks existed from their beginning in America in the late 18th c. After the panic of 1837 sentiment reached the stage of a movement to abolish banks, centered in the new Jacksonian states of the Mississippi Valley. Between 1845 and 1863, banks were abolished in seven states and on the Pacific Coast.

ANTIETAM, BATTLE OF (Sept. 17, 1862). In September Gen. R.E. Lee led his Confederate army across the Potomac R into Maryland. He took position at Sharpstown, on the Antietam Creek. He had Gen. Stonewall Jackson's corps to his left and Gen. James Longstreet's corps to the right. The attack by Union Gen. G.B. McClellan was uncoordinated and the Rebels stood fast. Nevertheless, Lee's drive was stopped, and on Sept. 19 he withdrew across the Potomac. It was the bloodiest battle of the war.

ANTIFEDERALISTS. Opponents of the adoption of the Constitution of the United States in 1787 and 1789. Antifederalism represented those who favored the retention of power by state governments, in opposition to those who wanted a strong central government. (See also DEMOCRATIC–REPUBLICAN PARTY.)

ANTI-HORSE THIEF ASSOCIATION. Organized at Fort Scott, Kansas, in 1859 to provide protection against bandits. The association spread as necessity arose, but by 1875 it had turned into a strictly social organization.

ANTI-IMPERIALISTS. Americans who opposed US colonial expansion after the Spanish-American War; most were members of the Anti-Imperialist League, founded in 1898. In 1900 the league claimed to have 30,000 members, but its influence quickly waned.

ANTI-MASONIC MOVEMENTS. In 1826 the author of a book revealing secrets about the Freemasons disappeared, causing widespread anti-Masonic reaction. Many Masons renounced their vows, and in 1831 a national Anti-Masonic convention was held at Baltimore, the first nominating convention of any party. It named William Wirt of Maryland as its candidate for president. This, the first third party, only drew support away from Henry Clay, thereby assuring the 1832 landslide for Andrew Jackson. Later in the decade, the party merged with the Whigs.

ANTIMONOPOLY PARTIES (1873–76). Sometimes called Independent or Reform parties, they were political organizations of farmers, especially Grange members. They demanded government reform, economy, and reduced taxation; most of them also demanded state regulation of corporations, particularly railroads. Some state parties eventually fused with the Democrats.

ANTINOMIAN CONTROVERSY (1636–38). Anne Hutchinson, a devout member of John Cotton's Boston congregation, gradually came to the belief that the accepted view of the covenant of grace, as preached by Cotton, denied the fundamental Protestant tenet of salvation by faith alone. The New England clergy regarded her view as a form of Antinomianism, a discarding of the moral law. Her teachings threatened to split the colony into factions; therefore, Gov. John Winthrop suppressed the movement. Hutchinson was found guilty of eighty erroneous opinions and was excommunicated and banished from the colony. She fled to Rhode Island.

ANTIRENT WARS (1839–46). Culmination of the resentment of farmers in New York state against the virtually feudal leasehold system, whereby the great landlords and land companies collected yearly tribute in produce, labor, or money, and exacted a share from the sale of a leasehold. In 1839 the militia was forced to put down the so-called Helderberg War. Antirent secret societies spread rapidly and elected John Young governor. The amended constitution of 1846 prohibited new feudal tenures. Old leases became fee simple (absolute) ownership.

ANTI-SALOON LEAGUE. Founded at Oberlin, Ohio, in 1893. Prior to the Eighteenth Amendment the league centered upon destroying liquor traffic by legislation. When in 1933 the Eighteenth Amendment was repealed, the league campaigned again for local option laws prohibiting liquor sales. Now called the National Temperance League.

ANTISLAVERY. Early antislavery in America consisted primarily of Quaker agitation. By the 1780s the opposition to slavery had spread. Because of its underlying republican ideology, the American Revolution encouraged antislavery sentiments. During these years all the states abolished the African slave trade and most moved toward the ultimate eradication of slavery. With the enactment of the Northwest Ordinance of 1787, slavery was confined to the area that increasingly became known as the South. Gradual emancipation in the northern states was not achieved without opposition; and the newly formed antislavery societies played a crucial role in these early achievements. Pennsylvania Quakers established the first such society in 1775. True abolitionism never gained a foothold in the South, although most states made manumisson more easily attained. After 1800 the tide turned. By 1830 nearly all the vocal abolitionists were forced to leave the South, although the movement was spreading rapidly through the North: In 1835 there were 225 auxiliaries of the Anti-Slavery Society (AAS); by 1840 there were 1,640. All-black National Negro Conventions focused the efforts of black abolitionists. In 1839 the abolitionists decided to establish a political party. The resulting Liberty, or Human Rights, party nominated presidential candidates in 1840 and 1844. After that the party split into faction, with the majority ending up in the FREE SOIL PARTY, which surfaced in 1848. The failure of both moral suasion and political action led many blacks and whites to greater militancy. In 1859 John Brown, with the aid of abolitionist groups, led his unsuccessful but galvanizing raid on Harpers Ferry. The final phase of antislavery activity was based primarily on hostility toward the slaveowner, a hostility encouraged by Harriet Beecher Stowe's *Uncle Tom's Cabin* (1851). Antisouthernism provided a vehicle through which the Republican party could unite all forms of northern antislavery feeling by 1860, when Abraham Lincoln was elected president.

ANTITRUST LAWS. Federal legislation aimed at the maintenance of competitive conditions in the American private enterprise economy. The SHERMAN ANTITRUST ACT (1896), the CLAYTON ANTITRUST ACT (1914), and the ROBINSON-PATMAN ACT (1936) are the principal legislative instruments by which the FEDERAL TRADE COMMISSION monitors suspected antitrust activities of American business.

ANZA EXPEDITION (Oct. 23, 1775–Jan. 4, 1776). Sent by New Spain (Mexico) to occupy Alta California in the face of English and Russian threats. A presidio was founded on the site of the modern city of San Francisco.

ANZIO. Town on the W coast of Italy, site of a World War II battle. British and American troops landed at Anzio and Nettuno on Jan. 22, 1944. The Germans rallied quickly, penned the invaders into a small beachhead, brought reinforcements, and almost drove the Allies into the sea. They held their precarious positions for four months. Sir Harold Alexander's spring offensive of May 11 broke the German Gustav line, and Gen. Mark Clark's units linked up with the beachhead two weeks later. Thus the liberation of Italy could proceed.

APACHE. Athapascan-speaking tribe that pushed into New Mexico in prehistoric times, later fanning out into Arizona, W Texas, and N Mexico. They were noted for the depredations they carried out against other Indian tribes and against white settlers. Their war orientation reached a climax under Cochise and Geronimo in the APACHE WARS. Some Apache adapted to a modified agriculture and others to hunting and fishing. In N New Mexico the Jicarilla Apache took on Plains traits (tipi and bison hunting). Other Apache tribes included the San Carlos, White Mountain, Tonto, Mescadero, Chiricahua, and Lipan. Remnants of the last still remain in Mexico.

APACHE PASS EXPEDITION (Feb. 4–23, 1861). Led by the Seventh Infantry against Cochise, a chief of the Chiracahua Apache, who was falsely accused of a kidnapping. Cochise went voluntarily under a flag of truce to deny the charges, but was seized by the army. He escaped and led attacks on the nearby stage station and on a wagon train. Six Apache hostages were hanged in retaliation, turning Cochise into an implacable foe.

APACHE WARS (1871–86). When President Grant's peace policy toward the Indians was announced, some 5,000 Apache were concentrated on the San Carlos Reservation in Arizona. The CAMP GRANT MASSACRE of over one hundred Apaches on April 30, 1871, began a series of repeated raids under such leaders as Victorio and Geronimo. Victorio was killed in a fight with Mexican troops in 1880. The Apache wars finally ended with Geronimo's surrender in 1886. He and his followers were sent to Florida as prisoners of war.

APALACHE MASSACRE (1704). Episode in Queen Anne's War in which 50 Englishmen and 1,000 Creek Indians invaded the Apalache district in W Florida. They defeated a force of 30 Spaniards and 400 Apalache, destroying all but one of the 14 Franciscan mission settlements and carrying off considerable loot and 1,400 Christian Indians.

APIA, DISASTER OF (March 6, 1889). British, German, and US warships were gathered in Apia harbor in Samoa preparing for hostilities because of Germany's attempt to set up a protectorate there. A hurricane destroyed three German ships; two US ships were destroyed and one blown ashore. A British ship escaped out to sea.

APPALACHIA. Largely mountainous region in the E United States, extending generally from SW Pennsylvania S through West Virginia and parts of Kentucky, Virginia, the Carolinas, Georgia, and Alabama. Early settlers built their log cabins and clapboard houses on land lying generally between the Blue Ridge Mountains and the southern extension of the Allegheny Mountains. Many descendants of the original settlers remained in the area, engaging in logging, coal mining, and farming. At least since the Great Depression, Appalachia has been the center of great poverty.

APPALACHIAN MOUNTAINS BOUNDARY.
See INDIAN BARRIER STATE; PROCLAMATION OF 1763; QUEBEC ACT.

APPEAL OF THE INDEPENDENT DEMOCRATS. Manifesto issued in 1854, inspired by the Kansas-Nebraska Act, then pending. Signers of the appeal, led by Sen. Salmon P. Chase, helped found the Republican party.

APPEALS FROM COLONIAL COURTS. In the latter part of the 17th c., all the new colonial charters reserved for the king-in-council the right to hear cases on appeal from provincial courts where the sum litigated exceeded a stated amount. In the New England colonies particularly, the appellate authority was at best grudgingly conceded; at times an order of the privy council was deliberately ignored. Pending appeals, executions of the colonial courts were suspended. Through this appellate procedure the privy council sought to bring the legal systems of the colonies into conformity with that of England.

APPOINTMENTS TO GOVERNMENT OFFICE. See CIVIL SERVICE; SPOILS SYSTEM.

APPOMATTOX. Village 20 miles ESE of Lynchburg, Virginia, scene of the surrender (Apr. 9, 1865) of the Confederate Gen. R.E. Lee to Union commander Gen. U.S. Grant. After the evacuation of Petersburg and Richmond, Grant surrounded the Rebels and addressed a proposal to Lee for surrender. Lee attempted to break out, but when he found that he faced impossible odds, he sent a flag of truce to Grant. Lee formally surrendered all forces then under arms in Virginia. It was the end of the Civil War and the Confederacy.

APPORTIONMENT.
Congressional Apportionment. The US Constitution as amended by the Fourteenth Amendment provides for the apportionment of seats in the US House of Representatives every ten years on the basis of population, except for the rule that each state shall have at least one representative. In 1929 Congress provided for a so-called permanent system of reapportionment, based on the national census and with the size of the House fixed at 435. Each state legislature could redraw district lines after gaining or losing seats. The 1929 act allowed for districts of grossly unequal distribution and for gerrymandering. Not until 1962, with the case of BAKER V. CARR, did the Supreme Court rule that federal courts could review apportionment cases. In 1964 the court ruled that congressional districts must be substantially equal in population.
Apportionment of State Legislatures. Until *Baker v. Carr,* constitutional standards by which apportionment should be measured were not established. In 1964 the court made these major points: the Fourteenth Amendment's equal protection clause "requires that the seats in both houses of a bicameral state legislature must be apportioned on a population basis"; apportionment must be "based substantially on population"; "the so-called federal analogy is inapplicable as a sustaining precedent for state legislative apportionments"; and deviation from the one-man, one-vote for both houses is unconstitutional.

APPRENTICESHIP. System of occupational training for a specific period under contract. In 1642 the Virginia legislature ordered that children of poor parents be apprenticed to learn "carding, knitting and spinning," while Massachusetts passed a similar law that became the prototype of legislation in the North. The voluntary contracts or indentures often included basic education. Such skills as carpentry, plumbing, and printing were typically learned by apprenticeship. The system even prevailed in the professions of law and journalism. With the expansion of educational opportunity, the apprentice system declined. Today the term "apprentice" is often used loosely to refer to any person learning a new trade.

APPROPRIATIONS BY CONGRESS. The congressional appropriations process begins each year with the president's budget requests. Currently about twelve separate appropriations bills are considered each year: customarily first by the subcommittees of the House Appropriations Committee, then by the full committee, and then by the full House. Similar units act in the Senate, and conference committees attempt to resolve House-Senate differences. Their recommendations return to each house for approval. The president then accepts or rejects each bill. Initially Congress acts in the context of the executive budget: it is free to accept, amend, or reject the president's proposals. Normally, Congress accepts them or amends them only incrementally.

AQUIDNECK ISLAND. Indian name for Rhode Island, largest island in Narragansett Bay and one of the components of the state whose official name is Rhode Island and the Providence Plantations. Purchased from the Narragansett Indians in 1638.

ARAB-AMERICAN RELATIONS. Before World War I the United States had no important political connections with the Arab world; and interest in the Arab world's strategic location and its vast oil reserves came mostly after World War II. The United States obtained air bases in Saudi Arabia, Morocco, and Libya, and backed American oil companies' efforts in Arab areas. Yet for several years after the war, the United States avoided deep involvement in Arab affairs, preferring to work through Britain and France to protect US interests. Meanwhile, deepening American association with European colonial powers and strong support for Israel produced the first serious strains between the United States and the Arabs. Nevertheless, Arab-American relations remained reasonably good. These relations took a turn for the worse in 1955 and 1956 after Secretary of State John Foster

Dulles refused to sell arms to Egypt and withdrew abruptly the US offer to help that country finance the building of the Aswan dam. Dulles's acts precipitated Egypt's nationalizing of the Suez Canal and the first major penetration by the Soviet Union into the Middle East (the USSR agreed to sell Egypt arms and to help finance the Aswan dam). American opposition to the British-French-Israeli invasion of Egypt in 1956 brought about some improvement in Arab-American relations, although the Eisenhower administration continued to back conservative, pro-Western regimes and oppose the more nationalistic, "socialist" governments. The Kennedy administration attempted a more even-handed policy toward the Arab world, but the Johnson administration's strong backing of Israel worsened US relations with the Arabs. The Nixon administration continued that policy, causing the worst rift in history between Arabs and Americans: the 1973 Arab oil embargo against the United States (lifted in 1974). Shortly after Jimmy Carter became president, he began a series of meetings with Arab and Israeli statesmen to bring about a settlement in the Middle East. His efforts bore fruit in 1978 when Israel and Egypt signed the CAMP DAVID AGREEMENT. That agreement was harshly criticized in other Arab quarters, as was Israel's more truculent policy toward its Arab neighbors. Israel's invasion of Lebanon in 1982 once again put a strain on Arab-American relations as American negotiators (and an international peace-keeping force, one part of which consisted of US marines) attempted to restore order among Christians, Jews, and various factions of Muslims in that country.

ARANJUEZ, CONVENTION OF (Apr. 12, 1779). Provided for the entrance of Spain into the revolutionary war as an ally of France, in case Great Britain should reject (which it did) Spain's offer of mediation.

ARAPAHO. Algonkin-speaking Plains tribe, who appear to have lived in the Red R valley in early historic times. They pushed into the Dakotas and Wyoming, adapted to bison hunting, and assimilated the Plains war pattern. Allied with the Cheyenne but warred intermittently with other Plains groups. The tribe was dispersed following US treaty and reservation allocation.

ARBELLA. Flagship on the fleet in which members of the Massachusetts Bay Company and Puritan emigrants sailed (1630) from England to Salem.

ARBITRATION. Labor-grievance arbitration as a part of the collective-bargaining procedure began in the 1930s with New Deal legislation. Since then it has become not merely a permissible activity but advocated as national policy. Commercial arbitration is a much older practice and ranges from automobile accident claims to international-trade arbitration involving many millions of dollars. The American Arbitration Association, founded 1926, is a leading tribunal for commercial arbitration.

ARBOR DAY. Originated in Nebraska in 1872 as a day to plant trees, it is now observed in virtually every state on the last Friday in April.

ARBUTHNOT AND AMBRISTER, CASE OF. In 1818 Gen. Andrew Jackson led a raid into the Spanish territory of East Florida, attacking the Seminole there. He captured Indian collaborators Alexander Arbuthnot and Robert Ambrister, British traders. Both were tried and shot.

ARCHAEOLOGY AND PREHISTORY, NORTH AMERICAN. Human beings entered the Western Hemisphere after millions of years of development in the Old World. Archaeologists recognize three major stages of North America's prehistoric cultures: the Lithic, the Archaic, and the Formative.

Lithic. Characterized by small bands of hunters and gatherers, exploiting the now-extinct Pleistocene environments about 10,000 years ago and earlier. Their tools consisted primarily of chipped stone artifacts. Early Lithic cultures are characterized by rough, percussion-flaked stone choppers, scrapers, and knives. No one site has been agreed upon as dating from this period, but several are intriguing possibilities. In contrast, the middle Lithic offers numerous examples in both number of sites and in dating control. For example, at Old Crow Flats, Yukon, a toothed skin flesher made on a caribou tibia, mammoth- and horse-bone artifacts, a few possible stone artifacts, and hundreds of apparently artificially broken bones were found among

several tons of vertebrate fossils. A series of human skulls also has been dated to this period. The late Lithic was a time of big-game hunting in the High Plains and Southwest. The Clovis culture, characterized by the use of fluted lanceolate projectile points and the exploitation of mammoth, was the earliest and most widespread of the late Lithic cultures, dating to about 11,250 years ago. Archaeologists generally agree that man's early movement into the Americas was across a dry land bridge that periodically stretched between Siberia and Alaska. Accumulating evidence indicates that man was in the Americas as a generalized Mongoloid physical type by at least 25,000 years ago.

Archaic. Emphasized exploitation of seasonally available resources. In the East the progressive adaptations to forest, riverine, and coastal conditions begun at the end of the Pleistocene culminated in the developed broad-spectrum hunter-gatherer lifeways some 5,000 years ago. This Eastern Archaic was characterized by polished and chipped stone artifacts and a semisedentary, or even sedentary, existence in some localities. West of the Rockies, the Western Archaic, or Desert, culture was essentially an adaptation to arid land with sparse vegetation, although semisedentary societies based on fishing and acorn-gathering emerged along the Pacific Coast. Typical artifacts were baskets and milling stones.

Formative. Molded by intensive plant cultivation. The Formative was not a continent-wide stage but was limited by climatic factors. The incipient domestication of native plants began about 3,000 years ago in the Mississippi Valley and other midcontinent riverine areas. This innovation was perhaps the result from a stimulus from the Desert Archaic, where corn had been cultivated 6,000 years earlier. The Eastern cultigens (sunflower, goosefoot, sumpweed, and pumpkin) were soon supplemented by Middle American domesticates that had already reached the Southwest between 3000 BC and 2000 BC. Primitive corncobs appear at Bat Cave, New Mexico, in a Desert culture context by this early period. Squash and gourd were apparently introduced into the East from the Southwest by about 1000 BC. A cultural florescence was experienced by the Adena and Hopewell peoples in the Eastern Woodlands between about 600 BC and AD 250. They made pottery, planted some domesticates, and constructed impressive mounds and earthworks. In general, Formative settlements can be distinguished by their greater size, complexity, and permanence; by expanded food storage capacity; and by new, more complex patterns of social organization. Such settlements are represented in the Southwest by the Anasazi, Mogollon, and Hohokam cultures. Strong and direct influence from Mexico is clearly evident in the presence of exotic artifacts, stepped pyramids, and ball courts. The town-and-temple, mound-and-plaza complex developed in the Mississippi drainage system sometime between AD 500 and AD 800; the complex reached its apex with the appearance of Mississippian cultures shortly afterward. The spectacular site of Cahokia in East St. Louis, Illinois, covered six square miles. Both Woodland- and Mississippian-influenced village-farming communities had become widespread throughout the East to the Plains periphery by AD 1000 to AD 1200. By about AD 1300, the cultural climaxes in the East and Southwest had waned under the impact of changing climatic and social conditions, although a village-farming lifeway continued to dominate both areas to the historic period.

ARCHANGEL, US TROOPS AT. In March 1918, after Russia had signed a separate peace with Germany, the Allies landed troops at the Russian ports of Murmansk and Archangel, where military supplies had been stockpiled by Allied ships. The unstable Bolshevik government at first welcomed the landings; but by August the Allied posture had become anti-Bolshevik, and Archangel was seized by an Allied force, 40 percent of which was American. Civil war was raging in Russia. Britain and France favored the Whites (i.e., non-Bolsheviks) and President Wilson's urge toward strict neutrality was compromised. By October the US force was responsible for a front of nearly 450 miles. Removal of the troops began in June 1919.

ARCHITECTURE.

American Indian. Indian house types varied so greatly that a general statement is impossible. Hunting peoples favored the movable skin tent, exemplified by the conical tipi. The domed wickiup was developed by seasonally moving peoples. Permanently settled gatherers depended basically on brush, straw, or matting. Thatched, round houses in central California contrast with multiple-family elongated tents of matting, each family occupying a single segment. The central Eskimo's igloo constituted the one native American instance of the keystone arch. Western Eskimo made sod houses with a central firepit. The beautifully elaborate plank houses of the Northwest appear to be variants of this pattern. The same semisubterranean style appears among the Pueblo in the ceremonial underground chamber, the kiva, center of all ritual. Pueblo dwellings were originally made of adobe and stone; adobe bricks are post-Spanish. The birch bark lozenge-shaped tent, the wigwam, generally appeared among the Algonkin-speaking peoples of the Northeast. The Iroquois offer a variation with elm bark covering. Wattle-and-daub houses appear in the round, rectangular, or L-shaped cabins of the Gulf peoples.

Spanish Colonial Styles. From the 1540s the Spaniards, employing Indian labor, combined Indian adobe techniques with baroque decorative forms from Europe. Forts and mission churches were built mainly of wood, but the greatest work was done in stone. The last phase of Spanish colonial architecture produced settlements in Texas (18th c.) and Arizona and California (18th and 19th c.); they incorporated the arch, vault, and dome, as well as rich Spanish baroque stone carving.

French Colonial Styles. New Orleans became (in the late 17th and early 18th c.) the greatest center of French architectural styles. Construction was primarily that of squared logs set upright and chinked with stone. Other buildings reflect the late medieval French traditions in form and construction: massive framing; well-developed support systems for high, sloping roofs, flared at the eaves and often heavy with tile coverings; and stucco or boarding over stone-chinked or brick-filled frames. The galerie is a prominent feature of these houses, on from one to four sides, usually covered by a second pitch from the eave flare. In lowlands, houses were frequently raised on an exposed basement, and thus the two-story galleried form of raised cottage or plantation house was developed. It became common all along the Gulf Coast.

Late Medieval and Early Renaissance Traditions. As soon as they could, the early settlers built houses as much like their former homes as possible: In New England, English-style half-timbered frames covered with clapboards or shingles; in New Netherlands, Dutch, Flemish, and Huguenot houses of brick, stone, and wood; in New Sweden, log, frame and stone buildings; and in Maryland, Virginia, and the Carolinas, brick and frame English houses. These houses contained a few Renaissance technical advances (developed flues and chimneys, plastered walls, glass windows), but they followed late-medieval traditions in the basic framing and covering techniques. At Williamsburg, Virginia, the town plan and capitol, college, and governor's palace represent the greatest single American monument to the Italian Renaissance style.

Later Anglo-Palladianism. Palladianism became the accepted "gentlemanly" style of architecture for the late 18th c. Many of the Anglo-Palladian ideas came to the English colonies in design books by eminent architects, notably James Gibbs's *Book of Architecture* (1728).

Neoclassicism and the Federal Style. Drawing primarily on the severest architecture of republican Rome and democratic Greece, romantic classicism provided the framework for the first great American national style. The plan for the new capital city of Washington provided a single focus for architects, including Thomas Jefferson, who had shown himself a master of the neoclassical style in his design of the Virginia state capitol (1785). Benjamin Latrobe, an English architect, working in the United States, produced impressive neoclassic buildings in Virginia, Philadelphia, and in Washington. President Jefferson appointed him architect of the capitol and surveyor of the public buildings. Charles Bulfinch succeeded Latrobe as architect of the capitol in 1817. Jefferson's own architecture continued to develop, in his rebuilding of Monticello as a Franco-Palladian villa and his brilliant design for the University of Virginia.

Growing Eclecticism. The period between 1825 and 1850 was dominated by the Greek revival, accompanied by an even stronger Gothic revival. Gothic became the "correct" style for churches, and the Gothic cottage became popular. In addition, there were Egyptian and Italian-villa styles. Around 1850 came the Romanesque and Renaissance revival. Technical change accelerated stylistic changes. Most important was the invention of the "balloon" frame, in which lightweight prefabricated members were nailed together, rather than heavy frame members dressed, jointed, and fitted by hand. The steel skeleton precluded the need for load-bearing walls, and the extensive use of cast iron revolutionized building practices as well as architectural possibilities.

Beaux Arts and the Rise of Modern Architecture. The École des Beaux Arts in Paris was the leading training ground for architects after ca. 1850. Architects trained there, including American practitioners, created trend-setting designs in academic French and English Gothic and Renaissance styles. Among the Paris-trained American architects were the highly influential Richard Morris Hunt, Henry Hobson Richardson, and Louis H. Sullivan. Sullivan's most celebrated pupil and disciple was Frank Lloyd Wright, often regarded as the father of modern American architecture. Two of Richardson's disciples, Charles McKim and Stanford White, were perhaps the most influential of all American architects. From their firm, McKim, Mead and White (and its chief rival Carèrre and Hastings) came the great turn-of-the-century Italian Renaissance style; it was a style especially appropriate to large public and commercial buildings. Domestic architecture remained eclectic. Wright was building his prairie houses, and detached houses and cottages were being built in the Queen Anne, Oriental, and Mission styles. Later Spanish colonial revival would sweep California and Florida.

International Style. The 1920s saw a blending of the native prairie architecture of Wright with the crisp, plain style favored by avant-garde European architects. It became known as the International style, and was especially evident in the work of Philip Johnson and Ludwig Mies van der Rohe. Most of the commercial buildings, especially skyscrapers, put up after World War II were variations of the International style. By the 1980s, however, there appeared to be a reaction to the austerity of the International style. Led by Philip Johnson himself, the new style, known as Postmodernism, revived some historical styles such as the Renaissance and projected a more "romantic" look.

ARCHIVES, NATIONAL. Created 1934 as an independent agency of the executive branch, to have custody of records transferred to the National Archives Building, Washington, D.C. The Federal Register Act of 1935 provided that all regulations intended to have the force of law must be filed at the National Archives and published in the *Federal Register* before being put into effect. Those of continuing effect are also printed in the *Code of Federal Regulations*. All but a few of the 19th-c. records and even greater quantities of 20th-c. records were in the building by 1945. The *Guide to the Records in the National Archives* (1948) describes more than 800,000 cubic feet of records accessioned by 1947. In 1949 the National Archives was made a bureau of the General Services Administration and renamed the National Archives and Records Service.

ARCHIVES, STATE AND LOCAL. State archival functions are variously assigned to a state historical society or commission, a state department of archives and history, a state library, or the secretary of state. Some states have modern, specially constructed buildings to house the archives. Most state archival agencies have some authority over the records of counties, municipalities, and other state-created local governing bodies. Municipal archival programs exist in some of the larger cities.

ARCTIC EXPLORATION. See BYRD'S POLAR FLIGHTS; POLAR EXPEDITIONS.

ARDENNES, BATTLE OF THE. See BULGE, BATTLE OF THE.

d'ARGES COLONY. In 1787 Pierre Wouves d'Arges acted as agent of the Spanish minister to the United States in proposing a plan to protect Louisiana and Florida from American encroachment by inducing Kentucky families to settle within the Spanish domain. Liberal terms were offered and a considerable number of Americans took advantage of the offer and became Spanish citizens.

ARGONAUTS OF CALIFORNIA. See FORTY-NINERS.

ARIKARA. Northern Plains tribe, river-bottom farmers in an area otherwise devoted to bison hunting. They had migrated N from the Caddoan focus of the lower Mississippi and thus were the northernmost of the Caddoan-speaking Indians. In the 1880s they were assigned to Fort Berthold Reservation, North Dakota.

ARIZONA. The forty-eighth state, it contains a northern plateau, central mountain belt, and dry, southern desert. In each of these regions, ancient cultures flourished from ca. 500 BC to ca. AD 1350 and then mysteriously decayed. The inhabitants that emerged later were the Pima, Papago, Apache, and Navajo. Fray Marcos de Niza ventured into the E mountains in 1539, followed in 1540 by Coronado, whose captains discovered the Grand Canyon and ascended the Colorado R to Yuma. Missionaries were in the area by the 1630s. In 1736 rich silver discoveries were made near present Nogales. That drew the first settlers. Spain established the first presidio-town Tubac in 1752 but moved the garrison N to Tucson in 1775. In 1821 Arizona became a part of Mexico and entered a period of extended neglect. In 1848 Arizona N of the Gila R passed to the United States (see GUADALUPE HIDALGO, TREATY OF). In 1850 it became part of New Mexico Territory; and by the GADSDEN PURCHASE of 1853, S Arizona was added to New Mexico. In 1856 Congress established the Arizona Territory. Gold and silver discoveries spurred population growth, the army forced hostile Indians onto reservations, a cattle industry developed, and the transcontinental railroad came through. In 1912 Arizona was admitted as a state, with Phoenix as the capital. The two world wars greatly increased the state's prosperity, with its great growth coming after World War II. During the 1960s Arizona enjoyed an unprecedented prosperity from mining (producing nearly 90 percent of the nation's copper), agriculture, manufacturing, and tourism. Pop.: 2,717,866 (1980).

ARK AND DOVE. The two vessels that brought the first colonists, about two hundred in number, to Maryland. Sailing from the Isle of Wight, Nov. 22, 1633, the two ships entered the Potomac during the first week of March 1634; they explored until March 25, when it was decided to make the first permanent settlement, still known as St. Marys.

ARKANSAS. First explored by de Soto in 1541 and claimed for France by the sieur de La Salle and Henry de Tonti in 1682; the first permanent settlement was founded in 1686 by Tonti. As part of Louisiana, Arkansas remained in French and Spanish hands until the Louisiana Purchase made it American territory in 1803. Originally part of Missouri Territory, it became a separate territory in 1819. Little Rock became the capital in 1821, and in 1836 it became a state. With some hesitancy, Arkansas joined the Confederacy, and by 1863 the N half of the state was in Union hands. The railroad age opened the rich coal, bauxite, and timber resources of Arkansas; and cotton became the main cash crop. Arkansas lost considerable population during the Great Depression but has been growing since World War II. Pop. 2,296,000 (1980).

ARKANSAS, DESTRUCTION OF THE (Aug. 5, 1862). After the Confederate ironclad *Arkansas* passed through the federal fleet before Vicksburg to cooperate in Gen. J.C. Breckinridge's attempt to recapture Baton Rouge, its machinery became disabled within five miles of its destination. The ship was run ashore and blown up to avoid capture.

ARKANSAS POST. Village on the N bank of the Arkansas R, near its junction with the Mississippi R. It was the earliest (1680) French settlement in the lower Mississippi Valley. When French Louisiana was divided in 1721, Arkansas Post became the administrative center for the Arkansas District. It remained an important center and the site of a Jesuit mission. It was captured by Union troops in 1863 and after the Civil War it declined.

ARKANSAS RIVER. Known to the early French as Rivière des Ark or d'Ozark, the 1,450-mile river was discovered and explored by de Soto in 1541. Jolliet and Marquette reached its mouth in 1673. Its early history centered around ARKANSAS POST. The headwaters of the Arkansas were in Spanish territory until a treaty with Spain in 1819 made the Arkansas R west of the 100th meridian a part of the W boundary of the United States.

ARKANSAS RIVER ROUTE. The mountain, or Pikes Peak, division of the Santa Fe Trail, which avoided the dangerous desert country. It followed the Arkansas R to old Bent's Fort and there turned SW to the mountains and crossed the Raton Pass.

ARKANSAS TRAVELER. Arkansas's best-known piece of folklore and a favorite old-time breakdown fiddle tune. The tune was first published in 1847, but the authors have never been determined. Newspapers, books, and articles of commerce have taken the title.

ARKS. Until 1860 arks—also known as flatboats, broadhorns, Kentucky boats, and Orleans boats—carried a large part of downstream traffic on rivers of the West. Cheaply constructed of green wood, shaped like boxes with raked bows, and sometimes roofed over, they were steered by a long oar and were sold for lumber or firewood at their destinations.

ARKWRIGHT MACHINERY. A spinning machine developed by Richard Arkwright in England ca. 1770. Samuel Slater smuggled its design to Providence, Rhode Island, and constructed a set of Arkwright machines carrying seventy-two spindles. These were installed in 1790 at Pawtucket, Rhode Island, introducing the modern factory to the United States.

ARLINGTON NATIONAL CEMETERY. In Virginia, across the river from Washington, D.C. Buried therein are the dead from every war since the Revolution and distinguished statesmen, including John F. Kennedy. The TOMB OF THE UNKNOWNS is there.

ARMAMENTS. See DEFENSE, NATIONAL.

ARMED MERCHANTMEN. See MERCHANTMEN, ARMED.

"ARM IN ARM" CONVENTION. See NATIONAL UNION ("ARM IN ARM") CONVENTION.

ARMINIANISM. See METHODISTS; REFORMED CHURCHES.

ARMISTICE DAY. In October 1918 Germany sued for peace; on Nov. 8, the Allies submitted their terms, based on the FOURTEEN POINTS. Germany accepted the terms and the armistice began on November 11. Until 1954 that date was observed as a legal holiday in the United States. Congress then officially changed the name of the holiday from Armistice Day to Veterans Day.

ARMORY ART SHOW (1913). One of the turning points in the acceptance of modern art by Americans, conducted from Feb. 15 to March 15 in the 69th Regimental Armory, New York City. It was the largest American display of contemporary art styles up to that time and was widely publicized.

ARMS MANUFACTURING. The manufacture of arms has been an important industry in the United States since colonial times. A key element in the success of the American revolutionary armies was the presence of many gunsmiths in the colonies. The key to modern machine making—the use of interchangeable parts—was demonstrated first in the arms industry by Eli Whitney and Samuel Colt early in the 19th c. Arms making requires precise workmanship to ensure that weapons can be fired accurately and safely. Some of the more famous American-made weapons were the Kentucky long rifle, the Colt six-shooter, the Winchester repeating rifle, and the Springfield Model 1903. During the 20th c., weapons became very complex and sophisticated, and weapon equipment began to include such devices as radar sights, heat-sensing projectiles, and proximity fuses.

ARMS RACE WITH THE SOVIET UNION. See RUSSIA, US RELATIONS WITH.

ARMSTRONG, FORT. One of a chain of frontier defenses erected after the War of 1812, located at Rock River, Ill., at the foot of Rock Island, in the Mississippi R.

ARMY, CONFEDERATE. A small regular force was established by the Confederate Provisional Congress on March 6, 1861, to consist of one corps of engineers, one of artillery, six regiments of infantry, one of cavalry, and four staff departments. This was soon overshadowed by the voluntary forces, or provisional army. By the end of April, President Jefferson Davis had called for 82,000 men. By August 400,000 volunteers were authorized. With the passage of the conscription act in April 1862, men were taken into the provi-

sional army directly. Serious difficulties were encountered in arming, clothing, and feeding the troops; those difficulties were to plague the Rebels throughout the war. The Confederacy was divided into military departments under commanders responsible only to the war department and the president. Other than President Davis himself, there was no commander in chief until Feb. 6, 1865, when Robert E. Lee was appointed. The number of enlistments in the Confederate armies has long been in dispute. Probably between 800,000 and 900,000 actually enrolled; but probably no more than 600,000 were actually under arms at any one time.

ARMY, UNION. When Fort Sumter was fired on, the United States had an army of only 16,000, and its effectiveness was soon lessened by the resignations of Robert E. Lee and other southern officers. Northern states feverishly raised volunteers, and by April 1962 the governors had offered some 300,000 troops. Starting in July 1861 Congress authorized a volunteer army of 500,000 men and authorized President Lincoln to call for 42,000 volunteers and 22,700 regulars. The regular army was used in the war for border defense against Indians, with the war being fought by volunteers. General officers were political appointees of the governors, with the lower ranked officers elected by the enlisted men. Thus discipline and efficiency suffered. By the middle of 1862 the army was so badly depleted by disease and battle losses that an additional 300,000 volunteers were called for; and in August a draft of 300,000 was required. Only about 65,000 were produced, and a further draft action was needed in March 1863. This threat of conscription stimulated volunteers. By the war's end the total strength of the army was about 1,000,000.

ARMY, UNITED STATES. The US army has traditionally consisted of a small professional force, the regular army, augmented in wartime by citizen soldiers: militia, national guard, organized reserve, volunteers, and draftees.

Revolutionary War (1775–82). The accepted birthdate of the US army is June 14, 1775, the day the Second Continental Congress appointed a committee to draw up rules and regulations to govern the New England army that had gathered near Boston and also voted to enlist ten rifle companies. Congress selected George Washington to be commander in chief. The Continental army, probably never more than 30,000 in strength, was composed mainly of infantry and artillery, with a small contingent of cavalry. At the end of the war, the army was almost entirely disbanded, reaching a nadir of 80 men guarding stores in 1784. The new Constitution gave Congress power to raise an army and levy taxes to support it and made the president commander in chief.

War of 1812. During the troubled years leading to the War of 1812, the regular army was expanded to about 6,000 men and reached a top strength of about 38,000 in 1814. Perhaps an equal number served in state volunteer units and even more in the short-term militia.

Peacetime Army (1815–45). After the War of 1812 the regular army developed the professionalism and efficient administration it had previously lacked. West Point became a vital force in creating a professionally trained body of officers. The army, nevertheless, was kept quite small for its tasks: policing the frontiers, a long war against the Seminole in Florida, and the manning of coastal fortifications. On the eve of the Mexican War, the army's strength stood at about 8,500.

Mexican War and After. The regular army underwent only limited expansion during the Mexican War, reaching to a peak of about 50,000. It showed a remarkable proficiency, particularly in the artillery. The immense new territories acquired by the war increased the army's responsibilities, and its peacetime strength reached 17,678 by 1858. In protecting emigrants to California and Oregon, the army encountered mounted Indians and the cavalry came into its own.

Civil War. See ARMY, CONFEDERATE; ARMY, UNION.

Post-Civil War Period. With the surrender of the South, the great Union army was hastily demobilized; by mid-1866 only a regular force of 57,000 remained. The strength was cut to 45,000 in 1869 and to 27,442 in 1876. The army played a major role in the occupation of the South, and the last troops were not removed until 1877. The army's major strength was again scattered at posts in the West, battling the Indians.

Spanish-American War. The army in 1898, scattered all over the continent, was poorly prepared for an overseas venture. The force was quickly strengthened to a final total of 247,717, consisting of an expanded regular army and volunteer units, mostly national guard. In Cuba and the Philippines, sickness and disease took a far higher toll than enemy bullets.

Postwar Reforms. After the Spanish-American War, the commanding general was replaced by a chief of staff heading up a general staff. The Army War College was established, and in 1903 the national guard was reorganized as the organized militia. The army between 1900 and 1916 ranged between 65,000 and 108,000. By the later date, it was equipped with new and destructive weapons, such as the machine gun, and was beginning to experiment with motor transport and the airplane. Its responsibilities included suppressing the Philippine Insurrection (1899–1902), relief duty in China during the Boxer Rebellion (1899), occupying Cuba (1899–1902), building the Panama Canal (1907–14), and conducting a punitive expedition to Mexico (1916).

World War I. The United States entered World War I with the army unprepared. A national selective service system was used to bring the army up to strength; even national guard units were drafted. The army was expanded from 210,000 to 3,685,000, of whom about 2,000,000 served in France as part of the AMERICAN EXPEDITIONARY FORCES. The army was again quickly demobilized at the end of the war, bringing its strength down to 202,394 by 1920.

World War II. In 1940 the entire national guard was called to federal service, a one-year draft was authorized, and most of the officers from the organized reserve were called to active duty. At the time of Pearl Harbor, the army numbered 1,643,500; but it was only semitrained and woefully short of modern equipment. The national army reached a peak strength of 8,300,000, more than 5,000,000 of whom served overseas.

After 1945. By 1949 rapid demobilization had reduced the army to 591,000 (not counting members of the air force, now a separate service). The outbreak of the Korean War in June 1950 reversed the trend toward demobilization. By July 1951 the army had been increased to a total of 1,500,000, accomplished by calling up national guard and reserve units and by expanded draft calls. Demobilization at the end of the Korean War was far more gradual than had been the case at the end of past wars. Nevertheless, by 1959 the army had been reduced to 862,000 men. The Berlin crisis in 1962–63 brought a call-up of reserves that increased army strength to 975,000. Expansion began again in 1965 as more troops were being sent to Vietnam. By 1968 army strength had risen again to the 1,500,000 level. The gradual withdrawal from Vietnam, starting in 1968, brought army strength down to 800,500 by July 1973. The draft was ended in 1973 and since then the army has been an all-volunteer force, as it had traditionally been in peacetime before World War II. In 1982 the army's strength stood at 788,026.

ARMY HOSPITALS. Primitive hospitals were provided for soldiers in the Revolution, War of 1812, and the Mexican War. The Civil War saw a considerable advance with the adoption of the system of evacuation to field hospitals set up in tents where the sick and wounded could get immediate attention and pavilion hospitals set up in permanent locations from which the seriously wounded could be evacuated. The Spanish-American War saw the introduction of permanent general hospitals. The main improvement in the Korean and Vietnam wars was the development of mobile surgical hospitals operating close behind the lines and the use of helicopters for evacuation of the wounded.

ARMY OF OCCUPATION (1918–23). The American Third Army crossed into Germany in December 1918, taking station in the N sector of the Coblenz bridgehead. Units were engaged in duties of occupation and training, including participation in civil administration, until July 2, 1919, when the Third Army was succeeded by the American Forces in Germany. At noon on Jan. 27, 1923, occupation was officially relinquished.

ARMY ON THE FRONTIER. The principal functions of the US army stationed near the frontier settlements were (1) guarding the settlements from hostile Indians; (2) developing and protecting the communication between the older settlements and the frontier, by exploring the West, constructing roads, and defending the overland trails, water routes, and later telegraph and railroad lines; and (3) policing the frontier until the civil governments could establish order. By ca. 1890 these functions had mostly come to an end.

ARMY POSTS. As the United States extended westward, army posts were usually established at the western fringe of settlement or beyond at strategic places in Indian country. They were often the most important points along routes of travel and were trading centers as well as refuges for settlers. Many towns that grew up around these forts still retain their names. Sites of newer army posts have been selected for such reasons as suitability as training centers or proximity to transportation and industrial facilities and the availability of a supply of labor. Political patronage has also often been a factor.

ARMY WAR COLLEGE. Established 1901 as the nucleus of a general staff. Its function has continuously been that of providing training of selected officers for higher command and general staff duties. Now located at Carlisle Barracks, Pennsylvania.

ARNOLD'S MARCH TO QUEBEC. In the summer of 1775 Col. Benedict Arnold laid before George Washington a plan for attacking Canada. The classic route by way of Lake George, Lake Champlain, and the Richelieu R was assigned to Gen. Richard Montgomery. Arnold went by sea and up the Kennebec R and Dead R and reached the St. Lawrence R on November 9. In the meantime, Montgomery had reached Montreal. Montgomery and Arnold assaulted Quebec on the night of December 31. The city was well fortified, however, and the effort failed. Montgomery was killed and Arnold wounded.

ARNOLD'S RAID IN VIRGINIA. In December 1780 the British sent an expedition into Virginia, mainly to block the mouth of the Chesapeake. The command was given to the traitor Benedict Arnold. Arnold seized boats on the James R and pushed up to Westover, Richmond, Westham, and Portsmouth, marauding and pillaging. In March 1781 he was joined and outranked by Maj. Gen. William Phillips. They led another devastating expedition through City Point, Petersburg, Manchester, and Warwick. Throughout these movements, the British were harassed by the inferior forces of the marquis de Lafayette and Anthony Wayne.

ARNOLD'S TREASON. Brig. Gen. Benedict Arnold of the Continental army had fought gallantly for the American cause from Ticonderoga (1775) to Saratoga (1777). But by the spring of 1779 several motives led him to treason: (1) repeated slights by Congress; (2) resentment at the authorities of Pennsylvania who had court-martialed him; (3) need for money; and (4) opposition to the French alliance of 1778. Throughout the rest of 1779 and 1780 he transmitted military intelligence to the British. On July 12, 1780, he accepted the British command at West Point and became a brigadier general in the British army. He went to England after the war and died there June 14, 1801.

AROOSTOOK WAR (1838–39). Confrontation occasioned by the failure of the United States and Great Britain to determine the boundary between New Brunswick and Maine. Both Maine and Massachusetts made grants to settlers along the Aroostook R, in territory claimed by the British. Attempts at compromise failed and by 1839, 10,000 Maine troops were dispatched there. Gen. Winfield Scott then negotiated a truce with the British. It resulted in a boundary commission, whose findings were incorporated into the WEBSTER-ASHBURTON TREATY of 1842.

ARPENT. Old French unit of land measure, still sometimes used in Louisiana. Standardized at 192 feet, or a square of that dimension (about five-sixths of an acre).

ARREST. The Fourth Amendment of the US Constitution guarantees against unreasonable seizures, and it is now established that an illegal arrest is an illegal seizure within the meaning of the amendment. Thus arrests based on mere suspicion or common rumor are illegal. The Fourth Amendment provides that "no Warrants shall issue but upon probable cause." Although the rule is otherwise with respect to searches, arrests for felonies may be made without warrants.

ARREST, ARBITRARY, DURING THE CIVIL WAR. Freedom from arbitrary arrest, synonymous in Anglo-Saxon tradition with civil liberty, has nevertheless often been abridged during times of "rebellion or invasion." The

Civil War, in particular, brought widespread abridgments. President Lincoln issued several proclamations in which the privilege of habeas corpus was suspended, the justification being the control of antiwar activities. Chief Justice Taney (and others) criticized the president's actions, holding that the legislative branch rather than the executive had this constitutional authority. Lincoln defended his actions against charges of dictatorship and no court action stopped him. The Confederacy likewise made summary arrests, and for the same reasons.

ARROWSMITH'S MAP. *A Map Exhibiting All the New Discoveries in the Interior Part of North America.* Published in London in 1795 by Aaron Arrowsmith. It was drawn from notes furnished by the Hudson's Bay Co. Editions continued to be published until 1850.

ARSENALS. Establishment for the manufacture, repair, and storage of armaments. Historically, US arms manufacture favored governmental control rather than private production to ensure quality and uniformity. The Springfield, Massachusetts, and Harpers Ferry, West Virginia, armories were established in 1794 and 1796, respectively. The expanded production needed in wartime was supplied by private industry. In modern times arsenals contribute only a small portion of the army's total ordnance requirements.

ART. See PAINTING; SCULPTURE.

d'ARTAGUETTE'S DEFEAT (1736). The French governor of Louisiana decided to exterminate the Chickasaw because of their long and successful opposition to the French. Maj. Pierre d'Artaguette was ordered to lead a force against the Indians. The resulting battle of Ackia was a disaster: d'Artaguette was wounded and he and a score of his men were captured and burned at the stake by the Chickasaw.

ART DECO. Artistic movement of the 1920s and 1930s; its primary expression was in design of architecture, furniture, art objects, and sculpture. It is characterized by elongated forms, geometric patterns, and the use of modern technology and materials. A major example of Art Deco architecture is the Chrysler building in New York City.

ARTICLES OF CONFEDERATION. After long debate, the Continental Congress adopted the

Articles of Confederation and sent them to the states for ratification on Nov. 15, 1777. The Articles finally became law on March 1, 1781. Although the Articles have been harshly criticized as inadequate, they were generally regarded in 1781 as offering a sound national constitution. They provided for a "perpetual union" between the states. Each remained sovereign and independent and retained every right not expressly ceded to the general government. A single agency of government, the Congress, was established; each state was to appoint from two to seven delegates annually to it, and each state was to have one vote. The states were to contribute to the upkeep of the government and to supply a quota of troops. To Congress was entrusted the management of foreign affairs, war, and the postal service; it was empowered to borrow money, emit bills of credit, and determine the value of coin; it was to appoint naval officers and superior military officers, and to control Indian affairs. But none of these powers was to be exercised save by a vote of a majority of all states; and more important, they could not be exercised save by a vote of nine (out of thirteen). It soon became evident that Congress was doomed to fail: it had no way of enforcing the Articles, and efforts began almost immediately to amend them. This proved impossible and by the close of 1786 they were in widespread discredit. Many leaders were eager to find a wholly new basis of government. Yet the articles, soon to give way to the Constitution, had preserved the idea of union until national wisdom could adopt a more efficient system.

ARTILLERY. The first artillery regiment of the Continental army was raised in January 1776; by 1777 four were operating. Artillerymen manned the country's first coast defenses in 1794, leading to a traditional classification of US army artillery into field, siege and garrison, and coast artillery. Between 1808 and 1901, artillery units served variously as light or horse artillery, infantry, or in coast defense, and grew to 98 batteries. In 1901 a major reorganization resulted in seven regiments being broken into separate numbered batteries and companies of coast artillery with the the corps of artillery. Coast and field artillery became fully separate branches in 1907. Reorganization has occurred regularly since that time.

ART NOUVEAU. Art movement of the late 19th c. that had its beginnings in Western Europe. Dealing mainly with the decorative arts, it was characterized by swirling forms from nature laid over classical structures. Leading American exponents of the style were Louis Sullivan and Louis Comfort Tiffany.

"AS GOES MAINE, SO GOES THE NATION." Saying based on the supposed accuracy of Maine voters in reflecting the national mood. The saying dates to the 1840 presidential election but is no longer considered seriously by political pollsters.

ASHBURTON TREATY. See WEBSTER-ASHBURTON TREATY.

ASHBY'S GAP. A pass in the Blue Ridge Mountains leading from the Shenandoah Valley into E Virginia. In June 1863 Gen. J.E.B. Stuart held the gap to prevent Gen. Joseph Hooker from interfering with Robert E. Lee's march to Gettysburg.

ASH HOLLOW, BATTLE OF. See HARY EXPEDITION.

ASHLAND. Industrial city in NE Kentucky. Founded 1815 by settlers from Virginia, it has been an important Ohio R port since that time. Coal, oil, natural gas, and limestone are available in the vicinity. The city has iron and steel mills and oil refineries. Pop.: 27,064 (1980).

ASHLEY EXPEDITIONS. Three expeditions sent out by W.H. Ashley aimed at launching the Rocky Mountain Fur Company to compete with the Hudson's Bay Co. and older American fur companies. Organized 1822, the first expedition was attacked by the Blackfoot and driven out. Ashley personally headed the second expedition, only to be attacked by the Arikara and forced to retreat. The third expedition, led by Jedediah Smith, pushed to the Yellowstone R and penetrated to the Green R valley, the Utah trapping grounds. The party returned with a rich cache of furs, and Ashley organized an annual fur-collecting rendezvous.

ASIA, TRADE WITH. At the end of the Revolution, American merchants were released from the restrictions of the British East India

Co., and trade with Asia burgeoned. Ships from Atlantic port cities brought back tea, silks, and cotton from China and India and spices and coffee from the East Indies. The Napoleonic Wars delivered a great part of Europe's extracontinental trade into American hands. American (and British) commerce in opium in Turkey, India, and China balanced payment for the first half of the 19th c. and brought China into the world economic and political picture. In 1854 Commodore Matthew C. Perry "opened" Japan; and thereafter commerce with other parts of Asia became less important, with Japan replacing China as America's chief Asian trading partner. Japan's extraordinary economic development in the 20th c. has rendered US trade with Japan even more important. After the Communist takeover of China in the 1940s, US trade ceased. By the 1980s, however, renewed contacts were made, and trade between the United States and China again assumed importance.

ASIENTO. Slave-trading license sold in 1713 to the English South Sea Company by the Spanish crown. The company was given the exclusive right to sell 144,000 African slaves in the Spanish colonies over 30-year period.

ASSASSINATIONS, POLITICAL. On Jan. 30, 1835, an unsuccessful attempt was made to kill Andrew Jackson; the assassination of President Lincoln on April 14, 1865, was the first of great political consequence in the United States. On July 2, 1880, Charles J. Guiteau, a disappointed office seeker, shot President Garfield, who died on Sept. 19. On Sept. 6, 1901, President McKinley was mortally wounded by Leon F. Czolgosz, an anarchist. Former President Theodore Roosevelt was wounded in the chest on Oct. 14, 1912, while making a campaign speech in Milwaukee, Wisconsin. Franklin D. Roosevelt was the target of an assassination attempt on Feb. 15, 1933, in Florida by Joseph Zangara. Huey P. Long was assassinated in Baton Rouge, Louisiana, on Sept. 10, 1935. On Nov. 1, 1950, two Puerto Rican nationalists attempted to kill President Truman. On Nov. 22, 1963, President Kennedy was shot and killed in Dallas, Texas, by Lee Harvey Oswald. Kennedy's brother, Robert F. Kennedy, was killed in Los Angeles on June 5, 1968, by Sirhan Sirhan while campaigning for the presidency. The turmoil of the 1960s led to a number of assassinations. In addition to the Kennedy murders, there were those of the black leaders Medgar W. Evers, Martin Luther King, Jr., and Malcolm X, and the American Nazi party leader, George Lincoln Rockwell. In 1972 and unsuccessful attempt was made on the life of presidential candidate George Wallace of Alabama, and he was left permanently crippled. There were two unsuccessful attempts on President Ford in September 1975. In April 1981 President Reagan was shot and wounded by John W. Hinckley, Jr. (later judged insane by a jury).

ASSAY OFFICES. Assaying of gold and silver is done at all federal mints, but special assay offices were established at New York in 1853; Boise, Idaho, 1869; Helena, Mont., 1874; Deadwood, S.D., and Seattle, Wash., 1896; and Salt Lake City, Utah, 1908. These plants could receive, test, melt, and refine gold and silver bullion and foreign coins. The early mints at New Orleans, La., Charlotte, N.C., and Denver, Colo., later became assay offices. Other than the federal mints, there are now only two assay offices, New York and San Francisco.

ASSEMBLY, RIGHT OF. The First Amendment of the US Constitution provides that Congress shall make no law abridging "the right of the people peaceably to assemble." Almost all constitutional clauses on the subject of assembly speak of "peaceful" or "orderly" assembly; thus the right of assembly is not absolute. To sustain a charge of unlawful assembly, it must be proved that the defendants intended to commit an unlawful act (such as intimidation, threats, boycott, or assault) or a lawful act in a violent, boisterous, or tumultuous manner. At the same time, it is clearly established in the law that a meeting cannot be prohibited merely because unpopular changes may be advocated.

ASSEMBLY LINE. System of manufacturing in which the work moves on a conveyor belt while each worker performs a specialized operation as the product goes by. In 1785 Oliver Evans built a gristmill near Wilmington, Delaware, in which a system of conveyors and chutes powered by waterwheels provided a continuous flow through the plant. This process became general in flour milling. Subsequently, conveyor systems were used in meat-packing plants and foundries. The machine manufacture of standardized and interchangeable parts was actually of European origin but was perfected in the US through the work of men like Eli Whitney and Samuel Colt. By the 1850s it was known in Europe as the American system. These various elements of the assembly line converged in the American automobile industry, notably the Ford Motor Co. This technological breakthrough was followed by other industries where large output at low unit cost was wanted. By the 1980s an increasing amount of assembly-line work was being done by computerized robots.

ASSESSMENT OF CANDIDATES. See POLITICAL ASSESSEMENTS.

ASSINIBOINE. Northern Plains tribe that dwelled in Saskatchewan and Montana in the 18th c. Numbering about 10,000 in 1780, they played an important part in trade between whites and Indians, channeling arms to the other tribes. The Assiniboine (also spelled Assinoiboine) gradually moved W to maintain contact with the Hudson's Bay Co. They adopted the horse, tipi, and related Plains traditons, waging war against their former Dakota relatives.

ASSINIBOINE, FORT. Founded on the Missouri R (1834–35) by the American Fur Co. near the present Montana-North Dakota border. It was also a depot for inland trade with the Assiniboine, Piegan, and Blackfoot tribes.

ASSISTANT. The Massachusetts Bay Co. charter (1629) provided for eighteen assistants to be elected yearly by the stockholders. Until deputies were admitted (1634), the Court of Assistants was the colony's sole legislature. The Connecticut charter (1662) provided twelve assistants.

ASSOCIATED LOYALISTS OF NEW ENGLAND (1776–79). Pro-British associations formed in Rhode Island during its British occupation. They made several naval raids in Long Island Sound.

ASSOCIATED PRESS. Formed in May 1848 by several New York City newspapers, who agreed to divide the expense of telegraphic transmission of news from Washington, D.C., and from Europe on its arrival by ship at Boston. By the Civil War, the AP reached out over the country through member newspapers that both collected and disseminated news. In 1900 the company was incorporated as a nonprofit cooperative. By 1980 the AP served 1,365 US daily newspapers and 3,600 US radio and TV stations. It had a worldwide membership of more than 10,000.

ASSOCIATIONS. Merchant societies and political clubs organized in the 18th c. for some specific purpose. The First Continental Congress adopted the famous "association," the members pledging themselves and their constituents not to import, export, or consume British goods until their grievances were addressed. After the outbreak of hostilities, associations (both patriot and loyalist) were spontaneously formed, pledging the signers to serve their cause with their lives. They became an effective device for recruiting troops.

ASSOCIATORS. Military organization formed by Benjamin Franklin in 1747 to defend Philadelphia. Revolting against the pacifist policy of the Quakers, they formed military companies and erected two batteries on the Delaware R. The Associators disbanded after the peace of Aix-la-Chapelle in 1748.

ASTOR FUR COMPANY. See AMERICAN FUR COMPANY; ASTORIA; PACIFIC FUR COMPANY.

ASTORIA. Fur trading post established by John Jacob Astor at the mouth of the Columbia R in Oregon in 1811 under Duncan McDougal. The War of 1812 sounded the doom of the enterprise and in 1813 the pro-British McDougal sold all the Astor interest on the Columbia to the North West Co. The post, renamed Fort George, was restored to the United States in 1818.

ASTOR PLACE RIOT. Took place in New York City on May 10, 1849, the outgrowth of a long-standing feud between the American actor Edwin Forrest and the English tragedian William Charles Macready. It was also essentially an expression of anti-British feeling. When police failed to disperse a pro-Forrest mob outside the Astor Place Opera House, where Macready was starring in *Macbeth*, the militia was called out. Twenty-two people were killed and 36 wounded.

ASTRONAUTICS. See SPACE EXPLORATION.

ASTRONOMY. The first major American observatories were the Harvard Observatory (1839) and the US Naval Observatory, Washington, D.C. (1842). The *Astronomical Journal* was founded in 1849. Until 1900, most American astronomers were occupied with visual observations or with calculation of orbits of solar-system objects. After that, interest shifted increasingly toward astrophysics and stellar astronomy. Photographic observation methods quickly superseded visual ones. At Lick Observatory in California, W.W. Campbell devised improved spectrographs for the 36-inch refractor. Frank Schlesinger perfected powerful new photographic techniques for measuring star distances. Harvard's programs of spectral classification culminated in the nine-volume *Henry Draper Catalogue* of stars (1918–24). Studies of the sun became prominent. The Mount Wilson Solar Observatory in California was built in 1904; its 100-inch reflector began operating in 1919. Edwin P. Hubble detected (1923) Cepheid variables in the great Andromeda nebula and later (1929) formulated the relationship between the distances and red shifts of galaxies. In 1949 powerful new equipment was installed in the Palomar Mountain observatory in California. It included the 200-inch Hale reflector, the 48-inch Schmidt telescope, and photoelectric devices for more accurate photometry of faint stars. During the 1950s and 1960s, electronic computers revolutionized theoretical astronomy. Especially notable were the calculations of stellar models and their evolutionary changes and the refined studies of the moon's motion. In 1951 H.I. Ewen and E.M. Purcell observed microwave line radiation emitted by hydrogen in interstellar gas clouds, and many observatories and laboratories built large radio telescopes to study it. Quasars remained a major unsolved mystery, and from 1968 on, much attention was given to pulsars. Instrumental artificial satellites launched by the National Aeronautics and Space Administration (NASA) from the mid-1960s observed the sun from new perspectives. The moon was mapped in detail and its surface inspected by landings, while Mars was viewed at close hand. Space probes surveyed Jupiter, Saturn, Venus, and Mercury.

ATCHISON. City established in Kansas on the Missouri R in 1854 as a center for efforts to make the territory a slave state. It later became the terminus for three railroads, including the Atchison, Topeka and Santa Fe. The city remains an important wholesale center. Pop.: 11,407 (1980).

ATCHISON, TOPEKA AND SANTA FE RAILROAD. See RAILROADS, SKETCHES OF PRINCIPAL LINES.

ATHAPASCAN. One of the major groupings of Indian languages. Tribes speaking Athapascan languages occupied a large part of C Alaska, W Canada, and the US Southwest (e.g., the Apache).

ATHERTON COMPANY. A syndicate headed by Maj. Humphrey Atherton and by Connecticut Gov. John Winthrop, the younger. They formed a company that, by purchase from the Indians (1659) and foreclosure of a questionable mortgage (1662), claimed title to all the Narragansett country. Jurisdiction was long claimed by both Rhode Island and Connecticut, until the English Board of Trade (1727) gave jurisdiction to Rhode Island, leaving the company's heirs no tenable claims.

ATKINSON, FORT. Early post built in Kansas on the Arkansas R along the Santa Fe trail in 1850. It was temporarily abandoned in 1853 and permanently abandoned in 1854. There were other Fort Atkinsons in Florida, Iowa, Nebraska, and Wisconsin.

ATLANTA. Capital and largest city of Georgia, key transportation, commercial, banking, and manufacturing city. Founded 1837 as Terminus, the W end of the railroad from Savannah. By the time of the Civil War, Atlanta was the nerve center of railroad and telegraph service for the whole Southeast. As such, it was a major objective in Civil War fighting (see ATLANTA CAMPAIGN). It was quickly rebuilt after the war and became the capital in 1868. Located there are Emory University, Georgia Institute of Technology, and Atlanta University. Pop.: 425,022 (1980).

ATLANTA CAMPAIGN (1864). By July 6, the Union troops of Gen. W. T. Sherman, numbering 110,000, had moved so near Atlanta that Confederate Gen. Joseph Johnston, with a defending army half that size, transferred his troops S of the Chattahoochie R, into prepared positions along Peachtree Creek. On July 17 Johnston was relieved by Gen. J. B. Hood. During August, Sherman edged closer to Hood's supply line and was soon across it. Hood evacuated Atlanta on September 1. Sherman completely destroyed the town.

ATLANTIC, BATTLE OF THE (1939–45). Struggle between Allied shipping and German submarines and Luftwaffe. By 1941, even before the US had entered World War II, the US navy was convoying ships to a line 400 miles W of Ireland. The Axis had sunk 2,162 Allied ships. The Germans met with particular success against north Russian convoys, and the Allies soon abandoned this run as too dangerous in the summer. But burgeoning US naval strength began to thwart the U-boats and their attack on convoys was virtually abandoned and never regained the initiative.

ATLANTIC AND PACIFIC RAILROAD. See RAILROADS, SKETCHES OF PRINCIPAL LINES.

ATLANTIC CABLE. See CABLES, ATLANTIC AND PACIFIC.

ATLANTIC CHARTER. Signed Aug. 14, 1941, by President Franklin D. Roosevelt and Prime Minister Winston Churchill at a meeting in Newfoundland. The United States was still technically a neutral in World War II. The charter expressed idealistic objectives for the postwar world, including the FOUR FREEDOMS, free trade, and self-determination for colonial peoples. It also laid the groundwork for the United Nations.

ATLANTIC COAST LINE RAILROAD. See RAILROADS, SKETCHES OF PRINCIPAL LINES; SEABOARD COAST LINE.

ATLANTIC COMMUNITY. A supposed feeling of community arising from a common culture, embracing North America and Western Europe. The area envisaged is sometimes viewed as having specific common interests sufficiently important to justify a common political and economic policy. To some extent

the North Atlantic Treaty Organization reflects this sentiment.

ATLANTIC FISHERIES DISPUTE. See FISHERIES DISPUTE, ARBITRATION OF.

ATOMIC BOMB. Weapon deriving its energy from the fission or splitting of the nuclei of certain isotopes of the heavy elements uranium or plutonium. Enrico Fermi achieved the world's first sustained nuclear chain reaction on Dec. 2, 1942; and the Manhattan District of the Army Corps of Engineers was responsible for the design and construction of plants in Oak Ridge, Tenn., and Hanford, Wash., for the production of uranium-235 and plutonium, and for the design, fabrication, and testing of the weapon at Los Alamos, N.M. A nuclear device was detonated there, under the direction of J. Robert Oppenheimer on July 16, 1945. A bomb was dropped on Hiroshima, Japan, on Aug. 6, 1945, and another on Nagasaki, on Aug. 9. They each released energy equivalent to about 20,000 tons of high explosive. More than 105,000 people died, and 94,000 were wounded. Their use brought World War II quickly to an end. Other nations soon produced atomic bombs, beginning with the Soviet Union in 1949. In 1952 the United States first tested the HYDROGEN BOMB.

ATOMIC ENERGY COMMISSION. See ENERGY RESEARCH AND DEVELOPMENT ADMINISTRATION; NUCLEAR REGULATORY COMMISSION.

ATOMIC POWER REACTORS. See NUCLEAR POWER.

ATTAINDER. A summary legal procedure whereby all ordinary civil rights of the defendant are waived, the state proceeding against him or her by bill, or legislative act. An attainted person suffered the loss of offices, property, and usually life, with heirs losing inheritance of the estate and noble rank, if any. The US Constitution specifically prohibits the enactment of bills of attainder.

ATTICA. New York state prison, site of the most violent prison riot in US history, on Sept. 9, 1971. About 1,000 out of the 2,254 inmates (85 percent of whom were black) at the prison seized control of part of the compound, taking about 30 hostages. The prisoners issued a long list of demands, including full amnesty for themselves. On Sept. 13, 1971, after four days of negotiations, Gov. Nelson Rockefeller sent in 1,500 heavily armed state troopers, sheriff's deputies, and prison guards. In the ensuing assault, 29 inmates and 10 hostages were killed. Three convicts and one guard had died prior to the attack.

ATTORNEY GENERAL. See JUSTICE, DEPARTMENT OF.

AUBURN PRISON SYSTEM. Designed to isolate convicts from each other in individual cells and to encourage them to penitence without sacrificing the value of their labor. Strict rules of silence were enforced. It was first used (1819) at a New York state prison at Auburn. Previously, inmates had been housed in large dormitories.

AUDUBON SOCIETY, NATIONAL. Devoted to wildlife protection and the conservation movement, founded 1885; by 1905 there were 25 state Audubon societies. The society was concerned primarily with campaigning for bird protection laws, but from its early days the society has also had broader wildlife and conservation interests. In 1980, it had 412,000 members and 448 local chapters .

AUGHWICK. An Indian villiage in Pennsylvania on the Juniata R near the site of Fort Shirley. In the 1750s it served as a trading post and a home for Indian refugees from the Fort Duquesne vicinity.

AUGUSTA. City in Georgia at the head of navigation on the Savannah R, founded in 1735 by Gen. James Oglethorpe. Until 1773 it remained the NW outpost of Georgia, dominating Indian trade and relations. Largely Loyalist, it fell twice into British hands. For a short period it was the state capital. Upland cotton and steam transportation made the city, temporarily, the greatest inland cotton market in the world. A government arsenal and a large powder mill made it a major source of supply for Confederate armies. Modern Augusta remains an important cotton trading center and is a major textile manufacturing city. Pop.: 47,532 (1980).

AUGUSTA. Capital city (since 1832) of Maine, located 45 miles from the open sea,
on both banks of the Kennebec R. It has been a seaport since its founding. Its site was used in 1628 as a trading post by the Pilgrims from Plymouth. During the 18th c., a fort was built against Indian and French invasions from Canada. The first permanent settlers arrived in the 1750s. Small settlements on both banks of the Kennebec merged to form Augusta in 1797. During the 19th c., Augusta grew as a shipping center. In earlier times, ice was cut each winter and shipped to other cities. Augusta produces cotton cloth, paper, and leather products and is a poultry marketing center. Pop.: 21,819 (1980).

AUGUSTA. British vessel that in 1777 led the attack against Fort Mercer on the Delaware R. The American fleet resisted, forcing a British retreat. The Revolutionists exploded the *Augusta*. Over 60 men were lost.

AUGUSTA, CONGRESS OF (Nov. 5–10, 1763). The governors of Virginia, North Carolina, South Carolina, and Georgia met with 700 representatives of the southern Indians at Augusta, Georgia, to inform them that the French and Indian War had ended, and bring about a general settlement on trade and boundary difficulties. They signed a treaty of friendship, thereby securing important land cessions in Georgia from the Creek.

AUGUSTA, FORT. Constructed at the forks of the Susquehanna R, by Pennsylvania in 1756, near the site of present Sunbury, to defend the frontier and to stall the French. Abandoned after 1780.

AUGUSTA, TREATY OF (1773). Made by Gov. James Wright of Georgia, and John Stuart, superintendent of Indian affairs in the Southern District, with chiefs of the Creek and Cherokee nations, at the suggestion of the Indians, who were hopelessly in debt to white traders. By this agreement Georgia was ceded two tracts of land comprising more than 2.1 million acres, and from the sale of these lands the traders were to be paid.

AUGUSTA COUNTY. Created by Virginia in 1738 from land lying beyond the Blue Ridge. It included parts of the present states of Kentucky, Ohio, Indiana, Illinois, and Pennsylvania, and nearly all of West Virginia. Here the Virginians came into conflict with Pennsylvania's claims. (See PENNSYLVANIA-VIRGINIA BOUNDARY DISPUTE.)

AURARIA. First settlement in Colorado, established 1858 at the juncture of Cherry Creek and the South Platte R, following gold discoveries. In 1860 it merged with Denver, on the opposite bank of the Cherry Creek.

AURORA. Philadelphia newspaper founded in 1790 by Benjamin Franklin Bache as the *General Advertiser,* becoming the Jeffersonian Republican mouthpiece. It was notorious for violent attacks on the administrations of George Washington and John Adams. It lost much of its effectiveness after 1800, when the national capital was moved from Philadelphia to Washington.

AUSTIN. Capital city of Texas. The first settlement on the site was named Waterloo, but the name was changed to honor the "Father of Texas," Stephen F. Austin, in 1839 when the site was selected as the capital of the Republic of Texas. The University of Texas is located in Austin as is the Lyndon B. Johnson Library. Pop.: 345,496 (1980).

AUSTIN COLONY. On Jan. 17, 1821, the Spanish authorities in Mexico granted Moses Austin permission to settle 300 families in Texas. The Mexican government later confirmed this concession to his son Stephen F. Austin, who obtained contracts to settle 900 additional families, most of whom he had introduced by 1833. Austin's colonies formed the nucleus of the Anglo-American occupation of Texas.

AUSTRALIAN BALLOT. See BALLOT.

AUTOMATION. In 1949 the Ford Motor Co. completed what was called the first automated factory, manufacturing automobile engines. The key elements of automation are automatic production machines; machines to transfer materials between, and feed materials into, production machines; and a control system that regulates the whole operation, including itself (feedback). Today, ROBOTS are playing an increasing role in automation.

AUTOMOBILE. The idea of substituting a motor for the horse occurred independently in several nations in the late 19th c. American accomplishment was most notable in steam-powered and electric-powered cars. Credit for the first successful American gasoline automobile is generally given to Charles E. and J. Frank Duryea, who began the manufacture of motors in 1896. In 1899, thirty US automobile manufacturers produced about 2,500 cars. Contrary to popular myth, there was great enthusiasm for the motor car from the beginning. Some 458,500 cars were registered in the United States by 1910. In 1908 Henry Ford introduced the Model T and William C. Durant founded what was to become General Motors. The $600, four-cylinder Ford Model N (1906–07) deserves credit as the first low-priced car with sufficient horsepower to be reliable. The Model T (1908–27) was even better adapted to the wretched rural roads of the day, and its immediate popularity skyrocketed Ford's share of the market for new cars to about 50 percent by the outbreak of World War I. Mass production techniques perfected by Ford in 1914, especially the moving-belt assembly line, progressively reduced the price of the Model T to a low of $290 by 1927, making the mass personal automobile a reality. By the mid-1920s automobile manufacturing ranked first in value of product and third in value of exports among US industries. The automobile industry was the life-blood of the petroleum industry; a chief customer of the steel industry; and the biggest consumer of many other industrial products, including plate glass, rubber, and lacquers. In 1929 there were 26.7 million motor vehicles in the United States. Improvements of the 1920s included the self-starter, the closed-car design, balloon tires, and syncromesh transmission. By the end of the decade, more than half the automobile manufacturers went out of business, and Ford, General Motors, and Chrysler represented about 80 percent of the industry's total output. Streamlined styling, the all-steel body, automatic transmission, and drop-frame construction were pioneered in the 1930s. Later innovations were power brakes, power steering, air conditioning, electronic fuel injection, rack-and-pinion steering, and front-wheel drive. Federal legislation affecting the industry proliferated from the New Deal era on. The National Labor Relations Act encouraged the unionization of the industry, with the United Automobile Workers union representing virtually all workers. Automobile design came to be regulated by the federal government with passage of the Motor Vehicle Air Pollution Act of 1965 and the National Traffic and Motor Vehicle Safety Act of 1966. In 1974 a national 55-mph speed limit was imposed. The phenomenal post-World War II proliferation of the automobile was abruptly halted in the winter of 1973–74 by a fuel shortage brought on by an embargo imposed by the Arab oil-producing nations. As the price of gasoline rose, the sale of small cars increased. By December 1973 for the first time in history, sales of compacts and subcompacts surpassed sales of standard-sized cars. The sales of foreign cars, especially Japanese imports, rose dramatically and severely cut into the sales of US manufacturers. Chrysler, the worst hit, faced bankruptcy but was kept in business by federally guaranteed loans. The sales of the other US manufacturers were also curtailed, especially in the recession of the early 1980s. By 1983, however, sales had improved and Chrysler had repaid its loans ahead of schedule.

AUTOSSEE, BATTLE OF (Nov. 29, 1813). During the Creek War, Gen. John Floyd, commanding 940 Georgia militia and several hundred friendly Creek Indians, crossed the Chattahoochee R into Mississippi Territory and attacked at Autossee, a Creek village near Tuckabatchee. They drove the Creek from their villages, burned their houses, and killed 200.

AVERY SALT MINE. Near New Iberia, Louisiana, crucial source of salt to the Confederacy. Destroyed by Union forces in April 1863. Reopened and worked continuously since 1883.

AVERYSBORO, BATTLE OF (March 16, 1865). W.J. Hardee's corps of Gen. J.E. Johnston's Confederate army, retreating through North Carolina, entrenched at the village of Averysboro and gave a portion of Gen. W.T. Sherman's Union army a determined resistance for several hours; but inferior numbers compelled retreat during the night.

AVERY'S TRACE. In 1787 the North Carolina legislature provided funds for Peter Avery to blaze and cut a trace across the Cumberland Mountains in the Tennessee country.

It went through the sites of the present towns of Harriman, Monterey, and Cookeville. The Cherokee claimed the region traversed by the trace and demanded toll. Guards of militia were often necessary.

AVIATION. See AIR TRANSPORTATION.

AVIATION ADMINISTRATION, FEDERAL (FAA). Agency of the Department of Transportation, charged with regulating air commerce. Prior to 1967 it was an independent agency.

AWAKENING, GREAT. See GREAT AWAKENING.

AYLLÓN EXPEDITION. In 1526 Lucas Vásquez de Ayllón sailed from the West Indies, with 600 prospective settlers and slaves and horses to the Carolina coast. His settlement, San Miguel de Gualdape, is recorded, but its site has yet to be determined. The Spaniards suffered malarial fevers, dissensions, and Indian assaults. After one year, the survivors returned to the West Indies.

AYUBALE, BATTLE OF (Dec. 14, 1703). A frontier engagement between a force of 50 whites and 1,000 Indians under former Gov. James Moore of South Carolina and the defenders of the Spanish mission at Ayubale, near Tallahassee. Moore took Ayubale, devastated a wide area, badly crippled the Spanish in Florida, and carried away a large number of Apalache Indians (or 600, according to the Spanish estimate), settling as Carolina dependents, on the E side of the lower course of the Savannah R, those not sold as slaves.

AYUNTAMIENTO (or *Cabildo*). A Spanish municipal council, with administrative, legislative, and judicial functions. Many cities in the Southwest were governed by them.

AZILIA, MARGRAVATE OF. The fantastic scheme of Sir Robert Montgomery to establish "a New Colony to the South of Carolina," between the Savannah R and the Altamaha R, known as the Golden Islands region. He received a grant in 1717 but the project never came about.

BACKLASH. Referred originally to the hostile reaction of conservative southerners to efforts to effect racial integration. By the 1960s the term was no longer limited to the South. As the national Democratic party adopted programs to upgrade the social, economic, and political status of blacks, there was a measurable hostile response among rank-and-file Democrats, especially among the white ethnic blocs and blue-collar workers. Much of the support of George C. Wallace's campaign for the presidency in 1968 mirrored this white backlash.

BACK TO AFRICA MOVEMENT. Founded by black leader Marcus Garvey (1914) as the United Negro Improvement Association. Garvey widely publicized the colonization idea through his weekly newspaper, the *Negro World.* Despite much publicity and a large subscribed fund from the black community, nothing was ever accomplished.

BACKWOODS AND BACKCOUNTRY. The term "backwoodsman" became common when pioneers began advancing the frontier into and beyond the mountains of Pennsylvania, Virginia, and the Carolinas, regions that came to be known as the backcountry. During the Revolution backwoodsmen under George Rogers Clark took Kaskakia and Vincennes from the British. An undisciplined but efficient army of backwoodsmen annihilated the British at the Battle of King's Mountain. Later, under their idol, Andrew Jackson, they fought the Creek War and won the Battle of New Orleans. Jackson's election as president represented the political zenith of the backwoodsmen.

BACON'S REBELLION (1676). Revolt in Virginia led by Nathaniel Bacon, Jr., a planter, against the unpopular rule of the royal governor, Sir William Berkeley. Bacon's volunteers drove Berkeley and his forces to the eastern shore of Virginia; but Bacon died within a few months, and Berkeley returned to the mainland. Commissioners sent by Charles II severely censured Berkeley's strict policies toward the defeated rebels and attempted to remove him from office. Berkeley returned to England to defend himself but died before seeing the king.

BACTERIOLOGY AND VIROLOGY. After the appearance of improved microscopes in the 1830s and 1840s, American medical investigators tried to establish a connection between the organisms they observed and epidemic diseases; but their failure led to an almost total halt in research until the 1880s, when new interest arose after the spate of advances in Europe brought on by the work of Joseph Lister, Robert Koch, and Louis Pasteur. Many American scientists went to Europe to learn about the demanding new laboratory methods and bacteriological techniques. By the mid-1880s, bacteriological instruction was being given at several universities. A few years later public health laboratories were established; early bacteriological activities included the testing of water supplies, the diagnosis of diphtheria, and the preparation of vaccines and sera. Much of the early bacteriological contributions were made in federal government laboratories. Daniel Salmon investigated the causal organism of swine cholera and in the 1890s organized a meat inspection service. In 1893 the cause of tick fever was discovered, one of the earliest demonstrations of the role of the insect vector. Important studies in the bacteriology of human diseases, particularly tuberculosis and hookworm, also came out of federal laboratories. Army scientists were responsible for the isolation of the pneumococcus in the early 1880s. The Yellow Fever Commission, under Walter Reed, made its electrifying demonstration of transmission of the disease by the mosquito. By the 20th c., bacteriologists began to organize societies and create journals and to spread out across the country to staff new university departments. The federal Hygienic Laboratory, founded in 1900, eventually became the National Institutes of Health. For much of the early 20th c., however, the nation's principal biomedical research center was the Rockefeller Institute for Medical Research (now Rockefeller University), founded in 1906. The remaining tasks of bacteriology were vigorously pursued, especially including virology. The most dramatic impetus to virology came with the introduction of the electron microscope just before World War II. With this instrument, the American study of such long-frustrating virus diseases as poliomyelitis and influenza greatly accelerated after the war, a study climaxed by the development of the successful Salk and Sabin vaccines. In the 1970s and 1980s much of the attention in the field was devoted to discovering the causes of the different forms of cancer.

BAD AXE, BATTLE OF (Aug. 3, 1832). The Sauk and Fox Indians, dissatisfied with lands to which the federal government had moved them, recrossed the Mississippi R under Black Hawk's leadership and attacked white settlers. They were defeated by an American force of 1,300 men at the mouth of the Bad Axe R.

BAD LANDS. A severely eroded area in South Dakota, created by water erosion. A vast number of fossils have been exposed. The federal government established the region as the Badlands National Monument in 1939.

BAGHDAD PACT (1955). Security and defense agreement between Iraq and Turkey; Britain, Pakistan, and Iran also joined, and considerable US financial aid was involved. The pact aroused the hostility of Egypt and was unpopular with Arab nationalists. It helped bring about the downfall of the Iraqi monarchy in 1958 and the new government withdrew from it. It was later (1959) replaced by the Central Treaty Organization (CENTO).

BAGOT-RUSH AGREEMENT. See GREAT LAKES DISARMAMENT AGREEMENT.

BAHAMA ISLANDS. Chain of 760 islands fifty miles off SE Florida. Formerly a British colony, they have been independent since 1973. Originally granted to the Carolina proprietors, they were a haven for pirates in the 17th and 18th c. Separated from the Carolinas in 1718, they were Loyalist during the American Revolution. During the Civil War, the islands served as a base for blockade runners; and during Prohibition they were a port for rum runners.

BAILEY V. DREXEL FURNITURE COMPANY, 259 US 20 (1922). The Supreme Court invalidated a 1919 act of Congress that had levied a tax on the products of businesses employing children under sixteen. The court held that the law was an attempt to bring under congressional control matters belonging to the states.

BAKER'S CABIN MASSACRE (April 30, 1774). The murder of six or seven unarmed Mingo Indians by a party of whites at Baker's Cabin, on the Virginia side of the Ohio R, near present-day Steubenville, Ohio. As a result, Chief Logan went on the warpath.

BAKER V. CARR, 369 US 186 (1962). Established the rule that the federal courts had the jurisdiction to review cases arising out of legislative malapportionment. Prior to *Baker v. Carr*, the Supreme Court had maintained that congressional districting was strictly a state responsibility. The impact of *Baker* was to open the doors to judicial consideration of issues related to apportionment. It stimulated immediate judicial, legislative, or referendum actions on the issue of apportionment in at least 43 states. It also led eventually to the one man, one vote rule of the Supreme Court.

BAKESHOP CASE. See LOCHNER V. NEW YORK.

BALANCE OF TRADE. The American colonies had an unfavorable balance of trade, depending as they did on England for capital and credit. After the Revolution, England's markets were closed to many American products and trade with the British West Indies was illegal. The new trade with China, treaties with Prussia and Sweden, and JAY'S TREATY improved matters, but the development of cotton growing and the outbreak of the Napoleonic Wars helped more. Both France and England bought heavily of US products. After 1806 Britain took successful steps to stop American commercial growth, a policy that eventually led to the War of 1812. After the war, foreign manufactured goods flooded the US market, hurting domestic industry and producing sentiment for high tariff protection. European investment in the United States picked up in the early 1830s but ended abruptly after the panic of 1837 eroded European confidence in the US economy. Between 1838 and 1849 the balance was slightly favorable. During the 1850s imports and exports both expanded rapidly until the Civil War. After the war, American foreign trade grew rapidly: from $405 million in 1865 to $1.2 billion in 1873. In general, the balance of trade remained favorable through World War I. Between 1914 and 1919 the US trade balance was favorable by $18.6 billion, and by 1916, the United States had ceased being a debtor nation and became a creditor.

The 1920s were prosperous. Since high tariffs made imports difficult, the only way to continue to sell abroad was to make heavy loans. The United States lent $12 billion during that decade, while foreigners invested $7 billion in the United States. After the 1929 crash, many of the borrowers were forced to default on their loans, and international trade went through a critical period. US foreign trade improved starting in 1934. Numerous reciprocal trade treaties lowered US tariff walls and encouraged freer trade. World War II stimulated exports enormously, mostly in lend-lease shipments to the Allies. Since much of this trade could not be paid for by the recipients, the United States had an unfavorable balance of trade during the war years. After the war, the nation exported vast quantities of goods to help rebuild a war-ravaged world, and a favorable balance of trade resulted until 1958. Starting that year, gold began flowing out of the country on a regular basis. In 1966 even the balance of merchandise began to shrink; in 1971 it turned unfavorable by $2 billion. Rising prices of American goods, increasingly efficient competition from abroad (especially Japan and West Germany), the costly Vietnam War, and the nation's increasing reliance on foreign oil, all tended to make the balance of trade unfavorable to the United States.

BALCONES ESCARPMENT. Geologic fault extending across Texas from Del Rio to the Red R near Denison. The region E of the fault is humid and contains nearly all of the most populous cities; the soil to the W is hard and dry.

BALIZE. Fortification built by the French in 1722 on the principal mouth of the Mississippi R, about a half mile from the Gulf of Mexico. Although planned as the first line of defense for Louisiana, it afforded slight protection because the mud would not hold strong works and other passes were negotiable by light craft. The Spanish maintained it, but the United States abandoned it for defenses 30 miles upstream.

BALLADS. The first collection of American folk songs was *Allen's Slave Songs of the United States,* (1867). American ballads, composed by coal miners, mountaineers, cowboys, sailors, railroad workmen, and lumberjacks are peopled with working-class characters. Undoubtedly the most popular are the occupational ballads ("Casey Jones," "The Erie Canal"), bad-man ballads (Jesse James), murder ballads (Pearl Bryant), and the bawdy barroom ballads popular in colleges. The Library of Congress has a continuing program of recording American ballads.

BALLINGER–PINCHOT CONTROVERSY (1909–11). A bitter contention over the conservation of natural resources during the administration of President Taft. Gifford Pinchot, chief of the Forest Service, publicly charged Secretary of the Interior Richard A. Ballinger with favoritism toward corporations seeking waterpower sites on public lands. Pinchot was dismissed, but Ballinger was forced to resign.

BALLOONS. In 1784—just a year after the success of the Montgolfier brothers in France—Peter Carnes raised a tethered 35-foot, hot-air balloon at Bladensberg, Maryland. The first free ascent in a balloon in America was made by Jean-Pierre Blanchard, a Frenchman, at Philadelphia in 1793. Not until 1830 did an American make a balloon ascent in the United States: Charles Ferson Durant, at Castle Garden on the S tip of Manhattan Island. The first aerial photographs in the United States were taken from a balloon in 1860, and the first telegraph message sent from the air in 1861. The Union used balloons in the Civil War. Captive balloons were used extensively for reconnaissance and fire control in World War I. In World War II Japan launched 9,000 unmanned bomb-carrying balloons to ride the jet stream toward the United States; about 10 percent reached America. The US Weather Bureau uses hundreds of small balloons daily to study atmospheric conditions. In May 1961 the US navy's Strato Lab V polyethylene balloon, with a capacity of 10 million cubic feet, carried two men to an altitude of 113,740 feet. Balloons are used to make celestial measurements with infrared telescopes and for cosmic ray studies. There were several unsuccessful attempts to cross the Atlantic in the 1970s, and finally in August 1978 three Americans, Max Anderson, Ben Abruzzo, and Larry Newman, completed the transatlantic crossing, lifting off from Maine and landing near Paris after 137 hours, 18 minutes aloft. In

May 1980 Max Anderson and his son Kris were the first to fly nonstop across North America.

BALLOT. In colonial times, voice voting was the usual procedure. Later the paper ballot emerged as the dominant voting method. Almost immediately the political parties started to print ballots, listing only the candidates of a single party. The parties were able to influence the vote by pressuring voters to take their ballot, virtually ensuring a straight-ticket vote, and forcing them to vote in public. Between 1888 and 1896 civic groups and "good government" people convinced over 90 percent of the states to adopt a new ballot patterned after one in Australia. The Australian ballot was official (being prepared and distributed by the government), consolidated (placing the candidates of both major parties on the same ballot), and secret. The same principles are employed in the voting machine.

BALL'S BLUFF, BATTLE OF (Oct. 21, 1861). A militarily inconsequential clash in Virginia in which Union Col. E.D. Baker, senator from Oregon and friend of President Lincoln, was killed. The public blamed Gen. G.B. McClellan for the Union defeat, and Congress inaugurated the Committee on the Conduct of the War to investigate such failures. McClellan arrested Gen. C.P. Stone for the defeat and for Baker's death. No formal charges were ever made. After six months' imprisonment, Stone was released.

BALTIMORE. Seaport at the upper end of Chesapeake Bay on the Patapsco R and Maryland's largest city. Founded 1729 and named in honor of the second proprietor of Maryland, Charles Calvert, Baron Baltimore. Always an important port, shipbuilding grew with the development of the Baltimore clipper. During the Revolution and the War of 1812 privateers built and manned in Baltimore played a conspicuous part. The tide of the latter war turned when the port was successfully defended against the British. In 1827 construction of the Baltimore and Ohio RR was begun, the first steam-operated railway in the United States. Baltimore's growth was stemmed in the second half of the 19th c. by political strife and the Civil War, climaxed in 1904 by a fire that destroyed 150 acres in the downtown area. After World War I the port revived; shipbuilding was continued but the city's industry was dominated by heavy industry, particularly represented by the largest tidewater steel mill in the nation. In the 1980s the port of Baltimore continued to thrive, and its urban renewal program was particularly noteworthy. Pop.: 786,775 (1980).

BALTIMORE, BATTLE OF (Sept. 12, 1814). After the burning of Washington, D.C., in the War of 1812, a British land force of 8,000 attempted to capture Baltimore. The city was successfully defended by a force of Maryland and Pennsylvania militia and volunteers.

BALTIMORE AFFAIR. An attack by a Chilean mob in Valparaíso on Oct. 16, 1891, upon 117 sailors on shore leave from the USS *Baltimore* left two Americans dead and several wounded. This hostility emerged from the mistaken feeling that during Chile's civil war the United States had sympathized with the Chilean authorities. After US protests, Chile apologized and paid indemnities.

BALTIMORE AND OHIO RAILROAD. See RAILROADS, SKETCHES OF PRINCIPAL LINES: CHESAPEAKE AND OHIO.

BALTIMORE CLIPPER. The topsail schooner developed around Chesapeake Bay in the revolutionary period and later similar square-rigged vessels. The *Ann McKim* (1833) was the ultimate expression of the type and is regarded by some as the link between the Baltimore clipper and the CLIPPER CHIPS.

BALTIMORE COUNCILS, PROVINCIAL AND PLENARY. Ecclesiastical legislation in the Roman Catholic church in the United States began with a synod of the priests under Bishop John Carroll of Baltimore in 1791. The regulations adopted served to administer church affairs until 1829, when the first Provincial Council of Baltimore was held. By 1852 the church had been divided into provinces, and provincial councils were established by their archbishops. Three plenary, or national, councils were held (1852, 1866, and 1884); they were concerned with a wide range of church matters.

BALTIMORE INCIDENT (Nov. 16, 1798). While convoying merchant vessels to Havana

51

during naval hostilities with France, Capt. Isaac Phillips in the US sloop *Baltimore* encountered a British squadron. Phillips, under protest, submitted to the removal of those of his crew without American papers. He was summarily dismissed from the navy, and stringent orders were issued requiring US vessels to resist forcibly any similar incidents. (See IMPRESSMENT OF SEAMEN.)

BANK, FEDERAL RESERVE. See FEDERAL RESERVE SYSTEM.

BANK DEPOSITS. Early banks had two basic ways of lending their credit: by issuing bank notes (the bank's demand promissory notes) or by creating deposits. After the National Banking System was set up in 1863, the use of checks drawn on demand deposits rapidly outdistanced bank notes. Between 1866 and 1913 the deposits of national banks grew from $565 million to over $6 billion, but their bank notes totaled only $727 million. Between 1914 and 1920 demand deposits rose from $10.1 billion to $19.6 billion. By 1929 the total had reached $22.5 billion, but by 1933 it had dropped to a low of $14.4 billion—figures that reflect, and had also helped cause, the boom and then the collapse of those years. The Banking Act of 1935 gave the Federal Reserve authority to double reserve requirements. During World War II demand deposits rose from $33.6 billion in 1940 to $88.8 billion in 1946. Demand deposits continued to rise through the Korean and Vietnam wars, and they reached a high of $435 billion in 1979. In 1981 they were at $385.5 billion.

BANK FAILURES. American financial history to 1934 was characterized by an appalling number of bank failures, because the majority of banks were uninsured local enterprises. The statistics of such failures between 1789 and 1863 are inadequate, but the losses were unquestionably large. Not until 1853 did banks' deposit liabilities exceed their note liabilities. The establishment of the National Banking System in 1863 introduced needed regulations for national banks. These were more numerous than state banks to 1894, and were larger on the average. But even their record left much to be desired. There were 515 national bank failures from 1864 to 1913,

while state banks suffered 2,491 failures. The worst year was the panic year of 1893, with almost 500 failures. The establishment of the Federal Reserve System in 1913 did little to improve the record. The bank holocaust of the early 1930s—of the 9,106 failures in four years, 1,947 were national banks—produced the needed reforms. Congress founded the FEDERAL DEPOSIT INSURANCE CORPORATION (FDIC), which insured each depositor. Thus virtually all individual accounts are fully insured. Today, bank failures average fewer than ten per year.

BANK FOR INTERNATIONAL SETTLEMENTS (BIS). International banking facility located at Basel, Switzerland. Established 1930 to aid the central banks of the major powers. It complements the operations of the INTERNATIONAL MONETARY FUND and the World Bank.

BANK HOLIDAY. See BANKING CRISIS OF 1933.

BANKING. Robert Morris founded the first commercial bank in the United States, the Bank of North America, in 1781. It greatly assisted the financing of the closing stages of the Revolution. By 1811 there were eighty-eight state-chartered banks. Secretary of the Treasury Alexander Hamilton's financial program included a central bank; accordingly, the first Bank of the United States was founded in 1791, with a twenty-year charter. Its huge $10 million capital and favored relationship with the government aroused much anxiety, especially among Jeffersonians. The bank's sound but unpopular policy of promptly returning bank notes for redemption in specie and refusing those of non-species-paying banks, together with a political feud, was largely responsible for its not being rechartered in 1811. Between 1811 and 1816 state banks increased to 246, and note circulation quadrupled. Nearly all but New England banks suspended specie payments in 1814 because of the War of 1812 and unregulated credit expansion. Congress established the second Bank of the United States in 1816, also with a twenty-year charter. The bank's $35 million capitalization and favored relationship with the Treasury likewise aroused anxiety. Instead of repairing the overexpanded credit situation, the bank aggravated it by generous lending policies, precipitating the panic of 1819. Thereafter, under Nicholas Biddle, it was well run. The bank's downfall grew out of President Jackson's prejudice against banks and monopolies; the memory of the bank's role in the 1819 panic; and most of all, Biddle's decision to let rechartering be a main issue in the 1832 presidential election. Jackson vetoed the recharter. After 1833, the government placed all its deposits with the "pet banks" (politically selected state banks) until it set up the Independent Treasury System in the 1840s. Between 1830 and 1837 the number of banks, note circulation, and loans all about tripled. The banks overextended themselves in lending to land speculators. The panic of 1837 resulted— bringing a suspension of specie payments, many failures, and a depression that lasted until 1844. For thirty years the country was without an adequate regulator of bank currency. Banks made many long-term loans, especially on real estate, and resorted to subterfuges to avoid redeeming notes in specie. Bankers had to consult weekly publications, Bank Note Reporters, for the current discount on bank notes and turn to the latest Bank Note Detectors to distinguish counterfeits and notes of failed banks. In this bleak era of banking, however, there were successful banking systems in Masaachusetts, New York, Indiana, Ohio, Iowa, and Louisiana. An improved banking system began with the National Banking Act of 1863. It set high reserve requirements for bank notes and forbade real estate loans and branch banking. In 1866 Congress levied a prohibitive 10 percent tax on state bank notes, which drove most of these banks into the new system. By 1866, there were 1,644 national banks, all required to use "National" in their name. Smaller banks continued to be state-chartered, however, and improvements in state banking laws began about 1887. Despite its improvements, the National Banking System had three major faults: the perverse elasticity of the bond-secured bank notes, of which the supply did not vary in accordance with the needs of business; the decentralization of bank deposit reserves; and no central bank to take measures to forestall crises or to lend to deserving banks in times of distress. Four times (1873, 1884, 1893, and 1907) panics highlighted the faults of the system. Improvised use of clearinghouse certificates in interbank settle-

ments somewhat relieved money shortages in the first three cases; "voluntary" bank assessments collected and lent by a committee headed by J.P. Morgan gave relief in 1907. The Owen-Glass Act of 1913 superimposed a central system on the existing national system. It required all national banks to join, which meant to buy stock equal to 3 percent of their capital and surplus, thus providing the funds to set up the Federal Reserve System (1914). State banks might also join, but few did. A majority of the nation's banks have always remained outside the Federal Reserve System, although the larger banks have usually been members. (Thus ended the need for the Independent Treasury System, which wound up its affairs in 1921.) Between the opening of the Federal Reserve System and the 1980s, the commercial banking system grew and changed, as might be expected in a fast-growing nation. The total number of banks actually declined, but the total amount of money in demand deposit grew from $10 billion to $435 billion (in 1979); and time deposits from $8.6 billion to $892 billion (in 1982). The 1930s witnessed many reforms growing out of the more than 9,000 bank failures between 1930 and 1933 and capped by the nationwide bank moratorium of March 1933. These laws gave the Federal Reserve System firmer control, especially over member banks. They set up the FEDERAL DEPOSIT INSURANCE CORPORATION to insure bank deposits, and soon all but a few hundred small banks belonged. During World War II, the banks converted their excess reserve into government obligations and increased their own holdings from $16 billion in 1940 to $84 billion in 1945. In 1951 the Federal Reserve System regained its freedom to curb credit expansion, and thereafter interest rates crept upward. That development improved bank profits and led banks to reduce somewhat their holding of government obligations. Term loans (five to ten years) to industry and real estate loans increased. Banks also encountered stiff competition from such rapidly growing rivals as savings and loan associations, personal finance companies, and money market funds. Interest rates rose spectacularly during the 1960s, prime commercial paper reaching 9 percent in 1970, then dropped sharply in 1971, only to rise once more, hitting a high of 20 percent in mid-

1980, and then lowering to about 12 percent in 1984.

BANKING, BRANCH AND GROUP. The first Bank of the United States had eight branches; the second, twenty-nine. The National Banking Act of 1863 forbade national branches. The Federal Reserve Act of 1913 permitted foreign branches to a limited degree; in 1918 state banks having branches and wanting to join the Federal Reserve System were authorized to keep them; and in 1927 national banks were allowed a limited number of branches in the parent bank's city, provided the states permitted branch banking. The Banking Act of 1933 permitted national banks to establish branches. By 1981, 15,355 banks had 43,995 branches and "additional offices." Where branch banking is prohibited or discouraged, resort has been made to chain or group banking: chains are owned by one or more individuals; groups by holding companies. Such uncontrolled concentration of financial resources caused public concern, and since 1956 the Federal Reserve's board of governors has had supervisory control in this field. Nevertheless, in 1981 there were 3,500 bank holding companies, with $939 billion in deposits, which represented 77 percent of all commercial deposits.

BANKING, STATE. State-owned banks began in the 18th c., when most colonies had loan offices or land banks. Interest payments from loans paid the expenses of the provincial governments. In the 19th c. sometimes the state was sole owner of a bank (South Carolina); more commonly it was part owner (Indiana). After the panic of 1819 public distrust of banks created the need for additional state-owned banks. Only some were profitable. The State Bank of Missouri was the most successful, surviving the panics of 1837 and 1857. In 1865 Congress imposed a 10 percent tax on state bank notes, thereby in effect forcing all state-owned banks to join the National Banking System. State-owned banks disappeared, but state-chartered private banks remained an important part of commercial banking.

BANKING ACTS OF 1933 AND 1935. The 1933 act created the FEDERAL DEPOSIT INSURANCE CORPORATION, increased the power of the Federal Reserve Board to control credit, and separated commercial and investment banking. The 1935 act reorganized the Federal Reserve Board, renaming it the board of governors of the Federal Reserve System, revised the deposit insurance provisions of the 1933 act, and increased the powers of the Federal Reserve System over discount and open market operations of Reserve banks.

BANKING CRISIS OF 1933. A large number of banks failed in 1931 and 1932, markedly weakening the banking structure. Efforts by the Reconstruction Finance Corporation to strengthen the banking industry were largely ineffectual. In 1933 bank moratoria were declared in twenty-two states by March 3; and on March 4, banks in the remaining states closed their doors. Congress, called in special session by President Franklin D. Roosevelt, passed an emergency banking act on March 9, providing machinery for reopening only sound banks, which were opened on March 13, 14, and 15. By March 15, banks controlling about 90 percent of the banking resources of the country were again in operation.

BANK OF NORTH AMERICA. America's first government-incorporated bank, chartered by the Continental Congress in 1781, commenced operations in Philadelphia on Jan. 7, 1782. Organized by Robert Morris, the bank supplied vital financial aid to the government during the closing months of the American Revolution,

BANK OF THE STATE OF SOUTH CAROLINA. See SOUTH CAROLINA, BANK OF.

BANK OF THE UNITED STATES, FIRST (1791–1811). As the result of a proposal by Secretary of the Treasury Alexander Hamilton, the creation of a central bank was effected in 1791. The bank, located in Philadelphia, had a capital of $10 million. One-fifth was subscribed by the government, the rest by private investors. Only US citizens might be directors. The bank was empowered to carry on commercial banking, was not permitted to deal in commodities or real estate, and was limited to a 6 percent interest charge on loans. The bank could issue circulating notes totaling up to $10 million. Through its main office and eight branches, the bank furnished the country with sound banking service for twenty years. It served as fiscal agent for the government and exerted a salutary controlling influence on the note issues of the state banks by refusing to accept state bank notes not redeemable in specie. Nevertheless, its charter was not renewed in 1811, due to doubt as to its constitutionality.

BANK OF THE UNITED STATES, SECOND (1816–36). After the demise of the First Bank of the United States, a brief period of relying on state banking proved unsatisfactory, and a second bank was incorporated in 1816. Capital and note issues were increased to $35 million, and the president of the United States could appoint five of the directors. The bank was badly managed until 1819, when a new bank president got it into a sound position. In 1823 Nicholas Biddle assumed the presidency, and the bank extended sound banking service through its main office and 25 branches. A dispute between Biddle and President Jackson made efforts to obtain a renewal of its charter futile, and the bank ceased to function in 1836.

BANK OF THE UNITED STATES V. HAL-STEAD, 10 Wheaton 51 (1825). Concerned the applicability of state legislation regulating the procedural processes to federal courts within the respective states. The Supreme Court upheld the power of federal courts to alter forms of proceedings to meet changing conditions on general (implied) grounds relating to the judicial power and from specific legislative grants.

BANKRUPTCY LAWS. Although authorized by the Constitution (Article I, Section 8), Congress did not immediately exercise the power to establish uniform bankruptcy laws. The first federal legislation (closely resembling English statutes) was enacted in 1800. It applied only to traders, merchants, and brokers. It was essentially a liquidating procedure, the assets of the bankrupt being sold to satisfy creditors. A bankrupt was permitted to retain a certain percentage of his assets and could be discharged from any unsatisfied indebtedness by the consent of the creditors. Public dissatisfaction led to its repeal in 1803. The second national bankruptcy law was passed in 1841, the direct result of the panic of 1837 and the ensuing depression. It was repealed as economic conditions im-

proved. The Civil War resulted in the third statute (1867) which was repealed in 1878, partly because of abuses by the courts administering it. During the intervals between the federal bankruptcy laws, state laws governed the debtor-creditor relationship. Such laws were limited because of the constitutional grant of power to Congress, were not uniform, and often discriminated against out-of-state creditors. The panic of 1893 rekindled interest in national bankruptcy legislation, and in 1898 Congress enacted a bankruptcy bill drafted primarily for various commercial interests. The act has continued to the present day, but has been amended almost 100 times.

BANKS, EXPORT-IMPORT. See EXPORT-IMPORT; BANK OF THE UNITED STATES.

BANKS, INVESTMENT. See INVESTMENT BANKS.

BANKS, NATIONAL. See BANKING.

BANKS, POSTAL SAVINGS. See POSTAL SERVICE, UNITED STATES.

BANKS, PRIVATE. Historically, private banks are the original form of banking. Like any private business, their obligations were originally protected by the personal liability of the individual or partnership. With the growth of social control of business, the number of private banks declined. Some states prohibit their operations, and there has been a tendency to subject them to the same control as corporations and curtail the field of their operations. Perhaps the most famous of private banks was that of J.P. Morgan.

BANKS, SAVINGS. The first savings bank in the United States was the Provident Institution for Savings in Boston, chartered Dec. 13, 1816. By 1820 there were ten mutual savings banks in the Northeast. By 1914 there were 634, with nearly 8,000,000 depositors and $4 billion in savings. In 1981 there were 442 savings banks, still chiefly in the Northeast, with $165 billion in deposits. In other parts of the country SAVINGS AND LOAN ASSOCIATIONS perform virtually the same services.

BANNOCK. A Great Basin tribe speaking a Shoshonean branch of the Uto-Aztecan linguistic family. The Bannock ranged from SE Idaho W into the Snake R region in Idaho and

E into Wyoming. Divided into small bands, the tribe moved widely, gathering wild seeds and insects and sometimes massing for communal rabbit and antelope hunts. Some adapted to horses but did not adopt the Plains war pattern. Their small population was reduced early by smallpox and reservation confinement.

BANNOCK WAR (1878). One of the last major uprisings among Indians of the Northwest. Threat of starvation impelled the Bannock to leave the Fort Hall Reservation in Idaho to find sustenance through gathering and hunting. They found the hogs of settlers rooting up the camass bulbs upon which they relied heavily for food, and under the leadership of Buffalo Horn, they began to attack settlers. Pursued by troops, the Indians suffered heavy losses, scattered in small groups, and gradually drifted back to the reservation.

BAPTIST CHURCHES. Roger Williams helped establish the first American Baptist congregation in Providence, Rhode Island, in 1639, but the center of the Baptist movement was in the Middle Colonies. The Philadelphia Baptist Association (1707) united churches from Virginia to Massachusetts. The Great Awakening led to the Ketochten Association in Virginia (1765) and the Warren Associaton in Rhode Island (1767). In the early 19th c. various general conventions were established to administer missionary work and to handle publications. These were voluntarily supported by the individual congregations. The Baptists split in 1845, largely over slavery. The Southern Baptist Convention adopted a more denominational pattern and empowered the central body to act semiautonomously. The Baptists in the north moved more slowly toward a centralized denominational organization, eventually becoming (in 1973) the American Baptist Churches in the USA. The Afro-American Baptists increased after the Civil War because of racial discrimination in the white churches. In 1880 the National Baptist Convention was formed, but it split in 1907, the largest faction becoming the Baptist Convention, USA, Inc. Tensions have always existed within all Baptist groups, but most have continued to believe in religious liberty, independence of the local congregation, and the doctrine of soul liberty. Most Baptists hold a theology derived from the Evangelical Calvinism of the 18th c. Although Baptists have adopted confessions of faith, these have been regarded as noncompulsory summaries of principles. There are 26 Baptist denominations in the United States as well as many independent congregations. Approximately 95 percent of all Baptists belong to the eight largest of those organizations: Southern Baptist Convention, 13.6 million (1980); National Baptist Convention, USA, Inc., 5.3 million members (1958); National Baptist Convention of America, 2.5 million members (1956); American Baptist Churches in the USA, 1.6 million members (1979); National Primitive Baptist Convention, 250,000 members (1975); Conservative Baptist Association of America, 104,000 members (1980); General Association of Regular Baptist Churches, 230,000 members (1981); and Free-Will Baptists, 228,000 members (1980).

BAR ASSOCIATION, AMERICAN. See AMERICAN BAR ASSOCIATION.

BARATARIA. A bay, village, and bayou on the Gulf Coast of Louisiana, headquarters of the smuggling operations of Jean and Pierre Laffite from 1810 to 1815. Though regarded as pirates by the United States, the Laffites claimed to operate as privateers under letters issued by the Republic of Cartegena (now part of Colombia), which had declared its independence from Spain in 1810.

BARBARY WARS. Two separate series of hostilities between the United States and the Barbary states (Morocco, Algiers, Tripoli, and Tunis) in the early 19th c.

Tripolitan War (1801–05). After the Revolution, the United States, following the example of European nations, made annual payments to the Barbary states for unmolested passage along North Africa's Barbary Coast. Nevertheless, difficulties ensued, and in 1801 Tripoli declared war and seized several US vessels. The war was feebly prosecuted until 1803, when Commodore Edward Preble was sent out with the *Constitution, Philadelphia*, and several brigs and schooners. Preble set up a strict blockade of Tripoli, but on Oct. 31, 1803, the *Philadelphia* ran on a reef and was captured. In February 1804 the US navy recaptured and burned it. During August and September Preble harassed Tripolitan shipping and fortifications. On September 4, the *Intrepid*, with a cargo of gunpowder and shells, was maneuvered into the harbor at night. Apparently the explosion occurred prematurely, for all participants were killed and little damage was done to Tripolitan shipping. By spring, with the DERNA EXPEDITION threatening Tripoli, the bey of Tripoli was ready to conclude peace. The treaty (June 4, 1805) abolished all annual payments, but provided a ransom for the men of the *Philadelphia*.

War with Algiers (1815). Although payments were continued to the other Barbary states, the absence of US naval war vessels preceding the War of 1812 encouraged Algiers to seize US merchantmen. In June 1815 Commodore Stephen Decatur was ordered to the Mediterranean, where he captured the Algerian flagship *Mashada* and secured a treaty: no future payments, restoration of US property, emancipation of Christian slaves who had claimed refuge on US ships, civilized treatment of prisoners of war, and an indemnity for a US merchantman recently seized. As Tunis and Tripoli were forced to equally hard terms and an American squadron remained in the Mediterranean, the safety of US commerce was assured.

BARBECUE. Meat cooked, often as whole carcasses, on racks over open pits of coals. Apparently originating in Virginia about 1700 in connection with local fairs, the barbecue became especially popular in the Southwest.

BARBED WIRE. Following various patents on barbed wire (twisted wire with barbs), in 1873 Joseph F. Glidden, a prairie farmer of Illinois, gave it commercial practicability and the next year sold the first piece, and factories soon developed. Before the plains were fenced into pastures, cowmen cooperated to build drift fences across long distances. By 1890 most private range land had been fenced. With fencing came wire-cutting wars in Texas and elsewhere; but barbed wire revolutionized the whole range industry, cutting off trail driving and free grazing, making improvement of breeds and watering of the range by wells and tanks inevitable.

BARGEMEN. Term used interchangeably with keelboatmen, bargers, and keelers, and applied to men engaged in operating river boats that traveled upstream as distinct from flatboats. Most full-time bargemen worked on the lower Mississippi R and Ohio R and its tributaries. After 1820 they gradually disappeared as the steamboat took over.

BARNBURNERS. Progressive faction of the Democratic party in New York state in the 1840s, after the breakup of the ALBANY REGENCY. Barnburners opposed further state expenditures for canals, favored a direct state tax, and opposed the extension of slavery. They seceded from the 1848 Democratic national convention and nominated Martin Van Buren for president. United with the Free Soilers, they defeated Lewis Cass, the Democratic candidate. They gradually returned to the Democratic party, but many of the younger Barnburners joined the newly formed Republican party.

BARNSTORMING. In the early 19th c. theatrical troupes traveled through the West, where they sometimes slept in barns and often played in theaters little better than barns. They brought contemporary farce and melodrama as well as Shakespeare to the frontier towns in the days before railroads. By analogy, the early itinerant fliers and stunt pilots were also called barnstormers.

BARNUM'S MUSEUM. Established in New York City in 1841 by P.T. Barnum. He exhibited thousands of curios and relics and also living curiosities. There was also a lecture room seating 3,000, in which plays were given. Fire destroyed the museum in 1865.

BARRON V. BALTIMORE, 7 Peters 243 (1833). The question was whether the Bill of Rights applied to state and local authority. Chief Justice John Marshall, speaking for a unanimous court, dismissed the case, concluding that the Bill of Rights restrained the federal government alone and was not binding on the states. The Fourteenth Amendment in effect overruled *Barron*.

BARTER. The exchange of goods without using money, such as obtaining furs from Indians for beads, liquor, and firearms. As settlers on the frontier usually lacked money they bartered horses, farms, tobacco, wool, and rice.

BARTLETT'S EXPLORATIONS. As US commissioner on the Mexican boundary question, John Russell Bartlett made explorations in 1850–53 into Texas, New Mexico, California, and adjacent Mexican states. Scientists accompanied the party, and the results were published with interesting illustrations in 1854.

BASCOM, FORT. Established on the Canadian R in New Mexico in 1868 to protect the frontier against the Cheyenne, Kiowa, Comanche, and Arapaho.

BASEBALL. Despite the myth that the game was invented by Abner Doubleday at Cooperstown, New York, in 1839, historians agree that a game in which a bat, ball, and bases were used was being played throughout the United States much earlier. Baseball scholars have demonstrated that Doubleday in fact had nothing to do with the game's founding or development. In any event, in 1845, a group of New York City sportsmen organized the Knickerbocker Baseball Club and drew up a set of rules. For the next few years baseball was played almost exclusively in and around New York City by gentlemen sportsmen. By 1860 more than 50 clubs belonged to the National Association of Baseball Players; several played regular schedules and charged admission. The Civil War broke up the clubs, but baseball became the most popular game among the troops. A short time after the war more than 200 clubs were organized. The first all-professional team was the Cincinnati Red Stockings, and in 1876 teams from eight cities established the National League of Professional Baseball Clubs, introduced regularly scheduled games, and formulated and codified most of the current rules. In 1901 the American League was organized. The first World Series was played in 1903. The World Series has been played every autumn since 1905. The All-Star Game is played in midseason between teams of the outstanding players of both leagues. Jackie Robinson became the first black man to play in the major leagues when he joined the Brooklyn Dodgers in 1947. Despite changes in popular tastes and customs, professional baseball has remained not only a business but also a monopoly. After a new league was announced in 1959, organized baseball absorbed some of the potential competitors and expanded each league from eight to ten teams. Franchises were shifted, and for the first time there were major league teams coast to coast. Later major league baseball expanded into Canada, when Montreal and Toronto were awarded franchises. Today the National League consists of 12 teams and the American League of 14. The 1970s saw the rise of a strong players' union. The players were successful in altering the so-called reserve clause, which bound a player to his club until he retired or was traded. In 1975 arbitrators in effect created free agents, that is, baseball veterans who can refuse to sign a contract and then enter the free-agent draft. This system has resulted in huge salary increases; today a number of major league stars are playing under multimillion-dollar contracts, which have been made possible largely from television revenues.

BASKETBALL. The only major sport of wholly American origin, basketball was invented in 1891 by James Naismith, a physical education instructor at the Springfield, Massachusetts, YMCA Training School. Naismith devised a game that forbade running with the ball and tackling, discouraged high-velocity throwing, and allowed each participant to share in ball handling and scoring. Within months, basketball was being played at other YMCAs, which began to form leagues in 1893. Women quickly took up the game, with Smith and Vassar colleges pioneering in the sport. Intercollegiate leagues began forming in 1901. The Amateur Athletic Union (AAU) joined with the Springfield YMCA to form a basketball rules committee and to control amateur and industrial teams. Professional, amateur, and industrial teams took form as well as intramural and competitive programs in public and private schools. Today basketball is second only to soccer in worldwide popularity. It has been an Olympic event since 1936; US teams have generally dominated Olympic basketball. A professional National Basketball League was formed in 1898 but lasted only until 1903. Players frequently played for several teams at once, the exclusive contract not becoming common until the 1920s. The National Basketball League (1938) and the Basketball Association of America (1946) merged in 1949 to form the National Basketball Association. It and the American Basketball Association (1967) now dominate professional basketball, regularly replenishing their ranks by organized drafting of outstanding college players.

BASTOGNE. A town in the Belgian Ardennes, scene of an epic defense by US troops during the Battle of the Bulge in World War II. See BULGE, BATTLE OF THE.

BATAAN-CORREGIDOR CAMPAIGN. Soon after the attack on Pearl Harbor, Dec. 7, 1941, Japanese landings in the Philippines trapped the forces of Gen. Douglas MacArthur on the Bataan Peninsula. His retreat was skillful. On Jan. 9, 1942, he retreated to a secondary line and held. By February the Japanese attack had been stopped, but MacArthur's men were gravely short of supplies. A tight Japanese blockade had isolated the Philippines. In early March, MacArthur was ordered to Australia. On April 9, Bataan surrendered; later many hundreds perished on the march to prison camps in central Luzon. Corregidor, a fortress island in Manila Bay, held out for three more weeks under Gen. Jonathan M. Wainwright. Japanese artillery and aircraft bombarded the island, forcing thousands to take shelter in tunnels. On May 5 and 6 Japanese troops gained a foothold, forcing Wainwright to surrender.

BATEAU. A keelless, flat-bottomed, sharp-ended craft, built of plank and propelled by oars, poles, or square sails. Large bateaux employed up to 20 rowers and carried 40 tons or more. Missouri bateaux were often called Mackinaw boats. Bateaux were superseded on the Ohio and Mississippi rivers before 1800 by keelboats.

BATHTUBS. First mentioned in the 1820s, the most advanced installation took place in Philadelphia in the early 1830s. By 1836, despite a high water rate and efforts to ban them as unsanitary, Philadelphia had 1,530. In 1845 Boston made their use illegal except on the advice of a physician. By 1860 most first-class New York hotels had bathtubs. The shower, or rain bath, was introduced about 1850.

BATON ROUGE. Capital city of Louisiana since 1849, located on the Mississippi R. Founded by the French ca. 1720 as a military and trading post. In 1822 the city became the site of the US military post and arsenal for the Southwest district. During the 20th c. Baton Rouge became an oil-refining center and an important river port. Louisiana State University is located there. Pop.: 219,486 (1980).

BATON ROUGE, BATTLE OF (Aug. 5, 1862). To regain control of the lower Mississippi R, the Confederates planned to recapture Baton Rouge. They attacked from the E and forced the Union troops to the levee, where their gunboats protected them. The Rebel forces were forced to withdraw.

BATON ROUGE, SEIZURE OF (Sept. 1810). Baton Rouge was in a portion of Spanish West Florida to which the US mistakenly asserted title as part of the Louisiana Purchase. In Sept. 1810, American settlers in West Florida seized the city, declared their independence from Spain, and invited the US to annex their territory. President Madison promptly gave orders for the occupation of West Florida as territory belonging to the US.

BATTERY. The 21-acre area at the S tip of Manhattan Island. Originally fortified by the Dutch; in 1693 the British installed a battery of cannon on the rocky island some 300 yards offshore. Construction of the large fort that dominates the present-day park was begun in 1808 and was later named Fort Clinton. By 1822 the offshore island had been connected to the mainland by landfill. In 1823 the fort was converted into an auditorium, Castle Garden, and became the center of one of New York's most popular recreation areas. Later it became the immigration station for New York and the New York Aquarium. In 1946 the fort was renamed Castle Clinton National Monument and was restored to its 19th-c. appearance.

BATTLE FLEET CRUISE AROUND THE WORLD. See GREAT WHITE FLEET.

"BATTLE HYMN OF THE REPUBLIC." American patriotic hymn. The words were written in 1861 by Julia Ward Howe to the music of "John Brown's Body," written by William Steffe in 1852. Printed in the *Atlantic Monthly* for Feb. 1862, it at once became popular and spread throughout the North.

BATTLESHIPS. See WARSHIPS.

BATTLESHIPS, DUMMY. On Feb. 24, 1863, a scow with turret of tar-smeared barrel staves, wooden guns, clay furnace, and pork barrel funnel was floated down the Mississippi R by federal seamen, causing Confederates below Vicksburg to destroy the newly captured ironclad *Indianola.* A similar dummy on Feb. 20, 1865, drew fire from Confederate batteries along Cape Fear R.

BATTS-FALLAM EXPEDITION (1671). First recorded crossing of the Appalachian Mountains. The expedition began at Fort Henry (site of Petersburg, Virginia). It was led by Capt. Thomas Batts and journalized by Robert Fallam. The party of five, including an Indian guide, crossed the Blue Ridge and Allegheny range and pushed down the valley of the New R to the West Virginia line.

BAYARD-CHAMBERLAIN TREATY. Drafted at Washington, D.C., Feb. 15, 1888, to clarify the respective powers and rights of Great Britain and the US in the waters of Newfoundland and adjacent provinces. The Senate rejected the treaty.

BAYARD V. SINGLETON. North Carolina superior court decision of 1787, the first reported decision under a written constitution overruling a law as unconstitutional. The defendant moved for dismissal according to an act of the legislature that required the courts to dismiss, upon affidavit, suits against persons holding forfeited Tory estates. The court overruled and declared that the state constitution gives every person a right to a decision concerning property by jury trial.

BAYNTON, WHARTON AND MORGAN. Philadelphia merchant firm that virtually monopolized the rich western trade after the French and Indian War. Before the legal opening of Indian trade, the firm sent the first cargo of goods westward (1765), infuriating Pennsylvanian frontiersmen known as Black Boys, who attacked the pack train and destroyed the shipment. Soon, however, the firm had 600 pack horses and wagons on the road between Philadelphia and Pittsburgh and some 300 boatmen on the Ohio R. It went into voluntary receivership in 1772, and its principals became part of the new INDIANA COMPANY.

BAY OF PIGS INVASION (April. 17, 1961). The attempt by Cuban exiles—organized, financed, and led by the US Central Intelligence Agency—to overthrow the government of Premier Fidel Castro in Havana. The landing of 1,453 men on the SW coast of Cuba was a total disaster as the Castro forces captured 1,179 and killed the rest. For the US and President Kennedy, the Bay of Pigs was a bitter political defeat and a monumental failure. It inspired the Soviet Union to install missiles with nuclear warheads in Cuba the following year, leading to the most dangerous postwar crisis between Washington and Moscow. In Dec. 1962, Castro released the 1,179 Bay of Pigs prisoners in exchange for $53 million worth of medical supplies and other goods.

BAYONNE DECREE. See NAPOLEON'S DECREES.

BAYOU. Along the Gulf Coast, numerous bays, creeks, sloughs, and small elongated lakes are called bayous. The word is more specifically used to distinguish the sluggish or stagnant offshoots of rivers that meander through the marshes or alluvial lowlands.

BAYOU TECHE EXPEDITION. A Union raid in Apr. and May 1863 from Brashear City (Barwick Bay) to Alexandria, Louisiana, on Red R, to disperse the Confederate state government at Opelousas and thus prevent Confederate reinforcements from being sent to Vicksburg, then besieged by Gen. U.S. Grant.

BAY PATH. A trail from the Connecticut R to Massachusetts Bay at or near Boston, sometimes called the Connecticut Path. From 1648 there was a route known as the New Path W through Weston and Brimfield to Springfield. After 1863 another path ran SW from the vicinity of Boston to Woodstock, Connecticut, and hence W to Hartford. Some claim that the second route was the Old Path used by the Thomas Hooker party in 1636 and by the other early colonists.

BAY PSALM BOOK. Hymnal used in Massachusetts Bay Colony, and the earliest book known to have been printed in the US. Begun in 1639 and finished in 1640, it was printed in Cambridge, Massachusetts, as the *Whole Booke of Psalmes* by Stephen Day (or Daye), the first printer of the English colonies. Eleven copies are known to exist.

BEALL'S RAID ON LAKE ERIE (Sept. 19, 1864). John Beall, a Confederate acting master in the navy, seized the steamer *Philo Parsons* on Lake Erie in an attempt to capture the Union revenue cutter *Michigan* and free Confederate prisoners on Johnson's Island, at the entrance to Sandusky Bay, Ohio. The plot failed when Beall's men revolted. He was captured three months later, tried, and executed.

BEAR FLAG REVOLT (1846). Unlike American residents of Monterey and Los Angeles those of NC California formed a community by themselves. Restive under Mexican rule, they believed the government planned to seize and expel all foreigners in the province. When the false rumor arose that 250 troops were advancing on Sacramento, the Americans immediately repaired to John C. Frémont's quarters at the Barysville Buttes. They seized a large band of government horses and captured Sonoma, the chief Mexican stronghold. Then followed the erection of the Republic of California under William B. Ide. Its flag featured a grizzly bear, which gave both the flag and the republic their names. Before the new government could get under way, Commodore John D. Sloat reached Monterey, claiming California for the US. On July 9, 1846, the US flag replaced the bear flag.

BEAR HUNTERS AND BEAR STORIES. When Lewis and Clark in 1806 returned from their historic expedition to the Far West, they published accounts of the grizzly bear, which is especially ferocious when cornered or thinks it is cornered. Stories of hand-to-hand fights with grizzlies and of fights between bulls and grizzlies became an enduring part of American lore. The discovery of the grizzly increased the fame of the more widespread black bear, known indeed to have killed a few men. Bear hunters became folk heroes as distinct as keelboatmen or Indian fighters.

BEAR PAW MOUNTAINS BATTLE (Oct. 1–5, 1877). At the end of their long campaign, the Nez Percé under Chief Joseph were surrounded by Gen. N. A. Miles's command in the Bear Paw Mountains of N Montana. After a brave resistance, Joseph surrendered, ending the NEZ PERCÉ WAR.

BEAR RIVER. Site in California of gold deposits, found in July 1848, six months after the strike at Sutter's Mill.

BEAR RIVER, BATTLE OF (Jan. 29, 1863). To subdue and control the Utah Indians, among the more peaceful of the area, Col. P.E. Connor led his troops to Bear R. With 200 effectives, he fought four hours against 300 well-armed Indians, smashing their villages, capturing their animals and stores, and killing over 200 of them. His own loss was 15 killed and 48 wounded.

BEATNIK. American literary movement of the 1950s, characterized by a rejection of establishment values and a determinedly "unliterary" writing style; leading exponents were Jack Kerouac and Allen Ginsberg.

BEAUBIEN LAND CLAIM. An effort to homestead a portion of the Fort Dearborn military reservation at Chicago. Jean Baptiste Beaubien had long lived on the tract as a trader, and in 1835 entered some 75 acres of it at the land office. A prolonged legal contest ended in rejection by the US Supreme Court in 1839.

BEAUFORT. Second permanent settlement in South Carolina, founded by the British in 1711 on Port Royal Island. First visited in 1521 by the Spanish, early attempts at settlement were made by the French (1562), English (1670), and Scots (1684). The city remains a port of entry. Preservation of colonial buildings and other historic landmarks have made Beaufort a tourist center. Pop.: 8,634 (1980).

BEAUHARNOIS, FORT. French post and Jesuit mission, erected in 1727 on Lake Pepin in Minnesota to keep the Sioux from attacking France's new line of communication between Lake Superior and the West. Abandoned ca. 1728.

BEAVER DAM CREEK, BATTLE OF. See MECHANICSVILLE, BATTLE OF.

BEAVER DAMS, BATTLE OF (June 24, 1813). Col. C.G. Boerstler with a detachment of about 600 men left Fort George, near Niagara, New York, under orders to march to the De Cou house above Beaver Dams to disperse James Fitzgibbon's British irregulars and Indians. Fitzgibbon was warned and ambushed the Americans a little E of Beaver Dams. After two hours of fighting, the Americans surrendered.

BEAVER HATS. Men's beaver hats were an important manufacture in America in the early 18th c. In 1732 Parliament forbade American makers to export hats, even among the American colonies. New England ignored or evaded the law. Silk hat manufacture began in earnest about 1835 and the beaver hat's economic importance disappeared.

BEAVER MONEY. Lack of currency in the Pacific Northwest led to private gold coinage called beaver money because a beaver was pictured on each coin (1849). Illegal but useful, they quickly disappeared from circulation because they contained 8 percent more gold than US coins.

BECKNELL'S EXPEDITIONS. William Becknell, the "father of the Santa Fe Trail," left Franklin, Mo., for Santa Fe, N.M., in 1821, on a trading expedition. He is believed to be the first American merchant to reach the New Mexican capital after Mexican independence. After a profitable trade, he returned to Missouri in 1822. Later in the year, he departed from the regular trail along the Arkansas R by crossing the Cimarron R, thus tracing out the Santa Fe Trail, and using wagons on the plains for the first time.

BEDFORD, FORT. Fort Raystown, Pa., built ca.1750, was enlarged and strengthened during the French and Indian War. Renamed Fort Bedford (1759), it was the main depot for supplies and troops between Carlisle and Fort Pitt. The fort withstood a six weeks' siege during Pontiac's conspiracy, but in 1769 was bloodlessly yielded to James Smith's Black Boys. It was abandoned before the Revolution.

BEDFORD ISLAND, BATTLE OF (1868). Col. G. A. Forsyth, leading 50 scouts in search of pillaging Indians, encamped on the Arikaree R near Wray, Colo. Attacked by about 1,000 Cheyenne and Sioux, the scouts moved onto Beecher Island. The Indians made several unsuccessful charges, then laid seige. The scouts held on until troops arrived on the ninth day and lifted the siege.

BEDINI RIOTS. Public demonstrations against the papal nuncio, Monsignor Gaetano Bedini, in Cincinnati, Ohio. On Dec. 31, 1853, a mob was dispersed after one citizen and one policeman were fatally injured.

BEE. Social gathering combining work, pleasure, and sometimes competition in frontier America. Corn husking, barn raising, log rolling, and threshing among the men; sewing, quilting, and apple paring among the women. These activities roused the competitive spirit, made sport of work, and gave recognition to champion workers. Educational counterparts were spelling bees and ciphering matches.

BEEF TRUST CASES. In 1902 three large meat packers —Swift, Armour, and Morris — formed the National Packing Company to secure control of packing houses in Kansas City, East St. Louis, and Omaha. The government charged monopolistic practices. In 1905 the Supreme Court upheld the government charges for the most part but failed to order dissolution of the company. The government sought an injunction, but the packers pleaded immunity because they had previously testified against themselves. In 1920, after a Federal Trade Commission investigation, the packers agreed to dispose of varied stockyard interests, retail meat markets, and the wholesaling of lines not directly related to meat packing.

BEEKEEPING. The honeybee, *Apis mellifera*, is not native to North America. The common black bees of Europe were imported to Virginia in 1621, followed by other strains. Beekeeping became important economically only after 1850, however. Books by L.L. Langstroth and by Moses Quinby in 1853 contributed greatly to the new industry. Among the innovations they described were the wax foundation, the movable-frame hive, the bee smoker, the honey extractor, and techniques of queen production.

BEEKMAN PATENT. A tract 16 miles square in Dutchess County, N.Y., embracing the present towns of Beekman, Union Vale, a portion of La Grange, and nearly all of Pawling and Dover. It was granted to Col. Henry Beekman in 1697 by the British governor.

BEER. See BREWING.

BEET SUGAR. The first successful beet sugar factory in the US was established at Alvarado, Calif., in 1870 (and continued in operation until 1967). Although Maine and Delaware have had some beet sugar production, mostly it has tended to concentrate in irrigated areas of the W. In 1981 about 3.2 million short tons of beet sugar were produced.

BELGIAN RELIEF. The means by which some 7.3 million Belgian civilians, inside the German lines durng World War I, received necessary food through the Allied blockade. Created in 1914 by a group of Americans, the Commission for Relief in Belgium (CRB) channeled more than 5.1 million tons of provisions into Belgium. From 1915 some 1.8 million French civilians in occupied N France were also included. Relief requirements were met by gifts of cash and kind collected in the US, the British Empire, and elsewhere; by British and French government subsidies totaling $314 million; and by US government loans.

BELKNAP, FORT. Built in 1850 in the Salt Fork of the Brazos R in C Texas to afford frontier protection and to guard the Lower Indian Reserve. Tribes on the reserve were the Caddo, Anadarkho, Waco, Tahwaccaro, and Tonkawa.

BELKNAP SCANDAL. During President Grant's second administration, the former wife of Secretary of War William W. Belknap secured a lucrative post tradership at Fort Sill for John S. Evans, reportedly receiving $6,000 per year for this service. After her death it was alleged that the money was paid to Secretary Belknap. In 1876 the House of Representatives voted unanimously to impeach the secretary and Belknap resigned.

BELLEAU WOOD, BATTLE OF (June 6–21, 1918). World War I confrontation between the American 2nd Division and the German 7th Army, which was approaching the Marne R at Château-Thierry. Against bitter resistance the Americans recaptured Bouresches, Vaux, and La Roche Wood. There were nearly 8,000 American casualties, and 1,600 German prisoners were taken.

BELLEFONTAI. The first permanent English-speaking settlement in the Old NW, near the present town of Waterloo, Ill. The settlers, mainly veterans who had served with George Rogers Clark, established themselves in 1779. In 1800 it was the third largest settlement in the Illinois Territory, but it gradually lost its identity.

BELLEFONTAI, FORT. Built in 1805 on the S side of the Missouri R, four miles from its junction with the Mississippi R. After the flood of 1810, the fort was moved to higher ground, where it served as military headquarters for the Middle West until the erection of Jefferson Barracks in 1826.

BELLE ISLE. Island in the James R at Richmond, Va., used as a prison by the Confederacy. It held about 10,000 men under harsh conditions by the end of 1863. The captives were then moved to a new prison at ANDERSON-VILLE, Ga.

BELLEVUE WAR. W.W. Brown, owner of a hotel at Bellevue, Ia., was believed to lead a gang of outlaws. Sheriff W.A. Warren attempted to arrest Brown and several of his men on Apr. 1, 1840. Four of the posse and three of the alleged bandits (including Brown) were killed, and thirteen of Brown's band captured. Citizens voted for hanging or whipping; the men were flogged and sent down the Mississippi R.

BELL TELEPHONE LABORATORIES. World's largest institution for organized industrial research, a subsidiary of AT&T. Bell Labs has provided much of the stimulus for the modern revolution in telecommunications based on solid-state electronics and information theory. Its prime responsibility has been the engineering of an integrated communications network for AT&T and for the operating companies (known as the Bell System) that were subsidiaries of AT&T until the 1984 divestiture. Bell Labs research has led to a wide range of techniques beneficial to many industries and to the military. A succession of fundamental contributions have emanated from there, including pioneer work in such areas as extraterrestrial radio waves, feedback amplifier theory, waveguides, electron diffraction, electronic circuits, information theory, artificial intelligence, radar, transistors, and the coaxial cable. Seven of its research scientists have been awarded the Nobel Prize. Headquarters are at Murray Hill, N.J.

BELMONT, BATTLE OF (Nov. 7, 1861). U.S. Grant's first Civil War battle and first defeat. Gen. J.C. Frémont ordered the attack on Belmont, Mo., to prevent Gen. Leonidas Polk at Columbus, Ky., from aiding Confederates in Missouri. Steaming from Cairo, Ill., on the Ohio R, Grant landed five miles above Belmont and drove Gen. G.J. Pillow's men to the river and set fire to their camp. Polk, crossing with reinforcements, and aided by the Columbus batteries, drove Grant to his transports and retreat.

BELTRÁN-ESPEJO EXPEDITION (1582–83). An expedition into New Mexico from Chihuahua led by Bernardino Beltrán to rescue two Franciscan missionaries. Upon reaching Pueblo and learning that the missionaries had been killed, he and his soldiers stayed to explore. Their favorable reports of the country and people strengthened the resolve of the authorities to colonize New Mexico and evangelize its inhabitants.

BEMIS HEIGHTS, BATTLES OF. See FREEMAN'S FARM, BATTLE OF.

BENEFIT OF CLERGY. In English common law, a plea exempting clergy from criminal process; later a commutation of the death sentence in certain felonies for all prisoners who could read. Statutes abolishing the privilege appear after the Revolution, but until the Civil War it was still used in southern states, sparing a master's valuable property in his slave.

BENNINGTON, BATTLE OF (Aug. 16, 1777). British Gen. John Burgoyne planned a raid on the American stores at Bennington, Vt., to encourage Loyalists, frighten New England, replenish his provisions, and mount a regiment of heavily equipped German dragoons. Led by German Col. Frederick Baum, about 800 men approached Bennington, where about 2,600 colonial troops were assembled. Despite reinforcements sent by Burgoyne, the Americans won the battle.

BENTON, FORT. Trading post on the Missouri R established in Montana by the American Fur Co. in 1844 as Fort Lewis. In 1846 it was moved to the site of the present town of Fort Benton, and in 1850 renamed in honor of Thomas Hart Benton.

BENTONVILLE, BATTLE OF (March 19–21, 1865). Gen. J.E. Johnston and a small Confederate force in North Carolina, hoping to prevent a junction of the Union forces of generals Sherman and Grant, attacked the left wing of Sherman's army. Though outnumbered, Johnston succeeded in fighting a drawn battle, but lost at least 2,000 men. By the night of Mar. 21, most of Sherman's army was concentrated at the spot, and Johnston retired.

BENT'S FORT. First known as Fort William, completed by William Bent and others c. 1832 on the N bank of the Arkansas R, seven miles E of present-day La Junta, Colorado. Fort Bent became the outstanding southwestern trading post in both the mountain fur trade and the overland commerce to Santa Fe. It was a military depot during the Mexican War. In 1849, Bent moved it 40 miles downriver, where it became known as Bent's New Fort. He leased it to the government until 1859 and retired. It was renamed Fort Wise and then Fort Lyon, and was moved again, 20 miles up the river to its present location.

BEREA COLLEGE V. KENTUCKY, 211 US 45 (1908). Involved the right of Berea College to teach black and white students together. Kentucky law declared it illegal and the state supreme court upheld the statute. The US Supreme Court dodged the major issue of interracial education and decided against the college on narrow grounds involving the right of the state to change or amend the charter of a corporation. The decision reinforced and expanded the separate but equal doctrine of PLESSY V. FERGUSON.

BERGEN PRIZES. The *Alliance*, a US vessel of John Paul Jones's squadron in European waters, captured three British merchantmen in 1779. When bad weather forced the vessels into Bergen, Norway, England requested and obtained restoration of its merchantmen from the Danish-Norwegian government. Jones demanded indemnification at Copenhagen. After years of negotiation, he was turned down.

BERING SEA DISPUTE. See PELAGIC SEALING DISPUTE.

BERING SEA FISHERIES. See SEALING.

BERKELEY. Home of the University of California, founded as a seminary town and named after George Berkeley, the English philosopher. It was incorporated in 1878. Pop.: 103,328 (1980).

BERLIN, TREATY OF (1921). Separate peace treaty between the US and Germany ending World War I. It was entered into after the Senate rejected the Treaty of Versailles. Its provisions accepted some of those of the Treaty of Versailles, including those dealing with colonies, disarmament, reparations, and responsibility for the war. The most important features rejected were the League of Nations, the International Labor Organization, and the boundary provisions.

BERLIN AIRLIFT. History's largest exclusively aerial supply operation. For eleven months in 1948 and 1949, US and British planes sustained more than 2 million West Berliners and occupation troops after the Soviet Union imposed the BERLIN BLOCKADE. A minimum of 140,000 tons of supplies were airlifted each month. The Soviets harassed some flights but stopped short of war. Hurt by reciprocal denial of imports from West Germany, they raised the blockade May 12, 1949, but the airlift continued into September.

BERLIN BLOCKADE. The Soviet blockade of Berlin, beginning June 23, 1948, and the responding BERLIN AIRLIFT were the most dramatic of the early cold-war confrontations. Initially seeking West Germany's recovery to promote the economic reconstruction and growth of Western Europe, the US in early 1948 imposed stringent German currency reforms and moved toward a West German constitution and government. This precipitated the Soviet blockade of the western half of Berlin, to prevent the revival of West German power. After 321 days of successful and British sustenance of West Berlin's population, the Soviets terminated the blockade.

BERLIN DECREE. See NAPOLEON'S DECREES.

BERLIN WALL. On Aug. 31, 1961, the East Germans ordered the building of a wall between East Berlin and West Berlin to put an end to the masses of East Germans defecting to the West. The wall succeeded in its purpose, and by the 1980s had seemingly become a permanent part of the Berlin landscape.

BERMUDA ADMIRALTY CASE. In April 1862 the Union navy captured the *Bermuda*, a British ship whose cargo included artillery, ammunition, small arms, and Confederate uniform insignia and postage stamps. A US court held that evidence proved the ship's cargo was intended for the Confederacy and that therefore the seizure was permissible. The US Supreme Court in 1865 upheld this position.

BERMUDA CONFERENCE (1957). After the deep Anglo-American rift caused by the Suez War in 1956, President Eisenhower and Prime Minister Harold Macmillan met in Bermuda to bring the two allies closer together again. The two leaders announced an agreement whereby the US would supply Britain with intermediate-range missiles.

BERMUDA ISLANDS. A cluster of more than 300 islands 570 miles E of Cape Hatteras, N.C. From 1612 to 1615 the islands were included under the Virginia Co. charter, but thereafter became a separate company colony and then a crown colony (1684). The settlers concentrated on tobacco, and there was considerable trade with the mainland. The inhabitants opposed British colonial policy and sent delegates to the Continental Congress to secure relief from the trade embargo against loyal colonies. They achieved their end by furnishing gunpowder and other supplies to the rebels. Bermuda is today a British dependency and a popular tourist area. Pop.: 54,893 (1980).

BERNARD, FORT. A small trading post between Horse Creek and Fort Laramie in Wyoming on the Oregon Trail. A trappers' trail from Bent's Fort in Colorado joined the Oregon Trail at this post. Taos and Santa Fe traders freighted flour here to trade to emigrants bound for the coast.

BETHABARA. The first town planted (1753) by German Moravians from Pennsylvania in Wachovia (now part of WINSTON-SALEM), N.C. Its early settlers were noted for advanced agricultural practices, especially their medicinal herbs. Bethabara grew slowly and is now only a small village, known locally as Oldtown.

BETHEL COMMUNITY (1844–77). Communist settlement in Shelby County, Mo., led by William Keil, who preached moral living but subscribed to no religious faith. The community prospered, and another Bethel was founded in Aurora, Ore., in 1855. Neither survived Keil's death in 1877.

BETHESDA HOUSE OF MERCY. Orphanage and school, founded by Rev. George Whitefield, near Savannah, Ga., in 1739. He died in 1770, and the project faltered before 1800. Savannah's present Bethesda dates from 1855.

BIBLE. The Geneva Bible (1560), the work of Protestant scholars who had fled to Geneva to escape the Catholic Queen Mary's persecutions, was the Puritan's Bible. Even after the appearance of the King James, or Authorized, Version in 1611, the Geneva Bible held its own. During the entire colonial period, the Bible was first among moral and cultural influences. The first book printed in the colonies was the *Bay Psalm Book*, which contained portions of the Bible. The first complete Bible was John Eliot's translation into the Algonkin language printed at Cambridge in 1663. Partly because the printing of the King James Version was an Oxford monopoly, three editions of Martin Luther's Bible in German appeared in America before any were printed in English. Robert Aitken published the first American Bible in English in Philadelphia (1781–82). Isaiah Thomas printed the first Greek New Testament in Worcester in 1800. The first printing of the Douay Version (Roman Catholic) was in Philadelphia in 1790. No single factor had a larger part in determining what moral direction the nation would take after the Revolution than the widespread distribution of the Bible throughout the West by such agencies as the American Bible Society (1816), the American Tract Society (1825), and the American Sunday School Union (1824). The Bible had an important role in advancing every reform movement in American history: antislavery, temperance, and peace movements.

BIBLE COMMONWEALTH. Applied by modern historians to the Puritan colonies of Massachusetts and New Haven, Conn., where the right to vote was limited to church members and an effort was made to bring all activities into harmony with the Bible.

BICAMERAL LEGISLATURES. Having as their antecedents the British Parliament and colonial legislatures, bicameral legislatures have been used by federal and almost all state governments since the adoption of the Constitution. Only Nebraska has (since 1934) a unicameral legislature. The bicameral legislature was developed to resolve political conflict through compromise. A heterogeneous group of voters selects the members of both chambers. On the national level, the Senate gives equal representation to each state, and the House of Representatives has members apportioned on the basis of each state's population.

BICYCLING. During the late 19th c., bicycling became one of the most popular American sports. Temporarily pushed into the background by the automobile, a revival occurred in the 1930s. Then in the 1960s and 1970s a major revival took place, partly because of the high cost of gasoline and partly because of the new interest in physical fitness and concern for the environment. An estimated 75 million people in the United States participate to some degree in bicycling.

BIDDLE MISSION (1836). Charles A. Biddle was sent by President Jackson to Nicaragua, Guatemala, and Panama to determine the expediency of a canal across the Isthmus of Panama. Instead, he secured from the government of New Granada (Colombia) for himself and his associates the right to build a road or a railway across the isthmus, as well as rights to steam navigation on the Charles R. Jackson was infuriated at the development and was planning a reprimand when Biddle died on Dec. 21, 1836.

BIDLACK TREATY (Dec. 12, 1846). Benjamin A. Bidlack, US representative in Bogotá, signed a treaty with New Granada (Colombia) removing tariff discrimination against American commerce and guaranteeing neutrality of the Isthmus of Panama and New Granada's rights of sovereignty over the isthmus. On thirteen occasions, US troops were landed to protect the transit route. When Panama seceded (Nov. 3, 1903), it was held by the US government that the covenant ran with this land. (See HAY-BUNAU-VARILLA TREATY.)

BIG APPLE. Term popularized in the 1970s to designate New York City. It is believed to have originated with jazz musicians in the 1940s.

BIG BLACK RIVER, BATTLE AT (May 16–17, 1863). After his defeat at Champion's Hill in Mississippi, Confederate Gen. J.C. Pemberton retreated to the Big Black R, hoping to hold the river's bridge long enough for the army to cross before Gen. U.S. Grant could attack. On May 17, Grant's advance troops appeared, and Pemberton was driven in retreat to Vicksburg.

BIG BONE LICK. Salt spring in Boone County, Ky., 1.5 miles E of the Ohio R. Large prehistoric animals, including the mastodon and the Arctic elephant, were attracted by the seepage of brine. Capt. Charles Lemoyne, found the lick in 1729; and in 1773 James Douglas, a Virginia surveyor, described the fossils. In 1806 Dr. William Goforth entrusted fossils to the English traveler Thomas Ashe, who removed them to Great Britain. Thomas Jefferson made a collection of the fossils, and natural history museums collected the remaining skeletons.

BIG BOTTOM MASSACRE (Jan. 2, 1791). Shawnee Indians surprised a new settlement on the Muskingum R in Ohio and killed fourteen people. Three settlers were captured; four escaped. The Ohio Company of Associates immediately provided greater protection for settlers.

BIG BROTHER MOVEMENT. Founded 1903 in Cincinnati, Ohio, to aid fatherless boys. The movement was formalized a year later. At present 400 member agencies are comprised by the national organization Big Brothers/Big Sisters, with headquarters in Philadelphia.

BIG HOLE, BATTLE OF (Aug. 9, 1877). During the NEZ PERCÉ WAR, Col. John Gibbon, with volunteers and mounted infantrymen, attacked Chief Joseph's camp on the Big Hole R in Montana. The Nez Percé drove the soldiers back and disabled or killed 69. Eighty Indians died, over two-thirds women and children.

BIG HORN MOUNTAINS. Range of the Rocky Mountains mainly in Wyoming but extending into Montana. Site of the Fetterman massacre (1886) and the Battle of Little Bighorn (1876).

BIG KNIVES. Also Long Knives. Used by western Indians to designate English colonists. George Rogers Clark spoke of himself and his men as Big Knives in speeches to Indians in 1778 after the capture of Illinois. Later the term came to designate Americans in general. Thought to have originated with the steel knives of the colonists, contrasted with stone implements of the Indians.

BIGLOW PAPERS. Originally, nine satiric poems by James Russell Lowell in Yankee dialect directed against the Mexican War; spoken by Hosea Biglow, they opposed the acquisition of additional slave territory. In 1848 and again in 1867 Lowell used the title *Biglow Papers* for collections of poems and essays (including the original nine poems), but the overall effect was no longer satiric.

BIG MOCCASIN GAP. In extreme SW Virginia; admitted Daniel Boone and other pioneers through the Clinch Mountains into Kentucky. Not far from it were the blockhouses, built by Capt. John Anderson in 1777, where the parties formed for the journey over the Wilderness Road. The line set by the Treaty of Lochaber (1768) and surveyed by John Donelson in 1770 crossed the road near this gap.

BIG STICK POLICY. President Theodore Roosevelt was fond of quoting an African proverb that if you speak softly and carry a big stick, you will go far. The Big Stick came to mean the power of the United States, especially the navy, which Roosevelt did not hesitate to show off. He used his Big Stick policy to take over and manage the affairs of several Latin American countries and to prevent similar actions by European countries.

BILLETING. Forced quartering of troops in private houses, a European practice rarely resorted to in America. Increased British troop arrivals during the French and Indian War made billeting an issue, arousing resistance in Charleston, New York, and Boston (leading directly to the Boston Massacre). Billeting was objected to in the Declaration of Independence and was prohibited in the Bill of Rights, in the Third Amendment.

BILL OF RIGHTS. At the Constitutional Convention in 1787 George Mason proposed that the Constitution be "prefaced with a bill of rights," but the motion lost. Accordingly, the constitution as submitted contained none. It did include some important guarantees of personal rights and liberties; the privilege of the writ of habeas corpus was not to be suspended except in cases of rebellion or invasion; no bill of attainder or ex post facto law was to be passed; all crimes were to be tried by jury; and no religious test could be required as a qualification to any office. When the Constitution came up for ratification, its opponents stressed the need for a bill of rights. The consequence was that the states sent along with their ratification more than a hundred amendments they wanted adopted by the new government. After nearly three months of deliberation (June–August 1789), the House of Representatives proposed seventeen amendments and sent them to the Senate. After a conference with the House, on Sept. 25, 1789, the Senate approved twelve of the original amendments. On Nov. 20, 1789, New Jersey became the first state to ratify the amendments. Virginia, on Dec. 15, 1791, was the eleventh, thereby completing the ratification process. On that date, the Bill of Rights became effective. Two amendments, those on the apportionment of representatives and the compensation of members of Congress, failed ratification. In some 400 words, the Bill of Rights provides for freedom of religion, speech, and assembly and the right of petition (First Amendment); a guarantee against unreasonable searches and seizures (Fourth Amendment); prohibitions of double jeopardy, of coerced testimony against oneself in any criminal case, of depriving any person of life, liberty, or property without due process of law, and of taking of private property for public use without just compensation (Fifth Amendment); the right to a speedy and public trial, the right to be confronted by accusing witnesses, and the right to assistance of counsel (Sixth Amendment); the right to trial by jury (Seventh Amendment); a prohibition against excessive bail or fines and against cruel and unusual punishment (Eighth Amendment). The Ninth Amendment is a statement of general principle that the provision of certain rights in the Constitution shall not imply the denial of other rights "retained by the people"; and so, too, the Tenth Amendment states that the powers not delegated to the federal government are reserved to the states or to the people. In 1833 the Supreme Court ruled that the first ten amendments protected the people against abuses of the federal government but did not apply to the states. However, the history of constitutional law in this country in the years following that decision has been largely a record of the watering down of that decision. The ratification of the FOURTEENTH AMENDMENT made much of the Bill of Rights applicable to the states, and the courts have over the years extended that applicability. Today, virtually all of the important principles of the Bill of Rights apply to the states as well as the federal government.

BILLS OF CREDIT. Noninterest-bearing government obligations that circulate as money; commonly applied to issues by the colonies and by the Continental Congress and states during the Revolutionary War. The bills became known as treasury notes or United States notes.

BILLS OF EXCHANGE. Paper orders, usually issued by a company in international trade, to pay out a specified sum of money at some future time and place. They were used in the colonial period for buying and selling goods in foreign markets. The term is still used in international trade.

BILLS OF RIGHTS, STATE. The bill of rights adopted by Virginia in 1776 was the model for the national Bill of Rights, the first ten amendments to the Constitution. The Virginia declaration, largely the work of George Mason, was in large part a restatement of English principles drawn from such sources as Magna Carta, the Petition of Rights, and the English Bill of Rights. It still stands in practically its original form in the Virginia constitution. The second great bill of rights, the Declaration of Rights of the Commonwealth of Massachusetts (1780), also remains in force today. The bills of rights in other states reflect more the results of local or contemporary events.

BILOXI. City in Mississippi on the Gulf of Mexico, the first settlement and first capital of the Louisiana Territory. Settled by Pierre Lemoyne, in 1699, with 200 French colonists, as Fort Maurepas on Biloxi Bay (near the present Ocean Springs). Relocated to the present site in 1719. Today commercial fishing is its chief industry. Pop.: 43,927 (1980).

BIMETALLISM. In 1792 Congress established a monetary standard under which both gold and silver served as a basis of coinage. The system was a failure, and by the 1830s adequate gold coinage had driven most of the silver coins from the market as the market value of silver was higher than its monetary value. In 1853 Congress confirmed this situation legally but left the silver dollar as a standard coin. In a revision of the law in 1873 the silver dollar was dropped, and the ratio of silver to gold fell below 16 to 1 for the first time in history. (See CRIME OF 1873.) This decline coincided with the opening of rich silver mines in the West, with the post-Civil War deflation, and with a deep depression that sorely afflicted the country. The consequence was a political movement, promoted by the silver interests and embraced by agrarian and pro-inflation elements for the restoration of bimetallism. Eventually there developed in the House a nonpartisan "silver bloc," led by members from the sparsely populated western states in which mine owners gained great political influence. In the 1870s, 1890s, and 1930s, the efforts of this pressure group, reinforced by the popular clamor for inflation, almost achieved bimetallism and succeeded in extracting from Congress legislation giving a cash subsidy of some sort to the producers of silver (see BLAND-ALLISON ACT OF 1878; SHERMAN SILVER PURCHASE ACT OF 1890). The depression of the 1930s restored interest in bimetallism, the gold standard, and the money supply. On April 5, 1933, President Franklin D. Roosevelt suspended the gold standard. The Thomas Amendment to the Agricultural Adjustment Act (May 12, 1933) authorized the president to restore bimetallism. During the 1960s the United States abandoned all but a small vestige of a metallic standard. The acts of March 3, 1965, and March 18, 1968, eliminated the gold reserve against Federal Reserve deposits and Federal Reserve notes. An act of July 23, 1965, put an end to minting standard silver coins; and an act of Aug. 15, 1971, temporarily suspended the international right to convert dollars into gold.

BINGHAM PURCHASE. In 1786 William Bingham purchased from Massachusetts 1 million acres of present-day Maine, then part of Massachusetts. He later acquired another million acres.

BIOCHEMISTRY. The first American studies were mostly concerned with agricultural problems involving plant growth and animal feeding. Proteins received a great deal of attention; agricultural chemists were concerned mainly with the protein content of feeds and their utilization by farm animals. In the late 19th c. T.B. Osborne at the Connecticut Agricultural Experiment Station carried out work on isolation and purification of plant proteins and sought to unravel their amino acid compostion. Other scientists did extensive studies on energy requirements of animals and energy values of various foods. Protein studies were followed in the early 20th c. by attention to vitamins and minerals. The work on vitamins A, B, D, and B-complex inaugurated a whole new understanding of nutrition and led, through practical application to food selection and fortification, to the virtual elimination of scurvy, rickets, beriberi, and pellagra. Composition and properties of body fluids received much attention from physiological chemists associated with medical schools and, especially, the Rockefeller Institute. American biochemists pioneered in the study of intermediary metabolism with the use of isotopic tracers. Radio isotopes were used extensively after World War II. Photosynthesis, enzymes, nucleic acids, and recombinant DNA, and gene-splicing are examples of areas of study of modern biochemists.

BIOLOGY. See BACTERIOLOGY AND VIROLOGY; BOTANY; ECOLOGY; FISH AND MARINE LIFE; GENETICS; HERPETOLOGY; MAMMALS; MOLECULAR BIOLOGY; ORNITHOLOGY; PHYSIOLOGY.

BIRCH BARK. Used by Indians of the Great Lakes country and adjacent Canada for covering canoes and wigwams. Small sheets of birch bark were used for picture writing with a stylus by some groups.

BIRCH SOCIETY. See JOHN BIRCH SOCIETY.

BIRDS. See ORNITHOLOGY.

BIRD SANCTUARIES. Natural areas set aside for birds, where they can nest, feed, and roost free from human harm. The first ones were established early in the 20th c. by the American Ornithologists' Union and the National Audubon Society. In 1903 President Theodore Roosevelt began setting aside government-owned lands as federal bird reservations. Today the Interior Department maintains about 400 units, covering 45 million acres. The Audubon Society maintains the nation's largest private refuge system, a string of more than sixty sanctuaries from Maine to California.

BIRD'S INVASION OF KENTUCKY (1780). From Detroit, British Col. Henry Bird led an army of mostly Indian troops against the settlers of Kentucky. Martin's Station and Ruddle's Station were easily overwhelmed, but lack of provisions compelled a retreat. Over 300 prisoners were taken to Detroit.

BIRD'S POINT. Early fortification in Missouri, opposite the mouth of the Ohio R where it joins the Mississippi. Of strategic importance in guarding both rivers, it was first fortified by the Spanish in 1795.

BIRMINGHAM. Largest city in Alabama. A major steel center, it is often called the Pittsburgh of the South. The city's industrial power is based on the high-quality iron ore, coal, and limestone within its immediate vicinity. The city was founded in 1871 and grew rapidly because of good railroad connections to national markets. Pop.: 284,413 (1980).

BIRTH CONTROL MOVEMENT. Birth control became a concern as early as the 1830s in the context of feminist and health reform agitation. From the beginning, the movement met with widespread disapproval and harassment. Nevertheless, there was some experimentation with contraceptive devices, plus a steady growth in demand for birth control information. Beginning in 1873 birth control pamphlets were classified as obscene by federal and state laws and were banned from the mails, which made it difficult even for physicians to write on the scientific aspects of contraception. Significant relaxation of anti-birth control legislation began with Margaret Sanger who defied the mail ban and, in 1916, opened a birth control clinic in Brooklyn, N. Y. The forerunner of the Planned Parenthood Federation was formed in 1917 and became the focal point for many legal battles during the following decades. After World War II, there was steady acceleration in public acceptance of family limitation, due partly to economic realities. This acceptance led to expanded educational and clinical programs by Planned Parenthood and other private organizations.; greater support for medical research in related fields, such as reproductive biology; extensive programs to produce cheap and effective contraceptive devices and drugs, particulary the birth control pill; and beginning in the 1960s federal involvement in birth control activities. (See also ABORTION.)

BISHOP HILL COLONY A theocratic communist colony, founded in Henry County, Ill., in 1846 by Erik Jansson, who settled there with some 1,500 Swedish Perfectionists. Dissolved in 1860.

BISMARCK. Capital city of North Dakota, located near an important crossing place on the Missouri R. Mandan Indian villages were located in the vicinity. The city was named in 1873 in honor of the German chancellor in the vain hope that German money would be forthcoming as an investment in a railroad line through the town. Bismarck is an important transportation center; live cattle, meat, and lignite are its main products. Pop.: 44,485 (1980).

BISMARCK SEA, BATTLE OF (March 2–4, 1943). To reinforce the Japanese garrison on New Guinea, a large Japanese convoy left New Britain on February 28. Hidden initially by bad weather, the convoy was spotted by Allied patrol planes in the Bismarck Sea. More than 300 US and Australian bombers and fighters and a strike by US torpedo boats sank all eight transports and four destroyers.

BISON. See BUFFALO.

BIT. Old term for one-eighth of a dollar, used chiefly in the South and Southwest, stemming from use of the Spanish real, a silver coin of that value. The term's use was limited to even multiples: two bits, four bits, and six bits.

BIZERTE. City in Tunisia, important in World War II. In November 1942, German and Italian troops occupied the area. On April 22, 1943, when Anglo-American troops attacked the Axis troops in the NE corner ot Tunisia, Bizerte was the objective of the US troops. The US Second Corps entered the city on May 7, the same day British units seized Tunis. This Axis defeat opened the way for future Allied operations across the Mediterranean into Europe.

BLACK AMERICANS. People of African descent first arrived in the New World with the Spanish in the 16th c. Other blacks were members of French expeditions that opened up the Mississippi Valley. But as the English came to be the chief colonizers, the introduction of Africans to fill the labor needs of the colonies linked the black experience in America to that of the Anglo-Americans. Between 5 million and 10 million Africans were transported to the Americas between 1619 and 1865. The 1980 census identified 26,488,218 black Americans in the United States, constituting slightly more than 11 percent of the total population. The first Africans introduced at Jamestown competed with indentured servants from Europe, although their presence as servants was not voluntary: they had been captured and sold. By 1670 servants of African descent were generally viewed as slaves, and the evolution of the institution of slavery had reduced Africans to the status of personal property. (See SLAVERY.)

The American Revolution and a declining profit from slaves led to the end of slavery in the North, but the invention of the cotton gin gave new impetus to slavery in the South. Thus, despite the ideals of the Declaration of Independence, slaveholding interests increased in influence well into the 19th c. The Constitution recognized the existence of slavery, and federal and state legislation protected property in slaves. Free blacks were discriminated against in both North and South. The DRED SCOTT CASE of 1857 articulated the position of the American black: The Supreme Court in effect denied that blacks were to be regarded as citizens. Blacks sought a variety of means to counter physical and psychological bondage. Conspiracies and revolts continued as long as slavery existed, among them those of Denmark Vesey (1822) and Nat Turner (1831). Opposition to slavery among free persons also existed, and in the 19th c. abolition became an influential force, largely through the activities of Frederick Douglass (who had fled slavery in Maryland), William Lloyd Garrison, and Theodore D. Weld. (See ANTISLAVERY.)

The effect of the Civil War was not evident at its start. Southern states were determined to maintain slavery, and President Lincoln announced that he had no intention of interfering with slavery in the states. Not until military conditions made it beneficial did Lincoln issue the Emancipation Proclamation (January 1863). That proclamation and the Thirteenth, Fourteenth, and Fifteenth amendments to the Constituition provided the legal basis for full citizenship for blacks, and for a brief period they enjoyed these benefits under federal protection; but several factors combined to prevent their new status from becoming permanent. First, blacks lacked education, economic independence, and political experience. Second, the opposition of southern whites to citizenship rights for blacks was virtually unanimous (and no broad base of support existed among northern whites). The mutual support that supposedly existed between Republicans and blacks disappeared completely in 1876. In that year the Republicans and southern Democratic conservatives struck a bargain: The Republican candidate, Rutherford B. Hayes, would be put in the White House, and in return federal troops would be withdrawn from the South and political power would be restored to the conservatives. Nevertheless, blacks made impressive educational and political gains. Blacks and their white supporters established a number of colleges and universities, including Fisk, Talladega, Morehouse, Atlanta, Johnson C. Smith, and Shaw. Economic progress was slower, with most of the former slaves and their offspring being reduced to the status of sharecropper, hardly an economic improvement over slavery.

World War I represents a watershed in the experience of black Americans. Most significant was the impetus given the urbanization of blacks by the needs of northern industry. Besides relief from the low wages and hardships of farming, the North offered less overt discrimination, better schools, suffrage, possibilities for justice in the courts, and access to public places. When war in Europe stopped the flow of immigrants for industrial labor, job opportunities for blacks increased and the trickle of blacks to the cities of the Northeast and West became a flood. By 1920 half a million southern blacks had relocated. Large numbers of black men (367,000 by 1918) served in the armed forces in World War I, virtually all in segregated units. Wartime gains made by blacks were largely eroded in the years following the war, however. The Ku Klux Klan revived and the number of lynchings turned upward. A series of race riots spread across the country. Despite the absence of appreciable progress economically and politically, there were significant cultural developments. Jazz had spread from New Orleans to all the northern cities and permeated American music, both popular and serious. The HARLEM RENAISSANCE, centered in New York City, was an important part of the cultural life of the 1920s. The Great Depression temporarily set back black progress in civil rights; for many blacks, as for poor whites, surviving economically was the only important consideration.

World War II affected blacks much as World War I had. More than a million black men served in the armed forces, and the increased demand for workers of all kinds greatly increased the economic well-being of virtually all blacks. The end of the war saw the stepping up of the activities of black civil rights groups, notably the National Association for the Advancement of Colored People (NAACP) and the National Urban League. Despairing of any action by Congress, these organizations focused on the judicial process as the likeliest route to improved civil rights for blacks. A series of court cases instituted by the NAACP led eventually to the 1954 and 1955 Supreme Court decisions in BROWN V. BOARD OF EDUCATION OF TOPEKA, KANSAS, which effectively outlawed school segregation. The mid-1950s also saw the beginning of more direct civil protests by blacks. The chief characteristics of black protest were a moderate, nonviolent approach, opposition to physical confrontation, and a willingness to suffer physically to make their point. The 386-day Montgomery, Alabama, bus boycott (1955–56) spawned the Southern Christian Leadership Conference (SCLC) and produced the foremost civil rights leader, the Rev. Dr. Martin Luther King, Jr. Black protest after 1960 became more confrontational in tactics, including sit-ins in restaurants and bus stations, stand-ins at segregated theater box offices, kneel-ins at segregated churches, and wade-ins at segregated beaches. A series of "freedom rides" was organized by the Congress of Racial Equality (CORE) to protest segregation in interstate travel, and voter registration drives and demonstrations were organized against discriminatory election practices. These demonstrations often resulted in violence, and the national guard had to be used to quell mobs attempting to prevent the implementation of court orders to desegregate schools in various southern states. Dozens of homes and churches were bombed and burned, and peaceful demonstrators were beaten and gassed. Both black and white civil rights workers were killed. Black frustration resulted in riots in a number of cities beginning in 1963; they included New York, Birmingham, Los Angeles (the Watts section), Detroit, Newark, Philadelphia, Chicago, Rochester, Atlanta, Nashville, and Boston. A second round of riots occurred in 1968 as a protest to the assassination of Martin Luther King.

The 1960s also saw the beginning of legislative remedies for discrimination against blacks. With the strong support of President Lyndon B. Johnson, Congress passed three historic civil rights bills: The Civil Rights Act of 1964, the Voting Rights Act of 1965, and the Civil Rights Act of 1968. Taken together, these acts removed virtually all legal impediments to full citizenship rights of blacks. Social, educational, and economic disparities persisted; and black activists continued to press for full equality in those areas. Black power in the political area became particularly notable in the 1970s and 1980s; voter registration drives greatly swelled the rolls of black voters, and the election of black mayors and city council members became commonplace all over the nation. In 1984, cities with black mayors included Chicago, Philadelphia, Atlanta, and Los Angeles.

BLACK BALL LINE. The first (1818) and most celebrated of the lines of translatlantic sailing packets operating between New York and (Liverpool) England. Monthly at first, the sailings were increased to twice monthly with eight ships in 1822. The line continued for sixty years.

BLACK BELT. Crescent-shaped area extending along the Alabama R in Alabama and up the Tombigbee R in NE Mississippi. It derives its name from the exceedingly rich black soil, which makes it one of the best agricultural regions of the South. From 1830 to 1860 the Black Belt was the leading cotton-producing region of the South and highly dependent on slave labor. Although it still produces cotton, today its farmers have diversified into food crops.

BLACK BOYS. Pennsylvania frontiersmen who under leadership of James Smith, defended the frontier against the Indians. In 1765, they burned a packhorse train belonging to a company engaged in the Indian trade. Disguised themselves by blackening their faces.

BLACKBURN'S FORD, BATTLE AT (July 18, 1861). Union Gen. Daniel Tyler's division found Confederate Gen. James Longstreet's brigade in position behind Bull Run at Blackburn's Ford, attacked, and was decisively repulsed.

BLACK CAVALRY IN THE WEST (1866–91). Established by Congress in 1866, the Ninth and Tenth Cavalry regiments spent over twenty-five years on the frontier fighting with distinction against Indians, bandits, horse thieves, and Mexican revolutionaries.

BLACK CODES. Legislation passed in the former Confederate states in 1865–66 to limit the freedom of recently freed blacks. Intended to replace the social controls of slavery. Typical were provisions for declaring blacks to be vagrants if they were unemployed and without permanent residence. They were subject to being arrested, fined, and bound out for a term of labor if unable to pay the fine. Persons encouraging blacks to refuse to abide by them were themselves subject to penalties. Northern reaction helped to produce the Fourteenth and Fifteenth amendments, which temporarily removed such legislation from the books. Following Reconstruction, many of the provisions of the black codes were reenacted in the Jim Crow laws that continued in effect in many cases until the Civil Rights Act of 1964.

BLACKFOOT. Plains tribe, the Siksika ("black feet") were so named because they wore black moccasins. The Blackfoot nation at its peak, between ca. 1700 and ca. 1870, had as many as 15,000 members. Spread from the North Saskatchewan R to the southern tributaries of the Missouri R in Montana, it formed a military federation significant in the balance of power in the NW Plains. The Blackfoot complex is classic Plains culture. They had the best-developed system of military associations (divisions of warriors) based on age-grading.

BLACK FRIDAY (Sept. 24, 1869). The climactic day of an effort by Jay Gould, James Fisk, Jr., and their associates to corner the gold market in the United States. A gold corner had not seemed difficult if governmemt nonintervention could be assured. Gould and Fisk began buying gold heavily and soon forced the price from $135 per ounce to $144, causing panic and fear in the markets. As the price rose to $160, the US Treasury ordered $4 million of the gold reserve to be sold. Gould had already begun selling, and the price soon dropped back to $135. The episode caused heavy losses to business, and scores of speculators were ruined. Gould and Fisk made $11 million.

BLACK HAWK WAR (1832). Conflict between the United States and Sauk (or Sac) and Fox Indians, mainly in Illinois and Wisconsin. Chief Black Hawk was the rival of Keokuk, who had ceded land to the whites in 1804 and had removed his people across the Mississippi R to Iowa in 1823. Black Hawk declined to evacuate his village at Rock Island, Ill. In 1831 white settlers preempted Black Hawk's village, and he was forced to withdraw across the Mississippi. Early in 1832, he and his people crossed back into Illinois. Gen. Henry Atkinson ordered Black Hawk to return to Iowa and Black Hawk's emissaries were shot in cold blood. Black Hawk retired up the Rock R, attacking and burning frontier settlements. On July 28 his force was massacred, and Black Hawk was captured by the Winnebago, who turned him in for a reward. He was taken to Washington, D.C., where, incongruously, he was honored by the US government and allowed to return to the remnant of his tribe in Iowa.

BLACK HILLS. Mountains in South Dakota and Wyoming, mainly in the Black Hills National Forest. More than 100 valuable minerals are present in commercial quantities. The Black Hills were within the great Sioux Reservation (Laramie Treaty of 1868) when gold was found in the hills by miners accompanying Gen. George A. Custer's expedition of 1874. Gold hunters rushed in, and this led to the BLACK HILLS WAR. The largest strike, the Homestead mine, yielded gold for over a century.

BLACK HILLS WAR (1876). Under the Laramie Treaty of 1868, the Black Hills were part of the Great Sioux Reservation, but gold seekers persistently trespassed. In 1874, the government sent troops into the Black Hills under Gen. G.A. Custer, ostensibly to establish sites for army posts. When Custer found gold, the gold rush was on. The Sioux refused to sell their land and in June 1876 Gen. George Crook mounted a three-pronged invasion of the Indian country. The Indians destroyed Custer's force at the Little Bighorn, but were unable to cope with renewed offensives. By spring most of the warriors had straggled in to the agencies to be disarmed. In 1877 the Sioux were obliged to cede the Black Hills for only a fraction of their value, and the area was opened to the miners.

BLACK HORSE CAVALRY. Corrupt members of the New York legislature in the late 19th c. They blackmailed corporations by introducing anti-business bills that would be killed if sufficient money were forthcoming.

BLACK INFANTRY IN THE WEST (1866–91). In 1866, Congress authorized six regiments of black regular army troops, four of which were infantry. In 1869, reorganized into two regiments, they were moved to border duty along the Rio Grande. In 1880, one was moved to Indian Territory, and later Arizona and New Mexico, and the other to Dakota Territory, where some units were assigned to guard Sitting Bull at Fort Randall.

BLACK JACK, BATTLE OF (June 2, 1856). Early engagement of the BORDER WAR. John Brown attacked a Missouri band, which held two of Brown's sons prisoner. The army dispersed both bands.

BLACK LAWS. Ohio statutes of 1804 and 1807, compelling registration of all blacks and denying validity to any black's testimony against whites. Repealed 1848–49.

BLACKLISTING. A practice of employers to exclude anyone from employment because of union activity or political beliefs. A widely used antiunion weapon until outlawed by the National Labor Act of 1935. Political blacklisting emerged during the cold war, especially against college professors and persons employed in the broadcasting and motion picture industries. Individuals with alleged Communist connections who refused to cooperate with congressional committees were branded as unfriendly witnesses and great pressure was exerted to deny them employment.

BLACK MUSLIMS. Religious movement, also known as the Nation of Islam, founded 1930 by Wali Farad, who is regarded by followers as the incarnation of God come to rescue blacks from the white race. In 1934 Farad disappeared and was succeeded by Elijah Muhammad. Black Muslims denounce Christianity as a tool of white oppression and preach black racial superiority.

BLACK NATIONALISM. Belief that the African origins and the American experiences of blacks have created in the United States a nation within a nation and that the interest of blacks can best be served by recognition of this ethnic unity and by a positive acceptance of blackness. (See also BLACK POWER.)

BLACK PANTHERS. Organized (1966) by Huey P. Newton and Bobby G. Seale. A synthesis of black nationalism and Marxism, the Panthers were founded on the principles of militant self-defense. Their insistence on arming themselves led to numerous arrests and police raids on branch headquarters during the 1960s. Newton and Seale themselves were convicted and imprisoned. In the early 1970s, the Panthers made a dramatic change in tactics, turning to electoral politics and community service. Membership was believed to have shrunk appreciably.

BLACK PATCH WAR (1907–08). Attempts of tobacco growers in Kentucky and Tennessee to overcome monopolistic control of markets and prices. In the Black Patch, or fire-cured, area of SW Kentucky and adjoining

Tennessee, aggressive methods of association members and retaliation by nonmembers resulted in much violence.

BLACK POWER. Control by black people of the political, social, economic, and cultural institutions that affect their daily lives. Black power is a concept that was particularly associated with the more militant black civil rights movement of the 1960s.

BLACKS. See BLACK AMERICANS.

BLACKSMITHING. The first colony at Jamestown, Virginia, in 1607 included a blacksmith, an important factor of all communities. Pennsylvania reported 2,562 blacksmith shops in 1810, and by 1850 the United States had about 100,000 blacksmiths, plus gunsmiths and machinists. The blacksmith not only made shoes for horses but also latches, hinges, andirons, farm tools, nails, and the various metal hand tools and equipment needed by an agricultural economy.

BLACKSTOCK'S HILL, BATTLE OF. See ENOREE, BATTLE OF.

BLACK SWAMP. Area in NW Ohio. Drainage difficulties and malarial diseases long retarded settlement. Drained after 1850, it became one of the richest farming sections.

BLACKWATER, BATTLE OF (Dec.18, 1861). Confrontation between Confederate Gen. Sterling Price and Union Gen. John Pope at the Blackwater R in Missouri. The Union forces won.

BLADENSBURG, BATTLE OF (Aug. 24, 1814).Confrontation between British troops under Gen. Robert Ross and American defenders at Bladensburg, Maryland. The British, headed toward Washington, drove back the Americans, who passed through Washington and settled in Georgetown. Thus the capital was left vulnerable to British occupation. (See WASHINGTON, D.C., BURNING OF.)

BLAND-ALLISON ACT (1878). The free-coinage bill sponsored by Rep. R.P. Bland of Missouri and Sen. W.B. Allison of Iowa. The act required the government to purchase $2 million to $4 million worth of silver bullion monthly and to coin it into legal tender at a

sixteen to one ratio to gold. It was replaced in 1890 by the SHERMAN SILVER PURCHASE ACT.

BLAST FURNACES, EARLY. The Puritans in Massachusetts established the first successful ironworks as early as 1644, but not until the 18th c. did iron smelting become important. By the American Revolution, American blast furnaces produced more pig iron and casting than England and Wales.

BLEASE MOVEMENT. Coleman L. Blease was elected governor of South Carolina by appealing to poor whites with his vehement attacks on blacks, aristocrats, and the clergy. His administration was bizarre. He pardoned extravagantly and answered opposition with abuse. He was reelected in 1912, but his conduct was more restrained in his second term.

BLEEDING KANSAS. See BORDER WAR.

BLENNERHASSETT ISLAND. In the Ohio R two miles S of Parkersburg, West Virginia. It is where Aaron Burr and Harman Blennerhassett are alleged to have plotted treason against the United States.

BLESSING OF THE BAY. Second seaworthy vessel built (1629) in the colonies.

BLIND. See HANDICAPPED, EDUCATION OF THE.

BLOCKADE. The closing of the ports of an enemy during wartime. At the onset of the Civil War, President Lincoln proclaimed a total blockade of the Confederacy. This blockade, a major factor in the Union victory, was scrupulously observed by the British, who viewed it as a valuable precedent. The United States extended the blockade to the doctrine of continuous voyage, which held that ships destined for a neutral country could be seized if it could be proved that their cargo was destined ultimately for a blockaded port. By World War I, submarines, mines, and long-range artillery had made the traditional close blockade militarily impossible. Britain resorted to a distant blockade, utilizing mine fields and patrols of cruisers on the high-sea approaches to Germany, and German U-boats blockaded the British Isles. In World War II the United States and Britain employed a long-range air and naval blockade against Germany, while the Germans again engaged in unrestricted submarine warfare against the Allies. During the Cuban missile crisis of 1962 the United States imposed a "quarantine" of Cuba to halt the delivery of weapons and force the removal of Soviet missiles installed there.

BLOCKADE RUNNERS, CONFEDERATE. The Union's total blockade of Confederate ports made trade with other countries by running the blockade highly lucrative. Cotton was run out and small arms and other munitions, provisions, clothing, hospital stores, manufactures, and luxuries were run in.

BLOODY ANGLE (May 12, 1864). The climax in the first phase of Gen. U.S. Grant's wilderness campaign in Virginia. Grant moved in force against the salient, or bloody angle, in Gen. Robert E. Lee's line. The Union advance was forced back. Neither side could advance, but Lee retired to prepared positions and the fighting ceased.

BLOODY ISLAND. Sand bar in the Mississippi R opposite St. Louis, long noted as a dueling rendezvous. Appearing first above water in 1798, its continuous growth menaced St. Louis harbor. A system of dikes and dams have eliminated the river's western shore and joined the island to the Illinois shore.

BLOODY MARSH, BATTLE OF (July 7, 1742). The decisive battle of the War of Jenkins' Ear. A Spanish force invaded Georgia but was defeated by James Oglethorpe.

BLOODY MONDAY (Aug. 6, 1855). Election riots in Louisville, Kentucky, growing out of the bitter rivalry between the Democrats and the Know-Nothings. Rumors started that foreigners and Catholics had interfered with the voting. A street fight occurred, twenty-two persons were killed, scores injured, and much property destroyed by fire.

BLOODY POND, BATTLE OF (Sept. 8, 1755). Confrontation at Lake George, New York, between the British and a French, Indian, and Canadian force. Bodies of Canadian and Indian fallen were thrown into a pool, hence the name of the battle.

BLOODY RUN, BATTLE OF (July 31, 1763). Attempt by forces under Capt. James Dalzel to

relieve Fort Detroit, which was under Chief Pontiac's siege. Pontiac's forces surprised Dalzel at Parent's Creek (ever since called Bloody Run). Dalzel was slain and sixty men killed or wounded.

BLOODY SHIRT. "Waving the bloody shirt" describes attempts in political campaigns (especially 1872 and 1876) by Radical Republicans to defeat Democrats by impassioned oratory designed to keep alive the hatreds and prejudices of the Civil War.

BLOOMERS. A loose-fitting costume of knee-length dress and pantaloons buttoned at the ankle, popularized by (ca.1851) and named for the feminist Amelia Bloomer. A form of bloomers survived to modern times as women's gym costumes.

BLOUNT CONSPIRACY (1796–97). Named for William Blount, US senator from Tennessee. The aim was to drive the Spaniards out of Louisiana and Florida by a land force of westerners and Indians with the aid of the British fleet. An incriminating letter exposed the plot, and Blount was expelled from the Senate.

BLUE AND GRAY. Familiar names for the armies of the North and South during the Civil War, derived from the colors of their uniforms.

BLUE-BACKED SPELLER. See WEBSTER'S BLUE-BACKED SPELLER.

BLUEBACKS. Confederate paper money. From an initial issue of $1 million, the treasury notes grew to $800 million by 1864, when deflationary measures were taken that reduced the outstanding currency to less than $500 million.

BLUE-COLLAR WORKERS. Members of the nonagricultural labor force who perform manual labor. In 1981 there were more than 31 million workers classified as blue-collar (as compared with 52 million WHITE-COLLAR WORKERS.)

BLUE EAGLE. See NATIONAL RECOVERY ADMINISTRATION.

BLUEGRASS COUNTRY. Some 8,000 square miles of EC Kentucky. The terrain, with some exceptions, has a gracefully undulating surface over a limestone foundation noted for the growth of bluegrass (*Poa pratensis*). The first settlers in Kentucky came to this region in one of the greatest migrations of US history, over the Wilderness Road, by way of Cumberland Gap.

BLUE LAWS. Originally, colonial laws regulating conduct, particularly on the Sabbath. In 1781 an account of these kinds of laws of Connecticut was published on blue paper; hence the name. Blue laws were most rigid in Puritan New England but existed to some degree in all the states. Stores and taverns were forced to remain closed on Sundays, and such activities as sports, entertainment, travel, and work were prohibited. Vestiges of blue laws persist in certain areas.

BLUE LICKS, BATTLE OF (Aug. 19, 1782). Engagement between Kentucky pioneers and Indians and Canadians in the British service, near the lower Blue Lick Springs on the Licking R. The attack was launched by the Kentuckians, who were ambushed and forced to retreat.

BLUE LODGES. Secret proslavery societies in W Missouri during 1854 to thwart efforts to make Kansas a free territory under the Kansas-Nebraska Act. They promoted the migration of proslavery settlers to Kansas and crossed the border to participate in the election of proslavery members to the territorial government.

BLUE RIDGE TUNNEL. Opened 1858 through the Blue Ridge Mountains under Rockfish Gap, between Afton and Waynesboro, Virginia.

BLUE SKY LAWS. Enactments designed to prevent fraudulent issuance of corporate stocks and bonds. Kansas enacted the first such law in 1911. Supplemented and to some extent superseded by the SECURITIES AND EXCHANGE COMMISSION.

BLUESTEM PASTURES. Prior to 1929, called Flint Hills, a region in EC Kansas. It was fenced in the 1880s and became the most important pasture country in the central prairie-plains area.

BLUFFTON MOVEMENT (1844). A short-lived attempt in South Carolina to invoke "separate state action" against the tariff of 1842. Though many Blufftonites undoubtedly contemplated secession, the object of their leader, Robert Barnwell Rhett, seems to have been a reform of the Union giving greater safeguards to southern interests.

BLUNDER, FORT. See ROUSE'S POINT BOUNDARY CONTROVERSY.

BOARD OF TRADE AND PLANTATIONS. The main British colonial office from its creation in 1696 until the American Revolution. It had charge of virtually all governmental and commercial affairs of the colonies.

BOARDS OF TRADE. See CHAMBERS OF COMMERCE.

BODY OF LIBERTIES. See MASSACHUSETTS BODY OF LIBERTIES.

BOG IRON MINING. Bog ore, a hematite deposited in pond and bog bottoms, was found in the coastal lowlands from Massachusetts to Delaware. The first important source of native iron, it was smelted with charcoal in small furnaces.

BOISE. Capital of Idaho, located on the Boise R. It provided an excellent base camp for gold prospectors in 1862, the year of its founding. Principal market and manufacturing center for SW Idaho. Major refineries for sugar beets. Pop.: 102,451 (1980).

BOISE, FORT. Fur trading post of the Hudson's Bay Company in Idaho. Built in 1834 on the Boise R, about seven miles above its mouth. Relocated in 1838 near the Boise's confluence with the Snake R. Famous as a stopping point on the Oregon Trail. Abandoned in 1855.

BOLL WEEVIL (*Anthonomus grandis*). A beetle that eats the buds and young bolls of cotton. It crossed from Mexico into Texas in the 1890s, and by 1923 it had reached the Atlantic coast. By 1930, 90 percent of cotton was infested. Since then the fight against it has decreased its ravages.

BONANZA KINGS. In 1871 John W. Mackay, James G. Fair, James C. Flood, and William S.

O'Brien organized the Consolidated Virgina Silver Mine near Virginia City, Nev. For twenty-two years its Comstock lode yielded $150 million in gold and silver. Bonanza was a large ore body in the lode.

BOND. A certificate stating that money has been loaned and that the issuer guarantees the money will be paid back at a certain time; meanwhile, a fixed rate of interest will be paid to the lender. Bonds are issued by corporations and government agencies,including the federal government (see DEBT, PUBLIC). Bonds issued by other government agencies are usually known as municipal bonds and are issued by states, cities, towns, and public corporations that have been created by those governments. Holders ordinarily do not pay US income tax on the interest they earn. Mortgage bonds are issued by companies (sometimes by individuals) that need capital.

BONHOMME RICHARD. Flagship of John Paul Jones, famous for its victorious encounter (Sept. 23, 1779) with two British warships off the E coast of England, the *Serapis* and the *Countess of Scarborough*. The battle is known for Jones's answer to the British demand for surrender:"I have not yet begun to fight."

BONITO. Large prehistoric pueblo ruin in Chaco Canyon, of Gallup, N. M., belonging to Pueblo III, the Grand period of Pueblo culture. Bonito was occupied ca. 919–1130. It was originally four stories high with 500 rooms. Excavated 1896–99 and 1921–23.

BONNEVILLE EXPEDITION (1832–34). Capt. B.L.E. Bonneville's party of trappers and traders from Missouri built Fort Bonneville on the Green R and then moved to the headwaters of the Salmon R. They then continued to cover the Rocky Mountains and the Columbia drainage basin. A branch expedition crossed Salt Lake Desert, descended Humboldt R, crossed the Sierras N of Yosemite Valley, and wintered at Monterey. They crossed the Sierras via Walker's Pass, rejoining Bonneville June I, 1834.

BONUS ARMY (1932). A gathering of about 15,000 unemployed World War I veterans who in May marched to Washington, D.C., seeking immediate payment of the bonus that

Congress had voted in 1924 but was not payable until 1945. They resisted all efforts to disband them and continued to live in their wretched hovels until July 28, when US troops dispersed them.

BONUS BILL, CALHOUN'S. In 1816 John C. Calhoun recommended that the profits from the second national bank be used to create a permanent fund for internal improvements. Legislation was passed by Congress but was vetoed by President James Madison, who thought it unconstitutional.

BONUS, MILITARY. Gratuity or benefit, usually paid in a lump sum, to veterans of military service, as distinguished from a pension, which is a continuing compensation. In 1776 the Continental Congress voted to reward the Continental army with grants of land, and military bonuses in the early 19th c. continued to take the form of land grants. Since the warrants could be sold or traded, most of the land ended up in the hands of speculators. Cash bonuses were paid to Civil War and World War I veterans. During World War II, Congress passed the Servicemen's Readjustment Act, commonly known as the GI Bill of Rights, a comprehensive veterans' aid bill. Similar laws covered veterans of the Korean and Vietnam wars.

BOOK COLLECTING. See COLLECTING: BOOKS AND MANUSCRIPTS.

BOOK PUBLISHING. In 1638 the first press arrived in Boston and was operated in Cambridge by Matthew Day. The BAY PSALM BOOK was the first book published, and by 1692, when the press wore out, more than 200 books had been published. Book publishing remained a cottage industry in the 17th and 18th c., and most print shops also turned out newspapers, magazines, and broadsheets. In the 18th c., the publishing industry became centered in New York. The long struggle for copyright was beginning, and specialized publishing was bringing new diversity. Children's books, textbooks, religious publications, and technical books were helping to broaden literacy. A technological revolution started ca. 1825 with the invention of the flatbed press and the revolving cylinder press. Thousands of volumes could be turned out in a short space of time. Cheap fiction, especially the dime novel, came out of this revolution. Between the Civil War and World War I, publishing influenced the national culture more than any other medium. The period also saw the rise of the university press. The 1930s saw the rise of the paperback book industry. After World War II, book publishing expanded greatly, especially in the area of textbooks. Publishing houses more and more came under the ownership of giant conglomerates. At the same time, small specialized publishing houses proliferated and at times prospered.

BOOKS, CHILDREN'S. Reading matter for colonial children consisted largely of works to instruct or improve. Most were English imports or American printers' reissues, some with slight Americanization. Among the most significant were John Newbery's *Little Goody Two Shoes* (1775) and *Mother Goose's Melodies* (1786). In the 1830s fantastic, didactic, geographical, and travel stories became popular. For decades, religious publishers poured out little books advocating religion and condemning vice. After the 1850s, authors specializing in children's stories produced a whole literature. They included Mary Mapes Dodge, Horatio Alger, Jr., Joel Chandler Harris, and Louisa May Alcott. In addition, Nathaniel Hawthorne, Thomas Bailey Aldrich, Jack London, and Mark Twain were among the leading authors of the day who wrote special stories for children. From the 1880s, formula-style dime novels became enormously popular, including boys' books that featured farm stories, sea stories, and westerns. Girls' stories often featured pious heroines, such as Elsie Dinsmore. The series continued their popularity into the 20th c. with such favorites as L. Frank Baum's Oz series, the Hardy Boys books, the Nancy Drew mysteries, and the Bobbsey Twins stories. The John Newbery medal (1922) and the Randolph Caldecott medal (1938) were established to honor quality children's literature.

BOOMER MOVEMENT (1879–85). Attempts to occupy the Oklahoma Panhandle area in Indian Territory. In 1866 some 2 million acres of fertile land, formerly belonging to the Five Civilized Tribes, was reclassified as "unassigned lands." Colonies of homesteaders, called boomers, attempted to settle the region but were ejected by soldiers. In 1889 the unassigned lands were opened to settlement by act of Congress.

BOOMTOWNS. Settlements that sprang up or rapidly increased in size as the result of some mineral, usually oil or gold, or industrial development.

BOONE-CALLAWAY KIDNAPPING (July 14, 1776). Three girls, Jemima, daughter of Daniel Boone, and two daughters of Col. Richard Callaway, were abducted by Indians near Boonsborough, Kentucky. A rescue party led by Boone rescued the girls on the third morning of their ordeal and the girls were escorted home in triumph.

BOONESBOROUGH. Former village on the south side of the Kentuky R, in the present county of Madison. Founded in 1775, by Daniel Boone. After 1777, Boonesborough was subjected to Indians attacks. The fiercest siege occurred Sept. 7–20, 1778, by a large body of Shawnee. The fort held, and the Indians withdrew.

BOONE'S STATION, KENTUCKY. The stockaded home of Daniel Boone from 1780 to 1786. Settled by Daniel's brother, Israel, in 1776, on Boone's Creek in Fayette County, near the present village of Athens.

BOONTON IRON WORKS. Important iron-making center, founded ca.1770 near Boonton, Morris County, New Jersey. It continued in operation until 1911.

BOONVILLE, BATTLE OF (June 17, 1861). In the first engagement of the Civil War in Missouri, pro-southern troops were defeated.

BOOT AND SHOE MANUFACTURING. Bootmakers and shoemakers operated in each of the colonies, and a nascent industry began to develop in E Massachusetts by the end of the colonial era. To supply the demands of a growing population after the Revolutionary War, merchant capitalists slowly reorganized the trade. Factories and mechanization came after 1850. Machines were perfected that imitated specific hand processes. By the 1980s American shoe manufacturers, suffering from foreign competition, provided work for about 150,000 people.

BOOTLEGGING. Derived from the early Indian traders' custom of carrying a bottle of liquor in the boot, especially applied to illicit deliveries of alcoholic beverages. The manufacture of illicit hard liquor is termed "moonshining." During Prohibition (1920–33), bootlegging came under the control of organized crime, and the consumption of bootleg liquor was about 100 million gallons a year.

BORAX (sodium tetraborate). Chemical compound with a wide variety of industrial uses. In 1880 production began in Death Valley, Calif., where for a decade the famous twenty-mule-team wagons carried borax to the railroad at Mojave, 160 miles away. Current production exceeds 1 million tons per year.

BORDER FORTS, EVACUATION OF (1796). At the end of the American Revolution, Great Britain agreed to evacuate all places held by its armies within the United States. These included Carleton Island (Fort Haldimand), Oswego (Fort Ontario), Niagara, Detroit, and Michilimackinac, guarding the trade route between Montreal and the West. For a decade, Britain delayed, exercising de facto control over the Northwest. In the 1790s, facing a war in Europe, the British did not want another in America, and by Jay's Treaty (1795), they transferred rule to the United States.

BORDER RUFFIANS. Term used by antislavery advocates to describe citizens in Missouri who endeavored to establish slavery in Kansas Territory.

BORDER SLAVE STATE CONVENTION (Feb. 4–27, 1861). Met in Washington, D.C., to attempt to satisfy the states of the far South on the slavery issue. Twenty-two states were represented, with the border states most active. The Crittenden Compromise plan, which formed the basis of discussion, was so modified that the convention satisfied no one. It was the last attempt at conciliation on the slavery issue in the territories.

BORDER STATES. Slave states separating North and South, consisting of Delaware, Maryland, Virginia, Kentucky, and Missouri. Although largely southern in sentiment, none seceded except Virginia, from which West Virginia separated. Most of them sent soldiers to the Confederacy.

BORDER WAR (1854–59). The opening of Kansas Territory to slavery in 1854 promoted emigration from the Northeast of antislavery groups and the arrival of squatters and speculators. There were recurring altercations between proslavery and antislavery factions, including sporadic killings and robberies. The Wakarusa War (December 1855), brought over 1,000 BORDER RUFFIANS into the territory. "Bleeding Kanasas" soon became a reality. The sack of Lawrence (May 21, 1856) and John Brown's massacre of five proslavery men at Pottawatomie three days later started four months of terror. Major conflict ended in 1859, but sporadic disorders continued until the Civil War actually began.

BORGNE, BATTLE OF LAKE (Dec. 14, 1814). Naval engagement preceding the Battle of New Orleans. The British prevailed , but the battle gave Gen. Andrew Jackson time to organize his successful defense.

BOROUGH. Numerous colonial towns were patterned after the English borough town with certain rights of self-government. They were chartered by the governor and governed by a mayor and recorder, appointed by the governor, and aldermen elected by the freemen. Later they were chartered by the state legislatures.

BOSQUE REDONDO. Reservation on the Pecos R in EC New Mexico to which Navaho and Mescalero Apache were removed in 1863. The government's plan to turn them into peaceful, sedentary farmers was not successful, but it did end the raiding. Eventually, the Navaho were allowed to return to their homeland.

BOSSES, POLITICAL. Bossism, a phenomenon dating from ca. 1850, has been linked with the immigration, urbanization, and machine politics of the times. Machine politics, and the bosses that ran the machines, concentrated on patronage, service, and favors in exchange for electoral loyalty. It maximized personal contact and organized access to government. Famous city bosses included William Marcy Tweed and Richard Croker (New York City), Frank Hague (Jersey City), James

Michael Curley (Boston), and Thomas J. Pendergast (Kansas City). Until his death in 1976, Richard J. Daley of Chicago was widely regarded as the last of the old-time political bosses.

BOSTON. Capital of Massachusetts, located on Massachusetts Bay. Capt. John Smith explored and mapped the vicinity in 1614, and in 1621 settlers located there and across the Charles R. In 1632 Boston was made capital of the Massachusetts Bay Colony. In 1639 the first post office was opened; in 1652, a mint; in 1674, a printing press; and in 1686, the first bank in the colonies. Boston thus became the largest and most important town in America. It was one of the earliest and chief centers of rebellion against the crown, and the first armed conflicts of the American Revolution took place in the environs. During the 19th c., Boston became the cultural center of the continent. It was the nation's leading port until New York overtook it. Since World War II, Boston's industry has spread throughout the metropolitan area, while commerce has remained centered in the city. Boston is still New England's main port. The home of twenty colleges and universities, it is a major research and medical center. Pop.: 562,994 (1980).

BOSTON, SIEGE OF (March 4–17, 1776). Gen. George Washington seized Dorchester Heights, from which his guns commanded Boston city and harbor. The British forces were thus in an untenable position, and on March 17 they evacuated the city.

BOSTON & MAINE. See RAILROADS, SKETCHES OF PRINCIPAL LINES.

BOSTON-BERCEAU ACTION (Oct. 12, 1800). Off Guadeloupe, the US frigate *Boston* captured the French corvette *Berceau* and towed it to Boston.

BOSTON COMMITTEE OF CORRESPONDENCE. Revolutionary body, convened Nov. 2, 1772, that was the precursor of other such committees calling for American unity and eventually for independence.

BOSTON COMMON. A forty-five-acre tract in Boston, bought by the city in 1634 as pasture and parade ground. In the Central Burying Ground lie many Bostonians and British soldiers killed at the Battle of Bunker Hill; monuments to famous citizens border the paths.

BOSTON MANUFACTURING COMPANY. Organized in 1813 by merchants engaged in the India trade, including Francis Cabot Lowell. It built at Waltham, Massachusetts, the first complete textile factory in America, combining power spinning and weaving.

BOSTON MASSACRE (March 5, 1770). British Grenadiers were beset by taunting civilians and fired into the crowd, killing five men. The British commander and several soldiers were tried for murder and acquitted.

BOSTONNAIS, or Bastonais. Term applied by French-Canadians to all Americans in the 18th c., although it means "people of Boston."

BOSTON NEWS-LETTER. First newspaper published without interruption in the colonial period, beginning in 1704. Its pro-British editor fled the city in 1776 when the British evacuated Boston.

BOSTON POLICE STRIKE (1919). Forbidden to unionize, three-fourths of the Boston police force went on strike on September 9. The police commissioner refused to work out a solution. Boston was left almost unprotected and riots, disorders, and robberies resulted. The mayor then called out the Boston militia, broke the strike, and restored order. With the city already under control, Governor Calvin Coolidge called out the entire Massachusetts militia, an action that gave Coolidge a reputation as a courageous defender of law and order.

BOSTON PORT ACT. The first of the Coercion Acts, passed by Parliament in 1774 to punish Boston for the BOSTON TEA PARTY. The port of Boston was ordered closed until the townspeople paid for the tea destroyed and proved they were peaceable subjects. The colonies rallied to Boston's aid, and the Continental Congress was called.

BOSTON RESOLUTIONS OF 1767. With a declining economy and the Townshend Acts threatening fresh British oppression, Samuel Adams secured the passage in the Boston town meeting of resolutions pledging the citizens to abstain from the use of many British manufactures. Outside New England the movement had little success and it was soon merged with the nonimportation agreement.

BOSTON RESOLUTIONS OF 1810. Condemnations by the Massachusetts legislature of President Madison's policy toward England. They forecast New England separatism in the approaching War of 1812.

BOSTON TEA PARTY (Dec. 16, 1773). Patriots dressed as Indians dumped 342 chests of tea belonging to the East India Co. into Boston harbor. The action marked the beginning of violence in the dispute between mother country and colonies, and it put the most radical patriots in command throughout America. The efforts of the British government to single out Massachusetts for punishment (see BOSTON PORT ACT) only served to unite the colonies.

BOSTON TEN TOWNSHIPS. Large tract of land near the Susquehanna R in New York state, claimed by both New York and Massachusetts. Ceded to New York in 1786.

BOTANICAL GARDENS. Among the earliest botanical gardens were John Bartram's Garden, established near Philadelphia in 1728, and those in Charleston and New York City.

BOTANY. The study of American plants began with the early explorers, who took specimens to Europe. John Banister, who came to America in 1678, was the earliest notable resident naturalist. *Florica virginica* (1739–43) was the first work devoted to Atlantic coastal flora. *Elements of Botany* (1803), written by Benjamin Smith Barton and illustrated mostly by William Bartram, was the first botany text published in the United States. The Englishman Thomas Nuttall botanized from Georgia to the mouth of the Columbia R and from San Diego to Michilimackinac. His *Genera* (1818) is a fundamental reference. François André Michaux explored W of the Mississippi and published *Histoire des arbres forestiers de l'Amérique septentrionale* (1810–13). Meanwhile, the plants of California were first collected in the 1790s by the Spanish botanists Thaddaeus Haenke, Martín Sessé, and José Mariano Mo-

ciño. Asa Gray became the leading American botanist of the 19th c.; he published *Flora of North America* in 1838–43 and later became an advocate of Darwinism. Regional floras for the West were often published by the federal government. Edward Charles Jeffrey, became the first professor of vegetable histology at Harvard in 1902. Plant physiology had been introduced by Joseph Priestly when he came to America in 1794, but little progress was made before the 20th c. Knowledge of photosynthesis and hormone actions progressed; tissue culture inspired research; and with the advent of the electron microscope, morphogenesis and ultrastructure were favored by plant physiologists. Molecular biology became a part of the study of higher plants. Plant pathology was first taught in 1873 and became a major focus in the 20th c., particularly in the study of viruses. The first American experiment in genetics, on Indian corn, was in 1716. It became a major subject in the 19th c., and with the rediscovery of Mendelian inheritance in 1900, attracted renewed interest. Cytogenetics, paleobotany, and the study of paleoclimates, fossil pollens, and the migration of floras are all example of modern botanical areas of interest.

BOUCHARD EXPEDITION (1816). Unsuccessful effort by Hippolyte de Bouchard and a force of Buenos Aires revolutionaries to take California from the Spanish.

BOUGAINVILLE LANDING (Nov. 1, 1943). One of the best-planned and executed amphibious operations of World War II. US marines quickly expanded the perimeter and accomplished their object, which was to create airfields.

BOUNDARIES OF THE UNITED STATES. When the United States and England made their peace treaty in 1783, the land recognized as the United States covered the territory of twenty-four of the present states. The N boundary was drawn through the Great Lakes and the St. Lawrence R, and across the N edges of New York, Vermont, and New Hampshire. The S edge was the boundary between Georgia and Florida, but secret clauses of the treaty set the boundary in two places. If Great Britain had to turn Florida back to Spain, the proper boundary of Florida lay at the line of 31 degrees N latitude. The United

States agreed to a more northerly border if the British continued to hold Florida. Spain got Florida back from Great Britain in 1783 and found that the 31-degree line had been set as the new border. This dispute led to Pinckney's Treaty of 1795; the border was agreed to where the peace treaty with Great Britain had drawn it.

Louisiana Purchase. In 1803 President Thomas Jefferson arranged for the largest single land additon to the United States through the LOUISIANA PURCHASE from France. The N border was to touch the border of British-owned Canada. However, French claims based in Louisiana and in Canada overlapped. Also, the correct NW boundary as of 1783 was still unsettled.The Convention of 1818 took up the question of the old NW boundary as well as the boundary between US-owned Louisiana and the W sections of Canada. A line was drawn directly S from the NW point of Lake of the Woods to the line of 49 degrees N latitude. From that point out to the Rockies, the 49th parallel was accepted as the boundary between the United States and Canada. (The Maine-New Brunswick border was not settled until 1842 with the Webster-Asburton Treaty.)

Florida Boundary and Transcontinental Treaty (1819). The Louisiana Purchase reopened boundary questions with Spain. French explorers and colonists had claimed parts of Florida. After the Louisiana Purchase, the United States acted as though these sections of West Florida were included in the Louisiana Purchase. In 1810, the United States announced that it regarded the Perdido R as the boundary of Florida and claimed the land between the Perdido and Mississippi. In 1812 the Territory of Mississippi was created with a strip of Gulf Coast from the Pearl R to the Perdido. Spain had neither the troops nor the power to cause any serious difficulty for US occupation. Today that section is divided between Alabama and Mississippi. The ADAMS-ONÍS Treaty took up the question of the W and S boundaries of Louisiana, where the former French possession touched on Texas and Spain's claims in the Rocky Mountains. The treaty lent further support to US claims to the Northwest and Pacific Coast.

Texas and the Mexican Cession. When the United States annexed the Republic of Texas, the question of boundaries between Texas and Mexico was inherited from the Lone Star Republic. The Mexican War, in fact, began in the disputed territory between the Rio Grande (which Texas claimed as the border) and the Nueces R (claimed by Mexico). After that war, an enormous new portion of North America came under US rule. The cession of land by Mexico included all of California, Utah, and Nevada, plus most of Arizona and New Mexico. In 1854 the GADSDEN PURCHASE treaty with Mexico added the S strips of Arizona and New Mexico.

Oregon Territory. Under the Louisiana Purchase, the United States claimed the Oregon Territory, which included modern Oregon, Washington, Idaho, parts of Montana, and much that lay farther N in what is now British Columbia. The Convention of 1818 said that the territory would be jointly occupied by Britain and the United States but owned by neither. American settlers moving into the territory in the 1840s created tension with Great Britain. In 1846 the extreme claims of Americans were withdrawn and a treaty was worked out with Britain, which extended the boundary line of the 1818 convention (49 degrees N latitude) to the Pacific, except for Vancouver Island, which remained British.

Alaska. The purchase of Alaska from Russia in 1867 brought with it one other major question about US boundaries. The coastline of Alaska is extremely irregular, so the question arose, whether the thirty-mile strip was to extend inland from the inlets or from "headland to headland" at the mouths of the bays and inlets. The question became important in the 1890s, when gold was discovered in the Klondike. Canadian interests tried to get the boundary drawn from headland to headland, so that Canada might have one open port. A settlement in 1903 found in favor of the United States.

BOUNTIES, COMMERCIAL. During the colonial period, Great Britain paid bounties to stimulate production. Loss of these bounties after the Revolution brought disaster. The state governments often offered bounties to build up domestic manufacturers by combining cash bounties, financial subsidies, and tariff protection. The practice declined in the 19th c. but has lived on in the form of tariffs, farm subsidies, and other forms of subsidy such as irrigation in the far West.

BOUNTIES, FISHING. See FISHING BOUNTIES.

BOUNTIES, LAND. See LAND BOUNTIES.

BOUNTIES, MILITARY. Practice of stimulating recruitment by payments of cash or land. Practiced during the Revolution both by Congress and the states, often competing with one another. Bounties were continued for the Indian campaigns and the Whiskey Rebellion and extending through the War of 1812. Bounties were abolished in 1833 but were resumed in 1847 during the Mexican War. In the Civil War, cash bounties only were granted.

BOUNTY JUMPER. A product of the system of military bounties, particularly in the Civil War. Aided and abetted by bounty brokers, men would enlist, collect their bounties, desert, and then reenlist elsewhere.

BOUQUET'S EXPEDITION (1763–65). At the outbreak of PONTIAC'S WAR, Henry Bouquet defeated the Indians at the Battle of Bushy Run, thereby relieving Fort Pitt. In October 1765, while parleying with the principal Indian chiefs, he kept them as hostages, demanding the release of all captives. He made peace with the Indians, thereby ending the terror on the border.

BOURBON COUNTY. Established by Georgia in 1785, on the Mississippi, N of the thirty-first parallel, extending to the mouth of the Yazoo R, above Natchez. As Spain had not yet evacuated this territory, and as the United States disputed Georgia's claim, the act was repealed three years later.

BOURBONS (Redeemers). White southern politicians who gained control of their state governments at the end of Reconstruction in the 1870s. Their detractors called them Bourbons, after the kings of France who were wedded to the past. Most were conservative Democrats who openly aligned themselves with the Republican, industrial North to exploit the natural resources of the South. In doing so, they sacrificed long-held tenets of agrarianism and states' rights.

BOURGEOIS. In the fur trade, the governor of the pack train, master of the canoe brigade, or despot of the trading post. His word was law and his orders were explicitly obeyed.

BOURGMONT'S EXPLORATIONS. Étienne Veniard de Bourgmont, first French scientific explorer of the Missouri R, commanded Fort Detroit in 1706. By 1712 he was exploring the lower Missouri Valley; and by 1717 he had reached the Platte R. Led expedition up the Mississippi and built Fort Orleans on the N bank of the Missouri.

BOUWERIES. When the Dutch West India Co. took over Manhattan Island in 1626, it divided a large tract of land in what is now the Lower East Side into six bouweries, or farms, leasing them to tenants. (See also BOWERY.)

BOWDITCH'S AMERICAN PRACTICAL NAVIGATOR. In 1799 Nathaniel Bowditch published an expanded and corrected edition of J.H. Moore's standard work, *The Practical Navigator*. By the third edition, the work was so changed that it bore Bowditch's name. It remains the standard work used by American seamen.

BOWERY. District in lower Manhattan in New York City that developed around a street first known as Bouwerie Lane, because it led from New Amsterdam to the bouwerie, or farm, of Peter Stuyvesant. Famous as a haven for derelicts.

BOWIE KNIFE. Devised by Rezin P. Bowie or his brother James, who died at the Alamo, it has been the subject of heroic folk tales. It was part of the regular equipment of frontiersmen, backwoodsmen, mountain men, Texas Rangers, and pirates. Its balanced blade made it a formidable throwing knife.

BOWLES'S FILIBUSTERING EXPEDITIONS. William Augustus Bowles, after living among the Creek in the early 1780s, incited them against Spain in three Florida filibustering expeditions (1788, 1791, and 1799), which were efforts to secure trading rights for his sponsors, an English trading company. In his last Florida exploit (1800), he captured the Spanish fort at St. Marks and held it for a few months. In 1803 he was captured and died in 1805 in Cuba.

BOWYER, FORT, ATTACK ON (Sept. 15, 1814). A British force of six ships and 1,300 men was defeated by an American force of 130 when they attempted to take this fort at the entrance to Mobile Bay.

BOXER REBELLION (1900). Uprising in China by a secret society known as Boxers; 231 foreigners and many Chinese Christians were murdered, and Peking was put under siege. The United States joined Great Britain, Russia, Gemany, France, and Japan in a military expedition for relief of the legations. The siege was raised and a punitive indemnity was imposed on the Chinese. The major nations were permanently to maintain legation guards at Peking and between the capital and the sea. The US share of the indemnity was reduced to $12 million and paid by 1924.

BOXING. See PRIZEFIGHTING.

BOYCOTTING. Collective refusal to purchase commodities or services from a manufacturer or merchant whose employment or trade practices are considered unfair. The boycott was held unlawful as early as 1886, and some were declared a conspiracy in restraint of trade. The Clayton Antitrust Act (1914), however, legalized some forms of union boycotting. The device has also been used to further social aims, such as the boycotts by various civil rights organizations.

BOYDTON PLANK ROAD, ENGAGEMENT AT (Oct. 27–28, 1864). A bloody battle on the Boydton Plank Road where it crossed Hatcher's Run, near Petersburg, Va., between Union Gen. Winfield S. Hancock's Second Corps and Confederate Gen. G.K. Warren's Fifth Corps.

BOYS' CLUBS OF AMERICA. Organization founded in the 1860s that sponsors about 600 clubs for boys in American cities. It supports programs of physical and social activities for boys aged eight to eighteen.

BOY SCOUTS OF AMERICA. Founded 1910 and based on principles established in England by scouting's founder, Lord Baden-Powell, in 1907. The purpose is to enhance character, teach the responsibilities of citizenship, and to develop physical and mental fitness. There are three programs: Cub Scouting, for boys who have completed the second grade or are eight to ten years old; Scouting, for boys who have completed the fifth grade or are eleven to seventeen years old; and Exploring, for young men and women who have completed the eighth grade or are fifteen to twenty years old. The scouting program depends on more than 1.5 million scoutmasters, den leaders, and Explorer advisers, who volunteer their time and talents. In 1980 the organization had 4.4 million members.

BOZEMAN TRAIL. Traced by John M. Bozeman, 1863–65, the shortest and easiest route to the gold fields of Virginia City, Mont. The trail continued the route from the South Platte R at Fort Sedgwick, Colo., past Fort Laramie, where it crossed the Oregon Trail, to the Powder R crossing at Fort Connor, Wyo. Thence it passed E of the Big Horn Mountains to the Yellowstone R, and W to Virginia City. Establishments of forts on the route led to war with the Sioux. After suppression of the Sioux in 1877, the Bozeman Trail became an important cattle trail.

BRADDOCK'S EXPEDITION (1755). During the French and Indian War, British Gen. Edward Braddock was dispatched to take Fort Duquesne by the route later called BRADDOCK'S ROAD. On the advice of Col. George Washington, his aide-de-camp, Braddock pushed on rapidly with some 1,200 men and a minimum of artillery, leaving a command to bring up the heavier goods. At Fort Duquesne the French and Indian troops were put to flight; but the Indians rallied, and Braddock ordered a retreat. Braddock was killed and the retreat became a rout.

BRADDOCK'S ROAD. From the Potomac R at Wills Creek (Cumberland, Md.) to the Monongahela R at Turtle Creek. In 1755 BRADDOCK'S EXPEDITION used it for their aborted attack on Fort Duquesne. Later it became a highway for western emigration and part was incorporated in the NATIONAL ROAD.

BRADSTREET'S FORT FRONTENAC EXPEDITION. After the disaster at Ticonderoga in July 1758, Col. John Bradstreet led a successful raid that went far to restore British morale during the French and Indian War. With 2,600 men Bradstreet crossed Lake Ontario and captured Fort Frontenac at Cataraqui (now Kingston) on August 27. He burned the post and the French ships used to supply the western forts. His action led to the evacuation of Fort Duquesne and the surrender of Fort Niagara.

BRADSTREET'S LAKE ERIE EXPEDITION (1764). Col. John Bradstreet led an expedition to the Great Lakes area to make peace with the Indians. At Lake Erie, Bradstreet revealed ignorance of Indian affairs by concluding treaties with unimportant delegations of Delaware and Shawnee. At Detroit he was only partially successful; he failed to move on mutinous Scioto villages. He later faced near mutiny due to severe hardships suffered by his troops. His reputation as a popular hero was ruined by the expedition.

BRADY PHOTOGRAPHS. Over 7,000 photographs taken by Mathew B. Brady and his associates during the Civil War. They represent an incomparable record of the war. The largest collections are in the National Archives and the Library of Congress.

BRAIN TRUST. A group of advisers drawn from universities by Franklin D. Roosevelt in the early days of the New Deal. Prominent among them were Raymond Moley, Rexford G. Tugwell, and Adolph A. Berle, Jr., all from Columbia University.

BRANDY STATION, BATTLE OF (June 9, 1863). The greatest cavalry engagement of the Civil War, with Gen. Alfred Pleasonton's Union cavalry and infantry and John Buford's Union cavalry clashing with J.E.B. Stuart's Confederates at Fleetwood Hill and Brandy Station, Va. The Confederates retained the field.

BRANDYWINE CREEK, BATTLE OF (Sept. 11, 1777). Fought in Chester County, Pa. British and Hessian troops composed a force of 18,000. The American army under Gen. George Washington numbered 11,000. Following a feint attack by the Hessians at Chad's Ford, the British crossed the E side of the creek at Jeffrie's Ford, continued S, and suddenly attacked near Birmingham Meetinghouse. The Americans were compelled to retire, and Washington withdrew his army toward Philadelphia.

BRANNAN PLAN (1949). Farm price-support plan using direct payments to farmers as a substitute for price supports. Proposed by Charles Brannan, President Truman's secretary of agriculture, the plan has been revived a number of times but never adopted.

BRATTLEBORO. See DRUMMER, FORT.

BRAZIL, CONFEDERATE EXPATRIATES TO. After the Civil War, about 5,000 southerners emigrated to Brazil. Most settled in wilderness colonies, as farmers and ranchers. Within a few years, most of the settlements had failed.

BRAZITO, BATTLE AT (Dec. 25, 1846). Gen. Alexander W. Doniphan, with 500 Missouri volunteers, encountered Mexican forces under Juan Ponce de León at the Rio Grande. In only thirty minutes the Americans triumphed.

BREDA, PEACE OF (July 21, 1667). Signed by England and France, it provided for restoration of Acadia to France and confirmed English possession of New Netherland.

BREED'S HILL. See BUNKER HILL.

BRETHREN (Dunkers or Dunkards). German evangelical Baptist sect that began to migrate to America in 1719. The Brethren lead a pacifistic and simple life. They became known as Dunkers because of their practice of triple-immersion baptism. The largest modern denomination is the Church of the Brethren. Membership:171,000 (1980).

BRETTON WOODS CONFERENCE (United Nations Monetary and Financial Conference). Held in New Hampshire, July 1–22, 1944, by forty-four nations, to plan postwar international economic cooperation. Agreement was reached for the INTERNATIONAL MONETARY FUND and for the WORLD BANK.

BREWING. Beer came to America with the earliest English settlers and brewing was carried on by farmers and tavern keepers. In the 19th c., German lager captured most of the beer market. The railroad made it possible for breweries to seek wide distribution, which required beer able to withstand temperature changes, bumping, and the lapse of time; and which operated against the small, local brewers. Pasteurization checked bacterial growth;

bottling became mechanized; and carbonation was controlled and artificial. After World War II, consolidation continued. The number of breweries fell from 229 in 1960 to 92 in 1980.

BRIAND-KELLOGG PACT. See KELLOGG-BRIAND PACT.

BRIAR CREEK, BATTLE OF (March 3, 1779). Col. Mark Prevost, British commander, trapped and routed a force of about 1,200 colonial troops at Briar Creek, Severn County, Ga.

BRICKER AMENDMENT. A series of proposals (1952–57) by Sen. John W. Bricker (Ohio) to amend the US Constitution, primarily to ensure that treaties and executive agreements inconsistent with the Constitution could not become effective in domestic law. The proposals were never enacted.

BRIDGEPORT. Second largest city in Connecticut, located on Long Island Sound, at the mouth of the Pequonock R. Bridgeport manufactures a wide variety of products from wire to plumbing supplies. Pop.: 142,546 (1980).

BRIDGER, FORT. Frontier trading post and army fort, located on Black's Fork, Uinta County, Wyo. Built by James Bridger, trapper and scout, with Louis Vasquez, in 1843. Best known as a way station and supply point for westward-bound emigrants. Taken over by Mormon colonists ca.1855, it was burned on the approach of US troops in the Mormon War of 1857. Rebuilt as a military post in 1858, it became famous as a mail, express, and telegraph station. Abandoned 1890.

BRIDGES

Timber and Masonry Bridges. The earliest bridges in the colonies were split logs or hewn timbers laid between timber cribs or rubble stone abutments. These were superseded by pile-and-beam structures of long stringers spanning between abutments and intermediate transverse rows of piles. The first timber truss span was built over the Merrimack R at Newburyport, Mass., in 1792–1806. Masonry bridges were extremely rare, because of the high cost of quarrying and dressing stone as well as laying up the blocks, until the advent of the railroad; the first, the Carrollton Viaduct at Baltimore, was built by the Baltimore and Ohio RR in 1829. It is still standing. The masonry arch was rapidly superseded by concrete around 1890.

Iron and Steel Truss Bridges. The first iron truss bridge was built in 1840 over the Erie Canal at Frankfort, N.Y. The iron railroad bridge at Manayunk, Pa., in 1845 was the first to contain both cast and wrought iron. The next decade was the heroic age of the iron truss. The rapid progress emboldened engineers to create massive iron and steel bridges required by broad waterways and heavy rail loads. The Ohio R proved to be the challenge; the first bridge to span it was built at Steubenville, Ohio by the Pittsburgh and Steubenville RR in 1863–65; it was 320 feet long. The first use of the cantilever truss for rail loads was in the Kentucky R bridge of the Cincinnati Southern Railway (1876–77).

Iron and Steel Arch Bridges. The iron arch bridge was slow to develop; the first built was at Brownsville, Pa. 1836–39. The Eads Bridge over the Mississippi R at St. Louis (1864–74), the triumph of James B. Eads, was the first in the United States built of steel and had the longest arch spans at the time.

Suspension Bridges. Chronologically, the suspension bridge antedates iron truss and arch forms, but these were derived from long-established timber and masonry prototypes. The suspension bridge with a rigid level deck carried by iron chains was invented by James Finley, who built the first one at Uniontown, Pa., in 1801. The wire-cable form was the achievement of Charles Ellet and John A. Roebling. Ellet's greatest bridge, at Wheeling, W. Va. (1846–49), failed in a storm and had to be rebuilt by Roebling. Roebling's triumphs came in stunning succession: Niagara Falls (1851–55), Cincinnati (1856–67), and Brooklyn (1869–83), which was the longest single span in the world at the time, 1,595 feet.

Steel and Concrete Bridges. The simple steel truss reached its greatest length, 746 feet, in the Chester Bridge, Chester, W. Va. (1977); and the longest of the continuous truss is the bridge over the Columbia R in Astoria, Oreg., with a span of 1,232 feet (1966). Cantilever trusses made it possible to stretch the New Orleans Public Belt Highway Bridge to 1,575 feet in 1958, and the Commodore Barry Bridge, Chester, Pa., to 1,644 feet in 1970. The longest steel arch, stretching 1,700 feet, is the New River Gorge Bridge at Fayetteville, W. Va. (1977). The Golden Gate Bridge at San Francisco (1933–37) was the longest clear span (4,200 feet) until the completion of the Verrazano-Narrows Bridge, New York City (1959–64; 4,260 feet).

BRIDGEWATER, BATTLE OF. See LUNDY'S LANE, BATTLE AT.

BRISTOE CAMPAIGN (Oct. 9–22, 1963). Gen. Robert E. Lee crossed the Rapidan R in Virginia turning the right flank of Union commander George G. Meade, and advanced toward Washington. Using parallel roads, Meade marched rapidly to cover the capital. His rear guard, under Gen. G.K. Warren, repulsed Gen. A.P. Hill's corps at Bristoe Station, October 14. Lee retreated to the Rappahannock R.

BRISTOL TRADE. In the early 16th c., Bristol found its location in SW England a great advantage in capturing trade with America; by the 17th c., it had become the foremost English port. It also became the port of departure for many colonists bound for America. In the 18th c., it still shared heavily in western enterprises, especially through slave trade and fisheries. On the eve of the American Revolution, it was the second city in England, and its merchants greatly influenced British colonial policy. Its member of Parliament, Edmund Burke, was the most eloquent pro-colonial voice in the House of Commons.

BRITISH DEBTS. Owed by American colonial merchants and planters to British merchants before the Revolution, totaling about £3 million in 1775. Wiping out the indebtedness by war was a contributing cause of the Revolution. During the war, all states enacted laws affecting these debts. Some laws confiscated Loyalist estates, including debts; some laws sequestered or confiscated the debts owed British merchants. These debts were an important problem in the peace treaty negotiations of 1782–83. Provisions of the final treaty called for the debts to be paid and for restoration of the confiscated estates of the Loyalists. Almost all of the states either delayed or refused compliance. With adoption of the Constitution, opposed by many debt-

ors, the federal courts facilitated collection, but the debt question was not finally resolved until after 1802, when special commissions settled the issue.

BROAD SEAL WAR. Following a close election in 1838, two groups sought admission to Congress from New Jersey. Both held commissions bearing the great, or broad, seal of the state, but only the Whig commissions were legally executed and signed by the governor. When fraud was proved against the Whigs, the House voted to seat the Democrats.

BROADSIDES. Political leaflets printed on one side only. In the American Revolution, they were an important medium for political information and opinion. Later used in antislavery and temperance campaigns; also for song sheets, memorials, obituaries, and accounts of trials and executions.

BROADWAY. Street in New York City running the length of Manhattan. In New Amsterdam, its first quarter mile was called the Heerewegh, or Heere Straat, anglicized to Broadway about 1668. Originally residential, by 1900 it had become the main business thoroughfare. Theaters congregated along it in the vicinity of Longacre (now Times) Square, until its name became a symbol for the professional theater. Brilliant lighting in the early 20th c. gave it the nickname of the Great White Way.

BRODHEAD'S ALLEGHENY CAMPAIGN (1719). Col. Daniel Brodhead set out from Fort Pitt with a force of 600 against the Seneca. A party of Indians coming down the Allegheny was defeated. The resulting provisional treaties for a short time saved the frontier from invasion.

BROOK FARM. Cooperative founded in West Roxbury, Mass., in 1841. Based on the ideals of TRANSCENDENTALISM and FOURIERISM. Manual and intellectual labor were to be united and men and women live in a simple but cultivated society. Members or supporters included Nathaniel Hawthorne, Ralph Waldo Emerson, and Margaret Fuller. The experiment came to an end in 1846.

BROOKINGS INSTITUTION. Founded 1928 by Robert S. Brookings in Washington, D.C. A pioneer in the organized, independent study of government problems and policies and the training of public-service personnel, its studies have had an immediate and direct impact on many federal programs, such as the Marshall Plan.

BROOKLYN. Borough of New York City at the SW extremity of Long Island. The earliest recorded land grants date from the mid-1630s, and the town of Breuckelen, named after a village in Holland, was established in 1646. Population growth was spurred by reliable steam ferries to and from New York City after 1814 and by Irish and German immigration. Although the fourth largest city in the nation, Brooklyn was dominated by neighboring New York City. The BROOKLYN BRIDGE in 1883 encouraged continued growth but also connected it more securely to Manhattan, thus facilitating the city's merger with New York City in 1898. Pop.: 2,230,936 (1980).

BROOKLYN BRIDGE. Opened May 24, 1883, making it the first bridge built across the East R between New York City and Brooklyn and the world's longest suspension bridge. John A. Roebling, the chief engineer, died in 1869, and his son Washington completed the task. One of the engineering marvels of the 19th c., it is also noted for the beauty of its Gothic arches and for the delicate tracery of its cabling.

BROOKLYN HEIGHTS, BATTLE OF. See LONG ISLAND, BATTLE OF.

BROOKS-BAXTER WAR. A dispute between Elisha Baxter and the Rev. Josiah Brooks, in the 1872 election for governor of Arkansas. Baxter won and was inaugurated, but Brooks contested the election and in 1874 secured a favorable state supreme court decision. President Grant ruled that the decision rested with the state legislature, which supported Baxter's claims.

BROOKS-SUMNER AFFAIR. Sen. Charles Sumner, in a speech on May 19, 1856, ridiculed Sen. Andrew P. Butler of South Carolina for his devotion to "the harlot, Slavery." Two days later Butler's nephew, Rep. Preston S. Brooks, also of South Carolina, attacked Sumner in the Senate chamber, causing severe injuries. The attack further inflamed the sec-

tional controversy, especially when attempts to expel Brooks from the House failed and he was praised in the South and reelected.

BROWN, FORT. Established at Brownsville, Texas, in 1846 by Gen. Zachary Taylor. Figured prominently in the notorious BROWNSVILLE AFFAIR. Closed in 1946.

BROWNISTS. Groups in England (ca.1580–ca.1660) that separated from the established church; derived from Robert Browne, who advocated an essentially Congregational polity, a church made up only of the visible elect who were to choose and install their own officers. The Pilgrims and Puritans of Massachusetts probably owed much to Browne.

BROWNSTOWN AND DETROIT TREATIES. At Detroit in 1807, Gov. William Hull negotiated cession of Indian claims to the SE quarter of Michigan, plus the portion of Ohio N of the Maumee R. Between this tract and the settled portion of the US lay extensive Indian possessions. At Brownstown, in 1808, Hull negotiated title to a roadway from Maumee Rapids to Lower Sandusky (modern Fremont) and thence S to the Greenville Treaty line to make possible land travel to Detroit without trespassing on Indian territory.

BROWNSVILLE AFFAIR. Around midnight on Aug. 13, 1906, in Brownsville, Tex., an armed group of men fired indiscriminately into homes and stores adjacent to Fort Brown, garrisoned by black soldiers. One townsman was killed and a policeman wounded. Witnesses alleged that those shooting were soldiers, but no evidence was ever offered against any of the soldiers. Nevertheless, President Theodore Roosevelt ordered all 167 enlisted men who had been garrisoned at Fort Brown cashiered. In 1972 all the discharges were changed to "honorable."

BROWN UNIVERSITY. Founded 1764 in Warren, as Rhode Island College. Moved to Providence in 1770, and in 1804 renamed in honor of Nicholas Brown, a benefactor. In 1891, Pembroke College, a school for women, was established.

BROWN V. BOARD OF EDUCATION OF TO-PEKA, KANSAS, 347 US 413 (1954). Landmark US Supreme Court decision whereby school segregation at all levels was declared unconstitutional. It reversed once and for all the separate but equal doctrine of PLESSY V. FERGUSON. The decision, written by Chief Justice Earl Warren, was unanimous. Oliver Brown sued the Topeka board of education when his daughter was denied admission to the school near her home because of her race. The case was combined with four other cases. The court held that to separate black school children by race induces a sense of inferiority that retards educational and mental development, that "separate education facilities are inherently unequal," and that the plaintiffs were "deprived of the equal protection of the laws guaranteed by the Fourteenth Amendment." Subsequently, the court mandated that local authorities proceed to integrate schools "with all deliberate speed." The decision limited its disapproval of separate but equal to education, but it was construed to mean that racial segregation was not permissible in other public facilities; and later court decisions supported such a view.

BRYAN-CHAMORRO TREATY. 1914 treaty between the United States and Nicaragua granting the United States rights in perpetuity to build an interoceanic canal across Nicaragua and to establish a naval base in the Gulf of Fonseca. Neither the canal nor the base was ever built.

BRYAN'S STATION. Village established in Kentucky (near Lexington) by four Bryan brothers from North Carolina. Scene of several Indian attacks, particularly in 1782, when it was besieged by about 300 Indians and Canadians. Battle of BLUE LICKS occurred three days later.

BUCCANEERS (Freebooters). Pirates who infested the West Indies in the 16th, 17th, and 18th c. Many were English privateers who plundered the treasure-laden ships en route to Spain from the Spanish Main.

BUCKBOARDS. Four-wheeled vehicles, drawn by horse or mule, widely used in the West. They had one seat resting on elastic boards fastened directly to the axles.

BUCKLAND RACES. Derisive Confederate name for a Union rout on Oct. 19, 1863, near Buckland Mills, Va.

BUCKSHOT WAR. In the 1838 Pennsylvania state elections, the Democrats and the Whig and Anti-Masonic opposition both claimed control of the Pennsylvania legislature. Two speakers were elected. A mob forced the Whig leaders to escape through a window. The governor called out the Philadelphia militia, requisitioning thirteen rounds of buckshot cartridges, whence the name Buckshot War. The impasse ended with three Whigs voting with the Democrats.

BUCKTAILS (1818–26). A faction of the New York Democratic-Republican party opposed to the Erie Canal policy of Gov. DeWitt Clinton. The name was taken from the deer's tail on the insignia of the Tammany Society.

BUDGET, FEDERAL. Drawn up each year by the US Office of Management and Budget, under the president's direction. The president presents a budget message to Congress, indicating what he recommends for government activity and the kinds of tax income he hopes to receive. The president cannot actually impose a budget on the country, however, since Congress has the constitutional right to approve budgeted items and to appropriate tax money. If the federal budget is unbalanced because there is too little income, this can be remedied by deficit financing: The government borrows the difference by the instrument of government bonds. (See also DEFICITS, FEDERAL.)

BUENAVENTURA RIVER. Early Spanish maps of North America showed a river flowing from the Rocky Mountains into Great Salt Lake and emptying into the Pacific Ocean. As late as 1844 John C. Frémont was searching for the mythical river.

BUENA VISTA, BATTLE OF (Feb. 22–23, 1847). During the Mexican War, Gen. Zachary Taylor had advanced his army to a mountain pass S of Saltillo. Near the hacienda of Buena Vista, he encountered Gen. Antonio López de Santa Anna with a force three times the size of his own. On the second day of the battle, the Americans won a brilliant victory.

BUFFALO. Common name for the American bison (*Bison bison*). They once ranged over about one-third of the continent from Canada to Mexico, and from Oregon to the Midwest. The chief habitat was the plains between the Missouri R and the Rocky Mountains. Easily hunted and of large size (the males reaching 2,500 pounds), the buffalo were a favorite food for Indians and frontier settlers. As civilization advanced W, the animals were exterminated and by 1850 few if any remained E of the Mississippi. The dry plains, however, still contained vast numbers, possibly more than 100 million. Plains Indians based their culture on the buffalo; every part was used. Natural increase kept pace with the slaughter until the advent of the railroad, when a systematic slaughter began. (The buffalo herds allegedly damaged railroad tracks and telegraph lines.) By 1889 one census showed only 1,091 bison still extant. In 1905 the American Bison Society was organized to preserve the remaining bison. Current population is estimated at about 20,000 head.

BUFFALO. Second largest city in New York state, on the E tip of Lake Erie. In 1799 Dutch land speculators bought most of the Phelps-Gorham purchase and commissioned Joseph Ellicott to survey and offer for sale lots in a village on Buffalo Creek. The village became the county seat in 1807. Burned by the British in 1813 but was rapidly rebuilt. Became the terminus of the Erie Canal in 1825. Buffalo is a major industrial city and port, connected to Canada by bridges. Its many industries, including steel, electric products, and grain storage, have access to the hydroelectric power supplied by nearby Niagara Falls. Pop.: 357,810 (1980).

BUFFALO CHIPS. Dried excrement of the American bison, widely used for fuel by American Indians and early white settlers in the Great Plains.

BUFFALO TRAILS. The tracks made by buffalo in seasonal migration and in quest of feeding grounds, salt licks, and water holes. Many of these routes were followed by the Indians to hunting grounds and as warriors' paths; they were invaluable to explorers and adopted by pioneers.

BUFFINGTON ISLAND SKIRMISH (July 19, 1863). The Confederate raider, Gen. John Morgan, was seeking to escape across the Ohio R at a ford opposite Buffington Island,

Meigs County, Ohio. Morgan's force was routed but he and his 1,200 men escaped. He was captured on July 26.

BUFORD EXPEDITION (April 1856). As part of the effort to make Kansas a slave state, Col. Jefferson Buford organized and equipped 400 southerners and sent them for settlement. Buford's men participated in many of the conflicts between the free and slave factions.

BUILDING AND LOAN ASSOCIATION. See SAVINGS AND LOAN ASSOCIATIONS.

BULGE, BATTLE OF THE. Last major German effort of World War II, so named from the large bulge created in US lines in the Ardennes region of Belgium, and the greatest pitched battle ever fought by US troops. As German armies retreated from France in late summer 1944, Field Marshal Gerd von Rundstedt secretly massed more than 200,000 men and 1,200 tanks in the wooded Eifel region opposite the Ardennes. On December 16, three German armies launched a major counteroffensive against seven US divisions; surprise was total. On the second day, US reinforcements were sent in, but German gains continued. On December 20, they surrounded Bastogne. On the 22nd the US Third Army began to drive to Bastogne's relief, and German panzer divisions striving for the Meuse R were slowed by gasoline shortages. On Dec. 23 the weather cleared, enabling Allied planes to attack German columns and drop supplies at Bastogne. Severe fighting continued into January 1945; the last of the bulge was not eliminated until January 28.

BULLBOATS. Tublike boats of the Mandan Indians, made of willow frames covered with raw buffalo hides. Early traders built boats similar in design.

BULL GARRISON HOUSE. On Tower Hill, South Kingston, Rhode Island. On Dec. 15, 1675, during King Philip's War, it was attacked and burned by Narragansett Indians.

BULL MOOSE PARTY. See PROGRESSIVE PARTY (1912-16).

BULL RUN, FIRST BATTLE OF (July 21, 1861). First major battle of of the Civil War, also known as the Battle of Manassas. The principal Union army, under Gen. Irvin McDowell, was mobilized about Washington. Union Gen. Robert Patterson, with a smaller army, was sent to retain Confederate Gen. Joseph E. Johnston in the Shenandoah Valley. Gen. P.G.T. Beauregard with his southern army occupied the line at Bull Run Creek, which lies across the main highways from Washington S. His advance force under Gen. M.L. Bonham was based at Fairfax Courthouse to watch McDowell's army. Public opinion compelled President Lincoln to order McDowell forward. The Union advance guard drove in Bonham's pickets on July 17. Bonham retired behind Bull Run. Eluding Patterson, Johnston reached Bull Run on Saturday, July 20, stationing his troops behind Beauregard's line. At dawn, McDowell attacked. Fierce fighting raged from Bull Run to the Henry house plateau to which the Confederates were driven. There Gen. T.J. Jackson won the nickname Stonewall. The arrival of another portion of Johnston's army turned the tide in favor of the Rebels. The Union troops were driven across Bull Run in disorder, pursued along the Warrenton Turnpike. The Union withdrawal turned into a rout as the troops streamed back toward Washington. From some 13,000 men actually engaged, the Union lost about 500 killed, 1,000 wounded, and 1,200 missing. The Confederates, with about 11,000 engaged, lost about 400 killed, 1,600 wounded, and 13 missing.

BULL RUN, SECOND BATTLE OF. Also known as the Battle of Manassas. Gen. R.E. Lee, Aug. 24, 1862, at Jefferson, Va., sent the 23,000 troops of Gen. Stonewall Jackson to break the communications of Gen. John Pope's Union army, unassailably positioned on the Rappahannock R. On Aug. 27, Jackson plundered Pope's base at Manassas Junction and proceeded to Groveton Heights. On Aug. 28, Pope attacked Jackson, who with difficulty beat off repeated assaults. Lee brought up the remainder of his army, 32,000 men, and formed them on Jackson's right. Lee swept Pope from his positions. Heavy rain on Aug. 31 delayed pursuit and made possible the retreat of Pope within the Washington defenses. Pope was not again trusted with field command. Losses were high for both sides.

BULLWHACKER. See MULE SKINNER.

BUNCOMBE. See BUNKUM.

BUNDLING. Mode of courtship in colonial times. Couples went to bed with their clothes on. This custom, inherited from Europe, came about because of unheated, crowded houses.

BUNKER HILL, BATTLE OF (June 17, 1775). To force the British from Boston, on the night of June 16 the American militia besieging the town sent 1,200 men to seize Bunker Hill, in Charlestown. Instead, the detachment built a small redoubt on Breed's Hill, which was nearer Boston. Attacks by the British infantry were bloodily repulsed but the provincials were soon out of ammunition and forced to retreat. After an engagement lasting less than two hours, the British were masters of the peninsula, but with heavy casualties. First regarded by the Americans as a defeat, Bunker Hill came to be regarded as a moral victory, leading to a dangerous overconfidence.

BUNKER HILL MONUMENT. Commemorating the Battle of Bunker Hill during the American Revolution, its cornerstone was laid by the Marquis de Lafayette in 1825. It was dedicated in 1843.

BUNKUM. A term that by 1828 had come to mean speechmaking designed for public applause and, later, insincere public talk or action. Reputed to have originated with a speech made by a Congressman to please his Buncombe County, N.C., district.

BURCHARD INCIDENT. On Oct. 30, 1884, the Rev. Samuel D. Burchard, the representative of several hundred Protestant clergymen supporting the Republican presidential candidate James G. Blaine, spoke in front of the candidate in New York City, describing the Democrats as the party of "rum, Romanism, and rebellion." Blaine's failure to offset the diatribe cost him Irish support and the election.

BUREAUCRACY. Generally pejorative term referring to all administrative organizations, both public and private. As commonly used, the term refers to the government agency of excessive size, impersonality, and unresponsiveness.

BURGESSES, HOUSE OF. See COLONIAL ASSEMBLIES.

BURGHERS. Citizens of an incorporated city who, under the Dutch (1657), enjoyed specific rights, and under the English were entitled by birth or admission by the magistrates to the designation of freemen. In New York and Albany, only freemen could do business or ply a trade.

BURGOYNE'S INVASION (1777). Crucial part of the BRITISH CAMPAIGN OF 1777. Gen. John Burgoyne was to invade New York from Canada by the Lake Champlain-Hudson R route. One expedition, under Col. Barry St. Leger, was to ascend the St. Lawrence R, cross Lake Ontario, and advance on Albany through the Mohawk Valley. Its principal objective was junction with Sir William Howe. In July, Burgoyne's own command proceeded up Lake Champlain, captured Ticonderoga, and proceeded up Lake George to force the Americans under Schuyler to retreat from Fort Edward. Meanwhile Howe, evidently believing the rebellion to be nearly crushed, left New York for Philadelphia. Burgoyne was overwhelmed at Bennington, Vermont; St. Leger, besieging Fort Stanwix, managed to repulse a body of militia under Gen. Nicholas Herkimer but at news of the approach of a patriot force under Benedict Arnold, abandoned his campaign. Gen. Horatio Gates, in command of the American army near the mouth of the Mohawk, reinforced by Gen. Daniel Morgan's Virginia Rifles, moved N and entrenched at Bemis Heights, S of Saratoga. Burgoyne, whose Indian scouts had fled, found himself dangerously close to the American army. He tried to retreat, was decisively defeated at the Battle of Saratoga, and was forced to surrender. It was the first decisive American victory of the war. (See FREEMAN'S FARM, SECOND BATTLE OF; SARATOGA, SURRENDER AT.)

BURKE ACT (1906). Provided that an Indian could become a citizen only at the end of a twenty-five-year trust period, when he received free title to his land. The secretary of the interior was given the right to abbreviate the probationary period in individual cases in which Indians had shown themselves competent to manage their own affairs. Accordingly, competency commissions were established to pass on the qualifications of Indian applicants.

BURLINGAME TREATY (1868). Between the United States and China, it acknowledged Chinese self-determination in a number of important areas and guaranteed nonintervention by the United States in Chinese domestic affairs. Named for Anson Burlingame, special envoy of the Chinese emperor.

BURLINGTON. Largest city in Vermont, on Lake Champlain. An important port city, with contact through Lake Champlain to the St. Lawrence Seaway in the N and with New York harbor to the S. Established 1773 on land chartered by New Hampshire. An important objective of British troops in the War of 1812, it was successfully defended and became a key American base. Pop.: 37,712 (1980).

BURLINGTON ROUTE. See RAILROADS, SKETCHES OF PRINCIPAL LINES: BURLINGTON NORTHERN.

BURLINGTON STRIKE (1888). Locomotive enginemen of the Burlington Railway went on strike for higher wages and improved conditions. Trains were wrecked, men shot, and property destroyed. The union finally gave in, and by Feb. 1, 1889, operations were normal.

BURMA ROAD. A 400-mile highway from Ledo, India, to join an existing 717-mile road to Burma from Kunming, China. Its construction was one of the largest engineering projects of World War II. In 1937 the Chinese began a crash program to get a passable military road between Kunming and Lashio, Burma, a railhead on a railway to the port city of Rangoon. By 1940 the Burma Road was a backcountry highway that could carry ten tons. Japan's conquest of Burma in 1942 blockaded China's land route to Rangoon. In June 1942 Gen. Joseph Stilwell, US theater commander in Burma, India, and China proposed to retake N Burma and build a 400-mile military highway to link up with the Burma Road at Wanting. The Ledo Road project started in October 1942, and the road gradually moved toward China. In January 1945 the Ledo and Burma roads were joined and named the Stilwell Road.

BURNS FUGITIVE SLAVE CASE (1854). In 1854 a vigilance committee in Boston freed

Anthony Burns, a fugitive slave, killing a US marshal in the process. Despite their efforts, Burns was remanded to his owner in Virginia, in compliance with the Fugitive Slave Law of 1850. Several citizens later bought Burns's freedom and returned him to Massachusetts. Following the Burns case, enforcement of the Fugitive Slave Law declined.

BURNT CORN, BATTLE OF (July 27, 1813). Encounter between Creek Indians and Alabama frontiersmen on Burnt Corn Creek.

BURR CONSPIRACY (1805–06). After his duel with Alexander Hamilton in 1804, Aaron Burr schemed to regain his lost political power by a filibustering adventure in Spanish territory W of the Mississippi, the details of which were never made public. It is generally believed that he planned to seize Texas from the Spanish and establish it as an independent nation. Having failed to attract England to his cause, he enlisted others who might help. One of them, Herman Blennerhassett, lived on an island in the Ohio R. Another co-conspirator, Gen. James Wilkinson, commanded the US army on the Mississippi. But as the time drew near for the expedition to start for New Orleans from Blennerhasset Island, Wilkinson declined to be involved further, and when Burr's advance flotilla reached the lower Mississippi he ordered its members arrested. Burr, too, was seized and then paroled. He attempted to escape to Spanish territory, but was again captured and returned east for trial. Burr was tried for treason and high misdemeanor but was acquitted for general lack of evidence. (See BURR TRIAL.)

BURR-HAMILTON DUEL (July 11, 1804). Burr challenged Hamilton to the duel ostensibly because Hamilton had made an insulting remark about Burr. In fact, the two men had been implacable enemies for a number of years, Burr blaming Hamilton for his defeat for the presidency in 1801. The duel took place at Weehawken, New Jersey; Hamilton was mortally wounded and died the following day. Charges against Burr were quashed, but he was permanently discredited in the public's mind.

BURR TRIAL (1807). As a result of the BURR CONSPIRACY, Aaron Burr was brought to trial for treason in federal circuit court in Richmond,

Virginia, with Chief Justice John Marshall sitting as circuit judge. In instructing the jury, Marshall gave an interpretation of the treason clause of the Constitution so restrictive that Burr was found innocent. Marshall was sharply criticized for his conduct at the trial, but his interpretation of the meaning of treason has generally prevailed.

BUSHWHACKERS. Originally, backwoodsmen; but during the Civil War, term applied to Confederate guerrilla fighters, especially border ruffians.

BUSHY RUN, BATTLE OF (Aug. 5–6, 1763). Encounter in the FRENCH AND INDIAN WAR. On an expedition to relieve Fort Pitt, the men under Col. Henry Bouquet were ambushed by an Indian force at Bushy Run, about twenty-five miles E of Pittsburgh. Bouquet feigned retreat, drawing the Indians forward and completely routing them; but the British lost more than 100 men.

BUSINESS, BIG. The first big business in the United States was the railroads, in the years after the Civil War. The extension of the transcontinental railroads and the consolidation of competing lines resulted in unprecedented economic power in the hands of the owners. Other industries soon followed into the category of big business: steel, automobiles, oil, chemicals, and telephone, telegraph, and radio. Public efforts to control the power of these businesses began early: The Interstate Commerce Act was passed in 1887, and the Sherman Antitrust Act in 1890. During the Progressive and New Deal eras further regulatory legislation was passed. Since the middle of the 20th c., much of the problem of size and concentration of economic power has manifested itself in the creation of conglomerate enterprises.

BUSINESS, PUBLIC CONTROL OF. The colonies inherited from England a penchant for competition in the production of goods and services, although certain types of proprietors (innkeepers, ferrymen, millers) were forced to offer their services to all applicants since their enterprises were affected with a public interest. The holders of a monopoly, such as a toll road, were also regulated in their charges. Railroads early came under state supervision. The Interstate Commerce

Act of 1887 forbade unreasonable rates and favoritism in rate-setting. In the 1880s the term "trust" came to be applied to business combinations that tended to shut out competition. The Sherman Antitrust Act of 1890 made illegal "every contract, combination in the form of trust or otherwise, or conspiracy in restraint of trade ... among the ... States, or with foreign nations." The powerful movement toward business consolidation continued, however, and the Clayton Antitrust Act of 1914 amended the Sherman law by punishing monopolistic practices. The Federal Trade Commission was set up the same year. The end of World War I also saw the end of the Progressive era, and the Republican administrations of the 1920s were content, for the most part, to give business its head. The end of that decade saw the collapse of the stock market and the beginning of the Great Depression. Once again, there was public clamor for control of big business. President Franklin D. Roosevelt's inauguration occurred in the dreary scene of banks closing, industrial production shrunk to less than half, staple farm crops at giveaway prices, and a third of the nation's workers jobless. He embarked on an unprecedented program of economic planning, including controls on businesses undreamed of by earlier generations. The National Industrial Recovery Act involved government in the day-to-day operations of industry; the Securities and Exchange Commission placed the securities market under tight federal control; and various banking laws were aimed at creating stability in the financial world. As is usual in wartime, the federal government assumed virtual dictatorship over industry during World War II, regulating the kinds of goods produced and price, wage, and profit limitations. After the war, fair employment practices were mandated on behalf of minority groups (and later for women). Consumer protection markedly increased by means of a reanimated Federal Trade Commission and the creation of the Environmental Protection Agency in 1970. The Federal Power Commission was concerned with energy sources, and the Department of Transportation was established in 1967 to embrace numerous existing agencies. Distress of the railroads promoted a public corporation, Amtrak. The Department of Health and Human Services alone has more than 300 programs to improve living conditions, each controlling some segment of industry. Ronald Reagan was elected president in 1980 on a platform that promised to decrease significantly the government's control over business. He appointed officials who were enthusiastic toward decontrol. Their efforts were to some extent thwarted by in-place legislation and agencies with strong mandates for control, but deregulation became the watchword of the 1980s.

BUSINESS CYCLES. The chronology of business cycles in common use in the United States was developed by the National Bureau of Economic Research, Inc. It charts annual fluctuations from 1834 and monthly and quarterly changes beginning in 1854. Since 1920, most of the business cycle contractions (recessions) in the United States have lasted about a year or less, a notable exception being the 43-month contraction beginning in 1929.

BUSINESS FORECASTING. Takes place at three levels: at the national level; at the industry or market level; and at the individual company level. Nearly all business forecasting in America is strongly quantitative. Numerical forecasts of the main national accounts, national economic indicators, industry time series, and firm accounting statements are regularly prepared. At a minimum businesses need annual forecasts; often quarterly or monthly forecasts are necessary. In addition, many industries make long-range forecasts, sometimes extending as far as five or ten years into the future. The growth of multinational corporations has made it imperative to forecast the outlook for the whole world economy. Overseas activity levels, world trade, US trade, and US balance of payments are the main items that command the attention of present-day business forecasters. By and large, there are two approaches to business forecasting. In the judgmental approach, economists with perceptive vision of the contemporary environment and prevailing trends fit the statistical magnitudes of the economy into future patterns that appear to be plausible. The other approach is through formal model building. Mathematical models with statistically estimated coefficients are fitted together into logical, dynamic systems. The development of readily available high-speed, sophisticated computer technology has greatly increased the potentialities of business forecasting.

BUSINESS MACHINES. The typewriter and the cash register, two US inventions, were the first commercially successful examples of business machines. Both came into use first in the 1870s, about the same time that Thomas A. Edison was developing his stock ticker (the parent of the teletyping machine), his mimeograph machine, and his phonograph (which was soon adapted as a dictating machine). They were quickly followed by the adding and calculating machine. By 1910 the accountant had available a bookkeeping machine that performed all four arithmetic operations. The first important calculating machine for science was the punched-card tabulating machine, first used in tabulating the 1890 census. The system's inventor, Herman Hollerith, formed the company that eventually became International Business Machines (IBM). In 1937 Chester F. Carlson invented an electrostatic system for reproducing documents. Known as xerography, since about 1950 it has been the most common method used in business reproducing machines. Today, the trend is toward the phasing out of mechanically operated business machines and the introduction of electronic typewriters, word processors, and small business computers, all made possible by solid-state technology.

BUSING. The transporting of children by bus to school to achieve desegregation or racial balance. In 1971 the Supreme Court decided in *Swann* v. *Charlotte-Mecklenburg Board of Education*, that busing was a legitimate instrument for achieving integration. It quickly became a controversial issue, with opinion polls showing that the public was overwhelmingly against it. Nevertheless, it has continued to be used, particularly in cases where all other efforts at achieving integration have failed.

BUSY BEES OF DESERET. The Mormon settlers (1848) in the territory that became Utah. Deseret is the "land of honeybee" of the Book of Mormon.

BUTE, FORT (Manchac Post). Established in West Florida in 1763 at the junction of the Iberville R (or Bayou Manchac) with the Missis-

sippi R. It remained an important British military and trading post until it was captured by the Spanish in 1779.

BUTLER'S ORDER NO. 28. (May 15, 1862). Gen. Benjamin F. Butler, the highly unpopular Union commander in occupied New Orleans issued an order that any female insulting or showing contempt for any US soldier should "be treated as a woman of the town plying her avocation." The ensuing uproar caused Butler to be removed from command later that year.

BUTLER'S RANGERS. Regiment of Loyalists recruited in 1777 by Col. John Butler to serve with the Indians against the colonists. From their headquarters at Fort Niagara, the Rangers embarked on forays that spread terror in New York and Pennsylvania. They perpetrated the Wyoming Valley invasion of July 1778 and raided Mohawk settlements in 1780. Disbanded June 1784.

BUTTE DES MORTS COUNCIL (1824). Meeting between the United States and three Indian tribes: the Chippewa, Menomini, and Winnebago. Held at Little Butte des Morts, N of Lake Winnebago. Treaty signed August 11, adjusting boundaries and the relations of these tribes with the Indians migrating to Wisconsin from New York.

BUTTERFIELD OVERLAND DISPATCH. Because of much travel to Colorado after the discovery of gold, D.A. Butterfield organized a joint-stock express and passenger service between the Missouri R and Denver. In July 1865, the route via the Smoky Hill R in C Kansas was surveyed. Soon coaches were in operation. Ben Holladay, acting for a competing organization, bought out the company in 1866.

BUTTERFIELD OVERLAND MAIL. See SOUTHERN OVERLAND MAIL.

BYRD'S POLAR FLIGHTS. In 1926 Commander Richard E. Byrd sailed on the USS *Chantier* for Kings Bay, Spitsbergen, in Norway. On board was a trimotor airplane. On May 9, at 9:02 AM, Byrd and his pilot, Floyd Bennett, reached the North Pole. On Nov. 29, 1929, Byrd took off from Little America, his base in Antarctica, for the South Pole. The pole was reached at 1:14 AM, Nov. 30.

CAIRO. City in S Illinois, at the juncture of the Ohio and Mississippi rivers, founded 1837. Completion of the Illinois Central RR attracted settlers, and by 1860 the population exceeded 2,000. Cairo was of great strategic importance during the Civil War. Pop.: 5,931 (1980).

CAIRO CONFERENCES (1943). On their way to the Teheran Conference, President Franklin D. Roosevelt and Prime Minister Winston Churchill met with Generalissimo Chiang Kai-shek in Cairo, Egypt (November 22–26) to discuss the war against Japan and other Far East matters. They agreed to take from Japan all the Pacific islands it had occupied since 1914; to restore to China all territory "stolen" from it by Japan; and to give Korea its independence. Returning from Teheran, Roosevelt and Churchill met with President Ismet Inonu of Turkey at the second Cairo Conference (December 4–6). No significant agreements were reached, and Turkey declined to enter the war.

CAJON PASS. Between the San Gabriel and San Bernardino mountains, the best route to Southern California. In 1776 it was traversed by Father Francisco Garces. The first American to discover the pass was Jedediah Smith in 1826. Shortly afterward, it became part of the route between California and Santa Fe.

CAJUNS. See ACADIANS.

CALAMITY HOWLER. A derogatory phrase used by opponents to describe Populists and agrarians of the late 19th c.

CALDER V. BULL, 3 Dallas 386 (1798). Case in which the Supreme Court defined an EX POST FACTO LAW.

CALHOUN'S DISQUISTION ON GOVERNMENT (1848). John C. Calhoun's treatise on the problems of minorities in a democratic government. Its keynote is the idea of a concurrent majority. Simple majority government always results in despotism over the minority unless some way is devised to secure the assent of all classes, sections, and interests.

CALHOUN'S EXPOSITION. John C. Calhoun's 1828 treatise asserting that the tariff of 1828 was unconstitutional. As remedy, he proposed NULLIFICATION. South Carolina should interpose the state's veto, to be binding upon its citizens and the general government unless three-fourths of the states should amend the Constitution.

CALICO RAILROAD. Derisive name for a proposed railroad between Lyons and Council Bluffs, Iowa. When the company halted work on the line for lack of funds, it was forced to pay its workers with supplies from the company store, including a supply of calico.

CALIFORNIA. Thirty-first state, admitted to the union on Sept. 9, 1850. The name California was first applied by the Spanish to Baja California; Alta California was discovered in 1542 by Juan Rodríguez Cabrillo. When a "sacred expedition" founded San Diego in 1769 and Monterey in 1770, Father Junípero Serra began what would ultimately be twenty-one Franciscan missions along El Camino Real from San Diego to Sonoma. New Spain tried to make Spanish colonists out of the native Indians through the mission system, but the attempt failed, and California remained weak and unprosperous under Mexico. At the end of the Mexican period in 1846, the non-Indian population was only about 7,000. Mexico ceded California to the US on Feb. 2, 1848, a consequence of the Mexican War. Gold had just been discovered at Sutter's Mill on the American R; and before the end of 1849 the gold rush had increased California's population above 60,000, the number required for statehood. Congress admitted California as a state as part of the COMPROMISE OF 1850. Mining remained the dominant industry until the 1870s, for the discovery of the great silver deposits of the Comstock lode in 1859 made up for the gradual decline in gold. A great drought in the 1860s nearly wiped out the cattle industry; but wheat began to flourish, and wine production increased in Northern California. The citrus industry developed phenomenally in Southern California. The first transcontinental railroad was completed in 1869. The Southern Pacific RR, as it was later called, dominated the economy and the government and politics of California. The 1870s were a time of depression and unemployment. Labor unrest was largely responsible for a new constitution (1879), which attempted important political and economic reforms, but conservative forces (the Southern Pacific and various public-utility corporations allied with corrupt politicians) negated much of its promise. In the first decade of the 20th c., a "good government" coalition took shape, electing Hiram W. Johnson governor in 1910. These progressives established effective regulation of the railroad and other public utilities, a workmen's compensation plan, and enacted the initiative, referendum, recall, and direct primary legislation. The warm winters and moderate summers of Southern California began to attract a great surge of new residents. The climate and varied landscape led the infant motion picture industry to move to Hollywood, and the movies in turn advertised Southern California. The first oil discoveries were made in Ventura County in the 1860s. By 1979 California had accounted for more than 11 percent of the nation's total output. The oil refining industry demanded enormous quantities of water; growing cities needed even more; and California's burgeoning agriculture depended on irrigation. Long aqueducts brought water to Los Angeles, the first from the Owens Valley in 1913. California was particularly vulnerable to the Great Depression of the 1930s. By 1934 nearly one-fifth of the people of the state were on relief, and one-fourth of its workers were unemployed. World War II not only ended the depression but launched the state into a period of unprecedented growth. California passed New York as the most populous state in the 1960s, its booming economy spurred by the aircraft, electronics, and aerospace industries. Pop.: 23,668,562 (1980).

CALIFORNIA ALIEN LAND LAW. Anti-Japanese law passed in 1913 (and amended three times). It restricted ownership of land to aliens who were eligible for citizenship. Repealed as unconstitutional in 1955.

CALIFORNIA BANK NOTES. In the 1820s Californians depended on Boston ships for all goods of foreign manufacture and generally paid for them with hides, known jocularly as California bank notes.

CALIFORNIA BATTALION. Naval battalion of mounted riflemen active in the Mexican

War, under the command of Capt. John C. Frémont.

CALIFORNIA TRAIL. Various routes to California, the earliest ones being up the peninsula (1769) and NW from Sonora (1774). From Santa Fe the Old Spanish Trail followed the Chama R, crossed Colorado into Utah, and later extended SW to Los Angeles. Early traders also went W through Zuni, then SW by Salt R and W by the Gila R, or (later) from Zuni W to the Mohave country. Others followed the Rio Grande S, then struck W to the headwaters of the Gila. In the 1840s gold-seekers converged in the Salt Lake Valley via the Platte R, Pueblo-Fort Bridger, and Frémont trails, then continued W into Northern California.

CALIFORNIA V. CENTRAL PACIFIC RAILROAD COMPANY (1888). The Supreme Court ruled that, under the commerce and other clauses, Congress has power to construct interstate means of transportation directly or by charter through corporations, and that California could not tax the franchise thus granted.

CALOMEL (mercurous chloride). First used by Benjamin Rush in the Philadelphia yellow fever epidemic of 1793, it was used throughout the 19th c. as a medication, especially for malaria.

CALUMET. See PIPE, INDIAN.

CALUMET AND HECLA MINES. Copper mines in the Keweenaw Peninsula of Lake Superior in NW Michigan, discovered 1859. Other mines were opened in the area and by 1923 most of them had consolidated with the Calumet and Hecla Co.

CALVINISM. Religious concepts arising from the teaching of John Calvin. Its fundamental principle is the conception of God as absolutely sovereign. The statement of Calvinism most infulential in America was the Westminster Confession (1647), accepted by New England Congregationalists and embodied in their Cambridge Platform (1648). American Presbyterians were sternly Calvinist; other Calvinistic bodies in America are the Dutch and German reformed churches.

CALVO DOCTRINE. Enunciated in 1855 by Carlos Calvo, Argentinian jurist; held that governments have no right to intervene in a foreign country in order to secure settlement of claims of their citizens. Latin American governments often include a Calvo clause in contracts. (Compare DRAGO DOCTRINE.)

CAMBODIA, BOMBING OF. See VIETNAM WAR.

CAMBRIDGE. City in Massachusetts, across the Charles R from Boston, founded in 1630. Harvard College founded there in 1636. In 1639 the first printing press in America was set up there, and since then the city has been a major cultural and literary center. The Massachusetts Institute of Technology, the Smithsonian Astrophysical Observatory, and Harvard have made it a center of scientific and industrial research. Pop.:95,322 (1980).

CAMBRIDGE AGREEMENT (Aug. 26, 1629). Puritan members agreed that if the Massachusetts Bay Company charter could be transferred to New England, they would migrate there with their families. The company thus shifted its emphasis from commerce to religion.

CAMBRIDGE PLATFORM (August 1648). Resolution sponsored by a synod of New England ministers and written by Richard Mather, which endorsed the Westminster Confession. Brought New World Presbyterianism into line with the mother country.

CAMDEN. A city in New Jersey, located on the Delaware R, across from Philadelphia,and founded 1681. Industries produce canned soup, radio and electronic equipment, chemicals, and leather goods. Pop.: 84,910 (1980).

CAMDEN, BATTLE OF (Aug. 16, 1780). Revolutionary War battle fought in South Carolina by Gen. Horatio Gates and his patriot army against Lord Conwallis' English army. Gates's men, exhausted by a long march, were soundly defeated by the British and fled to Hillsboro, N.C. Gates was replaced in command by Nathanael Greene.

CAMELS. In 1855 Congress appropriated $30,000 to purchase camels for use in the Southwest for mail and express routes through the desert. 76 camels were shipped to Texas and 28 to California. They did not thrive, and their use was soon discontinued.

CAMINO DEL DIABLO (Devil's Highway). An old, difficult trail connecting a series of desert water holes NW from Rio de Sonoita to the Gila R near its confluence with the Colorado R. It was traversed in 1699 by the Jesuit missionary Eusebio Kino and was later used by travelers to California.

CAMPAIGN SONGS. Partisan ditties in the 19th c. were usually new words set to established melodies. Perhaps the best known was "Tippecanoe and Tyler Too," in which words by A.C. Ross were adapted to the folk tune "Little Pigs." It swept the country and gave the Whigs a winning slogan in the 1840 presidential election. The most famous campaign song of the 20th c. is "Happy Days Are Here Again," used by Franklin D. Roosevelt in his 1932 campaign; it has become the unofficial campaign song of the Democratic party.

CAMPAIGNS, PRESIDENTIAL. Presidential campaigns have taken place every four years since 1788. After 1830, nomination has centered on national party conventions to choose individuals to run for president and vice-president and to adopt a party platform. Delegate selection to the conventions was for a long time wholly extralegal and controlled by local party traditions. Early in the 20th c., some states set up presidential primaries to choose delegates and record voter preferences. In the late 1960s further reform began to broaden the ability of party members to participate in delegate selection and reduce the influence of the party professionals. An incumbent president can usually (but not always) achieve renomination without a convention contest. If he does not want it or has already served two terms, the convention makes the final choice, sometimes after lengthy and bitter struggle. In recent years, most of that struggle has already taken place by the time the convention meets, for the most part in the various state primaries. In the 19th c., the candidate himself did little stumping, but the 20th c. saw increased candidate involvement. After the 1930s, radio figured prominently in getting the candidates' messages to the public and since the 1950s television has been the key medium.

Public relations experts and public opinion pollsters have also come to occupy crucial roles.

Campaigns of 1788 and 1792. After ratification of the Constitution, the Continental Congress fixed the first Wednesday in January 1789 for choosing electors, the first Wednesday in February for their voting, and the first Wednesday in March for starting the new government. Thirteen states could cast 91 votes; but two states had not ratified, and New York failed to elect or appoint electors; four electors failed to vote. George Washington received 69 votes, one of the two votes of every elector. John Adams received 34 of the second votes, making him vice-president. In 1792, fifteen states could cast 132 electoral votes. Washington's vote again was unanimous, and Adams defeated the Antifederalist George Clinton 77 to 50 for the vice-presidency.

Campaign of 1796. For the first time, the national election was contested by political parties. The Federalists agreed on John Adams and Thomas Pinckney. The Democratic-Republicans chose Thomas Jefferson and Aaron Burr. Adams received 71 electoral votes, Jefferson 68, Pinckney 59, Burr 30, and the remaining 48 votes were divided among 9 other candidates.

Campaigns of 1800 and 1804. In 1800, Jefferson and Burr each received 73 votes in the electoral college (see JEFFERSON-BURR ELECTION DISPUTE), John Adams received 65 votes, and Charles Cotesworth Pinckney, 64. Although he publicly disclaimed any intent to secure the presidency, Burr was put forward by the Federalists in order to defeat Jefferson. The vote was thrown to the House of Representatives, and it was only after 35 ballotings that Jefferson won. This narrow escape from frustrating the popular will led to the Twelfth Amendment to the Constitution, which separated the balloting for president and vice-president. In 1804 Jefferson covertly helped eliminate Burr from the ticket, Burr being replaced by George Clinton. The Federalists selected Pinckney as their presidential candidate and Rufus King for the vice-presidency. Jefferson and Clinton were elected.

Campaigns of 1808 and 1812. In 1808 James Madison was the choice of the Democratic-Republicans and George Clinton again was the vice-presidential nominee. The Federalists chose Charles Pinckney and Rufus King. Madison and Clinton won. In 1812 Madison was renominated by the party but with a tacit yielding to the demands of Henry Clay and the war hawks. Clinton had died in office, and Elbridge Gerry became Madison's running mate. Madison was opposed by DeWitt Clinton, a prowar Republican who won the support of the Federalists. Jared Ingersoll was nominated as his running mate. The electoral college gave Madison 128 votes, Clinton 89.

Campaigns of 1816 and 1820. There was no campaign in 1816 worthy of the name, and none at all in 1820. President Madison's choice was James Monroe and, despite some party support for William H. Crawford, he easily won the nomination. The Federalists, thoroughly discredited by now as a result of the HARTFORD CONVENTION, nominated Rufus King. Monroe was given 183 votes to 34 for King. In 1820 Monroe had virtually no opposition: He received all but one electoral vote.

Campaign of 1824. Marked the beginning of the transition from federalism to democracy. In general, the politicians supported William H. Crawford; John Quincy Adams represented business; John C. Calhoun, the South and the rising slave owners; Henry Clay, the rising West; and Andrew Jackson, the "people" everywhere. Calhoun withdrew and became the vice-presidential candidate on both the Adams and Jackson tickets. No candidate received a majority electoral vote. Jackson received the most, 99; Adams, 84; Crawford, 41; and Clay, 37. Selection was made by the House of Representatives. Clay threw his support to Adams, who was elected president.

Campaigns of 1828 and 1832. Adams' campaign for reelection in 1828 was fatally damaged by the charges that a "corrupt bargain" had been struck with Clay to win in 1824. Jackson won. There was a great increase in the popular vote cast: 647,286 for Jackson and 508,064 for Adams. The electoral vote was 178 for Jackson to 83 for Adams. Calhoun was again elected vice-president. Jackson ran for reelection in 1832, with Clay as his major opponent. The popular vote gave Jackson 687,502, Clay 530,189, and William Wirt (candidate of the Anti-Masonic party), 101,051. In the electoral college, the vote stood at Jackson 219, Clay 49, and Wirt 7. The South Carolina electors cast their votes for

John Floyd of Virginia. Martin Van Buren was elected vice-president.

Campaign of 1836. Martin Van Buren, Jackson's choice, was unanimously nominated at the Democratic National Convention, which also indicated that Van Buren, if elected, would continue "that wise course of national policy pursued by Gen. Jackson." This statement may be regarded as the first platform issued by the Democratic party. Van Buren was opposed by various anti-Jackson Democrats, Whigs, and Anti-Masons. He won the presidency with 170 electoral votes and a popular vote of 765,483 to 739,795 for his opponents. No candidate for the vice-presidency received a majority of the electoral vote, so the Senate chose the Democratic candidate, Richard M. Johnson.

Campaign of 1840. The new Whig party nominated Gen. William Henry Harrison for president and John Tyler for vice-president. The only bond uniting the Whigs was the desire to defeat the Democrats, in the person of President Van Buren, running for reelection. Harrison was adroitly celebrated as the "hard cider and log cabin" candidate running against the aristocratic Van Buren (actually, Harrison was himself a Virginia aristocrat). Slogans and songs ("Tippecanoe and Tyler Too") became an important part of the campaign. Harrison won with a popular vote of 1,274,624 to 1,127,781 for Van Buren and an electoral vote of 234 to 60.

Campaign of 1844. No outstanding Democratic candidate could muster sufficient strength to win at the national convention, so James K. Polk became the first "dark horse" candidate. George M. Dallas was his running mate. They ran on a platform of favoring the annexation of Texas and tariff reform. The Whigs nominated Henry Clay and Theodore Frelinghuysen; their platform favored a national bank and a protective tariff but quibbled on the Texas issue, which alienated some of the Whigs. Polk was elected, with 170 electoral votes to 105 for Clay. The popular vote was Polk, 1,338,464; Clay, 1,300,097. James G. Birney, running on the Liberal ticket, won 62,300 popular votes.

Campaign of 1848. The Whig candidate, Gen. Zachary Taylor, who sidestepped the burning issue of slavery, won on his military reputation. Millard Fillmore was his running mate. Taylor's Democratic opponent, Lewis Cass, was saddled with the slavery issue. The new Free Soil party, opposed to slavery extension, chose Martin Van Buren. He split the New York vote, assuring victory to Taylor. The popular vote was Taylor, 1,360,967; Cass, 1,222,342; and Van Buren, 291,263. The electoral vote was Taylor, 163; Cass, 127.

Campaign of 1852. The slavery issue had completely demoralized the Whig party. Neither President Fillmore, who had succeeded to office on the death of Zachary Taylor, nor Daniel Webster could win party support. Instead, the Whigs nominated another military hero, Gen. Winfield Scott. The Free-Soilers named the antislavery leader John P. Hale. After many ballots, the Democrats settled on another dark horse, Franklin Pierce. William R. King was named his running mate. Both major parties endorsed the Compromise of 1850, so there were no issues and little contest. Pierce carried all but four states. The popular vote was Pierce, 1,601,117; Scott, 1,385,453; Hale, 155,825. The electoral vote was Pierce 254; Scott, 42.

Campaign of 1856. The Republican party in its first presidential campaign nominated John C. Frémont. Its platform opposed slavery extension and condemned slavery and Mormonism. The American, or Know-Nothing, party nominated former president Fillmore. The Democrats nominated James Buchanan, with John C. Breckinridge as his running mate. Their conservative platform stressed states' rights, opposed sectionalism, and favored giving popular sovereignty to the territories. The electoral vote was Buchanan, 174; Frémont,114; Fillmore, 8. The popular vote was Buchanan, 1,832,955; Frémont, 1,339,932; Fillmore, 871,731.

Campaign of 1860. The Democratic party was not able to hold together over the slavery issue. Northern Democrats nominated Stephen A. Douglas for president, and the Southern Democrats picked John C. Breckinridge. They also adopted diametrically opposed platforms. The Know-Nothings and the Whigs coalesced into the Constitutional Union party and nominated John Bell. They attempted to ignore the slavery issue with a plea for the preservation of the Union. The Republicans nominated Abraham Lincoln as their candidate and Hannibal Hamlin as his running mate. The Republicans adopted a platform opposing the extension of slavery and advocating a homestead law and a protective tariff.

Lincoln won easily over the fragmented opposition; he won 180 electoral votes against 72 for Breckinridge, 39 for Bell, and 12 for Douglas. The popular vote was 1,865,593 for Lincoln; 1,382,713 for Douglas; 848,356 for Breckinridge; and 592,906 for Bell.

Campaign of 1864. The term "Republican" was carefully avoided in 1864, and it was the National Union Convention that met and renominated Abraham Lincoln. Andrew Johnson, a pro-Union southerner, was nominated for vice-president. The Democrats convened and called the war a failure and advocated the restoration of the Union by peaceable means. They named Gen. George B. McClellan for president. McClellan accepted the nomination but virtually repudiated the platform. The victories of the Union army rallied the people to the support of Lincoln and the Union. Lincoln carried every state that took part in the election but New Jersey, Delaware, and Kentucky, with 212 electoral votes to 21 for McClellan. But the popular vote was much closer: 2,213,665 for Lincoln to 1,803,237 for McClellan.

Campaigns of 1868 and 1872. Horatio Seymour and Frank Blair, the Democratic nominees, ran on a platform calling for a restoration of the rights of the southern states and the payment of the war bonds in greenbacks. The Republicans nominated Gen. Ulysses S. Grant, with Schuyler Colfax as his running mate. Their platform acclaimed the success of Reconstruction and denounced as repudiation the payment of the bonds in greenbacks. The Republican campaign was marked by "waving the bloody shirt," and there was personal vilification from both sides. Grant won 53 percent of the popular vote: 3,013,421 to 2,706,829 for Seymour. Grant received 214 electoral votes; Seymour, 80. There was a Republican split in 1872. The Liberal Republicans named Horace Greeley to oppose Grant's reelection. The Democrats accepted the nominees and platform of the Liberal Republicans. Grant received 286 electoral votes to Greeley's 66 and over 55 percent of the popular vote, receiving 3,596,745 votes to 2,843,446 for Greeley.

Campaign of 1876. At the Republican convention. James G. Blaine led the field for six ballots, but on the seventh a stampede to Rutherford B. Hayes resulted in his nomination. William A. Wheeler was named vice-president. The Democrat party chose Samuel J. Tilden. The platform denounced the scandals of the Grant administration and called for reforms. The electoral college gave Tilden 184 unquestioned votes, Hayes 165. The 4 votes of Florida, the 8 votes of Louisiana, the 7 votes of South Carolina, and 1 vote of Oregon were claimed by both parties. After a protracted, bitter dispute, Congress created an electoral commission to settle the matter. (See ELECTORAL COMMISSION.) Eventually all of the disputed votes were decided in favor of the Republicans, and Hayes was declared president, by the closest of electoral margins: 185 to 184. Tilden had won the popular vote, 4,284,020 to 4,036,572. It is generally believed that a deal had been struck: the southern Democrats would accept a Republican victory in return for which the last of federal troops would be removed from the South, thereby ending Reconstruction.

Campaign of 1880. The Republicans united behind a ticket of James A. Garfield and Chester A. Arthur. The Democrats named Winfield Scott Hancock. The popular vote was close: 4,453,295 for Garfield; 4,414,082 for Hancock. The electoral vote was Garfield, 214; Hancock, 155.

Campaign of 1884. James G. Blaine was the Republican candidate and Grover Cleveland the Democratic nominee. The campaign was one of the most vituperative in US history. Blaine favored big business and had raised suspicion that he had used his office of speaker of the House for his personal profit. To divert these attacks, Republicans accused Cleveland of having fathered an illegitimate son. There were virtually no serious issues. Cleveland won narrowly. The popular vote was 4,879,507 for Cleveland, 4,850,293 for Blaine. The electoral vote was 219 to 182.

Campaign of 1888. The tariff was the chief issue of this campaign. President Cleveland devoted his 1887 annual message totally to tariff reform; thereupon, the Republicans nominated a high-tariff man, Benjamin Harrison. He turned out to be an aggressive campaigner who made a deep impression on the country. The Democrats ran a dispirited campaign, losing by 233 electoral votes for Harrison to 168 for Cleveland. Once again a losing candidate had won the popular vote: Cleveland received 5,537,857 votes to 5,447,129 for Harrison.

Campaign of 1892. Cleveland and Harrison were again the candidates in 1892, and this time Cleveland won, by a surprising majority. President Harrison had estranged the professionals in the Republican party and had quarreled with Blaine, the party's most popular leader; furthermore, the Republican tariff act was not popular, nor were heavy federal expenditures. Cleveland, with a popular vote of 5,555,426, had 277 electors; Harrison, with a popular vote of 5,182,690, had 145.

Campaign of 1896. William McKinley was named by the Republicans, and they adopted a traditional, conservative platform. The Democrats were divided, but eventually chose William Jennings Bryan, after his sensational "Cross of Gold" speech. Other free silver groups, the Populist, the Silver Republican, and the National Silver parties endorsed his candidacy. Conservative Democrats named their own candidate, John M. Palmer. The campaign was highly spectacular. The Democrats exploited Bryan's oratory by sending him on speaking tours across the country. McKinley, by contrast, conducted a quiet, "front porch" campaign from his home in Canton, Ohio. They spent vast sums of money, however, and turned loose a flood of advertising. It was in many respects the first modern presidential campaign. The popular vote was unusually large. McKinley won with 7,102,246; Bryan received 6,492,559 votes. The electoral vote was 271 to 176.

Campaign of 1900. The candidates again were McKinley and Bryan, and in general the platforms were similar to those of four years earlier. At the Republican convention, McKinley accepted Theodore Roosevelt as his running mate. The popular vote was McKinley, 7,218,491; Bryan, 6,356,734. McKinley obtained 292 electoral votes to 155 for Bryan.

Campaign of 1904. Theodore Roosevelt had become president after the death of McKinley in 1901. Despite some misgivings from the more conservative Republicans, Roosevelt was nominated by acclamation. Charles W. Fairbanks was chosen for the vice-presidency. Democrats turned their backs on Bryanism and free silver by nominating Alton B. Parker, a conservative judge who pledged to maintain the gold standard. Roosevelt won by a landslide, 336 electoral votes to Parker's 140. He received a popular plurality of 2,544,238.

Campaign of 1908. Roosevelt, although at the height of his popularity, refused to run for a second elective term in 1908 and threw his support to William Howard Taft. The Democrats turned once more to William Jennings Bryan. Party differnces were not significant. Bryan received about 44 percent of the popular vote, 6,412,294 to Taft's 7,675,320. Taft's electoral vote was 321; Bryan's 162.

Campaign of 1912. The struggle for the Republican nomination became a battle between the progressive and conservative wings. Sen. Robert M. LaFollette against the incumbent, President Taft. Roosevelt now believed Taft to be too closely tied to the conservative Old Guard and threw his support to the progressives. The conservatives were in firm control of the convention and Taft was renominated. Roosevelt later accepted the nomination of the newly organized Progressive, or Bull Moose, party. The Democrats chose Woodrow Wilson. All three party platforms were unusually favorable to progressive policies. Wilson, backed by a united party, won easily. Wilson's popular vote was 6,296,547, Roosevelt's was 4,118,571, and Taft's was 3,486,720. The electoral vote was, respectively, 435, 88, and 8. Eugene V. Debs, the Socialist candidate, secured about 900,000 votes.

Campaign of 1916. The Republicans united behind Charles Evans Hughes, and there was no Democratic opposition to the renomination of Woodrow Wilson. The Republicans called for a stronger foreign policy, and Wilson pledged to keep America out of the World War. Wilson won with an electoral vote of 277, against 254 for Hughes. The popular vote was Wilson, 9,127,695; Hughes, 8,533,507.

Campaign of 1920. The Republicans nominated the dark horse Warren G. Harding for president and Calvin Coolidge for vice-president. The Democrats chose James M. Cox for president and Franklin D. Roosevelt for vice-president. The Republicans opposed membership in the League of Nations and attacked Wilsonian internationalism in general. Women were able to vote for the first time, swelling the popular vote to 26,733,905. Harding won over 60 percent of the vote. Cox received only 127 electoral votes to Harding's 404.

Campaign of 1924. The Republicans nominated Calvin Coolidge, who had succeeded to the presidency on the death of Harding in 1923. The Democrats took two and a half weeks to agree on a nominee. Finally the nomination went to John W. Davis, a compromise candidate acceptable to the supporters of both Alfred E. Smith and William G. McAdoo, who had effectively knocked each other out of the race. The result was another Republican landslide: Coolidge received 15,718,211 votes, and Davis 8,385,283. Coolidge received 382 electoral votes, Davis, 136. La Follette carried Wisconsin for 13 electoral votes.

Campaign of 1928. President Coolidge chose not to run for reelection, and the 1928 Republican convention chose Herbert Hoover as their candidate. The platform contained strong support for a protective tariff, sound business administration, and Prohibition. The Democrats named Alfred E. Smith, the first Roman Catholic to run for president and an advocate of repeal of Prohibition. The campaign was run mostly on personality, with a great deal of anti-Catholicism injected. Hoover won by a landslide, 444 electoral votes over Smith's 87. The popular plurality of Hoover over Smith was more than 6 million.

Campaigns of 1932 and 1936. The Republicans renominated President Hoover and Vice-President Charles Curtis. They adopted a platform praising the Hoover record in combating the depression. The Democrats nominated Franklin D. Roosevelt for president and John Nance Garner for vice-president. The platform pledged economy, a sound currency, old-age and unemployment insurance under state laws, the "restoration of agriculture," and repeal of Prohibition. After a campaign featuring Roosevelt's promise of a "new deal," the popular vote was Democratic, 22,809,638; Republican, 15,758,901; Socialist, 881,951. The electoral vote was 472 for the Democrats and 59 for the Republicans. In 1936 the Republicans chose Alfred M. Landon, on a platform strongly denouncing the New Deal. The Democratic convention turned out to be a ratification meeting for the New Deal. President Roosevelt and Vice-President Garner were renominated. The Democrats again won an overwhelming victory. The popular vote was Democratic, 27,752,869; Republican, 16,674,665. Democrats received 523 electoral votes; the Republicans only 8.

Campaign of 1940. The Republicans nominated Wendell L. Willkie, a liberal internationalist. The international crisis made the nomination of Roosevelt by the Democrats a practical certainty, even though his running for a third term was unprecedented. Both candidates promised aid to the Allies; both promised to keep the United States out of the war. Roosevelt and his new running mate, Henry A. Wallace, received 27,307,819 popular and 449 electoral votes. Willkie received 22,321,018 popular and 82 electoral votes.

Campaign of 1944. Thomas E. Dewey was nominated by the Republicans with little opposition. President Roosevelt, running for a fourth term, encountered even less opposition at the Democratic convention. The real struggle revolved around the vice-presidential nomination. Harry S. Truman was finally chosen. Roosevelt received 25,606,585 popular and 432 electoral votes to Dewey's 22,014,745 popular and 99 electoral votes.

Campaign of 1948. The Republicans, having gained control of Congress in 1946, expected to turn the apparently unpopular Truman administration out of power. Thomas E. Dewey was again the nominee. The Democrats unenthusiastically nominated Truman, who had succeeded to the presidency on the death of Roosevelt in 1945. Radicals left the party, nominating Henry A. Wallace on the Progressive ticket. Southerners, offended by the civil rights plank in the platform, seceded and formed the States' Rights Democratic, or Dixiecrat, party. They nominated J. Strom Thurmond as their presidential candidate. All the indicators, including the public opinion polls, saw Dewey and the Republicans as landslide winners. Truman won, however, in the greatest political upset in US history. The election was close. Truman polled 24,105,812 popular and 304 electoral votes against 21,970,065 popular and 189 electoral votes for Dewey. Thurmond polled 1,169,063 popular votes and 38 electoral votes. Wallace won 1,157,172 popular and no electoral votes.

Campaigns of 1952 and 1956. After a long and bitter struggle, the internationalist wing of the Republican party nominated Gen. Dwight D. Eisenhower against the opposition of Robert A. Taft. The Democrats turned to Adlai E. Stevenson. Eisenhower's appeal as a great war hero was enormous, and he won by a landslide. He and Richard M, Nixon, his running mate, polled 33,936,234 popular votes to 27,314,987 for Stevenson. The Republicans carried the electoral college, 442 to 89. Eisenhower and Stevenson were again the candidates in 1956, and again Eisenhower won by a landslide. In the election, the president polled 35,590,472 popular and 457 electoral votes to Stevenson's 26,022,752 popular and 73 electoral votes.

Campaign of 1960. The Democrats nominated John F. Kennedy for president and Lyndon B. Johnson for vice-president. The Republicans nominated Vice-President Nixon for president and Henry Cabot Lodge for vice-president. In a series of televised debates, the candidates submitted to questioning by reporters. Kennedy was generally believed to have "won" the debates. He also won an extremely close election: 34,227,096 votes for Kennedy to 34,108,546 for Nixon. Kennedy polled 49.7 of the popular votes cast; Nixon polled 49.6 percent. Kennedy won 303 electoral votes to Nixon's 219. Kennedy thus became the first Roman Catholic to become president.

Campaign of 1964. Lyndon B. Johnson assumed the presidency in November 1963, after the assassination of Kennedy. In 1964 the Democrats chose him by acclamation to be their presidential nominee, and Hubert H. Humphrey as the vice-presidential nominee. Conflict centered in the Republican party. Nelson Rockefeller, representing the moderate and liberal factions in the party, was pitted against Barry Goldwater, the leader of the conservatives. Goldwater won on the first ballot. Despite his popularity with the party professionals, Goldwater's extreme conservatism alienated many Republican voters, who either voted Democratic or not at all. Lyndon Johnson won a landslide victory, gaining 43,129,484 popular votes (61.1 percent), for 486 electoral votes. Goldwater won 27,178,188 votes (38.5 percent) and 52 electoral votes.

Campaign of 1968. By 1968 the Vietnam War had polarized the Democratic party. President Johnson chose not to run for reelection, causing a scramble for the nomination. Robert F. Kennedy was assassinated while campaigning in California, and Vice-President Humphrey was the eventual nominee. Richard Nixon was again the Republican nominee. A new party, the American Independent party, was largely formed in opposition

to racial integration. Its nominee was George C. Wallace. In the campaign, Humphrey defended the record of the Johnson administration, whose war policies were increasingly unpopular. The balloting brought Nixon a narrow victory. With 31,785,480 votes, he won 301 electoral votes. Humphrey won 31,275,166 votes and 191 electoral votes. Wallace gained 9,906,473 popular votes, or 13.5 percent of the total.

Campaign of 1972. Nixon and his vice-president, Spiro T. Agnew, were renominated in 1972. The Democrats, after a series of primary contests, chose George S. McGovern, a strong opponent of the Vietnam War. The election was a landslide for Nixon. He won 47,169,905 popular votes (60.7 percent) and 521 electoral votes from 49 states. McGovern won 29,170,383 popular votes (37.5 percent), but only 17 electoral votes.

Campaign of 1976. Gerald R. Ford was the Republican president in 1976, both President Nixon and Vice-President Agnew having been forced to resign office amidst unprecedented scandals. Ford was seriously challenged for the Republican nomination by the conservative Ronald Reagan. Ford was nominated, however, and Robert J. Dole was named his running mate. Jimmy Carter was the nominee of the Democrats. Walter F. Mondale was chosen as his running mate. Carter won a close victory at the polls, with 40,825,839 (50.4 percent) popular votes and 297 electoral votes. Ford received 39,147,770 (48.3 percent) popular votes and 240 electoral votes.

Campaign of 1980. President Carter was the Democratic nominee, and Ronald Reagan won the Republican nomination. John Anderson, a dissident Republican, ran as an independent. Capitalizing in particular on the public's impatience with the administration's handling of the problem of the hostages being held in Iran, Reagan won a landslide victory. He received 43,898,770 (51 percent) popular votes and 489 electoral votes. Carter got 35,480,948 (41 percent) popular votes and 49 electoral votes. Anderson received 5,719,222 votes.

CAMPBELLITES. See DISCIPLES OF CHRIST.

CAMP BUTLER. Located six miles E of Springfield, Ill., a training camp and prison camp during the Civil War.

CAMP CHASE. Located W of Columbus, Ohio, it was a training camp and military prison in the Civil War.

CAMP DAVID AGREEMENT. See ISRAELI-AMER-ICAN RELATIONS.

CAMP DOUGLAS. Located near the S limit of Chicago, a training camp and military prison in the Civil War.

CAMP FIRE GIRLS. Organization for girls through high school age, organized 1910. Its purposes are to enable girls to make suitable friends, improve their own health, and perform community service.

CAMP GRANT MASSACRE (April 30, 1871). The Arivaipa Apache, hoping to settle down and lead peaceful lives, were encamped near Camp Grant, Arizona. In an early morning attack, the Apache (almost all women and children) were slaughtered by a party of citizens of Tucson, assisted by Papago Indians. Of 108 Indians slain, only 8 were men. Twenty-nine children were sold as slaves. The perpetrators of the massacre were acquitted at once by a Tucson jury.

CAMP JACKSON AFFAIR (1861). After secessionists had set up Camp Jackson in St. Louis, Capt. Nathaniel Lyon, in command of the US arsenal in St. Louis, led a force of 8,000 men to seize the camp. While marching his captives to prison, Lyons' men encountered a large crowd sympathetic to the prisoners. The crowd was fired upon and about 28 persons were killed.

CAMP MEETINGS. Outdoor religious meetings were a feature of the evangelical revival from the 18th c. They usually lasted four days or longer, with several services each day, and with several ministers preaching.

CAMPOBELLO FIASCO (April 1866). An attempt by Irish Fenian nationalists to seize the island of Campobello, New Brunswick, for Ireland.

CAMP WILDCAT. A natural fortification in the Rockcastle Hills of Laurel County, Ky., where Union troops decisively repulsed a Confederate force on Oct. 21, 1861.

CANADA AND THE AMERICAN REVOLUTION. On Oct. 24, 1774, the Continental Congress appealed to the Canadians to join the Thirteen Colonies in their opposition to British rule, at the same time threatening to treat them as enemies if they chose not to join the Congress. When it became obvious that Canada would remain loyal, Congress decided to seize Canada by force. Congress authorized Gen. Philip Schuyler to undertake an invasion. After one ill-planned attempt against Montreal, the city was occupied Nov. 13, 1775. A similar assault against Quebec, led by Benedict Arnold and Richard Montgomery, failed. In May 1776 the first 10,000 regulars arrived from Britain, and after defeats at Cedars and Three Rivers, the Americans were forced to evacuate Montreal and St. Johns in June. British pursuit was delayed while they built a fleet, which destroyed Arnold's (see VALCOUR ISLAND, BATTLE OF), but it was too late in the season for further operations. Invasion of the colonies was postponed until 1777 (see BURGOYNE'S INVASION).

CANADA AND THE WAR OF 1812. Since the destruction of British power in Canada was a primary object of the War of 1812, it was inevitable that the United States would attempt the conquest of the colony. An 1812 attempt at the Detroit frontier was a disaster, and an enterprise on the Niagara was no more successful. The next year brought more success: Oliver Hazard Perry's victory in the Battle of Lake Erie permitted a successful invasion of W Upper Canada. The Detroit frontier region remained in American hands until the end of the war. Further E, the Americans successfully raided York (now Toronto), but initial successes on the Niagara were followed by a check at Stoney Creek, and no permanent foothold was gained. The campaign against Montreal was a total failure. In 1814 the United States again attempted to invade Canada on the Niagara, but no conquest of territory resulted.

CANADIAN-AMERICAN RELATIONS. The relationship between Canada and the United States, while generally amicable, has been marked by periods of sharp hostility tempered by an awareness of a shared continental environment and by the slow emergence of a Canadian foreign policy independent of either Great Britain or the United States. The original hostility arose from the four intercolonial wars in which the North American colonies of Britain and France were involved from 1689 until 1763. In the French and Indian War, Britain triumphed and Canada passed to the British (1763). The Canadians were caught up on the fringes of the American Revolution (see CANADA AND THE AMERICAN REVOLUTION). During that war, many American Loyalists fled to Canada and thereafter resented the loss of their American property and the renunciation by some states of debts to Loyalists. Furthermore, there were still evidences of American designs on Canada, particularly toward its western lands. This was one of the causes of the war against Britain in 1812. Unsuccessful invasions of Canada nurtured anti-Americanism, the burning of York (now Toronto) being especially resented. The Treaty of Ghent (1815) restored the status quo ante and the Rush-Bagot Agreement of 1817 neutralized the Great Lakes. A second period of strain began in 1837 and lasted until 1871. Rebellions in Canada were put down by the British government, but not before American filibusters provoked a number of border incidents. A dispute over the Maine boundary led to a war scare (see AROOSTOOK WAR); that dispute was settled in 1842, but the Oregon frontier remained in dispute until 1846. In the meantime, trade between the two countries flourished. During the US Civil War, Canadians feared invasion by the northern army; this led to the development of detailed defensive plans. Ultimately, however, Canada enacted its own neutrality legislation, in line with British policy. The American threat helped, in 1864, to bring the provinces together into a confederation, by the British North American Act of 1867. The Treaty of Washington of 1871 (between Britain and the United States) did much to ease tensions between the two countries, although it was resented by some Canadians as a denial of Canadian rights of self-determination. One more border quarrel had to be settled: the Alaska boundary question, which only took on importance after the discovery of gold in the Klondike in the 1890s. It was settled by treaty in 1903, and thereafter problems between the two neighbors were more economic and cultural than diplomatic. Although each nation erected trade barriers in the form of tariffs, the economies of the two nations continued to interlock more closely. Military cooperation was successfully pursued in both world wars; and both Canada and the United States were charter members of NATO in 1949. A collaborative series of early-warning defense systems was constructed across Canada during the cold war; and in 1957 the North American Air Defense Command (NORAD) was created. Trade tensions persisted, however. Canadians continued to be apprehensive of the growing American influence in Canadian industry. Disputes over the role of American subsidiary firms in Canada; over American business practices; and the effect of American television and magazines led to a resurgence of "Canada First" nationalism in the late 1950s and 1960s. Tensions eased somewhat in the 1970s and by the early 1980s, relations between the two were on the whole equable.

CANADIAN ANNEXATION MOVEMENT. In 1849 Canadian urban and industrial interests, particularly in Montreal, sponsored a movement to annex Canada to the United States to offset the economic depression then afflicting Canada. A circulated manifesto received over 1,000 signatures, including those of prominent political and financial leaders. Widespread opposition, counter manifestos, and a return to prosperity ended the movement within six months.

CANADIAN RIVER. Part of the Arkansas R system in the SW United States. It flows mostly E through New Mexico and the Texas Panhandle into Oklahoma, where it empties into the Arkansas. The name possibly was given to the river by traders who came from Canada. Early emigrants to California followed its S bank on their way to Santa Fe.

CANADIAN AND US BOUNDARY DISPUTES. See AROOSTOOK WAR; NORTHEAST BOUNDARY; NORTHWEST BOUNDARY CONTROVERSY.

CANAL BOATS. See CANALS.

CANAL RING. Corrupt contractors and politicians who conspired shortly after the Civil War to defraud New York by overcharging for repairs and improvement of the state's canal system. The group for years was powerful enough to prevent interference and to defeat unfriendly candidates for office.

CANALS. Since 1607, American river systems have provided an essential element in internal transportation. However, full-scale navigation ceased at the FALL LINE. The earliest canals—such as the one at Great Falls, Md. (constructed 1786–1808), and the one at Little Falls, N.Y. (1795) bypassed the fall line. The Middlesex Canal (1793–1804), connecting Boston with the Merrimac R, and the Santee and Cooper Canal (1790s), connecting these two rivers above Charleston, S.C., fully launched America into canal construction. The Erie Canal (1817–25) became the great school for American canal engineers and civil engineering in general. Erie engineers spread throughout the United States, working in all aspects of civil engineering, including the Pennsylvania Main Line Canal (1826–34), the Chesapeake and Ohio Canal (1828–50), and the Lehigh Canal (1827–29). When a canal would open up a large new territory and its chances for financial success were limited, the state tended to provide the necessary capital. When a canal focused on a single natural resource or was linked to an established trade route, it usually was privately financed. Except for the Erie Canal, most state systems were financial disasters. Private companies usually escaped the problems of poor construction based on contract favoritism, fiscal mismanagement, and pressures to locate in certain areas for political rather than sound engineering or business reasons. The principal engineering elements of a canal are the source of water supply, the canal bed, and locks to raise boats from one level to another. Other engineering elements are stop gates (to control water in long, open levels in case of a breach or during repairs), waste weirs, overflows, culverts, and aqueducts. Canal boats were basically of two types—packet (passenger) boats and freight boats. Packet boats lasted only until railroads developed. Towing power was furnished from towpaths along the shore by horses, mules, and later electric motors or steam engines. In large canals today vessels travel under their own power except when passing through locks. Sometimes tugboats are used. The Erie Barge Canal and the Chesapeake and Delaware Ship Canal are still vital transportation links. Canal landmarks are becoming the basis for parks, museums, and other recreational development and, in several cases, are being restored to their 19th-c. operating order. (See also ST. LAWRENCE SEAWAY; individual canals.)

CANAL ZONE. See PANAMA CANAL.

CANARY ISLANDS. Spanish islands off the NW coast of Africa, which served as a way station for Spain's New World voyages. The New England colonies early began a profitable intercourse with the Canaries and Portugal's Madeiras and Azores, involving mainly the exchange of lumber and fish for wine. Although illegal by the Navigation Act of 1663, trade with the Canaries continued until the early 19th c.

CANDLES. Candles lighted most American homes, public buildings, and streets until gas (1820s) and kerosene lamps (1850s) replaced them. Housewives made many kinds— bear grease, deer suet, bayberry, beeswax, tallow dip, and spermaceti. The homemaker was the only manufacturer until the 1700s when an itinerant candlemaker could be hired. Later, professional chandlers prospered in the cities. Although factories were numerous after 1750, home-dipping continued as late as 1880.

CANE RIDGE REVIVAL. The culmination of a great spiritual awakening in Kentucky (see GREAT REVIVAL). This occurred in Aug. 1801, at a camp meeting of about 20,000 near the Cane Ridge Meeting House in Bourbon County. The revivalists underwent fervid physical and vocal exercises that indicated an extraordinary religious experience. The Disciples of Christ developed from the intellectual quickening of the movement.

CANNING INDUSTRY. Nicolas Appert, a Parisian confectioner, is generally considered the father of the canning process (1809). Appert's method was based on submerging filled and corked bottles in boiling water for varying lengths of time. The tin can did not come into widespread use until 1839. In 1895, it was discovered that bacteria caused food spoilage, as shown earlier by Louis Pasteur, and that heating to temperatures above the boiling point was needed for sterilization of the product. Of the many developments since, that of the hydrostatic sterilizer stands out. In addition to providing consistent sterilization, this unit results in tremendous savings in steam and water costs and can adjust readily to different sizes of cans and bottles.

CANNONISM. Term common during Joseph G. Cannon's service as speaker of the House of Representatives (1903–11) when the powers of that office were used in the interest of the ultraconservative elements and to defeat progressive legislation.

CANOE. The Algonkin-speaking Indians of the Northeast made birchbark canoes long before the whites reached North America, and the pioneers quickly adopted them. Became chief vehicle for reaching much of the northern part of the continent.

CANTIGNY, AMERICAN ATTACK AT (May 28, 1918). Successful effort by US and French troops to take Cantigny, then a German stronghold.

CANTON. Industrial city in NE Ohio, producing a wide range of mechanical products. A major steel mill is operated there. Pop.: 94,738 (1980).

CANTON FUR TRADE. Developed from the search for a staple which American merchants could exchange for the teas and silks of China. The cargo of the first American vessel, the *Empress of China,* to Canton (1784) included such rare furs as otter, seal, beaver, and fox. Later, sea otter and fur seal skins were traded. After ca.1830, the importance of fur trading declined, becoming merely one aspect of a more general Pacific trade.

CAPE ANN. Eastern peninsula of Massachusetts, named for the wife of James I. In 1623 the Dorchester Company of merchants in England established a fishing station at the cape, to which came disaffected settlers from Plymouth and Nantucket. The enterprise failed in 1626, and for twenty years the settlement languished, until Rev. Richard Blynman arrived in 1642. The city of Gloucester, on Cape Ann, began to grow as a deep-sea fishing port and has never lost its eminence.

CAPE BRETON EXPEDITION. See LOUISBURG EXPEDITION.

CAPE CANAVERAL. A low sandy promontory on the E coast of Florida. The site, since 1950, for the assembling and launching of ballistic and space vehicles. Following the death of President John F. Kennedy in 1963 it was renamed Cape Kennedy, but it reverted to its original name in 1973.

CAPE COD. Peninsula in SE Massachusetts, possibly the Promontory of Vinland of the Norse voyagers (985–1025). Giovanni da Verrazano in 1524 approached it from the S. Bartholomew Gosnold gave it its present name in 1602. Samuel de Champlain charted its sand-silted harbors in 1606, and Henry Hudson landed there in 1609. Capt. John Smith noted it on his map of 1614, and the Pilgrims entered the "Cape Harbor" on Nov. 11, 1620. Whaling and cod fishing arose in the 18th c. Shipbuilding flourished before and after the Revolution. Whaling started the migration of Portuguese. During the summer months the fishing ports are exceptionally busy, and the villages and towns become heavily populated resorts. In 1961 Cape Cod was designated a national seashore.

CAPE FEAR, ACTION AT. See FISHER, FORT, CAPTURE OF.

CAPE FEAR RIVER SETTLEMENTS. Discovered by Giovanni da Verrazano in 1524, the Cape Fear region of North Carolina was the site of a short-lived Spanish colony in 1526. The first English settlement was made in 1662 by New England men under William Hilton. For unknown reasons the colony was abandoned, but Hilton returned the next year with a colony from Barbados to establish the county of Clarendon, which flourished until 1667. In 1713 Landgrave Thomas Smith of Carolina received a grant for Smith Island at the mouth of the Cape Fear R, and soon settlers from South Carolina and Albemarle, North Carolina, began to move into the region. In 1725 the town of Brunswick was laid out about fourteen miles from the sea. Wilmington was founded in 1733 and became the colony's chief port. From 1732 until 1775, thousands of Scottish Highlanders settled on the upper Cape Fear R. Naval stores, lumber, and rice became the most important products of the region.

CAPE GIRARDEAU. Bend in the Mississippi R sixty miles S of the French village of Ste. Geneviève in Missouri. In 1793 the Spanish granted Louis Lorimier, a French-Canadian, the right of establishing a trading post there. He prospered from land sales and the Indian trade.

CAPE HORN. Southernmost point of the Americas. Traditionally the most dreaded of ocean headlands because of its almost ceaseless storms and the fact that it lies within the southern ice line. First sighted by the Dutch navigators Jakob Le Maire and William Schouten in 1616, who named it after the town of Hoorn in Holland. The difficulty of making the westbound passage played a part in retarding the growth of California until the discovery of gold in 1848. This stimulus put American square-rigged ships in the forefront of the world. After the building of the Panama Canal, the importance of the route around Cape Horn rapidly declined.

CAPITAL, NATIONAL, LOCATION OF. Immediately after the Continental Congress adjourned (1783) from Philadelphia to New York, because of Pennsylvania's failure to protect it from the insults of mutinous soldiery, agitation was begun in Congress for establishing a permanent seat of government. Nearly every state offered a location. In 1790 Alexander Hamilton, secretary of the Treasury, supposedly acted upon the desire of the southern states to obtain the capital and traded, through Secretary of State Thomas Jefferson, Pennsylvania support for the Potomac R location, in return for Virginia support for his plan of the assumption of the states' Revolutionary War debts.

CAPITAL PUNISHMENT. Imposition of the death penalty for the commission of certain types of crimes, thereby known as capital crimes. Capital punishment was adopted from the English system. The colonies retreated from it during and after the American Revolution. During the Civil War some states reinstated the death penalty. The opponents of capital punishment renewed their attack at the turn of the century. A clear trend away from capital punishment became evident by the late 1960s. Executions dropped from a high of 152 in 1947 to 7 in 1965, and only 4 after 1967. In 1971, thirty-nine of the fifty-four US jurisdictions provided for the death penalty. In 1972 the Supreme Court ruled in *Furman* v. *Georgia* (408 US 238) that the

optional death penalty was unconstitutional because it violated the Eighth (cruel and unusual punishment) and Fourteenth amendments. One immediate effect was commutation of the death sentence to life imprisonment for all 600 prisoners awaiting execution, followed by a series of appellate court rulings that state laws imposing the optional death penalty were unconstitutional. By 1983 new legislation had restored the death penalty in thirty-seven states. Between 1977 and 1983 only seven persons were executed, although in 1983 there were 1,050 prisoners under sentence of death.

CAPITATION TAXES. The federal government is forbidden by the Constitution from levying a capitation (per capita) or other direct tax "unless in Proportion to the Census of Enumeration." The poll-tax restriction did not apply to states. Following colonial precedents, the state employed this tax, generally placed on all males above twenty-one, sometimes above sixteen. In southern states the poll tax was often made a prerequisite for voting, thus disqualifying both poor whites and blacks. Ratification of the Twenty-fourth Amendment in 1964 outlawed the poll tax in federal elections. In 1966 the Supreme Court ruled that the state poll tax was unconstitutional under the Fourteenth Amendment.

CAPITOL AT WASHINGTON. In a competition in 1791 of architectural plans for the capitol building, Stephen Hallet's, although not satisfactory, was judged the best. William Thornton submitted a more artistic design, and Hallet was employed to make working drawings of it and to superintend the construction. Accused of substituting his own plan, Hallet was dismissed in 1794 and James Hoban succeeded him. The cornerstone was laid with Masonic ceremonies by President Washington, Sept. 18, 1793; but the center portion had not been erected when the British burned the public buildings in 1814. Rebuilding commenced under Benjamin H. Latrobe, and the center portion of Acquia freestone with a low dome, designed by Charles Bulfinch, was finished in 1827. The present north and south wings of Massachusetts marble were begun in 1851, from designs of Thomas Ustick Walter, and finished in 1857–59. The present dome of cast iron was finished in 1865. It is surmounted by Crawford's heroic bronze of Freedom, 19.5 feet high. In 1959–60 the east front was extended over 30 feet.

CAPPER-VOLSTEAD ACT (Cooperative Marketing Act; Feb. 18, 1922). Authorized agricultural producers to form voluntary cooperative associations, exempt from antitrust laws, for producing, handling, and marketing farm products.

CAPRON TRAIL. An east–west trail in Florida, probably first run about 1850, the date of the establishment of Fort Capron (St. Lucie County). It passed from Fort Capron to Fort Brooke (Tampa), connecting all in-between forts. Named for Capt. Erastus A. Capron, a hero of the Mexican War.

CAPUCHINS. A branch of the Franciscan Friars Minor, founded in Italy in 1525. They were the first missionaries in Maine (1630) and established a central mission at Port Royal, Nova Scotia (1633). Placed in charge of missionary work in Louisiana in 1722, they expanded to the E bank of the Mississippi four years later. This latter area was ceded to the Jesuits in 1750.

CARACAS MIXED COMMISSIONS. Established after the 1902 Venezuelan debt crisis (see VENEZUELA, BLOCKADE OF). Protocols were signed in 1903 between Venezuela and ten creditor powers, including the US, providing for settlements of claims by commissions. Those commissions awarded sums ranging from over 10 million bolivars (francs) to Belgium to 174,000 bolivars to Norway-Sweden.

CARAVAN TRAFFIC ON THE GREAT PLAINS. Existed ca. 1825–75, reaching its peak after the Civil War. Included the Oregon movement (1842), the Mormon migration (1847), and the California gold rush (1848). The first important caravan traffic was via the Santa Fe Trail. William Becknell drove the first wagon from W Missouri to Santa Fe in 1822, a distance of almost 900 miles. Elm Grove, twelve miles SW of Independence, Missouri, was a favorite starting point for the Oregon Trail. Heavy freight caravans plied the routes between San Antonio and Chihuahua, between Santa Fe and Chihuahua, and from points in Nebraska, Kansas, and Colorado to the Far West by 1860. A well-known

road from Council Bluffs to the Great Salt Lake via Fort Bridger was traveled by thousands of Mormon pilgrims from 1847 to 1860. In 1869 the first transcontinental railway was completed, but caravan trade and travel continued for a decade.

CARDIFF GIANT. In 1868 George Hall had a human figure weighing 2,966 pounds carved from Iowa gypsum in Chicago. He transported the "giant" to Cardiff, N.Y., and secretly buried it on the Newell farm, where it was discovered by men digging a well. It was exhibited as a petrified prehistoric giant, creating much excitement and deceiving many people until the hoax was exposed by Othniel C. Marsh of Yale.

CAREY DESERT LAND ACT (1894). Unsuccessful effort by Congress to encourage settlers to reclaim desert lands by irrigation. It was replaced in 1902 by the NEWLANDS RECLAMATION ACT.

CARIBBEAN POLICY. Prior to the 1830s American policy focused chiefly on Cuba, in the hopes that the island would remain in Spain's weak hands and not fall to England or France. During the 1840s, US policy toward Cuba became more assertive, with attempts to buy or annex the island. Central America became an object of US interest in a projected interoceanic canal; treaties were signed with Colombia, Nicaragua, and Honduras to assure US rights to build a canal. The PANAMA CANAL was the outcome. The SPANISH-AMERICAN WAR left the Caribbean under US hegemony, with Puerto Rico as an American colony and Cuba under temporary occupation (the latter would assume quasi-protectorate status in 1902 under the Platt Amendment). The United States assumed the role of gendarme in the area, a policy expressed officially in 1905 in the ROOSEVELT COROLLARY to the MONROE DOCTRINE. Interventions under President Woodrow Wilson included takeovers of the governments in Haiti and the Dominican Republic. After World War I, US policy became less overbearing. In Central America there was a shift toward intraregional arbitration and joint action. In Cuba the Crowder Commission, a special board managing Cuba's public finances, completed its functions in 1924; and in the same year intervention in the Dominican Republic ended. The trend continued during the administration of Herbert Hoover with the abrogation of the Roosevelt Corollary, and culminated in President Franklin D. Roosevelt's GOOD NEIGHBOR POLICY, officially abandoning military intervention in Latin America. In 1934 the last troops were withdrawn from Haiti. By the early 1950s, policy once again assumed a more aggressive character, influenced by the cold war and the fear of Communist infiltration. Such considerations led to the overthrow of President Jacobo Arbenz Guzmán's leftist regime in Guatemala, with US support, in 1954. The aggressiveness became more pronounced in the 1960s after Cuba's gravitation toward the Soviet bloc. Accordingly, aid was given in 1961 to the abortive BAY OF PIGS INVASION of Cuba by anti-Castro exiles; in 1962, on US initiative, Cuba was excluded from the Organization of American States; and later in the year the island was blockaded during the CUBAN MISSILE CRISIS. The next assertion of US power occurred in 1965 in the Dominican Republic, where 42,000 US Marines were landed during a period of intense revolutionary unrest. An inter-American force soon replaced the marines and withdrew after elections the next year. In the late 1960s and the 1970s the United States paid scant attention to the Caribbean region. In 1978 a treaty was concluded with Panama according to which Panama would assume full control over the canal by 2000. But after a leftist, Sandinist junta took power in Nicaragua in 1979 and civil war intensified in El Salvador in the early 1980s, US policy became antagonistic again. In 1983 a leftist coup in GRENADA resulted in an invasion by US Marines.

CARILLION, FORT. See TICONDEROGA, FORT.

CARLISLE. Borough of S Pennsylvania, founded 1751; center of Scotch-Irish settlement in the Cumberland Valley. The crossroads of important Indian trails and site of Fort Louther, it was a trading center for pioneers.

CARLISLE COMMISSION. See PEACE COMMISSION OF 1778.

CARLISLE INDIAN INDUSTRIAL SCHOOL. First off-reservation school for American Indians; established in 1879 in Pennsylvania. Instruction covered farming, horticulture, dressmaking, cooking, laundering, housekeeping, and twenty trades. Its students included the great athlete Jim Thorpe. The school was closed in 1918.

CARLOTTA, CONFEDERATE COLONY OF. In 1865 many ex-Confederates left for Mexico, encouraged by Emperor Maximilian, and colonies were established along the railway between Veracruz and Mexico City. The best-known colony was Carlotta, 500,000 acres in the Cordova Valley, named for the empress. Among reasons for its failure were a hostile American press, lack of funds, improper colonization methods, forcible land seizure, political conditions in Mexico, local hostility, and opposition of the US government.

CARLSBAD CAVERNS. The largest underground chambers in the world, in SE New Mexico, were found by Jim White, a Texas cowboy, in 1901. The caverns became a national monument in 1923 and a national park (46,753 acres) in 1930.

CARMELITES. Catholic order believed to have been founded by St. Berthold about 1195 in Palestine. Their rule has stressed extreme asceticism, absolute poverty, abstinence from meat, and solitude. In 1452 the Order of Carmelite Sisters was formed. The friars were temporarily assigned the care of E Louisiana in 1622. Only one brother is known to have gone to the area, which was transferred to the Capuchins in 1726. The first sisters entered the US in 1790 and established a nunnery in Port Tobacco, Md.

CARNEGIE CORPORATION OF NEW YORK. Foundation created by Andrew Carnegie in 1911 to promote understanding between the US and the British Empire. From 1911 to 1917 it provided funds for for 2,509 library buildings. Today, the corporation concentrates on the improvement of education, especially among minorities and in developing countries.

CARNEGIE FOUNDATION FOR THE ADVANCEMENT OF TEACHING. Foundation established 1905 by Andrew Carnegie with an initial $10 million endowment. By 1973, teacher pension payments of $83 million had been paid out. The pension program was phased out in 1974. Several notable studies have been undertaken by the foundation in medical, legal, engineering, and dental education; college athletics; and teacher-training. Its program of entrance tests for graduate and professional schools evolved into the Educational Testing Service. The Council on Policy Studies in Higher Education, the foundation's principal organ, was formed in 1974 to report on various educational problems.

CARNEGIE HERO FUND COMMISSION. Created 1904 for making annual awards to recognize acts of heroism in the United States and Canada.

CARNEGIE INSTITUTION OF WASHINGTON. Founded 1902 by Andrew Carnegie to encourage original research by exceptional persons.

CARNIFEX FERRY, BATTLES AT (1861). Two encounters on the Gauley R in West Virginia. On Aug. 26 a Confederate brigade entrenched itself. On Sept. 10, a Union force dislodged them.

CAROLANA. In 1698 Daniel Coxe, British physician and land speculator, acquired title to the region west of the Carolina settlements, including the lower Mississippi Valley. The expedition sent to plant the colony landed at Charleston, South Carolina, but one ship sailed up the Mississippi for 100 miles, turning back when informed that the French occupied the region. The colony never materialized.

CAROLINA, FUNDAMENTAL CONSTITUTIONS OF. Pretentious and unsuccessful attempt (1669) to establish a feudal aristocracy in English America. Drawn up by John Locke for the earl of Shaftesbury. Provided for a provincial nobility having permanent ownership of two-fifths of the land and executive and judicial authority; an established Anglican church and religious toleration; and serfdom and slavery. Rejected by the assembly ca. 1700.

CAROLINA PROPRIETORS. Patent granted by Charles II in 1663 to eight joint proprietors. Their "Declarations and Proposals," the first organic law, promised land to settlers who emigrated within five years, representation of freeholders in a provincial assembly,

and liberty of conscience. The enterprise was not successful, and by 1729 all of Carolina was under the crown.

CAROLINA ROAD. See VIRGINIA PATH.

CAROLINE, FORT. Built at the mouth in 1564 of the St. Johns R in Florida, by French Huguenots. In 1565 a Spanish expedition was sent to settle Florida and expel the French. After establishing St. Augustine, the Spaniards captured Fort Caroline (Sept. 20), killing all its defenders. Renamed Fort San Mateo.

CAROLINE AFFAIR. After an abortive rebellion in Upper Canada in 1837, William Lyon Mackenzie and his followers fled to Navy Island in the Niagara R. Sympathizers on the American side of the river supplied them with food, arms, and recruits, using the steamer *Caroline*. On December 29, Canadian troops set afire and turned the vessel adrift, killing one American. A presidential protest was ignored by the British, and the case dragged on until 1842, when the British issued an official expression of regret as an adjunct of the Webster-Ashburton Treaty.

CAROLINE ISLANDS. Truk atoll, near the center of the Caroline Islands, was "neutralized" by a series of air strikes in April 1944. Key positions in the Palaus in the W Carolines, strongly fortified and defended by 13,000 Japanese, were assaulted on Sept. 15. Organized resistance ended on Nov. 27 at the cost of almost 10,500 US casualties.

CARONDELET. A converted Mississippi R steamboat which fought for the Union navy at Fort Henry and Fort Donelson. In April 1862, it forced the evacuation of Island Number Ten by running past the batteries at night.

CARONDELET CANAL. Constructed in 1794, it connected New Orleans to Bayou St. John, thus opening water communication between the city and Lake Pontchartrain and eliminating the necessity of a long Mississippi R voyage.

CARONDELET INTRIGUE. Attempt by the Spanish governor of Louisiana, Baron Francisco Luis Hector de Carondelet, to detach the western areas of the US from the Union.

The movement ended with ratification (1795) of Pinckney's Treaty.

CARPENTERS' HALL. Built in Philadelphia by the Carpenters' Guild in 1770. The first Continental Congress met there in 1774.

CARPETBAGGERS. Northerners who went to the South at the end of the Civil War and became active in politics as Republicans. So-called because they were said to have arrived with all their possessions in a carpetbag. The Reconstruction Act of 1867 offered them political opportunities by enfranchising blacks and disqualifying many former Confederate officeholders. They took an active part in shaping the new state constitutions. Hundreds of them were elected to office. At least 45 sat in the US House of Representatives and 17 in the Senate; 10 were governors. Their attitude toward black southern Republicans varied from close, dedicated alliance to open, hostile opposition. The resentment of white southerners led to their ouster with the end of Reconstruction.

CARPET MANUFACTURE. Carpetmaking in a factory system began in 1791 when William P. Sprague set up a carpet factory in Philadelphia. In 1828 the Jacquard system (for weaving intricate patterns) was introduced. Inventions by Erastus B. Bigelow and Halcyon Skinner between 1840 and 1875 made power weaving possible, and production was organized along modern lines in large plants. The last great innovation in the industry was the introduction of synthetic fibers after World War II.

CARRIAGE MAKING. Horse-drawn vehicles were made in the colonies from the earliest days of settlement. Prior to the Revolution, luxury vehicles were rare. Extensive road building and the westward migration increased demand. Builders of wagons and stagecoaches established themselves at strategic points (see CONCORD COACH). The most popular light vehicle for local transport was the two-wheel one-horse shay, or chaise. These were eventually superseded by the four-wheel buggy, which was simpler, lighter, stronger, and cheaper. Today, racing sulkies are virtually the only horse-drawn vehicles being produced.

CARRIAGE TAX. See HYLTON V. UNITED STATES.

CARRION CROW BAYOU, BATTLE OF (Oct. 14–15, 1863). Confederates attemped to turn back a federal raid up the Bayou Teche from Berwick Bay to Opelousas and Washington, La. Further skirmishes took place in November, when federal raiders returned from New Iberia.

CARRIZAL, SKIRMISH OF (June 21, 1916). Incident at Carrizal in Chihuahua, Mexico, between the US cavalry and a local force. The Americans were defeated and withdrew, leaving 45 men dead, wounded, or prisoner. Sharp notes were passed between the two governments, leading to the eventual withdrawal of US troops from Mexico. (See MEXICO, PUNITIVE EXPEDITION INTO.)

CARSON CITY. Capital of Nevada. Founded in 1858, it became the territorial capital in 1865 due to its proximity to the silver-mining district. Today it is a market center for stock-raising ranches. Pop.: 32,022 (1980).

CARTAGENA EXPEDITION. Organized 1741 in England to capture the great Spanish stronghold in the Caribbean. Its 120 vessels, 15,000 sailors, and 12,000 land troops, reinforced by 3,600 colonials, failed to take the fortress and about two-thirds of the land force was lost. (See KING GEORGE'S WAR.)

CARTER'S VALLEY SETTLEMENT. In 1770 John Carter located a trading house on the W side of the Holston R in Tennessee country a few miles S of the the Virginia line. In 1772 Indian raids forced him to give up, but he made another unsuccessful attempt in 1776. Other pioneers established a successful settlement in 1777, which continued to be known as Carter's Valley.

CARTER V. CARTER COAL COMPANY, 298 US 238 (1936). The Supreme Court ruled unconstitutional the Guffey Coal Act, regulating wages, hours, conditions of work, and prices in the coal industry. The court's ruling, that the coal industry did not come within the interstate commerce power of the federal government, was later effectively overriden.

CARTHAGE, BATTLE OF (July 5, 1861). Defeated at Boonville, Mo., secessionists retreated into SW Missouri, hoping for reinforcements. Near Carthage, they defeated the Union forces.

CARTOGRAPHY.

Commercial Mapping. Immediately after the Revolution, American mapmakers began compiling maps and atlases of states and regions. Prior to the introduction of lithography ca. 1830, maps were printed from copper engraving. Lithography expedited publication of maps in variant forms and at less cost. By midcentury, map publication was accelerated by the introduction of the rotary steam press, zinc plates, the transfer process, glazed paper, chromolithography, and application of photography to mapmaking. Late in the century, the fire insurance and underwriter map was developed and perfected in great detail. Commercial map publication during the 20th c. expanded to include the road map, generally available at every gas station.

Federal Mapmaking. In 1777 Robert Erskine was named geographer and surveyor to Gen. Washington's staff. Under him and his immediate successors, more than 130 manuscript maps were prepared. In 1785 Congress established the General Land Office, responsible for survey of the public domain. In 1807 a survey of the coasts was authorized, and the agency created for this project became the US Coast and Geodetic Survey. The rapid movement of population to the West and the large acquisitions of the Louisiana Purchase increased the need for mapping, much of which was accomplished by a topographical bureau established by the War Department in 1819. A cartographic office set up by the navy in 1842 was instrumental in mapping the Arctic and Antarctic regions and the Pacific Ocean. In the 1850s the Office of Explorations and Surveys was created for explorations, surveys, and maps of the West, especially for projected railroad routes. Army mapmaking techniques reached a high standard of excellence in the Civil War. US mapmaking agencies created after the war include the Bureau of the Census (1875), the Geological Survey (1879), the Hydrographic Office of the navy (1866), the Corps of Engineers (1870), and the Weather Bureau (1870). During World War I maps were made from aerial photographs for the first time. During the 1930s, many thematic and special-purpose maps were created for various New Deal agencies. Mapping agencies proliferated during World War II, producing topographic maps, aeronautical and nautical charts, and thematic maps. After World War II, large-scale mapping spread into the Arctic and Antarctic regions. The develoment of color-sensitive photographic instruments, highly sophisticated cameras in space vehicles, automated cartography combining electronics with computer technology, sensing by satellites, and a host of other kinds of instrumentation made possible almost instantaneous mapping of any part of the earth.

CARTOONS, POLITICAL. Benjamin Franklin printed his "Join or Die" snake cartoon in the *Pennsylvania Gazette* on May 9, 1754. Paul Revere and others depicted the Stamp Act and the Boston Massacre in separately issued engravings. The ratification of the Constitution was celebrated by Benjamin Russell with the rising columns of the "Federal Edifice" cartoon in the *Massachusetts Centinel* (1788). From the Jackson era through the Civil War many poster cartoons, wood engravings, and lithographs contained portraits of political figures, with lettering issuing from their mouths. Civil War cartoons appeared in periodicals such as *Harper's Weekly* and *Vanity Fair.* The modern cartoon, a pen drawing with effective caricatures, was the creation of Thomas Nast of *Harper's Weekly* following the Civil War. The first newspaper editorial cartoons were those of Walt McDougal used by the *New York World* in 1884. The comic strip with political content began with *Pogo* in the 1950s and was continued by *Doonesbury* in the 1970s.

CARVER CLAIM. A tract in NW Wisconsin embracing one-fourth of the modern state claimed by Jonathan Carver, who claimed that the Sioux had granted it to him in 1767. His claim was finally rejected in the early 19th c.

CARVER'S TRAVELS. The first person to visit and describe the upper Great Lakes and upper Mississippi was Jonathan Carver of Massachusetts. His tour (1766–68) was described in his *Travels*, first published in London in 1778. Many editions followed, but scholars today question its reliability.

CARY'S REBELLION. An uprising in colonial North Carolina. In 1707 Thomas Cary, deputy governor, was deposed at the solicitation of the Quakers, but he refused to abandon his office. In 1710 the proprietors sent Edward Hyde as governor, and Cary revolted. With aid from Virginia, Cary was captured and returned to England on a treason charge. He was never tried.

CASABLANCA CONFERENCE (Jan. 14–24, 1943). A World War II meeting between President Franklin D. Roosevelt and Prime Minister Winston Churchill to resolve military problems. The American proposal to assault the European continent was shelved in favor of the British plan for an invasion of Sicily and Italy.

CASCADES OF THE COLUMBIA. Falls and rapids in the Columbia R at the present site of the Bonneville Dam. Early explorers, fur traders, and settlers often crossed mountain passes to avoid them.

CASCO TREATY OF 1678. Ended war between the Indians of the Abnaki and Pennacook confederacies and the English settlers of Massachusetts Bay.

CASCO TREATY OF 1703. Unsuccessful attempt to halt the fighting at the N frontier of the Massachusetts Bay colony between the Abnaki and Pennacook Indians, in alliance with the French, and the English. At Casco, Maine, the Indians made professions of peace and disavowed any conspiracy with the French, but within two months were on the warpath again.

"CASH AND CARRY" PROGRAM. In 1939 the United States revised its neutrality laws to permit "cash and carry" purchase of military equipment by any power engaged in warfare. The law was designed to help the British and French, whose ships could easily sail to US ports during the opening months of World War II.

CASIMIR, PORT. See NEW CASTLE.

CASKET GIRLS. Women imported into Louisiana by the Compagnie des Indes as wives for settlers. The first consignments reached Biloxi in 1719 and New Orleans in 1727. Their name derives from the small chests in which they carried their clothes. Normally women were supplied to the colonists by raking the streets of Paris for undesirables or by emptying houses of detention. The casket girls, however, were recruited from charitable institutions and were practically guaranteed to be virtuous. It later became a matter of pride in Louisiana to claim descent from them.

CASTINE. Town on the E side of Penobscot Bay, Maine. Within the area of dispute between the French and English, it was a center of international rivalry in the 17th c. A trading post established there in 1630 alternated between English and French control. The Treaty of Breda (1670) gave it to the French, and English settlement of the area was effectively halted until 1763.

CASTLE THUNDER. A tobacco warehouse in Richmond, Va., used during the Civil War as a prison by the Confederates and, after Richmond fell, by federal authorities.

CASTORLAND COMPANY. Organized 1792 in Paris as the Compagnie de New York to colonize French aristocrats and others following the French Revolution. Land in Lewis County, N.Y., was bought and the first colonists arrived in 1796. Within four years the colony failed.

CATALINA. See SANTA CATALINA.

CATHOLICISM, ROMAN. Maryland was founded by the Catholic Calvert family as a sanctuary for English Catholics, but Maryland Catholics were deprived of their religious freedom after the Glorious Revolution of 1688. Nevertheless, a few became wealthy landowners. In the 18th c. a few Catholics also settled in Pennsylvania but were rare in the other colonies, where their religion was proscribed. Most colonial Catholics supported the American Revolution, yet only gradually did the Catholics acquire full civil rights. In 1784 Rome appointed John Carroll, a native Marylander, as superior of the US mission; five years later, he was elected first bishop of Baltimore. There were then about 35,000 Catholics in the US. Carroll became archbishop in 1808. Catholic education and charitable institutions in what is now the US date from 1727, when the first French Ursulines arrived in New Orleans. Georgetown Academy was opened in 1791; and the first seminary, St. Mary's, was founded in Baltimore. Elizabeth Bayley Seton founded the Sisters of Charity and founded a school for girls at Emmitsburg, Md., in 1809; Catholic orphanages and hospitals were opened, and by 1840 there were at least 200 Catholic schools. The first Catholic newspaper was founded at Charleston in 1822. To ensure uniformity of discipline and cooperation in solving common problems, bishops assembled regularly in the Provincial Councils of Baltimore. After 1890 the archbishops met annually in different cities. Between 1830 and 1860, the Roman Catholic population of the US grew from 318,000 to 3,103,000; nearly 2 million were immigrants. This sudden influx gave rise to the nativist, anti-Catholic movement that plagued US politics throughout the 19th c. and survived into the 20th. When the First Vatican Council convened in 1869, the American church was represented by forty-eight bishops and one abbot. In 1875 John McCloskey, archbishop of New York, became first American cardinal. Catholic education received its greatest impetus by the Third Plenary Council of Baltimore (1884). Catholic parents were commanded to send their children, if at all possible, to Catholic schools; and priests were ordered to erect an elementary school in each parish (a goal never attained). By 1900, the total Catholic population was more than 12 million. Since World War II certain forms of state aid to children attending Catholic schools have been upheld by the Supreme Court, but direct aid has been declared unconstitutional. Mainly because of the rising costs, the number of Catholic schools declined greatly in the 1970s. The Second Vatican Council (1962–65) wrought striking changes in the American church. In some respects, church discipline (over mixed marriage and fasting) was relaxed. The liturgy, revised and translated into English, was introduced everywhere but was not universally welcomed. Closer ties with other Christian denominations and with Jews were promoted. In some areas, unrest and decline overshadowed the renewal intended by the Vatican Council. Candidates for the priesthood declined alarmingly: from 596 seminaries and novitiates with 48,992 students in 1965 to 328 with 12,468 students in 1980.

The number of sisters dropped from 181,421 in 1966 to 122,653 in 1980. The number of Catholic newspapers and magazines declined, and many Catholic publishing houses went out of business. Finances were strained by diminished church attendance and by the burden of keeping up expensive inner city parishes and the system of parochial schools. Uncertainty about many Catholic doctrines increased, the church strictures against birth control, abortion, homosexuality, ordination of women, and political activism being prominent among them. Despite these conflicts, American Catholics ranks reached a new high of 50,449,842 in 1980.

CATSKILL MOUNTAINS. Mountains of the Appalachian system in New York. Since the 19th c., they have been a major resort area.

CATTLE. Cattle were brought to America before 1600 by Spanish settlers in Florida. In 1611 cattle raising began in Virginia, and the Pilgrims began with the Devonshire breed in 1624. By ca. 1650 cattle had been introduced to all the colonies. Cattle grazed on common or public lands, giving rise to brands and roundups early in American history. Since controlled breeding was impossible, the types of cattle intermingled and no distinction was made between dairy and beef cattle. The introduction of pure breeds came during the 19th c. During the Civil War, longhorn cattle, descendants of Spanish stock, grew up wild on the Texas plains. In 1867 began the great longhorn drives to the railhead in Abilene, Kans. By 1880 more than 4 million cattle had been driven north. Some of these had been held for breeding, giving rise to the range cattle industry in the northern plains. Overgrazing, disastrous weather, and settlement by homesteaders brought the range cattle industry to an end after 1887. The ranch cattle industry (based on owned and leased land, winter pasture and feed, and controlled breeding) led to more effective beef production. The Hereford and Angus continued to dominate the beef breeds, but after World War II the Charolais, Santa Gertrudis, Brahman, Brangus, and Beefmaster gained prominence. Although dairy herds have not changed to the same degree, productivity per cow has increased greatly. By 1978, 11 million dairy cows produced 122 million pounds of milk; and there were 116 million beef cattle in the US. About 40 million head were slaughtered in 1978.

CATTLE ASSOCIATIONS. 19th-c. organizations of cattle raisers in the western ranges. Brands were recorded with them, and they supervised sales and transportation. One of the largest, the Wyoming Stock Growers' Association, founded 1873, had a membership in 1886 of 400 from nineteen states with assets of $100 million.

CATTLE BRANDS. Peculiarly associated with ranching, as taken over from Mexico, the brand is a mark of ownership. They are burned on range horses as well. Brands are made up of letters, figures, and geometric designs, symbols, or representations of objects. Every legitimate brand is recorded by either state or county (or formerly cattle associations), thus preventing duplication within a given territory.

CATTLE DRIVES. Texans had a Beef Trail to New Orleans before they revolted from Mexico in 1835. In the 1840s they extended their markets N into Missouri. During the 1850s, emigration and freighting from the Missouri R to the West Coast demanded oxen, and Texas longhorn steers by the thousands were broken for work oxen. Herds of longhorns were driven to Chicago, and at least one to New York. During the Civil War, Texans drove cattle throughout the Confederacy, but a surplus still existed at the end of the war. In 1867 Joseph G. McCoy opened a regular market at Abilene, Kans., site of the railhead. The great cattle trails boomed. The Goodnight-Loving Trail opened up New Mexico and Colorado to Texas cattle. Tens of thousands were soon driven into Arizona. In the 1870s Texas longhorns were driven throughout the west by cowboys. The Long Trail extended into Canada. In the 1890s herds were still driven from the Texas Panhandle to Montana, but by 1895 trail driving was virtually ended by barbed wire and the railroads.

CATTLE TICK FEVER. The worst plague of the western range during the trail-driving days (1865–95). It caused widespread outbreaks of what was variously known as Spanish, Texas, or tick fever, and pleuro-pneumonia. For many years, the cause of the fever was unknown, but some locales established quarantines against the Texas longhorns. The cattle tick (*Boophilus annulatus*) has now been virtually eradicated.

CAUCUS. Political meeting of members of one particular party. Caucuses to nominate candidates for office were used as early as 1725, particularly in Boston, where several clubs endorsed candidates and came to be known as caucus clubs. Unregulated by law, by the middle of the 19th c., they were increasingly under the control of party bosses. Abuses were flagrant, and some attempt was made to regulate them. By the early 20th c., the caucus had given way to nominating conventions and later to the direct primary. A few states still permit the use of caucuses for nomination to local offices or selection of delegates to conventions. From 1796 until 1824 presidential candidates were chosen by a special congressional caucus; but many thought it contrary to the spirit of the Constitution, if not actually unconstitutional. After 1824, candidates began to be chosen by the nominating convention. The meetings of the respective party members in either house of the US Congress is also called a caucus. The Federalists held caucuses as early as 1796; the Jeffersonians followed suit. In general, this caucus has three functions: (1) to nominate candidates for speaker, president pro tem, and other House and Senate offices; and to elect party officers and committees, such as floor leader, whip, Committee on Committees, Steering Committee, Policy Committee; (2) to decide on policy or legislation; and (3) to censure party members for conduct detrimental to the party.

CAVALRY, HORSE. Branch of the US army, first used in the Revolutionary War. The four light cavalry regiments were then disbanded, and for the next fifty years the cavalry was only a minute part of the army. Indian troubles in the West revived the need for horse soldiers. In the 1830s Congress created two regiments of dragoons, which were trained to fight both mounted and dismounted. The second of these was formed to fight in the Seminole War. In 1846 a third dragoon unit was formed to fight in the Mexican War, and in 1855 the First and Second Cavalry were organized to fight in the West. There were ten regiments in the Civil War. Two were manned by black enlisted men and noncommissioned officers (but with white officers). When the Indian wars ended in the early 1890s, the horse cavalry again declined in importance. Some troops served as infantry during the Spanish-American War, but during World War I, only four regiments were sent to France. After that the mechanization of armies made the horse cavalry obsolete.

CAVALRY, MECHANIZED. See ARMORED VEHICLES.

CAVE-IN-ROCK. Cave in Hardin County, Ill., on the Ohio R, about thirty miles below the mouth of the Wabash R. Served as a rendezvous for outlaws who preyed on river traffic.

CAYUSE WAR (1847–50). A measles epidemic among the Cayuse Indians in SE Washington was blamed on the increasing number of white immigrants. The Indians attacked the Presbyterian mission at Waiilatpu, killing fourteen. Five Cayuse surrendered and were tried and hanged.

CEDAR CREEK, BATTLE OF (Oct. 19, 1864). Encounter between Union and Confederate forces, near Winchester, Va. Union forces, under Gen. P.H. Sheridan, were victorious. (See also SHERIDAN'S RIDE.)

CEDAR MOUNTAIN, BATTLE OF (Aug. 9, 1862). First encounter in the Second Bull Run campaign. Confederate troops repulsed Union troops, but withdrew.

CEDAR RAPIDS. Second largest city in Iowa, settled in 1838, when a trading post was built at the rapids of the Cedar R. Later it became a major railroad junction. Today, Cedar Rapids has factories that assemble and produce trucks and tractors, radios, and electrical equipment. Pop.: 110,243 (1980).

CÉLORON'S LEAD PLATES. In 1749 Pierre Joseph Céloron planted lead markers along the Ohio R proclaiming French title to the region.

CEMENT. Canvass White, later chief engineer of the Erie Canal, obtained a patent for the making of a true hydraulic cement (one that had to be pulverized after burning limestone to react with water). During the building of the canal (1817–25) and later railway building era, demand rapidly increased and suitable cement rocks were discovered in many localities. After the Civil War, Portland cements, because of their more dependable qualities, began to be imported from England. Domestic manufacture began at Copley, Pa., ca. 1870; A natural cement rock had been found that had about the same composition as the artificial mixture of the English Portland cement. Today, Portland cement is produced all over the country. In 1977 163 plants produced 76,340 tons.

CEMETERIES, NATIONAL. In 1862 Congress authorized the acquisition of land for national cemeteries for the burial of the war dead. Since the Spanish-American War, the kin of those who died in battle can request their return to the US for burial in a national cemetery, if they choose. About 12.5 percent of the World War I dead were reinterred in national cemeteries; more than half of the dead of World War II were returned. National cemeteries are administered by the Veterans Administration or the Department of the Interior. Permanent overseas cemeteries are under the control of the American Battle Monuments Commission.

CENSORSHIP.
The Press. Despite the First Amendment, in the early days of the republic, both Federalists and Republicans (Jeffersonians) prosecuted newspaper editors for seditious libel. But in 1836 Congress rejected President Andrew Jackson's efforts to bar "incendiary" abolitionist publications from the mails. Since ca. 1850, press censorship has more typically arisen from moral considerations than from political ones. In the turbulent post-Civil War era, "obscene" publications aroused great alarm, and antivice societies sprang up in major cities. Congress outlawed the mailing of "obscene," "lewd," or "lascivious" publications. In succeeding years, many states enacted legislation against their sale. Beginning in the 1920s, the obscenity laws came under increasing challenge, and the courts have progressively narrowed the criteria of what is censorable. Political censorship, other than in wartime, has been virtually nonexistent since World War I. In recent years, most of the efforts of the government to censor the press has centered on the unauthorized publication of classified material. Even here, the

government has met with only spotty success (see PENTAGON PAPERS).

Motion Pictures. In the early days of films, many cities and states established licensing boards to ban or cut any film deemed obscene, immoral, or otherwise objectionable. In addition, the Roman Catholic church established (1934) the Legion of Decency, to review films. The motion picture industry attempted various self-regulatory schemes, including the so-called Hays Office. It published specific standards to which all major film producers subscribed. This Production Code was almost universally adhered to through the 1940s but began breaking up in the 1950s, as the old film studios lost their preeminence in the industry and public attitudes became more permissive. In 1968, the film industry began assigning each movie a rating, which was supposed to indicate whether minors alone or accompanied by an adult could see the film. The 1970s saw the rise of a large-scale pornographic film industry; and despite local and state efforts, the products of this industry went largely uncensored.

Radio and Television. The Federal Communications Commission (FCC) has licensing and regulatory power over both radio and television broadcasting, although the law creating it contained the proviso: "Nothing in the Act shall be understood or construed to give . . . the power of censorship." Nevertheless, the FCC publishes standards to which all licensees must adhere. Most outright censorship has come from the industry itself; the television networks rigorously censor all material that goes over the air. The advent of cable television has seen the dissemination of programs that, by network standards, would be considered unacceptable and has resulted in new local efforts at censorship.

CENSORSHIP, MILITARY. Systematic military censorship began with the Civil War; it included army control of telegraph lines; post office confiscation of disloyal newspapers; imprisonment of newspaper editors; and confiscation of their presses. The Espionage Act of 1915 provided the government with the basis for World War I censorship, including examination of outgoing mail sent by troops in France and control of correspondents' dispatches sent from the front. A censorship board controlled domestic telephone and telegraph lines and overseas cables. Censorship in World War II was under the Office of Censorship. Radio, landlines, and overseas cables were subject to censorship, and censorship codes for press and radio were enforced. Overseas censorship imposed on mail and press communications was the strongest in US history. Mail from overseas was screened. During the Korean War, press dispatches from the combat zone were censored, but there was no screening of personal mail. There was no actual censorship during the Vietnam War, but press disclosure was controlled by security regulations that prevented the release of classified information.

CENSUS. The US Constitution provides for a decennial census to apportion the House of Representatives. The first census of 1790, however, went beyond what was required for that purpose. Census takers listed heads of families; number of persons in each household; and the number of free white males at least sixteen years old. With each census, additional categories of inquiry were added: data about domestic manufactures, social statistics (occupations, dependent persons, literacy, and schooling), data about economic institutions. After the 1870 census, the *Statistical Atlas* was published (1874). The 1880 census set the standard for all subsequent censuses. Statistics included detailed data about dependent and delinquent classes, the growth of cities, morbidity and mortality, police departments, benevolent and educational organizations, and religious bodies. Highly qualified special agents prepared reports on vital statistics, agriculture, major industries, use of power and machinery in industry, wages and prices, the factory system, and strikes and lockouts. The results were published in the ten-volume *Compendium of the Tenth Census*. In 1902 a permanent census office department was created, now part of the Department of Commerce. It publishes the annual *Statistical Abstract of the United States*, a compendium of statistics from its own censuses and from other sources.

CENT. The US cent came from the adoption of the dollar and its division decimally. A privately issued coin dated 1783 (the "Washington cent") had the word "cent" on it. Vermont and Connecticut issued cents in 1785 and Massachusetts in 1786. The first federal cent was the Fugio, or Franklin, of 1787. Cents, or pennies, have been minted regularly by US mints since 1793. They are also known as coppers, for the metal of which they are made.

CENTENNIAL EXPOSITION. Celebration in Philadelphia in 1876 commemorating the one-hundredth anniversery of the Declaration of Independence.

CENTRAL INTELLIGENCE AGENCY. Created 1947 to replace the Office of Strategic Services (OSS). It was placed under the National Security Council, and its function was to assemble intelligence information relative to the national security. It also included the clandestine collection of foreign intelligence information. The director of the CIA is the president's chief adviser on foreign intelligence and heads the US Intelligence Board (composed of the heads of the principal intelligence agencies). Since the 1950s, highly advanced scientific and technical methods of collection of intelligence have enabled the United States to negotiate and monitor adherence to agreements such as the Nuclear Test Ban Treaty and the Strategic Arms Limitation Treaty. In the 1970s and 1980s, critics charged that the CIA overstepped its power in its covert political actions overseas and at home. Among the clandestine operations directed, at least partly, by the CIA have included the Bay of Pigs invasion of Cuba (1961), the overthrow of the Allende government in Chile (1973), and the anti-Sandinista rebellion in Nicaragua in the early 1980s. The activities of the CIA are monitored by congressional committees, although practically speaking, the president is given a free hand in its operations.

CENTRALIZATION. The centralization of power in the federal government at the expense of the state governments has been a phenomenon since the adoption of the US Constitution in 1789. It has been stimulated mainly through congressional use of federal taxing power and by legislation regulating and protecting interstate commerce. Through its power to appropriate money and to prescribe conditions with which a state must comply if it wishes to share in federal funds, the national government is able to do indirectly what it cannot do directly. Centraliza-

tion is viewed with alarm by some, who fear that it will result in the reduction of the states to mere administrative arms of the national government, thereby negating the federal nature of the US. Conservatives, in particular, have decried the tendencies toward centralization.

CENTRAL OF GEORGIA RAILROAD. See RAILROADS, SKETCHES OF PRINCIPAL LINES.

CENTRAL OVERLAND CALIFORNIA AND PIKES PEAK EXPRESS. See PONY EXPRESS.

CENTRAL PACIFIC-UNION PACIFIC RACE. The Pacific Railway Act (1862) authorized the Central Pacific RR to build E from the California line and the Union Pacific RR to build W to the Nevada boundary. An amendment to that law (1865–66) authorized the roads to continue construction until they met. A race ensued because the company building the most track would receive the larger subsidy. Eventually, Congress passed a law stating that the two lines should join at Promontory Point, Utah. They met there on May 10, 1869.

CENTRAL ROUTE. The overland route used extensively after 1848 by immigrants bound for California. From Independence or other points on the Missouri R they followed the Platte R, went through South Pass in Wyoming, N of Great Salt Lake, along the Humboldt R to the sinks, and by different passes through the Sierras.

CERAMICS. See POTTERY.

CEREALS. In the United States, cereals ranking in importance according to acreage harvested are corn, wheat, oats, sorghum, barley, rice, rye, and sugarcane. Indians raised maize extensively long before the arrival of Columbus. European settlers quickly adopted it because it grew almost anywhere, required little attention, and yielded good returns. Columbus introduced wheat, barley, and sugarcane in 1493. New York and Pennsylvania produced wheat extensively in the 17th c. The "corn belt" developed in the 19th c. from Ohio to Nebraska after the mechanical revolution harnessed the horsepower necessary for extensive cultivation. Washington, California, and North Dakota also became important wheat-producing states. Since barley, oats, and rye withstand cold weather better than other cereals, they were grown in Montana, the Dakotas, and Minnesota. Besides being used as food, barley and rye were used to make alcoholic drinks. African slaves brought sorghum to America, but it remained unimportant until droughts and insect plagues ruined Great Plains farming in the 1880s. Texas has become the biggest producer. Rice culture began when South Carolina settlers imported rice from Madagascar in 1695. By 1808, Georgia farmers were raising African rice on dry land. In 1980 Arkansas, Texas, Louisiana, and California led in rice production. Sugarcane came to Louisiana from San Domingo in 1742, but commercial production did not develop until 1795. The states producing the most of America's sugarcane in 1980 were Louisiana, Florida, and Hawaii. In the 1970s US surpluses in cereal production, particularly wheat and corn, became an instrument of foreign policy: Grain sales to the Soviet Union became an important part of the expanding trade relations with the Eastern bloc.

CEREALS, MANUFACTURE OF. In 1854 Ferdinand Schumacher founded a company that ground and sold oats; it became the Quaker Oats Company, the precursor of a whole new industry, the breakfast foods manufacturers. Shredded wheat, probably the first ready-to-eat precooked cereal, appeared in 1893; it eventually became part of the National Biscuit Company. The Ralston-Purina Company also produced breakfast cereals but concentrated on the feed business. Two brothers, John H. Kellogg and William K. Kellogg, and Charles W. Post introduced various flaked-food products, including Post Toasties, Grape-nuts, and corn flakes. Post's company eventually became part of General Foods. General Mills, another large cereal company, introduced its most successful product, Wheaties, in 1921. Competition among the cereal manufacturers has remained keen, with all the companies constantly introducing new products and advertising and marketing them with great vigor.

CERRO GORDO, BATTLE OF (April 18, 1847). Confrontation between Mexican and US forces in the Mexican War, eighteen miles below Jalapa. US forces under Gen. Winfield Scott stormed two fortified hills and gained the rear of the position; the Mexicans fled.

CHAIN GANGS. Shackled convicts leased out to private businesses or working for the state, especially on roadbuilding projects. The introduction of road-making machinery largely eliminated the practice.

CHAIN STORES. Retail stores in the same general kind of business under the same ownership or management. Their success results from their ability to charge lower prices than independents, due chiefly to volume buying. In 1859, the Great Atlantic & Pacific Tea Company (A & P) was founded. Sears, Roebuck, the world's largest retailer, began as a mail-order business in 1886 but did not start to build its chain of stores until the 1920s. That decade saw the great growth of the chain-store phenomenon; by 1929 chain stores accounted for 22 percent of total US retail sales. Chains are more important in certain areas, accounting for 80 percent of total variety-store sales and 58 percent of total grocery-store sales in 1978.

CHAIRMAKING. Chairmaking was already regarded as a distinct branch of furniture making in the census of 1810. Rockers, said to be an American invention, were at an early date popular in Spanish America and were exported. Vessels leaving Baltimore on one day in 1827 carried 12,000 chairs. Philadelphia chair shops had steam-driven machinery before 1825. During the 19th c., Massachusetts was the leading producer. The most famous American chair, the Hitchcock, first produced in Connecticut has been in production since 1818. (See also FURNITURE.)

CHALMETTE NATIONAL HISTORICAL PARK. Located about five miles below New Orleans, on the E bank of the Mississippi R; site of the Battle of New Orleans (1815).

CHAMBERSBURG, BURNING OF (July 30, 1864). Confederate Gen. John McCausland, when refused a large ransom to spare Chambersburg, Pa., burned the town.

CHAMBERS OF COMMERCE. Voluntary associations of business and professional people approaching the problems of the community from the business viewpoint. The oldest, that of New York City, received its charter from King George III in 1768. Generally the chambers of commerce grew out of the older boards of trade, which were established for the purpose of regulating or supervising trading activities. Later, they were formed by businessmen for their common good or to foster some civic interest.

CHAMBLY, FORT. British fort built in 1775 at the foot of the Richelieu R rapids in Canada on the site of Fort St. Louis. Captured by the Americans in October 1775 and held until the spring of 1776. Evacuated and burned as the Americans retreated S to Ticonderoga.

CHAMPAIGN COUNTY RESCUE CASES (1857). Efforts to enforce the FUGITIVE SLAVE ACT, involving a conflict between state and federal laws in Ohio. Federal marshals were arrested by local authorities, irate over their efforts to return a fugitive slave to his owner. A federal judge ordered their release, finding that they had been rightfully performing their duty. The case became moot when local citizens paid for the manumission of the slave being held.

CHAMP D'ASILE. Built in 1817 by a group of Napoleonic exiles on the Trinity R in Texas. It was charged that they hoped to take Mexico and rescue Napoleon from St. Helena. The Spanish forced the colonists to withdraw to Galveston Island. Aided by the pirate Jean Lafitte, they made their way to the French settlements in Louisiana.

CHAMPION'S HILL, BATTLE OF (May 16, 1863). Gen. U.S. Grant's army met the Confederate army of John C. Pemberton defeating them and driving them toward Vicksburg.

CHAMPLAIN, LAKE. See LAKE CHAMPLAIN.

CHAMPLAIN'S INDIAN ALLIANCE. In 1608 Samuel de Champlain made an alliance with the Indians of the St. Lawrence and with the Huron, and between 1609 and 1615 he assisted them in campaigns against the Iroquois. The Iroquois soon allied themselves with the Dutch at Albany and became the natural enemies of New France.

CHAMPLAIN'S VOYAGES. Samuel de Champlain's first Canadian voyage (1603) was as observer for the expedition of Aymar de Chaste, authorized by Henry IV of France. His map of the St. Lawrence region resulted in a valuable account, *Des Sauvages*. In 1604 he explored Nova Scotia, and in 1605 he explored the New England coast, mapping 1,000 miles of coastline. He set out in 1608 with a group of settlers who founded Quebec. His final voyage was in 1633.

CHAMPOEG CONVENTION. Government established in 1843 at Champoeg, Oregon. The only such government in the Pacific Northwest until the Oregon territorial government was established by the US in 1849.

CHANCELLORSVILLE, BATTLE OF (May 1–4, 1863). Major Civil War engagement fought between 130,000 Union men commanded by Gen. Joseph Hooker and 60,000 Confederates under Gen. R.E. Lee. Lee's troops were entrenched behind Fredericksburg, Va. Hooker crossed the Rappahannock R and advanced to attack from behind Chancellorsville. Lee and Gen. Stonewall Jackson split their men, with Jackson taking his men around Hooker's right flank. Hooker, dazed by Jackson's attack, withdrew to the riverbank. Lee continued to advance and forced Hooker N of the river. Both sides suffered great casualties. It was the South's costliest victory, and Jackson himself was mortally wounded by his own troops.

CHANTIER. (from the French word for "shipyard"). In the fur trade of the Far West, the place near a trading post where lumber was made up, boats and canoes built, and other crafts necessary for the post performed.

CHANTILLY, BATTLE OF (Sept. 1, 1862). Occurred during Union Gen. John Pope's withdrawal to Fairfax Courthouse, Va., after his defeat at the second Battle of Bull Run. Confederate Gen. Stonewall Jackson, seeking to stop Pope, encountered federal troops protecting the line of retreat. Jackson failed in his mission, but Union losses were heavy.

CHAPARRAL. In the Southwest, any thick or thorny brush. In California, specifically the manzanita oak. In other parts the term includes granjenao, mesquite, allthorn, and huisache.

CHAPBOOKS. Cheap popular pamphlets, generally printed on a single sheet and folded to form twenty-four pages, often crudely illustrated with woodcuts. Published in the tens of thousands until ca. 1850, they were often the only literature available in the average home except the Bible, the almanac, and the newspaper. With their emphasis on the wonderful, the sad, and the humorous, they were the beginning of popular literature in the United States.

CHAPLIN HILLS, BATTLE OF. See PERRYVILLE, BATTLE OF.

CHAPULTEPEC, BATTLE OF (Sept. 13, 1847). During the Mexican War, US Gen. Winfield Scott, after a vigorous bombardment, launched a division against the Mexican garrison at Chapultepec, a rocky eminence and fortified castle on the W approaches to Mexico City. It fell to the US troops and Mexico City surrendered.

CHARITY SCHOOLS. During the colonial period, free education generally meant instruction for poor and underprivileged children. Schools were organized and supported by benevolent persons and societies. The system was gradually replaced by free public education.

CHARIVARI. See SHIVAREE.

CHARLES RIVER BRIDGE CASE, 11 Peters 420 (1837). The Supreme Court ruled against monopolistic power and held that corporate charters are to be construed strictly in favor of the public.

CHARLESTON. City in South Carolina, located on the peninsula between the confluence of the Ashley and Cooper rivers. Established in 1680 by the English, who had settled ten years earlier at Albemarle Point. By 1704 Charleston was a walled city, and in 1706 Fort Johnson was built on James Island at the mouth of the harbor. Served as capital of South Carolina until 1790. There was a large Indian trade, and rice and and indigo were exported to Europe and lumber to the West Indies. Manufactured goods were imported from England, household necessities from New England, and slaves from Africa. During the American Revolution, Charleston was three times successfully defended against the British; but it was held by the British from May 12, 1780, until Dec. 14, 1782. During the Napoleonic wars, Charleston had a new burst of commercial prosperity, giving rise to the many fine private houses and beautiful gardens. President Jefferson's embargo of 1808 and subsequent disorders, as well as the War of 1812 disrupted trade. The city never regained its commercial preeminence. The city came to be dominated by rice and cotton planters and was a center of anti-Union, secessionist sentiments in the 1850s. On Dec. 20, 1860, the convention that met at St. Andrew's Hall voted unanimously for secession from the Union. The first shot in the Civil War was fired from Fort Johnson upon Fort Sumter, at the mouth of Charleston harbor, on April 12, 1861. The fort fell to the Confederates, and the Union navy was kept out of Charleston harbor during the ensuing siege of Charleston. The city successfully kept Union troops at bay but finally fell on Feb. 17, 1865. A great fire in 1861, however, had done more damage than enemy bombardment. Today, the city has an oil-refining industry, major naval installations, and a profitable tourist industry. Pop.: 69,510 (1980).

CHARLESTON. Capital of West Virginia, founded at the junction of the Elk and Kanawha rivers in 1787. Here was located Fort Lee, a refuge and commercial center for wilderness settlers after the French and Indian War. In the Civil War, Charleston was under Confederate and Union control a half dozen times. Located close to deposits of soft coal and clays useful in making pottery and glass products, Charleston is a major producer of chlorine and dye products, synthetic fibers, and glass materials. Pop.: 69,968 (1980).

CHARLESTON AND HAMBURG RAILROAD. See SOUTH CAROLINA RAILROAD.

CHARLESTON HARBOR, DEFENSE OF (1776). On June 28, a British naval force headed by Sir Henry Clinton and Peter Parker failed to batter down the colonial force stationed on Sullivan's Island in Charleston harbor. The failure ended the planned British invasion of the South.

CHARLESTON RIOT (March 28, 1864). A fight in Charleston, Ill., between Union soldiers on leave and Copperheads. Nine were killed and fifteen wounded.

CHARLESTOWN. City in Massachusetts, now part of Boston, founded 1629. The Battle of Bunker Hill was fought at Charlestown in June 1775.

CHARLEVOIX'S JOURNEY (1720–22). Attempt by the French Jesuit Pierre François Xavier de Charlevoix to cross North America in order to discover a route to the Western Sea. Charlevoix went around the Great Lakes, entered Illinois, and voyaged down the Mississippi R to New Orleans and Biloxi. He wrote of his experiences in *Histoire et description générale de la Nouvelle France* (1744).

CHARLOTTE. Largest city in North Carolina and an important textile manufacturing center. Founded in the 1760s, it became the market town for the Piedmont area. Occupied by the British under Lord Cornwallis during the Revolutionary War. It was the home of a US mint in the 19th c., serving the goldfields of W North Carolina and N Georgia. Pop.: 314,447 (1980).

CHARLOTTE, FORT. English name for the French Fort Condé at Mobile after the French and Indian War in 1763. Captured by the Spaniards in 1780 and held until US troops took possession in 1813. (See MOBILE SEIZED.)

CHARLOTTE, TREATY OF CAMP (October 1774). Ended Lord Dunmore's War with the Shawnee, after the defeat of Chief Cornstalk. The site was in Pickaway County, Ohio.

CHARTER COLONIES. Colonies promoted through private enterprise, either by trading companies or lords proprietor, under charter from the crown. Colonies founded by trading companies either disappeared or changed their status early; thus the Bermuda Company was the only trading company in control of a colony through most of the 17th c. Connecticut and Rhode Island, founded as squatter colonies by dissenters from Puritan Massachusetts, received charters of incorporation early in the Restoration period. The predominant type throughout the 17th c. was the proprietary colony. Of this sort was James I's grant of all the Caribbean islands to the Earl of Carlisle. Other proprietary colonies were Maryland, Maine, the Carolinas, New York, the Jerseys, the Bahamas, and Pennsylvania. The Res-

toration government came to find charters an obstacle to the building of a colonial policy. Several colonies were royalized, and with the view to ultimate consolidation of all colonial possessions into a few large units, the Dominion of New England was established. It failed, but royalization progressed. By 1776 only two proprietaries, Maryland and Pennsylvania, and two corporation colonies, Connecticut and Rhode Island, remained.

CHARTERED COMPANIES. British joint-stock companies that were formed for purposes of trade in the New World. Since production of goods required the transportation of laborers, colonization became a by-product of the trading company. The Virginia Company, chartered in 1606, was the first such company to found a successful colony. A branch of the company, the Council for New England, established colonies in Massachusetts. Other colonies were developed by the Newfoundland Company (1610), the Massachusetts Bay Company (1629), and the Providence Island Company (1630). After the Puritan Revolution in England, the lord proprietor superseded the trading company as preferred sponsor of colonization, both king and colonists becoming increasingly distrustful of corporations.

CHARTER OAK. See CONNECTICUT CHARTER OF 1662.

CHARTER OF LIBERTIES. Drafted in 1683 by New York's first assembly, approved by James, Duke of York. It described the framework of government and the functions of governor, council, and a legislative assembly representative of the qualified freeholders, and guaranteed the freedom of the assembly, trial by jury, due process of law, protection of the property of women, freedom from feudal exactions, exemption from quartering of soldiers, and especially religious toleration for all Christians.

CHARTER OF PRIVILEGES. Granted by William Penn to Pennsylvania in 1701. It guaranteed freedom of worship to all who professed faith in "One almighty God." All who believed in Jesus Christ were eligible for office. A unicameral legislature was established and the council ceased to be a representative body.

CHARTERS, MUNICIPAL. Written instruments authorized or granted by the state by which cities or similar entities are given their corporate existence, powers, structure of government, and legislative and administrative procedures. In the colonial period, only royal and proprietary colonies were granted charters. With the Revolution, the granting of charters became a state function, and the power of the state legislature became paramount over a municipal charter, except to the degree that the legislature granted home-rule charters to the municipalities.

CHARTRES, FORT DE. Seat of French civil and military government in the Illinois country in the 18th c., located near Kaskaskia, Randolph County. The original fort, exposed to the flood waters of the Mississippi R, was begun in 1719 but quickly fell into disrepair and in 1732 a new fort was built some distance from the river. In 1747 the site was moved to Kaskaskia, where a completely new fort was completed ca. 1756. Transferred to the British in 1765, it was the last French post in North America to be surrendered under the Treaty of Paris. Renamed Fort Cavendish, it was the seat of British rule in the Illinois country until 1772, when it was abandoned.

CHARTRES, FORT DE, TREATY (1766). An agreement made by the British with the western Indians; the Indians acknowledged the authority of the king of England and agreed to return prisoners and stolen horses and to permit the establishment of trading posts. Peace lasted for the duration of British rule in the Illinois country.

CHASE IMPEACHMENT. Part of a concerted Jeffersonian Republican effort to curb the power of the federal bench. Samuel Chase, an arch-Federalist justice of the Supreme Court, was impeached by the House of Representatives in 1804 for unbecoming conduct and disregard of law. His acquittal in 1805 by the Senate was probably a distinct gain for judicial independence.

CHATEAUGAY, BATTLE OF (Oct. 25, 1813). Gen. Wade Hampton advanced along the Chateaugay R into Canada to Montreal with over 4,000 troops. On October 22 he halted about fifteen miles from the St. Lawrence R. Three days later he tried to dislodge a much smaller British force. He was soundly defeated and abandoned his drive to Montreal. He resigned his command.

CHÂTEAU-THIERRY BRIDGE, AMERICANS AT (1918). German troops entered Château-Thierry on May 31, having broken the French front on the Aisne. The US Third Division, aided by French colonials, prevented the enemy from crossing the Marne R, and on June 1 the German attacks ceased.

CHATTANOOGA. City in SW Tennessee, located on the Tennessee R at a strategic crossing used for centuries as an Indian trading place. About 1815 John Ross established a trading post there, known as Ross' Landing. In 1838 it was renamed Chattanooga, the original name for Lookout Mountain, meaning "rock rising to a point." It prospered from the coming of the railroad in the 1840s. It was fought over in some of the most critical battles of the Civil War and was the base from which Union Gen. W.T. Sherman marched through Georgia. In the 1930s the building of the Tennessee Valley Authority (TVA) was a great boon to the city. Today it is a major producer of electrical machinery and creates a wide range of other products, including chemicals, textiles, iron and steel, coal, and wood products. Pop.: 169,565 (1980).

CHATTANOOGA CAMPAIGN (October–November 1863). Before the Battle of Chickamauga, Confederate Gen. Braxton Bragg besieged Gen. W.S. Rosecrans's Union army at Chattanooga. Grant, placed in command of all Union forces in the West, replaced Rosecrans with G.H. Thomas and ordered him to hold Chattanooga "at all hazards." Reinforcements arrived, and on Nov. 24, 1863, Union Gen. Joseph Hooker captured Lookout Mountain, and on the next day Grant attacked all along the line. The Confederate center on Missionary Ridge gave way. The left had retreated; only the right held firm and covered the retreat into N Georgia. A rear-guard stand halted Grant's pursuit. The Union troops returned to Chattanooga; the Confederate army went into winter quarters in Dalton, Georgia.

CHAUTAUQUA MOVEMENT. Adult education programs that proliferated in the latter 19th c. Named for an assembly held at Lake Chautauqua, New York, in 1873 by leaders of the Sunday-school movement. Courses in the arts, sciences, and humanities were offered, and lecturers were sent out on what became known as the Chautauqua circuit. Home-study courses were also available. The movement continued into the 1920s.

CHECK CURRENCY. Bank deposits against which the owner may write a check. Although extensively used for making payments in New York and other large cities early in the 19th c., checks did not settle an amount of business equal to that settled by bank notes and coins until mid-century. The Civil War was a turning point in the use of checks. By the end of the century, almost 90 percent of all business was settled by checks.

CHECKS AND BALANCES. The separation of powers of government that was the underlying principle upon which the US government was created by the Constitutional Convention of 1787. This theory consists of setting off legislative and executive departments from each other and the courts against both. Each department is supposed to operate as far as possible within a separate sphere of administration. In order to prevent executive aggression, the system of checks and balances was introduced and provision was made for a federal judiciary. Furthermore, it was provided that the Senate and the House of Representatives should act as checks upon each other in the national Congress.

CHEMICAL INDUSTRY. In 1608 eight Poles and Germans "skilled in making tar, pitch, glass, and potashes" were sent to Jamestown, and some of these products were exported to London. There were early saltworks in Jamestown and Plymouth. The Dutch had a distillery at New Amsterdam in 1638, and Salem had one ten years later. Boston and Connecticut produced saltpeter and a variety of minerals and chemicals. Pennsylvania established a lime kiln (1681), a tannery (1683), and a paper mill (1690). Soap manufacture was undertaken in Boston in 1716, and sugar refining began in New York in 1730. These were all accomplished despite the English Navigation Acts of 1661, which were intended to discourage colonial manufacture of goods exported by the mother country. At the time of the Revolution, the Continental Congress urged the quick establishment of the whole

range of chemical industries, and some of the states offered bounties. By 1800 substantial quantities of salt, saltpeter, white lead, and sulfuric acid were being produced. The Du Pont powder works was established near Wilmington, Delaware, in 1802. Vitriol and alum works were opened soon afterward in Vermont and Maryland, respectively. In 1815, US chemical manufacturers initiated an often repeated appeal for tariff protection, alternately favored and rejected by the government into the 20th c. The manufacture of coal gas for illumination was introduced, and eventually nearly every town had its gasworks. The 1840s saw the recognition of phosphorous as a fertilizer and manufacturers began treating bones with sulfuric acid to produced superphosphate. Mineral sources of phosphorous were found in large deposits in South Carolina and Florida. In the 1860s the petroleum industry began its dramatic expansion, and with it grew a demand for sulfuric acid, necessary to the oil-refining process. Sulfur was in short supply until large supplies were discovered in the 1860s off the Louisiana coast and a method was perfected for pumping the sulfur out in a liquid state. Plastics were a peculiarly American specialty. Patent leather was first produced in 1819. A more famous process of creating plastic was Charles Goodyear's successful vulcanization (treatment with sulfur) of rubber in 1839. Celluloid, introduced ca. 1870, was made into dentures, collars, handles for toilet articles, and photographic film. Celluloid became a household word and ushered in the age of plastics. Bakelite was invented in 1909. Made of phenol and formaldehyde, it appeared just in time to fill the requirement of the new radio industry for insulating material. The complex Solvay soda process was introduced in the United States in 1884. A decade later, yet another process, consisting of the electrolysis of salt brine to yield sodium, chlorine, and their derivatives (such as soda), was refined; by 1909 the United States was self-sufficient in soda. The development of a practical dynamo in the 1870s led to the development of a commercially useful electric furnace in 1885. Other developments included the most important processes for making aluminum (1886), bromine (1889), carborundum (1891), and calcium carbide (1893). Fertilizer manufacture depended on foreign sources for potash and nitrate until the

1920s, when large underground deposits of potash were found at Carlsbad, New Mexico. Manufacture of synthetic chemicals, particularly nitrogen fixation, was spurred by World War I, when German supplies were cut off. By 1925 the United States had an important industry for nitrogen fixation; and by 1928, thanks in part to the confiscation of the German dye patents, it was largely self-sufficient in dyes. Thereafter, the US industry came to resemble that of Europe, with large firms producing diverse, but interrelated, products, with an emphasis on complex chemical synthesis instead of the simple processing of raw materials. The 1930s saw some spectacular chemical developments, especially the production of artificial rubber and synthetic gasoline from coal. New plastic materials were introduced, the most notable being the plastic fibers that ultimately supplanted cotton as the most popular textile material: viscose rayon and nylon. The element silicon began to yield its secrets in 1940, with the first of many hitherto unknown compounds called silicones. Ethyl gasoline, Freon, and fluorine were important discoveries. Following World War II, the fastest-expanding fields of the chemical industry have been plastics, pharmaceuticals, and petrochemicals.

CHEMICAL WARFARE. Gases, defoliants, and herbicides used as weapons of war. The Hague Convention of 1899 and the Geneva Protocol of 1925 placed restrictions on the uses of chemical weapons, and the latter forbade the employment of poisonous gases, widely used in World War I. That Protocol was not ratified by the US Senate until 1974, and US forces made widespread use of chemicals, especially defoliants, in the Vietnam War. "Incapacitating" gases are widely believed to have been used by a number of nations in small-scale wars of the 1970s and 1980s.

CHEMISTRY. In 1756 a course in natural philosophy, including some chemistry, was offered at what is now the University of Pennsylvania. Similar courses were offered at William and Mary in 1774 and at Harvard in 1787. The medical school of the University of Pennsylvania, founded 1765, offered a course in chemistry and materia medica; two years later, Kings College (Columbia) offered the same course. By 1800 Dartmouth and the College of New Jersey (Princeton) also had instruction in chemistry. In the half-century after independence, Philadelphia became the chemical center of the new nation. In addition to the manufacture of drugs, paints, bleach, sulfuric acid, and other acids, within fifty miles of the city mills and factories were turning out iron, glass, bleached paper, and gunpowder. The University of Pennsylvania maintained its preeminence in chemical education, but it was gradually overtaken by Yale, where the Sheffield Scientific School was established in 1847. The American Chemical Society was founded in 1877, and the *Journal of the American Chemical Society* took its place among the most important of its type in the world. The first decades of the 20th c. were of extraordinary importance to both practical and theoretical chemistry. The structure of the atom was being worked out. Exciting new research was beginning in radiochemistry, photochemistry, crystallography, pharmacy, spectroscopy, solution theory, acid-base theory, stereochemistry, polymer chemistry, and nutrition. The charge of the electron was measured, and covalent and ionic bonding were explained. In nuclear chemistry accelerators were pioneered for probing into the structure of atoms and for making artificial isotopes. This work evolved to the making of elements not naturally found on the earth. The first were neptunium and plutonium. Radioactive isotopes and deuterium proved invaluable in establishing reaction mechanisms and metabolic pathways. Willard F. Libby showed in 1946 how one could date ancient materials by the carbon-14 method. Scientists worked feverishly in secret during World War II to convert nuclear fission into an awesome weapon. Significant contributions to organic chemistry were made between 1920 and 1950 with the production of synthetic rubbers, numerous plastics, filaments like nylon, and epoxy cements. Other researchers determined the highly complex structure of various plant and animal components and secretions. Inorganic chemistry came alive in the 1930s with the intensive investigation of coordination and chelation compounds. Silicone was developed in the 1940s. In 1933 Linus Pauling predicted that the so-called inert gases could react with fluorine and other halogens, and this was accomplished in 1962. Geochemistry and cosmic chemistry have attracted many able researchers since the 1950s. The same is true for environmental chemistry, a field in which extremely sensitive methods of analysis have been devised. American analytical chemists have contributed substantially to spectroscopy, chromatography, ion exchange, and nuclear magnetic resonance procedures. But in both scientific and human importance, the greatest advances from the 1930s into the 1980s have been in the field of BIOCHEMISTRY.

CHEQUAMEGON BAY. On the S coast of Lake Superior, site of the first white settlement in what is now Wisconsin. French traders built a hut on the W shore, probably in 1658. Madeline, an island in the bay, was occupied by a fort built by Pierre Le Sueur; it was abandoned before 1700. In 1718 a French fort, La Pointe, was built on the island, and a French garrison was there until 1759. The first English trader was Alexander Henry, whose partner, Jean Baptiste Cadotte, founded a permanent trading post.

CHERBOURG. The capture of this French city on June 26, 1944, three weeks after the Normandy landings, gave the Allies their first great port in NW Europe.

CHEROKEE. See FIVE CIVILIZED TRIBES.

CHEROKEE NATION V. GEORGIA, 5 Peters 1 (1831). The Supreme Court allowed the state of Georgia jurisdiction over land that had been guaranteed to the Cherokee by treaty.

CHEROKEE RIVER. See TENNESSEE RIVER.

CHEROKEE STRIP. Popular name for an area of about 12,000 square miles in Oklahoma. Guaranteed to the Cherokee by treaties (1828, 1835). In 1891 the United States purchased the Cherokee Strip and opened it for settlement. In 1893 it became part of the Oklahoma territory.

CHEROKEE TRAIL. Laid out in 1848, it extended from Fort Gibson up the Arkansas R to the mouth of the Cimarron R and up the Cimarron to a point in NW Oklahoma. From there it ran W to the Santa Fe Trail, joining it at Middle Cimarron Spring. Also known as Trappers' Trail.

CHEROKEE WARS (1776–81). During the American Revolution, the Cherokee sided with the British and were soon engaged in a general war on the frontiers of the Carolinas, Virginia, and Georgia. Punitive expeditions converged on the Cherokee. Nearly all of their towns were plundered and burned, and several hundred Cherokee fled to British protection in Florida. Cherokee elders sued for peace in 1777, at the price of further cessions of Cherokee lands. A dissident faction, the Chickamauga, separated from the rest of the tribe, pushing down the Tennessee R and establishing new settlements on Chickamauga Creek, where they were joined by other dissident Cherokee. Again a Virginia-North Carolina expedition devastated the towns. In 1781 a treaty confirmed the land cessions of 1777; it was observed by all the Cherokee except the Chickamauga.

CHERRY VALLEY MASSACRE (Nov. 11, 1778). An attack by Col. John Butler's Rangers, a Loyalist regiment, and Indians under the Mohawk leader Joseph Brant, on the colonial outpost of Cherry Valley in the upper Susquehanna Valley. Thirty colonials were killed, and all the buildings were burned.

CHESAPEAKE AND DELAWARE CANAL. The canal connecting Chesapeake and Delaware bays was built 1825–29. It was over thirteen miles long, with three locks. A cut ninety feet deep through earth and stone was the heaviest engineering project yet undertaken in America. It is still in use.

CHESAPEAKE AND OHIO CANAL. A joint project of the federal government, Maryland, and Virginia; the legal successor of the Potomac Co. in the attempt to connect Chesapeake Bay with the Ohio R. The plan was to construct a series of locks and canals around the rapids and falls of the Potomac R from Georgetown to Cumberland. From there the Ohio was to be reached at Pittsburgh. Ground was broken in 1828, and the canal was completed to Cumberland by 1850. It never reached the Ohio; the Baltimore & Ohio RR made the connection before the canal's engineering problems could be solved. The completed portion is today a national historic park.

CHESAPEAKE AND OHIO RAILROAD. See RAILROADS, SKETCHES OF PRINCIPAL LINES.

CHESAPEAKE CAPES, BATTLE OF. See VIR-GINIA CAPES, BATTLE OF.

CHESAPEAKE-LEOPARD INCIDENT (June 22, 1807). Off Hampton Roads, Virginia, the US frigate *Chesapeake* was stopped by the British *Leopard* and ordered to surrender four deserters. Upon refusal, the British opened fire. The US vessel, unprepared for battle, was irreparably damaged; three men were killed and twenty injured. Its captain, James Barron, surrendered. Three US seaman and one deserter were removed from the *Chesapeake*, which was forced to creep back into port. In 1811 the British disavowed the act and returned the two surviving US seamen.

CHESAPEAKE-SHANNON FIGHT (June 1, 1813). Outside Boston harbor, the US frigate *Chesapeake* met the British frigate *Shannon*. The untrained US seamen were no match for the larger and more highly trained British. Within minutes all the American officers were dead or wounded and the men were in panic. The captain, James Lawrence, dying, gave the famous order, "Don't give up the ship." Nevertheless, the ship was quickly taken by the British.

CHEYENNE. Indian tribe that ranged in the 17th c. through W South Dakota, E Montana, N Wyoming, and into Colorado. By 1800 they had pushed to the Missouri R. In the high plains they abandoned farming and pottery making and, becoming superior horsemen, took over the classic Plains encampment organization. Between 1832 and 1851, some Cheyenne settled on the upper Arkansas R at Bent's Fort; others remained near the headwaters of the Platte and Yellowstone rivers. The southern groups fought the Kiowa but later allied with them, while the northern segment was involved with the Dakota, fighting Gen. George A. Custer.

CHEYENNE. Capital of Wyoming, established in 1867 by the Union Pacific RR. Became the chief outfitting point for gold seekers flocking into the area and for the cattle ranchers of the northern plains. The collapse of the cattle boom of the 1880s ended its great days. Pop.: 47,283 (1980).

CHICAGO. Second largest city in the United States, located on Lake Michigan, in NE Illi-nois, at the mouth of the Chicago R. The French explorers Louis Jolliet and Jacques Marquette were the first known white visitors, in 1673. The first permanent settlement was founded ca. 1790. With the Treaty of Greenville in 1795, a six-square-mile tract at the mouth of the Chicago R was ceded to the US, and in 1803 Fort Dearborn was erected. Its evacuation during the War of 1812 precipitated a massacre by the Potawatomi. A final treaty in 1833 secured US claims, and by 1837, when Chicago was incorporated as a city, the population was over 4,000. By the 1850s the railroads had established Chicago as the country's main freight transfer point. Soon there were blast furnaces and factories. Livestock, hauled to the Union Stock Yards, was slaughtered and processed at the city's packing plants. On Oct. 8, 1871, disaster struck with the great CHICAGO FIRE. Reconstruction began immediately. Expanding industries offered a breeding ground for strikes and labor unrest after the Panic of 1873 and the ensuing depression. Meanwhile architectural innovations transformed the city, while ghetto shanties housed a great wave of foreign immigration. During Prohibition, bootlegging, gang warfare, lawlessness, and municipal corruption gave the city a worldwide reputation. Today, Chicago is the Midwest's economic and cultural center. It remains a major center of food-processing and is the nation's leading producer of iron and steel. Also important are the manufacture of electrical equipment, machinery, metal products, and chemicals. It is a publishing and printing center. Pop.: 3,005,072 (1980).

CHICAGO AND NORTHWESTERN RAILWAY. See RAILROADS, SKETCHES OF PRINCIPAL LINES.

CHICAGO, BURLINGTON AND QUINCY RAILROAD. See RAILROADS, SKETCHES OF PRINCIPAL LINES.

CHICAGO DRAINAGE CANAL. Constructed 1893–1900, it reversed the flow of the Chicago R, converting it into a drainage canal connecting Chicago with the Illinois R at Lockport. City sewage, diluted with water from Lake Michigan was sent down the Illinois R. Diversion of the lake water provoked opposition from adjoining states and Canada, and finally the federal government induced Chicago to provide other means of sewage disposal (see CHICAGO SANITARY DISTRICT CASE). Today it is known as the Chicago Sanitary and Ship Canal.

CHICAGO FIRE. In 1871 a scorching wind blew up from the Southwest week after week, making the wooden structures of Chicago dry as tinder. Fire began on Sunday evening, Oct. 8, 1871. The legend is that Mrs. O'Leary's cow kicked over a lantern, thereby starting the fire. Whatever its cause, the fire consumed five square miles, including the central business district. The loss of human lives was estimated at between 200 and 300. Over 17,500 buildings were destroyed; 100,000 people were rendered homeless. Direct property loss was about $200 million. The city was quickly rebuilt and resumed its preeminent position.

CHICAGO, MILWAUKEE AND SAINT PAUL RAILWAY COMPANY V. MINNESOTA, 134 US 418 (1890). An act of the Minnesota legislature (1887) established the Minnesota Railroad and Warehouse Commission and defined its duties in relation to common carriers The US Supreme Court declared the act unconstitutional because it deprived a railroad of property without due process of law and deprived it of equal protection of the law.

CHICAGO, MILWAUKEE, SAINT PAUL AND PACIFIC RAILROAD. See RAILROADS, SKETCHES OF PRINCIPAL LINES.

CHICAGO PORTAGE. Traditional overland route between the Chicago and Des Plaines rivers, whereby travelers could transport their boats from the Great Lakes-St. Lawrence to the Mississippi system. In 1848 completion of the Illinois and Michigan Canal ended its importance.

CHICAGO ROAD. Early highway from Detroit to Chicago. It was originally an Indian trail, and Robert Cavelier, Sieur de La Salle, in 1680 was probably the first white man to travel it. It became an important link in the western migration, and from ca. 1830 thousands moved to the Northwest over the road.

CHICAGO SANITARY DISTRICT CASE (*Wisconsin* v. *Illinois*, 289 US 395, 710 [1933]). The increasing diversion of Great Lakes water by Chicago to carry off sewage through the CHICAGO DRAINAGE CANAL was claimed to be lowering lake levels, thus impairing transportation facilities of bordering states. The 1933 Supreme Court decision settled finally the authority of the federal government to intervene to force action by a state (in this case, to construct alternate sewage disposal works).

CHICAGO SEVEN (also Chicago Eight). Following the riots at the Democratic Convention of 1968, eight persons (Abbie Hoffman, Rennie Davis, John Froines, Tom Hayden, Lee Weiner, David Dellinger, Jerry Rubin, and Bobby Seale) were indicted for crossing state lines to riot or to conspire to use interstate commerce to induce rioting. Their trial became a marathon (1969–70). Judge Julius J. Hoffman's obvious bias provoked defiant behavior from the defendants, who saw the trial as a political forum. A mistrial was finally declared in the case of Bobby Seale. The jury ultimately acquitted all defendants on the conspiracy charge and found only five guilty of crossing state lines to riot. These convictions were reversed on appeal, and the government dropped the charges.

CHICAGO TREATIES. In 1821 the US government, meeting at Chicago with representatives of the Potawatomi and allied tribes, reached an agreement with the Indians to procure the southwestern part of Michigan. Again in Chicago in 1833, the government procured from the Indians living there several million acres lying between Lake Michigan and Rock R in NE Illinois and SE Wisconsin. The Indians were removed to new homes W of the Mississippi R.

CHICAGO, UNIVERSITY OF. Founded 1890–92 by John D. Rockefeller as a Baptist university. Growth was rapid under its first president, William R. Harper (1890–1906), and the university gained a reputation as a center of research. Under Robert M. Hutchins (1929–51), a progressive curriculum was instituted whereby students met the requirements for the bachelor's degree by passing, either through comprehensive examinations or placement tests, fourteen required courses. The system was largely abandoned in the 1950s.

CHICKAMAUGA, BATTLE OF (Sept. 19–20, 1863). A Civil War battle at Chickamauga

131

Creek, near Chattanooga. Both the Union army, under Gen. W.S. Rosecrans, and the Confederate army, under Gen. Braxton Bragg, made serious blunders. The larger Union forces eventually prevailed and withdrew into Chattanooga.

CHICKASAW. See FIVE CIVILIZED TRIBES.

CHICKASAW BLUFFS. The high bank of the Mississippi R at the mouth of the Wolf R where Memphis, Tennessee, was founded in 1820. The bluffs were the site of several forts dating from 1682. Much intrigue with the Chickasaw centered on this post, especially during the Spanish occupation of Louisiana.

CHICKASAW BLUFFS, BATTLE OF (Dec. 29, 1862). Union Gen. W.T. Sherman's attack was part of the threefold federal plan to capture Vicksburg. The repulse of Sherman's troops at Chickasaw Bluffs demonstrated the futility of the plan.

CHICKASAW COUNCIL HOUSE, TREATY OF (Sept. 20, 1816). Negotiated by Andrew Jackson and other commissioners, it promised an annuity to the Chickasaw Nation, money and land to chiefs and warriors, and exclusion of peddlers from their country. In exchange, the Chickasaw ceded land on both sides of the Tennessee R.

CHICKASAW-CREEK WAR. On Feb. 13, 1793, the Chickasaw declared war against the Creek, to avenge the murder of two hunters. Piomingo, a Chickasaw chief attributing the murders to Creek resentment at the Chickasaw refusal to join an alliance against the Anglo-Americans, sought US aid. The government promised support for the Chickasaw in return for peace and friendship but refused armed intervention. Spanish officials in Louisiana and West Florida engineered a treaty between the two tribes and other southern tribes with one another and with Spain.

CHICKASAW-FRENCH WAR (1736–40). Supplied with guns and ammunition by the English, the Chickasaw in 1734 had virtually halted French travel on the Mississippi. The governor of Louisiana, the sieur de Bienville, in 1736 planned a two-pronged attack against them. A French-Choctaw army noved N from Mobile, while another army descended the

Mississippi from Illinois. The latter was wiped out by the Chickasaw and Bienville's force was decisively routed at the Battle of Ackia. In 1739 a second campaign was mounted, again from both north and south. No attack was attempted, the French being stricken with fever; but the Chickasaw mistook a small party of French for the advance of a much larger force, and agreed to peace.

CHICKASAW OLD FIELDS. On the N bank of the Tennessee R, four miles below the mouth of the Flint R, in present Madison County, Alabama, where the Chickasaw fixed their easternmost villages when they migrated E to the Mississippi. Ceded to US 1805.

CHICKASAW TREATY (1783). Negotiated by Virginia's commissioners with the Chickasaw, at Nashborough (Nashville), removing the claim of the tribe to territory between the Cumberland R and the ridge dividing the waters of that river from those of the Tennessee R. Although failing to obtain a cession of W Kentucky, the commissioners, treating on North Carolina soil, cleared for North Carolina the Indian title to one of the most fertile stretches in the West and cemented friendship between settlers and the Chickasaw.

CHICORA. A legendary land in N Spanish Florida, in the present-day Carolinas, thought to have been inhabited in the 16th c. by Indians of great wealth but of strange form, some having tails, others having feet so large they could be used as umbrellas, and some having an eye in the middle of their chests.

CHIEF JOSEPH'S CAMPAIGN. See NEZ PERCÉ WAR.

CHIHUAHUA TRAIL. In the late 16th c., Spanish colonization had advanced from Mexico City N to Santa Fe. Until Mexican independence in 1821, all contact between New Mexico and the outside world was over this 1,500-mile trail. Superseded by railroads, today the route is a great automobile highway of Mexico.

CHILD LABOR. Juvenile employment probably existed in the spinning schools established early in the colonies. Textile mills founded after the Revolution are known to have employed children for excessively long hours. Two-fifths of the factory workers in New England in 1832 were reported to be children. Agitation for compulsory school-attendance legislation began about that time, and in 1840 Connecticut, Massachusetts, and Pennsylvania passed laws limiting the hours of employment of minors in textile mills. Nevertheless, the problem persisted for the rest of the 19th c., and it was not until 1920 that census reports began to reflect a decline in child labor. The Fair Labor Standards Act of 1938 set the minimum working age at fourteen for employment outside of school hours, sixteen for employment during school hours, and eighteen for occupations deemed hazardous. Amendments to the law passed in 1948, 1974, and 1978 regulated the use of child labor in agriculture.

CHILDREN'S COURTS. See JUVENILE COURTS.

CHILLICOTHE. One of the four tribal divisions of the Shawnee. The chief towns of the tribe also bore this designation. Three were located in Ohio. The first is the modern city of Chillicothe, on the Scioto R (Pop.: 23,420 in 1980). In 1800 it became capital of NORTHWEST TERRITORY and was later (1803–10, 1812–16) capital of Ohio. The others were "Old Chillicothe" on the Little Miami R, near present Xenia, and a town on the Great Miami at Piqua.

CHILLICOTHE JUNTO. A group of Chillicothe, Ohio, Jeffersonian Republicans who were responsible for bringing in Ohio as a state in 1803.

CHIMNEY ROCK. A landmark in Morrill County, Nebraska. The peak is 4,242 feet high and visible for forty miles.

CHINA, US ARMED FORCES IN. At the time of the Chinese Revolution of 1911 there was a battalion-sized US marine legation guard in Peking and an infantry regiment at Tientsin. Elements of the US fleet frequented the treaty ports, and a river patrol was established on the Yangtze R. These forces were increased in the 1920s; and Sino-Japanese hostilities beginning in 1931 caused the further deployment of US troops; by 1941 all US troops had been removed. World War II brought them back: Gen. Joseph W. Stilwell became the chief of staff to Chiang Kai-shek. Gen. Clair L.

Chennault, who had organized the American Volunteer Corps (the FLYING TIGERS), was given command of the US China Air Task Force, which later became the Fourteenth Air Force. In 1944 US B-29's were based in China, from which they could reach Manchuria, Korea, and Japan itself. At the end of the war, a 55,000-man marine force was sent into North China, but the size of the force was gradually reduced; finally, in June 1949, the last of them left.

CHINA, US RELATIONS WITH. In 1789 fifteen American vessels were carrying on trade with China, and that trade expanded greatly in the decades following (see CHINA TRADE). The first US emissary to China was Caleb Cushing, who in 1844 arrived with four naval vessels to formalize the first Sino-American treaty. It granted the US commercial privileges equal to those granted to Britain. In 1899 the US asked England, Russia, Germany, Italy, France, and Japan to observe trade equality for everyone, in the OPEN DOOR POLICY. In June 1900 the Boxers laid siege to Peking; by August an international relief expedition, including 2,500 US troops, was on its way to break the siege. A more equal relationship between China and the US began to develop during the tenure of the Nationalist government of Sun Yat-sen and Chiang Kai-shek. The US and China were allies in World War II, and it was mostly through the insistence of Franklin D. Roosevelt that China was regarded as a full member of the Allies. After the war, the US attempted to bring about a cessation of the civil war between the Nationalists under Chiang and the Communists under Mao Tsetung. A mission headed by Gen. George C. Marshall to mediate between Mao and Chiang failed; by 1949 the Communists had forced the Chiang government off the mainland and onto the island of Taiwan (Formosa). The US now regarded the Communist takeover as a victory of evil over good. This was reflected in the US government's determination for the next twenty-three years not to recognize the Communist regime, to oppose its entry into the UN, and to maintain a military alliance with the Chiang regime on Taiwan. During the KOREAN WAR Chinese Communist forces and US forces were in direct armed conflict. In 1972 President Nixon dramatically reversed US policy; he visited Peking and paved the way for full diplomatic relations. Exchanges between athletes, scholars, journalists, and commercial interests developed. Full diplomatic relations between the two countries were established on Jan. 1, 1979; diplomatic relations and a defense treaty with Taiwan were terminated, but more than fifty other agreements with Taiwan continued in effect. In the early 1980s, US-China relations continued to be businesslike, and there was a growing amount of trade between the two countries.

CHINA CLIPPER. Popular name for the Boeing 314 hydroplane made famous for its transpacific service in the 1930s. The first flight of this luxurious passenger and mail plane left for Manila from Alameda, near San Francisco, on Nov. 25, 1935.

CHINA INCIDENT. In February 1916 a British cruiser removed thirty-eight enemy aliens, including fifteen reservists, from the US ship *China* in the Yellow Sea. The prisoners were released on US demand, but the British assertion that enemy reservists were legally liable to seizure from neutral vessels remained untested.

CHINA TRADE. In 1787, John Kendrick in the *Columbia* and Robert Gray in the *Lady Washington* sailed from Boston for the NW coast of America. Then Gray, with a load of sea otter peltries, continued to Canton. For the next two decades, this trade continued. As sea otters became rare, traders shifted to seals. Sandalwood, obtained in Hawaii and other Pacific islands, also became an important trade item. American sea captains brought back tea, china, enamel ware, nankeens, and silks. After the Opium War (1840–42) between Great Britain and China, China was forced to open four additional ports to British trade. Similar rights for Americans were obtained in 1844.

CHINESE EXCLUSION ACTS. See CHINESE IMMIGRATION AND LABOR.

CHINESE IMMIGRATION AND LABOR. Chinese workers formed an important segment of the labor force of the American West (especially in California), and W Canada. Peak Chinese population in the 19th-c. US was about 125,000. Their presence aroused great antagonism among white workers, es-

pecially in the trade union movement in San Francisco. In 1880 a US commission signed a treaty with China permitting restrictions on the immigration of laborers. In the meantime, anti-Chinese sentiment filled the West, and the Chinese were systematically persecuted. The Exclusion Act of 1882, the first of many purely ethnic bars written into US immigration laws, suspended Chinese immigration for ten years (and made "permanent" in 1902). These restrictions were gradually reduced, but did not disappear completely until the immigration law of 1965.

CHINOOK JARGON. A patois used by traders, government agents, and missionaries in the Northwest in the mid-19th c. Given currency by Chinook Indian traders, it included elements of English, Spanish, French, and Russian.

CHINOOK WINDS. Seasonal winds of the Pacific Northwest which blow E and SE from the Pacific during winter and early spring, penetrating far into the interior, even to the E slope of the Rockies. They melt and evaporate snow and ice and bring sudden relief from the most severe winter weather.

CHIPEWYAN. A tribe of Canadian Indians, they were drawn into the 18th-c. fur trade. Their original habitat was around Great Slave Lake and Lake Athabasca.

CHIPPEWA (or Ojibwa). Tribe of the Eastern Woodlands, first encountered in the middle Great Lakes regions in the 16th c. by the French fur traders. Originally hunters, they became middlemen on the French trade routes. Today, they are scattered on what were formerly reservations in Minnesota, Wisconsin, Ontario, Oklahoma, and the Dakotas. They comprise the second largest tribe in North America, numbering about 80,000.

CHISHOLM TRAIL. A cattle trail from San Antonio, Texas, across Oklahoma to the railhead at Abilene (and later at Caldwell), Kansas. After the Civil War, Texas ranchers used it to drive large herds of cattle to market, and it remained an important cattle route until the railroads were extended into Texas.

CHISHOLM V. GEORGIA, 2 Dallas 419 (1793). Heirs of Alexander Chisholm of

South Carolina sued Georgia to enforce payment of claims against the state. Georgia refused to defend the suit; the Supreme Court, upholding the right of citizens of one state to sue another, ordered judgment by default against Georgia.

CHISWELL'S MINES. Iron mines in Wythe County, Virginia, first operated in 1758. During the Revolution a plot by Loyalists to seize the mines was thwarted.

CHIVINGTON'S MASSACRE. See SAND CREEK MASSACRE.

CHOCTAW. See FIVE CIVILIZED TRIBES.

CHOCTAW LAND FRAUDS. In 1830 unscrupulous speculators obtained illegally scrip that was intended for the new lands of those Choctaw who were being allowed to stay in Mississippi. The fraud was exposed and eventually resulted in an order postponing the land sales.

CHOCTAW TRADING HOUSE, TREATY OF. See INDIAN REMOVAL.

CHOCTAW TRAIL. Any of several Indian paths through Choctaw country, i.e., C and S Mississippi and W Alabama. Most important was a trail from Natchez to Mobile; another became part of the NATCHEZ TRACE.

CHOLERA. In June 1832 Asiatic cholera reached North America. It killed 3,000 in New York City; by October, it had reached New Orleans, where within three weeks it killed 4,340. Among major US cities, only Charleston and Philadelphia escaped this first onslaught, which traveled the inland waterways and reached the western frontiers. After 1833 it virtually disappeared until 1848, when it broke out again in US port cities, striking down more than 5,000 in New York alone. It spread rapidly, bringing death to even the remotest areas and lasting until 1850. The last major epidemic threatened American ports in 1865. Prompt work by the newly organized Board of Health kept the death toll to about 600 in New York, but other towns and cities were not so fortunate. The medical profession, however, developed improved techniques in treating it; and better public sanitation helped reduce both incidence and mortality. After 1873, only occasional cases of cholera were found aboard incoming vessels.

CHOUTEAU'S TRADING POSTS. Trading largely with the Osage Indians and operating under the authority of the Spanish government, Pierre and Auguste Chouteau in 1794 erected Fort Carondelet in what is now Bates County, Missouri. They established another fur-trading rendezvous on the Arkansas R ca. 1800. In 1809 Pierre and his son A.P. Chouteau became stockholders in the St. Louis Missouri Fur Company. Between 1822 and 1836, A.P. Chouteau established posts at present Salina and Purcell, Oklahoma. François G. Chouteau established a post on the Kansas R.

CHRISTIANA FUGITIVE AFFAIR. In 1851 Edward Gorsuch attempted to recover four runaway slaves being harbored by William Parker, a black man, in Christiana, Pa. Parker refused to turn them over, and Gorsuch's party threatened to burn his house. Gorsuch was killed, and thirty-eight of the neighbors were tried, but all were acquitted.

CHRISTIAN CHURCHES. See DISCIPLES OF CHRIST.

CHRISTIAN SCIENCE. See CHURCH OF CHRIST, SCIENTIST.

CHRISTINA, FORT. See WILMINGTON (Delaware).

CHRYSLER'S FIELD, BATTLE OF (Nov. ll, 1813). Bent on capturing Montreal, the US army halted a mile E of Chrysler's farm on the N bank of the St. Lawrence R. British gunboats began firing on the Americans, who retreated to their boats after sustaining heavy casualties.

CHURCH AND STATE, SEPARATION OF. See RELIGION.

CHURCHES, ESTABLISHED. See RELIGION.

CHURCH MEMBERSHIP SUFFRAGE. When the Puritans settled in Massachusetts with their trading-company charter, they established a theocracy, which they could maintain only so long as they could control the freemen, or stockholders, of the trading company. Thus they limited freemanship to those who approved the theocracy. When pressure from dissatisfied nonfreemen became too great, they accepted a limited number on condition of orthodox church membership. The colony of New Haven also adopted the principle of church membership suffrage. By the fusion of Connecticut and New Haven in the charter of 1662, the narrow suffrage ended in the latter colony, as it did in Massachusetts when the charter was annulled in 1684.

CHURCH OF CHRIST, SCIENTIST. A religious movement founded by Mary Baker Eddy in 1876; the Mother Church was founded in Boston in 1879. At the heart of Christian Science is its claim to be able to cure disease. The Christian Scientists have a large number of practitioners who heal through mental suggestion and personal influence. There are some 3,200 branches worldwide. The church publishes the *Christian Science Monitor*.

CHURCH OF ENGLAND. All the southern colonies, except Maryland, were founded under the leadership of members of the Church of England, the first successful colony being at Jamestown in 1607. Maryland was founded by a Roman Catholic proprietor, but the Protestants had established the Church of England there by 1702. In New York, the church was established in the four leading counties. During the 18th c., the Church of England advanced in the colonies where it was not established and lost ground in those where it was. The American Revolution confronted it with the problem of forming a national organization and obtaining a native episcopate. The Protestant Episcopal Church is the result.

CHURCH SCHISMS OVER SLAVERY. At the opening of the Civil War, the Presbyterian, Baptist, and Methodist churches had already divided into northern and southern branches over the slavery issue. The secession of the southern states also brought division to the Episcopalians. The Roman Catholics experienced no divisions and very little controversy as a result of either slavery or the Civil War. Others, like the Congregational, avoided splits because they were confined almost entirely to the North, while the Quakers excluded slave owners from the ranks.

CHURUBUSCO, BATTLE OF (Aug 20, 1847). After his victory at Contreras, Gen. Winfield Scott encountered Santa Anna's principal army at Churubusco, near Mexico City. The defenders were routed and retreated to the capital.

CIBOLA. Indian name for the villages of the Zuni in what is now W New Mexico, rumored in the early 16th c. to be fabulously wealthy. The Spaniards in Mexico in 1539 dispatched the expedition of the friar Marcos de Niza. His report inspired a stronger expedition the next year under Francisco Vásquez de Coronado.

CIMARRON. The Panhandle area of Oklahoma. Settled by squatters and cattlemen, the territory had no law (hence its other name No Man's Land). A movement was started to organize into the Cimarron Territory in 1887, but no formal action was ever taken.

CINCINNATI. City in SW Ohio, located on the Ohio R opposite the mouth of the Licking R. Part of the Miami Purchase of 1788, its original name was Losantiville, and it was the capital of the Northwest Territory, 1790–1800. Well located to command western and southern markets, it ranked third in manufacturing among US cities in 1860. Its leadership diminished as meat packing moved W and trunkline railroads reduced the importance of the Ohio R. Pop.: 385,457 (1980).

CINCINNATI, SOCIETY OF THE. Established in 1783 by officers of the Continental army about to disband. The name was an allusion to Cincinnatus, the Roman general who retired quietly to his farmstead after leading his army to victory. With a permanent fund for widows and the indigent, the founders also provided for the perpetuation of the society by making membership hereditary. There were thirteen state societies and an association in France for the French officers. The society soon entered a quiescent period but was revived in 1900. Current membership is about 1,800.

CINCINNATI RIOTS. On March 28, 1884, a mob lynched two youths convicted of manslaughter instead of murder; the mob's action stemmed from public dissatisfaction with the city's criminal courts, which were believed to have become corrupt. Troops were sent in and hard fighting ensued for several days. At least 45 persons died and 138 were injured.

CIO. See AMERICAN FEDERATION OF LABOR–CONGRESS OF INDUSTRIAL ORGANIZATIONS.

CIRCUIT COURTS. See JUDICIARY.

CIRCUIT RIDERS. Ministerial circuit riding was devised in England by John Wesley as a way of spreading Methodism. A circuit consisted of numerous preaching places scattered over a large district served by one preacher. By the end of the American Revolution, there were about 100 Methodist circuit riders in the colonies. The system was widely expanded, especially through the new western lands. Other religious bodies, especially the Cumberland Presbyterians, adopted circuit riding.

CIRCUITS, JUDICIAL. When the federal judicial system, under the Constitution, was established, the US was divided into three circuits (Eastern, Middle, and Southern) to each of which were assigned two justices of the Supreme Court. These justices were required to hold the courts twice a year, sitting with district judges. During the first three years of its existence, the Supreme Court had practically no business to transact and the chief justice and the associate justices found employment in riding the circuits. Some relief was granted in 1793 when only one justice was required to sit with a district judge, and the justices rode the circuit in turn. In 1869, circuit judges were appointed, most of whom traveled over several states. In the states, circuit courts existed, and in the early days the judge, accompanied by many lawyers, covered large circuits.

CIRCUS. John William Ricketts founded the first circus in America, in Philadelphia in 1793. The early circuses, predominantly shows of horsemanship, were more or less stationary. The first elephant was brought to America in 1796, and the traveling menagerie developed independently of the circuses. The two began to merge ca. 1825, and tents and portable seats were in use by 1828. By 1835 seventeen horse-drawn circuses existed. Triumphal entry into town by the entire caravan led by a band typifies the beginnings of the American circus street parade. Isaac A.

Van Amburg is credited with introducing the wild animal act in 1835, when he first entered a cage containing a lion, a tiger, a leopard, and a panther. The steam calliope arrived in 1857. Phineas T. Barnum's circus made its appearance in 1871 and it soon became rail-transported. In 1881 he merged with James A. Bailey, resulting in the Barnum & Bailey Circus. The five Ringling brothers founded their circus in 1884. In 1919 the two great circuses were merged and became Ringling Bros. and Barnum & Bailey, advertised as "the greatest show on earth." In 1956 economics forced it to give up tents in favor of appearing in permanent buildings.

CITIZENSHIP. Membership in a political community attended by certain privileges and responsibilities. In the US, virtually everyone holds dual citizenship of a special sort, federal and state. However, US citizenship is primary and state citizenship derivative. US citizenship can be acquired either by birth or by naturalization. Two basic rules govern citizenship by birth: place of birth and parentage. The only qualification is that the person must be born under US jurisdiction as well as in US territory. This qualification affects children of US diplomats, those born on foreign public ships in US territorial waters, those born of enemies during hostilities on American soil, children of American parents resident in foreign countries. The process of acquiring citizenship by naturalization may involve either collective or individual naturalization. The former is a conferring of citizenship on a group as a whole either by statute or by treaty. Individual naturalization involves a detailed process in which aliens themselves seek citizenship. Loss of citizenship is possible by the acquisition of citizenship in another country or by a variety of actions such as service in the armed forces of another country. Citizenship secured illegally or fraudulently may be revoked.

CITIZENSHIP, DUAL. A child born in the United States to foreign parents acquires US citizenship at birth; such children may at the same time acquire the citizenship of their parents, under the law of their country. The converse can arise when a child is born to American parents in a foreign country. Dual citizenship can also arise when a woman marries a citizen of another country and upon her marriage becomes a citizen of that country under its laws, or when a person becomes a naturalized citizen in a foreign country, but retains citizenship under the laws of the country of origin.

CITRUS INDUSTRY. Citrus fruit was introduced to the Americas by the Spanish *conquistadores* and early colonists. The citrus industry grew slowly in Florida and was of minor importance before the Civil War. During the Reconstruction period northern capitalists saw possibilities for profit in the citrus industry. With citrus stock imported from various parts of the world, the orange industry was transformed into a money-making business. Following World War II, Florida passed California in production of citrus fruit. Today citrus is Florida's most valuable crop; Florida groves constitute over 70 percent of the US citrus acreage. California leads in lemon production and ranks second in oranges and grapefruit. Arizona, Texas, and Louisiana also have significant citrus acreages.

CITY COUNCILS. The principal policymaking bodies for the nation's municipal governments are structured in four different ways. The most common form, the mayor-council, places both legislative and administrative power in the city council itself. The council-manager form allocates legislative power to the council and administrative power to a chief administrator, or manager. Infrequently found is the commission form, in which each council member serves as the head of an administrative department; and the fourth is New England's town meeting form. Early American cities were governed by unicameral city councils, which often were also entrusted with judical powers. After 1800, following the initiative of Baltimore and Philadelphia, many cities adopted the bicameral pattern of Congress and state legislatures; but this proved cumbersome, and by the 1980s virtually all US city councils were once again unicameral.

CITY GOVERNMENT. See LOCAL GOVERNMENT; MUNICIPAL GOVERNMENT.

CITY MANAGER PLAN. A form of municipal government in which the council appoints a city manager, who serves as the city's chief administrative officer. The plan originated in 1908 in Staunton, Virginia, but achieved widespread notice after being adopted in Dayton, Ohio, in 1913. Then it spread rapidly, particularly in smaller cities. In some cases a member of the council serves as titular mayor.

CITY PLANNING.
Colonial Towns. In 1638 New Haven, Connecticut, adopted a plan dividing the city into nine large square plots in rows of three, with the central square serving as the town common or green. This became a distinctive feature of colonial New England. In contrast, the architectural square was characteristic of the courthouse towns of Virginia, consisting of a smaller green square closely surrounded by private residences, shops, a stately courthouse, and usually one or two churches. It became standard throughout the South. Of the important seaport cities, Boston contained an unplanned maze of narrow winding streets, while Charleston, Philadelphia, Annapolis, Williamsburg, and Savannah contained axes, radials, diagonals, and squares patterned after monumental European Renaissance plans.

Post-Revolution and 19th-Century Plans. The growth of commerce following the American Revolution brought a new grandeur to city planning: sweeping radials and diagonals, squares, ovals, and circles, designed to provide nobler settings for imposing public buildings; notably, Pierre L'Enfant's plan for Washington. These plans were ultimately overshadowed by the simplicity of the gridiron pattern, notably that of New York City. The demand for textiles created the first planned company mill towns in New England, while wooden boomtowns of gridiron pattern were hastily developed in the eastern coal fields and the Plains states. The railroad promoted new railroad towns, while the Industrial Revolution created factory towns along the railroads in the East, designed as complete communities for industrial workers. In contrast to these notorious industrial slums, a few model company towns were designed. The Civil War hastened industrial growth and urbanization. Cities rapidly covered by the unimaginative gridiron pattern neglected environmental needs of residents in an effort to accommodate exploding urban populations. Improvements in urban mass transit caused rapid fringe expansion along main transportation routes, creating prototypes of today's suburban communities. Tall buildings appeared in the latter half of the 19th c. to relieve the monotonous horizontal pattern of urban development, while parks and landscaped residential avenues introduced much-needed open space.

City Beautiful Movement and Modern City Planning. In 1893 the World's Columbian Exposition in Chicago launched the City Beautiful Movement. Cities appointed civic art commissions to carry out vast self-improvement projects that yielded civic centers, tree-lined avenues, and waterfront improvements. A number of imaginatively planned housing developments emerged following World War I, financed by large corporations and insurance companies. They were designed on standard city blocks to demonstrate the advantages in appearance and open space over the traditional tight row-tenement development. In 1927 America's first garden city, Radburn, New Jersey, introduced the concept of the superblock—a large residential planning unit free from vehicular encroachment, providing uninterrupted pedestrian access from every building to a large recreation area within the center and pedestrian underpasses at major arteries. The legal framework for modern city planning practice began with the zoning ordinance, based on the police power to control land and thereby protect the interests of the individual and the community.

Federal Involvement. Under the New Deal, the federal government initiated strong leadership in housing programs and after World War II concentrated on slum clearance and urban renewal. The cabinet-level Department of Housing and Urban Development (HUD) was created in 1965, and the National Historic Preservation Act was passed in 1968. Federal assistance to housing was severely cut back in the 1970s, a trend continued by the Reagan administration in the early 1980s.

CIVIL AERONAUTICS ACT (1938). Law creating the five-member Civil Aeronautics Administration, which was given jurisdiction over commercial and private aviation. (See FEDERAL AGENCIES.)

CIVIL DEFENSE. Activities designed to minimize the effects of enemy attack upon the civilian population. During World War II, the Office of Civil Defense supervised civilian air-raid wardens, shelter maintenance, and firefighters. Later, proliferation of nuclear weapons made attempts at civil defense virtually useless; nevertheless, a system of shelters and plans for the evacuation of cities has been kept in place by federal and local authorities.

CIVIL DISOBEDIENCE. An overt action that goes beyond the traditional legal challenges to laws or institutions. Direct action attempts to force negotiations on the law or institution considered unjust. For example, persons denied service in a public facility may simply sit down and refuse to leave (a sit-in). Civil disobedience may also involve deliberate violation of the "unjust" law or resistance to other laws.

CIVIL ENGINEERING. A branch of engineering that deals with construction of buildings, roads, and other transportation systems, and public facilities such as water supply systems. The civil engineer deals with surveying, designing, and constructing reservoirs, sewage disposal systems, railroads, docks, bridges, and buildings for residential, commercial, or industrial purposes. Civil engineers cooperate with architects and with chemical, electrical, and mechanical engineers.

CIVILIAN CONSERVATION CORPS (CCC). New Deal agency created in 1933 to provide relief for unemployed young men. Nearly 3 million single men were placed on conservation tasks between 1933 and 1942. Reforestation was the most important, but enrollees were also engaged in erosion control, fire prevention, drought relief, land reclamation, and pest eradication. Abolished 1942 because of World War II.

CIVILIZED TRIBES, FIVE. See FIVE CIVILIZED TRIBES.

CIVIL RIGHTS, COMMISSION ON. See FEDERAL AGENCIES.

CIVIL RIGHTS AND LIBERTIES. Individual and group freedoms deemed to be so fundamental as not to tolerate government infringement. Among those guaranteed by the US Constitution are the right of habeas corpus; no bill of attainder or ex post facto law; jury trial; privileges and immunities; and no religious test for public office. The Bill of Rights guarantees certain substantive rights (notably freedom of speech, the press, assembly, and religious worship) and certain procedural rights in both civil and criminal actions (notably a speedy and public trial by an impartial jury). Throughout the 19th c., the courts held that these amendments did not apply to state and local governments. Beginning ca. 1925, however, the courts extended the protection of the Bill of Rights to the actions of states and localities.

CIVIL RIGHTS MOVEMENT. Nonviolent, direct-action campaign by black organizations and individuals and their white allies to achieve full racial integration. Generally dated from the Supreme Court's decision of 1954 in *Brown* v. *Board of Education of Topeka* to the passage in 1965 of the Voting Rights Act. Black expectations, particularly those of an expanding middle class, were significantly heightened by the Warren court's decision. A 1955 bus boycott in Montgomery, Alabama, was the first dramatic campaign of the movement. It was organized by Martin Luther King, Jr., who quickly became the leader of the entire movement. The eventual success of the Montgomery boycott not only publicized the deep-seated nature of American racism but significantly raised black consciousness. Furthermore, King's philosophy of nonviolence and civil disobedience was proven effective. There was determined opposition to integration, however; white citizens' councils and a revived Ku Klux Klan sprang up in numerous southern communities, ostensibly to protect the constitutional rights of whites, but actually to prevent the free access of blacks to public schools. President Eisenhower was compelled in 1957 by white mob violence to use federal troops to ensure the right of black children to attend the previously all-white Central High School in Little Rock, Arkansas. Soon a wave of student-led sit-ins, wade-ins, and sleep-ins directed against segregated public facilities engulfed the nation. Under the mounting black offensive, such places were desegregated with relative ease. To ensure cooperation between various student groups, the Student Nonviolent Coordinating Committee (SNCC) was formed in 1960; in 1961 it joined with the Congress of Racial Equality (CORE) to begin a series of "freedom rides" through the Deep South to test a Supreme Court decision banning segregation in interstate bus terminals. Their efforts were almost totally successful. By the end of 1961, SNCC and CORE, along with the Southern Christian Leadership Conference (Dr. King's group), were clearly in the vanguard of the movement, eclipsing the more conservative National Association for the Advancement of Colored People (NAACP) and the National Urban League, both of which had been responsible for most of the earlier civil rights advances of blacks. In 1963 King led large demonstrations to desegregate Birmingham, Alabama. The brutal force used by the police and the slaying of Medgar Evers, NAACP field secretary in Mississippi, a month later moved President Kennedy to ask Congress for a comprehensive civil rights law. Later that year, some 200,000 persons, led by King, participated in a march on Washington to demonstrate their support for the civil rights bill. The bill became law in July 1964, during the administration of Lyndon B. Johnson, who was also responsible for the enactment of the landmark Voting Rights Act of 1965. The passage of the Civil Rights Act of 1968, which outlawed discrimination in housing, also under Johnson's sponsorship, virtually ended all legal barriers to full black rights. Thereafter, the struggle for full rights moved to the social area and to the courts.

CIVIL SERVICE. The appointed civilian employees of a government unit, as distinct from elected officials and military personnel. Under early administrations, the federal civil service was relatively competent. Jacksonian egalitarian democracy saw the emergence of the SPOILS SYSTEM, which gave little or no consideration to competence. The unprecedented corruption and scandals of the post-Civil War era generated civil service reform and resulted in the creation of the US Civil Service Commission (1871). It remained ineffective until 1883, when Congress enacted the PENDLETON ACT, which is still the federal government's central civil service law. It created a merit system for many public offices based on competitive examinations. Over the years, the merit system has become almost all-encompassing; in a federal civil service of 3 million, there are fewer than 15,000 patronage posts of any consequence. Beginning in the late 19th c., civil service reform came to many state and local governments. In 1883 New York State adopted the first state civil service act. By the 1980s two-thirds of the states had them.

CIVIL WAR (1861–65). Sectional tension grew ominously in the 1850's and a major southern crisis followed the election of President Abraham Lincoln in November 1860. By early February 1861, the seven states of the Lower South (South Carolina, Mississippi, Florida, Alabama, Georgia, Louisiana, and Texas) had withdrawn from the Union and established the CONFEDERATE STATES OF AMERICA). The sending of an expedition by Lincoln to relieve the federal garrison at Fort Sumter in Charleston harbor precipitated a southern attack upon that fort, which was surrendered on Apr. 13. This was the opening of the war. Each side claimed that the other began it. After Sumter, Lincoln called for 75,000 militia to be furnished by the states. This policy, which called for troops from the four important states of the Upper South (Virginia, Arkansas, Tennessee, and North Carolina), caused them to withdraw from the Union and join the Confederacy. The Union had twenty-three states with 22 million people, as against eleven states and 9 million people (including 3.5 million slaves) within the Confederacy. In wealth and population, as well as in industrial, commercial, and financial strength, the Union was definitely superior to the Confederacy. The South had the advantage of bold leadership, gallant tradition, martial spirit, unopposed seizure of many federal forts and arsenals, interior military lines, and unusual ability among its generals. Its military problem was that of defense, which required far fewer men than offensive campaigns and widely extended hostile occupation. By the time Congress met in July 1861, the president had already taken those measures that gave to Union war policy its controlling character. Besides proclaiming an insurrection, declaring a blockade of all southern ports, and summoning the militia, he had suspended habeas corpus, expanded the regular army, directed emergency expenditures, and in general had assumed executive functions beyond existing law. A tardy ratification of his acts was passed by Congress on Aug. 6, 1861, and in 1863 these strongly contested executive measures were given sanction by the Supreme Court.

Militarily, both sides were unprepared. The first Battle of Bull Run (July 21) was the only large-scale engagement in 1861. Although a Union defeat, it was, like most of the battles, an indecisive struggle. Except during the generalship of Union officers G. B. McClellan, G. G. Meade, and U. S. Grant, the southerners had the undoubted advantage of military leadership on the main eastern front; R. E. Lee's notable but indecisive victories of second Bull Run, Fredericksburg, and Chancellorsville were won against John Pope, A. E. Burnside, and Joseph Hooker. At Antietam, however, McClellan stopped Lee's northern invasion of September 1862, while the ambitious Confederate offensive of 1863 was checked at Gettysburg. In the West most of the operations were favorable to the Union side. This was especially true of the "river war" (resulting in the capture of Columbus, forts Henry and Donelson, Nashville, Corinth, and Memphis); and the Union victories of 1863 at Vicksburg and Chattanooga. Later campaigns involved Confederate Gen. J. E. Johnston's unsuccessful operations against W. T. Sherman in upper Georgia, Sherman's capture of Atlanta and his famous march through Georgia and the Carolinas, Union Gen. P. H. Sheridan's devastating operations in the Valley of Virginia, the J.B. Hood–G.H. Thomas campaign in Tennessee, and final operations in the Petersburg and Appomattox areas, which culminated in the fall of Richmond and the close of the war. In the naval aspects, Union superiority was impressively shown in the blockade of southern ports, the capture and occupation of coastal positions, the cooperation of western flotillas with the armies, the seizure of New Orleans in April 1862, the complete control of the Mississippi R after the fall of Vicksburg and Port Hudson in July 1863, and the defeat and sinking of the Confederacy's proudest ship, the *Alabama,* by the *Kearsarge* (July 19, 1864). On the other hand, Confederate cruisers and privateers did considerable damage to Union commerce, the Union navy failed in the operations against Richmond, and several ports remained in southern hands until late in the war. War aims changed as the conflict progressed; the declaration of Congress on July 22, 1861, that the war was waged merely for the restoration of the Union was belied by the Radical Republicans, who by 1864 had determined in the event of victory to treat the

South as a subordinate section upon which drastic modifications would be imposed. The relation of the war to the slavery question appeared in various emancipating measures passed by Congress, in Lincoln's Emancipation Proclamation as well as his abortive compensated emancipation scheme, in state measures of abolition, and finally in the antislavery amendment to the Constitution. Confederate manpower is estimated to have been 600,000 to 700,000. Confederate dead have been estimated at 258,000; Union dead, at 360,000. The stupendous economic and material loss has never been more than roughly estimated. Aside from the obvious consequences of slaughter and destruction, the results of the war involved suppression of the "heresy" of secession, legal fixation of an "indestructible" Union, national abolition of slavery, overthrow of the southern planter class, rise of middle-class power in the South, ascendancy of the Republican party, inauguration of a high-tariff policy, far-reaching capitalistic growth associated with centralization of government functions, and adoption of the Fourteenth Amendment. (See also ARMY, CONFEDERATE; ARMY, UNION; CONFEDERATE STATES OF AMERICA; NAVY, CONFEDERATE; NAVY, US; and articles on specific battles by title.)

Civil War Diplomacy. The basic diplomatic policy of the US during the Civil War was twofold: to prevent foreign intervention on behalf of the Confederacy and to gain the acquiescence of England and France in the vast extension of maritime belligerent rights, which was considered necessary to crush the South. In the very beginning, Secretary of State W. H. Seward deliberately gave the British government the impression that he was willing to fight Great Britain should that country show undue sympathy for the Confederacy. The launching of the Confederate cruisers and the building of the Confederate rams in England and France gave the Union even stronger grounds for complaint, as did the sale of munitions and the colossal blockade-running business carried on with the Confederacy. French intervention in Mexico was an added score against France. The objective of Confederate diplomacy was to obtain foreign assistance in gaining independence. The Confederate government based its plans, first, upon European dependence upon southern cotton and, second, upon the well-known desire of England to see a powerful commercial rival weakened and of Napoleon III to see the champion of the Monroe Doctrine rendered impotent to frustrate his attempted annexation of Mexico. The Confederacy failed to obtain foreign intervention because the things to be gained by war on the part of England and France would not offset war losses.

Munitions. The standard equipment of the Union army was muzzle-loading Springfield or Enfield rifles and cannon. Many early regiments, however, went to the front with nondescript arms of their own procuring. Contractors sold the army thousands of antiquated, castoff, often dangerous weapons of European armies. Before 1861 various American companies had been making breech-loading repeating rifles that would fire fifteen times as rapidly as the best of muzzle-loaders, with equal accuracy and force, and with greater ease of manipulation. But the backwardness of the War Department and its staff prevented the use of such improved weapons until the closing months of the war. The munitions of the Confederacy were inferior to those of the North. Battlefield captures, raiding expeditions, imports from Europe, and an increasing production from newly built southern munitions plants kept the troops armed. By 1864, lead-smelting works, bronze foundries, a cannon foundry, and rifle, carbine, and pistol factories were operating. The big problem of supply was the lack of adequate transportation.

War Supply Contracts. In the first year of the war, the federal government and a score of states were bidding against each other for war supplies, with disgraceful consequences. Several of the great personal fortunes had their origins in Civil War contracts. Furthermore, goods of inferior quality often found readier sales than first-class products. The situation seems to have been not much better in the Confederacy.

Surrender of the Confederate Armies. The most important surrender after Lee's Appomattox (Apr. 9, 1865) was that of Confederate Gen. J. E. Johnston to W. T. Sherman near Durham Station, North Carolina, on April 26. Parole was granted to 37,047 prisoners on the same terms Grant had given Lee. The capitulation of the rest of the Confederate forces followed as a matter of course. On May 4, Gen. Richard Taylor surrendered to Gen. E.R.S. Canby at Citronelle, Alabama, thus ending Confederate forces E of the Mississippi. Six days later Jefferson Davis was captured by J.H. Wilson's cavalry near Irwinville, Georgia, and was imprisoned at Fortress Monroe. The final act was the surrender of Kirby-Smith and the trans-Mississippi troops to Canby at New Orleans on May 26. The total number surrendered and paroled from Apr. 9 to May 26 was 174,223.

Economic Consequences in the North. Despite its great destructiveness, the Civil War proved to be a great stimulus to the economic life of the North. Government contracts, paper-money inflation, and a new protective tariff system brought a rapid expansion of capital and a new prosperity to northern industry. Woolen manufacturing, munitions and war supplies, the petroleum industry, telegraphs and railways, the banking system, and agriculture experienced new gains. Labor turned new energies toward organizing national craft unions. The federal debt was over $2.6 billion at the end of the war; yet the national wealth had been greatly increased and a new era of American capitalism began.

Economic Consequences in the South. The Civil War brought economic suffering, devastation, and ruin to the South. As a result of the blockade, the interruption of intercourse with the North, and the strain of supporting the armed forces, the people were subjected to extreme privation. Large land areas were laid waste by military operations. Accumulated capital resources were dissipated. Railroads were either destroyed or deteriorated to the point of worthlessness. Livestock was reduced by almost two-thirds. Slave property valued at about $2 billion was wiped out. About a fourth of the productive white male population was killed or incapacitated. Land values were undermined; agricultural production was greatly retarded; trade was disrupted; banks and mercantile houses were forced into bankruptcy; the credit system was disorganized; and commercial ties with foreign nations were broken. The ending of slavery forced the plantation system to give way to sharecropper, tenancy, and small farm systems. The war and the policies of RECONSTRUCTION caused a diminution in the role the South played in the determination of national economic policies. Tariff, monetary, railroad, banking, and other such matters were generally decided without any consideration for the South. The result was economic exploitation of the South by other sections of the nation.

CLAIBORNE SETTLEMENT. William Claiborne established in 1631 a plantation on Kent Island in upper Chesapeake Bay, an outpost of Virginia represented in its general assembly. In 1638 Gov. Leonard Calvert seized Kent Island; during the civil war in England Claiborne temporarily regained control.

CLAIM ASSOCIATIONS. Frontier institutions designed to provide quasi-legal protection for settlers in areas where no land law existed. Such associations, also called claim clubs, appeared early in the 19th c. and were found in practically every part of the public land area that received settlers before 1870. Their heyday was in the 1840s and 1850s in Iowa, Kansas, and Nebraska. The squatters would come together and adopt a set of rules guaranteeing mutual protection of land titles to each claimant who met the simple requirements for improvement of the land. Claim jumpers were dealt with in summary fashion by these associations. The associations tended to go out of existence as governments were established within the settled areas.

CLAIM JUMPER. One who drove a squatter from his claim or, in his absence, seized it.

CLAIMS, FEDERAL COURT OF. Created by Congress in 1855, the court investigates contractual claims against the US by private parties or referred to it by an executive department or by Congress. In some cases the decisions of the court are final, subject to appeal to the Supreme Court; in others, the court merely reports its findings to Congress or to the department concerned.

CLARK, FORT. A frontier post built in 1813 where Peoria, Ill., now stands. Named in honor of George Rogers Clark, it was an effective restraint upon hostile Indians during the War of 1812. Unoccupied, it was destroyed by Indians in 1819.

CLARK, FORT, IN MISSOURI. See OSAGE, FORT.

CLARK'S NORTHWEST CAMPAIGN. During the early years of the Revolution, the British exercised undisputed control NW of the Ohio R. Their headquarters was Detroit, the key to the control of the fur trade and the Indian tribes. In an effort to protect Kentucky, George Rogers Clark, leader of harassed Kentucky settlers, directed his first blow against the French towns in Illinois. Kaskaskia was occupied in July 1778, and the remaining Illinois towns were easily persuaded to join the rebel standard. British Lt. Gov. Henry Hamilton of Detroit retook Vincennes on December 17; but instead of pushing on, he settled in for the winter. Clark, in turn, took Vincennes in February and thereafter maintained his grip upon the the southern end of the territory, although Detroit was never taken.

CLAYTON ANTITRUST ACT (1914). Outlawed certain monopolistic or restrictive trade practices not specifically covered by the SHERMAN ANTITRUST ACT (1890). Those two acts and the ROBINSON-PATMAN ACT (1936) and the Celler-Kefauver Act (1950) form the basis for federal antitrust activities.

CLAYTON-BULWER TREATY (1850). Provided that England and the United States would jointly control and protect any canal built across the isthmus of Central America. It was superseded in 1901 by the HAY-PAUNCEFOTE TREATY, which permitted the construction of a US-controlled canal.

CLEARINGHOUSES. In 1853 thirty-eight New York City banks organized the first US bank clearinghouse. The principle of clearing had been in use for centuries. It consists basically of matching offsetting items (e.g., bank checks) so that only the net result needs to be dealt with. By the end of the Civil War there were clearinghouses in all major US cities, and by 1920 the number had reached 198. Many clearinghouses assumed certain responsibilities for the banking community until the Federal Reserve period: they conducted examinations of their members, published reports of their condition, and aided those in difficulty by issuing loan certificates. Computerization has profoundly altered the methods of clearinghouses.

CLEVELAND. Port of entry and largest city in Ohio. In 1796 the Connecticut Land Company sent Moses Cleaveland to lay out a "capital" city and survey the Western Reserve lands it had purchased from Connecticut. Cleaveland chose the mouth of the Cuyahoga R, on Lake Erie, as the site. Cleveland gained access to the Atlantic Ocean with completion of the Erie Canal in 1825 and to the Ohio R with completion of the Ohio Canal in 1832. The Ohio Canal offered an outlet for agricultural products and provided the transportation necessary for industrial development, particularly iron and steel manufacturing. Allied industries, especially toolmaking, multiplied in the post-Civil War decades. Oil refining became significant after 1870. Pop.: 573,822 (1980).

CLEVELAND DEMOCRATS. Democrats who during President Grover Cleveland's second administration continued to support him after silverites, high-tariff men, and other dissident elements had broken from his leadership. Their defeat at the Democratic National Convention of 1896 led to the the formation of the National Democratic Party (Gold Democrats).

CLIFF DWELLERS. See ANASAZI.

CLINTON RIOT (Sept. 4, 1875). One of the worst disturbances during Reconstruction in Mississippi. Four whites and an undetermined number of blacks were killed. President Grant refused to send the army, thus allowing the whites to discard Radical Reconstruction.

CLIPPER SHIPS. Long, narrow wooden sailing vessels, with lofty canvas; from about 1843 to 1868, the greatest sailing ship in speed and beauty. Involved in the China trade and, after the discovery of gold in California and Australia, in the transport of prospectors to those areas. It was more than a quarter of a century before the steamship was able to break the record of the fastest clippers.

CLOCK AND WATCH INDUSTRY. The first clockmaker of record in America was Thomas Nash of New Haven in 1638. Throughout the 17th c., eight-day striking clocks with brass movements were produced in Connecticut. By 1745 Benjamin Cheney of East Hartford was producing wooden clocks; there is evidence that these clocks were being made as early as 1715 near New Haven. Benjamin Willard, founder of the Willard Clock dynasty of

Massachusetts, was apprenticed to Cheney. Eli Terry, the first to systematize clock production, commenced business at Plymouth, Connecticut, in 1794. After 1800 he began to produce wooden clocks in quantity. About 1814, Terry designed and manufactured the thirty-hour wooden shelf clock. Seth Thomas and Chauncey Jerome, both of whom worked for Terry, elaborated factory production and carried the industry into its modern phase. In 1825 Jerome designed the bronze looking-glass clock, and developed the commercial possibilities of the thirty-hour rolled-brass movement in 1838. By 1855 almost all common clocks in America were brass. The production of watches in some volume was begun in Massachusetts in the early 19th c. by men who had been apprenticed to the Connecticut clockmakers. Between 1836 and 1841, James and Henry Pitkin of East Hartford, Connecticut, made perhaps 800 movements, using the most elaborate tools known in America up to that time. Shortly before 1850, Aaron Dennison and Edward Howard made plans to manufacture watches on a volume basis, using a system of interchangeable parts. This venture resulted in the formation of Dennison, Howard, and Davis, predecessor of the Waltham Watch Company. An electric clock was patented in 1909, but its importance did not emerge until the 1920s. In the 1970s digital watches and clocks were first mass produced. The most accurate clocks and watches now contain a tiny vibrating quartz crystal.

CLOSED SHOP. A union-management system whereby it is stipulated that employees must be members of a specified union as a precondition for employment. It is opposed to the OPEN SHOP. Closed shop agreements were severely curtailed by the 1947 TAFT-HARTLEY ACT. (See also RIGHT-TO-WORK LAWS.)

CLOTHING INDUSTRY. Until the 19th c., shops produced custom-made clothing for the rich, while the average family wore homemade clothing of plain, durable wool or linsey-woolsey. After the 1830s, textile manufacture became an established industry, and the first clothing factory was established in New York City in 1831. But the output of ready-made clothing was inconsequential compared to the homemade amount. The Civil War demand for uniforms, which coincided with the widespread adoption of the sewing machine, led to standardized sizes. The sewing machine's low cost, portability, and simplicity promoted a decentralized industry based on unskilled labor (women and newly arrived immigrants especially), piecework, and low capital investment. The clothing worker's earnings were highly seasonal. Workers were jammed into tenement rooms with no adequate heat, ventilation, light, or sanitary conditions. In 1896 and 1897, New York State's new factory legislation banned families' living and working in the same quarters, but crowded working conditions persisted. In the early 20th c., efforts began at organizing both the men's and women's wear industries. Eventually most were organized into the Amalgamated Clothing Workers of America (men's wear) and the International Ladies' Garment Workers Union (women's wear). In 1937 they finally achieved industry-wide collective bargaining. Statistics on the growth of the ready-made clothing industry throughout the 20th c. attest to its increased importance in the economy. In the 1980s the United States produced more apparel than any other country in the world, but a substantial portion of ready-made clothing sold to American comsumers came from the Far East.

CLOTURE. Procedure used by the Senate since 1917 to curtail prolonged debate or filibuster in order to reach a final vote. Cloture must be proposed by sixteen senators; if approved, each senator thereafter is limited to one hour of speaking time. Also spelled closure.

CLOVIS CULTURE (or Llano culture). The earliest and most famous of the Late Lithic big-game hunting cultures, located in the High Plains and the Southwest; it existed in the Pleistocene environments with now extinct animal species 11,250 years ago. The relationship between the Clovis culture and contemporary cultures to the E and W is an unsolved puzzle, as is the origin of the culture.

COAHUILA AND TEXAS, STATE OF. On May 7, 1824, the Mexican Congress united the former Spanish provinces of Coahuila and Texas. The union was highly unpopular with the American colonists in Texas and was a cause of the Texas revolution.

COAL. A major US energy source, widespread throughout the country. The US Geological Survey ranks coal by chemical and physical characteristics. Anthracite, with the greatest percentage of carbon, ranks highest; lignite, with the smallest percentage, ranks lowest. Between them is a class called bituminous coals, which are the most abundant and most commonly used in the US. The Survey estimates that the potential recoverable reserves of coal are at least 400 billion tons, possibly much more. US coal production rose rapidly during the 19th c., from an annual production in 1800 of 120,000 tons to 265 million tons by 1900. Total production for 1978 was a bituminous and lignite coal output of about 665 million tons and an anthracite output of about 5 million tons. In the late 1960s, the industry was hampered by stiffening federal and state regulations designed to meet environmental considerations. The energy crisis in the 1970s led to renewed emphasis on coal.

COAL MINING AND ORGANIZED LABOR. Unionization of mine labor began in the 1840s, in response to dangerous working conditions, unsatisfactory wages, truck payments (payment in goods), abuses by company towns and privatized police, introduction of scab labor, blacklisting and yellow dog contracts, and unemployment. Unionization was complicated by the presence of thousands of immigrant workers in the pits; ethnic, cultural, racial, and linguistic barriers; the isolation of miners from one another; their relative immobility; and dual unionism and organizational mistakes. Since 1890, miners have been chiefly represented by the United Mine Workers of America (UMWA). Earlier, abortive unionization attempts were nearly all led by immigrants and, contrary to myth, were mostly moderate and conciliatory, favoring arbitration over strikes. The UMWA, in this tradition, rose to power under two of the most famous and conservative unionists of their generations, John Mitchell and John L. Lewis. In 1980, the UMWA had 245,000 members.

COAST AND GEODETIC SURVEY. Federal bureau, since 1970 absorbed into the National Oceanic and Atmospheric Administration. Congress in 1807 called for a survey of US coasts; F.R Hassler was appointed to supervise the project, as well as supervise US standards of weights and measures. Over the years, the bureau's functions were greatly expanded. Various operations of a geodetic survey were encompassed on land, including basic triangulations. Field data were accumulated for maps. A geodetic connection between the Atlantic, Gulf, and Pacific coasts was made. The Eastern Oblique Arc from the Bay of Fundy to New Orleans, started in 1816, was completed in 1889. The survey participated in several eclipse expeditions and boundary demarcations with Mexico and with Canada. Gravity observations have been conducted in various parts of the world. Hydrographic observations furnish navigational information and nautical charts. Aeronautical charts are produced; topographic operations are carried on along the coastline; hydrography and wire-drag surveys are made; ocean current studies, tidal observations and predictions, and certain features of oceanography are given attention. The geodetic survey itself investigates the size and shape of the earth. Geomagnetic studies determine the direction and intensity of the earth's magnetic field, and astronomical observations determine time, latitude, longitude, and azimuth in the mapping of stations used by the survey.

COAST GUARD, UNITED STATES. One of the armed forces and principal federal agency for marine safety and maritime law enforcement; operates under the Department of Transportation except during hostilities, when it is part of the navy. In 1790 Congress authorized Alexander Hamilton, secretary of the treasury, to construct and operate ten small cutters to ensure the collection of customs duties on imports. During the Quasi-War with France, there being no other US naval force, Congress in 1797 authorized the president to cause the cutters "to defend the seacoast and to repel any hostility to their vessels and commerce." The service soon began to distinguish itself as a fighting force. After the establishment of the navy (1798), Congress decreed that the cutters "cooperate with the Navy ... whenever the President shall so direct." In 1967, the Coast Guard was relocated from the Treasury Department to the new Department of Transportation. The modern Coast Guard performs a multitude of duties: search and rescue; maintaining ocean stations to furnish meteorological data; military readiness; enforcing laws of the high seas and customs, immigration, and conservation laws; merchant marine and boating safety; aids to navigation, such as lighthouses and buoys; ice-breaking; port security; oceanography; and research.

COASTING TRADE. Until the coming of the railroad ca. 1850, shipping along the coasts was the principal means of transportation and communication between sections of the new country. Manufactured goods of the Northeast were exchanged for the cotton and tobacco of the South, while agricultural products of the Mississippi Valley came to the Atlantic coast by way of New Orleans. Even after the coming of the railroad, such bulk cargoes as coal, lumber, ice, iron, steel, and oil were still shipped by sea. Colonial coasting trade was reserved to British and American vessels by the Navigation Acts of 1651 and 1660; with the formation of the Federal Union the policy was continued, a prohibitive tax being placed on foreign-built and owned ships in 1789, followed by their total exclusion from coastwise competition under the Navigation Act of 1817.

COASTWISE STEAMSHIP LINES. The first regular steamship lines operated in the sheltered waters of Long Island Sound and between Boston and Maine about 1825. Local services were established in the Gulf of Mexico in 1835; a regular line from New York to Charleston, Havana, New Orleans, and the Isthmus of Panama opened in 1848. In 1849 the route from Panama to the West Coast began. Competition from railroads and overland carriers resulted in the withdrawal of most service by 1937.

COCHISE INCIDENT. See APACHE PASS EXPEDITION.

CODE NAPOLÉON. The unification and simplification of French laws under Napoleon Bonaparte's direction, promulgated in 1804 as the French civil code. It served as model for the civil laws of Orleans Territory, and, much revised, remains the basic law of Louisiana.

CODE NOIR (Black Code). French edict of 1724 fixing the legal status of slaves in Louisiana. It also called for the expulsion of Jews from the colony and prohibited any religious creed other than Roman Catholicism. Essential provisions of the code remained in force in Louisiana until 1803, and many were embodied in later American Black Codes.

CODE, UNITED STATES. Publication of the general and permanent laws of Congress, in volumes arranged by fifty subject titles. The handiest source for statutory law in force at a given time.

CODES OF FAIR COMPETITION. The agreements that formed the basis of the NATIONAL RECOVERY ADMINISTRATION, established in 1933 as part of Franklin D. Roosevelt's New Deal economic recovery program.

COD FISHERIES. Fishermen from Spain, France, and England were attracted by the rich cod fisheries lying off the North American coast beginning in the 16th c. Within a few years of Capt. John Smith's successful fishing venture in 1614 off New England, fishing colonies were established in Massachusetts and Maine. France's defeats in the New World left England and its American colonies with most of the fishing privileges. Codfishing suffered severely from the Revolutionary War, but the US secured extensive fishing privileges from England in the 1783 peace treaty. The Peace of Ghent (1814) did not provide for continuance of US fishing privileges in British colonial waters, and the fisheries question remained a sore spot in Anglo-American relations until finally settled by the Hague Tribunal of Arbitration in 1910. During the 19th c., the European market declined, but the domestic market more than offset this loss. From ca. 1885 cod fisheries began to decline in relation to other American fisheries.

COERCION ACTS (Restraining Acts or Intolerable Acts). Four measures passed by the English Parliament in 1774, partly in retaliation for such incidents as the Boston Tea Party. They reduced Massachusetts to a crown colony; provided that judges, soldiers, and revenue officers indicted for murder in Massachusetts should be taken to England for trial; and removed all obstacles to the billeting of troops in Massachusetts.

COETUS-CONFERENTIE CONTROVERSY. A conflict in the 18th century between two factions in the Dutch Reformed churches. Two opposing assemblies, the *coetus* and the *conferentie*, evolved. In 1771 a plan of union brought from Holland reconciled the parties and established virtually complete independence of the church in America.

COEUR D'ALENE MISSION. A Roman Catholic Indian mission established (1842) near Cataldo, Idaho. In 1877 the mission was removed to the vicinity of Desmet, in present Benewah County.

COEUR D'ALENE RIOTS (1892). Clashes between union and nonunion workers (protected by the mine owners) in the lead and silver mines of N Idaho. A mill was dynamited, and a pitched battle was fought. State and federal troops took charge and martial law was proclaimed.

COFFEEHOUSES. Popular gathering places in the major ports and towns of the colonies. Such prominent coffeehouses as the London Coffee House (Philadelphia) and the Merchants' Coffee House (New York) assumed active roles in 18th-c. business and political life.

COFFEE'S TRADING POSTS. Two posts maintained by Holland Coffee and others in the 1830s, one on the N bank of Red R and the other on the same river above the mouth of Walnut Bayou in Oklahoma. Coffee exercised a strong influence over the Indians and ransomed numbers of white captives brought from Texas.

COHENS V. VIRGINIA, 6 Wheaton 264 (1821). The Supreme Court upheld its right to review the judgment of state courts in criminal cases.

COINAGE. The English denied their American colonies the right to mint coins, causing a severe shortage. Backward or poor areas were forced to use wampum, beaver skins, and other commodity money. Elsewhere the lack of an adequate amount of English specie was compensated by French, Dutch, Portuguese, and above all Spanish coins. The present US coinage system was established by the Coinage Act of 1792. The decimal system was decided on, the world's first. The dollar was divided into 100 "cents" (a new term) and also into half-dollars; quarter-dollars; "dismes" or dimes; and half-dismes. The actual coins were to be of silver, except for the copper cents and half-cents. In addition there were to be gold coins as multiples: "eagles," or ten-dollar pieces; half-eagles; and quarter-eagles. This gold-silver ratio was, however, difficult to maintain and led to the undervaluation of gold. For three decades after 1806 no silver dollars were coined; the many half-dollars that were struck tended to be hoarded or exported. By 1850 California gold was driving up the price of silver so rapidly that there was a severe decline in the already insufficient amount of silver coinage. After 1851 Congress authorized various mixed coinages, including a mixture of silver and copper, and copper and nickel coins. Gold production in California and Australia made it easy to supply the country with coins of large denomination, including "double eagles" ($20). As the use of notes increased, the volume of coinage shrank. Various laws attempted to force more silver into circulation by requiring the government to buy set amounts of silver each year. But apart from regions in the West, silver dollars never became popular except when the market price of silver jumped. Gold coins were removed from circulation after the United States went off the gold standard in the 1930s. In 1964–65, all silver coins were replaced by nickel-clad copper coins. A $1 coin with the image of Susan B. Anthony was introduced in 1979, but it proved so unpopular that it was abandoned in 1981.

COLD HARBOR, BATTLE OF (June 3, 1864). Following failures to smash and outflank Robert E. Lee at Spotsylvania, U.S. Grant on May 20 directed the Army of the Potomac SE on a turning movement. Lee retired behind the North Anna R. Grant continued sideslipping toward Richmond until the Confederates stood on a six-mile front without reserves.Grant's assault against well-entrenched lines cost 5,600 Union casualties and failed completely. Grant dug in, held Lee in position until June 12, then resumed sideslipping, and, crossing the James R, threatened Richmond through Petersburg.

COLD SPRING HARBOR BIOLOGICAL LABORATORY. Founded in 1890 at Cold Spring Harbor, New York, as a summer school in the biological sciences. As the Cold Spring Harbor Laboratory for Quantitative Biology (since 1963), it became one of the world's foremost centers for biological research.

COLD WAR. The struggle for world supremacy between the US and the Soviet Union following World War II. It was waged by diplomatic means, propaganda, and threats of force, rather than by outright military force—except in limited, local wars fought largely by proxies of the great powers—because the strains imposed by World War II and the threat of nuclear devastation deterred recourse to a "hot war." The US government has seen the hostility between the American and Soviet blocs and the American containment policy as the necessary results of a Soviet intention to impose Communist power wherever non-Communist weakness permitted. The USSR, on the other hand, has blamed the cold war on US imperialism. The threat of massive nuclear retaliation may well have been indispensable to keeping the contest merely cold as the superpowers confronted each other through the Korean War and a series of Berlin, Middle Eastern, and Eastern European crises in the 1950s. In the 1960s, however, not only did the end of the polarization of world power help force both superpowers into new diplomatic postures, but each superpower found habitual cold war policies leading it into frustration—the Soviet Union in the Cuban missile crisis of 1962 and the United States in Vietnam. As a result, more flexible policies and a Soviet-American détente could more readily recommend themselves. Détente culminated in the Helsinki agreements on European security and cooperation in 1975. In the late 1970s, US-Soviet relations again deteriorated, and during the Reagan administration reached a new low.

COLLECTIVE BARGAINING. A form of labor negotiation whereby both interested parties attempt to settle differences voluntarily. In the US it is the accepted method for settling labor disputes and is replaced by conciliation and compulsory arbitration only after it has failed.

COLLEGES AND UNIVERSITIES. American colleges and universities began in 1636 with Harvard College (now University). Other colonial colleges were the College of William and Mary, chartered in 1693; the Collegiate School (Yale University), founded in 1701; the College of New Jersey (Princeton University), chartered in 1746; King's College (Columbia University) chartered in 1754; the College, Academy, and Charitable School of Philadelphia (University of Pennsylvania), chartered in 1755; the College of Rhode Island (Brown University), chartered in 1764; Queen's College (Rutgers University), chartered in 1766; and Dartmouth College, chartered in 1769. At first, the colleges had a Protestant character, but with the advent of the Enlightenment the curriculum was modified by the addition of medicine, law, the sciences, and modern languages. State-controlled colleges and universities appeared in Georgia, North Carolina, and Tennessee by 1800. After the Civil War, the number of colleges and universities continued to increase. New institutions opened for women, blacks, American Indians, and members of various faiths. The opening of the Johns Hopkins University (1876) brought German standards of research and scholarship to American higher education. In 1862 the Morrill Act created the great land-grant colleges and universities, which have specialized in agriculture and engineering. During the 20th c., enrollment in colleges and universities climbed sharply upward, but in the late 1970s the rate of increase slowed, a reflection of birth rate statistics. By the 1980s, 43 percent of the 2,900 colleges and universities were under governmental (mostly state) control and accounted for 75 percent of the total enrollment. The private sector comprises institutions under denominational direction and those under the governance of self-perpetuating secular boards of trustees. A number of denominational colleges, though, have secularized the composition of their boards of trustees so as to qualify for much needed public funds. Colleges and universities by the 1980s faced increasing financial difficulties. The question of equal opportunity remains perplexing and controversial; although barriers to higher education for racial and ethnic minorities and for women have fallen, complaints of discrimination continue.

Black Colleges. A number of private and public institutions have drawn all or the majority of their students from among blacks. The private ones began with Lincoln University in Pennsylvania in 1854 and Wilberforce University in Ohio in 1856. Still extant in 1980 were Hampton Institute (1868), Fisk University (1866), Talladega College (1867), Howard University (1867), Atlanta University (1865), Johnson C. Smith University (1867), St. Augustine's College (1867), and Tuskegee Institute (1881). State-run colleges for blacks were established mostly in the 20th c. Although all state-run colleges have been legally integrated since the 1950s, many of these formerly all-black institutions still exist with predominantly black student bodies . The enrollment of black colleges in general, both private and public, has increased, even as blacks entered institutions from which they had previously been excluded.

Denominational Colleges. Of the approximately 900 colleges established in America by 1861, only 182 had survived. Most of these were founded by the major denominations: Presbyterians, Methodists, Baptists, Congregationalists, Roman Catholics, and Episcopalians. After the Civil War the church colleges' prominent position in American higher education was weakened by the impact of Darwinian ideas, industrial growth, development of modern science and technology, spread of humanistic and antireligious thought, declining financial status, and competition with prestigious secular institutions.

COLLOT'S JOURNEY. In 1796, French Gen. Victor Collot made an extensive journey to the Ohio R settlements and the Illinois country and along the Mississippi R to New Orleans. His journal shows an appreciation of the potentialities of the American West.

COLOMBIA–US CANAL CONTROVERSY. In 1903 the Colombian government authorized the US to build a canal across Panama (then part of Colombia); but the Colombian senate failed to ratify the agreement. The province of Panama, resentful over this failure, revolted, and with US aid established its independence. The US at once made a canal treaty with the infant republic (See HAY–BUNAU-VAR-ILLA TREATY). Colombia repeatedly demanded amends. Finally, in 1921, the United States paid Colombia $25 million.

COLONIAL AGENT. A representative of the colonies sent to England, who formed an indispensable link between the mother country and colony. In the 17th c. agents went to England only on special missions, usually representing the colony before the Board of Trade and the Privy Council. By the 18th c., when the business of colonial administration had greatly increased, the agent remained at his post year after year.

COLONIAL ASSEMBLIES. The first, the Virginia House of Burgesses, was called in 1619. It was composed of the governor, his council, and two burgesses elected for each of the towns, plantations, and hundreds. In the late 17th c. the elected element separated from the parent assembly, resulting in a bicameral legislative body. Plymouth colony set up a popular assembly of all qualified freemen. With the growth of out-settlements this evolved into a representative bicameral body. In Massachusetts Bay, Gov. John Winthrop and his supporters tried to concentrate legislative authority in the Court of Assistants. This failed, and a representative bicameral system eventually evolved. In Rhode Island, Providence, Portsmouth, Newport, and Warwick were empowered to initiate legislation that was thereupon referred to the assembly. Connecticut had the General Court, which was both a representative body and a primary assembly. The latter feature disappeared in the 18th c. in favor of local election of colonial officials. The Maryland proprietor, Cecil Calvert, Lord Baltimore, called an assembly of freemen. He attempted to establish the principle that the proprietor alone might initiate legislation, and sent over drafts of measures. The assembly rejected them, claiming sole powers of initiation, and passed a number of bills framed by its own members. Baltimore finally admitted the competence of the assembly to initiate laws but insisted they be submitted to him for approval. Lawmaking processes in Carolina were confused by the divergent aims of the eight proprietors and the settlers. The proprietors attempted to enforce the feudal Fundamental Constitutions with its extraordinarily complicated lawmaking machinery, designed to guarantee proprietarial control of legislation. New York under the Duke of York for many years had no popularly elected body. With the retirement of Gov. Edmund Andros to England in 1680, the settlers refused to pay imposts. The Duke of York granted an assembly, but the laws passed by the deputies were never ratified; under James II, assemblies were forbidden but reappeared under William III. Pennsylvania was provided with a popularly elected assembly. After the withdrawal of the charter of Massachusetts Bay in 1684, consolidation took place under the Dominion of New England; the assemblies were suppressed and lawmaking powers were centered in the appointed Dominion council. New York, East New Jersey, and West New Jersey, the last two with popularly elected assemblies, were also embodied in the Dominion before it collapsed in 1689. During the 18th c. the assemblies frequently came into collision with the governors, as a rule leaving the assemblies in a strongly entrenched position. With the approach of the Revolution, breaches took place between the assemblies and their governors in all but the two corporate colonies (Connecticut and Rhode Island).

COLONIAL CHARTERS. Royal charters represented the king's authorization of colonization under private enterprise. Charters to trading companies vested powers of government in the company in England, which determined officers, laws, and ordinances necessary for the colony. In proprietary charters, authority was granted to the lord proprietor. The charters of Connecticut and Rhode Island called for a government administered by governor, council, and house of representatives, with the house chosen directly, the governor indirectly, by the people. In the late 17th c. the king tried to substitute the royal province for corporation and proprietary governments. By 1776 there remained only two proprietary provinces, Maryland and Pennsylvania, and two corporation colonies, Connecticut and Rhode Island. Massachusetts operated under a charter but was governed in the 18th c. as a royal province.

COLONIAL COMMERCE. Several forms existed. There was the two-way commerce, between a colony and England, between two colonies, or between a colony and a West Indian port. Triangular trade was common, as between a colony, the African coast, and the West Indies, typified by Rhode Island's trade in rum, slaves, and molasses. Commerce was carried on, as a rule, in American-built ships. The two greatest commercial centers were Boston and Philadelphia. Colonial commerce involved not only barter, specie transactions in Spanish or Portuguese coins, and bills of exchange, but credit extensions on a great scale. Restrictions abounded. American woolens and beaver hats, for example, could not enter into commerce; certain other products could be carried directly only to the mother country or to another colony. Ships were required to have a British or colonial registry, to be commanded by British or colonial officers, to sail under British colors, and to import European commodities only through a British port, with the exception of a few specified articles.

COLONIAL COUNCILS. Existed in all the colonies. In general they represented the same control as the governor. They were appointed variously by the crown or the proprietor or were elected. They acted as the upper house of the legislature, and together with the governor, formed a supreme court of appeals in civil cases. Many of the governor's acts could be carried out only with the approval of the council.

COLONIAL CURRENCY. See COINAGE; MONEY.

COLONIAL DAMES OF AMERICA. Society of women, founded 1890, descended from ancestors who came to America prior to 1750. Membership in 1980 was about 2,000.

COLONIAL GOVERNORS. Chief civil officers in the American colonies before the Revolution, variously named by the king, the proprietor (and approved by the king), or (in chartered colonies) elected. Instructions issued in the king's name by the Privy Council to governors of royal colonies touched on nearly every subject involved in colonial government, but opposition by the colonists resulted often in the instructions not being enforced.

COLONIAL JUDICIARY. Every colony created a judiciary by act of the assembly and followed the general pattern of English procedure, including a system of local courts to try petty offenses; a county court presided over by a traveling superior judge; a superior court presided over by a chief justice; an attorney general. In the royal provinces the chief justice and the judges of the superior court were at first appointed directly by the crown. Governors were authorized to fill vacancies when they occurred. The death of George II in 1760 terminated all judicial commissions. The Board of Trade insisted that all renewals should be "at the pleasure of the Crown." This deprived Englishmen in America of rights guaranteed to Englishmen in England, and is one of the specific acts of tyranny charged against George III in the Declaration of Independence.

COLONIAL PLANS OF UNION. The separate founding of the colonies, coupled with difficulties of travel, prevented effective union until the Revolution. However, many proposals for union grew out of the common problems faced by the colonies. The chief plans, which varied widely in origin and the number of colonies to be included, were as follows: 1. The United Colonies of New England, 1643–84. Massachusetts Bay, Plymouth, Connecticut, and New Haven, united for frontier defense. 2. Dominion of New England, 1688. The British crown made Sir Edmund Andros governor-general of all the New England colonies, New York, and East and West Jersey. 3. Intercolonial Congress, 1689–91. New York, Massachusetts, Plymouth, and Connecticut entered a temporary military league for frontier defense. 4. William Penn's "Briefe and Plaine Scheam" for Union, 1697, a proposal for a loose confederation. 5. Union under the Earl of Bellomont, 1698–1701, governor of New York, Massachusetts, and New Hampshire, and commander of the military forces of Connecticut, Rhode Island, and the Jerseys. 6. Hamilton's Plan, 1699, for frontier defense and producton of naval supplies for the Royal Navy proposed by the deputy-governor of Pennsylvania. An intercolonial assembly was to levy a poll tax to finance the work, to be done by British regulars. 7. "A Virginian's Plan of Union," 1701, advocated uniting the colonies under a congress and governor-general. 8. Robert Livingston's Plan, 1701, proposed that the colonies be grouped into three units coordinated by the Council of Trade for frontier defense. 9. Earl of Stair's Plan, 1721, was to include all the continental colonies and the British West Indies. 10. The Lords of Trade Plan, 1721, was essentially a brief outline of the Stair plan. 11. Daniel Coxe's Plan, 1722, proposed a union of all the continental colonies under one governor, represented by a lieutenant in each colony. 12. The Kennedy-Franklin Plan, 1751, was published by Archibald Kennedy, receiver-general of New York, in a pamphlet on Indian trade and frontier defense. Benjamin Franklin added some details that closely resembled his later Albany Plan. 13. The Albany Plan, 1754. Largely the work of Franklin, it called for an intercolonial council with membership apportioned according to wealth and population. The president-general was to be appointed by the crown. Control of Indian affairs and frontier defense was to be administered by this royal officer and his council.

COLONIAL POLICY, BRITISH. The earliest English colonial policies are embodied in the 16th-c. patents to Sir Humphrey Gilbert and Sir Walter Raleigh; in 1606, patents were granted to the London and Plymouth companies of Virginia which embodied direct crown control; in 1624 Virginia became first "royal colony" under a system of government that permitted the survival of the colonial assembly. In 1629 appeared the corporate colony of Massachusetts Bay with a charter that permitted the transfer of the government of the company to the New World; 1632 saw the proprietaryship of Maryland. Thus, three types of colonial government appeared; royal, proprietary, and charter. With the outbreak of the English Civil War, the Long Parliament assumed control from the crown. Various regulations were passed favoring English shipping and manufactures. The Restoration added measures beginning with the Navigation Act of 1696. Colonial policy in the 18th c. was characterized by efforts to reduce the colonies to a uniform type, the royal colony, and by increased restrictions on colonial enterprise. An important modification of policy came with growing menace of French competition. Side by side with mercantilism, modern imperialism made its appearance. In order to secure direct revenue from the colonies, Parliament passed the Stamp Act of 1765 and the Townshend Acts of 1767, helping to bring on the Revolution.

COLONIAL POLICY OF THE UNITED STATES. See INSULAR POSSESSIONS.

COLONIAL SETTLEMENTS. Sir Humphrey Gilbert landed on Newfoundland in 1584. Sir Walter Raleigh in 1585 settled a few colonists on Roanoke Island (Carolina coast), but failed to keep the venture alive.(See RALEIGH'S LOST COLONY.) The close of war with Spain in 1604 freed England to turn to America. Joint-stock companies, combining capital and credit, entered into colonization. In 1607 the Plymouth Company tried a settlement on the Kennebec R (Maine), the London Company on the James R (Virginia). A rigorous winter and the death of the chief promoter soon sent the Kennebec settlers away. The London Company persisted. During its existence about 5,500 emigrants left England for Virginia. By 1625 there were only a thousand survivors. In 1624 the Dutch West India Company founded New Amsterdam and Fort Orange (Albany). In 1638 the New Sweden Company began Fort Christina on the Delaware (taken by the Dutch in 1655). The economic motive was not the only factor in colonial enterprise. The primary motive of the Pilgrims who planted the colony of Plymouth in 1620 was to establish a city of God. Similar motives led to the founding of Massachusetts, Rhode Island, and Connecticut. By 1700 the Bay province alone had over 50,000 people. Maryland owned its genesis to Lord Baltimore, who desired a refuge for Catholics. The circle of English colonies was completed in 1664 by the conquest of New Netherland, renamed New York and granted to the duke of York. He subgranted New Jersey to Sir George Carteret and Lord John Berkeley. Carolina, granted to eight men by charter in 1663, divided into North Carolina and South Carolina, settled by discontented planters from Barbados and persecuted Protestants from France and England. The Quakers established their own colonies on the Delaware. In 1674 Berkeley sold West Jersey, which the Quakers settled along the Delaware R at Burlington. East Jersey, purchased from the Carteret estate in 1680, went to a large board in which the Quakers were prominent. In 1681 William Penn received a charter for Pennsylvania, where he tried a "Holy Experiment" in Quaker principles. The province became a haven for the persecuted, welcoming English, Welsh, and Irish Quakers, and Germans. Delaware, granted to Penn by the duke of York and governed at first as part of Pennsylvania, in 1704 became a province with Penn as proprietor. Georgia came into existence in 1732 in response to humanitarian motives, harboring debtors from English jails.

COLONIAL SOCIETY. English settlers brought traditional concepts of the social order, in which deference was due the upper levels of society. But in America an abundance of land and a shortage of manpower created the opportunity for upward mobility and a large, open middle class of propertied farmers, artisans, merchants, and professionals. Newly freed indentured servants and casual laborers, the bottom rank of colonial society, were not permanently locked in that position. The instability resulting from such mobility, coupled with the attempt to tighten imperial authority after the Restoration, caused a series of violent challenges to established authority, but the indigenous elite reestablished their social and political leadership. By the 18th c., non-English emigrants were bringing with them a diversity of cultural, social, and religious ideas, a phenomenon that presaged the great influxes of the 19th c.

COLONIAL WARS. America's natural resources and the supposed advantages of controlling American markets led Europeans to seek vast holdings, and economic rivalries among the colonials themselves were intensified by racial and religious antagonisms. Louis XIV gave little practical support to offensives on America; thus, in KING WILLIAM'S WAR (1689–97), local French leaders had to resort to Indian allies in ruthless border raids. Similar raids were utilized, chiefly by the French, in QUEEN ANNE'S WAR (1702–13), KING GEORGE'S WAR (1744–48), and the FRENCH AND INDIAN WAR (1754–63); and by the English against the Spanish in the WAR OF JENKINS' EAR (1739–1742).

COLONIZATION MOVEMENT. Aimed at sending all or part of the black population in the United States to colonize Africa or Central America. As early as 1776, Thomas Jefferson proposed a plan to colonize US blacks in Africa. In 1815 Paul Cuffe, a black merchant, transported thirty-eight persons to Sierra Leone at his own expense. In 1817 the AMERI-

CAN COLONIZATION SOCIETY was established. It sent free blacks to Sierra Leone until 1821, when land that eventually became Liberia was purchased for the settlement. Various schemes emerged throughout the 19th c. and into the 20th. Most came to little, including the most famous, Marcus Garvey's "BACK-TO AF-RICA" MOVEMENT of the 1920s.

COLORADO. Visited by Francisco Vásquez de Coronado in 1541; Juan de Ulibarri took formal possession for Spain in 1706. Treaty of Paris (1763) recognized Spanish claims, but W Colorado was retroceded to France in 1800, and through the Louisiana Purchase in 1803, the US acquired it. The Spanish part went to Mexico and after the Mexican War and the Treaty of Guadalupe Hidalgo (1848) to the US. Trading posts were the first fixed habitations of white men in Colorado. The first towns in Colorado were founded in the 1850s by Spanish settlers from New Mexico, who developed irrigated agriculture and grazing. Need for protection from Indians caused the establishment in 1852 of Fort Massachusetts. In 1858 the Pikes Peak gold rush resulted in widespread settlement. Jefferson Territory became Colorado Territory in 1861. Colorado troops sustained the Union in the Civil War. Increased population helped bring statehood on Aug. 1, 1876. The range cattle industry, the extension of railroads, the discovery of great silver lodes at Leadville and Aspen, and the smelting industry furthered prosperity. Demonetization of silver and the panic of 1893 brought economic distress. Abrupt reduction in silver output was offset by the rise of the great gold camp of Cripple Creek. Coal and petroleum are also important. By 1960, farm products were valued at about thirty-five times the output of precious metals. Manufacturing now the leading industry. Colorado, with fifty-five named peaks higher than 14,000 feet, has a mean elevation of 6,800 feet. Scenic beauty and climate have fostered tourism as a leading industry. Pop.: 2,888,834 (1980).

COLORADO COAL STRIKES (1903–04; 1913–14). Caused by refusal of the mine operators in Trinidad, Colorado, to recognize the right to organize. Troops were called in. In 1904 the strikers returned to work without having won any material advantages, but in 1914 they won more satisfactory working conditions.

COLORADO RIVER PROJECTS. The Colorado R Compact (1922) apportioned the waters of the Colorado among the states of Arizona, California, Nevada, Colorado, New Mexico, Utah, and Wyoming (although Arizona failed to ratify the plan). In 1930 a program to coordinate Lower Basin power and water use was initiated by the US government. Initial operating contracts included the use of Hoover (Boulder) Dam power in California, reservation of waters for Arizona, and construction of the All-American Canal from hydroelectric-power revenues. Nine major and many smaller dams have been built, as well as reservoirs and water-diversion works. There have been long-standing differences between the Upper and Lower Basin states concerning release of water from the Upper Basin. The Colorado R Basin Project Act (1968) provided a ten-year moratorium on studies of any plan to import water into the Colorado R basin. Major additional facilities authorized by this act are the Central Arizona Project; the Southern Nevada Water Project; and the Dixie Project, which will supply southern Utah. Serious water deficiencies are predicted for the Lower Basin.

COLORADO SPRINGS. Second largest city in Colorado, situated in the E Rocky Mountains. A leading tourist city, it is the home of the US Air Force Academy and several other colleges. Established as a town in 1891, when silver and gold were discovered at Cripple Creek.

COLT SIX-SHOOTER. Invented by Samuel Colt and first manufactured in 1836, it revolutionized warfare and was an important link between the muzzle-loading musket and the magazine rifles and machine guns of today. Colt's original company failed in 1842. A few Colt arms used by army officers and Texas Rangers proved the worth of the "revolving pistol," and a supply was ordered by the government in January 1847. The first few thousand were made at the plant of Eli Whitney, son of the inventor, in New Haven, Conn. These .44-caliber revolvers soon became the standard of the US army and the Texas Rangers. Large quantities of Colt arms were used during the Civil War by both sides. Colt revolvers were originally made to use loose powder and lead bullets, the powder being ignited by a percussion cap. From ca. 1870, envelope cartridges, enclosing powder and bullet, were used until the advent of metallic ammunition.

COLUMBIA. One symbol of the US is a goddess-like figure called Columbia. First used in the 19th c., she has often been used on coins and stamps.

COLUMBIA. The capital and largest city of South Carolina and home of the University of South Carolina. Its industries include the manufacture of textiles, clothing, building materials, electronic equipment,and plastic products. The city was burned by the Union forces of Gen. W.T. Sherman on Feb. 17, 1865. Pop. 99,296 (1980).

COLUMBIA FUR COMPANY. Founded by Joseph Renville ca. 1822 and operated in the countries of the Sioux and Omaha, as far W as the Missouri R and as far E as the Great Lakes. After ca. 1827 part of the Astor American Fur Company.

COLUMBIAN EXPOSITION. See WORLD'S CO-LUMBIAN EXPOSITION.

COLUMBIA RIVER TREATY (1961) A water use agreement between the US and Canada. The construction of the Libby Dam on the Kootenay branch of the Columbia R (N Montana) was completed within five years after joint ratification. Canada built four dams in British Columbia. They supply hydroelectric power to Washington, Oregon, Idaho, Montana, British Columbia, and Alberta.

COLUMBIA UNIVERSITY. Private, nonsectarian institution, in New York City. Founded by royal charter as King's College in 1754, renamed Columbia College after the Revolution. The college expanded into a university in the 19th c. and moved to its present site on Morningside Heights in 1897. Barnard College offers women a four-year liberal arts curriculum.

COLUMBUS. Capital of Ohio and a a major industrial center: aircraft, auto parts, machinery, and coal-mining and oil-well equipment. Ohio State University is located there. The state capital since 1812. Grew rapidly with improved transportation, particularly the Ohio and Erie Canal (1831) and the Cumberland (National) Road (1833). Pop.: 564,871 (1980).

COMANCHE. Indian tribe of the Plains; dominated SW Texas and SW Oklahoma from their acquisition of the horse in the early 18th c. until their reservation confinement in the late 19th c. By 1719, independent bands occupied a section of SW Kansas on the N bank of the Arkansas R. Pushing south, they expelled the Jicarilla and Lipan Apache. The Comanche thereafter regarded the Apache as enemies. They also warred against Spanish and American settlers. Subdued and located with the Kiowa on two Texas reservations in 1854, ceding these in 1867 in favor of an Oklahoma parcel. Further uprisings in 1874–75 led to settlement on reservations.

COMBINE. A farm machine that combines harvesting and threshing. Developed by 1828 but not perfected until the 1870s. Between 1870 and 1873 the US Patent Office recorded the invention of six harvester-threshers; and by 1880 the combine was commercially established.

COMIC STRIPS. See NEWSPAPERS.

COMMERCE. See COLONIAL COMMERCE; TRADE.

COMMERCE, COURT OF. Created by Congress Mar. 4, 1913. Jurisdiction covered all civil suits arising under the Interstate Commerce Act and allied legislation. When Judge Robert W. Archbald, was impeached, convicted of corruption, and removed from the bench, Congress dissolved the court, Oct. 22, 1913.

COMMERCE, DEPARTMENT OF. Created 1913. The secretary of commerce is appointed by the president and is a member of the cabinet. The original mission of the department was "to foster, promote, and develop the foreign and domestic commerce" of the US. Now participates in the creation of national policy, promoting progressive business policies and growth; assisting states, communities, and individuals to achieve economic stability; improving use of the physical environment; assuring effective use and growth of scientific and technical resources; and acquiring, analyzing, and disseminating information concerning the nation and the economy.

COMMERCE CLAUSE. Article 1, Section 8, Paragraph 3, of the US Constitution gives Congress the power "to regulate Commerce with foreign Nations, and among the several States, and with the Indian Tribes." Beginning in 1824 (with *Ogden* v. *Utah*), the clause has given Congress, and thereby the federal government, almost complete control over all aspects of commerce. The Sherman Antitrust Act (1890) found constitutional justification in the clause, as it seemed to afford broad federal authority to prohibit combinations in restraint of trade and general market monopolization. The Supreme Court, however, continued to deny jurisdiction to the federal government in crucial areas; and regulation-minded Progressive leaders of the early 20th c. sought to expand the sweep of the clause. The Supreme Court itself, starting in 1913, began to expand its meaning. In the Shreveport Rate Case (1914), it took the position that "when interstate and intrastate activities are so related that the government of the one involves the control of the other, it is Congress and not the states that is entitled to prescribe the final and dominant rule." The Progressives also sought to use the clause to evolve a national police power, through far-reaching social and economic legislation. The court generally sustained such legislation. The major exception was the case of child labor legislation; the Court returned to limiting federal power. On this broad judicial view of the clause, New Dealers based the National Industrial Recovery Act (1933) and other broad economic measures. Judicial response was hostile and entailed a sharp return to older formulas. Franklin D. Roosevelt eventually induced the Court to embrace broad commerce precedents. In *National Labor Relations Board* v. *Jones and Laughlin Steel Corporation*(1937), the Court not only rejected the whole battery of narrow commerce formulas but also validated the clause as the principal constitutional base for later New Deal programs, authorizing broad federal control of labor relations, wages and hours, agriculture, business, and navigable streams. In the Civil Rights Act of 1964, Congress banned racial discrimination in all pub-lic accommodations. The constitutional foundations for it were the commerce and equal protection clauses of the Fourteenth Amendment.

COMMERCE COMMISSION. See INTERSTATE COMMERCE COMMISSION.

COMMERCIAL CABLE COMPANY. Founded in 1883 as principal competitor of WESTERN UNION. In 1884 laid two transatlantic cables. Land lines were operated in conjunction with the POSTAL TELEGRAPH COMPANY.

COMMERCIAL COMMITTEE. A principal standing committee of the Continental Congress, set up in 1775 to purchase powder. Functions gradually enlarged until it became the chief agency of Congress in the extensive business of exchanging American products for foreign arms.

COMMISSION GOVERNMENT. System of municipal government in which an elected commission serves both as executive and as legislature. Developed in Galveston, Texas, in 1900; by 1917 about 500 cities had adopted the system. Its popularity waned, and by the early 1980s only about one hundred municipalities had commission governments.

COMMISSION MERCHANTS AND FACTORS. Agents employed to purchase or sell goods on commission. System introduced soon after dissolution of the Virginia Company (1624) and probably was of most importance 1815 to 1860. Crops were produced in the South for markets in the Northeast and Europe, and commission merchants advanced money to planters in return for which products were consigned to them for sale. Development of commodity exchanges and expanded banking services ended the dominant position of the commission merchant.

COMMITTEE FOR INDUSTRIAL ORGANIZATION. See AMERICAN FEDERATION OF LABOR—CONGRESS OF INDUSTRIAL ORGANIZATIONS.

COMMITTEE GOVERNMENT IN THE REVOLUTION. See REVOLUTIONARY COMMITTEES.

COMMITTEE OF THE STATES. The Articles of Confederation empowered Congress to appoint a committee consisting of one delegate from each state to sit in the recess of Congress and to exercise such powers as Congress, "by the consent of nine states, shall from time to time think expedient to vest them with." The committee was called into existence only once (1784).

COMMITTEE OF THE WHOLE. Parliamentary device employed by the House of Representatives to expedite its deliberations. In effect, the House temporarily constitutes itself a committee, operating under more flexible rules; a quorum consists of only 100 members, and legislation is open to freer debate and amendment. All actions of the Committee must be approved by the House itself.

COMMITTEE OF THIRTEEN (1850). A select committee of the Senate set up to consider legislation pertaining to the slavery issue. The committee recommended two bills: an omnibus bill providing for the admission of California as a free state, the territorial organization of Utah and New Mexico, a settlement of the disputed Texas boundary, and a bill to end the slave trade in the District of Columbia. A lengthy amendment to the fugitive slave law was also submitted.

COMMITTEE OF THIRTEEN (1860). A select committee of the Senate constituted to consider proposed legislation concerning slavery in the territories. It was unable to agree on any recommendations.

COMMITTEE OF THIRTY-THREE (1860). A select committee of the House of Representatives composed of one member from each state and constituted to consider proposed legislation concerning the status of slavery in the territories. Like its counterpart in the Senate, it was unable to agree on any recommendations.

COMMITTEE ON PUBLIC INFORMATION (1917). Set up by order of President Woodrow Wilson, it consisted of the secretaries of state, war, and the navy, with journalist George Creel as chairman. Responsible for generating support for the war effort.

COMMITTEE ON THE CONDUCT OF THE WAR (1861–65). A joint committee of Congress to inquire into the management of

Union military and civilian policies in the Civil War.

COMMITTEES OF CORRESPONDENCE. Organized by the colonies to spread propaganda and coordinate the patriot activities. Samuel Adams persuaded Boston to establish the first standing committee of correspondence (1772).

COMMITTEES OF SAFETY. Carried on and extended the work of the revolutionary Committees of Correspondence. The Second Continental Congress, on July 18, 1775, recommended the establishment of such committees in the colonies to carry on the important functions of government. Committees supplied the armies with men and equipment and apprehended Tories. With adoption of state constitutions, the committees were largely replaced by constitutional agencies.

COMMODITIES AS MONEY. Used chiefly in the colonial period where there was a scarcity of coin or other suitable currency. By 1700 commodity currencies were giving way to coin payments in the towns and cities but remained common for some years in rural districts.

COMMODITY EXCHANGES. Enormous expansion of markets after 1850 required organizations that could handle exchanges of commodities on a large scale. The Chicago Board of Trade was organized in 1848. The New York Produce Exchange was formed in 1850. The Merchants Exchange of St. Louis had the characteristics of a modern exchange by 1854. The New York Cotton Exchange was organized in 1870 and the New York Coffee Exchange in 1882.

COMMODORES. See ADMIRALS AND COMMODORES.

COMMON LANDS. In early New England settlements, lands held in common by the proprietors, in which each owner had fractional rights and carried on farming in accordance with open field practices. More generally, undivided and unallotted land used for pasturage and woodland.

COMMON LAW. In Anglo-Saxon countries, principles of law established by tradition and previous court decisions and usually not incorporated in the constitution or written statutes of the country. The early English colonists were supposed to have brought with them their inherent common-law rights of person and property. The common-law rights of the individual were incorporated into the Declaration of Independence, the Constitution, and, especially, the Bill of Rights.

COMMON SENSE. A tract by Thomas Paine (1776), which maintained that, being of age, the colonies were qualified for independence and that their future interest demanded it. Over 120,000 copies circulated in three months.

COMMONWEALTH v. HUNT (1842). The supreme court of Massachusetts for the first time upheld the legality of a trade union.

COMMUNES. Communal-living experiments in the US antedate the Revolution, experiencing their greatest vitality in the early 19th c., when hundreds of planned communities, both religious and secular, were established. Most were of short duration. Among the best known were the AMANA COMMUNITY, BROOK FARM, NEW HARMONY SETTLEMENT, ONEIDA COMMUNITY, and the SHAKERS. The 1960s and 1970s saw a resurgence of communal living; but most of these communes were also short-lived.

COMMUNICATION INDUSTRIES. See BOOK PUBLISHING; MAGAZINES; NEWSPAPERS; PRINTING; RADIO; TELEGRAPH; TELEPHONE; TELEVISION.

COMMUNICATION SATELLITES. The launching of Sputnik I by the Soviet Union in 1957, and coincidental work in employing the moon as a passive reflector for communications, stimulated US development of artificial satellites. In 1960, the US launched Echo I, a giant balloon reflector that relayed voice and some television signals. Telstar I (1962) provided the crucial test for superiority of the active satellite and the capability of COMSATS in providing multichannel, wideband transmission. Syncom 2 (1963) achieved a geostationary orbit synchronous with the earth's rotation. In 1962 the US established the Communications Satellite Corporation (COMSAT) as part of a worldwide commercial satellite system. The International Telecommunications Satellite Consortium (Intelsat) developed the first commercial synchronous satellite, Intelsat I (Early Bird) in 1965. By 1980 five series of Intelsat satellites served almost 100 nations. A keen competition developed in the American domestic satellites field. In 1981 the North American domestic series included Westar, Satcom, Anik (Canadian), Comstar, and Communications Technology Satellite (joint US-Canadian). Two main types of systems emerged: one serving a large number of customers and the other tailored to specialized needs, such as the SBS-I satellite (1980). Sixty-four international, domestic, and military communications satellites orbited earth in 1980.

COMMUNIST PARTY UNITED STATES OF AMERICA. In 1919 a schism split the Socialist party (SP) and the more radical Bolsheviks, who rejected the progressive gradualism of the SP. The Bolsheviks then split into Communist party (CP) and the Communist Labor party (CLP). Both went underground as the federal government pursued its repressive antisubversive policy. In 1920 the United Communist party (UCP) was created; but the split persisted until unity was imposed by the Communist International (Comintern) in 1921. The Communist Party of America was formed and the Comintern urged it to operate in the open. The Workers Party of America was created and the Communist Party of America formally dissolved in 1923. In 1925 the name was changed to Workers (Communist) Party of America, and in 1929 it became the Communist Party United States of America (CPUSA). The change in 1929 was more than a change in name. In the American party a leftist tendency appeared under James P. Cannon, and a rightist faction, under Jay Lovestone, which argued that conditions in the US justified modification of Communist policy. Both factions were expelled in 1928–29, and the Stalinist element prevailed. The rigid alienation of all dissenting factions continued until 1935. The Nazi menace caused the Comintern in Moscow to lay down a new Popular Front policy of making common cause with liberal elements, even capitalists. The period of the Popular Front (1935–39) was the time of the party's greatest vogue. Leaders manipulated hundreds of front organizations. Instead of fighting the trade-union movement, the Communists joined it and established strong centers of influence. In 1939

Stalin negotiated a nonaggression pact with Hitler, and thousands in the party and front organizations left the party. In 1941, Germany invaded the Soviet Union, and World War II found the US and the USSR on the same side. Thus, from 1941 to 1945 the CPUSA was in the forefront of patriotic striving. In 1943 the Soviet Union, in a gesture of amity, abolished the Comintern; and in 1944 the CPUSA became the Communist Political Association. With the end of World War II the international Communist line changed again and the cold war began. The CPUSA was reestablished. The party was brought to the point of collapse chiefly as the result of strong pressure from the federal government. The Smith Act of 1940, which made it a crime to advocate or teach the violent overthrow of the government, was vigorously enforced. Party leaders were imprisoned and only a skeleton public organization was maintained. The party again went underground. The denunciation of Stalin by Nikita Khrushchev in 1956 traumatized many American party members. Contrary to the dogma of the past, it was also said that war with the capitalist states was not inevitable and that peaceful coexistence could obtain. Once again, the communist movement fell into factionalism. Between 1930 and 1955, party membership fluctuated greatly, with peaks of 55,000 in 1938 and 65,000 in 1945. In 1978 the party claimed a membership of 18,000.

COMMUNITIES. Mennonite and other religious communities were founded on Delaware Bay, in N Maryland, and in Pennsylvania in the 17th c. The 18th c. saw the founding of Dunker, Shaker, Separatist, and other religious communities. By the 19th c. they had been established as far west as Indiana and Ohio. Other religious communities were Perfectionists at Oneida, N. Y., Brooklyn, N. Y., and Wallingford, Conn.; the Hopedale Community, Massachusetts (1842–57); the Amana Community, in New York and, later, in Iowa (1842–1932); the Bishop Hill Colony in Illinois (1848–62); the Mormon Community at Orderville, Utah (1874–84), and the Hutterian Brethren. Among the nonreligious communities, based on experimental economic or social philosophy, was Robert Owen's unsuccessful experiment at New Harmony, Ind., purchased from the Rappists in 1825. In 1841, Boston intellectuals established the West Rexburg Community, which later became the Fourierist BROOK FARM. Fourierist communities were also established in Wisconsin and New Jersey. Other settlements founded on social or economic communism were at Teutonia, Pa. (1843), Icania, Iowa (1848–98), Equity, Ohio (1839–32), Eutopia, Ohio (1847–51), and Modern Times, Long Island, N. Y.(1851–60).

COMMUNITY ACTION PROGRAM. Established 1964 as part of President Lyndon B. Johnson's War on Poverty. Provided funds and a rationale for about 1,000 community action organizations formed within the next three years and expected to attack social problems at the community level, using federal funds administered and controlled locally. It was the most controversial of the Great Society programs, its critics charging waste, mismanagement, and personal political aggrandizement by local leaders. It was severely curtailed after 1967 and virtually ended after Richard M. Nixon became president.

COMPAGNIE DE L'OCCIDENT. Also known as the Western Company, the Mississippi Company, or Mississippi Bubble. A French trading company organized by John Law in 1717 for exploiting the resources of Louisiana. In 1719 became Compagnie des Indes (Company of the Indies). Retained control of Louisiana until 1731.

COMPANY OF ONE HUNDRED ASSOCIATES. Formed 1627 in France for the colonization of New France (Canada). Its charter was revoked in 1663.

COMPROMISE MOVEMENT OF 1860. An unsuccessful attempt to avert secession and the Civil War. No agreement could be reached on the status of slavery in the territories.

COMPROMISE OF 1790. In return for Alexander Hamilton's agreement to provide the congressional votes needed to locate the national capital on the Potomac R, Thomas Jefferson and James Madison promised enough votes to assure enactment of Hamilton's plan for assumption of the revolutionary war debts of the states by the federal government.

COMPROMISE OF 1850. Concerning the issues of states' rights and slavery. Concluded that California was to be admitted as a free (non-slave) state, that the question of slavery in Utah and New Mexico territories would be decided by popular sovereignty, and that the slave trade would be abolished in the District of Columbia. Texas border disputes were settled and the Fugitive Slave Act was amended.

COMPROMISE OF 1890. The Republican majority in the US Senate agreed to scuttle a law protecting black suffrage in return for passage of the Sherman Silver Purchase Act and the McKinley Tariff Act.

COMPROMISES OF THE US CONSTITUTION. The Constitutional Convention of 1787 was presented with the VIRGINIA PLAN to create a national government that would largely disregard the autonomy of the separate states. The NEW JERSEY PLAN provided for a revision of the Articles of Confederation and an increase in the powers of the extant national government. But that government was to operate only on the states as such. Congress would consist of two houses: In the Senate the states would have equal representation; in the House representation based on population. Slaves would be counted as part of the population but each slave would be counted as three-fifths of a person. The slave trade was allowed to continue for twenty years, in return for which the southern states consented to allowing the national Congress to pass navigation acts and regulate commerce.

COMPROMISE TARIFF OF 1833. See TARIFF.

COMPTROLLER GENERAL OF THE UNITED STATES. Head of the General Accounting Office (GAO), an independent agency formed to assist Congress in providing legislative control over the receipt, disbursement, and application of public funds. Appointed by the president for a fifteen-year term.

COMPTROLLER OF THE CURRENCY. Created by Congress on Feb. 25, 1863. The comptroller is appointed by the president for a term of five years, to provide administrative regulation and supervision over the country's national banks, numbering 4,437 in 1980.

COMPUTERS. In 1835 Charles Babbage developed an automatic calculator surprisingly similar to the modern computer. It contained a memory, performed all four arithmetic operations, and made use of a punched card or printed output. Major developments, however, did not occur until the 1930s. In 1937, Howard Aiken designed a calculating device based on conventional punched-card machines. Completed in 1944, it went into immediate operation on war-related calculations. George Stibitz at Bell Telephone Laboratories constructed the first relay-calculating device, the Complex Calculator, in 1939. The first electronic computer, ENIAC, was a result of the collaboration of John Mauchly and J. Presper Eckert at the University of Pennsylvania. By 1945, ENIAC was working on ballistics tables, atomic energy problems, and assorted mathematical problems. The collaboration of John von Neumann with the ENIAC project resulted in the first electronic computer in which the program could be stored and modified. EDVAC took another quantum jump beyond ENIAC — an internally stored program, general-purpose computer. Limited memory remained the foremost problem. This limitation was overcome with Eckert's development of an acoustic delay-line memory. This enabled the designers to think in terms of building a memory of, say, 512 or 1,024 words with only a few tubes, in contrast to the large tube requirement for ENIAC's small memory capacity. The first internally stored program computer, the EDSAC, was designed and built at Cambridge University by Maurice Wilkes. BINAC, a computer built by the Eckert-Mauchly Corporation (formed 1946) had its first successful run in 1949. Two other forms of memory commonly used by first-generation computers were electrostatic tubes and magnetic drums. The electrostatic-tube memory was developd in England by F.C. Williams of Manchester University. Some of the postwar computers owed their importance chiefly to the offspring they spawned. One of the most prolific was built at the Institute for Advanced Study. Its progeny included MANIAC, ILLIAC, JOHNNIAC, ORDVAC, AVIDAC, SILLIAC, and WEIZAC. Another major computer of this period was Whirlwind, built at the Massachusetts Institute of Technology. The project began in 1944 when Gordon Brown was asked to build an aircraft simulator for the navy. This project eventually led to the first digital computer and the first effective magnetic-core memory. With the delivery of UNIVAC I in 1951 to the Bureau of the Census by Eckert-Mauchly, individual computers lost their uniqueness. They also began to be recognized as having a variety of practical applications. IBM's entry into the electronic digital computer field came in 1951, followed by Raytheon, Bendix, and Burroughs. The years 1955–65 saw many new accomplishments. One of the most significant was the development of computer languages. The first was FORTRAN, developed at IBM. In 1959 the first automated computerized process control system was installed (at a Texaco refinery); the banking industry adopted MICR (Magnetic Ink Character Recognition); and transistors began to replace vacuum tubes. The transistor enabled the size of electronic devices to be reduced by a factor of 100,000 by the 1980s. Major external stimuli for the astonishing achievements in miniaturization were provided by the aerospace programs, in missile guidance systems, and by the telephone industry. By the mid-1970s the impact of microelectronics on consumer products was already substantial, as in the pocket-sized electronic calculator. Miniaturization of electronic components in the late 1970s and early 1980s led to the introduction of desktop and home computers.

COMSTOCK LODE. One of the richest deposits of precious ores ever discovered, in Virginia City, Nev. From its discovery in 1859 to its decline in 1879, more than $500 million in silver and gold were recovered.

CONCESSIONS AND AGREEMENT (1664–65). Issued to encourage immigration to New Jersey. Provided for a liberal government, freedom of conscience, and land on reasonable terms.

CONCILIATION, LABOR. The settlement of industrial disputes either by conference between employers and employees or by joint boards representing them, without the assistance of outside agencies. When an outside agent intervenes, the procedure is known technically as mediation.

CONCORD. Capital of New Hampshire, on the Merrimack R. Concord is an agricultural market center. There is granite quarrying nearby. The town was settled as early as 1725.

In the 19th c., it was a leading supplier of coaches and wagons. Pop: 30,400 (1980).

CONCORD GROUP. Coterie of writers living in Concord, Mass., in the 19th c., including Henry David Thoreau, Ralph Waldo Emerson, Nathaniel Hawthorne, A. Bronson Alcott, and William Ellery Channing.

CONDÉ, FORT. Erected 1711 by the French under the sieur de Bienville on the site of the present Mobile, Ala. Transferred to the British in 1763 and renamed Fort Charlotte.

CONESTOGA MASSACRE. See PAXTON BOYS.

CONESTOGA WAGON. Huge, heavily built wagon with broad wheels, famous for conveying settlers to the West. A precursor of the prairie schooner.

CONFEDERACY. See CONFEDERATE STATES OF AMERICA.

CONFEDERATE AGENTS. Purchasing representatives of the Confederacy in Europe, Mexico, and Canada.

CONFEDERATE ARMY. See ARMY, CONFEDERATE.

CONFEDERATE FLAG. The Stars and Bars was the first officially adopted; more famous is the so-called Southern Cross (mistakenly also referred to as the Stars and Bars), with thirteen white stars imposed on a blue St. Andrews cross over a red background.

CONFEDERATE NAVY. See NAVY, CONFEDERATE.

CONFEDERATE STATES OF AMERICA. A confederacy of eleven southern states founded primarily to preserve slavery and protest against centralizing tendencies of the federal government, which was perceived to advance the economic interests of the North to the disadvantage of the agrarian South.

Constitution. Adopted Feb. 8, 1861. Preserved most of the provisions of the US Constitution but omitted the general welfare clause, which tended toward centralization. Safeguarded the sovereignty of member states and forbade the Confederate congress from passing any law impairing property rights in slave trade. Guaranteed the right to take slaves into the territories; but it prohibited the African slave trade and permitted non-slaveholding states to join the new Confederacy.

Executive Department. The constitutional convention elected Jefferson Davis of Mississippi president and Alexander H. Stephens of Georgia as vice-president. Robert Toombs of Georgia became secretary of state; Christopher Memminger of South Carolina, secretary of the treasury; Leroy Pope Walker of Alabama, secretary of war; Stephen Mallory of Florida, secretary of navy; John H. Reagan of Texas, postmaster general; and Judah P. Benjamin of Louisiana, attorney general.

Judicial System. Relied primarily on the state courts, there being no provision for a Confederate supreme court. District courts were active in trying federal cases and sustaining the central government.

Congress. The capital was removed early in the war from Montgomery, Ala., to Richmond, Va., where the Congress met thereafter. Largely ineffective, both houses became bitterly divided into anti-Davis and pro-Davis factions.

Decision Leading to War. Faulty intelligence led the Confederate government to believe that US forces would evacuate Fort Sumter, at Charleston. Instead, President Lincoln sent reinforcements. Davis and his cabinet decided to fire on the approaching expedition, thus starting the war he had hoped to avoid. Lincoln responded by issuing the order for a blockade of the southern coasts and the raising of 75,000 troops.

Manpower. The disproportion in manpower (about two to one) and economic resources between the North and South in 1860 was so great that the Confederacy had little chance to win the war.

Diplomacy. The first objective of the Confederacy was to secure recognition by France and England. Their only success was that England and France recognized the belligerency of the Confederacy. Russia, wishing to see a strong United States as a counterbalance to the British Empire, was hostile to the Confederacy.

Blockade-Runners. Although Europe refused to recognize the Confederacy or to break the blockade, it rendered it great material aid. This was accomplished by furnishing crews and financial backing for the block-ade-runners, the swift, small steamers that slipped into southern harbors on dark nights. They operated principally from Nassau and Bermuda; their main port of entry was Wilmington, N.C. The Union navy was largely ineffective in stopping the traffic, without which the Confederacy could not have survived. At least 1.5 million bales of cotton were exported by the blockade-runners through Matamoros, Mexico. Blockade-runners brought into the Confederacy 600,000 stands of arms, principally Enfield rifles.

Ordnance. Although the Confederacy relied largely on Europe for small arms, it made remarkable progress in manufacturing gunpowder and cannons.

Clothing and Food. In 1860 the eleven states that became the Confederacy produced only 10 percent of the manufactured goods of the country. Shoes, in particular, were in chronic scarcity and civilians in southern cities suffered from lack of food. There seems to have been adequate food in the country; the great trouble was distribution, largely because of the destruction of the railroads.

Finance. During the four years of war, the Confederacy operated on only $27 million in cash. The bullion in US customhouses and mints within the Confederacy, amounting to $718,294, was seized; sequestration of enemy property and appropriation of the gold and silver of the New Orleans banks just before the capture of the city brought $11,661,082. So recklessly did congress authorize the issuance of treasury notes and bonds that high inflation was a constant problem. The total Confederate debt is conservatively estimated at $2.3 billion.

Taxation. The financial disaster of too much paper money leading to high inflation might have been avoided but not until after two years of war did congress pass a drastic tax law. The belief existed that future generations should share the expense of winning independence through longterm bonds. The Confederacy raised only about 1 percent of its income in taxes.

Peace Movements. After the defeat at Gettysburg and the fall of Vicksburg in 1863, many southerners thought the cause was lost and a serious peace movement developed. The peace advocates were often organized into secret societies, notably the Heroes of America, that elected local officers, protected deserters, and tried to sabotage the Confederate cause by various activities. President Davis appointed Vice-President Stephens, Sen. R.M.T. Hunter of Virginia, and former Supreme Court Justice Campbell as commissioners to carry on peace negotiations. They met on Feb. 3, 1865, with Lincoln and Secretary of State Seward on the *River Queen* at Hampton Roads, Va. Lincoln insisted on the restoration of the Union and the abolition of slavery as indispensable terms of peace. The Confederacy refused.

The Final Collapse. The end of the Confederate states came with the surrender of Lee at Appomattox, Va., Apr. 9, 1865; the surrender of Gen. J.E. Johnston at Durham, N.C., Apr. 26; the flight of the cabinet; the arrest of Davis at Irwinville, Ga., May 10; and the surrender of Gen. Edmund Kirby-Smith in the trans-Mississippi West, May 26. The collapse of the Confederacy was caused by the conjunction of adverse circumstances mentioned above and the questionable leadership of President Davis as compared with the superior leadership of President Lincoln.

CONFEDERATION. The period from 1781 to 1788 and the government under the ARTICLES OF CONFEDERATION, the nation's first constitution. On Mar. 1, 1781, the Articles became the framework of central government in the new country. A unicameral legislature with one vote per state, no power of taxation, no power to regulate commerce, and no authority to coerce a state, all indications that Americans intended to prevent a recurrence of their problems under the British. Congress adopted the administrative structure developed under the Second Continental Congress: a secretary for foreign affairs, a secretary of war, and a superintendent of finance. One issue had delayed adoption of the articles, control of the domain W of the Appalachian Mountains. The Confederation had committed itself to creating new states there that would eventually be equal with the original thirteen. Thomas Jefferson's proposals became the basis of the ORDINANCES OF 1784 AND 1785. The former divided the West into territories with much self-government and provided for each territory's entrance into the union on a basis of equality with the original thirteen once it reached the population of the smallest state. The Ordinance of 1785 provided for the orderly disposition of lands to settlers. Congressional hopes for revenue from land sales depended on speculators rather than settlers, and the more restrictive ORDINANCE OF 1787 (the Northwest Ordinance) replaced Jefferson's 1784 one. At first, Congress would appoint territorial officials; when 5,000 males inhabited the territory, they would elect an assembly that would nominate candidates for the governor's council; when 60,000 free adults lived in the territory, it could apply for equal statehood. The Confederation's inability to regulate either foreign or domestic commerce left the new nation at the mercy of the major trading nations. America competed against the mercantilistic systems of England, France, and Spain without imposing any restrictions in retaliation. Individual states competed economically with one another, and Congress could do nothing about it. The Confederation also had no power to resolve diplomatic difficulties with other nations. Spain presented problems to the United States as westward expansion brought the two close to one another on the Gulf Coast. Lacking a reliable source of revenue, the Confederation found itself in dire straits. It could not tax but could only requisition funds from the states, which rarely met their quotas. Moreover, the Continental Congress was forced to assume debts that had been contracted during the Revolution from private individuals, states, and foreign governments; state governments, with strong tax powers, did not face the same dilemma. Continental currency thus became virtually worthless. Fears of more frontal assaults on property rights, such as SHAYS'S REBELLION, led conservatives to demand a reformation of the central government, leading directly to the CONSTITUTIONAL CONVENTION of 1787 and to the eventual adoption of the US Constitution.

CONFEDERATION, ARTICLES OF. See ARTICLES OF CONFEDERATION.

CONFEDERATION, FORT. Spanish post, built in Alabama in 1794 on the Tombigbee R on the site of a French fort erected in 1736. Named to commemorate a new union with local Indian tribes. The fort was dismantled in 1797, in accordance with Pinckney's Treaty of 1795. US troops rebuilt and occupied it soon afterward.

CONFIRMATION BY THE SENATE. The constitutional requirement that appointments by the president be made "by and with the Advice and Consent of the Senate." By 1980 there were over 300 office titles whose holders require confirmation by the Senate.

CONFISCATION OF PROPERTY. Property has been confiscated in the US during wartime since the Revolution, when the property of Loyalists was subject to seizure. During the Civil War both the North and South confiscated property. During both world wars, Congress enacted laws enabling the confiscation of millions of dollars worth of alien property. Most property was returned after each war, after war claims of US citizens were satisfied.

CONFISCATION OF US PROPERTY ABROAD. See NATIONALIZATION OF US PROPERTY ABROAD.

CONGLOMERATES. Business organizations built on acquisitions of firms in businesses usually not directly related to each other. Conglomerates proliferated in the 1950s and 1960s. In 1969, antitrust indictments challenged some of them, and they were more closely scrutinized by the Securities and Exchange Commission. The recession of the late 1970s and early 1980s gave evidence that many conglomerates were far less efficient than supposed. By the 1980s, business mergers and acquisitions had decreased, and some conglomerates were divesting themselves of less profitable components

CONGREGATIONAL CHURCHES. The Non-Separating Puritans who originally settled the New England colonies accepted the Calvinist Westminster Confession of Faith and affirmed the policy of admitting to the sacraments only those who could relate a conversion experience. After considerable controversy, the Halfway Covenant, which included those who could not relate a conversion experience, was adopted in 1662. The AWAKENING of the 18th c. was a period of crisis for Congregationalism. The early 19th c. saw the splitting off of the Unitarian churches, primarily in Boston. During the second half of the 19th c., Congregationalism continued in a more liberal direction. In 1913 a liberal confession of faith was adopted, and in 1931 the Congregationalists merged with the Christian Churches to become the Congregational Christian Churches. This denomination in turn merged with the Evangelical and Reformed Church to form the United Church of Christ in 1957 (1,745,533 members in 1980). The Unitarians who withdrew from orthodox Congregationalism in the early 19th c., have moved progressively away from distinctively Christian affirmations, and now stress an intellectual humanism rooted in the values of all religions. John Murray gathered the first Universalist church in Gloucester, Mass., in 1779, but the greatest influence on American Universalism was Hosea Ballou, who, a generation later, moved Universalism in a more Unitarian direction. In 1961 the Unitarians and the Universalists formally merged in the Unitarian Universalist Association, which in 1980 had 139,052 members.

CONGREGATION DE PROPAGANDA FIDE. Founded 1622. After the pope, the highest court of appeal for the church in the US to 1908, when the US ceased to be a missionary territory.

CONGRESS, CONTINENTAL. See CONTINENTAL CONGRESS.

CONGRESS, UNITED STATES. The 1787 CONSTITUTIONAL CONVENTION created a Congress of two houses, a Senate in which each state would have equal representation and a House of Representatives in which states would be represented according to population. The Constitution created a legislative branch coequal in stature and authority with the executive and judicial branches.

Functions and Powers. (1) Through the passage of bills that become law, Congress determines national policies to be carried out by the executive branch. (2) Congress raises and appropriates the money to carry out these policies. (3) Congress oversees the executive branch to determine whether such national policies are being carried out. (4) Members of Congress enhance public understanding of national issues. (5) Congress seeks to bring justice out of conflicts between citizens and their government. (6) Congress seeks solutions to the issues that divide the nation. The basic powers are to tax, spend, and borrow; to regulate foreign and interstate commerce; to maintain a defense establishment; to declare war; to admit new states; and to propose constitutional amendments. Congress also has an almost unlimited power of investigation. Congress may not tax exports, grant titles of nobility, or pass ex post facto laws. The Bill of Rights prohibits Congress from abridging freedom of speech, the press, the free exercise of religion, the right of peaceful assembly, the right of petition, and other freedoms. Since it has the constitutional power to ratify treaties and confirm cabinet and ambassadorial nominees, the Senate regards itself as the president's chief foreign policy adviser; not all presidents have agreed to such a role for the Senate. Congress has other nonlegislative powers in connection with the presidency. If no candidate receives a majority of the electoral votes, the House of Representatives determines the president and the Senate determines the vice-president. If the vice-presidency becomes vacant, the House and Senate must both confirm the president's nominee to fill the vacancy. In the case of presidential disability, Congress has grave, complicated duties. Congress alone has the power to impeach and remove from office the president and all federal civil officers.

Membership. First Congress (1789–91) consisted of 26 senators and 65 representatives; the Ninety-seventh (1981–83) had 100 senators and 435 representatives. The Constitution provides that representation in the House be kept up to date through a federal census every ten years. The Supreme Court in *Westberry* v. *Sanders* (1964) laid down the one-man, one-vote doctrine, ruling that congressional districts must be substantially equal in population. Representatives have a two-year term; senators, six. Minimum age for House members is twenty-five; for senators, thirty. All must be citizens and, at the time of election, must reside in the state from which elected.

Rules and Procedures. Under the Constitution, the Congress must meet every January; the president may call special sessions of either body. The Constitution provides that the vice-president shall preside over the Senate without a vote except in case of a tie. The House chooses its own presiding officer, the Speaker of the House, from its membership. Any member may introduce a bill or resolution on any subject except that all bills for raising revenue must originate in the House but may be amended freely by the Senate. The House and Senate must make a journal of their proceedings except for secret matters. Recent procedural reforms have made voting, both on the floor and in committee, a matter of public record. Of great historical importance is the *Congressional Record,* a record of debate with much additional material.

Committee System. Not envisioned by the makers of the Constitution, the committee system, evolved through trial and error, is still evolving. The committees have specific, written jurisdictions. Working usually through hundreds of subcommittees, committees choose which bills to consider, amend, rewrite, kill, or recommend for passage, with or without public hearings. The House committee system is more powerful than that of the Senate. The House performs most technical work through committees; committee recommendations have an excellent chance of being adopted by the entire House, usually without major amendments. The smaller Senate, with historic pride in its freedom of debate, more often makes major changes in committee recommendations.

House and Senate. A notable difference in House and Senate operating methods is debate. For decades senators regarded themselves as answerable to no one save their constituencies.. This created the tradition of unlimited debate. As it rapidly grew in numbers, the House found it necessary to put rigid limits on debate. Despite frequent references to the Senate as the upper house, the Constitution clearly created two equal, coordinate bodies, neither superior to the other. No bill can be sent to the president until it passes both houses in identical form; and neither house can adjourn for more than three days without permission of the other.

CONGRESSIONAL APPORTIONMENT. See APPORTIONMENT.

CONGRESSIONAL RECORD. A daily, unofficial publication of the proceedings and official records of Congress. Published since 1873, it was preceded by the *Annals of Congress* (1789–1824), *Register of Debates* (1824–37), and *Congressional Globe* (1834–73), all privately published.

CONGRESSIONAL REGULATORY POWERS. Powers granted Congress by the Constitution to enact controls in certain areas and to make laws or regulations needed to implement such powers. Most regulatory legislation is passed by Congress in pursuance of the delegated power to tax, spend for the general welfare, and regulate interstate commerce. In recent years, Congress has passed on to administrative agencies the power to issue specific regulations controlling social and economic activities. Congress spells out broad operating boundaries subject to alteration for practical or political reasons. Domestically, the power of Congress to control law is virtually unlimited. Control over foreign policy is shared with the president. Congress is given the power to declare war and to appropriate all monies expended in war efforts; but since the Constitution assigns the president the power to command the armed forces, the deployment of such forces can virtually commit the Congress to support undeclared war efforts, such as those in Korea and Vietnam. Historically, Congress has granted the president authority to act according to his judgment during periods of domestic and international conflict.

CONGRESS OF INDUSTRIAL ORGANIZATIONS. See AMERICAN FEDERATION OF LABOR–CONGRESS OF INDUSTRIAL ORGANIZATIONS.

CONGRESS OF RACIAL EQUALITY (CORE). Founded in 1942, CORE was in the forefront of the civil rights battles of the 1960s. It became nationally famous with its "freedom rides" of 1961, in which interracial groups dramatically challenged southern segregation while traveling in Alabama and Mississippi. By the mid-1960s, CORE reversed its goal from integration to racial separatism, and membership and influence declined sharply.

CONNECTICUT. The Connecticut R valley and the shoreline of Long Island Sound were thickly settled by Indians when Adriaen Block, a Dutchman, sailed up the river in 1614. In the 1630s, settlers from Massachusetts Bay arrived at Windsor, buying land from Indians. They displaced a Dutch trading post at Hartford and also settled Wethersfield. To these three "river towns" were added a military settlement at Saybrook (1635) and a Puritan colony at New Haven (1638). Connecticut Colony was organized under the Fundamental Orders (1639), the first organic document of government in US history. The orders were superseded by the royal charter of 1662. In 1818 a genuine constitution was adopted. (With numerous amendments the constitution continued in force until a new constitution was adopted in 1965.) Agricultural changes due to hostile topography, soil depletion, and a growing livestock production led to vast migrations from the state during the half-century following the Revolution, and population became fairly stable until the development of the industrial sector. Metals (especially brass), rubber products, small arms, machine tools, clocks, electrical equipment, and aircraft and other military production have dominated Connecticut industry. Urbanization continued steadily to about 1920. The dominant movement since the depression, however, has been suburban. Connecticut vies year after year with one or two other states for the highest per capita wealth in the country. Pop.: 3,107,576 (1980).

CONNECTICUT, FUNDAMENTAL ORDERS OF. As founded in 1635, Connecticut consisted of the three river towns— Windsor, Hartford, and Wethersfield — with Springfield temporarily included. The planters, with neither patent nor title, established a court that, from 1636 until 1638, exercised political jurisdiction. In 1639 they established the Fundamental Orders. The document recognized no higher authority than the freemen of the three towns and provided for the calling of general assemblies; the election of a governor and magistrates; and the qualification of voters. It specified how deputies to the court were to be elected; how elections were to be called; how courts were to be organized and empowered; and how taxes were to be apportioned.

CONNECTICUT, OLD PATENT OF. The first grant to Connecticut, known from what purports to be a copy of a deed made by the earl of Warwick, in 1632, of a strip of land including part of the present state of Connecticut. Warwick had no right to make the grant, and the grantees only moved to take possession in 1635, when they began erecting a fort at the mouth of the Connecticut R. In 1644 the fort and, presumably, the rights under the patent were sold to the planters of the river towns Patent played a large part in securing for Connecticut the limits set forth in the Charter of 1662.

CONNECTICUT CHARTER OF 1662. Following the accession of Charles II, the settlers of Connecticut were granted a new charter, dated Apr. 23, 1662. In 1687, under James II, the colony was formally annexed by Sir Edmund Andros to his Dominion of New England. According to tradition, the colonists refused to surrender their charter, secreting it in a hollow tree (the Charter Oak). Then, with the overthrow of King James, Connecticut resumed its charter government. The charter continued as the basic law until 1818.

CONNECTICUT COMPROMISE. In the Constitutional Convention of 1787, the small states demanded a legislature with each state having an equal vote (see NEW JERSEY PLAN), whereas the large states wanted a system whereby representation was based on population (see VIRGINIA PLAN). Roger Sherman of Connecticut proposed a compromise: two houses, the one with equal and the other proportional representation. His plan was adopted.

CONNECTICUT CONSTITUTIONAL CONVENTION. Two hundred and one delegates met at Hartford, Conn., on Aug. 26–Sept. 16, 1818, to frame a constitution to replace the CONNECTICUT CHARTER OF 1662. As finally ratified (On October 5), all Christian sects were put on an equal basis, small-town control of the lower house of the legislature was continued, the governor was given slightly more power, and an independent judiciary was established.

CONNECTICUT WESTERN LANDS. The CONNECTICUT CHARTER OF 1662 granted the territory that the state now occupies plus a seventy-mile-wide strip from the Delaware R to the Pacific Ocean. In 1786 Connecticut ceded to the US all its western territories except the Western Reserve (an area extending 120 miles from Pennsylvania's western boundary along Lake Erie), most of which it sold in 1795 to the Connecticut Land Company. It retained a half-million-acre tract in the western part of the Reserve, the Firelands, set aside to compensate Connecticut families for losses in the Revolution.

CONNECTICUT WITS. See HARTFORD WITS.

CONNOLLY'S PLOT (1775). John Connolly, a Loyalist officer, proposed to Lord Dunmore that he should capture Fort Pitt and join Lord Dunmore in putting down the rebellion in Virginia. George Washington had been warned, however, and Connolly was captured Nov. 20, at Hagerstown, Maryland.

CONQUISTADORES (conquerors). Leaders of the Spanish conquest of the Americas. Juan Ponce de León, in search of the fabled fountain of youth, had landed on the shores of Florida (1513) before Hernando Cortes took Mexico in 1519. Immediately thereafter, other conquistadores began exploring and subduing lands northward. Notable among them were Pánfilo de Narváez, Álvar Núñez Cabeza de Vaca, Hernando de Soto, Francisco Vásquez de Coronado, Antonio de Espejo, and Alonso de León and Juan de Oñate.

CONSCIENCE WHIGS. Dissident New England members of the Whig party, so-called because of their vigorous opposition to slavery. In 1848 most of them bolted the Whig national convention and joined the Free Soil Party.

CONSCIENTIOUS OBJECTORS. Originally persons of various religious and social sects who opposed war as contrary to their faiths and creeds. Since the Civil War the government has broadened the definition to include persons objecting to participation in, and support of, all wars on moral and intellectual grounds.

CONSCRIPTION. US laws before and after independence required able-bodied males to enroll in the militia. The Continental Congress in 1778 recommended the states draft men from their militias for one year's service in the Continental army, but this failed to fill the ranks. Both sides resorted to conscription during the Civil War, which worked effectively for neither. In 1917, Woodrow Wilson decided to rely on conscription, rather than enlistment, for World War I. The Selective Service Act of 1917 was carefully drawn to remedy earlier problems. In 1917–18, 24 million men were registered and nearly 3 million inducted into military services, with little resistance. In 1940, the Selective Service and Training Act instituted national conscription in peacetime for the first time, requiring registration of all men between twenty-one and forty-five, with selection for one year's service by national lottery. In 1941 that service was extended by another year, and after Pearl Harbor, to the duration of the war plus six months, requiring all men between eighteen and sixty-four to register. After World War II, except for a brief period in 1947 and 1948, registration and conscription laws were in effect at all times until 1973, when the draft was ended. In 1980 a new draft registration law was passed, but no conscription was contemplated short of a national emergency.

CONSERVATION. The prudent use of resources, including land, the people living on it, water, wildlife, and minerals. Little was done with respect to conservation by the US government until in 1849 the Department of the Interior was established. Federal forest reservations were established in the 1870s, and the Forest Reserve Act of 1891 set aside 13 million acres as reservations. Yellowstone National Park was established in 1872, Yosemite in 1891. Societies and clubs emphasizing conservation were formed, including the Sierra Club in 1892 and the National Audubon Society in 1905. Conservation of public lands was greatly aided by the policies of President Theodore Roosevelt. The National Park Service Act was passed in 1916; the Migratory Bird Treaty Act with Canada, restricting hunting of migratory species, became law in 1918; and the Mineral Leasing Act, regulating mining on federal lands, and the Federal Water Power Act, giving the Federal Power Commission authority to issue licenses for hydropower development on public lands, were both passed in 1920. The period 1933–39 has been called the "golden age of conservation." The primary conservation emphasis during the administration of Franklin D. Roosevelt was on land planning. The Soil Erosion Service, Civilian Conservation Corps, Tennessee Valley Authority, Soil Conservation Service, and Resettlement Administration were established. In 1963 the Clean Air Act appropriated funds for an attack on air pollution. The Council on Environmental Quality was established in 1969 to oversee efforts in dealing with pollution and to make environmental policy recommendations to the president. The Environmental Protection Agency (EPA) proposed several national quality standards pursuant to the mandates of such legislation as the Clean Air Act of 1967 and the Water Quality Improvement Act of 1970. In 1980 President Carter signed a bill designating over 104 million acres in Alaska national conservation areas. The Reagan administration initiated a policy of encouraging the commercial development of public lands, a policy that placed it in direct conflict with the various conservation groups.

CONSERVATISM. The American Revolution and the Declaration of Independence have been traditionally regarded as anticonservative by nature. But the Constitution, written in 1787, is regarded as a blunting of the edge of revolutionary radicalism. In the early Republic, Federalists represented conservatism, whereas the Jeffersonian Republican-Democrats represented liberalism. The Republican party, which later came to be the only effective conservative political institution in American public life, was founded on a thoroughly nonconservative principle: the abolition of slavery (i.e., the taking of private property by government decree). After the Civil War, the Republican party allied itself with big business and inaugurated a period of conservative rule lasting until 1932, when Franklin D. Roosevelt was elected and instituted his New Deal. Even the revival of the Republican party under Presidents Eisenhower, Nixon, and Ford after World War II made no fundamental change in New Deal social and economic planning, although all three paid lip service to the principles of conservatism and were, in fact, more conservative than postwar Democratic presidents. In 1980 Ronald Reagan became the first Republican president since Hoover to represent true conservative principles. He instituted a policy of dismantling or severely curtailing many social and economic programs originating in the New Deal and accepted by his Republican predecessors.

CONSPIRACIES ACTS OF 1861 AND 1862. Attempts to suppress antiwar activities in the North during the Civil War. Provided fines and imprisonment for those who would obstruct or overthrow the government and identified antiwar activity as treason.

CONSTELLATION-INSURGENTE ENCOUNTER (Feb. 9, 1799). During naval hostilities with France, American Commodore Thomas Truxtun in the frigate *Constellation* defeated the French frigate *Insurgente* in a sharp engagement in the West Indies. Victory gave vigorous backing to the US policy of commerce protection and set high standards for its new navy.

CONSTELLATION-VENGEANCE ENCOUNTER (Feb. 1–2, 1800). The *Constellation,* heading for Guadeloupe, sighted the French frigate *Vengeance.* Commodore Thomas Truxtun of the *Constellation* ordered his men to aim at the hull. The French fired into the American ship's rigging to prevent chase; they suffered about four times the losses of the Americans. When the *Constellation's* mainmast fell, the French escaped.

CONSTITUTION. An American 44-gun frigate launched Oct. 21, 1797; flagship in the naval war with France and in the Tripolitan War. Notable victories in the War of 1812 earned it the nickname "Old Ironsides." Rebuilt in 1833, it served as a training ship at Portsmouth, Va., from 1860 to 1865, was partially rebuilt in 1877 and again in 1925, and, except for one cruise, has been docked at the Boston navy yard since 1897.

CONSTITUTIONAL APPORTIONMENT. See APPORTIONMENT.

CONSTITUTIONAL CONVENTION. The US Constitution was the work of a convention that sat at Philadelphia from late May 1787 until mid-September, the culmination of a lengthy campaign for constitutional reform staged by those who regarded the ARTICLES OF CONFEDERATION as hopelessly deficient. All states except Rhode Island sent delegates to the convention; the participating states named seventy-four delegates, of whom fifty-five were present. Dominant was a group of delegates intent on creating a genuinely national government possessed of powers adequate to promote the security, financial stability, commercial prosperity, and general well-being of states: George Washington, James Madison, James Wilson, Gouverneur Morris, Rufus King, Charles Cotesworth Pinckney, John Rutledge, Benjamin Franklin, Edmund Randolph, and Alexander Hamilton. They were mostly supported by a moderate group that accepted the necessity for strong

central government but was willing to compromise substantially with the convention's states' rights bloc: Elbridge Gerry, Oliver Ellsworth, Roger Sherman, and Abraham Baldwin. A small bloc of states' rights delegates was firmly opposed to the creation of a sovereign national government and wanted to maintain a confederation type of government. Its leaders included William Paterson, author of the NEW JERSEY PLAN; John Dickinson; Gunning Bedford; John Lansing; and Robert Yates. Each state had one vote in the convention. The nationalist faction demonstrated its power at the very outset of the proceedings. Randolph presented the VIRGINIA PLAN, which called for a genuinely national government rather than one based upon state sovereignty. This meant junking the Articles of Confederation outright and erecting a powerful national government, federal only in that it would still leave to the states a separate if unspecified area of sovereignty. The most serious conflict between the nationalist and states' rights factions came over the composition of the legislature. The nationalists demanded that both houses of Congress be apportioned according to population and that the lower house, at least, be elected directly by the people of the several states. The states' rights faction demanded state equality and offered the NEW JERSEY PLAN, which called for a one-chamber legislature based on state equality— in effect a continuation of the Confederation Congress. The ultimate solution was found in the CONNECTICUT COMPROMISE, which provided that the lower house of Congress be apportioned according to population, that each state have one vote in the upper house, and that all bills for raising revenue originate in the lower house. The debate on the executive proved to be protracted and difficult, but it too was a victory for a strong national government. The delegates accepted a plan whereby the president would be chosen by an ELECTORAL COLLEGE made up of delegates chosen by the states. Equally nationalistic was the convention's resort to the judiciary to guarantee federal sovereignty and national supremacy against incursion by the states. The document declared that the laws of national government are to be the "supreme law of the respective states" and bound state courts to enforce them as such. The convention established a national judiciary and vested in the federal courts, especially the Supreme Court, the ultimate power to settle questions involving state and federal sovereignty. Meanwhile, in a concession to the states' rights party, the convention resorted to a specific enumeration of the powers of Congress; but it incorporated an important clause giving Congress the power to enact "necessary and proper" legislation in fulfillment of its delegated powers, and it accepted a vaguely drafted "general welfare clause" that, with the "necessary and proper" provisions, was to serve as the basis for a tremendous expansion of federal power. In mid-September 1787 the convention put its various resolutions and decisions into a final draft and submitted the Constitution to the states for approval. (See CONSTITUTION OF THE UNITED STATES.)

CONSTITUTIONAL UNION PARTY. Made up of old-line Whigs and members of the American (Know-Nothing) party., In 1860 chose John Bell and Edward Everett as candidates for president and vice-president. Polled 590,000 votes and carried only Kentucky, Virginia, and Tennessee.

CONSTITUTION-CYANE AND -LEVANT ENGAGEMENT (Feb. 20, 1815). The *Constitution,* captured the British frigate *Cyane* and sloop of war *Levant* 200 miles NE of the Madeiras.

CONSTITUTION, FORT. Erected in 1775 on what is now Constitution Island in the Hudson R opposite West Point. Early in 1776 was abandoned. Later part of the old works were restored as redoubts.

CONSTITUTION-GUERRIÈRE ENGAGEMENT (Aug. 19, 1812). The capture of the British frigate *Guerrière* by the *Constitution* was the first important naval victory of the War of 1812 and did much to win enthusiasm for the war from New Englanders.

CONSTITUTION-JAVA ENGAGEMENT (Dec. 19, 1812). After a two-hour battle, the British *Java* surrendered to the US *Constitution*, after having suffered five times the losses of the American ship.

CONSTITUTION OF THE UNITED STATES. Since 1789, the basic frame of the government of the United States. It came out of the CONSTITUTIONAL CONVENTION of 1787. For complete text see *Appendix.*

Ratification. The convention provided for ratification of the Constitution by state conventions, with the constitution going into effect when nine of the states had ratified. The proponents of the constitution, known as the Federalists, met with overwhelming success, primarily because the Antifederalists could offer no constructive alternative.

Dates of Ratification by States: December 1787: Delaware (unanimous); Pennsylvania (vote 46–23); New Jersey (unanimous). January 1788: Georgia (unanimous); Connecticut (128–40). February 1788: Massachusetts (187–168, with a request for a bill of rights). April 1788: Maryland (63–11). May 1788: South Carolina(149–73). June 1788: New Hampshire (57–47, with request for twelve amendments). *June 1788: Virginia (89–79, with a request for a bill of rights); New York (30–27). *November 1788: North Carolina (194–77, after a bill of rights had been proposed). *May 1790: Rhode Island (34–32). *Ratified Constitution after the ninth state adoption.

Amendments. Twenty-six amendments have been adopted since 1789. The first ten were drafted to meet the protests in numerous state ratifying conventions against the absence of a bill of rights in the Constitution. On the initiative of James Madison, the First Congress submitted twelve amendments to the states; ten of these were ratified in 1791 and constitute the BILL OF RIGHTS. The subsequent sixteen amendments are discussed in separate articles (e.g., FOURTEENTH AMENDMENT).

CONSTITUTIONS, STATE. See STATE CONSTITUTIONS.

CONSULAR CONVENTION. In 1782, Benjamin Franklin signed a convention with the French foreign minister that departed materially from instructions from Congress. It contained the threat of extraterritoriality. John Jay advised against ratification. Negotiations resulted in the more favorable treaty of 1788.

CONSULAR SERVICE. See FOREIGN SERVICE.

CONSUMER PROTECTION. Among the early protective consumer laws was a mail fraud law passed in 1872. State and local governments also early provided "sealers" to inspect the accuracy of weights and measures and inspectors to check on sanitation standards. By 1906 the Pure Food and Drug Act was passed. In 1914 the Federal Trade Commission was created to monitor advertising. Self-policing attempts by Better Business Bureaus were only partially successful; consumers were often bewildered by rival product claims. In 1928 Consumers Research was founded. A private nonprofit organization designed to substitute the publication of laboratory test results for partisan advertising claims, it was soon overshadowed by Consumers Union (1936). The CU had 2.8 million subscribers for its magazine *Consumer Reports* in 1981. National, state, and local consumer organizations were formed in the 1960s and 1970s to assist in handling buyers' complaints, to lobby for legislation, and to introduce consumer education into the schools. Prominent among these were the various organizations sponsored by Ralph Nader. Consumerism became a national cause.

CONTEMPT OF CONGRESS. The Supreme Court has held repeatedly that either the House of Representatives or the Senate may hold private persons in contempt. Under an 1857 statute, Congress passes a resolution on the contempt charge, which is then turned over to the US attorney for the District of Columbia for grand jury action and prosecution. Any resulting punishment is judicially imposed.

CONTI, FORT. Two redoubts built on the E bank of the Niagara R at Lake Ontario in 1679 by the sieur de La Salle to protect the base of supplies for his expedition. Destroyed by fire within the year.

CONTINENTAL. Word used variously to describe colonies on the mainland as opposed to island colonies (such as Bermuda); certain members of the American army during the Revolution; and paper money used during the Revolution.

CONTINENTAL ASSOCIATION (1774). Short-lived attempt by the American colonies to force Great Britain to recognize political rights by means of economic coercion (i.e, limiting trade).

CONTINENTAL CONGRESS. Body of delegates during the Revolutionary War that served as an advisory council of the colonies. After independence, it continued to be the central government of the new republic under the ARTICLES OF CONFEDERATION until it was superseded on Mar. 4, 1789, by the new government under the Constitution. The First Continental Congress, which sat at Philadelphia from Sept. 5 to Oct. 26, 1774, consisted of delegates from all colonies except Georgia. Adopted the DECLARATION OF RIGHTS (Oct. 14), the CONTINENTAL ASSOCIATION (Oct. 20), and a resolution calling for a new congress if grievances were not redressed. Grievances were not redressed. The Second Continental Congress met in Philadelphia in May 1775 and resolved to come to the aid of Massachusetts where armed conflict had broken out. It took over the provincial army at Boston and appointed George Washington commander in chief. The idea of independence by now was firmly entrenched, and on July 4, 1776, it adopted the DECLARATION OF INDEPENDENCE and set about framing an instrument of union. A year and a half later (Nov. 15. 1777). the Articles of Confederation were finally agreed upon (although ratification by the thirteen states was not completed until March 1, 1781). After the war, support for the Congress from the states dwindled; and Congress grew progressively weaker. Pressure for change grew, and the result was the ANNAPOLIS CONVENTION of 1786, which in turn led to CONSTITUTIONAL CONVENTION of 1787.

CONTINUOUS VOYAGE DOCTRINE. See ENEMY DESTINATION.

CONTRABAND, SLAVES AS. Union policy early in the Civil War to treat fugitive slaves as contraband property. Reversed by CONFISCATION ACT OF 1861, but "contraband" as a slang term for "slave" was widely used.

CONTRABAND OF WAR. A term in international law deriving from a belligerent's claim of right to prevent an enemy from receiving goods of value in waging war and to declare such goods shipped by neutrals as liable to seizure and condemnation, usually on the high seas. In the wars of the 1790s, both Britain and France arbitrarily seized hundreds of US ships, charging contraband violations. The NAVAL WAR WITH FRANCE (Quasi-War) resulted. During Civil War, US cruisers captured British ships with cargo bound for the Confederacy.

During World War I, Britain imposed broad categories of contraband on neutral shipping destined for the enemy, virtually ending US trade with Germany. Germany's submarine warfare against Allied shipping hastened US entry into the war. In November 1941, Congress passed a law allowing US merchant ships to carry any cargo, including contraband, through war zones to and from Great Britain. The 1949 Geneva convention called for free passage of medicine, religious objects, foodstuffs, clothing, and tonics for children and maternity cases.

CONTRACT CLAUSE. Article I, Section 10, of the US Constitution provides that no state shall pass any law "impairing the Obligation of Contracts." Broad interpretation of this clause by the Supreme Court under Chief Justice John Marshall made it the basic constitutional instrument for the protection of private property in the 19th c. Beginning in the 1890s, the more flexible due process clause of the Fourteenth Amendment progressively replaced the contract clause as the constitutional bulwark of property. Complexities of urban, technological society have necessitated legislative modification of absolute property rights.

CONTRACT LABOR, FOREIGN. During the Civil War a labor shortage led the Union government to allow foreign workers to enter into agreements providing their services to private employers in return for prepaid transportation to the United States. During the economic recession of the mid-1880s craft unionists demanded curbs on foreign contract labor. In 1885, Congress passed a law prohibiting the prepaid passage of immigrants in return for a promise of their services. The statute specifically exempted actors, artists, lecturers, singers, domestic servants, and skilled labor required for new industries. The exemptions were changed periodically by amendments.

CONTRERAS, BATTLE OF (Aug. 19–20, 1847). Gen. Winfield Scott's troops, after severe fighting, drove the Mexican troops from the heights of Contreras and captured Churubusco.

CONVENTION, DIPLOMATIC. A binding agreement between countries to follow a particular course of action, not quite as solemn an agreement as a treaty.

CONVENTION OF 1787. See CONSTITUTIONAL CONVENTION.

CONVENTION OF 1800. Signed by the United States and France, it ended the NAVAL WAR WITH FRANCE, or Quasi-War, with mutual restoration of captured naval vessels and liberalization of the treatment of US ships in French ports.

CONVENTION OF 1818 WITH ENGLAND. Treaty giving US citizens the right to fish portions of the Canadian coast and settling Anglo-American boundary disputes in the Northwest. Also set up arbitration procedures for indemnification claims.

CONVENTIONS, PARTY NOMINATING. Held at both state and and national levels to nominate party candidates and conduct other party business. Common in all states during the 19th c.; but most states now have primary elections. National conventions to nominate candidates for president were first held at Baltimore in preparation for the election of 1832.

CONVICT LABOR SYSTEMS. In the early 1800s, private entrepreneurs began to contract for prison labor. The state received money for the prisoners' services. The lease system allowed convicts to work outside the prison, most often as railroad construction laborers and in mines, sawmills, and brickyards. Later, convicts were more generally used directly by the state, notably as road construction gangs.

CONWAY CABAL (1777–78). Efforts by a New England coterie to wrest control of the army and the Revolution from Gen. George Washington. Generals Thomas Conway and Horatio Gates were among the leaders of the cabal. Public revelations rallied support for Washington, overwhelming conspirators both in Congress and the army.

COOCH'S BRIDGE, BATTLE OF (Sept. 3, 1777). Confrontation near Elk Ferry, Maryland, between patriot forces and a contingent of British and Hessian troops. The Americans won.

COOKE, JAY, AND COMPANY The leading US banking house during the Civil War. Agent for selling US treasury bonds. Failed in 1873 after bad railroad investments.

COOK'S SEARCH FOR THE NORTHWEST PASSAGE (1776–80). Capt. James Cook of the British navy sailed along the American coast N into the Arctic Ocean until his way was blocked by ice. Sailing along the Alaska coast, he passed through the inlet named for him and found his way through the Aleutian Islands, the Bering Strait, and far into the Arctic Ocean. Proved that there was no navigable northwest passage. Wintered during 1779 in the Hawaiian Islands, where the natives killed him.

COOPERATIVES. Associations formed for the purchase or sale of goods and services for the benefit of members. One of the earliest was fire insurance cooperative formed by Benjamin Franklin in 1752. Modern consumer cooperatives purchase goods, most often food, for their members at beneficial prices. The commonest form of consumer cooperatives are the credit union associations, which in 1980 had about 43 million members. Farmer associations market products, purchase farm supplies and equipment, and provide credit and insurance. Can also be effective political lobbyists for agricultural interests.

COOPER UNION FOR THE ADVANCEMENT OF SCIENCE AND ART. Institution for free instruction of men and women in applied science, art, and social and political science, established in New York City in 1859 by Peter Cooper. It is especially noted for its architecture and engineering programs.

COPPAGE V. KANSAS, 236 US 1 (1915). The Supreme Court held that statutes allowing employers to discharge workers who joined unions violated the Fourteenth Amendment.

COPPERHEADS. Northerners who opposed the war policy of President Abraham Lincoln. Advocated a union restored by negotiation rather than war. The successful termination of the war discredited the Copperheads, and the Democratic party was handicapped for some years because of its Copperhead affiliates.

COPPER INDUSTRY. In 1709 copper production began at Simsbury, Connecticut. English colonial law forbade smelting in the colonies, so most ore was shipped to England. Exploration of the rich ore deposits of the Upper Peninsula of Michigan began in the 1850s. By 1880 production had increased to 30,000 tons annually. The first discovery of copper in Montana was at Butte in 1866. Later, the Anaconda Copper Mining Company gained control of most of the mining properties in the area. Introduction of the Bessemer steel converter for smelting copper in the late 1880s made it possible to treat much lower-grade ore, leading to the exploitation of huge bodies of ores in Arizona. In 1980 output was 1.2 million tons. In 1979 imports accounted for 13 percent of the domestic supply.

COPPOC CASE. Edwin and Barclay Coppoc were members of John Brown's attack on HARPERS FERRY in 1859. Edwin was executed, but Barclay escaped.

COPYRIGHT. Provides protection to authors of literary, dramatic, musical, and other artistic and intellectual work. Article 1, Section 8, of the US Constitution gives Congress the power to enact copyright laws. Congress passed the first federal copyright legislation in 1790; the law has been amended regularly since then. Microfilm, photocopying, audio and video tapes, and electronic information storage and reproduction were incorporated into the 1976 law. It extended the copyright protection to the lifetime of the author plus fifty years; imposed copyright liability on public broadcasters, cable television, and jukebox operators; and codified the fair use doctrine for photocopying.

CORAL SEA, BATTLE OF THE (May 7–8, 1942). History's first aircraft carrier battle and the first large naval battle in which the surface ships did not exchange fire. The Americans lost more ships, but the Japanese lost more planes. It was a US strategic victory in that the Japanese were forced to replan their efforts to isolate Australia.

CORINTH, BATTLE AT (Oct. 3–4, 1862). After the battle of Shiloh, the Union troops occupied Corinth, Miss. Confederate troops broke through the advance lines of Union Gen. W. S. Rosecrans and assaulted his main position. After heavy losses, the Confederates retreated to Holly Springs, Miss..

CORN. First cultivated by American Indians in prehistoric times. By the time Europeans arrived, corn, or maize, was widely grown in both North and South America. Jamestown and Plymouth owed their survival to the grain, which could be eaten green or dried and ground into meal, to be made into bread. Corn was excellent feed for livestock, and could be distilled into whiskey, to be consumed or sold. Prior to the Civil War, corn rather than cotton was the most valuable crop in the South. Later, the Midwest became the corn belt, one of the most productive agricultural areas in the world, particularly after hybrids were introduced in the 1920s. In 1979 the US produced one-half of the world total. Of the 60 million acres of corn harvested annually, 86 percent is used for grain; the rest for forage and silage.

CORN BELT. The uniquely fertile region of the upper Mississippi Valley, stretching from Ohio to Nebraska, in which farmers specialize in growing corn. In 1979 about 65 percent of US corn was raised in the corn belt states: Nebraska, Iowa, Missouri, Illinois, Indiana, and Ohio.

CORN BORER, EUROPEAN. Introduced into the US ca. 1910; by 1949 it had spread over nearly all major corn-growing areas and caused a loss of more than 300 million bushels of grain corn each year. Since then, bore-resistant hybrids and new insecticides have materially reduced the loss caused by the pest.

CORNELL UNIVERSITY. Coeducational land-grant institution of higher learning, founded by Ezra Cornell in 1865 at Ithaca, New York. The College of Agriculture, Veterinary College, College of Home Economics, and School of Industrial and Labor Relations are state schools. The other colleges are privately run.

CORNET. Lowest-ranking commissioned officer in a cavalry troop; after 1799 generally designated a second lieutenant.

CORN-HOG ECONOMY. Raising hogs for sale to market, and raising corn to feed the hogs. The system was once prevalent in the corn belt, but today agriculture is more diversified.

CORNING LETTER. A public letter from President Lincoln, dated June 12, 1863, to Congressman Erastus Corning and other New York Democrats. Replying to charges that his arrest of the leading Copperhead was illegal, Lincoln asked rhetorically: "Must I shoot a simpleminded soldier boy who deserts, while I must not touch a hair of a wily agitator who induces him to desert?"

CORONADO'S EXPEDITION (1540–42). Francisco Vásquez de Coronado started N from Mexico looking for the fabled Seven Cities of Cibola. He crossed Arizona into New Mexico; another branch of his expedition discovered the Grand Canyon. Lured by tales of the wealthy country of Quivira, Coronado in 1541 pushed E into the Plains. The expedition found the Quivirans, who were Wichita, in what is now Kansas, but they had no treasure. His expeditions acquainted the Spanish with the Southwest and opened the way to future settlement.

CORPORATIONS. The trading companies chartered in the 16th and 17th c. by the English crown were the first corporations in American history. By the 18th c. corporations had become primarily trading companies, their governing functions having been taken over by royal governors. From 1780 to 1801, US states chartered 317 business corporations, almost all for such public purposes as supplying water, transport, insurance, or banking. During the 19th c., corporations were used more for general business purposes, and states enacted statutes facilitating their formation. Multistate business entities arose in the form of trusts. In several industries, trustees exercised control by holding the stock of a number of corporations operating throughout the country. In 1890, Congress enacted the Sherman Antitrust Act, which severely restrained their activities. Although the US Constitution makes no reference to corporations, it gives Congress the power to regulate commerce between the several states and with foreign nations. Congress used this power in chartering national banks and transcontinental railroads in the 19th c. Since 1890, the federal government has constrained the power of state-chartered corporations to centralize control of economic acitivity throughout the nation and the world. In addition to regulating such specific industries as transportation (although some deregulation has taken place there), broadcasting, and atomic energy, the federal government polices all corporations through the Securities and Exchange Commission.

CORPUS CHRISTI. City on the Gulf Coast of Texas, on a well-protected harbor in Corpus Christi Bay, which was named by Spanish explorers in 1519. Founded 1839, the town became an important center for the cotton and wool trade, and later for oil- and chemical-refining. Pop.: 231,999 (1980).

CORREGIDOR. Fortified island in Manila Bay in the Philippines, important in World War II. In May 1942 US forces were overrun and surrendered to the Japanese. On Feb. 27, 1945, the island fortress was retaken by American troops.

CORRUPT BARGAIN. Charge made by Jacksonians in 1825 that Henry Clay had supported John Quincy Adams in the House presidential election in return for being made secretary of state.

CORRUPTION, POLITICAL. Corruption has been a constant feature of US politics since the birth of the Republic. The 19th c. witnessed corruption on a grand scale, generally in connection with the spoils system. Among prominent instances were the Indian land frauds, the scandals of the Grant administration, and the murky bargaining after the 1876 choice of Rutherford B. Hayes as president. The House of Representatives and Senate were rife with corruption and scandal; bribery and influence peddling among state legislators was equally widespread. The TEAPOT DOME OIL SCANDAL and WATERGATE are the most significant examples of political corruption in the 20th c.

CORRUPT PRACTICES ACTS. The Pendleton Act of 1883 and similar state laws of the time attempted to assure fairness in political campaigns and elections. Such laws regulate contributions and expenditures and look for improper activity in the conduct of elections, such as illegal registration, bribery, and fal-

sification of returns. The Hatch Act of 1939, with later amendments, restricts political activities of federal government employees.

COSMETICS For approximately two decades following the American Revolution only a sparing application of powder and rouge was considered fashionable. Except for light applications of scent and hair oil, use of cosmetics by men remained socially unacceptable. The domestic production of cosmetics continued to expand after 1800; growth was relatively slow throughout the 19th c. Demand was largely confined to wealthy, fashion-conscious women in urban areas. Output of the cosmetics industry moved up sharply during the 20th c. Among major contributors to this trend were further urbanization, higher income levels, a relaxation of standards of social behavior, and the introduction of medium- and low-priced products. In addition, there were extensive advertising and sales promotion campaigns.

COST OF GOVERNMENT. Growing populations, the demand for better public services, and wars and depressions have produced ever-increasing governmental expenditures. The federal government spent $5 million in 1792; in 1978, more than $400 billion. Collectively, national, state, and local governments spent $10.59 billion in 1927; in 1978, over $745 billion. The largest single federal program has been for national defense and international relations. Education and highways accounted for more than half of state and local budgets before the depression; education, welfare, and highways have accounted for more than half subsequently. In 1979 the national government provided $53.5 billion in grants to states and $19.6 billion to local governments. States provided their local governments with $61.1 billion and grants and shared revenues in 1977. The already substantial transfer of funds from the national to state and local level was augmented in 1972 by passage of the first national revenue-sharing act, providing for the return by the federal government of more than $5 billion annually to state and local governments for general expenditures for the five-year term of the act, which was extended in 1976 and again in 1980.

COST OF LIVING. Wage earners during the colonial era must have suffered declines in real income, since commodity prices were highly unstable. Inflation during the Revolution also undoubtedly hurt those in urban centers. In the early 1790s, prices began another sharp rise, leading to the earliest US strikes on record, among Philadelphia craftsmen. Continuous urban retail price quotations for the years 1789–1850 are practically nonexistent. According to one estimate, real consumption expenditures per capita tended to rise at an average of 1.3 percent per annum, going from $46 in 1789 to $106 in 1850. Over the interval 1850–1913 the general cost-of-living pattern resembled that of the consumption price index of 1789–1850. Civil War inflation saw wages lagging far behind living costs, a disparity particularly severe in the South. Real consumption per capita reached $301 by 1913, which represents an average annual increase of 1.67 percent since 1850. US Bureau of Labor monthly Consumer Price Index has improved coverage and, by the 1980s, provided quotations in twenty-three selected areas on about 304 commodities and services. Except for the years of the Great Depression, the Index has consistently risen. Fortunately, productivity also advanced rapidly during the same period, which permitted wage rates to keep up with the cost of living, and in the long run to surpass it. From $301 in 1913 to $971 in 1973, real consumption increased at an average of 2 percent per annum. Cost of living escalated markedly thereafter, and inflation was in the "double digits" by 1980. The Reagan administration brought the rate down but at the cost of increased unemployment and high interest rates.

CÔTE DES ALLEMANDS. A forty-mile area along the Mississippi R named for German settlers who were given land grants there in 1721 by the sieur de Bienville.

COTENTIN PENINSULA. Half of the US forces invading Normandy on June 6, 1944, entered into the Cotentin. By the end of the month, troops that had landed elsewhere reached the Cotentin W shore and sealed off and captured Cherbourg. From July 3 to 18, they moved S about seven miles at a cost of 40,000 casualties. On July 31, they seized Avranches.

COTTON. Although grown in the South since the founding of Jamestown in 1607, cotton did not become a cash crop during the colonial period. But by the late 18th c. revolutionary inventions in the English textile industry began the process that transformed the South into the "cotton kingdom." Planters in South Carolina and Georgia found a lucrative market for their cotton when trade with England reopened after the Revolution. When in 1793 Eli Whitney invented his cotton gin, which quickly and cheaply separated the seeds from the staple, the cotton belt rapidly expanded westward into Alabama, Mississippi, Louisiana, Arkansas, Tennessee, and Texas. In 1860, the US produced more than 2 billion pounds (4.5 million bales) of cotton. About 75 percent was exported, mainly to England. The Civil War was a disaster to cotton raisers. The Union blockade separated the South from its markets, and at war's end most cotton farmers were destitute, their fields and equipment in neglect or ruin, their black labor force free. Gradually the South returned to cotton but under a much altered system. Land was rented out in small parcels, usually under the sharecropping system. In 1880, 36 percent of cotton farmers were tenants; in 1935 it had risen to over 60 percent. Meanwhile, production increased. The prewar high was soon equaled, reaching 10 million bales by 1900 and 16 million by World War I. By that time, there were signs of serious trouble in the southern cotton belt. Declining prices, production inefficiencies, competition from abroad, the boll weevil, and, finally, the Great Depression, wreaked havoc on older cotton producers. The market improved after the Depression but never equaled predepression levels: production declined from 16 million bales in the 1920s to 14.6 million bales in 1979. The cotton belt had shifted west; in 1979, Texas was the largest producer, followed by California, Mississippi, Arizona, Louisiana, and Arkansas. The US share of world production was 17 percent in 1980.

COTTON CONTROL ACT. See BANKHEAD COTTON ACT.

COTTON GIN. Machine used to pull cotton fibers from the seed, invented by Eli Whitney in 1793, thereby turning cotton an important cash crop in the South. Whitney's gin used spiked teeth set into a wooden cylinder to pull the cotton fibers through the slots in a metal breastplate; the slots were too small to allow the seeds to pass through. A second cylinder with brushes freed the fibers from the teeth. Patented improvements of the original gin continued throughout the 19th c.

COTTON KINGDOM. Between 1830 and 1860, the region reaching from South Carolina to Texas. Characteristic of the Cotton Kingdom were the plantation system and slavery. The plantation system developed because cotton was most cheaply produced on a large scale. Slavery supplied a cheap and abundant supply of unskilled labor.

COTTON WHIGS. See CONSCIENCE WHIGS.

COUNCIL, CITY. See CITY COUNCILS.

COUNCIL BLUFFS. City in SW Iowa on the Missouri R; began as a Potawatomi village clustered about an army blockhouse built in 1837. Mormons arrived in 1846 and named the town Kanesville. Wagon trains were organized there for the long journey to Great Salt Lake and to the goldfields of California. In 1853 its name was changed to Council Bluffs. It became a major railroad terminus. Pop.: 56,449 (1980).

COUNCIL FOR FOREIGN PLANTATIONS. Appointed by Charles II in 1660 to secure a more uniform system of colonial government and to enforce the new Navigation Act. After various vicissitudes, it finally became (1675) the Committee for Trade and Plantations.

COUNCIL FOR NEW ENGLAND. Branch of the Virginia Co., chartered 1606, to colonize and govern land extending from Long Island to the Bay of Fundy. A closed corporation of forty members, it consisted of nobles and landed gentry more interested in developing the land along feudal lines than in trade. Sir Ferdinando Gorges was president, and his son Robert was the first governor-general. The enterprise was a failure; New England was colonized by non-members.

COUNCIL OF APPOINTMENT, NEW YORK. Body created 1777 to check the appointive power of the governor, it became the nucleus of a powerful political machine that by 1821 could dispense patronage of 14,950 offices. Abolished 1821.

COUNCIL OF ECONOMIC ADVISERS. See FEDERAL AGENCIES.

COUNTERFEITING. Counterfeit notes prior to the Civil War had to be distinguished not only from ordinary legal tender but also from legitimate paper money circulating at a discount, because it represented obligations of broken or failed banks and was therefore only fractionally valuable. This complication gave rise to pamphlets known as Bank Note Reporters and Counterfeit Detectors, which gave up-to-date information on the validity and value of notes currently in use. This necessity came to an end in 1867, with the effective end of state banknote issues. Today the prevention of counterfeiting is the responsibility of the Secret Service, an agency of the Treasury Department.

COUNTRY STORE (general store). Dominant in the early years of US settlement. Because the isolation of the community compelled farmers to obtain most things locally, storekeepers carried a varied assortment of goods: groceries, livestock feed, clothing, medicine, books, and hardware. In accepting farm products for store goods, the merchant acted as a marketing agent. Many country merchants also served as local postmasters and informal bankers. The store was often a social center for the community.

COUNTY. See COUNTY GOVERNMENT.

COUNTY FAIRS. Annual events in rural areas that arose in the early 19th c. Unlike earlier fairs, which were primarily buying and selling events, these fairs focused on the exhibition of farm produce and livestock, with prizes awarded for the best in different categories. Once an important feature of rural society, their importance declined as the farm population shrank.

COUNTY GOVERNMENT. County governments, which are substantially unchanged in form since colonial days, exist in all states except Rhode Island, Connecticut (which abolished counties in 1959), and Alaska, whose boroughs differ from counties in some respects; in Louisiana counties are called parishes. The typical county operates through an elective governing body, whose functions are largely administrative, and a set of elective officers— such as sheriff, attorney, treasurer, registrar of deeds, and coroner. Commissioners commonly number three to five. A small number of counties have an administrative head, usually called the county executive, who is analogous to the mayor of a city. In a few instances, county governments furnish services usually provided by municipalities — such as libraries, parks, and airports — in addition to functioning as administrative agencies. State laws largely determine county government structure, functions, and authority. Property tax is the principal local source of county budgets, but a large and increasing part of county budgets comes from state and federal aid, from shared state taxes, and, since 1972, from federal revenue-sharing funds.

COUREURS DE BOIS (or bushrangers). Men who left 17th-c. French settlements in Canada and took to the wilderness, actuated by adventure and the fur trade. This large exodus seriously weakened the colony of New France. Despite government edicts, bushrangers flourished. They were accused of debauching the Indians but did render valuable service as explorers and pioneers in the fur trade.

COURTESY OF THE SENATE. Time-honored custom observed by the Senate when considering presidential nominations to federal offices (including judgeships). If a nominee is objected to by one or both of his home-state senators, the Senate will generally refuse to confirm the appointment if the objecting senator belongs to the same party as the president.

COURTHOUSE ROCK. Landmark on the Oregon Trail, located about five miles S of Bridgeport, Nebraska. It is about 250 feet high and covers an acre.

COURT OF INTERNATIONAL JUSTICE, PERMANENT. See INTERNATIONAL COURT OF JUSTICE.

COURTS-MARTIAL. Military courts established to try individuals subject to military jurisdiction. Primarily based on the British courts-martial system, American courts-martial derive authority from the constitutional authority of Congress "to make Rules for the Government and Regulation of the land and naval forces."

COURTS OF THE PLAINS. Under Mexican law, a judicial system of *jueces del Campos* (judges of the plains). They were circuit riders attending stock roundups on the great ranches to settle conflicting claims of ownership, who also acted as general peace officers. Also applied to impromptu popular tribunals set up along emigrant trails across the Great Plains before a formal judicial system was established.

COUTUME DE PARIS. Judicial system of French colonial Canada and Louisiana, based on customary feudal law of Paris. Although the English criminal code was introduced to Canada by the Quebec Act of 1774, French civil law was retained until 1792. Similarly, the American system introduced in the Illinois country and the Northwest Territory guaranteed to French inhabitants existing *coutumes* in family relations and in descent and conveyance of property. In Louisiana, *coutumes* remained in force until Spanish law was imposed in 1769.

COUTURE'S OPERATIONS. Jean Couture, a French defector from the Arkansas Post, guided (1700) an English expedition from Charleston through the Cherokee country and down the Tennessee, Ohio, and Mississippi rivers to the mouth of the Arkansas.

COVENANT, CHURCH. In all early New England churches, the founders agreed to abide by a set of religious principles. Later recruits were also required to abide by this covenant. At times of revival the covenant was often "renewed."

COVERED WAGON. Wagon box with a framework of hoop-shaped slats over which a canvas tent was stretched; the primary means of transportation in the settlement of the West. They were built in numerous designs and sizes, the two most famous being the Conestoga wagon and the prairie schooner. Each was drawn by several teams of horses, mules, or oxen. Some were boat-shaped with oarlocks so that they might be floated over streams, the animals swimming across.

COVODE INVESTIGATION (1860). A partisan committee, headed by Republican Rep. John Covode of Pennsylvania, to investigate irregularities in President Buchanan's administration. Its major purpose was to obtain campaign material for the 1860 election; this was realized in a voluminous report denouncing the Democratic administration.

COWBOYS. The cowboy began his career when the Spanish brought cattle to the continent in the early 16th c. Later, when settlers began moving into Texas in the 1820s, they adopted Mexican methods for herding and handling cattle. The heyday of the cowboy began in 1867, with the founding of the first real cow town, Abilene, Kansas. Texas cattle, several million strong after years of neglect because of the Civil War, could then be trailed to a railhead without encountering farmers. The cowboy who drove these cattle to market captured the popular imagination partly because of his unique working gear, most of it borrowed from the Mexican vaquero. Furthermore, the cowboy represented courage and devotion to duty. So dangerous was the life that seven years was the average limit to his riding life. Discovery of the cowboy by "penny dreadfuls" (popular novels of violent adventure that originally cost a penny) gave the nation a hero who represented an ideal of physical prowess and courage that accorded well with the mores of the day. He was further idealized in motion pictures and television.

COWBOYS AND SKINNERS. Bands of irregular cavalry and guerrillas who operated chiefly in the "Neutral Ground" of Westchester County, New York, during the American Revolution. The Cowboys were a Loyalist light horse battalion. The Skinners were separate bands of mounted banditti who plundered, burned, and ravished the "Neutral Ground" from 1778 to 1783, and sold their plunder to both sides. They were sometimes employed as scouts and spies, although both sides hanged or shot them whenever they were caught.

COW COUNTRY. Vast region in the West, its central portion being the Great Plains area. At its height, after 1880, it included most of the region from Mexico to Canada and from the central part of the second tier of states west of the Mississippi nearly to the Pacific coast. After ca. 1885, farmers began encroaching on cow country, and by the 20th c. a definite cow country ceased to exist.

COW CUSTOM. The unwritten law of the range in the 19th c., dealing with such matters as prior rights to grazing areas, boundaries of ranges, roundups, movements of cattle on trails, branding of unmarked animals, rights to water, erection of drift fences, and cooperative measures in preventing prairie fires, protecting a neighbor's cattle, or caring for stray animals. Much was later translated into statutory law by such states as Wyoming and Texas.

COWPENS, BATTLE OF (Jan. 17, 1781). Revolutionary encounter at Cowpens, South Carolina; a brilliant American victory. After the first encounter, the British thought they had won, advanced in disorder, and were met by a deadly fire and bayonet attack.

COW TOWNS. As the great cattle drives began in 1867, the railheads that were their destination developed into the gaudy cow towns of legend. The first was Abilene, Kansas. As the railroad network spread out, cow towns were established in other parts of Kansas and in Missouri, Nebraska, Wyoming, Montana, the Dakotas, Texas, Arizona, Colorado, and New Mexico. The later towns acted as distributing points for vast range areas; cattle owners also made these towns headquarters for buying and selling.

COXEY'S ARMY (1894). A protest march on Washington, D.C., led by Jacob Sechler Coxey, who wanted two bills enacted to relieve the depression caused by the panic of 1893. They would provide for large issues of legal-tender currency to be spent for good roads and other public improvements, thus providing work to the unemployed. He attempted to assemble a "living petition" of the unemployed, who would march from Massillon, Ohio, to the capital. His army set out on Easter Sunday, arriving in Washington on May Day with 500 men. When he tried to speak from the Capitol steps, he was arrested, fined, and sent to jail for carrying banners and walking on the grass in the Capitol grounds. Meanwhile, "industrial armies" larger than Coxey's had been formed by the unemployed on the Pacific coast and elsewhere, planning to join Coxey in Washington. Many disintegrated before reaching Washington, and only about 1,200 straggled in. The District of Columbia finally paid their way home.

COX'S INSURRECTION (1798). Zachariah Cox, a land speculator, embarked down the Ohio R from Smithland, Kentucky, with an armed force of eighty. He was arrested on a charge of plotting insurrection, presumably against Spain. He escaped, was rearrested, all the time claiming his innocence. In 1803, Congress declared his arrest illegal but denied his claim for damages.

CRAB ORCHARD. Station on the Wilderness Road in Kentucky, near Logan's Fort in what is now Lincoln County. Here travelers formed parties for protection against Indians as they prepared for journeys over the Cumberland Gap.

"CRACKER LINE." In Civil War parlance, a food-supply line. Especially applied to the steamboat line that brought foodstuff up the Tennessee R to Union troops in Chattanooga.

"CRACKERS." Derogatory term for poor whites of the rural South, especially those of Georgia.

CRAIG V. STATE OF MISSOURI, 4 Peters 410 (1830). Supreme Court decision declaring unconstitutional a Missouri law which established a loan office that could issue paper money.

CRANEY ISLAND. Fortified island at the mouth of the Elizabeth R in Virginia, scene of a battle in the War of 1812. A powerful British fleet, hoping to capture Norfolk, Portsmouth, and Gosport, attacked but was repulsed by Virginia militia.

CRATER LAKE NATIONAL PARK. In SW Oregon; surrounds Crater Lake, which fills the core of a long-dead volcano, Mount Mazama. The lake is the deepest in the US (2,000 feet) and is six miles wide. Crater Lake includes several islands created by later volcanic ac-

tion: Wizard Island is a cone itself, rising to almost 2,000 feet.

CRAWFORD, FORT. Built 1816 at Prairie du Chien, Wisconsin, it commanded the junction of the Wisconsin and Mississippi rivers. Scene of several important Indian treaty-signings.

CRAZY SNAKE REBELLION (1900–1901). Creek uprising, led by Chief Crazy Snake, over the US government's plan to allot their tribal lands. Eventually the leaders were arrested, tried, and released after pledging to make no further trouble.

CREDIT. What credit existed in the colonies and in the young Republic was usually extended by individuals or by merchants as a part of their commercial activities. Early banks filled credit needs of the mercantile community. They also issued bank notes in exchange for commercial paper. After 1865 the creation of demand deposits (checking accounts) largely replaced note issue. In the 19th c., local banks were the dominant institution in the short-term credit market in the North and West; in the South a combination of merchants and cotton factors provided similar service. Commercial paper houses were the only instrument for interregional movement of credit; they began in the East in the 1840s and moved into the Midwest in the 1870s and to the Pacific coast ca. 1900. They were simple arbitragers, buying commercial paper from banks in high-interest regions and reselling it to banks in lower-interest areas. The emergence of capital-intensive transportation and manufacturing firms and a new finance-intensive technology in agriculture increased demand for long-term credit. At first these demands were partly met by commercial banks and the new industrial banks. But the panic of 1837 and the ensuing depression convinced some bankers that long-term loans were unsafe. New legislation made it difficult for commercial banks to make these loans, and other institutions emerged as major suppliers. The first savings bank opened in 1816, and it quickly became the major source of long-term credit in the Northeast. Life insurance companies met this need for the rest of the country. Rapid industrialization produced a need for a new source of credit. The New York Stock Exchange was organized in

1817, followed by local markets in other major cities. These exchanges moved into transportation securities in the early 19th c. and into public utilities shortly thereafter. By 1900 they were handling manufacturing securities, and by World War I the market served to mobilize credit for almost all branches of American activity (agriculture was an exception). Although the system suffered a temporary setback after the 1929 crash, it rebounded during World War II and remains a major route for the extension of long-term credit.

CREDIT ISLAND, BATTLE OF (Sept. 5–6, 1814). Confrontation during the War of 1812 on the Upper Mississippi R. US troops were attacked on the island (now part of Davenport, Iowa) by a British and Indian force and retreated to St. Louis.

CRÉDIT MOBILIER OF AMERICA. Company used by major stockholders of Union Pacific RR to strip that company of its assets. When in 1867 a congressional investigation loomed, a leader of the company distributed at least 160 shares of stock among various members of Congress. Although some were censured and many reputations were ruined, no convictions ever resulted.

CREEK INDIANS. See FIVE CIVILIZED TRIBES.

CREEK WAR (1813–14). Disagreements over how to cope with white intrusions split the Creek into two factions. The Upper Creek, or Red Sticks, were hostile; the Lower Creek, or White Sticks, remained loyal to the US. Prophets arose among the Red Sticks, inciting them to war. On March 27, 1814, Gen. Andrew Jackson defeated the Red Sticks at Horseshoe Bend on Tallapoosa R in E Alabama. Although the White Sticks aided Jackson in the war, they were compelled to sign the Treaty of Fort Jackson (Aug. 9, 1814), ceding more than 20 million acres.

CREOLES. Originally, Europeans born in the American colonies, as distinguished from their fellow nationals born in the mother countries. Usually restricted to individuals of French, Spanish, or Portuguese ancestry. In modern Louisiana, the term is usually applied to all persons with French or Spanish ancestry.

CREOLE SLAVE CASE. In 1841, the 135 slaves of the *Creole,* en route to New Orleans, overpowered the crew and sailed the vessel into Nassau. The US demanded the return of the slaves, but the British, who had abolished slavery, refused. In 1853, an Anglo-American commission agreed on an indemnity of $110,330 to the United States.

CRESAP'S WAR (1774). Desultory warfare, under Capt. Michael Cresap, with the Ohio River Indians. Among other incidents, the family of Logan, a noted chieftain, were brutally murdered, prompting ravages by Logan and his followers. Later it was shown that Daniel Greathouse, not Cresap, was the leader in the massacre.

CRÈVECOEUR, FORT. Built by La Salle in 1680 on the Illinois R opposite present-day Peoria, Ill., for protection against the Iroquois. First French fort in the West. Destroyed that same year.

CRIME. Criminal proscriptions in colonial New England derived from the English common law and the ascetic Christianity of the Puritans. Intoxication, sexual irregularities, irreverence, and other departures from biblical strictures were the commonest crimes; heresy and witchcraft were the ultimate offenses. Punishment was swift and relied heavily on corporal pain and public humiliation. Adding to the problem, courts in England transported to the southern colonies convicts who had been offered the alternative of indentured servitude on plantations. In post-Revolution American cities, gangs carried on their predations; river pirates terrorized inland waterways; large numbers of runaway youths and vagrants supported themselves by theft. The expansion of the western frontier in the 19th c. created notorious outlaws, cattle rustlers, and resolute law officers. Prostitution and gambling flourished. Gun-carrying became commonplace; homicide and armed robbery thrived. Countermeasures were severe: lynch law, perfunctory trials, and harsh punishments were dispensed by peace officers as remorseless as the criminals. Massive immigration during the century set the stage for gangster-controlled organized crime. (See CRIME, ORGANIZED.) In modern America, the common varieties of property and assaultive crimes have had their highest incidence in settings of low socioeconomic status, characterized by family instability, unemployment, low educational attainment, and migrant population. Official crime statistics published annually since 1930 in the *Uniform Crime Reports* indicate a striking increase generally in rates of serious crime. Historical studies of police records of major urban centers, however, contest the popular view that the actual current crime rate is higher than it was in the 19th c. FBI statistics actually show a decline in criminal homicide rates. Changes in technology and social organization have created new patterns. The vulnerability of air transportation has posed fresh challenges to law enforcement. White-collar crime, violations committed in the course of performing business and professional duties, has become more common (and largely undiscovered). The widespread use of credit cards and computers has produced new varieties of crime.

CRIME, ORGANIZED. Enterpreneurial activities that provide customers with illegal goods or services, including prostitution, gambling, bootlegging, and the sale of narcotics. Such activities go back to the colonial period, but organized crime is generally considered a 20th-c. phenomenon. In the decade preceding World War I, a movement to enforce gambling laws closed racetracks in all but five states and thus virtually eliminated ontrack bookmaking, thereby driving all gambling underground and placing it in the hands of organized crime. The real beginning of organized crime, however, dates from the passage in 1919 of the Eighteenth (Prohibition) Amendment to the US Constitution. With sale of alcoholic beverages illegal, a market for illicit enterprise opened up. Those who rose to prominence as bootleggers were primarily distributors. They often opened their own distilleries and breweries and operated their own import services. Because of the rapid rise of bootlegging gangs and their efforts to expand, violent gang wars and bloody massacres often resulted. The level of violence persisted well beyond the end of Prohibition in 1933. Bootlegging gangs moved into other areas, particularly gambling, loan-sharking, and labor racketeering. New ethnic groups entered organized crime. Although Jews and Italians had made important inroads into the operation of red-light districts before World War I, bootlegging greatly accelerated their rise. The creation of black ghettos in northern cities during World War I allowed the formation of black-controlled policy and numbers rackets. Bookmaking, including the betting on sports as well as horse races, remained for the most part under the control of the old established crime families. After World War II, organized crime turned increasingly to traffic in narcotics, especially heroin. Italian, especially Sicilian, influence in organized crime was strengthened as the old Jewish and Irish crime leaders failed to produce heirs. In the 1930s and 1940s, Italian criminals in the New York–New Jersey region coalesced into some five of six major "families." In Providence, Buffalo, Detroit, Chicago, New Orleans, and Kansas City coalitions that were primarily Italian achieved important positions within organized crime. Investigations into these groups led to the popular myth that a Mafia or Cosa Nostra maintained tight control over crime throughout the nation. By the 1980s, however, there were indications that the Italian influence on organized crime was far from complete. The widespread use of heroin, especially in black ghettos, meant that new gangs, chiefly black, controlled that traffic. Cocaine, which is smuggled into the country from Central and South America, brought Latin-American gangs, especially Cubans and Colombians, into its traffic.

CRIME AGAINST KANSAS. See BROOKS-SUMNER AFFAIR.

CRIME OF 1873. Derogatory term for the Coin Act of 1873. The omission of the standard silver dollar and the general decreased use of silver as a monetary metal led to a depressed silver market. The result was the movement for the free coinage of silver that dominated US politics in the decades that followed. The "silverites" traced much of their discontent to the 1873 legislation, although that law in fact merely codified policies already in operation.

CRIPPLE CREEK MINING BOOM. In 1891 a promising gold vein was discovered SW of Pikes Peak in Colorado, leading to the founding of the town of Cripple Creek. The district's gold output reached its peak of $50 million in 1900; more than $500 million worth of gold has been taken from mines there.

CRIPPLE CREEK STRIKES (1893-1904). Series of bloody labor disputes at the Cripple Creek, Colorado, gold mines. Strikes by the miners resulted in loss of life, property destruction, abuse of the state militia power, and the eventual defeat of the unions.

CRISIS. Series of patriotic pamphlets written by Thomas Paine during the American Revolution. The first appeared in 1776 and began with the famous sentence "These are the times that try men's souls." In all, *Crisis* comprised sixteen pamphlets.

CRITTENDEN COMPROMISE (1860). Unsuccessful effort, sponsored by Sen. J. J. Crittenden of Kentucky, to avert the Civil War. The heart of the compromise provided that slavery would be prohibited N of 36° 30′, the line of the Missouri Compromise, but would be protected south of that line, extending all the way to California. Proposal defeated after President Lincoln refused to yield on prohibition of slavery in the territories.

CRITTENDEN RESOLUTION (July 22, 1861). House of Representatives resolution stating that the North's objective in the Civil War was to preserve the Constitution and not to interfere with slavery or subjugate the South. A similar resolution passed the Senate.

CROGHAN'S EXPEDITIONS TO ILLINOIS (1765, 1766). Two attempts by George Croghan, a renowned Indian agent, to pacify Indians in the Illinois country, which had recently been ceded to the British by the French. Proceeding from Fort Pitt down the Ohio R in 1765, Croghan was attacked and captured by the Kickapoo and Mascouten. He was released due to his captors' fear of British reprisals. Although the Indians formally accepted British authority, Croghan made a second expedition down the Ohio in 1766 to hold conferences with the tribes and confirm their acceptance of the British.

CROSS KEYS, BATTLE OF (June 8, 1862). Engagement near Harrisonburg, Virginia. Outnumbered Confederate forces, under Gen. Richard Ewell, repulsed an attack by John Frémont's Union troops.

"CROSS OF GOLD" SPEECH. "You shall not press down upon the brow of labor this crown of thorns, you shall not crucify mankind upon a cross of gold." So William Jennings Bryan concluded his attack on the single gold standard before the Democratic Convention at Chicago on July 8, 1896. The free-silver delegates enthusiastically nominated him as party candidate for president.

CROSWELL LIBEL SUIT (1802). In his defense of Harry Croswell, who had been convicted of criminal libel, Alexander Hamilton argued the truth of the allegation should be considered, a judicial novelty at the time. Hamilton's argument was incorporated in a New York state libel law passed in 1805, thus representing an outstanding victory for freedom of the press.

CROWBAR LAW OF OHIO (1819). Taxed branches of the Bank of the United States. Declared unconstitutional by the Supreme Court.

CROWN POINT. Promontory on the W shore of Lake Champlain in N New York, claimed by both New France and the English colonies. In 1731 France built Fort St. Frederic there; the English forced its destruction in 1759. A new Fort, Crown Point, was built. It in turn was destroyed by Patriot forces in the Revolution. It is a state park today.

CROWN POINT TO NO. 4. Historic road, built in 1759 by the British from Fort Crown Point through the Vermont wilderness to old Post No. 4 on the Connecticut R. An important roadway during the Revolution.

CROW WING, BATTLE OF. See SIOUX–CHIPPEWA WAR.

CROZAT GRANT. France, in 1712, granted Antoine Crozat a charter of government and monopoly over Louisiana. He was responsible for all expense of government. His venture proved unprofitable, so Crozat relinquished his grant in 1717.

CRUISERS. See WARSHIPS.

CRYSTAL PALACE EXPOSITION (1853). International fair held in New York City. Inspired and named for the London exhibition of 1851, it was the first such fair held in the US. It was held in a glass-and-iron structure built on what is now Bryant Park. The exhibition was not a financial success but was the prototype of later world fairs.

CUBA, AMERICAN RELATIONS WITH. American economic relations with Cuba antedate the Revolution. Strategic and political relations evolved from its status as a Spanish colony. The US was content with a weak Spain controlling Cuba, with the expectation that it would gravitate toward US control once Spain lost it. Consequently, the US discouraged Cuban independence during the Spanish-American independence wars, fearing British domination. In 1853 President Pierce offered to buy Cuba but was sharply refused. In response, the US issued the OSTEND MANIFESTO (1854), which claimed the right of the US to buy or take Cuba with or without Spanish consent. Southerners pressed for the admission of Cuba as a slave state. The Civil War effectively ended efforts to buy Cuba. In 1868 the Cuban wars of independence began. They dragged on until 1898, when the sinking of the US battleship *Maine* in Havana harbor offered the US the excuse to invade and occupy Cuba. At the end of the SPANISH-AMERICAN WAR, the US permitted Cuban independence, but with important provisos: US naval bases could be established in Cuba and the US could intervene in Cuban affairs in order to preserve independence or internal order. In the decades that followed, Cuba was, to all intents, a US colony. The US intervened militarily several times, and American capital poured into the country. In 1934, Fulgencio Batista Zaldívar, an army strongman, assumed power. His rule was to the liking of the US. Cuba was assigned a highly profitable sugar quota and preferential treatment for other products. American capital was welcomed and protected, and no objections were raised to the US naval base at Guantánamo Bay. In 1959, Fidel Castro overthrew Batista, and established a revolutionary government. Relations with the US quickly deteriorated. American-owned property in Cuba was confiscated; the US canceled Cuba's sugar quota; and formal diplomatic relations were ended. Castro's government became increasingly orthodox Marxist, and he formed a close alliance with the Soviet Union. Relations deteriorated further under the Kennedy administration, re-sulting in an economic blockade, the disastrous BAY OF PIGS INVASION, and the more successful CUBAN MISSILE CRISIS. Relations remained strained during the 1970s. In 1980 Castro let some 120,000 Cubans, including about 1,800 criminals, emigrate to the US, an act regarded as hostile by the US. Tensions increased in the early 1980s, when the Reagan administration accused the Cubans of attempting to export their Marxist ideology to other Caribbean and Latin-American republics.

CUBAN MISSILE CRISIS (1962). In August it was ascertained that the Soviet Union was engaged in a large military buildup in Cuba, including the placing there of missiles capable of targeting the United States. On October 21, President Kennedy demanded the removal of the missiles and announced a strict quarantine on all offensive military equipment being shipped to Cuba. On October 24, the deadline for compliance with the quarantine passed quietly. Soviet ships approaching Cuba changed course, thereby averting a US-Soviet showdown. Later the Soviet Union agreed to the removal of the missiles from Cuba.

CULLOM COMMITTEE. Senate Committee, headed by Sen. S.M. Cullom of Illinois, that led to the establishment of the Interstate Commerce Act of 1887.

CULPEPER'S REBELLION (1677-79). Insurrection in the Carolina colony by tobacco planters over the navigation acts. Its leader, John Culpeper, imprisoned the royal governor, established courts, and administered the colony for two years. Culpeper went to England, promising submission to proper authority, but was arrested and charged with treason. The earl of Shaftsbury, a proprietor of Carolina, came to his support and he was acquitted.

CUMBERLAND, ARMY OF THE. In the Civil War, it played an important part in many battles and in Sherman's Atlanta campaign. Originally called the Army of the Ohio.

CUMBERLAND, FORT. Series of fortifications at the junction of the Potomac R and Wills Creek, at Cumberland, Maryland. A storehouse was built in 1750, a small fort in 1754, and a larger fort in 1755. Abandoned 1765. Reoccupied during Whiskey Rebellion.

CUMBERLAND COMPACT. See CUMBERLAND SETTLEMENTS.

CUMBERLAND GAP. A pass in the Appalachian Highlands about forty-five miles NE of Knoxville, Tennessee. In use for centuries by Indians and buffalo herds, in the 18th c. it was the route by which thousands of hunters, traders, and settlers entered Kentucky. A mail route was established through the gap in 1792, and in 1797 a tollgate was erected. During the Civil War, it passed back and forth between Union and Confederate hands. Railroads crossed the gap in 1889 and today a major highway uses the gateway.

CUMBERLAND PRESBYTERIAN CHURCH. Offshoot of the Presbyterian Church founded 1810, it grew rapidly in Tennessee and Kentucky. In 1906 they merged with the Southern Presbyterian Church. In 1980 it had a membership of 94,574.

CUMBERLAND ROAD. Also called the United States Road, National Road, National Turnpike. First national road in the US, authorized by Congress in 1806 to be built from Cumberland, Maryland, to the Ohio R. By 1818 it reached Wheeling, now in West Virginia. In 1825 Congress authorized extending it from Wheeling to Zanesville, Ohio. This part followed Zane's Trace, which at Zanesville turned SW to Lancaster, Chillicothe, and the Ohio R. Its parts were turned over to the states in the 1830s, and under their control was extended to Vandalia, Illinois, its final western terminus. Today it is US Route 40.

CUMBERLAND ROAD, TENNESSEE. Ran from E Tennessee through Cherokee territory to Fort Blount on the Cumberland R. Opened in 1795; not to be confused with the national Cumberland Road.

CUMBERLAND SETTLEMENTS. The Transylvania Co., headed by Richard Henderson, beginning 1775, constructed several forts on land acquired from the Cherokee along the Cumberland R. Settlements grew up around the forts, and after it was determined that they were in North Carolina and not Virginia, Henderson set up a government at French Lick (Nashville, Tennessee). Known as the Cumberland Compact, it was later declared void by the North Carolina legislature, which provided Henderson and his associates a consolation grant of 200,000 acres of land on Clinch and Powell rivers.

CURRENCY. See COINAGE; MONEY.

CURRENCY, CONTINENTAL. Bills of credit issued by the Continental Congress and the states to finance the American Revolution. The Congress issued a total of about $241 million and the states a total of $209 million. This was far more than was prudent, and by 1781 the bills had virtually no value; thus came the phrase "not worth a Continental." In 1790, the new government redeemed them at 1 percent of their face value.

CURRENCY, RED DOG AND BLUE PUP. Nicknames applied to state bank notes in the era following the end of the Bank of the United States (1836), when the circulating medium was largely badly secured and fluctuating in value. The name probably comes from engraved designs on some of the notes.

CURRIER & IVES. New York City lithography firm. Nathaniel Currier began it in 1835; James M. Ives joined it in 1850. The firm's prints, which cover virtually all subject matter, were tremendously popular and are regarded today as an important source of social history of the era. The firm went out of business sometime after 1907.

CUSHING'S TREATY (1844). Opened political relations between the US and China by giving the US trading privileges equal to those afforded England and introduced the principle of extraterritoriality.

CUSTOMS. The Constitution gives Congress the power "to lay and collect Taxes, Duties, Imposts, and Excises [and] to regulate Commerce with foreign nations." Consequently, the first Tariff Act was passed July 4, 1789, establishing customs districts and ports of entry and authorizing customs officers. During the first year of operation, the Customs Service collected duties of over $2 million. Until 1860, customs receipts represented 80 to 90 percent of the government's revenue; thereafter, until 1910, 45 to 55 percent. Following passage of the personal income tax legislation in 1913, customs revenue became only a fraction of total federal receipts. Customs revenues totaled about $7.5 billion in 1980.

CYCLES, BUSINESS. See BUSINESS CYCLES.

CYCLONES. See TORNADOES.

DADE MASSACRE (Dec. 28, 1835). During the Seminole War, an attack on a US force en route from Tampa Bay to Fort King, 130 miles to the NE. The Indians surprised the 112 Americans, killing 108.

DAIRY INDUSTRY. Cattle were imported to the colonies in the 17th c. By the 1840s dairy manufactures were reported in all thirty states, with New York, Pennsylvania, and Massachusetts the largest producers. The perishable nature of milk limited the industry until the introduction of milk trains ca. 1850. But adulteration and contamination remained a problem, despite corrective state and local laws. Gail Borden began to make patented condensed milk in 1859; Dr. H. D. Thatcher developed a sanitary dairy bottle in 1884. The real solution, pasteurization, developed only after 1893. By the 1920s, milk from tuberculin-tested herds was on the market. Factory cheesemaking began in Oneida County, N.Y., in 1851. By 1880 annual output was 172 million pounds. Wisconsin displaced New York as the principal cheese producer, with cheddar-type being the overwhelming product. The first butter factory, or creamery, was established in 1861. In 1878 the centrifugal cream separator was invented; and by the 1880s refrigerator cars were being placed in service. Advances in dairy husbandry began in the 1880s with the practice of feeding the animals ensilage, thereby extending the milking season. Dairies adopted milking machines in the 1920s and later installed cooling equipment. Milk output doubled between 1900 and 1960, and peaked at 124 billion pounds in 1979.

DAKOTA. Group of Plains Indians, mostly in Minnesota, the Dakotas, Wyoming, and Montana in the 19th c. Siouan-speaking, it included the Hidatsa, Teton, Assiniboine, and Mandan. In 1780 there were about 25,000, one of the larger Plains groups. With the horse, the Dakota moved as bands across their vast territory, exploiting the bison in the grasslands and engaging in warfare. Their religion featured the vision quest, Sun Dance, Ghost Dance, and medicine bundles or fetish objects. The gold rush of the 1870s into the Black Hills, their territory, created solidarity among the Dakota peoples and allied them with the Cheyenne. The alliance culminated in the 1876 battle at Little Bighorn. A revival of the Ghost Dance movement resulted in the Battle of Wounded Knee in 1890. Dakota are currently on former reservations in North and South Dakota.

DAKOTA EXPEDITIONS OF SIBLEY AND SULLY (1863–65). US army campaigns against the Dakota tribes, led by Gen. H. H. Sibley and Gen. Alfred Sully. Their general purpose was to subdue the Dakota militarily and make the Dakota Territory suitable for settlement. The Indians were defeated and scattered.

DAKOTA GOLD RUSH. See BLACK HILLS.

DAKOTA LAND COMPANY. In 1858 it secured several town sites on the Big Sioux R, set up a provisional government at Sioux Falls, elected a legislature, and chose a representative to Congress. Federal recognition was denied, and the election of President Lincoln cut off their patronage. Indian hostilities in 1862 ended the project.

DALLAS. Second largest city in Texas, located in N Texas at the forks of the Trinity R. French traders operated there in the 18th c.; a trading post was set up in 1840. Confederate forces used it as a base in the Civil War, but it was not involved in combat. Railroads came in 1872, and it became a cotton and wheat center. Rebuilt after a major flood in 1908. Modern Dallas is a financial and insurance center. Textiles, oil and chemical refineries, aircraft factories, and electrical manufacturing establishments are its industrial base. Pop.: 904,078 (1980).

DALLAS-CLARENDON CONVENTION (1856). Anglo-American agreement in which Britain agreed to withdraw from Nicaragua and Honduras, while the US conceded an enlarged British Honduras.

DALLAS REPORTS. First four volumes of Supreme Court decisions, 1790–1800.

DALLES, THE. Stretch of Columbia R, about 70 miles E of Portland, Or. A dangerous point in the early fur trade due to navigation difficulties and Indian hostilities. The city of The Dalles, founded 1857, is a busy inland port, with ships moving through the locks of the Dalles Dam (built 1957). Pop.: 10,820 (1980).

DAME SCHOOLS. Colonial schools, usually conducted by a woman in her home, in which young children were taught basic subjects.

"DAMN THE TORPEDOES." Reply by Union Adm. D. G. Farragut to a warning of submerged torpedoes (mines) during the Battle of Mobile Bay (Aug. 5, 1864). Farragut led his fleet safely through the mine fields.

DANBURY, BURNING OF (April 27, 1777). A depot of patriot stores at Danbury, Conn., was attacked and burned by British Col. William Tryon. Part of the stores had been saved by retreating Continental troops.

DANBURY HATTERS' CASE (*Loewe* v. *Lawlor*, 208 US 274 [1908]). The Supreme Court ruled that unions were subject to the Sherman Antitrust Act and awarded damages to the company. Individual union members were deemed liable, and the homes of 140 workmen were ordered sold to pay the damages.

DANCE.
  American Indian Dance. Simplest was the round dance of the Great Basin, a social event with dancers shuffling in a circle. Among the Pueblo and California groups, dancing was a religious ritual. The masked impersonations of the rain beings marked the ceremonial highlight of a complex ritual calendar. The Plains Indians were noted for their GHOST DANCE and SUN DANCE.
  Theatrical Dance. Although there were a few European dance companies touring in the 19th c., theatrical dance in America had its real beginning in the 1920s. The companies of Anna Pavlova and Sergei Diaghilev exposed US audiences to the classical ballet. Members of those companies established ballet schools in the larger cities and eventually developed companies. Modern dance, with a native tradition going back to Isadora Duncan and Ruth St. Dennis, prospered under the influential figures of Martha Graham and Doris Humphrey. Ballet companies thrived in the 1930s in Chicago, Philadelphia, and New York. George Balanchine and Lincoln Kirstein began the company that developed into the New York City Ballet. Ballet Theatre (now American Ballet Theatre) began performances in 1940. After World War II, the lines between modern dance and ballet became blurred as choreographers such as Martha Graham, Merce Cunningham, Alvin Ailey, Glen Tetley, and Twyla Tharp created dances for both media. Jerome Robbins and Agnes De Mille were the most influential of the native classical choreographers. Ballet burgeoned in the 1970s, and by the early 1980s, there were professional companies in most major cities, including Philadelphia, Chicago, Houston, and San Francisco. Among national touring companies were those of Robert Joffrey and Alvin Ailey. The Dance Theatre of Harlem was founded as a primarily black classical ballet company. Dance in the movies dates from the 1930s musicals of Fred Astaire and Ginger Rogers. Beginning in the 1940s, Gene Kelly exerted great influence. On the Broadway stage, De Mille, Robbins, and Bob Fosse sparked the development of a high level of professionalism and artistry in the popular theater.
  Social Dancing. Until the 20th c., ballroom dances, such as the waltz, polka, and schottische, were European imports. Ragtime was the first native music to create native dances to go with it. In the 1920s and 1930s, the Charleston, the black bottom, the Lindy, and the foxtrot commandeered dance floors. Latin rhythms—the rhumba, tango, samba, and the cha-cha-cha—alternated with the native dances. The rock-and-roll revolution of the late 1950s brought with it a whole new type of dance, beginning with the twist. In the 1970s, discotheques replaced traditional dance halls; and disco dancing, often accompanied by lavish video systems and light shows, became the rage.

DANCING RABBIT CREEK, TREATY OF (Sept. 27, 1830). Provided for the end of Choctaw claims to land in Mississippi and for the nation's removal W of the Mississippi R. Almost 8 million acres were surrendered.

DANISH SPOLIATION OF AMERICAN COMMERCE (1807–11). Danish attempts to capture British merchantmen flying false American flags resulted in a number of legitimate American vessels being captured. After US protests and long negotiations, the Danes paid indemnities in 1830.

DANISH WEST INDIES. See VIRGIN ISLANDS.

DANITES. Secret Mormon order (the Sons of Dan) founded ca. 1838. Members were reputed to be pledged to follow the Prophet regardless of law and public morality.

D'ARGES COLONY. See ARGES.

DARK AND BLOODY GROUND. Name given Kentucky in the 18th c., as battles raged amongst the various Indian tribes and settlers. Feuds and civil outbreaks continued the sobriquet into the 19th c.

DARK DAY (May 19, 1780). In New England, the sun rose clear and bright, but by mid-morning darkness had developed. That evening the moon appeared blood red, and the earth was wrapped in darkness. Religious people thought these phenomena a fulfillment of biblical prophecy. Scientists conjecture they were caused by smoke from fires on the frontier.

DARK HORSE. Compromise candidate selected by a party convention when a deadlock arises among leading candidates. Warren G. Harding was a famous dark horse candidate.

D'ARTAGUETTE'S DEFEAT. See ARTAGUETTE.

DARTMOOR PRISON. English establishment where US naval prisoners were held during the War of 1812. On April 6, 1815, they rioted to protest being held after peace had been restored. Seven were killed and sixty wounded. The British eventually paid indemnities. The prisoners were released at the end of April 1815.

DARTMOUTH COLLEGE. Founded 1755 as an Indian charity school in Connecticut. Moved to Hanover, N.H., in 1769 and was renamed for the earl of Dartmouth. It stayed open through the Revolution, and by 1780 had graduated about one hundred. Its greatest growth has been in the 20th c.

DARTMOUTH COLLEGE CASE (*Trustees of Dartmouth College* v.*Woodward,* 4 Wheaton 518 [1819]). The Supreme Court ruled that a state could not alter the obligations of a contract. It established the Constitution as a powerful instrument for the protection of property rights.

DAUGHTERS OF THE AMERICAN REVOLUTION (DAR). Patriotic society organized 1890. Membership requires an ancestor who served in the American Revolution. Membership in 1980 was 209,000.

DAUGHTERS OF THE CONFEDERACY. See UNITED DAUGHTERS OF THE CONFEDERACY.

DAVENPORT. City in Iowa, on the Mississippi R., founded 1836. An important commercial center, it built the first bridge across the Mississippi and had the first railroad service in Iowa. Industries include aluminum manufacturing and food-processing plants. Pop.: 103,264 (1980).

DAVIS, FORT. Established in W Texas in 1854 to protect settlers and mail along the Overland Trail. Changed hands several times during the Civil War. Abandoned 1891.

DAVIS, IMPRISONMENT AND TRIAL OF. In late April 1865, the Confederacy having collapsed, Jefferson Davis made plans to escape to Europe. On May 10, he was captured by Union forces, and soon imprisoned in Fortress Monroe, Va., charged with treason and complicity in the assassination of Abraham Lincoln. He was incarcerated for two years, released on bail, and finally brought to trial in November 1868 on a new set of charges. On Christmas Day, President Andrew Johnson issued a general amnesty proclamation, and charges against him were dismissed.

DAWES COMMISSION. Appointed by President Cleveland in 1893 to negotiate with the FIVE CIVILIZED TRIBES and induce them to give up their tribal governments and come under state and federal laws. Abolished 1905 after successfully reached agreement.

DAWES GENERAL ALLOTMENT ACT (1887). Broke up Indian nations and opened part of their land to white settlement. Resulted in most of the best land falling into white hands, a situation the Indian Reorganization Act of 1934 tried to rectify.

DAWES PLAN (1924). After the German default on World War I reparations, this plan operated successfully until replaced by the Young Plan in 1930.

DAYLIGHT SAVING TIME. Utilizes summer daylight by advancing the clock one hour in spring and turning it back one hour in fall. Movement originated in England and was adopted by the US Congress in 1918. There was much opposition, and the law was repealed; after that, daylight saving time became a matter of state and local option. In World War II, Congress again imposed it on the nation, calling it "war time." After 1945, state and local option again prevailed until 1966, when the Uniform Time Act called for all states to adopt daylight saving time unless they specifically exempted themselves by legislative act. Clocks are advanced on the last Sunday in April and turned back on the last Sunday in October.

DAYTON. Industrial city in SW Ohio. Best known as the home of the Wright brothers, who developed their airplane in their bicycle shop. Dayton is a center for the manufacture of precision tools and machinery, including cash registers, electrical ignition systems for automobiles, and weighing scales. Pop.: 203,588 (1980).

D DAY. US military term designating the target date for an operation; commonly used to refer to June 6, 1944, date of the Allied invasion of Normandy.

DEARBORN, FORT. Founded 1803 at the mouth of the Chicago R, where Chicago now stands. Destroyed by Indians during the War of 1812 and rebuilt, it was garrisoned off and on until the city of Chicago was founded in 1833. Evacuated 1836, its site becoming Grant Park.

DEARBORN WAGON. Light, four-wheeled vehicle, usually with a top and pulled by one horse. In almost universal use in America ca. 1819–50.

DEATH VALLEY. Desert valley about 140 miles long, in California near the Nevada line. The driest and hottest area in North America, it is the bottom of a volcanic fault and the lowest point in the US (282 feet below sea level). Proclaimed a national monument in 1933.

DEBATABLE LAND. That part of SE North America that came to be Georgia, so called because of the long disagreement between Spain and England over its ownership. England won uncontested rights in 1763.

DE BOW'S REVIEW. Influential journal in the antebellum South, published in New Orleans after 1846. Supported slavery and secession. Resumed after the war, it devoted itself to the economic recovery of the South. Ceased publication 1880.

DEBT, IMPRISONMENT FOR. Practice imported to the colonies from England. Opposition began ca. 1775 and mostly abolished in the 19th c.

DEBT, PUBLIC. In 1789 the new national government assumed the foreign debts of the Continental Congress amounting to $11.7 million. Alexander Hamilton, the first secretary of the treasury, recommended that the government also assume the domestic debt, another $40 million (including accrued interest). Despite strong opposition, this took place, and the federal government also assumed some $18.2 million in state debts. From 1790 through the 19th c., the public debt fluctuated widely, with heavy increases resulting from the War of 1812. From just over $45 million in 1812, it rose to $2.3 billion in 1866. It then was reduced to $585 million in 1892, and averaged $1 billion until World War I. In 1917, the issuance of Liberty Bonds raised the debt to $25 billion, reduced to $15 billion by 1930. The huge increase in both the debt and the gross national product (GNP) in World War II clarified the relationship between the two, and economists came to consider them together (e.g., the federal debt exceeded the GNP by 20 percent in 1945). By 1980 the debt was about 36 percent of the GNP, a ratio lower than in the depression years of the 1930s but higher than the 25 percent level of the prosperous years of the 1920s. The federal indebtedness in 1982 was $1,142,035,000,000 or $4,909.15 per person in the US.

DEBT AND INVESTMENT, FOREIGN. The net of all the claims on people or governments of foreign nations held in the US, less the reverse claims held by foreigners, is the foreign debt owed to or by this country. Before the Revolution, Americans had been deeply indebted to English merchants, and during the war the Continental Congress borrowed heavily from Holland and France. After the Napoleonic Wars, European capital flowed to America, particularly into state bonds. Later, American railroads and other utilities were able to borrow from Europe and to market their common stock there. By 1914, there was $7.2 billion of foreign capital in the US, and Americans owned about $3.5 billion in foreign obligations. World War I reversed these relations. By 1920, European governments owed the US government $12 billion. European investors had drawn their US balances down to $3 billion, while American private interests had sent an additional $4 billion abroad. Debts of European governments proved more than they could handle, and arrangements were made in the 1920s for gradual repayment and low interest rates. The Great Depression and World War II ended the hope of substantial collection of those debts. Financial assistance by the US in the war took the form of lend-lease, a euphemism for outright gifts, so that no large burden of current indebtedness remained at the close of the war. To make capital available, the United Nations set up the International Monetary Fund and the International Bank for Reconstruction and Development, with the US the largest subscriber to both. The MARSHALL PLAN was carried out without increasing the debt of European nations to the US. In 1950 total foreign investment was only $19 billion, of which $11 billion represented direct ownership. Europe prospered, and by 1965, American private investment abroad was $81 billion, of which nearly $50 billion was direct ownership. Consequently, the US began showing large deficits in the balance of international payments. The federal government discouraged this capital outflow, as did the recession of 1969–71. The US remained by far the leading creditor nation, with foreign claims reaching $168 billion in 1980; these claims were balanced by expatriated currency, chiefly in the hands of bankers and oil-exporting nations.

DEBTS, STATE. After the federal government assumed most Revolutionary debts of the states (see DEBT, PUBLIC), nearly all the states found themselves debt-free. Between 1820 and 1840, the states entered into extensive borrowing for canals, turnpikes, railroads, and manufacturing enterprises. The panic of 1837 and the ensuing depression caused many of these issues to default. As a result, it became common practice to write rigid debt limits into state constitutions. Between the Civil War and the 1930s, most state borrowing financed construction of public buildings and highways. The Great Depression saw states borrowing to finance general relief expenditures. Overall, though, the 1930s period was one of repayment of state debts. State indebtedness was $3.59 billion in 1940, dropped to $2.4 billion in 1946, but rose to nearly $5.3 billion in 1950. During the 1960s, most states more than doubled their debts, to $39.5 billion in 1969. By 1978, it had reached $103 billion. Expanded programs of public works and construction of penal institutions, hospitals, educational facilities, and recreational facilities led to the increase. Despite these large increases, the state component in local government debt—including counties, municipalities, school districts, and special districts—remains the smallest.

DECIUS LETTERS. Anonymous attack on Patrick Henry for his opposition to the Constitution. Published in 1788 and 1789 in a Richmond newspaper, they were written by either James Montgomery or John Nicholas.

DECLARATION OF INDEPENDENCE. Evolved from a resolution by Richard Henry Lee to the Continental Congress on June 7, 1776. Thomas Jefferson was named chairman of a committee that included Benjamin Franklin, John Adams, Roger Sherman, and Robert R. Livingston and was assigned the task of drawing up the declaration. Jefferson completed his draft, incorporated changes requested by the committee, and laid it before Congress on June 28. After some negotiations, Congress voted unanimously (with New York abstaining) for independence. Jefferson's paper was edited for two days by Congress, which nevertheless left the document mostly intact. Congress completed its revision of the Declaration in the early evening of July 4. Few facts are known about the signing of the document. On that date it bore only the signatures of John Hancock, as president, and Charles Thomson, as secretary of Congress. On July 19, after learning New York had approved the Declaration, Congress voted that the document be "engrossed . . . on parchment." On August 2, the *Journal* of Congress notes, "The Declaration of Independence being engrossed and compared at the table was signed by the members." The names of the signers were kept secret until Jan. 19, 1777, when they were released to the world. (For the text of the Declaration of Independence, see APPENDIX.)

DECLARATION OF RIGHTS (1774). Resolution by American colonists to the British government embodying their complaints that their rights as Englishmen were being denied them. Specifically, they cited their opposition to the STAMP ACT of 1765, the TOWNSHEND ACTS of 1767, and the COERCIVE ACTS and QUEBEC ACT of 1774.

DECLARATORY ACT (1766). Intended by the British to be an important constitutional compromise with the American colonies, it became instead a cause for further grievance. The act asserted that the colonies were subordinate to the crown and Parliament; declared the king and Parliament had full power and authority to make laws binding to the colonies; and declared all votes, resolutions, and proceedings of the colonies calling into question the authority of Parliament as null and void.

DECORATION DAY. See MEMORIAL DAY.

DECORATIONS, MILITARY.
Medal of Honor. Highest US decoration for valor during war, awarded by the president in the name of Congress. Authorized in the Civil War. Only US decoration to include a pension ($100 a month).
Distinguished Service, Navy, and Air Force Crosses. Ranking next below the Medal of Honor. Established for the army 1918, for the navy 1919, and for the air force 1960. Awarded for combat heroism.

Distinguished Service Medal. Awarded since World War I for meritorious service in any capacity, not necessarily in combat.
Silver Star. The third highest award for combat heroism, it dates from World War I and is awarded in all the services for gallantry in action.
Legion of Merit. Awarded since World War II to members of the US armed forces and friendly foreign nations for meritorious conduct.
Distinguished Flying Cross. Awarded for heroism or extraordinary achievement while participating in aerial flight. Authorized 1926, but made retroactive to 1918.
Soldier's Medal, Navy and Marine Corps Medal, and Airman's Medal. Awarded for personal bravery usually indicating risk of life in a noncombat situation. Date from 1926, 1942, 1960, respectively.
Bronze Star. May be awarded to any person who, while serving in any capacity in the services, distinguishes himself by heroic or meritorious achievement. Dates from 1944; replaced the Combat Infantry Badge and Combat Medical Badge.
Air Medal. Established 1942, it is given to any person who distinguishes himself by meritorious achievement while participating in aerial flight.
Purple Heart, Order of the. America's oldest military decoration, established by George Washington 1782 for meritorious service and extraordinary fidelity; originally called the Badge of Military Merit. Since 1942, awarded to members of the armed forces (and to some civilians) for injuries received in action.

DEERFIELD MASSACRE (1704). French soldiers and their Indian allies from Canada overcame sleeping inhabitants of the snow-drifted stockade at Deerfield, Mass. About 50 were killed, 137 escaped, and 111 were taken captive. On the journey to Canada, 17 others died. After several years of negotiations, 60 captives were allowed to return home; some, however, elected to remain in Canada.

DEFENSE, DEPARTMENT OF. Created 1947 in order to unify the armed forces; replaced the War and Navy departments. Headed by the secretary of defense, the third ranking member of the president's cabinet, and made up of three subordinate departments: army, navy, and air force. These are headed, respectively, by the secretaries of the army, the navy, and the air force. The joint chiefs of staff, the nation's top military officers representing the respectives services, serve directly under the secretary of defense and are the department's principal military advisers.

DEFENSE, NATIONAL. The US Constitution gave the federal government powers to provide for the common defense, balanced by state control of militia and the right of the citizenry to bear arms. Congress was empowered to levy taxes, declare war, raise armies, and provide for a navy. The president was named commander in chief.

DEFIANCE, FORT. Built 1794 at the junction of the Auglaize and Maumee rivers, within the present Defiance, Ohio.

DEFICIT, FEDERAL. The American Revolution was financed largely by domestic loans and issues of paper money, most later repudiated or redeemed at very low rates. Since then, the federal government as often as not has operated at a deficit. All wars and most major depressions have caused deficits; there were eighty-nine annual deficits during 1791–1980. The War of 1812 caused a four-year deficit of $68 million. The Mexican War produced a three-year deficit of $53 million. The Civil War resulted in a four-year deficit of $2.6 billion. The Spanish-American War caused a two-year deficit of $127 million. World War I produced a three-year deficit of $24.9 billion. Not until 1929 was deficit spending used to speed recovery from a depression. By 1941, federal deficits totaled about $50 billion. World War II produced a deficit of $183 billion and precipitated a price inflation which almost doubled consumer costs from 1939 to 1952. The Korean War, the cold war, and foreign aid to nations devastated by World War II were largely responsible for the next deficit, $16.6 billion in 1952–54. Another large federal deficit began in 1961, caused by the Vietnam War, extensive social welfare reforms, the cold war, and space exploration. At the end of fiscal 1973, there was a deficit of $14.4 billion. After a relatively small deficit of $3.5 billion in 1974, federal deficits soared to unprecedented levels, including a record high in

1976 of $65.6 billion. Conservative economists and politicians have long blamed the high federal deficits for high inflation and interest rates. In 1980, Ronald Reagan was elected president on a platform promising an end to deficit spending. He failed to accomplish this, however, and during his administration deficits rose to new highs. It was estimated that the 1984 deficit would reach $200 billion.

DEFINITIVE TREATY OF PEACE (1783). Marked the end of the Revolutionary War and assured American independence. Britain agreed to evacuate troops "with all convenient speed," prewar debts owed to British individuals were to be paid, boundaries were set, and fishing rights in the Atlantic were established.

DE HAVEN'S EXPEDITION (1850–51). Unsuccessful attempt by US navy expedition to rescue Sir John Franklin, a British explorer lost in the Arctic. The expedition, led by Lt. E. J. De Haven, searched Baffin Bay, sailed into Barrow Strait, and discovered and named Grinnell Land.

DEISM. Belief in the existence of a supreme being, but rejecting revelation and the supernatural doctrines of Christianity; introduced into America in the 18th c., its influence was particularly felt during and immediately after the Revolution. Thomas Jefferson is usually regarded as a deist.

DELAWARE. Middle Atlantic state on the Delaware Peninsula, which it shares with Maryland and Virginia. Settled in 1631 by the Dutch, superseded briefly by Swedes in 1638. The Dutch regained control in 1655, only to be overthrown by the English, who gave it its present name. Originally three counties in William Penn's grant, it became a separate state 1776. It was the first to ratify the Constitution. Industrialization began early in the north, with agriculture predominating in the south. The Du Pont Company and the Du Pont family have long played an important part in Delaware. Capital city is Dover. Pop.: 595,225 (1980).

DELAWARE (Indians). Algonkin-speaking tribe originally located in New Jersey, and on Manhattan, Long, and Staten islands, they eventually migrated to Oklahoma. First contacted by the Dutch in 1609; reputedly sold Manhattan Island in 1626. As they were forced westward, they became involved with the French and Spanish, fought the British, and converted to Moravian Christianity.

DELAWARE, WASHINGTON CROSSING THE (1776). On Christmas Day, 1776, troops under Gen. George Washington crossed the Delaware R from the Pennsylvania side north of Trenton, defeating the British the following day (see TRENTON, BATTLE OF). Emanuael Leutze's *Washington Crossing the Delaware* has become a symbol of this exploit, the turning point of the Revolution.

DELAWARE AND HUDSON. See RAILROADS, SKETCHES OF PRINCIPAL LINES.

DELAWARE AND HUDSON CANAL. Built 1825–28 to connect the Delaware and Hudson rivers, principally to carry coal from Pennsylvania to New York. Once enormously profitable, by 1900 the railroads had destroyed its usefulness.

DELAWARE AND RARITAN CANAL. Built 1830–34 to connect Philadelphia and New York directly by water. It was of enormous economic importance. Taken over by the Pennsylvania RR 1871, its traffic had almost ceased by 1930.

DELAWARE BAY. Discovered by Henry Hudson 1609. Called South Bay by the Dutch and originally Godyn's Bay by the English. Named for Thomas De La Warr, the governor of Virginia.

DELAWARE COUNTIES ACT OF UNION (1682). Pennsylvania action that accepted as part of the colony counties constituting the modern state of Delaware.

DELAWARE, LACKAWANNA AND WESTERN. See RAILROADS, SKETCHES OF PRINCIPAL LINES: ERIE LACKAWANNA.

DELEGATION OF POWERS. Traditionally, courts have held that Congress cannot delegate its powers, which are derived from the people, to other agencies of government. However, some delegation has proved necessary and the courts have not prohibited it. For example, Congress's power to regulate interstate commerce has been for the most part delegated to the various regulatory commissions. Also, Congress often delegates to the president the power to change tariff rates in negotiation with foreign nations. In all cases, Congress must define the subject to be regulated, and delegation must be to public officials, not to private groups or individuals.

DELIMA V. BIDWELL. See INSULAR CASES.

DEMOCRACY. Democracy developed gradually in the course of American history. As the colonial period progressed, democratic tendencies were most pronounced in the popularly elected legislatures that grew in power in most of the colonies. The Revolution eliminated the monarchy and a hereditary titled aristocracy and broadened the base of social, economic, and political power. The right to vote and hold office without regard to property qualifications was greatly expanded during the Jacksonian period. The right to vote was extended to free blacks by state action in only six states by 1860, but the Fifteenth Amendment (1870) forbade the denial of the right to vote because of race or color and gave Congress the power to enforce this concept by appropriate legislation. The long struggle to translate this commitment into reality culminated in the Voting Rights Act of 1965. By 1920, fifteen states had extended the suffrage to women, and the right to vote was nationalized by the Nineteenth Amendment in 1920. Finally, the voting age was reduced in 1971 to eighteen by the Twenty-sixth Amendment.

DEMOCRACY, JACKSONIAN. See JACKSONIAN DEMOCRACY.

DEMOCRACY, JEFFERSONIAN. See JEFFERSONIAN DEMOCRACY.

DEMOCRATIC PARTY. The party conventionally is traced to the Anti-Federalists, those who opposed ratification of the Constitution. During the Washington and Adams administrations, they coalesced into the Republican, or Jeffersonian, faction, which became known as the DEMOCRATIC-REPUBLICAN PARTY and after the Jacksonian era simply as the Democratic party. Thus Thomas Jefferson and Andrew Jackson are both regarded as founders of the party. The party was originally identified with strict or narrow construction of the Constitution, favoring expanded states' rights and a minimal national government. During the Jacksonian era, a democratic populism was added to states'-rights posture. The party was enormously successful in the first half of the 19th c., particularly as the more populist states of the frontier entered the Union, but foundered badly over slavery. It split into northern and southern wings. From the Civil War until Woodrow Wilson was elected in 1912, the Republicans were firmly in control of the national government except for the two administrations of Grover Cleveland. Wilson was succeeded by another series of Republican administrations. The impact of the Great Depression provided the basis for Franklin D. Roosevelt's landslide victory of 1932. His coalition-building skills brought urban labor, southern conservatives, and blacks and other ethnic minorities all under the umbrella of the New Deal. That coalition, for the most part, endured through the administrations of Harry S. Truman, John F. Kennedy, and Lyndon B. Johnson, although Republicans held the White House throughout the 1950s. The Johnson administration, under the Great Society, produced sweeping social and economic reforms, the most comprehensive since the New Deal. The Voting Act of 1965 in effect enfranchised millions of southern blacks, most of whom could be expected to support the Democratic party. Despite his successes, Johnson saw his party seriously divide over the Vietnam War. A Republican, Richard Nixon, was elected in 1968 and 1972. Jimmy Carter, economically more conservative than his immediate predecessors, was elected in 1976; he was defeated overwhelmingly in 1980 by the conservative Republican Ronald Reagan. At the state and local level, the Democratic party remained strong. Although the South, so heavily Democratic traditionally that it became known as the Solid South, was no longer a one-party section, it still remained strongly Democratic. Labor unions and minorities remained loyal to the party, but the old coalitions had diminished by the 1980s.

DEMOCRATIC-REPUBLICAN PARTY. Offshoot of the Anti-Federalist party and ancestor of the modern Democratic party. Organized around Thomas Jefferson, who led the opposition to the policies of Alexander Hamilton in the 1790s. Jefferson's Republican party, as it came to be known, was based on a number of "Republican" and "Democratic" clubs already formed in different states. It opposed a strong central government, the economic policies of Hamilton, and support for England during the Napoleonic Wars, advocating an agrarian democracy, strict construction of the Constitution, and reforms eliminating aristocratic control of government.

DEMOGRAPHY. The quantitative, statistical analysis of populations focusing on birth, marriage, death, and geographical mobility. The first serious US contributions in the field were made by historians of early America whose work began to appear in the 1960s. Focusing on specific communities, colonies, or groups, these historians made use of modern demographic methods in order to demonstrate what actually happened to people living in the 17th, 18th, and 19th centuries.

DEMOLOGOS. Robert Fulton's steam warship, designed during the War of 1812 to defend New York harbor. Launched 1814, it cruised the harbor in 1815 but never saw battle.

DENONVILLE, FORT. Wooden fortress built on the E bank of the Niagara R in 1687 to protect French trade. Abandoned the next year.

DENONVILLE'S INVASION (1687). Expedition against the Seneca by the French governor of Canada, marquis de Denonville. Leaving Montreal for Irondequoit Bay, Denonville's troops destroyed several Seneca villages before returning.

DENTISTRY. The earliest dental specialists were itinerants, and apprenticeship was the common method of learning. In the early 19th c., books on dentistry began appearing; some medical schools included courses on dentistry. The Society of Surgeon Dentists was organized in New York City 1834. In 1839 the *American Journal of Dental Science* appeared. In 1840 a college opened in Baltimore (now the Dental School of the University of Maryland). The Ohio College of Dental Surgery followed in 1845 and other colleges in the 1850s. Various dental associations coalesced into what is today the American Dental Association (ADA). From the beginning, the professional associations looked to the improvement of educational standards. Dental schools were rated, and requirements for practice of dentistry continued to rise until a university education was necessary. Mechanical breakthroughs were impressive. New drills and other instruments were devised. The foot-operated, cord-driven dental engine, introduced 1871, proved of fundamental importance. Artificial teeth were improved when porcelain replaced ivory. The discovery of anesthesia 1846 made extraction relatively painless, and the invention of vulcanite in the 1850s made cheap dentures widely available. Early in the 20th c., the use of careful antiseptic techniques, proper techniques of cavity preparation, and stable amalgams for filling cavities were important improvements. Increasing use of X rays helped diagnosis.

DENVER. Capital of Colorado, in the NE part of the state; founded 1858 by a gold-seeking party. Located near the foot of the Rocky Mountains, it became the supply depot for the mines, and grew rapidly after the coming of the railroad 1870. Great silver camps formed; agriculture flourished nearby. The closing of the mines ruined its smelting business, but the coming of World War II brought large war industries. It became an important distribution, trade, tourist, and cultural center. Pop.: 491,396 (1980).

DENVER AND RIO GRANDE WESTERN. See RAILROADS, SKETCHES OF PRINCIPAL LINES.

DEPARTMENT STORES. In the 1880s large retail establishments, divided into departments and selling clothing, soft goods, furniture, and home appliances, became centerpieces of the retail districts of all major cities. In 1899 their share of the total retail trade was 2 percent; it grew to 8 percent in 1929 and to 10 percent in 1980. In 1977, the Census Bureau classified 8,800 establishments as department stores. Of these, only 600 were independent units; the rest were parts of chains. In the 1950s, department stores opened branches in suburban shopping malls. These branches proved highly profitable, and by the 1980s many department store chains had closed their original urban stores to concentrate on their suburban outlets.

DEPORTATION. Governmental expulsion of an unwanted alien. Governments have always considered it their right to expel aliens as they see fit, often under harsh and unfair procedures. The first such law in the US, the Alien Act of 1798, one of the ALIEN AND SEDITION LAWS, expired in 1800, never having been enforced. An alien act of 1888 provided for the expulsion of contract laborers (typically Chinese) and the Immigration Act of 1891 extended the penalty to all illegal immigrants. The law has been amended many times, but the right of the government to expel those it considers undesirable has never been successfully challenged. In the 1920s, deportation centered on those deemed politically subversive, or mentally or physically defective. In the 1930s, illiterates, prostitutes, and criminals were the chief deportees. Deportation of narcotics violators reached a high in the 1960s. In the 1970s, the emphasis in deportation was on illegally present laborers from Mexico, the Caribbean, and Central America. In 1980, the Cuban government sent 1,800 criminals to the US in "freedom flotillas." Unable to deport them back to Cuba, they were held in overcrowded detention centers, as were thousands of Haitian refugees who reached the US each year.

DEPOSIT, FORT. Built on the Tennessee R in Alabama 1813 by Andrew Jackson as his base during the CREEK WAR.

DEPOSIT, NEW ORLEANS. In 1795 Spain granted the US free navigation on the Mississippi R. For three years, US citizens were given the privilege of depositing and reexporting their property duty-free in New Orleans. From 1798 the New Orleans deposit was extensively used. It was closed by Spain in 1802, but threat of war forced its reopening in 1803, and it remained open until the US took possession of New Orleans by the LOUISIANA PURCHASE.

DEPOSIT ACT OF 1836. Provided for distribution of the US Treasury surplus to the states, on the basis of their representation in Congress. Distribution was halted after the PANIC OF 1837 turned the surplus into a deficit.

DEPRESSION, GREAT. See GREAT DEPRESSION.

DEPRESSION OF 1920. Rumors of a buyers' strike caused commodity prices to decline rapidly, money to become extremely tight, and gold to be taken out of the country; and led to a 30 percent decline in industrial stocks. Depression lasted through 1921.

DERNA EXPEDITION (1805). During the Tripolitan War, William Eaton led a US force from Alexandria across 500 miles of desert to Derna. He hoped to overthrow the bey of Tripoli. He captured Derna, but a peace treaty had already been signed.

DESERET, STATE OF. Name given the provisional state formed by the Mormons in 1849; included the immense area of land, acquired in the Mexican War, between the Sierra Nevadas and the Rockies. Salt Lake City was chosen capital and Brigham Young named governor. Congress declined to go along with the scheme, creating instead the Territory of Utah, which the Mormons accepted as a temporary measure. (See also UTAH.)

DESERT, GREAT AMERICAN. See GREAT AMERICAN DESERT.

DESERT CULTURE (Western Archaic culture). Stage of Indian development in prehistoric western North America. Among its features are small social units, seed harvesting, fur cloth, woven sandals, basketry, flat milling stones, and a wide variety of small tools. Radiocarbon dating places its beginnings at between 11,000 and 9,000 years ago. The desert culture persisted into the historic period in some areas.

DESERTION. Absence without authorization from military service. Traditionally a serious problem to armies after reverses have destroyed morale, when food and supplies run out, or when pay has not been forthcoming. In the Revolution, desertion depleted the forces after the British capture of New York. Widespread desertion, even in the midst of battle, plagued the military during the War of 1812. During the Mexican War, nearly 7 percent of the troops deserted. The Civil War produced the highest American desertion rates, 11 percent on the Union side and 10 percent on the Confederate side. Since then, rates of desertion have dropped. The rate was fewer than 1 percent in World War I (not counting draft evaders). It rose somewhat

during World War II and the Korean War; but even during the unpopular Vietnam War reached high of only 7.4 percent in 1971.

DESERT LAND ACT (1877). Allowed settlers to acquire a total of 1,120 acres of public lands in western areas where large tracts were needed to justify dams and ditches for irrigation. The law was widely abused by speculators, but it remained in force into the 20th c.

DES MOINES. Capital and largest city in Iowa, located at the confluence of the Raccoon and Des Moines rivers. A fort was founded there in 1843, and the city that grew up around it became a stopping place for wagon trains headed west. Industries are food processing, magazine publishing, insurance, and farm products. Pop.: 191,003 (1980).

DE SOTO EXPEDITION (1539–43). Hernando de Soto, a Spanish conquistador, secured a royal grant for the conquest of Florida. Sailing from Havana, he landed at Tampa Bay and began a four-year journey in search of riches, on which he pillaged and massacred thousands of Indians. In 1541 he crossed the Mississippi R into NE Arkansas. In 1542 he headed down the Arkansas R to the Mississippi once more. He fell ill and died near Natchez, May 21, 1542. His men fought off Indians in E Texas, built barges to float down the Mississippi, finally reaching the Gulf of Mexico. On Sept. 10, 1543, 320 survivors (out of the original 600) landed at the mouth of the Pánuco R in Mexico.

DESTROYER DEAL. In 1940 President Franklin D. Roosevelt agreed to turn over to the British fifty old US destroyers to help them defend themselves against German submarines. In return, Britain gave the US the right to build naval and air bases on some of its Western Hemisphere territories. Isolationists in Congress attacked the agreement, but Roosevelt contended it lay within his powers as commander in chief of the military.

DESTROYERS. See WARSHIPS.

DÉTENTE. Term used to describe efforts to reduce tensions between the US and the Soviet Union in the 1970s.

DETROIT. City located on the Detroit R in SE Michigan. Founded 1701 as Fort Detroit, a

French garrison and fur-trading post. In 1760, Fort Detroit surrendered to a British military force. Prosperous under the British, it was included within the new US in 1783. The British, however, continued to administer Fort Detroit until, by Jay's Treaty, their troops withdrew in 1796. In 1805, newly designated as capital of the Michigan Territory, it burned and was rebuilt, only to be captured by the British in the War of 1812. It grew throughout the 19th c., and in the early 20th c. became the automobile capital of the nation. Its economy is still dependent on the automobile industry; the slump in car production in the late 1970s led to an unemployment rate almost double the national rate. Pop.: 1,203,339 (1980).

DETROIT, SURRENDER OF (Aug. 16, 1812). Gen. William Hull surrendered to the British without a fight and was subsequently court-martialed and found guilty of cowardice and neglect of duty. President Madison remanded the sentence because of Hull's service during the Revolution.

DEVIL'S HOLE, AMBUSCADE OF (Sept. 14, 1763). Attack by the Seneca at the Niagara R on John Stedman, the keeper of the portage, and twenty-four men. Except for Stedman and one or two others, all were killed. The Seneca continued to control the portage, thus closing a source of supply for Fort Detroit.

DEWITT'S COLONY. In 1825 Green DeWitt obtained from the governor of Mexico a contract to settle 400 families in Texas. DeWitt settled 181 land titles at Gonzales, where the first shot of the Texas Revolution was fired, Oct. 2, 1835.

DEW LINE. On Sept. 27, 1954, the US and Canada agreed to establish a third radar line, "Distant Early Warning" (DEW) Line, across Arctic Canada from Alaska to Greenland. This supplemented the Pinetree Chain of radar stations extending across the continent north of the US-Canadian border and the "Mid-Canada Line." DEW Line began operation on July 1, 1957.

DIAMOND ISLAND FIGHT (Sept. 23, 1777). Colonial troops fought British defenders of Diamond Island at Lake George, N.Y., in an unsuccessful attempt to cut British Gen. Burgoyne's communications on the lake.

DICTIONARIES. The first American dictionaries, *Compendious Dictionary of the English Language* (1806) and the two-volume *An American Dictionary of the English Language* (1828) by Noah Webster, were strongly nationalistic and often idiosyncratic in spellings and punctuations. Webster's dictionaries were continued by his publishers, George and Charles Merriam. Their major work is the *International* series, published in successive editions in 1890, 1909, 1934, and 1961. Its abridged editions, beginning in 1898, set the pattern for desk dictionaries. Competition for the Merriam-Webster dictionaries has been sporadic. The six-volume *Century Dictionary* (1889–91), the nearest analogue to the *Oxford English Dictionary*, was last published in 1909. For many years Funk and Wagnall's various dictionaries were the chief competition for Merriam-Webster. Its *New Standard College Dictionary,* the latest version, appeared in 1963. Other outstanding competitors have been published including the *Random House Dictionary* (1966) and the *American Heritage Dictionary* (1969).

DICTIONARY OF AMERICAN BIOGRAPHY. A cooperative reference work sponsored by the American Council of Learned Societies, originally published between 1928 and 1936 in twenty volumes containing 13,633 biographical sketches. No person who died after Jan. 1, 1935, was included. Since 1936 several supplementary volumes have been published.

DIGHTON ROCK. A petroglyph on the Taunton R in Massachusetts, first observed in 1680. Its intricate and not easily decipherable inscriptions have been attributed to Phoenicians, Norsemen, and some thirty other unprovable sources. It is now certain that most of its designs were relatively meaningless scribblings by Indians in colonial times. The first inscription may have been made by the lost Portuguese explorer Miguel Corte-Real in 1511.

DIME. Coin of US currency having the value of ten cents, or one-tenth of a dollar. First spelled "disme," it was so marked when first put into circulation in 1796.

DIME NOVELS. Mrs. Ann S. Stephens wrote the first novel of record published in paper covers to sell for ten cents, *Malaeska: The Indian Wife of the White Hunter.* Published 1860, it was followed by others that quickly fell into the style that the dime novel was to maintain throughout its existence, with continuous suspense, violent action, and bloodshed, but a high standard of morals. By 1880 dime novels were denounced as a menace to youth. Nevertheless, circulation increased; one story is known to have sold nearly 500,000 copies. By 1910 pulp paper magazines were replacing dime novels, the character of the fiction remaining much the same.

DIPLOMACY, SECRET. Diplomats of all nations practice secret diplomacy; but the US Constitution provides for ratification of treaties by the Senate, which usually means immediate publication of texts as well as public hearings and debates. After World War II the US concluded an ever-increasing number of executive agreements as compared to treaties. There were also over 400 secret agreements, the nature of which the State Department declined to reveal. Moreover, thousands of other executive agreements were evidently concluded by other government agencies, particularly by the Defense Department. After discovery of secret executive agreements signed in the 1960s with Ethiopia, Laos, Thailand, South Korea, and Spain, legislation was passed providing that all international agreements must go to Congress for its information.

DIPLOMATIC MISSIONS. The use of special diplomatic missions has varied throughout American history. By and large, 18th- and 19th-c. presidents conducted diplomacy through regularly appointed envoys, usually local American ministers and ambassadors. In the 20th c. presidents have often negotiated through special envoys, rather than through regularly accredited representatives.

DIPLOMATIC SERVICE. See FOREIGN SERVICE.

DIRECT PRIMARY. See PRIMARY, DIRECT.

DIRECTORIES, CITY. Philadelphia had the first city directory in 1785; it assigned numbers to houses and lots and made possible a uniform system of residential identification. The second appeared in New York in 1786; Boston followed 1789. Most contained advertising, historical information, directions and advice to visitors, data on mails and import duties, and statistics. Today no city is without a directory.

DIRIGIBLES. Motor-driven lighter-than-air craft that can be flown against the wind and steered; first constructed in America by Caesar Spiegler 1878. Thomas Scott Baldwin built the first dirigible for the US government in 1908, 96 feet long with a 20-horsepower engine. During World War I, the US navy ordered sixteen dirigibles of the nonrigid type, developed from a British model used for antisubmarine patrols. The English nickname, "blimp," was adopted by US navy personnel. At war's end the navy had thirty blimps. In 1919 Congress authorized the procurement of two rigid airships. Meanwhile, the army concentrated on the semirigid type and blimps. In 1921 the army purchased *Roma*, an Italian semirigid airship which during a trial flight in 1922, flew into a high-voltage electrical transmission line, burst into flames, and crashed. In 1925 the army procured the semirigid *RS-1*, fabricated by the Goodyear-Zeppelin Corporation and erected by the army at Scott Field, Ill. After some use it was seriously damaged and dismantled in 1928. Both services began designing dirigibles inflated with nonflammable helium rather than highly dangerous hydrogen. Weather remained a threat, however; in 1925, for example, the navy blimp *Shenandoah* broke up in a violent thunderstorm. In 1928 Goodyear-Zeppelin built two rigid airships for the navy, the *Akron* and *Macon*, the largest airships ever built, until exceeded by the German *Hindenburg* in 1936. They could carry five fighter planes in their hulls and could launch and retrieve planes in flight. In 1933, the *Akron* was lost in a violent electrical storm over the Atlantic; the *Macon,* suffered a structural failure and crashed in the Pacific in 1935. Their loss ended the navy's development of the rigid airship. But the blimp was widely used during World War II, especially for antisubmarine patrols. In 1957 a navy antisubmarine blimp made a nonstop circumnavigation of the North Atlantic, being in the air for 264 hours. In 1961 the navy's blimp squadrons were decommissioned. Today only blimps operated (for advertising purposes) by the Goodyear Tire & Rubber Co. survive.

DISARMAMENT. Reduction of the number and type of weapons with which wars can be fought, usually arrived at by agreement between nations. In 1817 the US and Great Britain agreed that only small craft should be stationed in the Great Lakes, and since 1871 the US-Canadian border has been unguarded. Attempts at disarmament were made after both world wars. The naval forces of the major nations were limited in size by various agreements made in the 1920s. Poison gas, widely used in World War I, was outlawed by international convention and played no important part in World War II. Since World War II, the UN has been especially active in limiting nuclear weapons. In 1963, the US, USSR, and Great Britain agreed to limit the testing of nuclear devices. In 1967 the nuclear powers agreed not to use nuclear weapons in outer space, nor to construct military bases on the moon. The Strategic Arms Limitations Talks (SALT) between the US and USSR began in 1969. A SALT treaty was completed in 1972, but relations between the two powers deteriorated and little further progress was made in the 1970s and early 1980s. An emerging issue in the early 1980s was the so-called nuclear freeze on existing weapons.

DISCIPLES OF CHRIST. Religious denomination, also known as the Christian Church, founded ca. 1795 by Alexander Campbell, a dissident Baptist. Followers originally called Campbellites. Membership: 1.2 million (1980).

DISSENTERS. Originally, those who disagreed with the doctrines of the Church of England. Most important were Congregationalists, Baptists, Quakers, Presbyterians, and Methodists. Also called nonconformists.

DISTILLING. The settlers at Roanoke Island brewed a crude ale from maize, the New Englanders made wine from wild grapes, and commercial distilleries were operating in New Amsterdam in 1640. Rum, distilled from West Indian sugar, was an important colonial industry. On the frontier, whiskey was distilled from corn, rye, and barley. By 1791, farmers had enough economic interest in

whiskey to oppose the federal taxation (see WHISKEY REBELLION). In the 19th c., distilleries were for the most part small family-run businesses, and Kentucky remained famous for its Bourbon whiskey. Distilleries were closed by the Eighteenth Amendment, but after repeal of Prohibition in 1933, most distilling became big business. By the 1980s, most liquor was produced by a half dozen major corporations.

DISTRIBUTION ACT. See DEPOSIT ACT OF 1836.

DISTRICT, CONGRESSIONAL. The electoral unit by which members of the US House of Representatives are selected. The total number of House seats to which each state is entitled is set by the federal government after each census (reapportionment), but state legislatures set boundary lines for districts (redistricting), often creating great inequalities (see GERRYMANDER.) In 1964, US Supreme Court held that districts must be substantially equal in population and not so eccentric in shape as to create political advantages for any party. Consequently, federal courts have declared invalid numerous state plans for redistricting.

DISTRICT OF COLUMBIA. Established 1790 in order that the nation's capital city could be built on territory outside the control of any one state. The original hundred-square-mile site was carved out of Virginia and Maryland. In 1846, Virginia requested the government to restore its land, and the District was reduced to sixty square miles. Today, the District is contiguous with WASHINGTON, D.C.

DIVINE PROVIDENCES. New England theologians believed that the age of miracles had passed, but that divine providences were events based on natural causes but specifically ordained by the will of God. Emphasized by Increase and Cotton Mather as a device to arouse the sluggish emotions of what they believed to be a backsliding generation.

DIVISION ACT OF 1800. Separated the Indiana Territory from the original Northwest Territory. Vincennes and Chillicothe were made the capitals of the respective territories.

DIVORCE. The New England colonies, not considering marriage a sacrament, removed divorce to the secular courts. The adversary system prevailed, with one party being guilty of any of various charges, the most common being adultery, neglect, and physical cruelty. Some states, especially those with a strong influence from the Church of England or the Roman Catholic church, did not readily accept judicial divorce. South Carolina permitted no divorce until 1949; New York recognized only adultery as grounds until the 1960s.

DIXIE. Unofficial name for the southern states of the US. Its source is unknown and appears to have been first used in the 1850s. "Dixie," by Daniel D. Emmett was a minstrel song that became the Confederate anthem and marching song.

DODGE CITY. City in S Kansas on the Arkansas R; site of several temporary army camps before Fort Dodge was built in 1864. A center for buffalo hunters, became rendezvous for cowboys and shipping station for cattle after the arrival of the railroad in the 1870s. Pop.: 18,001 (1980).

DODGE CITY TRAIL. Cattle trail from W Texas to the railhead in Kansas. Herds crossed the Red R near Vernon, continued through Fort Supply in W Oklahoma to Dodge City.

DODGE-LEAVENWORTH EXPEDITION (1834). Mission under Col. Henry Dodge to persuade the Plains tribes to accept the Osage, Cherokee, Delaware, and Seneca tribes, which were being displaced to the west. Treaties were concluded in 1835 and 1837, but bitter warfare ensued.

DOHRMAN'S GRANT. Section of land (23,040 acres) granted to A. H. Dohrman in 1787 in Tuscarawas County, Ohio, in appreciation for his services during the Revolution as agent in Portugal.

DOLLAR. The standard unit of US currency, which under the decimal system is divisible into one hundred cents or ten dimes. The word itself is a corruption of the German *thaler*, a coin widely circulated in the colonies. The French écus and the Spanish pieces (pesos) of eight, or eight reals, were also called dollars. (See also COINAGE.)

DOLLAR-A-YEAR MAN. Practice begun during World War I, and revived during the New Deal and World War II, in which prominent business and professional persons served the government for the token salary of a dollar a year, plus expenses.

DOLLAR DIPLOMACY. Pejorative term for the use of US economic power to further foreign policy.

DOLLAR SIGN ($). Used as early as 1788, most likely a combination of the letters *p* and *s*, standing for "pesos."

DOLPHIN ADMIRALTY CASE (1863). The contraband-laden *Dolphin,* obviously destined for the Confederacy, was captured between neutral ports of call. A federal judge, elaborating on the continuous voyage doctrine, held that all segments of such voyages are illegal.

DOMESTIC RELATIONS, COURTS OF. Judicial innovation of the early 20th c. Courts deal with family maladjustments, desertion, immorality, child abuse and neglect, illegitimacy, and similar problems.

DOMINICAN REPUBLIC. US interest in the Dominican Republic has been manifest since Dominican independence from Haiti in 1844. Presidents Andrew Johnson and Grant sought annexation but failed, but US control over the nation's affairs remained strong. In 1916 President Wilson declared martial law and placed a US naval officer in charge of the government. US rule ended in 1924, and in 1930 Rafael Trujillo began his long one-man rule. His despotic administration was supported by the US until he was assassinated in 1961. In 1965, US troops invaded to end a revolution. The UN and the Organization of American States offered strong protests, and the troops were finally withdrawn in Sept. 1966. Thereafter, the US gave the Dominican Republic substantial economic assistance. There was renewed strife in the early 1970s but no US intervention.

DOMINICANS, or Order of Preachers (O.P.). The first community of Dominicans in the US was established at Springfield, Ky., in 1806. Four Dominican provinces remained in the US in 1980.

DOMINION OF NEW ENGLAND. See NEW ENGLAND, DOMINION OF.

DOMINION THEORY. A theory, given currency by John Adams, that the colonies were not part of the British realm, but were individual realms subject directly to the king. Parliament thus had no authority.

DONATION LANDS. Given by state or federal governments to reward citizens for services or to encourage settlement. In 1842, 1850, and 1854, Congress passed donation acts for the territories of East Florida, Oregon, Washington, and New Mexico.

DONELSON, FORT, CAPTURE OF (Feb. 15, 1862). A Confederate stronghold on the Cumberland R, which commanded the approach to Nashville. On his second attempt, Union Gen. U.S. Grant took the fort, with 14,000 Confederate troops surrendering.

DONELSON'S LINE. Boundary separating Virginia and Cherokee territory; run in 1771 by Col. John Donelson. The line was dishonestly fixed and reported to run with the Kentucky R., thus giving Virginians encouragement to settle on land that by treaty belonged to the Cherokee.

DONGAN CHARTERS. Beginning in 1686, New York Gov. Thomas Dongan issued new charters for New York City, Harlem, and towns on Long Island.

DONIPHAN'S EXPEDITION (1846–47). During the Mexican War, Col. A.W. Doniphan, led an expedition into Chihuahua, defeating 600 Mexicans at Brazito and 3,000 at the Battle of Sacramento. He then occupied Chihuahua City.

DONNER PARTY. California-bound emigrants, whose nucleus was the Donner and Read families, became snowbound in the Sierra Nevadas in Nov. 1846. The survivors escaped starvation only by cannibalism of the dead. Forty-seven of the original 87 survived.

"DON'T FIRE TILL YOU SEE THE WHITE OF THEIR EYES." Alleged command, presumably to conserve powder, given the patriots at Bunker Hill, June 17, 1775.

"DON'T GIVE UP THE SHIP." Spoken by James Lawrence, commmander of the US frigate *Chesapeake,* after he fell mortally wounded in engagement with British frigate *Shannon,* thirty miles off Boston harbor, June 1, 1813. The *Chesapeake* was captured.

DORCHESTER. Residential district in south Boston, founded 1630. A town-meeting form of government was set up, reportedly the first of its kind in the colonies.

DORCHESTER COMPANY. Joint-stock company formed 1624 in Dorchester, England, for the purpose of establishing a colony in New England. By 1627, fifty men had been left at Cape Ann, augmented by some dissidents from Plymouth Colony. Replaced by the New England Company.

DORR'S REBELLION (1841–42). In 1841, Rhode Island still barred more than half the adult male population from voting. Thomas W. Dorr led a faction that drew up a People's Constitution, while a legal convention drew up another known as the Landholders' Constitution. Both provided for enlargement of the suffrage. The People's Constitution was ratified and a new government was organized with Dorr as governor. The incumbent governor ordered the state militia against the Dorrites. Dorr was sentenced to life imprisonment, later rescinded. A later constitution adopted many of the features of the People's Constitution.

DOUBLOON. A widely circulated Spanish gold piece, so called because its value was double that of a pistole.

DOUGHBOY. Popular term for US army enlisted man in World War I.

DOUGHFACES. Contemptuous term for northerners who, before the Civil War, supported southern slavery policies.

DOVE. See ARK AND DOVE.

DOVER. Capital of Delaware, founded 1717. Replaced New Castle as capital in 1777. Pop.: 23,512 (1980).

DOVES. Those who opposed American participation in the war in Vietnam, based on the symbolic "dove of peace." Supporters of the war were called hawks.

DRAFT. Compulsory militia laws were used sporadically during the Revolution both for local defense and for the Continental army. Service could be avoided by hiring a substitute or by paying a fee. From the end of the Revolution until 1863, American military service was entirely voluntary. Both Union and Confederate armies were organized on the basis of voluntary regulars supplemented by state militia augmented by drafted troops. Manpower shortages forced both the North and South to a federal draft. Substitutes and fees in lieu of service again were authorized in the North. Bitter opposition to the draft developed, leading to widespread DRAFT RIOTS. After the Civil War, a federal military reserve was created, the state militia became the national guard, and the the foundation was laid for a regular army that could be fleshed out by a federal draft, which was done by the Selective Service Act of 1917. Substitutes and bounties were outlawed, and enrollment and selection were to be done by local civilian boards, who established the categories of deferment and acted on appeals. Requirements were developed by the army general staff and apportioned as state quotas. The order of induction was determined by lottery. The program was generally accepted by the public as fair and reasonable and was revived as World War II approached, although the renewal of the Selective Service Act passed by only one vote in Congress. The impact of the World War II draft was pervasive. Over 10 million men were inducted. Draftees were assigned to all the armed services. With the exception of one year (1947–48), the draft was in continuous operation from 1940 to 1973. Requirements of the Korean and Vietnam conflicts were much smaller. During the latter war, a liberal schedule of exemptions resulted in virtually all married men, members of the national guard and reserve units, men in exempt occupations such as teachers, and students being exempt from the draft. Inequities led to a return to the lottery, but most discriminatory features of the law remained. In 1973 the Nixon administration ended the draft and returned to an all-volunteer military. In 1980, registration of all males again became mandatory, but no draft was envisioned.

DRAFT RIOTS (1863). Minor riots occurred in Rutland, Vt.; Wooster, Ohio; Boston, Mass.; and Portsmouth, N.H.; but none equaled those in New York City. Objection to the draft rested chiefly on the provision for money payments in lieu of service. Shortly after the drawing of lots commenced on July 13, a mob, mostly of foreign-born laborers, began a protest that led to four days of rioting that resulted in a thousand casualties and $1.5 million in property loss. On July 15, militia regiments restored order, and after troops from the Army of the Potomac were brought in drawings began again on Aug. 19 and proceeded peaceably.

DRAGO DOCTRINE. Adopted by the Second Hague Conference in 1907, it forbids armed intervention by a nation as a means of collecting debts owed by a foreign country. Named for an Argentinian foreign affairs minister. Often incorporated into trade agreements; especially favored by Latin American countries.

DRAKE AT CALIFORNIA. In 1579, after plundering the Pacific coast of South America, Sir Francis Drake sailed northward in the *Golden Hind* and entered Drake's Bay, Calif., to repair his ship. Claiming the land for England and naming it New Albion, he spent thirty-six days exploring and establishing friendly relations with the Indians. In 1936 a brass plate he had erected as evidence of England's claim was discovered near San Francisco.

DRAKE'S OIL WELL. In 1859 oil was discovered at Titusville, Pa. by E. L. Drake, marking the beginning of the petroleum industry in the US. The discovery precipitated a rush to the oilfield.

DRAMA. See THEATER.

DRAPER'S MEADOWS. First settlement W of the Allegheny divide, on the present site of Blacksburg, Va.; founded 1748 by Scottish and Irish immigrants from Pennsylvania. Destroyed by Shawnee Indians 1755.

DREADNOUGHT. Class of battleship that derived its name from the British warship *Dreadnought* (1906). Its size, speed, turbine engines, and armament made obsolete every battleship afloat, inaugurating a race in building battleships of its class by all naval powers, including the US (who built seventeen before World War I). Later, the smaller and faster destroyer became the focus of warship building.

DRED SCOTT CASE *(Dred Scott* v. *John F.A.* Sanford, 19 Howard 393). The Supreme Court in 1857 ruled that Scott, because he was a slave, was neither a citizen of Missouri nor a citizen of the US and had no constitutional right to sue in federal courts. The decision stirred inflammatory reactions, helping to precipitate the Civil War. After the war, the Thirteenth and Fourteenth amendments superseded the Dred Scott decision.

DRESS. Early American colonists dressed in an approximation of the prevailing English mode. In Jamestown, Va. (1607), women's bodices and men's doublets were long waisted, boned, and stiffly padded with high, starched, fan-shaped whisk collars or ruffs. Men wore padded trunk hose and tights, sometimes with boots to mid-thigh, and leather jerkins. Women dressed in full skirts over a hoop. Both sexes wore wide-brimmed hats with high crowns and shoes with heels. Pilgrim attire was plain and somber, with woolen stockings and heavy shoes. Dutch clothing was made of satin and velvet, with jewelry accessories. By 1630, male garb consisted of a skirted doublet with slashed sleeves over a full-sleeved linen shirt with wide, lace-edged collar. Gathered breeches, heeled boots with turned-down cuffs, swords, broad-brimmed hats with plumes, mustaches, and pointed chin beards underlined the dashing effect. Women wore high-waisted bodices with low necklines and three-quarter-length sleeves. They covered their full skirts with silk aprons; added jewelry, fans, and muffs; and adorned their faces with beauty patches. About 1670 the three-piece suit (coat, waistcoat, and breeches) came into existence. Throughout the 18th c., a fitted knee-length coat with flared skirt and matching breeches was worn over a vest, often embroidered in colored silks. Powdered wig, cravat, silk stockings, and heeled shoes with buckles completed the costume. Men wore three-cornered hats and greatcoats with capes. A scarlet woolen cape was popular with both sexes. Women's dresses had low necks, tight elbow-length sleeves edged with deep ruffles, and

full skirts worn over hoops. Sheer white fichus crossed over the bodice. A deep bonnet was worn out of doors. Wealthy men and women imported silk brocades and velvets for their clothing. The less wealthy wore homespun and buckskin breeches or coarse woolens and linens of English maunfacture. After the American Revolution the new country copied everything French. Extravagant dress was abandoned for simplicity and natural lines. Men wore high-waisted, double-breasted, cutaway coats with wide lapels and high collars over tight midcalf breeches. The top hat of beaver appeared, worn over unpowdered hair. Women wore high-waisted neoclassic gowns of lightweight embroidered muslins and short coiffures with ringlets, plumes, or turbans; carried beaded purses; and walked in flat-heeled slippers. By 1820, men had adopted full-length trousers, wool cutaways of skirted frock coats, patterned velvet vests, and stiff black cravats. By 1830, women's clothing was made of warmer silks and woolens, the waistline had descended to its natural place, and vast leg-of-mutton sleeves appeared, along with enormous hats and cashmere shawls. Cone-shaped, gored skirts reached to the ankle, revealing shoes with small heels. Toward 1840 a deep oval bonnet concealed the face, the sleeve diminished, and the skirt began to expand. In the 1850s, the crinoline appeared, a cage of metal hoops joined by vertical cotton tapes. By the mid-19th c., Americans could purchase a variety of woven textiles and, ultimately, ready-made clothing. Elias Howe patented the sewing machine (1846); during the Civil War machine-sewn uniforms were issued. By the late 1860s, mass-produced clothing for men was widely accepted. Women purchased ready-made capes and underwear but made their own dresses from paper patterns. The most significant indigenous innovation of the 1850s was the blue denim work pants made by Levi Strauss. Originally worn during the California gold rush, Levis were adopted by lumberjacks, railroad workers, and cowboys. Men began to wear neckties, caps, straw hats, and black silk top hats. The 1860s saw the matching three-piece suit and the sack jacket. In 1860, women's skirts reached their maximum circumference, and in 1865 the fullness began to move to the rear, evolving into the bustle and train. Tightly laced corsets culminated in the hour-glass figure of the 1890s. In the first decade of the 20th c., the silhouette was an S-curve, with bosom thrust forward and hips back. High, boned collars and lace trimmed the popular shirtwaist. Just before World War I, women wore narrow hobble skirts, ostrich boas, and enormous plumed hats. During the war many served in uniform. Their roles necessitated drastic reforms; corsets and floor-length skirts were abandoned. In the 1920s, hems rose to the knee, legs were encased in flesh-colored silk stockings, arms were bare, and hair was short under cloche hats. Dresses were tubular and low waisted. With the depression the hem dropped to midcalf. Slacks became popular, and Hollywood was an important influence. Adrian, who dressed many of the stars, popularized the square, padded shoulders, which remained in style until 1947. It was accompanied by upswept hair and high-heeled platform shoes with ankle straps. The classic sportswear look appeared in the 1930s. Women wore sweaters and skirts; men wore pullover sweaters or tweed jackets with flannel trousers. Nylon stockings were introduced in 1940; at the end of World War II, nylon, the first completely artificial fiber, started a trend to synthetics that all but eclipsed natural fibers by the 1970s because of their low cost and ease of care. Skirts remained short during the war, but in 1947 Christian Dior created the New Look; hemlines dropped, full skirts appeared over stiff petticoats, and cinched waists and rounded shoulders replaced angularity. Ten years later, the loose chemise was in vogue. The extremely short minidress was introduced in the mid-1960s, accompanied by white plastic boots, enormous sunglasses, and long, straight hair. Hats were no longer fashionable. Pants were worn by women of all ages for every occasion. In the 1960s, the demarcation between the sexes diminished in dress. Both wore long hair, platform sandals, shoulder bags, jewelry, and decorated blue jeans. Leather and handcrafted clothing became popular. The 1970s saw a partial return to a more tailored, conventional look, a trend continued in the popular "prep school" look of the early 1980s. Blue jeans, the symbol of the counterculture of the 1960s remained as popular as ever with both sexes, while designer jeans became status symbols for some.

DREWRY'S BLUFF, BATTLE AT (May 12–16, 1864). Union troops under Gen. B. F. Butler, operating from Yorktown peninsula in Virginia, were defeated by Confederate forces under Gen. P.G.T. Beauregard.

DRIED FRUITS. Until canning techniques were perfected in the 19th c., drying and the use of salt and sugar were principal methods of preserving fruits. Maine became the nation's supplier of dried apples, exporting great quantities. By the early 20th c., 83 percent of all dried fruit came from California. Canning and freezing, and wide availability of fresh fruits, soon reduced the necessity for dried fruits, and they became delicacies.

DROGHER TRADE. Type of commerce between American firms, mostly in Boston, and Spaniards in California, from ca. 1825 to 1834. New England manufactures were exchanged for cattle hides. "Drogher" is a West Indian word applied to slow and clumsy coast vessels.

DROUGHTS. Transitory droughts, affecting comparatively small areas or lasting for a single season, may be expected every year in some areas, but annual droughts, when rainfall is abnormally low for several years, over a long period of time are infrequent. Rainfall records show that an extended drought in the midwestern area culminated in the 1840s, after which more abundant precipitation reached a maximum phase in the 1870s and 1880s. Again, in 1886–95 an extensive drought prevailed, followed by years of abundant rainfall. Another dry phase began ca. 1930 and continued through 1941. Especially affected were the interior valleys, the Southwest, and the Great Plains. In 1950 a drought began in the Southwest; after it ended with heavy rains in summer 1957, a long drought started in the Atlantic coast states, and by the mid-1960s water tables, rivers, and reservoirs reached dangerously low levels. A series of hurricanes raked the Appalachins during 1967–72, bringing rivers and water tables back to the level of the pre-drought years. A very widely spread drought plagued the country in 1976–77. California and the Pacific Northwest suffered the most but crop damages in the Atlantic states were also considerable. After two wet years, a hot dry wave in 1980 resulted in a moderate drought and water shortages in the Northeast.

DRUG ADDICTION. In the 19th c., opium derivatives, especially morphine, were easily available in the US, since legal restrictions were not widely enacted until the end of the century. By the 1890s opium importation reached about a half-million pounds annually. In 1898 diacetylmorphine, under the trade name Heroin, was marketed as a cough suppressant, but soon its addictive nature became apparent. Within a few decades heroin was preferred over morphine by addicts. Commercial production of cocaine began in the late 19th c., and it became popular in many forms. Besides the stimulating and euphoric qualities it imparted to tonics, soda pop, and elixirs, cocaine had various medical uses as an anesthetic and painkiller. By 1900, its dangers were apparent and its use generally outlawed. The Pure Food and Drug Act (1906) sought to ensure that proprietary medicines would be labeled as to narcotic content. At about the same time, the US began cooperating in various international efforts to control traffic of illegal drugs. After decades of relative stability, use of drugs burgeoned in the 1960s and continued through the 1970s and into the 1980s. Smoking marijuana became acceptable in many social circles; and use of the so-called hard drugs, heroin and cocaine, increased alarmingly. Abuse of prescription medicines increased, especially among older persons. International trafficking in narcotics became a major industry. In 1970 the Comprehensive Drug Abuse Prevention and Control Act was passed, and state laws were toughened. Special forces were employed in attempts to halt entry of narcotics into the country. Treatment centers were instituted and preventive programs were begun. Despite all efforts, drug abuse, including alcoholism, remained at a high level.

DRY DOCKS. The first federal dry dock in the US was a 253-foot graving dock completed at Boston 1833. The New York Navy Yard's 307-foot dock (1851) boasted the world's first all-metal cofferdam. Following the Spanish-American War, 740-foot graving docks were constructed at Portsmouth, Boston, Philadelphia, and Mare Island (California). Subsequently, the navy established dry docks at Puget Sound and Pearl Harbor. During World War I, 1,005-foot dry docks equipped with massive traveling cranes were built at Norfolk, Philadelphia, and San Francisco. In World War II, graving docks with reinforced concrete walls over 20 feet thick were constructed at Norfolk and Philadelphia. During 1942–45, twenty-seven LSDs (landing ship docks) were launched as combined dry docks and landing craft carriers.

DRY FARMING. Conducting agricultural operations without irrigation in a dry climate involves raising crops that are drought resistant or drought evasive (maturing in late spring or fall). In California in the 1850s, Americans began to raise such crops as winter wheat, whose principal growing season coincided with the winter rainfall season. By the 1860s dry farming had spread to Utah and the Pacific Northwest. In the Great Plains, dry farming methods were encouraged by the US Department of Agriculture, which created the Office of Dry Land Agriculture in 1905. The drought cycles of the 1930s intensified experimental work and the invention of machinery for special soil cultural processes.

DUAL CITIZENSHIP. See CITIZENSHIP, DUAL.

DUBUQUE. City in NE Iowa, founded 1833 as a lead-mining center. Later a lumber center and an important port on the Mississippi. Pop.: 93,745 (1980).

DUBUQUE MINING DISTRICT. See GALENA-DUBUQUE MINING DISTRICT.

DUCKING STOOL. A rude armchair used from the 17th c. to the early 19th c. as punishment by public humiliation for certain offenses, including witchcraft, scolding, and prostitution. The offender was strapped into the chair and immersed repeatedly in a pond or stream.

DUELING. The first recorded duel in the colonies occurred at Plymouth 1621. Dueling lost favor in the North after the Revolution but spread in the antebellum South. Most states outlawed it, and by the late 19th c. public opinion and ridicule brought an end to the custom.

DUE PROCESS OF LAW. The US Constitution provides that neither the federal nor any state government may "deprive any person of life, liberty, or property, without due process of law." The original Bill of Rights, including the Fifth Amendment, was held to be a limit only on the federal government. The Fourteenth Amendment, with its due process clause, was expressly intended as a limit on the states. For the first thirty years after ratification of the latter in 1868, the Supreme Court was reluctant to use its powers to enforce the amendment, believing that the original federal equilibrium ought to be maintained. State courts stressed the substantive, rather than the procedural, aspects of the state due process clauses. The result was the doctrine of freedom of contract, which read a laissez-faire ideology of private enterprise into the due process clauses of the Fifth and Fourteenth amendments. Beginning ca. 1925, the Supreme Court increasingly held that the concept of "liberty" in the Fourteenth Amendment puts the same restraints on the states that the First Amendment does on the federal government. By the 1980s, the court was applying to state criminal procedures virtually all of the requirements spelled out in the Bill of Rights.

DUGOUT. Temporary home of the Plains, built in the side of a ravine or hill. Three sides were made of earth. The front, made of logs or sod, had a door and a window. (See also SOD HOUSE.)

DUG SPRINGS, BATTLE AT (Aug. 2, 1861). Gen. Nathanial Lyon, operating near Wilson Creek, Mo., defeated a Confederate force of the Missouri State Guard under Gen. James S. Rains.

DUKE OF YORK'S LAWS (1665). Elaborate code of laws, based on those of Massachusetts and New Haven, drawn up to govern the towns of Long Island, N.Y.

DULL KNIFE CAMPAIGN (1878–79). Two bands of Northern Cheyenne, led by the chiefs Dull Knife and Little Wolf, fled their reservation in INDIAN TERRITORY and started for their home in Montana. Federal troops were sent to return them. On Jan. 22, 1879, Dull Knife's band was captured, but the chief escaped to the Sioux. Little Wolf's band was in-duced to surrender on March 25 but was permitted to remain in Montana.

DULUTH. Third largest city in Minnesota, located at the W end of Lake Superior, where the St. Louis R empties into the lake; also the farthest point inland that ships can reach through the St. Lawrence Seaway and Great Lakes. Named for the Sieur Duluth who visited 1679. His interest, fur-trading, remained important in the area until the 1840s. Later, Duluth became a railroad center. Discovery of iron ore in the Mesabi Range made it a major Great Lakes port; also an important grain center. Pop.: 92,811 (1980).

DULUTH'S EXPLORATIONS. Commissioned in 1678 by the governor of New France to find a route to the western sea, Daniel Greysolon, Sieur Duluth (Dullhut), set out to explore westward from Lake Superior. He had a rendezvous with the Sioux near the site of present Duluth 1679, and accompanied them through the Savanna portage to Lake Mille Lac, near the source of the Mississippi. In 1680 he unsuccessfully sought a new route to the Mississippi by pushing westward from Sioux country on Big Stone Lake. Thereafter his efforts were utilized in the Iroquois wars and in safeguarding the French in the West. In 1683 he built a post on St. Croix portage, the first interior fort in Wisconsin.

DUMBARTON OAKS CONFERENCE (Aug. 21–Oct. 7, 1944). Held in Washington, D.C., to make preliminary plans for what turned out to be the United Nations. Participants were the US, Great Britain, the Soviet Union, and China. Arrangements were made for a full UN conference to agree on the final charter. Proposals were published by the four governments on Oct. 9, 1944.

DUMMER, FORT. First permanent English settlement in what is now Vermont, erected 1724 at present-day Brattleboro by Massachusetts colony as a trading post and for protection of its northern frontier.

DUMMER'S WAR (1724–25). Boundary dispute between Abnaki Indians and Maine and Vermont settlers. Superior Indian forces were defeated. Named for William Dummer, Massachusetts governor.

DUMPLIN CREEK, TREATY OF (June 10, 1785). Between the governor of the state of Franklin (E Tennessee) and chiefs of the Overhill Cherokee. Permitted white settlement between French Broad R and the ridge dividing the Little Tennessee and Little rivers.

DUNBAR'S EXPEDITION (1804-05). President Jefferson asked William Dunbar to explore the Red River of the South. Expedition left from Natchez, entered the Red from the Mississippi but higher up turned into its confluent, the Ouachita (Washita). After penetrating into Arkansas as far as Hot Springs, they returned to Natchez.

DUNBAR'S LINE. Sometimes applied to the thirty-first parallel between the Mississippi and Chattahoochee rivers, recognized by the Pinckney Treaty of 1795 as the international boundary between the US and Spanish West Florida. Surveyed by Andrew Ellicott for the US and William Dunbar for Spain 1798.

DUNKARDS. See BRETHREN.

DUNMORE'S WAR (1774). Expedition against the Shawnee in the Ohio country led by Lord Dunmore, royal governor of Virginia. After a decisive defeat at Point Pleasant, the Indians sued for peace. Dunmore established Camp Charlotte, made a treaty, and returned to Virginia.

DUQUESNE, FORT. French fort at forks of Ohio R; before capture originally belonged to the Ohio company. Troops left from there to defeat George Washington's force at Great Meadows (1754) and to rout Gen. Edward Braddock's expedition (1754). The French then held undisputed possession of the Ohio Valley until 1758, when they destroyed the fort and retreated upon the approach of an expedition led by Gen. John Forbes.

DUST BOWL. Great Plains area devastated by the great drought of the 1930s, including parts of New Mexico, Texas, Oklahoma, Kansas, and Colorado. Many of its ruined sharecroppers, known as Okies, migrated to California.

DUTCH BANKER'S LOANS (1782, 1784). Financial assistance offered the colonies by Amsterdam banking houses. Negotiated by John Adams, they assured financial independence of the colonies during the Revolution.

DUTCH FORK OF SOUTH CAROLINA. District about forty miles long between the Broad and Saluda rivers. Settled by Germans between 1740-60, it kept the German language for a century.

DUTCH GAP CANAL. Cut across the neck of a loop in the James R, near Bermuda Hundred, Va. Begun by Union Gen. Gen. B. F. Butler during the Civil War as a way of saving miles of travel up the river and avoiding powerful Confederate batteries. Militarily, the channel was a failure and was never used; after the war it was enlarged and used by river steamboats.

DUTCH-INDIAN WAR (1643-45). Brought on by the brutal Indian policy of Willem Kieft, director-general of New Netherland. In Feb. 1643, Kieft attacked Indians at Pavonia and murdered about eighty in their sleep. The tribes rose in fury, and soon Long Island, Westchester, and Manhattan were laid waste. With the exception of distant Fort Orange and Rensselaerswyck, safety was to be found only in the immediate vicinity of Fort Amsterdam on Manhattan Island. 1,500 Indians threatened attack and the colonists faced starvation. The Indians had no sustained plan of attack, however, and after a year, a general peace was signed.

DUTCH MERCHANTS AT ALBANY. In 1614, agents of the United New Netherland Co. erected Fort Nassau on Castle Island; in 1624 the Dutch West India Company built Fort Orange. A lucrative fur trade developed. In addition, private merchants and traders operated in the area. The Dutch continued profitable operations long after the English conquest 1664. (See ALBANY.)

DUTCH WEST INDIA COMPANY. Organized by Dutch merchants and chartered by the States General 1621, the company's enormous powers included the exclusive right to trade on the W coast of Africa, in the West Indies, on both coasts of America, and in Australia. In 1624 the company planted a settlement at Fort Orange (Albany) and, in 1625, on Manhattan Island, the colony of New Netherland. Strict obedience was imposed on all colonists. Director and council acted under instruction from the company. Continued despotic control and the company's interest in trade rather than colonization were detrimental.

DUZINE. Form of government by which descendants of the twelve original Huguenot patentees of New Paltz, N.Y., continued to rule the town. Begun 1728, it existed to some degree until ca. 1820.

EADS BRIDGE. First bridge across the Mississippi. A steel and iron structure at St. Louis, completed 1874; named for its designer, J. B. Eads.

EADS GUNBOATS. Seven Union ironclad gunboats, built by J. B. Eads. Used to blockade southern ports and attack Confederate forts along the western rivers.

EADS JETTIES. System of jetties designed by J. B. Eads to maintain the depth of the Mississippi R at its mouth. Completed 1879.

EAGLE, AMERICAN (the bald eagle, *Haliaeetus leucocephalus*). Probably first appeared as an American symbol on a Massachusetts coin 1776. Placed on the Great Seal of the US 1782. On the reverse of some US coins since the beginning of coinage. The bald eagle is an endangered species and is protected in every state under the National Emblem Act (1940).

EARTHQUAKES. First recorded earthquake in the US in New England 1638. The W US exhibits the greatest seismic activity in the country, especially Alaska, California, Nevada, Utah, and Montana. The great SAN FRANCISCO EARTHQUAKE of Apr. 18, 1906, was associated with rupture of the San Andreas fault, which is still the cause of seismic activities on the West Coast. In New Madrid, Mo., large earthquakes occurred in 1811–12. An earthquake near Charleston, S.C., killed about sixty people 1886.

EASTERN ARCHAIC CULTURE. Hunting and gathering lifeway in forests and river valleys of prehistoric E North America, particularly in Kentucky, Georgia, Tennessee, Alabama, S Illinois, and S Missouri between 7000 and 5000 BC. Characterized by hunting a variety of animals, extensive utilization of wild plants, fishing, and shellfish gathering. Technologically versatile tools such as axes, and wedges were evident, as were large notched and stemmed projectile points. Bone, horn, ivory, and shell artifacts became abundant. Copper was pounded into knives, projectile points, and various utilitarian tools in the Old Copper culture of Wisconsin and neighboring states. Burial mounds, pottery, sedentism, and cultigens first appear in E North America. Semisedentary and even sedentary existence became possible, giving rise to the Riverine Archaic culture. Archaic was eventually replaced throughout warmer and moister areas of the East by the Formulative culture, a lifeway sustained primarily by domesticated plant foods, ca. AD 500.

EASTERN ORTHODOXY. First American Eastern Orthodox churches were the 19th-c. Russian missions in Alaska. Main growth in the US due to heavy immigration from E Europe at the end of the 19th and beginning of the 20th c. The history of these churches in America as elsewhere has been one of division and controversy; there are indications that this period is ending. The patriarch of Moscow healed some schisms among American Russian Orthodox in 1970 and various Greek churches also moved toward unity. In the late 1970s twenty-one Orthodox churches had combined membership of more than 4 million. The two largest churches were the Greek Orthodox Archdiocese of North and South America (1.95 million members) and the Orthodox Church in America (1 million members).

EASTERN SOLOMONS, BATTLE OF (Aug. 24, 1942). To reinforce Guadalcanal, in the Solomon Islands, the Japanese dispatched 1,500 troops from Truk, in the Carolines. US reconnaissance picked up the movement; a naval task force met the oncoming reinforcements, taking a heavy toll of planes and pilots. No reinforcements reached Guadalcanal. American losses were light.

EAST FLORIDA. See FLORIDA.

EAST INDIA COMPANY, ENGLISH (1600–1874). In order to rid itself of an oversupply of tea, the company gained the right (1773) to export tea directly to America. Required

Americans to pay a tax on the tea and precipitated anti-British activities, particularly the BOSTON TEA PARTY, leading to the Revolution.

EAST INDIES TRADE. Voyages began from Salem, Mass., 1784, with provisions to the Cape of Good Hope and Mauritius. From there ships sailed to Bombay, Mauritius, Madras, Calcutta, Canton, Mocha, and other ports. Cotton was traded for teas, iron, wine, ginseng, spices (especially pepper), and coffee. End of the East India Co.'s monopoly in 1813 and end of the Napoleonic wars in 1814 increased competition until it was sometimes cheaper to buy Indian goods in London. By 1840, American merchants were importing Calcutta goods from Manchester, England, and shipping cloth from Lowell, Mass., to India.

EAST JERSEY. Separate province awarded 1676 to Sir George Carteret, identified as land lying east of "the most southwardly point of the east side of Little Egg Harbor" to the Delaware R at the forty-first parallel. In 1682, bought by William Penn. Perth Amboy became capital in 1686. Population included Puritans, Scottish Presbyterians, and Quakers. Government came under the crown 1782.

EASTON, TREATY OF (Oct. 26, 1758). Between Pennsylvania and the Delaware and Iroquois Indians. The Iroquois abrogated a treaty ceding most of their land in the W Susquehanna Valley to the English. They also agreed to let the Delaware live and hunt in those lands. The Delaware were thus diverted from helping the French.

EAST TEXAS MISSIONS. Spanish border institutions designed to check French aggression and Christianize Indians. Two were founded on the Neches R 1690; abandoned 1693. Five were founded 1716 near Nacogdoches, and one on the lower Trinity R 1756. Unsuccessful, three were moved to San Antonio 1730; shortly after transfer of Louisiana to Spain 1762, the others were suppressed.

EAST TEXAS OILFIELD. Located 140 miles from the Gulf coast, its discovery was made 1930 by C.M. ("Dad") Joiner. Within a year, there were 1,815 wells with a production of 295,000 barrels. By late 1935 there were 19,507 wells producing 820 million barrels,

over a field covering about 137,000 acres. The field is still producing.

EATON AFFAIR. Sen. John H. Eaton, later to be secretary of war under President Jackson, married a widow, Margaret ("Peggy") O'Neale, in 1829. According to Washington scandalmongers, she had been Eaton's mistress while her first husband was still alive. When Eaton was appointed to the cabinet, the social status of his wife became a political issue. Some cabinet members attempted to ostracize her. Martin Van Buren was the only cabinet member to support the Eatons. The Eaton affair contributed to the break between Jackson and John C. Calhoun in 1830, followed the next spring by a cabinet reorganization, which brought the Eaton affair into the open; Van Buren and Eaton resigned, and three pro-Calhoun cabinet members were forced to do the same.

ECHO. Slave ship captured 1858 with 300 native Africans on board and brought to Charleston, S.C. The would-be slaves were sent to Liberia; the *Echo* was condemned as a slaver and sold. The captain and crew were tried but acquitted, despite a conclusive case.

ECOLOGY. The main activity of naturalists during the 18th and 19th c. was describing species and their distribution, noting how distributions were correlated with topography, soil, climate, and associated species. Practical aspects of man's relation to nature stimulated considerable interest in agricultural insect pests during the 19th c., and economic entomology was strengthened by discovery that certain species are important vectors of diseases. Limnology was the first ecological science to be formally organized; physical attributes of lake waters as influences on lake organisms were investigated in the 1890s in Illinois, Wisconsin, Michigan, Indiana, and Ohio, accompanied in each case by establishment of a biological research station. Marine research stations have an earlier origin in America and have provided important impetus for ecology. Woods Hole, Mass., has been the site of such study since 1885. Plant ecology began primarily in response to the work of Europeans at the universities of Chicago and Nebraska. Animal ecology had a broad origin. Its early history was partly built upon limnology and plant ecology and partly upon pure and applied zoology.

ECONOMIC ADVISERS, COUNCIL OF. Three economists appointed by the president with approval of the Senate, responsible for providing him expert opinion on economic matters and help in preparing his annual economic report.

ECONOMIC ROYALISTS. Term of opprobrium used by Franklin D. Roosevelt in 1936 during his reelection campaign to describe those persons prominent in finance and industry who opposed New Deal programs.

EDENTON. Town in North Carolina on Albemarle Sound laid out 1712; known as "the town on Queen Anne's Creek" until 1722, when enlarged and incorporated as Edenton (named for Charles Eden, former governor). Capital of the colony from 1722 until about 1743; a center of shipbuilding and trade. Pop.: 5,357 (1980).

EDGE HILL, BATTLE OF (Dec. 5–7, 1777). Series of small skirmishes in which Gen. William Howe tested the strength of Gen. George Washington's fortified camp near Whitemarsh, three miles above the present Philadelphia city limits. The British took Edge Hill, but Howe decided that Washington could not be displaced, and on Dec. 8 withdrew to Philadelphia.

EDUCATION. In 1647 the General Court of Massachusetts passed the Old Deluder Satan Act, requiring instruction in reading and writing. All New England colonies enacted similar laws, except Rhode Island, where education remained private. In the 18th c., the "moving school" arose, a teacher being located a few months at a time in each of the villages surrounding a town. Secondary education in New England began with the Boston Latin School 1635. Such schools featured Latin and Greek. During the mid-18th c., the academy, offering nonclassical and practical subjects, was increasingly attended. Higher education was inaugurated 1636; Massachusetts alloted funds "towards a schoole or colledge," later named Harvard College, chartered 1650. Yale opened 1701, Brown 1764, and Dartmouth 1769. Education varied in the middle colonies. The Dutch in New Netherland set up public elementary schools. The English in the 18th c. taught the poor in Anglican church schools. Grammar schools were founded in New York, including one that prepared students for King's College (now Columbia University), 1754. In New York, Pennsylvania, New Jersey, Rhode Island, Maryland, and Delaware, various religious sects established their own elementary schools. In secondary education Pennsylvania led the middle colonies, founding the Friend's Public School of Philadelphia 1689 (now the William Penn Charter School); secondary schools to train ministers; and the Academy in Philadelphia, proposed by Benjamin Franklin 1743 and opened 1751. The Maryland General Assembly established a free public school at Annapolis 1696. In addition to King's College, higher education in the middle colonies comprised the College of New Jersey (Princeton University), founded 1746; the College of Philadelphia (University of Pennsylvania), the new name for Franklin's Academy by rechartering 1755; and Queen's College (Rutgers University), chartered 1766. Southern colonial school policy was laissez-faire. In the South there was a system of apprentice training; charity schools; private schools and tutorial training for the wealthy; and so-called Old Field Schools, elementary schools established on abandoned wasteland. Privately endowed elementary schools also came into being. Some education was provided for black children; plantation owners were interested in teaching them Christianity. The only college in the South during the colonial period was the College of William and Mary in Williamsburg, Va. (1693). After the Revolution, most state constitutions included educational provisions. Georgia, in 1785, North Carolina, in 1789, Vermont, in 1791, and Tennessee, in 1794, granted charters for state universities. The US Constitution makes no reference to education, which was reserved to the states. But the federal government has spent billions of dollars on education. Earlier aid consisted of land grants; today, direct grants of money are made both to institutions and individuals. Until the early 19th c., New England was the only region that could lay claim to anything resembling a public school system. A Massachusetts law of 1789 legally established the district school system and the district school system was made compulsory 1827. New York state set up a decentralized school system, 1784, fully operative by 1812. Considerable effort was expended all over the country to create educational systems. Textbooks emphasized moral training based on religious principles, often to such an extent that Catholics, Jews, and various Protestant minorities were forced to open schools. The Latin grammar school gave ground to the English grammar school, to the academy, and finally to the high school. The academy had a curriculum of astronomy, geology, and other theoretical and practical sciences; foreign languages; philosophy, art, and music; rhetoric and oratory; and English language and literature. American colleges inaugurated a broader curriculum in response to social demands. Natural and physical sciences, modern foreign languages, law, and social sciences appeared as well as studies for the profession of medicine. Gradually religious influence was replaced by the secular. Professional schools opened for the training of engineers, physicians, clergymen, and lawyers. Many private and denominational schools were founded; state legislatures established their own colleges and universities. The elective system began in the early 19th c. and soon became general. Teacher training received impetus before 1830 through publication of several treatises on pedagogy; opening of private teachers' seminaries in the 1820s; and publication of teachers' journals. In 1852, Massachusetts enacted legislation making school attendance compulsory. Kindergartens became increasingly common after the 1850s. The elementary school founded by John Dewey at the University of Chicago (1896–1904) served as a model for progressive education. The testing movement began in the 1890s. The high school grew in prestige throughout the 19th c., taking the place of the academy and becoming the typically American school of the people—free, public, universal, comprehensive in curriculum, and both academic and vocational. Teacher training became the province of state normal schools, which later became teachers' colleges. In many areas, it was the only kind of higher education available to women. By the end of the 19th c., various female "academies" and colleges had been established. After the Civil War, schooling of all kinds, almost entirely racially segregated, was made available to blacks; but only a small minority achieved anything beyond the most rudimentary training. The legality of segregated schools was established 1896, when the Supreme Court ruled that "separate but equal" schools for blacks could coexist with white schools, a decision not reversed until 1954. The elementary school grew rapidly in the 20th c. The junior high school appeared ca. 1910 and the nursery school ca. 1920. State teachers' colleges became general liberal arts colleges and eventually full universities. Professional education flourished, sometimes in separate universities, such as the Massachusetts Institute of Technology, but more typically as separate parts of general universities, such as medical and law schools. School reform has been a recurrent phenomenon; progressive education, a reform movement of the early 20th c., itself came under attack as reformers called for return to traditional methods of pedagogy. Scientific education received new attention in the 1960s, partly as a result of the new awareness of the scientific level of Soviet education. In the 1970s, reformers concentrated on ridding curricula of what were considered biases favoring the white, male, middle class at the expense of women, minorities, and the poor.

EDUCATION, BOARDS OF. Boards of education go back to the founding of the universities of the state of New York 1784 and Massachusetts 1837. Since then, state, county, and local government units have appointed, or citizens have elected, committees or boards of citizens to conduct public educational institutions and affairs. State boards of education define the educational policies for administrative and teaching staffs from nursery school to graduate school. On the local level, there are some 15,000 school districts.

EDUCATION, LAND GRANTS FOR. See LAND GRANTS FOR EDUCATION.

EDUCATION, UNITED STATES OFFICE OF. Established 1867 to collect statistics and facts on the condition and progress of education in the US and to diffuse such information, promoting the cause of education; renamed the Office of Education 1869 and placed under the Department of the Interior. Known as the Bureau of Education 1870–1929; became a constituent division within the Department of Health, Education, and Welfare 1953.

Ceased as a separate entity 1979 when absorbed by the new Department of Education.

EDWARD, FORT. Built 1755 at the Great Carrying Place on the Hudson R fourteen miles S of Lake George during the French and Indian War. Abandoned 1777.

EDWARDS, FORT. Frontier post built (1816–17) at present site of Warsaw, Ill., replacing a fort built 1814 and destroyed 1815. Abandoned 1824.

EFFECTIVE OCCUPATION. Spain's claims in the New World, based on prior discovery, were refuted by the English, French, and Dutch who admitted Spain's claims only in those areas where Spain had "actually settled and continued to inhabit." With the TREATY OF MADRID 1670, Spain formally recognized the principle, which remains an important doctrine in international law.

EGG HARBOR ENGAGEMENT (Oct. 15, 1778). Heavy losses were visited on colonial troops under Polish Gen. Casimir Pulaski. The colonial force had attempted to harm British shipping at Egg Harbor, N.J.

EGYPT. Colloquial term for southernmost quarter of Illinois, probably resulting from the delta-like character of the Cairo region and several Egyptian place names; used at least as early as 1855.

EIGHTEENTH AMENDMENT, also known as the Prohibition Amendment (1919–33). Prohibited manufacture, sale, transportation, import, and export of intoxicating liquors. The Anti-Saloon League campaigned for national prohibition 1913; finally successful on Jan. 13, 1919, when Nebraska became the thirty-sixth state to ratify, thereby making the amendment effective. The VOLSTEAD ACT was passed to enforce the amendment. By 1932 public support of the amendment was definitely waning. The Republican platform demanded return to state option; the Democratic platform favored repeal. The repeal process began, culminating in the TWENTY-FIRST AMENDMENT, which went into effect in 1933.

EISENHOWER DOCTRINE. Enunciated 1957 by President Eisenhower, it declared that US military and economic power would be used to protect the Middle East against communist aggression. Took the form of a congressional resolution, which was signed into law.

ELBE RIVER. The Elbe R and a tributary, the Mulde, served as a dividing line between Soviet and Allied forces of the West when World War II in Europe ended. American troops of the Second Armored Division were first to reach the river, on Apr. 11, 1945. Yet Allied high command had already decided to forgo a drive on Berlin and to use the Elbe and Mulde as readily discernible terrain features to avoid clashes between converging Western and Soviet troops. Patrols from other American units along the Mulde subsequently pushed to the upper Elbe in hope of being first to contact the Soviets. On April 25 a patrol met the Soviets at Torgau.

EL CANEY, BATTLE OF. See SAN JUAN HILL AND EL CANEY, BATTLES OF.

EL DORADO OIL FIELD. Oil was first struck at the El Dorado Oil Field, Kansas, in 1915. Peak production of 30 million barrels was in 1918. The field is still producing.

ELECTION LAWS. Traditionally, laws governing elections have been within the province of states, although the original Constitution set some guidelines. Various amendments have given the right to vote to women, to persons over eighteen, and to those who had never paid a poll tax. Federal statutes, such as the various civil rights acts of the 1960s, have also limited authority of the state to exclude categories of persons from voting. States still establish the general basis for voting. Election of local and state officials, representatives to state legislatures, members of Congress, and presidential electors takes place at state level. Fraudulent voting, improper electioneering, misuse of campaign funds, and bribery and intimidation of voters are subject to state legislation if committed in state elections. State law establishes machinery for conduct of elections. Contested elections are usually settled by court order under state legislation. Control over party primaries and state conventions is exercised by states.

ELECTION OF THE PRESIDENT. After prolonged discussion, the drafters of the Constitution provided that the president would be chosen by electors, especially selected as the legislature of each state should prescribe. Each state was to be entitled to "a number of electors equal to the whole number of Senators and Representatives to which the State may be entitled in the Congress." (In 1962 the Twenty-third Amendment added three electoral votes for the District of Columbia.) Each elector was to cast two votes; the candidate who received the largest number was to become president and the runner-up was to become vice-president, provided the largest number of votes constituted a majority. Should no candidate receive a majority, selection was to fall to the House of Representatives, where each state would be entitled to one vote. Early development of a two-party system in the US produced notable changes in the projections of the framers of the Constitution. Consequently, the Twelfth Amendment was passed in 1804, requiring electors to vote once for president and vice-president. During the first decades of the Republic state legislatures selected electors. By 1828 the present practice of selecting electors by popular, partisan vote was nearly universal. All electoral votes of each state go to the candidate receiving the most votes in the state, allowing designation of a president who has received fewer popular votes than his opponent. The electoral college has twice elected such presidents: Rutherford B. Hayes in 1876 and Benjamin Harrison in 1888. Nominations for president and vice-president are made at national party conventions whose delegates have been selected through party primaries, state party conventions, or state party central committees. National committees of each party raise campaign funds, develop organizations to influence the voter, and assist in research and public relations.

ELECTIONS. The US Constitution requires a congressional election every two years to elect all 435 members of the House of Representatives for two-year terms and one-third of the Senate for six-year terms. Every four years a presidential election must be held. Each state constitution contains provisions for what officers are to be elected, the requirements of the secret ballot, times of elections, and qualifications of voters. Various amendments and laws ensure that virtually every adult who is is a citizen may vote. In

earlier times, the franchise was limited to propertied people and blacks and women were excluded. Most state and county elections are held in the fall and even-numbered years at the same time as presidential and congressional elections, which are held on the first Tuesday after the first Monday in November. Usually, two judges of election representing the two major parties, one inspector, and several clerks are required in each precinct. The clerks check the voter's name against the registration list. Votes are cast on an automatic voting machine or registered on blank ballots, both in the privacy of a voting booth. Absentee voting is allowed if specific conditions are met. The cost of elections is borne by both the government and the private sector. The government pays for the administration of elections and keeping election records. Presidential campaigns are also partly paid for by federal funds. Money spent by the private sector amounts to hundreds of millions of dollars each year donated to specific candidates' election committees or to a particular party. Despite agitation on the part of Congress and concerned citizens' groups to limit the amount that can be contributed to campaigns, there is still no ceiling.

ELECTORAL COLLEGE. The electoral college plan that emerged from the Constitutional Convention provided for the selection of the president and vice-president by electors from each state, equal to the number of senators and representatives in Congress. The electors were selected by state legislators, but with the development of a party system in the 1820s, voters were asked to choose from among slates of electors put forth by the parties and generally pledged to particular candidates. Under the present system, voters designate their presidential choice by voting for a slate of electors pledged to a party's candidates for president and vice-president. The party receiving the most popular votes in a state receives all the electoral votes of that state. The winning slate of electors of each state convenes in December and the electors cast their votes. In January, the electoral votes are counted before a joint session of Congress. If an absolute majority of votes is not received by any candidate, Congress decides: The House of Representatives elects the president, and the Senate elects the vice-president. The electoral college generally ratifies the results of the popular vote, but it has failed three times to elect a president (1800, 1824, 1876). In the first two, the decision was made in the House. In 1876, Congress established an electoral commission to rule on disputed sets of electoral returns from several states. In two cases, the candidate selected in the electoral college had fewer popular votes than his opponent (1876, 1888), producing a "minority" president.

ELECTORAL COMMISSION (1876). Established by Congress to adjudicate the disputed Hayes-Tilden election. Four states reported conflicting sets of voting returns. Only one vote from the four states would have made Democrat Samuel J. Tilden president over Republican Rutherford B. Hayes. Reconstruction was nearly over, but military units were guarding polling places in Florida, Louisiana, and South Carolina, where Reconstruction governments reported Republican victories. The other dispute was in Oregon. The commission was to consist of two members each from the two parties and one impartial member, who turned out to be a Republican. The commission declared Hayes the winner. It was widely believed that a deal had been struck: the southern Democrats would accept Hayes as president if the Republicans would end Reconstruction in the South.

ELECTRIC POWER AND LIGHT INDUSTRY. The arc-lighting industry was the first sector of the electric light and power industry to achieve a substantial commercial success. Philadelphia installed arc lights in 1878, and other cities quickly followed. Thomas A. Edison was largely responsible for the successful incandescent lighting system; the first commercial central station, in New York City, began operation in 1882. In 1892, the Edison companies merged to form the General Electric Co. George Westinghouse introduced an incandescent lighting system using alternating current, which proved to have decisive advantages over Edison's direct-current system. The Westinghouse Electric Co. was formed in 1886 to manufacture transformers, alternators, and other alternating-current apparatus. The first commercial installation (at Buffalo, N.Y.) opened in 1886. Urban streetcars were electrified in the late 1880s, and the decades that followed saw the gradual electrification of long-distance railways as

well. High-speed turboelectric generators in central power stations were introduced in the first decade of the 20th c. and made it more economical for consumers to purchase electric power than to install their own generating plants. The growth of the industry brought the realization that even further economies could be achieved through power pools. The establishment in the 1930s of the federal Tennessee Valley Authority (TVA) and the Rural Electrification Administration (REA) accelerated the spread of power into outlying areas. A federal program to develop nuclear reactors for power production was launched in 1954; the first installation opened in Shreveport, La., in 1957. Many others went on line; but by the 1980s, the early predictions of an industry dominated by nuclear energy had been proved wrong. Both economics and public fears of the dangers of nuclear plants assured that fossil-fueled plants would continue to produce most of the nation's electricity.

ELECTRIFICATION, HOUSEHOLD. Began in the 1880s as the incandescent lamp and the telephone were developed. Full electrification did not come until the 1920s. Utility companies concentrated on electrifying industry, but it became clear that morning and evening power needs of households complemented perfectly the peak loads supplied to industry. Speeding the process were the invention of a low-cost, nondegradable electrical resistance and the high-speed, fractional horsepower electric motor adaptable to household appliances. Electric heat research began in the 1890s; by 1914, seven companies were manufacturing cooking and heating appliances. Much of early technology came from General Electric. At the same time, the Maytag Co. was making innovations in electric washing machines (the automatic washer appeared after World War II). The earliest domestic refrigerator was patented in 1908, but practical models were not developed until the 1920s, by Frigidaire, another division of General Electric. Kelvinator specialized in converting iceboxes into electric refrigerators; at the same time the company was developing the use of sulfur dioxide as a refrigerant. Freon later became the standard refrigerant. W. H. Hoover began selling his electric vacuum cleaners in 1907. The Great Depression saw the dissolution of many of the smaller electrical appliance companies; consolidations and mergers concentrated production in the hands of major full-appliance line manufacturers, such as General Electric, Westinghouse, Philco, and RCA. The end of World War II saw the trend toward the almost total electrification of the American home, which declined in the 1970s and 1980s because of the greatly increased cost of electric power and search for more economical sources such as solar energy.

ELECTROCHEMICAL INDUSTRY. Mechanical generators of electricity (dynamos) appeared in the late 1870s, making an electrochemical industry possible. The electric furnace, which utilized the passage of a current through resistant materials, such as carborundum, artificial graphite, and carbide, to generate intense heat, was developed after 1885. The Aluminum Co. of America was founded on an electrolytic process to extract aluminum from bauxite. The tremendous hydroelectric power source developed at Niagara Falls in the 1890s and by the Tennessee Valley Authority (TVA) in the 1930s gave the US great importance in electrochemistry. All major metals except iron and steel are now made or refined electrically. The polished metallic surfaces on appliances are electroplated. Dow Chemical Co. began (1915) producing metallic magnesium from seawater. Electrochemical methods were also introduced during World War II for the isotope separation of uranium, for which additional hydroelectric sites were constructed.

ELECTRONICS. The electron was discovered in 1897, and Guglielmo Marconi first demonstrated wireless telegraphy in the 1890s. Thus began the era of electronics. In 1906, Lee De Forest invented the triode, or thermionic vacuum-tube amplifier; its ability to amplify electric signals, while not immediately appreciated, was to be crucial in the development of electronics. The development of the telephone industry was based on it, as was radiocommunications. The formation of the Radio Corp. of America (RCA) in 1919 marked the practical beginning of the radio industry. Broadcasting began soon afterward. During the period between the two world wars, American broadcasting developed into a giant industry. "Talking" motion pictures were introduced in 1927, and the change

from mechanical to electronic phonograph recording and reproduction in the 1920s led to a new level of quality unsurpassed until development of the long-playing record, magnetic tape, high-fidelity stereophonic and digital recording. World War II gave a tremendous push to the American electronics industry. The proximity fuse and atomic weapons depended heavily on electronics for their development. Anti-aircraft fire control and the exigencies of artillery tables led, respectively, to the development of servomechanism and mechanical computers. Wartime radar and other telecommunications advances found ready applications in civilian fields; this great leap forward in electronics has been labeled the Second Industrial Revolution. Preeminent among the new developments was the invention, at Bell Laboratories, of the transistor, which contributed substantially to the extension of the communications arts to television, telemetry, and space flight; the spread of electronics in the economy; and the development of computers. Progress in medicine, industrial control, food technology, and a host of consumer fields ranging from materials processing to the printing of books was made possible by the introduction of electronic methods. The most pervasive development was the electronic computer, which made it possible to enhance and multiply the capabilities of the human brain.

ELECTRONIC SURVEILLANCE. Since 1934, telephone wiretapping in the United States has been illegal but widely engaged in by law enforcement officials as well as by private parties. Bugging is not illegal, per se, but has been made subject to various constitutional restrictions based on the laws of trespass. In 1968 Congress authorized federal and state officials to wiretap for a wide variety of suspected offenses if they first obtained a court order. Electronic surveillance played a significant part in the WATERGATE scandals of the Nixon administration.

ELEMENTARY AND SECONDARY SCHOOL EDUCATION ACT (1965). Passed by Congress as part of Lyndon B. Johnson's Great Society program; the first general federal financial assistance to elementary and secondary schools. Major aim was education of poor children. Established a number of categories under which aid was available to states.

ELEVATED RAILWAYS. First line opened in New York City in 1867. Electrification began ca. 1903. The noise and unsightliness led to replacement mostly by underground railways or subways. Since World War II, there has been some resurgence in popularity, the monorail, for example.

ELEVATORS. Early hoists and elevators functioned by winding a rope on a drum to raise the platform. They were not used to carry passengers. In 1854, Elisha Otis demonstrated a safety device that would grip the elevator guide rails if the hoist ropes parted, thus making the passenger elevator possible. His first passenger elevator was installed in a New York City store in 1857. Drum-machine elevators were restricted to low-rise buildings. By 1870, a rope-geared hydraulic system was developed, eliminating the winding drum. Modern high-speed elevators appeared ca. 1900, when the traction machine was developed. It could serve buildings of any height. Later developments provided automatic landing of the elevators at floor level and automatic floor selection.

ELEVATORS, GRAIN. In 1842, a Buffalo grain merchant built an elevating apparatus for unloading grain directly from vessels into his warehouse. By the 1880s, railroads encouraged construction of grain elevators at stops throughout the grain belt. Grain elevators consist of enormous clusters of concrete silos or steel tanks, receive grain carried by trucks from farms, and handle the grain by pneumatic machinery.

ELEVENTH AMENDMENT (1798). Declared that "the judicial power of the United States shall not be construed to extend to any suit in law or equity, commenced or prosecuted against one of the United States by citizens of another state, or by citizens or subjects of any foreign state."

ELGIN-MARCY TREATY (June 5, 1854). Also known as Reciprocity Treaty. Established Canadian-US reciprocity over fishing rights.

ELIZABETH. City in NE New Jersey; important port city and manufacturing center. Settled in the 17th c. by the ELIZABETHTOWN ASSOCIATES. Capital of the province until 1676 and of East Jersey until 1686. Pop.: 106,201 (1980).

ELIZABETHTOWN ASSOCIATES. First group granted permission (1644) to settle in New Jersey. Purchased 400,000 acres from the Indians and settled Elizabethtown (now ELIZABETH). The original settlers were Puritans from New England and Long Island.

ELK HILLS OIL SCANDAL. In 1921, A. E. Fall, secretary of the interior under President Harding, "borrowed" $100,000 from E. L. Doheny, president of the company to which he had leased important oil reserves on public lands at Elk Hills, Calif. The company was forced to pay back all monies made from the deal. Fall was convicted (1931) of bribery and sentenced to a year. (See also TEAPOT DOME OIL SCANDAL.)

ELK RIVER, BATTLE OF (May 1–2, 1862). Louisiana cavalry, operating in the vicinity of Elk River, Ala., defeated Union forces, capturing many stores and inflicting severe casualties.

ELLENTON RIOT (Sept. 16–19, 1876). Bloodiest Reconstruction incident in South Carolina. White riflemen in pursuit of a black criminal terrorized other blacks. Federal troops intervened but two whites and several blacks were killed.

ELLIS, FORT. Defense against the Sioux; built in 1867 on the East Gallatin R, near Bozeman, Mont. Abandoned 1886.

ELLIS ISLAND. In New York harbor, reception center for immigrants between 1892 and 1954. More than 16 million immigrants passed through Ellis Island, almost three-fourths of all immigrants during this period.

ELLSWORTH'S ZOUAVES. Union volunteer force in the Civil War, named for its founder, E. E. Ellsworth of Chicago.

ELMIRA, BATTLE OF (Aug. 29, 1779). Iroquois Indians and Loyalists made an unsuccessful stand against patriot forces.

ELMIRA PRISON. Union prison camp in Elmira, N.Y. Established 1864, it held over 12,000 prisoners. More than 25 percent died.

EL PASO. City in Texas and port of entry from Mexico; Juárez lies just across the Rio Grande. Discovered and named El Paso del Norte in 1598; Franciscan mission established 1659. Became US territory in 1849; Fort Bliss was established against the Apache. Major commercial and manufacturing center in area noted for cattle, cotton, and minerals. Pop.: 425,259 (1980).

EMANCIPATION, COMPENSATED. Plan to eliminate slavery by having the government buy and free the slaves. Proposed by Virginia in 1829 and revived by the Republican platform of 1860. President Lincoln approved the plan, but war ended all efforts.

EMANCIPATION MOVEMENT. Efforts to free slaves and send them to Liberia began in 1817; after 1830, the aggressive American Anti-Slavery Society urged immediate emancipation. Although unsuccessful, their plans kept the issue constantly before the public.

EMANCIPATION ORDERS, FRÉMONT AND HUNTER. On Aug. 30, 1861, Gen. J. C. Frémont, commander of the Department of the West, declared free the slaves of all persons in Missouri supporting the Confederacy. Gen. David Hunter, commander of the Department of the South, did the same in South Carolina, Georgia, and Florida, on May 9, 1862. President Lincoln, eager not to alienate border states, voided both orders.

EMANCIPATION PROCLAMATION (Jan. 1, 1863). President Lincoln's grant of freedom to slaves in all states then in rebellion. Admonishing the freedmen to abstain from violence, it invited them to join the Union armed forces. Although it did not free slaves in border states, the mere fact of its promulgation ensured the death of slavery in the event of a northern victory.

EMBARGO ACT (1807). Measure taken by President Jefferson to deal with abuses to US shipping by England and France in the early stages of the Napoleonic Wars. Prohibited trade with either country. Generally regarded as a failure, it was effectively repealed as soon as Jefferson left office.

EMBASSIES. Missions of the highest rank, headed by an ambassador. Until 1893, when the first ambassador was appointed, only ministers represented the nation abroad. By 1981, the US was exchanging ambassadors with 144 countries.

EMBLEMS, PARTY. Symbols of political parties since the black cockade of the Federalists. They often appear at the top of a party ballot. A crowing rooster or a star usually serves for the Democrats, an elephant or an eagle for the Republicans, clasped hands for the Socialists, the hammer and sickle for the Communists. The donkey is also a symbol for the Democrats.

EMIGRANT AID MOVEMENT. 1854 plan to promote free-state migration in Kansas Territory. Founded a few towns but results were negligible. (See also NEW ENGLAND EMIGRANT AID COMPANY.)

EMINENT DOMAIN. The Fifth Amendment of the Constitution implicitly acknowledges the right of eminent domain by stating that private property shall not "be taken for public use, without just compensation." By Supreme Court interpretation, the same right and limitation have been attributed to state governments.

EMORY'S MILITARY RECONNAISSANCE (1846). Lt. W. H. Emory of the US Topographical Engineers supervised first US survey in the Southwest, from the Rio Grande and Gila R to the California coast. Was part of military planning for Mexican War.

EMPLOYERS' LIABILITY LAWS. During the 18th and early 19th c., common law recognized the duties of the "master" both to provide the "servant" a reasonable safe place to work and to establish safety rules; but many accidents were not traceable to negligence but to the inherent risk of the work. Beginning in the mid-19th c., states began passing laws increasing employer responsibility. First federal legislation (1908) covered workers in interstate commerce; a 1915 law protected seamen. Beginning in 1902, in Maryland, workmen's compensation laws have been enacted to ease financial strain of the injured employee. Standard provisions ensure that an injured or sick employee will receive cash or medical benefits without proof of fault. Compensation is awarded by administrative, not judicial, bodies and according to definite payment schedules, so that money is received a short time after injury or death. By 1973 all fifty states had comprehensive workmen's compensation statutes.

EMPLOYMENT SERVICE, UNITED STATES (USES). Established during World War I to mobilize the work force. Made a permanent part of the Labor Department in 1933. Sets minimum standards, develops uniform administrative and statistical procedures, publishes employment information, and promotes a system of cooperation between states. Works cooperatively with the 50 state employment services by providing testing and counseling, expanding job placement, and providing guidance.

EMPRESARIO SYSTEM. Method to encourage settlement in Mexican Texas. Each empresario received large sections of land for each hundred families he introduced as settlers. Only Catholics of good moral character could settle, and the empresario was expected to establish schools and churches.

EMPRESS AUGUSTA BAY, BATTLE OF (Nov. 2, 1943). Naval encounter fought some fifty miles W of Bougainville, the Solomon Islands. After an hour, the Japanese withdrew with heavy losses.

ENABLING ACTS. Legislation by which Congress admits new states.

ENCOMIENDA SYSTEM. A Spanish modified feudal institution, introduced into the New World. The king granted individuals an estate and the right to receive and collect for themselves the tributes of the Indians who lived on it, who were given them in trust, for their life and the life of one heir.

ENCYCLOPEDIAS. The *Encyclopaedia Britannica*, first published in Edinburgh in 1768, was pirated in the US in 1798. Since the early 20th c., it has been an American publication. The *Encyclopedia Americana* first appeared in 1829 as a translation of a German one. Publication lapsed in 1858; the contemporary work by that name dates from 1902. Modern children's encyclopedias include *The Book of Knowledge, World Book, and Merit Students Encyclopedia*. The *New*

Columbia Encyclopedia is the preeminent one-volume encyclopedia. Specialized reference sets include the *International Encyclopedia of the Social Sciences, Dictionary of American Biography, Dictionary of Scientific Biography, Dictionary of American History, Encyclopedia of Philosophy*.

ENEMY ALIENS. The Alien Enemies Act of 1798 authorizes the president to expel from the country any alien whom he regards as dangerous to the public peace or safety. Since then, various espionage and internal security laws have expanded the government's power to deal with enemy aliens. The two world wars saw the greatest utilization of such laws, often unfairly and in many cases illegally. (See JAPANESE-AMERICANS IN WORLD WAR II.)

ENEMY DESTINATION. Doctrine legalizing the seizure of contraband cargoes carried in neutral ships between neutral ports when there is evidence of ultimate enemy destination. In the 18th c., British courts held neutral ships to be part of the enemy merchant marine when neutral trade exceeded limits customary in times of peace. Americans carried goods from the French West Indies to American ports and reshipped them to France. The British then held that such shipments constituted continuous voyages between the enemy ports of origin and ultimate destination. This rule was applied to contraband by 1761 and to blockade by 1804. The US denied and rejected the rule; but later embraced it during the Civil War.

ENERGY, US DEPARTMENT OF. Created 1977 by consolidating the major federal energy functions into one cabinet-level department. The department provides the framework for a comprehensive and balanced national energy policy and is responsible for research and development of energy technology.

ENFORCEMENT ACTS. See FORCE ACTS.

ENGINEERING EDUCATION. The earliest engineering school in America was the US Military Academy at West Point (1802). The Rensselaer School (1824) was by the late 1840s transformed into a polytechnic school based on French and German models. Professional technical instruction was begun at Harvard (1847), Yale (1847), the University of Pennsylvania (1847), Dartmouth (1851), and the University of Michigan (1852). The Massachusetts Institute of Technology (MIT) was founded in 1859; most of the agricultural and mechanical colleges founded after passage of the Morrill Act of 1862 used MIT as an example. The increasing demand for skilled technicians resulted in a proliferation of engineering schools in the second half of the 19th c.: Stevens Institute of Technology (1870), Case Institute (1880), Georgia Institute of Technology (1888), and the California Institute of Technology (1891).

ENGINEERS, US ARMY CORPS OF. Fulfills both civil and military functions. Acts as a combat arm, a technical service, and as a national construction agency. Built breastworks at Bunker Hill, the Cumberland Road, the Panama Canal, and the Manhattan Project. The present organization dates from 1802, when President Jefferson decreed that the US Military Academy at West Point be constituted as an engineering school (the first in the nation). Most of West Point's top graduates went into the corps. In the 19th c., the corps built roads, canals, piers, and lighthouses, and took part in surveys and explorations. From 1824, Congress assigned the corps increasing responsibility for river and harbor projects, flood control, water conservation, and recreation facilities. Often at the center of controversy, particularly with conservationists.

ENGLISH SETTLEMENT. A colony founded in Edwards County, Ill. (1818), for English artisans and laborers. Two towns were established: Wanborough, which soon died, and Albion, which had a 1980 population of 12,285.

ENLISTMENT. In colonial times, service in the militia was mostly compulsory, but forces raised for long expeditions depended on enlistments, which was also the method by which Continental forces were raised. In 1783, the country began a peacetime dependence on voluntary enlistment in the armed forces that endured down to the passage of the first peacetime conscription act in 1940. Enlistment was the primary method of raising forces in all American wars until 1917. In 1973, the postwar draft came to an end. All

services now depend solely on enlistment for terms that generally are from three to five years. (See also CONSCRIPTION.)

ENOREE, BATTLE OF (Nov. 20, 1780). Patriot forces under Thomas Sumter won an engagement in South Carolina against British forces under Sir Banastre Tarleton.

ENSIGN. Lowest commissioned rank in the US navy and coast guard. Army officers also once carried the rank.

ENTAIL OF ESTATE. Under feudal law the grantee of an estate could not sell or dispose of any property. On his death, it was inherited by his eldest son. Common law favored free disposition of such tenures. Entail estates were common in the colonial South and middle colonies. By the Revolution there was considerable opposition to entail, which tended to perpetuate an aristocratic class. Virginia led in abolition of the custom.

ENTANGLING ALLIANCES. A phrase used by Thomas Jefferson (not George Washington; Washington advised against "permanent alliances "). At his first inauguration (1801), Jefferson declared his devotion to "peace, commerce, and honest friendship with all nations, entangling alliances with none."

ENUMERATED COMMODITIES. Colonial products permitted to be exported only to certain destinations, generally Great Britain or its colonies, the object being to prevent important products (especially tobacco) from reaching European markets except by way of England. (See also NAVIGATION ACTS.)

ENUMERATED POWERS. Powers specifically given to the federal government by the Constitution, as opposed to IMPLIED POWERS.

ENVIRONMENTALISM. Organized efforts to preserve and improve the quality of the air, water, and land and to establish controls over the use of such pollutants as smoke, insecticides, and industrial waste. The Environmental Protection Agency, created 1970, has federal responsibilities over such efforts.

EPHRATA. Religious community founded 1735 near Lancaster, Pa., by German Seventh

Day Baptists. Included were two monastic orders, Sisters and Brethren. The monastic features of the community had died out by 1800, but the congregation survived until ca. 1890. Now a museum.

EPIDEMICS. In the colonial period, the chief epidemic diseases were smallpox, yellow fever, and diphtheria, which first swept the colonies in 1735. Periodic outbreaks of measles, scarlet fever, and influenza also aroused concern. Smallpox was brought under some control in the 19th c. by vaccination, and the incidence of diphtheria declined. A series of yellow fever epidemics, beginning in Philadelphia in 1793, struck at every major city for the next twelve years. The attacks on southern ports peaked in the 1850s; in New Orleans, three epidemics killed 14,000 residents. Yellow fever then spread up the inland waterways but tapered off after the Civil War, the last outbreak occurring in New Orleans in 1905. A second major epidemic disease of the 19th c. was Asiatic cholera; as a filth disease, it fell before the advancing sanitary movement. In the 20th c., a comparable outbreak of disease was the great influenza epidemic of 1918–19, with a death toll of 450,000. In the later 20th c., poliomyelitis was a scourge of younger people until vaccination brought it under control. In the early 1980s, acquired immune deficiency syndrome (AIDS) became a serious health threat to certain segments of the population identified as high risk groups, the most prominent being male homosexuals.

EPISCOPAL CHURCH. The Revolution left the Anglican church divided and weakened. The more High Church New England wing and the more moderate Southern wing met in 1785 and ironed out their differences. The result was the adoption of a modified Book of Common Prayer and a church government that united the historic values of episcopacy with considerable local and lay control. In the 19th c., there were clashes between the new Anglo-Catholic theology of the Oxford, or Tractarian, movement and more traditional understandings of the episcopal position. The last serious eruption of the controversy occurred in 1873; a small party withdrew to establish the Reformed Episcopal church. In the 20th c., the Protestant Episcopal church has maintained a moderately liberal theological position. Heavily influenced by so-called Social Gospel, it has stressed social services and urban ministries. In the 1970s, the church began ordaining women and revised the prayer book, causing some dissension. Membership: 2,800,000 (1980).

E PLURIBUS UNUM ("From the many, one"). Motto on the seal of the United States, selected by Benjamin Franklin, John Adams, and Thomas Jefferson (1776).

EQUAL EMPLOYMENT OPPORTUNITY COMMISSION. Federal agency founded by Civil Rights Act of 1964, which prohibits discrimination in employment based on race, color, religion, sex, or national origin. Mandate covers all employment conditions.

EQUALITY, DOCTRINE OF. In *Leviathan* (1651), Thomas Hobbes reasons that the right of self-preservation is the fundamental natural right, and the equality of that right makes men equal in the most fundamental respect. In his *Second Treatise of Government* (1690), John Locke asserts that the equality of humans rests in their being members of a single species; thus, no man is by nature governor over another and all men are free. From these two sources, comes the assertion in the Declaration of Independence that "all men are created equal." That assertion is regarded as a self-evident truth; and the rights to life, liberty, and the pursuit of happiness are seen to be derived from it.

EQUAL PROTECTION OF THE LAW. The Fourteenth Amendment of the US Constitution, which provides that no state shall deny any person the equal protection of the law, was designed to protect newly emancipated blacks of the South. The Supreme Court, in the *Civil Rights Cases* (1883), confined the clause's applicability to state-enacted discriminations. In *Plessy v. Ferguson* (1896), the court sanctioned state-imposed segregation, provided that the separate accommodations were substantially equal. In 1938, the court began moving toward a more literal reading of the equal protection clause. In *Brown v. Board of Education of Topeka* (1954), the court reversed itself on *Plessy* and stated that segregated schools are inherently unequal. During the next twenty years Congress passed civil rights acts that declared that any kind of racial segregation or discrimination violates the Fourteenth Amendment.

EQUAL RIGHTS AMENDMENT (ERA). Proposed constitutional amendment stating that "Equality of rights under the law shall not be denied or abridged by the United States or by any state on account of sex." First introduced in 1923; not passed by Congress until 1972. Became one of the most emotional political issues of the day. By 1975, thirty-five states (of the thirty-eight needed) had ratified the proposed amendment. Ratification deadline extended to June 30, 1982, but amendment failed.

EQUAL RIGHTS PARTY. A minor political party, in existence from 1884 to 1888; advocated enfranchisement of women.

ERA. See EQUAL RIGHTS AMENDMENT.

ERA OF GOOD FEELING (1817–24). The two administrations of James Monroe. The demise of the Federal party gave the appearance of political union in strong nationalism, illustrated by the tariff act of 1816, the second National Bank, and western development. Monroe received all but one electoral vote in 1820.

ERIE. City in Pennsylvania, located on Lake Erie; an important business and manufacturing center, with paper mills and machinery-making and electrical-equipment factories. A vital industrial center after the completion of the Erie and Pittsburgh Canal in 1844. Pop.: 119,123 (1980).

ERIE, FORT. British fort erected 1764 on the Niagara R at Lake Erie. Destroyed 1779 and rebuilt 1791. In the War of 1812, changed hands several times. Fortifications destroyed by the Americans in 1814.

ERIE, LAKE. Fourth largest of the Great Lakes. The first white man on its waters was Louis Jolliet (1669). Claimed for France. In 1669 La Salle launched the first ship. Rivalry between French and English over the fur trade gave the lake a strategic importance. The French held Detroit and Niagara until the end of the French and Indian War. The British and Indians maintained control of the lake until Jay's Treaty (1794), which placed the international boundary in the center of the lake. American settlements spread along the southern shore. In the War of 1812, the British fleet was defeated in the Battle of Lake Erie. The British yielded the lakes, which were neutralized in 1818. The completion of the Erie Canal and the Ohio canal sytem greatly increased commercial traffic. Part of the St. Lawrence Seaway, important economically to Buffalo, N.Y., Erie, Pa., the Ohio lake ports, and Detroit, Mich.

ERIE, LAKE, BATTLE OF (Sept. 10, 1813). The major naval engagement on the Great Lakes in the War of 1812. Commander O. H. Perry commanded the American fleet, which blockaded Malden, the British base. Victory assured US control of the lake and free entry to Canada. Perry sent the celebrated message "We have met the enemy, and they are ours."

ERIE CANAL. Built by New York state between 1817 and 1825 to connect New York City and Buffalo. The 4-foot-deep ditch was 363 miles long, with 83 locks lifting boats a total of over 600 feet; it cost over $7 million to build. Its success led to a national "canal mania." The New York legislature constructed branches all along the route. It was largely responsible for the development of Great Lakes area before the coming of the railroad. By the 1870s, railroads began to supplant it. Now part of the New York State Barge Canal System.

ERIE LACKAWANNA. See RAILROADS, SKETCHES OF PRINCIPAL LINES.

ERIE RAILROAD. See RAILROADS, SKETCHES OF PRINCIPAL LINES.

ERIE TRIANGLE. About 200,000 acres bounded by Lake Erie, New York, and the forty-second parallel; part of the territory ceded to the United States by New York and Massachusetts in 1781 and 1785, respectively. Pennsylvania bought it in 1788.

ESCALANTE-DOMÍNGUEZ EXPEDITION (1776–77). A 2,000-mile expedition from Santa Fe through Great Salt Lake Valley, Arizona, and Colorado by two Spanish priests. Extended Spanish claims nearly to the forty-second parallel.

ESKIMO. The Eskimo, or Inuit, one of the most widely distributed peoples of the world, inhabit the area from SE Alaska around the Arctic coasts to E Greenland. They speak Eskaleut, a unique language. Social organization based on hunting whale, seal, and caribou. Environment has made them especially inventive: the igloo for quasi-permanent residence, the harpoon with detachable shaft, the kayak, and special footgear, boats, sleds, and sledges. Chief organizational arrangement based on lines of kinship. Population never seems to have exceeded 60,000, not including 16,000 Aleuts, a linguistically related people.

ESOPUS WAR (1659–64). Between the Esopus, a division of the Delaware Confederacy, and Dutch settlers near the present Kingston, N.Y. Conflict worsened after Peter Stuyvesant sold some Indians into slavery.

ESPIONAGE ACT (1917). World War I legislation that authorized severe punishments for transmitting information regarding the war effort. In 1918 amendments were added (the Sedition Act), providing for heavy punishment for anyone who should, during war, "utter, print, write, or publish any disloyal, profane, scurrilous, or abusive language" about the flag, the armed forces, the Constitution, or the form of government. More than 1,500 persons were arrested, including socialist leader Eugene V. Debs. Modified in 1940, in the postwar years it was employed against Ethel and Julius Rosenberg, who were executed in 1953. The law has been much amended since then.

ESSEX JUNTO. A group of influential Essex County, Mass., public figures who supported the adoption of the Constitution and the Federalist party. Called the British faction because of opposition to the embargo and the War of 1812. Led in the calling of the HART-FORD CONVENTION.

ESSEX WILDCAT BANK. Founded in Vermont in 1832, it was one of numerous banks that issued large amounts of irredeemable currency before the National Banking Act of 1863.

ESTABLISHED CHURCHES. The Congregational church was established (supported by public funds) in several New England colonies and the Church of England in part of New York and some southern colonies. Practice ended with the Revolution.

ETERNAL CENTER. The first large crude oil strike in present West Virginia (1860).

ETHNOLOGY, BUREAU OF AMERICAN. Established by Congress 1879. Became foremost center for study of American Indians. Produced works on linguistics, ethnology, archaeology, physical anthropology, and history. In 1964 merged with other agencies of Smithsonian Institution.

EUTAW SPRINGS, BATTLE OF (Sept. 8, 1781). The last important Revolutionary engagement in South Carolina. Americans successfully prevented British troops there from going to the aid of Cornwallis at Yorktown.

EVANGELICAL ALLIANCE. Early attempt (1846) at cooperation among Protestant groups. Existed until 1908, when the Federal Council of the Churches of Christ replaced it.

EVANGELINE (1647). Long poem by Henry Wadsworth Longfellow telling of lovers separated during the expulsion of the Acadians by the British in 1755. Its heroine has become a mythic figure among the Acadians, or Cajuns, of Louisiana.

EVANS'S GENERAL MAP OF THE MIDDLE BRITISH COLONIES IN AMERICA. Published 1755 in Philadelphia and London. Had seventeen reissues and many plagiarisms.

EVANSVILLE. City in SW Indiana, an important port on the Ohio R. Settled 1812, when a ferry service was begun. With the steamboat, became a prosperous river port. Industries include a large aluminum factory and distribution of agricultural equipment. Pop.: 130,496 (1980).

EVERGLADES NATIONAL PARK. Located in SW Florida, it is a swampy region famous for a wide variety of wildlife, especially the alligator and many species of birds.

EXCESS PROFITS TAX. Enacted 1917 to capture excess wartime profits; repealed 1921. In 1933 and 1935, two mild excess profits taxes supplemented a capital stock tax. New laws were passed during World War II; tax increased to 95 percent by 1943. Repealed 1946 but reimposed during Korean War.

EXCHANGE, BILLS OF. Originally, a promise to pay that was incurred in one currency and to be paid in another currency. As such, it was a way of coping with the early mercantilist prohibition on the exportation of gold and silver and of avoiding the risk of transporting bullion. The use of bills of exchange declined in the late 19th c. with the increased self-financing of industry, the growing tendency to eliminate the wholesale merchant with increasing industrialization, and the increased use of telegraphic transfers of funds.

EXCHANGE OF PRISONERS. An established practice by the time of the American Revolution, British soldiers were exchanged for Massachusetts militiamen after the battles at Lexington and Concord, thereby setting precedent for the rest of the war. Battlefield exchanges took place during the War of 1812, but none was negotiated during the Mexican War. Although an exchange plan was in place during the Civil War, it proved largely ineffective. Virtually no exchanges took place during the Spanish-American War. In World War I, exchanges took place after hostilities ended, which has become the general pattern.

EXCHANGES. Since the 16th c., exchanges have provided a permanent, institutionalized auction market for buying and selling paper commodities (company shares, bank stock, and governmental obligations). The New York Stock Exchange dates from the late 18th c.; the Chicago Board of Trade was founded in 1848 to deal in grains and provisions. Specialized exchanges were established to deal in flour, sugar, coffee, rubber, silk, hides, and mine products. Originally self-regulating, they have come increasingly (since 1916) under government supervision. The Securities Act (1933) and the Securities Exchange Act (1934) were the principal federal statutes.

EXCHANGE STUDENTS. Colonial and early Republic Americans studied abroad, especially in medicine. These exchange students and their 19th-c. successors brought back not only German doctorates but German ideas for raising standards of higher education and of academic freedom. During the 20th c., attendance by Americans at foreign universities increased greatly under the stimulation of Rhodes and Fulbright scholarships. Foreign study in American universities has increased sharply since World War II. In 1980, 286,000 foreign students were enrolled in US institutions.

EXCISE TAXES. Internal taxes on items or services produced and sold within the country. One of the earliest was the tax on whiskey, which led to the WHISKEY REBELLION.

EXECUTIVE AGENT. A representative of the president of the US whose purpose is to conduct negotiations or investigations dealing with foreign countries. Began when George Washington sent Gouverneur Morris to London to investigate US-British relations.

EXECUTIVE AGREEMENTS. International agreements concluded by the president; as distinguished from treaties, which must be ratified by the Senate. They are as effective as formal treaties in conferring rights and obligations and are mentioned in the Constitution obliquely as "agreements" and "compacts." The president has considerable leeway in deciding whether to negotiate an executive agreement or a treaty.

EXECUTIVE AND CONGRESS. The Constitution created a strong executive and a strong legislature, endowed each branch with independent power, and provided a minimum of structuring of the relations between them. Some key functions, such as appointments, lawmaking, and treaties, are shared; and few functions not deliberately designed to be shared are the exclusive province of one branch. Congress declares war, but the president initiates it. The history of relations between the two branches has been one of struggle, with the predominant share of successes, and therefore of enlarging power, accruing to the executive. The most sweeping assertion of presidential power occurred when President Lincoln expanded the armed forces, drew unappropriated funds from the Treasury, instituted censorship over the mails, and suspended the writ of habeas corpus. In opposite pattern, Congress can also be ascendant. The Senate refused to follow President Wilson's commitment to the League of Nations. Congress and the executive can also draw together in consensus and cooperation, as in Franklin D. Roosevelt's New Deal in the 1930s, Harry S. Truman's and Dwight D. Eisenhower's foreign policy of the post-World War II era, and Lyndon B. Johnson's Great Society program of the 1960s.

EXECUTIVE OFFICE OF THE PRESIDENT. Established 1939 to assist the president in effectively controlling and coordinating the executive branch. Today, it includes the White House Office, the Office of Management and Budget, the Council of Economic Advisers, the National Security Council, the Office of Emergency Preparedness, National Aeronautics and Space Council, Office of Science and Technology, Office of the Special Representative for Trade Negotiations, Office of Consumer Affairs, Officer of Economic Opportunity, Office of Intergovernmental Relations, Council on Environmental Quality, Domestic Council, Office of Telecommunications, Council on International Economic Policy, and Special Action Office for Drug Abuse Prevention.

EXECUTIVE ORDERS. Deal with a wide variety of internal administrative matters of the executive branch, such as departmental reorganization and the promulgation of civil service rules and regulations, and are based on the president's constitutional powers or derive from statutory authority. The courts have regularly ruled that executive orders have the force of law, but only if they have a basis in constitutional or statutory law. Thus, President Truman's seizure of steel mills during the Korean War was held unconstitutional. Since 1907, executive orders have been numbered. Published in the *Federal Register*.

EXECUTIVE PRIVILEGE. From the very beginning of the US government, presidents and other executive officials have maintained that they are not required to disclose matters involving confidential relations within the executive department; furthermore, presidents have asserted that they are not answerable to any judicial process except impeachment. This position has often collided head-on with

the power of Congress to investigate all matters within its legislative capability. Congress has tended to go along with presidents who invoke presidential privilege. But during the WATERGATE controversy of 1974, the US Supreme Court required President Nixon to surrender taped White House conversations. The interests of fairness in the administration of justice were held to outweigh Nixon's claim of absolute presidential authority to determine the application of claimed executive privilege.

EXETER COMPACT. Agreement (based on the Mayflower Compact) signed by a group of settlers in Exeter, N.H., in 1639. An attempt to provide government for the town.

EXPANSIONISM. The Louisiana Purchase (1803) and expansion of the country from the Appalachians to the Missouri Valley are the earliest examples of the enduring tendency of the American republic to increase its territory, followed by the prolonged (1810–19) effort to annex Florida. Missionary zeal, known as Manifest Destiny, was important in territorial acquisitions of the 1840s, when the boundary of the US reached the Pacific Ocean. Except for the acquisition of S Arizona with the Gadsden Purchase (1853) and the purchase of Alaska (1867), continental boundaries of the US were completed with the Treaty of Guadalupe Hidalgo in 1848. The expansion of the 1890s and early 20th c. (Puerto Rico, Hawaii, the Philippines, the Canal Zone, the Pacific islands, the protectorate over Cuba) was imperialistic in tone, colonial in method, and insular in direction. Although cold war competition after World War II inspired the establishment of US bases and military and economic aid programs throughout the globe, the US has seemingly rejected the association of mission with territorial conquest.

EXPATRIATION. Right of a citizen to transfer allegiance from one political state to another. In the US, all persons are recognized as possessing that right; in the past, however, other nations have claimed that natives of their country, even after assuming American citizenship, were still subject to their laws. These conflicts were usually settled eventually by treaty.

EXPORTS. See TRADE, FOREIGN.

EXPORT TAXES. Both federal government and states are prohibited by the Constitution (Article I, Section 9; Article I, Section 10) from imposing export taxes.

EX POST FACTO LAW. Legislation that retroactively makes an action a crime. The US Constitution specifically prohibits such laws (Article I, Section 9).

EXTRADITION. Surrender by one sovereign government to another of a fugitive from justice. In the US federal system, it also refers to the surrender of a fugitive from one state to another. The Constitution (Article IV, Section 2) requires that each state honor extradition requests of others; in practice governors have much discretionary power when such requests are made.

EXTRA SESSIONS. The Constitution (Article II, Section 3) gives the president power to call Congress into special, or extra, sessions. Congress is not required to act on the matter for which it is called into session; nor is it limited to action only on that matter. Fewer extra sessions are called today, because Congress sits for longer terms than previously.

EXTRATERRITORIALITY, RIGHT OF. Immunity to laws of a country granted to nationals of another country. In Oriental countries, extraterritorial courts were set up to administer Western law for Westerners. An 1830 treaty between Turkey and the US exempted US citizens from Islamic law. The US had extraterritorial privileges in China, Japan, Muscat, Siam, and Persia. American and British formed the Foreign Settlement in Shanghai (1863) a municipal administration, exempt from Chinese jurisdiction. In 1906, the US Court for China was established. Extraterritoriality treaties have been abrogated; all sovereign nations today are assumed to be on equal footing as far as their domestic laws are concerned.

EZRA CHURCH, BATTLE OF (July 28, 1864). Unsuccessful attempt, near Atlanta, by Confederate troops to halt southward march of Gen. W. T. Sherman.

FACTORY SYSTEM, INDIAN. Chain of government-owned and operated stores that existed in Indian areas between 1795 and 1822. There were twenty-eight stores in all, but only seven or eight existed at any one time. Stores were located in Georgia, Tennessee, Michigan, Wisconsin, Indiana, Illinois, Mississippi, and Louisiana. Purpose of the system was to strengthen military policy, promote peace, protect Indians against exploitation by private traders, and offset influence of the British and Spanish. Factors sold goods to Indians in exchange for furs, bear oil, beeswax, and other products, which were sold at auction or in foreign markets. System did not work as planned.

FAIR DEAL. Domestic policies of President Truman; essentially an extension of the NEW DEAL of the 1930s.

FAIR EMPLOYMENT PRACTICES COMMITTEE (FEPC). Government agency during World War II to ensure equal access to jobs for qualified people, regardless of race or national origin. In 1948, President Truman proposed the FEPC be permanent, but this was rejected by Congress; in time most of its basic purposes became accepted elements of national labor practice.

FAIRFAX PROPRIETARY. Patent issued to Thomas, Lord Culpeper, by King James II in 1688; counter to wishes of the inhabitants of Virginia, he was given rights to the region between the Rappahannock and Potomac rivers, which later passed to Thomas, Lord Fairfax. After the American Revolution and the Definitive Peace of 1783, Fairfax heirs sued to resume ownership of the more than 5 million acres. Eventually, Virginia agreed to relinquish claims to all lands specifically appropriated by Fairfax for his own use, in return for all lands that were "waste and unappropriated" at his death.

FAIR LABOR STANDARDS ACT (1938). Also known as the Wages and Hours Bill; regulated hours of labor, wages, and child labor in industries involved in interstate commerce. A minimum wage was established, certain hazardous occupations were prohibited to youths and time-and-a-half pay was required for overtime. Upheld by Supreme Court 1941.

FAIR OAKS, BATTLE OF (May 31–June 1, 1862), also known as the Battle of Seven

Pines. Union forces under Gen. G. B. McClellan fought Confederate troops under Gen. J. E. Johnston, who was wounded in battle, and Gen. G. W. Smith, who replaced him. The Rebels were initially successful but eventually forced to retire.

FAIR-TRADE LAWS. Legislation protecting manufacturers from price-cutting of brandname merchandise by retailers. California passed the first such legislation 1931; most states followed. In 1937, federal legislation supported state laws. Initially courts approved fair-trade agreements signed between suppliers and retailers; but by the 1950s, many such agreements had been invalidated.

FALKLAND ISLANDS. Both Argentina and Great Britain have claims to the Falklands (or Malvinas) from the 18th c. After Britain colonized the islands in the 1830s, the US persistently refused to consider Argentinian claims. In 1982, during stalemated talks with Britain on its sovereignty in the Falklands, Argentina seized the islands. A large British force retook them after several weeks of fighting. The fiasco caused the collapse of Argentina's military junta.

FALLEN TIMBERS, BATTLE OF (Aug. 20, 1794). Between US forces under Gen. Anthony Wayne and British-led Indian forces in NW Ohio. Decisive American victory paved way for frontier enforcement of JAY'S TREATY and British evacuation of border forts.

FALLING WATERS SKIRMISH (July 13–14, 1863). Between retreating Confederate forces and Union cavalry, on the Potomac R near Williamsport, Md. Confederate Gen. J. J. Pettigrew was mortally wounded, but the Rebels retired safely to Virginia.

FALL LINE. Division roughly parallel to the Atlantic coast, separating coastal plain from Appalachian foothills; produced sectionalism in colonial South. The tidewater area, conducive to a large-plantation economy, was home to wealthy, conservative slaveowners, who controlled local governments. The back country nurtured a small-farm economy; its people were rougher in manner, more turbulent in politics, and more egalitarian in social mores.

FALMOUTH, BURNING OF (Oct. 18, 1775). In retaliation for aid it had given besieged Boston, the British burned Falmouth, then part of Portland, Me.

FANEUIL HALL. Public market and meeting hall erected in Boston 1742. Site of public protests against the British before the Revolution; known as the Cradle of Liberty. Declared a national historic landmark 1967, and focus of a large urban renewal project.

FAR EASTERN POLICY. US policy in the 18th c. was directed toward protecting its businessmen and missionaries and their property; the right of EXTRATERRITORIALITY was a major instrument in that pursuit. Treaties with China recognized its territorial and administrative integrity in 1844 and 1858. Policy with Japan, opened to the West by Commodore Matthew Perry in 1854, also concerned extraterritoriality and commercial privileges. The US promulgated treaties and gentlemen's agreements with both China and Japan that halted emigration to the US. In 1899–1900, the Open Door was declared; it pledged (and asked other nations to pledge) equality of trade opportunity and the territorial and administrative integrity of China. Japan's rise as an eastern power resulted in US-Japanese agreements, some of which condoned Japan's imperialistic designs on Manchuria. Despite this, the US continued to trumpet its Open Door policy toward China. Japan's invasion of Manchuria in 1931 caused the US to invoke the Kellogg-Briand pact and resulted in the doctrine of nonrecognition (1932). Thereafter, policy tended to favor China and exhibited apprehension about Japan's aspirations, especially toward French and Dutch possessions in Southeast Asia. After World War II, US policy in China tried to maintain the Nationalist government in power, despite overwhelming strength of the Communists. When the Nationalists were forced off the mainland to Taiwan, the US continued to recognize them as the legal government of China. Resulting tension saw the buildup of North Korea by the Soviet Union and China, while the US supported South Korea. The Korean War brought China into direct conflict with the US. In Japan, the US, as occupying power after World War II, imposed a Western-styled democratic constitution and oversaw reindustrialization. A 1954

Geneva settlement temporarily divided Vietnam, formerly part of French Indo-China, into North Vietnam and South Vietnam; it was to be reunited by national elections. The US, fearing a communist victory, was reluctant to allow the elections. Complex maneuvers were also designed to keep Laos out of communist hands. A military commitment begun by President Kennedy led to a full-scale war under Presidents Lyndon B. Johnson and Richard Nixon. Eventually, the US withdrew from Vietnam, and the country was reunited under the communists. Meanwhile, Nixon reestablished relations with the communist government of mainland China, leading to recognition of that government and to the downgrading of US protection of Nationalist Taiwan.

FARGO. Largest city in North Dakota, founded 1872 at a ferry crossing of the Red R. An important shipping point for rich wheat farmland; also a center for livestock trade. Pop.: 61,308 (1980).

FARMER-LABOR PARTY OF MINNESOTA. Coalition of agrarian and labor organizations; an important factor in state politics from 1918 to 1944, displacing the Democratic party as major political force. Elected a number of US senators and members of the House. In 1930, elected Floyd B. Olson governor; reelected twice, he served until his death in 1936. Elmer H. Benson was elected governor 1936 but was defeated 1938 by the Republican candidate, Harold E. Stassen. Never regaining its momentum, the party merged with the Democratic party 1944. Supported Franklin D. Roosevelt in 1932, 1936, and 1940.

FARMER-LABOR PARTY OF 1920. Effort in 1920 to create a national party based on idea that workers and farmers should exercise controlling power in government. Hoped to nominate Robert M. La Follette for president, but he declined; nominee Parley P. Christiansen polled fewer than 300,000 votes. Doomed when it failed to secure endorsements of the American Federation of Labor and of Eugene V. Debs, the Socialist leader.

FARMERS' ALLIANCE. Either of two agricultural organizations of the late 19th c., one formed in the Northwest and one in Texas, Louisiana, and Arkansas; both were populist movements opposed to railroads, land sharks, and banks. Unification efforts failed because of divergent economic interests and the formation, mainly under the auspices of the Northwestern Alliance, of the People's or Populist, party 1892.

FARMER'S ALMANAC. Published continuously since 1793, its homely presentation of weather and planting information, scientific subjects, along with its moral and literary character were widely imitated.

FARMERS INSTITUTES. Founded late 19th c. and usually sponsored by a county agricultural society, a county grange, or a farmers club, institutes held two-day meetings to discuss farm problems in light of scientific and practical knowledge. Household economy was added for farm women. National attendance reached a high of 4 million; after 1914, absorbed by agricultural extension.

FARMER'S LETTERS, DICKINSON'S. The most effective presentation of colonial objections to the Townshend Acts of 1767, written by John Dickinson, a Pennsylvania farmer. Widely circulated, they helped bring colonists to the position that Parliament had no right to legislate them.

FARMERS' ORGANIZATIONS. Two scientific agricultural societies were founded 1785, one in South Carolina and one in Philadelphia; members were mostly landowners interested in finding the best kinds of plants and animals to raise. In 1867, the semi-secret Patrons of Husbandry was founded; members met in local groups soon referred to as Grangers, prominent in the 1870s and 1880s. Two separate groups, each known as the FARMERS' ALLIANCE, were founded in the 1880s; cooperative farmers' stores were soon found in many communities, run by farmers for their own benefit. In 1902, the National Farmers Union was established as an agency mainly of small-farm owners; it hoped to achieve united action with the trade union movement. Several attempts have been made to form farmers' political parties; the most successful one was the FARMER-LABOR PARTY OF MINNESOTA. More successful has been the American Farm Bureau Federation, which is not a political party but exerts great political influence in farmers' interests.

FARMING. See AGRICULTURE.

FAR WEST. Town in Missouri, founded 1836 by Mormons. In 1838, its population of some 10,000 Mormons was expelled by the governor during the anti-Mormon crusade.

FAR WEST. Stern wheeler on the Yellowstone R; after the Battle of the Little Bighorn, it carried out Maj. Marcus A. Reno's wounded.

FATHER OF HIS COUNTRY. Descriptive designation of George Washington, dating from at least 1778; used in *Nord Americanische Kalender* 1779.

FATHER OF WATERS. Inexact translation of Algonkin name for the Mississippi R ("great water" is a more exact translation).

FAVORITE SON. Presidential candidate proposed by his own state political delegation; often used as a holding action until the delegation can cast its vote for the likely winner.

FAYETTE, FORT. Built 1792 on the Allegheny R, immediately above Fort Pitt, in what is now Pittsburgh; staging area for the Battle of Fallen Timbers (1797) and recruiting station in the War of 1812. Abandoned ca. 1816.

FEATHERBEDDING. Pejorative term for union practice of insisting that workers be employed or paid even though management claims they are not performing any useful tasks.

FEDERAL AGENCIES. Created by statute and executive order to execute or administer national legislation. The Executive Reorganization Act of 1949, an outgrowth of the HOOVER COMMISSION, authorized the president to create, abolish, transfer, or modify any part of the executive branch. Congress may overrule a change. Closest to the president is the EXECUTIVE OFFICE OF THE PRESIDENT, followed by the thirteen executive agencies, known as the cabinet departments. In order of rank they are: State, Treasury, Defense, Justice, Interior, Agriculture, Commerce, Labor, Health and Human Services, Housing and Urban Development, Transportation, Energy, and Education. There are a number of important federal agencies similar in structure to cabinet-level departments but smaller or relatively less im-

portant, including the National Aeronautics and Space Administration (NASA), Veterans Administration, US Information Agency, Federal Reserve System, Smithsonian Institution, National Science Foundation, Small Business Administration, and General Services Administration. Regulatory agencies include the Interstate Commerce Commission, Federal Communications Commission, Civil Aeronautics Board, Federal Power Commission, Federal Trade Commission, Securities and Exchange Commission, and Food and Drug Administration. There are numerous even smaller, more specialized agencies, ranging from the Tax Court of the United States to the Railroad Retirement Board.

FEDERAL AID. Prior to the Great Depression, most federal aid was in the form of money or land given to states for canals, railroads, education, and roads. In the 1930s, New Deal philosophy held that only national rescue could relieve the hunger and homelessness of one-fifth of the population and the collapse of agriculture, industry, and credit. Aid thereafter grew in complexity and scale, taking the forms of cash payments, tax credits, payments in kind, and low-interest loans. Federal aid to state and local governments and to individuals took another large jump during the 1960s with the Great Society program of President Lyndon B. Johnson; vast sums were dispensed to rid the nation of illiteracy, poverty, and racial injustices.

FEDERAL-AID HIGHWAY PROGRAM. The Federal Highway Administration is responsible for construction and maintenance of the 42,500-mile National System of Interstate and Defense Highways. Federal funds support 90 percent of the interstate system and usually 75 percent of primary, secondary, and urban roads and streets. Most funds come from special taxes on highway users, deposited in the Highway Trust Fund.

FEDERAL AVIATION ADMINISTRATION (FAA). Promotes civil aeronautics, with particular attention to safety and efficient use of navigable airspace; promulgates safety regulations and air traffic rules; operates aids to navigation and communication; administers grants-in-aid for airport development; and engages in air safety research.

FEDERAL BUREAU OF INVESTIGATION (FBI). Established 1908 as investigative arm of the Department of Justice. Jurisdiction covers a wide range of federal investigative matters in the criminal, civil, and security fields, including espionage, sabotage, and subversive activities. Generally responsible for enforcing most federal criminal statutes. Its National Crime Information Center (NCIC), founded 1967, is the nation's largest collector and disseminator of crime statistics. Longtime head (1924–72) J. Edgar Hoover was one of the more controversial public servants of the 20th c. Idolized by many as the nation's top crime fighter, he was opposed by liberals and civil liberties advocates for the secret and sometimes vindictive activities of the FBI.

FEDERAL COMMUNICATIONS COMMISSION (FCC). Independent agency that regulates interstate and foreign communications by radio, television, telegraph, wire, and cable. Responsible for development and operation of broadcast services and for efficient telephone service at reasonable rates. Seven members are appointed, with Senate approval, for seven-year terms by the president and a chairman who serves at his pleasure.

FEDERAL DEPOSIT INSURANCE CORPORATION (FDIC). Established 1933 to provide bank depositors insurance against loss of deposits. All members of the Federal Reserve System must be insured, and other banks may be: in 1978, 97.8 percent of all banks were FDIC members.

FEDERAL ELECTION CAMPAIGN ACT (1972). Limited the amount candidates or their families could spend on campaigns. Set rigorous standards for the reporting of campaign receipts and expenditures, including the name and address of any person contributing more than $100.

FEDERAL EMERGENCY RELIEF ACT (1933). Created the Federal Emergency Relief Administration (FERA) and alloted $500 million to be used as direct relief by states.

FEDERAL EXPENDITURES. When the federal government began operation, its functions were few and expenditures small. As new functions were added and old functions expanded, federal expenditures vastly increased. Thus, in 1791, expenditures amounted to only about $3 million; but in 1982 it was estimated at $725 *billion*. Wars have been the chief cause. During the Vietnam War, for example, federal expenditures nearly tripled, from $87.8 billion in 1962 to $246.5 billion in 1973. Traditionally, national defense has taken the largest percentage of expenditures; but in 1973 for the first time since before the Korean War, the largest allocation went to an area other than defense: human resources.

FEDERAL GOVERNMENT. The national political system created by the US Constitution: the institutions of government (Congress, the presidency, and the Supreme Court); the basic roles and powers of each of the three branches; the federal system, which divides power between national and state governments; the principle of separation of powers; and the checks-and-balances system, designed to protect the jurisdiction of each branch from the other two.

FEDERAL HOME LOAN BANK. Established 1932, it authorized creation of eight to twelve banks in different parts of the country with a total capital of $125 million. Created a system somewhat like the Federal Reserve System; members are building and loan associations, savings banks, and insurance companies. Directs the Federal Home Loan Banks System and the Federal Savings and Loan Insurance System.

FEDERALIST. Collection of essays written by James Madison, Alexander Hamilton, and John Jay following the Constitutional Convention of 1787, to encourage ratification of the Constitution by New York state. Appearing over the signature Publius, the papers are regarded as the most trenchant explanation of the philosophy of the new federal constitution.

FEDERALIST PARTY. Began as a cluster of nationalists within the Continental Congress (including Robert Morris, James Madison, George Washington, and John Jay) who were instrumental in calling the Constitutional Convention of 1787. Believing in strong national government, virtually all members of the First Congress counted themselves Federalists; so did the president and all the cabinet. Opposition soon developed, however, centered around the agrarian philosophy of Thomas Jefferson. In all areas except Virginia the established elite remained Federalist; the party's position reflected the interests of northern merchants, commercial farmers, and those who had a particular interest in maintaining close relations with Great Britain. In the election of 1796, the Federalist candidate, John Adams, barely won the presidency; in 1800, the Federalist party lost the presidency to Jefferson. After that they did not again win a national election, but continued to show strength at state and local level and to offer opposition to the DEMOCRAT-REPUBLICAN PARTY (as the Jeffersonians were by now known). Disintegrated during the 1820s.

FEDERAL MEDIATION AND CONCILIATION SERVICE. Replaced US Conciliation Service 1947 as Department of Labor's chief agency for minimizing or preventing interruptions of commerce by labor-management disputes. Lends assistance in mediating differences over new contract terms or over grievances arising under existing contracts; has no law enforcement authority.

FEDERAL POWER COMMISSION. Regulatory agency in the field of hydroelectric power and natural gas. Works with other agencies in planning multipurpose river-basin development; licenses construction of power projects on navigable waters or government lands; and regulates rates, securities, accounting practices, and the mergers of companies transmitting or wholesaling electrical energy. Exercises similar controls over interstate commerce in natural gas.

FEDERAL REGISTER. Official journal of the US government; publishes all presidential proclamations, executive orders, and regulations having general application or legal effect, and such other documents as the president or Congress may direct.

FEDERAL RESERVE SYSTEM. Central bank of the US, founded 1913; comprising twelve regional banks, coordinated by a central board in Washington, D.C. At its creation, all national banks had to subscribe 3 percent of their capital and surplus for stock; state banks might also become members. The 1913 law also supplied an elastic note issue of Federal Reserve notes based on commercial paper; re-

quired member banks to keep half their legal reserves (after 1917, all of them) in district Federal Reserve banks; and improved the check-clearing system. At first, chief responsibilites were to create credit to carry on the nation's part of World War I. The Federal Reserve did too little too late to stop the speculative boom that culminated in the 1929 crash and subsequent wholesale (more than 9,000) bank failures, which brought on congressional investigations and demands for reform. In 1932, Congress temporarily permitted the Federal Reserve to use federal government obligations, as well as gold and commercial paper, to back Federal Reserve notes and deposits. Subsequent laws increased powers of the Federal Reserve System. The board was reorganized, without the secretary of the Treasury; was given more control over member banks and over open-market operations; and received important new credit-regulating powers. In World War II, the Federal Reserve assisted with bond drives and saw to it that the federal government and member banks had ample funds for the war effort. Its regulation limiting consumer credit, price controls, and the depression before the war were mainly responsible for there being somewhat less inflation with somewhat more provocation than during World War I. By 1945, the system's holdings of Treasury obligations were $24 billion. In 1979, members of the Federal Reserve System included 5,425 banks of 14,738 in the US; they held about 75 percent of all US bank deposits. (See also BANKING.)

FEDERAL SAVINGS AND LOAN INSURANCE CORPORATION. Established 1934 to guarantee mortgages and insure savings accounts. Capital stock was financed by the Home Owners Loan Corporation; directed by the Home Loan Bank Board. State member associations are not obliged to belong to it, although most do.

FEDERAL SECURITIES ACT (1933). Compelled full disclosure to investors of information relating to new securities issues offered publicly or through the mails or in interstate commerce. Required most new issues to be registered with the Federal Trade Commission.

FEDERAL-STATE RELATIONS. The Constitution defined federal powers but did not make clear the extent of state powers. To remedy this, the Tenth Amendment was added 1791 as part of the Bill of Rights, specifically reserving to the respective state or the people "the powers not delegated to the United States by the Constitution, nor prohibited by it to the States." The amendment helped establish the principle of dualism: matters of local concern should be handled by states, while affairs of general importance should be handled by the federal government. Federal authority gradually extended into fields previously reserved to states; since the defeat of the Confederacy there has been little effective resistance to this centralizing trend. The federal constitution itself limits states in many ways, especially in the area of financial autonomy. Given those restrictions, federal-state relations in the area of finance have become more and more important. With passage of the first Social Security legislation 1935, federal grants-in-aid to states for the first time became substantial. By the 1980s financial responsibilities had become a serious issue, as state governments had become more and more dependent on federal grants.

FEDERAL TRADE COMMISSION (FTC). Created 1914 to investigate evidence of unfair business competition between companies engaged in interstate commerce. Consists of five members, no more than three of whom belong to a single political party. An independent federal agency whose decisions have the force of law, it can require a company to stop unfair practices and impose criminal penalties on firms when fraudulent intent or harm to health can be proved. Also controls radio and television advertising.

FEMINIST MOVEMENT. See WOMAN'S RIGHTS MOVEMENT.

FENCE VIEWERS. Local officers in New England who verify property boundaries and administer laws relating to them.

FENCE WAR. Struggle that ensued when ranchmen began using barbed wire in the cattle country. In the early 1880s fence cutting became so serious in Texas that the full state ranger force was required to supplement local authorities.

FENCING AND FENCING LAWS. Virginia, Maryland, and North Carolina in the 17th c.

had laws requiring that crops be fenced. Fencing laws advanced with the movement of the frontier. Settlers insisted upon using unsold public land, and as settlement increased, the demand for fencing of pasture, rather than crops, arose and spread westward. The zigzag, or Virginia rail, fence spread; as timber became more scarce, post-and-pole, picket, and board fences became common and wire fencing came into use. In the treeless plains, cattlemen took possession of large areas, and were driving cattle to the railroad (see CATTLE DRIVES); settlers could not protect crops until the advent of barbed wire, when the frontier again began to move. Advancing settlers fenced their farms; free open range began to disappear. Cattlemen fenced their own land, and until curbed by federal legislation in 1885, they frequently enclosed government land. In areas of mixed husbandry, the woven wire fence came into use near the close of the century.

FENIAN MOVEMENT. Originated 1858 among Irish-Americans to raise money, supply equipment, and provide leaders to aid the Irish uprising against Great Britain. Membership reached 250,000. In 1865 the Fenians established an "Irish Republic" in New York and ordered bond issues. A group called "the men of action" broke from the parent organization and conducted raids into Canada. Opposed by the federal government and Roman Catholic church, members deserted to join the Land League and Home Rule movements. Last congress was held 1876.

FERGUSON IMPEACHMENT. In 1917, Gov. James E. Ferguson of Texas was charged by the state house of representatives with twenty-one impeachment charges, including misappropriation of state funds. He was found guilty on ten charges, removed from office, and disqualified from holding public office. Politically vindicated 1924 when his wife, Miriam A. Ferguson, was elected governor.

FERRIES. Used to cross all large streams in colonial days; gradually replaced by bridges or tunnels. The island position of Manhattan necessitated ferry connections in all directions. Ferries were also important in Boston and across the Delaware R between Philadelphia and Camden, N.J. Virtually all major rivers were crossed by ferry service.

FERRIS WHEEL. A noted feature of the 1893 Chicago world's fair. Invented by G.W.G. Ferris, it was a huge upright steel wheel with passenger cars swung around its rim. Continues to be a popular ride at amusement parks and fairs.

FERROUS METALS. Iron leads all metals produced in the US. First used probably by Indians, mostly for coloring purposes. American colonial ironmaking began in the 17th c. at sites near iron ore deposits; first successful operations were in Massachusetts. Mining of a vast iron ore district in the Lake Superior region began 1846; by 1892 the Mesabi Range was the leading domestic source. (See also IRON AND STEEL INDUSTRY.) The mining of **manganese** dates from 1837, when ore was produced for coloring earthenware. Mined in quantity for use in steelmaking in the late 19th c. Although manganese deposits are widespread, they are either small or of very low grade; domestic production is insignificant in comparison to imports. Chromite, the principal **chromium** mineral, was first found in the US in Maryland (1827) and used for pigment. Later deposits were found in California, Montana, and Oregon; but mostly imported from the Middle East. No domestic ore mined since 1961. Small amounts of **nickel** have been found in Pennsylvania and Missouri; but until 1954, when a mine was opened in Oregon, domestic primary nickel was produced mainly as a by-product of copper refining. **Cobalt** is a relatively rare element in the earth's crust. In the past, small amounts were found in Idaho, Utah, and Pennsylvania; but since 1971, all domestic needs have depended on imports. **Columbium**, used in steel alloys, is found in western states; but demand outstrips domestic supplies, and imports are relied upon. Production of **molybdenum** is centered in the US, where more than 50 percent of world resources are located. The principal US source is a vast deposit at Climax, Colo. **Vanadium**, used as a steel additive, was discovered in the early 20th c. in Colorado; other deposits were later found in the Southwest. By 1960, the US was the world's principal source. **Tungsten** deposits were discovered 1872, but demand did not develop until the early 20th c. Produced between the Rocky Mountains and the Pacific coast; US deposits estimated to be about 10 percent of world total.

FERTILIZERS. Colonists farmed poor soils that were rapidly depleted in fertility. Through necessity, animal manure, waste fish, seaweed, tannery wastes, and slaughterhouse by-products were used as fertilizers. Gypsum and lime were introduced in the late 18th and early 19th c. When European chemists revealed that phosphorus, potassium (potash), and nitrogen were of critical importance in plant growth, America turned to chemical fertilizers. Superphosphate was first produced 1849. In 1850, a mixed fertilizer was patented consisting of bones, sulfuric acid, ammoniacal liquors, and residues of chemical processing industries. US phosphate deposits were developed, mostly in South Carolina, Florida, and Tennessee. As the 19th c. progressed, synthetic fertilizers became widely used. Important among them are ammonium sulfate, calcium cyanamide, and anhydrous ammonia. By the 1980s, the fertilizer industry faced serious problems with respect to future sources of raw materials (phosphate rock, potash salts, and hydrogen from petroleum and natural gas for synthesis of ammonia). Fertilizers were also criticized by environmentalists, since water runoff from fertilized lands caused serious eutrophication of nearby lakes and streams. Use of chemical fertilizers in the US was 51.1 million tons in 1979, double that of 1960.

FETTERMAN MASSACRE (Dec. 21, 1866). Chief Indian victory of the SIOUX WARS. Crazy Horse lured Capt. William Fetterman and eighty men onto Lodge Trail Ridge, near Fort Phil Kearney, Wyo. Every man in Fetterman's command was killed.

FEUDALISM. One motive prompting New World colonization was desire on the part of proprietors to establish feudal domains. Maryland, the Carolinas, New Jersey, Delaware, and Dutch settlements along the Hudson R represent efforts to transplant feudalism. Most such experiments were short-lived.

FEUDS, APPALACHIAN MOUNTAINS. Law enforcement was long virtually nonexistent in the mountainous regions of Kentucky, Tennessee, North Carolina, Virginia, and West

Virginia. Bitter disputes arose (and remained unsettled) between mountaineers over even trifling matters. Greatest single cause for dispute was the division of sentiment over the Civil War, when armed bands attempted to intimidate people on both sides of the national issue. Most outstanding of such feuds was that of the Hatfield-McCoy families (1880–87).

FFV. Initials of "First Families of Virginia," a pejorative term in the 19th c. referring to aristocratic families of the state.

FIELD MUSEUM OF NATURAL HISTORY. Begun as the Columbian Museum, part of the 1893 Chicago world's fair; funded largely by Marshall Field, with departments of geology, botany, zoology, and anthropology. Noted for expeditions, publications, and public education programs.

FIFTEENTH AMENDMENT. Ratified 1870, an attempt to guarantee the franchise to newly emancipated slaves. Forbidding federal or state governments to deny or abridge the right to vote "on account of race, color, or previous condition of servitude," it evoked endless countermeasures in the South; not fully implemented until after the passage of the Voting Rights Act of 1965.

FIFTHS MINING TAX. Provision that one-fifth of all metals mined belonged to the crown is found in Spanish and Mexican law as well as English colonial charters. The Continental Congress in 1785 reserved a third for the government. The US does not apply this principle; it was specifically rejected in the Mineral Patent Law of 1866.

"FIFTY-FOUR FORTY OR FIGHT." Slogan of the expansionist Democrats in the 1840s, referring to the line (54° 40′) claimed by the US as the boundary between Oregon and Canada.

FIGUREHEADS. Used on American ships as early as the Revolution. John Paul Jones is credited with designing a goddess of Liberty for the *America*, the first ship-of-the-line of the US. In 1909 the navy ordered removal of figureheads from fighting ships.

FILIBUSTER, CONGRESSIONAL. Practice in the US Senate of prolonging debate and using other delaying tactics to prevent action,

thereby forcing the body to end consideration of a proposal. Traditionally, every senator has unlimited speaking time; but in 1917, the Senate adopted cloture provisions for ending debates, stipulating that two-thirds of the senators present must vote in favor of cloture before the filibuster can be ended. More than fifty major filibusters have been recorded on such measures as civil rights bills and draft reform.

FILIBUSTERING. In the 19th c., American adventurers engaged in armed expeditons against countries with which the US was at peace, especially Spanish possessions in the New World. The BURR CONSPIRACY was widely believed to be a filibustering attempt against Spanish Louisiana, Texas, and, perhaps, Mexico. There were numerous other filibustering attempts in Texas, California, and Cuba. In 1853, William Walker sailed from San Francisco with a small force and landed in Lower California, which he then proclaimed an independent republic; shortly thereafter, he "annexed" neighboring Sonora. In 1855, Walker turned his attention to Nicaragua (see WALKER FILIBUSTERING ATTEMPT). Filibustering was halted by the Civil War and never again became a problem.

FILLMORE, FORT. Established 1851 in New Mexico, about thirty-six miles N of El Paso, Tex.; held by both sides during the Civil War.

FILMS. See MOTION PICTURES.

FILSON'S MAP. Map of Kentucky published 1784; drawn by John Filson and based on surveys of Daniel Boone and others.

FINCASTLE COUNTY. Name given by Virginia Assembly in 1772 to the part of the colony W of the Kanawha R and S of the Ohio R; included all of present Kentucky. Divided 1776 into three counties, Kentucky being the name of one.

FIRE-EATERS. Southern proslavery extremists, who early advocated secession and formation of a confederacy.

FIRE FIGHTING. Some larger colonial cities owned hooked ladders; smaller towns had no protection. In 1730, New York City imported from Holland two hand-pumping machines.

Companies were all volunteer, and water was pumped from wells, ponds, or streams. First telegraph fire-signal system was put into operation in Boston 1852. Steam fire engine introduced 1829; Cincinnati introduced the first salaried steam fire department 1853. In the later 19th c., fireproof or fire-resistant buildings began to be built, the chemical fire extinguisher was developed, and the sprinkling system came into use. In the 20th c., fire departments were motorized. By 1910, high-pressure hydrant systems were introduced. By the 1950s, the super pumper, capable of pumping 8,000 gallons of water per minute, was in wide use. Other innovations included the snorkel truck, equipped with a cherry picker boom to replace the traditional ladder; and foam, for fighting oil fires.

FIRELANDS. 500,000 acre tract in the Western Reserve (Huron and Erie counties) awarded by Connecticut to citizens of nine "suffering towns" for losses resulting from British raids during the Revolution. Lands were partitioned in 1808, and settlement began.

FIRESIDE CHATS. Radio addresses by President Franklin D. Roosevelt during his first administration; aimed at boosting public confidence during the depths of the Great Depression, and the first effective political use of the new medium of radio.

"FIRE WHEN YOU ARE READY, GRIDLEY." Order given by Commodore George Dewey to Capt. C. V. Gridley at the beginning of the Battle of Manila Bay in the Philippines (May 1, 1898).

"FIRST IN WAR, FIRST IN PEACE, AND FIRST IN THE HEARTS OF HIS COUNTRYMEN." Words written by Gen. Light-Horse Harry Lee and offered by John Marshall in Congress, on the death of George Washington. Repeated in Lee's memorial oration in Philadelphia, Dec. 26, 1799.

FIRST LADY OF THE LAND. Unofficial title of "First Lady" as applied to the wife of the president originated in the first half of the 19th c.; does not appear to have achieved wide currency until the 20th c.

FISH AND MARINE BIOLOGY. The history of study of American fishes can be roughly divided into two periods: the first, primarily one of exploration and description, and the second (from ca. 1870) one of biology and management. Thomas Harriott's *Briefe and True Report of the New Found Land of Virginia* (1588) contained two paragraphs on fish and one on fishing. That work was followed by numerous descriptive scientific works in the 17th and 18th c. Carl Linnaeus included the description of forty new American species in the 12th edition of his *Systema naturae* (1766–68). J. D. Schoepf, a surgeon with Hessian troops during the American Revolution, wrote the first ichthyological paper written in America and the first concerned solely with American species (1787). Native research soon began appearing. The Lewis and Clark expedition to the West (1803–06) brought back twelve new species of fish. Useful works on fishes of particular areas were published by Constantine Rafinesque (1820), J.V.C. Smith (1833), J. E. De Kay (1842), J. E. Holbrook (1855–60), and Louis Agassiz (1860). Institutional research improved considerably after the establishment of the Smithsonian Institution (1846), the Museum of Comparative Zoology at Harvard University (1859), and the American Museum of Natural History (1869). S. F. Baird led natural history research at the Smithsonian; Louis Agassiz trained many outstanding natural historians at Harvard, including ichthyologists C. F. Girard, D. S. Jordan, and A. A. Jordan. The last was the foremost American ichthyologist from the 1870s to the 1920s. The American Fisheries Society, founded 1870, has played a leading role in the development of fishery biology. The US Fish Commission was founded 1871. It made the first, not always successful, efforts at large-scale fish-stocking programs. Down to the end of World War II, the management of American fisheries steadily worsened; after the war, however, state and federal funds were more generously invested in management and management research. Fishery training programs were greatly expanded in universities across the country. Congressional interest in the development of **marine biology** can be traced to establishment 1807 of the Coast and Geodetic Survey. From its beginnings, the US navy encouraged voyages of exploration and publication of results. In 1838, Congress authorized the US Exploring Expedition, which included a philologist, conchologist, botanist, horticulturist, mineralogist, two naturalists, and two draftsmen. Beginning 1850, the Coast and Geodetic Survey assisted in extended biological surveys of the East and Gulf coasts. In 1877 it sponsored an expedition to examine physical and biological conditions of the Gulf Stream and waters around Cuba, Key West, and the Gulf on the steamer *Blake*, which carried on marine studies into the early 20th c. In 1882, the Bureau of Fisheries built the *Albatross*, the first ship specially built for marine research by any government. It amassed one of the greatest collections of marine organisms made by a single ship. It was followed by a number of research vessels, most notably *Albatross IV*, which operated after the mid-1970s out of the Marine Biological Laboratories at Woods Hole, Mass. By the late 1970s, the US Fish and Wildlife Service operated thirteen fish-and-wildlife laboratories and ninety-one fish hatcheries.

FISHDAM FORD, BATTLE OF (Nov. 9, 1790). A British force attacked a patriot encampment in NW South Carolina commanded by Gen. Thomas Sumter. Sumter's men repelled the attack, capturing Maj. James Wemyss, the British commander.

FISHER FORT, CAPTURE OF (1864–65). Fort Fisher, N.C., on Cape Fear R, was a stragegic Confederate port. Unsuccessfully attacked December 1864 by a Union fleet of sixty vessels. In January 1865, the fleet again bombarded it two days and nights. About 2,000 sailors and marines landed and attacked; after severe fighting, the fort was taken.

FISHERIES DISPUTE, ARBITRATION OF. Rights of American citizens to fish in waters off the Canadian coast were a longtime source of dispute between the US and Great Britain. Various treaties, including the Treaty of Washington (1871), stipulated fishing and landing rights of American fishermen. Controversies remained, however, and in 1909 both governments referred the argument to the Permanent Court of Arbitration at The Hague, which laid down (1910) definitive decisions and regulations.

FISHERIES DISPUTES. Independence from Great Britain led to disputes over the right to fish in waters off the Canadian coast (see FISHERIES DISPUTE, ARBITRATION OF). Disputes have also taken place with other powers. Since World War II, a number of Russian and Japanese fleets have operated in the same areas as US fishing boats; disagreement has arisen over the proper way to control the catch of certain species to ensure that the fish will not be exhausted as a resource. There have also been serious disputes, sometimes even open warfare, in the Gulf of Mexico between Texan and Mexican shrimp boats; in 1980, Mexico renounced its fishing accords with the US. Canada seized several US fishing boats in the late 1970s, and efforts to effect a comprehensive US-Canadian fishing treaty stalled.

FISHER'S HILL, BATTLE AT (Sept. 22, 1864). Union forces under Gen. P. H. Sheridan defeated a Confederate force under Gen. J. A. Early at Winchester, Va.

FISHERS ISLAND. Between the S coast of Connecticut and the E coast of Long Island; discovered by Adrian Block 1614. Claimed by both New York and Connecticut from the 17th c. until 1879, when ownership finally went to New York.

FISHING AND FISHERIES. Fishing boats were active off North America during the earliest explorations, and Europeans were drying fish ashore before taking it back to Europe for sale. Fishing grounds off New England and Canada provided an enormous resource for early colonists. Extensive fishing industry also developed early in Chesapeake Bay and off Cape Hatteras. In 1978, the US stood fourth among the world's fishing nations, behind Japan, the Soviet Union, and China, catching and processing over 6 billion lbs. annually. The northeast coast produces cod, mackerel, flounder, and shellfish. The Gulf Coast is particularly rich in shrimp. The Pacific coast produces salmon and tuna.

FISHING BOUNTIES. From 1797 the federal government levied duties on imported salt and paid allowances, amounting to a bounty, on fish or meat cured with foreign salt and then exported; it affected chiefly the cod industry. A cod bounty of one sort or another continued until 1866.

FISHING CREEK, ACTION AT (Aug. 18, 1780). A British force under Col. Banastre

Tarleton routed a patriot encampment (near the Catawba R, in South Carolina) under Gen. Thomas Sumter. This defeat laid South Carolina open to royalist troops.

FISHING CREEK CONFEDERACY. Disturbances around Fishing Creek Valley (mainly in Columbia County, Pa.) during the Civil War by draft resisters. Union forces were dispatched to find and destroy a fort constructed by resisters in the mountains; it was never found, but a few citizens were arrested and convicted by court-martial.

FISK OVERLAND EXPEDITIONS (1862–66). In 1862, Congress authorized army escort for emigrant trains going through Indian country. Capt. J. L. Fisk led a number of such escorts. His route through Montana to Helena was later followed by the Great Northern RR system.

FISK UNIVERSITY. Founded 1865 in Nashville as a school for blacks; integrated in the 1960s.

FITCH'S STEAMBOAT EXPERIMENTS. John Fitch claimed to have considered use of the steam engine for ships before he heard of similar plans by other inventors. In 1786, he formed a company, having secured exclusive rights to operate steamboats in the waters of New York, New Jersey, Virginia, Delaware, and Pennsylvania. Tried out his first vessel at Philadelphia, with the Continental Congress looking on. He built several steamboats but failed to earn expenses.

FIVE-AND-TEN-CENT STORES. Also known as variety stores; the first opened in Utica, N.Y., in 1879 by F. W. Woolworth; by 1899 Woolworth had 54 such stores, and by 1919 there were 1,081. Other large chains of variety stores were Kresge, Kress, Green, Grant, and Newberry. By the 1980s, most such stores carried a wide variety of merchandise.

FIVE CIVILIZED TRIBES. Choctaw, Chickasaw, Creek, Cherokee, and Seminole tribes; so-called because of their readiness to adapt to Europeanized institutions at the time they were moved to the Indian Territory of Oklahoma. The Cherokee spoke a language related to that of the Iroquois and occupied regions in what is now Tennessee and North Carolina.

The four other tribes are linguistically assigned to the Muskhogean grouping, which had a tradition of western origin and may have fanned into the Southeast in late prehistoric times. In 1539–42, Hernando de Soto found the Creek, Choctaw, Chickasaw, and Cherokee in locations that remained fairly fixed until the exodus in the 19th c. (The Seminole were a composite tribe that developed in the late 18th c.) None of the tribes was very large: The largest was the Cherokee, with a population of 22,000 in 1650; by 1715, it had been reduced by half by smallpox. Even the earliest accounts report federations and political organizations; one of these, the Creek Confederacy, was a political and military organization made up of several tribes. All five tribes were intensively agricultural, planting maize and vegetables. All practiced a religion based on fertility and world renewal. The Choctaw allied themselves with the British; the others tended to independence. By the early 19th c., many Indians had abandoned their former modes of life and taken on European patterns of social and economic organization. Beginning with the Jackson administration, attempts were made to dispossess them and move them to Indian Territory; their removal was effected 1835–42 and involved the forced migration of the Cherokee, the so-called Trail of Tears. It was not accomplished without rebellion, notably the second Seminole War (1835–42). A few fled to the Florida Everglades, where their descendants live today. A few were finally allowed to remain in W North Carolina. In Indian Territory, the five tribes established autonomous states, employing the constitutional model of the US. It was the presence of these states that gave rise to the term "civilized." The five tribes retained their autonomy until Oklahoma acquired statehood in 1907.

FIVE FORKS, BATTLE OF (April 1, 1865). Fought about twenty-five miles S of Richmond. Union Gen. P. H. Sheridan successfully attacked Confederate force of Gen. G. E Pickett. Evacuation of Richmond began the next day.

FIVE NATIONS. The five original tribes of the Iroquois Indian Confederacy: Mohawk, Oneida, Onondaga, Cayuga, and Seneca, all based in C and W New York. In 1722, a sixth "nation," the Tuscarora from North Carolina, was accepted.

FIVE-POWER NAVAL TREATY (1922). Limited aggregate battleship tonnage as follows: 525,000 each to the US and Great Britain; 315,000 to Japan; and 175,000 each to France and Italy.

FIVE VILLAGES. Large fortified villages of the Mandan and Hidatsa, on the Missouri R between the Heart R and the Little Missouri R, in North Dakota. Existed as early as 1738; conducting business with the Hudson's Bay Co. by 1772. The smallpox epidemic of 1837 caused survivors to rebuild further up the river. By 1858, the villagers were dispersed.

FLACO'S RIDE (Sept. 24–30, 1846). John Brown, called Juan Flaco ("Lean John"), rode 500 miles from Los Angeles to San Francisco in less than five days' time to alert Americans there that Los Angeles was being besieged.

FLAG DAY (June 14). Presidents Wilson and Coolidge suggested that June 14 be celebrated as Flag Day, the anniversary of the day on which the flag was adopted (June 14, 1777). Congress gave it official status 1949.

FLAG OF THE CONFEDERATE STATES. See CONFEDERATE FLAG.

FLAG OF THE UNITED STATES. On June 14, 1777, the Continental Congress resolved "that the flag of the thirteen United States be thirteen stripes, alternate red and white; that the union be thirteen stars, white in a blue field, representing a new constellation." Changed over the years as new states have come into the Union; today, there are thirteen stripes, representing the original states, and fifty stars, one for each state.

FLAG, PRESIDENTIAL. First designed 1882, the present flag consists of a blue field with a slight modification of the Great Seal of the United States, surrounded by a circle of fifty stars, in the center.

FLAGS, MILITARY. The navy assigns personal flags to admirals and pennants to various commands. The US marine corps has distinct colors, regimental flags, and flags for general officers on ships or post. The army provides personal flags for the chief of staff and generals on the general staff; also distinctive flags for the various departments (e.g., quartermaster, infantry, ordnance).

FLAPPERS. Young women of the 1920s who broke with tradition by wearing loose (flapping) dresses and by cutting their hair short.

FLATBOATMEN. Men who worked on flatboats, the roughly made rafts that carried goods downstream, especially on the Mississippi, and then were broken up for timber. Usually farmers or laborers out to see the country or to sell farm products. They bore a reputation for thievery, debauchery, and quarrelsomeness. (See also STORE BOATS.)

FLETCHER V. PECK, 6 Cranch 87 (1810). The Georgia legislature authorized (1795) the issuance of grants of certain public land along the Yazoo R. A later legislature (1796) annulled these grants as fraudulent. Case involved Peck, who conveyed his lands to Fletcher with a covenant that the title had not been impaired by the subsequent act of the Georgia legislature. Fletcher sued Peck, when it appeared he would lose title. The Supreme Court held that the original grant was binding; the term "contract" applies to a grant from a state as well as those between individuals. First example of a state law being invalidated as contrary to the Constitution. (See also DARTMOUTH COLLEGE CASE.)

FLINT. A city in Michigan, fifty miles NW of Detroit. Center of automobile manufacturing. Scene in 1936 of the first sit-down strike (in the Buick factory). Most wage-earners work for General Motors and belong to the United Auto Workers; the average wages are among the highest in the country. Educational institutions include a branch of the University of Michigan, the Michigan School for the Deaf, and General Motors Technical Institute. Pop.: 159,611 (1980).

FLOATING BATTERIES. Heavily armed vessels with protective armor but with comparatively weak motive power, used in the US as early as 1776 (on the Delaware R in the defense of Philadelphia). First steam warship the *Demologos*, built by Robert Fulton in 1814–15, was a floating battery.

FLOGGING. A common form of punishment during the colonial period, whipping has been outlawed in all states except Delaware, where it may be administered for twenty-five different crimes.

FLOOD CONTROL ACT (1936). Extended the Flood Control Act of 1928, which had authorized $325 million for levee work in the Mississippi Valley, to cover all US river basins. Asserted federal responsibility for controlling floods and assigned responsibility to Army Corps of Engineers.

FLOODS. During great floods, the economic and human losses exceed those of most other disasters. The most notable flood of the 19th century was the JOHNSTOWN FLOOD in 1889. Flooding caused by the GALVESTON STORM of Sept. 8–9, 1900, killed an estimated 6,000 people. The most widespread flood in American history was the great Lower Mississippi Valley flood of March–June 1927, in which 313 lives were lost and $300 million damage was inflicted. The region has suffered great floods about every decade since the earliest settlements. One of the longest floods occurred during the three-month period form March to May 1965 in the upper Mississippi, when deep snow melted over a wide area. Record floods have also occurred in the region of the Potomac R and adjacent basins (1889, 1936, 1937, 1942, and 1972). In the US the average annual loss of life from flooding during 1925–70 was only 83; but property losses in the 1951–70 period rose to $450 million annually, with some 75,000 people driven from their homes each year.

FLOOR LEADER. The senator or representative in Congress who acts as leader of his party on the floor of the chamber of which he is a member. Originally only in the House of Representatives and only for the majority party, his function being to assist the speaker of the House in arranging and pushing through the legislative program. Informally designated by the speaker until the reduction of the speaker's power in 1910–11. Now chosen by party caucus. Thus, both chambers now have a majority leader and a minority leader, whose chief function is to direct the parliamentary strategy of their parties.

FLORIDA. Southernmost state of the US, bounded on the N by Alabama and Georgia, on the E by the Atlantic, and on the W by the Gulf of Mexico and Alabama. Discovered by Juan Ponce de León in 1513; explored by Lucas Vázquez de Ayllón, Pánfilo de Narváez, and Hernando de Soto. Jean Ribault landed near St. Augustine in 1562 with 150 colonists and claimed territory for France, but moved on to near present-day Beaufort, S.C. Two years later René Goulaine de Laudonnière, who had accompanied Ribault, came to Fort Caroline. In 1565, Ribault returned with 300 colonists but was driven off by Spaniards. Starvation drove the Frenchmen toward the Spanish settlement of St. Augustine, where most of them were massacred. Dominique de Gourgues avenged the French in 1568 by wiping out the Spanish garrison at San Mateo (Fort Caroline). Menéndez established St. Augustine, San Mateo, and a number of garrisons along both coasts of the peninsula. Spanish settlement also consisted of a Franciscan mission system (see FLORIDA, SPANISH MISSIONS IN). In 1698 a fort was erected at Pensacola to block French expansion in the Mississippi region. English pressure from the north led to the destruction of the Spanish missions, frontier warfare over land between Florida and Georgia, and the eventual cession of Spanish Florida to England by the Treaty of Paris (1763) in exchange for Cuba. The Proclamation of 1763 established colonial government and divided the region at the Apalachicola R into East Florida and West Florida. After 1775 thousands of Loyalists poured into East Florida; it was the objective of several attacks by the Americans (1776–78) and assisted the southern campaign of the British in 1778. West Florida was part of the Anglo-Spanish Mississippi rivalry. The region became involved in the Revolution through the efforts of Americans to get supplies at New Orleans (see GIBSON-LINN EPISODE; WILLING EXPEDITION) and Spain's declaration of war against England (1779). By the Definitive Treaty of Peace (1783), both East Florida and West Florida were returned to Spain. West Florida was claimed as part of the Louisiana Purchase in 1803 and was occupied in 1813; Spain ceded the rest of Florida under the Adams-Onís Treaty (1819). Gen. Andrew Jackson, first American governor, restored semicivil government. The appointive legislative council, authorized by Congress for the Florida territory in 1822, became elective in 1826. In 1824, Tallahassee was chosen as the capital.

Numerous cotton plantations developed between the Suwannee and the Apalachicola; oranges, lumber, sugarcane, tobacco, corn, and rice were also produced. Economic development came to an abrupt halt in 1837: the second Seminole War (1835–42) and the panic of 1837 closed every bank and wiped out most white settlements south of St. Augustine (see SEMINOLE WARS). In 1845 Florida was admitted as a slave state; first elections for state officials were held in May. The Internal Improvement Act of 1855 encouraged generous land subsidies to private companies engaged in construction of railroads. Cattle ranches multiplied on the open range, and population doubled by 1860. On Jan. 10, 1861, Florida seceded. Only major Civil War battle was Olustee (Feb. 20, 1864); Confederates successfully defended the interior of the state. In May 1865 a mixed garrison of Union soldiers and emancipated slaves introduced Reconstruction. New state constitution did not provide ballots or other civil rights for blacks. State was then placed under military rule in March 1867. A new constitution (1868) revised the criminal code and made public education the responsibility of the state. Florida Reconstruction was brought to an end with the election of conservative Democrat George F. Drew as governor in 1876. Drew ushered in an era of "Bourbon democracy," so called because it was dedicated to commercialization and industrialization of the state, even avowing a willingness to cooperate with Yankee investors. Encouraged by land subsidies from the Bourbons, the railroad tycoons came to Florida, and railroads brought a rapid influx of settlers and tourists. Promotional literature was partially responsible for the expansion of citrus groves from Jacksonville south to Biscayne Bay in the 1880s. The Great Freeze of 1895 destroyed most of the trees, but it resulted in improved techniques of citrus production that brought exports up to 5 million boxes by 1905. Phosphates were found in the Peace R near Bartow in 1885 and by 1900 Florida was exporting 5.5 million tons of phosphate. Significant 20th-c. developments have been the land boom (1921–25); selection of Cape Canaveral as the site for the US space program; and the opening of Disney World near Orlando in 1971, boosting the economy of central Florida, and attracting more than a million visitors in its first year. Population grew from 500,000 in the early 1900s to 9.7 million in 1980.

FLORIDA, JACKSON'S SEIZURE OF. See ARBUTHNOT AND AMBRISTER, CASE OF.

FLORIDA, SPANISH MISSIONS IN. First were the abortive attempts prior to 1565; then Jesuit missions, 1566–71; and finally the Franciscan missions, 1573–1763. The martyrdom of the Dominican Luis Cancer de Babastro occurred in 1549 and the unsuccessful expedition of Tristán de Luna in 1559–61. In 1565 the Jesuits were called upon. The first expediton (1566) resulted in the martyrdom of Father Pedro Martínez. A second expedition (1568) produced few converts, but one of the lay brothers compiled the first catechism and grammar (both now lost) in the Yamasee language. In 1570 an attempt was made to missionize the region called Ajacan (Virginia), but eight fathers and brothers were massacred in 1571. In 1573 the first Franciscans arrived. Extended their work north, south, and west from St. Augustine. (See also GEORGIA, SPANISH MISSIONS IN.) They made and kept thousands of Indian converts. The decline of the missions came with the founding of Charleston, S.C. (1670) and English aggressiveness (see APALACHE MASSACRE). All had disappeared by 1763, when Florida was ceded to England.

FLORIDA BOUNDARY. The 16th-c. La Florida included all Spanish North America E of the Mississippi R. In 1670 the Treaty of Madrid recognized British occupation as far south as Charleston, S.C., and in 1743 British conquest reached the St. Marys R. In 1719 Spain accepted the Perdido R (the present western limit of Florida, where it adjoins Alabama) as the Florida-Louisiana boundary. In 1763 England set up East Florida and West Florida, the latter extending from the Apalachicola to the Iberville (almost to New Orleans); in 1764 the northwestern limit was placed at the mouth of the Yazoo R, on the Mississippi. Spain regained the Floridas in 1783, and the southern boundary of the United States was drawn along the thirty-first parallel, from the Mississippi to the Apalachicola, down the Apalachicola to the Flint, eastward to the head of the St. Marys R, and thence to the Atlantic. US claimed West Florida as part of the Louisiana Purchase (1803).

The portion west of the Pearl R was included in the state of Louisiana in 1812; the part east to the Perdido was added to the territory of Mississippi in 1813 (both were legally Spanish). The ADAMS-ONÍS TREATY of 1819 evaded defining the previous ownership of West Florida and left East Florida's limits unchanged. The latter was made a territory in 1821, and a state in 1845.

FLORIDA EAST COAST RAILROAD. See RAILROADS, SKETCHES OF PRINCIPAL LINES.

FLORIDA RANGERS. A Tory corps formed at St. Augustine (1776). In 1778 captured Ft. Barrington in Georgia and burned Ft. Tonyn.

FLORIDA WAR. See SEMINOLE WARS.

FLOUR MILLING. Colonists in the 17th c. introduced European grains along the eastern seaboard, built windmills and water mills, and developed New York as a milling and marketing center for flour. The Erie Canal cut freight costs between the Genesee Valley and New York by 90 percent per ton. By 1843 automatic machinery was installed in mills at Buffalo and steam power was used in grain storage elevators. By 1870, millers were experimenting with high grinding, which produced a finer flour and more flour per bushel. Minneapolis flour shipments rose from 1 million to 5 million barrels between 1876 and 1884. Hard spring wheat, grown increasingly in the Dakotas and Minnesota after 1865, required special techniques because of its higher gluten content and more easily shattered bran. Electric power came into use as early as 1887, but steam and water power predominated until about 1920. During World War II flour for military use was vitamin-enriched; thereafter, practice became common, reducing some vitamin-deficiency diseases and eliminating others.

FLYING CLOUD. A clipper ship built at East Boston (1850). An extreme type of its class, it long held top place for beauty and speed. Set records from New York to San Francisco (89 days) and to Hong Kong (127 days).

FLYING THE HUMP. US officials in 1941 saw a vital need to keep China in the war; yet Japan's early conquests had cut off all means of supplying China other than by air. Route led over the 10,000-foot Patkai Range and the 14,000-foot Kumon Range; the main "hump," which gave its name to the massif and the air route, is the 15,000-foot-high Satsung Range between the Salween and Mekong rivers. A monthly maximum of 71,042 tons was reached in July 1945. The Hump was the proving ground of massive strategic airlift.

FLYING TIGERS (American Volunteer Group). The most ambitious and famous undertaking to promote China's air effort against Japan. US furnished pilots, planes, and support personnel. Conceived by Claire L. Chennault, an American military aviator, who in 1937 retired to accept employment as an adviser to the Chinese. First engaged the Japanese on Dec. 20, 1941. The Chinese technically owned and controlled the group, but in mid-1942 it came under US control and was redesignated China Air Task Force. During seven months of fighting destroyed approximately 300 Japanese aircraft.

FOLK ART. The term most often used to describe artistic efforts of those who have little or no training in the principles of academic art; other terms include "naive," "primitive," "provincial," "popular," and "nonacademic." Folk art flourished especially between the Revolution and the Civil War. It was created by, and for, ordinary people. Some motifs indicate a response to national events, George Washington's death, for example. Other patriotic emblems included the Indian; the closely related figures of Liberty and Columbia; carved portraits of Thomas Jefferson, Andrew Jackson, and Abraham Lincoln; and the eagle. In painting the emphasis is on color, decorative surface patterns, and flat, unmodeled, two-dimensional shapes; in sculpture, bold and simple forms are used to produce unique creations. Lack of sophistication or technical skill is outweighed by simplicity of line and form, often combined with deliberate attention to details, a straightforward utility of purpose, and an engaging originality of design or decoration. Even today untutored individuals still produce works of considerable aesthetic accomplishment.

FOLKLORE. Europeans who colonized the Atlantic seaboard related wonders of natural history and repeated accounts of magical feats performed by Indian sorcerers. Afro-American folk expression covers a spectrum of interrelated forms: animal and "Old Marster" tales; spirituals, blues, work songs, and hollers; toasts; hoodoo practices; dance steps; and formulaic sermons. These undercover spoken, sung, and recited traditions are indebted less to African sources than to American conditions. From the Tennessee backwoods of Davy Crockett; across the Mississippi of Mike Fink; to the Rockies of Jim Bridger, the westering frontiers created a breed of ring-tailed roarers who could put a rifle ball through the moon, tote a steamboat on their backs, and whip their weight in wildcats. These boasters echoed the midcentury spirit of Manifest Destiny. The waves of immigrants produced an ethnic lore comprising Old World survivals, such as belief in the evil eye, and New World forms, such as the humorous dialect stories. In ballads of death at the steam engine's throttle, in a cave-in deep underground, in a log jam, or in a cattle stampede, or in anecdotes of oil field, cow camp, and lumber shanty, one common figure emerged: the skilled and dedicated workman, faithful to his employer, to his fellows, and to the free-enterprise system. In the 1920s and 1930s a pantheon of pseudo heroes, led by Paul Bunyan, the giant lumberjack, and Pecos Bill, the giant cowboy, caught the public fancy.

FOLK MEDICINE. The American colonists found the Indians using an effective system of natural medicine, which they were quick to adopt. Perhaps the most influential folk-medical chapbook in America was the *Long Lost Friend* of John George Hohman, published in German at Reading, Pa., in 1820; along with the so-called *Egyptian Secrets* ascribed to Albertus Magnus, it spawned many recipe books.

FOLKSONGS. See BALLADS; MUSIC.

FOLSOM CULTURE COMPLEX. A Paleo-Indian culture (9000–8000 BC), named from the initial discovery at a kill site near Folsom, N.M. (1926); other sites were found in an area extending from Saskatchewan to N Mexico. Evidences of Folsom man include distinctive fluted lance points, scrapers, knives, gravers, and other tools; remains are almost always found with bison, especially *Bison taylori,* an animal typical of the Late Wisconsin period.

FONDA'S EXPEDITION. Led by John H. Fonda (1823) from the vicinity of Fort Towson in SE Oklahoma, to Santa Fe, N.M.

FONTAINEBLEAU, TREATY OF (Nov. 3, 1762). France ceded the Isle of Orleans and all Louisiana (see PARIS, TREATY OF).

FOOD. Maize (Indian corn) was the staple of the Indian diet. It was eaten raw, cooked, or popped. Generally dried to be cooked as hominy or crushed into meal for grain. Eastern tribes cultivated corn, beans, peas, red peppers, onions, pumpkins, squash, sweet potatoes, and melons. Maple sap, nut oils, fish oils, bear grease, and fats were used to flavor foods. Nuts, grapes, berries, and wild game were sought in the woods. Wild rice, which was harvested by the Indians, has become a modern delicacy. The waters yielded fish, eels, and shellfish (on which the Pilgrims survived until their first crop came in). Indians of the Great Plains relied on a diet of bison, antelope, and wild hog. Meat was preserved by slicing the meat into thin strips and drying it, making jerky, a process also used by the Northwest Coast Indians to preserve salmon. The so-called Digger Indians foraged for grasshoppers, field mice, grubs, roots, wild grass seed, and acorns. Columbus introduced barley, grapes, sugarcane, and horses to the New World. Cattle were introduced by the Spanish in 1525. Sheep were taken to Virginia in 1609. New Englanders liked to corn (cure in brine) beef, eating it boiled with root vegetables. By the mid-17th c., cattle were numerous enough to permit a limited slaughter. New England traders brought cargoes of sugar, molasses, and tea. In the South in preplantation days, corn was the primary food and remained important as hoecake, hush puppies, corn pone, and bourbon whiskey. In the early 1800s the rise of cities meant that fewer Americans were growing their own food; many poor in the cities could not afford wheat grain and were lucky to eat meat once a week. On the frontier, however, there was a plethora of meat, especially beef. European visitors marveled at the variety of foods available, especially the amount of meat in the diet. Pineapples, coconuts, and bananas had begun to be imported. The new railroad network was instrumental in distribution. After the Civil War, canning helped vary the American diet even further. Federal legislation (1906) helped ensure purer foods. The Great Depression of the 1930s left the country with more food than people could buy, and various New Deal programs were initiated to correct the situation. The Federal Surplus Commodity Corporation bought excess commodities and distributed them to the needy. During the mid-1940s, farm output expanded rapidly. Technological improvements afforded over a 50 percent increase in total output, using less acreage and labor. Food for Peace programs, school lunches, food stamps for the poor, and many other programs resulted from a food surplus.

FOOD AND DRUG ADMINISTRATION (FDA). Created 1927 to enforce the various pure food and drug acts. Has responsibility for safety and appropriate labeling.

FOOD PRESERVATION. Early English settlers subsisted on dry corn and beans from the Indians. Western explorers found the Plains Indians cutting buffalo meat into thin strips and drying it in the sun. Commercial canning began with pickles and catsup in 1819. The cooking in boiling water took took five or six hours, but the invention of the pressure cooker, in 1874, led to rapid processing and revolutionized commercial and home canning. In the 1840s, American families began using the icebox for food storage and preservation, and the refrigerated rail car came into use after 1850. The mechanical refrigerator began to replace the icebox ca. 1920. In 1923, Clarence Birdseye perfected a machine for quick-freezing food. Frozen foods became prevalent after World War II, and the deep-freeze unit became common. Freeze drying developed in the 1950s.

FOOD STAMP PROGRAM. Program for better nutrition among low-income families. Families taking part in the program purchase (or are given) food coupons, which are used to buy food for human consumption. Retailers redeem the coupons through banks. The program began in 1964 and was sharply expanded in the 1970s. By the early 1980s, some 23 million Americans were receiving food stamps. Long criticized by conservatives for alleged waste, fraud, and abuse, the program was cut by the Reagan administration. Benefits were reduced and about 1 million persons dropped from the program.

FOOTBALL.
Amateur Football. In 1869, Princeton and Rutgers met in the first intercollegiate game, actually a type of soccer. English rugby became popular and was soon transformed into American football. The changes were codified in 1880, and a virtually new game was established. By World War I, the game was the leading US intercollegiate sport. College teams play in regional leagues, or conferences, and the leading teams from each conference often meet in postseason bowl games (e.g., Rose Bowl, Cotton Bowl, Orange Bowl). Football is also played at the high school level, where competing teams also play in regional leagues.
Professional Football. Professional football originated in the industrial towns of Ohio and W Pennsylvania in the early 20th c. The American Football Association (later National Football League, or NFL) was formed in 1920, and by the 1930s most major cities had obtained league franchises. A rival league was established in 1946, but it collapsed. The American Football League was formed in 1959; merged with NFL in 1964. The NFL consists of two conferences (American and National), with fourteen teams in each. The winners of each conference meet for the championship in the Super Bowl. In 1983 a competing group, the United States Football League (USFL), was formed. Television revenues have greatly increased the profitability of professional football.

FORBES EXPEDITION (1758). Major campaign of the French and Indian War. Gen. John Forbes led British colonial forces against the French at Fort Duquesne, which fell on Nov. 25.

FORBES ROAD. Built 1758 across W Pennsylvania for use of the FORBES EXPEDITION. Became chief highway to Ohio Valley.

FORCE ACTS. Various federal statutes passed to enforce certain national laws and constitutional amendments, particularly in the South. An 1833 law authorized force to collect customs in South Carolina, which was defying federal tariff acts. During Reconstruction several acts were aimed at enforcing political and civil rights of newly freed slaves.

FORD'S PEACE SHIP. In 1915, Henry Ford financed an unsuccessful, unofficial mission, on board *Oscar II*, to induce European neutrals to force an end to World War I.

FOREIGN AFFAIRS, COMMITTEE FOR. See REVOLUTIONARY COMMITTEES.

FOREIGN AID. Instrument of US foreign policy, beginning with World War II, when about $50 billion worth of aid was transferred to US Allies, chiefly through LEND-LEASE. Afterward much aid was channeled through various international bodies, particularly the United Nations Relief and Rehabilitation Agency (UNRRA). The 1947 TRUMAN DOCTRINE resulted in $400 million in aid being given to Greece and Turkey. The MARSHALL PLAN, also 1947, resulted in some $17 billion for reconstruction and rehabilitation of Europe and to halt expansion of communism. In 1949, President Truman proposed the POINT FOUR program for underdeveloped countries. Military assistance was also offered to the French in Indochina and to the Nationalist Chinese on Formosa. Vast amounts also went for military aid to European allies through the NORTH ATLANTIC TREATY ORGANIZATION and similar military pacts were established in other parts of the world, all of which were based on US military aid. President Eisenhower established (1957) the Development Loan Fund for poorer countries. President Kennedy instituted the ALLIANCE FOR PROGRESS, a plan to spend $20 billion over a ten-year period for economic development in Latin America. By the late 1970s, some $125 billion had been expended in foreign aid since the end of World War II. Military aspects of foreign aid came increasingly under criticism from the public and members of Congress, particularly in Southeast Asia, the Middle East, and Latin America.

FOREIGN POLICY.

Beginnings: 1776 to 1825. Early policy was concerned with establishing the viability of independence. Aid from France during the Revolution had helped assure independence, but in his farewell address George Washington warned against permanent alliances and urged an independent course in foreign affairs. The address became a foundation stone of American isolationism, a given in US domestic politics, which has ebbed and flowed for two centuries. Thomas Jefferson attempted to win respect for US trading rights, which led to the War of 1812. But the Napoleonic Wars brought one advantage to the United States: the LOUISIANA PURCHASE. The MONROE DOCTRINE (1823) declared that the US would not intervene in European matters and that European powers, in return, would not extend their possessions in the Western Hemisphere.

Nationalist Expansion: 1825 to 1898. With a weak Canada and Mexico at its borders, the US began a period of expansion. The doctrine of MANIFEST DESTINY encouraged President Polk to demand all of Oregon from Britain; he settled for the area south of the forty-ninth parallel. He pursued war with Mexico in order to bring all of the Southwest, including Texas and California, into the Union. Alaska was purchased from Russia in 1867, and French and Spanish influence was effectively decreased in Latin America.

Emergence as a World Power: 1898 to 1945. The Spanish-American War (1898) gave Puerto Rico, Guam, and the Philippines to the US. Hawaii was added by congressional resolution (1898), and the PLATT AMENDMENT (1901) gave the US its first protectorate in Cuba. US commercial interests in the Far East were protected by the OPEN DOOR POLICY and through a most-favored-nation treaty with China. US involvement in World War I represented a clear break with traditional isolationism, but the Senate refused to approve US membership in the League of Nations. The KELLOGG-BRIAND PACT (1928) outlawed war as an instrument of national policy, but it had no enforcement mechanism. German and Japanese aggressions in the 1930s severely tried US neutrality, despite the series of neutrality laws passed by Congress. In Latin America, the GOOD NEIGHBOR POLICY attempted to end the more blatant examples of what Latin Americans had begun to call Yankee imperialism. At the outbreak of World War II, Franklin D. Roosevelt rejected neutrality laws; he leased destroyers to Britain and created lend-lease aid to the Allies, thereby committing the US to the Allied side.

Post-World War II Policy: 1945 to 1962. At first the US sought to maintain wartime cooperation and build the United Nations. It proposed international control in nuclear affairs and signed peace treaties with Eastern Europe that were highly favorable to the USSR. The early cold war (1947–53) marked the initiation of the containment policy, which extended aid to people resisting communist expansion. President Truman responded to the Berlin blockade with a giant airlift, created the North Atlantic Treaty Organization (NATO), and intervened in Korea when the communist North Koreans invaded South Korea. President Eisenhower brought West Germany into NATO and installed missiles in Europe. President Kennedy continued the Truman-Eisenhower policy of containment. He forced a confrontation with the Soviet Union in Cuba in 1962 but signed a Nuclear Test Ban Treaty in 1963. He also substantially expanded US involvement in South Vietnam.

Vietnam and After. Lyndon B. Johnson continued containment policies of his predecessors. He escalated involvement in Vietnam, a policy authorized by Congress with the TONKIN GULF RESOLUTION (1964). As US troop involvement grew, with no discernible results, public opposition to the war grew; and it was that opposition that caused Johnson to decide not to run for reelection in 1968. Richard Nixon, elected to succeed him, began a policy of gradually reducing US ground troops in Vietnam, although he expanded the bombing raids on North Vietnam and Cambodia. In 1973, the war finally came to an end with the total collapse of the South Vietnamese government and failure of US objectives there. Meanwhile, Nixon had opened relations with Communist China and signed a strategic arms limitation treaty (SALT) with the Soviet Union. President Ford vowed to continue the Nixon policy of détente with the Soviets. The HELSINKI ACCORDS were signed in 1975. President Carter made human rights a centerpiece of US foreign policy. He successfully concluded the Panama Canal treaties (1978), broke diplomatic relations with Taiwan and established formal relations with mainland China, and, most importantly, engineered the CAMP DAVID AGREEMENTS (1978) between Israel and Egypt. The collapse of the monarchy in Iran and the subsequent holding of fifty American hostages proved the major problem of the Carter administration. US foreign policy under Ronald Reagan continued

to focus on attempts to settle disagreements in the Middle East, particularly an American presence in Lebanon, marked by the deaths of over two hundred Marines who were part of a peace-keeping force. In Latin America, continued American intervention in El Salvador and Nicaragua raised serious questions about the US role in the region and the degree of Cuban and Soviet involvement. The invasion of Grenada and the overthrow of a Marxist regime was generally hailed by the US public. However, relations with the Soviet Union deteriorated to a level not seen since the cold war. Installation of cruise missiles in Europe exacerbated the situation.

FOREIGN SERVICE. The American colonies were represented by high-quality emissaries to Europe during and immediately after the Revolution. But quality faded when the spoils system took hold. Improvement came after 1856, when an act was passed that established administrative control over principal consular positions and increased salaries: a small move toward a merit system and professional foreign service officers. Congress reorganized the consular service in 1906 but failed to remove it from politics. President Theodore Roosevelt extended the merit system to consular officers. Major reform came with Rogers Act (1924), which amalgamated various diplomatic and consular services into the Foreign Service of the US (an agency of the Department of State); raised salaries and increased living allotments; and created a ranking of diplomatic officers. Replaced by the Foreign Service Act of 1946 although philosophy remained intact. The principal change in the foreign service after World War II lay in its enlargement: In 1982 there were representatives in 136 embassies, 64 consulate generals, 35 consulates, 3 branch offices, and 34 consular agencies.

FOREIGN TRADE. See TRADE, FOREIGN.

FORESTRY. During the 1880s, several states established forest commissions, and the American Forestry Association launched an effort for the study and protection of forests. In 1891, Congress authorized the president to establish forest reserves from the public domains. Gifford Pinchot became chief forester in 1898 and assumed control in 1905 of the newly organized Forest Service. National forests were expanded, research in forestry began, and a forestry profession emerged. Milestones were the establishment of the National Park Service (1916) and designation of the first wilderness area (1924). During the 1930s, the Civilian Conservation Corps enrolled some 2 million youths in forestry programs. Beginning in the 1960s, the renewed interest in protecting the natural environment saw increased forest protection and a new awareness of the importance of wilderness areas.

FOREST SERVICE, UNITED STATES. A Division of Forestry was set up in 1881. Reorganized as Forest Service (1905) with Gifford Pinchot as director. Placed under Department of Agriculture. In 1982, the Forest Service managed 154 national forests and 19 national grasslands, comprising 188 million acres, under the principles of multiple use and sustained yield: recreation and natural beauty, wildlife habitat, livestock forage, and water supplies.

FORGES, COLONIAL. In the 17th c., a few ironworks were established in New England but not until the early 18th c. did the iron industry become important. By 1775, there were more forges and greater production of bar iron in the colonies than in England and Wales.

FORMAN'S MASSACRE (1777). Col. William Forman and twenty companions were killed by Indians while on a scouting expedition near present-day Wheeling, W. Va.

FORSYTH'S FIGHT. See BEECHER ISLAND, BATTLE OF.

FORT. *See under identifying name of fort* (e.g., RECOVERY, FORT), except where the designation has become attached to a city (e.g., FORT LAUDERDALE).

FORT BENTON. Town in Montana, founded on the Missouri R in 1846 as Fort Lewis by the American Fur Co. A main port of entry during Montana gold rush.

FORT HILL LETTER. John C. Calhoun's definitive statement of his nullification doctrine, written 1832.

FORT LAUDERDALE. Florida city established 1838 as a military post. Famous for canals and riverfront, it is a prominent resort and a citrus and dairy products center. Port Everglades is two miles south. Pop.: 153,256 (1980).

FORT WAYNE. City in Indiana, founded 1794 as a frontier fort by Gen. Anthony Wayne. The Miami Indians and the French had occupied the site, where the St. Joseph and St. Mary rivers combine to form the Maumee R. Important outpost in the War of 1812. Later became a major rail center. Pop.: 172,196 (1980).

FORT WORTH. Texas city, founded 1845 as a frontier fort. A major cattle shipping point after 1874 and a center of meat-packing industry. Today oil-producing and aviation manufacturing are major industries. Pop.: 385,141 (1980).

FORTY ACRES AND A MULE. Slogan common among blacks in the South after the Civil War, describing the homestead that each family expected from the confiscation of plantations.

FORTY-EIGHTERS. German immigrants to US after Revolution of 1848.

FORTY FORT. Frontier fort erected 1772 in present Forty Fort Borough, Wyoming Valley, Pa. Named for the first forty settlers.

FORTY-MILE DESERT. Between the sink of Humboldt R and the Carson and Truckee river routes, in Nevada. Worst stretch of the journey for the goldseekers traveling to California.

FORTY-NINERS. Gold-seekers who trekked to California in 1849, after gold was discovered there in 1848.

FOUNDATIONS, ENDOWED. Benjamin Franklin set up two funds, both still in existence, to lend money to "young married artificers." The Peabody Education Fund was established in 1867, but most foundations have 20th c. origins. John D. Rockefeller and Andrew Carnegie each set up several foundations; and the Milbank Memorial Fund (1905) and the Russell Sage Foundation

(1907) are other early examples. Foundations proliferated after World War II, chiefly because of tax advantages. Trend slowed after tax reforms of 1969 which set up more stringent rules. The Ford Foundation (1936) is the nation's largest. Education, the arts, and medical and scientific research are major recipients of foundation grants.

FOUNDING FATHERS. American political leaders during the years of the Revolution and the writing of the Constitution.

FOUR FREEDOMS. Ideals for a postwar world expressed by President Franklin D. Roosevelt in 1941: (1)freedom of speech and expression; (2) freedom of worship; (3) freedom from want; and (4) freedom from fear.

4-H CLUBS. Rural youth movement founded 1902; the H's stand for head, heart, hands, and health. The clubs sponsor competitions among farm boy and girls in various fields of agricultural endeavor. Membership in 1980 was about 4 million.

FOUR HUNDRED. The social elite of New York City, so-called because Mrs. William Astor's ballroom in the 1890s could accommodate only 400 guests.

FOURIERISM. Social philosophy based on the theories of Charles Fourier (1772–1837), a French socialist. Some forty Fourier communities, based on an idealistic communism, were established in US after 1834, including BROOK FARM, the most famous. All failed.

FOUR-MILE STRIP. Strip of land on each side of the Niagara R from Lake Ontario to Lake Erie. Ceded to the British by the Seneca (1764).

FOUR-POWER TREATY. Arms limitation treaty signed 1921 by the US, Great Britain, France, and Japan. Each agreed to respect the others' "insular dominions . . . in the Pacific Ocean." Followed by six other armament treaties.

FOURTEEN POINTS. America's terms for peace after World War I, as set forth by President Wilson: (1) "open covenants of peace openly arrived at"; (2) freedom of the seas;

(3) removal of economic barriers and equality of trade conditions; (4) reduction of armaments to the lowest point consistent with domestic safety; (5) impartial adjustment of colonial claims; (6) evacuation of Russian territory and Russian self-determination; (7) evacuation and restoration of Belgium; (8) evacuation of France and restoration of Alsace-Lorraine to France; (9) readjustment of Italian frontiers; (10) autonomous development for the peoples of Austria-Hungary; (11) readjustments in the Balkans; (12) autonomous development for the non-Turkish nationalities of the Ottoman Empire and the opening of the Dardanelles; (13) restoration of an independent Poland with access to the sea; and (14) establishment of a general association of nations. Generally accepted by the Allies, they became the basis for the ensuing peace treaties.

FOURTEENTH AMENDMENT (1868). One of the three Civil War amendments to the Constitution. Defines US citizenship and has clauses guaranteeing all citizens due process and equal protection of the laws. Has served as the basis for many landmark Supreme Court decisions, particularly in civil rights cases.

FOURTEENTH COLONY. Designation variously used for Transylvania (western Virginia), Franklin (in what is now eastern Tennessee), and Vermont.

FOURTH OF JULY. See INDEPENDENCE DAY.

FOWLER EXPEDITION (or Glenn-Fowler expedition). Exploration in 1821 by Jacob Fowler and Hugh Glenn to open a road to Santa Fe.

FOWLTOWN, BATTLE OF (Nov. 21, 1817). Beginning of the Seminole War. When Indians refused to be removed, US troops attacked them at Fowltown, near Fort Scott, Ga.

FOX. Tribe that originally possessed a Woodland culture and were traditionally allied with the Sauk (with whom they shared an Algonkin language). With the Kickapoo, they moved into Michigan in the 17th c. In conflict with both the French and Chippewa (see FOX-FRENCH WARS). With the Sauk fought in the Black Hawk War of 1832. Moved to Kansas.

Separated from the Sauk and returned to a reservation in Iowa.

FOX-FRENCH WARS. After 1671, the Fox attempted to block French expansion. In 1712, the French armed the Chippewa, and the Fox mounted an unsuccessful attack on Detroit. The surviving Fox fled to Wisconsin and incited other tribes against the French. A French punitive expedition in 1716 captured hostages and extracted a Fox promise to end the war. Ten years later the Fox again attacked the French; in 1728 a large French-Indian expedition destroyed two Fox villages, and forced the Fox to merge with the Sauk. Guerrilla warfare continued until 1738.

FOX-WISCONSIN WATERWAY. Ancient portage route from the upper Great Lakes to the Mississippi R, through what is now Wisconsin. Between a bend of the Wisconsin R and the upper Fox R, now connected by a canal, there was a level-ground portage of about a mile and a half. First used by the French (1673). British built towns at each end. Later the Americans secured it by building Fort Howard at the E end and Fort Crawford at the W end.

FRANCE, AMERICAN JOINT COMMISSION TO (1776). Silas Deane, Arthur Lee, and Benjamin Franklin sought arms and other aid from France and Spain. Spain refused, and the French kept the commission waiting until 1778. After a treaty was signed, the commission stayed on in Paris; Franklin was made minister plenipotentiary to France.

FRANCE, CONVENTION WITH. See CONVENTION OF 1800.

FRANCHISE. In political context, the right to vote. Persons on whom the right are conferred are voters or electors; collectively, they make up the electorate. Qualifications for voting laid down by federal and state constitutions. Laws have dealt with such matters as age, sex, race, nationality, literacy, property holding, payment of taxes, and periods of residence. In the US the movement toward universal (white male) suffrage began in 1789 and received its great impetus under Jacksonian democracy. Efforts to gain the franchise for blacks begin at the end of the Civil War and did not end until the passage of the civil rights acts of the 1960s. The Nineteenth Amendment (1919) gave women the franchise; the Twenty-sixth (1971) lowered the voting age to eighteen. The proportion of the total population that possessed the franchise increased from 6 percent in 1789 to about 70 percent in the 1980s.

FRANCISCANS. Roman Catholic order founded by St. Francis of Assisi in 1209. Important in both Spanish and French North America and were active in Maryland after 1672. Later, they labored chiefly in the West and Northwest. In 1973 there were 3,326 Franciscans in the US.

FRANCO-AMERICAN ALLIANCE OF 1778. Two treaties between France and the Thirteen Colonies during the Revolution. French aid brought the conflict to a victorious end.

FRANCO-AMERICAN MISUNDERSTANDING. France, angered by the Anglo-American JAY'S TREATY of 1794, nullified a 1778 treaty with the Americans and decreed that American ships carrying British goods would be seized and the crews treated as pirates. In 1798, President John Adams sent a special mission to Paris to negotiate, but it was unsuccessful. After the XYZ AFFAIR, America entered into the Quasi War, or NAVAL WAR WITH FRANCE. The CONVENTION OF 1800 ended most of the problems.

FRANCO-AMERICAN RELATIONS. France's help to the Thirteen Colonies was an essential element in the American victory in the Revolution. Relations deteriorated after the end of the war, leading to the Franco-American Misunderstanding. Relations improved with the Convention of 1800, and the sale of Louisiana to the United States by Napoleon ended one source of conflict between the two nations. The establishment of the Second Republic in 1848 was well received in the United States, but America's unsympathetic attitude toward the Crimean War (1854–56) and general contempt for Napoleon III was matched by Napoleon's proposed mediation in the US Civil War, his sympathy for the South, and his intervention in Mexico when the United States was occupied in the war. The French presence in Mexico was removed in 1867, and thereafter Franco-American relations improved. They generally remained good through World War I. During World War II, relations were uneasy between Charles De Gaulle and Roosevelt and Churchill who were reluctant to accept him as the leader of the Free French; but differences were subordinated to liberation of the country and the defeat of Germany. After World War II, relations were on the whole good. The US-funded Marshall Plan was essential in the reconstruction of France, which joined the North Atlantic Treaty Organization (NATO) in 1949. Tensions increased after Gen. Charles De Gaulle became president in 1958. Dissatisfied with America's refusal to give France equality in the Atlantic alliance, he undertook a diplomatic and economic offensive against both the United States and Great Britain. He withdrew French forces from NATO in 1966 and mounted an attack on the US dollar. Relations improved after De Gaulle's retirement in 1969, and they remained generally good through the 1970s and early 1980s.

FRANCO-AMERICAN WAR PRIZE CASES. The Convention of 1800 between the United States and France released France from responsibility for the FRENCH SPOLIATION CLAIMS. Thus Americans turned to their government for settlement. Congress finally (in 1885) agreed to pay the claims, and between 1885 and 1925, claimants and their descendants finally received a total of $5 million.

FRANKFORT. Capital of Kentucky, located on the Kentucky R. Laid out 1786, originally known as Frank's Ford. A marketing and shipping town, with several liquor distilleries. Pop.: 25,973 (1980).

FRANKING. The privilege of sending material through the mails without charge, in general limited to members of Congress, other authorized officials, and government agencies.

FRANKLIN, BATTLE OF (Nov. 30, 1864). Confederates rashly attacked Union forces at Franklin, Tenn. Federal troops repulsed them but retired to Nashville.

FRANKLIN, STATE OF. Dissidents in W North Carolina met at Jonesboro, now in Tennessee, 1784, and declared the area a state. North Carolina immediately repealed the cession act, which had turned over the area to the federal government. Franklin maintained a precarious existence until North Carolina reestablished jurisdiction in 1789.

FRANKLIN STOVE. Invented by Benjamin Franklin in 1742, it consisted of a low stove, equipped with loosely fitting iron plates, through which air might circulate and be warmed before passage into the room. Did not resemble the so-called Franklin stove of today.

FRANQUELIN'S MAPS. Twenty maps of the New World done between 1678 and 1708 by J.B.L. Franquelin, a French hydrographer.

FRAUNCES TAVERN. A reconstructed 18th-c. house in New York City, operated as a public house by Samuel Fraunces after 1762. Site of Gen. Washington's farewell to his officers (1783). Now a restaurant and museum.

FRAYSER'S FARM, BATTLE OF (June 30, 1862). One of the Seven Days' Battles in PENINSULAR CAMPAIGN.

FRAZIER-LEMKE FARM BANKRUPTCY ACT. Enacted 1934 to relieve farmers threatened by foreclosure. Authorized courts to grant a five-year moratorium. Ruled unconstitutional 1935 by Supreme Court. A modified version was unanimously sustained.

FREDERICA. Fortified town in Georgia, laid out in 1736 by James E. Oglethorpe as a defense against the Spanish in Florida.

FREDERICK. Town in Maryland, laid out in 1745. During the Civil War, several important battles were fought in the vicinity. Pop.: 27,557 (1980).

FREDERICKSBUG, BATTLE OF (Dec. 13, 1862). Major battle between Confederate Gen. R.E. Lee (with 78,000 troops) and Union Gen. A.E. Burnside (with 122,000 troops). Burnside withdrew N of the Rappahannock after suffering over 10,000 casualties (versus 5,000 Confederate casualties).

FREDONIAN REVOLT. In 1826, Haden Edwards, an EMPRESARIO in East Texas, at odds with the Mexican authorities, proclaimed the Republic of Fredonia. The revolt was suppressed in 1827 without bloodshed.

FREE BLACKS. The 1790 census counted approximately 60,000 free blacks; by 1860, there were approximately 500,000. Some were descendants of those who had never been slaves; others had been freed. All northern states abolished slavery shortly after the Revolution. In the South, some slaves were given their freedom and others managed to buy it. Still others ran away to the North. The Civil War ended the peculiar legal status of the free black.

FREEBOOTERS. See BUCCANEERS.

FREEDMAN'S SAVINGS BANK. A bank for newly freed blacks, founded in Washington, D.C., in 1864. Closed 1874.

FREEDMEN'S BUREAU. Established by Congress in 1865 to provide emergency food and shelter to those dislocated by the Civil War, especially former slaves. Established schools, conducted military courts to hear complaints, and supervised the arrangements for work made by the freedmen. Agents established in all former slave states. Most important contribution was education. Eleven colleges and universities and sixty-one normal schools were founded. Also registered black voters under the Reconstruction plan.

FREEDOM OF RELIGION. A fundamental guarantee embodied in the very first clause of the First Amendment: ''Congress shall make no law respecting an establishment of religion, or prohibiting the free exercise thereof. . . .'' Issue has been a continuing one, most notably in aid to religious schools and school prayer, both of which have been ruled against by the Supreme Court.

FREEDOM OF SPEECH. A basic right protected by the First Amendment. No clear analogue or predecessor in English or colonial common law. Its application has been most seriously tested where persons holding unpopular views are concerned. The Supreme Court has tended to strengthen the principle.

FREEDOM OF THE PRESS. A basic right protected by the First Amendment. Press freedom has never held to be absolute: The sedition acts of 1798–1801 sent antigovernment editors to prison; antislavery publications were suppressed in the South before the Civil War; and during World War I, the Espionage Act of 1917 resulted in a frenzy of prosecution of persons and publications opposed to the war. Nevertheless, the principle of a free press has generally been upheld by the courts.

FREEDOM RIDERS. Blacks and whites who traveled in buses in the South in 1961 to protest racial segregation in bus terminals.

FREEHOLDER. The owner of a land or estate, either for life or with inheritance rights. Seven colonies restricted the suffrage to freeholders; others permitted persons with other forms of property to vote.

FREE LAND. Designation for the American frontier; squatters could settle there and eventually expect either to acquire title by purchase or to sell their claims to others. Free grants were given in the colonial period, and in Oregon and Florida before 1862. After 1862, all public land that was surveyed and opened to settlement was free, with some exceptions, under the Homestead Act. This law, last applied to Alaska, was repealed in 1974.

FREEMAN'S EXPEDITION. Exploration of the Red R of Louisiana and Texas in 1805 by Thomas Freeman. Organized by President Jefferson after the Louisiana Purchase.

FREEMAN'S FARM, FIRST BATTLE OF (Sept. 19, 1777; also known as the first Battle of Bemis Heights, or Stillwater). British Gen. John Burgoyne was defeated by Americans under Gen. Horatio Gates just below Saratoga, N.Y.

FREEMAN'S FARM, SECOND BATTLE OF (Oct. 7, 1777; also known as the second Battle of Bemis Heights, or Stillwater). British Gen. John Burgoyne was defeated for the second time by American forces under Gen. Horatio Gates. The British retreated.

FREEMASONS. Masonic lodges were established in the American colonies in the 1730s. Masons were active in Revolutionary activities, many of the Founding Fathers being members, and continued to be an active force in American politics. Influence led to ANTI-MASONIC MOVEMENTS of the 1820s and 1830s.

FREEMAN. In colonial times, the same as FREEHOLDER.

FREEPORT DOCTRINE. Stephen Douglas' view that slavery could be excluded from the territories. It secured him reelection to the Senate but angered the South, thereby losing him presidential support.

FREE SHIPS, FREE GOODS. Refers to the claim of neutrals that cargoes in neutral ships, except contraband, are not subject to seizure by belligerents. Not accepted by England at the time of the War of 1812.

FREE SILVER. Political slogan of the late 19th c. urging the unlimited coinage of silver by the US government. Favored by those looking for a large increase in the money supply. Ended in 1900 with the passage of the Gold Standard Act.

FREE SOCIETY OF TRADERS. Commercial company to which William Penn sold 20,000 acres of land in Pennsylvania in 1681. Little came of the scheme.

"FREE SOIL, FREE SPEECH, FREE MEN AND FRÉMONT." Free Soil party platform of 1848, adopted by the Republicans in 1856.

FREE SOIL PARTY. Organized 1848 in opposition to extending slavery into the western territories. Presidential nominee Martin Van Buren polled only 291,263 votes, but a dozen members of Congress and a number of state legislators were elected. Later absorbed into the new Republican party.

FREE-STATE PARTY. See KANSAS FREE-STATE PARTY.

FREETHINKING. Religious thought based on reason as opposed to established religion. Important in America in the 18th c., as evidenced by Thomas Paine's *Age of Reason* (1794–96). In the 19th c., W.E. Channing, R.W. Emerson, and Theodore Parker advocated forms of free thought. Later that century, the "higher criticism" of biblical scholarship introduced a form of freethinking into Christianity.

FREE TRADE. The concept that goods should be traded in international markets without governmental control.

FREMONT. City in California, on San Francisco Bay, established 1956 by the consoli-dation of several residential towns. Pop.: 131,945 (1980).

FRÉMONT'S EXPLORATIONS. Five expeditons by J.C. Frémont into the Far West from 1843 to 1854. The first three were officially sponsored attempts to chart what is now Wyoming, Utah, Oregon, California, and Nevada. The last two were privately financed and were looking for a railroad route across the Rocky Mountains.

FRENCH ALLIANCE. See FRANCO-AMERICAN ALLIANCE OF 1778.

FRENCH AND INDIAN WAR (1754–63). Final stage of the struggle (began 1689) between the French (in alliance with various Indian tribes) and English for control of North America. Last part of the war was American counterpart of European Seven Years' War. French forts on the Great Lakes and the Ohio and Mississippi rivers encroached on land claimed by Virginia. George Washington was sent to warn the French. He was met by superior force and forced to retire. In 1755 Gen. Edward Braddock was defeated in trying to take Fort Duquesne. The British were more successful in upper New York, where Fort Edward was established on the Hudson R., but 3,000 British colonials died of illness at Albany. The French swept the English from Oswego, and an inept British attempt to take Quebec was a disaster. In 1759, a new government in London was determined to drive the French out of North America. Gen. James Wolfe captured Quebec. The attempt on Montreal was stymied, but the capture of Niagara cut French water communication to Louisiana and opened the back door to Montreal. That city finally fell to the British in 1760, thereby winning Canada. Fighting continued in the West Indies. The Treaty of Paris (1763) confirmed the British gains.

FRENCH CREEK, ACTION AT (Nov. 1–2, 1813). British flotilla was defeated at Clayton, N. Y., by an American shore battery.

FRENCH DECREES. French efforts to blockade English shipping during the Napoleonic Wars. Ordered capture of all provisions going to England. At first US ships were exempted but were included after 1795. Struck particularly at American commerce and led US to retaliate unsuccessfully with the EMBARGO ACT (1807), the NONINTERCOURSE ACT (1809), and MACON'S BILL NO.2 (1810).

FRENCH FORTS. Fort Frontenac was built at Kingston, Ont., in 1673, Fort Miami (St. Joseph, Mich.) in 1679, Fort St. Louis and Fort Crèvecoeur (in Illinois) in 1680–82, Fort Biloxi (Mississippi) in 1699, Mobile in 1702, and New Orleans in 1717. New France now extended from the Gulf of St. Lawrence to the Gulf of Mexico; and to protect it, strategic intermediate points were occupied: Fort Pontchartrain (Detroit) in 1701; Fort Michilmackinac (Michigan) ca. 1715; Fort de Chartres (Illinois) in 1717; and Fort Niagara (New York) ca. 1721. Attempts to secure the upper Ohio Valley were less successful. Forts included Presque Isle, Le Boeuf, Machault, Venango, and Duquesne. The FRENCH AND INDIAN WAR began here and ended in the complete downfall of New France. The forts passed into English hands or were abandoned.

FRENCH GRANTS. Land given to French settlers in America by the US government, 1795 and 1798, in Scioto County, Ohio, as recompense for worthless deeds bought from Scioto Co. Few actually settled the land.

FRENCH PRIVATEERS. In 1797 the US government claimed that 32 US merchant ships had been captured by French privateers (newspapers claimed that over 300 had been captured). The Americans retaliated in 1798 in what became known as the NAVAL WAR WITH FRANCE. About 84 French privateers were captured.

FRENCH REFUGEES. French Protestants (Huguenots) settled in colonial South Carolina, Virginia, and other British colonies. French-speaking Walloons went early to New Netherland, and French-Swiss groups settled in Pennsylvania and North Carolina. French Revolution brought a succession of political refugees: aristocratic emigrants, former plantation owners from Santo Domingo, exiled revolutionaries, and, after Waterloo, many Bonapartists.

FRENCH SPOLIATION CLAIMS. Claims made by US citizens for losses sustained by French blockade during the Napoleonic Wars. Some were settled by the Compromise of 1800 and others by the Louisiana Purchase Treaty of 1803. A second, more controversial group of claims grew out of French seizures between 1806 and 1810. Not settled until 1836; France paid about $5.5 million.

FRIENDLY ASSOCIATION. An extralegal Quaker organization established in Pennsylvania in 1756 for the purpose of promoting friendly relations with the Indians. Opposed by the proprietary interest, probably ended ca. 1764.

FRIENDS, SOCIETY OF. See QUAKERS.

FRIES'S REBELLION (1799). Armed insurrection in Pennsylvania against federal tax on land and houses. Also called Hot Water Rebellion because housewives scalded would-be assessors. Suppressed by federal troops.

FRINK AND WALKER STAGE LINES. Operator of most of the stages in Illinois and adjoining states ca. 1836–55.

FRITCHIE, BARBARA, AND THE FLAG. Apocryphal story that Stonewall Jackson ordered his troops to fire on a Union flag displayed in Barbara Fritchie's window in Frederick, Md., but rescinded the order when she waved the flag defiantly. The 96-year-old widow actually waved a flag from her porch at Confederate troops six days after Jackson had passed through town.

FRONTENAC, FORT. French fort at Kingston, Ont., 1673. Captured by English 1758; demolished 1819.

FRONTENAC EXPEDITION (1696). Punitive expedition against the Indians by the comte de Frontenac to punish them for raids and interfering with trade.

FRONT ROYAL, BATTLE AT (May 23, 1862). Part of JACKSON'S VALLEY CAMPAIGN. Gen. Stonewall Jackson defeated Union forces at Front Royal, Va.

FROST-BITTEN CONVENTION (Dec. 14, 1836). Irregular assembly, meeting at Ann Arbor, that agreed to the terms by which Michigan was admitted to the Union.

FRUIT GROWING. By 1566, Spaniards were planting olives, dates, figs, and citrus fruits on the Georgia coast; by 1769 they had planted fruit orchards all the way from Texas to California. In 1629 residents of Jamestown were growing apples, pears, peaches, and apricots. The orange became a commercial crop in Florida ca. 1821 and by the 1980s was the largest fruit industry in the US. Grape growing was second. Apples were being exported from New England to the West Indies by 1741 and from Virginia to England by 1759. Apple-growing followed the frontier westward, and commercial centers eventually grew up in Ohio and the Northwest. Commercial fruit growing was seldom profitable until the railroad made transportation to population centers possible.

FRUITLANDS. Cooperative community established in 1843 by Bronson Alcott in Massachusetts. Ten families settled on eleven acres, but severe weather forced them out after seven months.

FUELS. The first fuel used in the colonial era was wood; it heated homes and, later, powered early steam locomotives and steamships. Charcoal made from it was used in iron forges. During the 19th c., coal supples were tapped and became the basic fuel for locomotives and industry, as well as for home heating. Petroleum and natural gas came into widespread use in the 20th c. The demand became so great that the US became an importer of oil, which led to great economic and political upheavals in the 1970s and 1980s. After World War II, nuclear fuels became available, but their promise was not fully realized: high costs and fear of nuclear accidents held back their development. Major sources of energy in the US are petroleum, natural gas, and coal.

FUGIOS. Also known as Franklin cents. Earliest coins issued by the US, dated 1787.

FUGITIVE SLAVE ACTS. Series of local, state, and federal laws aimed at discouraging runaway slaves and those who aided them. Such laws date from colonial times, but the federal Fugitive Slave Act of 1850, part of the COMPROMISE OF 1850, figures most prominently. Provided for US commissioners to issue warrants for the arrest of fugitives and orders for their return to their owners. Called for harsh penalties for anyone aiding fugitives. Served to galvanize the anti-slavery movement.

FULBRIGHT ACT AND GRANTS. Program sponsored in 1946 by Sen. J.W. Fulbright to finance international educational exchange programs. Initially funded from sale of property abroad considered surplus after World War II. The program was expanded over the years and became the largest program in history of international exchange grants made to individuals.

"FULL DINNER PAIL." Republican campaign slogan in the 1900 presidential election campaign, used to emphasize the prosperity of William McKinley's first term and to appeal to the labor vote.

FULTON. Wooden side-wheeled steamer built 1837 for New York harbor defense. Given new engines in 1852, it took part in PARAGUAY EXPEDITION. Burned during Civil War.

FULTON'S FOLLY. Derisory name for the *Clermont*, the steamboat built in 1807 by Robert Fulton. Made 150-mile run from New York to Albany in thirty-two hours, beginning new era in transportation

FUNDAMENTAL CONSTITUTIONS. English colonists carried to the New World the concept of a supreme and fundamental constitution to which all laws must conform. Patents and royal charters, however, usually offered no more than local autonomy. In the Restoration period, the proprietors of the Carolinas and Jerseys granted concessions and agreements followed by fundamental constitutions (see CAROLINA, FUNDAMENTAL CONSTITUTIONS OF); these, with William Penn's Frame of Government, were an attempt to compromise with the new concept of sovereignty in the people that had developed in the northern colonies. The precursor was the MAYFLOWER COMPACT. The FUNDAMENTAL ORDERS OF CONNECTICUT, and PROVIDENCE AGREEMENTS are similar except that they were made to be permanent; these two corporation colonies were much more independent of the mother country than colonies of any other type and furnished the pattern on which the state constitutions of the new US were modeled.

FUNDAMENTAL ORDERS OF CONNECTI-CUT. See CONNECTICUT, FUNDAMENTAL ORDERS OF.

FUNDING OF THE REVOLUTIONARY DEBT. See ASSUMPTION AND FUNDING OF REVOLUTIONARY DEBT.

FUNSTON'S CAPTURE OF AGUINALDO (March 14–25, 1901). During the PHILIPPINE INSURRECTION, the insurgent president, Emilio Aguinaldo, was captured at Palanan by a force headed by Gen. Frederick Funston. Aguinaldo took the US oath of allegiance, thereby effectively ending the insurrection.

FURNITURE. Stylistically, American furniture has always been closely related to Old World models, but with pronounced regional characteristics.

17th Century. Simple board furniture was nailed together by house carpenters. More sophisticated pieces were made by joiners, including heavy, low, rectangular chests, tables, chairs, bedsteads, and cupboards of oak. Pine and maple were used for interior parts. Much early furniture was painted strong earth colors.

Restoration and William and Mary Styles (1690–1730). The 1690s brought lighter new forms and classical proportions. Innovations included dovetail construction, moldings around drawers, and teardrop or chased-brass mounts instead of iron escutcheons and wooden knobs. Most furniture was made of native walnut or maple, occasionally ornamented with more exotic materials. New forms included cane-back, banister-back, slatback, leather-back, and upholstered chairs; tall clocks; high chests of drawers and matching dressing tables; slant-top desks; and gateleg and butterfly tables.

Queen Anne and Chippendale Styles (1730–90). In the Queen Anne style case furniture in particular was highly architectural, with molded cornices, scroll pediments, dentils, and flutes and reeds as well as proportions based on Palladian principles. Chairs featured backs with solid, vase-shaped splats and bow-shaped crests. Sometimes the knees of cabriole legs were carved with scallop shells and volutes, but usually there was little ornament. Increasingly comfortable furniture was made; card and tea tables, firescreens, and desks and bookcases were popular new forms. With the Chippendale style, ca. 1760, came mahogany, although walnut, maple, and cherry continued to be used, especially in rural areas. Chippendale splats were pierced, case pieces continued in the Palladian mode, with the addition of carved ornament in French, Chinese, or Gothic style. Newport, Boston, and Philadelphia became the center for American Chippendale design. Manufacture of the Windsor chair began in Philadelphia ca. 1750. It was lighter and stronger than its English model and became the forerunner of inexpensive 19th-c. painted and stencilled fancy chairs.

Federal Furniture in the Neoclassical Style (1790–1825). American adaptations of Hepplewhite and Sheraton styles were widely accepted by the 1790s. The urn, anthemion, bellflower, and swags of drapery were common elements in ornament. Griffins, steer skulls, busts and figures of ancients, and the new United States seal, the American eagle, and columns and pilasters were widely used.

Victorian Styles (1835–1901). About 1835, revival styles were introduced with elements of several styles often combined. J.H. Belter of New York pioneered in the use of laminated wood for curved forms that were elaborately carved. Michael Thonet's Viennese bentwood chairs of unadorned surface and clean outline were widely copied by domestic manufacturers. C. L. Eastlake's "sincere" simplified designs were influential in the 1870s and 1880s. Design was further simplified by the Mission oak style. Metal used increasingly in furniture.

Twentieth Century. The International school of architecture was accompanied by a parallel furniture style, simple and unadorned. Designers exploited technology and new materials, including stainless steel, chrome, glass, plastic, and leather. In contrast, the Art Deco style, which flourished after ca. 1925, is one of ornament with exotic motifs from many sources, including Egyptian, Aztec, and Southwest Indian art. In 1940 Charles Eames and Eero Saarinen began work in molded plywood, a form that proliferated after World War II. George Nelson introduced the storage-wall room divider with interchangeable parts in 1945. Scandinavian modern, with simple, cleancut lines and mostly bleached woods, was popular in the 1950s and 1960s. The 1970s saw the introduction of what came to be known as high tech, which was furniture modeled after commercial and industrial designs. The 1980s saw a more eclectic fashion return: Victorian, Art Deco, high tech, and Italian contemporary often mixed together.

FURNITURE INDUSTRY. The export of furniture began in the 18th c., giving rise to a US furniture industry beyond the individual craftsmen common in earlier furniture making. Active in the export trade was a consortium of Salem, Mass., cabinetmakers and allied craftsmen. Cabinetmakers and chairmakers established shops in Charleston, Savannah, and New Orleans. By 1820, the New York shop of Duncan Phyfe alone required the services of 100 workmen. By the 1850s, the largest furniture firms were true factories, using steam-powered mortising, tenoning, and carving machines; steam-powered lathes; and steam-powered jig, scroll, band, and circular saws. New techniques of bending wood and pressing wood scraps into molds were also perfected. Grand Rapids, with its proximity to western timber stands, became the manufacturing center. In the 20th c., a new center of furniture, based on supplies of hardwood and cheap labor, grew up in W North Carolina, with the major marketing center at High Point.

FUR TRADE. Traffic in furs and skins began with the first contacts between European explorers and Indians along the shores of North America and has continued without interruption. Almost the only New World commodity that afforded immediate returns.

New England. Trade with the Indians continued throughout the colonial period, declining in importance after KING PHILIP'S WAR. The geographical situation prevented any considerable expansion; there were no great waterways leading to the interior of the continent.

Middle Atlantic States. The trade of the New York area, which dominated the Hudson-Mohawk route to the Great Lakes and the Northwest, was established by the Dutch, monopoly rights being granted in turn to the New Netherland Co. and the Dutch West India Co.; important posts were established at Fort Orange (Albany) and the House of Hope on the Connecticut R. The Dutch laid the foundations of trade with the Iroquois, who became the middlemen for tribes further west. The English continued the fur trade, after taking over New Netherland in 1664 but soon came into conflict with the French. The fur trade became a vital factor in the Anglo-French rivalries that did not end until 1763. By 1750 trade had reached the Wabash and Maumee rivers, where the English clashed with the French. Pennsylvania enjoyed the advantage of position in exploiting the Ohio region; Philadelphia and Lancaster were trading centers.

Great Lakes Region. One of the richest fur regions, peltry trade flourished for 200 years. Beaver most important, but raccoon, otter, mink, muskrat, and fox were also sought. New France had its genesis largely in the fur trade in the area. Quebec was founded in 1608, and the fur trade rapidly extended to the interior. Export rights to France were vested in a succession of companies, and trading posts were established at Niagara, Detroit, Michilimackinac, Sault Ste. Marie, La Baye, St. Joseph's, and Vincennes. Following the capitulation of Montreal in 1760, there was an influx of British merchants and a rapid expansion of the trade. Government monopoly, common under the French, gave way to company monopoly. The North West Co. became the most powerful. The British refused to surrender the Northwest posts to the US until 1796 (see BORDER FORTS, EVACUATION OF). In 1795 the United States inaugurated unsuccessful system of government factories (see FACTORY SYSTEM, INDIAN) to undermine British influence. From ca. 1815 to 1834, J.J. Astor dominated the Great Lakes fur trade with his AMERICAN FUR COMPANY.

Rocky Mountains. During the early 19th c., most attractive fur-trading area. The St. Louis Fur Co. (founded 1809) and the Missouri Fur Co. (founded 1814) extended their operations as far west as Montana. In 1824 traders of the Rocky Mountain Fur Co. struck out boldly into the mountains and inaugurated the famous rendezvous (see TRAPPERS' RENDEZVOUS) at such places as Jackson's Hole and Pierre's Hole. The Rocky Mountain Fur Co. eventually lost out to Astor's American Fur Co., which thereafter dominated the area.

Southeast and Lower Mississippi. The English were already on the Cumberland and Tennessee rivers when La Salle claimed the Mississippi Valley for France in 1682, but by 1717 the French had won over all important

Indian tribes except the Cherokee and had deprived the Carolina traders of half their Indian traffic. By the 1730s the English had recovered some of their lost trade. After French expulsion from the Mississippi Valley in 1763, British traders controlled the trade until American independence. The Louisiana Purchase (1803) brought the fur trade in New Orleans under US control, the War of 1812 loosened the hold of the British traders at Mobile and Pensacola, and the acquisition of the Floridas in 1821 brought the entire southeastern fur trade into American hands.

FUTURE FARMERS OF AMERICA. Youth organization, founded 1928, to encourage young people to enter farming, to develop knowledge and skills useful in agriculture, and to encourage good citizenship.

GABRIEL'S INSURRECTION (1800). A conspiracy of Gabriel and other slaves near Richmond, Va., to seek freedom; the conspirators were arrested before they could strike.

GADSDEN, FORT. Built by Gen. Andrew Jackson on the E bank of the Apalachicola R near its mouth, during his invasion of Florida (1818). Maintained by US through the rest of the Spanish occupancy.

GADSDEN PURCHASE (1853). Strip of land bought by the US from Mexico; comprises S Arizona and S New Mexico. Named for James Gadsden, US ambassador, who negotiated the treaty.

GAG RULE, ANTISLAVERY (May 26, 1836). Adopted by the House of Representatives to hold back the flood of antislavery petitions being introduced.

GAINES, FORT. Erected 1822 in Mobile Bay. Seized (1861) and held by the Confederacy until recaptured by Union troops in 1864. Abandoned 1898.

GAINES CASE. One of America's longest lawsuits, instituted 1834 by Myra Clark Whitney (later Gaines) to recover property in New Orleans from the estate of her father. Settled (1894) after her death; heirs received almost $2 million from the city.

GAINES' MILLS, BATTLE (June 27, 1862). Engagement near Mechanicsville, Va. Confederate forces forced the withdrawal of Union troops to the S side of the Chickahominy R.

GAINES' TRACE. Indian trail made into a highway (1810) to connect Tennessee and Tombigbee rivers and bypass Spanish revenue officers at Mobile.

GALENA-DUBUQUE MINING DISTRICT. Lead was first mined in SW Wisconsin, NW Illinois, and Iowa in 1690. From 1788 to 1810, the Fox Indians permitted mining. Lead ore was floated downstream on flatboats. In first quarter of 19th c., output was 472 million pounds, valued at $14.2 million.

GALLEY BOATS. Small shiplike craft of the Ohio R, designed to use both sails and oars and used for military purposes. Originally built by the French and Spanish, they were adopted by the Americans.

GALLIPOLIS. Ohio settlement founded 1790 by French immigrants known as the French Five Hundred, who held fraudulent land titles from the Scioto Land Co. On Ohio R about three miles below mouth of Great Kanawha R. (See FRENCH GRANTS.)

GALLOWAY'S PLAN OF UNION. Submitted 1774 by Joseph Galloway to the Continental Congress. Called for settling problems with England by establishing an American legislature with a president-general appointed by the king. Narrowly rejected by Congress.

GALVANIZED YANKEES. Confederate prisoners of war who were given their freedom in exchange for taking an oath of allegiance and enlisting in the Union army. About 6,000 enrolled in six regiments, which served on the western frontier.

GALVESTON. Texas island city, an important seaport on the Gulf of Mexico. A piratical center in the early 19th c., became the base for the Texas navy during the republic and later was a US naval base. Pop.: 61,902 (1980).

GALVESTON, LOSS AND RECAPTURE (1862–63).The Union navy ousted the Confederates from Galveston island in late 1862. Confederate forces retook the port city on Jan. 1, 1863.

GALVESTON PIRATES. Operated in the Gulf of Mexico in the early 19th c. Claiming to be privateers engaged by the revolutionary government of Mexico, they were in fact pirates and slave traders. Jean Lafitte was the most famous. US navy ended their activities in 1821.

GALVESTON STORM (Sept. 8, 1900). Tropical cyclone and tidal wave that devastated Galveston, Tex., killing 7,000 persons.

GAMBLING. By 1750 lotteries were an integral part of public financing, being used by municipalities, churches, public utility companies, and schools. Most were abolished after 1830 and were not generally used again until the 1960s, when New Hampshire and New York, followed by other states, introduced state lotteries. Horse-racing betting both at the races and off-track is an important source of revenue in a number of states. Nevada legalized all forms of gambling in 1931, with Las Vegas and Reno becoming major centers. New Jersey legalized it in Atlantic City in the late 1970s. Illegal gambling has long been an important activity. Faro, roulette, poker, and craps entered America through New Orleans, where the first houses were opened ca. 1803. Gambling and the professional sharper spread throughout the West, the most spectacular being the riverboat gamblers. In 1850 an estimated 2,000 sharpers worked the boats between New Orleans and St. Louis. Saratoga Springs, N. Y., was a noted gambling center in the 19th c.

GARCÍA, MESSAGE TO. President McKinley, during the Spanish-American War, used Lt. A.S. Rowan to find the Cuban revolutionary general Calixto García Íñiguez. Rowan succeeded and returned with messages *from* García. Exploit came to symbolize overcoming great odds to achieve a goal.

GARDENING. Early settlers quickly adapted Indian forms of gardening to achieve self-sufficiency. Greenhouse gardening began in the early 18th c. but achieved commercial importance only in the 19th c., with the production of lettuce, cucumbers, and tomatoes. During wartime, the government often has encouraged family gardening; in World War II, 43 percent of fresh vegetables were grown in "victory gardens." Organic gardening (i.e., without use of pesticides or other chemicals) increased in the 1970s.

Settlers adapted European models for their flower gardens: Spanish walled patio gardens in the Southwest and Florida and formal English gardens in New England and Virginia. Shipments of roses to America predate 1700, and American growers, including George Washington, developed new varieties.

GARDINER AWARD. Treaty of Guadalupe Hidalgo (1848), granted about $600,000 to G.A. Gardiner and his associates for claims against Mexico. They were later proved fraudulent, and Gardiner committed suicide. (See also AMERICAN-MEXICAN MIXED CLAIMS COMMISSIONS.)

GARDINERS ISLAND. Lies between the north and south forks of eastern Long Island, N. Y. Bought by Lion Gardiner in 1639 from the Indians; later confirmed by proprietary grant. Island still owned by the Gardiners.

GARFIELD-BLAINE-CONKLING CONTROVERSY. Patronage dispute involving President Hayes, his spokesman and successor, James A. Garfield, Garfield's secretary of state, James A. Blaine, and Sen. Roscoe Conkling of New York. Conkling accused the others of reneging on campaign promises and resigned his seat and vainly sought vindication by reelection. It was to avenge this "injustice to Conkling" that C.J. Guitreau assassinated President Garfield.

GARLAND CASE, 4 Wallace 333–39 (1867). Supreme Court ruled unconstitutional a federal law requiring attorneys to swear that they had not borne arms against the US or served in a government hostile to it. Court said law was a bill of attainder and ex post facto.

GARRISON MOB (Oct. 14, 1835). Abolitionist editor William Lloyd Garrison was attacked by mob in Boston and nearly killed.

GARY. Steel-producing city in Indiana, founded on Lake Michigan in 1906 by the United States Steel Corporation. Mills were largest in the world for thirty years. Pop.: 151,953 (1980).

GAS, NATURAL, INDUSTRY. See NATURAL GAS INDUSTRY.

GAS IN WARFARE. See CHEMICAL WARFARE.

GASOLINE TAXES. First imposed in 1919 by Oregon, Colorado, and New Mexico to fund highway building. By 1930, all the states had imposed them, and in 1932 the federal government levied them. In 1956, the Highway Trust Fund was created as a repository and disbursing agent for the tax monies.

GASPÉE, BURNING OF THE (June 9, 1772). Citizens of Rhode Island burned the British ship which was involved in antismuggling operations.

GASTONIA RIOTS (1929). Labor strife in Gastonia, N.C., resulted in the death of the chief of police and, reportedly, seven strikers. Union leader Fred E. Beal and six others were convicted of murder. All fled to Russia.

GATLING GUN. Patented 1862 by Richard J. Gatling. First conspicuous use in Spanish-American War. Its six to ten barrels, arranged in a circle, were revolved by a crank. Could fire up to 400 rounds per minute. Superseded by the machine gun.

GAUNTLET, RUNNING THE. When a captive warrior was brought to an Iroquois village, the women and children, armed with sticks, formed two lines between which the prisoner was required to run; if he survived the ordeal, he was often permitted to live. First reported in 1647.

GENERAL ARMSTRONG. In 1814, during the War of 1812, US privateer *General Armstrong* was destroyed by the British while in port in the Azores. US pressed claims for damages against Portugal. Settled later by Napoleon III, acting as arbitrator, who found for Portugal.

GENERAL COURT, COLONIAL. Governing body of Massachusetts Bay colony, consisting of the governor, eighteen assistants, and the freemen of the colony. Met four times a year to exercise mostly legislative powers. Other New England colonies adopted variations.

GENERAL ELECTRIC RESEARCH LABORATORY. Established Schenectady, N. Y., 1900, under the auspices of the General Electric Co. Research gave General Electric a powerful position in the lamp industry and encouraged the establishment of similar laboratories

by other companies. By 1975, the laboratory had staff of 1,000.

GENERAL ORDER NO. 38 (April 13, 1863). Issued by Union Gen. A.E. Burnside, forbade expressing sympathy for the Confederacy within Department of the Ohio. C.L. Vallandigham, the Copperhead leader, was convicted under it. (See VALLANDIGHAM INCIDENT.)

GENERAL ORDER NO. 100. See CIVIL WAR GENERAL ORDER NO. 100.

GENERAL TIME CONVENTION. See AMERICAN RAILWAY ASSOCIATION.

GENERAL WELFARE CLAUSE. Article 1, Section 8, of the US Constitution grants to Congress the "Power to lay and collect Taxes, Duties, Imposts and Excises, to pay the Debts and provide for the common Defence and general Welfare of the United States." Whether the welfare clause has a content independent of the other enumerated powers has long been in dispute. Since the 1930s, the courts have generally given Congress wide latitude in how it defines the clause.

GENESEE ROAD. Built in 1797 to cross New York from Fort Schuyler to Geneva. Later became part of the Mohawk route to the West.

GENETICS. First used to describe fields of heredity, variation, and evolution, has come to encompass cytological and biochemical aspects of heredity. Major 20th-c. developments, largely in the US, include the chromosome theory of heredity, the theory of the gene, the chemical basis of heredity, the double-helix model of the gene, the genetic control of protein synthesis, the genetic code, the regulation of gene action, and gene splicing.

GENETICS, APPLIED. Following the rediscovery of the Mendelian theory, a vigorous eugenics movement sprang up (ca. 1900) to try to improve national heredity. Feeblemindedness became the object of reform of the eugenicists, many of whom defined heredity in terms of middle-class values and racial strains. Becoming identified with racist and anti-immigration campaigns, the eugenicists were scientifically discredited by the 1920s. H.J. Muller's discovery (1926) that genes could be altered by external application of radiation gave new scientific impetus to applied genetics. The possibility of applying knowledge of genetics took on a new dimension with the discovery of the chemical processes involved in heredity. Moral and religious considerations have caused genetic engineering to be approached warily by the scientific community, particularly gene splicing.

GENÊT MISSION. Citizen Edmond Charles Édouard Genêt, appointed minister from revolutionary France to the US in 1792, became involved in the domestic quarrel between Alexander Hamilton and Thomas Jefferson, the latter his friend. Violated neutrality by outfitting privateers. US government demanded his recall but permitted him unofficial residence.

GENEVA ACCORDS OF 1954. Series of agreements reached between France and the Vietnamese communist forces led by Ho Chi Minh. Ended first Indochina War. Called for a cease-fire and temporarily divided Vietnam into two zones separated by a demilitarized area. French and Vietminh forces were to be removed from Laos and Cambodia, who were to pledge to remain neutral. The "temporary" zones of Vietnam solidified into North Vietnam and South Vietnam. Their continued enmity led to VIETNAM WAR.

GENEVA CONFERENCES. Various international meetings held at Geneva, Switzerland. The first such was the GENEVA THREE-POWER NAVAL CONFERENCE of 1927. In 1932–34 there was a general disarmament conference attended by fifty-eight nations; it concentrated on land armaments. Virtually nothing was accomplished. In 1947 an international tariff conference resulted in the General Agreement on Trade and Tariffs (GATT). The GENEVA ACCORDS OF 1954 came out of an international conference aimed at ending the Indochina War. A summit conference of 1955 among the major powers resulted in President Eisenhower's proposal for an "open skies" aerial reconnaissance system for the verification of arms reductions. No agreements came out of the conference. In 1961 a conference met to try to resolve the conflict in Laos; it resulted in the establishment of a neutral coalition government. The US also participated in a series of conferences on the international control of nuclear weapons, held intermittently since 1958; they helped prepare the way for the Nuclear Test Ban Treaty (1963), the Nuclear Nonproliferation Treaty (1968), and the SALT I Treaty (Strategic Arms Limitation Treaty, 1972).

GENEVA CONVENTIONS. International agreements for the humane treatment of prisoners of war, especially the sick and wounded. The first Geneva Convention (1864), ratified by most western nations, dealt only with field armies. An 1868 convention expanded the earlier agreement to include naval warfare. Revised and expanded regularly since; the 1949 revision increased the coverage to include noncombatants in wartime.

GENEVA THREE-POWER NAVAL CONFERENCE (1927). Called by President Coolidge, included Great Britain and Japan. (France and Italy declined.) Attempted unsuccessfully to impose a limit on the tonnage of naval ships.

GENIZARO. Non-Pueblo Indians who lived in the Spanish style in 18th-c. New Mexico. Many were Plains Indians who had been captured and turned into servants. Adopting Christianity and the Spanish language, they were settled in Santa Fe and in separate villages.

GENTLEMEN'S AGREEMENT. In diplomatic circles, an informal agreement between two countries, not formalized by a written treaty. A famous example was the 1907 agreement under which President Theodore Roosevelt promised good treatment for Japanese residents in the US in return for a promise that Japan would prevent further immigration to the US.

GENTRIFICATION. Process whereby housing in rundown urban neighborhoods is bought, rehabilitated, and occupied by members of the middle class. The practice became prevalent in the 1970s as former slums were reclaimed. Opponents have argued that the process displaces the poor, minorities, and the elderly.

GEOGRAPHER'S LINE. Begun 1785 by Thomas Hutchins, geographer of the US, it began at the point at which the Pennsylvania boundary intersected the Ohio R and ran due W for forty-two miles. Every six miles, at right angles to the line, the meridians marking the boundaries of the Seven Ranges were drawn, while parallel to it, at six-mile intervals, east-west lines were drawn to complete the township boundaries.

GEOLOGICAL SURVEY, UNITED STATES. Bureau of the Department of the Interior, established 1879. In 1882 launched program to make a national map; goal remains unattained as the demand for maps of larger scale and greater accuracy has diverted funds from the general project. The survey has made important contributions to both theoretical and practical geology. Broad objectives of the bureau include survey, investigations, and research covering topography, geology, and the mineral and water resources of the US.

GEOLOGICAL SURVEYS, STATE. North Carolina began a geological survey in 1824; South Carolina sponsored an examination of its minerals and strata in 1825. Other states initiated their own surveys in the 1830s; by the beginning of the Civil War, nearly every state had a geological survey done or in progress. State geologists were responsible for the establishment (1848) of the American Association for the Advancement of Science. Before the rise of universities, offered significant employment to American scientists.

GEOPHYSICAL EXPLORATION. In the 19th c., geophysics represented an informal alliance of three scientific groups. Planetary astronomy addressed such problems as the formation, age, and structure of the earth; "dynamical" geology attempted to explain earth processes in terms of mechanics and physical laws; and mining engineering provided technical training in metallurgy, mathematics, and physics. In the exploration of the American West, G.K. Gilbert framed geological observations into rational systems of natural laws organized on the principle of dynamic equilibrium. C.E. Dutton conceived the idea of isostasy, or the gravitational equilibrium of the earth's crust. Others applied geochemical and geophysical analysis to the problems of orogeny and igneous ore formation. G.F. Becker specifically attempted mathematical and mechanical models to describe ore genesis and the distribution of stress in the earth's crust. Glacial movements were related to astrophysical cycles, thereby providing common ground for geology, geophysics, astronomy, and meteorology. After World War II, new techniques and instruments were developed for mining and military purposes. Oceanography, with a theoretical topic (continental drift) to organize its research, thrived. Exploration after the 1950s was exemplified by specific projects, such as the International Geophysical Year, Project Mohole (for drilling into the interior of the earth), the Joint Oceanographic Institutes Deep Earth Sampling Program, the International Upper Mantle Project, and the Geodynamics Project (an international attempt to discover the force behind crustal movements).

GEORGE, FORT. On the Canadian side of the Niagara R at its entrance into Lake Ontario. Captured by the Americans in 1813 as part of the plan to capture York (now Toronto) but forced to evacuate after failure of expedition against Montreal.

GEORGE WASHINGTON. Arriving in Algiers in 1800 with the annual tribute paid to the dey of Algiers, the *George Washington* was ordered to carry gifts to the sultan of Turkey. After this humiliation, President Jefferson issued orders for defensive and offensive measures against the dey (SEE BARBARY WARS).

GEORGIA. Youngest of the original colonies, Georgia was founded as a buffer against Spanish Florida and French Louisiana; to produce silks and other special raw materials; to rehabilitate the debtors of London; and to offer a refuge for persecuted Protestants. Chartered 1732, the colony comprised that territory between the Savannah and Altamaha rivers and lines drawn due west from their headwaters to the Pacific. Savannah was settled in 1733 and opposition by Spain led to the WAR OF JENKINS' EAR (1739–44). The British captured Savannah in 1778, and much of Georgia remained in British hands during the Revolution. Georgia ratified the Constitution on Jan. 2, 1788; but until the 1838 removal of the Indians it argued with the federal government over the rights of the Creek and Cherokee and its boundaries. Chattahoochee R accepted as western boundary. For a time the world's greatest cotton-producing region. Seceded Jan. 19, 1861; but escaped the war until 1864, when Gen. W.T. Sherman made his devastating march from Atlanta to the sea. Readmitted to the Union in 1868, but its expulsion of blacks from the legislature led to a second Reconstruction phase, which ended only in 1870. After Reconstruction, a conservative machine, known as the Bourbon triumvirate, dominated the state until 1890. A registration law of 1908 effectively eliminated the black voter and consolidated the power of the Democratic party. Political control of the state remained in the hands of conservative, rural, white voters until the elimination of the white primary in 1945. Thereafter, there was a rapid increase in the number of black voters, most of whom became Democrats. The civil rights acts of the 1960s solidified black voting, and the number of black officeholders increased. Economic recovery was slow following Reconstruction. Until World War II, Georgia's industries were largely engaged in primary processing, particularly in lumber and textiles. Cotton began to lose its hegemony under the New Deal, and after ca. 1950, livestock, grain, poultry, and forest products became dominant in the state's agriculture, as mechanization increased and landholdings grew in size. Many new industries appeared, particularly in the Atlanta area, which became the symbol of the so-called New South. Pop.: 5,464,265 (1980).

GEORGIA. Confederate cruiser purchased in Scotland in 1863. In seven months captured or destroyed nine vessels. Eventually sold at Liverpool.

GEORGIA, PURITAN MIGRATION TO. Descendants of the Puritans who arrived in Massachusetts in 1630. In 1695 moved to South Carolina and from there to a grant at Dorchester, Georgia, in 1752. Consisted of about 350 whites and 1,500 slaves.

GEORGIA, SOUTHERN BOUNDARY OF. By its original charter, Georgia's southern boundary was the Altamaha R; but in 1763 the boundary was extended S to the St. Marys R and to a straight line joining the source of the river with the confluence of the Flint and Chattahoochee. Spain accepted the boundary in PINCKNEY'S TREATY of 1795. But Georgia rejected the boundary and claimed 2,500 square miles more to the south. Accepted original survey in the 1860s.

GEORGIA, SPANISH MISSIONS IN. Beginning in 1569, seven missions were founded, including ones at Apalache (1632) and Sábacola on the Chattahoochee (1681). Attacks by Indians, slave traders, and Caribbean pirates were a constant threat. In 1702, South Carolina began a drive against the missions and by 1703 they had effectively been destroyed.

GEORGIA, WAYNE'S OPERATIONS IN (1782). After the British surrender at Yorktown (October 1781), Gen. Anthony Wayne was sent south to eliminate the British in Georgia. Savannah was surrendered to the Americans on July 12, 1782, peace having been voted by Parliament.

GEORGIA COMPACT (Apr. 24, 1802). Provided for the cession of Georgia's western lands on several conditions, chiefly that the US would pay Georgia $1.25 million out of the proceeds of the land sales and extinguish the Indian title to land in Georgia (see CHEROKEE NATION V. GEORGIA).

GEORGIA LAND LOTTERY SYSTEM. Method by which Georgia disposed of its public land 1803–31. In general, all Georgia men twenty-one years of age, widows, and orphans were eligible for the draw and war veterans were awarded an extra draw. The land was divided into lots, generally of 202.5 acres, and the drawer was entitled to pay a fee of from $15 to $20 per lot.

GEORGIA-MISSISSIPPI COMPANY. In 1795 was granted 12 million acres between the Mississippi and Tombigbee rivers. In 1796, sold out to Massachusetts speculators, who organized the New England Mississippi Co. Chief contender with Congress for a settlement of the dispute of ownership (see YAZOO FRAUD).

GEORGIANA. Proposed colony (1763) to be established on the Mississippi R, S of the Ohio R, to be settled by veterans of the French and Indian War. A few hundred families from New England settled around Natchez, but they secured only squatters' rights. No charter ever issued.

GEORGIA PLATFORM. Adopted 1850, it accepted the Compromise of 1850 but warned against further encroachments on the rights of the South.

GEORGIA RAILROAD. See RAILROADS, SKETCHES OF PRINCIPAL LINES: WESTERN AND ATLANTIC RAILROAD.

GEORGIA V. STANTON, 6 Wallace 50 (1867). The Supreme Court ruled in favor of the military government of Georgia, thereby upholding the Reconstruction Acts of Congress.

GERMAINE GIRL CAPTIVES. Four children captured by the Cheyenne. Two were recaptured in Texas on Nov. 8, 1874. Gen. N.A. Miles threatened annihilation if the other two were not returned. The Cheyenne obeyed.

GERMAN-AMERICAN BUND. Founded 1932 among German-Americans, it became blatantly pro-Nazi in the late 1930s.

GERMAN-AMERICAN DEBT AGREEMENT. Settlement in 1930 of Germany's World War I debts. The US accepted noninterest-bearing bonds totaling $247 million. After making payment of $65 million, Germany suspended payment.

GERMAN COAST. See CÔTE DES ALLEMANDS.

GERMAN FLATS. Area in New York state, near the present village of Herkimer, granted ca. 1723 for settlement to the Palatines as a protection against the French. In 1757, about 200 residents were killed by an attack by the French and Indians. Ten miles were laid waste in 1778.

GERMAN MERCENARIES (or Hessians). In the American Revolution, troops hired by Great Britain from several German princes. Almost 30,000 fought against the colonists.

GERMANTOWN. Town in Pennsylvania, founded 1683 by German Quakers and Mennonites, who purchased 25,000 acres near Philadelphia.

GERMANTOWN, BATTLE OF (Oct. 4, 1777). Early encounter in the American Revolution between Gen. George Washington and the British force of Gen. Charles Cornwallis, which was occupying Philadelphia. Washington's daring and strategy impressed Europe and helped gain the aid of France.

GERMANY, AMERICAN OCCUPATION OF. Begun when US troops crossed the German border (Sept. 11, 1944) and lasted until May 5, 1955, when occupation powers were relinquished to West Germany. In 1945, Germany was partitioned into four occupation zones: British, American, French, and Russian; Berlin, in the Russian zone, was also divided. Gen. Dwight D. Eisenhower became US military governor. Later the military governor was replaced by a high commissioner.

GERONIMO'S CAMPAIGNS. See APACHE WARS.

GERRYMANDER. Political machination whereby the party in power can redraw district lines so as to strengthen its own positions. Often accomplished by creating eccentrically shaped voting districts. Term first used in Massachusetts in 1812 when Gov. Elbridge Gerry sponsored a redistricting that gave the Jeffersonian Republicans a distinct advantage in the election of state senators. One such district was said to be in the shape of a salamander, derisively renamed a gerrymander.

GETTYSBURG, BATTLE OF (July 1–3, 1863). Encounter that marked the turning point in the Civil War and marked the defeat of Confederate Gen. R.E. Lee's attempt to invade Pennsylvania and reach Washington, D.C. On July 1, Union forces held Cemetery Hill, S of Gettysburg. The Confederates were unable to dislodge them. On July 3, sensing this was his only hope for victory, Lee ordered Gen. G.E. Pickett's cavalry to charge the Union center. The charge failed and the Confederate retreat began. Left dead or wounded were 20,000 Confederate and 23,000 Union troops.

GETTYSBURG ADDRESS (Nov. 19, 1863). Delivered by President Lincoln at the dedication of the national cemetery at Gettysburg, Pa. Legend has it that Lincoln wrote the speech while traveling by train, but actually it was completed in Washington; only minor changes were made en route to Gettysburg. One of the great speeches in history.

GHENT, TREATY OF (1814). Ended the War of 1812. American rights in the Newfoundland fisheries were acknowledged; both parties agreed to discourage the slave trade; and commissions were appointed to settle outstanding boundary disputes.

GHOST DANCE. A nativistic movement that originated in 1869 among the Paiute Indians of Nevada. A prophet named Wodziwob predicted that the world would end, after which all dead Indians would return to rebuild the world. His followers danced in a circle and sang divinely revealed songs. The movement spread throughout the West, but subsided. Resurgence in 1889, when the prophet Wovoka announced that by singing and dancing the Indians would make the white man disappear. It spread among the Plains tribes and became a militant movement among former warriors confined on reservations.

GI. American servicemen in World War II, derived from the initials for "government issue" stamped on uniforms and other equipment supplied by the army.

GIBBONS V. OGDEN, 9 Wheaton 1 (1824). In a monopoly dispute involving conflicting state and federal laws, Chief Justice John Marshall interpreted the term "commerce" so broadly as to give Congress the right to regulate interstate commerce.

GI BILL OF RIGHTS. Popular name for the Servicemen's Readjustment Act of 1944. It provided World War II veterans with vocational rehabilitaion; loans for housing, farms, and businesses; veterans' hospitals; and fees and living expenses for up to four years of education. Variations of the GI Bill were passed for veterans of the Korean and Vietnam wars.

GIBSON, FORT. Established 1824 in Indian Territory (Oklahoma) on the Neosho R near its confluence with the Arkansas. Abandoned 1891.

GIBSON GIRL. Idealized American woman as depicted by artist Charles Dana Gibson at the turn of the century.

GIBSON-LINN EPISODE (1776–77). Successful effort by two American officers (George Gibson and William Linn, posing as traders) to buy gunpowder secretly from the Spanish authorities at New Orleans for use by colonial troops.

GIDDINGS RESOLUTIONS (1842). A series of antislavery resolutions proposed by Congressman J.R. Giddings. When censured by the House, he resigned his seat and was reelected.

GIDEON SOCIETY. Organization for Christian travelers, founded 1899. Best known for placing Bibles in hotel rooms.

GIDEON V. WAINWRIGHT, 372 US 335 (1963). The Supreme Court ruled that in all felony cases, the defendant is entitled to counsel.

GILA TRAIL. Early trade route to the West. There were several alternate courses, following the Gila R and its branches. Used by early Spanish explorers, trappers, and by emigrants to California. The Southern Pacific RR laid out on some of the routes.

GILBERT ISLANDS. Occupied by the Japanese early in World War II. Recaptured by US marines in November 1943 in one of the bloodiest operations of the war.

GILBERT'S PATENT. Issued by Queen Elizabeth I to Sir Humphrey Gilbert in 1578. He failed in his attempt to plant a colony in Newfoundland and was lost at sea (1583). His half-brother, Sir Walter Raleigh, inherited the patent.

GILDED AGE. Period between the end of the Civil War and the Panic of 1873, exemplified by widespread speculation, loose business and political morals, and flashy life styles. Title came from an 1873 novel by Mark Twain and Charles Dudley Warner.

GINSENG, AMERICAN (*Panax quinquefolium*). Relative to the Oriental root to which the Chinese impute extraordinary powers. From the 18th c., it has been exported to China. Wisconsin principal US producer.

GIRL SCOUTS OF THE UNITED STATES OF AMERICA. Founded 1912 by Juliette Gordon Low. Girls share in activites that emphasize development of awareness, values, relating to others, and contributing to the betterment of society. Programs are arranged in four ascending age groups: Brownies, Junior Girl Scouts, Cadettes, and Senior Girl Scouts.

GIST, TRAVELS AND JOURNALS OF. Christopher Gist explored the Ohio Valley from 1750–52 and published a journal of his exploits. He also kept a journal of his expedition with George Washington to Fort Le Boeuf in 1853.

"GIVE ME LIBERTY OR GIVE ME DEATH!" Cry made by Patrick Henry in 1775 urging Virginians to organize a militia preparatory to fighting for independence.

GLACIER NATIONAL PARK. Established 1910 in the Rocky Mountains, in N Montana. Its 1 million acres include extensive areas for the preservation of wildlife. Adjoins Canadian Waterton Lakes National Park.

GLASGOW, ACTION AT (Oct. 15, 1864). During Confederate Gen. Sterling Price's expedition into Missouri, his forces captured the Union garrison and supplies.

GLASSBORO SUMMIT CONFERENCE (June 1967). Between Soviet Premier A.N. Kosygin and President Lyndon B. Johnson. Held at Glassboro State College, N. J. Chief topic was the Middle East.

GLASSMAKING. There were successful glass houses in the 18th c. in Pennsylvania, New Jersey, and Maryland. Improved techniques for pressed glass in the early 19th c. at factories in Pittsburgh, Boston, and Sandwich, Mass., resulted in lower prices, making glass accessible to everyone. By the 1850s, European processes were emulated by US manufacturers, and new methods were introduced, notably by Michael Owens, whose bottle machines (developed 1899–1903) revolutionized the beverage industry. Plate glass made possible a change in architectural styles. The Corning Glass Works developed the ribbon machine, capable of producing up to 2,000 light bulbs per minute. Safety glass was developed for the automobile industry. Art glass was chiefly represented by the studio of Louis C. Tiffany and the factory of the Steuben Glass Co.

GLASS-STEAGALL ACT (1932). An emergency banking measure aimed at saving banks at the beginning of the Great Depression. The Banking Act of 1933 is also sometimes known as the Glass-Steagall Act.

GLEBES. Lands set aside for the clergy in the American colonies, in pursuance of English tradition.

GLIDERS, MILITARY. Weapon system unique to World War II, first used by Germans in 1940 and adopted by British and American operations. Gliders made possible the delivery of armed troops and heavy material that could not be dropped by parachute. The largest Allied glider mission (Sept. 1944) employed 2,596 gliders to secure a bridgehead across the Rhine at Arnhem.

GLORIETA, BATTLE OF (March 28, 1862). Encounter on the Santa Fe Trail, a turning point for the Civil War in the Far West. Union forces attacked from the rear, destroying the Confederate baggage and supply train. Survivors forced to retreat to Santa Fe and down the Rio Grande.

GNADENHUTTEN. A Delaware village on the Tuscarawas R in Ohio. Founded 1772 by Christian Indians and Moravian missionaries. Colonials were suspicious of the pacifism of the village and in attempting to destroy it and remove the Indians, March 7, 1782, militiamen executed about a hundred men, women, and children.

GNP. see GROSS NATIONAL PRODUCT.

GODEY'S LADY'S BOOK. Influential woman's magazine published 1830–92, dealing in matters of fashions, etiquette, and home economics.

GOEBEL AFFAIR. After a close election, the Republican W.S. Taylor was declared governor of Kentucky over the Democrat William Goebel. Goebel's mountaineer supporters marched on the capital in protest. On Jan. 30, 1900, Goebel was shot by an unidentified rifleman. The legislature declared him elected, and he was sworn in on January 31 but died on February 3.

GOLD ACT (June 17, 1864). Aimed at speculators, made it unlawful to buy or sell foreign exchange to be delivered after ten days. Caused great fluctuation in price of gold and was repealed on July 2.

GOLD BUGS. Free silverites' name for those in favor of the gold standard in the 1896 presidential campaign.

GOLD CLAUSE CASES. After the US government went off the GOLD STANDARD in 1933, suits were brought demanding that notes be paid in gold, as specified by contract. Supreme Court ruled in favor of Congress' right to abrogate the gold clause and "coin money and regulate the value thereof."

GOLD DEMOCRATS. Faction rejecting the radical free-silver platform of William Jennings Bryan in the 1896 election. J.M. Palmer, their presidential candidate, received only 134,635 votes.

GOLDEN GATE BRIDGE. Completed 1937, crosses entrance of harbor at San Francisco. The central span is 4,200 feet long.

GOLDEN HILL, BATTLE OF (Jan. 19, 1770). Clash between Liberty Boys and British soldiery in New York City.

GOLDEN HIND. Ship of Sir Francis Drake that circumnavigated the globe (1577–80).

GOLD EXCHANGE. Gold market in New York City, founded 1862. Traded gold certificates of deposit until US resumed gold redemption in 1879.

GOLD HOARDS, FEDERAL. In 1933, gold coin was recalled from circulation. Federal Reserve banks were required to exchange gold for credits or noncirculating gold certificates. Safeguarding of the entire gold reserve fell to the federal government, which created the Fort Knox gold depository (1936).

GOLD IN CALIFORNIA. Gold was discovered at Sutter's Mill in 1848, setting off rush to California and the gold fields.

GOLD MINES AND MINING. Between 1799 and 1848, about $24.5 million in gold was mined in North Carolina and Georgia. The first decade of California mining, 1848–58, saw some $550 million in gold extracted. The California mines were placer deposits of gold mixed with sand and gravel. In 1859 the Comstock lode was discovered in Nevada. Gold camps were established in Idaho, Montana, South Dakota, and Colorado. The Alaska mines were first worked in the 1880s. New chemical processes were developed to extract the ore, and such new explosives as nitroglycerine and dynamite used. Production reached its highest levels in the decade 1905–15; an average of more than 4 million fine ounces was produced yearly. In 1980, 951,000 fine ounces were produced, most of it from Nevada, South Dakota, Utah, and Arizona.

GOLD PURCHASE PLAN (1933). The Reconstruction Finance Corporation was authorized to buy gold newly mined in the US at prices to be determined in consultation with the president and secretary of the treasury. The initial price was $31.36 per ounce and had risen to $34.45 by 1934, when the price was fixed at $35 per ounce.

GOLD REPEAL JOINT RESOLUTION (June 5, 1933). Congress canceled the gold clauses in public and private debts, which had required the debtor to repay the creditor in gold dollars.

GOLD RESERVE ACT (Jan. 30, 1934). Congress nationalized all gold by ordering the Federal Reserve banks to turn over their supply to the US Treasury, receiving gold certificates in return. The act also authorized devaluation of the gold dollar, which was fixed at 59.06 cents.

GOLD STANDARD. The Redemption Act of 1875, by making paper dollars redeemable in gold by 1879, formally put the nation on the gold standard. The unit of value was the gold dollar, which contained 23.22 grains of pure gold; an ounce of gold could be coined into $20.67, the "mint price" of gold. The gold standard was strengthened by the Gold Standard Act of 1900. Remained basic system until end of gold standard in 1933. Gold far from stable in value. But more stable than silver; its historical record was much better than that of paper money. A worldwide shortage of gold meant that most nations could not afford to go on a gold standard; instead, they utilized the gold exchange standard, which in effect made them dependent on the gold-standard central banks of Great Britain, France, and the US. The entire system began collapsing in the early 1930s; bank failures in the US in 1932 severely shook public confidence in the economy and the public began to hoard gold. On March 6, 1933, President Franklin D. Roosevelt declared a bank moratorium for four days and forbade banks to pay out gold or to export it. In April the government called in all outstanding gold coins, issuing in their place gold certificates. President Roosevelt was given the power to reduce the gold content of the dollar as much as 50 percent. In 1935 the price of gold was fixed at $35 an ounce, but the actual coinage of gold was prohibited. Thus the nation went on a "qualified gold-bullion standard." After World War II, the regulations of the International Monetary Fund resulted in the US dollar being redeemable in gold, the universal reserve currency. As foreign nations demanded that their dollars be exchanged for gold, US gold reserves fell to less than $12 billion; this created unbearable pressure on the $35 per ounce price lid for gold. Finally, in 1971, President Nixon announced that the US Treasury would no longer redeem dollars in gold for any foreign treasury or central bank; that effectively took the nation off any semblance of a gold standard.

GOLD STAR MOTHERS. Organization founded 1928 by mothers of men or women who had died in military service during wartime.

GOLF. The first golf club in America was established in 1786 in Charleston, S.C. The oldest continuing golf club is St. Andrews, founded in 1888 in Westchester County, N. Y. The US Golf Association (USGA) was established 1894. Americans began dominating the international competitions in the 1920s with such champions as Bobby Jones and Walter Hagen. The Masters Tournament, played at Augusta, Ga., became a major world competition.

GOLIAD, MASSACRE AT (March 27, 1836). Col. J.W. Fannin, Jr., of the Texas army surrendered his force of about 400 men near Goliad, Tex. The Mexicans regarded them as pirates and executed them.

GONZALES, BATTLE OF (Oct. 2, 1835). First battle of Texas Revolution. Mexican force sent to capture a cannon at Gonzales, Tex., was routed a few miles away.

GOOD NEIGHBOR POLICY. Latin American policy enunciated by President Franklin D. Roosevelt in 1933. Its most important point was the US pledge not to intervene militarily in countries of the Western Hemisphere.

GOODNIGHT-LOVING TRAIL. Cattle trail starting near Fort Belknap, Tex., running SW and W to the Pecos R and then up the Pecos to Fort Sumner, N. M., where the cattle were sold. An extension continued N to Denver and Cheyenne. In use after 1866.

GORE-MCLEMORE RESOLUTIONS (1916). Proposed congressional resolution warning US citizens against traveling on armed vessels because of German intentions to attack them. President Wilson considered the resolution an intrusion, and it was tabled.

GORGES' PROVINCE OF MAINE. Grant awarded Ferdinando Gorges in 1639. Unsuccessfully attempted to establish a feudal regime. Incorporated Agamenticus as market and borough town in 1641 and the city of Gorgeana in 1642. Province neglected after Gorges' death (1647). In 1678 his heirs sold out to Massachusetts Bay Colony. Province became York County.

GORTONITES. Rhode Island disciples of Samuel Gorton, who in 1643 was banished from Massachusetts Bay for teaching a form of Antinomian mysticism.

GOTHIC LINE. In June 1944, the Germans gave up Rome to the Allies and assumed a defensive stand 150 miles north, protecting the Po Valley. Consisted of a belt of fortifications 10–12 miles deep in naturally strong defensive terrain, about 200 miles long, roughly from Carrara to Pesaro. In April 1945, US troops broke the line. Entered the valley and took Bologna on April 21. Germans surrendered on April 29.

GOVERNMENT CORPORATIONS. Public enterprises incorporated in the manner of private companies (composed of a board of directors, a general manager, and so forth) and to a large extent independent from traditional governmental supervision. (See TENNESSEE VALLEY AUTHORITY; FEDERAL DEPOSIT INSURANCE CORPORATION; US POSTAL SERVICE, for example.)

GOVERNMENT NEWSPAPERS. Private newspapers in the Washington area that benefited from government printing business before the establishment of the Government Printing Office in 1860. The contracts were part of the patronage system.

"GOVERNMENT OF THE PEOPLE, BY THE PEOPLE, AND FOR THE PEOPLE." Definition of democracy that President Lincoln incorporated in the Gettysburg Address, Nov. 19, 1863.

GOVERNMENT OWNERSHIP (sometimes called public ownership). The theory that land and natural resources belong to the whole people or to the ruler as representative of the people predates history. Eminent domain, enshrined in state and federal law, represents the principle that government may buy privately owned property for public purposes.

GOVERNMENT PRINTING OFFICE. Printing and distribution of government publications was at first undertaken by commercial publishers on a contract basis. The Government Printing Office (GPO) was established in 1860 and has gradually come to monopolize virtually all federal publishing.

GOVERNOR. Chief executive of the state governments. Early state constitutions generally called for weak governors as a result of the unpopularity of colonial, especially royal, governors. In the 20th c., most states have seen fit to increase the power of the governor, with the result that the modern governor generally has great power and responsibility.

GOVERNORS, CONFERENCES OF. The National Governors' Council was founded in 1908 and holds annual meetings. Committees decide the agenda. There are six standing committees, and there are also five regional conferences.

GOVERNORS ISLAND. Small island in New York Bay, near the S tip of Manhattan. Part of military area of New York City since 1698. Fortification built 1776. Ceded to the federal government in 1800 and Castle William and Fort Columbus (later named Fort Jay) erected. Since 1966 US coast guard headquarters for the eastern area.

"GO WEST, YOUNG MAN, GO WEST." Advice made famous by Horace Greeley in the *New York Tribune* in an editorial, July 13, 1865. The phrase had actually originated with J.B.L. Soule in 1851.

GRADUATION ACT (Aug. 3, 1854). Reduced the price of government land from $1.25 per acre to $1, graduated down in some cases to 12.5 cents per acre.

GRAFTON V. UNITED STATES (1907). Supreme Court ruled that military tribunals were equal in authority to civil courts and that thus servicemen cannot be tried in both systems for the same offense.

GRAND ARMY OF THE REPUBLIC (GAR). Association of Union veterans of the Civil War, founded 1866. Powerful lobby for benefits to veterans and their families. Its peak membership was 409,489 in 1890. The last member died in 1956.

GRAND BANKS. Undersea tableland between Newfoundland, Canada, and deep water, reaching to the latitude of Boston and E for 500 miles. By 1578, Europeans were fishing the area. Still a major world fishing ground.

GRAND CANYON. A 280-mile-long gorge of the Colorado R in Arizona, 4 to 18 miles wide and in places more than a mile deep. The Grand Canyon National Park, established in 1919, is one of the nation's premier tourist attractions.

GRANDFATHER CLAUSE. A device in southern state constitutions to prevent blacks from voting. It exempted from literacy tests lineal descendants of anyone who had the right to vote in 1867. Declared unconstitutional in 1915.

GRAND GULF, BATTLE AT (April 29, 1863). To secure a landing for army near Vicksburg, Miss., Union ironclads bombarded Confederate shore batteries to no avail. Forced to land farther downstream.

GRAND OHIO COMPANY. Formed 1769 to purchase 2.4 million acres of land ceded to the British by the Six Nations and to plant a colony on the Ohio R to be known as Pittsylvania (later changed to Vandalia). After the Revolution, reorganized as the Vandalia Co.

GRAND PORTAGE. The nine miles in Minnesota between Lake Superior and navigable waters on the Pigeon R. The name also came to be applied to the post (ca. 1780) at the lake end of the portage.

GRAND PRAIRIE. A geographical division of N Texas extending about 200 miles S from the Red R, two to three counties in width. Settlement began 1848. First important cattle-grazing region of Texas.

GRAND RAPIDS. City in Michigan, settled 1826 as a Baptist Indian mission on the site of an Indian village and trading post. Settled largely by Dutch immigrants, some of whom began the manufacture of furniture. Name synonymous with mass-produced American furniture. Pop.: 181,843 (1980).

GRAND RIVER MASSACRE. See MESSIAH WAR.

GRAND TRUNK WESTERN. See RAILROADS, SKETCHES OF PRINCIPAL LINES.

GRANGER CASES. Between 1869 and 1874, several Midwestern states passed so-called Granger laws, which regulated railroads and grain elevators within their respective boundaries. In 1877, Supreme Court ruled that such laws were within the rights of the states. In 1886, the court restricted state regulation to strictly intrastate business.

GRANGER MOVEMENT. Farmers' clubs, especially in the grain-growing region of the Middle West. By 1873, they had become the farmers' chief political lobby, especially aimed at the regulation of railroads and grain elevators (see GRANGER CASES.). Hardly less important were their business ventures: cooperative elevators, creameries, and general stores. Their efforts to manufacture farm machinery was a costly failure that contributed to the movement's decline in the late 1870s.

GRANT'S HILL, BATTLE OF (Sept. 14, 1758). British defeat at Fort Duquesne. Major James Grant, on the hill in Pittsburgh that now bears his name, was overwhelmed by French and Indian troops.

GRANTS-IN-AID. Federal grants of money to state and local governments. The first large grants (1862) were public lands, and broad use of money grants began with the New Deal. Federal grants are rarely unconditional, even REVENUE SHARING, which was devised to rid local governments of federal bureaucracy in applying for grants. Federal grants total more than $50 billion annually.

GRANVILLE GRANT. Large tract, approximately one-half of the royal colony of North Carolina, received by Lord John Carteret, later Earl Granville, in 1728. Efforts by the Granville heirs to regain the property after the American Revolution ended with an adverse Supreme Court decision in 1817.

GRASSHOPPERS. Both migratory (locusts) and nonmigratory grasshoppers have been serious problems, especially in New England in 1743, 1749, 1754, and 1756. California, Missouri, and Minnesota suffered heavily in the 1820s; the Great Plains were attacked in 1855 and particularly in the great plague of 1874–76. The plague of 1936 afflicted the Midwest, South, and especially the Great Plains. Poison bran was the chief control until the development of chlordane in the 1940s. Since then, new insecticides have kept grasshoppers in check.

GRATTAN INCIDENT (Aug. 19, 1854). Attack during the SIOUX WARS by a military detachment from Fort Laramie, Wyo., on Sioux villages. Led by Lt. J.L. Grattan, it was annihilated by the Indians.

GREAT AMERICAN DESERT. The myth that a great desert existed between the Rocky Mountains and the Missouri and Mississippi rivers persisted until the 1840s.

GREAT AWAKENING. See AWAKENING.

GREAT BASIN. A 189,000-square-mile region lying between the Wasatch Mountains on the E and the Sierra Nevada on the W, including most of Nevada and the western third of Utah.

GREAT BRIDGE, BATTLE AT (Dec. 9, 1775). The Virginia militia defeated a Loyalist force near Norfolk.

GREAT DEPRESSION. Period between 1929 and 1940. Actually began in Europe, but is usually dated from the stock market crash on Oct. 24, 1929. Businesses and banks failed, and production of goods and services dropped almost 30 percent by 1932. Unemployment rose from 1.5 million to 12.1 million. A major crisis had developed by the time Franklin D. Roosevelt initiated his NEW DEAL program.

GREAT EASTERN. Ship completed in England 1858, the largest in the world at the time. In 1866 laid first transatlantic cable.

GREAT LAKES. Largest group of lakes in the world, consisting of lakes Superior, Huron, Erie, Michigan, and Ontario. The US-Canadian border runs through all but Lake Michigan, which is entirely within the US. The French first effected a lodgment on the lower St. Lawrence R but were long barred from access to the lower lakes by hostile Iroquois. By the end of the 17th c., the French had explored and mapped all five lakes. The French founded Detroit in 1701, largely to block English access to the lakes. By the surrender of Canada in 1760 in the FRENCH AND INDIAN WAR, the British became masters of the Great Lakes. After the American Revolution, they agreed to share control with the US. During the War of 1812, the US government established naval dominance of all the lakes. The Great Lakes Disarmament Agreement of 1817 established limitations on naval forces on the lakes. Commerce and industry in the region burgeoned after the opening of the Erie Canal in 1825. Products are transported across the lakes, through the St. Lawrence Seaway and the New York State Barge Canal to Canada and the Atlantic Ocean. Commercial fishing has declined since 1945, due chiefly to industrial pollution.

GREAT LAKES, NAVAL POWER ON THE. In 1761 and 1771 the British built shipyards on the lakes and thereafter operated a navy. After 1796, both the British and the Americans maintained armed vessels. Major area of conflict during War of 1812. To prevent reoccurrence, two nations signed the Great Lakes Disarmament Agreement, limiting naval forces on the lakes (1817). It is still in force.

GREAT LAW OF PENNSYLVANIA (Dec. 7, 1682). Enacted by freeholders called together by William Penn, it established liberty of conscience, extended the suffrage, limited the death penalty, and attempted to legislate a perfectly moral state. It remained the basis of law for colonial Pennsylvania.

GREAT MASSACRE (April 1622). Inflicted on the English in Virginia by Opechancanough, Powhatan's brother and successor. Only Jamestown was saved.

GREAT MEADOWS. Site near Uniontown, Pa., the first battle of the French and Indian War. On May 27, 1754, Maj. George Washington decisively defeated a French and Indian force and erected Fort Necessity. In July it was attacked by a large enemy force. Washington capitulated and retreated to Virginia.

GREAT MIGRATION. Emigration of 60,000 persons from England during the reign (1625–49) of Charles I. About a third went to New England, where they founded Massachusetts Bay, Connecticut, and Rhode Island. Others settled in the Caribbean. Major cause was Puritan discontent, but depression in agriculture and the cloth trade contributed.

GREAT NINE PARTNERS' PATENT. Large New York land grant secured by speculators in 1692–98. Included most of the northern half of Dutchess County.

GREAT NORTHERN RAILROAD. See RAILROADS, SKETCHES OF PRINCIPAL LINES: BURLINGTON NORTHERN.

GREAT PLAINS. Region lying between the ninety-eighth meridian and the Rocky Mountains. Before white occupation, the home of the Sioux, Cheyenne, Arapaho, Pawnee, Comanche, and Apache. In the 1850s, commissioners and Indian agents made treaties with the Indians by which the tribes ceded territory, agreed to move, or gave permission for laying out roads and establishing military posts. Emigrants, including Mormons on their way to Utah and gold seekers rushing to California, poured west over its roads. By the end of the Civil War, the area was aflame with the

SIOUX WARS. During the same period, the Union Pacific and other railroads were built. Beginning in the 1860s, the region was the scene of the great range cattle industry, which declined because of the pressure of settlers, who narrowed the open range until it disappeared by the 1890s. During the 1930s, dust storms devastated large sections. Between 1930 and 1980, the rural population of the area decreased by one-third, although agricultural production increased greatly.

GREAT REVIVAL (1801). Western religious revival movement, centered in Kentucky, involving Presbyterians, Methodists, and Baptists. It was characterized by enormous camp meetings, one of which was estimated at having up to 25,000 participants. Emphasis was on emotion. Strengthened Baptist and Methodist churches, but the Presbyterians suffered schisms. Cumberland Presbyterian church dates from the period.

GREAT SALT LAKE. Located in NW Utah; 51 by 83 miles in area, averaging 25 to 30 feet in depth. Salt content ranges from 20 to 27 percent. Discovered 1824 by Jim Bridger.

GREAT SERPENT MOUND. Prehistoric Indian mound in Ohio, now a state park. It represents a crawling serpent 1,330 feet long and from 2 to 3 feet high.

GREAT SMOKY MOUNTAINS. A group of the Appalachian Mountains along the North Carolina-Tennessee border, about fifty miles in length. So-called because of the blue haze characteristic of the area.

GREAT SOCIETY. Theme of President Lyndon B. Johnson's domestic program. It included massive efforts to reduce poverty, improve education, and ameliorate the effects of racial discrimination. The program was reduced by the demands of the Vietnam War, and many of its projects were dismantled by succeeding administrations.

GREAT SPIRIT. Religious idea of a single divine being usually associated with the Algonkin-speaking peoples of the Eastern Woodlands; it may have been a Christian idea integrated into native religious pattern.

GREAT SWAMP FIGHT (Dec. 19, 1675). Engagement of KING PHILIP'S WAR at South Kings-

town, R.I.; the combined forces of Massachusetts Bay, Plymouth, and Connecticut decisively defeated the Narraganset Indians.

GREAT TRADING AND WAR PATH. Indian path that ran down the Shenandoah Valley, connecting with the warpath of the Creek Indians in Tennessee country. One of its prongs ran through the Cumberland Gap and another through Boone's Gap. A great stream of white migration flowed along it to the Southwest after 1770.

GREAT TRAIL. Indian thoroughfare leading from the Forks of the Ohio R to Detroit, passing through the present towns of Wooster, Fremont, and Toledo. During late 18th c. most important trail north of the Ohio.

GREAT VALLEY. Large area in California between the Sierra Nevada and the Coast Ranges. First explored by Jedediah Smith 1822. Today the agricultural heartland of California.

GREAT WHITE FLEET. Sixteen US battleships painted white and sent on a cruise around the world by President Theodore Roosevelt (1907–09) as a demonstration of US might.

GREELY ARCTIC EXPEDITION. Three-year (1881–84) expedition to Grinnell Land for exploration and scientific observation, led by Lt. A. W. Greely. Became marooned but a rescue mission found seven survivors, including Greely, at Cape Sabine.

GREENBACK. Popular name for the type of US note issued during the Civil War as legal tender for all but tariff duties and interest on the public debt. Depreciated during the war, they were brought to par by the Resumption Act (1875).

GREENBACK MOVEMENT. Political efforts to have the GREENBACK accepted as complete legal tender and be issued freely. It opposed the gold standard, and its strongest appeal was to debtor farmers, who had an interest in cheap money; both major parties gave it some support in their 1868 conventions. By 1872, only minor parties supported the movement and in 1876 they had coalesced into the GREENBACK PARTY. The movement was a significant predecessor of many agrarian and populist movements.

GREENBACK PARTY. Founded 1876 by members of the Greenback Movement, the Labor Reform party, and several Granger groups. Peter Cooper of New York became its candidate for president; received 80,000 votes. More than 1 million votes were cast for party candidates in 1878, by which time the party had come out in favor of free silver, a limit on the hours of labor, and reform of public land grants. James Weaver, the candidate in 1880, received 300,000 votes. Public approval of the gold standard worked against the party and its last presidential candidate was Benjamin F. Butler (1884). Members drifted into the new POPULIST PARTY.

GREEN BAY. City in Wisconsin, site of the earliest white settlement W of Lake Michigan. The French built Fort St. François Xavier in 1684. Later called Fort La Baye, it was abandoned 1760. British arrived 1761. The considerable settlement, although pro-French, took oath of allegiance to Britain. Became important fur-trade emporium. The town was pro-British in the War of 1812 and disliked the coming of the Americans and the building of Fort Howard in 1816. Modern Green Bay is an agricultural and lumbering center and produces large quantities of dairy, lumber, and paper products. Pop.: 87,889 (1980).

GREENBRIER COMPANY. Land company organized 1745, receiving a grant of 100,000 acres in the Greenbrier Valley in West Virginia. Rival to the more famous Ohio Co.

GREEN MOUNTAIN BOYS. Military company, headed by Ethan Allen, formed 1770 to protect the claims of settlers on New Hampshire grants in what is now Vermont. New York state was asserting claim over the area. Settlers under New York jurisdiction were terrorized, rude fortresses were built, and New York sheriffs were driven off. Green Mountain Boys espoused the patriot cause; declared Vermont an independent republic in 1777. In 1790, New York relinquished its claim and Vermont (the Green Mountain State) entered the Union.

GREEN RIVER. Tributary of the Colorado, in WC Wyoming. Between 1824 and 1840, a favorite meeting place of various tribes who assembled for annual exchange of pelts for trade goods.

GREENSBORO. City in NC North Carolina, center of the state's largest metropolitan area. Named in honor of Gen. Nathanael Greene, who during the American Revolution fought the Battle of Guilford Courthouse nearby. Insurance and textile center. Pop.: 155,642 (1980).

GREENVILLE, FORT (1793). One of a line of fortifications built between Cleveland and Lake Erie for protection against the Indians. In 1795 the Northwest tribes signed the Treaty of Greenville. Abandoned soon after.

GREENVILLE, TREATY OF (Aug. 3, 1795). Sequel to Gen. Anthony Wayne's defeat of the Indians at Fallen Timbers, Ohio. Negotiated by Wayne and chiefs of the Delaware, Shawnee, Wyandot, Miami Confederacy, and others; established a definite boundary between Indian lands and those open to white settlement. Much land was ceded to the US, allowing greatly increased immigration into the Northwest Territory.

GREENVILLE ACT (1764). Also known as the Sugar Act. Passed by Parliament, it imposed duties on sugar, coffee, wine, and other items imported into the colonies from foreign countries. Generally called for stricter enforcement of customs laws.

GRIERSON'S RAID (April 17 to May 2, 1863). Union Col. B.H. Grierson led a cavalry raid from La Grange, Tenn., through Mississippi, to Baton Rouge, La., to disrupt Rebel communications and transportation and to draw forces away from Vicksburg, which Gen. U.S. Grant was attacking. He covered 600 miles in 16 days.

GRIFFIN, FORT. Built 1867 on the Clear Fork of the Brazos R, in Sheckelford County, Tex., to protect border settlements from the hostile Comanche and Kiowa. In the 1870s, a trading center for buffalo-hide buyers and cattlemen; abandoned 1881.

GRIFFON. First sailing ship on the upper Great Lakes, built 1679 by the sieur de La Salle; it carried him to Green Bay. Later that year it was sent back to Niagara laden with furs; vessel and crew disappeared and their fate remains a mystery.

GROSJEAN V. AMERICAN PRESS COMPANY, 297 US 233 (1936). Supreme Court found a Louisiana license tax on newspaper advertising a violation of freedom of the press guarantees of the Constitution.

GROSS NATIONAL PRODUCT (GNP). Figure showing the value of all US goods and services produced in a given year. Includes at market prices the purchases by consumers and government organizations, private investments in US business and farm activities, and the value of all exports.

GROS VENTRE. French name for Indians of the Atsina and Hidatsa tribes.

GROVETON, BATTLE OF (Aug. 28–29, 1862). Gen. Stonewall Jackson destroyed Union stores at Manassas Junction, Va., massed his forces behind the railroad at Groveton, and attacked a Union division at Warrenton pike, allowing Gen. R.E. Lee to assemble his troops for the second Battle of Bull Run on August 30.

GUADALCANAL. Largest of the Solomon Islands, site of one of the bloodiest battles of World War II, lasting from August 1942 to February 1943, when Japanese survivors evacuated.

GUADALUPE HIDALGO, TREATY OF (Feb. 2, 1848). Between the US and Mexico, it ended the Mexican War. By its terms, virtually all of the Southwest, including Texas and California, became part of the US.

GUAM. Southernmost of the Mariana Islands, a US possession since 1898. During World War II, Guam was occupied by the Japanese until 1944. By the Organic Act of 1950, its administration placed under the Interior Department, with a governor appointed by the president. Has a unicameral legislature and a court system. Its people have been US citzens since 1950. Pop.: 105,816 (1980).

GUANTÁNAMO BAY. US naval base in Cuba. The Platt Amendment of 1901 gave the US the right to lease naval stations in Cuba. A new treaty in 1934 reasserted US rights there. Fidel Castro, after coming to power in 1959, denied the validity of the treaties; but the US retained the base.

GUFFEY COAL ACTS. Integral part of President Franklin D. Roosevelt's efforts to create federal regulatory power under the National Industrial Recovery Acts. The first one, the Bituminous Coal Conservation Act (1935), was declared unconstitutional by the Supreme Court. Congress passed a second act, the Guffey Coal Act (1937), which regulated the coal industry by creating a commission with the most comprehensive administrative power ever granted a regulatory agency in peacetime.

GUILFORD COURTHOUSE, BATTLE OF (March 15, 1781). Gen. Nathanael Greene met British Gen. Charles Cornwallis in a battle near present-day Greensboro, N.C. The British held the field, but the battle was a strategic victory for the Americans: Cornwallis soon withdrew to Wilmington, abandoning most of North Carolina.

GUINN AND BEAL V. UNITED STATES, 238 US 347 (1915). Supreme Court declared unconstitutional Oklahoma's attempt to include a permanent GRANDFATHER CLAUSE into its state constitution.

GUION'S EXPEDITION (1797). A detachment commanded by Capt. Isaac Guion was sent to occupy Chickasaw Bluffs and Walnut Hills, Miss., in accordance with PINCKNEY'S TREATY, which gave the US the right to occupy Spanish posts along the Mississippi R.

GULF, MOBILE AND OHIO. See RAILROADS, SKETCHES OF PRINCIPAL LINES: ILLINOIS CENTRAL GULF.

GULF STREAM. Current system that carries warm water from the Gulf of Mexico northeastward to the Grand Banks of Newfoundland. East of the Banks is an ill-defined, weaker current alleged to carry warmth to western Europe. By 1519, Spanish seafarers had learned how to navigate the Gulf Stream. In 1775, Benjamin Franklin began a series of surface temperature measurements across the Atlantic. In 1844 the US Coast Survey began a major study of the Gulf Stream; results strongly supported the notion that it is driven primarily by the prevailing winds rather than by density differences. A 1948 study showed theoretically that the currents result from variation of the deflecting force of the earth's rotation. Later theories have accepted parts of both density difference and wind-stress theories.

GULLAH. Also known as Geechee, a dialect spoken by blacks in coastal Georgia and South Carolina.

GUNBOATS. Tiny men-of-war overgunned in proportion to size first appeared in the Battle of Valcour Island on Lake Champlain, 1776. Such boats were effective only along a coast, being unstable in the open sea; became widely used to suppress West Indian piracy and in the Seminole Wars. In the Civil War, improvised gunboats were found on embattled rivers everywhere. Ironclads were more useful against forts than against other boats. By the time of the Spanish-American War, gunboats were larger and ocean-worthy. The inshore fighting of World War II called for small gunboats, with emphasis on a multiplicity of automatic weapons and on rocket launchers for shore bombardment. The gunboat concept of enormous firepower in a small vessel received new impetus from rocket weaponry. The Vietnam War spawned a variety of tiny types used to police shoreline or to penetrate riverways.

GUNDELOW. Small vessel used in the 1870s mostly for lightering coal and cotton from ships in Portsmouth, R.I., and Newburyport, Mass., to the mills on the rivers. Also sometimes applied to a small gunboat used by the colonial army on Lake Champlain.

GUNNISON MASSACRE (Oct. 26, 1853). Capt. J.W. Gunnison and seven colleagues, who were surveying for a railroad, were slain near Deseret, Utah. Although the Mormons were blamed, the attack was made by Ute Indians to avenge the death of a warrior by emigrants.

GUTIÉRREZ-MAGEE EXPEDITION (1812–13). Filibuster attempt to wrest Texas from Spanish control led by Bernardo Gutiérrez de Lara, a Mexican, and A.W. Magee, a former US army officer. The Spanish governor of Texas at San Antonio and twelve of his staff were cap-

tured and killed. In August 1813, the filibuster force of 3,000 was ambushed by the Spanish and destroyed.

GWYNN'S ISLAND. Site in Chesapeake Bay where in 1776 Lord Dunmore, the royal governor of Virginia, built a stockade, having fled Norfolk. He was soon forced to abandon it.

HABEAS CORPUS, WRIT OF. Legal process through which someone who is being detained may secure a quick judicial inquiry into the lawfulness of the detention. The writ is traceable to the Magna Carta (1215), and its availability as a remedy against the crown dates from the 15th c. In the colonies, was part of common law and is guaranteed in the Constitution, except it may be suspended if "the public Safety may require it" in times of rebellion or invasion. President Lincoln did so during the Civil War.

HAGUE COURT OF ARBITRATION. See PERMANENT COURT OF ARBITRATION.

HAGUE PEACE CONFERENCES (1899, 1907). The first conference, attended by twenty-six nations, including the US, reached modest agreement on rules of land and maritime warfare but failed to make headway on limiting arms. Set up Convention for the Pacific Settlement of International Peace and Permanent Court of Arbitration. The second conference was attended by forty-four governments. Armament discussions again failed. Conventions appeared on laws of war, naval warfare, and neutrality. Also renounced right to use force to collect debts. Conferences important to development of League of Nations, United Nations, and international courts of justice.

HAGUE V. COMMITTEE ON INDUSTRIAL ORGANIZATION, 207 US 496 (1939). Supreme Court ruled that a city cannot deny permits for public meetings nor forbid the distribution of printed matter through fear that public order might be endangered. Regarded as an important statement on the meaning of civil liberty.

HAIDA. Indian tribe of the Northwest Coast. Possessed a generally uniform culture with the Tlingit and Tsimshian, characterized by potlatch, totem poles, exquisite carving and painting, and large communal houses.

"HAIL COLUMBIA." First national anthem of the US.

HAINES' BLUFF. Overlooking the Yazoo R, about fourteen miles NW of Vicksburg, Miss. Fortified by Confederacy to protect Vicksburg. Union troops forced its evacuation May 18, 1863.

HAITI, INTERVENTION IN. On July 28, 1915, after counterrevolutionaries killed the country's ruling general, US marines occupied the island. The legislature elected a puppet president, and appointees of President Wilson ran all important government offices. US in control until 1930, when a popularly elected government took over. US military occupation ended in 1934.

HAKLUYT'S VOYAGES. Richard Hakluyt's collection of original records of English voyages before 1600. Covers virtually every voyage of importance, with a full narrative by a participant and official documents and private letters.

HALDIMAND NEGOTIATIONS. Talks during the American Revolution between Vermont leaders, including Ethan Allen, and the British commander at Quebec, Frederick Haldimand. The Vermonters wanted to perpetuate Vermont, which had been denied admission to the US, and safeguard its landed interests regardless of who won the war. Basic agreement by both sides, which was considered treasonous by some, but the end of the war put an end to all such plans.

HALE, EXECUTION OF (Sept. 22, 1776). Nathan Hale, acting as a spy for the Americans, was executed by the British. His last words are said to have been, "I only regret that I have but one life to lose for my country."

HALF-BREEDS. Persons of racial intermixture, specifically children with one white parent and one Indian parent. French voyageurs and fur trappers often married Indian women, and their offspring were known as *métis*.

HALF-BREED TRACT. Tract of land consisting of 121,000 acres in the triangle between the Mississippi and Des Moines rivers in SE Iowa, set aside for the use of half-breeds by treaty with Sac and Fox (1824). Allowed to sell after 1831, and the land fell into hands of speculators and white squatters, who were given legal title after much legal battling.

HALF MOON. The ship on which Henry Hudson explored the Hudson R in 1609.

HALFWAY COVENANT (June 1657). Children of the founders of Massachusetts and Connecticut were given membership in the church pending spiritual regeneration of their own. Participation in the Lord's Supper and voting in the church were withheld until they could give acceptable proof of their conversion.

HALIFAX, FORT. Built in Maine in 1754 at the confluence of the Sebasticook and Kennebec rivers. One of the last forts erected by the British.

HALL, FORT. Built in 1834 Idaho on the Snake R. A fur-trading center and stopover point for Oregon Trail immigrants. Abandoned 1855.

HAMBURG RIOT (July 8, 1876). Confrontation in Hamburg, S.C., between Radical Republicans and Democrats for control of the state. One white and seven blacks were killed.

HAMILTON, FORT. Built 1791 on the Miami R in Ohio, first of a line of posts between Fort Washington (Cincinnati) and Fort Defiance (Maumee Valley).

HAMILTON'S FISCAL POLICIES. Alexander Hamilton set forth a conservative economic policy based on confidence in American credit, both at home and abroad, a sound currency, an integrated system of manufactures, the revival of foreign trade, and the establishment of a national bank and a mint.

HAMILTON'S REPORT ON MANUFACTURES (1791). Alexander Hamilton insisted that development of the nation required mercantilist policies rather than pursuit of laissez-faire. He proposed protective duties and bounties and premiums on domestic manufactures. Largely ignored by Congress, which regarded it as inimical to agriculture and as providing special favor to a small economic class.

HAMLET CASE (1850). James Hamlet, a free black in New York City, was arrested and taken to a Baltimore jail, in strict accordance with the new Fugitive Slave Act. Redeemed through the intervention of abolitionists.

HAMMER V. DAGENHART, 247 US 251 (1918). The Supreme Court declared unconstitutional an attempt by Congress to outlaw CHILD LABOR.

HAMPDEN EXPEDITION (1814). Effort by the British during the War of 1812 to take possession of NE Maine. US militia defeated at Hampden; Bangor and Frankfort surrendered.

HAMPTON. City in Virginia on Chesapeake Bay opposite Norfolk. Established 1610. Claims to be oldest continuously occupied English settlement in the New World. Military objective in the Revolution, War of 1812, and Civil War. Pop.: 122,617 (1980).

HAMPTON ROADS CONFERENCE (Feb. 3, 1865). Attempt to end the Civil War, held on board the *River Queen* in Hampton Roads, Va. President Lincoln offered peace on the basis of reunion, emancipation, and the disbanding of Confederate troops. Confederate delegates were not empowered to accept any terms except independence, and so the conference adjourned.

HANDICAPPED, EDUCATION OF THE. In 1817 T.H. Gallaudet opened a private school for the deaf in Hartford, Conn.; his method of sign communication was later used in several other schools. In 1864, his son, E.M. Gallaudet, established the National Deaf-Mute (now Gallaudet) College in Washington, D.C. By 1979, abut 86,000 deaf and hard-of-hearing pupils received special educational assistance. S.G. Howe established schools for the blind in Boston (1832), New York, and Philadelphia. The American Printing House for the Blind, founded 1855, received annual federal grants after 1879. Library facilities for the blind were made available in Boston (1868), New York state (1896), and the Library of Congress (1897). In 1979, about 33,000 blind pupils received special assistance. Chicago provided special schools for the crippled in 1899 and New York in 1906. Today, children homebound with serious physical defects are aided by radio, television, and telephone; those in regular schools benefit from specially designed buildings, furniture, and buses. Wheelchairs are made available. In 1979, about 178,000 crippled children received special aid in public schools. The largest category of physically handicapped in schools is that of the speech-impaired. In 1979, about 1.2 million speech-impaired children received special education. In 1980, the needs of handicapped children became the responsibility of the Office of Special Education and Rehabilitative Services within the new Department of Education.

HANDSOME LAKE CULT. An Iroquois nativist movement founded by Seneca prophet Handsome Lake in 1799. Combining native Iroquois beliefs with the pacifistic ideals of the Quakers, it spread rapidly to the other tribes of the Six Nations. Still survives in altered form.

HANGING. Method of execution brought from England. Primary method of effecting capital punishment until electrocution and lethal gas. In 1981 four states still maintained the practice.

HANGING ROCK, ACTION AT (Aug. 6, 1780). Engagement at Hanging Rock, S.C., between patriots and a large contingent of British regulars and Tories. The British were defeated.

HANNASTOWN. Settlement in Westmoreland County, Pa., founded 1733; an important rendezvous for expeditions against the Indians, who attacked and destroyed it on July 13, 1782.

HANNASTOWN RESOLUTION (May 16, 1775). Frontier inhabitants of Westmoreland County, Pa., declared it the duty of Americans to resist English oppression.

HANNIBAL AND ST. JOSEPH RAILROAD. See RAILROADS, SKETCHES OF PRINCPAL LINES.

HAPPY HUNTING GROUND. Concept of afterlife among the Algonkin-speaking Indians. Suggestive of Christian beliefs, it perhaps stemmed from Jesuit contacts.

HARD LABOR, TREATY OF (Oct. 14, 1768). Signed at Hard Labor, S. C., between Virginians and Indians. Fixed the boundaries of Indian country in the western lands. Colonial dissatisfaction led to the line being shifted farther west by the Treaty of Lochaber.

HARD MONEY. Gold or silver coin, as opposed to paper money. The Constitution says that "no State shall ... make any Thing but gold and silver Coin a Tender in Payment of Debts," which put the United States on a hard money basis. Intent modified numerous times until, in 1971, the United States took the final step in establishing an irredeemable paper money standard. (See also GOLD STANDARD; MONEY.)

HARDWARE TRADE. Domestic production of hardware did not outpace imports until after 1860; by 1900, US hardware exports exceeded imports. The general store was the major retail outlet until the middle of the 19th c., when the more specialized hardware store became common. Their number peaked at about 35,000 in the 1950s; in 1977, there were about 26,500.

HARGIS-CALLAHAN-COCKRELL FEUD (1899–1912). Dispute in Breathitt County, Ky., between the Hargis-Callahan family and the Cockrell family, stemming from a contested county election. Resulted in more than 100 deaths.

HARLEM. Community in New York City, settled by the Dutch in the early 17th c. and named for the Dutch city of Haarlem. Merged with New York City in 1873. A community of wealthy whites in the 19th c., the mass settlement of blacks there began ca. 1900. By 1920, it was an almost completely black area and was regarded as the cultural capital of the black world and the center of the HARLEM RENAISSANCE. Much of the housing degenerated as new arrivals overcrowded the community, creating great economic and social problems. After World War II, public housing projects replaced many of the old slums but created their own social problems. By the 1980s,

New York blacks had also settled in other areas, but Harlem still contained about half the million-plus black population.

HARLEM, BATTLE OF (Sept. 16, 1776). After the Battle of Long Island, George Washington withdrew to Manhattan and established a line from the mouth of the Harlem R across to Morningside Heights. About 1,000 British attackers were repulsed. This small victory greatly heartened the American troops, who held position for another month.

HARLEM RENAISSANCE. Black cultural movement during the 1920s, centered in HARLEM, New York City. Under the influence of W.E.B DuBois and novelist James Weldon Johnson, the movement was characterized by racial pride and interest in African culture. The burst of black creativity in the literary and visual arts attracted white financial backing, which disappeared with the Great Depression. Nevertheless, the movement had a broad impact on American literature, music, and theater.

HARMAR, FORT. Built 1786 in Ohio at the junction of the Muskingum and Ohio rivers. Furnished protection to surveyors and later to nearby Marietta. After Treaty of Greenville (1795), the troops were withdrawn.

HARMAR, FORT, TREATIES OF (Jan. 9, 1789). Between the US and the various Indian tribes in the Northwest Territories. Set limits of Indian territory and paid the Indians to relinquish any further claims.

HARMAR'S EXPEDITION. In 1790, Gen. Josiah Harmar conducted two excursions from Fort Washington (Cincinnati) against Indian towns near present-day Fort Wayne. In both cases, the Indians won.

HARMONY SOCIETY. Established 1804 in Butler County, Pa., by German Separatist immigrants. In 1825 moved to permanent home at Economy, Pa. Agriculture and commerce highly successful until late in the century when bad management dissipated their wealth. Adopted celibacy in 1807 and thereafter depended on converts for growth. Dissolved in 1903.

HARNEY EXPEDITION (1855). Gen. W.S. Harney led a campaign against the Sioux from

Fort Leavenworth, Kans. Defeated Little Thunder. Reached the Missouri R at Fort Pierre in Dakota country. Built Fort Randall downriver.

HARO CHANNEL DISPUTE. Boundary between Washington state and British Columbia set in middle of channel that separated Haro and Rosario straits. Two channels existed necessitating an arbitral decision in 1872.

HARPERS FERRY. Town in West Virginia, founded 1747 where the Shenandoah R joins the Potomac; site of a federal arsenal after 1796. The arsenal was the objective of John Brown's raid in 1859 and a principal objective of both Confederate and Union forces in the Civil War. Union forces took the town early in the war, but Confederate Gen. Stonewall Jackson won a major victory with his capture of Harpers Ferry on Sept. 15, 1862.

HARPER'S WEEKLY. Pictorial magazine founded 1857; of great political influence during the Civil War and was famous for the cartoons of Thomas Nast. Later was converted into a literary and public affairs journal.

HARRISBURG. City in Pennsylvania, on the Susquehanna R, capital since 1812. Iron and coal are mined in the area, and steel products, food packing and processing plants are important industries. Pop.: 53,264 (1980).

HARRIS' FERRY. Original settlement at present Harrisburg, Pa., ca. 1718.

HARRISON, FORT. Built 1811 on the Wabash R where Terre Haute, Ind., now stands to protect against raids by Techumseh and the Prophet.

HARRISON LAND ACT (1800). Amended the LAND ACT OF 1796 by facilitating individual purchases of public land in the Northwest and by creating a more flexible credit system.

HARRODSBURG. Earliest white settlement in Kentucky, founded 1774.

HARTFORD. Capital and largest city in Connecticut. Established forty miles up Connecticut R by the Dutch (Fort Good Hope) in 1633. In 1662, an English charter issued to Connecticut caused the original "river towns" to absorb New Haven colony. Modern Hartford is an insurance and firearms center. Pop.: 136,392 (1980).

HARTFORD, TREATY OF (1650). Between the Dutch of New Netherland, headed by Peter Stuyvesant, and the English United Colonies of New England. Fixed borders between the colonies but left open the ownership of the Delaware Valley.

HARTFORD CONVENTION (Dec.15, 1814–Jan. 5, 1815). Called by New England opponents to War of 1812. Sought to revise Constitution so as to reduce southern influence in the federal government. The convention met in secrecy during wartime, giving rise to charges of treasonable intent. Movement died with end of war.

HARTFORD WITS. Young writers of the late 18th c., chiefly Yale graduates, who belonged to an informal literary club in Hartford, Conn. Principal members were Timothy Dwight, Theodore Dwight, Richard Alsop, and Lemuel Hopkins.

HARVARD UNIVERSITY. Oldest college in the nation, founded 1636 at Cambridge, Mass. In 1780 it became a university; in 1782, a medical school was established; and in 1817, a law school was added.

HASTINGS' CUTOFF. A route to California that crossed the Great Salt Desert and the Sierra Nevada instead of proceeding N to Fort Hall, Idaho, and then branching S. It was shorter but the desert was threatening.

HATCH ACT (Aug. 2, 1939). Expanded the Pendleton Civil Service Act of 1883 by restricting political activity by all federal employees except those in policy posts. A 1940 amendment brought under the act all state and local employees paid in full or in part by federal funds.

HATFIELD-MCCOY FEUD. Family dispute in West Virginia and Kentucky. Animosity dated from the Civil War, but the feud proper began in 1880, when a Hatfield was accused of stealing a McCoy hog. Raged throughout the 1880s with several murders and executions.

HAT MANUFACTURE, COLONIAL RESTRICTIONS ON. In 1732 Parliament, to protect British manufacturers, forbade the colonial exportation of hats, even to another colony. Also required a seven years' apprenticeship, excluded blacks, and limited manufacturers to two apprentices.

HATTERAS INLET, CAPTURE OF (Aug. 28–29, 1861). Union steam warships destroyed the weak Confederate forts protecting Pamlico Sound.

HAUN'S MILL MASSACRE (Oct. 30, 1838). An armed mob in Caldwell County, Mo., attacked a Mormon colony, killing seventeen.

HAVANA, ACT OF (July 30, 1940). Approved by the Pan-American Union, it was designed to prevent the transfer to Germany of any European colonies in the Western Hemisphere.

HAVASUPAI. Indian tribe of Arizona. Along with the Walapai and Yavapai, they numbered about 1,000. They took over river-bottom farming of maize, and maintained an isolated and marginal culture.

HAWAII. Group of Pacific islands, became the fiftieth state in 1959. Named the Sandwich Islands by their discoverer, James Cook (1778). American merchants, missionaries, and whalers reached the islands in the early 19th c. and established near complete control over the economy and law and government. The monarchy was overthrown in 1893 by a US-backed revolution after the queen had tried to lessen US influence in her government. The new republic petitioned Washington for annexation, and in 1900 the Terrritory of Hawaii was established. By then sugar and pineapple production were the mainstays of the islands' economy. Pearl Harbor became the prime US naval base in the Pacific, and during World War I, Schofield Barracks became an important army post. After the Japanese attack on Dec. 7, 1941, Hawaii was a major command center for the Pacific war. Hawaii's long campaign for statehood was realized in 1959. Tourism is its single most important industry. Pop.: 965,000 (1980).

HAWKS. Term applied to those who enthusiastically supported the US war effort in Vietnam, contrasted to the doves, who opposed the war.

HAWK'S PEAK EPISODE (March 6–9, 1846). When J.C. Frémont was ordered by the Mexican authorities to leave California, he raised the US flag on Gavilan, or Hawk's, Peak, near Monterey, and stayed there for three days. Regarded as a direct cause of the BEAR FLAG REVOLT.

HAWLEY-SMOOT TARIFF. See SMOOT-HAWLEY TARIFF.

HAW RIVER, BATTLE OF (Feb. 25, 1781). Col. Henry defeated a Loyalist force in North Carolina, thereby deterring many local Tories from espousing the Loyalist cause.

HAY-BUNAU-VARILLA TREATY (1903). Between the US and the new Panama republic. The United States, in return for $10 million, was given "perpetual" rights to the Canal Zone.

HAYBURN'S CASE (1792). The first Supreme Court case involving the constitutionality of an act of Congress. Arose from a pension claim; relief was otherwise provided and the court did not have to act on the matter.

HAYFIELD FIGHT (Aug. 1, 1867). Engagement of the SIOUX WARS between the Miniconjou Sioux and the US army; no decisive victory for either side.

HAY-HERRÁN TREATY (Jan. 22, 1903). Between the US and Colombia; gave the United States the right to build a canal across the isthmus of Panama.

HAYMARKET RIOT (May 4, 1886). Seven policemen were killed and seventy injured when a bomb exploded as the police tried to break up a labor rally in Chicago. Eight alleged anarchists were convicted; four were hanged. In 1893, Gov. J.P. Altgeld pardoned the three surviving prisoners, saying that the trial had been a farce.

HAY-PAUNCEFOTE TREATIES (1900, 1901). Between the US and Great Britain. Britain agreed to let the US build a transisthmian canal under its own auspices. US agreed that the canal should be open to vessels of all nations.

HAYS, FORT. Built 1867 in Kansas to combat hostile Plains Indians. Became Hays City after the railroad reached it. Wild Bill Hickok was frontier marshal there in 1869.

HAYWOOD-MOYER-PETTIBONE CASE (1905). The main officers of the Western Federation of Miners were tried for the assassination of the governor of Idaho. Two were acquitted and the other released without a trial.

HAZELWOOD REPUBLIC. Organized 1856 in the Sioux Agency of Minnesota. Had eighty-two members by 1858. Adoption of the dress and habits of white men offended their fellow Indians, and by 1860 the movement had failed.

HEADRIGHT. System in the English colonies in the 17th c. of granting a certain number of acres (usually fifty) for each settler. System also found in the early land laws of Texas.

HEALTH AND HUMAN SERVICES, DEPARTMENT OF. Created 1979 after the Department of Education was split away from the Department of Health, Education, and Welfare. It administers the federal government's health services, including Medicare and Medicaid, and the social security programs.

HEALTH, PUBLIC. See PUBLIC HEALTH.

HEATH PATENT (1629). Grant by Charles I to Sir Robert Heath of the region S of Virginia, to be called Carolana, later Carolina. In 1663 the patent was declared forfeited because no settlement had been planted.

HELDERBERG WAR. See ANTIRENT WAR.

HELENA. Capital of Montana, settled 1864 at a gold site known as Last Chance Gulch. In 1875 it became capital of the Montana Territory and developed quickly after silver and lead mines were developed in the area. With the coming of the railroad, it became a major shipping center and supply center for ranchers and farmers. Pop.: 23,938 (1980).

HELENA, BATTLE OF (July 4, 1863). Unsuccessful attempt by Confederate forces to take Helena, Ark.

HELICOPTERS, MILITARY. In World War II, about 500 helicopters were used for lifesav-ing missions. The Korean War saw increasing use of helicopters in rescue and supply missions; in 1951 the marines employed them as assault transports to move troops into battlefield positions over inaccessible terrain. During the Vietnam War, helicopters equipped with machine guns, rockets, and small guided missiles were developed for armed escort of transports and ground interdiction.

HELPERITES. Persons subscribing to the theories of H.R. Helper, a North Carolinian who wrote *The Impending Crisis of the South* (1857); it maintained that slavery was an economic fallacy responsible for the South's failure to keep pace with the North. Widely circulated by the Republicans, the report was publicly burned in the South and Helperites persecuted.

HEMP. England encouraged the colonies to grow hemp, important for rigging in sailing ships, but it never became an important crop. After the Revolution, was a staple crop in Kentucky and Missouri. After advent of steel for cordage, demand lessened. Production ceased after World War II.

HEMPSTEAD. Town on Long Island, N.Y., settled 1643 on land granted to settlers from Connecticut by the local Indians. In the early 20th c., the coming of the Long Island RR turned it into a suburb of New York City. Pop.: 40,404 (1980).

HENING'S STATUTES. A collection of the laws of Virginia from 1619–1792, compiled 1808 by W.W. Hening. A supplement later brought the collection down to 1808.

HENNEPIN NARRATIVES. Louis Hennepin was a friar who accompanied the sieur de La Salle on his voyage to Illinois (1675) and was sent (1680) to explore the upper Mississippi R. Captured by the Sioux, he was rescued and returned to France. His successful narratives, largely truthful, gave European readers an account of the flora and fauna of North America.

HENRY, FORT. Built 1774 as Fort Fincastle on the Ohio R on the site of what is now Wheeling, W. Va. On Sept. 10, 1782, it was attacked by Indians and British in what is claimed to be the last battle of the American Revolution. Another Fort Henry, on the Tennessee R, was captured on Feb. 6, 1862, by Union Gen. U.S. Grant, beginning his Mississippi campaign.

HENRY LETTERS. In 1809, John Henry, a British agent investigating secessionist sentiment in New England, sold his correspondence to President Madison; its publication in 1811 was aimed at discrediting New England Federalist opponents.

HEPBURN ACT OF 1906. Legislation aimed at increasing the powers of the Interstate Commerce Commission.

HERD LAW VERSUS FREE GRASS. Conflict in the newly settled West in the late 19th c. between ranchers and homesteaders. Stock raisers favored allowing herds to roam at will, following the pastures. The homesteaders favored fencing. The controversy often erupted in violence; but increased population led to fencing becoming common.

HERMITAGE. Estate of Andrew Jackson near Nashville, Tenn., bought in 1795. Original brick house (1819) burned in 1834. Present house built on the site.

HERMOSA CASE. In 1840, slaves of the American schooner *Hermosa* were freed in Nassau; slavery was not recognized in British territories. US claimed that the slaves were still the owner's propery because the ship had been forced into British waters. Owners eventually paid $16,000 indemnity.

HERPETOLOGY. Early contributions to the study of American reptiles were contained in the works of Mark Catesby (1731–43) and William Bartram (1791) and there were descriptions of American reptiles by Carolus Linnaeus in his *Systema Naturae* (1758). By the early 19th c., there was considerable information made available by European scientists, who had traveled as far west as the Rocky Mountains. J.E. Holbrook, a Charleston physician, produced the first native contribution to the subject: *North American Herpetology* (1836, 1842). Numerous scientists accompanied government-sponsored expeditions to the West. Since the 1920s, American universities have become the primary centers for herpetological studies.

HERRIN MASSACRE (June 22, 1922). Forty-seven nonunion workers in a strip mine in Williamston County, Ill., were captured by union men during a coal strike. They were ordered to run for their lives under fire; twenty-one were killed. A grand jury returned indictments, but local sentiment prevented convictions.

HESSIANS. See GERMAN MERCENARIES.

HESTER CASE. In 1698, the *Hester* was seized at Perth Amboy, New Jersey, by New York customs agents. In their successful lawsuit, the proprietors were awarded damages and the right for New Jersey to have ports of its own confirmed.

HEXING. A form of witchcraft practiced by the Pennsylvania Dutch.

HICKSITES. Followers of Elias Hicks, a Long Island Quaker, who split away from the Society of Friends in 1827. They formed Swarthmore College.

HIDE AND TALLOW TRADE. In Spanish California, in the early 19th c., missions and ranchers depended chiefly on the sale of hides and tallow for a livelihood. Boston ships did a direct commerce between California and the eastern seaboard. On the Great Plains, buffalo hide was an important article of commerce.

HIGH COMMISSION, COURT OF. English court established in the 16th c. to protect the crown against heresy and treason. The court became the principal means of rooting out Puritan nonconformity, thereby causing many Puritan ministers to flee to Holland and the New World.

HIGHER CRITICISM. The historical and textual study of the Bible, introduced into America in the late 19th c.; bitterly condemned by fundamentalists, who looked upon the Bible as infallible.

HIGHER EDUCATION FACILITIES ACT (Aug. 14, 1963). Authorized a program of federal grants and loans for the construction of public and private higher educational facilities.

HIGHLANDS OF THE HUDSON. A rugged land mass extending along the Hudson R in the area of West Point, N.Y. Fortified against the British in the Revolution. Sir Henry Clinton captured Fort Constitution in 1777. In 1778, Gen. Thaddeus Kosciusko was placed in charge of colonial defenses. A massive chain was stretched across the river between West Point and Constitution Island, and redoubts and forts on the hills inland assured protection against a land attack.

HIGHWAY ACT (June 29, 1956). Authorized $32 billion to construct an interstate highway system, for which the federal government would pay 90 percent. The act placed a tax on gasoline and created the Highway Trust Fund to help finance construction costs.

HIGHWAYS. See ROADS.

HIJACKING, AERIAL. Piracy of aircraft, principally commercial airlines; also called skyjacking. Hijackers included both political malcontents (especially Cuban refugees) and persons demanding ransom. It became a serious problem in the late 1960s, causing tough security measures to be put into effect in 1971. Various international treaties were put into effect setting up procedures for the apprehension, extradition, and punishment of air pirates. Hijackings decreased dramatically.

HILLABEE TOWNS. Five Creek towns in E Alabama. The Hillabee Creek, numbering about 800, took part in the Creek War; their towns were devastated in November 1813 by a combined force of Cherokee and Tennessee militia, with 316 inhabitants killed or captured.

HINDMAN, FORT. See ARKANSAS POST, BATTLE OF.

HIPPIES AND YIPPIES. The term "hippy" originated with jazz musicians' "hip," meaning sharp and aware of things. In the 1960s, the term was adopted by young people attempting to lead a life outside the American middle-class conventionality. Among certain characteristics were the rejection of materialistic values, adoption of bright and bizarre clothing, long hair and untrimmed beards, and a life characterized by rootlessness. Yippies were an outgrowth. The term stands for Youth International party. The Yippy philosophy was to satirize all conventional institutions, particularly the political. The Yippies were most prominent during the 1968 Democratic Convention in Chicago. Both movements died out in the 1970s.

HISE TREATY (1849). Unauthorized treaty made with Nicaragua by Elijah Hise, a diplomat sent to Central America by President Polk. In return for US right to build a trans-isthmus canal, the US guaranteed the territorial integrity of Nicaragua, including its claim to the town of San Juan, a British protectorate. Although not adopted, the treaty helped turn American public opinion against Great Britain.

HISTORICAL SOCIETIES. Founded by state and local groups in the years after the American Revolution. The first was the Massachusetts Historical Society (1791), followed by New York City in 1804. The first attempt to organize a national society was the American Antiquarian Society (1812). The American Historical Association was founded in 1884, the Southern History Association in 1895 (disbanded 1905), and the Mississippi Valley Historical Association in 1907, which in 1964 became the Organization of American Historians. There are numerous special-interest societies (e.g., the Railway and Locomotive Historical Society, the Steamship Historical Society of America, the American-Swedish Historical Museum, and the Association for the Study of Negro Life and History). The most important activity of all historical societies is the collection and preservation of manuscripts, documents, books, pamphlets, newspapers, and artifacts.

HISTORIOGRAPHY, AMERICAN. Sagas of Norse voyages to America were written down by Adam of Bremen in *Northerly Lands* (ca. 1070). Great English compendiums include Richard Eden, *The Decades of the Newe Worlde (1555)*; Richard Haklyut, *The Principal Navigations, Voyages and Discoveries of the English Nation* (1625); and Samuel Purchas, *Hakluytus Posthumus, or Purchas, His Pilgrims* (1625). Many firsthand accounts of early colonial settlements include Capt. John Smith, *The General History of Virginia, New England and Summer Isles* (1624). William Bradford, governor of Plymouth Colony, wrote its history between

1630 and 1651; John Winthrop did the same in his journal for the Massachusetts Bay Colony. Two 18th-c. writings include Thomas Prince, *Chronological History of New England* (1736), and William Smith, *The History of the Province of New York* (1757). An early history of the Revolution was Mercy Otis Warren, *History of the Rise, Progress, and Termination of the American Revolution* (1805). With the establishment of the Constitution, there developed a consciousness that generated the founding of historical societies and the publication of documents. The most famous of the editors of such publications was Jared Sparks, who published in twelve volumes the *Diplomatic Correspondence of the American Revolution* (1829–30). Government agencies too began publishing select portions of their records, but it was not until the National Archives Act of 1934 established the National Archives and a historical publications commission that there was any systematic means of location and publication of historical materials on a national scale. Biography served as a popular form of history in the early republic. Sparks published twelve volumes of *The Writings of George Washington* (1834–37) and edited the works of Benjamin Franklin in ten volumes (1836–40). He also published the twenty-five volume *Library of American Biography*, which gave accounts of local heroes. The capstone of such compendiums was *The Dictionary of American Biography* (1928–36, with several supplements), sponsored by the American Council of Learned Societies. The 19th c. saw several examples of what might be called the literary history, including George Bancroft, *History of the United States from the Discovery of the American Continent* (1834–74), and Henry Adams, *History of the United States During the Administrations of Jefferson and Madison* (nine voumes, 1889–91). In 1913, Charles A. Beard published *An Economic Interpretation of the Constitution*, and it set the standard for a new kind of critical history that was to characterize the 20th c. After World War II and during the cold war, historians began to look for continuities in their past. This characterized in the work of Daniel Boorstin, Clinton Rossiter, and Arthur Schlesinger, Jr. Another approach which came to the fore in some circles was the so-called revisionist school, which seeks to reevaluate traditional views of American history.

HISTORY, AMERICAN, SOURCES OF.

Material. Archives, manuscripts, newspapers, and printed government documents are four basic types of literary sources. Archives constitute the official records and working papers of an organization. Manuscripts are the private records of individuals. Because of the availability of newspapers from virtually every period and place in American history, historians have found them important, if often unreliable sources. Printed government documents reflect a great deal more than the workings of the government: The reports of many agencies deal with the multiple economic and social facets of American life. Much of the quantitative data used by historians is generally from government documents, especially those emanating from the census bureau. Artifacts also constitute an important research source. Houses, furniture, tools, handicrafts, and machine-made products tell much about the American experience. Similarly, maps, prints, photographs, and paintings can furnish contemporary visual conceptions of the past.

Locations. Governmental records are found in capital cities, and county or city records in city halls or county courthouses. Churches most often maintain archives, recording births, baptisms, weddings, and funerals. Federal records are administered by the National Archives and Records Service; it maintains the National Archives in Washington, D.C., and twelve regional archives and the various presidential libraries. Much of the National Archives' material is available on microfilm. The Library of Congress contains 30 million manuscript items related to American history. University libraries, archives, and special collections are also good sources of American history. Great private libraries have important source material. Historical societies constitute an important resource. Most such societies, along with university libraries, have cooperated with the National Historical Publications and Records Commission in microfilming collections of national importance. A detailed finding aid accompanies each publication.

Guides. The *Guide to Archives and Manuscripts in the United States* was published in 1961; arranged geographically, it printed responses from repositories throughout the nation. In 1962 the Library of Congress began publishing the *National Union Catalog of Manuscript Collections*. It has entries for individual collections and an extensive index, combining names, repositories, and subjects. Many repositories have published their own excellent guides to their collections.

HITCHCOCK RESERVATIONS (1919). Proposed exceptions to the Treaty of Versailles and the League of Nations sponsored by Sen. G.M. Hitchcock, the Democratic leader, in an attempt to reconcile Republican opposition. Would have given Senate veto power over US military actions for the league; equality of vote in the league with the British Empire; exemption of domestic questions from the league's jurisdiction. Republicans instead embraced LODGE RESERVATIONS.

HOBKIRK'S HILL, BATTLE OF (April 25, 1781). Colonial forces were defeated by the British near Camden, S.C.

HOCKEY. In the late 18th c., British soldiers in Canada played a rudimentary version of hockey with the Mohawk on frozen lakes and ponds. Standardized rules were adopted at McGill University in 1879, based largely on those of lacrosse and rugby. In 1885, the Canadian Amateur Hockey Association was formed. Hockey was introduced into the US in 1893, the year in which the Stanley Cup, named for the then governor-general, was put up for competition in Canada. Since 1926, only professional teams have competed for this trophy. The National Hockey League (NHL) was founded in Canada in 1917, and US teams were admitted after 1924. In 1981, the league had twenty-two teams, fourteen of them US teams. Traditionally, most NHL players have been Canadians. The World Hockey Association (WHA) was founded in 1972 as a second professional league; in 1979, it merged with the NHL. Yale and Johns Hopkins universities both claim to have introduced hockey as a game to the United States in 1893. By 1980, hundreds of amateur high school, college, and community hockey teams existed. The governing body of amateur hockey in the United States is the Amateur Hockey Association of the US; it holds membership in the International Ice Hockey Federation, and it sponsors the US Olympic

team in the winter games. The 1980 Olympic winter games were the scene of US amateur hockey's most spectacular triumph: the US team unexpectedly defeated its more highly ranked rivals to win the gold medal.

HOG REEVE. A town officer in colonial New England, with the duty of impounding swine that strayed from the common lands and appraising any damage done by them.

HOGS. Hernando de Soto introduced hogs into North America. In the thirteen colonies, hogs accompanied the first settlement at Jamestown in 1607; by late 17th c., were well established in all colonies, as was the practice of finishing them for market by feeding them on Indian corn. American breeds developed from these early sources, but more significant development resulted from European importations in the early 19th c. The eight leading breeds in the 1980s included the Chester White, Duroc, Hampshire, Poland China, and Spotted, all dating from the 19th c. The Berkshire and Yorkshire, developed mainly in England; and the American Landrace, developed from the Danish Landrace. Since the 1930s, a meat-type hog has provided an increased yield of preferred lean cuts and reduced the yield of fat. During the 19th c., herds of swine were driven to market in cities on the eastern seaboard. Later, with population shifts and the development of transportation systems, packing centers were established at Cincinnati and Chicago. By the 1980s, the production of hogs was a major US agricultural enterprise. In 1979, the total gross sale of hogs, pork, and pork products amounted to almost $9 billion.

HOHOKAM. A prehistoric culture that thrived along the Salt and Gila rivers in S Arizona and New Mexico by 100 BC and climaxed between AD 1200 and 1400. Evidences of the culture are best represented at the Snaketown site. Sedentary village life and irrigation systems were well established by AD 500. During the climactic period, multistoried great houses with mud walls up to 2 meters thick were built, and the canal system reached its greatest extent (about 150 miles). A widespread drought is thought to have contributed to the downfall of the culture. Plant cultivation supported the economy, supplemented by hunting and gathering; large numbers of chipped stone and bone tools, grinding stones, stone bowls, axes, and painted ceramics litter the settlements.

HOLDEN PEACE MOVEMENT (1863–64). W.W. Holden, editor of a Raleigh newspaper, sought to detach North Carolina from the Confederacy and make a separate peace with the Union. Holden ran for governor in 1864, and his resounding defeat ended the movement.

HOLDING COMPANY. "Pure" holding companies confine their operations to the ownership and management of other firms and are not themselves operating companies. Holding companies emerged as a common form of business organization ca. 1900, some decades after such companies were formed in the railroad industry (1853) and the communications industry (1832). The Public Utility Holding Company Act of 1935 and the Bank Holding Company Act of 1956 restricted their activities.

HOLES OF THE MOUNTAINS. Mountain valleys where fur trappers camped and met for annual rendezvous. Famous were Jackson Hole and Pierre's Hole of the Teton range in Wyoming, and Ogden's Hole in the present city of Ogden, Utah.

HOLLADAY OVERLAND STAGE COMPANY. By 1866 operated over 2,760 miles of western road, used 6,000 horses and mules, 260 coaches, and employed hundreds of men. The federal government paid proprietor Ben Holladay $650,000 annually to carry mail over his lines. He sold out to Wells, Fargo and Co., 1866.

HOLLAND LAND COMPANY. Formed 1796 by Dutch banking houses after purchasing huge land tracts in the Genesee Valley and Pennsylvania. Unsuccessful, its assets were liquidated in the 1830s and 1840s.

HOLLAND PATENT (1769). Land grant of 20,000 acres in Albany County, N.Y., to Henry Fox, Lord Holland, who sold the tract to others.

HOLLAND SUBMARINE TORPEDO BOAT. Early submarine, designed by J.P. Holland; purchased by US navy 1900. 53 feet long, including armament of one torpedo tube.

HOLLY SPRINGS. On Dec. 20, 1862, Confederate troops attacked and destroyed Union stores at Holly Springs, Miss., forcing Gen. U.S. Grant to approach Vicksburg from the river.

HOLLYWOOD. Section of Los Angeles, first settled 1853; center of the motion picture industry since the 1920s.

HOLMES COUNTY REBELLION (June 1863). Civil War draft resistance incident in Ohio. Two resisters were wounded by troops, and thirteen men surrendered for trial.

HOLMES V. WALTON (1780). New Jersey supreme court decision, sometimes cited as a precedent for the doctrine of judicial review. The court passed on the constitutionality of a legislative act.

HOLSTON TREATY (July 2, 1791). Fixed the Cherokee-US boundary in the Southwest Territory (now Tennessee).

HOLT'S JOURNAL. Patriot newspaper, published by John Holt in upstate New York; after 1783 in New York City.

HOLY CROSS, PRIESTS OF. Roman Catholic order introduced into America 1841; founded Notre Dame University in South Bend, Ind.

HOLY EXPERIMENT. William Penn's term for the ideal community he founded in Pennsylvania 1681.

HOMEOPATHY. Pharmacotherapeutic technique relying on the ability of medicinal substances to act curatively when administered in accordance with the "law of similars." Originated in Europe; brought to the US 1820; throughout the century, the American school was the world leader. Centered in the Northeast and Middle Atlantic regions, homeopathy attracted rich, prominent clients and new German immigrants. In the mid-19th c., homeopathic physicians were expelled from medical societies and ostracized by orthodox (allopathic) physicians. Nevertheless, some medicines introduced by homeopathy were eventually adopted by allopaths and manufactured by leading drug companies. In 1903, homeopathic physicians were admitted to the American Medical Association. Today, there are about 1,000 practicing homeopathic physicians in the US.

HOME OWNERS' LOAN CORPORATION (HOLC). Created 1933 to assist homeowners unable to meet mortgage payments during the Depression. Made loans totaling $3 billion by 1936.

HOME RULE. Policy permitting cities and counties to draft charters, establish governmental structures, and control matters local in nature. Achieved through state legislation, its primary impact has been to permit variations in governmental structure.

HOME RULE IN THE SOUTH, RESTORATION OF. Virginia, by a quick appeal to Congress, escaped the rigors of RECONSTRUCTION. In Tennessee, a new constitution was ratified 1870 and a Democratic governor elected 1871. In Georgia, Democrats gained control of the legislature in November 1871 and impeached Gov. R.B. Bullock. In North Carolina, the legislature impeached Gov. W.W. Holden 1871, but the Democrats did not gain complete control of the state government until 1876. Texas was under carpetbag rule until 1874, when the Radical governor, failing to get federal support, surrendered his office to a Democrat. In Arkansas, a Democratic-Conservative governor took office 1874. In Mississippi, the lieutenant governor was impeached, the governor resigned, and Radical control came to an end 1876. In South Carolina, the 1876 election saw much irregularity on both sides, and each side claimed victory. The Republicans were forced to give way (April 11, 1877) after President Hayes withdrew federal troops. In Florida, a state supreme court decision allowed Gov. George F. Drew to assume office on Jan. 2, 1877. In Louisiana, President Hayes sent a commission to negotiate an agreement, and on April 24, 1877, home rule was established under Gov. F.T. Nicholls.

HOMESTEAD ACT (1862). Provided that Americans could get title to 160 acres of public land for use as a "homestead," to develop agriculture in the West. The homesteader was required to build a house on his land and to begin to farm it; after five years, he would own it free and clear. By 1900, about 80 million acres had been homesteaded.

HOMESTEAD MOVEMENT. Political agitation aimed at making public lands available at no cost, or at minimum charges, to persons willing to establish farms. The Free Soil party was founded (1848) to further aims of the movement. Major opposition came from the South, which feared creation of new antislavery states; from eastern conservatives, who feared labor shortage in the East; and from the Know-Nothing movement, which opposed giving land to immigrants. In 1860, the Republican party endorsed homesteading and in 1862, President Lincoln signed the HOMESTEAD ACT.

HOMESTEAD STRIKE OF 1892. Violent confrontation between iron, steel, and tin workers' union and Carnegie Steel Co., at Homestead, Pa. H.C. Frick, chairman of the company, determined to break the union and demanded members accept decreased wages. When workers went on strike, he brought in nonunion labor. Ensuing violence resulted in militia being brought in to break the strike, and organized labor's first struggle with large-scale capital ended in failure.

HONEY ISLAND. Refuge at Pearl River, Miss., for Confederate deserters. In April 1864, the Confederate army cleared the area.

HONEY WAR (1839). Popular name for hostilities in NE Missouri over a border dispute with Iowa. After disagreement over ownership of bee trees, the two governors ordered militia to enforce respective state laws. Compromise prevented armed conflict.

HONOLULU. Capital and largest city of Hawaii, on the island of Oahu. During the 19th c., Honolulu became the "crossroads of the Pacific"; an important port for trading ships and whalers, and shipping center for Hawaiian products. An essential naval and air base during World War II. Pop.: 365,048 (1980).

HOOD'S TENNESSEE CAMPAIGN (October–December 1864). Confrontation between Union Gen. W.T. Sherman and Confederate Gen. J.B. Hood. Early in October, Hood waited at Tuscumbia, Ga., on the Tennessee R for Sherman's attack. When Sherman ignored him, Hood pushed into Tennessee to scatter Union forces gathering at Nashville. On November 29, he assaulted forces of Gen. J.M. Schofield, nearly cutting them off; but the next day, Hood suffered heavy losses. On December 15, Gen. G.H. Thomas's cavalry attacked Hood and crushed his left, successfully renewing attack the next day at the Battle of Nashville. He was unable to disperse Hood's army, however, which crossed the Tennessee R and turned toward Corinth, Miss.

HOOKWORM. Intestinal parasite prevalent in warm climates; first noted in Puerto Rico 1899. By 1900 a new American variety was attacking victims in the South. In 1909, John D. Rockefeller funded a commission to eradicate the disease itself, to strengthen public health administration, and to educate the public in hygiene. Work was carried on after 1914 by local public health agencies. No longer a serious threat in the US.

HOOSAC MILLS CASE (*United States v. Butler*, 297 US 1 [1936]). The Supreme Court ruled that part of the Agricultural Adjustment Act (1933) was unconstitutional, representing an effort by Congress to regulate agricultural production, a matter solely within jurisdiction of the states.

HOOSIER. Nickname for inhabitants of Indiana since pioneer days, of uncertain derivation.

HOOVER COMMISSIONS. Two nonpartisan commissions on organization of the executive branch. The first was named by President Truman 1947 and chaired by former President Herbert Hoover. Ended 1949, another body was formed during the Korean War. More than 70 percent of its recommendations were put into effect, including the Military Unification Act of 1949; creation of the General Services Agency; and formation of the Department of Health, Education, and Welfare.

HOOVER DAM. Completed 1936 across the Colorado R at Boulder, Colo. Noted for its height (726 feet), its generating capacity (1.3 million kilowatts), and for the size of the lake, Lake Mead, largest artificial lake in the country. Originally called Boulder Dam.

HOPEDALE COMMUNITY. Founded 1842 in Milford, Mass., as an "experiment in the science of a divine order of society." Shifted from extremes of communism and individualism, failing 1856.

HOPEWELL. First great cultural complex in prehistoric North America, from ca. 300 BC to AD 250. Developed in Illinois and spread to S Ohio, where impressive earthworks were constructed. Corn was apparently never a staple; harvesting a wide variety of wild plants and animals sustained the population. Raw materials used in ornamental and ceremonial objects included mica, copper, shell, pipestone, meteoric iron, shark and alligator teeth, bear teeth, obsidian, and tortoiseshell.

HOPEWELL, TREATY OF (Nov. 28, 1785). First general Indian treaty made by the US; at Hopewell, S.C. with the Cherokee, and followed by similar treaties made with the Choctaw and Chickasaw. The treaties fixed boundaries between Indians and whites.

HOPEWELL IRON WORKS. Two apparently independent enterprises built in Pennsylvania in the 18th c. The Hopewell forge began in present Lebanon County 1742, and the Hopewell Furnace and Forge in present Berks County 1744.

HOPI. Classic representatives of Pueblo culture, occupying three mesas at the edge of the Painted Desert in NE Arizona. Numbered about 6,500 in the early 1980s, with each of seven towns forming a basic social unit; there is no tribe as such. The Hopi speak a Shoshonean language. It is suggested that they are deeply rooted in their present location. They are divided into maternal clans; ownership of property passes from mother to daughter. Ceremonial activity aims at agricultural fertility, world renewal, and societal stability. Like other Pueblo, they have adopted the pattern of intensive agriculture, despite desert conditions. The Hopi have successfully maintained their culture despite many outside pressures.

HORNBOOK. Primer, or first reading book, used in colonial schools; transplanted from

England, so-called because it was a sheet of paper mounted on a board and covered with transparent horn. Hornbooks contained the alphabet; vowel combinations; the Lord's Prayer; and Roman numerals.

HORNET-PEACOCK ENGAGEMENT (Feb. 24, 1813). Off British Guiana, the US sloop *Hornet* captured the British brig *Peacock*. Soon afterward the *Peacock* sank.

HORNET-PENGUIN ENGAGEMENT (March 23, 1815). The US sloop *Hornet* engaged the British brig *Penguin* in the south Atlantic, damaging it so badly it had to be destroyed.

HORSE. Single-hoofed *Equus caballus*, native to America, emerged about one million years ago and became extinct approx. 10,000 years ago. Reintroduced into the Western Hemisphere by Christopher Columbus, who landed twenty-five on Hispaniola. Spanish horses acclimated quickly, and by the mid-16th c., there were horse breeders and traders in Cuba, Jamaica, Chiapas, and Oaxaca. Horse ranches were established in New Mexico ca. 1607, and by 1700 there were numerous ranches in Arizona. From there, horses were taken to California, where they increased prodigiously. In the late 1600s, the horse spread north from Spanish Florida into the English colonies. On the outskirts of Virginia, they multiplied in a feral state, like the mustangs of the Southwest, until they were a menace to crops. Before settled agricultural systems developed, oxen were preferred for draft purposes; the horse was used for inland travel and military excursions. Later, horses and mules drew canalboats and railcars. The western pony served hunter, trapper, and miner; and later the cow horse provided mounts for the cowboy. New England carried on the first extensive horse breeding, chiefly for speed and agility. In Pennsylvania, horses were bred for size, strength, and endurance, qualities needed for draft animals; such breeds made possible the agricultural revolution of Middle America after the Civil War. The corn belt from Ohio to Iowa was the center of the draft horse supply. The development of the internal-combustion engine resulted in the displacement of horses for power and transportation. From about 26 million farm horses and

mules in the US in 1920, the number dropped to about 3 million in the 1970s.

HORSEHEAD CROSSING. Two river crossings. In Texas, the Goodnight-Loving Trail crossed the Pecos R near the present town of Ficklin at Horsehead Crossing; in Arizona, travelers bound for Concho and Fort Apache crossed the Puerco R just below its junction with the Little Colorado R, at Horsehead Crossing.

HORSE MARINES. Ordinarily referred to cavalry doing the work of marines, or vice versa; by extension may designate almost any naval or military incongruity. Associated especially with an episode (1836) during the Texas Revolution; a troop of Texas Rangers sighted and captured three Mexican supply ships, becoming known as the Horse Marines.

HORSE RACING. Course racing began on Long Island, N.Y., 1665; races were also run in other colonies in the 17th c. In early colonial races, the owner of each horse put up a stake, and stakes combined made the purse. Auction pools (in which the contestants were auctioned off and the purchaser of the winner collected the pool less a commission by the pool seller) were developed after the Civil War. Bookmakers made their appearance about the same time. Adoption of the pari-mutuel system 1908 gave racing a new aspect: once a semiprivate sport, it became a vast public entertainment business in which racing associations, horse breeders and trainers, and state governments derived income directly proportionate to the volume of wagering. Total revenue to racing states from racing in 1980 amounted to approx. $713 million. New York, Connecticut, and Nevada have legalized off-track betting. Pari-mutuel betting is legal in about half the states. More than half the nation's thoroughbreds are raised in five states: California, Kentucky, Florida, Maryland, and Virginia.

HORSESHOE BEND, BATTLE OF (March 27, 1814). After a six-months' campaign during the War of 1812, Gen. Andrew Jackson decisively defeated the Creek at Horseshoe Bend on the Tallapoos R in present-day Alabama. The Indians refused to surrender and all but about 50 of the 800 warriors were killed. The battle broke forever the military power of the southern Indians.

HORSE STEALING. In the West and Southwest, one of the more serious capital crimes; horse thieves were usually unceremoniously executed, usually by hanging. During the lawless decades following the Civil War, gangs of horse thieves operated out of Texas into the Old South and West.

HORTALEZ AND COMPANY. Dummy company set up 1776 by the French as a way of sending military stores secretly to the American colonists.

HOSPITALS. The Pennsylvania Hospital in Philadelphia, founded 1751, was the first permanent British-American institution created solely for care of the sick. (The French had already founded hospitals in Mobile 1713 and New Orleans ca. 1722.) After the Revolution, general hospitals appeared in urban centers (New York Hospital, 1791; Massachusetts General in Boston, 1811); they were privately supported charitable institutions designed for short-term care. Persons with incurable or terminal illnesses were sent to public almshouses. To care for the insane, custodial institutions developed. To fill military needs, the federal government created special hospital systems, the oldest being the Marine Hospital Service (1798). Throughout the 19th c., America had a mixture of city, state, and federally supported institutions and private philanthropic hospitals, the latter often established by ethnic, religious, or benevolent societies. Until midcentury the private patient scarcely existed; those with private means were cared for at home. St. Vincent's Hospital in New York (1849) was among the first to provide private rooms; since the mid-20th c., private and semiprivate rooms have predominated. Scientific laboratories and special therapy areas began to appear ca. 1890. X rays, discovered in 1895, furthered the trend toward making the hospital the workshop of medicine. An 1873 survey showed that there were 149 hospitals, one-third of which were for mental patients; fifty years later there were 6,762 hospitals, a growth resulting as hospitals' role changed from that of a hospice for the sick poor to that of diagnostic and treatment center of all

classes. After World War II, the hospital began to assume the role of community health center, as a substitute for the rapidly vanishing general practitioner.

HOT OIL CASE (*Panama Refining Company v. Ryan*, 293 US 388 [1935]). Cases in which the Supreme Court struck down New Deal legislation, ruling that Congress had delegated essential legislative power to the president.

HOT WATER, BATTLE OF (June 26, 1781). Skirmish near Williamsburg, Va., between colonial and British troops. Also called the Battle of Jamestown and Battle of Green Spring.

HOUMA. Indian tribe originally in Mississippi; migrated to Louisiana in the 18th c. Today, the Houma are a French-speaking group of mixed ancestry: Indian, black, and white, numbering approx. 2,500.

HOUSATONIC. Sloop of war of the Union fleet, blockaded Charleston in 1863–64. A hand-operated Confederate submarine torpedoed and sank it on Feb. 17, 1864.

HOUSE COMMITTEE ON UN-AMERICAN ACTIVITIES (HUAC). Founded 1938, chaired by Rep. Martin Dies, Jr., of Texas. Renamed the Internal Security Committee 1969 and abolished 1975. Firmly under control of conservatives, it concentrated on ferreting out alleged subversives in government, labor unions, the press, religious bodies, and Hollywood.

HOUSE OF HOPE (or Fort Good Hope). First European settlement in Connecticut; founded 1633 by the Dutch on the Connecticut R within the territory of modern Hartford. Soon overwhelmed by English settlements.

HOUSE OF REPRESENTATIVES. See CONGRESS, UNITED STATES.

HOUSING POLICIES, FEDERAL. In 1917, the government found it necessary to build housing projects for war workers. With the Great Depression came disaster in the private housing market, and in response many kinds of federal measures, including subsidies for low-rent public housing. The National Housing Act of 1934 established the Federal Housing Authority (FHA), which guaranteed mortgages for private housing. A series of national housing acts (1937, 1954, 1958, 1968) authorized construction of public housing for low-income groups and subsidized housing for the middle class. The Housing and Community Development Act of 1974 shifted much responsibility for low-income housing to local communities.

HOUSING AND URBAN DEVELOPMENT, DEPARTMENT OF (HUD). Cabinet-level department created 1965; brought together all housing and community-development activities of the federal government.

HOUSTON. Largest city in Texas and fourth largest in the nation; founded 1836 on Buffalo Bayou, fifty miles from the Gulf of Mexico; first capital (1837–39) of the Republic of Texas. Thrived as a timber and agricultural center; first railroad center of Texas. After 1900 an oil town and after 1919, when the Houston Ship Channel opened, an important port city. Refineries, tank farms, and chemical plants were located along the waterway. The nation's space headquarters in the 1960s with establishment of the Manned Spacecraft Center. In the 1970s a worldwide center for the petroleum industry. Also a major medical center. Pop.: 1,594,086 (1980).

HOWARD, FORT. Built 1816 at Green Bay, Wis., on the site of earlier French and British forts; first American fort on Green Bay.

HOWARD UNIVERSITY. Established 1867 in Washington, D.C., as a school for blacks. Nonsegregated today, it consists of sixteen schools and colleges; partly funded by the federal government.

HUBBARDTON, BATTLE OF (July 7, 1777). The British defeated a colonial force under Seth Warner at Hubbardton, Vt., as it retreated from Ticonderaga, N.Y.

HUDSON RIVER. Giovanni da Verrazano was probably the first white man to see the Hudson R, 1524; French traders traversed it during the 16th c., trading with the Mohawk, and founded 1540 a small fort near the site of Albany, N.Y. Henry Hudson, exploring for the Dutch West India Co., ascended the river 1609 as far as Albany and sent a party twenty-five miles further upstream, past the mouth of

the Mohawk. It thereupon became an artery for Dutch colonization, with Albany founded as a fur-trading station 1614. The British took over Dutch possessions along the river 1664. Completion of the Erie Canal 1825 added to the river's position as the chief avenue of trade and transportation from upper New York State to New York City. Robert Fulton's *Clermont* was tested on the Hudson 1807, ushering in a new era of steamboat traffic on the river. Completion of the Hudson River RR 1851 along the E bank brought about a steady diminution of the river's traffic.

HUDSON RIVER CHAIN. In 1778, a chain was stretched across the Hudson R from West Point to Constitution Island as a barrier to British shipping. The individual links were slightly over 2 feet long and 2.5 inches thick and weighed 140 pounds. The chain, weighing 180 tons, was attached to huge blocks on either shore, supported by protecting batteries; it was buoyed at frequent intervals in midstream.

HUDSON RIVER LAND PATENTS. Both the Dutch and the English made large grants along the Hudson R. The great manor of Kileaen Van Rensselaer, called Rensselaerswyck, lay on both sides of the river. Other large manors included those of Robert Livingston, Henry Beekman, Frederick Philipse.

HUDSON'S BAY COMPANY. Founded 1670; during the heyday of the fur trade, it had posts in most parts of modern Canada and a few on US soil.

HUERTGEN FOREST. Woodland near Belgian border of Germany, SE of Aachen; site of intense fighting in World War II. Stalwart German defense was attributable in part to German plans for a counterattack (see BULGE, BATTLE OF THE).

HUGUENOTS. French Protestants during religious struggles of the 16th c. Many fled to America, settling all along the Atlantic coast, especially in New York, Boston, Pennsylvania, and Maryland. In South Carolina, Huguenots began arriving 1670 and played a large part in the founding of Charleston 1680. Their religion was Calvinistic in theology and presbyterian in government.

HULL, COURT-MARTIAL OF (1814). Gen. William Hull was charged with treason, cowardice, and unofficerlike conduct for surrendering Detroit in the War of 1812. After an unfair trial, he was acquitted of treason but convicted of the other charges and sentenced to death. President Madison pardoned him.

HULL HOUSE. Settlement house founded 1889 in Chicago by Jane Addams; became the prototype of the neighborhood settlement house.

HULL'S TRAIL. Cut by Gen. William Hull through the forest and swamp on his 1812 march to Detroit. Began at Urbana, Ill.

HULL TREATY (Nov. 17, 1807). Between the US and the Ottawa, Chippewa, Wyandot, and Potawatomi. Much land in the SE Michigan Territory was ceded by the Indians.

HUMAN RIGHTS. As early as 1639, the Maryland General Assembly decreed that all freemen should "have and enjoy all such rights liberties immunities privileges and free customs ... as any natural born subject of England hath or ought to have or enjoy." In 1789, when the US Constitution was ratified, Congress undertook to add a bill of rights, which became the first ten amendments (ratified 1791). The Fourteenth Amendment, adopted after the Civil War, has had the effect of extending the human rights guarantees of the Bill of Rights to state governments. Human rights were recognized on an international scale after World War II with the adoption of the United Nations declaration of human rights. Human rights became an issue during the administration of President Carter; he restricted US foreign aid to those nations meeting minimum standards in the protection of their citizens' human rights.

HUNDRED DAYS (March 9–June 16, 1933). Special session of the 73rd Congress during which it enacted much legislation of the first New Deal.

HUNKERS. Conservative faction of the New York Democratic party after the breakup of the ALBANY REGENCY in the 1840s. Progressives were known as the Barnburners.

HUNTERS AND CHASERS OF THE EASTERN FRONTIER. Secret society formed in the US 1833 of those agitating for Canadian independence from Great Britain. Membership probably reached 40,000 in 1839. With headquarters at Cleveland, they launched several unsuccessful attacks against Windsor and Prescott, Canada. Began to disintegrate after 1841.

HUNTING GROUNDS. Limited and fairly well-defined regions recognized as the exclusive preserve of a particular tribe; also referred to a vast area, like the Great Plains, where buffalo hunting was shared by many tribes.

HUNTSVILLE. First town in Alabama; originally called Twickenham, renamed 1811. Soon became a thriving commercial center. Burned by Union forces, it regained its position after the war. Experienced phenomenal growth after World War II, when population was just over 16,000, to 142,513 by 1980.

HURON, LAKE. Second largest Great Lake, bounded by Ontario and Michigan. Discovered by Father Joseph Le Caron 1615; became the route for explorers, missionaries, and fur traders to the Mississippi R and the Plains.

HURRICANES. Intense revolving storms that occur in tropical and subtropical waters and frequently extend over land. Long a major threat to the Gulf Coast and Caribbean; occasionally they travel up the Atlantic coast as far as New England. In the past, many thousands were killed in hurricanes, but modern weather forecasting has aided authorities in evacuating areas in storm paths. Property damage remains high, however. Hurricane Agnes, for example, in 1972, caused damage totaling more than $2 billion; it was the greatest natural disaster in American history, but only 130 lives were lost in comparison with the Galveston hurricane of 1900 in which 7,000 persons were drowned.

HUTCHINSON LETTERS. Thomas Hutchinson, British governor of Massachusetts, wrote a series of letters urging abridgment of American rights and soliciting troops. Benjamin Franklin made them public, causing the Massachusetts legislature to call for Hutchinson's removal. Franklin was denounced before the Privy Council and punished by the loss of his post of deputy postmaster-general.

HYDROELECTRIC POWER. A small water-driven dynamo was installed at Niagara Falls 1880, providing power for two arc lamps in a nearby park. The first installation utilizing alternating current was located on the Willamette R in Oregon 1889; the first three-phase hydroelectric plant was located on Mill Creek in California 1892. From 1902 to 1907, hydroelectric power capacity grew from 438,472 horsepower to 1,349,087 horsepower. The Federal Power Commission was established 1920 to regulate further development of hydroelectric power. A major limitation of most hydroelectric plants, the wide annual fluctuation of stream flow, was overcome by creation of power pools, which integrated large numbers of hydroelectric and steam-generating stations into a single distribution network. In 1928, the output of hydroelectric power plants reached 43 percent of the total electric power generated in the US. The Tennessee Valley Authority (TVA) was developed in the 1930s; hydroelectric power generated by TVA was almost 10 percent of total national production of hydroelectric power by 1978. A crucial innovation since World War II has been pumped storage. During periods of slow demand, water may be pumped from one reservoir to another at a higher elevation, and then released to generate electricity during a period of high demand.

HYDROGEN BOMB. Only modest theoretical research on thermonuclear fusion was done until the Soviet Union first detonated an atomic bomb in September 1949. During the next six months, debate took place in the Truman administration over whether to develop the hydrogen bomb; on Jan. 31, 1950, Truman announced his decision to accelerate work on the bomb, thereby ending the debate. In February, S.M. Ulam and Edward Teller devised a new design principle incorporated in the first test device detonated at Eniwetok Atoll in the Pacific Ocean, Oct. 31, 1952.

HYGIENE. By 1832, most large cities had boards of health; twenty states had adopted licensure regulations for medical practitioners. Only a few individual physicians, beginning with Benjamin Rush, evinced special interest in hygiene; nor as a profession did physicians honor traditions of hygienic practices. The American Physiological Society was founded 1837 to promote public hygiene, but by the 1870s there was still no comprehensive treatise on hygiene. The situation changed abruptly with the growth of bacteriology and emergence of preventive medicine begun by Louis Pasteur and continued by many others. With the surge of scientific knowledge in the 20th c. hygiene assumed its rightful position as an integral component of medical education. (See also MENTAL HYGIENE MOVEMENT; PUBLIC HEALTH.)

HYLTON V. UNITED STATES, 3 Dallas 171 (1796). The Supreme Court ruled that a tax on carriages, imposed by Congress, was not a direct tax and therefore was constitutional; first instance of the Supreme Court passing on the constitutionality of an act of Congress.

HYMNS. Probably the only book of hymns before the Revolution was one issued at Newport 1766 by Baptists. A Methodist selection of English origin appeared 1790 and had an American supplement by 1808. By ca. 1833 collections of hymns were published by most American Protestant churches, but few hymns by Americans were included. Samuel Davies (1723–61) was the first American to write hymns that have survived. American missionary hymnody had its beginnings in Asahel Nettleton's *Village Hymns* (1824). Soon the great surge of camp meetings, Sunday schools, and prayer meetings stimulated hymn writing. In the 20th c., the ecumenical movement and the Hymn Society of America, founded 1922, have encouraged hymn writing.

IBERVILLE RIVER. Named for the sieur d'Iberville, who traversed it 1699; now called Bayou Manchac. Leaves the Mississippi fifteen miles below Baton Rouge and empties into the Amite R about twenty-five miles to the east. A link in the Spanish-French boundary after the TREATY OF PARIS (1763); Spain regarded it as the boundary between Louisiana and Spanish West Florida after the LOUISIANA PURCHASE.

ICARIA. The perfect commonwealth described by the French Communist Étienne Cabet in *Voyage en Icarie*, 1840. Cabet attempted to put the theory in practice in two US settlements: one in Fannin County, Tex.,

1848, and one in Nauvoo, Ill., 1849. There were later efforts in Missouri, Iowa, and California. None prospered.

ICELAND, US FORCES IN. Fearing a German takeover, the British and then Americans occupied Iceland during World War II.

ICHTHYOLOGY. See FISH AND MARINE LIFE.

IDAHO. First seen by white men when Lewis and Clark reached the continental divide 1805. After 1808, trappers and traders explored the area, which became a disputed borderland between Canada and the US; under British control from the War of 1812 until 1848 when it became part of the Oregon Territory. In 1863, Congress created the Idaho Territory (which included present-day Montana). Idaho, with Montana separated from it, became a state 1890. Gold was discovered 1860; the railroad came in the 1870s; and important lead and silver deposits were discovered. Farming expanded rapidly. Timber covers 40 percent of Idaho's area; lumbering is an important industry, as is tourism. Pop.: 943,935 (1980).

"I HAD RATHER BE RIGHT THAN BE PRESIDENT." Expression used by Sen. Henry Clay of Kentucky 1839; he opposed abolitionism, a position that was unpopular outside the South and injurious to his presidential chances.

ILLINOIS. The French constructed numerous forts and trading posts in the 17th and early 18th c. In 1763, control passed to Great Britain, who annexed it to the Province of Quebec 1774. George Rogers Clark captured Kaskaskia and Cahokia 1778 in the name of Virginia and later seized Vincennes, Ind., assuring American control of the Illinois Country. A county of Virginia until 1784; became part of the Northwest Territory 1787; became a state 1818. Indians relinquished their last Illinois lands after the Black Hawk War of 1832. By 1870, ranked first in wheat and corn production and livestock, and second in hog production. Still a leading agricultural state. Manufacturing has continued to expand; in 1880, manufactured products had five times the value of agriculture; the ratio was eight to one 1977. Springfield is the capital, and CHI-

CAGO has long been its commercial and financial center.

ILLINOIS, BRITISH ATTEMPTS TO REACH. The Illinois Country passed to Great Britain from France 1763; but Pontiac, chief of the Ottawa, opposed the British and blocked eastern access to the area. In 1764, the British began ascent of the Mississippi from New Orleans, but were again frustrated by Indian attacks. In 1765 Pontiac promised to abandon resistance and the French surrendered Fort Chartres.

ILLINOIS, GREAT VILLAGE OF THE. Large Indian settlement in the 17th c. on the Illinois R. Extended by 1680 along the river for three miles with a population of perhaps 7,000, made up of eight tribes. Later that year, it was attacked and destroyed by the Iroquois; its inhabitants were dispersed.

ILLINOIS AND MICHIGAN CANAL. Completed by Illinois 1848; connected Lake Michigan and the Mississippi R by a channel from Chicago to La Salle on the Illinois R. Of vast commercial importance, its use dwindled in the 20th c.

ILLINOIS AND WABASH COMPANY. Formed 1779 by the merging of two earlier companies, both of which held claims to land in the Illinois Country. Sought to establish settlements but apparently went out of business after Virginia ceded its western lands to the federal government 1784.

ILLINOIS CENTRAL RAILROAD. See RAILROADS, SKETCHES OF PRINCIPAL LINES: ILLINOIS CENTRAL GULF.

ILLINOIS COUNTRY. Term commonly applied in the 17th and 18th c. to the region that became the state of Illinois.

ILLINOIS COUNTY. Created by Virginia 1778 for the government of the Illinois Country; survived until 1784, when the federal government created the Northwest Territory.

ILLINOIS FUR BRIGADE. Annual (after 1816) trading expedition sent out by the American Fur Co. from Mackinac; traveled down Lake Michigan, through the Chicago portage and Des Plaines R to the Illinois R, where it fanned out to barter with Indians for furs.

ILLUMINATI OF NEW ENGLAND. Alleged secret cult, espousing doctrines of the French Revolution, that existed in New England ca. 1798. Alarmists regarded it as a threat to religious and civil institutions. The Freemasons were suspected of being involved. The alarm soon died out.

I'M ALONE CASE. In 1929, the US coast guard sank the Canadian vessel *I'm Alone*, which was engaged in smuggling liquor into the US. A crew member was killed, setting off an outcry in Canada. In 1935, a special commission ordered the US to offer apology and pay indemnities.

IMBODEN-JONES RAID (April 20–May 14, 1863). Two-pronged raid into West Virginia near the Maryland border by Confederate generals W.E. Jones and J.D. Imboden; railroad bridges were destroyed, and supplies and livestock were taken to Virginia in preparation for the Gettysburg campaign.

IMMEDIATISM. Movement begun ca. 1831 for the immediate abolition of slavery in the South.

IMMIGRATION. Flow of immigrants to the North American continent constitutes the greatest movement of people in Western history. In the years 1820–1979, the total of immigrants was 49,125,413. Germany sent 14.2 percent of the total; Italy, 10.8 percent; Great Britain, 10 percent; Ireland, 9.7 percent; and Sweden, 2.6 percent. France, Greece, Norway, Poland, China, and the West Indies each sent between 1 percent and 1.9 percent.

Colonial Immigration (1607–1776). The Dutch colony of New Netherland for fifty years separated the English colonies of New England from those of the South. In addition, by 1776 there were large settlements of Scotch-Irish and Irish (350,000) and Germans (225,000) on the frontier; there were smaller numbers of Huguenot French, Welsh, Swedes, Danes, Scotch, and Finns.

The Old Immigration (1776–1890). After the Napoleonic Wars, the rapid modern growth of Europe's population suddenly made itself felt. Peasants, artisans, and intellectuals became expatriates out of dissatisfaction with conditions and a belief that they would be favorable in the US. Whole regions fell victim to "America fever."

The Irish Wave. Increased rapidly from about 55,000 in the 1820s to almost 1.7 million in the 1840s and 1850s. Thereafter until 1890, Irish immigration averaged about 500,000 per decade. Most were of the artisan, small-farmer class, many the victims of land clearances and consolidations. Many settled in the large cities of the Northeast, accounting for the rapid growth of cities and providing cheap labor necessary for incipient industries. The number of new immigrants dropped drastically in the 20th c., hitting a new low of only 10,000 in the 1970s.

The German Wave. From 1820 to 1979 the total of immigrants from Germany was almost 7 million. Many came as a result of the political upheavals of 1830 and 1848. Agricultural America had a special appeal for rural Germans whose homeland was in the process of industrial development. They distributed themselves throughout the US; favored areas were in the northern Mississippi Valley.

The Scandinavians. From 1820 to 1979, immigration from Sweden totaled 1.2 million; that of Norway amounted to 856,000. Peak period for both countries was the decade between 1901 and 1910.

The Italians. In 1930, New York City had more people of Italian stock than Rome. 1907 was the peak year of Italian immigration. Since 1890 more than half have settled in New Jersey, New York, and Pennsylvania; about 15 percent settled in New England; and slightly less than 15 percent in Illinois, Indiana, and Ohio.

The Mexicans. Since 1900 the number of Mexican immigrants has risen dramatically: the first decade there was a total of 49,642; between 1971 and 1980, the number was 583,700. Most have settled in the Southwest. Total recorded for the entire period from 1820 to 1980 is 2,177,100.

The Canadians and French Canadians. Statistics are incomplete and unreliable, but it is estimated that there were 370,000 Canadians in the US in 1930. Most settled in highly industrialized regions of New England.

The Iberians. Immigrants from Portugal began to arrive in the 1870s, settling primarily along the New England coast. Peak Spanish influx was 1911 to 1920, when 68,000 were counted.

The Peoples of Eastern Europe. To the year 1900, immigration from Balkan states and eastern Europe was ascribed in official US reports either to Russia, Poland, European Turkey, or Austria-Hungary; the latter two designations embraced a number of distinct nationalities and ethnic groups. In the decade 1901–10, 2,145,261 Austro-Hungarians migrated, but national affiliation or province of origin cannot be specified. Many were undoubtedly Czechs. Over half a million Polish immigrants to the US were counted between 1820 and 1979, but the figure is known to be low. In 1950, the Russian component in the foreign-born white population was 8.8 percent. Many of these were displaced Jews, who had fled the various Russian pogroms. Immigration from the Soviet Union was 32,500 for 1971–79. The largest concentration of Russian-born immigrants, Jewish and non-Jewish, have settled in the Middle Atlantic region.

Asia. Between 1820 and 1951, 954,230 immigrants were recorded from Asiatic countries, by far the largest group Chinese (399,217). Immigration acts of 1921, 1924, and later had the direct effect of suppressing migration to the US from Asiatic lands. In the years 1954–79, refugees admitted from Asia show a total of 196,216, over half of these coming from Vietnam. Located principally in the Middle Atlantic, the Pacific coast, the Gulf Coast, and New England.

Trends of the 1960s and 1970s. Work regulations specified in the Immigration Act of 1965 tended to curtail the flow of laborers from northern Europe and South America; and the high priority given relatives increased the influx from southern Europe (especially Greece), Mexico, Canada, and Asia.

IMMIGRATION RESTRICTION. The Chinese Exclusion Act of 1882 prohibited immigration of Chinese; Japan, responding to pressure from the US government, agreed to stop emigration of unskilled workers 1908. The first quota law, the Immigration Act of 1921, limited immigration substantially and favored northwestern Europeans. The Johnson-Reed Act of 1924 further reduced quotas, setting the annual quota of immigrants at 150,000 (over 800,000 had immigrated in 1921); maintained a national-origin formula; but repealed Chinese and Japanese exclusion laws.

A 1952 update of the law maintained the formula but raised the annual quota to 160,000. A 1965 law (amended 1974) raised the quota to 170,000 and removed the worst excesses of the national-quota system. High priority was given to persons desiring reunification with their families and special consideration to political refugees and displaced persons. Effective 1968, the annual ceiling figure of 120,000 immigrants went into effect.

IMPEACHMENT. The US Constitution provides that the president, vice-president, and all civil officers (including federal judges) may be removed from office for "Conviction of Treason, Bribery, and other high Crimes and Misdemeanors." The House of Representatives has "sole Power of Impeachment" and the Senate "the sole Power to try all Impeachments." Impeachments have been voted and tried on a number of occasions, primarily involving judges. The two-thirds vote of the Senate necessary for conviction has been obtained in only three cases. Serious impeachment proceedings against the president have only occurred twice. In 1868 President Andrew Johnson was impeached by the House of Representatives but acquitted by the Senate (see IMPEACHMENT TRIAL OF ANDREW JOHNSON).

In October 1973, proceedings were begun against President Nixon. In July 1974, the House Judiciary Committee recommended three articles of impeachment to the House of Representatives; but Nixon resigned before a full House vote could be taken (see WATERGATE).

State Impeachments. State legislatures also have the right of impeachment, but have not used it extensively. Judges (often for partisan reasons) have been impeached and removed from office; and governors of three states, New York, Texas, and Oklahoma, have been impeached and removed.

IMPEACHMENT TRIAL OF ANDREW JOHNSON. Johnson succeeded to the presidency upon the death of President Lincoln and set about to put into effect Lincoln's Reconstruction program. He alienated the Radical Republicans, who favored a tougher policy toward the former Confederacy. They wanted continuance of E.M. Stanton as the secretary of war, which was the object of the Tenure of Office Act of 1867, passed over Johnson's veto. Johnson fired Stanton anyway, on Feb. 21, 1868. Three days later the House of Representatives, by a vote of 126 to 47, impeached the president for defying the Tenure of Office Act. On March 13, 1868, Senate trial began. Evidence for the prosecution consisted largely in establishing that Johnson had in fact removed Stanton. The defense was that under the Constitution, the president had the right to do so and that the Tenure of Office Act, in seeking to deprive him of that right, was unconstitutional. Johnson did not personally appear at the trial. When the vote was counted, thirty-five senators had voted guilty and nineteen not guilty; two-thirds not having pronounced, the chief justice, who was presiding, declared the president acquitted.

IMPERIALISM. The purchase of Alaska (1867) ended the period when all new US territory was assumed to be on the path to eventual statehood, and thereafter expansionism took forms more properly labeled "imperialistic." Before the Civil War, there was southern sentiment to annex Cuba as a slave-holding territory. In the post-Civil War period, there were moves to annex or control the Dominican Republic, the Danish West Indies (Virgin Islands), Samoa, and Hawaii. The Spanish-American War (1898) resulted in Guam, Puerto Rico, and the Philippine Islands becoming outright colonies, while Cuba was made a self-governing protectorate. Hawaii, which later gained old-style territorial status 1900, was also annexed during the war. Establishment of a protectorate in Cuba (1901) was followed by similar actions in Panama (1903), the Dominican Republic (1905, 1916), Nicaragua (1912), Haiti (1915), and the purchase of the Virgin Islands (1917). The Open Door notes (1899, 1900) marked a US attempt to impose its own commercial and diplomatic guidelines upon the great-power rivalry in China. The Good Neighbor policy of the 1930s involved a general abandonment of formal protectorates. In 1934, Congress voted for eventual independence for the Philippines.

IMPLIED POWERS. Doctrine holding that the Constitution gives the federal government powers, by implication, beyond the specific ones stated in the various articles; based on the clause (in Article I, Section 8) stating, "The Congress shall have Power ... to make all Laws which shall be necessary and proper for carrying into execution the foregoing Powers, and all other Powers vested by this Constitution ..." Proponents of strong central government have argued for almost unlimited implied powers, while states'-right advocates and persons who fear strong federal government, have argued the opposite. In general, the Supreme Court has upheld broad interpretations of the implied power doctrine.

IMPORTS. See TRADE, FOREIGN.

IMPRESSMENT, CONFEDERATE. Confederate policy of seizing supplies for the army from producers and slaves for work on fortifications. Criticism of administration of the law and the law itself increased with the growing suffering. Abandoned toward the end of the war.

IMPRESSMENT OF SEAMEN. The drafting of men into a navy, it caused bad relations between Great Britain and the US between 1790 and 1815. The British, in the midst of the Napoleonic Wars, claimed the belligerent's right to search foreign neutral ships and to remove any seamen deemed British (about 20,000 British seamen were serving on American ships). They left determining of nationality to press gangs and boarding officers; native-born American seamen were returned without indemnity if their citizenship could be proved, but each separate case had to be established by the US government. Three times the US tried to negotiate a treaty in which each party would deny itself the right to impress persons from the other's ships. In 1812, Congress alleged impressment to be the principal cause of the war against Great Britain.

INAUGURATION OF THE PRESIDENT. The Constitution requires that the elected president be inaugurated by taking an oath (or affirmation) of office. The vice-president takes a similar oath. Usually administered by the chief justice on the steps of the Capitol. Until 1933, inauguration was on the March 4 following the election; since then, January 20 has been inaugural day.

INCOME TAX CASES (*Pollock v. Farmer's Loan and Trust Company*, 157 US 429; *Rehearing*, 158 US 601 [1895]). Supreme Court ruled unconstitutional an 1894 income tax of

2 percent on incomes over $4,000. Not until 1913, after adoption of the Sixteenth Amendment, could a federal income tax be levied.

INCOME TAXES. See TAXATION.

INDEMNITIES. Payments exacted to recoup military costs of a victor state or to compensate for damages suffered by a state or its nationals from injuries by another state or its nationals. Efforts to collect German reparations after World War I and World War II showed the impracticability of full compensation for losses in major wars. The 20th c. has brought many repudiations of national debts by revolutionary regimes and large-scale nationalizations of alien property, despite international law demanding prompt and adequate compensation to previous owners. Use of force to collect such debts has been largely abandoned.

INDENTURED SERVANTS. In colonial America, for the most part adult white persons bound to labor for a period of years. There were three classes: the free-willers, or redemptioners; those who were kidnapped or forced to leave their home country because of poverty or for political or religious reasons; and convicts. Most colonies regulated treatment of servants. Runaways were compelled to return to their masters. Indentured service ceased after the Revolution.

INDEPENDENCE. City in Missouri, founded 1827 on the Missouri R. At the head of the Santa Fe and Oregon-California trails, the jumping-off place of the American frontier. Home of Harry S. Truman and site of the Truman library. Pop.: 111,805 (1980).

INDEPENDENCE DAY. Adoption of the Declaration of Independence on July 4, 1776, has caused that day to be celebrated as the birth date of the US since the early days of the Republic. Declared a national holiday 1941.

INDEPENDENCE HALL. Structure in Philadelphia where the Declaration of Independence, Articles of Confederation, and Constitution were signed. Built (1732–57) as Pennsylvania's state house; meeting place of the Continental Congress during the Revolution.

INDEPENDENCE ROCK. Granite boulder on the N bank of the Sweetwater R in Wyoming; landmark on the Oregon Trail.

INDEPENDENT TREASURY SYSTEM. Alternative to a central bank, supported by Democrats. Congress set up the system 1846 to receive and pay only in specie at subtreasuries located in major cities. It worked badly, and the government made increasing use of banks, which promptly loaned money left in their hands. In 1914, the Federal Reserve System, a central bank, went into operation; in 1921 the Independent Treasury System ended.

INDIANA. First sighted by the French as early as the 1670s. Small settlements were established, notably Fort Miami ca. 1704. After the French and Indian War, the region was ceded to the English. After the Revolution, it became part of the US, and settlement began; in 1788 it became part of the Northwest Territory. The Americans defeated the Indians at the decisive Battle of Tippecanoe in 1811, thereby opening the territory to unimpeded colonization. Became the nineteenth state 1816. From 1800 to 1830, most settlers came from Kentucky, the Carolinas, Maryland, and Tennessee. Thereafter, most settlers came from Ohio and the Middle Atlantic; there was an influx of immigrants, particularly Germans. Traditionally an agricultural state, manufacturing began after the coming of the railroads. By 1980, when the state had 5.5 million residents, more than two-thirds were urban dwellers.

INDIANA COMPANY. A group of Indian traders lost goods at the hands of Indians in 1763. As compensation, the chiefs of the Six Nations presented them with a large tract of land. On the outbreak of the American Revolution, the Indiana Co. was reorganized and proceeded to sell this land; but operations were blocked by Virginia, which claimed the land. The Continental Congress recognized the claims of the Indiana Co., but Virginia refused to recognize Congress's jurisdiction. After the Constitution became effective 1789, the company brought suit against Virginia; the court ruled it had no jurisdiction.

INDIAN AFFAIRS, BUREAU OF (BIA). Principal federal agency responsible for Indian programs. Under one name or another, in existence since 1824. Part of the War Department until 1849; later transferred to the Interior Department. Principal responsibilities are land and resource management and development; education, vocational training, and placement; law and order; and social welfare. Since the 1970s, the BIA has transferred authority and responsibility wherever possible to the various tribes.

Indian Agencies. Local administrative units of the BIA that most directly affect reservation Indians. An agency may have jurisdiction over a single reservation, part of a reservation, or several reservations. Each is headed by an agent or a superintendent. Agency personnel may be specialists in several fields, including education, law enforcement, social welfare, forestry, adult vocational training, employment assistance, and housing.

INDIANAPOLIS. Capital and largest city of Indiana; marketing center for very rich farmland; industries include meat and food processing, precision tool works, and chemical works. An insurance and financial center. Founded as the capital city 1820 by the legislature, who located it at the center of the expected state population. Pop.: 700,807 (1980).

INDIAN BARRIER STATE. A neutral barrier state closed to white settlement but open for Indian trade was first proposed 1755, to settle French and British claims to the Ohio Valley. Similar plans were proposed after that; but once independent, the US asserted its authority over Indian lands, and the idea was dropped.

INDIAN BIBLE, ELIOT'S. 1200-page translation into Algonkin by John Eliot, composed 1650–58 and printed on the hand press at Harvard; published 1663. Eliot not only had to learn the language but also to invent an orthography.

INDIAN BRIGADE. Three Union regiments in the Civil War composed largely of Cherokee, Creek, and Seminole, which fought many minor engagements in NE Indian Territory.

INDIAN CLAIMS COMMISSION. Established 1946 by Congress to hear and settle claims by Indian tribes for compensation for lands taken from them. Expired 1978; remaining claims transferred to the Court of Claims. By 1980 almost $400 million had been awarded to claimant tribes.

INDIAN COMMISSIONS. In 1865 President Andrew Johnson named a commission to negotiate treaties with the Indians of the Great Plains and Southwest; it met with only minor success. Several other commissions were named in the 1860s to handle specific Indian problems. In 1869 Congress authorized a permanent Board of Indian Commissioners to exercise joint control with the secretary of the interior over a fund to promote peace and civilization among the Indians. Abolished 1933.

INDIAN COUNTRY. Generally, a territory to which Indian title had not been extinguished; specifically, the area set aside in pursuance of the Indian removal policy formulated 1825. By 1840, Indian Country extended from Texas to Canada and included much of the territory in between. Gradually reduced over the years until 1854, when it became known as the Indian Territory, roughly equivalent to modern Oklahoma.

INDIAN CULTURE, AMERICAN. Ethnologists agree that American Indians are descended from people of NE Asia who made a series of migrations across the Bering Strait and into North America, beginning as early as 25,000 years ago. Different groups fanned out from an original point of entry in Alaska, became isolated, and began to assume both cultural and linguistic identities. Physically, the American Indian peoples relate to a general East Asian Mongoloid strain; but there is great diversity in physical types. The skin color of Indians has been popularly designated "red," believed to stem from the practice of those first seen by Europeans of applying red ochre dye to their bodies. Indians speak 600 separate languages, none of which have been proven related to a Eurasian speech family. Languages were unwritten until Europeans introduced variously conceived phonetic alphabets. Two primary patterns are discernible beneath the diversity. (1) In N North America and S South America, initial arctic and subarctic hunting adaptation persisted. Both areas used the transportable skin tent and similar modes of dressing skins, tailoring clothes, and working stone; food and its preparation and weapon assemblage were similar; and social, political, and religious structures appear also to have much in common.(2) In the temperate, subtropical, and tropical regions, the migrants became settled, their cultures based on various forms of wild-seed gathering; from this gathering adaptation, centered in Middle America, the basic agricultural inventions of the Indians proceeded. The most intensive cultural developments occurred in Mexico, Peru, the American Southwest, and the lower Mississippi. There was superficial contact with Norsemen in NE North America and probably some exchange between South American Indians and Polynesia. The wheel and the wheeled vehicle were unknown to the American Indian. The population in both North and South America in 1492 has been estimated at 8.5 million. The population north of Mexico is estimated at 1.1 million. Diseases and epidemics brought by the white man caused the native populations to decline. Native American cultural diversity broadly reflects the adaptations of farmers, gatherers, and hunters to their natural surroundings.

Eskimo Culture Area. So distinct are the Eskimo (or Inuit) culturally that they are often accorded an identity all their own. They may have been the last arrivals in North America, spreading out from the W American arctic ca. AD 1000, moving as far E as Greenland. They all speak a mutually intelligible language. Their subsistence is gained basically through hunting, on both sea and land. The Eskimo lack any tribal or political sense, stressing familial relationships. Inventions include the harpoon with detachable head, the saucerlike lamp fueled by seal oil, tailored skin and fur clothing, and several types of boats, including the kayak. Sod and stone houses were in general use, although a few groups lived in the domed ice lodge. The basic element in their religion was a world view according to which the inhabitants of the animal world were seen as morally superior to men, allowing themselves, if the proper rituals were carried out, to be taken for food. A second element was shamanism, marked by the presence of curers or doctors.

North American Subarctic Culture Area. Not easily defined, because residents in the interior both of Alaska and of N Canada were influenced by the more vital cultures nearest them. Characterized by an inland adaption to tundra and boreal forest and the hunting of caribou, moose, and deer. Both exploited game resources to the full, though fur trapping did not come into its own until after the 17th c. Principal designations of tribal groups depend on language; subarctic groups had no political sense. The socioeconomic band was the primary functioning unit, usually based on kinship. They moved about in the course of a year for hunting, trapping, and fishing. Inventions include the round and tailed snowshoe, pemmican, and a portable skin tent that presaged the Plains tipi. Religion was similar to that of the Eskimo, with recognition of animal spirits, shamanism, and group ceremonies involving hunting. Girls were secluded for a year following the onset of the menses; the bringing of such young women back into the band was the major ceremonial event.

Northwest Coast Culture Area. Stretching from SE Alaska to Puget Sound, an exclusively maritime culture, especially dependent on salmon. Aboriginal population appears never to have been large. Small villages were the rule, groups federated by communality and kinship. A tribal sense evolved, which allowed for cultural and linguistic distinctiveness. Villages were composed of cedar-plank extended-family houses inhabited by as many as forty people. Prestige and social status were achieved through dissemination of property; potlatch gift-giving originated: one village feasted another, or there was exchange feasting between groups within a village. Among the tribes were the Kwakiutl, Haida, Tlingit, and Tsimshian. A modified maternal system existed (for example, property was inherited from the mother's brother). There were chiefs, but political power rested with the group. Salmon and other fish were netted, seined, and lured. Horn and antler wedges were used to split cedar logs into planks. Elaborate dugout canoes were common. The totem pole, a familial device, was erected at the center of the house front, the mouth of one of the figures on the pole being used for the entrance. The principal ceremonial was the First Salmon Rite. Animals represented on the totem pole were those with which an ancestor had had a mystical experience.

Western Culture Areas: Plateau, Basin, and California. Although topographically isolated by mountains and deserts, they had a common dependence on wild-seed gathering. Only among the Mohave and Yuma did the strong agricultural development of the Southwest manifest itself. Plateau peoples were divided into fairly distinct tribal-linguistic units; a sense of village and tribal autonomy existed. The office of the chief, dependent on force of personality and speaking skills, assumed some importance in village affairs. Economically, they depended on the gathering of various wild root crops; on hunting; and on salmon, taken in large quantities. In the Basin, often under desert conditions, hunting deer and rabbits was interspersed with gathering juniper berries and pine nuts; a wide variety of insects was obtained for food. After 1700, Eastern Basin and Plateau tribes took on the horse and the Plains manner of warfare. California was characterized by the gathering of acorns, supplemented with hunting and fishing, and this dependency on the acorn gave the area its distinctive separatism; a single tribe inhabiting a single village might renounce all contact with other groups, and warfare might result from trespass. Of the three areas, the Basin had the simplest technology; inventions and adaptions were made by the Californians especially, including leaching baskets (for the acorns) and stone points for both the dart and the arrow. Housing varied widely, from the wickiup of the Basin to the plank houses of the Yurok and Hupa, pale reflections of those of the Northwest, to a great range of tentlike shelters, brush houses, and semisubterranean dwellings. The rabbitskin blanket was widely used for warmth; basketry and matting were the high points of artistic achievement in the Basin area; geometric designs were created. Religion was simple among the Basin peoples. Ceremonial dancing, shamanism, and the girls' rites were all less elaborate among them than in California and the Plateau.

Plains Culture Area. Before the advent of the horse, Plains tribes encompassed a number of largely undifferentiated cultures, moderately nomadic. The portable skin tent was dragged by dogs on the travois. Bison were hunted and often stampeded over cliffs. Horses that had escaped the Spanish thrived on the Plains and were captured and domesticated by the Indians. Plains culture and its associated war patterns had come into their own by 1780, by which time the equestrian

development had been fully integrated. A twofold ecological system arose; sedentary eastern Plains groups, such as the Omaha and Osage, although strongly influenced by the horse and by bison hunting, developed maize farming, contrasting with the exclusively equestrian tribes, such as the Crow, Blackfoot, Kiowa, and Comanche. Tribal entities in the Plains were definable by territory, language, and common cultural convention. Hunting and war patterns created the basic band unit, although the bands cooperated at times, especially at times of intensive bison hunting. Strong maternal clan institutions appeared in the northeast, while eastern tribes such as the Omaha developed equally strong paternal stress. There were no paramount chiefs but rather leaders for various activities: hunt chiefs, war leaders, priests, and curers. In hunting, the Plains Indians acted as though at war; the hunt was rigorously policed, groups of warriors acting to keep other hunters in line. Status was achieved on the basis of a system of formal counting of acts of bravery, or coups. Every part of the bison was used: the skins for robes, the sinew for thread, the paunch as a cooking vessel. Flesh was jerked, pounded with berries, dried, and boiled. Religious life was a mixture of acts of war and benign ceremonies for tribal good. In the Sun Dance, for example, a common ritual throughout the area, accompanied by the display of related fetish objects, there was a vague sense of tribal benefit to be obtained from the sun; yet at the same time the dance was a vow of vengeance. The quest of a vision was the major religious preoccupation; fasting, humbling, and self-torture were all employed toward that end.

Eastern Culture Areas: Eastern Woodlands (Northeast) and Southeast. A unified cultural focus was evidenced in the area from the Great Lakes to the Gulf of Mexico and from the Atlantic coast to the Mississippi. Strong Mexican influences contributed to intensive farming and construction of elaborate earthworks in prehistoric times. The Southeast was apparently the source of a series of population movements that took place before European contact. Many Northeastern Algonkin-speaking tribes were an extension of Southeast culture. The hallmark of the Southeast culture area was its political organization. The tribal sense amounted almost to nationalism. Groups such as the Creek,

Cherokee, Choctaw, and Iroquois developed strongly defined political systems involving well-defined official positions and political federations. From such federations derive the peace pipe, wampum, the sachem, and the tomahawk. The Southeastern peoples tended to build palisaded villages, a pattern that extended to the Northeast. A town had fields, cabins (L-shaped houses of wattle and daub), and game yard, a virtual stadium. In addition, some tribes of the Gulf region had a ceremonial structure, a temple-like circular building, often on a mound. Among the Creek and their neighbors, men were warriors, hunters, and farmers; women owned land and house. The men married into the woman's community. Office was obtained by inheritance through females; women as a group achieved a virtual gynocracy. The Eastern Woodland peoples were less well defined in tribal estate and social structure, but many developed federations out of fear of the Iroquois. They stressed the patrilineal family. Tribalism existed as a force, related to hunting territory. There was no formalized structure of chieftainship. In the Southeast, tobacco was strongly developed. Corn was ground in mortars. Beans and persimmons were staples. Poisons were used in fishing and war. Nonagricultural groups made extensive use of birchbark for canoes, housing, and containers. Southeastern religon was based on agriculture, stressing fertility and rituals designed to enhance the growing of food. Animal spirits were not unknown, and there is some parallel to the vision quest of the Plains tribes. There were shamanistic curers, and rituals included purification, fasting, ritual emetics, and solemnity. Groups to the west had an elaborate mythology, including the Hiawatha legend, Manebush, and the "Great Spirit."

Southwestern Culture Area. The Southwest shows considerable cultural diversity and linguistic variation, with two major foci in the prehistoric past: the Pueblo of N Arizona and New Mexico and the Hohokam culture of S Arizona. The prehistoric Basket-Maker culture arose to a peak of development between AD 1000 and AD 1300. The Athapascan-speaking Navaho and Apache reached the area in late prehistoric times. Most remarkable about the area is the intensive agriculture that was developed in the face of desert conditions. The Spanish term *pueblo* refers to the permanent villages of adobe and stone, with multistoried houses, sometimes having 200 to 300 rooms. The towns, with populations ranging from 250 to 3,000, were arranged according to local tradition. The Hopi and Acoma towns were built on mesa tops, the houses aligned to the contours of the mesa itself. In the Rio Grande Valley, several blocks of houses might be put together in rows, sometimes with a central plaza. The important structure was the kiva, the ceremonial chamber. The Pueblo possessed a tightly knit society and well-defined kinship relationships. Among the Hopi and Zuni, a matrilineal clan system was paramount. In the central Pueblo area, among the Keresan Pueblo, matriarchy was less strong; and in the east, among the Tanoans, the paternal dual system arose. The Spanish, especially after the Pueblo revolt of 1680, introduced elected secular officials with some success. Most pueblos had an official peacemaker, an obscure and mystic figure often designated the cacique. He was required to concentrate on communal good, acting as the bearer of peace. Pueblo agriculture centered on maize, although tobacco, corn, beans, and squashes were also basic. Men wove textiles; women made pottery. Footgear was generally a buckskin moccasin. Rug-weaving developed into a notable art. Religion was the major cohesive element in Pueblo society, directed principally toward a reaffirmation of a tie with traditional supernatural beings.

Twentieth-Century Indian Culture. The 1980 census reported 1,418,000 Indians and Alaska natives in the US, compared with 523,591 in 1960, making them the most rapidly increasing group in the US. More than 50 percent live in urban areas, particularly Chicago, Los Angeles, the San Francisco Bay area, and Minneapolis-St. Paul. Indians who have not migrated live on about 200 reservations. The Navaho, living mainly in Arizona and New Mexico are by far the largest tribe, with a population of 140,000. The best-preserved Indian cultures are those of the Hopi, Zuni, and Navaho. More than fifty languages are still alive, despite the inroads of acculturation. The Pan-Indian movement became strong in the 1970s; it was based on maintaining an Indian identity. Other Indian groups were involved in political action of various kinds, all aimed at improving the condition of the Indian. As a group, Indians remain the most deprived in the nation. In 1970, the average annual income per Indian family was only $1,500, while the unemployment rate was ten times the national average. Life expectancy was 33 percent lower than the national average. The educational level of all Indians remained below that of the nation as a whole. Although modern Indians by no means speak with one voice, there are many issues on which most agree. Most wish to retain their Indian cultures and their identity as Indians. They want the right to determine their own destinies rather than have decisions made for them by non-Indians. At the same time, they insist that the nation honor its treaty obligations and continue to assist them financially and in other ways. (See also INDIAN MEDICINE; INDIAN POLICY, COLONIAL; INDIAN POLICY, NATIONAL; INDIAN RESERVATIONS; INDIAN TERRITORY.)

INDIAN FACTORY OF VIRGINIA. Attempted trade system between the English and the Cherokee during the French and Indian War, in 1757. Factors, or traders, were to barter supplies with the Indians, at the same time recruiting warriors. The first cargo was recalled from the Indian Country because of the Cherokee War; later the plan was dropped.

INDIAN MEDICINE. The Eskimo and other native American hunting groups developed the concept of the shaman, popularly termed a medicine man, calling him to restore the soul, and thereby good health, by ritual and magic. Hunting cultures recognized that such illnesses as toothache, broken bones, sleeplessness, and constipation could be treated by more prosaic means: potions, infusions, and poultices. The Navaho built a religious system based on curing by chants and rituals. Gulf tribes, such as the Creek, gave special training to curers. Sweat bathing was used for cures. "Medicine bundles," buckskinwrapped sacred objects, were thought to have curative powers among the Plains tribes; but their primary function was ceremonial. Native South Americans contributed more to medical knowledge than did native North Americans. From tropical forests came curare, originally a poison; rubber products, including tubing and the enema syringe; and quinine, coca, and ipecac.

INDIAN MISSIONS. During the colonial period, efforts to Christianize Indians were made by the Spanish in Florida and the Southwest; French Jesuits in the South and New York; Roger Williams, John Eliot, and David Brainerd in New England and the Middle Atlantic; and the Moravians among various tribes. Missionary and gospel societies were organized both before and after the Revolution by various Protestant denominations.

INDIAN POLICY, COLONIAL.
British Policy Prior to 1755. The British viewed Indian title to land as one of occupancy, with the ultimate fee in crown and colony. Indian affairs were largely controlled by individual colonies, resulting in their being robbed of land and cheated in trade. Many tribes, therefore, allied themselves with the French during the French and Indian War.

British Policy After 1755. To win Indian support, the British inaugurated a system of imperial management 1755, creating two separate Indian departments. By 1761, the right to buy Indian lands had been denied the American colonies. A proclamation in 1763 guaranteed to the Indians "for the present" the lands between the Appalachians and the Mississippi. A new proposal 1764 provided that the Indian superintendents be given the right to regulate such Indian affairs as treaties, trade, land purchases, and matters pertaining to peace and war. All Indian traders were to be placed in their control. In 1767, a compromise between imperial and colonial control was effected: regulation of Indian trade was transferred to the colonies and plans made for a definite Indian boundary. Westward colonization, when and if it came, would be under imperial control. The real problem then was to prevent encroachments upon the frontier land. The Indians were paid very little for land cessions. The British, nevertheless, succeeded in retaining the friendship of the major tribes during the Revolution.

INDIAN POLICY, NATIONAL.
Indians in the American Revolution. Indians generally took the British side. The Iroquois aided the British on the Canadian front; to the south, the Shawnee, Creek, Delaware, and Cherokee were active.

Early Federal Policy. The Articles of Confederation placed affairs firmly in the hands of the federal government; the Constitution generally did the same. Before the War of 1812, Indian policy had two principal objectives: to keep them pacified and to gain control of their trade. Both the French and the British tried to incite them against the Americans and to win their fur trade. In 1806, a superintendent of Indian trade was named. Trade fell increasingly into private hands; the office of superintendent was abolished 1830.

Land Cessions and Treaties. For nearly a century after the founding of the US, Indian land cessions were accomplished by means of treaties couched in the formal language of international covenant. These treaties were negotiated with Indian chieftains by appointees of the executive branch of the federal government and ratified by the US Senate. Compensation to Indians for ceded land consisted of livestock, various kinds of merchandise (often guns and ammunition), and annuities. By 1880, the federal government had expended more than $187 million for the extinguishment of Indian land titles. But in return it had gained title to virtually all of the contiguous US.

Removal Policy. The predominant theme in Indian policy in the first half of the 19th c. was that of transferring to lands in the West all those Indians east of the Mississippi R who wished to continue their tribal status, the so-called removal program. In 1802, when Georgia was asked to cede lands from which the states of Alabama and Mississippi were later created, its officials insisted that in return the federal government promise to obtain for the state title to all Indian lands within its borders. In 1804, Congress authorized the president to work out an exchange of eastern lands for those in the West. By 1809, substantial opposition to removal had developed among the eastern tribes, motivated by the experiences of the Cherokee, Delaware, and Shawnee, who had voluntarily gone westward in the late 18th c. President Monroe in 1817 called for the resettlement of nearly 100,000 eastern Indians. Andrew Jackson as president espoused a vigorous policy of Indian removal, with the full support of Congress, which passed the Indian Removal Act of 1830. It created the INDIAN TERRITORY for tribes agreeing to land exchanges and created a mechanism for securing the permission of the indigenous tribes of Indian Territory, who were being asked to accept strangers onto their lands. Virtually all the tribes of Ohio, Illinois, and Indiana gave up their lands under that law and were moved westward. The greatest resistance to removal came from the tribes of the Southeast; even the small Seminole tribe chose to fight rather than consent to removal. The most tragic story is that of the Cherokee (see TRAIL OF TEARS). By 1850, the period of removal was essentially over. The 1850s and 1860s saw the holdings of the relocated Indians further reduced as new states were created out of lands once "permanently" set aside for Indian occupancy. By 1850, the federal government had acquired more than 450 million acres by 245 separate Indian treaties. As the Civil War neared, new features of Indian policy were developed. Important among them was land allotment. The treaty of 1854 with the Omaha contained the first comprehensive provision for division of Indian lands into individual holdings and provided a model for later treaties. During the Civil War, the FIVE CIVILIZED TRIBES, were subjected to pressures from both sides, despite their preference for neutrality. Consequently, there were Indian contingents fighting on both sides.

Assimilation Policy. The major thrust of federal policy following the Civil War was toward subduing still-hostile western tribes and placing them on reservations. In 1871, Congress decreed that the federal government would not enter into any further treaties with Indian tribes. In the 1870s, many missionary groups began to advocate policies aimed at Indian assimilation. Efforts were made to break up the communal holdings of each tribe and distribute the land among its members, making Indian yeoman farmers more similar to their white neighbors. In 1887 a federal allotment act was passed providing for the breakup of the reservations. It also called for the creation of off-reservation boarding schools for Indian youngsters; it was widely believed that they could be educated in the ways of whites, thereby solving the "Indian problem." By midcentury there were more than 100 schools financed in part from the "civilization fund," all operated by religious organizations, except for the Five Civilized Tribes, who administered their own. Religious influence waned after 1870, when the federal government undertook to operate Indian schools. The first federal boarding school was established 1879 at Carlisle, Pa.

In the 1890s, the Bureau of Indian Affairs began contracting with local public school districts for educating Indian youngsters.

Citizenship Policy. Some early Indian treaties, such as that of 1830 with the Choctaw, provided for grants of citizenship to individual Indians. Later treaties conditioned citizenship on the acceptance of an allotment of land or on the approval by an administrative body, which was empowered to determine fitness for citizenship. Several Indian naturalization acts were passed after the Civil War. By 1924, approximately two-thirds of the Indians in the US had become citizens; in that year, Congress passed a general Indian citizenship act, as a result of which all native-born Indians came to enjoy full citizenship status.

Twentieth-Century Policy. The 1920s were years of confusion as new policy proposals were made and considered. Various proposals were contained in the Indian Reorganization Act of 1934, which provided for an end to the allotment program; continuance of federal trusteeship over lands already alloted; construction of local schools; democratic local governments on the reservations; and a policy of Indian preference with respect to employment in the Bureau of Indian Affairs. A 1946 law made it easier to bring claims against the federal government. The dominant policy theme during most of the 1950s was that of withdrawing special federal services from Indians and elevating the Indian to a status of equality with other citizens. This policy produced protest from Indian groups, who were united in their effort to have it overturned. It ceased to be a major policy in the 1960s and 1970s, when the principal trend was toward placement of administrative responsibility for reservation services in the hands of Indians, while the federal government continued to finance these services. Special legislation to permit the Bureau of Indian Affairs to contract with Indian tribes and make grants to them was passed by Congress 1975.

INDIAN RESERVATIONS. Although some states have created small Indian reservations, the vast majority are under the supervision of the US Bureau of Indian Affairs, which administers more than 400 discrete Indian land units. Reservations may be inhabited by a single tribe or by several tribes. The Indian Reorganization Act of 1934 provided legal authority for the residents of a single reservation, regardless of how many tribes they might represent, to establish a unified local government. Although the lands in some reservations, especially those of the Southwest, are still held in common ownership, it is more usual for reservations to be a combination of tribally and individually owned lands. In the latter instance, the federal government is the trustee for both tribal and individual owners and enforces restrictions against mortgage and sale. In some areas, notably the Great Plains and the Pacific Northwest, much land inside the original boundaries of reservations was acquired by non-Indians prior to passage of the 1934 act. A confusing combination of state, tribal, and federal jurisdiction prevails within the boundaries of such reservations.

INDIAN SPRINGS, TREATIES OF (1821, 1825). The Creek ceded all their lands in Georgia and agreed to migrate west of the Mississippi. Superseded by the 1826 Treaty of Washington.

INDIAN STREAM REPUBLIC. Settlers in the extreme northerly part of New Hampshire established their own government and adopted their own constitution 1832. Their claim of independence, or, failing that, of belonging to the US, but not to New Hampshire, was rejected by both state and federal governments. Despite some sentiment to join Canada, in 1836 the people voted to join New Hampshire.

INDIAN TERRITORY. Originally included all of Oklahoma except the panhandle; never an organized territory, but set aside as a home for the Five Civilized Tribes, who were removed to it in the period 1820–42. In 1866, they ceded the western part as a home for other tribes.

INDIAN TRADE AND INTERCOURSE ACT (1834). Set aside a "permanent" INDIAN COUNTRY, from which white settlers were to be rigidly excluded. Trading was permitted only under federal license and safeguards were established to protect the Indians. Guarantees remained in effect only so long as whites were not interested.

INDIAN TRADE AND TRADERS. Explorers and settlers arriving in America saw vast potential wealth in furs and skins. In the north, Indian trade was almost synonymous with the beaver trade; in southern latitudes, trade was mainly in coarse skins and hides, such as deer, bear, and buffalo. See also FUR TRADE.

INDIAN TRIBAL COURTS. Created in the late 19th c. and consisting usually of one to three Indian judges; held on various reservations. They try minor cases in which Indians are party; sometimes called courts of Indian offenses.

INDIGO CULTURE. Introduced into South Carolina 1744. Stability was given the industry by the granting (1748) by the British government of a bounty; became after rice the colony's most important crop. Production declined after the Revolution.

INDUSTRIAL BROTHERHOOD. Organized 1868, an early effort to fuse a national labor organization. Did not survive the depression of the 1870s.

INDUSTRIAL MANAGEMENT. In the early 20th c., a term used interchangeably with SCIENTIFIC MANAGEMENT. By the 1940s, the term primarily meant factory management; hardly used by 1980s. In general, the pertinent courses being taught in schools of business administration were known as "systems analysis," "production and operations management," and so forth.

INDUSTRIAL RELATIONS. Also known as personnel management, human resources management, and employer-employee relations. Can be traced to Robert Owens, British textile-mill owner and utopian socialist, who discovered that productivity could be increased if workers were treated with dignity. He influenced men like Ordway Tead, who promoted the organization of personnel departments in corporations in the early 20th c. Areas of concern include selection of workers to fit various jobs; studies of appropriate organization structures into which workers should be fitted to work most effectively; motion-and-time studies which standardize and measure performance; and the corporation's overall policy toward trade unions to which its workers belong.

INDUSTRIAL RESEARCH. As a systematic pursuit did not generally appear until late in the 19th c. A typical industrial scientist of the period was C.B. Dudley, who conducted studies for the Pennsylvania RR on the composition of rails and establishing standards and specification for mechanical equipment used by that railroad. In 1901 Congress established the US Bureau of Standards, which assisted manufacturers in devising uniform specifications for products and processes. Entrepreneurs became aware that the application of science could be used for profitable innovation and product development. The Standard Oil Co. devised a process that made it possible to utilize profitably sulfurous petroleum deposits. Leo Baekeland invented a synthetic plastic (Bakelite), the forerunner of many such inventions later in the century. Thomas A. Edison had founded a company in 1870s for the primary purpose of conducting industrial research; Arthur D. Little founded a similar company 1886. Such firms inspired large manufacturing companies to establish their own research laboratories; notable were those of General Electric, Du Pont, Eastman Kodak, and, most famous of all, Bell Laboratories, founded by American Telephone and Telegraph. In the 1920s, automotive research came of age, notably that done for General Motors by C.F. Kettering. After World War II, industrial research came into its own, much at the level of pure scientific research, often done in cooperation with the federal government and universities. Such corporate giants as IBM, Xerox, and all the companies based on utilizing the semiconductor can trace their growth directly to their research efforts.

INDUSTRIAL WORKERS OF THE WORLD (IWW). Radical labor organization founded 1905 as an alternative to the American Federation of Labor. From 1909 to 1918, achieved success and notoriety as the most militant institution on the American left, appealing to all workers regardless of skill, nationality, race, or sex, and seeking to organize them into giant industrial unions that would seize control of industry and abolish the capitalist system. Members were known as Wobblies. Virtually destroyed by federal action during World War I, when leaders were charged with sedition; only forty-two groups in existence 1980.

INDUSTRIES, COLONIAL. During the colonial period, most Americans were involved in agriculture; but there were other economic pursuits: naval stores, including tar, pitch, resin, and turpentine; planks, boards, shingles, and even house frames; and potash and pearl ash, were exported. New England port cities became shipbuilding centers, which stimulated such allied industries as the making of sails, rope, nails, spikes, anchors, and chain-plates. In New England, fishing and whaling developed into major industries. Textile-making was largely a household industry, but a few shops in New England produced rough serges and linsey-woolseys. Other home manufactures were furniture, tools and other implements, wagons, harnesses, and nails. Ironmaking reached large proportions. Other industries were tanneries and leatherworking, fulling mills, gristmills, powder mills, brick kilns, saltworks, paper mills, printing shops, firearm shops, and breweries and distilleries.

INDUSTRY, FORT. Located on the Maumee R, on site of present-day Toledo, Ohio; here the Indian tribes ceded (1805) 2.7 million acres of land in the Western Reserve.

INFLATION. Prior to the Revolution, inflation occurred in many colonies where bills of credit were issued by the government and made legal tender. During the Revolution, bills of credit were put into circulation on a large scale by both the states and the Continental Congress. By January 1781, the currency was valued at 100 to 1 in relation to specie (gold), and by May it had no value. With establishment of the new Republic, prices remained moderate until the War of 1812, when another inflation occurred, caused by the overissuance of bank notes; after 1815, the price level receded sharply until 1821. Major inflation occurred during the Civil War, again fueled by the issue of paper money. The price level dropped rapidly after 1865 until 1880. With the outbreak of World War I, prices again began to rise, peaking in spring 1920, when the wholesale price index stood at 244 percent of the prewar level. Because of direct controls introduced in 1942, official price indexes in World War II rose only moderately (between 10 and 15 percent); with removal in 1946, the unleashing of monetary purchasing power drove prices up again. Beginning in the late 1950s, the US suffered from disturbingly high annual rates of inflation. The Vietnam War and a series of extremely unbalanced federal budgets carried inflation into the 1970s. From 1971 to 1974, the Nixon administration entered into price and wage controls by administrative decrees and commissions. The Arab oil embargo of 1973–74 raised energy and petrochemical costs to heights that disrupted the entire price structure. Market forces set in motion produced both recession and an 11 percent inflation in 1974. In 1976, inflation dropped to 5.8 percent, but in 1977, a four-year increase began, from 6.5 in 1977, to 13.5 in 1980. President Reagan's extensive budget cuts and a prolonged economic recession resulted in a decrease to 6.7 percent in 1982.

INFLATION IN THE CONFEDERACY. By the end of 1861, the Confederate congress had issued a total of $105 million in treasury notes, without much resorting to taxes. Confederate bonds did not sell well. The government tried to meet expenses by issuing still more treasury notes; by the end of 1864, the amount of currency had risen to $1 billion, and the gold quotation was 40 to 1. State, city, and private issues of notes complicated the currency, as did large issues by banks, which had been freed from the compulsion to redeem notes in specie early in the war. Although collapse of the currency came with Confederate defeat, it would have occurred shortly in any event.

INFLUENZA. First epidemic in the colonies occurred 1647. Widespread in Europe and America in 1830, 1837, and 1847; eased up for a long period; broke out on a worldwide scale 1889–93. In the summer of 1918, the worst pandemic in world history began, killing an estimated 15 million; about 28 percent of the US population was attacked; death toll was 450,000. During later scattered outbreaks mortality gradually dropped until outbreaks of a new strain (the "Asian flu") in 1957, 1958, and 1960. During additional outbreaks in 1963, 1968, and 1969 mortality rates were much lower than in previous epidemics.

INFORMATION AGENCY, UNITED STATES (USIA). Government agency under the president with task of presenting accurate information about the US to foreigners. Work ranges from setting up libraries in foreign cities, to operating the Voice of America radio system; works in close cooperation with the State Department. From 1978 to 1983, known as the International Communication Agency.

"IN GOD WE TRUST". Motto that appears on most issues of US coins; practice began during the Civil War.

INHERENT POWERS. Powers expressly conferred on national agencies by the Constitution, though the Supreme Court has on occasion described as inherent those powers arising out of the federal government's character as a sovereign state. Specifically, they include the power of the president to restrict sale of arms to warring nations, power to expel undesirable aliens, and power to acquire territory by discovery and occupation. (Compare IMPLIED POWERS.)

INHERITANCE TAX LAWS. The federal government adopted an estate tax 1916 that became a permanent part of the federal tax system; it had resorted to temporary inheritance taxes on several earlier occasions. By 1902 half the states had adopted inheritance taxes; all except Nevada ultimately did so. The federal estate tax until 1976 was on estates in excess of $60,000, later liberalized so that by 1987 estates of less than $600,000 would be exempt.

INITIATIVE. Process by which citizens, either directly or indirectly, propose legislation or constitutional amendments; operative only within the context of state or local governments, there being no provision for the initiative at federal level. Traditionally used in conjunction with RECALL, and REFERENDUM.

INJUNCTIONS. Restraining court orders, which have played a major role in labor history. Prominent for the first time in the Pullman strike of 1894, when strikers were issued a "blanket injunction" not to interfere with train operations. Thereafter often used in labor disputes, even though the Clayton Antitrust Act of 1914 was supposed to limit its application in labor disputes. The Norris-La Guardia Act of 1932 effectively ended such use; but the Taft-Hartley Act of 1947 allowed

federal courts to issue an injunction against a union if an actual or threatened strike endangered the nation's health or safety.

INQUISITION, SPANISH (or Holy Office). Sporadic activity in the New World began as early as 1524; established permanently in Mexico City, 1571; jurisdiction extended into the Spanish borderlands now within the US. Suppressed 1813, restored briefly, and abolished 1820. Took cognizance of heresy, blasphemy, perjury, forgery, bigamy, and book censorship. Indians and non-Catholics were exempt. The death sentence was rare; punishment included fines, flogging, confiscation, and imprisonment.

INSANE, TREATMENT OF THE. See MENTAL HYGIENE MOVEMENT.

INSCRIPTION ROCK (or El Morro). A varicolored sandstone rising 200 feet in Valencia County, N.M.; named for inscriptions carved by early Spanish explorers, the earliest in 1605. A national monument.

INSECTICIDES AND HERBICIDES. Use of arsenical compounds dates from the 17th c.; commonly used in the 19th c. Pyrethum, nonpoisonous to humans, was used against household insects in the 1880s. Lead arsenate was first used against the gypsy moth in 1892 and against the cotton boll weevil until the development of calcium arsenate in 1916. In 1906, the Department of Agriculture began using arsenical dips against the Texas fever-carrying cattle tick. DDT was developed during World War II, quickly becoming the most widely used insecticide until its use was banned 1972. Systemic insecticides were developed to protect both plants and animals, while 2,4-D, a systemic growth regulant developed 1944, brought about a new era of chemical weed control. By the 1980s, increasing concern over residual dangers of insecticides and herbicides led to new research in the use of biological (predators and parasites) and cultural (planting and cultivation) control methods.

INSPECTION, COMMITTEES OF. Bodies formed in the colonies in retaliation to the TOWNSHEND ACTS OF 1767. The first one, formed 1768 in New York City, was ordered "to inspect all European importations," with the aim of restricting such imports, thereby forcing repeal of the Townshend Acts.

INSPECTION, GOVERNMENTAL. The federal government has traditionally used an inspection system to assure enforcement of laws covering immigration, migrant labor, voting procedures, the armed services, national parklands, forests, and timber management. Some of the older federal inspection agencies are the Steamboat Inspection Service (1838), the Interstate Commerce Commission (1887), and the Food and Drug Administration (1927). States have inspection laws governing operation of factories, mines, hospitals, schools, public utilities, buildings, and restaurants. Inspection of agricultural products began in the late 19th c.; the federal government also inspects meat products.

INSTALLMENT BUYING. Consumer installment selling was first introduced 1807 by a furniture company. Automobile buying on the installment plan, the largest component, began 1910. The modern revolving charge account, allowing partial payment over a period of time, was introduced by Wanamaker's of Philadelphia in 1938. Originally offered at no charge, such plans now charge interest on the unpaid balance. Bank credit cards, which also permit partial payment, began 1951 and are a significant part of outstanding credit today. The Truth-in-Lending Act (1969), a federal law, requires disclosure of finance charges as annual percentage rates; the Fair Credit Billing Act (1974) protects consumers against inaccurate and unfair credit billing and credit card practices.

INSTITUTE FOR ADVANCED STUDY. Educational and research center founded 1930 at Princeton, N.J., noted especially for its school of mathematics. A haven for scholars; has no students as such. Noted scholars who have been connected with the institute include Albert Einstein, Oswald Veblen, J. Robert Oppenheimer, and George Kennan.

INSTITUTE OF ARTS AND LETTERS. See AMERICAN ACADEMY AND INSTITUTE OF ARTS AND LETTERS.

INSULAR CASES (1901–22). Succession of cases where Supreme Court determined the status of outlying (or insular) US possessions.

It held that Hawaii and Alaska were incorporated territories, thereby binding Congress to all provisions of the Constitution when legislating for those territories. The Philippine Islands and Puerto Rico were held to be unincorporated territories; Congress had more leeway in legislating for them.

INSULAR POSSESSIONS. Outlying territories of the US. They have consisted of the following: Hawaii, Puerto Rico, the Philippine Islands, Guam, American Somoa, the Virgin Islands, the Trust Territory of the Pacific Islands, Midway, Wake Island, and Canton and Enderbury islands (the last two administered jointly with Great Britain).

INSURANCE.
   Marine Insurance. English underwriters insured American vessels in colonial years. The Insurance Co. of North America, the first stock insurance company in the nation, was founded 1792. Marine premium receipts increased over 300 percent between 1843 and 1858, due to tremendous underwriting created by the clipper trade. Civil War insurance rates handicapped merchantmen carrying the American flag; and after the war, foreign carriers carried 75 percent of US cargo, forcing many marine underwriters to seek new forms of business. Congress limited coastal trade to American carriers in 1893; US marine underwriters again prospered. Greatest growth came with World War I; federal legislation made it possible for companies to quote stable rates. After the war, Congress encouraged risk spreading among underwriters and exempted them from antitrust, allowing them to compete in world markets. In 1980, the premium volume of US ocean marine insurance was more than $1 billion.
   Inland Marine Insurance. Originally insured cargo on inland waterways; has expanded to include movement on land. Premiums grew from $196 million in 1948 to more than $2 billion in 1979.
   Aviation Insurance. Covers the hull and liability hazards of both commercial airlines and private aircraft. In the late 1970s, a thousand US companies participated in aviation insurance; premium volume was $171 million in 1980.
   Fire Insurance. First fire insurance company founded 1752; in 1794 the Insurance Co. of North America first marketed insurance

on both the building and its contents. In 1835, the first factory mutual insurance company was organized. In 1866, fire companies formed the National Board of Fire Underwriters. In 1909, Kansas became the first state to regulate rates. In 1948, almost $1.3 billion in premiums were written; in 1979, $4.8 billion.

Workmen's Compensation Insurance. Traditionally, injured workers' legal rights were based on common law, which hinged on establishment of fault. In the early 20th c., most states adopted some form of compensation laws, which recognized industrial accidents and disease as hazards of industry; cost of insurance was incorporated into the cost of doing business. In 1933, only 33 percent of the total work force was covered; in the mid-1970s, about 75 percent was included. 1979 premiums were $13.2 billion. (See also EMPLOYER'S LIABILITY LAWS.)

Automobile Insurance. First issued 1898, by 1979 automobile insurance premiums reached $36.6 billion. In many states, liability insurance is mandatory.

Life Insurance. Earliest life insurance policies were sideline policies written by marine underwriters on the lives of sea captains. Annuity funds for ministers go back to the 18th c., as does the TONTINE PLAN, a life insurance lottery. Life insurance companies, as such, began early in the 19th c. and expanded rapidly. Massachusetts became (1855) first to regulate the industry through an insurance department. The first mortality table based on the experience of insured lives in America was published 1868. The late 19th c. was a period of great competition among companies; failure rate was high. Beginning ca. 1900, various state investigations and new legislation resulted in reforms aimed at protecting policyholders. Entry into mutual funds and variable annuities by companies made them subject to federal securities laws. Nearly 1,950 legal reserve life insurance companies owned assets of $480 billion in 1980. The first group life insurance policy was issued by the Equitable Life Assurance Co. in 1911. By the 1980s, low-cost group life, health, and disability coverages were available through companies and professional associations.

Health Insurance. The Travelers Insurance Co., founded 1863, was the first company to write health insurance providing a schedule of stated benefits payable to the insured for each illness or injury. The Massachusetts Health Insurance Co., founded 1847, was the first to write individual health insurance policies. Workmen's compensation laws stimulated interest in group health insurance contracts for illness and nonwork injuries not covered by the law; in 1914, the Metropolitan Life Insurance Co. issued the first group health contract, covering its home office employees. Blue Cross had its beginnings in 1948; to compete with Blue Cross, traditional insurance companies developed reimbursement policies for hospital and surgical care. Perhaps most significant was the development of major medical insurance, in the mid-1970s, by using deductibles and coinsurance to control claim cost and claim frequency. During the 1950s, the health insurance industry also began to provide long-term disability income coverage. The advent of Medicare in 1966 caused many companies to modify coverages to avoid duplicating Medicare benefits. Dental insurance plans developed in the 1970s.

INSURRECTIONS, DOMESTIC. Most insurrections before 1861 were in one of two categories: agrarian or frontier uprisings directed against a tidewater government controlled by a planter or mercantile establishment; or insurrections by slaves. Most important of the former were BACON'S REBELLION (1675–76) in Virginia; the REGULATORS OF NORTH CAROLINA (1760s and 1770s); SHAYS'S REBELLION (1786–87); the WHISKEY REBELLION (1799); FRIES'S REBELLION (1799); and DORR'S REBELLION (1841–42). Large slave uprisings were rare; it is believed that there were only two or three in the colonial period: those in New York City in 1712 and 1741, and the large uprising at Stono, S.C., in 1739. In the early 19th c., at least three serious black uprisings took place: the Gabriel uprising in Virginia (1800), the abortive Denmark Vesey uprising in Charleston (1822), and the insurrection led by Nat Turner in Virginia (1831). All failed, as did John Brown's insurrection in 1859, a white-led uprising aimed at freeing the slaves.

INTEGRATION. Chattel slavery, though rigidly subordinating the position of the slave, was basically incompatible with racial segregation; racial mixing and miscegenation were widespread in the South. The Jim Crow pattern first emerged in the North, where free blacks were disfranchised in New Jersey, Pennsylvania, and Connecticut. Blacks were not allowed to testify in court against whites in Illinois, Ohio, Indiana, Iowa, and California. Black ghettos existed in most large cities. In the South, the Civil War destroyed slavery physically; the Thirteenth, Fourteenth, and Fifteenth amendments destroyed it constitutionally. The period also produced a battery of enforcement acts and civil rights laws designed to guarantee civic equality; but the laws' narrow interpretations by a conservative Supreme Court resulted in blacks in the South (and in many northern and border states) being denied the intended benefits of emancipation. When poor black and white southerners threatened to coalesce in the Populist revolt of the 1890s, southern state regimes successfully disfranchised almost all blacks and masses of poor whites also, and adopted the full range of Jim Crow ordinances, which segregated blacks in schools, public conveyances, hotels and restaurants, and made legal the all-white neighborhood. Churches were also rigidly segregated, as were the armed forces. The trend toward integration began in the 1940s, when the Supreme Court ordered first graduate schools, and then undergraduate colleges to integrate. Public schools were ordered integrated in 1954. Covenants protecting all-white neighborhoods were declared unconstitutional. The armed forces were integrated in 1948. The civil rights acts of the 1960s banned segregation in transportation and recreation and in such privately owned facilities as hotels and restaurants. The 1965 Voting Rights Act led to the massive enfranchisement of blacks. By 1970, school integration in the South, based on the 1954 *Brown v. Board of Education of Topeka* decision and later ones, had outstripped that in the North and West, where de facto segregation, based on neighborhood makeup, remained common. Federal judges made use of various stratagems, including busing, to integrate such schools. Most resistant to integration were the areas of jobs, because unions and seniority blunted integration drives, and housing, because whites fled integrating city neighborhoods for the suburbs (which were almost entirely white). Black discontent with slow integration in these vital areas fueled the urban rioting of the late 1960s. Despite controversy over school busing and the rhetoric of black separatism, integration in sports and the communications media was dramatic, and public opinion surveys continued to indicate that white acceptance was growing.

INTELLIGENCE, MILITARY AND STRATEGIC. Intelligence gathering has always been a function of the services; but only in 1885 did the War Department form a section to supervise intelligence activities. Since then, intelligence staffs have existed in each of the services. The World War II Joint Chiefs of Staff Intelligence Committee became the J-2 section after the war. In 1947, Congress created the NATIONAL SECURITY COUNCIL and the CENTRAL INTELLIGENCE AGENCY; since then, military intelligence has been largely subsumed under the concept of strategic, or national, intelligence. The State Department has its own intelligence board, and the National Security Agency (NSA) deals in communications, cryptology, and the information gleaned from breaking or monitoring foreign coded transmissions. In 1959, the US Intelligence Board was created to coordinate all federal intelligence efforts.

INTELLIGENCE TESTS. American psychologists began ca. 1910 to adapt tests originated by French physician Alfred Binet in order to deal with the great social problem of "feeble-mindedness"; the resulting Stanford-Binet intelligence test became the standard intelligence quotient (IQ) test for many decades. Its usefulness was first demonstrated in World War I, when all army recruits were tested. There have been many adaptations of the IQ test over the years; for decades, critics have pointed out class and ethnic biases of the tests and bewailed harmful effects of typing pupils by IQ when they might with proper training improve their scores. Since the 1950s, attempts have been made to devise tests that do not depend on environmental factors.

INTERCHANGEABLE MANUFACTURE. System by which components may be made so similar in size and shape that they can be assembled to close limits without fitting. Thomas Jefferson tried to introduce the principle to the US. The first US contract specifying interchangeable parts was issued 1813; the principle was fully realized at the Springfield Armory between 1844 and 1848. Interchangeable clock parts had been produced as early as the 1790s. Widely adopted by industries in the late 19th c., it made the modern assembly line possible.

INTEREST LAWS AND INTEREST RATES. A usury law was first enacted in Massachusetts in 1661; by 1791, such laws had been enacted by the thirteen original states, initial limitations ranging from 6 percent to 10 percent. Federal banking laws of 1864 and 1933 tied national bank rates to state usury laws. In 1969 Congress passed the Truth-in-Lending Act, which regulates most commercial lenders and has extensive disclosure requirements, including a showing of the total cost of borrowing as an annual percentage rate. Payment of interest on deposits has been the primary method used by banks to attract private funds. Traditionally, the interest-paying instruments have been savings accounts and certificates of deposit; but occasionally banks have paid interest on checking accounts.

INTERIOR, DEPARTMENT OF THE. Founded 1849, the guardian of the nation's natural resources. Composed of six units: Management, Program Development and Budget; Fish, Wildlife, and Parks; Land and Water Resources; Energy and Minerals; and Congressional and Legislative Affairs. Subsidiary organizations include the Bureau of Land Management, caretaker of 450 million acres of public domain; Geological Survey; Bureau of Indian Affairs; Fish and Wildlife Service; Bureau of Outdoor Recreation; Bureau of Mines; and Mining Enforcement and Safety Administration.

INTERIOR DECORATION. In the 19th c., decorating ideas were included in architectural handbooks, a prime example being *The Architecture of Country Houses* (1840), which has one section devoted to furnishing interiors. By the end of the century, the more affluent began seeking professional help in furnishing their houses. No documentation exists to suggest when the first professional decorator began, but in 1904 a magazine called *The Interior Decorator* appeared on the market, listing individual interior decorators. Today, the basic purpose of the interior decorator, or designer, is to provide an interior environment congenial to householder and guests. Interior decoration has become a profession supplying business and middle-class domestic needs as well those of the affluent.

INTERMARRIED CITIZEN. A person who, through marriage to an Indian, became a citizen of the tribe, especially applied to the Five Civilized Tribes. Intermarried citizens shared equally with citizens by blood in lands and other tribal property.

INTERMEDIATE CREDIT BANKS. Twelve district banks established 1923 by Congress to increase the supply of credit available to farmers. In 1968 their assets were transferred to the PRODUCTION CREDIT ASSOCIATIONS.

INTERNAL REVENUE. See TAXATION.

INTERNATIONAL COURT OF JUSTICE. Also known as the Hague Court and the World Court; established under the United Nations in 1946 as successor of the Permanent Court of International Justice. Composed of fifteen members, each from a different country. Only nations may be parties in cases before the court; in general it hears cases only with consent of the states that are parties before it.

INTERNATIONAL GEOPHYSICAL YEAR (IGY: July 1, 1957–Dec. 31, 1958). Geophysical observations by approx. 30,000 scientists and technicians from more than seventy countries in eleven fields: cosmic rays, geomagnetism, glaciology, gravity, ionospheric physics, latitude and longitude determination, meteorology, oceanography, seismology, and solar activity. Two prominent achievements of the IGY are the discovery of the Van Allen radiation belts, and the calculation of a new, pear-shaped model of the shape of the earth. A one year's extension (to Dec. 31, 1959) of the IGY was officially called International Geophysical Cooperation.

INTERNATIONAL HARVESTER COMPANY. Consolidation in 1902 of the leading manufacturers of farm machinery; C.H. McCormick was head of the consortium. Ordered broken up by the federal government 1914 as an illegal combination in undue restraint of trade under the antitrust laws.

INTERNATIONAL JOINT COMMISSION. US-Canadian body created 1909; has jurisdiction over cases involving use of boundary waters or of rivers crossing the US-Canadian border. May also settle any problem of any nature that the two governments agree to refer to it.

INTERNATIONAL LABOR ORGANIZATION (ILO). Intergovernmental agency established 1919 and now a specialized agency of the United Nations. Sets international labor standards and sponsors a broad range of technical assistance programs to help less-developed countries improve their services in the labor field.

INTERNATIONAL LAW. The US Constitution authorized Congress "to define and punish Piracies and Felonies committed on the high Seas, and Offenses against the Law of Nations" (Article I, Section 8, Clause 10). Courts routinely apply international law in litigations within the US that present issues within its rules, such as acquisition and delimitation of territory, conflicts of nationality, and rights of aliens. Rules of international law stem from the customary practice of nations, evidenced by diplomatic documents and determined by courts, or from positive lawmaking treaties.

INTERNATIONAL MONETARY FUND (IMF). Founded 1947 to promote stability of currencies and international cooperation on a multilateral basis. In 1981, there were 141 members. Each nation subscribes an amount appropriate to its economic importance; and from this fund any member may temporarily draw out monies to help meet its international trade deficits. In 1969, the IMF established a new monetary facility, the Special Drawing Rights (SDR's), which by the late 1970s became one of the principal reserve assets of the international monetary system.

INTERSTATE COMMERCE COMMISSION (ICC). Oldest federal regulatory commission, founded 1887. Consists of eleven commissioners appointed by the president and confirmed by the Senate. Principal task of the ICC has been the regulation of railroads, and, since 1935, motor carriers. Traditionally has had almost complete regulatory power over these common carriers; in the late 1970s,

however, a trend away from regulation caused its authority to diminish.

INTERSTATE COMMERCE LAWS. Although the Constitution specifically grants the federal government power to regulate "Commerce ... among the several States," for a century there was little federal regulation of interstate commerce other than transportation and communications. The Interstate Commerce Act of 1887, creating the INTERSTATE COMMERCE COMMISSION, was the first major federal statute. The SHERMAN ANTITRUST ACT of 1890 was aimed at curbing monopolies and supported in 1914 by the CLAYTON ANTITRUST ACT and creation of the Federal Trade Commission. In the decades that followed, a wide variety of federal laws were enacted, including food and drug acts, the Securities and Exchange Act, the Federal Communications Commission of 1934, the Shipping Act of 1916, the National Labor Relations Board of 1935, the Taft-Hartley Act of 1947, and the Truth-in-Lending Act of 1969.

INTERSTATE COMPACTS. Although the Constitution states that "no state shall, without the consent of Congress ... enter into any Agreement or Compact with another State, or with a foreign Power," interstate agreements of various kinds have existed since colonial days. Only those that are deemed to affect the balance of the federal system must receive the approval of Congress. In 1979, there were 176 interstate compacts in effect. Most significant are river development compacts, dealing with irrigation, pollution control, fishing, and navigation. A large number of compacts deal with social questions. A notable economic compact is the Port Authority of New York and New Jersey, established 1921, which does a multibillion dollar business involving the port facilities of the New York City-New Jersey area, as well as its management of airports, bridges and tunnels, office building complexes, and mass transit.

INTERSTATE TRADE BARRIERS. Commercial blockages between colonies were widened and intensified by states under the Articles of Confederation; they were a principal reason for calling the Constitutional Convention of 1787. The Constitution expressly forbade such blockages, and for a century and a half the US had the most extensive free trade area in the world. During the Great Depression, various states attempted to protect their home industries by putting up barriers. The Supreme Court struck down undisguised discriminations but was tolerant of others.

INTERURBAN ELECTRIC LINES. By 1900 there were more than 2,100 miles of interurban railroad lines in the US, most of them built to improve local and branch line passenger service. When the peak mileage of 15,580 miles was reached in 1916, almost two-thirds was located in Illinois, Indiana, Michigan, Ohio, Pennsylvania, and New York. They were unprofitable, and expanding automobile traffic caused their extensive abandonment after World War I. By 1960, only 200 miles of interurban lines remained.

INTERVENTION. Traditionally, international law permitted nations to intervene in other sovereign states to protect the lives and property of their own citizens. Throughout its early history, US forces bombarded foreign towns in reprisal for offenses to US traders and missionaries, and landed marines in nations to protect Americans during upheavals. Nevertheless, the new Republic attempted to forge a policy of nonintervention. In 1796, President Washington, in his farewell address, enunciated the principle of "extending our commercial relations, to have as little *political* connection as possible." Nonintervention was the cited reason for recognizing the new republics of Latin America; it was also the basis of the Monroe Doctrine of 1823. US presidents found little difficulty, however, in intervening in Spanish Florida and later in other former Spanish colonies in the New World, including Cuba, Colombia, Nicaragua, Haiti (a former French colony), the Dominican Republic, and Mexico. In the Good Neighbor Policy of 1933, the US agreed that "no state has the right to intervene in the internal or external affairs of another." After World War II, the US returned to a policy of "protective intervention," but extended it worldwide. Citing its determination to contain communism, the nation intervened in Greece (1947–49), Korea (1950–53), Lebanon (1958, 1983–84), and Vietnam (1965–73); and resumed intervention in Latin America: the blockade of Cuba in 1962, the Dominican Republic in 1965, the clandestine overthrow of the government of Chile in 1973, and efforts to prop up "friendly" governments in Central America in the early 1980s.

INTOLERABLE ACTS (1774). Also known as the Coercion Acts. Five acts of Parliament intended to restore peace and order in America and to isolate Massachusetts after the Boston Tea Party. Although aimed at reinforcing royal authority at the expense of personal liberty, they had the effect of throwing the colonies into ferment and becoming the justification for calling the first Continental Congress.

INTREPID. A Tripolitan ketch that had been captured by Stephen Decatur during the war with Tripoli, the *Intrepid* was used by him in burning the *Philadelphia*, which had been captured. Decatur later exploded the ketch in Tripoli harbor in an unsuccessful attempt to blow up Tripolitan gunboats.

INVESTIGATING COMMITTEES. Power of legislative bodies to conduct investigations was considered inherent in the performance of legislative functions; as early as 1792, the House of Representatives named a committee to investigate an army defeat in the Indian wars. Both houses have generally given committees power to compel testimony and to punish recalcitrant witnesses; courts have generally upheld Congress's right to investigate. In the mid-20th c., attention was concentrated on abuses of committees, especially the House Un-American Activities Committee and the Senate Permanent Committee on Investigations (the so-called McCarthy Committee). Congressional committees have often come into conflict with the Executive Department, as presidents have refused to cooperate, invoking the doctrine of separation of powers.

INVESTMENT BANKS. Early in the 19th c., brokerage houses and commercial bankers sold securities (chiefly governments') to wealthy clients or to investment houses overseas. During the Civil War and afterward, Jay Cooke and Junius Morgan and his son, J.P. Morgan, dominated investment sales. Morgan's attempt to form a monopoly in his Northern Securities Co. resulted in the trust-busting activities of the Theodore Roosevelt administration. During the 1920s, giant commercial banks developed large investment affiliates to market securities, and their irresponsible management contributed to the 1929 panic. After 1933, investment banks were severely regulated. By the 1980s, investment firms were performing a greater variety of services, such as advising investors, evaluating securities, and arranging direct placements themselves.

INVESTMENT COMPANIES. Financial organizations that sell their shares, called mutual funds, to public investors in order to place the proceeds in a diversified investment portfolio. Main advantages to the investor in mutual funds are diversification, liquidity, and continuous professional supervision. They proliferated in the 1920s, when they were known as investment trusts. Many participants lost their investments in the 1929 market collapse, giving the trusts a bad name; this in turn led to their reorganization as "investment companies." By 1980, 564 mutual funds had 12 million stockholders and assets of $135 billion.

IOWA. Iowa was claimed by the French in 1673; ceded to Spain 1762; restored to France 1800; and acquired by the US by the LOUISIANA PURCHASE of 1803. Part of the Territory of Missouri in 1812; an unorganized territory from 1821 to 1834; attached to the Michigan Territory 1834; and in 1836 formed part of the Wisconsin Territory. Permanent settlement began 1833, and the Territory of Iowa, including present Iowa, Minnesota, and parts of North and South Dakota, was established 1838. Admitted to the Union in 1846 with its present area. An agricultural state, the value of its livestock and livestock products exceeds that of any other state, although by 1980, industrial production slightly exceeded farm income. Pop.: 2,913,387 (1980).

IOWA BAND. Eleven ministers, members of the American Home Missionary Society, who came to Iowa 1843. Founded Congregational churches and Iowa College (1848).

IPSWICH PROTEST (1687). Refusal by citizens of Ipswich, Mass., to pay taxes levied by the colonial governor; one of the earliest organized protests against the British.

IRAN, US RELATIONS WITH. Until World War II, Iran was considered within the British sphere of influence; after the war, US policy was dominated by its interest in Iran's vast oil reserves, and by its commitment to keep the shah, Mohammed Reza Pahlavi, in power. He was overthrown in 1952 and the oil industry nationalized; the US was largely responsible for his return to the throne in 1953, and through a vast program of economic and military aid, Iran became America's strongest ally in the Middle East. Discontent with the shah within Iran grew, partly because he was looked upon as a puppet of the US. In 1979, he was deposed by militant Muslims led by Ayatollah Khomeni and US embassy personnel were held hostage for 444 days (see IRANIAN CAPTIVITY); after they were released, relations between Iran and the US remained tense.

IRANIAN CAPTIVITY (Nov. 4, 1979–Jan. 20, 1981). Iranian militants seized the US embassy in Teheran and took some ninety people hostages, about sixty of whom were Americans. The militants announced that the Americans would be held until the US returned the deposed shah to Iran to be tried for crimes he committed while in office. The Carter administration refused to extradite the shah and retaliated with various economic sanctions. On November 19 and 20, the Iranians released thirteen women and blacks but continued to hold fifty-three others. On April 24, 1980, with all diplomatic efforts stymied, a rescue mission was mounted; it failed and eight US servicemen were killed in a helicopter crash. One hostage was released July 11 due to illness. On July 27, the shah died. Negotiations continued, clouded by the US presidential campaign. Finally, with Algerian diplomats as intermediaries, the fifty-two Americans were released, on the day that Ronald Reagan replaced Jimmy Carter as president.

IRISH TRACT. That portion of the Valley of Virginia and the bordering region to the NW settled by Scotch-Irish.

IRON ACT OF 1750. Action by Parliament allowing colonial pig iron and bar iron to enter Britain free of duty; specified that certain kinds of mills and furnaces could not be built in the colonies, a restriction which was not observed.

IRON AND STEEL INDUSTRY. Founded in the 17th c. by British capitalists; by the time of the Revolution, the colonies were producing almost 15 percent of the world's iron. Ironworks had been built in every colony but Georgia, with Pennsylvania the leader in production. The typical unit was an iron plantation, containing the owner's house, houses for the workers, and an estate with abundant timber. Blast furnaces consumed vast quantities of charcoal. The colonies also produced steel by the cementation process that involved prolonged heating of wrought iron with carbon. From the Revolution to the Civil War, America lagged behind in the transformation of the iron industry taking place in Europe; it finally switched to coke in the 1860s, the same time that the Bessemer process, invented in England, was widely adapted. Also developed was the open-hearth, or Siemens-Martin, process, which by the 1890s had supplanted the Bessemer process. From 1875 to 1920, steel production increased from 380,000 tons to 60 million tons annually, and America became the world leader in the manufacture of iron and steel. Technological improvements, a protective high tariff, and abundant natural resources were factors. From 1855 to 1900, the axis of the iron industry shifted from the East to the Midwest. Iron was brought to ports on Lake Michigan and Lake Erie, and great steel centers grew up in Pittsburgh, Youngstown, and Gary. Birmingham, Ala., became the center of southern iron and steel production. After the 1950s, US steel production lost ground relative to the rest of the world, especially Japan. By the 1980s, steel producers were especially hurt by importations; many plants closed.

IRONCLAD OATH. Reconstruction requirement of 1867, imposed by RADICAL REPUBLICANS, by which every person elected or appointed to any federal office, civil or military, had to swear allegiance to the Constitution and to declare that he had never voluntarily borne arms against the US. Effectively disqualified most white southerners from office.

IRONCLAD WARSHIPS. Thickening a ship's sides with armor against penetration was done as early as the 1840s but not extensively until the Civil War. The Confederates fitted the captured Union frigate *Merrimack* (renamed *Virginia*), followed by similar operations on both sides. The Union also built new ships, especially designed with armor. The first was the *Monitor*; its success against the *Merrimack* on March 9, 1862, led to the construction of many others of the same type. The Rebels used ironclads extensively on inland waters, especially the Mississippi; but the Union navy eventually prevailed over them.

IRON CURTAIN. Phrase made popular by Winston Churchill, who announced at Fulton, Mo., on March 5, 1946, that an iron curtain had descended between Western and Eastern Europe, behind which Soviet control was increasing.

IROQUOIS. Large collection of tribes that inhabited the Mohawk Valley and the lake region of New York, including the Seneca, Cayuga, Oneida, Onondaga, and Mohawk. Formed a political union, the League of the Iroquois, or Five Nations, that for two centuries dominated their Algonkin neighbors. Joined by the Tuscarora in 1712, they became known as the Six Tribes. Each tribe had a council to regulate its own local affairs, and a great council, consisting of fifty peace chiefs, or sachems, who met yearly at Onondago, N.Y. Judicial, legislative, and military questions were resolved within the individual tribes and passed on to the representative body. Ambassadors traveled to advise of decisions, questions, and times of meeting. Decisions of the sachems, who achieved their positions matrilineally, were highly susceptible to public opinion. Tribes lived in stockaded villages, in communal housing; their maize cultivation and matrilineal descent emphasize their connection with Indians of the Southeast. The league ceased to be effective after the Revolution, when the tribes were forced to disperse. A flurry of messianism began 1799 with the appearance of the prophet Handsome Lake. In 1979, about 8,800 Iroquois lived on six reservations in New York state.

IROQUOIS BEAVER LAND DEED. In 1701 the Iroquois tribes deeded "in trust" their lands in Canada in return for English protection against the French; they had not intended to transfer title to the land itself.

IROQUOIS THEATER FIRE (Dec. 30, 1903). Fire in this supposedly fireproof theater resulted in the deaths of over 600 people in Chicago, leading to a wave of safety legislation around the country.

IROQUOIS TREATY (1684). Between the Iroquois tribes and the governors of New York, Virginia, and Massachusetts. Indians agreed to live in peace with the English.

IRRIGATION. Irrigation on a large scale in the US was first practiced by the Mormons in Utah; by 1850, they had 16,333 acres under cultivation. In California, irrigation ditches were dug in 1857, diverting water from the Santa Anna R to a new settlement at Anaheim. Canals were dug in Colorado on a large scale from 1870 to 1900. Thereafter, conflicts among water-users and companies became common. In 1887, California invented the irrigation district, which had power to levy taxes and issue bonds. Within thirty years, each of the western states had authorized creation of such districts. Because most rivers flowed through several states, interstate agreements had to be effected for an equitable apportion of available water, as mandated by the Supreme Court. After 1940, there was a spectacular rise in the use of deep-water wells in irrigating fields. Texas, New Mexico, Louisiana, and Arkansas made especial use of digging wells. In 1978, the irrigated land in the US comprised 51 million acres.

ISLAND NUMBER TEN, OPERATIONS AT (March 15–April 7, 1862). A combined Union army and naval force captured Island Number Ten, located in the Mississippi R fifty-five miles below Cairo, Ill. The first achievement in the campaign to divide the Confederacy by gaining control of the Mississippi.

ISLE OF ORLEANS. Tract of land near New Orleans, at the mouth of the Mississippi R. In the 18th c., it was a French and then Spanish possession, and a serious barrier to American navigation of the Mississippi. Came to the US with the LOUISIANA PURCHASE.

ISOLATIONISM. Nonintervention in European affairs was a policy in the early Republic; efforts by John Adams to avoid war with France were part of the isolationist tradition. President Jefferson advised against "entangling alliances" in his first inaugural address.

The Monroe Doctrine (1823) advised America "not to interfere in the internal concerns" of Europe. Efforts to stay out of World War I and rejection of the League of Nations afterward were consistent with isolationism. When World War II erupted in Europe, many isolationists worked through the America First Committee, the leading noninterventionist pressure group before Pearl Harbor. With American entry into World War II, isolationism lost its strong position, nor was it regained after the war. The controversies and frustrations of US involvement in Vietnam gave some renewed currency to the arguments of isolationists.

ISRAELI-AMERICAN RELATIONS. President Truman immediately recognized Israel after it declared its independence 1948; in 1949 the US began aiding Israel with loans, grants-in-aid, and technical assistance. In 1950, the US joined with Great Britain and France in guaranteeing the boundaries of Israel and its Arab neighbors and placed a limited arms embargo on the region. Relations between the US and Israel deteriorated because of US denunciation of the Israeli-British-French attack on the Suez in 1956. Israel later was pressured to return the Gaza Strip and the Sinai Peninsula to Egypt. In return, President Eisenhower guaranteed Israel access to the Gulf of 'Aqaba. Israel's victory over Egypt, Jordan, and Syria in the Six-Day War of 1967 surprised the world; afterward Israel resisted pressure to withdraw to its prewar boundaries. The US chose not to force the issue even after it became the sole supplier of military aircraft to Israel after the cooling of Franco-Israeli relations. Major US support continued in 1973, when a combined Syrian-Egyptian attack on Israel began the fourth Arab-Israeli war. President Nixon's request for emergency military aid was quickly approved by Congress. That support led, in turn, to the Arab oil embargo in 1974; thereafter the US attitude was marked by an increasing effort to pressure Israel to make concessions to the Arabs. A major breakthrough occurred 1978 when President Carter engineered the Camp David agreement between Egypt and Israel, culminating in the 1979 peace treaty between the two countries. Egypt's initiative was not followed by other Arab nations. In the late 1970s, increased terrorist activities of the Palestinian Liberation Organization (PLO) resulted in massive retaliations by Israel, including four incursions into Lebanon (1975, 1978, 1980, and 1982). Those incursions and the Israeli policy of establishing new settlements in the occupied areas led to disagreements with the US. Relations improved somewhat in 1983 and 1984 after the US began to view Syria, rather than Israel, as the major source of the political deterioration of Lebanon.

ISTHMIAN CANAL. See PANAMA CANAL and CANAL ZONE.

ITAMI. Prehistoric big-game-hunting people of the North American High Plains; divided into two phases: the Folson (9200 BC–8000 BC) and the more widespread and culturally diffuse Plano phase (8000 BC–5000 BC). The most important campsites and kill sites, with impressive bones and weapons deposits, have been unearthed in Colorado and New Mexico.

ITEM VETO. Process by which a governor is able to veto a single item in a bill while approving the rest of it; often limited to appropriation bills. First appeared in the Confederacy.

IUKA, BATTLE OF (Sept. 19, 1862). Union generals W.S. Rosecrans and E.O.C. Ord planned a coordinated attack against the force of Confederate Gen. Stirling Price at Iuka, Miss., who was positioned on a dangerous salient. Rosecrans's attack was beaten back by Price and, due to bad communications, Ord never attacked. Price was able to remove his army to a safer position.

IWO JIMA, BATTLE OF (Feb. 16–March 17, 1945). Iwo Jima, an island 750 miles S of Tokyo and heavily fortified by the Japanese, gave them an important two hours' warning of US B-29 raids from the Mariana Islands. To reverse the situation, the US marines were ordered to take the island. Following three days' bombardment, they landed February 19. Because of massive preparation, beach casualties were moderate, but capture of the remainder of the island required the most bitter battle of the Pacific. Heavy casualties were inflicted by both sides. Seizure of Mount Suribachi (Feb. 23) gave the marines the dominant terrain, from which was carried on a ten-day struggle to capture the ridges, buttes, and deep caves in which the Japanese made their last desperate stand. Officially declared secured on March 17, but another nine days were required to extinguish all resistance. The battle cost the US 4,590 dead and 24,096 wounded; more than 20,000 Japanese were killed.

JACKSON. Capital (since 1821) and largest city of Mississippi. Natchez Trace crossed the Pearl R at the site, a trading post called Le Fleur's Bluff since the 1790s. Severe fighting in Civil War destroyed much of the city. Pop.: 202,895 (1980).

JACKSON, BATTLE OF (May 14, 1863). Gen. U.S. Grant defeated a small Confederate force at Jackson, Miss.

JACKSON HOLE. Valley in W Wyoming, E of the Teton Range and S of Yellowstone Park; location of a trappers' rendezvous.

JACKSONIAN DEMOCRACY. Term signifying the rise and triumph of popular democracy during Andrew Jackson's presidency and immediately afterward. Term did not achieve currency until the late 19th c.

JACKSON'S VALLEY CAMPAIGN (1862). Gen. Stonewall Jackson was left with a small force in the Shenandoah Valley after most of the Rebel forces were removed for the PENINSULAR CAMPAIGN. Assigned to harass Union troops there, thus tying up troops to defend Washington, at the expense of their Richmond campaign. Succeeded in creating much alarm and pinning down a considerable Union force. In thirty-five days, he marched 250 miles, fought four battles, and won them all. On June 21, he began to transfer his command to R.E. Lee's army at Richmond.

JACKSONVILLE. Largest city in Florida, located on the St. John's R; an important port and commercial and industrial center. Major industries include wood products, chemicals, and food products. Site of one of the earliest attempted settlements in America, Fort Caroline, established 1564 by the French. Later, British and Spanish forts were located there. Andrew Jackson's supply base during Seminole War; city renamed in his honor 1822. A center for Confederate blockade runners, it was occupied several times by Union troops.

Later became Florida's first resort city. Pop.: 540,898 (1980).

JACOBIN CLUBS (also called Democratic Societies). Modeled after the Jacobin clubs in Paris; organized in Philadelphia and other cities after arrival (1793) of French minister Edmond Charles Genêt (Citizen Genêt). Sought to propagate democratic views in American politics and arouse support for French Revolution. Generally opposed the Federalist policies.

JAMES EXPEDITION (1820). Led by botanist and geologist Edwin James through the trans-Missouri country; concluded that the Great Plains were unfit for habitation.

JAMES RIVER AND KANAWHA COMPANY. Founded 1785 by George Washington as the James River Co. to build canals and locks around its rapids and falls. In 1832 began canal to connect the James with the Ohio. Never completed. In 1880 its rights of way bought by Chesapeake and Ohio RR.

JAMESTOWN. Colony established 1607 by the Virginia Co. of London on a marshy island in the James R estuary in Virginia. The settlers built a fort and planted grain; disease appeared quickly, probably malaria and dysentery, and many died during the first summer. Friendly Indians supplied the survivors with corn and wild meat, enabling forty to survive the winter. Tobacco became the most important crop. The colony began to thrive and became the seat of the first legislative assembly in the New World. By 1624, there were 124 settlers. Colony had twenty-two houses, three stores, and a church. Burned during BACON'S REBELLION (1676). Never regained its vitality; government moved to Williamsburg 1699.

JAPAN, US RELATIONS WITH. In 1853, Commodore M.C. Perry led a US navy squadron into Tokyo Bay and negotiated a trade treaty with the Japanese, thereby ending Japan's traditional isolation. Japan realized the advantages of Western manufacturing, military organization, and trading customs; trade with the US, in particular, increased. In 1905, in the treaty ending the Russo-Japanese War, Japan recognized US rule over the Philippines; the US recognized Japanese control of Korea. Discrimination against Japanese immigrants led to a crisis; but in the 1907 GENTLEMEN'S AGREEMENT Japan promised to keep its nationals from emigrating to America. By the 1920s, Japan had become an important naval power and was involved in serious disputes with the US and Great Britain over disarmament treaties. In 1931, the Japanese government fell into the hands of military leaders who invaded Chinese territory. The US supported China and announced that it would not recognize any land captured by the Japanese. Japan then announced that it would no longer honor commitments to limit the size of its navy. Tension increased during the late 1930s and culminated in the Japanese attack on PEARL HARBOR in 1941. After Japan's defeat, the US became the chief occupying power and the country was run by Gen. Douglas MacArthur. He encouraged development of a new constitution that prohibited military forces, and helped rebuild industries. A peace treaty was signed between the US and Japan in 1951. US bases were allowed to remain on Japanese territory by special treaty. Trade agreements closely tied the countries' economies. As the industrial strength of Japan burgeoned, trade relations between the two countries were marked by vigorous competition in the fields of electronic equipment, textiles, and automobiles. A continuing problem for the two governments has been how much of each other's products each will admit to home markets.

JAPANESE-AMERICAN RELOCATION. In 1942, military authorities designated the West Coast a restricted zone and ordered all persons of Japanese extraction, including US citizens, out of the area. They were sent inland to "relocation centers," in California, Arizona, Idaho, Utah, Wyoming, and Arkansas, and allowed to return to their homes only at the end of the war. About 112,000 persons were involved, more than 70,000 of whom were US citizens.

JAPANESE CHERRY TREES. In Potomac Park, Washington, D.C.; a gift of the Japanese government in 1912.

JAPANESE EXCLUSION ACTS. After the Chinese Exclusion Act of 1882, efforts were made to exclude Japanese immigrants. In 1907, President Theodore Roosevelt negotiated the GENTLEMEN'S AGREEMENT, whereby Japan agreed to prohibit its nationals from emigrating to the US. In 1924, legislation barred the immigration of Japanese. Only after World War II were such restrictions repealed.

JAVA SEA, BATTLE OF (Feb. 27, 1942). Unsuccessful attempt by a combined Allied fleet to halt Japanese invasion of Java.

JAY-GARDOQUI NEGOTIATIONS (1785). Unsuccessful attempt by the US and Spain to settle boundary disputes and rights to navigation on the Mississippi R.

JAYHAWKERS. Bands of free-staters involved in the Kansas border war between 1856 and 1859, some of whom fought on the Union side in the Civil War. Today, the term is a nickname for a Kansan.

JAY'S TREATY (Nov. 19, 1794). Between Great Britain and the US, to settle disputes arising out of the treaty that ended the American Revolution. Principal issues were Britain's refusal to evacuate frontier forts in American territory; obstacles to collection of prewar debts by British creditors, despite guarantees of the 1783 treaty; status of former Loyalists in the US; and refusal of Britain to allow US merchant ships into its ports in the West Indies. Negotiated by Chief Justice John Jay. Britain agreed to evacuate the frontier forts, the US guaranteed prewar debts to Britain, and various other issues were to be submitted to special commissions.

JAZZ AGE. Term used to describe the period between World War I and 1929.

JEFFERSON, FORT (Illinois). Begun 1780 by George Rogers Clark on the Mississippi R, twelve miles below the mouth of the Ohio R. Evacuated 1781.

JEFFERSON, FORT (Ohio). Built 1791, six miles S of the present Greenville, as a depot in the campaign against the Indians.

JEFFERSON BARRACKS. Built 1826 on the Mississippi R ten miles S of St. Louis as an infantry school for the US army; still active.

JEFFERSON-BURR ELECTORAL DISPUTE (1800). Both Thomas Jefferson and Aaron Burr received seventy-three votes for president in the electoral college, although Burr had been running for vice-president. The election was thrown into the House of Representatives, where Jefferson's Federalist opponents schemed against him. No deciding vote could be effected, and for weeks intrigue went on amid rumors of forcible resistance should the scheme succeed. Jefferson elected on the thirty-sixth ballot. The TWELFTH AMENDMENT was ratified 1804 to prevent a similar occurrence.

JEFFERSON CITY. Capital of Missouri, on the Missouri R; designated capital city 1821. Occupied by Union troops during the Civil War because of its Confederate sympathies. Pop.: 33,619 (1980).

JEFFERSONIAN ARCHITECTURE. Palladian-type classical building planned or under the influence of Thomas Jefferson.

JEFFERSONIAN DEMOCRACY. Thomas Jefferson's philosophy of a democracy based on a citizenry of small, educated, independent freeholders. He opposed primogeniture and entail; feared emergence of a landholding aristocracy; believed in universal, state-supported education; advocated freedom of religion, speech, and the press; and reserving to the states as much power as possible.

JEFFERSONIAN REPUBLICAN PARTY. See REPUBLICANS, JEFFERSONIAN.

JEFFERSON'S PROPOSED STATES. Thomas Jefferson's plan for future disposition of western lands was submitted to Congress; variously amended, it was enacted as the Ordinance of 1784. It provided for the dividing of the western country into convenient units, and for statehood once a unit attained 20,000 free inhabitants. Slavery (after 1800), nullification, and secession were forever prohibited. States to be carved from the Virginia cession were to be named Cheronesus, Metropotamia, Saratoga, Pelisipia, Sylvania, Michigania, Assenisipia, Illinoia, and Polypotamia. The Ordinance never went into effect, being superseded by the Ordinance of 1787. (See also ORDINANCES OF 1784, 1785, AND 1787.)

JEFFERSON TERRITORY. Settlements that grew up in the Denver area after discovery of gold were technically in the jurisdiction of faraway Kansas. Delegation to Congress requested formation of Jefferson Territory; but Congress was unable to act because of the slavery issue. In the meantime, conventions and elections were held in the territory, a constitution was adopted, and officials chosen. Two sessions of the legislature met and passed laws. Ended with creation of Territory of Colorado in 1861. (See also COLORADO.)

JEHOVAH'S WITNESSES. Apocalyptic sect founded 1871 by C.T. Russell; known by several names until present one adopted 1931. Since 1879, its principal means of spreading its message has been the *Watchtower*. Witnesses hold to the nontrinitarian belief that Christ was an archangel and believe in the imminence of the millennium. In that golden age, 144,000 will share in the kingly rule of Christ; others who have followed Witnesses' strictures may escape destruction. Claim to exemption from military service and its proselytizing activities have involved the sect in a number of court cases, most of which they won. US membership: 565,309 (1981).

JENKINS' EAR, WAR OF (1739–43). Struggle between England and Spain over the ownership of Georgia, part of the War of the Austrian Succession. Named for a British seaman who lost an ear in a brush with the Spanish off the Florida coast. Conflict centered along the border between Florida and Georgia, and on the isthmus of Panama, where the British tried to take Cartagena, Colombia's main port city. Ended with no decisive results.

JENKINS FERRY, BATTLE AT (April 30, 1864). Site of a severe setback for Confederate forces, on the Saline R about fifty miles S of Little Rock, Ark.

JERSEY CITY. City in New Jersey, founded 1629 by the Dutch. A major industrial and shipping center, located across the Hudson R from New York City. Pop.: 223,532 (1980).

JESUIT MISSIONS. When Spain suppressed the order in 1767, Jesuits controlled 70 percent of New Spain's one million mission Indians. Eusebio Kino (1645–1711), the Apostle of Arizona, had founded twenty-four missions in the American Southwest. French Jesuits from Canada penetrated Maine, New York, and the Great Lakes area, missionizing

Indian tribes. Others came up the Mississippi to missionize the southern tribes. The western Sioux were reached ca. 1730. There were in all twenty-two Jesuit martyrs. When the pope reestablished the Jesuits in 1805, they again resumed their activities among US Indians. A dozen Jesuits flatboated down the Ohio in 1823, opened an Indian school in St. Louis (1824), and opened missions among the Miami, Potawatomi, Osage, and Kickapoo. From these missions, they fanned out into most of the other western tribes, even spreading into Alaska. By the 1870s, they had expanded into Indian Territory.

JESUIT RELATIONS. Jesuit missionaries in frontier America sent regular reports to their superiors. These reports, covering activities from 1610 to 1791, were published in 1896 in seventy-three volumes as *Jesuit Relations and Allied Documents*.

JESUITS. Jesuits, or members of the Society of Jesus, were an influence in colonial America and later in frontier America (see JESUIT MISSIONS). They were involved in the founding of Maryland (1634), and their Maryland Mission became the headquarters for the spread of the order throughout the West. They founded Georgetown University, in Washington, D.C., in 1789 and went on to found numerous other educational institutions. By the 1980s, there were more than seventy Jesuit schools in the US. In 1980, there were 7,600 members of the order in the US.

JESUP, FORT. Established at Natchitoches, La., 1822, between the Red and Sabine rivers. Abandoned after 1848.

JET PROPULSION LABORATORY. Federally owned installation at Pasadena, Calif., primarily engaged in applied research and development related to the exploration of deep space. Pioneer rocketry, radio telemetry, missile systems, and lunar and planetary exploration.

JEWS. See JUDAISM, AMERICAN.

JIM CROW LAWS. Enacted in southern (and some border) states in the late 19th c. to separate the races in public conveyances; came to embrace racial segregation in all categories. (See SEGREGATION.)

JIMSONWEED CULT. Religious group among Indians of southern California in the late 18th c. Centered on the drinking of a narcotic brew made from the jimsonweed (*Datura stramonium*). Lasted into 19th c.

JOB CORPS. Antipoverty program, established by President Lyndon B. Johnson in 1964 as part of his Great Society policy. Dedicated to providing general and vocational education, technical training, and useful work experience for young people from poor backgrounds. In the peak year of 1967, there were over 42,000 young people enrolled in the program. After 1973, Job Corps activities came under the Comprehensive Employment and Training Act (CETA).

JOCKEY HOLLOW. Site near Morristown, New Jersey, where Gen. George Washington's Continental army encamped during the winter of 1779–80.

JOHN BIRCH SOCIETY. Semisecret ultraconservative organization founded 1958, whose declared aim is to fight communism. Advocates return to minimum federal government. Publishes *American Opinion*.

JOHNS HOPKINS UNIVERSITY. Founded 1876 in Baltimore, Md., modeled after the German universities. It included the first graduate school in the nation and has long been noted for its medical school and hospital.

JOHNSON AND GRAHAM'S LESSEE V. MCINTOSH, 8 Wheaton 544 (1823). Established the constitutional principle that grants of land made to private individuals by Indian tribes are invalid.

JOHNSON COUNTY WAR. See RUSTLER WAR.

JOHNSON DOCTRINE. Expansion of the Roosevelt Corollary of the MONROE DOCTRINE. Enunciated by President Lyndon B. Johnson in 1965 in justification of his military incursion into the Dominican Republic. It stated that the "American nations ... will not permit the establishment of another Communist government in the Western Hemisphere."

JOHNSON'S ISLAND. In Lake Erie, used during the Civil War to house Confederate prisoners.

JOHNSTOWN FLOOD (1889). Resulted from the collapse of the Conemaugh Reservoir dam in Pennsylvania. It inundated the valley below it, killing more than 250 in Johnstown and its suburbs.

JOINT COMMITTEE ON RECONSTRUCTION. Established 1865 by the Senate and House of Representatives to determine the conditions by which the former Confederate states would be received back into the Union. Formulated Fourteenth Amendment and the laws that set up RECONSTRUCTION.

JOINT OCCUPATION. Agreement reached by the Convention of 1818 whereby the US and Great Britain could jointly trade and establish settlements in the Oregon country for ten years. Joint occupation ended by treaty 1846.

JOINT RESOLUTIONS. See RESOLUTIONS, LEGISLATIVE.

JOINT-STOCK LAND BANKS. Chartered 1916 with private capital to make agricultural loans, chiefly in the Middle West, Texas, and California. Prospered until late 1920s when many failed. Liquidated 1933; replaced by Land Bank Commission.

JOLLIET AND MARQUETTE DISCOVERY. In 1673, Louis Jolliet and Jacques Marquette set out from the N shore of Mackinac Stait to explore Lake Michigan, Green Bay, the Fox R, the Wisconsin R, and the Mississippi R as far S as Arkansas. On their return trip, they ascended the Illinois and Des Plaines rivers, portaging at Chicago to Lake Michigan. Marquette published his journal of the trip.

JONATHAN (or Brother Jonathan). Common nickname for a patriot during the American Revolution; used derisively by the British and Loyalists. Later it became a synonym for a country bumpkin and for an American in general.

JONES ACT (1916). Organic Act of the Philippine Islands passed by Congress; committed US to eventual independence of the islands and established its government as a US dependency.

JONES COUNTY, SECESSION OF. Center of antisecession sentiment; supposedly seceded from the state of Mississippi during Civil War. No written record of secession exists, but a company of raiders did cooperate with Union troops.

JONESTOWN MASSACRE (Nov. 18, 1978). In the mid-1970s, Jim Jones, a charismatic churchman, moved most of his cult, the People's Temple, from San Francisco to Guyana, where he established a commune. Continuing complaints of abuse there led US Representative Leo Ryan of California to lead an investigating party to the commune in 1978. As Ryan's party prepared to leave, five of them were killed by members of the cult. Then Jones, who had become increasingly paranoid, told his followers that they were threatened by outsiders and must commit suicide. They were ordered to drink a poisoned punch, and those who refused were shot or injected with cyanide. When Guyanese troops reached Jonestown the next day, they found 913 members of the commune dead, including Jones.

JONES V. VAN ZANDT, 5 Howard 215 (1846). Sustained the Fugitive Slave Law of 1793, by declaring that slavery was a political question for each state to settle; also required each state to allow the restoration of slave property of other states.

JORNADA DEL MUERTO ("journey of death"). A ninety-mile desert road from Valverde, N.M., to El Paso, Tex.

JOUETT'S RIDE (June 3, 1781). Capt. John Jouett, Jr., rode forty-four miles in one night from Louisa, Va., to Charlottesville, where the Virginia legislature was in session, to warn them of an impending attack by British troops. Among those saved from capture were Thomas Jefferson, Richard Henry Lee, Thomas Nelson, Jr., Benjamin Harrison, Patrick Henry, and Edmund Randolph.

JOURNALISM. See NEWSPAPERS.

JOURNAL OF CONGRESS. The official record of the proceedings of Congress, kept since 1774. The journals are substantially incorporated in the *Journals of the Continental Congress*, published 1904–37 by the Library of Congress in thirty-four volumes; the *Annals of Congress*(1789–1824); *Register*

of Debates (1824–37); *Congressional Globe* (1833–73); and in the *Congressional Record* since 1873.

JUCHEREAU'S TANNERY. Established 1702 near Cairo, Ill.; included a mission, more than a hundred tradesmen, and many Mascouten hunters. Abandoned 1704, after an epidemic.

JUDAISM, AMERICAN. In 1654, twenty-three Sephardim (Spanish and Portuguese Jews) arrived in New Amsterdam from Brazil, from which they had been forced to migrate; it was the first Jewish community in North America. Other Jews arrived soon after, mostly from northern Europe. By the mid-1700s, Jews enjoyed greater freedom in the English colonies than anywhere else in the world. The Sephardim continued to dominate Jewish spiritual life in the colonies, although the number of Jews of Germanic descent (Ashkenazim) constituted the majority of American Jews in the 18th c. Prior to 1840, there were no rabbis in America, and services were led by a cantor. By the mid-18th c., there were between 2,000 and 3,000 American Jews; many were involved in mercantile activities and several had amassed considerable wealth. Immigration from Germany increased quickly in the early 19th c.; by 1850, there were 50,000 Jews in the United States. By 1880, the number was 250,000. The Ashkenazim migration had included many educated middle-class laymen and scholarly rabbis. Reform Judaism took hold, and there were extensive changes made in the tone and content of services, prayers, and traditional rituals. Rabbi I.M. Wise, the most influential of the Reform scholars, established himself in Cincinnati in 1854, issued a modern Hebrew prayer book in 1857, and helped organize the liberal Union of American Hebrew Congregations in 1873 and the Hebrew Union College in 1875. Attempts by traditionalists to stem the tide and organize parallel institutions met with scant success. Mass migrations from the Russian empire resulted from the giant pogroms in the 1880s. The new arrivals were characterized by religious orthodoxy, political radicalism, and Zionist leanings. The great majority settled in congested slums. In New York City—where 46 percent of American Jews still lived in 1939—the largest urban community of Jews in history was consolidated. Anti-Semitism was making its first noticeable appearance in the United States. In the city slums, Jews formed a proletariat, particularly in the garment industry; such Jews took the lead in establishing powerful trade unions to ameliorate sweatshop conditions. A fusion of the Germanic and Eastern European Jewish community was accelerated by the increasing anti-Semitism, the growing proclivity toward Zionism, and the rise of Adolf Hitler in the 1930s. As the Democrats became the party of urban-oriented reform, Jews flocked to its support. The newcomers expanded the cultural and religious horizons of American Jewry. A vital, secularist Yiddish literature, press, and theater flourished from the 1910s to the 1930s. Jews began also to play an important part in the mainstream of American popular culture, especially in the areas of motion pictures and popular music. Despite the inroads of reformist Judaism, Orthodoxy maintained its adherents; in 1887, the Orthodox established a talmudic academy in New York, evolving into Yeshiva University. They also formed various unions of Orthodox congregations and rabbinical councils. The newcomers also gave vitality to Conservative Judaism, which permitted change within traditional continuity. Jewish education began to reflect a new synthesis of religion, modern Hebrew culture, and Zionism. American Jews played a crucial role in obtaining support for the state of Israel, founded in 1948 as the culmination of Zionist hopes. In the aftermath of World War II, the American Jewish community was augmented by over 200,000 German and Eastern European Jews, including many Hasidim. Anti-Semitism, which had come to be associated with nazism, came to be considered anti-American; by the 1950s, virtually all legal sanctions of anti-Semitism had been removed. Jews flocked into the professions, notably law, medicine, accounting, and teaching. By the 1970s, however, the New Left supported the Palestinians in particular and the Arabs in general, and consequently attacked Israel and Zionism as their primary opponents. Moreover, many young Jews criticized the American Jewish community for its growing conservatism and materialism. Nevertheless, there were signs that the Jewish community was on the threshold of a cultural, and perhaps spiritual renaissance. Newer and older forms of worship and social organization were being experimented with.

The Israeli experience, moreover, exercised a highly beneficial impact on the Jews' self-image, and there was strong support for aiding the beleaguered Soviet Jews.

JUDICIARY.

Colonial and Constitutional Origins. Basic to the colonial judiciary was the office of justice of the peace, which dealt in minor civil and criminal matters. Above that was the county court; and in some colonies, a right of appeal existed to the colonial assembly. In some cases a further appeal could be directed to the judicial committee of the Privy Council in England. After the colonies became independent states, the court systems remained fundamentally the same, except for the development of courts of appeals with full-time professional judges. All proposed plans submitted to the Constitutional Convention of 1787 called for a national judiciary distinct from the state systems. The Constitution as adopted introduced two major breaks with the past: state judiciaries were subordinated to the federal judiciary, and an independent judiciary was explicitly created under the doctrine of separation of powers. It created a Supreme Court and such inferior courts as Congress might establish and called for, in effect, lifetime tenure for federal judges. The Judiciary Act of 1789 effected the judicial provisions of the Constitution. It created a Supreme Court composed of a chief justice and five associate justices; three circuit courts, which were to be conducted by two Supreme Court justices and a district judge; and thirteen district courts, over each of which a district judge was to preside.

Federal Judiciary. The federal judiciary has seen a steady expansion. The district courts assumed in 1891 all the trial court responsibility originally allocated to both them and the circuit courts. The circuit court system was modified repeatedly after 1801. The membership of the Supreme Court was increased to an all-time high of ten in 1863 and established at nine in 1869. In 1891, the Supreme Court justices were relieved of obligations to ride circuit and much of their appellate jurisdiction. To enable the Supreme Court to keep up with the growing stream of cases, jurisdictional reductions have been made from time to time limiting the classes of cases that might be taken to the court. Provisions with respect to appellate jurisdiction, set by Congress, are complex. Congress has created other specialized tribunals, for example, those that have jurisdiction over the territories, the Court of Claims, the Court of Customs and Patent Appeals, and the Tax Court. Finally, the independent regulatory agencies exercise functions that are essentially judicial in character.

State, County, and Municipal Courts. State judicial systems vary greatly in matters of appointment, tenure, jurisdiction, organization, and procedure. State judges may be chosen by the legislature, by cooperation between governors and legislatures, by popular election, or by a nonpartisan appointive-elective methods. Tenure varies from lifetime appointment to specific terms of service to mandatory retirement at a certain age. In the 1920s and 1930s, a number of states made significant reforms in their judiciaries. The replacement of justice-of-the-peace courts with municipal courts within cities was a step toward increased efficiency and consistency. In the 1960s, the states began to establish unified state court systems, with central administrative authority vested in the state's chief justice and highest court; over half the states had adopted such a system by 1973. Jurisdiction of general trial courts, both criminal and civil, is usually organized on a county or multicounty basis, while municipal courts are organized on the basis of the city or borough. General trial courts have jurisdiction over felony criminal cases, all juvenile, domestic relations, and probate cases, and civil actions involving claims in excess of $5,000. Municipal courts generally have jurisdiction over the remainder of state cases, including criminal misdemeanors, local ordinances, and minor civil cases.

JUDICIARY ACT OF 1789. Implemented judiciary clause in the Constitution. Provided for a Supreme Court of six members, three intermediate circuit courts comprising two Supreme Court justices and a district judge, and thirteen district courts, corresponding roughly to state boundaries, with a judge for each. Established principle of judicial review of state courts by assigning the Supreme Court jurisdiction on writs of error in cases of conflict between state and federal authority.

JUDICIARY ACT OF 1801. Passed by the Federalists immediately before they left office, it was regarded by the Democratic-Republicans as an attempt to retain Federalist control over the judiciary. The Democratic-Republicans repealed the act in 1802 and restored the Judiciary Act of 1789 to full force.

JUDICIARY ACT OF 1925. Gave the Supreme Court substantial control of the cases it would hear through a writ of certiorari granted or denied at the court's discretion; also changed the route of bills from federal district courts to appeals courts. Sometimes called the Judge's Bill of 1925.

JUKES FAMILY. Pseudonym for a family reported in 1875 by sociologist Richard Dugdale as having a two-century record of various kinds of crimes and antisocial behavior.

JUMPING-OFF PLACES. Towns along the US frontier where pioneers completed their outfitting for the journey west in the 1840s and 1850s. Independence, Mo., was the best known.

JUNEAU. Capital of Alaska since 1900. Founded 1880 during gold rush. Pop.: 19,529 (1980).

JUNIUS, LETTERS OF. Published in a London newspaper from 1769 to 1772 by a disaffected British official, possibly Sir Philip Francis. Highly critical of the British colonial policies, they were frequently reprinted in American colonial newspapers.

JURY TRIAL. The characteristic mode of determining issues of fact at common law was transplanted from England to the American colonies and became an integral part of their legal system in both civil and criminal common law cases. The Constitution as proposed in 1787 contained the provision that "the Trial of all Crimes, except in cases of Impeachment, shall be by Jury," but there was no provision for jury trial in civil cases. The Sixth Amendment elaborated on the subject of jury trial in criminal cases by providing that "the accused shall enjoy the right to a speedy and public trial, by an impartial jury of the State and district wherein the crime shall have been committed." Some states, however, have not adhered rigidly to the old common law requirement that the jury be composed of not more or less than twelve persons and the requirement that the verdict be unanimous. Jury trial has not been required in cases involving petty offenses, and in all cases, including cases involving serious crimes, the right of trial by jury may be waived by the parties.

JUSTICE, DEPARTMENT OF. Established 1870; the office of attorney general had been created by the Judiciary Act of 1789. For many years the attorney general served as the legal counsel to the president and had no department as such; but by the Civil War he was conducting most federal cases and had a growing staff. Direction of US attorneys and US marshals had been transferred from the courts to his office. This trend was formalized by the act that created the Department of Justice under the attorney general. In 1871 the federal prison system was placed under the department's jurisdiction. The Criminal Division was added in 1909 and the Lands Division (later the Land and Natural Resources Division) in 1910. In the extensive departmental reorganization of 1933, several offices were made into divisions, including the Antitrust Division, the Tax Division, and the Claims Division (later the Civil Division). The Internal Security Division was created in 1954 and the Civil Rights Division in 1957. As legislation for the protection of the public continued to increase, the Pollution Control Section in the Land and Natural Resources Division (1970), the Consumer Affairs Section in the Antitrust Division (1971), and the Economic Stabilization Section in the Civil Division (1971) were created. Meanwhile, enforcement duties were added. The Bureau of Investigation (later the Federal Bureau of Investigation) was created in 1908. The Immigration and Naturalization Service was transferred from the Department of Labor to Justice in 1940. Antinarcotics enforcement was concentrated in the Department of Justice with the creation of the Bureau of Narcotics and Dangerous Drugs in 1968. In 1972 the president created the Office for Drug Abuse Law Enforcement and the Office of National Narcotics Intelligence. The Community Relations Service, created by the Civil Rights Act of 1964 and charged with assisting minority groups, was transferred from the Department of Commerce to Justice in 1966.

JUSTICE OF THE PEACE. A local official authorized to keep the peace and try felonies and trespasses. The office flourished in the colonies, exercising sweeping local executive and administrative powers. Drew up the levy, collected the tax, appointed road commissioners and supervised highways, made disbursements, granted licenses to keep taverns and retail liquors, and appointed and controlled administrators, executors, and guardians. They generally took acknowledgments of deeds and depositions and performed marriage ceremonies. While the office still exists in some states, the justice is in the main a committing magistrate, generally popularly elected.

JUVENILE COURTS. The first specialized juvenile court in the United States was created in Chicago in 1899; reformers sought to separate children and youth from the ugly conditions in prisons and improve their opportunities for contructive citizenship. By 1925, a juvenile court existed in every state except two. Constitutional challenges to juvenile court practice and procedure were consistently overruled. Concerns that children were denied a right to bail, counsel, public trials, jury trials, and immunity against self-incrimination, and that they could be convicted on hearsay testimony or by only a preponderance of the evidence, were swept aside. Legislative reform in California and New York in 1961 and 1962, respectively, began to place a more regularized procedure on the historically informal juvenile court practices. In 1967 the US Supreme Court ruled that constitutional due process protected the juvenile and mandated formal fact-finding hearings, together with the juvenile's right to be represented by an attorney and to avoid self-incrimination. The court ruled in 1970 that the criminal system's principle of proof beyond a reasonable doubt must be utilized in juvenile court trials, but also in 1971 that juveniles were not entitled to a jury trial under the Constitution. In 1984 the court approved pretrial detention of juveniles on the order of a judge.

KADIAK ISLAND. See KODIAK ISLAND.

KALAMAZOO. City in Michigan, founded 1829 on the Kalamazoo R. Paper manufacturing began in 1867 and remains the major industry. Pop.: 79,722 [1980]

KALAMAZOO CASE (*Charles E. Stuart et al v. School District No. 1 of the Village of Kalamazoo,* 30 Michigan 69 [1874]). The Michigan supreme court confirmed the right of the state to establish, at public expense, a complete system of education, thus setting an important precedent.

KALLIKAK FAMILY. Pseudonym for two New Jersey kinship groups investigated by the psychologist H.H. Goddard (1866–1957). A detailed genealogical history of the family showed a large percentage of its "bad blood" group displayed various kinds of antisocial behavior; while the "good blood" group consisted almost entirely of normal individuals, many superior or prominent. The study concluded that feeblemindedness is inherited as a recessive unit character. Later investigations of the study regarded it as underplaying the influence of societally conditioned and environmentally determined factors in mental ability.

KANAWHA SALT WORKS. Located on the Kanawha R near present Charleston, W. Va., on site of Indians works. First deep well dug in 1808. By 1817, there were twenty brine wells producing 600,000 to 700,000 bushels annually.

KANSAS. Coronado reached C Kansas in 1541; it was then the home of the Kansa, Osage, Wichita, Pawnee, and Pueblo Indians and was frequented by other hunter tribes. England, France, and Spain claimed the area at various times, but real interest in exploration came after the Louisiana Purchase (1803). Pioneers came through via the Santa Fe Trail. Fort Leavenworth (1827) was the first to be established. Indian removal acts of 1830 and 1850 set nearly one-fourth of the area aside as a permanent home for Indians. Became territory in 1854 under the Kansas-Nebraska Act. Center of extreme rivalry between North and South, over the extension of slavery and the route to be taken by the transcontinental railroad. Thus began the six-year period when the area was referred to as "Bleeding Kansas." The Indians' land vanished rapidly as lands were opened to white settlement. In 1861, Kansas was admitted to the Union as a free-soil state. After the Civil War, the Indians were removed to Indian Territory, but Kansans were harassed by Indian raids until the late 1870s. The first railroad arrived in 1860. Railway towns became the western terminals for the Texas cattle drives. Hard winter wheat became a major crop, and industrial expansion kept pace with agriculture. By the 1980s, Kansas produced about one-fifth of the nation's wheat. Livestock production was of even greater value. Airplanes and farm machinery were among the state's major manufactures. Its industrial income is derived mainly from oil, natural gas, coal, salt, clay, and stone. Pop.: 2,363,208. (1980).

KANSAS BORDER WAR. See BORDER WAR.

KANSAS CITY. City in W Missouri at the confluence of the Missouri and Kansas rivers, founded as a trading post 1800. Several settlements preceded the present city, which by 1846 was competing for the Santa Fe trade with nearby Independence. Became a railroad and packing center after the Civil War; separated from Kansas City, Kans., only by the state line. Pop.: 448,159 (1980).

KANSAS COMMITTEE, NATIONAL. Organization founded 1856 to provide aid for free-soilers (those opposed to slavery) in Kansas Territory. (See also FREE SOIL PARTY.)

KANSAS FREE-STATE PARTY. Founded 1855 by a consolidation of antislavery groups in Kansas Territory. Became part of the Republican party 1859.

KANSAS-NEBRASKA ACT (1854). By repealing the MISSOURI COMPROMISE, it made real the possibility of slavery in both territories, stating that the question of slavery should be settled by the people living in them. Kansas and Nebraska were opened for settlement 1854. Nebraska remained relatively quiet; settlers came to Kansas not only to develop the frontier but also to lend their weight in the determination of whether Kansas would be free or slave.

KAPOSIA, BATTLE OF (1842). Also called the Battle of Pine Coulie; at South St. Paul, Minn., between the Chippewa and the Sioux. The Sioux won.

KASKASKIA. Town founded 1703 by French Jesuits on the Kaskaskia R above its junction with the Mississippi R in the Illinois Country. A British garrison was established there 1767. By 1770 contained almost a thousand inhabitants. When the Illinois Territory was established 1809, it became the territorial capital; in 1818, the first state capital. Decline set in when the capital was moved to Vandalia 1820. A disastrous flood almost destroyed it 1844; and in 1881 the Mississippi and Kaskaskia rivers began changing their courses. By 1910, their waters had obliterated the ancient settlement.

KASSERINE PASS, BATTLE OF (Jan. 30–Feb. 25, 1943). World War II battle in Tunisia between the Allies and German and Italian troops under Gen. Erwin Rommel. After setbacks, the Allies eventually took the pass.

KAYODEROSSERAS PATENT. Contested grant of 300,000 acres along the Mohawk R in New York state. The patent was granted to thirteen persons in 1703 but disputed by Mohawk tribal leaders, who alleged fraud. In 1763, a compromise was effected: the patentees gave up some land, the Mohawk received some compensation.

KEARNEYITES. Followers of Denis Kearney, a California labor agitator, who, in 1877, organized the Workingmen's party in California as a protest against unemployment, Chinese coolie labor competition, and other economic and political evils. The new California constitution (1879) partially met the group's demands. By 1880, the party had practically disappeared.

KEARNY, FORT. Established 1846 on the Missouri R, removed 1848 to a location on the Platte R near the present city of Kearney, Nebr. Protected emigrants on the Oregon Trail; in use until 1871.

KEARNY-FRÉMONT QUARREL (1847). Col. John C. Frémont continued to act as governor of California after Gen. S.W. Kearny was ordered to set up a new government. Frémont was court-martialed, found guilty in 1848; President Polk pardoned him, but Frémont refused the restoration of his rank and resigned from the army.

KEARNY'S MARCH TO CALIFORNIA (1846). Gen. S.W. Kearny left Santa Fe on Sept. 25 to conquer California. His party learned that Commodore R.F. Stockton and Col. J.C. Frémont had already taken it; but later he learned that Mexicans had expelled the Americans from several places, including Los Angeles and Santa Barbara. He drove off the Mexicans in a battle at San Pasqual on Dec. 6, and soon reached San Diego.

KEARNY'S MISSION TO CHINA (1842). Commodore Lawrence Kearny was sent to Canton at the close of the ANGLO-CHINESE WAR to gain assurances that US merchants would be able to operate in China on the same footing as other Western traders. His success led to the later Open Door doctrine.

KEARSARGE AND ALABAMA ENCOUNTER (June 19, 1864). Battle off Cherbourg, France, between the Confederate ship *Alabama* and the Union ship *Kearsarge*. The *Kearsarge* enjoyed every advantage of condition and forced surrender of the sinking *Alabama*.

KEELBOAT. Used on American rivers, chiefly in the West. A long narrow craft built on a keel and ribs, with a long cargo box amidships; steered by a special oar and propelled by oars or poles, or fitted with sails.

KEFAUVER INVESTIGATIONS (1950). Sen. Estes Kefauver, chairman of a special crime committee, instituted intensive investigations into crime in the nations' major cities; his adept use of the new medium of television made the public aware of the extensive nature of organized crime.

KEITH CONTROVERSY. In 1691, George Keith, a Quaker leader in Pennsylvania, criticized the Friends' Meetings for doctrinal and disciplinarian laxity. He formed his own "Christian Quakers" sect, and went to England to defend himself after being forbidden to preach. He was disowned 1695.

KELLOGG-BRIAND PACT (1928). Also called the Pact of Paris. Signed by fifteen nations, who agreed to renounce war as an instrument of national policy and called for settlement of disputes by pacific means.

KELLY'S FORD (Nov. 7, 1863). The Union army under Gen. G.G. Meade successfully attacked the Confederate works on the Rappahannock R at Kelly's Ford, Va.

KELLY'S INDUSTRIAL ARMY. Organized by C.T. Kelly in California in 1894; consisted of 1,500 unemployed men who traveled east by railroad boxcar to join COXEY'S ARMY in Washington, D.C., in a mass protest against unemployment. In Iowa, they were forced off the train, and started on foot to Washington. Only a remnant reached the capital.

KEMPER RAID (1804). After the US failed to take possession of West Florida after the Louisiana Purchase, three brothers, Reuben, Nathan, and Samuel Kemper, led an abortive attempt to seize control of the area for the US.

KENESAW MOUNTAIN, BATTLE OF (June 27, 1864). As he approached Atlanta, Union Gen. W.T. Sherman met a Confederate army occupying the crest of Kenesaw Mountain. Sherman made an unnecessary and unsuccessful attempt to assault the mountain, one of his few serious errors.

KENNEBEC RIVER SETTLEMENTS. In 1607 the Popham plantation was established in Maine at the mouth of the Kennebac R, but was abandoned the next year. In 1626, Abraham Shurt settled on Monhegan; the Pilgrims established a trading post at Cushenoc, far up the Kennebac; and by 1630 there were eighty-four families near the river's mouth. A stout fort was at Pemaquid. Several others were founded in the decades ahead. They flourished until the Indian wars, when most were destroyed and had to be rebuilt.

KENNEDY, JOHN F., ASSASSINATION (Nov. 22, 1963). At 12:30 PM (central standard time), President Kennedy was shot while riding in a motorcade in Dallas, Tex. Three shots were fired from the sixth floor of the Texas Public School Book Depository. The president was shot twice, in the lower neck, and, fatally, in the head. Texas Governor John B. Connally was also hit and seriously wounded. Within an hour, Lee Harvey Oswald, a twenty-four-year-old former defector to the Soviet Union, was arrested as a suspect in the murder of a Dallas policeman; before midnight, Oswald was charged with Kennedy's murder. Within forty-eight hours of his capture, he was fatally shot by Jack Ruby, a Dallas night-club owner. The WARREN COMMISSION concluded that Oswald was Kennedy's sole assassin.

KENNEDY, ROBERT F., ASSASSINATION (June 5, 1968). At 12:16 AM (Pacific standard time) in the Ambassador Hotel in Los Angeles, Sen. Kennedy was shot three times. He died the next day. The senator's assailant was a twenty-four-year-old emigrant from Jerusalem and an Arab nationalist, Sirhan B. Sirhan. He was convicted and sentenced to death; the sentence was commuted to life imprisonment in 1972, and he remained in prison in California.

KENSINGTON STONE. Found at Kensington, Minn., in 1898; it bears a long inscription in runic characters telling of a journey of exploration "from Vinland to the west." Purported to have been created in the 14th c. by Norsemen; most experts today regard it a 19th c. hoax.

KENT STATE PROTEST (May 4, 1970). The Ohio national guard, ordered to break up a political protest meeting (opposing President Nixon's ordering of an invasion of Cambodia) at Kent State University, Kent, Ohio, fired sixty-one shots point blank into a crowd of students, who had thrown rocks and shouted abuse at them. Thirteen students were wounded and four were killed. A state grand jury exonerated the guardsmen but brought in thirty-one indictments against the young people. Public opinion eventually forced the state to drop all charges. The tragedy galvanized the antiwar movement; some 700 colleges and universities were closed down in sympathy for the Kent victims.

KENTUCKY. Fifteenth state of the Union, formed from the trans-Appalachian territory of Virginia. Settlement coincided with the Revolution. Scene of considerable fighting, it was caught in constant Indian raiding from both above and below the Ohio, much of it stimulated by the British. By 1790, the availability of abundant virgin land had attracted more than 70,000 settlers. From 1782 to 1792 the pioneers engaged in a political struggle to establish local county governments, to separate the region from the political control of Virginia, and to establish an independent commonwealth (see KENTUCKY CONVENTIONS). Kentucky entered the Union 1792. The state thrived, even during the War of 1812; though the state banking system went bankrupt in the depression of 1819, it prospered again after 1820. The Civil War placed a severe strain on Kentucky; technically the state was neutral, but actually it was sharply divided internally. Approximately 35,000 volunteers fought with the Confederacy; and more than twice that number with the Union. An appreciable number of officers of general rank fought on both sides, and both Abraham Lincoln and Jefferson Davis were born in Kentucky. In the post-Civil War era, Kentucky made sectional political adjustments, exploited its rich timber and mineral resources, and reestablished trade and industry. Since 1920, its agrarian economic base has shifted to a more highly industrialized one. On the Ohio R frontier, Kentucky has become highly industrialized. Among the significant industries are whiskey, tobacco, textiles, automobiles and trucks, and chemicals. Pop.: 3,661,433 (1980).

KENTUCKY, INVASION OF (1862). Confederate Gen. Braxton Bragg moved his army from Chattanooga into Kentucky, arriving at Bowling Green in mid-September. He was opposed by Gen. D.C. Buell, who concentrated his forces at Louisville. On Oct. 8, the two forces met in a bloody battle at Perryville. Bragg achieved a tactical success, but two days later it was decided that he should leave Kentucky rather than chance defeat in enemy territory.

KENTUCKY AND VIRGINIA RESOLUTIONS. See VIRGINIA AND KENTUCKY RESOLUTIONS.

KENTUCKY CONVENTIONS. A series of ten meetings from 1784 to 1792 in which Kentucky called for more assistance from Virginia in opposing Indian attacks and made provisions for more self-government. In the tenth convention (April 1792) a democratic state constitution was drafted.

KENTUCKY COUNTY. Created by the Virginia assembly on Dec. 31, 1776. Included all of FINCASTLE COUNTY S of the Ohio R and W of the Big Sandy R and Cumberland Mountains; divided into three counties 1780.

KENTUCKY'S NEUTRALITY DOCTRINE. In May 1861, the legislature resolved that the state would "take no part in the civil war now being waged ..." and the governor warned all armed forces against entering Kentucky. Nevertheless, warring forces swamped it from all sides.

KERNSTOWN, BATTLE AT (March 23, 1862). Obeying orders to detain Union forces in the Shenandoah Valley, Confederate Gen. Stonewall Jackson engaged a division at Kernstown, Va. He was repulsed and forced to retreat.

KEROSINE OIL. First distilled from coal 1846; produced commercially 1854; by 1859 the country had more than fifty companies making kerosine, and the business was crowding out such older illuminants as whale oil and camphine. Soon it was distilled from petroleum, and use of coal declined. By 1860, more than 200 patents had been granted on kerosine lamps. In 1860, a kerosine stove was perfected. In the 20th c., new uses for kerosine developed, most notably as a jet engine fuel.

KETTLE CREEK, BATTLE OF (Feb. 14, 1779). After Savannah had fallen to the British, British troops overran Georgia until they were rebuffed at Kettle Creek; there patriots surprised and scatterd a large Loyalist force. The British retired from Augusta, and loyalism in Georgia and South Carolina was severely checked.

KEY WEST. Southernmost city in the US, in Florida. The first settlers, chiefly from South Carolina and St. Augustine, arrived 1822. Long a key military point for the US; also a popular resort community. Pop.: 24,292 (1980).

KIDDER MASSACRE (June 29, 1867). Lt. L.S. Kidder, with eleven men, left Fort Sedgwick, Colo., with dispatches for Gen. G.A. Custer. They were ambushed and killed by Cheyenne.

KIDNAPPING OF FREE BLACKS. Despite laws to the contrary, it was common practice for free blacks in northern states to be kidnapped and sold as slaves in the South. Fugitive slave laws, empowering federal officers to seize runaway slaves and return them to their owners, made it easy to seize free blacks and hasten them into slavery under pretext of law.

KILBOURN V. THOMPSON, 103 US 168 (1880). Supreme Court declared that Congress had no "general power of making inquiry into the private affairs of the citizens."

KILLDEER MOUNTAIN, BATTLE OF (July 28, 1864). Gen. Alfred Sully, leading the northwestern Indian expedition on the Knife R in North Dakota, successfully attacked some 5,000 Sioux occupying Killdeer Mountain.

KING, MARTIN LUTHER, ASSASSINATION (April 4, 1968). The Rev. Dr. Martin Luther King, Jr., leader of the nonviolent civil rights movement, had gone to Memphis, Tenn., to support striking sanitation workers. He was shot while waving to a crowd from a hotel balcony and died an hour later. The assassination was followed by rioting, looting, and arson in black districts of more than a hundred cities. Thousands were injured and forty-six people were killed; ten died in extensive rioting in Washington, D.C. On June 8, James Earl Ray was arrested for King's murder; he pleaded guilty and received ninety-nine years in prison. In 1979, a congressional investigation stated that the assassination was "probably" the result of a conspiracy of right-wing St. Louis businessmen.

KING COTTON. Expression much used before the Civil War; it signified the southern belief that cotton was so essential that those who controlled it might dictate economic and political policies.

KING GEORGE, FORT. Blockhouse built 1721 on the Altamaha R in Georgia, to offset French expansion. Burned 1725.

KING GEORGE'S WAR (1744–48). Confrontation between England and France over the boundaries of Canada and northern New England; the New World extension of the War of Austrian Succession. The English captured Louisburg (Cape Breton Island) but failed in their efforts to take Quebec and Montreal. The Peace of Aix-la-Chapelle, which ended the war, restored Louisburg to France.

KING PHILIP'S WAR (1675–76). Philip, sachem of the Wampanoag, rejected the peace treaty that had been signed by his late father Massasoit. He launched devastating raids in Massachusetts, Maine, and New Hampshire. The British in turn destroyed the Narragansett. In 1676, the Indians threatened the major cities of Plymouth and Providence; but by May the tide had turned. Philip was killed, and peace was restored.

KING'S COLLEGE. See COLUMBIA UNIVERSITY.

KING'S MOUNTAIN, BATTLE OF (Oct. 7, 1780). Confrontation between a British force, largely Loyalist, under Maj. Patrick Ferguson and an army of "mountain men" from the back country at King's Mountain in present York County, S.C. The British, who were occupying the mountain, were attacked from all sides by the patriots. Virtually all the British were killed, wounded, or captured.

KING'S PROVINCE. Portion of mainland Rhode Island, the present-day Washington County, that was known as the Narragansett Country and claimed by Rhode Island, Connecticut, and Massachusetts. A royal commission in 1665 gave it to Rhode Island.

KINGSTON. City in New York, on the Hudson R; settled 1652 and soon a trading center. During the Revolution, it became the capital 1777 after New York City was taken by the British. The government moved after the British burned the town. Pop.: 24,481 (1980).

KING'S WOODS. In colonial New England, the king's surveyors marked the best pines for use as masts for the royal navy. When this timberland had passed into private hands, taking of this timber continued, thereby contributing to colonial discontent.

KING WILLIAM'S WAR (1689–97). First of the French and Indian wars. The French in Canada and their Indian allies attacked British border forts and settlements. A New England force failed to take Montreal, and a French squadron failed to take Boston. The Treaty of Ryswick ended the fighting but did little to settle the dispute.

KINKAIDERS. In 1904 Congress passed the Kinkaid Act, which allowed homesteads of

640 acres in W Nebraska. A rush of home-steaders, known as Kinkaiders, met disap-pointment; unproductive soil, drought, dust storms, and warfare with cattlemen and sheepmen defeated them.

KINSEY REPORT. In 1948, Alfred C. Kinsey and his associates at Indiana University, pub-lished their results of a comprehensive survey of the sexual habits of American men, *Sexual Behavior in the Human Male.* It was widely discussed and created great controversies. In 1953, he published a similar report on women.

KIOWA. Small Plains tribe that moved from the Black Hills to the Arkansas R. In alliance with the Comanche, they raided far into Mex-ico and terrorized sections of present Okla-homa and Texas in the 1860s and 1870s. Fiercely resistant to the inroads of settlers.

KIOWA, FORT. Built ca. 1822 by the Ameri-can Fur Co. on the Missouri R about ten miles above present Chamberlain, S.D. Abandoned after the decline of the fur trade.

KITCHEN CABINET. Derisive title for Presi-dent Andrew Jackson's informal group of ad-visers who held no official positions in government.

KITTANNING CAMPAIGN (1756). During the French and Indian War, Kittanning, a Del-aware village on the Allegheny R was used as an Indian base for attacks on Pennsylvania farmers. To prevent further raids, the Penn-sylvania militia burned the village, destroyed ammunition and supplies, and killed about forty Indians.

KLAMATH-MODOC. Two Indian tribes that shared a language and certain cultural tradi-tions. The Klamath lived in lakes and marshes in SC Oregon, and the Modoc lived at the edges of the Basin in NE California. Contact with the white man came after 1830; in 1864 both tribes were moved to a reservation in Or-egon. The Modoc War of 1872–73 resulted from tensions surrounding that removal.

KLONDIKE RUSH. Gold was discovered along the Klondike R in 1896 in Canada's Yukon Territory. Between 1897–99, some 100,000 persons left for Alaska. By 1900, $27 million in gold per year was being taken; but the richer deposits were soon exhausted.

KNIGHTS OF LABOR. Secret labor league founded 1869; by 1886, membership was be-tween 600,000 and 700,000. Its aim was to weld the whole labor movement into a single disciplined army. Soon overshadowed by the American Federation of Labor.

KNIGHTS OF THE GOLDEN CIRCLE. Secret proslavery order organized 1855 and active during the Civil War among Indiana COPPERHEADS.

KNIGHTS OF THE WHITE CAMELIA. Secret organization founded in New Orleans in 1867 to oppose Radical Reconstruction; much like the Ku Klux Klan.

KNOW-NOTHING PARTY. Founded 1849 in New York; a secret patriotic society. Members were sworn not to reveal its mysteries, and their universal answer to questions was "I know nothing about it." They pledged to vote only for native Americans, to work for a twenty-one-year probation period before nat-uralization, and to combat the Roman Catho-lic church. As the American party, it did well in the 1854 and 1855 New England, New York, and Delaware state elections; but split over the slavery issue. Former President Mil-lard Fillmore, its 1856 presidential candi-date, carried only Maryland. This defeat brought about the party's end.

FORT KNOX (Indiana). Built 1788 at Vin-cennes, Ind. Previous forts on the site had been named Fort Sackville and Fort Patrick Henry.

FORT KNOX (Kentucky). Army post estab-lished 1918, thirty-one miles SW of Louis-ville. In 1937 the US gold repository was lo-cated there.

KNOXVILLE. Major city in E Tennessee, field headquarters for the TENNESSEE VALLEY AUTHORITY (TVA) and home of the University of Tennes-see. Settled 1787, it was capital of the Terri-tory South of the Ohio River, which entered the Union as Tennessee in 1796. Served as state capital twice. Held by Union troops dur-ing the Civil War; besieged and partly destroyed by the Confederates. Pop.: 183,139 (1980).

KODIAK. City on Kodiak Island, Alaska. The oldest city in Alaska, it was founded 1792 by Russians as a fur-gathering station. Fishing became its major industry in the 19th c. Pop.: 4,756 (1980).

KODIAK ISLAND. Located in the Gulf of Alaska. The habitat of the Kodiak bear and the king crab. Also site of a US naval base.

KOREA, WAR WITH (1871). In 1866, an American armed schooner grounded on a sandbar in the Ping-yang river in Korea. The Koreans, who regarded violation of their traditional seclusion as a capital offense, burned the ship and murdered the crew. Two punitive expeditions were sent. In one encounter 250 Koreans were killed; American loss was 3 killed and 9 wounded. No treaty was secured until 1882.

KOREAN WAR (1950–53). Conflict between the communist forces of North Korea, aided by China, and the noncommunist forces of South Korea, aided by the US-led United Nations force. At the end of World War II, Korea had been "temporarily" divided along the 38th parallel. Tensions developed when North Korea refused to participate in free elections supervised by the UN in 1947, and culminated in the invasion by North Korea of the south in June 1950. President Truman authorized Gen. Douglas MacArthur to commit US troops to aid South Korea. They were placed, along with contingents from fifteen other nations, under formal command of the UN. Seoul, the South Korean capital, quickly fell. MacArthur exploited UN sea and air supremacy by executing an end run around the North Koreans; he landed an amphibious force at Inchon, behind enemy lines. Seoul was retaken, and MacArthur pursued the North Koreans into their own territory above the 38th parallel. Pyongyang, the capital, fell and the UN forces moved near the Yalu R, which separates North Korea from China. In November 1950, an overwhelming Chinese army crossed that border and entered the war on behalf of North Korea. The UN forces were forced back to a defensible line immediately north of the 38th parallel. MacArthur's insistence on carrying on the war above the Yalu

R caused President Truman to replace him with Gen. M.B. Ridgway in April 1951. Peace negotiations began July 1951 and dragged on until an armistice was signed on July 27, 1953. Basically, the *status quo ante bellum* was restored, and the basic problem of Korean unity was left unresolved. Both sides claimed victory. The US had put 1.6 million servicemen into the war zones. Losses were 54,246 killed, 4,675 captured, and 103,284 wounded. The US cost was about $20 billion.

KU KLUX ACT (1871). One of the Force Acts, it gave extraordinary power to the president in order to destroy the Ku Klux Klan and other "conspiracies" in the South. Declared unconstitutional 1882.

KU KLUX KLAN.
19th Century. Post-Civil War secret organization of southern whites aimed at recouping their prestige and countering Reconstruction polices. Sought to protect whites from what they felt was humiliation by freedmen (former slaves) and to reassert white supremacy. Klansmen wore white robes and masks and rode robed horses with muffled feet. They rode at night, intimidating blacks, carpetbaggers, and scalawags. Responsible for lynchings, floggings, and other acts of violence. In 1871 the KU KLUX ACT outlawed the Klan, but it did not cease operations until the 1870s, by which time whites were again firmly in control of local and state governments.
20th Century. In 1915, the Klan was reborn, again a secret vigilante organization for native-born, white, Protestant Americans. By the mid-1920s, it had spread nationwide and had perhaps 3 million members. Its particular enemy was Roman Catholics. In the 1930s, Jews and communists were targets. It all but died out in World War II but was revived again in the 1950s; again, blacks were its chief target, but its influence was at best marginal. There were an estimated 10,000 members in 1980.

LA BALME'S EXPEDITION (1780). French raid, led by a Col. La Balme, against the British at a Miami village where Fort Wayne, Ind., now stands. La Balme's intention was to take Detroit. He was pursued by the Miami and killed; his men were dispersed.

LA BAYE. See GREEN BAY.

LA BELLE FAMILLE, BATTLE OF (July 24, 1759). A large force of French and Indian troops on its way to relieve FORT NIAGARA was intercepted by the British at La Belle Famille (Youngstown, N. Y.) and utterly routed; only 200 out of 1,200 soldiers escaped capture or death.

LABOR. Common interests of artisans resulted in some organization in the 17th c., but it was not until the late 18th c. that unionism came into being. In 1792, Philadelphia shoemakers formed a protective organization; in 1794 the Typographical Society of New York was formed.

19th Century. Despite its 18th-c. beginnings, trade unionism is basically a 19th-c. phenomenon. Democracy under President Jackson gave an impetus to labor's rights to organize; in 1842 a Massachusetts case, *Commonwealth v. Hunt*, recognized the legality of unions and their right to strike for a closed shop. Ten-hour legislation was passed in seven states in the 1840s, although loopholes allowed workers to toil longer if they contracted for a longer workday. By 1860, the ten-hour day was widely accepted for skilled craftsmen, but not for the unskilled. The Civil War caused a labor shortage, which benefited the labor movement. The National Labor Union was formed 1866; its primary aim was the eight-hour day. In 1872, it converted into a political party and ran a presidential candidate. It failed shortly after that. Only ten of thirty labor unions survived the panic of 1873. One casualty was the mining union; in its wake came a secret organization called the Molly Maguires; its members were accused of fomenting violence. Wage reductions led to a general railroad strike 1877. Socialism had some influence after 1876, and the headquarters of the First International was moved from Basel to New York City. The Marxist Socialist Labor party had its beginnings 1876. Antagonism to the labor movement throughout the depression years led to secret societies. The KNIGHTS OF LABOR, founded 1869, was for a short time the most powerful labor organization in the nation. The eight-hour-day movement reached its climax in 1886, when labor demonstrations in Chicago led to a bombing in which seven policemen were killed. Branded as radical, the eight-hour movement suffered a serious setback. Samuel Gompers and Adolph Strasser of the cigarmakers union

formed the Federation of Organized Trades and Labor Unions in 1881, based on British union models. Reorganized 1886 as the AMERICAN FEDERATION OF LABOR (AFL). Membership increased from 200,000 in 1886 to more than 1.75 million in 1904. Through collective bargaining, strike, boycotting, and picketing, the AFL sought to improve the economic status of its members. It rejected independent political action, and organized the skilled crafts into national unions. Only the UNITED MINE WORKERS (UMW) was initially organized along industrial lines. Labor strife was common. The HOMESTEAD STRIKE (1890) against the Carnegie Steel Co. resulted in a number of deaths. The Coeur d'Alene district of Idaho was the scene of bitter miners' strikes in 1892, 1894, and 1899. Socialists, unable to impose their ideology on the AFL, formed what in 1900 became the Socialist Party of America. The American Railway Union was founded 1893 as an industrial union open to all railroad workers, including the unskilled. In 1894, it led a nationwide strike against the Pullman Co. Another industrial union, the International Ladies' Garment Workers ' Union (ILGWU) was formed 1900. Strong antiunion activity followed the formation of the NATIONAL ASSOCIATION OF MANUFACTURERS (NAM) 1895. NAM sponsored an open-shop movement, during which unions were dealt a heavy blow by court rulings that boycotts were violations of the SHERMAN ANTITRUST ACT. The AFL was also challenged by the left; in 1895 the INDUSTRIAL WORKERS OF THE WORLD (IWW) was formed; it called for abolition of the wage system and stressed direct action, the general strike, boycotts, and sabotage.

Early 20th Century. Woodrow Wilson's election as president in 1912 and his use of Gompers as his labor adviser meant that organized labor for the first time had access to a sympathetic administration. Under Wilson's sponsorship, Congress passed several laws favorable to labor. State laws limited child labor, set wage and hours standards for women, provided controls over sanitary and safety conditions, and attempted to establish accident insurance. The Department of Labor was created 1913; its first secretary was a former trade union official. Labor's opposition to the Sherman Antitrust Act led to its modification in 1914; the resulting CLAYTON ANTITRUST ACT was called by Gompers the "Magna Carta of labor." It generally made legal most union activities; judicial interpretations watered down its effect, however. The 1920s, a decade of massive economic growth, saw real wages and per capita income rise, except for textile workers and coal miners. Union membership went down during the decade, and lost another 500,000 members in the depression years of 1929 to 1933.

New Deal. Labor reform began in 1932 with the NORRIS-LA GUARDIA ACT, which curtailed the courts' power to issue injunctions against peaceful strikes and made antiunion employment contracts unenforceable in the courts. When Franklin D. Roosevelt came into office in 1933, he set in motion a wide variety of prounion laws and regulations. His NEW DEAL sponsored several programs to put the nation's unemployed laborers back to work. Included was the NATIONAL RECOVERY ADMINISTRATION, which prescribed minimum wages and maximum hours and eliminated child labor. In 1938, these provisions became statutory law with the passage of the FAIR LABOR STANDARDS ACT. The SOCIAL SECURITY ACT of 1935 created a national pension plan for workers. The union movement began a massive organizational drive, increasing noncompany membership from 3 million in 1933 to 20.5 million in 1978. Nevertheless, the old split between the craft and industrial unions surfaced again. In 1935, the three industrial unions within the AFL, the UMW, the ILGWU, and the Amalgamated Clothing Workers of America, broke away to form what became the Congress of Industrial Organization (CIO), with John L. Lewis of the UMW as head. Both the AFL and the CIO continued to grow and sign up new members. President Roosevelt extracted a no-strike pledge from union leaders during World War II.

Postwar World. Antiunion sentiment grew after the end of the war; among its causes were the inflationary spiral, increasing power of the unions, existence of corrupt labor officials, and communist influence in some unions. The major result of this hostility was the TAFT-HARTLEY ACT, passed by a Republican Congress over President Truman's veto. A rapprochement between the AFL and CIO led to their merger 1955. George Meany of the AFL became president and Walter Reuther of the CIO became head of the industrial union department. Public-sector employment grew spectacularly after World War II, and unionization soon began. The American Federation of State, County, and Municipal Employees (AFSCME) became the fastest growing union in the nation. By the 1980s, the AFL-CIO continued to dominate the US labor movement, despite defections from its ranks. (The UMW disaffiliated itself in 1947; the Teamsters were expelled for corruption in 1957; and the United Automobile Workers disaffiliated themselves in 1968.) It became more directly involved in politics, endorsing candidates and contributing large sums of money to their campaigns.

LABOR, DEPARTMENT OF. Established 1913 to "foster, promote and develop the welfare of wage-earners, to improve their working conditions, and to advance their opportunities for profitable employment." Includes the Bureau of Labor Statistics, the Bureau of International Labor Affairs, the Women's Bureau, the US Employment Service, and the Occupational Safety and Health Administration.

LABOR DAY. Thirty-two states had individually declared the first Monday in September a holiday when President Cleveland signed a law in 1887 designating the day a national holiday.

LABOR PARTIES. The National Labor Union formed a short-lived party in 1872, the first such in the nation. The Greenback Labor party, founded nationally 1878, received the support of the KNIGHTS OF LABOR, whose president, Terence Powderly, was elected mayor of Scranton, Pa., on its ticket. Powderly was also a founder of the POPULIST PARTY in 1889; by that time, the AMERICAN FEDERATION OF LABOR (AFL) was replacing the Knights of Labor as the chief organization. Socialist trade unionists founded the Socialist Labor Party in 1877, and later sought organized labor support. In 1920 the National Labor party formed an alliance with farmer groups and together they founded the FARMER-LABOR PARTY. The AFL, continuing its practice of remaining aloof from direct political action, did not actively support the new party, and it survived only in Minnesota (today's Democratic-Farmer-Labor party is its descendant). During the 1930s, various socialist and left-wing parties vied for support from organized labor; but labor gave most of its support to the Democratic party.

LABOR UNIONS. See LABOR.

LABRADOR FISHERIES. Important cod-fishing grounds since colonial days. The DEFINITIVE TREATY OF PEACE gave American fishermen liberal privileges along the Labrador coast.

LACONIA GRANT (1629). John Mason and Sir Ferdinando Gorges were awarded large tracts of land in W Maine. The grant was never utilized, and their company was dissolved 1634.

LAFAYETTE, FORT. Built 1812 at the entrance to New York harbor; used during the Civil War to hold political prisoners.

LAFAYETTE ESCADRILLE. Squadron of volunteer American airmen who fought for France in World War I. Abosorbed by the US Air Service, 1918.

LAFAYETTE'S VISIT TO AMERICA (1824–25). The marquis de Lafayette, a hero of the American Revolution, made a triumphant tour of the US by invitation of the president and Congress, visiting virtually every part of the country.

"LAFAYETTE, WE ARE HERE." Words spoken by Col C.E. Stanton at the tomb of the marquis de Lafayette on July 4, 1917; referred to the presence of US troops at the side of French troops in World War I.

LA FOLLETTE PROGRESSIVE PARTY. Federation of various progressive groups, such as the NONPARTISAN LEAGUE, the FARMER-LABOR PARTY, the SINGLE TAX LEAGUE, and labor groups formed to support Sen. Robert M. La Follette of Wisconsin for president in 1924 and to elect progressives to Congress. La Follette received about 17 percent of the vote, but carried only Wisconsin.

LA GALETTE, FORT. Built by the French 1749 near present Ogdensburg, N.Y., to protect Montreal from Indian attack. Captured by the British 1760.

LAIRD RAMS. Two ironclad naval vessels ordered 1862 by the Confederate navy from John Laird and Sons, English shipbuilders. The British government would not allow delivery; eventually sold to the royal navy.

LAISSEZ-FAIRE. Designates the economic doctrine that the well-being and progress of society are assured when individuals are free to apply their capital and labor without hindrance from the state.

LAKE CHAMPLAIN. Strategically located on the US-Canadian border, it was discovered 1609 by Samuel de Champlain; used by both the French and English; a prime military objective of the British in 1754. Fighting on and over the lake only ended with the fall of Montreal in 1760. During the Revolution, both Americans and British were determined to control the lake. The British were more successful. Again the center of hostilities in the War of 1812. Today, Lake Champlain is a link in the Hudson-St. Lawrence waterway; the surrounding region is a noted resort area.

LAKE GEORGE, BATTLE OF (Sept. 8, 1755). Confrontation between the New York militia and a French and Indian force. Both sides suffered serious losses.

LAKERS. Great Lakes bulk carrier steamships: long, narrow, and deep vessels. Transported iron ore, coal, limestone, and wheat. Date from 1816; by 1927, there were 765 in use.

LAKES, GREAT. See ERIE, LAKE; GREAT LAKES; HURON, LAKE; MICHIGAN, LAKE; ONTARIO, LAKE; SUPERIOR, LAKE.

LAKES-TO-GULF DEEP WATERWAY. A canal connecting the Great Lakes with the Mississippi R via the Des Plaines and Illinois rivers was envisioned as early as 1673. First section completed 1848; final connection made 1933.

LAME-DUCK AMENDMENT. The Twentieth Amendment to the Constitution, ratified 1933, abolished lame-duck sessions of Congress. Before then, Congress met in the December after an election and sat until the following March 4, even though many of its members may have been defeated in the November election (lame ducks). The amendment called for the new Congress to convene January 3, and for the president to be inaugurated January 20 rather than March 4.

LAMP, INCANDESCENT. In 1879 Thomas A. Edison made the first successful high-resistance carbon lamp. The lamp was improved over the years, most notably by the General

Electric Co. Although fluorescent lamps provide more light with greater efficiency, incandescent lamps continue to be used because of their simplicity and low cost.

LANCASTER, FORT. Trading post on the South Platte R, Colo., in use between 1843 and 1857.

LANCASTER, TREATY OF (1744). Settled disputes between Maryland and Virginia and the Six Nations. The Indians ceded much of W Maryland and agreed to support the British in KING GEORGE'S WAR.

LANCASTER PIKE. Privately subscribed toll road completed 1794 in Pennsylvania; first turnpike in the US. Little used after the Pennsylvania RR was built parallel to it.

LAND ACT OF 1796. Reenacted the rectangular system of survey embodied in the ORDINANCE OF 1785. Offered public lands for sale in 5,120-acre blocks; the smallest unit that could be bought was 640 acres, at a minimum price of $2 per acre. Failed because of these high minimums. (See also LAND ACT OF 1820.)

LAND ACT OF 1800. See HARRISON LAND ACT.

LAND ACT OF 1820. Minimum price of public lands was reduced from $2 to $1.25 per acre, the entire amount payable at the time of purchase. Smallest purchasable unit of land was 80 acres.

LAND BOUNTIES. The colonies and, after the Revolution, the states and the federal government offered land bounties instead of cash subsidies to reward military service. Such grants were awarded in every war up through the Mexican War. (See also LAND SCRIP.)

LAND GRANT ACT. See MORRILL ACT.

LAND GRANTS.
Colonial. By English law, title to all of English America was in the king, and from him all later claims stemmed. Royal land grants took the form of charters, and the whole Atlantic seaboard, except Florida, was parceled out to various land companies and individual proprietors. From these in turn came grants to individuals and groups, which were eventually incorporated into regular colonial governments. In New England the general court in each colony granted a tract, called a township, to a body of settlers, who in turn issued deeds to individuals. In New York, Maryland, and South Carolina there were vast individual grants and extensive engrossment. In New York, the practice had begun under the Dutch by the creation of patroon estates, which were recognized as valid by the British. In Virginia, there was at first a headrights system, fifty acres for each person arriving. This system degenerated, and under it large plantations grew up that were far too big to be fully cultivated. Land grants as bounties for military service began 1750; much of such land was in the west. The British made extensive military grants in the Floridas after their acquisition from Spain. In most cases, Indian titles were presumed to be extinguished by the local colonial government; the practice of frontiersmen buying land from Indians was stopped after 1763; only the colonies could negotiate with the tribes over land. Spain and France made grants similar to those made by England. When new areas came under the control of England, or later of the US, earlier foreign land grants were accepted as valid.

Spanish and Mexican. Title records to these early grants before US control were in poor shape, some of them being entirely lost. Often grants had been made on conditions never fulfilled. Conflicting claims were common, and these had to be tested in the courts with American judges attempting to apply Spanish and Mexican law and American equity. In some cases forged documents and fabricated grants had to be assessed. In all, 20,059 claims were confirmed for a total of 30 million acres.

For Education. The ORDINANCE OF 1785 stipulated that one thirty-sixth of the acreage of the public land states should be granted to states for public schools. New states after 1848 were given 1,280 acres in each township; and Utah, Arizona, New Mexico, and Oklahoma were given twice that for each township. Land was also set aside for the founding of state universities. In 1862 the MORRILL ACT gave each state 30,000 acres of public land for each representative and senator it had in Congress, to aid in establishing colleges of agriculture and mechanical arts. As a result, A & M colleges were established in every state, with two each in the southern states because of their insistence on segregation.

For Railways. Beginning 1850, Congress awarded large tracts of land as inducements to railroad companies to build a nationwide railway system. By 1871, land grants totaled 176 million acres. Most went to the transcontinental companies; the Northern Pacific, for example, was given 39 million acres. Railroads undertook advertising campaigns to attract immigrants, who would settle on their lands and purchase them. Reformers condemned the land grants as inconsistent with the free homestead policy; and in 1871 they succeeded in halting further grants. Continued agitation over the large amount of land claimed by railroads led to the General Forfeiture Act of 1890, which required the return to the government of land along projected lines never built.

LANDGRAVE. German title proposed for the second order of provincial nobility provided for in the Fundamental Constitutions of Carolina by the lords proprietors. Mostly ceremonial meaning.

LANDMARK. Designation of a building or public space specifying that it has important historic or aesthetic significance. Landmark status usually means that owners may not demolish or alter the building without permission from an official body, usually a landmark commission.

LANDS OFFICE, US GENERAL. Created 1912 to manage more than a billion acres of public land. Transferred to the Bureau of Land Management, 1946. By 1978, it administered 417 million acres of public lands and the leasing and sale of mineral rights on an additional 169 million acres. Chiefly preserves public lands for economic use, recreation, wildlife, and scenic beauty.

LAND ORDINANCES. See ORDINANCES OF 1784, 1785, AND 1787.

LAND POLICY. The LAND ORDINANCE OF 1785 provided that public lands be sold to raise revenue. As late as 1855, this income was 17 percent of the total federal income. Advocates of free land won their objective with adoption of the HOMESTEAD ACT, 1862. Congress had previously aided in the building of ca-

nals, roads, and railroads by generous grants of land. It had also made grants of land for public schools, public buildings, state universities and agricultural colleges, and other public institutions, on the assumption that such grants enhanced the value of the remaining lands and encouraged sale and development. Consequences of this speedy transfer of lands to private ownership were not considered until the threatened exhaustion of timber lands raised fundamental questions about the wisdom of past disposal practices. By the beginning of the 20th c., conservation of the remaining resources under federal ownership was vigorously advocated. National forests were set aside as permanent reservations. Places of scenic beauty were made national parks. In 1934, the remaining rangelands in public ownership were organized into management districts under the Taylor Grazing Act, thereby virtually ending the era of free land. (See also LAND GRANTS.)

LANDRUM-GRIFFIN ACT (1959). Designed to suppress corruption and the influences of organized crime in labor organizations.

LAND SCRIP. Land scrip, along with land warrants, were exchangeable for public lands. Scrip was used primarily to reward veterans; the greatest volume was given to soldiers of the American Revolution, the War of 1812, and Mexican War. A total of 68 million acres were conveyed to more than 400,000 veterans, their heirs, or their assignees. Also an integral part of treaties with Indians; much scrip fell into the hands of speculators, who used it to acquire valuable timberland in Minnesota and California. Another issuance of scrip followed the Civil War; five years' service entitled a veteran to a 160-acre homestead. Although sale of public lands was halted in 1889, holders of land scrip could exchange it for such lands. By the 1960s, there was still scrip outstanding.

LAND SPECULATION. Began with the first settlements; the proprietors of Virginia gave themselves vast tracts of land from which they hoped to derive substantial incomes. Similarly, the Penns and Calverts in Pennsylvania and Maryland and the early proprietors of New York, New Jersey, and the Carolinas speculated in lands. Speculators bought both title and political control over great tracts in the Mississippi Valley. Struggles of rival companies for charters and grants played an important part in British colonial policy; company rivalries were matched by the rival land claims of the colonies. When the public domain of the US was created by donations of states with western land claims, speculative interests converged on Congress with requests to purchase tracts in the Ohio country. Great companies were formed. For example, the New York and Boston Illinois Land Co. acquired 900,000 acres in the Military Tract of Illinois. By the 1840s, sales were restricted to small tracts, and after 1862, very little new land was opened to unrestricted entry and large purchases could be made only in areas previously opened to sale.

LAND TENURE. The status of the occupant of land, whether owner (landlord) or tenant (lessee) is based, in general, on English common law. In colonial America, lands were held in entail and passed by primogeniture, and were subject to payment of quitrents. But abundance of land available for settlement and increased liberality in granting to small owners weakened this system. Many estates disappeared in the Revolution; and in general the laws of primogeniture were abolished. By the mid-19th c., most land was owned outright and could be sold at will. Tenant farming continued to be an economic problem, particularly in the South, where sharecroppers in some areas represented up to 94 percent of the total number of farmers.

LANGLEY AERONAUTICAL LABORATORY. US agency founded 1920 to do basic research in aviation and aerodynamics; located near Hampton, Va. Played a major role in the US space program as part of the National Aeronautics and Space Administration (NASA).

LANSING. Capital of Michigan and an important commercial and industrial center. Pop.: 130,414 (1980).

LANSING-ISHII AGREEMENT (1917). Between the US and Japan; reaffirmed agreement on the territorial integrity of China and the OPEN DOOR POLICY.

LAOS, INTERVENTION IN (1954–74). The US opposed the coalition, neutralist govern-ment of Souvanna Phouma, which came into power after the partition of French Indochina, 1954. Aid was frequently suspended in an effort to turn Laotian policy toward an anti-communist path. In 1958, it began to be channeled to right-wing army leaders; in 1963 Souvanna received US support when he turned against the Pathet Lao, the Laotian communist faction. During the Vietnam War, official policy was to respect a neutral Laos; nevertheless, for seven years a secret war was waged. The Ho Chi Minh Trail and communist positions in N Laos were bombed. In 1974, a new coalition government formed; it ordered all foreign troops out of the country and reduced American influence.

LA POINTE, TREATY OF (1842). The Chippewa ceded half of the upper peninsula of Michigan and a tract in N Wisconsin.

LAPWAI MISSION. Established 1836 near Lewiston, Idaho. Location of first printing press in the Pacific Northwest. Closed 1847 when its leader, the physician-missionary Marcus Whitman, and twelve associates were murdered by Indians.

LARAMIE, FORT. Wyoming post established by fur traders 1834; used by emigrants on the Oregon Trail as a supply and refitting depot. Purchased by the US government 1849 and converted into a military post. Abandoned 1890; now a national historic site.

LARAMIE, FORT, TREATY OF (1851). The Plains Indians agreed to forts and roads in their country in return for annuities; never ratified by the Indians.

LARAMIE, FORT, TREATY OF (1868). Ended Red Cloud's War; the US agreed to withdraw forts and recognize as Indian land all that part of present South Dakota W of the Missouri R. (See also SIOUX WARS.)

LARNED, FORT. Founded 1859 on the Arkansas R in Kansas; used as a base against the Cheyenne. Abandoned 1878.

LA SALLE, EXPLORATIONS OF. Robert Cavelier, sieur de La Salle, arrived in Canada 1666, and explored Niagara, Green Bay, Lake Michigan, and the rivers of the area. In 1682 he reached the Mississippi R, which he descended to the Gulf of Mexico. He claimed the entire Mississippi Valley for France and named it Louisiana. In 1684, he attempted to bring a shipload of colonists to Louisiana but was unable to find the mouth of the Mississippi. He was murdered 1687 by mutineers on the Texas coast.

LA SALLE, SPANISH SEARCHES FOR. The Spanish, alarmed by the sieur de La Salle's incursion into the Gulf of Mexico, sent several expeditions to destroy his colony. In 1689, the fourth such expedition found the remains of his colony in Texas, after it had been destroyed by Indians.

LAS ANIMAS LAND GRANT. In 1843, the Mexican government granted two entrepreneurs 4 million acres in present-day Colorado. Congress confirmed only 97,651 acres of the grant, and dissatisfied claimants long sought restoration unsuccessfully.

LASSEN'S TRADING POST AND RANCH. Important center in NE California for early explorers and gold seekers.

LAS VEGAS. Largest city in Nevada, home to a large number of gambling casinos, luxurious hotels, and restaurants. Pop.: 164,674 (1980).

LATIN AMERICA, US RELATIONS WITH. The US in the 1820s recognized the independence of the new nations of Latin America and opposed, through the MONROE DOCTRINE, any efforts by European powers to reestablish colonial rule in the Western Hemisphere. Relations focused on establishment of US hegemony in the Caribbean. War with Mexico (1846–48) concluded with the annexation of the US Southwest, including Texas and California. US preeminence in the Caribbean was firmly established by the Spanish-American War (1898–99), which concluded with the annexation of Puerto Rico and the creation of a protectorate over Cuba. Long-standing dispute with Great Britain over the building of a canal across the Central American isthmus was resolved when the US built the Panama Canal. Security of that waterway made it imperative that states in its vicinity not fall under the dominance of a hostile power; the US undertook to eliminate political disorder and financial mismanagement in states whose internal difficulties exposed them to European intervention. In the early 20th c., troops were sent into Cuba, Haiti, the Dominican Republic, Nicaragua, and Mexico. These incursions created fear and distrust of US intentions.

In the 1920s American capital found new opportunities in Latin American mines, railroads, and public utilities. A number of governments became heavily indebted to American banks. Anti-Americanism reached new heights, symbolized by the long-standing occupation of Nicaragua by US marines. President Hoover removed them 1933, and President Franklin D. Roosevelt inaugurated the GOOD NEIGHBOR POLICY, which repudiated intervention into Latin American affairs. The military protectorates over Panama and Cuba were ended, and by the time World War II arrived, more cordial relations prevailed. Except for Argentina, which had a pro-Axis government, all the Latin American republics joined the Allies. The ORGANIZATION OF AMERICAN STATES (OAS) was created 1948. Latin American relations remained cordial, despite concern with a leftist Guatemalan government between 1951 and 1954 (and which was overthrown by a US-aided junto). Creation of a Soviet-backed communist government in Cuba after Fidel Castro came to power in 1959 created new strains. The US broke relations and supported an abortive invasion of counterrevolutionary forces in 1961, which undercut Latin-American sympathy for the US position. The 1962 CUBAN MISSILE CRISIS created further adverse opinion. The US intervened militarily in the Dominican Republic in 1965, and in 1973 a left-wing Chilean government was overthrown with the backing of the US Central Intelligence Agency. Such actions did little to improve US standing.

Relations improved during President Carter's administration, partly because of his concern with human rights, and partly because he was able to achieve Senate ratification of the Panama Canal treaties, which stipulated a gradual takeover of the canal by Panama. But as the 1980s began, turmoil in Central America provoked new antagonism. Worried by socialist Sandinist rule in Nicaragua and the civil war in El Salvador, President

Reagan initiated a very active stance in the affairs of those countries and in Honduras.

LATIN SCHOOLS. Patterned after English schools, Latin schools appeared in all the colonies except Georgia, but were commonest in New England. Most renowned was the Boston Latin school, founded 1635. Schools were privately run, with tuition charged; curriculum was confined to Latin, Greek, religion, and mathematics.

LATTER-DAY SAINTS, CHURCH OF JESUS CHRIST OF, or Mormons. Religious sect founded 1830 by Joseph Smith, who claimed to have discovered and translated the Book of Mormon on the basis of visions from heaven. The Book of Mormon purports to be the history of certain lost tribes of Israel, who ended up in America. In 1831, Smith attempted to found an ideal community in Kirtland, Ohio; his followers moved to Missouri in 1837, where they became unpopular with the non-Mormon population and were forced to flee again, this time to Nauvoo, Ill. There Smith promulgated further revelations, which separated them decisively from Christian denominations; most radical was that of polygamy. The Mormons were forced to move again, to Carthage, Ill., where Smith was murdered 1844. Brigham Young assumed leadership and led the sect across the Great Plains to form the state of DESERET in the valley of the Great Salt Lake. Tightly organized by Young, they became virtually an independent nation. After the Mexican War, Mormons were forced to abjure polygamy and admit non-Mormons to the territory, which became the state of Utah. By the 1980s, they were one of the fastest-growing religious groups in the US, and their membership had become international. There were four separate denominations. The main body had a 1978 membership of 2,592,000.

LAUD COMMISSION. Established by the PRIVY COUNCIL 1634 to supervise the American colonies, named for its president, William Laud, the Anglican primate. Given broad powers but accomplished little. Abolished 1641 by the Long Parliament.

LAURENS, FORT. Erected 1778 on the Tuscarawas R in NW Ohio as an advance base for an expedition against Detroit. Abandoned after prolonged siege by Indians.

LA VÉRENDRYE EXPLORATIONS. In 1728, the seiur de La Vérendrye hoped to create an overland route from Lake Superior to the Pacific Ocean, thereby opening a route of commerce from the Far East. He obtained a trade monopoly in this vast territory, and established posts from Lake Superior to Lake Winnipeg. Looking for a westward-flowing river, he led a party to Star Mound in Canada. His two sons traveled 1743 to Big Horn Mountain, near the North Platte R (which they thought was the Missouri) where they buried the La Vérendrye Plate, claiming the Upper Missouri Valley for France. The plate, inscribed with the names and dates of the party, was recovered 1913.

LAWRENCE, SACK OF (May 21, 1856). Early in the Kansas BORDER WAR, a proslavery mob burned antislavery newspaper offices and a hotel which they believed to have been built as a fort by the antislavery New England Emigrant Aid Company. News of the attack galvanized the North and gave rise to the issue of "Bleeding Kansas."

LAWRENCE STRIKE (1912). Successful effort by textile workers in Lawrence, Mass., to stop the imposition of a wage cut; first success of the INDUSTRIAL WORKERS OF THE WORLD (IWW), who had organized the workers.

LAW SCHOOLS. The first US lawyers were trained by apprenticeship. By the 19th c., however, there were a dozen law schools. By 1860 there were twenty-one schools. Most taught by the case method. As schools developed, it became clear that the case method was useful in teaching common law but inadequate for statutory law. Various pedagogical reforms were instituted. Courses oriented toward problems rather than cases were introduced; special areas, such as administrative law, labor law, consumer law, poverty law, tax law, and civil liberties, were added to the curriculum. In the 1960s, enrollment rose sharply; in 1979, 25,180 men and 10,026 women received degrees at 175 institutions.

LEAD INDUSTRY. French trappers discovered lead 1693 in the Upper Mississippi Valley; it was also mined in New York and Virginia.) Demand in the Revolutionary War opened small mines in several states. In 1797, a lead mine and furnace was established at Mine La Motte, Mo.; by 1819, it was producing 3 million pounds of lead per year. Peter Lorimier built a Scotch hearth in 1834 near Dubuque, Iowa; this new technology greatly lowered costs. Development of the lead region from Galena into S Wisconsin and Dubuque proceeded rapidly, so that by 1845 the district produced about 55 million pounds of lead. Completion of the transcontinental railroad 1869 gave impetus to the growth of western lead mining (in Montana, Idaho, Utah, Nevada, California, and Colorado). Rich silver-lead ore was discovered at Leadville, Colo., in 1876; for a time this was the world's largest lead-producing area. In the 1880s, Coeur d'Alene, Idaho, was developed as an important lead-silver-zinc producing area. New refining techniques in the late 19th c. gave the industry a boost. The industry was revitalized by the discovery in the 1950s of the New Lead Belt, or the Viburnum Trend, in SE Missouri. Recycling of lead also became important. In 1980 the US used 1.2 million short tons of lead, which was supplied by 745,000 tons recycled from scrap and 560,000 tons from domestic mines; the remainder was imported.

LEAGUE OF NATIONS. International body formed at the end of World War I. President Wilson was one of the League's foremost backers, but the Senate failed to ratify the VERSAILLES TREATY setting it up and the US never became a member. Henry Cabot Lodge, Republican of Massachusetts, led the opposition. Despite minor successes in the 1920s and 1930s, the League was unable to halt the aggressions of Italy and Germany and could not prevent World War II. Replaced afterward by the UNITED NATIONS.

LEAGUE OF WOMEN VOTERS. Founded 1920 to help the newly enfranchised women make intelligent use of voting privileges; an outstanding agency for nonpartisan political education and a sponsor for legislation and policies. In 1980 it had a membership of 122,000.

LEARNED SOCIETIES. The American Philosophical Society was founded 1743 in Philadelphia and based on a club set up 1727 by Benjamin Franklin. Followed by the American Academy of Arts and Sciences, founded 1880 in Boston. Early societies include the Massachusetts Historical Society (1791), the Chemical Society of Philadelphia (1792), the New-York Historical Society (1804), and American Antiquarian Society (1812). Specialized societies proliferated after the Civil War. Among them were the American Chemical Society (1876), the American Historical Association (1884), the American Economic Association (1885), and the American Anthropological Society (1902). Two honorific societies were the National Institute of Arts and Letters (1898) and the American Academy of Arts and Letters (1904), which merged in 1976. Three coordinating councils were formed: the National Research Council (1916), the American Council of Learned Societies (1919), and the Social Science Research Council (1923).

LEASEHOLD. System of land tenure characteristic of the SE portion of the colony and state of New York. The tenant was bound to a perpetual payment of rent in money, produce, labor, or all three. Abolished in the middle of the 19th c., largely as a result of the ANTIRENT WAR.

LEATHER INDUSTRY. Early colonists much admired the Indian processing of raw hides by the chamois method; Massachusetts and the Middle Colonies had tanneries employing that method by the end of the 17th c. In the South, the tannery was a common feature of plantations. By 1840, the census of manufactures reported 8,229 tanneries. Later, many procedures were mechanized, and steam power turned most of the machinery. Tanning became a profitable adjunct of Midwestern meatpacking. The industry boomed in both world wars and suffered at the end of each; reduced demand, excess capacity, and competition from substitute materials curtailed production. In 1977 3,077 leather tanning and finishing establishments employed 243,000 people.

LEAVENWORTH. City in Kansas, on the Missouri R, near the site of Fort Leavenworth. Squatters moved into the area 1854, and the town was incorporated 1855. Terminus for the overland mails and a freighting headquarters. Pop.: 33,656 (1980).

LEAVENWORTH, FORT. Built 1827 on the Missouri R to protect traders headed west; starting point for military expeditions, meeting place for Indian councils, and supply depot for forts on the frontier. The Army of the West was organized there at the beginning of the Mexican War (see KEARNEY'S MARCH TO CALIFORNIA.) Occupied a strategic position in the West during the Civil War. To the military post was added the army general staff school in 1881 and a federal penitentiary in 1895.

LEAVENWORTH AND PIKES PEAK EXPRESS. Created to serve the Pikes Peak region of Colorado after discovery of gold in 1858.

LEAVENWORTH EXPEDITION (1823). After thirteen US soldiers were killed at the Arikara villages on the Upper Missouri R, Col. Henry Leavenworth led a large force up the river from Council Bluffs, Iowa. His army attacked the Arikara fortified villages, forcing their submission.

LEBANON. In 1958, at the request of President Camille Chamoun of Lebanon, who feared civil war, President Eisenhower dispatched marines and army troops to Lebanon. They secured (July 15 and 16) port facilities and the international airport at Beirut. Presence of the forces apparently forestalled a coup d'etat by Gen. Fuad Shehab; but the Lebanese legislature elected him president. Chamoun refused to resign for several weeks, but by October 25, Shehab was firmly in office, order was restored, and the troops had departed.

In 1982, after an Israeli invasion of Lebanon and the subsequent defeat and withdrawal of the Palestine Liberation forces in Beirut, President Ronald Reagan dispatched a force of U. S. Marines as part of a multinational peacekeeping force. Repeated attacks on the force culminated in a terrorist bombing of the barracks and the death of 241 men.

LEBOEUF, FORT, WASHINGTON'S MISSION TO. In 1753 the governor of Virginia selected George Washington to deliver a message to the commandant of Fort LeBoeuf in NW Pennsylvania, demanding that the French evacuate that fort and Fort Presque Isle.

Washington delivered the message; he and his companions noted the strength of fort and garrison and the large number of canoes there, indicating a contemplated exdedition down the Ohio. After a dangerous return voyage, Washington delivered his intelligence to Dinwiddie on Jan. 16, 1754.

LECOMPTON CONSTITUTION (1857). Proslavery advocates in Kansas met at Lecompton and adopted a state constitution favorable to slavery. It was approved by the proslavery legislature but rejected by the opposition legislature. President Buchanan recommended that Kansas be admitted as a state under the Lecompton Constitution, but Congress refused to go along. A compromise provided for a referendum in which Kansans voted on the issue; statehood, under the Lecompton Constitution, was rejected.

LEDERER'S EXPLORING EXPEDITIONS (1669–70). John Lederer explored western Virginia and upper South Carolina, visiting Indian tribes, whose customs he recorded in a book published in London in 1672.

LEE, FORT. Built 1776 on the summit of the New Jersey palisades; opposite Fort Washington, on Manhattan Island. The two forts were built by Gen. George Washington to prevent passage of enemy vessels up the Hudson R; but they failed to do so. Fort Lee was abandoned after the fall of Fort Washington. Present borough of Fort Lee was incorporated in 1904. Pop.: 32,449 (1980).

LEECH LAKE UPRISING (1898). Federal troops were called out to quell an uprising of previously friendly Pillager Indians, a band of Chippewa, in N Minnesota. There were several injuries before the Pillagers surrendered.

LEGAL TENDER. Between 1776 and 1789, the problem was whether the states should be permitted to print currency and require its acceptance by creditors regardless of its severe depreciation in value. Just after the Civil War, the question was whether Congress had power to issue paper money (greenbacks) that would be legal tender in payment of private debts. (See LEGAL TENDER CASES.)

LEGAL TENDER ACT (1862). To finance the Civil War, Congress issued fiat money and put in circulation $450 million in paper money.

These notes were declared legal tender, even though no specific gold reserve was set aside; nor was any date announced for their redemption. Constitutionality of the 1862 act was decided by the LEGAL TENDER CASES.

LEGAL TENDER CASES. In *Hepburn v. Griswold* (8 Wallace 603, 1870), the Supreme Court declared the LEGAL TENDER ACT of 1862 unconstitutional, holding that Congress had no power to enact legal-tender provisions. At the ensuing term of the court, with two new members, the court reheard the arguments and reversed the *Hepburn* decision, in *Knox v. Lee* and *Parker v. Davis* (12 Wallace 457, 1871).

LEGISLATURE. Law making bodies on the national, state, and local levels. Congress has provided the norm for state, and to some degree, local legislatures. All state legislatures, like the federal Constitution, provide for separation of powers. All except Nebraska have bicameral legislatures. Local governments have departed furthest from the national model. The CITY MANAGER PLAN provides for a chief executive chosen by, but not from, the legislature. The majority of local governments have abandoned bicameralism.

LEHIGH VALLEY RAILROAD. See RAILROADS, SKETCHES OF PRINCIPAL LINES.

LEISLER REBELLION (1689). The Glorious Revolution in England was followed by uprisings in America. On May 31, Capt. Jacob Leisler usurped control of southern New York. At his suggestion, representatives of Massachusetts, Connecticut, and New York met in New York City to concert measures for a united offensive against Canada. The operation failed; Leisler was tried for treason and executed.

LEND-LEASE. A subsidy for America's allies that provided the economic and military aid they needed during World War II. By the close of the war, a total of $47.9 billion of lend-lease aid had been extended to thirty-eight countries; most had gone to Great Britain, the Soviet Union, and China. Military supplies, agricultural goods, raw materials, and manufactured goods were dispensed.

LEWES, BOMBARDMENT OF (1813). British attempt to stop shipping on the Delaware

R during the War of 1812. British vessels in Delaware Bay threatened to destroy the town unless provisions were supplied. The subsequent bombardment missed the town; shortly afterward the British withdrew.

LEWIS AND CLARK EXPEDITION (1804–06). After the Louisiana Purchase in 1803 President Jefferson authorized an expedition for western exploration. Meriwether Lewis and William Clark shared its leadership. The party left St. Louis in the spring of 1804, traveling up the Missouri R by flatboat and keelboat; it consisted of twenty-six soldiers and various servants and interpreters, including Sacajawea, a Shoshone who became known as the Bird Woman. On Nov. 7, 1805, the explorers gazed upon the Pacific Ocean. They had ascended the Missouri and its Jefferson branch to the mountains, which they had crossed to the Snake and Columbia rivers to the sea. Winter was passed in a shelter near present-day Astoria, Oreg.; in March 1806 the return journey was begun. After crossing the Rockies, the explorers separated into three groups to make more extensive examination of the country. Thus, both the Missouri and Yellowstone rivers were descended, near whose junction the groups reunited. The party passed rapidly downriver to St. Louis, where on Sept. 23, 1806, the expedition ended.

LEXINGTON. Second largest city in Kentucky; center of the bluegrass region, one of the most important horse-breeding and horse-trading areas in the world. Settled 1775; first horse race 1787. A major agricultural shipping center and leading tobacco auction center. Location of the University of Kentucky. Pop.: 204,165 (1980).

LEXINGTON. Name of several American ships, from the Revolutionary War to World War II. In the latter war, an aircraft carrier damaged so badly in the Battle of the Coral Sea (1942) that it had to be sunk by a US destroyer.

LEXINGTON, SIEGE OF (Sept. 12–20, 1861). Confederate troops surrounded Lexington, Mo., occupied by Union troops. Eventually, the Union force surrendered.

LEXINGTON AND CONCORD (Apr. 19, 1775). Opening battles of the American Revolution. A British detachment was sent from Boston to capture military supplies at Concord, Mass. The detachment was attacked by patriot forces at Lexington, who were unable to halt the drive. Another battle took place at Concord; the patriots were more successful, and the British returned to Boston with heavy losses.

LEXINGTON AND OHIO RAILROAD. See RAILROADS, SKETCHES OF PRINCIPAL LINES.

LEXOW COMMITTEE (1894). New York state senate investigation that uncovered widespread graft in the New York City police department, which was under political control of TAMMANY HALL.

LEYTE GULF, BATTLE OF (Oct. 23–25, 1944). Major sea battle of World War II; crucial step in the recapture of the Philippines from the Japanese. The American armada, under the commands of Adm. T.C. Kinkaid and Adm. W.F. Halsey, totaled about 800 ships and 1,500 airplanes. A great American victory destroyed the Japanese fleet as an effective fighting force.

LIBBY PRISON. Notorious Confederate prison in Richmond, made up of vacant tobacco warehouses. After Union raids on Richmond aimed at freeing the prisoners, the Confederates moved the prison to Macon, Ga. (See also DAHLGREN'S RAID.)

LIBEL. English political libel suits were paralleled in colonial courts. The most celebrated prosecution was that of John Peter Zenger, New York printer, in 1735. The prosecution contended that only the fact of publication could be determined by the jury, while the court was to determine whether the publication was libelous. Andrew Hamilton, counsel for the prisoner, persuaded the jury to judge both law and fact and secured Zenger's acquittal. Later trials established this case as a precedent; in 1805 New York enacted a statute embodying the Zenger decision. It permitted the defendant to give truth in justification, provided it was published with ''good motives and for justifiable means.'' That principle has tended to become part of American jurisprudence, making libel suits difficult to prosecute.

LIBERALISM. Believing in the rationality of man and the dignity of the individual, committed to freedom, equal justice, and equal opportunity, liberals have always been reformers with little reverence for tradition and great faith in the power of human intelligence to establish a more just society. They have distrusted power and privilege, felt sympathy for the exploited and deprived, and relied upon rational and enlightened social and economic policies to rehabilitate even the lowest elements of society. The Anglo-American liberalism of the 18th and 19th c., traceable to John Locke and Adam Smith, was a reaction against powerful monarchies. It espoused a strictly limited, decentralized government. The natural rights of the individual (life, liberty, property, and the pursuit of happiness) had to be protected from the state. This supposition underlay the American Revolution, the Bill of Rights, Jeffersonian Democracy, Jacksonian Democracy, and the antislavery movement. The Populist movement of the late 19th c. advocated a number of classic liberal reforms. The multifaceted Progressive movement of the early 20th c. struggled to curb corporate power through trust-busting and social welfare reforms. The New Deal went much further in social planning and social welfare. Since that era, liberalism has tended to be associated with the Democratic party, whereas conservatism has generally been associated with the Republicans. (See also REVOLUTION, AMERICAN; BILL OF RIGHTS; JEFFERSONIAN DEMOCRACY; JACKSONIAN DEMOCRACY; POPULIST PARTY; PROGRESSIVE PARTY; NEW DEAL.)

LIBERATOR. Antislavery newspaper edited by W.L. Garrison and published in Boston from 1831 to 1865. Important in the antislavery movement, despite small circulation.

LIBERIA. Republic on the W Coast of Africa, founded in the 19th c. by the AMERICAN COLONIZATION SOCIETY for the repatriation of freed American slaves. Originally a colony, it declared itself independent in 1847, although the US, embroiled in the controversy over slavery, did not recognize it until 1862. Became seriously overextended financially in the late 19th c.; by 1912 badly in default to European creditors. In return for a US loan, it agreed to accept American customs officers and a military mission. Heavy investment by the Firestone Tire and Rubber Co. after 1925 partially alleviated financial strains. Became even more fully under US control during World War II, when its capital, Monrovia, became a major supply depot. After the war, exports of high-grade iron gave the country a higher degree of economic independence. European and Asian influences began competing heavily with American. The Liberian constitution, which replicated the US Constitution, was abrogated 1980; a military coup installed a People's Redemption Council and forced the ruling oligarchy out of office.

LIBERTY, SEIZURE OF THE (June 10, 1768). Incident in the Boston agitation against the SUGAR ACTS. British customs officials, realizing that John Hancock's sloop *Liberty* had not paid duty on the Madiera wine it was carrying, seized the vessel. A crowd assaulted the officials on the dock, forcing them to flee.

LIBERTY BELL. Ordered from London by Philadelphia in 1751, the bell was cracked in testing and was repaired locally; installed in the Philadelphia state house and proclaimed American independence following the reading of the Declaration of Independence there on July 8, 1776 . Hidden during the Revolution, it was damaged tolling the death of Chief Justice John Marshall in 1835; fatally cracked during Washington's Birthday celebrations in 1846. Housed in Independence Historical Park, Philadelphia.

LIBERTY LEAGUE. Conservative organization founded in the 1930s in opposition to Franklin D. Roosevelt's New Deal programs. Many of its members, which included Alfred E. Smith, were wealthy Democrats. In 1936, the league supported the Republican candidate, Alfred M. Landon.

LIBERTY LOANS. Borrowing by the US Treasury in 1917 to provide funds for European allies in World War I and US war activities. Issues were sold directly to the public; all were oversubscribed.

LIBERTY PARTY. First antislavery political party, formed 1839. Ran candidates for president in 1840 and 1844. In 1848 its candidate withdrew, and the party merged with the FREE SOIL organization.

LIBRARIES. A few libraries were founded in America in the 17th c., including ones at Harvard (1638), Boston (1655), and William and Mary (1693), but most colonies had none until well into the 18th c. Benjamin Franklin founded the first subscription library, in Philadelphia, in 1731. Other social libraries were founded in Durham and Lebanon, Conn. and in Newport, R.I. Between 1733 and 1850, more than 1,000 social libraries were opened; they were subscription (i.e., members paid an annual fee) or proprietary (i.e., joint stock companies aimed at making a profit). A free public library for juveniles was established in Salisbury, Conn., in 1803, and another in Lexington, Mass., in 1827. Peterborough, N. H., founded the first (1833) general public free library. The Boston Public Library opened 1852; it became the model for free city libraries around the country. By the Civil War, the nation boasted more than 500 public libraries. The American Library Association was founded 1876, and Melvil Dewey, one of its founders, devised the first widely used classification system, the Dewey Decimal System. In 1900 the library school at Columbia College produced its first graduates. Within a few years, every major type of library was represented in the US and most were well established, including the LIBRARY OF CONGRESS. University libraries dominate the field of research libraries. Elementary and secondary school libraries, the largest category of libraries, were greatly aided by federal funds. In 1981, there were 14,831 public libraries (including branches) in the US.

LIBRARY OF CONGRESS. Founded 1800, its original collection of 3,000 volumes was burned by the British 1814. To replace it, Congress purchased Thomas Jefferson's library, more than 6,000 books. In 1865 Congress passed an act requiring deposit in the library of a copy of all books and other materials on which copyright was claimed. In 1866, the library of the Smithsonian Institution (40,000 volumes) was incorporated. Further appropriations and acquisitions followed; by 1897 it had grown to nearly a million volumes. It moved into its own building and later expanded into two annexes. During the 20th c., the library emerged as the nation's preeminent research library; by 1981, the collections totaled over 78.6 million items and constituted unparalleled resources.

LICENSE CASES, 5 Howard 504 (1847). The Supreme Court permitted states to require licenses for certain goods imported from other states, representing a weakening of the doctrine of exclusive federal control of interstate commerce.

LICENSES TO TRADE. Licenses to trade granted in the colonies reflected the English common law, which recognized the power of the sovereign to regulate the "common callings," such as innkeeping, carrying goods and persons, or operating a bridge. Most licensing power has since fallen to state and local governments. The Supreme Court has sometimes limited the right to license businesses, holding that the due process clause of the Constitution is a bar to much of such state action. Federal licensing is found in banking, telecommunications, fuel, and transport industries.

LIFE EXPECTANCY. In the 17th c., life expectancy at birth is believed to have been between 25 and 30 years. During the colonial period, half of all children died before the age of 10. Average length of life in the 1770s was probably about 35 years. Between 1820 and 1850, rising death rates were reported from large cities, a consequence of immigration, poverty, and rapid urban growth. Estimates place life expectancy ca. 1850 at about 40 years. Beginning ca. 1870 improved living conditions, sanitary reform and application of microbiological discoveries caused a downward trend in mortality, as did a decline in the frequency of such communicable diseases as smallpox, diphtheria, typhoid and typhus fevers, tuberculosis, and malaria. Mortality of children under 5 years of age did not decrease materially until ca. 1900; improper feeding, poor sanitation, overcrowding, poverty, and the common infant killers, diarrhea and pneumonia, kept rates high until then. Increase in life expectancy since 1900 has been striking. That year life expectancy at birth was 49.2 years, with women living an average of two years longer than men; in 1979 it was 70.6 years for men and 78.3 for women. In 1900, life expectancy for nonwhites was 33 years, 14.6 years less than that of whites. By 1979, it had risen to 69.9 years, 4.5 years below that of whites. This difference resulted from higher infant and maternal mortality among blacks, as well as higher death rates from certain infectious diseases.

LIFESAVING SERVICE. In 1837 Congress authorized the employment of ships to render aid to distressed navigators. Lifesaving stations were set up along the East Coast. This service was merged 1915 with the Revenue Cutter Service to form the COAST GUARD.

LIGHTING. Domestic lighting in America prior to ca. 1815 included lamps fueled by oil from animal or vegetable sources, tallow or bayberry candles, and pinewood torches. After an efficient means of producing inflammable gas from coal was discovered, a new era of lighting began; Baltimore was the first American city to employ gas streetlights (1816). The electric light industry emerged during the late 19th c. Improvements such as the Welsbach mantle kept gas lighting competitive until World War I. Rural residents relied upon candles or oil lamps throughout most of the 19th c. because coal gas could not be economically distributed in the countryside. Discovery of petroleum 1859 soon led to the development of the kerosene lamp. The period after 1880 was a time of intense market competition between the gaslight, arc light, and incandescent light industries and between the alternating-current and direct-current systems. Incandescent lighting with alternating current emerged the winner. The fluorescent lamp, introduced 1938, presented several advantages over the incandescent lamp; it has since come into wide use, especially in commercial space. High-intensity mercury-vapor lamps came into general use for street lighting after World War II.

LIGONIER, FORT. Founded 1758 in Pennsylvania as a link between E Pennsylvania and Fort Pitt. During Pontiac's War, Ligonier was the only fort W of the mountains in Pennsylvania that did not fall; its retention made possible the relief of Fort Pitt by Col. Henry Bouquet's forced march 1763.

LINCOLN. Capital of Nebraska since 1867, when the town of Lancaster was renamed in honor of the recently assassinated president. An important trading and food processing center. Pop.: 171,932 (1980).

LINCOLN, ASSASSINATION OF (April 14, 1865). While attending a play at Ford's Theatre in Washington, D.C., President Lincoln was shot in the back of the head by John Wilkes Booth. Lincoln died in a lodging house across the street from the theater the following morning. Although Booth broke his leg in jumping from the presidential box to the stage, he escaped and, with David E. Herold, fled to Virginia. They first went to the house of Dr. Samuel A. Mudd, who set Booth's leg, and hid in a pine thicket, where a farmer, Thomas A. Jones, brought them food. On April 26, Booth and Herold were captured near Port Royal, Va., on a farm owned by Richard H. Garrett. Herold surrendered, but Booth defied his captors and was shot and killed. The government implicated eight persons in addition to Booth in the assassination. They were tried before a military commission and found guilty. Four (Herold among them) were hanged July 7, two (including Mudd) were sentenced to life in prison, one was given six years, and charges against another dismissed. Jones and Garrett were not indicted. In 1869, President Andrew Johnson pardoned those imprisoned.

LINCOLN COUNTRY WAR (1876–78). Struggle between two rival groups of ranchers and businessmen in SE New Mexico. A series of murders and depredations culminated in July 1878 in a three-day battle at the town of Lincoln. Billy the Kid was a participant.

LINCOLN-DOUGLAS DEBATES (1858). Between Abraham Lincoln, Republican candidate for the US Senate from Illinois, and Stephen A. Douglas, the Democratic candidate. The first was held at Ottawa, Ill., on Aug. 21; the seventh and last took place at Alton on Oct. 13. Slavery and its various ramifications were the foci. Lincoln lost the election, but gained nationwide attention.

LINCOLN HIGHWAY. The idea of a coast-to-coast highway originated 1912 with leaders of the new automobile industry. Funds were collected, aided by federal grants after 1921. From Jersey City the route chosen passed through Pennsylvania to Fort Wayne, Ind., then near Chicago; through Omaha, Cheyenne, Salt Lake City, Sacramento, and ended in San Francisco. Work on the 3,339 mile course began 1914; in 1925 the road became US Highway 30.

LINDBERGH KIDNAPPING CASE. On March 1, 1932, the infant son of Charles A. Lindbergh was abducted from his parents' home in Hopewell, N.J. A ransom demand for $50,000 was paid, but the baby's body was found May 12. On Sept. 15, 1934, Bruno Hauptmann, a carpenter, passed a bill from the ransom at a New York filling station. He was arrested and convicted, and executed on April 3, 1936.

LINDBERGH'S ATLANTIC FLIGHT (May 20–21,1927). First nonstop flight between New York and Paris and the first one-man crossing of the Atlantic by air, made by Charles A. Lindbergh in the *Spirit of St. Louis*, a monoplane. Lindbergh was received enthusiastically by the French and became an international hero.

LINEN INDUSTRY. Flax was the principal textile fabric in colonial America, where it was raised and made into linen on the family farm. Some colonies subsidized its manufacture into sailcloth; for two centuries flax and yarn were common barter items. LINSEY-WOOLSEY, made of flax and wool, was a common clothing fabric. Cotton replaced linen as the basic fabric in the 18th c., but small linen mills persisted. Most produced canvas or thread. Many linen products now sold in the US are imported.

LINGAYEN GULF. On the NW coast of Luzon Island, the Philippines; site of two invasions during World War II, the first by Japanese in 1941 and the second by returning Americans in 1945.

LINSEY-WOOLSEY. Stout homespun cloth made of wool and flax, extensively manufactured in the American colonies and on the frontier.

LIQUOR LAWS. As early as 1619, the colony of Virginia outlawed drunkenness. Beginning 1633, Massachusetts passed progressively stricter laws against drunkenness. Other colonies soon did the same. Simultaneously colonies began to reap considerable income from liquor taxes. The temperance movement began ca. 1800; in 1829, Maine was the first state to adopt a local-option law, which permitted local jurisdictions to prohibit liquor sales within their borders. In 1846 Maine initiated statewide prohibition. By 1918, twenty-eight states were dry. The violent PRO-HIBITION era lasted from 1920 until 1933. Today, a diversity of legislation exists among the states; none is completely dry any longer. All states prohibit sale of liquor to minors; all prohibit driving while intoxicated, though definitions of "intoxication" vary; some have established a government monopoly on liquor sales.

LISA, FORT. Established ca. 1813 near the present site of Omaha, Neb., by LISA AND COMPANY. Most important post on the Missouri R, controlling the trade of the Omaha, Pawnee, Oto, and neighboring Indians.

LISA AND COMPANY. In 1802, Manuel Lisa and associates took over the fur trade monopoly from the CHOUTEAU AND COMPANY interests along the Missouri and Osage rivers. The monopoly ended with US assumption of control of the area after the Louisiana Purchase.

LITCHFIELD LAW SCHOOL. Founded 1784 in Litchfield, Conn., by Tapping Reeve; first law school in the nation. Closed 1833.

LITERACY. The US enjoys a high rate of literacy as a result of a strong interest in schooling and emphasis on the printed word as a means of communication. Today, educators classify as "functionally illiterate" individuals who lack skills at the fourth- to sixth-grade level. An estimate of the number of functional illiterates in the US was about 20 million adults (1980). Estimates of complete illiterates run to about 1 million.

LITERACY TEST. Used by the federal government as an adjunct to its immigration and naturalization laws and for induction into the armed forces; many states use it as a device to determine qualifications for voting. In its latter use the tests gained notoriety, as states, especially in the South, used it to deny the franchise to blacks; this practice was ended by the VOTING RIGHTS ACT OF 1965.

LITERARY SOCIETIES. Common in rural districts throughout the West in the 19th c. and into the 20th c.; objectives were social, as they sought not only to create interest in literature but to provide entertainment and opportunity for social contacts. Meetings were generally held once or twice a month, usually at a schoolhouse, and consisted of readings; short plays; debates; and sometimes music.

LITERATURE. Discovery, exploration, and settlement were the subjects of the first writings about the New World, beginning with Richard Hakluyt's *Principal Navigations, Voyages, Traffiques and Discoveries* (1589). A library of narratives by John Smith, William Bradford, John Winthrop, and others describes and interprets the first ventures of the English people into the New World. Theological writing became the dominant literary medium; Cotton Mather and Jonathan Edwards were the most impressive examples. In Virginia, William Byrd practiced a more secular art; his journals (written in the 1740s but not found and published until the 1940s) reveal a humorous, light-hearted writer. Benjamin Franklin was the first American writer to achieve international acclaim; his autobiography, letters, satires, bagatelles, almanacs, and scientific writings are the work of a citizen of the world and were so recognized in his time. Other 18th-c. writers of note include Thomas Jefferson, Thomas Paine, and Charles Brockden Brown.

In the early 19th c., William Cullen Bryant, Washington Irving, and James Fenimore Cooper were the leading literary figures of the new Republic. They were followed by the New England poets and essayists: James Russell Lowell, Oliver Wendell Holmes, Henry Wadsworth Longfellow, Ralph Waldo Emerson, Henry David Thoreau, and Nathaniel Hawthorne. A bit apart from this group were John Greenleaf Whittier, Emily Dickinson, and Herman Melville. Only one antebellum author of the South was of comparable stature: Edgar Allan Poe. History as literature was represented by Francis Parkman and William Hickling Prescott; stylistic craftsmanship is most evident in the work of Henry Adams. Harriet Beecher Stowe's *Uncle Tom's Cabin*, partisan, sentimental, and melodramatic, went around the world. Walt Whitman's *Leaves of Grass* is generally considered the most original American poetry of the 19th c. Henry George, Andrew Dickson White, and William James were all influential in scholarly writing.

American fiction came of age in the late 19th and early 20th c., especially in the works of Mark Twain. Other eminent American writers of the period were Hamlin Garland, Stephen Crane, Frank Norris, and William Dean Howells. Henry James, followed by Edith Wharton, opened the modern manner of fiction by concentrating on the subjective world. Willa Cather and Ellen Glasgow were other influential novelists of the period. Poetry was represented by Vachel Lindsay, Edgar Lee Masters, Edwin Arlington Robinson, Carl Sandburg, and Robert Frost. Foreign influences were evident in the works of T.S. Eliot and Ezra Pound, which diverted poetry into the more difficult styles of Wallace Stevens, Hart Crane, and Marianne Moore.

The 1920s began with the smashing success of Sinclair Lewis's *Main Street* (1920) and saw the rise of such world-renowned writers as F. Scott Fitzgerald, Ernest Hemingway, Gertrude Stein, Thomas Wolfe, William Faulkner, John Dos Passos, and Thornton Wilder. The 1930s, with the Great Depression, was represented by the voices of Katherine Anne Porter, John Steinbeck, James T. Farrell, Erskine Caldwell, and James M. Cain.

World War II produced powerful novels by Norman Mailer, James Jones, James Gould Cozzens, and Joseph Heller. The 1940s and 1950s produced such novelists and shortstory writers as Eudora Welty, Carson McCullers, Flannery O'Connor, Truman Capote, Gore Vidal, and James Baldwin. Deriving from the works of Nathanael West and Henry Roth in the 1930s, the postwar Jewish novel flourished in the fiction of J.D. Salinger, Saul Bellow, Bernard Malamud, Philip Roth, and Isaac Bashevis Singer. Virtuoso novelists and storytellers such as Vladimir Nabakov, John Updike, John Cheever, and Joyce Carol Oates have kept the genre alive by sheer linguistic agility. Postwar poets include Robert Lowell, Randall Jarrell, Theodore Roethke, John Ashbery, and Allen Ginsberg. Eugene O'Neill and Tennessee Williams represent the apex of American dramatic writing, followed by Thornton Wilder, Arthur Miller, and Edward Albee. Leading literary critics have included Edmund Wilson, Lionel Trilling, Leslie Fiedler, and Alfred Kazin.

LITTLE AMERICA. Name given by Richard E. Byrd to the Antarctic base he established 1929.

LITTLE BIGHORN, BATTLE OF (June 25, 1876). Confrontation between the Sioux of the Dakota Territory and the US cavalry force under Col. G.A. Custer. The Sioux bitterly resented the opening of the Black Hills to white settlers in violation of an 1868 treaty. Due to official graft and negligence, they were facing starvation in the fall of 1875. They left their reservations and, joined by tribesmen from other reservations, engaged in their annual buffalo hunt; the movement took on the proportions of a serious revolt. The army ordered the Indians to return to their reservations; cavalry sought to capture or disperse those bands hunting. In June, Custer found the Sioux camped on the bank of the Little Bighorn R. He split his regiment into three, putting Major Marcus Reno and Major Frederick Benteen in charge of two detachments and assuming command of the third himself. The actions of Benteen and Reno have long been the subject of controversy; Reno became confused and ordered his men to fall back at a critical stage, and this probably caused Custer's command to suffer the full concentration of the Indians' attack. His force was totally annihilated.

LITTLE ROCK. Capital and largest city of Arkansas; business and processing center for cotton and general farming activities. Became capital of Arkansas Territory in 1820; captured by the Union army during the Civil War; scene of bitter confrontation over the integration of its public schools in 1957. Pop.: 158,461 (1980).

LIVESTOCK INDUSTRY. Importation of livestock began 1609; extensive animal husbandry was long characteristic of the frontier. Animals grazed with little attention paid to them; they were rounded up periodically, marked to indicate ownership, and herded and trailed to market. More intensive husbandry was required in areas of denser settlement; animals were fenced, fed, and sheltered. After 1900, the industry became more intensive and productive. Most processing of animal products was done on the farm before 1800. Slaughtering, processing, and marketing soon became a specialized industry. In colonial times, Philadelphia was the center for meat-packing and export to the West Indies and Europe. Processing shifted westward; Cincinnati was a great processing center by the 1840s, and Chicago by the 1870s. Improved refrigeration on railroads and ships allowed packers to reach vaster markets. By the 1930s, the truck was replacing the railroad, and decentralization of meat-processing accelerated. The Chicago Union Stock Yards closed 1971 for lack of business.

LOBBIES. In the 19th and early 20th c., the typical political lobbyist focused on the legislative arena and used high-pressure methods, including bribery, to influence legislators. By the 1980s, most lobbyists had widened their focus to include the executive department and especially the regulatory agencies. The division between lobbying government officials and influencing public opinion was blurred. Most lobbyists act for associations with an economic interest: business, farm, labor, and the professions. Over half the registered lobbyists in Washington are specialized business associations, such as the AFL-CIO, the Farm Bureau Federation, and the National Association of Manufacturers. A large category of lobbyists represents groups with a particular social or political end in view; prominent among these are anti-gun control groups like the National Rifle Association; civil rights groups like the National Association for the Advancement of Colored People; good government groups like Common Cause; and peace groups like the National Peace Action Committee. Congress began regulating lobbyists as early as 1913; and 1946 legislation requires that all lobbyists be registered and that they make public disclosures of all their activities. Lobbying at the state government level is less controlled than at the federal level.

LOCAL GOVERNMENT. In the original colonies towns and counties played the most significant government role. The town was of central importance in New England; counties were dominant in the South. Increasing urbanization shifted the emphasis to municipalities. By the late 20th c., more than 70 percent of the population lived in incorporated urban places. Functions of local government include law enforcement, fire protection, public health (including waste disposal), education, and the construction and maintenance of roads. City governments have traditionally followed the English model of mayor and council but some have experimented with a commission structure in which the legislative and executive functions are com-bined in one body. Others have adopted the council-manager form of government, which has a strong professional executive branch under a city manager. A prominent feature of local governments in the 20th c. has been the rise of single-purpose government authorities, such as independent school districts, airport and port authorities, and water and sewage districts.

LOCHABER, TREATY OF (Oct. 18, 1770). Between Virginia and the Cherokee; allowed white settlement in areas previously denied.

LOCHNER V. NEW YORK, 198 US 45 (1905). Supreme Court ruled unconstitutional a New York law regulating the labor hours of workers, ruling that the law violated the Fourteenth Amendment right of the individual to sell his labor.

LOCHRY'S DEFEAT (Aug. 24, 1781). Col. Archibald Lochry and a detachment of Pennsylvania volunteers were attacked about twenty miles below the site of Cincinnati by a band of Indians under Joseph Brant and Alexander McKee. A third of Lochry's men were killed, the rest captured; several captives, including, Lochry, were later killed.

LOCKE'S POLITICAL PHILOSOPHY. John Locke, one of the leading English philosophers of the 17th c., had a profound effect on American political thinking of the 18th c., reflected in the Declaration of Independence and the US Constitution. His most characteristic contribution was his doctrine of natural rights; he maintained that life, liberty, and property were the inalienable rights of every individual and that the happiness and security of the individual were the ends for which government came into being. He believed that the social contract was a means of securing not only political authority but also political and social liberty. Accordingly, revolution is justified when government oversteps the bounds of the social contract.

LOCKOUT. Temporary withholding of work by an employer, generally used as retaliation for the activities of a labor union; often used to forestall a strike. Some forms are illegal.

LOCKS AND WATERWAYS. In the late 18th c., dams and locks were employed to make rough rivers navigable for arks and flatboats, for example, around the rapids of the James R at Richmond; along the Potomac, Connecticut and Merrimack rivers. For economy, walls of early canals were wood; they often began to warp soon after completion. With the advent of cement, locks were both stronger and higher; in 1830, one with a lift of seventeen feet was built on the Delaware Division of the PENNSYLVANIA CANAL SYSTEM. Larger rivers were canalized: the Monongahela in Pennsylvania for a hundred miles in 1826; nearly a hundred miles of the Muskingum in Ohio were made large enough for steamboats. With increased steamboat traffic, improvement of small rivers and creeks by locks became a favorite form of congressional patronage. The practice died out with the coming of the railroad. (See also CANALS.)

LOCOFOCO PARTY. Jacksonian faction of the Democratic party in New York state began after 1835.

LOCOMOTIVES. In 1825, John Stevens built the first experimental locomotive in the US; in 1827, Peter Cooper built the Tom Thumb, an experimental locomotive, for the Baltimore and Ohio RR. The B&O sponsored a design competition, won in 1831 by Phineas Davis with his York, the predecessor of the vertical-boilered locomotives called grasshoppers. The Best Friend of Charleston, the first locomotive intended for commercial service, was built in West Point, N.Y., for the South Carolina Canal and Railroad Co. Locomotives were also imported from England, but they proved ill adapted to the sharp curvature and heavy grades of American rail lines. Matthias W. Baldwin successfully adapted the steam locomotive to American topography; soon the Baldwin works in Pennsylvania were the nation's largest locomotive builder. Several smaller locomotive builders merged into the American Locomotive Co., second of the country's great locomotive builders. The Pennsylvania RR built locomotives in its own shops and also pioneered in standardization. Steam locomotives attained the speed of 60 miles per hour in 1848. Hauling capability developed more slowly; the typical locomotive for freight and passenger work in the 1870s had four driving wheels and a tractive effort of between 8,000 and 12,000 pounds. The Consolidated type freight locomotive was built for six or eight driving wheels. By the turn of the century, tractive efforts had reached 46,000 pounds. The most important technical improvement was superheating, which allowed very hot, dry steam to be delivered to the cylinders. By 1920, tractive effort had reached 120,000 pounds, and the mechanical stoker, necessary for firing such locomotives, had been perfected. In 1925, the first "superpower" locomotive was completed by the Lima Locomotive Works. It became the prototype for hundreds of locomotives. Locomotive building came to a virtual halt during the Great Depression. By World War II, progress in diesel locomotives, first introduced 1925, was so great that many railroads bought no more steam locomotives. Baldwin built its last steam locomotives 1949. Straight electric locomotives were never used extensively on American railroads; approaches to cities, tunnels, and suburban lines were the most often electrified. The Milwaukee electrified 641 miles over the Rocky, Bitter Root, and Cascade ranges, and the Pennsylvania electrified its line between New York and Washington, D.C. By the 1970s, except for short electric lines, virtually all railroads were powered by diesel-electric locomotives.

LODE MINING. Gold, silver, and other metals are generally found in streaks, called lodes, veins, or ledges, that range from a few inches to many feet in width, and frequently a mile or more in length. Mining is conducted underground, with the ore being reached by shafts or tunnels. The discoverer of a new lode could, by local law, stake out two claims along the lode; others, one claim. In 1872 Congress fixed the size of lode claims at 600 feet wide and 1,500 feet long.

LODGE RESERVATIONS. Henry Cabot Lodge, Republican senator from Massachusetts, objected (1919) to the Treaty of Versailles and the covenant of the League of Nations by sponsoring several sets of reservations to the agreements. President Wilson refused to accept the reservations, and the Senate never ratified them.

LOEWE V. LAWLOR. See DANBURY HATTERS' CASE.

LOGAN ACT (1799). Arose after efforts by Quakers to mediate the NAVAL WAR WITH FRANCE;

made it a high misdemeanor subject to fine and imprisonment for any citizen to carry on correspondence with a foreign government in any controversy in which the US is involved.

LOGAN'S FORT. Also known as St. Asaph Station; built at Stanford, Ky. ca. 1775. In 1776, it was attacked by Indians and successfully defended by founder Benjamin Logan.

LOG CABIN. Often asserted to have been introduced by the Swedes in the lower Delaware Valley in 1638; but a log blockhouse in Maine built ca. 1640-45 indicates that New Englanders had learned log construction for themselves. Construction increased rapidly in the 17th c., and the one- and two-room log cabin became the typical pioneer home.

LOG COLLEGE. Established at Neshaminy, Pa., in 1726 by a Presbyterian minister. Provided the impetus for the Presbyterian Synod to organize a college at Princeton, N.J., (later PRINCETON UNIVERSITY), in 1746.

LOGROLLING. Practice among members of Congress of trading votes for each other's bills. Term is derived from frontiersmen's practice of helping one another in cutting down trees and rolling up the logs for building.

LOGSTOWN. Indian village eighteen miles below the forks of the Ohio, near the present Ambridge, Pa.; probably founded by the Shawnee ca. 1728. The most important Indian village on the upper Ohio from 1747 to 1753.

LOGSTOWN, TREATY OF (June 13, 1752). Between Virginia, and the combined chiefs of the Iroquois, Delaware, Shawnee, Wyandot, and Miami Indians; permitted Virginians to settle south of the Ohio R and to build two fortified trading houses on the river.

LOGWOOD TRADE. Logwood comes from the leguminous tree *Haematoxylen campechianum*, found in Central America and the West Indies. Chiefly used in black and blue dyes. Important trade item in the 18th c.

LONDON, DECLARATION OF (Feb. 26, 1909). Tentative agreement by ten naval powers to codify and standardize laws of maritime warfare. Never ratified, but the US tried to make it an important instrument of policy.

LONDON, TREATY OF (1604). Ended warfare between England and Spain. Spain believed that it prohibited English merchants from trading in its New World colonies, but England gave it the opposite interpretation. Fighting recommenced.

LONDON COMPANY. See VIRGINIA COMPANY OF LONDON.

LONDON ECONOMIC CONFERENCE (1933). President Hoover had committed the US to participate, but in the meantime Franklin D. Roosevelt had assumed the presidency and begun reforming monetary policy, including abandoning the gold standard. He would not support a currency-stabilizing program offered by the gold-bloc nations and recalled the US delegation.

LONDON NAVAL TREATY OF 1930. Attempt by the naval powers (US, Great Britain, Japan, France, and Italy) to limit the size and number of warships. A compromise agreement was reached, but it did not survive the 1930s.

LONDON NAVAL TREATY OF 1936. Called after Japan had abrogated agreements made at the WASHINGTON NAVAL CONFERENCE of 1921–22. The US, Great Britain, and France agreed to limit the size of their warships, but Italy refused to sign the treaty. Soon rendered meaningless by World War II.

LONG, HUEY, ASSASSINATION (Sept. 8, 1935). Sen. Huey P. Long was shot at the state capitol at Baton Rouge, La., by Carl A. Weiss, son-in-law of an anti-Long state judge. Weiss was shot dead by Long's bodyguards. Long died two days later.

LONG BEACH. California port city, located on San Pedro Bay; part of the Los Angeles metropolitan area. Discovery of oil in the harbor and under much of the city has made it an important petroleum center. Industries include shipyards and aircraft factories. Pop.: 361,334 (1980).

LONG EXPEDITION. James Long of Virginia led a filibustering expedition to Texas in

1819 to protest US cession of the area in the ADAMS-ONÍS TREATY with Spain. Once there he declared Texas free and independent of Spain and set up a provisional government with himself as president. Failing to receive expected help from the pirate Jean Lafitte and facing an overwhelming Spanish force, he fled. He returned 1821 and captured La Bahia, near San Antonio. The newly independent government in Mexico City invited him to visit; he accepted and was killed there in 1822.

LONGHORNS, TEXAS. Descended from cattle that strayed from Mexico from the 16th c., the Texas longhorn had achieved its own characteristics by the early 19th c. Long of leg, body, and tail, its horns spread from 3 to 5 feet and occasionally to 8 feet. For CATTLE DRIVES, the breed was ideal.

LONG ISLAND. Part of New York state, 118 miles long; lies parallel to the shore of Connecticut and is bounded on the north by Long Island Sound and on the south by the Atlantic Ocean. In 1620, it was included in the grant given by James I to the Virginia Co. of Plymouth. During the same period, Dutch settlements were formed along its western tip, across the East R from Manhattan. English settlers from Connecticut and Massachusetts settled the eastern end. The Treaty of Westminster (1674) finally established all of Long Island as part of the English colony of New York. In 1683, the island was divided into three counties: Queens, Kings, and Suffolk. Eventually most of Queens County became the Borough of Queens, New York City (the rest became Nassau County); Kings County became Brooklyn, New York City. Agriculture, oystering and fishing were important industries until the mid-20th c. Today aircraft manufacture and electronics are major industries. Much of Nassau County has been developed into suburban communities. The eastern end is made up of numerous summer resort areas.

LONG ISLAND, BATTLE OF (Aug. 27, 1776). Confrontation between forces of Gen. George Washington and British forces under Gen. William Howe. Washington's line was at Brooklyn Heights when Howe came across from Staten Island. The patriots were badly mauled; through expert strategy Washington was able to retreat to Manhattan Island.

LONG ISLAND FLATS, BATTLE OF (July 20, 1776). The Overhill Cherokee, in alliance with the British, attacked Fort Watauga, Eaton's Station near Long Island of Holston, and Carter's Valley, all in E Tennessee and SW Virginia. Near Long Island, on level lands, or flats, a sharp battle was fought. The Indians were routed, with more than forty killed.

LONG ISLAND OF HOLSTON, TREATY OF (1777).The Virginia and North Carolina militia made successful raids against the Cherokee after the Battle of Long Island Flats. In the treaty that followed, the Cherokee ceded lands to the whites.

LONG'S EXPLORATIONS. In 1819, Maj. Stephen H. Long in the steamboat *Western Engineer*, explored the Yellowstone R. Because of expense and delays, Congress refused more funds, but authorized him to explore the Rocky Mountains. In 1820, Long and twenty men set out for the Platte, Arkansas, and Red rivers. He discovered Long's Peak, Colo., and a member of his party made the first ascent of Pike's Peak. In 1823, he made another exploration, up the St. Peter's (Minn.) R to establish the location of 49° north latitude and take possession of all territory below this boundary in accordance with the CONVENTION OF 1818 WITH ENGLAND. Returning, the party went down the Red R to Lake Winnipeg and thence eastward through the Great Lakes to Niagara.

LOOKOUT MOUNTAIN, BATTLE OF (Nov. 24, 1863). Union forces, under Gen. Joseph Hooker, cleared Lookout Mountain, Tenn., of Confederate troops, who had held the position since the Battle of Chickamauga two months earlier.

LOOM. Primitive English looms were brought to America by early settlers. Power looms were invented in England, but American types were perfected in New England ca. 1825. These were able to weave both wool and cotton and to make patterns. Looms to weave ingrain carpets and eventually Brussels and Wilton carpets were developed. After the Civil War, improvements were introduced that automatically changed shuttles and stopped a loom when a single warp thread broke. Automated looms were introduced in the 20th c. to offset the rising costs of labor and to handle synthetic yarn. One important development was the shuttleless loom; a jet of water is used to force the weft between the warp. (See also TEXTILES.)

LOOMIS GANG. Six Loomis brothers terrorized Madison County, N.Y., during the 1850s and 1860s. Burglary, horse stealing, and even murder finally aroused the community. Vigilantes killed the oldest brother, burned the Loomis farmhouse, and frightened the rest of the gang into quiescence.

LOOSE CONSTRUCTION. Liberal interpretation of what the US government is allowed to do under the Constitution. A loose construction view of the Constitution permits a use of more power by Congress than a strict constructionist view, which permits only the use of powers specifically granted by the Constitution.

LÓPEZ FILIBUSTERING EXPEDITIONS (1850–51). Armed attempts by Cuban revolutionists led by Narciso López and American annexationists to free Cuba from Spain. The first expedition captured the Spanish fort at Cárdenas before being dispersed and forced to leave the island. The second expedition was captured; members were either executed or imprisoned.

LORAMIE'S STORE. Trading post on the Miami-Maumee portage in W Ohio; founded by Pierre Louis Lorimier (anglicized to Peter Loramie) ca. 1769. Destroyed 1782 by George Rogers Clark. A fort was erected on the site in 1794.

LORDS OF TRADE AND PLANTATION. Twenty-one members of the PRIVY COUNCIL who were given authority over the New World colonies by Charles II in 1675. Developed a complex system of colonial administration, complete with salaried staff. Dissolved 1696.

L'ORIENT. Now Lorient, an important French port on the Bay of Biscay. During the American Revolution, American frigates brought prizes into L'Orient and sold them; the port became a place of departure for American munitions and of entry for products sold to the French during the war.

LORIMER CASE. In 1909 William Lorimer, a Republican, was elected to the Senate from Illinois. After an investigation of bribery and corruption charges, the Senate declined to unseat him. New evidence was produced; the Senate again investigated his election and on July 13, 1912, ousted him from his seat.

LOS ADAES. Spanish garrison in Louisiana established E of the Sabine R in 1718 to prevent French encroachment from Natchitoches. Surrendered to the US in the Louisiana-Texas boundary settlement of 1821.

LOS ANGELES. Largest city in California and third largest (behind New York and Chicago) of the US. Explored by the Spanish in the 1760s; a mission was established outside the modern city limits by Father Junipero Serra in 1771 (Mission San Gabriel). Grew slowly under Spanish rule; when Mexico declared its independence 1822, it passed under Mexican rule. Became a center for the cattle trade in the early 19th c. Seized by US marines at the start of the Mexican War, who fled after the city was surrounded by California Mexicans; retaken after the Battle of La Mesa, 1847. After the war, the city, along with all of California, was turned over to US rule. Discovery of oil in the area and the coming of the railroad assured steady growth. The combination of good climate, fruit raising, and easy connections with the Middle West brought the population to 100,000 by 1900. During the 20th c., the automobile became the key to travel within the city. Through improvements in San Pedro Bay, Los Angeles became a major port city. In 1907, work was begun on the Owens Valley aqueduct, which brought water from the Sierras across the desert. Early in the century, the motion picture industry moved from the East Coast to Hollywood, a part of Los Angeles. World War II spurred growth in the aircraft industry, which remains strong today. Also an electronics center. Pop.: 2,966,763 (1980).

LOST BATTALION. Misnomer for part of the US 77th Division in the Meuse-Argonne offensive in World War I. From Oct. 3–12, 1918, it was encircled by German troops, whom it fought off valiantly, until relief arrived.

LOST CAUSE. Symbolic term for the ideals, aspirations, and memories of the southern Confederacy.

LOST COLONY. See RALEIGH'S LOST COLONY.

LOST GENERATION. Term, probably coined by Gertrude Stein, for the American writers of the 1920s who had exiled themselves from the mainstream of American life. They included Ernest Hemingway, F. Scott Fitzgerald, William Faulkner, Thomas Wolfe, Thornton Wilder, E.E. Cummings, and Hart Crane.

LOTTERIES. First authorized by King James's third charter of Virginia (1612); so widespread by 1699 that a New England ecclesiastical assembly denounced them. Used throughout the 18th c. in most states to fund schools, roads, bridges, canals, and other expenses. Antilottery societies gained strength in the 1830s; during the next two decades one state after another ended lotteries, until they survived only in Louisiana. In 1890, Congress forbade the use of the US mails to advertise or distribute tickets; two years later, Louisiana abolished its lottery. Despite the mail embargo, state lotteries had a rebirth in the 1970s. By 1980, fourteen states had lotteries, with total revenues of more than $2 billion.

LOUDON, FORT. Built 1756 on the Little Tennessee R in Tennessee by the English of South Carolina. Besieged by French-incited Cherokee in 1760 and forced to surrender. Many of its occupants, including civilians, were massacred; the fort was burned.

LOUISBURG EXPEDITION (1745). During KING GEORGE'S WAR, Gov. William Shirley of Massachusetts mounted a large expedition against the French fortress and naval station at Louisburg, Nova Scotia, on Cape Breton Island. Land forces laid siege to the town, which capitulated, and captured the French fleet upon arrival. The colonists were embittered when, by the Treaty of Aix-la-Chapelle of 1748, the British sacrificed Louisburg for Madras, India. (See also AIX-LA-CHAPELLE, TREATY OF.)

LOUISIANA. Explored by the Spanish beginning 1520. In 1682 the sieur de La Salle followed the Mississippi to its mouth and claimed the entire valley for Louis XIV of France. First permanent French colony in 1699 at BILOXI. In 1718, John Law, a Scottish banker, was given control of Louisiana. He organized the Company of the Indies, but his company failed (see MISSISSIPPI BUBBLE). Louisiana reverted to royal control. France undertook to connect New France (Canada) and Louisiana by erecting forts to exclude the English from the Mississippi Valley. The resulting wars (see KING GEORGE'S WAR and the FRENCH AND INDIAN WAR) culminated in the expulsion of the French from the mainland of North America. Louisiana west of the Mississippi and the Isle of Orleans were ceded to Spain in 1762; the remainder of Louisiana was surrendered to England in 1763 (see FONTAINEBLEAU, TREATY OF; PARIS, TREATY OF). Experienced a steady development under Spanish rule. Disputes between the US and Spain over navigation of the Mississippi and the northern boundary of West Florida were settled by PINCKNEY'S TREATY OF 1795. In 1800, Spain retroceded Louisiana to France; but before France took possession, Napoleon sold it to the US in 1803 (see LOUISIANA PURCHASE).

Admitted to the Union in 1812. Agriculture (especially sugar culture) and commerce expanded rapidly. The steamboat made New Orleans the commercial emporium of the Mississippi Valley; the 1850s brought railroad and levee construction. The sixth state to secede from the Union; New Orleans was captured by Union forces in 1862, and vital sections of the state remained in federal hands throughout the war. Emerged from the war with virtually no capital and an impoverished population. Radical Reconstruction led to corruption, violence, racial animosity, and political cynicism. Industrial development began ca. 1900, with exploitation of petroleum and natural gas resources, as well as salt, sulfur, and timber. A mild spirit of progressivism entered politics ca. 1920 and became militant when Huey P. Long was elected governor in 1928. His elaborate program of public improvement and social amelioration, put into effect with ruthlessness, dominated Louisiana politics even after his assassination in 1935. State politicians continued to be characterized as either "Longites" or "anti-Longites." Louisiana boomed during World War II and prospered after, through industrialization and a mechanized agriculture. Between 1970 and 1980, its population increased by 15 percent (to 4,203,972).

LOUISIANA, UPPER. Spanish designation for that part of Louisiana stretching northward from Hope Encampment on the Mississippi R to Canada and westward to the Rocky Mountains. After 1770, St. Louis was its capital, presided over by a lieutenant governor subordinate to the governor in New Orleans. The US called Upper Louisiana the District of Louisiana, distinguishing it from Lower Louisiana, which was called the Territory of Orleans. Upper Louisiana was divided after the Louisiana Purchase of 1803 into five districts.

LOUISIANA PURCHASE (1803). Ceded to Spain by France in 1762 (see FONTAINEBLEAU, TREATY OF), which soon turned to diplomacy as a means of recovering it. In 1800, Napoleon Bonaparte acquired Louisiana for France in return for placing the son-in-law of the Spanish king on the newly erected throne of Etruria. President Jefferson, worried over Spanish harassment of US shipping on the Mississippi, sent James Monroe to Paris to assist Robert R. Livingston in negotiating American rights. Monroe was authorized to offer $10 million for the Isle of Orleans, on which New Orleans stood, and the Floridas. By the spring of 1803, Napoleon's plans for an American empire had gone astray; Spain refused to round out his possessions by ceding the Floridas. War was imminent; Napoleon decided to reap a profit and placate the Americans by selling them all of Louisiana. After negotiations, the US agreed on April 30 to pay $11.25 million for Louisiana, set aside $3.75 million to pay the claims of its own citizens against France, and place France and Spain on an equal commercial footage with the US and the colony for twelve years.

LOUISIANA REVOLUTION OF 1768. French inhabitants of Louisiana keenly resented being transferred to Spain in 1762; Spain's tardiness in taking possession of the colony induced them to hope that actual transfer would never take place. Economic distress, loyalty to France, and the unpopularity of the first Spanish governor of Louisiana, culminated in his expulsion from the colony.

LOUISVILLE. Largest city in Kentucky, located on the S bank of the Ohio R at the Falls of the Ohio. Laid out 1773 but not occupied until a fort was erected in 1778. Opening of the LOUISVILLE AND PORTLAND CANAL around the falls in 1830 made it one of the busiest river ports in America. During the Civil War, an im-

portant supply base for the Union army. Industries include farm machinery, electric appliances, and liquor. Pop.: 298,451 (1980).

LOUISVILLE AND NASHVILLE RAILROAD. See RAILROADS, SKETCHES OF PRINCIPAL LINES.

LOUISVILLE AND PORTLAND CANAL. Completed 1830 around the Falls of the Ohio at Louisville. Federal government assumed control in 1872, ending tolls in 1880. Rebuilt 1927.

LOVEJOY RIOTS. Elijah P. Lovejoy, an abolitionist, was threatened by proslavery men for the editorials in his newspaper, the *Observer*, published at St. Louis. He moved his press to Alton, Ill., but mobs destroyed three successive presses and killed him when he tried installing a fourth. Considered a martyr by abolitionists.

LOVELY'S PURCHASE. W.L. Lovely, Cherokee Indian agent in Arkansas, negotiated an agreement whereby the Osage ceded land at the confluence of the Verdigris and Arkansas rivers in E Oklahoma.

LOVEWELL'S FIGHT. Occurred at Pigwacket (Fryeburg), Maine, May 9, 1725. Capt. John Lovewell led a company on a scalp-bounty expedition; they were ambushed by a force of Pequawkets, who killed twelve of the white men, including Lovewell.

LOWELL. City in Massachusetts located at the juncture of the Merimack and Concord rivers. Site of thriving textile industry by the early 19th c. and regarded as a model industrial city. Declined when the industry began moving south in the 1930s. Pop.: 92,418 (1980).

LOWER CALIFORNIA. Also known as Baja California. Discovered by the Spanish in 1533 and separated from Spanish Upper (Alta) California in 1772. Sought by the US in the 1840s and 1850s; scene of futile filibustering exploits of William Walker. James Gadsden failed to obtain it as part of the Gadsden Purchase in 1853.

LOWER COUNTIES-ON-DELAWARE. Comprising the present state of Delaware, the counties evolved from Swedish and Dutch settlements and were conveyed by the duke of York in 1682 to Pennsylvania. The Lower Counties seceded from Pennsylvania in 1704 and formed their own assembly.

LOYAL, FORT, CAPTURE OF (May 20, 1690). At the beginning of King William's War, a mixed force of French and Indians compelled the surrender of Fort Loyal on Casco Bay, Maine. Many of the captured were tortured and murdered.

LOYALISTS. Also known as Tories. Those loyal to Great Britain during the American Revolution comprised about one-third of the colonial population. After the Battle of Lexington, they organized militia companies. Although they probably contributed 60,000 soldiers, their military service was not commensurate with their numerical strength. As the struggle progressed, all who refused to take an oath of allegiance to the new government were denied rights of citizenship and could not vote, hold office, or enjoy court protection. In many cases, they were forbidden to pursue professions or to acquire or dispose of property. The more ardent were jailed, put on parole, or sent to detention camps. Nearly all the new state governments enacted legislation banishing those who refused to swear allegiance. About 200,000 Loyalists died, were exiled, or became voluntary refugees.

LOYAL LAND COMPANY. In 1748, Virginia granted 800,000 acres of western land to the company; by 1754 settlers had bought land in the Tennessee and Kentucky country. Thomas Walker negotiated the treaties of Fort Stanwix (1768) and Lochaber (1770), whereby the Indians ceded their rights to the lands. (See also STANWIX, FORT, TREATY OF; LOCHABER, TREATY OF.)

LOYALTY OATHS. Immigrants to the colonies were forced to take loyalty oaths to the crown and the colonial regime. In the American Revolution, oaths were used to enforce boycotts against Loyalists. The Constitution requires a loyalty oath of federal and state officers. During the Civil War, loyalty oaths were required in both the North and South, and were central in Reconstruction policies. Oaths did not play a primary role in the world wars, but were required of both civilian and military personnel of the federal government.

In the agitation over communists in the period after World War II, loyalty testing was prominent in the executive establishment. Many state legislatures and municipal bodies required loyalty oaths of teachers and governmental employees, most of which were upheld by the Supreme Court.

LOYALTY REVIEW BOARD. Created 1947 by the Civil Service Commission to review evidence and conclusions in cases concerning the loyalty of federal employees. Abolished 1953.

LUBBOCK. City on the high plains of W Texas in a cattle-raising and cotton-producing area. A center for the W Texas oil industry. Pop.: 173,979 (1980).

LUDLOW'S CODE. Body of laws compiled 1650 by Roger Ludlow for the commonwealth of Connecticut. Remains the foundation of the laws of the state.

LUMBEE. Or Croatan Indians. Centered in Robeson County, N.C., with a population of about 40,000; of mixed ancestry of white, Indian, and black strains. Claim descent from Sir Walter Raleigh's lost colony intermarried with the Hatteras Indians.

LUMBER INDUSTRY. The white pine, found in the Northeast, was the earliest species of tree favored by lumbermen. As the nation expanded, other species were cut, including the Norway pine, southern pine and cypress, redwood, Douglas fir, and Port Orford cedar. The ax was replaced by various kinds of saws, culminating in the band saw. Important developments since the mid-19th c. include the making of paper from wood pulp, the burgeoning of the plywood industry, and the use of wood fibers for insulating materials and wallboard. Many large companies maintain tree farms, practice conservation measures and plan for future cuttings. Many timber reserves are in national forests and subject to rules established by the US Forest Service.

LUNDY'S LANE, BATTLE AT (July 25, 1814). The most sharply contended engagement of the War of 1812; in Ontario, near Niagara Falls. The Americans, pushing into Canada from Fort Erie, were met by superior British forces. After intense fighting, the

Americans retreated, but the battle indicated that the American army could hold its own against the British.

LUSITANIA, SINKING OF THE (May 7, 1915). The *Lusitania*, a British passenger liner, was sunk without warning by a German submarine, with 1,198 deaths. Of these, 128 were Americans. Created intense indignation in the US even though the Germans had warned American passengers of travel on British liners. A large cargo of small-arms ammunition may have exploded and contributed to its rapid sinking.

LUTHERAN CHURCHES. Lutherans from Salzburg began settling 1734 in Georgia; large numbers soon immigrated to Pennsylvania. The Ministerium of Philadelphia was created 1748, and a national organization, the General Synod, was formed 1820. Dissension arose over doctrinal matters, and Lutheranism divided into several denominations. By the 1980s, about 95 percent were members of three synods: the Lutheran Church in America (2,925,188 members), the American Lutheran Church (2,352,431 members), and the Lutheran-Missouri Synod (2,719,319 members). In 1982, the first two agreed to merge.

LUTHER V. BORDEN, 7 Howard 1 (1848). The Supreme Court ruled that existing state government was legally empowered to use martial methods to maintain itself against violence.

LYCEUM MOVEMENT. Early adult education movement in the US. First Lyceum society was organized 1826 at Millbury, Mass. Town lyceums, estimated at 3,000 in 1835, had increased to 12,000 by 1915. In the 1920s some degenerated into programs of semipopular music and "sanitized vaudeville"; others developed into historical or literary societies, public museums, and libraries.

LYGONIA. Grant, commonly called the Plough Patent, made by the Council of New England in 1636 of a large area west of the Kennebec R in Maine. Settlement failed; title fell to Sir Alexander Rigby in 1643, whose claim was contested for many years. Eventually (1691), a new Massachusetts charter put an end to the Province of Lygonia.

McALLISTER, FORT, CAPTURE OF (Dec.13, 1864). Captured by Union troops; located eighteen miles SW of Savannah, Ga., it controlled the mouth of the Ogeechee R and had held up Gen. W.T. Sherman's March to the Sea.

McCARDLE, EX PARTE 7 Wallace 506 (1869). Marked the summit of Radical Republican power over RECONSTRUCTION. Republicans in Congress passed a law depriving the Supreme Court of the power to declare Reconstruction acts unconstitutional. McCardle, a Mississippi editor, had been jailed and denied benefit of habeas corpus. The Court unanimously decided it had no jurisdiction because of the new restriction and dismissed his case.

McCARRAN-WALTER ACT (1952). Basic, comprehensive immigration law, passed over President Truman's veto. Retained the national origins system of the 1924 law but removed race as a bar to immigration; gave preference to aliens with needed skills; provided for a rigorous screening of aliens in order to eliminate security risks and subversives; and called for broader grounds for the deportation of criminal aliens.

McCARTHY-ARMY HEARINGS (1954). Grew out of Sen. Joseph R. McCarthy's charges that the army was lax in discovering communist spies. The army retaliated by claiming that McCarthy and his subcommittee's chief counsel, Roy Cohn, had intervened to obtain special treatment for Private G. David Schine, a good friend of Cohn's; and, not succeeding, were using the hearings to harass the army. The hearings, shown daily on national television, turned into a shambles, with McCarthy indulging in rambling, seemingly irrelevant speeches. His behavior became the object of widespread exasperation and derision. His major blunder came late in the hearings, when he blurted out that he had information that the army's counsel, Joseph N. Welch, was harboring in his law firm a member of a left-wing lawyers' organization. In a statement redolent of sadness and bitterness, Welch lashed out at McCarthy and his methods, making him appear a vicious bully. For the first time, many Americans gained an insight into the kind of human tragedy McCarthy's investigations had caused; he was discredited in the eyes of most. Eventually, the Senate initiated hearings to censure McCarthy; by a vote of sixty-seven to twenty-two, the Senate voted to "condemn" but not to "censure" McCarthy. It was the effective end of McCarthyism.

McCORMICK REAPER. Although there were earlier patents, the 1834 reaper of Cyrus H. McCormick invaded the Middle West, which was ready for an efficient harvester that would make extensive wheat growing possible.

McCULLOCH V. MARYLAND, 4 Wheaton 316 (1819). Two questions were involved: first, whether Congress had power under the Constitution to establish a bank and, second, whether Maryland could impose a tax on this bank. A unanimous court upheld the power of Congress to charter a bank as a government agency and denied the power of a state to tax it. Chief Justice John Marshall's discussion broadly interpreting the powers of Congress remains a classic statement of implied powers.

McDONALD'S EXPEDITION (1774). Angus McDonald, acting for Lord Dunmore, colonial governor of Virginia, led an attack against the hostile Shawnee in Ohio. (See also DUNMORE'S WAR.)

MACDONOUGH'S LAKE CHAMPLAIN FLEET. US naval force in the War of 1812 under the command of Lt. Thomas Macdonough. On Sept. ll, 1814, he met the British fleet at Cumberland Head, near Plattsburgh, N.Y., and won.

McDOWELL, BATTLE AT (May 8, 1862). Combined Confederate forces of Gen. Stonewall Jackson and Gen. Edward Johnson gained a decisive victory in the engagement at McDowell, Va., compelling Union forces to retreat toward Franklin.

McGILLIVRAY INCIDENT (Aug. 7, 1790). Alexander McGillivray, the Creek Indian chief, signed two treaties with the US that abrogated the Treaty of Pensacola. In 1792, under salary to the Spanish, he abrogated the US treaties. His death in 1793 left both Spanish and US treaties unratified.

McGUFFEY'S READERS. Series of textbooks by W. H. McGuffey that molded American literary taste and morality from 1836 until the early 20th c. Known as the Eclectic Series; contained lessons with accompanying pictures and taught principles of religion, morality, and patriotism. By 1920, total sales had reached 122 million copies.

MACHAULT, FORT. Built 1754 by the French on the site of Franklin, Pa.; one of a link of forts from Lake Erie to the Ohio R. Abandoned 1759.

McHENRY, FORT. Built 1799 on a small island in Baltimore harbor. Its attack during the War of 1812 inspired Francis Scott Key to write "The Star-Spangled Banner."

MACHINE, PARTY. Arose in the 19th c. as professional politicians, operating under the spoils system, took advantage of the presence of large unassimilated immigrants in the nation's large cities. In return for votes, precinct and ward leaders provided rent money, fuel, food, and jobs for needy families and aided groups when they got into trouble with the state. At the apex of the party machine were the city or state bosses. Not all bosses ran their organizations for selfish motives; many entered the political arena solely in public service, but there were those whose political machine was built on the spoils system, corruption, fraud, waste, and graft. Boss Tweed of New York City's TAMMANY HALL is the archetypical machine boss. Decline began in the mid-19th c., when the new civil service reduced the sources of patronage, voters became more independent and sophisticated, and various social programs alleviated the worst of the conditions on which the machine thrived.

MACHINE GUNS. In 1862, R.J. Gatling patented a gun with six barrels that rotated around a central axis by a hand crank. H.S. Maxim patented the first automatic machine gun 1884; powered by recoil energy, it was smaller, lighter, and easier to operate. In 1890, J.M. Browning introduced the principle of gas operation; his guns remained standard equipment for US forces through the Korean War. Browning's .30-caliber gun was replaced in the mid-1950s by the M-60.

MACHINE TOOLS. Early in the 19th c., British engineers and machinists developed the main categories of modern machine tools: engine lathes equipped with slide rests, boring machines, planers, and shapers. All were quickly transferred to America; by the 1840s the demand was so great that manufacture of machine tools became a specialized industry. By 1914, there were more than 400 machine-tool manufacturers in the US. America's chief contribution to design was in specialized, high-speed machinery devoted to production of standardized components.

McINTOSH, FORT. Built 1778 on the Ohio R within the limits of present Beaver, Pa., as a base for a projected expedition against Detroit. Headquarters for a time of the Western Department of the Continental army.

McINTOSH, FORT, TREATIES OF (1785). Agreements whereby the Wyandot, Delaware, Chippewa, and Ottawa tribes ceded much of Ohio. Later repudiated by the Indians; peace was not secured until the Treaty of Greenville of 1795.

MACKENZIE'S TREATY (1831). Kenneth Mackenzie, a director of the American Fur Co., arranged a peace between the warring Blackfoot and Assiniboine, at the same time opening a large section of the upper Missouri country to exploitation by his company.

MACKINAC, STRAITS OF, AND MACKINAC ISLAND (formerly Straits of Michilimackinac and Michilimackinac Island). Lakes Michigan, Superior, and Huron are connected by the straits and the St. Marys R. In the middle lies Mackinac Island, once a strategic military and commercial center. French rule was established there in the 1660s. British rule began in 1761. During the American Revolution, the British moved their fort from Mackinaw City to Mackinac Island. The US gained possession by the 1783 treaty ending the Revolution. The British took possession in War of 1812 and held it until 1815. Later became fur-trading center. Present population about 500.

MACKINAW BOAT. A light, strongly built, flat-bottomed boat, pointed at both ends, adapted from the Indian canoe.

McKINLEY TARIFF (1890). William McKinley, as chairman of the House Ways and Means Committee, was the sponsor of this strongly protectionist law. Increased tariffs to about 48.4 percent and allowed the president to increase tariffs even higher in retaliation against other countries' tariffs.

McMAHON ACT (1946). First Atomic Energy Act. Created five-man Atomic Energy Commission to conduct atomic research and to hold title to all atomic equipment in the US.

McNAMARA CASE (1910–11). Three labor leaders, James B. McNamara, his brother John T. McNamara, and Ortie McManigal, were charged with the bombing of the *Los Angeles Times*. McManigal confessed but the two brothers pleaded not guilty and became symbols of labor's struggles against management. Clarence Darrow became their attorney, and during the course of the trial was accused of trying to bribe jury members. The brothers later confessed, dealing a serious blow to the labor movement.

MACOMB PURCHASE. In 1791 Alexander Macomb contracted for the purchase of 3.6 million acres in upstate New York. Financial difficulties forced him to deed the tract to William Constable and others.

MACON. City in Georgia; an Indian village on the site was visited by Hernando de Soto in 1540; its central location made it a valuable trading post. Present city founded 1820 and became a railroad center. Today, its principal industry is textiles. Pop.: 121,122 (1980).

MACON'S BILL NO. 2 (1810). Enacted to compel Great Britain and France, at war with each other, to stop their illegal seizures of American commercial vessels by banning all trade with either country. Replaced the unsuccessful Nonintercourse, or Embargo, Act.

MADISON. Capital city of Wisconsin. Founded in 1836 and was the capital of Wisconsin Territory. The seat of the University of Wisconsin, it is in the center of the dairy farming area, and there are important food-processing and meat-packing industries. Pop.: 170,382 (1980).

MADISON, FORT (sometimes called Fort Bellevue). Built 1809 on the Mississippi R where the city of Fort Madison, Iowa, now stands. Its purpose was to protect the Indian trade. It was attacked in the War of 1812 by Indians supporting the British.

MADISON COUNTY ANTISLAVERY WAR (1859–60). The antislavery Berea School (now College) was founded in 1855; and Kentucky slaveowners were alarmed over the aboliton doctrine of its founders and its policy of educating blacks alongside whites. An armed mob forced the antislavery families to leave the state.

MADISON SQUARE GARDEN. Four separate sports arenas in New York City. The first, originally known as Gilmore's Garden, located on Madison Square, was replaced in 1890 by a new building, designed by Stanford White; it housed musical and theatrical performances, horse and dog shows, political conventions, circuses, and athletic events, particularly boxing. White was murdered in its roof garden in 1906. In 1925, a third garden was built at Eighth Avenue and Fiftieth Street. It became the world's most famous sports arena. The fourth Garden was opened in 1968 in a complex on the site of Pennsylvania Station.

MADRID, TREATY OF (1670). By implication, Spain for the first time recognized the legal existence of British colonies in the New World.

MADRID CONFERENCE (1880). International conference involving the imperialistic rivalries in Morocco. Little was accomplished, but it was the first time the US had participated in an international conference.

MAFIA. See CRIME, ORGANIZED.

MAFIA INCIDENT (1890–92). Nineteen members of a Sicilian secret society, the Mafia, were indicted for the murder of the New Orleans police chief. Despite the overwhelming case against them, all were found innocent. A public protest followed, and eleven persons were lynched by a mob. Three were Italian subjects, and the Italian government protested and demanded protection for the New Orleans Italian community. Unsatisfied with the US response, Italy recalled its minister. President Benjamin Harrison offered indemnities to the families of the slain men

and expressed official regrets. Diplomatic relations were resumed.

MAGAZINES. In 1741, America's first two magazines appeared: *American Magazine, or Monthly View* and Benjamin Franklin's *General Magazine and Historical Chronicle*. Neither magazine lasted a year. Later, more successful magazines included *Godey's Lady's Book, New York Ledger, Century, Scribner's, Atlantic,* and *Forum*. Also successful were reprints of popular British reviews. A number of factors led to the burgeoning of magazines in the late 19th and early 20th c.: improved printing processes, large profits from national advertising, and cheap mailing privileges. Mass circulation, popular magazines included *Reader's Digest, Saturday Evening Post, Life, Liberty, Look,* and *Collier's*. After World War II, television drew off great numbers of readers and advertisers. Of the mass-circulation magazines, only *The Reader's Digest* survived intact. Only two new mass-circulation magazines appeared: *TV Guide* and *People*. News magazines (*Time, Newsweek, US News and World Report*) continued to prosper, as did all sorts of specialized journals. Among the most successful of the latter are *The New Yorker, Sports Illustrated,* and *Playboy*.

Children's Magazines. The first American juvenile periodical was the *Children's Magazine* (Hartford, 1789). *Youth's Friend and Scholar's Magazine* (Philadelphia, 1823) was a product of the Sunday-school movement and the first aimed at teaching religious truth to young people. The most important children's magazines of the 19th c. were *Youth's Companion* (Boston, 1827–1929), *Harper's Young People* (1879–95), *Riverside Magazine* (1867–73), and the most influential of them all *St. Nicholas,* founded in 1873 and edited for more than thirty years by Mabel Mapes Dodge. Among the more successful periodicals of the 20th c. have been *Youth's Companion, American Boy, Boys' Life, American Girl, Scholastic, Cricket, Jack and Jill,* and *Sesame Street*.

MAGDALENA BAY RESOLUTION (1912). Also known as the Lodge Corollary. Aimed at blocking the purchase of a large tract of land in Baja California, Mexico, by a Japanese syndicate. The purchase was deemed a threat to California and the Panama Canal. It was the first time that the Monroe Doctrine was applied to an Asiatic power.

MAGEE-KEARNEY EXPEDITION (1820). Army force sent to lay out a route up the Mississippi R to the mouth of the St. Peters (Minnesota) R. They reported the route impracticable and returned to St. Louis by boat.

MAINE. The most northeasterly of the states, it has an extremely long and irregular coastline, with numerous bays and inlets. Maine is believed to have been visited by French, British, and Portuguese explorers in the 16th c. Settlement was attempted by the French in 1604 on an island in the St. Croix R; it failed after one winter. In 1607, the English planted a colony on the Kennebec R, but it too expired. In 1622, Sir Ferdinando Gorges and John Mason received a grant for all lands between the Merrimack and the Kennebec. Massachusetts assumed control in 1677, and in 1691, William and Mary granted a charter to Massachusetts, thereby confirming its claim. After the Revolutionary War, a boundary dispute arose between Maine and Canada; settled by Webster-Ashburton Treaty (1842). Agitation for separation from Massachusetts had begun in the 18th c. and reached its culmination in 1820 when Maine was admitted as a free state as part of the Missouri Compromise. Democratic during most of the early 19th c., Maine became a Republican state in the 1860s and remained so until well into the 20th c. Primarily a state of farmers, lumbermen, and fishermen, Maine's pulpwood and paper industry mushroomed after 1880. Early in the 20th c., the state had an important textile industry, but most of that moved to the South. The loss of the textile industry and the decline in lumbering have combined to make Maine one of the nation's most economically depressed states. Tourism is a major industry. Pop.: 1,125,000 (1980).

MAINE, DESTRUCTION OF THE (Feb. 15, 1898). The US battleship *Maine* was positioned in Havana harbor during Cuba's revolt against Spanish rule. The ship was totally destroyed by two explosions, and 260 men were killed. The Spanish claimed that an internal explosion had been the cause; the Americans claimed the original cause had been an external explosion. News of the disaster stirred up national feeling in the US, fanned by the hys-

terical journalism of the newspapers of William Randolph Hearst and Joseph Pulitzer. The slogan "Remember the Maine" was a major factor in bringing the US to a declaration of war against Spain. No conclusive evidence was ever offered as to the cause of the destruction of the *Maine*.

MAINE BOUNDARY DISPUTE. See AROOSTOOK WAR; NORTHEAST BOUNDARY; WEBSTER-ASHBURTON TREATY.

MAIZE. See CORN.

MAJORITY RULE. A fundamental American concept, evolved from the principle of the sovereignty of the people. Majority rule is limited somewhat by the Constitution; civil liberties are fundamental law and cannot be suppressed by a temporary majority. The Constitution itself cannot be amended without the consent of two-thirds of both houses of Congress and three-fourths of the states.

MAKAH. Indian tribe occupying the Olympic Peninsula of the state of Washington, where they still have lands. Their native culture was a variation of the rich Northwest Coast development; but the Makah did not achieve the cultural sophistication of the Haida, Tlingit. or Kwakiutl-Nootka.

MALARIA. Long prevalent in Europe and Africa, by 1700 malaria had become established in America all along the east coast. It spread to the Mississippi Valley with the American settlers. Reached its height in New England in the 18th c. and in the Midwest ca. 1875. Associated wtih marshes since antiquity, malaria tended to rise with the initial clearing of the land and fall with cultivation and drainage. The synthesis of quinine (from cinchona bark) in 1820 made rational therapeutics more practicable. Around 1900, the role of the mosquito became established; extended antimalaria campaigns began in 1912, especially in the South. After World War II, the Public Health Service, chiefly by the use of DDT, inaugurated a campaign to eradicate malaria. By the 1980s, the US was free of significant indigenous malaria.

MALLET BROTHERS EXPLORATIONS 1739-42). Pierre and Paul Mallet, French traders, led the first expedition that crossed the Plains from the Missouri R. In 1740, they explored the Arkansas R from the Rockies to the Mississippi. They made a second Santa Fe expedition from New Orleans by boat up the Mississippi, Arkansas, and Canadian rivers into central Oklahoma.

MALMÉDY MASSACRE (Dec. 17, 1944). German troops captured about 100 US troops near Malmédy, Belgium, and executed them. A few feigned death and survived; eighty-six died. It was the worst single atrocity against US troops in Europe during World War II. A US tribunal sentenced forty-three Germans to death and thirty to life imprisonment. The death sentences were commuted, and none of the convicted served a full prison sentence.

MALVERN HILL, BATTLE OF (July 1, 1862). Last of the Seven Days' battles, it ended Union Gen. G.B. McClellan's PENINSULAR CAMPAIGN.

MAMMALOGY. Progress in describing American mammals was slow during the 18th c. Thomas Jefferson included in his *Notes on the State of Virginia* (1785) tables that compared the weights of European and American species. He also encouraged the successful recovery of mammoth bones by Lewis and Clark. Activity picked up in the 19th c., much of it under state sponsorship. An outstanding example was *Zoology of New York* (four volumes, 1842–44). The federal government sponsored a series of exploratory expeditions, especially after 1850 when S.F. Baird assumed responsibility for the program within the new Smithsonian Institution. The latter 19th c. saw the rise in phylogenetic studies, aroused by interest in evolution and paleontology, and with a concern for wildlife management. C. Hart Merriam dominated the science from the 1890s to the 1920s. He was first head of the Department of Agriculture's Division of Economic Ornithology and Mammalogy (created 1888). Under his direction, the divison (renamed the Bureau of Biological Survey in 1905) studied the economic importance of many species.

MAMMOTH CAVE. In Edmonson County, Kentucky. Evidences of Indian occupation were found for miles inside its entrance by early explorers. Source of saltpeter during the War of 1812. Center of 50,000-acre national park.

MANASSAS, BATTLE OF. See BULL RUN, FIRST BATTLE OF; BULL RUN, SECOND BATTLE OF.

MANCHAC. A British trading post established shortly after 1763 at the junction of Bayou Manchac (Iberville R) and the Mississippi R. It was captured by the Spanish in 1779.

MANCHESTER. Largest city in New Hampshire, located on the Merrimack R., on the site of an early settlement called Derryville. In 1807 a canal was opened that skirted the Amoskeag Falls to permit barges to reach the area from Boston. Its industries include the manufacture of shoes and clothing, light machinery, and metal products. Pop.: 90,757 (1980).

MANCHURIA AND MANCHUKUO. Manchuria was important to US exporters at the time of Russian economic penetration in the 1890s; from 1901 to 1903, the Roosevelt administration quarreled with the Russians over the status of US traders. Japanese military successes in Manchuria led to a parceling of spheres of influence, to which Roosevelt acquiesced. Later, the Taft administration tried unsuccessfully to internationalize the railroads, driving Japan and Russia together. The US conceded Japanese hegemony there; the Chinese republic never exercised more than nominal control. In 1932, Japan cemented its control by creating the puppet state of Manchukuo, which was not accepted by the US. A secret agreement at the Yalta Conference in 1945 gave the Soviet Union hegemony over the area in return for its intervention in the war against Japan. The Red Army occupied Manchuria in 1945. In 1950, an agreement between Mao Tse-tung and Joseph Stalin led to complete Chinese Control.

MANDAN, FORT. Built 1805 by the Lewis and Clark expedition at Five Villages, now Stanton, N.D. It was an advantageous wintering place because of neighboring Mandan and Hidatsa villages.

MANDAN, HIDATSA, AND ARIKARA. Three Indian tribes of the northern Plains that practiced river-bottom maize cultivation along the Missouri R in the general area of North Dakota. They spoke mutually unintelligible languages. Used the tipi and shared other elements of the bison-hunting culture but tended toward permanent villages. Greatly reduced by smallpox in mid-19th c.

MANDATES. After World War I, conquered German and Turkish colonies were assigned for administration to individual Allied powers. The US was not a party to the treaties but insisted on equal rights with other powers. US claims were finally granted, and ten treaties were negotiated, securing for the US all the rights it would have had if it had joined the League of Nations.

MANGAS COLORADAS WARS. Series of Apache hostilities led by Mangas Coloradas, chief of the Apaches in SW New Mexico. In 1861, he allied himself with Cochise after the US cavalry had ordered the hanging of Apache hostages. He was wounded at Apache Pass on July 15, 1862, but recovered. He was taken prisoner in January 1863. Killed while allegedly trying to escape.

MANHATTAN. An island and borough of New York City. It was discovered by Giovanni da Verrazano in 1524 and visited by Henry Hudson in 1609. The name is derived from the Manhattan Indians who lived there. There were Dutch settlers by 1613, and in 1626 Peter Minuit, an agent for the Dutch West India Co., bought the island from the Canarsie Indians for, according to legend, $24. New York City spread rapidly over the island in the 19th c. The city was confined to this island alone until Greater New York was created in 1898. (See also NEW YORK CITY.)

MANHATTAN PROJECT. The World War II project that led to the development of the atomic bomb. So-called because the early research was conducted at Columbia University in New York City. For security reasons, the project was moved to the University of Chicago. Oak Ridge, Tenn., was the site chosen for separation of the fissionable uranium-235 isotope. In December 1942, Enrico Fermi succeeded in producing and controlling a chain reacton in the pile, or reactor, at Chicago. That reactor also produced uranium-238, the second path to the bomb. Five giant reactors were constructed at Hanford, Wash. to produce plutonium. In 1942, J. Robert Oppenheimer was put in charge of the weapons laboratory at Los Alamos, N. M. There a uranium weapon was tested on July 16, 1945.

The first atomic bomb was dropped on Hiroshima, Japan, on Aug. 6, 1945, and the second against Nagasaki, Japan, on Aug. 9, 1945. Japan quickly capitulated.

MANIFEST DESTINY. Concept of the 1840s and 1850s suggesting the supposed inevitablility of the continued territorial expansion of the United States. The phrase first referred specifically to the annexation of Texas, but it was quickly utilized in the controversy with Great Britain over Oregon and in the demand for annexations of territory as a result of the Mexican and Spanish-American wars.

MANILA BAY, BATTLE OF (May 1, 1898). The fleet of Commodore George Dewey attacked the Spanish squadron at Manila, in the Philippines. At about noon, the shore batteries were silenced and every Spanish ship was destroyed. Manila fell on August 13.

MANITOULIN ISLANDS. Stretched across northern Lake Huron, they were first sighted by French Jesuits ca. 1640. After the War of 1812, Drummond Island (now part of Michigan) was awarded to the US; the remainder went to Canada. The islands are popular resorts and fishing grounds.

MANN, FORT (also known as Fort Atkinson). Troops were quartered here in the Mexican War, but its exact location in Kansas is in doubt.

MANN ACT (1910). Aimed at the suppression of the white-slave traffic, it made interstate travel or transportation for illegal purposes (such as prostitution) illegal.

MANORS. At the time of colonial settlement in the New World, the self-sufficient manor was the prevailing mode of agricultural life in England. Because the country gentlemen wanted to secure landholdings in the New World, the manorial system was established in the proprietary colonies, especially in New York, Maryland, and Carolina. In New Netherland, numerous patroonships, virtually manors, were authorized; but only Rensselaerwyck was successfully established. The early English governors of New York created manors in Westchester, on Long Island, and elsewhere. Their legal and political characteristics were feudal, but they could not withstand the encroachments of town and county authority, or the opposition of tenants. The tenants on Rensselaerwyck manor agitated against their leasehold estates and perpetual rents, and the controversy erupted into the ANTIRENT WAR of 1839–46. Although the Fundamental Constitutions of Carolina of 1669 set up an aristocratic system of landholding, there is no evidence of any manor actually having been founded. Over a hundred proprietary manors were set up by William Penn for his colony in Pennsylvania, but in no case does it appear that manorial jurisdiction was ever exercised. The abolition of PRIMOGENITURE by all the states after the American Revolution effectively ended any possibility of a manorial system surviving in the US.

MANUEL'S FORT. The first American outpost in present-day Montana, built by Manuel Lisa, a fur trader, at the junction of the Yellowstone and Bighorn rivers in 1807. Hostility of the Blackfoot caused its abandonment in 1811.

MANUFACTURES, RESTRICTION OF CO-LONIAL. English manufacturers felt it imperative to eliminate competition from the colonies. A 1699 law forbade export of wool from any colony; colonies could only manufacture woolen goods for consumption within their own borders. A similar prohibition against hat manufacturing was passed in 1732, and the Iron Act of 1750 prohibited further erection of most kinds of mills. However, the law encouraged production of colonial pig iron, which was needed in England.

MANUFACTURING. In the early Republic, the only power-using plants were mills for making flour, lumber, paper, and gunpowder and for grinding plaster. During the next quarter of a century, spinning and weaving mills were introduced; nearly 200 cotton mills were erected. The use of steam to move machinery became common. The growth of manufacturing was encouraged by a rapidly expanding market protected by tariffs and held together by canals and steam transportation on land and water. Inventors designed textile machinery that enabled inexperienced operatives to make plain fabrics cheaply and efficiently. Other manufactures included hats, footwear, axes and nails, plowshares, hoes, pressed glass and porcelain, plated met-alware, lamps, and numerous minor conveniences once considered luxuries. At the same time, growing demands led to the establishment of shops and foundries to build such large-scale products as steamboat machinery and locomotives and machine tools. Most manufacturing was concentrated in the North, and that was largely responsible for the North's victory in the Civil War. The end of that war inaugurated a period of high protection during which new branches of manufacture were brought to the US from Europe. The introduction of the Bessemer steelmaking process, the opening of new mines, the growth of inland industrial cities, and a great influx of immigrants turned the nation's energy increasingly to manufacturing. New inventions and scientific discoveries multiplied. The electrical industry arose when the incandescent lamp and alternating current changed illumination and power distribution and substituted electric power for shaft and belt transmission in large plants. Petroleum appeared at the opportune moment to provide lubricants for millions of machine-age bearings and subsequently suggested the development of internal combustion engines, which made oil an indispensable source of power. By 1890, the US had surpassed its nearest rivals, England and Germany, and was the leading industrial nation. The 20th c. brought unprecedented research and development of new processes and products, beginning with the automobile. Plastics such as celluloid film led to the motion picture industry and photography in general. Synthetic fibers, beginning with rayon, revolutionized the textile industry. Telecommunications progressed from the telegraph to the telephone to radio and television. Electrical appliances for the home began in earnest in the 1920s and proliferated after World War II. World War II aided research in aircraft and scientific instruments, and that research led to sophisticated manufactures in the postwar world. Electronics in particular introduced a whole new world of manufactured products. Outwardly, the most striking change in US industry between 1945 and the 1980s was its relocation. The movement was away from the Northeast and Middle West to the South and West. Florida, Texas, and California in particular became major manufacturing centers. By the 1980s, however, foreign competiton, especially from Japan, was becoming a major threat to many areas of American manufacturing, especially steel production, small electrical appliances, and automobiles.

MANUFACTURING, HOUSEHOLD. Through the 19th c., most articles of home consumption were made by members of the family. Wool cards, flax hatchels, spinning wheels, hand looms, and dye tubs were in almost every home. Later, the sewing machine was equally ubiquitous. Maple sugar, cheese, cider, soap, candles, shoes, harness, furniture, woodenware, plows, harrows, tools, and nails wre commonly homemade. But the output of local factories, blacksmith shops, and workshops increasingly displayed household products and the total value of family-made goods began a steady decline.

MANUMISSION. The formal liberation of a slave by means of an instrument of writing, such as a will or a deed of manumission, as prescribed by state law. Manumission was advocated by moderate antislavery groups in opposition to the extreme abolitionist program for immediate, unconditional emancipation. Personal considerations, such as religion or belief in natural rights, influenced the slaveowners to free their slaves.

MAPLE SUGAR. In the late 17th c., the English settlers took up the Indian practice of boiling down maple sap into syrup and sugar, usually in bark troughs. Maple sugar quickly became an article both of food and commerce. In the 19th c., less expensive cane sugar began to replace it. Production now confined to the New England states, on a small scale.

MAPPING OF AMERICAN COASTS. In 1500 Juan de la Coas compiled a large map of the world incorporating the known Spanish, Portuguese, and English discoveries in America. Only four maps are known to have been actually printed between 1492 and 1510. The earliest, by Giovanni Contarini (1506) was closely followed in 1507 by a globe and large wall map by Martin Waldseemüller. The text accompanying his globe suggested for the first time that the New World be called America. The fourth map, printed by Johann Ruysch, appeared in 1508. Oronce Fine, whose map appeared in 1531, assumed that America was attached to Asia. After the circumnavigation of the globe and several expeditions in the Pacific, the western coast of America began to take shape. It was first drawn on a map in 1529; but there was no other good map of the coast until 1544, when a master chart, maintained under the supervison of the Casa de Contraction, was supposed to have added to it all new discoveries as soon as they were made. The first authentic map of the coast of California, undated, but based on the Cortes discoveries of 1535, was followed by a map of the same region by Alonso de Santa Cruz (1542–45). In 1538, Gerhardus Mercator separated America from Asia and rejected the Asiatic names commonly used for the New World. With the publication of Mercator's large-scale chart of the world in 1569, the science of cartography came into its own, and mariners were able to navigate with a degree of certainty. In the 17th c., maps of the Atlantic coast made the first attempts to lay down the latitudes and longitudes of the region. In the 18th c., a survey of the Atlantic coast was sponsored by the British; those charts, published as they were completed, were eventually issued as *The Atlantic Neptune* (1774–81). Surveys of the Pacific coast were climaxed by the works of Alexander von Humboldt and Aimé Bonpland. In the 19th c., the mapping of the US was completed by the Coast Survey (later the Coast and Geodetic Survey.) (See also CARTOGRAPHY).

MARAIS DES CYGNES MASSACRE (May 19, 1858). An incident of the Kansas Border War. Charles A. Hamilton, a proslavery settler, arrested and shot eleven free-staters in a ravine near the Marais des Cygnes R. Five survived.

MARBURY V. MADISON, 1 Cranch 137 (1803). The US Supreme Court declared that the court would rule unconstitutional and void acts of Congress in conflict with the Constitution. By this decision, the doctrine of judicial review was firmly established and the judiciary was strengthened in the balance of powers among the legislative, executive, and judicial branches of the national government. The opinion, written by Chief Justice John Marshall, was a highly technical one involving the right of the court to issue writs of mandamus.

MARCH TO THE SEA, SHERMAN'S. See SHERMAN'S MARCH TO THE SEA.

MARCY'S EXPLORING EXPEDITION (1852). Capt. R.B. Marcy, under orders from the War Department, led an expedition to explore the Red R to its source. His 1853 report disclosed that there were two main branches of the river. The valuable lands between them were the object of litigation between the US and Texas in 1896. Marcy also brought back much valuable scientific information.

MARDI GRAS. An elaborate series of street pageants and indoor festivities held in New Orleans on Shrove Tuesday, the day before Lent.

MARE CLAUSUM. In international law, the principle of the "closed sea" as against *mare liberum,* or "open sea." The United States has been traditionally in favor of the free sea; though in 1866, it asserted the principle of *mare clausum* in trying to protect its sealing rights in Alaskan waters. But America had to surrender the principle; it had invoked the principle of *mare liberum* too often.

MARIA MONK CONTROVERSY. In 1836 a book claiming to be the autobiography of a nun named Maria Monk was published in New York. Written actually by a group of Protestant clergymen, its stress on priestly immorality aroused a storm of anti-Catholic feeling.

MARIANA. Territory in Massachusetts between the Salem and Merrimack rivers from the sea to their heads and including Cape Ann. Originally granted in 1622 to John Mason, but neither he nor his heirs could make good their title. In 1629, it was incorporated into the Massachusetts Bay Colony.

MARIETTA. First settlement (1788) in the Ohio country, where the Muskingum R empties into the Ohio.

MARIN, EXPEDITION OF (1753). Moving by water from Montreal, Paul Marin established French authority in W Pennsylvania by occupying Presque Isle (now Erie, Pa.), Fort LeBoeuf, and Venango. The expedition alarmed the Indians and precipitated British-American resistance.

MARINE BIOLOGICAL LABORATORY AT WOODS HOLE. Established 1888 at Woods Hole, Mass. The federal government is the laboratory's largest single supporter. Important research is done in cytology, genetics, developmental biology, nerve conduction, invertebrate zoology, marine botany, general physiology, and embryology. Woods Hole is also the site of the US Fish Commission's laboratories and the Woods Hole Oceanographic Institution.

MARINE CORPS, UNITED STATES. Founded 1775 by the Continental Congress but disbanded after the Revolutionary War. Reinstated in 1798, the marines fought in virtually all sea actions during the Naval War with France (1798–1800) and in the Barbary Wars (1801–15), which included the famous march "to the shores of Tripoli." The marines saw limited action in the War of 1812; and the next three decades saw operations in the Caribbean, the Falkland Islands (1832), and Sumatra (1831–32), and patrolling off West Africa to suppress the slave trade (after 1820). Marines were heavily involved in the Mexican War, landing at Veracruz and accompanying Gen. Winfield Scott on his march to Mexico City; they helped storm Chapultepec, and in the West marine squadrons were repeatedly used in the conquest of California. In the Civil War, most service was with the navy, overshadowed by the larger scope and drama of the land campaigns. From 1865 to 1898, there were some thirty-two marine landings in foreign countries, especially Latin America. In the Spanish-American War, a marine battalion seized Guantánamo Bay and accepted the Spanish surrender of Guam. A marine regiment fought in the Philippine Insurrection (1899–1904); marines were also part of the relief column sent to Peking in the Boxer Rebellion (1900). In World War I, marines fought throughout France. After the war, there was large-scale involvement in Nicaragua (1926–33) and China (1926–41). In World War II, marine action was mostly in the Pacific. Marines were involved in the defense of Pearl Harbor, the Philippines, and Guam, Wake, and Midway islands. Beginning with Guadalcanal (August 1942), marine divisions or corps made numerous amphibious assaults. In the Korean War, marines executed the assault at Inchon and subsequent capture of Seoul (September 1950). At the time of the Chinese invasion, the marines were near the Chosin Reservoir in NE Korea and fought their way back to Hungnam. Two years of trench warfare followed. Marine involvement in Vietnam began in 1954; ground forces and helicopter units were involved there throughout the war. A brigade-size force was landed in Lebanon in July 1958; in 1983, another detachment was part of a multinational force aimed at keeping the peace in Lebanon. After suffering more than two hundred deaths from terrorist attacks, they were removed by President Reagan in 1984.

MARION, FORT. Spanish-built fort at St. Augustine, Fla. (1756). Named after Gen. Francis Marion after US acquired Florida in 1819.

MARIPOSA LAND GRANT. A large tract of land, roughly equivalent to modern Mariposa County, Calif.; first given to the Mexican governor and was purchased by John C. Frémont in 1847, even though there were grave questions as to its validity. Frémont's claim was eventually confirmed by the US Supreme Court, and the discovery of gold on the land made him rich. He lost the property, however, and died in poverty. It was said that $20 million in gold was taken from it in 1872.

MARITIME COMMISSION, FEDERAL. Independent regulatory agency, established 1961 to protect the interests of the public by regulating waterborne shipping in foreign and domestic offshore commerce of the US.

"MARK TWAIN." On the old Mississippi R steamboats, the leadmen called the soundings, thus "quarter twain," indicating 2 1/4 fathoms; "mark twain," indicating 2 fathoms, or 12 feet. It was made famous as the pen name of Samuel L. Clemens.

MARQUE AND REPRISAL, LETTERS OF. The Constitution gives Congress power to "grant Letters of Marque and Reprisal, and make Rules concerning Captures on Land and Water." Marques and reprisals were papers from a belligerent government authorizing privateers to engage in warfare against enemy ships. During the American Revolution, such letters were issued both by the Continental Congress and by state governments to 1,150 vessels. In the War of 1812, privateers numbering 515 captured about 1,450 prizes. It was practiced only briefly by the South during the Civil War. Since then, the destruction of enemy commerce has been limited to government-owned vessels.

MARSHALL CONVENTION. A gathering of the governors of Texas, Louisiana, Mississippi, and Arkansas at Marshall, Tex., in May 1865. Called to obtain more favorable terms of surrender to the Union, it was not successful.

MARSHALL ISLANDS. A group of coral atolls and reefs located 2,000 miles SW of Hawaii. They became a Japanese mandate after World War I. They were strategically important in World War II, and US efforts to take them focused on Japanese headquarters on Kwajalein atoll. Taken in February 1944. The capture of Eniwetok atoll followed. In 1947, the Marshalls became part of the US Trust Territory of the Pacific.

MARSHALL PLAN. Formally the European Recovery Program (1948–52), named for Secretary of State George C. Marshall, who proposed it. It was designed to revive the European economy by massive US financial and technical aid. Amounted to $12 billion in aid (plus $1.5 billion for assistance on credit terms). The combined gross national products of the seventeen European nations who participated in the plan rose 25 percent, or 15 percent over prewar levels.

MARTHA'S VINEYARD. Island off the SW coast of Cape Cod, Mass. Discovered 1602 by Bartholomew Gosnold, and granted to Thomas Mayhew, who founded Edgartown in 1642. Formerly an important whaling center, it is now a well-known summer resort.

MARTIAL LAW. President George Washington used martial law when he dispatched troops to quell the WHISKEY REBELLION in 1794. Thereafter, martial law was rarely invoked. Andrew Jackson declared martial law in New Orleans in the face of imminent British attack in 1814. It was declared in Indiana in 1864 in the face of Copperhead threats; that led to the important Supreme Court decision in *Ex parte Milligan* (1866) protecting civilians from being arbitrarily tried by military authorities when civil courts are still functioning. Martial law has been invoked to stop a race riot (Detroit, 1943) and to preserve the peace during the civil rights confrontations of the 1960s.

MARTIN-TOLLIVER FEUD (1884–87). Family vendetta in Morehead, Ky. Twenty-three men had died when, on June 22, 1887, the Tolliver leaders were all killed.

MARYLAND. The Proprietary Province of Maryland was granted in 1632 by Charles I to George Calvert, Lord Baltimore, a recent convert to Roman Catholicism. The first settlement was established in 1634 at St. Marys City. Although a Catholic colony, after the Anglican Church was established there in 1689 Catholics could not practice their religion openly. The colony's economy was based on tobacco, and its plantation system was based on slavery. Although there were divided loyalties at the time of the Revolution, Maryland declared its independence by the adoption of the first state constitution in November 1776. After the Revolution, Maryland ceded the land that became the District of Columbia. During the War of 1812, Maryland's troops defended Baltimore with the siege of Fort McHenry (1814) and at the Battle of North Point. During the Civil War, S Maryland and the Eastern Shore favored the Confederacy, but a quick takeover of the state by federal troops preserved Maryland for the Union. Marylanders fought on both sides. The major battles of Antietam (or Sharpsburg) and South Mountain (or Boonesboro) were fought on Maryland soil. After the war, Maryland converted to a commercial and industrial economy. The Chesapeake and Ohio Canal and the Baltimore and Ohio, the nation's first railroad, connected Chesapeake Bay with the Middle West. After 1865, Baltimore became a center of banking and the steel and copper industries. Its port in 1979 was the eighth largest US port in tonnage. Commercial fishing is an important industry. Pop.: 4,216,000 (1980).

MASON, FORT. Established 1851 in Mason County, Tex., as a frontier protection against the Comanche and Kiowa. There were also forts by that name in Missouri and Pennsylvania.

MASON-DIXON LINE. The Pennsylvania border with Delaware, Maryland, and West Virginia; best known as the symbolic border between North and South. Surveyed 1760–1763 by two English surveyors, Charles Mason and Jeremiah Dixon.

MASSAC, FORT. Built by the French in 1757 in Illinois Country. Originally named Fort Ascension, it was renamed in 1758. In 1794, the US army erected a new fort on the site. It was where George Rogers Clark landed at the outset of his Illinois campaign.

MASSACHUSETTS. Bartholomew Gosnold landed on Cape Cod in 1602 and Martin Pring at Plymouth in 1603. Samuel de Champlain mapped Massachusetts harbors in 1605–06; and in 1614 Adriaen Block and John Smith charted Cape Cod and Massachusetts Bay. In 1620, the first settlement was made at Plymouth by English Pilgrims. Competitive English merchants built trading bases at Weymouth, Wollaston, and Gloucester; plantations were formed at Medford, Charlestown, Boston, Salem, and Gloucester. In 1629, a group of wealthy Puritan merchants secured a royal charter for the Massachusetts Bay Co., and in 1629 and 1630 the first ships reached Boston. By 1640, there were 18,000 Bay Co. planters occupying thirty towns, compared to Plymouth Plantation's nine towns with 3,000 people. Theocratic intolerance exiled from the Bay Co. to neighboring colonies the harshly persecuted Quakers, Baptists, and other dissenters. After the Restoration in 1660, a royal commission was dispatched to New England (1664). Its clashes with local authorities led to the annulment of the Bay Co. in 1684. Massachusetts was placed under the Dominion of New England, but after the Glorious Revolution, King William abolished the Dominion and joined Plymouth, Maine, and the Massachusetts Bay Colony. Peaceful years followed, and new settlements were founded in W Massachusetts. Shipbuilding, overseas commerce, and waterpower industries developed a wealthy, moderate merchant leadership that replaced the theocrats. Boston became America's leading seaport. Quarrels with England became more serious; imperial taxes such as the Stamp Act (1765) brought merchants, small landholders, and debtors into boycotts, riots, and attacks on tax collectors. The Committees of Correspondence and the Sons of Liberty were so effective that the Stamp Act was repealed; but the English initiated the Townshend Acts (1768).

Massachusetts groups petitioned other colonies to oppose what they called an English usurpation of power. Anti-English activities increased, culminating in an armed clash (April 19, 1775) between the Minutemen and three British companies at Concord Bridge. Thus began the American Revolution. The British evacuated Boston on March 17, 1776. Postwar depression hit Massachusetts especially hard. England closed its ports to Yankee ships and poured European goods into American harbors. Inflation bankrupted farmers and shopkeepers and landed them in debtors' prisons; this produced the abortive SHAYS'S REBELLION. Many pioneer families moved westward. But with the opening of the China trade in 1784, the economy improved. Profits built shipyards in every river mouth. When the War of 1812 was declared, Massachusetts Federalists repudiated it as "Mr. Madison's War" and occasionally collaborated with the enemy. After the war, the textile industry burgeoned in Fall River, New Bedford, and Lowell. Industrial cities were founded all over the state, their personnel formed by the 50,000 Irish immigrants who flooded the state after the potato famine of 1846. Massachusetts was a great center of abolitionist sentiment; and during the Civil War, Massachusetts sent 146,00 men to fight for the Union. After the war, Massachusetts prospered. The movement of the textile industry to the South left many industrial cities in a depressed state. By 1940 only diversified industries using skilled labor could survive; these included electronics, machinery, metal fabrication, paper specialties, chemicals, tools, and airplane engines. Service industries, notably finance and insurance, thrived. In the 1980s, the state's activities included nuclear physics, chromatography, lasers, solar energy, and computers. Massachusetts's population increased slightly between 1970 and 1980 (to 5,737,037), but most of its cities lost population.

MASSACHUSETTS, FORT (Colorado). Built 1852 in the San Luis Valley to protect settlers on the Upper Rio Grande against the Ute. In 1858, the post was moved six miles south and the name changed to Fort Garland.

MASSACHUSETTS, FORT (Massachusetts). Built 1744 in Williamstown, one of the three Province Forts for the protection of the Deerfield Valley. In 1746, it was attacked by a party of French and Indians and destroyed; it was rebuilt in 1747.

MASSACHUSETTS BAY COMPANY. The royal charter of 1629 confirmed to a group of Puritan merchants power to trade and colonize New England between the Merrimack and Charles rivers. The group was given the right to limit the franchise to members of the church. Dissent within the theocracy resulted in the exile of the groups that founded Connecticut and Rhode Island. The company remained neutral during the Puritan Revolution in England but suffered with the Restoration. It opposed the new colonial policies, especially the Navigation Acts. The company's charter was withdrawn in 1684.

MASSACHUSETTS BODY OF LIBERTIES (1641). Code of law promulgated by the Massachusetts general court and submitted to the towns; it was to be in force for three years and, if found satisfactory, made perpetual. Based on the common law, it left much authority to the magistrates. It was replaced in 1648.

MASSACHUSETTS CIRCULAR LETTER. On Feb. 11, 1768, the Massachusetts House of Representatives, opposing the Townshend Acts, petitioned George III and drafted a letter describing the petition to the other colonial legislatures. This step toward colonial unity was punished by dissolution of the general court on July 1, 1768.

MASSACHUSETTS GOVERNMENT ACT. Also called the Regulating Act, second of the COERCION ACTS, was passed by Parliament in 1774 with the intention of quelling disturbances created by the tea tax. Transferred executive power from the colonists to the crown. Crystallized public opinion in favor of an armed revolt, if need be, to safeguard the liberties of the colony.

MASS PRODUCTION. A system of production based on interchangeable parts and characterized by the moving-belt assembly line. When Henry Ford applied the moving-belt principle to the manufacture of the Model T automobile in 1903, the increase in productivity was immediate and spectacular. The increase resulted partially from the more minute division of labor and automatic materials handling; in addition, a good part of the increase in productivity came simply from forcing workers to work faster. Mass production has been almost invariably accompanied by integration, that is, control by one company of every stage of the productive process from raw materials to the marketing of the finished product. Modern management was revolutionized at the turn of the century by Frederick W. Taylor; he used the stopwatch to analyze and measure work and developed such innovations as routing, cost accounting, and the organization of management along functional lines. Since World War II, systems analysis and computer technology have become dominant.

MASS TRANSPORTATION. Mass transportation systems developed along with the growth of cities. The earliest systems involved horse-drawn street cars. Generally, it was found that cars could run more smoothly on rails than over regular street pavements. Some street railways were extended beyond the city limits, employed regular locomotives, and became links in major railroad systems. Trolley cars employed electric engines that drew current from overhead wires. In heavily populated cities, the tracks were often either elevated above the streets or lowered into tunnels or open cuts. The gasoline engines made bus service possible, and trolley systems were generally dismantled, as were some elevated trains. Although formerly privately owned, virtually all mass transit systems are now publicly owned and often heavily subsidized. The US Department of Transportation has a major responsibility in assisting local governments in planning and developing new systems of mass transportation.

MATAMOROS EXPEDITION (1836). During the Texas Revolution, the provisional government vacillated over launching an expedition to seize Matamoros. The Mexicans seized the advantage and destroyed the troops assembled for the raid.

MATANZAS, FORT. Built in St. Augustine, Florida, by the Spanish in 1743 as a defense against the British.

MATILDA LAWRENCE CASE (1836). Matilda Lawrence, a slave, left a steamboat at Cincinnati and later claimed her freedom on the ground that her master had brought her to free soil. The local court remanded her to slavery.

MAUMEE INDIAN CONVENTION. Conference held in 1793 by the confederated Indian tribes of the Northwest Territory (Delaware, Wyandot, Miami, and Shawnee). Encouraged by the British, they demanded that the US give up all of the Northwest Territory. As a result, the US army carried out its final campagn against these tribes.

MAUREPAS, FORT. Erected by the French in 1699 on the Bay of Biloxi. It was the seat of the first French colony in Louisiana. Destroyed by fire in 1719.

MAURY'S CHARTS. Beginning in 1847, Matthew Maury, in charge of the Depot of Charts and Instruments of the Navy Department, published charts of the world's oceans. To explain the charts, he published what eventually became a comprehensive work, *Sailing Directions*.

MAUVILLA, BATTLE OF (October 1540). Between the Spanish forces of Hernando de Soto and those of the Indian chief Tuscaluza, near the present site of Montgomery, Ala. Mauvilla, a fortified Indian town, was burned and Tuscaluza committed suicide. De Soto was seriously wounded.

MAVERICK. An unbranded animal, especially cattle roaming loose with no apparent owner; named for S.A. Maverick, a Texas rancher. Mavericking, that is, rounding them up and claiming them, became an occupation that at times bordered on thievery.

MAXENT, LACLEDE AND COMPANY. A firm established in New Orleans in 1762 to trade with Indians W of the Mississippi R. The company established a post at St. Louis , and its operations ranged as far N as the St. Peters R. (Minnesota).

MAXIM GUN. Invented by H. S. Maxim in 1884; it was the first automatic, quick-firing gun.

MAXWELL LAND GRANT. In N New Mexico and Colorado, made in 1841 by the Mexican government to Guadalupe Miranda and Carlos Beaubien. In 1860, Congress confirmed the title to Beaubien's son-in-law, Lucien Maxwell. He eventually acquired 1,714,765 acres.

MAYFLOWER. Three-masted merchant ship that was chartered in 1620 to take the Pilgrims to America. They left Plymouth harbor on September 16 with 102 passengers and crew. They sighted Cape Cod on November 19 and reached the site of Plymouth, Massachusetts, on December 21. The *Mayflower* remained until houses could be built for the new settlement. It sailed for England on April 5, 1621. After 1624, its history is uncertain.

MAYFLOWER COMPACT. An agreement signed on Nov. 11, 1620, by the male passengers on the *Mayflower*, before coming ashore, that they would submit to the will of the majority in whatever regulations of government were agreed upon. The Pilgrims had no patent to settle in New England, and some of the passengers had threatened to strike out for Virginia. The compact established a local government that could maintain order until a patent could be obtained. The government was, in effect, a theocracy.

MAYO FOUNDATION. Nonprofit corporation that runs the Mayo Clinic in Rochester, Minn.; incorporated 1919 by Dr. William J. Mayo and his brother, Dr. Charles H. Mayo. The foundation conducts the Mayo Graduate School of Medicine, the Mayo Medical School, and a broad program of medical rsearch.

MAZZEI LETTER (1796). A letter from Thomas Jefferson to an Italian friend, Philip Mazzei, in which he attacked the Federalists and, by extension, George Washington. Precipitated permanent break between Washington and Jefferson.

MEAT-PACKING. Commercial meat-packing came into existence ca. 1818 in Cincinnati, followed soon by plants in Chicago, Louisville, and St. Louis. During the Civil War, Chicago reached front rank but had competition from Kansas City, Omaha, Sioux City, and St. Paul. By the 1870s, such giant Chicago meat-packing companies as Armour, Swift, and Libby, McNeill and Libby dominated the industry nationally. Meat-canning got a considerable boost during the Civil War, and after 1868, Armour and others developed a canned corned beef and roast beef trade. Other companies packed ox and pork tongues and potted meats, chicken, rabbits, hams, and soups. A European market was created, and the demand for canned corned beef became so great in the US that it affected the sale of fresh cuts. Considerable quantities of meat were still smoked in the US in 1900, especially such pork cuts as ham, bacon, and shoulder. The introduction of efficient railroad refrigerator cars ca. 1880 made possible the transportation of fresh meat from as far west as Omaha to New York City without spoilage.

MECHANICS' INSTITUTES. Along with lyceums and apprentices' libraries, mechanics' institutes emphasized self-improvement through education. A New York institute was founded in 1822, and others quickly followed. Their mission was to provide low-cost technical education to the poor. By mid-century, however, evening lectures tended increasingly to be patronized by the middle classes; by that time, technical education was being more generally carried out in formal classroom situations. In time, some of the mechanics' institutes merged with temperance societies or lyceums or disappeared for lack of purpose.

MECHANICSVILLE, BATTLE OF (June 26, 1862). Sometimes called the Battle of Beaver Dam Creek. The Union force was entrenched behind Beaver Dam Creek, E of Mechanicsville, Va., when it was attacked by Confederate forces under A.P. Hill and James Longstreet. The Rebels were repulsed.

MECKLENBURG DECLARATION OF INDEPENDENCE. Document purportedly adopted by the citizens of Mecklenburg County, North Carolina on May 20, 1775, in which they declared themselves independent of England. Most historians agree that the declaration is spurious.

MECKLENBURG RESOLVES. On May 31, 1775, a committee of safety meeting at Charlotte, Mecklenburg County, North Carolina, drew up as set of resolves that suspended all British governmental agencies in the county. It provided for nine militia companies to be held in readiness but stopped short of declaring independence.

MEDICAL EDUCATION. Of the 3,500 physicians in the colonies in 1776, no more than 400 had medical degrees, principally from schools in Edinburgh, London, and Leiden. The College of Philadelphia established a medical school in 1765 and King's College (now Columbia University), in 1767. By 1800, only ten colleges had instituted any kind of medical instruction. The two-year curriculum typically included courses in anatomy, materia medica, chemistry, and theory and practice of physic; practical clinical lectures, and one year attending the practice at a hospital. Then, after three or more years of experience and preparing and defending a thesis in Latin, a candidate was eligible for the M.D. degree (after 1792, the M.B. degree was abolished). Between 1820 and 1850, state legislatures chartered proprietary medical schools, made up of independent self-appointed professors. Although there was virtually no control over such schools, their standards were not uniformly low; but the pressures of competition and the absence of detached governing boards forced standards downward. The American Medical Association was formed in 1847 to improve medical education. Little was accomplished until after the Civil War, when a renaissance in medical education began. It was largely brought about by returning scholars from European, especially German, medical schools. Progress was slow; by 1900, only about 15 percent of 25,000 matriculates in medical schools held a baccalaureate degree, and many students entered medical school with less than a high school diploma. Most influential was the opening of Johns Hopkins Hospital (1889) and Johns Hopkins Medical School (1893), both patterned after the German system. Major reforms set in after 1910, after the Flexner Report called public attention to the existence of numerous diploma-mill schools and the large number of mediocre institutions. Medical schools were classified as either A, B, or C schools, and most states refused to certify graduates of C schools. More than half of US medical schools closed. By 1929 the classification system was dropped as no longer required. Basic training constituted two years of preprofessional college education, a four-year graded curriculum, and an approved internship. Medical schools maintained a substantial full-time clinical faculty and residency teaching program. Postwar medical education was aided by government grants and subsidies through the National Institutes of Health and other federal agencies. Also important were the vast resources of the nation's private foundations.

MEDICAL RESEARCH. Important early examples of medical research are the work of W.W. Gerhard on the distinction between typhoid and typhus (1837) and Oliver Wendell Holmes on the contagiousness of puerperal fever (1843); the experimental studies of gastric function by William Beaumont (1833); the introduction of ether anesthesia (1846) through the work of T.G. Morton and Horace Wells; and the clinical experiments of J.M. Sims leading to the discovery of a technique for the repair of vesicovaginal fistula (1852). Early medical laboratories include the ones opened by H.P. Bowditch in 1871; by the New York City Health Department in 1893, and by the medical department at Johns Hopkins in 1905. Progressive medical schools and hospitals opened pathological, bacteriological, and clinical laboratories. In 1906, John D. Rockefeller opened the Rockefeller Institute for Medical Research (now Rockefeller University); its research activities set the standards for the new century. Medical schools, both private and state, established research arms both independent of and closely tied with their teaching programs. During and after World War II, the federal government emerged as the major source of support of medical research, especially through the research arm of the US Public Health Service, the National Institutes of Health, and the various agencies of the Department of Health and Human Services.

MEDICAL SECTS. The 19th c. produced a wide spectrum of unorthodox systems of medicine, including botanical practitioners, homeopaths, hydropaths, and osteopaths. Samuel Thomason used sweat-producing, emetic, and purgative herbs as well as steam baths and enemas in treating all diseases. He attracted a wide following. Homeopathics based their system on the belief that drugs would cure if they caused the same symptoms as the disease being treated. By 1900 there were twenty-two homeopathic schools; but only a few practitioners were still active in the 1980s. Water was employed in cure treatments, and hydropathic colleges, societies, and journals were established. Water-cure establishments appeared throughout the country, and thousands of patients "took the cure." Osteopathy was based on the belief that diseases result from malalignment of bones, especially those of the spine. By 1910, there were twelve schools of osteopathy, and doctors of osteopathy were eventually licensed in all states. The requirement for education and practice are similar to those of orthodox medicine.

MEDICARE. National program of health insurance for the aged, enacted 1965, as part of President Lyndon B. Johnson's GREAT SOCIETY program. Finances much of the cost of hospital and nursing-home care for persons over sixty-five years of age through the SOCIAL SECURITY SYSTEM. Also provides voluntary reduced-cost insurance covering doctors' bills.

MEDICINE AND SURGERY. When the US came into being, MEDICAL EDUCATION was rudimentary. Malaria, scurvy, dysentery, and respiratory diseases were prevalent in New England, the South, and the West. Tuberculosis was, throughout most of the 19th c., the leading cause of death. Against repeated outbreaks of cholera and yellow fever, physicians were no more effective, but epidemics did spur sanitary improvements. In the early 19th c., during the heyday of heroic medicine, vigorous dosing with drugs, bleeding with the lancet and by leeches, and use of calomel or castor oil to induce copious diarrhea, were preferred; such measures, believed to redistribute the maldistributed basic humors of the body, added further insult to the patient already weakened by fever. Some effective drugs were administered, including cinchona, opium, and digitalis. By the 1830s, important discoveries were being made: typhus and typhoid were differentiated, the physiological aspects of digestion had been discovered, and, in 1846, ether anesthesia was employed with immediate acclaim. American scientific medicine came into its own in the 1890s and grew in importance in the 20th c. Discoveries were made in the leading centers of research, at medical schools, or at privately endowed institutes, the most famous being Rockefeller University. Practitioners have become increasingly specialized; hospitals and their use have increased. By 1973, there were more than 7,000 hospitals with 1.65 million beds. Along with changing patterns of medical care have come changing patterns of disease and a slowly rising life expectancy (see LIFE EXPECTANCY). By the late 20th c., heart disease, cancer, stroke, and accidents accounted for the majority of deaths. The age distribution of the population had changed; the elderly and the very young came to constitute larger percentages, with implications for medical care, because it is these two groups that require it the most.

MEDICINE CREEK COUNCIL (October 1867). Between the US government and the Kiowa, Comanche, and Apache tribes and parts of the Arapaho and Cheyenne, on Medicine Creek, in South Dakota. The Indians ceded large tracts of land and accepted removal to new reservations.

MEDICINE SHOW. Beginning ca. 1830, self-styled physicians, botanists, and showmen began selling patent, cure-all medicines through traveling shows that featured blackface comedians, songs, and jokes, while they hawked their product.

MEEKER MASSACRE (1879). Ute uprising at White River, Colo., against the arbitrary rule of the US Indian agent N. S. Meeker. A cavalry detachment sent to aid the beleagured agency was ambushed, with ten men killed. Other Ute attacked the agency, killing Meeker and seven others. The agency was eventually relieved.

MEIGS, FORT. Built 1813 by Gen. William Henry Harrison on the Maumee R opposite the present town of Maumee, Ohio. From April 28 to May 9, 1813, unsuccessfully besieged by a force of British, Canadians, and Indians.

MELLON INSTITUTE OF INDUSTRIAL RESEARCH. See CARNEGIE-MELLON UNIVERSITY.

MELTING POT THEORY. Term used to express one theory of the development of American society. Suggests the culture is a mixture of elements drawn from the different immigrant groups, and the native Indians where they survived, and that these different groups have fused together into a new culture.

MELUNGEONS. Part-Indian people who have long lived in a remote mountain section of Hancock County, Tenn.

MEMORIAL DAY. Celebrated on the last Monday in May; began 1868 as Decoration Day (then observed on May 30), originally to decorate the graves of Union soldiers killed in the Civil War. It has since become the day on which the US honors the dead of all its wars.

MEMPHIS. City in SW Tennessee on the E bank of the Mississippi R, on the lowest of the Chickasaw Bluffs. The Chickasaw fixed it as the place where they crossed the Mississippi. Fort Assumption was built 1739 on the bluff by the French and used for the campaign against the Chickasaw. In 1795, the Spanish erected a fort, which stood for two years. The town was laid out in 1819. Rail and river transportation aided rapid development as a cotton center; in Union hands throughout the Civil War. Pop.: 646,356 (1980).

MEMPHIS, NAVAL BATTLE AT (June 6, 1862). Confrontation between a Union flotilla and the Confederate river defense fleet for control of the Mississippi R. The Union fleet broke through the Rebel ships; Memphis immediately surrendered.

MEMPHIS AND CHARLESTON RAILROAD. Begun at Charleston in 1829, by 1845 its western terminus was Atlanta; completed to Memphis in 1857, thereby breaking the monopoly of New Orleans on the lucrative export trade of the Mississippi Valley.

MENÉNDEZ EXPEDITION IN FLORIDA AND GEORGIA. Between 1565 and 1615 Pedro Menéndez de Avilés, with a large Spanish force, drove the French out of Florida and Georgia, and established more than twenty missions, including ones at St. Augustine, Tampa, and as far N as South Carolina.

MENNONITES. Descendants of an Anabaptist group based on the teachings of Menno Simons. The first Mennonite settlers came to the New World (to Pennsylvania) in 1683; later became known as the Pennsylvania Dutch. Generally pacifists, they maintain a high de-gree of community discipline. The Amish, a conservative body of Mennonites, are particularly notable because they maintain strict customs of dress and advocate separation from the world. In 1978, there were 97,142 Mennonites.

MENOMINEE IRON RANGE. Situated mainly in the Menominee Valley in Michigan and Wisconsin. Mining dates from the 1870s.

MENTAL HYGIENE MOVEMENT. Dates from the publication in 1908 of *A Mind That Found Itself* by C.W. Beers, after which various state societies were set up; they conducted educational campaigns and recommended reforms in mental illness treatment and did much to popularize psychiatry.

MERCANTILE AGENCIES. Established after the panic of 1837 to supply credit information to would-be lenders. The two best known merged 1933, forming Dun and Bradstreet, Inc.

MERCANTILISM. Economic theory in which a country regulated trade, production, and manufacture. England chiefly regarded the colonies as producers of raw materials and markets for its goods. Colonial manufacture for an export trade that competed with its own was discouraged by legislation. On the other hand, colonial production of articles needed within the empire was encouraged; bounties were paid to promote their colonial production. Both sides profited from this policy; there was little opposition to the system among colonial Americans, so long as measures were purely regulatory and did not levy taxes on them. The system was specifically approved by the First Continental Congress in the Declaration of Rights of 1774.

MERCER, FORT, ENGAGEMENTS AT (Oct. 22 and Nov 20, 1777). British Gen. William Howe dispatched Hessian troops against a smaller colonial force at Fort Mercer, Red Bank, N.J.; they were repulsed but attacked a month later with greater numbers. The fort was then dismantled.

MERCHANT MARINE. The New England colonies began began trading with the West Indies upon formation; lumber and fish were traded for sugar, molasses, and rum.

England's NAVIGATION ACTS benefited the colonies; by 1700 Boston ranked third (after London and Bristol) among all English ports in the tonnage of its shipping. The Revolution brought a short-lived dislocation of trade. The long Napoleonic Wars, starting in 1793, put a premium on the neutral status of American-flag shipping, which could visit ports where the British or French belligerent flags could not. American registered tonnage tripled from 1790 to 1810, as did combined exports and imports, about 90 percent of which was carried in American bottoms. After the War of 1812, the US merchant marine experienced the rapid changeover to steam navigation. New York became the principal port. The ability of steamboats to ascend the Mississippi R and its tributaries quickly revolutionized and promoted traffic on western waters. Permanent transatlantic steam navigation dates from 1838; and by the 1840s, immigration, Britain's repeal of its corn and navigation acts, and the discovery of gold in California combined to bring the American merchant marine to its golden age. By the 1850s, it almost equaled Britain's shipping in tonnage. Trade suffered during the Civil War from naval raiders and blockading. Due to high insurance rates during the war, many American square riggers were transferred to foreign registry. From 1860 to 1910 the share of US imports and exports carried in American bottoms shrank from 66 percent to 8 percent. World War I made the US aware of the importance of shipping flying its own flag. An ambitious shipbuilding program was instituted; by 1921, the US had overtaken Great Britain for first place among the world's merchant fleets, with some 700 new large steel freighters and 575 smaller ones. The Great Depression again threatened US shipping. Congress passed in 1936 the Merchant Marine Act, setting up the Federal Maritime Commission and establishing a system of operating subsidies for lines sailing in "essential trade routes." During World War II, the subsidized merchant marine fully demonstrated its high value; the federal government embarked on a tremendous emergency building program, which produced 5,777 vessels. Foreign services on the essential trade routes were fairly successful after the war; domestic shipping fell off sharply in the coastal and intercoastal trades, because of competition from railroads, trucks, and eventually, air express.

Congress revised the Merchant Marine Act in 1970, with little long-term effect. Jet airplanes had virtually driven out regular ocean passenger service. Containerization, with truck bodies, railroad freight cars, and other preloaded containers carried aboard ships were efforts to cut labor costs. Oil tankers increased more than tenfold in size, special ships were developed for natural gas, and bulk carriers were developed to carry iron and other ore.

MERCHANTMEN, ARMED. In the colonial and post-Revolutionary periods, shipping interests armed their merchant vessels against piracy and privateering. In 1856, privateering was abolished, and this, combined with less piracy, made arming virtually obsolete. During wartime, some merchant vessels have been armed, but in general they have been protected by armed convoys.

MEREDITH CRISIS (Sept. 30–Oct. 10, 1962). James Meredith, a black student, was admitted to the University of Mississippi under federal court order. Attempts to prevent him from enrolling, led by the governor, resulted in a riot in which two were killed and federal troops, along with the national guard, were called up by President Kennedy.

MERIDIAN CAMPAIGN (February 1864). Union Gen. W. T. Sherman proceeded from Vicksburg, Miss., to Meridian, for the purpose of destroying Confederate supply depots and railroads. Confederate Gen. N. B. Forrest cut off his cavalry support; he was forced to return to Vicksburg.

MERRILL'S MARAUDERS. A 3,000-man, all-volunteer unit in World War II, so-called after its commander, Gen. F. D. Merrill. Assigned 1943 to retake N Burma and reopen the BURMA ROAD. Made an extremely costly five-month, 500-mile trek to take the crucial town of Myitkyina. Its siege left 123 Marauders dead.

MERRIMAC, SINKING OF (June 3, 1898). In the Spanish-American War, the US navy, in an effort to block the harbor of Santiago, Cuba, sank the collier *Merrimac* across its entrance. The project failed; the eight-man crew was taken captive.

MERRIMACK. See MONITOR AND MERRIMACK, BATTLE OF.

MERRYMAN, EX PARTE (1861). Supreme Court decision in which Chief Justice Roger B. Taney, writing for the majority, ruled that the writ of habeas corpus could be suspended constitutionally only by Congress, not by the president.

MERRY MOUNT. Also known as Mount Wollaston; site of an Indian trading post established 1625 in Quincy, Mass. Its proprietor, Thomas Morton, was several times arrested and put out of business by the Puritans for providing liquor to the Indians. His humorous book, *New English Canaan*, made fun of the New Englanders.

MESABI IRON RANGE. In NE Minnesota; contained the richest deposit of iron ore in the US when it was discovered in the 1890s. Since then, more than 2.5 billion tons of ore have been removed. By the 1960s, the richest of the hematite ore had been mined, but large deposits of taconite remained.

MESA VERDE, PREHISTORIC RUINS OF. In Colorado; the most extensive and best preserved of pre-Columbian cliff dwellings and temples, made of stone, clay, and supporting poles. Predecessors of the present Pueblo, cliff dwellers flourished in the 11th and 12th c. It is supposed that they were forced to abandon the mesa canyons by a severe drought in 1276.

MESILLA. Unincorporated town in New Mexico, originally on the W side of the Rio Grande but since 1865, because of a change in the river's channel, on the E side. In 1861–65, the capital of the Confederate territory of Arizona.

MESQUITE. Small tree of the dry Southwest; produces a bean valuable as cattle food and from which the Indians make brew and bread. Trunks are used for fence posts and limbs and roots for fuel.

MESSIAH WAR (1890–91). Outgrowth of the GHOST DANCE excitement among the Sioux Indians; culminated in the Battle of Wounded Knee, the only important battle of the war. (See also WOUNDED KNEE, BATTLE OF.)

METHODISTS. Protestant sect founded ca. 1738 by John Wesley in England, brought to America in 1771 by Francis Asbury. After 1784, completely separated from the Church of England, or Protestant Episcopal Church. Methodism grew rapidly in America; the system of circuit riders met the need for clergymen in outlying regions and allowed relatively uneducated men to enter the ministry. The combination of simplicity, discipline, organization, and lay participation soon made it the largest Protestant denomination. The church split into groups over the slavery issue, many of which were reunited in 1968 as the United Methodist church, with almost 10 million members.

MEUSE-ARGONNE OFFENSIVE (Sept. 26–Nov. 11, 1918). Culminating campaign of World War I; in the Argonne forest and the marshes of the Meuse R in France. The American army attacked and destroyed German defenses, which were four lines ten miles deep. During the offensive, the US commander, Gen. J. J. Pershing, deployed twenty-one divisions, comprising some 1.2 million men, of whom one-tenth were casualties in capturing 48,800 prisoners and 1,424 guns.

MEXICAN BOUNDARY. Provided by the Adams-Onís Treaty of 1819; not finally settled until the Gadsden Treaty of 1853. The boundary runs from the Gulf of Mexico up the Rio Grande to the S boundary of New Mexico. The line W from the Rio Grande runs from 31°47′ north latitude due W one hundred miles then S to 31°20′ north latitude, and from there along that parallel to 111° west longitude, then going in a straight line to a point on the Colorado R twenty English miles below the junction of the Gila and Colorado, and, finally, up the middle of the Colorado some twenty miles to a point nearly seven miles to the W of the junction of the Gila and Colorado and about ten miles by water below that junction, meeting at that point the boundary from the Colorado to the Pacific. The last boundary dispute between the two countries was settled 1963; it had resulted from a change in course of the Rio Grande. After the settlement, an artificial riverbed was dug to prevent the river from again changing course.

MEXICAN CESSION. See GUADALUPE HIDALGO, TREATY OF.

MEXICAN DECREE (April 6, 1830). Sought to save Texas for Mexico by stopping immigration from the US. Garrisons were sent to Texas to enforce the law, but the Americans already in Texas ignored its provisions and eventually (in 1836) declared themselves independent of Mexico.

MEXICAN GULF PORTS, BLOCKADE OF (1846–48). In the Mexican War. Frontera, Tampico, Veracruz, and Alvarado were taken by the US navy, and thereafter squadrons under the command of Capt. M. C. Perry cruised up and down the Gulf coast of Mexico, blockading the ports.

MEXICAN OIL CONTROVERSY. In 1938, Mexico expropriated US and British oil companies. The US companies were more intransigent than the British; the Mexican president ordered all their concessions expropriated. Although the companies claimed a worth of $500 million, after long negotiations, Mexico paid them $24 million.

MEXICAN WAR (1846–48). Its immediate cause was US annexation of Texas. After the Mexican government had refused to receive a US delegation (sent to negotiate the purchase of New Mexico and California), President Polk ordered Gen. Zachary Taylor to advance to the Texas–Mexican border. Clashes between Mexicans (who crossed the border) and Americans inevitably resulted; Polk sent a message to Congress stating that war existed and that it was begun by Mexico on American soil. Congress authorized a declaration of war. An expedition under Col. S. W. Kearney was dispatched to take New Mexico and California; Taylor occupied the immediate regions to the S of the Rio Grande pending the major invasion of Mexico by sea from Veracruz. The Kearney and Taylor campaigns were successful and in March 1947, Gen. Winfield Scott captured the fortress at Veracruz and began the march to Mexico City. After severe fighting, he captured Mexico City on September 14, and President Santa Anna fled the country. A peace treaty was completed on Feb. 2, 1848, at Guadalupe Hidalgo. By its terms, Mexico ceded all claims to Texas; the US agreed to pay $15 million for New Mexico, Arizona, and California.

MEXICO, CONFEDERATE MIGRATION TO. After the Civil War, an estimated 2,500 Confederate leaders moved to Mexico. Colonies were planted in several provinces and encouraged by the Mexican government, but various economic and political difficulties caused most to fail. Most successful was the Cordova Valley Colony (see CARLOTTA, CONFEDERATE COLONY OF).

MEXICO, FRENCH IN. In 1862, a French army, representing the ambitions of Napoleon III, captured Mexico City. Napoleon chose Ferdinand Maximilian, archduke of Austria, to head a monarchy. The US refused to recognize him, and continued to support Benito Juárez. The US, involved in the Civil War, made protests against French intervention in the New World, and after the war, brought strong pressure on the French. Finally, on March 12, 1867, the French left. The soldiers of Juárez soon captured Maximilian, who was deserted by his Mexican supporters. He was court-martialed and shot on June 19, 1867.

MEXICO, GULF OF. Strategically important since the early Spanish search for a possible water passage through the continental barrier, the Spanish settlement of Cuba, Mexico, and the Gulf Coast of Florida, and the French settlement of Louisiana. Later important primarily as the receiver of traffic from the Mississippi R and trade outlet for the US midlands. Location of vast oil and gas reserves and great supplies of fish and sulfur.

MEXICO, PUNITIVE EXPEDITION INTO (1916–17). In 1916 Pancho Villa, with about 500 men, crossed the border from Mexico and raided Columbus, N.M. Gen. J. J. Pershing was ordered into the state of Chihuahua in N Mexico in retaliation. The Mexican government protested this infringement of its sovereignty; the US protested Mexican inability to control bandits at its border. For a time war seemed imminent, and President Wilson mobilized the national guard. Negotiations proved fruitless, but in 1917, the US withdrew its forces.

MEXICO, RELATIONS WITH. By 1830, some 20,000 Americans had settled in Texas. When Mexico tried to restrict immigration and impose tighter control over Americans already there, the Texans rebelled; they won independence in 1836 and declared themselves a republic. US annexation of Texas in 1845, along with US designs on New Mexico and California led to the MEXICAN WAR. In 1853, the US bought 54,000 square miles of the Mesilla Valley in the GADSDEN PURCHASE. After the Civil War, US protests resulted in end of French occupation begun in 1862 (see MEXICO, FRENCH IN). US–Mexican relations were particularly cordial during the long (1876–1911) dictatorship of Porfirio Díaz, who welcomed foreign capital. US investments in mining, land, and manufacturing rose to more than a billion dollars, earning huge profits but arousing resentment among Mexican liberals. The 1910 revolution produced a generation of conflict between the two countries, culminating in the American occupation of Veracruz in 1914 and the punitive raids (1916–17) against Pancho Villa. In 1917, a new constitution contained severe restrictions on foreign economic activities, thereby arousing new animosities in the US. Major US petroleum holdings were expropriated 1938, but a peaceful solution was arranged (see MEXICAN OIL CONTROVERSY). A Mexican-American general agreement signed 1941 settled most outstanding issues. Mexico joined the war against the Axis in World War II. Afterward, relations between the two countries were mostly cordial, the most persistent problem being Mexico's displeasure over treatment of its migrant laborers in the US.

MIAMI. City in SE Florida, located on Biscayne Bay. Surrounded by several other municipalities that together make up one of the largest resort areas in the nation. Also a commercial and financial center, with a large garment industry. A few Americans settled in the area during the 1870s, planting orange groves; the city did not thrive until the coming of the railroad in 1896. A boom in the early 1920s collapsed, but growth resumed after World War II; today the city has the largest Cuban population in the nation. Miami Beach, a separate city (Pop.: 96,298 in 1980), is located on a long island between Biscayne Bay and the Atlantic Ocean proper, and connected to Miami by causeways. Pop.: 346,931 (1980).

MIAMI, FORT (Indiana). Also called Fort Miamis. Built by the French ca. 1749, at present-day Fort Wayne. Replaced an older fort by the same name. Garrisoned by the British in 1763, who shortly thereafter were forced to evacuate it during Pontiac's uprising.

MIAMI, FORT (Ohio). At the foot of the Maumee rapids, built by the British in 1794. Its position, nearly forty miles within American soil, was protested by George Washington and Thomas Jefferson. Yielded to the US by Jay's Treaty (1796); retaken by the British during the War of 1812.

MIAMI PURCHASE. J. C. Symmes of Morristown, N.J., a member of the Continental Congress, led a group sold title to 1 million acres between the Miami and Little Miami rivers, eventually reduced to about 300,000 acres. First permanent settlement in the area was in 1788 at Columbia, at the mouth of the Little Miami. The second, also 1788, at the mouth of the Licking R, eventually became Cincinnati. Population of the area increased after the Treaty of Greenville (1795).

MIAMI TRAIL. Indian trail, with several branches, running from the valleys of the Miami and Little Miami rivers of SW Ohio to the Cherokee country of the South. Much used in Indian invasions of Kentucky.

MICHIGAN. Claimed by the French in 1671; Detroit founded 1701 as a fur-trading center. Possession passed to the British in 1763; in 1774 attached to Quebec. At the close of the American Revolution, Michigan was ceded to the US, but the British retained jurisdiction until 1796. Then became part of the newly created Northwest Territory; in 1805, Congress created the Michigan Territory, with Detroit its capital. The British briefly occupied the territory during the War of 1812. Completion of the Erie Canal in 1825, and growth of steamer transport on the Great Lakes, assured important water transportation between Detroit and the East. Admitted to the Union in 1837. In the 1840s, vast mineral resources on the upper peninsula were discovered. At the beginning of the 20th c., when industrialization began, agriculture and lumbering were the great sources of the state's wealth. By the 1920s, Detroit was the automotive capital of the nation. The Great Depression was unusually severe in Michigan; but in World War II, Detroit and the other industrial cities became great production centers. The state thrived in the postwar years;

but by the 1980s, the depressed condition of the automobile industry caused high unemployment once again. Pop.: 9,258,344 (1980).

MICHIGAN, LAKE. One of the Great Lakes, discovered by Jean Nicolet in 1634. In the 18th c., a highway for explorers and traders; in the 19th c., American settlers poured into the area and such thriving cities as Milwaukee and Chicago were founded. Now part of the Great Lakes–St. Lawrence Seaway; handles a vast amount of international commerce, particularly in coal, iron ore, limestone, and grain.

MICHIGAN TERRITORIAL ROAD. Laid out 1830; ran from Detroit to the mouth of the St. Joseph R, an important route for immigrants to the lower peninsula of Michigan. A stage line over the road was established 1834.

MIDDLE-OF-THE-ROAD POPULISTS. In the presidential campaign of 1896, those members of the People's (Populist) party who objected to fusion with either of the older parties. Unable to prevent their party from endorsing the Democratic presidential candidate, William Jennings Bryan. (See also POPULIST PARTY.)

MIDDLE PASSAGE. The trip from Africa to the West Indies, the second leg of the triangular voyage of a slave ship (see TRIANGULAR TRADE).

MIDEWIWIN. Also known as Grand Medicine Lodge. Secret society of medicine men (and women) among the CHIPPEWA. Members possessed an extensive pharmacopoeia, practiced bloodletting and simple surgery, and used songs and formulas of exorcism. A principal means of transmitting legends, songs, and religious lore.

MIDNIGHT JUDGES. Judicial appointments made by John Adams just before he was succeeded in the presidency by Thomas Jefferson. Congress legislated most of the judges out of their commissions. (See JUDICIARY ACT OF 1801; MARBURY V. MADISON.)

MIDWAY, BATTLE OF (June 4–6, 1942). Major engagement in the Pacific during World War II; the first important American victory.

The Japanese, determined to take Midway Island, assembled one of the greatest fleets (185 warships) in modern history. The US navy attacked the armada as it steamed toward Midway, destroying in particular all four Japanese aircraft carriers as their planes were refueling on deck. The battle effectively turned the tide of the naval war in the Pacific.

MIDWAY ISLANDS. Located 1,200 miles NW of Honolulu; annexed by the US in 1867. Attacked by the Japanese in World War II.

MIER EXPEDITION. Abortive counterexpedition into Mexico ordered by Texas President Sam Houston in 1842. Only 250 Texas troops crossed into Mexico; they surrendered at Mier on the lower Rio Grande. One-tenth were shot, the others imprisoned.

MIFFLIN, FORT. Originally built as Mud Fort in 1762 on Mud Island, Delaware R, below the mouth of the Schuylkill R. The most important of Philadelphia's defenses, it was besieged by the British in late 1777, and abandoned by the patriots. Rebuilt after the British evacuation of Philadelphia; in use until shortly after World War II.

MIGRANT WORKERS. Agricultural laborers who move from area to area, usually at harvest time. They (and their families, who generally travel with the workers) suffer many problems: economic, health, and educational. In the Southwest, many are illegal aliens from Mexico. Their plight was dramatized in the 1960s by César Chavez, who successfully organized a union of migrant workers.

MILITARY ACADEMY, UNITED STATES. Founded 1794 at West Point, N.Y., as a school for artillerists and engineers; became a true military academy in 1802, although actual training did not begin until after 1812. Greatest period of growth occurred under Maj. Sylvanus Thayer, superintendent from 1817–33, who expanded the curriculum and introduced a new system of order, organization, and discipline. Long the only engineering school in the country; its graduates, working both as civil and military engineers, were largely responsible for planning and building many major canals, roads, and railroads before the Civil War. In that war, West Point graduates dominated the commands on both sides. In World War I, again, the academy's graduates nearly monopolized the higher ranks, furnishing all commanders of armies and above and about 90 percent of those of corps and divisions. Dominance has been less in later wars, but graduates continue to dominate higher army commands. After every war, there have been extensive changes in organization and curriculum to keep abreast of new developments in military art and technology. Women cadets now train alongside men.

MILITARY AID TO THE CIVIL POWERS. The president is empowered to employ federal troops under Article IV, Section 4, of the Constitution and under the "insurrection" statutes, which allow him to make use of troops to maintain the Constitution, to support federal law enforcement, or to protect interstate commerce and federal property. As commander in chief, the president can also employ troops in humane tasks, such as aiding disaster victims. Troops have been used to break strikes, and during the 1950s and 1960s were employed to enforce court-ordered desegregation of schools.

MILITARY LAW. Regulates the military establishment. The Uniform Code of Military Justice, enacted by Congress, is the source of military law. The US Court of Military Appeals is the final appellate tribunal for military cases.

MILITARY POLICY. During its early history, the US maintained a minimum of military forces in peacetime, rapidly expanding them in time of war and just as rapidly demobilizing them at the end of each conflict. America's emergence as a world power after the Spanish-American War brought some modifications: both the army and navy were modernized, and the militia was converted into the national guard. After World War I, in a wave of isolationism, the traditional services were cut back drastically; the new service, airpower, remained ill-defined and controversial. After World War II, the military structure was dismantled as hastily and almost as completely as after earlier wars. But growing tensions with the Soviet Union made clear the necessity for military strength, including maintenance of a nuclear striking force capable of deterring attack on the US or its allies.

In addition, such international agreements as the North Atlantic Treaty Organization (NATO) kept large numbers of American troops on foreign soil. These forces and the expanding technology of modern armaments required a maximum level of expenditure, causing postwar administrations to accept defense budgets representing a large percentage of total federal expenditures.

MILITARY ROADS. See ROADS, MILITARY.

MILITARY TRACTS. Land bounties offered by the states and federal government to attract men into the armies or to reward soldiers for their services. New York, North Carolina, and Virginia were among states that set aside special tracts to satisfy the warrants given to veterans of the Revolutionary War and the War of 1812. The US also created such tracts, the first being in C Ohio, adjacent to the VIRGINIA MILITARY RESERVE IN OHIO; three others were in Missouri, Illinois, and Arkansas. In these, veterans of the War of 1812, who received 160 acres each, were required to locate their warranties by lottery. Most veterans sold their warrants to speculators for prices as low as 10 cents an acre, creating a high percentage of absentee owners; squatters settled on the absentee-owned lands and flouted all efforts to make them pay rent. Local governments frequently leveled discriminatory taxes on absentee-owned land. Thus many speculators were eventually forced to give up their lands to tenants. (See also LAND BOUNTIES.)

MILITARY WARRANTS. See LAND BOUNTIES; MILITARY TRACTS.

MILITIA. Early American colonists faced Indian attack, and survival dictated that every male be both settler and soldier. Out of this tradition grew the militia. Southern colonies made the county the basic militia unit, each supervised by a lieutenant. In other areas, the town was the basic unit. As the American Revolution approached, the patriot faction gained control of the militia, which reinforced the Continental army, provided local security, and harassed British detachments. About 41 percent of the troops employed in the war were members of the militia. In 1792, in an attempt to make the militia the focus of the nation's military policy, Congress passed the Militia Act; it subjected all white, able-bodied male citizens between the ages of eighteen and forty-five to service in the militia. The law was virtually unenforceable, and the militia declined. Militiamen performed poorly in the War of 1812 and had no part in the Mexican War. During the Civil War, volunteer units performed the function of a militia. After the Civil War, they generally adopted the name national guard. In 1903, Congress in the Dick Act in effect transformed the NATIONAL GUARD into a militia; in 1933 the guard was given the status of a reserve component of the army. In 1956, the regular army took over the basic training of all guardsmen, although when not on active federal service they remain under state control.

MILLERITES. See ADVENTIST CHURCHES.

MILLER-TYDINGS ENABLING ACT (1937). Amendment to the Sherman Antitrust Act that permitted manufacturers to force retailers to sell trademarked merchandise at a price determined by the manufacturer. (See FAIR TRADE LAWS.)

MILLIGAN, EX PARTE, 4 Wallace 2 (1866). Supreme Court decision that held that neither the president nor Congress has the power to set up military tribunals except in the actual theater of war, where civil courts are not functioning. Regarded as a setback to the military governments established by the Radical Republican Congress in the former Confederate states.

"MILLIONS FOR DEFENSE, BUT NOT ONE CENT FOR TRIBUTE." Slogan of those who opposed appeasing France (1798) in negotiations to end that country's hostile actions against US shipping.

MILL STREAMS. When dams and short canals with locks began to be built in the late 18th and early 19th c., the fall of the water at the locks was often employed to operate mills and factories. Such important industrial centers as Manchester, N.H., Woonsocket and Pawtucket, R.I., and Paterson, N.J., were built around mill streams.

MILWAUKEE. Largest city in Wisconsin, located on Lake Michigan; settled 1835. Attracted many immigrants, especially Germans, who opened breweries, which rapidly

became a major industry. A leading port, manufacturing center, and grain market. Pop.: 636,212 (1980).

MIMS, FORT, MASSACRE AT (Aug. 30, 1813). Attack by about 1,000 Creek on the stockade on Lake Tensaw, near Mobile, Ala. Families in the vicinity had taken refuge in the unprotected stockade. All but 36 of the fort's 553 inhabitants were massacred.

MINA EXPEDITION (1817). Attempt to liberate Mexico by Francisco X. Mina, a Spanish exile in the US. Landed at Soto la Marina, Tamaulipas, in April 1817, and marched into the interior. Captured by the Spanish and executed on Nov. 11, 1817.

MINERALOGY. The main development of mineralogy and geology took place in the 19th c. The leading figure was Benjamin Silliman, professor of chemistry and natural science at Yale after 1802. His students in particular were important in the development of the geological sciences. In the mid-19th c., courses in analytical chemistry were introduced into many colleges and medical schools. The publications of the US Geological Survey, organized 1879, and of the state geological surveys carried much descriptive mineralogical and petrographic material. Numerous professional societies were founded, including the Mineralogical Society of America in 1919. (See also GEOLOGICAL SURVEY, UNITED STATES; GEOLOGICAL SURVEYS, STATE.)

MINERAL PATENT LAW. The mining laws of 1866, 1870, and 1872 adopted the idea of open mineral exploitation of public lands. A claimant who discovered a mineral lode or a placer (surface deposit) could secure a patent from the US on the lands covered by his claim. Locations based on discovery of a lode were limited to 1,500 feet by 600 feet, and placer claims to 20 acres. Under a 1920 law, rights of exploration and production of oil and gas came to be leased, not patented, with royalty paid to the US as landowner. Coal mining on public lands is also on a lease arrangement.

MINES, US BUREAU OF. Established 1910 to alleviate working conditions in coal mines, which accounted for 2,000 deaths per year. A division of the Department of the Interior;

primarily a research and fact-finding agency. Its goals are to ensure that the nation has adequate mineral supplies for security and other needs and to develop the technology necessary for the extraction, processing, use, and recycling of mineral resources at a reasonable cost without harm to the environment or the workers involved.

MINESWEEPING. After World War I, during which the US and Britain laid the immense North Sea barrage of some 56,000 mines, 230 miles long and from 15 to 35 miles wide, minesweepers spent months clearing mines, with no assurance that all of them had been removed. An estimated 500,000 mines were laid during World War II. In European waters alone, after the war ended, more than 1,900 minesweepers spent two years clearing mines. US minesweepers cleared some 17,000 square miles of Japanese waters. The North Koreans laid mines off the Korean coasts during the Korean War; the US air force mined the Haiphong harbor during the Vietnam War. Both areas were swept after the end of hostilities.

MINGO BOTTOM. Region of Ohio about three miles S of Steubenville, named for the Mingo Indians. In 1782, the rendezvous for the frontiersmen under Col. David Williamson who marched to Gnadenhutten and massacred nearly 100 Christian Indians.

MINIMUM-WAGE LEGISLATION. After 1900, several states passed minimum-wage laws. Some repealed their laws, and beginning 1923, the Supreme Court ruled such laws unconstitutional, violating both the Fifth and Fourteenth amendments. New state laws were passed in the 1930s; in 1938 the court ruled them constitutional. In 1938 Congress passed the FAIR LABOR STANDARDS ACT, amended several times since and covering those involved in interstate commerce. By the 1980s, it had been made applicable to a large majority of the nation's work force. Originally aimed at establishing a 40 cents per hour minimum wage, by 1982 the minimum wage was $3.40.

MINING CAMP, LAW OF THE. Extralegal code in the early western mining camps where the US had not yet established civil government. When miners found a promising spot, they quickly formed a mining district, defined its boundaries, passed laws regulating the filing and working of claims, and elected officers, including a sheriff who preserved order. This born-of-necessity law was partially recognized by the US in the MINERAL PATENT LAW of 1866.

MINISINK PATENT. Granted 1704 by the royal governor to Stephen De Lancey and associates. A vast tract in Orange and Sullivan counties, New York, bounded on the south by Pennsylvania.

MINNEAPOLIS. Largest city in Minnesota, located at the joining of the Minnesota and Mississippi rivers. One of the Twin Cities, the other being St. Paul. The army built Fort Snell on the present-day site in 1819; it was the first army post established W of the Mississippi. Chartered 1856, the city grew rapidly, using waterpower to operate sawmills and flour mills. Precision-tool making is a major industry. Pop.: 370,951 (1980).

MINNESOTA. Occupies the Lake Superior highlands, a portion of the prairie plains, and the upper limits of the Mississippi Valley. More than 11,000 lakes are the state's most distinctive feature. Occupied mostly by Sioux when white men arrived in the 17th c. In 1679, the Sieur Duluth claimed possession for Louis XIV; Minnesota passed to Spain when France ceded its area W of the Mississippi. By the time of the War of 1812, the North West Co., a British firm, was in practical control of the area, with at least twenty-four posts. After the War of 1812, the Sioux accepted the sovereignty of the US. In 1819, Fort Snelling (Minneapolis) was established, and became the center of a fur-trading region; in 1849 Congress created the Minnesota Territory. Further treaties with the Indians opened vast areas to settlement. In 1858, Minnesota was admitted to the Union. War with the Sioux continued intermittently until after the Civil War. Then, great waves of immigration began: the largest group was German, followed by Scandinavians. By the 1880s, wheat and dairy products led the state's economy. Discovery of great deposits, particularly the MESABI IRON RANGE in 1891, made Minnesota the primary US source of iron ore. Lumbering, flour milling, and livestock remained important. After 1900, Minnesota became an urban, industrial commonwealth. Electronics, adhesives, and abrasives added to its industrial growth. Pop.: 4,094,000 (1981).

MINNESOTA MORATORIUM CASE or *Home Building and Loan Association v. Blaisdell et al.,* 290 US 398 (1934). Minnesota passed a law forbidding foreclosures on mortgages (in order to relieve property owners during the Great Depression). The act was upheld by the Supreme Court.

MINORITY RIGHTS. American history has been characterized by an almost constant struggle to protect minority rights against encroachments. In 1798, for example, the Alien and Sedition Acts imposed restrictions on freedom of speech and the press, and were vigorously opposed. As the 19th c. progressed, increasing social and economic complexities, expanded government regulatory power, and several wars posed new problems and dramatized old ones. Attempts by workers to form unions were restricted; only in the 1930s were these restrictions somewhat abated. Political minorities were jailed during World War I and investigated by constitutionally and morally questionable methods in the 1920s and 1950s; often kept off ballots by state statutes; and punished for allegedly conspiring to organize the Communist party and to teach and advocate the overthrow of the government. During World War II, without trial and solely on the grounds of race, the US government forced thousands of Japanese-Americans to leave their homes and reside in camps. Blacks were long relegated to racially segregated schools, housing, and public facilities. The *Brown v. Board of Education of Topeka, Kansas* case (1954) and the great civil rights acts of the 1960s did much to secure the rights of racial minorities in the nation; and court decisions, legislation, and executive orders since then have tended to buttress the rights of various minorities, including the poor, elderly, handicapped, prisoners, homosexuals, and Indians. The rights of women are often classified with those of minorities, although women, in fact, represent a majority of the population.

MINOR V. HAPPERSETT, 21 Wallace 162 (1875). Supreme Court ruled that the Fourteenth Amendment did not give women the constitutional right to vote; held that suffrage is not coextensive with citizenship.

MINSTREL SHOWS. Popular form of entertainment of the 19th and early 20th c. By 1857, shows had settled into a standard pattern of white performers impersonating blacks. There were dances, comic sketches, and acrobatic turns. Died out ca. 1930.

MINT, FEDERAL. Established 1793 in Philadelphia. Over the years, Congress has established various branches: New Orleans; Charlotte, N.C.; Dahlonega, Ga.; San Francisco; Denver; and Carson City, Nev. Today, there are two mints, Philadelphia and Denver, and two assay offices, San Francisco and New York City.

MINTS, PRIVATE. Frequently appeared in new gold-producing areas when there was a scarcity of US minted coins. Their coins, of original design, circulated freely. Existed at various times in California, Oregon, Utah, and Colorado. With establishment of the US mint in San Francisco in 1854, the need for private mints disappeared.

MINUTEMEN. Popular name for the Massachusetts militia at the time of the American Revolution. Other states (Maryland, New Hampshire, Connecticut) also called their militia minutemen. The famous Massachusetts militia developed when reorganized 1774 to rid it of Tories; members were ready for any emergency "at a minute's notice." Fought the British at Concord and Lexington and were part of WASHINGTON'S EIGHT MONTHS ARMY.

MIRANDA'S INTRIGUES. Francisco Miranda, an exiled Venezuelan in the US after 1783, tried to interest the government in liberating the Spanish Indies. President John Adams opposed the scheme. Miranda made two attempts (1805 and 1806) to liberate Venezuela but his force was repulsed by the Spanish. He was captured and imprisoned by the Spanish in 1812.

MIRANDA V. ARIZONA, 384 US 436 (1966). Supreme Court case in which it ruled that the prosecution may not use statements obtained by "custodial interrogation" (questioning initiated by officers after a person has been taken into custody) unless the person has been warned prior to any questioning that he or she has a right to remain silent and a right to the presence of an attorney. The case was both praised as a civil liberties landmark and bitterly criticized for unduly restricting law enforcement. Reading the "Miranda rights" to a prisoner has become standard practice for arresting officers.

MIRO, FORT. Spanish post established on the Ouachita R in 1785, on the site of present-day Monroe, La. First called Ouachita Post; renamed Monroe in 1819.

MISCEGENATION. The first statutes against interracial marriage were enacted in Maryland (1661) and Virginia (1691). Other states followed suit. As late as 1950, some thirty states still had such laws on their books. In 1967, in *Loving v. Virginia*, the Supreme Court unanimously ruled such laws unconstitutional.

MISSILES, MILITARY. World War II saw development of missilery by the major participants: the US handheld bazooka antitank weapon; the artillerylike Soviet Katyusha and US naval barrage rocket; a variety of antiaircraft missiles for air and ground forces; the innovative German V-1 pulse-jet buzz bomb; and the German supersonic, liquid-fuel V-2 ballistic missile with a 200-mile range, launched by the hundreds against London and Antwerp. After the war, both East and West began developing intercontinental ballistic missiles (ICBMs) and 1,500-mile intermediate-range ballistic missiles (IRBMs). The first-generation of US ICBMs (Atlas and Titan 1) and IRBMs (Jupiter, Thor, and nuclear-powered submarine-carried Polaris A1) were quickly followed by subsequent generations. Soviet missiles followed a similar pattern. Second-generation ICBMs in the mid-1960s included a solid-propellant and silo-sited Minuteman 1 and 2. In the third generation, the Minuteman 3 with MIRV (multiple, independently targeted reentry vehicle) warheads and the submarine-based Polaris A3 (2,500-mile range) were developed. They were followed by the Poseidon (2,500-mile-range MIRV warhead, for an advanced Trident submarine). By 1979, the US had 1,700 missiles. Development of a new MX missile (land-based mobile missile) began in the early

1980s; these weapons would be supposedly secure from attack. (See also STRATEGIC ARMS LIMITATION TALKS.).

MISSIONARY RIDGE, BATTLE OF (Nov. 25, 1863). Union victory near Knoxville, Tenn. The Confederate force, under Gen. Braxton Bragg, was stationed at the foot of Missionary Ridge and at its crest. Union Gen. G. H. Sherman took the foot of the ridge, then drove the disorganized Rebels from the hilltop. Bragg could only withdraw to Chickamauga Station and Dalton. A week later he relinquished command of the Army of the Tennessee.

MISSIONARY SOCIETIES, HOME. Voluntary associations, usually under denominational control, for the advancement of religion in needy parts of the US. Presbyterian, Baptist, and Congregational churches began such activities as early as the 18th c.; revived interest in evangelical religion in the 19th c. saw establishment of many local societies. Their chief aim was to maintain churches on the western frontier; later, attention was paid to the foreign-born in cities, and to blacks. During the 1930s, many missionary societies were transformed into social agencies, deemphasizing church programs and intensifying efforts to increase the immigrant's social and economic well-being.

MISSION INDIANS OF CALIFORNIA. Between 1769 and 1823, a chain of twenty-one Franciscan missions was established in California by Father Junípero Serra. The Indians living nearby were forcibly Christianized by the Spaniards and taught agriculture and trades. Soon they came to be known by the names of the missions at which they lived. In 1833, the missions were closed for lack of funds. The Indians, much reduced in numbers due to epidemics, were turned out to shift for themselves; for years they drifted around in misery on the margins of the expanding white settlements. Between 1870 and 1907, small parcels of land were purchased for these Indians by the government. Principal surviving groups in southern California are the Diegueño and the Cahuilla.

MISSIONS, FOREIGN. American Protestant churches began trying ca. 1810 to convert the non-Christian world through missionary societies. The American Bible Society undertook the translation of the Bible into virtually every language of the world. Foreign mission activities were particularly notable between 1850 and 1930. Unrest in mission lands, opposition from foreign cultures and religions, and a reappraisal by the churches of the gospel in relation to non-Christian faiths have caused a cutback in foreign missions, although many continue to be active.

MISSIONS, SOUTHWEST. The Spanish mission was meant to be temporary; after training Indians for citizenship and economic self-dependence, the mission regime was to give way to civil and parochial administration. Along with the mission went the presidio, or military guard. During the 1570s, the Franciscans established missions among the Pueblo in Arizona and New Mexico; later missions were established in Texas and California. By 1630, there were twenty-five, with a Christian population of some 60,000. In 1680, the thirty-three New Mexico missions and the three in Arizona were destroyed in the great PUEBLO REVOLT. With reconquest at the end of the 17th c., the missions were restored. They declined during the 18th c. and, by the 19th c., were practically nonexistent.

MISSISSINEWA, BATTLE OF (1812). Gen. William Henry Harrison captured and burned the villages of the Miami, in the service of the British, along the Mississinewa R.

MISSISSIPPI. Prior to European exploration, the region was inhabited by the Chickasaw, Choctaw, Natchez, Biloxi, Tunica, and Pascagoula Indians. The sieur de La Salle claimed the region for the French in 1682. Biloxi was founded in 1699, but the region fell to the British after 1763 and to the US after the American Revolution. The Mississippi Territory was created in 1798; to it was later added Tennessee and part of Florida. In 1817, Mississippi (minus Tennessee and Florida) was admitted to the Union. Indian cessions opened it to white settlement; speculation drove land and slave prices to unrealistic levels. The panic of 1837 caused severe depression and repudiation of state bonds and drove many residents to seek refuge and fortune in Texas. During the 1840s, Mississippi developed a one-crop (cotton) economy, and by 1860 the slave population was larger than the white population. Mississippi was the second

state to secede and provided the Confederacy with its president, Jefferson Davis. During the war, more than 100 battles and skirmishes took place within the state, the most important being the Battle of Vicksburg. Mississippi experienced a decade of strife under Reconstruction, but by 1875 the prewar power elite (known as the Redeemers, later Bourbons), capitalizing on racial prejudice and hatred of Reconstruction, managed to restore itself to power. Their power was almost complete until the 1890s, when small farmers and laborers achieved a degree of political strength with the adoption of a new constitution. Blacks remained disenfranchised until the mid-1950s; schools were desegregated in the late 1950s. Large-scale black voter registration in the 1960s changed Mississippi politics profoundly. After the mid-1950s came the shift from a one-crop cotton economy to a diversified agricultural and industrial system. The percentage of the labor force employed in agriculture dropped from 43 percent in 1950 to 7.3 percent in 1970. Pop.: 2,520,638 (1980).

MISSISSIPPIAN CULTURES. The prehistoric Mississippian cultures dominated the lower and middle Mississippi Valley from ca. AD 700 to the historic period. Settlements ranged from small villages to Cahokia, Illinois, with an estimated population of 30,000. Its economic base was the intense cultivation of corn, beans, and squash. Society was characterized by centralized political organization, social stratification, and a highly developed religious cult.

MISSISSIPPI BUBBLE (1720). John Law, a Scot, organized the Mississippi Co. in 1718 to assume control of Louisiana. Speculation in company stock drove up prices without any sound basis in tangible assets. In 1720 the company failed and the stockholders lost their entire investment. Law's connection with the venture ceased, but the company retained control of Louisiana until 1731.

MISSISSIPPI COMPANY OF VIRGINIA. Organized 1763 by a group that included George Washington to procure a large tract of land at the junction of the Ohio and Mississippi rivers. The American Revolution terminated the hopes of the company.

MISSISSIPPI RIVER. The greatest of the North American rivers and one of the world's busiest commercial waterways. It has two main lateral branches, the Ohio R to the east and the Missouri R to the west. The length of the river is 2,348 miles, and the waters of the system pass through two Canadian provinces and thirty-one states into the Gulf of Mexico. Hernando de Soto discovered it for the Europeans in 1541, but major exploration began in 1673, when Louis Jolliet and Jacques Marquette proceeded down the river from the Wisconsin R to the Arkansas. In 1682 the sieur de La Salle explored the river from the Illinois R to its mouth and claimed its valley for France and named it Louisiana. In 1699 the French established themselves first at Biloxi, then at Mobile Bay, and finally (in 1718) they founded New Orleans. Thereafter, for half a century, the Mississippi was used and controlled by the French. When France lost its New World possessions in 1763, the Mississippi became an international boundary. According to the Definitive Treaty of Peace of 1783, the United States was to extend to the Mississippi between Spanish Florida and Canada, and Americans were to have free navigation of the river. The Spanish, who controlled the mouth of the river, were not party to the treaty and imposed duties regarded as prohibitive by Americans in the Ohio Valley. In 1800, however, Spain ceded Louisiana back to the French, who promptly (1803) sold it to the United States. Thereafter, the Mississippi R served as the great artery of trade and commerce for the whole midcontinent. By 1860, more than 1,000 steamships were plying the river. Its vital importance was recognized by both sides in the Civil War, and the struggle for its control was one of the principal aspects of the war (see MISSISSIPPI RIVER, OPENING OF THE). After the war, the railroads diminished its importance and commercial traffic dwindled. In 1879, Congress established the Mississippi River Commission to supervise maintenance and improvement of the river, chiefly by deepening and widening its channels and creating flood-control mechanisms. In 1970, traffic on the river was 230 million tons annually.

MISSISSIPPI RIVER, NAVIGATION ON. Indian craft used on the Mississippi were the bull boat, or coracle, made of buffalo hide stretched on a frame, and the pirogue, or dugout canoe. The French introduced the bateau, a large flat-bottomed skiff propelled by oars, and the barge, which was propelled by sails, oars, or cordelle. The Spanish patrolled the river by a fleet of galleys, probably large barges or small ships. The Americans introduced the flatboat, or ark, which handled much of the downstream transportation until the advent of steam. (The flatboat was dismantled and sold as timber at the end of the voyage.) The keelboat was another American adaptation; it was a long, narrow craft built on ribs and keel and propelled by setting poles or cordelle. The first Mississippi steamboat was the *Orleans* or *New Orleans*, built at Pittsburgh; it entered the Natchez–New Orleans trade in 1811. Steamboats multiplied rapidly after 1820; this necessitated improvements, including dredging of sandbars and clearing channels. By 1840, steamboat traffic had reached its zenith, but railroads soon began sapping trade from the steamboats. The navigation of the river remains important to carry bulky freight (petroleum, coal, steel) much of it on barges.

MISSISSIPPI RIVER, OPENING OF THE. The strategic importance of the Mississippi R was recognized by both sides in the Civil War, and the Union set a high priority on controlling it, thereby splitting the Confederacy in half. Union forces captured New Orleans (May 1, 1862) and other points as far up as Baton Rouge. The Confederates strongly fortified the high bluffs at Port Hudson, twenty-five miles above Baton Rouge, and at Vicksburg, 200 miles to the north. After a siege of nearly two months, Vicksburg surrendered on July 4, 1863. When the news reached Port Hudson, that post also surrendered since it was no longer of value to the Confederates. This completed Union control of the river.

MISSOURI. Settlement began in the present state of Missouri ca. 1735, with the establishment of Ste. Genevieve, a few cabins across from the mouth of the Kaskaskia R. St. Louis was founded in 1764. The French villages and fur traders became pawns of European politics: France handed over all of Louisiana to Spain in 1762, and during Spanish rule, settlements were made at St. Charles (1769), Carondelet (1767), New Bourbon (1793), Cape Girardeau (1793). In 1780, the British and Indians mounted an unsuccessful attack on St. Louis. After the American Revolution, American settlers poured into Missouri, creating new threats to Spanish control. American hegemony was established in 1803 with the Louisiana Purchase. In the early 19th c., a mass of immigrants, mostly from the South, crowded into Missouri, many bringing slaves. The Missouri Territory was established in 1812, but its admittance as a state was delayed over the bitter quarrel over the slavery issue. The MISSOURI COMPROMISE finally settled the issue, and Missouri entered the Union as a slave state in 1821. Economically, the state thrived. St. Louis was the gateway to the West, the fur trade continued to prosper, and corn and wheat raising dominated the state's agriculture. The struggle over slavery persisted, however. During the 1850s, Missouri again became divided over the slavery issue. In 1861, Missouri had three elections, but each time the moderates, who were for peace and compromise, won overwhelmingly. The Union armies threw out the pro-Confederate state government in 1861, and thereafter in the Civil War, Union strength prevailed. Nevertheless, the state suffered from guerrilla warfare for four years; more than 400 skirmishes were fought before the end of the war. The state prospered after the war, particularly as a rail hub. Farming was productive, and manufacturing supported the immigrant labor that began to flow into the state, largely from Germany and Ireland. Growth continued as the cattle and wheat of the Great Plains flowed into Missouri cities, particularly St. Louis and Kansas City, to be converted into beef and flour. In the 20th c., economic development was marked by increasing farm mechanization and expanding industrial production. Pop.: 4,917,444 (1980).

MISSOURI, THREE FORKS OF THE. A picturesque and strategically important spot in Montana, so named because three principal source streams of the Missouri R unite there: the Jefferson, the Madison, and the Gallatin. Lewis and Clark camped at the junction in 1805.

MISSOURI COMPROMISE (1820–21). First effort of the US Congress to deal with the extension of slavery into new areas. In 1819, there was an equal number of slave and free states, and when Missouri petitioned for statehood, the House of Representatives passed an amendment to the statehood bill prohibiting further introduction of slaves into Missouri and providing that all children born of slaves to be freed at the age of twenty-five. The Senate rejected the House amendment. A compromise was reached: Missouri was to be admitted as a slave state and Maine as a free state. Slavery was to be prohibited in the remainder of the Louisiana Purchase N of 36° 30'. Missouri's efforts to exclude free blacks and mulattoes from the state caused a second compromise to be effected in 1821. The Missouri Compromise was repealed in 1854 by the KANSAS-NEBRASKA ACT.

MISSOURI-KANSAS-TEXAS RAILROAD. See RAILROADS: SKETCHES OF PRINCIPAL LINES.

MISSOURI PACIFIC RAILROAD. See RAILROADS: SKETCHES OF PRINCIPAL LINES.

MISSOURI RIVER. A major tributary of the Mississippi R and the longest river in the US (2,466 miles). It is formed in Montana by the junction of the Jefferson, Gallatin, and Madison rivers. It winds through one of the most fertile valleys in the world, to its junction with the Mississippi (ten miles N of St. Louis). The lower Missouri was known to French traders by 1705, and in 1720 a Spanish caravan was sent from Santa Fe to the Missouri to drive back the French. The Missouri was first explored from its mouth to its source by Lewis and Clark in 1804–05. It became the great highway to the West; the first steamboat ever to ascend the river was the *Independence* in 1819. Steamboating on the river reached its peak in the late 1850s and declined following the completion in 1859 of the Hannibal and St. Joseph RR. Over the years, the Missouri has seen a number of flood-control, irrigation, and navigation improvement programs. By the 1970s, there were seven dams on the Missouri.

MISSOURI RIVER FUR TRADE. In the early days of the West, the Missouri R and its tributaries constituted one of the great sources of furs. Forts, posts, and houses were scattered along the Missouri in the wilderness long before the tide of immigration set in. After some earlier penetrations by the French, Cedar Post was established in 1800 in the Sioux country, thirty-five miles below the present site of Pierre, S.D. The most important early post,

Fort Lisa, was that of the St. Louis Missouri Fur Co.; it was located in Nebraska, near Council Bluffs, Iowa. The most important of the American Fur Co. forts was Fort Union, in present-day North Dakota. St. Louis was the center of the fur trade. In 1853, there were 150 fur trading posts.

MITCHELL'S MAP (1755). Published in London under the auspices of the Board of Trade by John Mitchell, a Virginian. His map went through numerous revisions before 1792 and figured in nearly every boundary dispute involving the US or parts thereof. On it were laid down the first boundaries of the US following the Treaty of Paris (1783).

MIWOK. Californian Indians spread through the central river valley and to the north of San Francisco Bay.

MIXED COMMISSIONS. Instruments of international law composed of members of differnt nationalities for the purpose of achieving the peaceful settlement of disputes. Jay's Treaty of 1794 set up a mixed claims commission to settle damages, debts, boundary disputes, and other matters. Among later ones were the Mexican Commission (1868), which disposed of over 2,000 claims; and the US-German Mixed Claims Commission created after World War I to settle war damage claims. Since World War II, nearly 200 commissions of conciliation have been established to settle international disputes.

MOBILE. City in SW Alabama, located on Mobile Bay. In 1702, the sieur de Bienville established a fort nearby, but flooding forced removal to the present site in 1711. It passed to the British in 1763 and to Spain during the American Revolution. The Americans took it in the War of 1812. During the Civil War, Mobile was one of the most important Confederate ports, strongly fortified and much used by blockade runners until the Battle of Mobile Bay (Aug. 5, 1864) closed it. After the war, Mobile burgeoned as a major port, exporting lumber, cotton, and naval stores. It is also a shipbuilding center. Pop.: 200,452 (1980).

MOBILE ACT (1804). After the Louisiana Purchase, Spain contended that it owned all territory on the Gulf of Mexico E of the Mississippi R. Congress, at President Jefferson's insistence, passed the Mobile Act, which claimed that area for the US. The region (eastward from the Mississippi to the Perdido R, and bordering on the Gulf, but not including Mobile) was not actually occupied until 1810 (see WEST FLORIDA, ANNEXATION OF).

MOBILE BAY, BATTLE OF (Aug. 5, 1864). A Union fleet, commanded by Adm. D. G. Farragut, forced an entrance into Mobile Bay through a narrow, highly fortified passage. "Damn the torpedoes!" cried Farragut, as his *Hartford* took the lead. His vessels eventually reached the bay, despite the heroic fight put up by the Confederate ironclad *Tennessee*.

MOCCASIN. Most Indian tribes wore footwear called moccasins, often decorated with beads and quills. The eastern moccasin had a soft sole and was made by folding a piece of soft tanned skin up over the foot. The Plains Indians preferred a moccasin with a hard sole. Moccasins were adopted by the whites and were universally worn by early trappers.

MODEL CITIES PROGRAM. Slum rehabilitation, part of President Lyndon B. Johnson's Great Society program. Sixty-three model cities were chosen to draw up urban renewal plans that were to emphasize slum rehabilitation rather than clearance. The program was mostly dismantled by the Nixon administration.

MODOC WAR (1872–73). Last of the Indian wars in N California and S Oregon. The Modoc had been removed in 1864 to the Klamath reservation in Oregon, a move that angered their more aggressive elements. A young chief, Captain Jack (Kintpuash) led a group back to their former habitat near the Lost R in California. Although they included only 75 warriors (accompanied by 150 women and children), it took more than 1,000 US cavalrymen to dislodge them. Captain Jack and three others were captured and hanged; the rest of the band was exiled to Indian Territory.

MOGOLLON. Also called the Western Pueblo; a prehistoric culture developed in S New Mexico and SE Arizona. Their distinctive culture, centered on the raising of corn, squash, and beans, appeared ca. 1000 BC.

Their large settlements, containing multi-room pueblo dwellings appeared ca. AD 1000; some contained over 100 rooms. Their mountain habitat lacked the high agricultural yields that supported the later Hohokam and Zuni cultures.

MOHAVE. Indian tribe settled along the lower reaches of the Colorado R; the largest (about 3,000 in 1680) of the so-called River Yumans. They raised corn and collected mesquite beans. They were led by a war chief, who organized formalized battles, war games that the tribes of the area carried on among themselves. Religious ceremonies centered on individual dream experiences. Contact had taken place as early as 1540, but they remained essentially apart from outsiders and entered into no treaties.

MOHAWK AND HUDSON RAILROAD. Opened 1831, when the first steam locomotive in New York state, the *De Witt Clinton*, was put into service. The line connected Albany with Schenectady; in 1853, it became part of the New York Central system.

MOHAWK VALLEY. The only natural east-west passage through the Appalachian barrier. From the earliest, the fur trade moved along this route to Albany. Inevitably there was a clash with the Iroquois and the French. In 1701, the Iroquois signed a treaty deeding their hunting grounds to the king of England. During the colonial wars, the valley settlements suffered cruelly. A part of the only continuous water route from the Atlantic to the Great Lakes, the valley became the natural route along which highways, railroads, and canals were built. A stream of immigration and trade moved through the valley westward with the opening of the Erie Canal in 1825.

MOHEGAN AND MAHICAN. Two Indian tribes speaking differing Algonkin languages but culturally much alike and easily confused with each other. The Mohegan were spread through the upper Thames Valley in Connecticut and often identified with the Pequot. After King Philip's War (1675), the Mohegan were the dominant Algonkin in S New England. Their fame through this period rests largely on their paramount chief, Uncas. The Mahican inhabited the upper Hudson Valley and area around Lake Champlain. Under pressures from the Mohawk and Europeans, they gradually shifted westward and to the Housatonic in Massachusetts. They are best known through James Fenimore Cooper's *The Last of the Mohicans*.

MOHEGAN CASE. Deeds given in 1640, 1659, and later by Uncas, chief of the Mohegan, to Connecticut colony conveyed virtually the whole Indian country and were renounced by the later Mohegan. In 1703, Queen Anne set up a commission, which decided that Connecticut should restore all the land to the Mohegan; but later commissions decided in favor of the colony.

MOHONK, LAKE, CONFERENCE. Held annually between 1883–1912 at Lake Mohonk, N.Y., to consider Indian affairs. Attended by clergymen, educators, government officials, ethnologists, and other interested parties, its most important recommendations were that Indians be assimilated into the mainstream of American life and that the tribal lands be alloted to individual Indians.

MOLASSES ACT (1733). Passed by Parliament, it laid a prohibitive duty on rum, molasses, and sugar imported from foreign colonies into Great Britain's American colonies. Smuggling on a large scale minimized the act, which probably served as a mildly protective tariff in favor of the British West Indies. Repealed 1764 by the Sugar Act.

MOLASSES TRADE. The keystone of colonial commerce, supplying as it did a product that enabled the colonists to offset their unfavorable balance of trade with England. Molasses provided a money cargo almost as current as cash. Served as the basis for the triangular trade in which rum sent to Africa brought slaves to the West Indies, where they were exchanged for cash or bills of exchange and more molasses. In 1704, Parliament confined the exportation of molasses to England or its colonies. In 1733 the MOLASSES ACT unsuccessfully attempted to eliminate trade with the foreign West Indies. Modifications of the law permitted the direct importation of molasses, but the Navigation Acts continued to limit American shipping until 1830.

MOLINO DEL REY, BATTLE OF (Sept. 8, 1847). At the beginning of the storming of

Chapultepec hill, near Mexico City, Gen. W. W. Worth stormed a stone building, the Molino del Rey ("king's mill") at the base of the hill. Although the building did not contain the expected store of armaments, it furnished cover for the assault on Chapultepec.

MOLLY MAGUIRES. A secret society of Irish labor agitators in the anthracite region of Pennsylvania. Active from ca. 1865 until broken up in a series of sensational murder trials in the late 1870s. Settled labor disputes by intimidation and murder. In 1874, railroad and mine owners hired James McParlan, a Pinkerton agent, to infiltrate the organization. He rose quietly in the organization, and the murder prosecutions that resulted were largely based on his testimony.

MONEY. Any generally accepted medium of exchange, standard of value, or store of value. Today the definition of money includes demand deposits in commercial banks; commercial bank time deposits and other assets that can be turned readily into cash (US Treasury bills and deposits in savings and loan associations) are considered "near money."

During the colonial period, many commodities served as money; wampum in New England, beaver skins in the Middle Colonies, and tobacco and many kinds of foodstuffs in the South. Individual colonies issued paper currency. In 1791, Congress established a bimetallic standard at a rate of 15 ounces of silver to 1 ounce of gold. Silver was undervalued at that ratio, however, and quickly disappeared from circulation; by the 1830s, the nation was in effect on a monometallic gold standard. During the Civil War, the right to redeem paper money in specie was suspended, and gold was traded on the free market. The value of paper money, therefore, fluctuated from day to day. The suspension lasted until 1879. Bimetallism officially came to an end in 1900 when the Coinage Act officially established gold as the standard. A series of executive orders and acts of Congress in 1933 compromised the gold standard by abrogating the right to redeem paper money in gold. The last vestiges of a metallic standard disappeared in 1965 and 1968, when two acts eliminated the gold reserve against Federal Reserve deposits.

In the colonial period, English pounds, shillings, and pence circulated in small amounts; most colonial money consisted of commodities, non-English (especially Spanish dollars) coins, and paper money. Each colony set its own legal value for current coin, giving rise to an extraordinary confusion of values. The given value of the different paper issues was even more confusing. During the Revolution, the Continental Congress authorized $241 million worth of bills of credit between 1775 and 1779; in addition, the states issued bills worth $209 million. Only a negligible quantity of it was ever redeemed, although the Funding Act of 1790 provided for its redemption for specie (gold and silver) at a ratio of $1 in gold or silver for each $100 in Continental notes; the term "not worth a Continental" dates from that period.

The Mint Act of 1792 authorized the establishment of a mint to coin gold eagles ($10 gold pieces), half eagles, and quarter eagles; dollars, of pure silver, half dollars, quarter dollars, dimes, and half dimes; and cents, of copper, and half cents. The coins quickly disappeared because their metal content was undervalued; in any event, coins proved too cumbersome to circulate in everyday transactions. Instead, Americans used a hodgepodge of paper money issued by state-chartered banks, by the two US banks (1791–1811 and 1816–36), and occasionally by nonbank corporations. From the 1830s through the 1850s, Congress made several efforts to value its coinage in accordance with the market price of raw bullion, but met with only marginal success.

To help pay for the Civil War, Congress authorized $450 million in paper money, officially known as US notes but popularly called greenbacks. This was the first paper money printed by the federal government. The greenbacks were quickly devalued in the marketplace, and in 1863 Congress passed the National Bank (or Currency) Act. It established a federally chartered banking system; each national bank was authorized to issue bank notes against federal bonds. In 1866, Congress imposed a 10 percent tax on nonnational bank notes, driving them out of circulation. Late in the 19th c., farmers, silvermine owners, and some businessmen called for the reinstatement of bimetallism. Bankers and other sound-money adherents resisted, and much political dissension resulted. The issue was settled by the Gold Standard Act of

1900, which adopted a gold standard. The Federal Reserve Act of 1913 made additional basic changes in the currency by providing for a Federal Reserve note secured by gold and commercial paper and a Federal Reserve bank note secured by government bonds. The Great Depression created a new flurry in currency and banking. In 1933, President Franklin D. Roosevelt recalled gold coins, bullion, and certificates, in effect taking the country off the gold standard. In 1934 the dollar was devalued, and in 1935 the issuance of national bank notes was ended. In 1965, the silver certificate was also discontinued. By the 1980s, the currency system consisted of fractional subsidiary silver and copper currency, a few outstanding silver dollars, and paper money issued by federal reserve banks. By far the greatest part of the money supply was in demand deposits in commercial banks. Thus, the evolution of the American money system has been from bimetallism through a monometallic gold standard to "managed money." The payments mechanism has evolved from a hodgepodge of currencies in the 19th c. to a standard fiat money. Checks drawn against demand deposits constitute 75 percent of the money supply and cover well over 90 percent of the dollar value of transactions.

MONHEGAN ISLAND. A small, rocky island off Penobscot Bay, Me.; an early sailing objective of voyagers to New England. It was described in 1569 and visited by George Weymouth in 1605. Between 1614 and 1622, it became the largest fishing and trading post in New England and the frequent resort of ships from Virginia, Plymouth, and other settlements. The fishing industry died off quickly; the modern settlement of the island dates from 1790.

MONITOR AND MERRIMACK, BATTLE OF (March 9, 1862). Confrontation between two ironclads during the Civil War. The Confederates refitted the captured Union *Merrimack* with a double layer of 2-inch-thick iron. It was rechristened the *Virginia*, a name that did not gain usage. On March 8, 1862, the *Merrimack* sortied from Norfolk and easily sank two wooden ships that were protecting the Union position at Newport News. Meanwhile, the Union navy's own ironclad, the *Monitor*, had made a dramatic dash from New York. On March 9, the *Monitor* successfully

engaged the *Merrimack* until tide and cumulative damage required it to head for Norfolk. By naval semantics, both antagonists won: the *Monitor* tactically because it kept the *Merrimack* from destroying the USS *Minnesota*, which had been its aim; the *Merrimack* strategically because the Union navy thenceforward stayed out of Hampton Roads until the *Merrimack* was destroyed by its own crew when the Rebels evacuated Norfolk on May 11, 1862.

MONITORS. The original *Monitor* was completed in 1862 and took part in the historic engagement against the *Merrimack* at Hampton Roads, Va. The US government built a number of monitors all patterned on the original, but their performance was disappointing. However, the success of the original ironclads gave a worldwide impetus to the adoption of the revolving armored turret.

MONMOUTH, BATTLE OF (June 28, 1778). The British army, under Sir Henry Clinton, evacuated Philadelphia and arrived at Monmouth Courthouse (Freehold, N. J.) on June 26 on its march to New York City. Gen. George Washington assigned Gen. Charles Lee to command the advanced corps and attack the British rear. Lee failed, and his entire division was in retreat until halted by Washington. One of the fiercest battles of the war followed, engaging some 10,000 men on each side. During the night, Clinton's army quietly withdrew, leaving 249 dead. Lee was court-martialed and convicted on charges of disobeying orders and making an unnecessary retreat.

MONMOUTH PURCHASE. Including that part of present-day New Jersey extending "west from Sandy Point (Sandy Hook) along the coast and up the Raritan River and south for twelve miles from any part of this northern line." The original settlers were Quakers and Baptists from Long Island and Newport, who established Middletown and Shrewsbury. The duke of York annulled the treaty in 1672 as being in conflict with his prior grant of the territory to John Berkeley and George Carteret.

MONOCACY, BATTLE OF THE (July 9, 1864). A confederate army of approximately 11,000 men, advancing on Washington, D.C., encountered about 6,000 Union troops strongly posted on the E bank of the Monocacy R, SE of Frederick, Md. The Union force was routed at heavy cost, and the Rebels resumed the march.

MONONGAHELA, BATTLE OF THE (July 9, 1755). Between a British force under Gen. Edward Braddock at Braddock, Pa., and a French and Indian force marching from Fort Duquesne. It was a complete rout for Braddock's forces, caused more by incompetence than cowardice, as was charged at the time. Most of the officers, including Braddock, were killed or wounded. Lt. Col. George Washington, one of Braddock's aides, survived.

MONONGAHELA RIVER. A tributary of the upper Ohio R, it drains the western slopes of the Alleghenies in West Virginia, Maryland, and Pennsyvania. Its great importance dates from 1750 and 1752, when Christopher Gist explored the region for the Ohio Co., and a path was blazed from the Potomac to the Monongahela.

MONOPOLY. American public policy against monopoly derives in part from early English laws against the practice of purchasing essential commodities to influence their prices and to reap considerable profits from resale. Efforts to create industrial monopolies were common in the late 19th and early 20th c. The US Steel Corp. and the Standard Oil Co. are the most famous examples. Such monopolies, or trusts, eventually resulted in the SHERMAN ANTITRUST ACT of 1890 and the Clayton Antitrust Act of 1914.

MONROE, FORTRESS. At Hampton, Va., commanding the entrance to Chesapeake Bay; completed 1834. It remained in Union hands during the Civil War, the Confederates making no attempt to capture it. Gen. G. B. McClellan began the Peninsular Campaign there 1862.

MONROE DOCTRINE. President Monroe's message to Congress of Dec. 1, 1823, laid down the principle that European governments could establish no new colonies in the New World. The message was enthusiastically received in the US, but it had little immediate practical value. It remained virtually unnoticed by European powers, and minor violations of it occurred in Britain's encroachments in Central America and its acquisition of the Falkland Islands. The first great revival of interest in the doctrine came in 1845 with the intrigues of Great Britain and France to prevent the annexation of Texas, the dispute over Oregon with Britain, and the fear of British purposes in California. President Polk reiterated the principles of Monroe (see POLK DOCTRINE). Again, the immediate results were not important, but the principle had begun to sink into the American mind. During the Civil War, Spain intervened in Santo Domingo and France established a puppet empire in Mexico (see MEXICO, FRENCH IN). While other circumstances contributed to the fall of that empire, there can be no question that two major factors were the diplomatic pressure exerted by the US government in 1865 and French fear of the United States.

The doctrine was cited in the 1880s as reason for forbidding the construction by Europeans of a transisthmian canal and as implying that such a canal must be under the exclusive guarantee of the US. This point of view was accepted by Great Britain in the first Hay-Pauncefote Treaty (1900). In 1895, President Cleveland asserted that the doctrine compelled Great Britain to arbitrate a boundary dispute with Venezuela over the limitations of British Guiana. Eventually a peaceful solution of the problem was devised.

The growing nationalism of the US in the early 20th c. continued to have its effect on the doctrine. The Theodore Roosevelt administration, beginning moderately, gradually moved to the position that the US must assume a measure of control of the more unruly of the Latin American republics in order to prevent European action against them. The Roosevelt Corollary to the Monroe Doctrine, as his policy came to be known, asserted that wrongdoing by a Latin American state might compel intervention by the US. The doctrine has figured as justification in the not infrequent interventions in the affairs of Caribbean states.

The nations of the Western Hemisphere adopted the Act of Chapultepec (1945), which broadened the Monroe Doctrine by incorporating the principle that an attack on one country of the hemisphere was to be considered an act of aggression against all countries of the hemisphere. In 1948, the Organization of American States (OAS) was formed, through which the principles of the Monroe Doctrine could be effected by a system of Pan-Americanism. Despite this emphasis on hemispheric unity, US fear of communist infiltration in Latin America led it to take action unilaterally in Guatemala (1954), Cuba (1960–61), the Dominican Republic (1965), and Grenada (1983). The Monroe Doctrine has never obtained a true international status, and in the US itself there has been some degree of reaction against extreme interpretations of its principles.

MONROE MISSION TO FRANCE (1794–96). James Monroe, a known friend of the French republic, was US minister there when the terms of JAY'S TREATY with Great Britain became known. Monroe had previously assured the French that the treaty when completed would not weaken US ties with France. Monroe tried to palliate what seemed to him the ill faith of Washington's cabinet. Federalist leaders were able to convince Washington that Monroe's conduct was disloyal to the administration and the president recalled him.

MONROE–PINKNEY TREATY (1806). Proposed commercial treaty with Great Britain, intended to replace Jay's Treaty. President Jefferson disapproved of its terms and never submitted it to the Senate.

MONTANA. At the time of the early explorers, the area was inhabited by the Sioux, Blackfoot, Gros Ventres, Flathead, and Crow. Montana came to the US with the Louisiana Purchase, and its early growth was linked with the fur trade. A spectacular mining period opened in the 1860s; emphasis shifted from placer mining to quartz veins and to silver mining in the 1870s, and to copper and zinc deposits in the 1880s. Politically, it became part of Idaho Territory in 1863 and was created Montana Territory in 1864. The homestead acts brought an influx of settlers, both farmers and cattle and sheep ranchers. Montana became a state in 1889. After the great mining period, its principal source of income has been agriculture. Petroleum and natural gas were developed after 1915, and enormous coal deposits, suitable for strip mining, have been discovered. Pop.: 786,690 (1980).

MONTE CASSINO. Mountain and abbey, about fifty miles N of Naples, scene of a bloody battle in World War II. The Germans had incorporated the hill and abbey into their defenses, which were in the way of the Allies' drive north to Rome. On Feb. 15, 1944, the Allies destroyed the abbey buildings and their artistic and cultural treasures, but they were unable to take the mountain until May. The abbey was rebuilt after the war.

MONTEREY. City on the central coast of California, capital of Spanish and Mexican California from 1777 to 1845. Permanent US control came during the Mexican War (July 7, 1846). Today it is a popular resort area. Pop.: 27,558 (1980).

MONTERREY, BATTLES OF (Sept. 21–23, 1846). In the Mexican War, Gen. Zachary Taylor's invading army attacked Monterrey (in NE Mexico) and conquered it within three days.

MONTGOMERY. Capital city of Alabama, established 1817 on a site occupied by the Alabama Indians. It became an important shipping and warehousing center for Alabama cotton before the Civil War. It was briefly the capital of the Confederacy but was almost completely destroyed in the war. Today, it continues to be the commercial center of an agricultural area and manufactures furniture and cotton fabrics. Pop.: 178,157 (1980).

MONTGOMERY BUS BOYCOTT (1955–56). Considered the beginning of the modern CIVIL RIGHTS MOVEMENT, the boycott began when Rosa Parks, a black woman, refused to relinquish her seat on a Montgomery, Ala., bus to a white man. She was arrested, and the Rev. Martin Luther King, Jr., organized a boycott of the city buses by Montgomery's black population. As a result, the bus company lost 65 percent of its income. Following a Supreme Court decision of Nov. 13, 1956, the boycott ended when the bus service began a policy of desegregation.

MONTGOMERY CONVENTION (1861). Assembled at Montgomery, Ala., to organize the CONFEDERATE STATES OF AMERICA. Represented were South Carolina, Georgia, Alabama, Mississippi, Florida, and Louisiana. Jefferson Davis was named president and the government sat in Montgomery until it moved to Richmond later that year.

MONTICELLO. Home of Thomas Jefferson, near Charlottesville, Va. Jefferson was his own architect and designed the house in the Palladian manner. He is buried on the grounds.

MONTPELIER. Capital city of Vermont, settled in 1787. The state government is its chief economic interest. Pop.: 8,241 (1980).

MONTREAL, CAPTURE OF (1760). The British victory over the French at Quebec in 1759 was followed by a spirited effort by the French to hold onto Montreal. But in May 1760, English ships appeared on the river below Quebec and leisurely prepared for the final stroke. On Sept. 8, 1760, the French governor surrendered Montreal, and with it Canada.

MONTREAL, CAPTURE OF (1775). On November 13, without encountering resistance, American troops marched into Montreal and occupied the city until June 15, 1776, when the British retook it.

MONTREAL, WILKINSON'S EXPEDITION AGAINST (1813–14). Badly managed attempt by US Gen. James Wilkinson to take Montreal during the War of 1812.

MOONEY CASE. In 1916 in San Francisco, Thomas J. Mooney, a minor labor leader, was convicted of planting a bomb that killed ten people. He was sentenced to death on evidence that was both weak and questionable, and the presiding judge began a campaign to save him. President Wilson persuaded the governor of California to commute his sentence to life imprisonment. In 1939 Mooney was pardoned and freed.

MOON HOAX. In 1835, the *New York Sun* announced wonderful new discoveries on the moon; included were batlike beings, temples of polished sapphire, and a beautiful inland lake. The hoax convinced even some Yale scientists and put the *Sun* on the road to prosperity.

MOON LANDING. On July 16, 1969, three astronauts (Neil A. Armstrong, Edwin E. Aldrin, Jr., and Michael Collins) began their voyage to the moon. On July 20, Armstrong and Aldrin, in their lunar module, cut loose from the space ship Apollo II and landed on the surface of the moon. Six and one-half hours later, Armstrong climbed down and set foot on lunar soil, and Aldrin soon followed. Half a billion people watched on television as the two astronauts moved about on the lunar surface. They raised the US flag, collected rock and soil samples, and set up scientific equipment that would remain on the moon. After two hours, they returned to the lunar module and prepared for the return flight. They splashed down in the Pacific on July 24.

MOONSHINE. Illicit whiskey, that is, liquor on which excises have not been paid. The unauthorized selling of whiskey has been a legal problem since the early Republic (see WHISKEY REBELLION) and reached its zenith in the 1920s during Prohibition. (See also BOOTLEGGING.)

MOORE'S CREEK BRIDGE, BATTLE AT (Feb. 27, 1776). A decisive victory of North Carolina Patriots over Loyalists, fought eighteen miles N of Wilmington. Although the battle lasted only three minutes, 1,600 Loyalists were overwhelmed by 1,100 Patriots. It prevented a British invasion of the colony that year.

MORAL MAJORITY. An organization of fundamentalist Christians, headed by the Rev. Jerry Falwell. It has been a prominent supporter of conservative political candidates, most notably Ronald Reagan in the 1980 presidential election, and opposes such causes as the Equal Rights Amendment, school busing, abortion, and gay rights. It has particularly favored school prayer.

MORAVIAN BRETHREN. Protestant sect tracing its ancestry to the Hussites of 15th-c. Bohemia. The first attempted Moravian settlement in America was in Georgia in 1735. Permanent settlements were made at Nazareth, Pa., in 1740, and at Salem, N.C., in 1753.

MORGAN-BELMONT AGREEMENT (1895). A contract between the US Treasury and the banking houses of J. P. Morgan and August Belmont. The financiers agreed to buy $62 million worth of government bonds and pay for them in gold, thus replenishing the government's rapidly diminishing gold reserve.

MORGAN'S RAIDS (1862–64). Confederate Col. J. H. Morgan led a series of spectacular dashes into Ohio from Kentucky and Tennessee. He was killed in E Tennessee in September 1864.

MORGAN'S TRIALS (1827–31). William Morgan of Batavia, N.Y., disappeared in 1826, just as he was about to publish a book revealing the secrets of Freemasonry. Several Masons pleaded guilty of conspiracy in abducting him and were given prison sentences and fines. Others were imprisoned for contempt. Mason's fate was never determined. The suspicion aroused contributed to the anti-Masonic movement.

MORMON, BOOK OF. According to Mormons, a translation by Joseph Smith of the sacred history of white ancestors of the American Indians who were descendants of the ancient Hebrews. Smith claimed that this record was delivered to him in the year 1827 by an angel who gave him instructions for translating it. The Book of Mormon is regarded by Mormons as equal in authority with the Bible as the word of God.

MORMON EXPEDITION (1857–58). US army campaign to subdue the Mormons, who were refusing to obey federal laws. President Buchanan ordered artillery troops to Utah, but the oncoming winter forced the expedition to winter at Ft. Bridger, Wyo. By spring, promises of amnesty had induced the Mormons to submit, and the expedition marched into Salt Lake City without bloodshed.

MORMONS. See LATTER-DAY SAINTS, CHURCH OF JESUS CHRIST OF.

MORMON TRAIL. After their expulsion from Nauvoo, Ill., in 1846, the Mormons took a westerly route along a well-beaten trail, through what is now Iowa, to the Missouri R. By permission of the Omaha Indians, they crossed into Nebraska Territory, where they wintered. In April 1847, they started W, following the Platte R to Fort Laramie, Wyo. There they followed the Oregon Trail to Fort Bridger, Wyo.; traveling to the SW through Echo Canyon to the Weber R, they ascended East Canyon, crossed the Big and Little mountains of the Wasatch Range, and entered the valley of the Great Salt Lake in Utah through Emigration Canyon on July 24, 1847.

MORMON WAR. (1844–46). A series of conflicts between the Mormons of Nauvoo, Ill., and their non-Mormon neighbors. Armed forces were assembled by each side, and on June 27, 1844, the Mormon leader Joseph Smith and his brother Hyrum were murdered. Violence erupted again in 1845, and the militia was called out. The Mormons agreed to leave the state. Anti-Mormons nevertheless moved in force against Nauvoo; peace was patched up, and the Mormons hastened their exodus. By mid-December 1846, nearly all had gone.

MORRISTOWN, ENCAMPMENT AT (1776–77, 1779–80). Winter site for the Continental army during the Revolution. During the first winter, Gen. George Washington located the general camp SE of Morristown, N. J. Two years later, the army camped at Jockey Hollow, four miles SW of the general's headquarters at the Jacob Ford Mansion.

MORSE GEOGRAPHIES. In 1784, Jedediah Morse brought out the first geography to be published in the US, causing him to be called the father of American geography. More than twenty-five editions of *Geography Made Easy* were published.

MORTARS, CIVIL WAR NAVAL. Heavy guns designed to throw shells with a high angle of fire were built at Pittsburgh in 1862 for use by the Union navy. Used to bombard the principal defenses below New Orleans and crucial in the siege of Vicksburg which was bombarded for forty-two days with 7,000 shells. At the end of the war, the navy had twenty-six such guns.

MORTGAGE RELIEF LEGISLATION. In the 1870s and 1880s and again in the 1920s in the Plains states, there was a large-scale overextension of farmer indebtedness, primarily in land mortgages. Agitation for debtor relief included demands of inflation of the money supply (such as the Free Silver movement) and for public regulation of business monopolies. Two kinds of mortgage relief legislation emerged: (1) the establishment of statutory periods of redemption that continued after foreclosure sale; and (2) the requirement that mortgaged property be sold for fair value. At the beginning of the Great Depression of the 1930s, mortgage distress became a national concern. By 1936, twenty-eight states had passed mortgage relief legislation. A federal moratorium act was passed in 1937, but more effective were the actions of the federal farm-credit agancies offering refinancing to the farmers.

MOSBY'S RANGERS. Confederate troops commanded by Col. J. S. Mosby; their main activities consisted of sudden attacks on Union outposts, followed, when pursued, by quick dispersion. Highly successful, they were a thorn in the side of Union generals.

MOSQUITO FLEET. Small naval squadron assembled 1823 to wipe out West Indian pirates. By 1829, the fleet had captured about sixty-five pirate craft, virtually destroying their power.

MOSQUITO QUESTION. Mosquito comprised the present coast of Nicaragua, strategically located for an isthmian canal. In 1844, Britain established a formal protectorate, which the US regarded as a violation of the MONROE DOCTRINE. Incorporated into Nicaragua in 1860.

MOST-FAVORED-NATION PRINCIPLE. An agreement between two parties that each will extend to the other terms at least as good as those given any third country. In US history, it first appeared in 1778 in a treaty with France. It became a standard part of 19th-c. treaties, but its application after World War II has been complicated by such regional economic arrangements as the Common Market.

MOTION PICTURES. In 1893, Thomas A. Edison received patents for his Kinetograph camera and for his viewing apparatus. His motion pictures went on public view in 1894 in New York, London, and Paris. Several other processes were patented and displayed at about the same time. The first movies were only brief sequences, inserted in a vaudeville show. Before long, productions became more elaborate as pictures began to tell a story. Initial production centers were in the New York City area, Chicago, and Philadelphia. In 1913, the lure of good weather called producers west, and Hollywood, Calif., became the American production headquarters. Corporate headquarters remained in New York. Hollywood during the golden age of silent film became the international center of motion picture production. In 1928, the industry shifted to talking pictures, and to some extent Hollywood lost its international flavor. Technicolor was the first successful color process, and from the release of the record-breaking *Gone With the Wind* in 1939, an increasing proportion of important motion pictures were in color. After World War II, the motion picture went through a difficult period, as television increasingly took its place as the nation's primary entertainment medium. The output of feature films was drastically cut, but eventually an informal merger of the motion picture and television industries occurred: films made for movie houses were sold to the television networks after their initial runs, and special films were produced for television.

MOTOR TRUCK TRANSPORTATION. In 1917, the first long-distance truck shipments were made with trucks hauling military supplies to ports of embarkation. At that time, too, pneumatic tires capable of withstanding heavy truck loads were being developed; the improved tires enabled trucks to double their former speed, an enormous economic advantage. Interstate trucking increased steadily in the 1920s and 1930s, although railroad transportation continued to dominate the long-distance movement of goods. In World War II, trucks served as a mobile assembly line on the home front and were often the decisive factor in theaters of war. After the war, the trucking industry resumed a steady and rapid growth. An important development of the late 1950s was piggybacking, or long-distance moving of loaded semitrailers on railway flatcars; in 1970, there were almost 1.3 million semitrailers loaded on flatcars. By 1977, there was a truck total of 26,213,000, which was more than quintuple the 1941 figure.

MOULTRIE, FORT, BATTLE OF (June 28, 1776). Colonial forces at Fort Moultrie, in Charleston harbor, successfully beat off a British attack. The British sustained heavy losses and were kept out of the South for the next two years.

MOUNDS AND MOUND BUILDERS. The General Mound Area of the eastern US corresponds approximately with the basins of the Mississippi R and its tributaries, particularly those to the east, and the Gulf and southeastern seaboard regions. Conical mounds, reaching up to 70 feet in height, are artificial hillocks of earth or stone or a combination of both. Built for interment or as monuments, truncated mounds occur mostly in the Mississippi Valley; they are flat-topped pyramids, sometimes 100 feet high and may cover 16 acres of ground. Effigy mounds, so-called because they were built in the image of animals, birds, and human beings, are concentrated in S Wisconsin and adjacent parts of Iowa, Minnesota, and Illinois. The greatest is the Serpent Mound, in Adams County, Ohio; this effigy, following the sinuous coils of a serpent, measures 1,330 feet in length. Remains of defensive earthworks have also been discovered, in particular those of the Hopewell Indians of Ohio. Explorers of the 16th c. found certain tribes in the South using, if not actually building, mounds. Some of the mounds date back as far as 5000 BC, although the height of the mound builder culture ranged from 1000 BC to the historic period. The mound-building peoples had achieved a considerable degree of advancement: copper was hammered into implements and ornaments; very creditable potteryware was made; and woven fabric of several types was produced.

MOUNTAIN MEN. Fur trappers of the Rocky Mountains who mingled with the Indians, adopting their manner of life, food, clothing, shelter, morals, and frequently their superstitions. Beaver and buffalo hides were the major items of commerce. As immigrants arrived in the West, the mountain men became scouts and guides.

MOUNT DESERT. Island off NE Maine. Jesuit missionaries arrived ca. 1611. Their small settlement was wiped out in 1613 by a raid of Virginians. The French relinquished the island in 1713, and it changed hands frequently for the rest of the 18th c., eventually being given outright to Sir Francis Bernard, royal governor of Massachusetts. Today, it is a summer resort.

MOUNT HOLYOKE COLLEGE. Located in South Hadley, Mass., it is the oldest US woman's college (1836).

MOUNT HOPE. A hill in the present town of Bristol, R.I., it was the home of Wampanoag sachem Metacom (King Philip). During King Philip's War, he was killed at the foot of the hill, on Aug. 12, 1676.

MOUNT RAINIER NATIONAL PARK. In the state of Washington, includes the 14,410-foot-high Mount Rainier, an inactive volcano covered with glaciers and surrounded by extensive forests of Douglas fir and hemlock.

MOUNT RUSHMORE NATIONAL MEMORIAL. Located in South Dakota. Four gigantic sculptures, were carved beginning 1925 into the rock face of Mount Rushmore by Gutzon Borglum and his son Lincoln, of George Washington, Thomas Jefferson, Abraham Lincoln, and Theodore Roosevelt.

MOUNT VERNON. Home of George Washington on the S bank of the Potomac R, near Alexandria, Va. The Washington family acquired title to Mount Vernon in 1690. The central part of the existing house was built ca. 1743. Washington returned to Mount Vernon at the close of his presidency in 1797 and died there on Dec. 14, 1799. He is buried there.

MOURT'S RELATION. Book printed in London in 1622, a valuable source of information on the Pilgrims' arrival and first months in America. G. Mourt, who signed the preface, is identified as George Morton, who settled in Plymouth in 1623. William Bradford and Edward Winslow generally have been considered the chief authors of the work.

MOWING MACHINE. As early as 1812, wooden horsedrawn rakes were used in the East. In 1856 Cyrenus Wheeler put on the market a two-wheeled mower with a hinged cutter bar that could operate on rough and uneven ground. By 1860, several machines were being manufactured that did not differ essentially from the mowers in use today.

MOYNIHAN REPORT. *The Negro Family: The Case for National Action*, by Assistant Secretary of Labor Daniel P. Moynihan, attempted to define the plight of black Americans in 1965. Commissioned by President Lyndon B. Johnson and intended as a prelude to formulating national policy, it provoked bitter controversy instead. Most of it centered on the book's attention to the alleged deterioration of the black family.

MRS. O'LEARY'S COW. According to popular legend, the great Chicago fire of 1871 was started when a Mrs. O'Leary's milk cow upset a lantern. Mrs. O'Leary denied the story.

MUCKRAKERS. At the beginning of the 20th c., a group of reformers who sensationally laid bare in popular magazine articles and books the abuses that permeated American political, social, and economic life. Lincoln Steffens's *The Shame of the Cities* and Ida M. Tarbell's *History of the Standard Oil Company* (both 1903) set the pattern. Of the novels, *The Jungle* (1906) by Upton Sinclair was the most important; it revealed the unsavory conditions in the Chicago meat-packing plants. Despite their sensational manner of presentation. the muckrakers were responsible for much of the progressive legislation of the period.

MUGWUMPS. Derisive term for those liberal, or independent, Republicans who bolted the party in 1884 to support Grover Cleveland, the Democratic candidate.

MULE. The mule, a hybrid offspring of a jackass and a mare, became important in America in 1785, when George Washington crossed European jacks with native horse stock, creating a mule stock that found ready favor with fellow planters. Mules proved particularly adapted to farm needs and were extensively used as pack animals, both in the army and in overland supply trains. As mechanization grew, the demand for mules decreased; in 1960, the Department of Agriculture stopped counting the number of mules in use.

MULE SKINNER. The mule driver flourished from the 1850s to the 1870s, when millions of tons of freight were being pulled by mules and oxen across the Great Plains. Mules and mule skinners were probably as numerous as oxen and bullwhackers (oxen drivers) at that time.

MULLAN TRAIL. Wagon trail to the Pacific Northwest, laid out 1860. It ran for 624 miles from the head of navigation of the Missouri R (Fort Benton, Mont.) to Walla Walla, Wash. It was built primarily for military purposes but played an important part in opening the Montana mines.

MUNICIPAL GOVERNMENT. The governmental structure of US municipalities derives from English models introduced in the colonial period. Councillors and aldermen were elected but the mayor was appointed by the colonial governor. Later, the mayor was typically elected. In the early 20th c., in medium- and small-sized cities, there was a major movement toward council-manager governments, with a few cities adopting the commission government. The elected mayor and elected council type of municipal government remains the most widely used form.

MUNICIPAL REFORM. A movement in American local government that was traditionally focused on achieving the goals of honesty in public officials and efficiency and economy in government. It became a clearly identifiable movement at the end of the 19th c., when the corruption of machine-dominated big cities brought about reforms in the electoral system. At the same time, malpractices in the private sector resulted in the municipal ownership of such vital services as the provision of water, gas, electricity, and transit system. Port facilities and ferries were often taken over by the municipal reformers as well. Much political reform emphasized the introduction of professional management personnel in the executive branch and a nonpolitical civil service. As a result of reforms, much of the power has shifted from the political machine to the mayor, who is generally directly accountable to the electorate.

MUNITIONS. During the American Revolution, the first American innovations in muskets, the Pennsylvania, or Kentucky, rifles, for example, were already apparent. The principal artillery pieces were cast-iron, bronze, and brass cannon and siege mortars. The Colt revolving rifle was introduced in 1858. Despite the demonstrated success of repeating rifles, US soldiers still carried single-shot Springfields until 1890, when the Danish-designed Krag-Jörgenson magazine rifle was adopted. It was the standard shoulder weapon of US forces in the Spanish–American War. In World War I, the US army used mainly an adaptation of the British Enfield.

During World War II and the Korean War, the eight-shot Garand, or M-1, a semiautomatic rifle, was standard. In Vietnam, the M-16, a lighter rifle that used .22-caliber ammunition, was favored.

Artillery improvements during the Civil War were mostly in the direction of greater size and strength and in the introduction of rifled cannon on a large scale. The greatest limitation on artillery, the lack of a good recoil mechanism, was overcome before World War I. By far the best recoil system and recuperators were those on the French 75-millimeter gun the Allied forces used as their main field artillery weapon. It fired a 16-pound shell over a range of three miles at a rate of thirty rounds per minute. Many guns were mounted on railroad cars for long-range bombardment.

The machine gun (the Browning .30-caliber, recoil-operated, belt-fed, water-cooled weapon) was regarded as the "best of all machine guns" in World War I. The Browning automatic rifle was widely used in World War II. Both the tank and the airplane were widely used in World War II, which was fought largely with the improved weapons of World War I. Jet fighters came into use in the Korean War, and helicopters were being used for supply and medical evacuation. In Vietnam, the jet bomber, carrying a weapons load of 75,000 pounds, was the chief instrument of heavy aerial bombing.

Naval vessels have gone through periods of heavy change. Steam power came into use during the Mexican and Civil wars, and the ironclad was introduced in the latter. The 1906 British *Dreadnought*, carrying ten 12-inch guns, established a new standard for battleships. The greatest innovation of World War I in naval warfare was the submarine, which in World War II became a major weapon. Development has been spectacular since the advent of nuclear propulsion; today, they are not only propelled by nuclear power, but they carry nuclear warheads.

The most spectacular development of all in munitions has been the intercontinental ballistic missile with its nuclear warhead. By 1979, the US had about 7,300 nuclear warheads, while the Soviet Union had 8,100; the combined force of this arsenal could easily destroy both the superpowers and much of the rest of the world.

MUNN V. ILLINOIS, 94 US 113 (1877). A Supreme Court decision that allowed Illinois to continue fixing maximum rates for storage of grain; the warehouse business was "affected with a public interest" and therefore public control was justified.

MURFREESBORO, BATTLE OF (Dec. 31, 1862–Jan. 2, 1863). Civil War encounter near Nashville, Tenn. Confederate forces, under Gen. Braxton Bragg, held early advantage, but a spectacular Union counterattack forced Bragg to retreat toward Chattanooga.

MUSCLE SHOALS SPECULATION (1783–89).The Muscle Shoals region on the Tennessee R was thought to have great potential value as it might afford westerners an outlet via Mobile at a time when Spain was denying Americans use of the Misssissippi R. Three unsuccessful efforts were made to colonize Muscle Shoals. (See also SPANISH CONSPIRACY.)

MUSEUMS. The 1769 by-laws of the American Philosophical Society called for collecting items for a "cabinet," as museums in the 18th c. were often called. One of the purposes of the Massachusetts Historical Society (founded 1791) was the "collection and preservation of material for a political and natural history of the United States." Books, manuscripts, and maps were the primary accessions. The Peabody Museum of Salem, Mass., specializing in maritime history and dating from 1799 is the oldest museum in continuous operation in the country. The Smithsonian Institution was founded in 1846. With the founding of the American Museum of Natural History (1846) and the Metropolitan Museum of Art (1870) in New York and the Museum of Fine Arts (1870) in Boston, the term "museum" replaced "cabinet." During the 20th c., the establishment of museums of art, history, and science in all parts of the US accelerated rapidly, notable examples being the Museum of Modern Art and the Guggenheim Museum in New York City. In 1975, there were 5,225 museums in the nation. They vary from the great general museums like the Metropolitan to the specialized. Entire villages and towns, such as Williamsburg, Va., and Mystic, Conn., have been turned into museums; and individual houses, such as Mount Vernon and Monticello, have the status of museums.

MUSIC. From ca. 1720, informal singing schools were organized in New England to promote group singing, especially hymns. After 1770, several hundred tunebooks were published; the composers were mostly Americans, and the tunes were mostly religious. Secular music was published after ca. 1800; mostly it was marches, dances, and sentimental, humorous, patriotic, and topical songs. From ca. 1820, the vogue of minstrel shows created many pseudo-black songs, the most famous being those of Stephen Foster and D.E. Emmett (who wrote *Dixie*). Afro-American music influenced the style of America's first internationally famous composer, Louis Moreau Gottschalk. The first American opera was W. H. Fry's *Leonora* (1845), followed by G. F. Bristow's *Rip Van Winkle* in 1856. Both Fry and Bristow composed symphonies, cantatas, and oratorios. Musical societies were also being formed, and the first permanent symphony, the New York Philharmonic Society, was formed in 1842. By the end of the century, many American composers were at work cultivating the traditional European forms. The most noted was Edward McDowell, who was also the first head (1894–1906) of the music department of Columbia University. The 20th c. has seen more reliance on American popular and folk music by serious composers; they include John A. Carpenter, George Gershwin, Marc Blitzstein, Aaron Copland, and Leonard Bernstein. The music of Douglas Moore, Virgil Thomson, and Roy Harris is all identifiably American. Charles Ives, John Cage, Elliott Carter, Milton Babbitt, Gian-Carlo Menotti, Samuel Barber, and Philip Glass have been especially influential.

The most original and creative currents in American popular music came from Afro-American roots (ragtime, jazz, blues, rock), but both whites and blacks participated in its development. Scott Joplin at the beginning of the 20th c. was the great popularizer of ragtime. The blues are a personal expression of feeling. W. C. Handy wrote the most famous blues song, "The St. Louis Blues," and Ma Rainey, Bessie Smith, Leadbelly, B.B. King, Ray Charles, and Arethra Franklin have been notable blues singers. Jazz began in New Orleans, spread north to Chicago, Kansas City, and New York, and forever changed the sound of American popular music. King Oliver, Louis Armstrong, Fletcher Henderson, Benny Carter, Duke Ellington, Benny Goodman, and their contemporaries influenced an entire world of music. Rock and roll developed out of rhythm and blues, an urban form of the blues aimed at blacks. Rock and roll, beginning in the 1950s, reached the white population, particularly the young. Bill Haley and the Comets, Elvis Presley, Buddy Holly, and Chuck Berry were among the most influential (as was the British quartet, the Beatles).

The rural South, especially the mountains, has long been a fertile ground for American folk music. A kind of urban, often politicized folk music developed in the 20th c., based on the old southern traditions. Woody Guthrie, Pete Seeger, Bob Dylan, Joan Baez, Arlo Guthrie (Woody's son), and Judy Collins have been especially influential.

Southern folk music is also the root of country and western music. The commercialization of hillbilly (as it was then called) music began in the 1920s with the advent of radio, especially the Grand Ole Opry. Jimmie Rodgers, the Carter family, and Uncle Dave Macon were among the early popular country singers; they were followed by Bob Wills and His Texas Playboys, Ernest Tubb, and Roy Acuff. By the 1980s, country music had become highly varied, and its leading performers achieved a nationwide popularity. Among such stars were Eddie Arnold, Loretta Lynn, Johnny Cash, Willie Nelson, Kris Kristofferson, Dolly Parton, and Merle Haggard.

Although it grew out of the European operetta, American musical comedy early developed a characteristic American expression. Victor Herbert's essentially European operettas (*The Red Mill,* 1903; *Naughty Marietta,* 1910) soon gave way to the wholly American works of George M. Cohan, Irving Berlin, Jerome Kern, George Gershwin, Cole Porter, Vincent Youmanns, Richard Rodgers, Frank Loesser, Frederick Loewe, Jule Styne, and Stephen Sondheim.

MUSSEL SLOUGH INCIDENT (May 11, 1880). Gun battle near Hanford, Calif., between settlers on railroad lands and a US marshal accompanied by representatives of the Southern Pacific RR, which was trying to evict the settlers. Seven men were killed. Tensions relaxed after the killings, and both sides made concessions.

MUSTANGS. Horses in the American midlands that strayed from Spanish herds and became wild. Their range extended from the plains of Alberta, down the corridor between the Mississippi R and the Rocky Mountains, and along the Mesa Central of Mexico. In the early 19th c., there were millions of them, and mustangers used various methods to capture them and sell them for domestication. But many were killed off as a nuisance, as ranching took over the countryside.

MUTINY. Two significant mutinies took place during the American Revolution. On Jan. 2, 1781, six regiments mutined at Morristown, N.J., and marched on Philadelphia (see PENNSYLVANIA TROOPS, MUTINIES OF). On Jan. 20, 1781, three New Jersey regiments sought to imitate the Pennsylvania troops, but they were quickly put down and two of the ringleaders hanged. There were minor mutinies in the War of 1812, but since that time, mutinies have never been of significance in the armed forces.

"MY COUNTRY 'TIS OF THEE". Patriotic hymn written in 1832 by S. F. Smith to the melody of the British national anthem, "God Save the King (Queen)." Rechristened "America" it quickly became popular and an unofficial national anthem.

MYERS V. UNITED STATES, 272 US 52 (1926). The Supreme Court ruled that the president may remove appointed executives without the consent of the Senate.

MY LAI MASSACRE (March 16, 1968). An incident during the Vietnam War when at least 450 Vietnamese civilians, mostly women, children, and old men, were gunned down by US infantrymen in the village of My Lai, South Vietnam. Lt. William L. Calley, Jr., was convicted in 1971 for the premeditated murder of at least twenty-two Vietnamese. His sentence of life imprisonment caused a public outcry, and President Nixon ordered Calley placed merely under house arrest. His sentence was later reduced to twenty years, and in 1976, he was paroled.

MYSTICISM. Anne Hutchinson's particular kind of mysticism was regarded as dangerous by the Puritans, and in 1637 she was exiled from the Massachusetts Bay Colony. The early Quakers attempted to combine a mystical emphasis on the Inner Light with the traditional Puritan sects; but these two elements frequently pulled them in opposite directions. Jonathan Edwards, primarily a traditional theologian, displays many elements of mysticism in his writings. The Roman Catholic church has always found a place for mysticism; and the mystical experience had been especially described in the 20th c. by Thomas Merton. The tradition of Jewish mysticism has been largely represented by Hasidism. Mysticism has always been an important part of American Indian religion, perhaps best exemplified by the Native American church.

NACOGDOCHES. The oldest town in East Texas; founded 1779, it was a strategic frontier outpost for Anglo-American immigrants to Texas. A center of revolutionary disturbances, notably the Fredonian Revolt of 1826.

NADER'S RAIDERS. Colleagues of Ralph Nader, a noted consumer advocate, who after 1968, investigated various government agencies and private corporations, stimulating reform.

NANTUCKET. An island S of Cape Cod, Mass.; discovered 1602 by Bartholomew Gosnold and settled by the English in 1659. Whaling became a major industry in the 19th c. Today, it is a summer resort.

NAPOLEON'S DECREES. Napoleon's economic struggle with Great Britain had the effect of cutting off burgeoning American trade with the Continent and with Britain. In 1807, he declared lawful prey ships submitting to the British Orders in Council. The Jefferson administration retaliated with the EMBARGO ACT of 1807.

NARCOTICS TRADE AND LEGISLATION. In 1905, the US government's first antinarcotic legislation went into effect. Reducing the large number of narcotics addicts after the easy availability of drugs in the 19th c. was complicated by constitutional conflicts between federal and state powers; eventually the federal government became the chief policing agent against the illegal use of drugs. Smuggling has remained the focus of attention in the control of narcotics; the amount of drugs smuggled into the country, like the number of drug users, has been impossible to determine objectively. In 1955, Congress passed both mandatory minimum sentences for many narcotics-related offenses and the death penalty, at the jury's discretion, for some heroin violations. Heroin addiction became a major public issue in the mid-1960s, as addiction came to be popularly construed as the cause of a large percentage of both property and violent street crime. Reliance on therapy or other alternatives to prison for drug abuse did not dramatically reduce the crime rate by the 1980s; neither did the widespread use of methadone as a legal replacement for heroin. Public frustration at the failure led to enactment of severe prison penalties in several states, most notably New York, the state having perennially the largest addict population.

Federal efforts to stem the tide of addiction and trafficking concentrated on agreements with producing nations and border and customs patrols. Neither effort was notably successful, and by the 1980s educating the public against the dangers of narcotics and drug abuse became an important cause. The center of the drug trade was identified as Central and South America which supplied billions of dollars worth of cocaine, in particular, to the US market.

NARRAGANSETT BAY. An inlet of the Atlantic Ocean in SW Rhode Island. A major US harbor, it was visited in 1524 by Giovanni da Verrazano.

NARROWS. A strait connecting the upper and lower New York bays and separating Staten Island from Long Island; it was entered by Giovanni da Verrazano in 1524, and today the Narrows is spanned by the Verrazano-Narrows bridge, the world's longest suspension bridge (4,260 feet). Fortifications on both sides of the Narrows long provided for an effective defense of New York harbor.

NARVÁEZ EXPEDITION (1528–36). Pánfilo de Narváez, with 600 men, landed at Tampa Bay. Marching N along the coast, he lost contact with his ships, and after famine and battles with the Indians, the surviving 247 men ollowed the Gulf coast in crude flatboats as far as Texas, where the flotilla broke up near Galveston Bay, and Narváez died in 1528. The few survivors included Álvar Núñez Cabeza de Vaca, who went on to his own adventures.

NASHOBA. A communistic settlement of slaves near Memphis, established in 1825 by Frances Wright, a Scottish social reformer. She fell ill, and her plans for a number of such communities never materialized. Nashoba was abandoned within five years.

NASHVILLE. A port city on the Cumberland R and capital of Tennessee, founded 1779 as Fort Nashborough and incorporated as Nashville in 1784. The fertility of the Cumberland Basin attracted settlers, and the town developed into a commercial and manufacturing center. Occupied throughout the Civil War by Union troops, it suffered little and made a speedy recovery after the war. It burgeoned after the creation of cheap power by the Tennessee Valley Authority in the 1930s. Religious publishing is a major industry, and it is the center of the country and western music business. Pop.: 455,651 (1980).

NASHVILLE CONVENTION (1850). Meeting of the slave-holding states in which states' rights and the legality of slavery were affirmed. Its first session called for secession, but the second session ended in a fiasco.

NASSAU, FORT. Built 1623 by the Dutch on the Delaware R in Gloucester County, N.J., to give Dutch fur traders dominance. Abandoned and replaced by Fort Casimir in 1651.

NAST CARTOONS. Thomas Nast's cartoon, appearing in *Harper's Weekly* between 1862 and 1886, were a great force in contemporary politics. He exposed Boss Tweed and Tammany Hall in 1870, creating the Tammany tiger. He also invented the symbolic Republican elephant and the Democratic donkey.

NATAQUA, TERRITORY OF. An abortive movement of citizens of Honey Lake Valley, Calif., in 1856, to organize an independent territory.

NATCHEZ. City in SW Mississippi, situated on the lowest of several bluffs of the Mississippi R. The sieur de Bienville established Fort Rosalie there in 1716; destroyed in 1729 by Natchez Indians. In 1763, came into possession of the English, who renamed it Fort

Panmure. Captured for Spain by Bernardo Galvez in 1779; surrendered to US in 1798. It became a commercial center in the early 19th c. as the southern terminus of the newly built Natchez Trace, which originated at Nashville. Its planter economy went into decline after the Civil War, but it later regained its economic health as it capitalized on timber and oil. Today, it is a large tourist center. Pop.: 22,015 (1980).

NATCHEZ INDIANS. The largest of the native tribes of the lower Mississippi in the 17th c. Suffered depredations at the hands of the French and the Choctaw. Segments of the tribe were assimilated into Creek and Cherokee, but the culture and the language (Muskogean) were destroyed.

NATCHEZ CAMPAIGN OF 1813. Waged by US forces against the Creek on the frontier of Mississippi Territory. An important segment of the CREEK WAR.

NATCHEZ TRACE. A road running more than 500 miles from Nashville, Tenn., to Natchez, Miss., roughly following an old Indian trail. Its building was authorized in 1806 by Congress, and in a few years it had achieved great economic and military importance.

NATCHITOCHES. Town established by the French on the Red R in Louisiana in 1713 as a defense against Spanish establishments in Texas. It figured in inconclusive Franco-Spanish boundary controversies until 1806, when it passed into US hands. A military post during the Texas Revolution and the Mexican War, it lost its commercial importance after 1850, when the main river channel shifted. Pop.: 16,664 (1980).

NATIONAL ACADEMY OF SCIENCES. Established by Congress in 1863 as a private organization to investigate and report on any subject of science or technology. Today, its primary purpose is to promote scientific research, both pure and applied.

NATIONAL AERONAUTICS AND SPACE ADMINISTRATION (NASA). Established 1958 to assume responsibility for all space activities except those with military requirements. Beginning in 1959, NASA launched hundreds of instrumented satellites and space probes. During the 1960s, a network of such satellites with commercial possibilites was transferred to the private Communications Satellite Corporation (COMSAT). Overshadowing all NASA's operations was the manned spaceflight program. Numerous suborbital and four orbital missions were flown in the early 1960s, and the first MOON LANDING took place in July 1969. NASA's most ambitious project of the 1970s was the space shuttle. The shuttle *Columbia* was successfully orbited in 1981 and was proclaimed operational in 1982. NASA's next project was establishing a permanent manned orbital station.

NATIONAL ANTHEM. See "STAR-SPANGLED BANNER."

NATIONAL ASSOCIATION FOR THE ADVANCEMENT OF COLORED PEOPLE (NAACP). Founded 1909 by white progressives and black militants, with a program demanding equal educational, political, and civil rights for blacks. Attorneys for the NAACP won important court victories as early as 1915; during the 1920s and 1930s, the organization focused its attention on antilynching legislation. The NAACP increasingly directed its attention to voting rights, housing, and school desegregation. With Thurgood Marshall as its chief lawyer, the NAACP figured prominently in a series of pro-black Supreme Court decisions, culminating in the landmark *Brown v. Board of Education of Topeka, Kansas* in 1954. The NAACP was a leading and effective participant in the civil rights movement of the 1960s, in spite of feeling on the part of many younger and more activist blacks that it was too benign.

NATIONAL ASSOCIATION OF MANUFACTURERS (NAM). Organized in 1895, comprises manufacturing firms that produce 75 percent of the nation's goods. The NAM has traditionally espoused an ideology of laissez-faire, antiunion sentiments, and disseminates its opinions by vigorous lobbying.

NATIONAL BANK NOTES. In 1863 Congress authorized the issuance of bank notes by national banks, using US bonds as guarantees. They were never a satisfactory currency, but they represented the sole US bank note currency until 1914, when the Federal Reserve

System was established. Some remained in circulation until 1935.

NATIONAL BUREAU OF STANDARDS. Established by Congress in 1901. Charged with the responsibility of maintaining the standards of weights and measures, as well as their multiples and subdivisions as required by science, education, and commerce. The bureau has developed thousands of new standards of quality, safety, performance, and precision measurement. They were fundamental to the development of virtually every technological innovation of modern times.

NATIONAL COMMITTEES. Each of the major US political parties maintains a national committee with representatives from each state organization. Most of its activities are concentrated on presidential elections, particularly the national nominating conventions that choose the presidential and vice-presidential candidates and adopt party platforms.

NATIONAL CONFERENCE OF CHRISTIANS AND JEWS. Organized 1928 as a formal organization for effecting a spirit of brotherhood between the two religions.

NATIONAL DEBT. See DEBT, PUBLIC.

NATIONAL DEFENSE EDUCATION ACT (1958). Major federal legislation for the disbursement of money to education. Originally intended to promote mathematics and science, it now covers a much wider area.

NATIONAL EDUCATION ASSOCIATION (NEA). The largest (1.7 million members) professional educational organization in the US; created in 1871 to promote educational efforts and excellence and to secure teachers' rights. Also lobbies for education legislation and acts as a bargaining unit at the local level.

NATIONAL ENVIRONMENTAL POLICY ACT (1969). Made the protection of the environment a matter of national policy by requiring all federal agencies to consider the effect on the environment of all major activities and to include in recommendations for legislation environmental impact statements. The act created the Council of Environmental Quality, which oversees the nation's efforts in dealing with pollution.

NATIONAL GUARD. The modern counterpart to the militia; the modern national guard began with the Dick Act of 1903; the National Defense Act of 1920 established a three-component army: the regular army, the organized reserves, and the national guard. Individual national guard units are under the command of the state governors until they are called into active duty by the president. National guard units undergo at least forty-eight drills and fifteen days of field training annually. Aside from being used in wartime, guard units give aid in times of natural disasters and maintain order during civil disturbances.

NATIONAL INDUSTRIAL RECOVERY ACT. See NATIONAL RECOVERY ADMINISTRATION.

NATIONAL INSTITUTES OF HEALTH (NIH). An agency of the Department of Health and Human Services, NIH has the mission of improving the health of all Americans. It conducts biomedical research and provides grants for outside research. Its ten component institutes are Cancer; Heart and Lung; Allergy and Infectious Diseases; Dental Research; Arthritis, Metabolism, and Digestive Diseases; Neurological Diseases and Stroke; Child Health and Human Development; General Medical Sciences; Eye; and Environmental Health Sciences. Headquarters are at Bethesda, Md.

NATIONALIZATION OF US PROPERTY ABROAD. Beginning with the Russian Revolution, it became an increasing practice in the 20th c. for nations to expropriate the property of aliens. Between the two world wars, many US nationals lost their property in this fashion. After World War II, the communist nations of Eastern Europe entered into lump sum payments for expropriated property, usually well under 50 percent of value. After the 1960s, many nationalizations took place, particularly in Latin America. The US, while acknowledging the right of all countries to nationalize the property of foreigners in the course of making structural changes in their economies, has insisted in all such cases that US claimants be paid in accordance with international law.

NATIONAL LABOR RELATIONS ACT (NLRA; 1935). Also known as the Wagner Act; it guarantees the rights of workers to organize, bargain collectively with their employers, and strike (subject to the law). It encourages collective bargaining. The National Labor Relations Board was established by the law to administer its provisions. The NLRA is the cornerstone of national labor policy, and its passage as part of Franklin D. Roosevelt's New Deal represented the culmination of at least a half century of effort by the labor union movement. Amended in 1947 by the TAFT-HARTLEY ACT, which placed some restraints on unions not present in the NLRA.

NATIONAL ORIGINS QUOTA ACT (1924). The basic US IMMIGRATION law until superseded by the 1965 law. It limited US immigration to 150,000 person per year, parceled out according to a factor based on the 1890 census. It was seen as discriminatory against Eastern Europeans.

NATIONAL RECOVERY ADMINISTRATION. Created by the National Industrial Recovery Act (NIRA) of 1933, a New Deal emergency measure. It was aimed at stimulating the economy, and provided for codes of fair competition, for exemption from antitrust laws, and for the government licensing of businesses. It guaranteed the right to collective bargaining and stipulated that the codes should set minimum wages and maximum hours. Participating companies displayed the Blue Eagle emblem. The code-making provisions of the act were declared unconstitutional by the Supreme Court in SCHECTER POULTRY CORPORATION V. UNITED STATES, thereby rendering it virtually powerless. The NRA was terminated on Jan. 1, 1936.

NATIONAL REPUBLICAN PARTY. Political faction created in 1824 by a split in the Jeffersonian Republican party. Primarily the followers of John Quincy Adams and Henry Clay. Eventually, the National Republicans were absorbed into the new Whig party.

NATIONAL RIFLE ASSOCIATION (NRA). Lobbying group of sportsmen and marksmen. Opposes gun control legislation. It has more than one million members.

NATIONAL ROAD. Section of the Cumberland Road extending W from Wheeling, W.

Va. Construction was begun in 1825, and by 1833 had reached Columbus, Ohio. The road eventually reached St. Louis. Today, US Route 40 follows its course.

NATIONAL SCIENCE FOUNDATION (NSF). Created 1950 to establish science policy for the government. Its board is made up of prominent scientists and educators appointed by the president.

NATIONAL SECURITY ACT (1947). The act integrated the armed forces by creating the Department of Defense, with the departments of Army, Navy, and Air Force subsidiary to it. The act also created the National Security Council and the Central Intelligence Agency.

NATIONAL SECURITY COUNCIL. A five-member council consisting of the president, vice-president, chief of the National Securities Resources Board, and secretaries of State and Defense. The council administers the planning, developing, and coordinating of all functions concerned with the defense of the United States. It advises the president on foreign policy decisions and security problems.

NATIONAL TRUST FOR HISTORIC PRESERVATION. A private, nonprofit organization created by Congress in 1949 to encourage the preservation of sites, buildings, and objects significant in historical and cultural aspects of American life.

NATIONAL UNION FOR SOCIAL JUSTICE. Created in 1935 by C. E. Coughlin, a Roman Catholic priest and popular radio speaker. Denounced the New Deal policies and advocated the nationalization of banks and utilities. Disbanded in 1936 but continued to operate independently in many areas. Its magazine *Social Justice* was barred from the mails at the beginning of World War II because of its pro-Nazi and anti-Semitic statements.

NATIONAL URBAN LEAGUE. Founded 1911 for the purpose of dealing with the problems of blacks. It attacked the color line in organized labor and lobbied for the equal employment policies in the national government. In the 1960s, the league embraced direct action and community organization and helped organize massive demonstrations in support of civil rights and economic justice and concentrated on building political power within the black community.

NATIVE AMERICAN CHURCH. The principal religion of Indians living between the Misssissippi R and the Rocky Mountains. It is also represented among the Navajo of the Great Basin, in California, and in Canada. Incorporated 1918 as an amalgamation compounding Christian elements with others of Indian derivation. It features as a sacrament the ingestion of the peyote cactus, which may induce hallucination.

NATIVISM. The policy of favoring native inhabitants of a country as against immigrants, particularly those espousing Roman Catholicism. Anti-Catholic sentiment became pronounced in the 1820s, brought on by the mounting Catholic immigration. The Protestant churches took up the cry against Rome, and nativists formed the American Republican party and, in 1854, the Know-Nothing, or American, party. Its brief popularity was halted as Americans became absorbed over the slavery conflict and forgot their fears of Rome. Nativism had a revival in the 1880s, again brought on by mounting immigration. The country was flooded with anti-Catholic documents; newspapers bent on exposing the machinations of Rome were founded; and a fraudulent document alleged to be a papal bull calling for the massacre of all Protestants was widely circulated. New anti-Catholic organizations were founded, but again the movement was halted by the intervention of World War I. The last great burst of nativistic excitement occurred during the 1920s and culminated with the bitter nativistic propaganda engendered by the presidential campaign in 1928 of the Catholic Democrat, Alfred E. Smith.

NATIVISTIC MOVEMENTS, AMERICAN INDIAN. Variously termed messianic cults, reversion or amalgamation religions, and revitalization movements, they have been common among American Indians since the 17th c., when the Pueblo in Arizona and New Mexico rebelled and temporarily expelled the Spanish. In 1762, the Delaware Prophet appeared in the Lake Erie region, preaching a return to the old customs and helped bring on Chief Pontiac's uprising. Other prophets appeared in numerous tribes; a Seneca prophet, Handsome Lake, started a cult in 1799 that has survived among the Iroquois to the present. Numerous nativistic movements cropped up among the West Coast Indians. The most famous of the messianic cults was that of the Ghost Dance, which began in 1869 when a Paiute of Nevada named Wodziwob began to prophesy supernatural events. A resurgence of the Ghost Dance in 1889, led by Wovaka, another Paiute messiah, became a more militant movement when it spread into the Plains area; it came to a climax in 1890 at the Battle of Wounded Knee.

NAT TURNER'S REBELLION (1831). The most significant American slave uprising. Turner, a thirty-one-year-old slave and religious mystic, felt that God had ordained that he strike against slavery. In Southampton County, Va., Turner and six other slaves killed Turner's owner and the owner's family. They gathered arms and enlisted other slaves. The force grew to about seventy-five, and they killed about sixty whites. Turner was caught and hanged, and vindictive whites began a reign of terror against blacks.

NATURAL GAS INDUSTRY. Gas springs were found near Charleston, W. Va., in 1775, but they were primarily a curiosity. A natural gas well discovered in Fredonia, N.Y., in 1824 powered streetlights, and natural gas wells were developed in Ohio and Indiana. By 1900 the value of gas produced in the US was $24 million annually. As a by-product, natural gas became more available as petroleum industry developed. The most serious problem lay in the transporting of the product until, ca. 1930, engineers developed seamless pipes that transmitted gas cheaply and efficiently. World War II inaugurated a tremendous boom in natural gas consumption and production. Thousands of miles of new pipelines were built from the natural gas fields of the Southwest to cities. Natural gas quickly displaced coal and fuel oil in residential and commercial buildings . By 1970, producers supplied more than 42 million individuals and corporations, who paid $11 billion for the product. By 1980, there were 175,000 gas wells in the country.

NATURALIZATION. The US Constitution provides that Congress alone shall have power to "establish an uniform Rule of Naturalization." Three principal methods of granting citizenshp to aliens are through collective naturalization, judicial naturalization, and derivative naturalization. Collective naturalization entails the simultaneous grant of citizenship to groups of aliens, ordinarily following acquisition of territory in which they reside. Derivative naturalization results from the naturalization of another person, usually a parent or spouse; like collective naturalization, it does not depend on the beneficiary's application. Judicial naturalization, the most widely used and recognized form, entails an individual application by each alien seeking naturalization. Provisions for judicial naturalization have been on the statute books since 1790, always entrusted to the courts. Today, naturalization courts have jurisdiction. To qualify, an alien must have been lawfully admitted to the US for permanent residence for five years. The Immigration and Naturalization Service processes applications for naturalization. When the applicant has completed the procedure, the court orders the applicant admitted to citizenship, directs that he or she take the oath of allegiance, and issues a certificate of naturalization.

NATURAL RIGHTS. Concept of rights generally thought to have been brought to the colonies through the writings of John Locke (see LOCKE'S POLITICAL PHILOSOPHY). The idea permeates the Declaration of Independence. Modern political theory has not adhered to this idea of individuality before organization; the dominant view is that natural rights have, at most, ethical significance and no place in political science.

NAUTILUS. A "diving boat" armed with a torpedo, designed and built at Rouen, France, by Robert Fulton and launched 1800. Napoleon Bonaparte advanced some funds after the boat had submerged itself several times successfully. In an 1801 exhibition, Fulton blew up a French sloop with the *Nautilus*; but no further funds were forthcoming from Napoleon, and Fulton had the ship dismantled.

NAVAHO. Or Navajo. An Indian tribe of the Southwest, of the Athapascan language group. They constitute the largest contemporary Indian tribe, with a population of about 145,000 (1980), situated mostly in Arizona and New Mexico. They migrated from Canada and Alaska ca. 1375–1475, and they may have displaced the Pueblo from their great sites in Colorado and New Mexico. They spread out over a large area, developing small family plots and moving on, depending on the availability of water and wood. They adapted customs and practices readily from other groups. Much of the Navaho culture is clearly of Pueblo, and especially Hopi, origin. They acquired sheep from the Spanish and assumed a mixed farming-pastoral mode. They also adapted European weaving, but their designs are southwestern. They learned silver working from the Mexicans. The paraphernalia of their religion is clearly Pueblo: corn pollen, rain symbolism, ritual curing, altars made of multicolored sands, and masks. But while Pueblo religion aimed at fertility and rain, Navaho ritual was directed toward curing and the establishment of communal good through the restoration of the health of the ill. Navaho social organization is based on a network of about sixty maternal clans.

Always at war with the Pueblo, the Navaho also vigorously opposed white settlement. Despite treaties, their opposition to the whites continued, and in 1863 Col. Kit Carson led a punitive expedition against them. They were rounded up and forced into captivity at Bosque Redondo, N.M. Continued resistance led the federal government to set aside for them a reservation of nearly 4 million acres in New Mexico and Arizona.

NAVAL ACADEMY, UNITED STATES. Established 1845 at Annapolis, Md. It offers a four-year course leading to a bachelor of science degree. Its fundamental mission is educating professional officers rather than technicians. Women students were first admitted in 1976.

NAVAL OBSERVATORY AND NAUTICAL ALMANAC OFFICE. The Depot of Charts and Instruments was founded in 1830 to test and maintain navigational measuring instruments. From the beginning, it was also involved in purely astronomical research. In 1842 name changed to the US Naval Observatory; observations were begun in preparation for a nautical almanac and wind and current charts for improved navigation were published. Congress established Nautical Almanac Office in

1849, and the first volume of the *American Ephemeris and Nautical Almanac* was published in 1855. The two agencies merged in 1893. The prime function remains to provide accurate time and the astronomical data necessary for safe navigation at sea, in the air, and in space. A master clock that determines standard time for the US is maintained at the observatory.

NAVAL OIL RESERVES. Public lands with petroleum deposits set aside in 1912 for the use of the navy. The three sites were at ELK HILLS and Buena Vista, Calif.; and TEAPOT DOME, Wyo. In 1921, the Harding administration transferred them from the navy to the Interior Department, and in comparative secrecy, leased them to private interests. Investigations eventually disclosed that Secretary of the Interior Albert B. Fall had received $100,000 from the president of the company that had leased Elk Hills and had engaged in involved financial dealings with the company that leased Teapot Dome. Through the ensuing litigation, the leases were canceled and Fall was convicted of bribery, but the others were acquitted.

NAVAL RESEARCH LABORATORY (NRL). Beginning operations in 1923, its early research concentrated on sound and radio. Sonar was developed in 1935 and put into production in 1938. Radar was proposed in the laboratory as early as 1922, and by 1932 early tests were carried out. Three important programs after World War II concerned upper-atmosphere research, guided missiles, and nuclear power. The NRL is divided into four fields: space, oceanography, electronics, and materials.

NAVAL STORES. The resinous products of pine (tar, resin, pitch, and turpentine) used aboard ships. Because of their vital importance to trade, the British Board of Trade arranged for a bounty to be paid to colonial producers. The main sources were North Carolina and later Georgia.

NAVAL WAR WITH FRANCE. Also known as the Quasi-War. In 1798, during the Napoleonic Wars, France began to plunder and seize American merchant ships, and Congress ordered the US fleet to retaliate. George Washington was called from retirement and appointed commander of the army; the American navy was rapidly increased from three ships to fifty-five. Action centered in the West Indies. Aside from encounters with privateers (on which France placed much of its reliance), US ships met the French in only four engagements, each an American victory. In September 1800, the Americans dislodged the French from the Dutch island of Curaçao. On Sept. 30, 1800, a peace was concluded with the CONVENTION OF 1800.

NAVIGATION ACT OF 1817. Stated that all cargo between American ports must be carried on ships entirely owned by American citizens. (See COASTING TRADE.)

NAVIGATION ACTS. English laws of the 17th c. that protected British shipping against competition from foreign shippers. No goods could be imported into or exported from any British colony except in English vessels. In addition, certain commodities could be imported into the colonies only from England. Closely related were the Trade Acts, mostly enacted after 1700. They gradually developed into a complicated system of trade control and encouragement. Colonists were largely limited to buying British manufactures, but an elaborate system of export bounties was provided so that British goods were actually cheaper to the colonies than similar foreign goods. Colonial production of commodities desired in the British markets was similarly encouraged by a variety of measures. Although mutually profitable to colonies and mother country, the system sometimes was subverted by parliament to protect home industries from colonial competition.

NAVIGATOR. A handbook for western emigrants, with descriptions of river towns, published by Zadok Cramer in Pittsburgh ca. 1801. It had gone through twelve editions by 1824. The early editions contained instructions for navigating the Ohio R; later editions gave directions for the Mississippi, Missouri, and Columbia rivers.

NAVY, CONFEDERATE. The Confederacy had ample naval personnel, as 321 officers resigned from the US navy and offered their services. Two US shipyards fell to the Confederacy: Norfolk and Pensacola. All shipping in the Norfolk yard had been destroyed, but the

Confederates raised the hull of the *Merrimack* and converted it into an ironclad ram. Much ordnance was also secured from Norfolk. The Pensacola yard was of little value. Lack of all necessary facilities, however, and the increasing effectiveness of the Union blockade presented grave obstacles to the building of a Confederate navy. The Confederacy never possessed a mobile fleet, although the ships it secured from the British did much damage to the Union navy.

NAVY, DEPARTMENT OF THE. Created as a cabinet-level department in 1798, it remained so until 1947, when the National Security Act created the Department of Defense, thereby unifying the armed forces. The Navy Department was subsumed under Defense.

NAVY, UNITED STATES. The navy was founded by the Continental Congress in 1775; eleven colonies also had navies that, when totaled, exceeded national numbers. During the Revolution, all maritime branches brought in about 800 prizes; but, despite its prowess, it was the French navy that was decisive in the victory. American navies vanished in peacetime, but Barbary pirates and warring British and French preyed on US commerce. Consequently the Navy Department was founded in 1798 and a buildup was begun. The first man-of-war afloat was the 44-gun frigate *United States.* In the NAVAL WAR WITH FRANCE, the US navy was greatly expanded through the conversion of merchantmen. The navy gave a good account of itself both in that war and in the Tripolitan War.

In the early 19th c., the navy concentrated on the building of light gunboats. They proved worthless in the War of 1812, while twenty-two seagoing vessels won glory, including the *United States* and *Constitution.* Also significant were the victories on the inland waters, including the battles of Lake Erie and the defense of New Orleans. The war stabilized the navy, and its participation in the Algerian War (1815), suppression of West Indian pirates (1816–29), and antislavery patrols (1820–50) provided training for the Mexican War. Unchallenged in that war, the navy conducted blockade and amphibious operations, the latter exemplified by the landing at Veracruz and the maintenance of the lifeline for the triumphal march to Mexico City.

During the Civil War, the Union navy had two main missions: to blockade southern ports and to take the Mississippi R, thereby splitting the Confederacy in half. Both missions were accomplished. Altogether, 1,504 blockade runners were captured and destroyed, and the Confederacy was virtually isolated from Europe. The US navy took New Orleans in April 1862, and assisted the army in taking Vicksburg in 1863.

A small new navy of twenty-one modern craft was far readier than Spain for the Spanish-American War of 1898, which was distinguished by the easy victory of Commodore George Dewey at Manila. The navy won national support and began a great expansion, dramatized by the Great White Fleet of sixteen battleships (1907–09).

The navies of the major participants played a relatively insignificant role in World War I. The chief mission of the US navy was transporting troops to France. Besides the portents of the submarine and the airplane, the war unveiled the amphibious potential that the navy had in combat readiness and the excellence of the marines. Both were to play a major role in World War II.

The US Pacific fleet was virtually destroyed at Pearl Harbor, but the navy rebounded with a strength of 3 million men and women serving on 8 battleships, 48 cruisers, 104 aircraft carriers, 349 destroyers, 203 submarines, 2,236 convoy-escort craft, 886 minesweepers, 4,149 large and 79,418 small amphibious craft, 1,531 auxiliaries, and 22,045 other type vessels. The supplying of America's Allies was made possible by the navy convoys, and the landing on the Continent by Allied land armies was made possible by the navy's amphibious capability. In the Pacific war, the navy was the major combatant. Prominent were such great naval encounters as the Battle of the Coral Sea, the Battle of Midway Island, and the Battle of the Philippine Sea. Marines stormed and secured the "stepping-stone" islands on the way to Japan: Guadalcanal, Iwo Jima, Saipan, Guam. When atomic attacks on Hiroshima and Nagasaki ended the war, the navy was preparing for the invasion of Japan.

The navy furnished close air support from carriers and amphibious craft during the Korean War, particularly at the Inchon landings. Naval gunfire prevented free North Korean and Chinese use of the coasts, and 16-inch battleship guns were unexpectedly useful in interdicting enemy positions far inland. American warships appeared in Vietnamese waters in 1961, with minesweepers helping Vietnamese patrols find infiltrators among coastal fishing craft. In 1965 US destroyers started an anti-infiltration patrol-and-search operation that used conventional warships. Broadened to include shore bombardment, this inshore blockade continued until the US withdrawal in 1973. After 1966, another naval operation patrolled the numerous outlets of the Mekong R.

By the 1980s, the Atlantic fleet contained the second and sixth fleets, the latter in the Mediterranean, while the Pacific fleet had the third and seventh fleets, the latter in Southeast Asian waters. Each fleet had force subdivisions, such as amphibious, antisubmarine, cruiser-destroyer, hunter-killer, mine, naval-air, and submarine. The battleship enjoyed a revival in the 1980s in duty off the coast of Lebanon. The active fleet in 1982 consisted of 448 vessels, including 13 aircraft carriers, 94 surface combatants, and 94 submarines (all except 3 nuclear).

NAZARENE, CHURCH OF THE. Formed 1908 by the merger of three Pentecostal or Holiness churches. The church adheres to the teachings and ecclesiastical structure of 19th-c. Methodism. The Nazarenes believe that regeneration and sanctification are different experiences. They practice faith healing and abstain from the use of tobacco and alcohol. Membership: 484,276 (1980).

NEAR V. MINNESOTA, 283 US 697 (1931). Supreme Court found a Minnesota law that provided for the quashing of a "scandalous" periodical unconstitutional, declaring that freedom of the press means freedom from prior restraint and the right to criticize public officials is a fundamental principle of free democratic government.

NEBRASKA. Principal Indian tribes of the area were the Omaha, Oto, Ponco, Missouri, Pawnee, Cheyenne, and Sioux. US interest in the area began with the Louisiana Purchase (1803) and the Lewis and Clark Expedition (1804–06). Fort Lisa (on the site of Omaha), Fort Atkinson, and Belleville were all established before 1820. Nebraska Territory was organized under the KANSAS-NEBRASKA ACT of 1854. Reduced to approximately its present size by creation of the Colorado and Dakota territories in 1861. Admitted 1867 to the Union, with Lincoln its capital. Its agricultural economy was, until development of extensive irrigation in the 1930s, subject to frequent damage from drought. In 1981, it ranked third in cattle raising. Pop.: 1,570,000 (1980).

NEEDHAM-ARTHUR EXPEDITIONS (1673–74). James Needham and Gabriel Arthur were first Englishmen to explore the Tennessee country. Needham was slain (1673) by an Indian guide, but Arthur journeyed on to Florida, South Carolina, the Ohio R vicinity, and apparently down the Tennessee R. Probably the first white man to navigate that stream and to visit the Kentucky country.

"NEGRO PLOT" OF 1741. Widespread fires broke out in New York City in 1741; a hysterical populace attributed them to a plot by blacks supported by the Spanish, who aimed to establish the Roman Catholic church in New York. Despite lack of evidence, thirty-nine blacks and four whites were executed.

NELSON, FORT. Built 1782 at the Falls of the Ohio in present-day Kentucky; incorporated into the town of Louisville in 1785.

NESTERS (1867–86). With open-range cattle grazing the major industry from Texas to Montana, cattlemen divided the land into large grazing tracts, some of which they fenced. When farmers, known as nesters, attempted to settle on the range, the cattlemen kept them out by intimidation and violence. In 1885, Congress passed a law making it illegal to interfere with settlers. Of greater potency was the great blizzard of 1886 which ruined most of the cattle barons. Homesteaders then more easily occupied the public domain of the Plains.

NEUTRAL GROUND. (1) During the American Revolution, Westchester County, New York (which then included the Bronx), because it was not consistently occupied either by the British or by the Americans. (2) After 1806 the region between the Arroyo Hondo, near Natchitoches, La., and the Sabine R, near Nacogdoches, Tex., as the result of an agreement between Spain and the US. (3) Twenty miles of land along a line from the Mississippi R to the Des Moines R., ceded by the Sioux, Sauk, and Fox Indians in 1830. In this neutral ground, largely in Iowa, the three tribes could hunt but must remain peaceful.

NEUTRALITY. George Washington's administration rejected alliance with any foreign power. Neutrality proved to be precarious; there were recurring threats of war with Great Britain and the undeclared NAVAL WAR WITH FRANCE (1798–1800). During the Napoleonic Wars, Thomas Jefferson attempted to protect US neutral rights through embargoes against violators. The War of 1812 was fought supposedly to protect US neutrality rights against British violations, but the end of the Napoleonic Wars in 1815 left a legacy of generally successful violation of neutral rights by the great maritime powers. America's posture as a proponent of neutral rights was considerably tarnished by the MONROE DOCTRINE, the Mexican War, and, most especially, by the Civil War. Enforcement of the blockade of the Confederacy involved adoption of practices earlier objected to by the US. World War I, the first modern total war, began with the law of neutrality in disarray. The US attempted in vain to maintain a policy of neutrality and to protect its neutral rights. German attacks on US shipping in particular caused US public sentiment to shift to the side of the Allies. In the interwar period, American reaction against war, power politics, foreign entanglements, and the Allies who did not pay their war debts contributed to renewed interest in isolationist policy and a neutral stance in world affairs. Congress passed the Neutrality Acts of 1935, 1936, 1937, and 1939; but later in 1939, the Roosevelt administration was veering from strict neutrality to the side of the Allies. The concept of neutrality was replaced with that of the arsenal of democracy and open support of Great Britain. Arguments over neutrality ended on Dec. 7, 1941, with the Japanese bombing of Pearl Harbor. The issue has never been raised seriously since then.

NEUTRAL RIGHTS. See NEUTRALITY.

NEVADA. Prior to the 19th c., the area's principal inhabitants were the Paiute, Shoshone, and Washo Indians. Mexico claimed the territory after becoming independent from Spain in 1821 but ceded it to the US after the Mexican War (see GUADALUPE HIDALGO, TREATY OF). In 1850, Congress created Utah Territory; most of what is now Nevada was part of it. The Mormons settled in the Carson Valley in 1851 but moved on to Salt Lake Valley in 1857. A large number of miners were attracted to Virginia City in 1859 with discovery of silver. Congress created the separate Nevada Territory in 1861 and admitted Nevada as a state in 1864. After decline of the COMSTOCK LODE in 1879, Nevadans turned to cattle and sheep raising. New mineral discoveries (silver, copper, gold) in the early 20th c. set off a new mining boom. In 1931, gambling was legalized, setting the stage for the great boom in the tourist industry that was to follow World War II. Between 1950 and 1980, population rose from 160,083 to 799,184.

NEW AMSTERDAM. Founded 1625 when the Dutch West India Company moved its settlement on Nut (now Governors) Island to lower Manhattan Island; grew when settlers moved from Fort Orange (now Albany) because of Indian troubles in 1626. The colony was ruled autocratically by the director of NEW NETHERLAND province and his council; despite difficulties, the new town prospered. In 1637, the brutal Indian policy of Director Willem Kieft resulted in a war that threatened to wipe out the town. Peter Stuyvesant, his replacement in 1647, reformed the colony's administration, had the streets surveyed, and took steps to raise the money for repairing the fort and building a school. In 1656, there were 120 houses and 1,000 inhabitants. As a result of the Dutch Wars, New Amsterdam passed to the English, becoming New York City, in 1664. After the recapture of the colony by the Dutch in 1673, it was called New Orange; then renamed New York after the restoration of the colony to England in 1674.

NEWARK. Largest city in New Jersey, founded by Puritans from Connecticut in 1666 under the leadership of Robert Treat. Ravaged during the American Revolution by British troops who followed George Washington's retreating army across New Jersey. Completion of the Morris Canal in 1832 and opening of the New Jersey RR in 1835 brought growth to the city's economy. Its labor force was swelled by an influx of German and Irish immigrants. A diversified industrial and manufacturing center in the post-Civil War period, with leather its principal product. In the 20th c., a major transportation and shipping center, and a leading insurance center. Since World War II, it has had a major influx of black residents. A major racial disturbance in 1967 resulted in the death of twenty-six people and more than $10 million in property damage. In 1980 its population of 329,248 was 58 percent black and 19 percent hispanic.

NEW BEDFORD. Major fishing port in Massachusetts; home of several textile and machinery companies. Once the largest whaling port in the world. Its ships made Hawaii a standard calling place and established the first US presence there. After kerosine replaced whale oil as a lighting fuel in the late 19th c., its industry died. Since the 1930s, much of its textile industry has moved away. Pop.: 98,478 (1980).

NEWBERRY V. UNITED STATES, 256 US 232 (1921). Supreme Court decision that held that a party primary was not an integral part of an election and hence did not come under federal law; had the effect of giving southern states a constitutional basis for excluding blacks from voting in primary elections. Overturned in 1944 and 1953.

NEWBURGH ADDRESSES (March 11, 1783). Long unpaid officers of the continental army, meeting at Newburgh, N.Y., circulated an unsigned address that urged direct attention by the Congress to their grievances. Gen. George Washington, who was present at the camp, denounced the "irregular invitation" and a second, less vehement address then appeared. Washington advised patience, and his enormous influence calmed the agitation.

NEW CAESAREA. Alternate name for New Jersey, given in the original deed of 1664 to territory leased to John Berkeley and Sir George Carteret. "Jersey" is a corruption of Caesar's-ey ("Ceasar's island"). The hybrid form, New Caesarea (or sometimes latinized to Nova Caesarea), was rarely used.

NEW CASTLE. Strategic settlement on the Delaware R founded by the Dutch in 1651 as Fort Casimir; captured by the Swedes in 1654, recaptured in 1655 and renamed New Amstel. Captured by the English in 1664 and named New Castle. In 1682, William Penn first landed on American soil at New Castle, and under his proprietorship it was the seat of the assembly of the Lower Counties. With the outbreak of the American Revolution, it became the capital of Delaware. Because of British invasion in 1777, the capital was moved to Dover. (See also LOWER COUNTIES-ON-DELAWARE.)

NEW DEAL. Social and economic policies of the administration of Franklin D. Roosevelt; primarily aimed at relieving hardships caused by the Great Depression and bringing about the recovery of the national economy. Among Roosevelt's first actions was the "bank holiday," in which he ordered the banks closed, suspended all transactions of the Federal Reserve and other banks, and embargoed the export of gold (see BANKING CRISIS OF 1933). The CIVILIAN CONSERVATION CORPS was established to provide work for men in reclamation projects and in national parks and forests. The FEDERAL EMERGENCY RELIEF ACT authorized federal funds to match those allotted for the relief of the unemployed by state and local governments. The Home Owners' Loan Association was authorized to issue bonds to refinance the mortgages of owners who were about to be foreclosed. The Agricultural Adjustment Administration was empowered to pay cash subsidies to farmers who voluntarily curtailed production. The NATIONAL RECOVERY ADMINISTRATION (NRA), empowered various industries to limit production in order to raise prices. Employees were promised collective bargaining and minimum wages and hours. The PUBLIC WORKS ADMINISTRATION was created to provide employment by the construction of public works. The TENNESSEE VALLEY AUTHORITY (TVA) was created to erect dams and power plants and improve navigation and flood control. The SECURITIES AND EXCHANGE COMMISSION (SEC) was created to regulate the stock market. The FEDERAL DEPOSIT INSURANCE CORPORATION was authorized to guarantee all bank deposits. A reciprocal trade agreement act was aimed at stimulating foreign commerce. SOCIAL SECURITY created a federal tax on employers' payrolls to be used to build up funds for unemployment, retirement, and disability benefits. The RURAL ELECTRIFICATION ADMINISTRATION (REA) was established to bring electric power to the nations' farmers through cooperative power plants. The NATIONAL YOUTH ADMINISTRATION was aimed at keeping young people in school and out of the labor market. The Federal Theatre Project and Federal Writers' Project provided work for many writers and professional theater personnel. The Wealth Tax Act levied taxes on large individual incomes. The Public Utilities Holding Act was designed to prevent abuses in that field. The NATIONAL LABOR RELATIONS ACT proposed to outlaw employer-dominated unions and assure labor of its right to collective bargaining and created the National Labor Relations Board (NLRB).

New Deal programs, taken together, were unprecedented in American political life. The constitutionality of much of this innovative legislation became a central issue of 1935. A conservative Supreme Court began to declare individual acts unconstitutional. With Roosevelt overwhelmingly reelected in 1936, he attempted to reorganize the judiciary to make it more tractable to his New Deal. He was accused of attempting to "pack" the Supreme Court, and his plan was defeated. Nevertheless, the court on its own came round and in general began approving New Deal legislation. Roosevelt's second-term proposals were considerably tamer, and fewer, than those of the first. In general, they were revisions of previous legislation. One important new law was the FAIR LABOR STANDARDS ACT OF 1938.

NEW DEPARTURE POLICY. Segments of the Democratic party in 1871 accepted the constitutional amendments adopted after the Civil War in order to attract Liberal Republicans who opposed the Radicals then in power. The New Departure Democrats supported Horace Greeley in the presidential campaign of 1872.

NEW ECHOTA, TREATY OF (1835). The Cherokee agreed to give up their territory east of the Mississippi R and to remove to the West. (See also TRAIL OF TEARS.)

NEW ENGLAND. Maine, New Hampshire, Vermont, Massachusetts, Rhode Island, and Connecticut formed a distinct section from the beginning of European settlement in America. It is largely cut off from the rest of the continent by the northern spurs of the Appalachian mountain range, and has no navigable river system to give it access to the hinterland. New England was settled by Puritans. Massachusetts set up a theocracy that was practically independent of England for a half-century; Rhode Island and Connecticut never had royal governors. Immigration almost ceased in New England for two centuries. Poor soil and broken terrain lent itself only to subsistence farming; large estates (and slavery) never developed. It became a region of small farms, with overseas traders and fishermen along the coast.

NEW ENGLAND, DOMINION OF. Established 1686 by the English government to include the colonies of Massachusetts, Plymouth, Rhode Island, Connecticut, New Hampshire, Maine, the county of Cornwall (northern Maine); and King's Province (a disputed region in S New England). They were consolidated into one province with Edmund Andros named governor. New York and New Jersey were added in 1688, making the unit too large to administer. Andros's autocratic rule was unpopular; upon hearing that James II had abdicated, the colonists revolted and overthrew Andros in 1689.

NEW ENGLAND ANTISLAVERY SOCIETY. Founded 1832 in Boston; first group in America organized for the immediate freeing of slaves without compensation to slaveholders.

NEW ENGLAND COMPANY (1628). Unincorporated, joint-stock venture to continue settlement in the Massachusetts Bay region. Dispatched a fleet with prospective settlers and supplies and appointed John Endecott governor of the tiny settlement at Naumkeag (later Salem). Secured a royal charter 1629 and thereafter became known as the Massachusetts Bay Co.

NEW ENGLAND EMIGRANT AID COMPANY. Organized 1854 to promote antislavery immigration to Kansas. A profit-making enterprise, it sent about 2,000 settlers to Kansas and was blamed by President Pierce and the proslavery leaders for all the troubles there. Its friends believed it had saved Kansas from becoming a slave state.

NEW ENGLAND PRIMER. First published ca. 1690; combined lessons in spelling with injunctions of Calvinistic piety. For half a century the only elementary textbook in America, and for another half century it continued to be used.

NEW ENGLAND WAY. Theocratic practices of the Massachusetts Bay Colony, taken from the title of a book by John Cotton published 1645. Massachusetts religious leaders regarded it as an example for the Puritan reconstruction of the Church of England. The church (which developed into Congregationalism) was a body of professed regenerates (the elect) who subscribed to a covenant. They selected officers, chose and ordained ministers, and allowed no interchurch organizations. They admitted to the church only persons who approved the covenant and whose piety and deportment recommended them to the congregation. They were supremely intolerant of others; citizenship in the colony depended on church membership.

NEW FRANCE. French possessions in the New World, generally extending from the Eastern Seaboard to the Great Lakes and down through the entire Mississippi Valley. During the period 1689–1760, there was great rivalry between France and England over the colonies. In 1763, Canada was surrendered to England; the remainder of New France was divided between England and Spain.

NEW FREEDOM. Political and economic philosophy of Woodrow Wilson, calling for reforms that would restore the government to the people. Growth of corporate power, he argued, had rendered obsolete many traditional concepts of American democracy.

NEW FRONTIER. Political and economic philosophy of John F. Kennedy. His administration made innovations at home in economic and defense projects and called for such new international endeavors as the ALLIANCE FOR PROGRESS and the PEACE CORPS.

NEW HAMPSHIRE. In 1629 John Mason was granted what he called New Hampshire. Massachusetts, objecting to the dissenters settling there, assumed control of the area 1641. Farming, lumbering, shipbuilding, fishing, and fur trade were chief occupations. In 1679, New Hampshire was created a separate royal province; after the fall of the Dominion of New England, it once again came under Massachusetts rule. In 1692, it became permanently separate. After the Indian Wars (1689–1725), the province grew rapidly, but by 1776 its northern half was still unsettled. In 1776, the citizens drove out the royal governor and created a new government, the first colony to do so. It was an active participant in the Revolution. A long dispute with New York was settled 1777 by the creation of Vermont (see NEW HAMPSHIRE GRANTS). The state was Federalist in its early days, then turned to Jeffersonian Republicanism and never embraced the Whigs; generally Republican since that party was founded. In the 19th c., cotton mills and other factories were built, notably at Manchester; but in the 20th c., a more diversified industry has taken over. Sheep raising, dairying, lumbering, and tourism are major industries. Pop.: 920,610 (1980).

NEW HAMPSHIRE GRANTS. Early name for what is now Vermont. Both New York and New Hampshire claimed the area; and in 1765, New York began chartering townships, claiming all previous titles invalid. But the settlers, determined to keep their land, formed the GREEN MOUNTAIN BOYS, declared themselves (1777) independent, and entered the Revolution as the separate state of Vermont.

NEW HARMONY SETTLEMENT. Founded in Posey County, Ind., in 1825 by Robert Owens, the English industrialist, on the site of the earlier Harmony Society. The community initially attracted notable scientists, educators, and writers, but failed to prosper and went out of existence in 1827.

NEW HAVEN COLONY. In 1637, John Davenport and Theophilus Eaton, with a group of Londoners and additional recruits from Massachusetts and from the Connecticut Valley settlements, planted a colony at Quinnipiac, later known as New Haven. Without royal charter, the group purchased land from the Indians, founded churches, established a government, and eventually founded Stamford, Southhold on Long Island, Branford, Guilford, and Milford. In 1643, an official colonial government was established; political privileges were limited to members of the Congregational church. In 1664, New Haven merged with Connecticut in order to protect itself from New York.

NEW JERSEY. In 1665, James, duke of York, granted all his lands between the Hudson and Delaware rivers to Lord Berkeley and Sir George Carteret. Berkeley's interests were sold, and in 1676 the area was split. Carteret remained proprietor of East Jersey; and Quaker leaders became proprietors of West Jersey. The proprietors willingly surrendered their political power; in 1702 the province was ruled by a royal governor. Until 1738, the governor of New York was also the governor of New Jersey. In 1775, after the closing of the port of Boston, the colony formed a provincial congress to assume all power. Few states suffered as much in the Revolution. Both British and American armies swept across it, and Loyalists returned in armed forays and foraging expeditions. The battles of Trenton, Monmouth, and Springfield helped ensure American independence. At the Constitutional Convention of 1787, New Jersey assumed the role of advocate for the smaller states (see NEW JERSEY PLAN.).

In the Federalist era, industry and transportation began to remold the state; from 1800 to 1830, improved roads, notably the Morris Turnpike (1801), invigorated the economy. The advent of canals and railroads completed the transformation. By 1860, New Jersey was an urban, industrial state. Newark and Jersey City held concentrations of industry, while Hoboken and Camden were created by ship and rail facilities. After the 1840s, there was an influx of immigrants. In the 20th c., blacks from the South and hispanics swelled the urban population. Principal industries include tourism, particularly along the Jersey shore, scientific research, chemical and mineral refining. Pop.: 7,364,158 (1980).

NEW JERSEY PLAN. Proposed by William Paterson of New Jersey at the CONSTITUTIONAL CONVENTION in June 1787. Expressing the views of the smaller states, it suggested that the existing Articles of Confederation be simply amended: a one-chamber legislature, in which each state, regardless of size, would have one vote; and it did not provide for a chief executive. The plan met prompt defeat.

NEW JERUSALEM, CHURCHES OF THE. Also known as Swedenborgians. Members follow the teachings of the 18th-c. Swedish mystic Emanuel Swedenborg, believing that all reality is filled with the spirit and the true nature of reality will be revealed at the second advent, or New Jerusalem. Swedenborg's followers included many of the 19th-c. transcendentalists; not all of his contemporary followers are members of the New Jerusalem churches.

NEW LIGHTS. Cult that split the New England churches in the 1740s and helped bring on the Great Enlightenment. Based on the preachings of the English evangelist George Whitefield, members believed in the old doctrine of sanctification by faith alone. Many leaders were forced out of their parishes.

NEW LONDON, BURNING OF (Sept. 6, 1781). A British fleet landed Gen. Benedict Arnold and about 800 men near New London, Conn. Fort Trumbull was quickly taken; most of the warehouses and residences of the town were burned.

NEW MADRID. Settlement founded in Missouri, then part of Spanish Louisiana, under the leadership of George Morgan in 1789. Spain hoped to make Spanish Louisiana a buffer state between Mexico and the US by settling it with discontented Americans (see WESTERN SEPARATISM). Morgan soon grew discouraged by the Spanish authorities and removed himself and left administration to the Spanish.

NEW MARKET, BATTLE OF (May 15, 1864). Confederate victory in the Shenandoah Valley of Virginia. Gave Confederate Gen. R.E. Lee the opportunity to concentrate all his resources on the defense of Richmond.

NEW MEXICO. Archaeological discoveries indicate the presence of Sandia and Folsom man in the state more than 10,000 years ago. When the Spanish first arrived in 16th c., they found some twenty Indian pueblos concentrated along the Rio Grande. The Pueblo civilization, totaling approximately 20,000, was built around the culture of corn and was one of the most highly developed of the cultures of native North American Indians. Conquest and settlement began 1598 as Franciscan friars converted the Pueblo to Christianity. Many natives resented the intrusion of the Spanish; in 1680 they drove the white men out in a bloody uprising (see

PUEBLO REVOLT). Reconquest was accomplished by 1696, and the rest of the Spanish era saw the Pueblo living peacefully with their conquerors. Throughout the 18th c., it was the nomadic Apache, Navaho, Ute, and Comanche that threatened both the Spanish and the Pueblo.

Anglo-American intrusion was begun in the early 19th c. by hunters; continued with the opening of the Santa Fe trade in 1821; was increased when the area became part of the US as a result of the Mexican War. Territorial status was granted 1850, and the long subduing of the Indians began. The Apache were the last to capitulate, in 1886. During the Civil War, a Confederate force gained control of much of the territory but were driven out in 1862. After the war, the Texas cattle frontier expanded into New Mexico. The coming of the railroad in the 1880s fed an already existing mining boom and brought Anglo-American farmers in large numbers. Statehood was granted 1912. Industries produce petroleum, natural gas, potash, and uranium. Tourism is also a leading industry. Pop.: 1,299,968 (1980).

NEW NATIONALISM. Economic and political philosophy of Theodore Roosevelt. Advocated use of the federal government to achieve political, social, and economic reforms, such as regulation and control of corporations, better working conditions, and conservation of natural resources.

NEW NETHERLAND. Dutch province in what is now New York and New Jersey. The Dutch West India Co. in 1624 settled a small group at the mouth of the Hudson R; but their main settlement was up the river at Fort Orange, where Albany now stands. In 1626, Indian troubles forced the settlers at Fort Orange to remove themselves to the Manhattan Island settlement, then known as NEW AMSTERDAM. Peter Minuit was governor and had purchased the island from the Indians, paying the value of 60 guilders ($24) in trinkets. New Amsterdam was only moderately profitable for the company, and in 1629 a new charter was offered. It provided for the grant of great estates, called patroonships. The patroonships were (except for Rensselaerswyck) unsuccessful. In 1637, Willem Kieft was appointed director general, but his brutal and unwise Indian policy created such a dan-

gerous situation that he was replaced by Peter Stuyvesant in 1647; he was able to effect the required reforms, and introduce burgher government. Indian troubles persisted; he had to fight three Indian wars, extending from Kingston to Long Island. Gradual encroachment of settlers from New England on Dutch territory had been a source of trouble from the beginning; the question of boundary was finally settled by the Treaty of Hartford (1650) (see HARTFORD, TREATY OF), but encroachments continued. The last year of the Dutch regime in New Netherland was fraught with grave fear of Indian wars, rebellion, and British invasion. Stuyvesant tried vainly to put the province in a state of defense, but on Aug. 29, 1664, he was forced to surrender to an English fleet, which claimed the province in the name of James, duke of York.

NEW ORLEANS. Located between Lake Pontchartrain and the Mississippi R about 100 miles from the Gulf of Mexico, the town was founded 1718 by the French governor of Louisiana, the sieur de Bienville. An unprofitable port, it was transferred to Spain as part of Louisiana Territory W of the Mississippi in 1763 and then returned to France in 1800. In 1803, it was sold to the US as part of the Louisiana Purchase. By 1800, New Orleans had become an important transshipment point to ocean vessels for flatboats and keelboats; by 1812, steamships were traveling the Mississippi. With defeat of the British in the War of 1812, New Orleans became the leading port city of the South; by 1840, it led the nation in value of exports and handled more of exported western produce than all other ports together. But railroads began tapping the Mississippi Valley trade; by 1860 New Orleans's share of total volume handled had dropped precipitously. Recovery began during World War I; the petrochemical industry after World War II spurred further economic revival; and by 1979, the New Orleans port once again handled more tons of goods than any other US port. Pop.: 557,482 (1980).

NEW ORLEANS. First steamboat on western waters; built 1811–12 at Pittsburgh by Nicholas J. Roosevelt under patents held by Robert Fulton and Robert R. Livingston. A sidewheeler, it plied the New Orleans–Natchez trade until it sank in 1814.

NEW ORLEANS, BATTLE OF (Jan. 8, 1815). In the autumn of 1814, a British fleet of over fifty vessels, carrying 7,500 soldiers, appeared in the Gulf of Mexico preparatory to attacking New Orleans, the key to the entire Mississippi Valley. Gen. Andrew Jackson, commandant of the American army in the Southwest, reached New Orleans on Dec. 1, 1814, and immediately prepared its defense. Instead of coming up the river, the British unloaded their troops down river and marched them across the swamps to a spot several miles below New Orleans, where Jackson's troops were encamped. The British attempted to take the Americans by storm, but so effective was the American defense that the British were repulsed in less than a half hour, losing over 2,000 men. They retired to their ships and departed. The battle came two weeks after the War of 1812 had officially closed (see GHENT, TREATY OF). The only unalloyed American triumph of the war, it had tremendous effect on the political fortunes of Jackson.

NEW ORLEANS, CAPTURE OF (May 1, 1862). Union Adm. D. G. Farragut successfully passed two Confederate forts that guarded the Mississippi R below New Orleans, cut the heavy chain cable that stretched across the channel, and shortly thereafter entered New Orleans. The small Confederate force there was forced to withdraw upriver, and the city fell.

NEW ORLEANS RIOTS (1873–74). The Republican candidate for governor, W.P. Kellogg, who had federal support, and the Democratic candidate, John McEnery, both claimed to have won the election. McEnery's partisans stormed two police stations, causing two deaths; his legislative supporters were arrested and jailed. Clashes between citizens and Republican officials also occurred in other parts of the state and were checked by the intervention of US troops. In September 1874, McEnery took over the government but the army restored Kellogg. The uprising paved the way for the overthrow of the Republican regime in Louisiana three years later.

NEW PLYMOUTH COLONY. Founded by about one hundred English Separatists who came to New England on the *Mayflower* in 1620. Some had come from the Netherlands, where they had been living for more than a decade. They sailed from Plymouth, England, Sept. 16, 1620. On December 26, after five weeks exploring Cape Cod, the *Mayflower* anchored at Plymouth, Mass. During the winter, despite the help of friendly Indians, more than half the settlers died. By spring, there had come a turn for the better; in a few years the menace of food shortage was permanently removed. The undertaking had been financed by London merchants, who in 1627 sold their interest to the settlers and withdrew. Other villages were established nearby, and the town of Plymouth widened into the colony of New Plymouth. Although they had no clear right to form a government, they had, before landing, organized themselves into a body politic by entering into a covenant, the MAYFLOWER COMPACT. William Bradford was the colony's governor for thirty years. New Plymouth was not economically well placed, was soon overshadowed by the Massachusetts Bay Colony, and absorbed by it 1691.

NEWPORT. City in SE Rhode Island on Aquidneck Island, founded 1639 by dissidents from Massachusetts. Site of the second Baptist church in America, the city subscribed to the same principle of religious freedom that animated Roger Williams' settlement at Providence. Newport became an important seaport. Shipbuilding began ca. 1646; by the mid-18th c., the city was at the height of its commercial glory. During the Revolution, the city was held by the British from 1776–79; after that it became headquarters for the French troops under the comte de Rochambeau. The flight of rich Loyalists during the war led to decline, but about a century later it revived as a summer resort for the rich. Pop.: 29,259 (1980).

NEWPORT BARRACKS. Established ca. 1805 as an arsenal on the Kentucky side of the Licking R, opposite Cincinnati. Menaced during the Civil War; later moved inland and renamed Fort Thomas.

NEWPORT NEWS. Seaport city in Virginia situated at the mouth of the James R. Founded ca. 1620. In the late 1800s became a leading shipbuilding center. Pop.: 144,903 (1980).

NEW SMYRNA COLONY. Founded 1767 by immigrants from Greece, Italy, and Minorca near the present city of Daytona Beach, Fla. After seven or eight years of farming sugarcane, rice, indigo, and cotton, colonists were to receive tracts of land. In 1776, 600 survivors of the original 1,400 marched to St. Augustine, petitioned the British for relief from their indentures, and settled there when released by the governor.

NEWSPAPERS. Earliest colonial paper was *Publick Occurrences Both Foreign and Domestic*; it appeared for one issue only in Boston on Sept. 25, 1690, and was immediately suppressed for not having secured official permission to publish. Next recorded newspaper was the *Boston News-Letter*, which published in one form or another from 1704 to 1776. The *Pennsylvania Gazette*, made famous by Benjamin Franklin, was founded 1728 and taken over by Franklin the next year. His innovations, which made the paper a great success, included the first weather report, an editorial column, the first cartoon, and humor. It lasted until 1815. The outstanding colonial case involving freedom of the press centered on John Peter Zenger and his *New-York Weekly Journal*, the first newspaper to be the organ of a political faction. By 1750, there were newspapers in Boston, New York, Philadelphia, Charleston, Annapolis, Williamsburg, and Newport. On the eve of the Revolution, there were thirty-seven papers in the colonies.

After the Revolution, newspapers tended to become highly politicized. The Federalist mouthpiece, the *Gazette of the United States*, espoused the principles of George Washington and John Adams. Secretary of State Thomas Jefferson subsidized the competing *National Gazette* by appointing its editor translator in the State Department. The *New York Evening Post* became linked to Alexander Hamilton, and the *American Minerva* became associated with John Jay and Rufus King. The Alien and Sedition Acts of 1798 were particularly hard on newspapermen: ten journalists were found guilty, fined, and in several instances jailed for alleged seditious utterances. Most charges were dropped after Jefferson became president in 1800.

Venturesome printers soon moved west from the seaboard; by 1800, at least 500 new papers were started in the original thirteen states alone. Soon newspapers appeared in

Kentucky, Tennessee, and Ohio. The so-called penny press made its appearance in 1833 with the *New York Sun*, which soon had the largest circulation in the world. The older, well-established, generally dignified dailies sold for six cents; and they were quick to denounce the upstarts as catering to low public tastes. Without question, the penny press was directed at the common people; often they promoted sensationalism to the point of outright faking. They capitalized on street sales, giving rise to the newsboy who ran about the city, calling out the headlines.

After the Civil War, the sensationalism introduced by the penny press was revived and extended by new reliance on advertising. By 1880, advertising met a major part of the costs of publishing a daily. A consequence was hard-fought competition for both subscribers and street sales. The two greatest competitors were Joseph Pulitzer and William Randolph Hearst. Pulitzer introduced the "Yellow Kid," the first comic strip. The comic strip was lured away by Hearst; soon most newspapers were running full pages of comics. Pulitzer and Hearst also competed in their lurid coverage of the Cuban problem, the sinking of the *Maine*, and the Spanish-American War.

The history of newspapers in the 20th c. can be largely understood through a study of the growth of the newspaper chain. Hearst had newspapers from coast-to-coast, as did the Scripps-Howard chain. By the 1980s, important chains included Gannett, Knight-Ridder, Cowles, Newhouse, and Murdoch. In addition, many newspaper companies are highly diversified corporations. The New York Times Co., for example, publishes, in addition to newspapers, books, magazines, and teaching materials; and the company owns radio and television properties and interests in papermills.

Production techniques changed radically in the 19th c. The steam-powered press was introduced in 1822; the cylinder press, imported in 1824, took a larger sheet of paper. The stereotype was developed in the 1830s, and by 1863, newsprint was delivered in rolls instead of cut sheets. By 1876, presses were equipped with folders so that a newspaper of several sections could be printed and folded and assembled for delivery. The linotype was introduced in 1886, and by 1895, there were more than 3,000 in operation around the country. The linotype itself fell prey to progress; by the 1980s, many newspapers had retired their last linos, as offset printing and then computerized typesetting replaced it. Notable advances came, too, in color printing, and some newspapers used color in their run-of-the-press sections.

Despite the technical advances, newspapers in the 1980s continued to operate in a precarious economic situation. Television was generally blamed for the decline in the number of newspapers being published; the new medium drained away both audience and advertising dollars. Whereas a century earlier, many cities had as many as ten dailies, in 1981 only New York had three general dailies. Philadelphia, Chicago, Boston, and Los Angeles two each; and Washington, D.C. only one.

NEW SWEDEN COLONY. First permanent settlement in the Delaware R valley; only Swedish colony in the New World. Established by the New Sweden Co. as Fort Christina in 1638 at the present site of Wilmington, Del. Small outlying forts were added on the New Jersey side of the Delaware, near the present site of Philadelphia and Chester, Pa. In 1654, New Sweden captured the Dutch fort at New Castle, Pa., thereby establishing control of the entire valley. The Dutch retaliated with a large force that wiped out Fort Christina and established a Dutch fort in its place.

NEW YORK. The New York Provincial Congress voted for independence in May 1776. George Clinton was elected governor in 1777; he served for six terms (until 1795), and during the Revolution he directed the militia and harassed the Tories. He championed states' rights but failed to prevent ratification of the Constitution in 1788. He was succeeded by the Federalist John Jay. Clinton returned to office in 1800 for one last term, and thereafter one faction or the other of the Democrats ruled in the state. In 1825, due to the promotion of Governor De Witt Clinton, the Erie Canal was opened. It proved to be of great economic importance to the state and was largely responsible for the growth of New York City into a world-class city. Advent of the railroad further advanced the growth of New York, both state and city. Upstate and

Long Island farming also prospered; dairying was foremost upstate, and potatoes and vegetables the main crops on Long Island. In 1861, the state enthusiastically answered the Union call for men and supplies, but by 1863 war weariness and an unfair draft had triggered riots, which were put down. The Civil War had a mixed effect on the economy, in general slowing the rate of growth.

New York's economic preeminence was reflected in its politics. Anticorruption and political reform were the hallmarks of a long list of distinguished governors: Samuel Tilden (1875–76), Grover Cleveland (1883–85), Theodore Roosevelt (1899–1900), Charles Evans Hughes (1907–10), Alfred E. Smith (1919–20, 1923–28), Franklin D. Roosevelt (1929–32), Herbert H. Lehman (1933–42), Thomas E. Dewey (1943–54), W. Averell Harriman (1955–58), and Nelson A. Rockefeller (1959–73). In 1980, New York residents had a per capita income 8 percent above the national average. The state's leading industries are printing and publishing, apparel, food, chemicals, and primary metals and fabricated metal products. Having reinforced its early population growth by heavy influxes of European immigrants in the late 19th c., of southern blacks after World War I, and Puerto Ricans after 1940, New York lost its population lead to California in 1963. Pop.: 17,557,288 (1980). (See also NEW NETHERLAND; NEW YORK COLONY.)

NEW YORK CENTRAL RAILROAD. See RAILROADS, SKETCHES OF PRINCIPAL LINES.

NEW YORK, CHICAGO AND ST. LOUIS RAILROAD. See RAILROADS, SKETCHES OF PRINCIPAL LINES.

NEW YORK CITY. Consists of five boroughs: Manhattan, the Bronx, Queens, Brooklyn, and Staten Island. Its importance has historically rested on the excellence of its ice-free, sheltered harbor and the attendant volume of its commerce, which has made it the premier port of the world. In 1664, during the first Anglo-Dutch War, the Dutch surrendered the city of New Amsterdam to the English, who renamed it in honor of James, duke of York, later King James II. In 1673, the city was briefly recaptured by the Dutch, but it was returned to English rule 1674. The colonial city prospered under a surprisingly liberal and tolerant administration that ensured the loyalty of the Dutch subjects and promoted commercial prosperity. In 1689–91, a rebellion helped check the increasing tyrannical policies of James II; its leader was executed, but the Glorious Revolution in England led to a return to more liberal government in New York City. In 1731, Harlem, at the northern end of Manhattan Island, was annexed. The city was the site of the Stamp Act Congress of 1765; Whig leadership drove the colony relentlessly toward revolution. With outbreak of hostilities, New York was vital to both British and American strategy. Although the New York state remained in American hands, the city early (August 1776) fell into British hands and remained under occupation for the remainder of the war.

The city returned to prosperity after the war and grew in commercial importance. From 1785 to 1790, it was the nation's capital. It suffered little from the War of 1812, and in the decades following enjoyed its greatest period of growth. The opening of the Erie Canal in 1825 turned the city into a major market and the leading port city. By 1830, it had surpassed Philadelphia as the nation's largest city, and by 1860 its population had reached 814,000.

New York was divided over the Civil War, and the Draft Riots of 1863 caused extensive loss of life and property. After the war, New York became the unquestioned symbol of a complex urban enclave and the marketplace of a maturing finance capitalism that had been stimulated by the war. In 1898, the present five boroughs were incorporated into the Greater City of New York. The city has been a traditional bastion of Democratic power. Aaron Burr was an early Democratic leader of the Jeffersonian Republicans, and after 1861 the city was dominated by the often corrupt Tammany Hall; its power was effectively broken by the fusion mayoralty of Fiorello H. La Guardia in the 1930s. Since La Guardia, however, it has reverted to being a Democratic city. New York is regarded as the cultural capital of the country, with world-famous opera and ballet companies, symphony orchestras, libraries, museums, and theaters. It is also the center of publishing, fashion, and broadcasting. It is a world finance and banking center and the home of the nation's two largest stock exchanges. The United Nations headquarters are located in the center. Tourism and conventions are important industries. Pop.: 7,071,030 (1980).

NEW YORK CITY, PLOT TO BURN. On Nov. 25, 1864, a Confederate attempt was made to burn New York City. Various hotels and places of entertainment were torched, but the damage was trifling.

NEW YORK COLONY. In 1688, the colony of New York was added to the Dominion of New England (see NEW ENGLAND, DOMINION OF); but the accession of William and Mary in England created great unrest in that dominion, including the arrest of William Andros, its governor. In New York, Jacob Leisler seized control of the government, and Schenectady was burned by the French and Indians. The new governor of New York tried and executed Leisler and his chief lieutenant; but Leislerian and anti-Leislerian factions continued to disturb the colony for many years. In 1692, conciliation was reached with the Five Nations, and this alliance became a cardinal point of British policy in New York. In 1701, the Iroquois ceded much of the western part of the colony to the British crown. Edward Hyde, Viscount Cornbury (a cousin of Queen Anne), made extravagant grants during his governorship (1702–08). His arrogance and corruption greatly antagonized the assembly and hastened the contest over the power of the purse, which was to agitate the province for the remainder of the colonial period. There was also constant pressure from the French along the colony's northern border. Finally, in 1759 Jeffrey Amherst, British commander in chief in North America, compelled the French to abandon Ticonderoga, Crown Point, and Niagara; but until the reduction of Montreal by Amherst in 1760, the western frontier of New York suffered cruelly. New York opposed both the Stamp Act and the Townshend Acts. The Sons of Liberty became active. In 1774, a committee of correspondence was named to write to the other colonies. Local and state revolutionary committees took over the government of the colony. On July 9, 1776, the Provincial Congress of New York approved the Declaration of Independence, and on the following day declared New York a free state.

NEW YORK, NEW HAVEN AND HARTFORD RAILROAD. See RAILROADS, SKETCHES OF PRINCIPAL LINES: PENN CENTRAL.

NEZ PERCÉ WAR (1877). The Nez Percé Indians, occupying the region where Washington, Oregon, and Idaho meet, had been on friendly terms with the whites until the gold rush of 1860 brought swarms of miners and settlers onto their lands. In 1863, some of the Nez Percé chiefs agreed to remove to a reservation in Idaho, but Chief Joseph and the southern Nez Percé refused to leave, and hostilities broke out. US troops moved against the Indians, who initially defeated the soldiers. But eventually Chief Joseph was forced to surrender as he attempted a retreat into Canada.

NIAGARA, CARRYING PLACE OF. Portage road fourteen miles in length on the E bank of the Niagara R, connecting lakes Ontario and Erie. Built by the French in 1720 as a detour around Niagara Falls, and in 1751 Fort Little Niagara was built to protect it. The British captured the fort 1759 and controlled the portage until relinquished by the terms of JAY'S TREATY in 1796.

NIAGARA, FORT. Built by the French in 1726 on the E shore of the Niagara R, 6.5 miles N of the Niagara Carrying Place. Became the principal guard of the coveted gateway to the rich fur lands of the West. During the French and Indian War, the English captured it and made it a British fortress (1759). Relinquished to the Americans in 1796 by Jay's Treaty but captured by the British during the War of 1812. Returned to the US at the end of the war.

NIAGARA, GREAT INDIAN COUNCIL AT (1764). Between the British and the Ottawa, Huron, Seneca, Menomini, Chippewa, Iroquois, and other Indian groups. The Huron and Seneca signed treaties ceding land to the British; the other nations made no formal treaties.

NIAGARA CAMPAIGNS. During the War of 1812, Gen. Stephen Van Rensselaer unsuccessfully attacked (1812) the British at Queenston, opposite Fort Niagara. In 1813, Col. Winfield Scott captured Fort George, adjacent to Queenston, and the British abandoned the entire Niagara frontier. In 1814, the Americans captured Fort Erie, defeated the enemy at Chippewa, and fought the Battle of Lundy's Lane.

NIAGARA FALLS. In the Niagara R between lakes Ontario and Erie, composed of the American Falls and the Canadian, or Horseshoe, Falls, separated by Goat Island. Descends 167 feet to the lower river.

NIAGARA FALLS POWER. Niagara Falls was recognized early as an attractive source of power. In 1885, a tunnel was designed that would divert enough water to drive a number of mills. By 1902, Niagara power stations were producing one-fifth of the nation's total electrical energy. During the 1920s, increased transmission voltages permitted the power to be transmitted economically to locations hundreds of miles from the falls and created a regional power source. In 1950, the US and Canada signed a treaty that would at once protect the scenic beauty of the falls and equalize the usable flow of water between the two countries. The generators at Lewiston, N.Y., have a capacity of almost 2 million kilowatts.

NIAGARA MOVEMENT. Black civil rights movement founded in 1905 by W.E.B. Du Bois and W.M. Trotter. Reflected black opposition to the accommodation and gradualism advocated by Booker T. Washington. Forerunner of the NATIONAL ASSOCIATION FOR THE ADVANCEMENT OF COLORED PEOPLE.

NICARAGUA, RELATIONS WITH. In 1867, a US-Nicaraguan treaty was signed; earlier, several US corporations had been issued charters to do business in Nicaragua. In 1911, the US backed the conservative Adolfo Díaz for president and concluded with him arrangements for New York bankers to lend money to Nicaragua and to control Nicaragua's customs collections, national bank, and railroads until loans were paid. When the Díaz presidency was threatened in 1912, US marines were sent into the country. The US continued to control Díaz's successors; the loans were repaid 1924, and the marines withdrawn in 1925. They returned the next year, however, after a civil war broke out. Díaz was returned to the presidency, and it was agreed that the marines would train a constabulary. Two generals succeeded Díaz to the presidency, but another, Augusto César Sandino, opposed US involvement in the country. The head of the Nicaraguan constabulary, Anastasio Somoza García arranged the murder of Sandino and his own election to the presidency in 1936. With US backing, Somoza and members of his family continued to rule Nicaragua. In 1979, Gen. Anastasio Somoza-Debayle was forced into exile by a Sandinista guerrilla uprising. A socialist regime was inaugurated, and shortly thereafter all US aid to Nicaragua was halted, the reason given being that the Sandinistas were supplying arms to left-wing Salvadoran guerrillas. The US began giving military aid, at first secretly and then openly, to anti-Sandinista forces across the border.

NICARAGUAN CANAL PROJECT. The idea of a waterway along the San Juan R and Lake Nicaragua to connect the Atlantic and Pacific oceans was first considered in the 18th c. In 1887, an American corporation undertook a survey for construction of such a canal, but political considerations and other factors resulted in the adoption of the Panama route instead.

NICOLET, EXPLORATIONS OF. Jean Nicolet, a French explorer, went to Canada in 1618 and in 1634 became the first white visitor to Wisconsin, Michigan, and Lake Michigan.

NINE-POWER PACT (1922). Between the US, Belgium, the British Empire, China, France, Italy, Japan, the Netherlands, and Portugal; guaranteed China's territorial integrity and the Open Door principle.

NINETEENTH AMENDMENT (1920). Gave women the right to vote.

NINETY-SIX. Village in South Carolina and a British post during the Revolutionary War. Besieged by the Americans in 1781; although the fort withstood the siege, it was too far inland, and the British abandoned it.

NITRATES. Achieved importance with invention of gunpowder, which is four-fifths potassium nitrate (saltpeter). During the Revolution, the colonial governments paid a bounty for it, but most had to be supplied by France. Large quantities were discovered in Kentucky and Tennessee in the 19th c. and were exploited by the Confederate army. Later, a process was developed to convert sodium nitrate to potassium nitrate, and Chile became the chief source. As use in fertilizer increased, there was intensive competition to develop a process that would convert atmospheric nitrogen to nitrate. The most efficient method developed was the Haber process, which has come to supply most of the world's requirements.

NIXON, RESIGNATION OF (Aug. 9, 1974). Nixon's resignation, the first presidential one in the history of the Republic, was rooted in WATERGATE and other scandals that plagued his second term and eroded the political strength derived from his overwhelming reelection in 1972. Two specific events forced Nixon to resign: In late July 1974, the House Judiciary Committee adopted three articles of impeachment delineating many specific charges against the president. On July 24, the Supreme Court ruled that he must provide quantities of tapes of White House conversations required in the criminal trials of his former subordinates. The tapes disclosed that Nixon had participated as early as June 23, 1972, in the cover-up of the Watergate burglary. By resigning, Nixon avoided the disgrace implicit in a successful impeachment, and he preserved the pension rights and other perquisites of a former president that would have been lost. On Sept. 8, 1974, his successor, Gerald R. Ford, pardoned Nixon of any crimes he may have committed while president.

NOBILITY, TITLES OF. Although sundry traces of feudalism appear in American colonial law and governmental practice, the Revolution committed the country to a republican system. Conferring of titles is prohibited by the Constitution in Article I, Sections 9 and 10.

NOLAN, EXPEDITIONS OF. At least four filibustering expeditions (1792–94, 1794–96, 1797, 1798–1801) into Texas were made by Philip Nolan, a Kentuckian. Nolan penetrated as far as the Rio Grande in his ostensible search for wild horses and skins. He was killed in a skirmish with a Spanish detachment near the present Waco, Tex.

NOMINATING SYSTEM. In the US, the three chief methods of nominating candidates for public office have been the caucus, the convention, and the direct primary. Beginning early in the Republic, members of the legislature (state or national) belonging to the same party would meet, or caucus, to recommend candidates for office, including for the presidency and vice-presidency. The last congressional caucuses, to nominate presidential candidates, were held 1824. Meanwhile, the states had been developing the delegate convention system. By 1830, state conventions prevailed everywhere except in the South. In 1831, the Anti-Masonic party inaugurated the national nominating convention. The National Republicans and the Democrats followed the example, with the result that the nominating convention became the accepted method of nominating party candidates for the presidency and vice-presidency, while state conventions controlled the election of candidates for state office. Party conventions, however, were prone to control by political bosses, and to counteract that tendency, the direct primary system was developed. Originated in Wisconsin in 1903, the primary election system provides for the direct selection of party candidates by popular vote under state supervision. By 1915, the primary system was adopted in some form in all but five states; today it is established as the most important nominating method.

NONFERROUS METALS. Of the major nonferrous metals (aluminum, copper, lead, zinc, nickel, and tin), all except tin are produced in commercial quantities in the United States. Lead production came first; both the English and French exploited the small deposits of lead in eastern North America in the 18th c. The Missouri lead mines, developed by the French in 1798, have been in continuous production since then. The Lead R district in Wisconsin and Illinois was developed in the early 19th c.; by the late 19th c., the US was the leading lead producer in the world. After World War II, domestic lead production averaged about 1 million tons annually, about 80 percent of domestic consumption.

Zinc was first produced commercially in the late 19th c. The Joplin, Mo., zinc ore district, opened in 1871, proved the nation's most important. Until World War II, the US continued to be a net exporter of zinc; since then, US demands have outstripped production.

Copper was worked by the American Indians, but commercial copper production did not come until the 1840s, with the discovery of the great western mines, particularly at Butte, Mont. By the 1880s, the US was the principal producer of copper in the world, a position it has retained.

The demand for aluminum accelerated rapidly after World War II, after new refining methods made it competitive with other nonferrous metals. In the 1970s, the US produced and consumed 40 percent of the world output.

NONIMPORTATION AGREEMENTS. Chief economic weapon used by the colonies against Great Britain from 1765. It was first used by New York merchants, who declared they would order no more British goods until the Stamp Act was repealed; their example, was quickly followed by Boston and Philadelphia merchants. British merchants and manufacturers, in turn, lobbied so vigorously in Parliament that the Stamp Act was repealed. The same weapon was later used to force repeal of the Townshend duties, and in 1770, the British government repealed all Townshend duties except on tea. The colonial boycott on tea collapsed after New York merchants accused their Newport counterparts of flouting the agreement.

NONINTERCOURSE ACT (March 1, 1809). The act designated France and Great Britain as countries that the US would not do business with in retaliation for depredations against American shipping. It was a considerable weakening to the previous embargo policies; it in turn was further weakened in 1910 by Macon's Bill Number 2.

NONPARTISAN LEAGUE, NATIONAL. An agrarian movement of the early 20th c. It called for state-owned elevators, mills, and packing plants and for state hail insurance and credits. The league won the governorship of North Dakota in 1916 and quickly spread through the western states. By 1924, the movement had almost died, but the Farmer-Labor party descended from it.

NONRECOGNITION POLICY. Nonrecognition has often been used by the US government to express its displeasure with a foreign nation's regime. It was first used in 1913, when President Wilson refused to recognize the regime of Victoriano Huerta in Mexico.

NORFOLK. City in Virginia, founded 1682; in the 18th c., it became the chief port for the Chesapeake region. During the Napoleonic Wars, it prospered through trade with the West Indies. After the Civil War, Norfolk became the terminus of several railway systems, making it an important exporter of coal, tobacco, and cotton. The navy yard and other military facilities are important industries. Pop.: 266,979 (1980).

NORFOLK AND WESTERN. See RAILROADS, SKETCHES OF PRINCIPAL LINES.

NORMANDY INVASION (June 6, 1944). Allied landings in France on D Day, the prelude to the defeat of Nazi Germany in World War II. It involved 5,000 ships, the largest armada ever assembled, and about 150,000 American, British, and Canadian troops; they were under the command of Gen. Dwight D. Eisenhower, with Gen. Bernard L. Montgomery as ground commander. The landings took place on beaches extending from the mouth of the Orne R near Caen to the base of the Cotentin Peninsula.

British and Canadian division landed near Caen with relative ease and quickly established contact with British airborne troops that had captured bridges over the Orne. By nightfall, the troops held beachheads from two to four miles deep.

US troops went ashore at Utah Beach, north of Carentan, and at Omaha Beach, between Bayeux and Carentan. The presence of a powerful German defense was catastrophic. But inch by inch, the troops forced their way inland, so that when night came, the beachhead was approximately one mile deep. By the end of the first week, all Allied beachheads were linked and sixteen divisions had landed; only thirteen Geman divisions opposed them. By the end of June, a million Allied troops were ashore.

NORSEMEN IN AMERICA. While Norse acquaintance with North America is acknowledged, its extent is debatable and its duration uncertain. A fixed point is that there were Norsemen at L'Anse aux Meadows ca. AD 1000 according to archaeological excavations. Norsemen made many unrecorded but vaguely traceable voyages for at least 350 years thereafter and must have at times wintered away from home, but that they established a single long-lasting colony anywhere in America is not proven. (See also VINLAND.).

NORTH AFRICAN CAMPAIGN (1942–43). In November 1942, Allied forces under US Gen. Dwight Eisenhower landed in Morocco and Algeria. Italian and German troops put up a strong defense and prevented the Allies from quickly taking Tunis and Bizerte. Field Marshal Erwin Rommel's Italo-German army, defeated at El Alamein, retreated across Libya; Rommel took up a defensive position at Mareth, Tunisia, halting the pursuing British under Gen. B.L. Montgomery. In February 1943, the Axis inflicted severe damage and panic among British and American troops; but in March, the Allies pushed Rommel's army into the northern corner of Tunisia. The final offensive started on April 22, and Bizerte and Tunis fell on May 7. The last Axis resistance ended on May 13.

NORTH ATLANTIC TREATY ORGANIZATION (NATO). Founded 1949 by Belgium, Canada, Denmark, France, Iceland, Italy, Luxembourg, Netherlands, Norway, Portugal, United Kingdom, and the United States; Greece, Turkey, Spain, and West Germany joined later. In the cold war following World War II, the Western democracies found themselves increasingly in contention with the Soviet Union and its communist-bloc allies. A single defense system was deemed necessary, and NATO was the result. It consists of a council and a military committee of three European commands and a Canadian-US regional command. Paris was its original headquarters; but after France withdrew its forces from the integrated NATO commands in 1967, NATO was moved to Brussels. In the late 1960s and early 1970s, when East-West détente seemed to be growing, most of the members placed less stress on NATO. But beginning in the late 1970s, Soviet involvement in Africa, Afghanistan, and Poland led to a reassessment of NATO's importance. Most members increased their military spending, adding to NATO forces' strength.

NORTH CAROLINA. The first English colony in America was planted on Roanoke Island in

1585; the settlers soon returned to England, and the second attempt (1587) became known as the Lost Colony. Virginia settlers began locating along Albemarle Sound ca. 1650, and in 1664 eight lords proprietors, under patent of Charles II, created two counties: Albemarle and Clarendon (Cape Fear region). Efforts to settle Clarendon were soon abandoned, and until 1711 North Carolina, as the northern portion of Carolina came to be called, was ruled by a deputy governor from Charleston, although it had its own legislature. In 1729, North Carolina became a royal colony. Five towns had been founded during the proprietary period: Bath (1706), New Bern (1710), Edenton (1712), Beaufort (1715), and Brunswick (1725). After 1729, government improved, population increased and spread, agriculture and industry developed, many churches and a few schools were established, and a new and more permanent capital (Edenton) was designated. The Cape Fear region was settled, and thousands of Scotch-Irish and Germans moved from Pennsylvania into the Piedmont. By 1775, settlers had reached the mountains.

North Carolina patriots crushed the Tories at Moores Creek Bridge in 1776, ending British plans to occupy the South early in the war; the Battle of Guilford Courthouse was the most important Revolutionary battle in the state. The state ceded its western lands in 1789, and Tennessee was created from them. The University of North Carolina, the first state university in the Union, opened its doors in 1795. Although North Carolinians held over 300,000 slaves in 1860, Union sentiment was strong, and it was late in seceding, and during the war a strong peace movement developed in the state. Battles were fought at Plymouth, New Bern, Fort Fisher, Bentonville, and elsewhere. North Carolina was readmitted to the Union in 1868. Farm tenancy replaced the old plantation economy. Tobacco and furniture manufacturing became major industries; the textile industry expanded; and peanuts became an important crop. It has also become center for industrial research. Pop.: 5,874,429 (1980).

NORTH CAROLINA RAILROAD. Completed 1856, it connected Goldsboro and Charlotte (232 miles). By connecting with several roads in E North Carolina, it gave the state its first east-west rail connection. It later became part of the Southern Railway system.

NORTH DAKOTA. Formed by a division of Dakota Territory in 1889, the state is largely a cool, semiarid grassland. The northern region was settled in the late 19th c., and the rest of the state at the beginning of the 20th c. The peak of homesteading came in 1906, and in 1910, with settlement nearing completion, 71 percent of the population was of foreign stock. Wheat farming was the overwhelming industry and remains so today. Cattle and cattle products rank second. Pop.: 652,695 (1980).

NORTHEAST BOUNDARY. Although the Definitive Treaty of Peace of 1783 designated with great precision the boundary between Maine and New Brunswick (hence between the US and Canada), controversy lasted for almost sixty years. It was finally fixed at its present boundaries by the Webster-Ashburton Treaty of 1842.

NORTHERN PACIFIC RAILROAD. See RAIL-ROADS, SKETCHES OF PRINICIPAL LINES: BURLINGTON NORTHERN.

NORTHERN SECURITIES COMPANY V. UNITED STATES 193 US 197 (1904). A Supreme Court decision upholding the government's contention that the company in question, which controlled the Great Northern, Northern Pacific, and Burlington railroads, was in violation of the Sherman Antitrust Act.

NORTHFIELD BANK ROBBERY (Sept. 7, 1876). Eight men, including Frank and Jesse James and the three Younger brothers, in holding up the bank in Northfield, Minn., killed the teller and engaged in a wild gun battle with citizens. Two bandits and a bystander were killed. Most of the gang was later arrested, but the James brothers escaped.

NORTHWEST ANGLE. A projection of land on the northern border of Minnesota. Separated by the rest of Minnesota by a bay of the Lake of the Woods, its is the northenmost territory of the US proper.

NORTHWEST BOUNDARY CONTROVERSY. The Definitive Treaty of Peace of

1783, in setting the border between the US and British North America, used a map drawn in 1755 that did not accurately depict the course of the Mississippi R. Thus, a serious boundary gap was left, and it was settled by the Convention of 1818. It also decreed that lands west of the mountains claimed by either party were to be free and open. The controversy resulting from this was finally terminated by the Oregon Treaty of 1846, which created the present boundary line.

NORTH WEST COMPANY. Major fur-trading firm, organized during the American Revolution; it established posts over much of Canada and the northern US. Its chief inland depot was Grand Portage until 1804 and Fort William thereafter. Excessive competition with the Hudson's Bay Co. led to warfare. In 1821, the two companies merged as the Hudson's Bay Co.

NORTHWEST CONSPIRACY (1863–64). An unrealized Confederate effort to overthrow the governments of Ohio, Indiana, Illinois, and Missouri by liberating Rebel prisoners of war in those states.

NORTHWEST ORDINANCES. See NORTHWEST TERRITORY; ORDINANCES OF 1784, 1785, AND 1787.

NORTHWEST PASSAGE. Until 1800, it was widely believed that there was a sea route across North America by which ships could reach the Orient. Finding that passage was the goal of many explorers. In the 19th and 20th c., the explorations shifted to the north: In 1906, Roald Amundsen, a Norwegian, was the first to sail from the Atlantic to the Pacific through the Arctic. Of the five possible routes through the Canadian Arctic archipelago, only two are practical and only one is deep enough for large ships. Atomic submarines have navigated an under-the-sea route across the North Pole.

NORTHWEST TERRITORY. Comprising the modern states of Ohio, Illinois, Michigan, Indiana, and Wisconsin, it was established by Congress in 1787. Public lands were to be surveyed in townships and into sections of 640 acres, which would be sold to settlers. The first settlement established under the law's terms was at Marietta, Ohio, in 1788. In 1800, the Indiana Territory was split away

and the diminished Northwest Territory was further decreased in 1803, when Michigan was annexed to Indiana. The Northwest Territory gave place to the state of Ohio on March 1, 1803.

NORUMBEGA. Indian name for the New World north of Florida, appearing on 16th- and 17th-c. maps. In 1604, Samuel de Champlain used it for the Penobscot R.

NUCLEAR NONPROLIFERATION TREATY (1969). Signed by the US, the Soviet Union, and sixty other nations; it banned the spread of nuclear weapons; the nations with nuclear capabilities pledged not to furnish nuclear weapons to nations not having them.

NUCLEAR POWER. Industrial interest in nuclear power grew after World War II, and the Atomic Energy Commission (now the Nuclear Regulatory Commission) by 1957 had put seven experimental reactors in operation. By 1979, the total nuclear gross generating capacity of the US provided 54 million kilowatts in seventy-five operating plants. Many more were in the planning state. The Three Mile Island accident of March 1979, in which some radiation was released, provided a rallying point for antinuclear protests and led to numerous investigations and to an immediate closing of seven similar reactors. By 1984, the controversy over nuclear power had not died down. No new nuclear plants were being planned, and some plants ready to go on stream were having their openings delayed as power companies studied their viability.

NUCLEAR REGULATORY COMMISSION. (NRC). Successor agency to the Atomic Energy Commission; responsible for the regulation of civilian uses of nuclear energy, including setting safety standards.

NUCLEAR TEST BAN TREATY (Aug. 5, 1963). The US, Great Britain, and the Soviet Union signed an agreement calling for an end of nuclear tests in the atmosphere, in space, and underwater. More than 100 other nations later acceded to the treaty.

NUECES RIVER. Although Texas had never extended W of the Nueces R as a Spanish or a Mexican province, the Texas Republic claimed the Rio Grande as its boundary. After annexation, the US also claimed the Rio Grande; it was certified by the Treaty of Guadalupe Hidalgo in 1848.

NULLIFICATION. The act by which a state suspends, within its territory, a federal law. The doctrine evolved from the theory that the Union represents a compact between sovereign states and that the states are not bound by laws that go beyond the constitutional limits of the Union. In 1822, South Carolina declared the tariff act of 1832 void within its borders. President Jackson denounced nullification as rebellion and treason and asked for passage of a force bill that would enable him to enforce the law by use of force. However, he also called for a more moderate tariff act. Both acts passed the Congress, but a constitutional crisis was avoided when South Carolina rescinded its nullification order. The Supreme Court has denied the power of a state to nullify federal law or policy.

NUMBER 4. Now Charlestown, N. H., it was founded in 1740 as the most northerly English post in the Connecticut Valley. Attacked frequently by the French and Indians, it was of great military importance in protecting Massachusetts.

NUREMBERG TRIALS (1945–46). After World War II, many leading German military and governmental circles were put on trial by the Allies, at Nuremberg, Germany, for crimes against humanity. Hermann Goering and twelve others were condemned to death, three were acquitted, and six received jail sentences.

OAKLAND. City in California, located on the E shore of San Francisco Bay and connected with San Francisco by the Bay Bridge and a rapid transit system. It was founded as a supply point for gold miners during the 1849 Gold Rush. Today, Oakland engages in manufacturing, specializing in machinery and shipbuilding. Pop.: 339,288 (1980).

OATS. First planted in North America ca. 1600. Long the outstanding feed for horses, oat production declined sharply with the disappearance of horses from America's streets and farms. Oats can be grown from Alaska to Texas; Arkansas, Minnesota, Wisconsin, and Oregon are the leading producers.

OBERLIN MOVEMENT. An evangelical anti-slavery movement, founded 1834 in Cincinnati, with most of its adherents later moving to Oberlin College, Ohio. These evangelists converted much of Ohio and the West to abolition.

OBLONG, THE. A narrow strip along the E borders of Dutchess, Putnam, and Westchester counties traded to New York by Connecticut in 1731 for a rectangular strip along Long Island Sound.

OBSERVATORIES, ASTRONOMICAL. During the first fifty years of the Republic, about twenty-five notable observatories were equipped for viewing celestial bodies. The US Naval Observatory, Washington, D.C., established in 1842, served as the national observatory. In the late 19th and early 20th c., observatories proliferated in the US, particularly on college campuses. The largest and most sophisticated are in place at Mount Palomar and Mount Wilson, California.

OCALA PLATFORM. Adopted by Florida farmers in 1890, it demanded abolition of national banks, a graduated income tax, free and unlimited coinage of silver, low-interest loans for farmers, and the popular election of US senators.

OCEANOGRAPHY. The US Coast Survey after 1844 conducted extensive explorations of oceantides, currents, and bottom deposits, and participated in research in deep-sea biology. The Hydrographic Office and the Naval Observatory later joined in such pursuits. The exploration of the sea bottom benefited greatly from the invention of a sounder that brought substantial samples back to the surface. The production of trade-wind charts, thermal charts, whale charts, and storm and rain charts was begun in the 1840s. M.F. Maury wrote *The Physical Geography of the Sea* in 1855, and it became the basis of modern oceanography. The sinking of the *Titanic* in 1912 and the development of submarines during World War I jointly stimulated research into underwater sound. Sonic depth-finders, photogrammetry, and aerial photography were introduced in the 1920s. In 1927, the Rockefeller Foundation began a major effort in oceanography. The result was the founding of the Woods Hole Oceanographic

Institution in 1930 and the strengthening of ongoing programs, principally at the University of Washington and the Scripps Institution of Oceanography of the University of California. After 1945, Texas A&M, Miami, Rhode Island, Columbia, New York, Oregon State, and Johns Hopkins universities began substantial programs of teaching and research. Federal programs were also stepped up: The National Oceanic and Atmospheric Administration was established in 1970, as was the National Oceanographic Instrumentation Center.

OFFICE OF ECONOMIC OPPORTUNITY (OEO). The coordinating agency for the War on Poverty begun by President Lyndon B. Johnson in 1964. Among the programs under OEO were the Job Corps, Neighborhood Youth Corps, VISTA, community action programs, work training and work study programs, and Head Start. OEO was under congressional attack almost from the beginning, and many of its programs were transferred to other agencies. It was abolished during the Nixon administration.

OFFICE OF MANAGEMENT AND BUDGET (OMB). Superseded the Bureau of the Budget in 1971 as presidential agency for formulating government fiscal policy. OMB prepares the annual budget that the president submits to Congress each year. The director has cabinet-level status.

OFFICE OF PRICE ADMINISTRATION (OPA). A World War II agency created to set ceiling prices on most commodities and handle rationing of staples.

OFFICE OF STRATEGIC SERVICES (OSS). A World War II agency charged with centralizing the collection and analysis of strategic information and the planning and performing of special operations, especially in the realms of espionage and sabotage. Precursor of CENTRAL INTELLIGENCE AGENCY, founded 1947.

OFFICERS' RESERVE CORPS. Established 1916, its primary function has been to provide school-trained officers. Its members are assigned to units of the Organized Reserve Corps and to inactive regiments of the regular army. The Reserve Officers' Training Corps (ROTC) has been the major means of filling the corps.

OGALLALA. Nebraska town on the South Platte R; established 1869 as the terminus for one of the important Texas cattle trails. It was a stop on the Union Pacific RR and became a cow town with a lively reputation. Pop.: 5,638 (1980).

OGDEN PURCHASE. In 1826, the Ogden Co. purchased large amounts of land in New York state from various Iroquois chiefs.

OGDENSBURG. Industrial city and port in New York state on the St. Lawrence R. A French Indian mission, La Présentation, was founded on the site 1749. The British garrisoned it in 1760, naming it Fort William Augustus and later Fort Oswegatchie. Permanent settlement began in 1792, and the British captured it during the War of 1812. In the 19th c. an important port of entry and railroad center. Pop.: 12,375 (1980).

OGDEN'S HOLE. A rendezvous for fur trappers near the NE shore of Great Salt Lake, Utah. The present town of Ogden stands on the site.

OHIO. The Indians inhabiting Ohio in the historic era were descendants of the prehistoric MOUND BUILDERS. La Salle claimed the whole region for France in 1699, but by the beginning of the 18th c., both French and British fur traders were moving in and out of the area. The British, disputing French claims, established the Ohio Co. in 1747 and placed it under Virginia. French attempts to destroy British posts met with some success, but at the end of the French and Indian War (1763), the British were in control. It became known as the Old Northwest. In 1774, Britain attempted to make all of Ohio part of Canada, one of the grievances leading to the American Revolution. The Treaty of Paris (1783) ceded all of the Old Northwest, including present Ohio, to the US. The Ordinance of 1787 created the Northwest Territory, gave full citizenship rights to settlers there, and guaranteed them eventual self-government. Land companies were formed and settlement began, the first being at Marietta in 1788. Losantiville (Cincinnati) was formed later the same year. The Connecticut Land Co. was formed to settle the Western Reserve, and in 1796 Cleveland was established. With the support of the British,

Ohio Indians kept up a relentless guerrilla war until 1794, when a decisive battle was won by US troops at Fallen Timbers and Ohio was more or less pacified. In 1800, the western part of the Northwest Territory became the Indiana Territory, and in 1803, Ohio was admitted as the seventeenth state.

The British invaded N Ohio during the War of 1812, but were repulsed; the Treaty of Ghent (1814) ended British hopes in the Ohio country. Ohio then entered into its greatest period of growth. Settlements prospered from the rich farmlands, and immigrants began arriving from Europe. The state's population doubled between 1820 and 1830. During the 1830s a great transportation-building program began: canals connected the natural waterways, a statewide road system was developed, the National Road was opened, and the first railroads were built. During the second half of the 19th c., Ohio became a great commercial and industrial center. Cleveland, Youngstown, and Canton became centers of the iron and steel and other heavy industries. Akron was the national center for the rubber industry; Toledo was a glassmaking center; and Cincinnati was one of the great meat-packing centers in the nation. Politically, the state became a bastion of conservative Republicanism; it produced seven presidents: Ulysses S. Grant, Rutherford B. Hayes, James A. Garfield, Benjamin Harrison, William McKinley, William Howard Taft, and Warren G. Harding. Ohio prospered during the 1920s but suffered greatly during the Great Depression. It was the center of much labor strife. The state regained prosperity during World War II and maintained it after the war. The opening of the St. Lawrence Seaway in 1959 made Cleveland and Toledo seaports. Pop.: 10,797,419 (1980).

OHIO, FALLS OF THE. Rapids on the Ohio R opposite Louisville, Ky. Flatboats could go down the rapids in high water, but they were an impediment to steamboats; freight and passengers had to be portaged. The LOUISVILLE AND PORTLAND CANAL was built around the falls in 1830.

OHIO, FORKS OF THE. The junction of the Allegheny and Monongahela rivers at PITTS-BURGH. A fort was built by the Ohio Co. there in 1754, but it was captured by the French, who renamed it Fort Duquesne. Captured and renamed Fort Pitt, it remained under British supervision for more than a decade.

OHIO COMPANY OF ASSOCIATES. Organized in Boston in 1786 by a group of Revolutionary War officers for the purpose of settling the Ohio country. By skillful lobbying, it secured 1.7 million acres N of the Ohio R at very favorable terms (the acreage was later diminished after the company ran into financial difficulties). It founded Marietta 1788.

OHIO COMPANY OF VIRGINIA. Organized 1747 by petition to the crown for large tracts of land W of the Appalachian Mountains. A road was opened across the mountains ca. 1752, and a settlement was planted in what is now Fayette County, Pa. In 1754, the company erected a fort at the Forks of the Ohio. The French and Indian War ended the company's activities.

OHIO-MICHIGAN BOUNDARY DISPUTE. Long controversy over the cape on Maumee Bay in Lake Erie. The dispute reached its climax in the bloodless Toledo War of 1835–36. Congress gave the strip (some 400 square miles) to Ohio Territory but compensated Michigan Territory with statehood and another tract of land on the Upper Peninsula.

OHIO NATIONAL STAGE COMPANY. The company operated stagecoaches on the western division of the National Road after 1833. Its headquarters were in Columbus, and it had branch lines to all parts of Ohio and W Pennsylvania, and by 1844 had a near monopoly. The railroads ended its importance in the 1850s.

OHIO RIVER, DISCOVERY OF. In 1669, the sieur de La Salle, having heard of the "great river" ("Ohio" in the Iroquois tongue), found his way to the marshy country below the Falls of the Ohio, near Louisville. Whether La Salle abandoned the expedition before it reached the river is an unanswered question. News of La Salle's voyage quickly spread. Louis Jolliet's map in 1674 gave the general course of the Ohio as far as the falls, and Franquelin's map in 1682 showed that it flowed into the Mississippi R. According to unverified reports, Abraham Wood, a fur trader at Fort Henry (now Petersburg) between 1654–64, discovered several branches of the Ohio and Mississippi. If so, he preceded La Salle.

OHIO STATE CANALS. In 1825, two major canals were begun, the Ohio and Erie from Lake Erie at Cleveland, to the Ohio R at Portsmouth; and the Miami and Erie from the Ohio at Cincinnati to Dayton, with a later extension to Lake Erie. By 1832, the 308-mile Ohio and Erie was open. The extension of the Miami and Erie Canal to Toledo and Lake Erie was begun in 1833, but completed only in 1843. The canals were of enormous importance to the industrial and commercial growth of Ohio, but by the 1850s, they were being replaced by the railroad.

OHIO VALLEY. A natural link between the Appalachians and the Mississippi Valley. In the 17th c., there developed a flourishing trade with the Indians. The French established a series of forts in the upper Ohio Valley, and in 1758 the English captured Fort Duquesne at the Forks of the Ohio, renaming it Fort Pitt, the strategic center of the valley.

OJIBWA. See CHIPPEWA.

OKANOGA, FORT. Built 1811 at the juncture of the Columbia and Okanogan rivers in Washington by the Pacific Fur Co.; eventually taken over by the Hudson's Bay Co.

OKEECHOBEE, BATTLE OF (Dec. 25, 1837). The bloodiest engagement of the second Seminole War and an important factor in the removal of the Indians from Florida. Gen. Zachary Taylor commanded US troops.

OKINAWA. Japanese island important in World War II as a staging point for projected US invasion of Japan. On April 1, 1945, US forces began a struggle that ended on June 21 with more than 115,000 Japanese defenders defeated. It had been one of the bloodiest battles of the Pacific war; many of the Japanese were burrowed into caves, and the invading US troops eliminated them at heavy cost.

OKLAHOMA. In the historic period, it was peopled by bands of nomadic Osage, Kiowa Apache, and Comanche, who wandered the W plains. Except for its panhandle, Oklahoma was part of the Louisiana Territory. Between 1817 and 1842, the FIVE CIVILIZED TRIBES were forced to leave their homes in the Southeast and settle on assigned tracts in what became known as the Indian Territory. The five tribes adopted slavery and joined the Confederacy during the Civil War. Later they lost half their lands as the federal government began moving other tribes into Oklahoma. They included the Arapaho, Osage, Comanche, Cheyenne, Pawnee, Seneca, Shawnee, and Wyandot. White interest in the Indian Territory also increased. The movement of vast cattle herds from Texas through Oklahoma encouraged organized use of the rich western grazing lands. The coming of the railroad introduced thousands of whites to the economic potential of these lands. After 1879, attempts were made by organized immigrant groups called boomers to settle on the unassigned lands. Beginning in 1889, much of Indian Territory was opened to white settlers (see OKLAHOMA OPENINGS).

The western part of Indian Territory was made Oklahoma Territory in 1890; it came under territorial government, while Indian Territory was governed by the Indian nations. Pressure developed from the whites for statehood; finally, in 1907, the twin territories entered the Union as Oklahoma. After 1904, the state prospered after oil was discovered. Boom towns flourished, but many soon became ghost towns. The Great Depression hit Oklahoma especially hard as the drought of 1934–36 turned much of W Oklahoma into the Dust Bowl. Many of the dispossessed, known as Okies, left for California and Texas. In the postwar period, Oklahoma continued to be a major producer of petroleum and natural gas. The manufacturing of transportation and farm equipment and clay and glass items, as well as a large cattle industry, gives the state a diversified economy. Pop.: 3,025,266 (1980).

OKLAHOMA CITY. The capital of Oklahoma, it began suddenly on April 22, 1889, when 10,000 settlers, waiting for their land claims, set up camp there in tents, turning it into a frontier metropolis. It became the state capital in 1910. During the 1920s, Oklahoma City became a great oil center. Grain elevators and stockyards, cottonseed oil plants, and food processing factories are also located in the city. Pop.: 403,213 (1980).

OKLAHOMA OPENINGS. At high noon, April 22, 1889, the former Indian lands of W Oklahoma were opened to white settlement. This resulted in a run in which some 50,000 people took part, each seeking to be the first to settle on one of the 160-acre homesteads. Other land openings took place in 1901 and 1906.

OKLAHOMA SQUATTERS. White settlers on Indian lands before they were officially open to white settlement. Some were removed by the military, and all were warned not to occupy unassigned lands. Those who entered lands before they were open to white settlement came to be known as Sooners.

OLD DOMINION. When Charles II was restored to the throne in 1660, in response to the loyalty of the Virginia burgesses, he elevated Virginia to the position of a dominion. Thus, Virginia became known as the Old Dominion.

OLD FUSS AND FEATHERS. Nickname for Gen. Winfield Scott. It referred to his love of pageantry and meticulousness in military procedure and etiquette.

OLD HICKORY. Nickname for Andrew Jackson, because of his endurance and strength.

OLD IRONSIDES. Nickname for the CONSTITUTION.

OLD NORTH CHURCH. Common name for Christ Church, Boston, erected in 1723. It was in its steeple that two signal lights were hung to indicate to Paul Revere that the British were approaching Lexington on the night of April 18, 1775.

OLD NORTHWEST. Vast area between the Ohio and Mississippi rivers and the Great Lakes. The Definitive Treaty of Peace of 1783 awarded this territory to the US. After the states had ceded their claims to the WESTERN LANDS, it became a public domain organized as the NORTHWEST TERRITORY.

OLD ROUGH AND READY. Nickname for Gen. Zachary Taylor, earned by him during the Seminole War of 1841.

OLD SOUTH CHURCH. Built in Boston in 1729. Here was held the Boston Massacre town meeting that forced the royal governor to withdraw British troops from Boston in 1770; and here also was held the Boston Tea Party.

OLD SOUTHWEST. Region lying W of Georgia, South Carolina, and North Carolina and extending to the Mississippi R. Tennessee, Alabama, and Mississippi were formed out of the Old Southwest.

OLEANA. Colony in N Pennsylvania established in 1852 by Norwegians on 120,000 acres of land. A "New Norway" was planned, but the colony soon collapsed.

OLIVE BRANCH PETITION (1775). Sent by the Continental Congress to King George III, setting forth the grievances of the colonies. Richard Penn, a staunch Loyalist, was sent as their messenger; but the king refused to see him or receive his petition.

OLUSTEE, BATTLE OF (Feb. 20, 1864). Confederate victory that thwarted Union hopes of getting possession of the interior of Florida.

OLYMPIA. Capital of the state of Washington. First settled in 1846, it soon became the largest settlement of the Puget Sound area. Pop.: 27,447 (1980).

OMAHA. Plains tribe who inhabited NE Nebraska on the Missouri R. They were sedentary and agricultural, except for the annual bison hunt. The tribe spoke Siouan and was most closely related to the Ponca, Kansa, and Osage. There were an estimated 2,800 of them in 1780.

OMAHA. The largest city in Nebraska and one of the most important transportation and food-processing centers in the United States. It became a key railroad town in 1865 when th Union Pacific RR chose it as the eastern terminus for the first major rail line across the Great Plains. Earlier, it was an important stopping place for wagons moving westward. Pop.: 311,681 (1980).

OÑATE'S EXPLORATIONS (1598–1608). Appointed to colonize a new settlement to be founded on the Rio Grande, the Spanish explorer Juan de Oñate advanced with 400 men

430

and took formal possession near El Paso in 1598. In the following years, he explored and subjugated what are now New Mexico and NE Arizona, went as far west as the Gulf of California, and perhaps traveled as far north as Kansas.

ONEIDA COLONY. A radical experiment in social and religous organization, established 1848 in Oneida, N. Y. The colony promulgated communism, rejected monogamy for complex marriage, and encouraged the eugenic breeding of children. A branch colony was established at Wallingford, Conn. The colonies were successful, but outside pressures forced them in 1879 to adopt monogamy. Communism was replaced by joint-stock ownership. In its new form, the Oneida Co. became noted for its production of fine silver and stainless steel flatware.

ONION RIVER LAND COMPANY (1773–75). In 1773, the company bought 77,000 acres of land from New Hampshire in what is now Vermont. Ethan Allen, one of the partners, began the settlement of Burlington, even though it was known that New York state also held claims on the land. To destroy the New York claims, the company resorted to mob violence and the destruction of property, and the use of the Green Mountain Boys, commanded by Allen. New York ceased to press its claims after the outbreak of the American Revolution, and Vermont became a separate state. The company's affairs were badly managed, however, and its partners benefited little financially.

ONIONS. First brought to America by the colonists. Commercial production of Bermuda onions began ca. 1900 in Texas, California, and Louisiana. In 1980, the US produced 1.67 million short tons of onions, valued at $346 million.

ONTARIO, LAKE. The smallest of the Great Lakes; discovered by Champlain and Brulé in 1615. Fort Frontenac was built in 1673 where the city of Kingston now stands; it was destroyed by the English in 1758. Fort Toronto was built in 1750, where the city of Toronto now stands. The lake was a principal water thoroughfare of the fur trade. Fort Oswego was built in 1727, destroyed by the French in 1756, and rebuilt by the British in

1759 and renamed Fort Ontario. Fort Niagara, built in 1678 by La Salle, was surrendered by the English to the US after the American Revolution. Lake Ontario became important in the 19th c. for the shipping of grain and lumber from the Middle West and Canada, and of coal from Pennsylvania. With the opening of the St. Lawrence Seaway in 1959, shipping through Lake Ontario increased greatly.

OPEN DOOR POLICY. Basic US policy toward China from ca. 1900. It stated the intention of the US to press for equal commercial and industrial rights in China with the major powers there (Great Britain, Germany, and Russia).

OPEN-RANGE CATTLE PERIOD. After ca. 1866, open-range grazing of cattle began in the central and northern plains as a steady stream of cattle poured north out of Texas. Mature cattle were shipped to market, but yearlings were driven to new ranges, the boundaries of each rancher's pastureland being determined by unwritten law. Cattle were branded so they could be identified at roundups. Great profits were derived from the open-range cattle industry, and eastern cattle companies were formed to take advantage. By ca. 1885, most of the open range was fully stocked and much of it overstocked. In the terrible winter of 1886–87 hundreds of thousands of cattle perished, and virtually every open-range rancher faced ruin. The open-range cattle industry never recovered; in addition, the range area was being rapidly settled and enclosed.

OPEN SHOP. See CLOSED SHOP.

ORANGE, FORT. The Dutch settlement, trading post, and fort on the site of modern Albany, N.Y.; founded 1624, but two years later Indian troubles forced the families to move downriver to New Amsterdam.

ORDERS IN COUNCIL. Edicts in Great Britain issued by the king and having the force of law. Two orders in council, issued during the Napoleonic Wars, are of primary interest in US history. The order of Jan. 7, 1807, placed French commerce under a blockade and forbade neutrals (which included the US) to trade from one port to another under Napoleon's jurisdiction. The orders of Nov. 11,

1807, stipulated that neutral ships, again including American, might not enter any ports "from which ... the British flag is excluded." The orders were superseded in 1809 and were actually repealed in 1812, but too late to avert the War of 1812.

ORDINANCES OF 1784, 1785, AND 1787. At the end of the American Revolution, seven states had western land claims and six had none. The latter refused to join the Confederation until the former should cede their lands to the new government for the common benefit of all. New York, in 1780, led the way by giving up all claims to the western lands, whereupon Congress passed a resolution pledging that the lands the states might cede would be erected into new states. The Ordinance of 1784 provided for an artificial division of the entire West into sixteen districts, each district to become eligible for statehood upon reaching a population of 20,000. The 1785 Ordinance provided a scientific system of surveying and subdividing land. In 1787, Congress enacted an ordinance for the government of the territory N of the Ohio R. It provided for the future division of the territory into not less than and not more than five states; it contained compacts that established religious freedom, prohibited slavery, and guaranteed the fundamental rights of English liberty and just treatment of the Indians.

OREGON. The region may have been reached by sea by the Spanish Bartolomé Ferrelo in 1543. Capt. James Cook's tremendous profits from sea otter furs sold in Canton led many British and American traders to the coast. Thomas Jefferson sent Lewis and Clark with instructions to find the River Oregon, which they identified as the Columbia. In 1811, John Jacob Astor founded Astoria on the Columbia, the first settlement in Oregon. The Columbia District was first referred to officially as Oregon in 1822, when a bill was introduced into Congress to set up the Territory of Oregon. Under an 1818 treaty with Great Britain, the Northwest (which included British Columbia, Washington, Oregon, Idaho, and parts of Montana and Wyoming) was jointly occupied without formation of a government. Great Britain claimed all land N of the Columbia R, and US politicians felt that the US should have all the coast. The militant slogan "Fifty-four Forty or Fight" was used by those advocating the ouster of Great Britain. President Polk negotiated the treaty of 1846, which established the present boundary.

Man first arrived in the Oregon region ca. 10,000 years ago. The Chinook Indians were the dominant group in the historic period. White settlement began in the 1830s; each year saw larger numbers coming over the Oregon Trail to obtain donation lands, primarily in the fertile Willamette Valley. They guaranteed their squatters rights by organizing a provisional territorial government at Champoeg in 1843. Official territorial status came in 1849, and Washington Territory was separated from Oregon in 1853. Oregon was granted statehood in 1859. The Indians were placed on reservations in 1855. Gold rushes of the 1850s produced the Rogue River War (1855–56). Similar rushes to Oregon during the Civil War and afterward produced wars that resulted in the confinement of the rest of the Indians to reservations. Today, agriculture, lumbering and wood products, and stock raising are important industries. Pop.: 2,632,663 (1980).

OREGON. US battleship that traveled from San Francisco to Cuba during the Spanish-American War. Dramatic evidence of the need for quicker communication by water between the Pacific and the Atlantic.

OREGON PAROCHIAL SCHOOL CASE (*Pierce v. Society of the Sisters of the Holy Names of Jesus and Mary,* 268 US 510, 1925). The Supreme Court invalidated an Oregon law under which all children would have been required to attend public schools.

OREGON QUESTION. In the early 19th c., the Pacific Northwest was the subject of conflicting claims of ownership of Spain, Great Britain, the US, and Russia. Until the final division of the territory between the US and Britain, the Oregon question was the subject of intermittent correspondence between the two countries. By 1844, popular feeling found expression in the political slogan "Fifty-four Forty or Fight," widely used in the campaign in which James K. Polk was elected president. After Polk's election, the OREGON TREATY OF 1846 settled the Oregon question by continuing the boundary E of the Rockies (forty-ninth parallel) to the sea.

OREGON TRAIL. First traced from the Missouri R to the Columbia R by explorers and fur traders. Independence, Mo., was the most frequent place of departure. Traffic during the 1840s and 1850s became so heavy that the road was a clearly defined and deeply rutted way; generations later, hundreds of miles of the trail could still be traced.

OREGON TREATY OF 1846. Fixed the boundary between the US and British America at the forty-ninth parallel W of the Rocky Mountains except at the western terminus of that line, where it swerved southward around Vancouver Island. Settled the OREGON QUESTION.

ORGANIZATION OF AMERICAN STATES (OAS). Founded 1948 to foster better relations among the American nations. It succeeded the Pan-American Union. The OAS has sought to settle disputes among its twenty-eight members, has fostered economic and social progress in the hemisphere, and has concerned itself with human rights.

ORISKANY, BATTLE OF (Aug. 6, 1777). A bloody encounter near Rome, N.Y., between an army of Tories and Indians and a patriot force under Gen. Nicholas Herkimer. The Americans were ambushed but rallied and sent their attackers into retreat.

ORLEANS, FORT. First fort built on the Missouri R, by the French in 1723 at the mouth of Grand R as part of their plan to open a trade route to Santa Fe.

ORLEANS, TERRITORY OF. Probably first visited by the survivors of Hernando de Soto's expedition in 1543; claimed by La Salle for France in 1682. Bienville founded New Orleans in 1718 and made it capital in 1722. Passed to US in 1803 as part of LOUISIANA PURCHASE.

ORNITHOLOGY. Alexander Wilson is known as the father of American ornithology, even though his *American Ornithology* (1808–14) has long been overshadowed by J.J. Audubon's *Birds of America* (1827–38). Scientific ornithology thrived in the late 19th c.; birds were found, named, described, and classified. The American Ornithologists' Union, founded 1883, began publishing a checklist of of North American birds (760 species by 1957).

ORTHODOX CHURCHES. See EASTERN ORTHODOXY.

OSAGE. Siouan tribe found in historical times in Missouri in two principal bands, the Great Osage and the Little Osage. In 1808, the Osage ceded all their lands in Missouri and Arkansas and subsequently were found in Oklahoma.

OSAGE, FORT. Built 1808 on the Missouri R, nineteen miles E of present-day Kansas City. Most important US western outpost until 1827.

OSAGE HEDGE (*Maclura*). A thorn-bearing tree that produces a pale green fruit, the osage orange. Millions of these trees were used on the treeless prairies as hedgerows. Its thorn inspired barbed wire.

OSAWATOMIE, BATTLE OF (Aug. 30, 1856). Osawatomie, Kans., was attacked and sacked by a force of proslavery men. The town's defense was commanded by John Brown.

OSGOODITES. A New Hampshire sect, followers of Jacob Osgood (1777–1844). In 1812, they left the Freewill Baptists, claiming special powers of prophecy and healing. By 1890, the movement had died out.

OSTEND MANIFESTO (1854). After US efforts to buy Cuba from Spain had failed, President Pierce's negotiators at Ostend, Belgium, issued a manifesto declaring that should the US consider Spain's further possession of Cuba inimical to US interests, forcible seizure would be fully justified. The manifesto created a storm of denunciation, and the US was forced to disavow it.

OSTEOPATHY. The general application of manipulative methods based on the recognition of the importance of the structural integrity of the body and linked with general application of the science of natural immunity; developed by Andrew T. Still (1828–1917). By 1980, there were eight US colleges offering degrees in osteopathy, and there were about 14,000 practicing osteopaths.

OSWEGO. City in New York on Lake Ontario; founded as an Indian trading post in 1722 by English and Dutch traders. Site of important English fort trading post in the 18th c. In the War of 1812, Oswego was a US naval base and was attacked and captured by the British. The city is a center of hydronuclear electric power. Pop.: 19,793 (1980).

OTSEGO LANDS. A tract of 100,000 acres on the Susquehanna R and Otsego Lake, in New York state. It was purchased from the Indians in 1769, and Cooperstown was laid out on the tract in 1789.

OUIATENON, FORT. Built 1720 by the French on the N bank of the Wabash R near present-day Lafayette, Ind., as a point on the fur-trading route. Abandoned 1791.

"OUR COUNTRY RIGHT OR WRONG." Motto that formed part of a toast offered on April 4, 1816, by Capt. Stephen Decatur. It reflected the nationalism resulting from the War of 1812.

"OUR FEDERAL UNION! IT MUST BE PRE-SERVED!" Part of a toast offered on April 13, 1830, by Andrew Jackson. The words rallied Unionists and contributed to the successful conclusion of the nullification crisis of 1833.

OUTER SPACE TREATY (Jan. 27, 1967). Signed by the US, the Soviet Union, Great Britain, and fifty-seven other nations. It established general principles for the peaceful exploration of outer space and banned the employment and testing of weapons in outer space.

OVERLAND COMPANIES. Parties that traveled from the East to the Pacific coast by wagon trains, as opposed to those who went by ship around Cape Horn or by the Isthmus of Darien. The first great overland movement was to the Oregon country in the 1840s, quickly followed by those headed for the California gold fields after 1849.

OVERLAND FREIGHTING. The movement of goods, after the 1840s, over the Overland Trail from points on the Missouri R to the Rocky Mountains or California. Hauling began after Salt Lake City was founded (1847) and gold was discovered in California (1849). The outfitting towns along the Mis-souri, especially INDEPENDENCE, were the eastern terminus for the traffic that generally crossed the Platte Valley or the Kansas Valley. The trains averaged about twelve miles per day, and the time required for a trip from Kansas City to Salt Lake City was about fifty days. The railroads put an end to overland freighting.

OVERLAND MAIL AND STAGECOACHES. Monthly government mail services began in 1850 between Independence, Mo., and Salt Lake City and Santa Fe. A similar service began between Salt Lake City and Sacramento in 1851. In 1858, a government-subsidized southern mail route, via El Paso and Tucson, was inaugurated. In 1860, the Pony Express was established along a central route. Operations were continued until the completion of the transcontinental railroad in 1869.

OVERLAND TRAIL. A shorter variation of the Oregon Trail. It followed the South Platte R to Latham, near present-day Greeley, Colo., up the Cache la Poudre R, across the Laramie Plains, over Bridger's Pass (in Wyoming), and thence W to Fort Bridger, Wyo. Highways US 30 and Interstate 80 now follow approximately the Overland Trail through W Wyoming.

OXEN. Used by the early settlers as draft animals and for plowing. Their slowness was counterbalanced by their great strength and endurance. Oxen drew in enormous numbers for freighting in the West. Two large loaded wagons were often hooked together and drawn by as many as ten yoke (twenty) of oxen.

PAC. See POLITICAL ACTION COMMITTEE.

PACIFIC FUR COMPANY. Organized 1810 by John Jacob Astor as a subsidiary of the American Fur Co., with chief depot, Astoria, on the Columbia R. Bad management and the War of 1812 caused it to fail.

PACIFIC NORTHWEST. Region of the United States comprising the states of Oregon, Washington, and Idaho, all part of the old Oregon country.

PACIFIC RAILROAD. See RAILROADS, SKETCHES OF PRINCIPAL LINES: UNION PACIFIC.

PACIFIC REPUBLIC MOVEMENT. Various groups of westerners advocated the formation of an independent nation of the lands W of the Rockies in order to remain neutral in the North-South dissension that was splitting the rest of the country in the years before the Civil War.

PACIFICUS AND HELVIDIUS. After President Washington issued (April 22, 1793) a proclamation of neutrality during the war between France and England, he was defended by Alexander Hamilton, who wrote a number of articles under the pseudonym Pacificus. James Madison refuted them in a series of articles under the name Helvidius.

PACIFISM. Traditionally, pacifism has been associated with such religious denominations as the Quakers and Mennonites who hold war to be in fundamental contradiction to their faiths. Male members have generally been conscientious objectors. Pacifist movements have been in existence since the early 19th c., but they have never attracted a large following.

PACKETS, SAILING. The packet, or sailing line, as distinguished from the transient, or tramp, was one of a line of privately owned vessels sailing in regular succession on fixed dates between specified ports. The Black Ball Line began monthly transatlantic service between New York and Liverpool in 1818; by 1822, several more lines were competing for the traffic, and service between New York and London and Le Havre began. Until 1838, sailing packets conveyed most of the new, cabin passengers, and fine freight. After that, steamships began cutting into those lucrative fields; and packets began carrying chiefly immigrants and freight. The last ocean packet sailed in 1881.

PACK TRAINS. Organized by the trans-Allegheny pioneers as a way of getting goods to eastern markets. A caravan of packhorses laden with goods for barter, mainly peltry, potash, flax, whiskey, and feed were sent over old Indian trails. The trains returned with salt, iron, sugar, lead, and such urban luxuries as crockery. Later the trails were widened to accommodate wagon trains.

PAINTING. The earliest pictures done in America were watercolors and drawings by explorers. The artist recorded flora and fauna or made topographical views. A few painters settled and worked in New England in the 17th c. Several anonymous limners were active in the Boston area and in the Dutch colony of New Netherland in the late 17th c.

American painting in the 18th c. was highly imitative of European, especially English, style. A number of European painters emigrated and contributed important works, mainly portraits. They include Justus Englehardt Kühn (German), Gustavus Hesselius (Swedish), and three important English emigrants: Peter Pelham, Charles Bridges, and John Smibert. Benjamin West and John Singleton Copley were the two most famous American painters of the 18th c. West went to England in 1760, where he became a leading painter and president of the Royal Academy. Copley, who incorporated a high degree of realism in his work, also emigrated to Europe (in 1774) and never returned. The late-18th c. saw a flowering of American painting. Among the best known of the artists were Charles Willson Peale, John Trumbull, Ralph Earl, and Gilbert Stuart.

Although romanticism began in the 18th c., it saw its fullest expression in the 19th. Artists began turning away from the works of man; nature, especially in its wilder aspects, was used as a vehicle of expression. Narrative painting assumed a romantic character as painters of religious, historical, and genre subjects gave greater emphasis to the drama of the setting. Monumental, ambitious historical paintings were especially appreciated; Emmanuel Leutze's *Washington Crossing the Delaware* (1851) is the most famous example of romanticized, sentimental historical painting. Two leading portraitists of the period were Samuel F.B. Morse and Thomas Sully. The Hudson River school, represented especially by Thomas Doughty and Asher B. Durand, emphasized landscapes of gentle, often imaginary romanticism.

Naturalism also was an outgrowth of the 19th c. As early as 1810, Charles Wilson Peale and his brother James were offering paintings remarkably free of sentiment and allegory. Winslow Homer and Thomas Eakins created paintings that were highly realistic, yet partook of the romantic impulse. Many of Morse's portraits provide uncompromising likenesses and place him among the pioneers of naturalism.

The years 1880–1930 are generally called the American Renaissance because all the arts, including painting, flourished as never before. Among the leading painters were Homer, Eakins, John Singer Sargent, James McNeil Whistler, Mary Cassatt, and Childe Hassam.

American painting in the 20th c. can be seen as a series of revolutions against previous styles. The Ash Can school, which included John Sloan, Maurice B. Prendergast, and Robert Henri, brought forth a revolution in subject rather than style. Georgia O'Keefe, Charles Sheeler, and Charles Demuth simplified sometimes almost to a geometric core. The American regionalists (Grant Wood, Thomas Hart Benton, and John Steuart Curry) focused on authentically American types. The theme of the city was taken up by Edward Hopper, Charles Burchfield, Ben Shahn, and William Gropper. Abstract expressionism asserted itself in reaction to the social realism of the 1930s. William de Kooning, Mark Rothko, and Jackson Pollock were its leaders. By 1960 a reaction to abstract expressionism had set in. Jasper Johns was painting a series of American flags and the pop artists Andy Warhol, Roy Lichtenstein, and James Rosenquist were painting in a highly representational style. On the other hand, Robert Rauschenberg and Frank Stella continued in the nonrepresentational tradition. Optical illusions and photo realism were genre of other painters of the 1970s and 1980s.

PAIUTE. Indian people inhabiting the Great Basin, from SE Oregon through S California. They numbered about 7,500 in 1845. Dependent on the gathering of wild seed and fruit, their tribal development was minimal. They spoke two main languages of the Shoshonean family. It was a northern Paiute, Wovoka, who in 1880 originated the second GHOST DANCE movement. In the 1980s, the northern Paiute numbered about 4,000 and the southern Paiute about 1,800.

PALATINES. German Protestants from the Lower and Rhenish Palatinates who emigrated to America in 1709. Most settled in Herkimer County, New York; others settled in New Jersey and Pennsylvania.

PALEONTOLOGY. Because of Thomas Jefferson's paleontological interests, the White House had one of the first scientific exhibitions of fossils. During the early 19th c., the study of fossils was put on a firm geologic base by the concepts of stratigraphic succession and correlation. State geological surveys regularly included paleontological materials. Beginning in 1838, the federal government assumed a role in the investigations of natural history and natural resources and sponsored a series of expeditions exploring the western territories. In 1879, four territorial surveys were combined under the US Geological Survey. Eventually, specimens went to the Smithsonian Insitution. Vertebrate fossils have aroused the most interest, but invertebrate fossils have received more scientific investigations, if less public attention. Plant fossils, until recently, have received little attention, but today paleobotany is a thriving field. Micropaleontology, the study of one-celled organisms, and especially palynology, the study of spores and pollen, are important new disciplines. New techniques have been used to push the record of life back. Today it is known that some simple organisms are more than 3 billion years old.

PALMER'S DISCOVERY OF ANTARCTICA. According to the logbook of the sloop *Hero*, Capt. Nathaniel Brown Palmer, an American, discovered the mainland of Anarctica on Nov. 18, 1820, about eighty days before the reputed date of discovery by Capt. John Davis. He made his initial landfall on what is now known as Palmer Peninsula and discovered, with George Powell, the South Orkney Islands in 1821.

PALMITO RANCH, BATTLE OF (May 13, 1865). The last land battle of the Civil War. On May 12, a Union force drove a small group of Confederates from Palmito Ranch, near the mouth of the Rio Grande in Texas. The following day the Rebels moved back into their former position with reinforcements and forced the Union troops into retreat.

PALO ALTO, BATTLE OF (May 8, 1846). The first battle of the Mexican War. Gen. Zachary Taylor's army defeated a much larger Mexican force twelve miles NE of Brownsville, Tex.

PAMPHLETEERING. Pamphlets were an inexpensive, effective method used by colonial Americans to propagate new and unpopular ideas. Leaders of the Revolution wrote many pamphlets to justify their cause, the most noteworthy being Thomas Paine's *Common Sense* and *The Crisis*. The multiplication of newspapers in the early federal period made pamphlet warfare less common, but religious groups and social reformers continued to make use of them.

PAN-AFRICANISM. Movement begun among American blacks in the early 20th c. aimed at ridding Africa of colonial rule and unifying it under self-determination. W.E.B. Du Bois was an early leader and presided over several Pan-African Congresses. After World War II, active leadership in the movement passed to local African leaders. The main theme became national independence, and the Organization of African Unity was formed toward that end. Nationalism within the various black African countries became a stronger force than political unity, and the creation of regional economic organizations represented the main thrust of the unity movement.

PANAMA CANAL. A fifty-one mile waterway through the Isthmus of Panama, connecting the Atlantic and Pacific oceans and one of the world's most strategic waterways. In 1855 a railroad was constructed across the isthmus by an American company; it was an immediate success, and the long-held idea of a canal connecting the two oceans took on a new urgency. In 1881, under a concession granted by Colombia, of which Panama was then a part, a French company commenced construction of a canal; Ferdinand de Lesseps, the engineer of the Suez Canal, was in charge. A substantial amount of excavation had been completed before work was abandoned in 1889, when the company went bankrupt. In 1902, Congress authorized the United States to complete the canal if the assets of the French company could be acquired and if Colombia's permission was forthcoming. Colombia refused its permission, and Panama (with the tacit support of the United States) revolted and declared its independence in 1903. The United States recognized the new government and promptly signed a treaty with it for the construction of the canal. The treaty granted to the United States in perpetuity a zone of land for the transisthmian canal. Within that zone, Panama granted the United States all rights, power, and authority.

The threat posed by tropical diseases, which had contributed to the French failure, was eliminated by a brilliant and energetic program. In 1905, John F. Stevens was named chief engineer and under him the successful implementation of the first phases of actual construction was completed. After Stevens resigned, Lt. Col. G.W. Goethals was named (1907) to replace him. Congress in 1906 resolved a bitter dispute by directing the construction of a lock canal rather than a sea-level one. The completion of the canal was one of the engineering and construction marvels of the age; it opened on Aug. 15, 1914. Its success was immediate.

Panama's dissatisfaction with its original treaty with the United States began manifesting itself almost immediately. New agreements were made in 1928, 1934, 1936, and 1953, all aimed at meeting some of Panama's objections and generally increasing the amount of money the country received. Serious political unrest in Panama began in the 1960s, aimed at the returning of the Canal Zone to Panama's sovereignty. In 1977, after long negotiations, President Carter reached an agreement with Panama, and the two nations signed two treaties. They transferred the Canal Zone to Panama's control; provided for administration of the canal by a joint US-Panamanian body; and stipulated that US military forces would remain in Panama until the year 2000 and would guarantee the canal's neutrality thereafter. After a bitter fight, the Senate ratified both treaties in April 1978.

PANAMA RAILROAD. Built (1849–55) by a US company under commission from the Colombian government. It went across the Isthmus of Panama connecting the Atlantic and Pacific oceans. Until the building of a transcontinental railroad across the United States, the Panama Railroad carried thousands of passengers from the East Coast to California. After completion of the Panama Canal, the railroad was operated by the same company that ran the canal. In 1979, it became part of the government-owned system.

PANAMA REVOLUTION. In 1912, after the Colombian senate refused to ratify a treaty granting rights to US to build a transisthmian canal, a group of dissident Panamanians seized control of Panama City and declared Panamaniam independence. The US navy intervened and the US quickly recognized the insurgents, who signed a new agreement giving the US exclusive rights to build and control a canal. The US guaranteed Panama's independence. (See HAY-BUNAU-VARILLA TREATY.)

PAN-AMERICAN GAMES. A series of contests conducted at four-year intervals and open to athletes from all the American nations.

PAN-AMERICAN UNION. International agency of Western Hemisphere nations founded in 1890. It was subsumed under the Organization of American States (OAS) in 1948.

PANIC OF 1785. Put an end to the boom following the Revolution and ushered in a three-year period of hard times. Aggravated by the absence of any central mechanism for promoting interstate trade, by state laws interfering with interstate trade, and by the British refusal to conclude a commercial treaty. One consequence was SHAYS'S REBELLION.

PANIC OF 1792. Collapse resulting from the speculative boom of 1791, brought on by schemes for internal improvements and speculation in bank scrip and western lands.

PANIC OF 1819. Brought on by a sharp contraction of credit initiated by the second Bank of the United States in its efforts to curb speculation in commodities and western lands following the War of 1812. Southern and western states particularly hard hit.

PANIC OF 1837. Brought on by the enormous state debts resulting from the construction of canals and railroads and the chartering of new banks. To curb the excesses, President Jackson ordered that all payments for public lands be made in specie (gold), thus cramping the operations of banks that were deeply involved in speculation in western lands. The panic was aggravated when most banks suspended specie payments. An Independent Treasury System was established in 1840; but the depression, particularly bad in the South and West, lasted until 1843.

PANIC OF 1857. Followed the boom decade after the Mexican War. Speculation and ex-

pansion ran riot in railroad construction, manufacturing, the wheat belt, and land. State banking was poorly regulated, and the failure of a large insurance company in Cincinnati pricked the bubble. Unemployment grew, breadlines formed, and ominous signs of social unrest appeared. Eastern industrial cities were particularly hard hit.

PANIC OF 1873. Precipitated by the failure of a number of large eastern firms, particularly Jay Cooke and Co. Causes were worldwide: a series of wars, excessive railroad construction, commercial dislocation caused by the opening of the Suez Canal, speculation, and industrial overexpansion. The depression that followed was one of the worst in US history: By 1875, a half million men were out of work. Wage reductions caused strikes in coal mines and textile mills and among railroad workers (see RAILROAD STRIKES OF 1877). Improvements began in 1878.

PANIC OF 1893 The uneasy state of the British security market in 1890 stopped the flow of foreign capital into America and the resale of European-held securities caused a stock market collapse in New York and substantial exports of gold. By the end of 1893, about 4,000 banks and more than 14,000 commercial firms had failed. It was feared that the US government, in the light of declining gold reserves, would be forced off the gold standard. The imports of gold stabilized the monetary situation somewhat, but the winter of 1893–94 saw the beginning of widespread unemployment, strikes met by violence, and the march of COXEY'S ARMY on Washington, D.C. The depression did not lift until the poor European crops of 1897 stimulated US exports and the importation of gold.

PANIC OF 1907. Sometimes called the "rich man's panic." When Standard Oil had to pay 8 percent interest to float a $20 million bond issue, a sharp drop in the stock market took place, the so-called silent panic. To halt the panic, the Treasury authorized large deposits in several banks. Investment banker J.P. Morgan headed a banking group that used a borrowed emergency fund of nearly $40 million to rescue banks and firms they deemed savable and whose survival was crucial. Although only big financiers were, in general, affected by the panic, many questioned the desirability of letting one private citizen wield such power in a crisis. Congress initiated a number of monetary reforms and made the initial steps in setting up the Federal Reserve System.

PANIC OF 1920. See DEPRESSION OF 1920.

PANIC OF 1929. See GREAT DEPRESSION.

PANTON, LESLIE AND COMPANY. Organized in East Florida during the American Revolution by Loyalists to build up trade and influence with the Creek Indians. Created trouble between the Creek and US, but after ca. 1795 confined itself to business and was allowed to continue in operation. Its successor, Forbes and Co., handled most Indian trade until ca. 1817.

PAOLI, BATTLE OF (Sept. 21, 1777). Confrontation at Paoli Inn, Pa., between colonial troops under Gen. Anthony Wayne and the British. Tory spies had revealed Wayne's position, and he was surprised and defeated.

PAPER AND PULP INDUSTRY. In 1609, a paper mill making use of rag fibers was established at Germantown, near Philadelphia. By 1810, there were 202 mills in sixteen states. Technical developments between 1828 and 1890 made straw and then wood usable as raw materials. The 20th c. created a forest-based, capital-intensive industry. After World War II, American paper production led the world; in the 1970s, more than 60 million tons of paper was produced, about 90 percent domestically consumed.

PARAGUAY EXPEDITION. In 1858 a US squadron was sent to Paraguay to seek redress for an 1855 incident in which a US sailor was killed during an encounter with Parguayan ships. They secured an indemnity for the man's family.

PARAPSYCHOLOGY. Organized psychical research began in America with the founding in 1885 of the American Society for Psychical Research. William James was its most noted supporter. In the 20th c., the most notable research in parapsychology was done at Duke University by J.B. Rhine.

PARATROOPS. Paratroops were first used by the French in World War I. Between the wars,

the US did little to develop an airborne arm, but German success with paratroops early in World War II spurred the formation of five airborne divisions. The first one supported Allied amphibious landings in North Africa; others followed in Sicily, Normandy, southern France, the Netherlands, and Germany. There were two airborne operations during the Korean War and one during the Vietnam War.

PARCEL POST. The delivery of packages by mail began in 1913, after years of argument over whether the US Post Office ought to provide such service or to leave the business with private express companies.

PARIS, DECLARATION OF (1856). The major European powers outlawed privateering, but the US declined to adhere to the declaration. Later, during the Civil War, the US endeavored to adhere to the ban, in order to outlaw Confederate privateering; but the Europeans declined.

PARIS, PACT OF. See KELLOGG-BRIAND PACT.

PARIS, PEACE OF (1783). Following the American Revolution, preliminary articles were signed at Paris between the US and Great Britain and between the Netherlands and Great Britain. Later that year, three definitive treaties were signed between Great Britain, the US, France, and Spain.

PARIS, TREATY OF (1763). Between Great Britain and France, a result of the British victory in the French and Indian War. France ceded all of Canada to Britain, and Britain's American colonies' boundaries were extended westward to the Mississippi.

PARIS, TREATY OF (1899). Terminated the Spanish-American War. Spain relinquished all claims to Cuba and ceded Puerto Rico, the Philippines, and Guam to the United States.

PARIS CONFERENCES. A series of lengthy conferences aimed at settling European problems at the end of World War II. In 1946, the twenty-one nations that had fought Germany agreed to peace treaties with the Axis satellites (Finland, Bulgaria, Romania, Hungary, and Italy). The major powers were unable to agree on a German peace treaty, and in 1949 the Western powers refused a Soviet plan for German reunification, and the Soviets rejected extension of the new West German constitution to East Germany.

PARISH. In Louisiana, the civil or political unit corresponding to the county in other states.

PARITY. A principle in naval defense used as a basis for the limitation of naval armaments adopted at the Washington Conference of 1921–22. It established the allowed relative strength of the capital ships of the participating nations. Japan refused to renew the limitation treaties in 1936, which effectively ended the parity agreements.

PARKER'S FORT. Established 1835 at the headwaters of the Navasota R in Limestone County, Tex. In 1836, attacked by the Comanche and Caddo; only one person survived.

PARKS, NATIONAL. Of the 70.9 million acres of federal land in the National Park System in 1980, 15.8 million were in forty-eight national parks and 50.2 million in seventy-eight national monuments. National parks can be established only by Congress, but national monuments can be established by presidential decree. Congress established the National Park Service as part of the Department of the Interior in 1916. Over the years, the areas managed by the park service came to include recreational and cultural areas as well as natural wonders and historical monuments and became known informally as the national park system, a name formalized by Congress in 1953. In 1980, the National Park Service included 333 areas, in every state except Delaware.

PARSON BROWNLOW'S BOOK. Short title of a powerful antisecessionist book, published in 1862 by William G. Brownlow, a Tennessee Unionist.

PARTIES, POLITICAL. See POLITICAL PARTIES.

PASADENA. City NE of Los Angeles in the San Gabriel Mountains. Largely residential, it is noted for its nearby scientific resources, including the California Institute of Technol-

ogy, the Huntington Library, and the Mount Wilson Observatory. Pop.: 119,374 (1980).

PASS CHRISTIAN. Early French settlement in Mississippi. Passed to US in 1811 after the annexation of West Florida. Site of battle in War of 1812. Pop.: 5,014 (1980).

PASSES, MOUNTAIN. Early hunters and pioneers were dependent on natural outlets through the mountains. In the Appalachians, these were generally called gaps. In the Rockies, they were called passes. The most important pass in the Kentucky approach to the West was the Cumberland Gap, followed by Flower Gap, Blue Ridge Gap, and Moccasin Gap. On the Forbes Road, leading from Philadelphia to Pittsburgh, Miller's Run Gap was crossed. The river valleys unlocking the southern route to the West were the Gila and the Colorado. The Colorado trail, known as the Spanish trail, went N from Taos, crossed the Wasatch Mountains and Mojave Desert, and entered California by the Cajon Pass. The Gila route was the shorter trail from Santa Fe, going W across the mountains, and by way of Warner's Pass, eventually reaching San Diego. The Arkansas R route W to Pueblo, Colorado, led to three or four different passes: the Williams of Sandy Hill, the Roubideau or Mosca, and the Sangre de Cristo or Music passes. This route crossed the Great Basin of Utah and Nevada and surmounted the Sierra Nevada passes in California. After the eastern escarpment had been scaled, there still remained mountain folds in the Sierra Nevada. The Tehachapi Pass into San Joaquin Valley crossed one such fold. The central approach to the Rockies was by way of the Platte R.

PASSPORTS. Issued by local authorities and notaries as well as the secretary of state until 1856 when issuance was confined to the State Department. Except for the Civil War period, passports were not required of foreign travelers in the US until 1918. The requirement was made permanent in 1921.

PATENTS AND US PATENT OFFICE. Patents and monopolies have been granted since colonial times as a way of encouraging invention and the growth of industry. The Articles of Confederation made no mention of patents, so the individual states continued to grant them. The Constitution gives to Congress the right to issue patents. First patent law in 1790, and in 1802 the Patent Office was created. An 1836 law gave the Patent Office responsibility for examining petitions and for ruling on the validity of the claims for an invention, its usefulness, and its workability. The law provided that the fourteen-year monopoly could be extended under certain circumstances. In 1861, Congress increased the monopoly period to seventeen years. Today, the Patent Office is part of the Department of Commerce.

PATERSON. An industrial city in New Jersey founded 1791 on the falls of the Passaic R, where a waterfall almost 70 feet high provided power for early factories. Paterson's principal activities have been in thread making and textiles; and from 1840 to ca. 1910, it was the center for the US silk industry. Pop.: 137,970 (1980).

PATRIOT WAR (1837–38). Confrontation between the British and Canadian rebels who wanted to free Canada from British rule and their American supporters. International complications were averted by the strong stand taken against the rebels by the US government, which sent federal troops to the frontier. British and Canadian authorities brought the rebellion under quick control.

PATRONAGE, POLITICAL. First implemented on a national scale during the administration of President Jackson (1828–36), and quickly spread to state and local government. By 1880, governments were in many cases mere appendages of political machines that grew out of the excesses of the spoils system. Some reform resulted from the PENDLETON ACT of 1883. Most state governments have some sort of merit system in operation, but they continue to use the patronage system to a much larger extent than does the federal government. Traditionally, counties and cities have been the strongholds of political parties and, as such, have been slow to adopt a strong civil service system.

PATROONS. In 1629, The Dutch West Indies Company provided for the grant of great feudal estates, called patroonships, in New Netherland. The system never worked; and at the close of Dutch rule, only Rensselaerswyck, a large estate on the Hudson R., could be properly called a patroonship.

PAWNEE. Great Plains tribe living in Nebraska at the time of the first contact. Three main bands spoke a single Caddoan language, and a fourth spoke Skidi, a variant dialect. The Pawnee stressed both the permanent farming village and forays far afield for horses and military honors. They were known for the ceremony of the morning star, a ritual involving human sacrifice for communal good. The Pawnee enjoyed fairly benign relations with Europeans and were often employed as US army scouts.

PAWNEE ROCK. A landmark of uplifted sandstone on the old Santa Fe Trail near what is now Pawnee Rock, Kans. Scene of warfare between the Pawnee and Cheyenne, and it was used by various marauding bands of Plains Indians to launch attacks on wagon trains. Most of it has been quarried away.

PAWTUCKET. Mill city in Rhode Island, located at Pawtucket Falls on the Blackstone R, four miles N of Providence. The first permanent settlement was begun in 1671, and ironmaking was the chief industry until 1793 when Samuel Slater installed the first Arkwright machinery for spinning cotton in America. Pawtucket continued as a textile center until well after World War II, when most of the industry moved south. Pop.: 71,204 (1980).

PAXTON BOYS. In 1763, a band of rangers from Paxton, Pa., were responsible for killing twenty Conestoga Indians. Efforts to bring the culprits to justice were of no avail and exacerbated the tensions between the frontiersmen and the easterners. In 1764, some 600 armed "back inhabitants" marched on Philadelphia, and Benjamin Franklin was chiefly responsible for quelling the insurrection. Thereafter, under Lazarus Stewart, the Paxton Boys removed themselves to the Wyoming Valley, near present-day Wilkes-Barre, from where they carried on intermittent warfare.

PAYNE'S LANDING, TREATY OF (1832). Made on the Oklawah R in Florida by the US and the Seminole. One of the causes of the second Seminole War.

PEACE COMMISSION OF 1778. The surrender of Gen. John Burgoyne at Saratoga in 1777 led the British to propose peace with the colonies. Their offer included the repeal of the obnoxious parliamentary legislation since 1763 and a constitutional arrangement of home rule. Even though the terms offered would have been satisfactory earlier, the Continental Congress refused to meet with the delegates sent to make the offer.

PEACE CORPS. Established 1961 as part of President Kennedy's New Frontier program. The Peace Corps was based on the idea that underdeveloped countries could be helped most when individual Americans with special skills lived and worked with the people and trained them in the use of their own resources. Volunteers in dozens of countries worked at tasks ranging from sanitary engineering through school teaching to child care and nutrition. In 1971, the Peace Corps was combined with a number of other agencies to form a new federal organization known as ACTION, but in 1981, the Peace Corps was again made an independent agency. In 1982, there were about 5,000 volunteers.

PEACE MOVEMENT OF 1864. Various efforts made to end the Civil War within the terms stipulated by President Lincoln: reunion and emancipation. Horace Greeley, Jeremiah Black, James F. Jacquess, and James R. Gilmore, all carried on unsuccessful talks with Confederate emissaries.

PEACE MOVEMENTS. Virtually every war in which the United States became engaged was opposed by one or more peace groups. The War of 1812 was opposed by conservative Federalists of New England, who flirted with the idea of seceding from the Union in the Hartford Convention of 1814. The Mexican War was opposed most strongly by northern critics of slavery, who attacked the war as a slaveholders' plot to add new land for the extension of slavery. Opposition to the Civil War was generally of a conservative, often racist, nature, based on opposition to the use of the federal government's power to take action against slavery. Opposition to the Spanish-American War was directed at the decision of President McKinley's administration to keep the Philippines and suppress the Filipinos by force. Such opposition saw imperialism as contrary to American ideals. Most opposition to US involvement in World War I was more or less isolationist in nature; that war was regarded as a European dispute that America had no business involving itself in. American isolationism reasserted itself in the years between the wars, expressed formally by the series of neutrality acts passed by Congress in the 1930s. Once the United States entered the war, however, the peace movement collapsed and US participation in World War II received a more nearly unanimous domestic support than any previous war.

The Korean War in 1950 saw pacifist groups reduced to the lowest point of their peacetime influence in at least half a century. Pacifist organizations emerged in the 1950s, particularly those opposed to nuclear testing. The National Committee for a Sane Nuclear Policy was formed in 1958 by pacifists and liberals. The US involvement in Vietnam elicited a strong and ultimately effective peace movement. Millions of persons took part in peace marches across the country, and college campuses became the center of draft-resistance movement. The anti-Vietnam War movement led Congress to pressure the Nixon administration to end the war. The administration signed a peace treaty in Vietnam in January 1973. The early 1980s saw a resurgence of the peace movement, aimed particularly at forcing the world's powers to embrace a policy of nuclear nonproliferation.

PEACE RESOLUTIONS OF BRITISH PARLIAMENT. In 1782, the House of Commons passed a resolution praying that the American Revolution might be brought to an end without reducing the colonists to obedience by force.

PEACHTREE CREEK, BATTLES ON (July 1864). Attempts by Confederate forces under Gen. John Bell Hood to defend Atlanta by attacking Union forces as they crossed Peachtree Creek. The second encounter was the bloodiest of the Atlanta campaign; Union casualties were 1,600, Confederate, about 2,500.

PEA RIDGE, BATTLE OF (March 7–8. 1862). Also known as the Battle of Elkhorn Tavern. Engagement in NW Arkansas near the Missouri border for control of the trans-Mississippi. Superior leadership and equipment finally brought victory to the Union army and ended organized fighting in the trans-Mississippi.

PEARL HARBOR. On Dec. 7, 1941, Japanese bombers attacked Pearl Harbor, the US naval base on Oahu, Hawaii, six miles W of Honolulu. Virtually the entire US fleet of ninety-four vessels, including eight battleships, was concentrated there; and the dispositon of troops, airplane, and antiaircraft guns made effective defense nearly impossible. Not a single US plane in the area could be got into the air except a fighter squadron at Haleiwa, which the Japanese had overlooked. At the end of the Japanese attack, Pearl Harbor was a smoking ruin, with most of the fleet and planes destroyed or severly damaged. Fortunately, three aircraft carriers were not in the harbor. On December 8, President Roosevelt, calling Pearl Harbor Day a day that would "live in infamy," asked Congress for a declaration of war. Various official commissions and private investigators have over the years attempted to place the blame for the unpreparedness of the Americans at Pearl Harbor, but it remains a controversial subject.

PEARY'S POLAR EXPEDITIONS (1891–1909). In 1891, Robert E. Peary explored N Greenland, wintered at McCormick Bay, and on April 30, 1892, crossed the ice cap to Independence Bay on the NE coast of the island. The following year, he returned to Greenland. He repeated the feat in 1895. In 1898 Peary undertook to discover the North Pole. He wintered at Cape d'Urville and spent 1899 exploring Ellesmere Island. Proceeding along the Greenland coast in 1900, he reached what is now Peary Land, where he struck northward over the ice to latitude 83°52′. Here he was forced back. In 1902 he made another attempt, this time stopped by the snow at 84°17′. In 1907, he made another attempt. He wintered at Cape Sheridan, and in the following year started northward from Point Moss. In six weeks, he reached latitude 87°6′. when open water forced him back. After wintering again at Cape Sheridan, Peary in 1909 made another attempt. Finally on April 6, 1909, he reached the North Pole.

PECK, FORT. Built 1867 as a trading post on the Missouri R, about 2.5 miles above the Big Dry, in Montana. It was taken over by the federal government in 1874 and maintained as an Indian agency until 1879.

PECOS TRAIL. See GOODNIGHT-LOVING TRAIL.

PECULIAR INSTITUTION. Euphemism for slavery, in general use in the 1830s.

PEGGY STEWART, BURNING OF (Oct. 19, 1774). A mob at Annapolis, Maryland, burned the *Peggy Stewart*, which was loaded with about a ton of tea.

PEKING CONGRESS (October 1900–September 1901). Met to settle the questions arising out of the BOXER REBELLION. China agreed to punish the officials responsible for the murder of the foreigners, allowed the diplomatic corps the right to a fortified legation quarter, and agreed that alien troops might be maintained in China to protect communications lines. China also agreed to pay an indemnity.

PELAGIC SEALING DISPUTE. To protect the pelagic seal herd in the Bering Sea, in the late 19th c. the US announced that the Bering Sea was under its control. A treaty was eventually worked out that sharply limited seal hunting.

PELELIU. One of the Palau Islands under Japanese control during World War II. In mid-1944, a massive US effort was made to seize it and two other Palaus. They were taken at great cost, and their usefulness to the US forces was limited.

PEMAQUID PAVEMENTS. Extensive stone remains at Pemaquid Point, Me. May have been a 16th-c. Spanish fishing base. Most of the stones were removed for local building in the mid-19th c.

PEMAQUID POINT. Peninsula on the Maine coast between the Kennebec R region and Penobscot Bay. The Abnaki inhabited the area when the first Europeans arrived in 1605. In 1616, John Smith sent a dozen European fishing ships there, and the English settled there in 1625. A palisaded post was built in 1634. It was the most vital eastern outpost against the French colonization of Maine. After 1664 administered as part of New York. Reclaimed by Massachusetts after 1685.

PEMBINA. A strategic fur trade point in North Dakota for the North West Co. in its war with the Hudson's Bay Co. and one of the best-known outfitting points for the buffalo hunters. In 1812, the first permanent settlement in North Dakota was made there.

PEMBROKE RESOLVES. Drawn up by the citizens of Pembroke, Mass. (1772) protesting the plan of the British ministry to have Massachusetts judges' salaries paid by the crown.

PENDERGAST MACHINE. A Democratic political club founded by James Pendergast in Kansas City, Mo.,in 1890. Harry S. Truman's early political career was under the aegis of the machine, although it is generally agreed that he avoided involvement in corruption. James died in 1911, and his brother Thomas took charge and controlled the machine until he went to prison for tax fraud in 1939.

PENDLETON ACT (1883). The federal government's basic civil service law; it established the Civil Service Commission and decreed that competitive examinations were to determine the qualifications of applicants for federal jobs.

PENINSULAR CAMPAIGN (1862). Unsuccessful effort by the Union army under Gen. G.B. McClellan to take Richmond, the Confederate capital, by way of the peninsula formed by the York and James rivers. On June 26, Gen. Robert E. Lee attacked the Union right at Mechanicsville, thus beginning the Seven Days' Battle. On July 1, the Union army withdrew and the campaign ended.

PENITENT BROTHERS (Los Hermanos Penitentes). A secret religious organization in New Mexico. The group's purpose is the celebration, by reenactment, of the Passion of Jesus Christ. They were driven underground by the physical suffering they inflicted on themselves, chiefly through flagellation.

PENNAMITE AND YANKEE WARS. See YANKEE-PENNAMITE WARS.

PENN CENTRAL. See RAILROADS, SKETCHES OF PRINCIPAL LINES.

PENN'S FRAME OF GOVERNMENT. Charter issued by William Penn in 1682 enumerating the rights of settlers in his American colonies. Penn assured religious liberty, established a governor and council with large governing powers, including the sole power of originating laws, and an assembly limited to approval of laws. Both bodies were to be elected by freemen. It was revised in 1701, when the assembly was given complete control over legislation and taxation.

PENN'S HOLY EXPERIMENT. See HOLY EXPERIMENT.

PENNSYLVANIA. When settled by Europeans in the early 17th c., Pennsylvania was inhabited by 15,000 Delaware, Susquehanna, and Shawnee Indians. The Dutch, English, and Swedes were in early competition. Henry Hudson entered the Delaware R in 1609 and subsequently the Dutch established trading posts. In 1638, the Swedes built Fort Christina, and in 1643, the first permanent settlement on Tinicum Island at the mouth of the Schuylkill R. The Dutch seized New Sweden in 1655, only to lose it to the English in 1664. It was placed under the governance of the duke of York, who in turn in 1681 made Quaker leader William Penn its governor and proprietor. Penn made his colony a haven for persecuted Quakers and others under a liberal charter. After his death in 1718, the colony was at first governed by his widow, Hannah Penn, and then by his sons John, Richard, and Thomas. At the time of the American Revolution, when the proprietorship ended, it was being governed by William Penn's grandson, John Penn. By that time, the original English Quakers had been joined by Germans and Scotch-Irish. Philadelphia was the largest and richest city in the colonies and the second largest in the British Empire.

The Penns had boundary disputes with Maryland, Connecticut, and Virginia because of the vague "sea-to-sea" charters of the colonies. The French were also encroachers on the western lands claimed by the Penns. Forts were built by the French at the present sites of Erie, Waterford, Franklin, and Pittsburgh; the most famous was Fort Duquesne, site of present-day Pittsburgh. In 1758, it was captured by the English and renamed Fort Pitt. The English defeat of the French in 1763 ended the French threat to Pennsylvania.

The first Continental Congress met in Pennsylvania throughout the Revolution, and both the Declaration of Independence and the US Constitution were written there. Pennsylvania became the second state to ratify the Constitution, and Philadelphia was the national capital from 1790 to 1800, when it was moved to Washington, D.C. After the Revolution, Pennsylvania thrived and its population grew. The Philadelphia-Lancaster Turnpike, the nation's first, was completed in 1794; many miles of state canals were constructed and linked by the Allegheny Portage RR over the Alleghenies in 1835. Pioneer railroads were built in the mining regions, and a great growth of commerce and shipbuilding took place. Oil was discovered near Titusville in 1859, and the later 19th c. saw a continued growth of industry, with steel and iron, textiles, and leather and lumber industries predominating. It led the nation in bituminous and anthracite coal mining. It was the scene of great labor strife in the late 19th c., climaxed by the great anthracite strike of 1902. The Great Depression hit Pennsylvania especially hard; and much of its industry continued to suffer after the end of World War II. Pop.: 11,866,728 (1980).

PENNSYLVANIA, INVASION OF (1863). After the Confederate victory at Chancellorsville, Va., in May 1863, Gen. R.E. Lee began moving into Pennsylvania, with Union Gen. G.G. Meade in hot pursuit. The two armies met in the greatest battle of the Civil War at Gettysburg on July 1–3. Casualties were great on both sides, but the Rebels were forced to retire to Virginia. Assuming the blame for the disaster, Lee offered his resignation to President Jefferson Davis, who refused.

PENNSYLVANIA, UNIVERSITY OF. Founded 1740 as a charity school, it was restructured in 1749 by Benjamin Franklin as a purely secular institution of higher learning. In 1755, it was designated a "College and Academy." The first medical school (1765) and the first department of botany (1768) were established there. Control was taken over briefly in 1779 by the Pennsylvania state government, but it was returned to private hands in 1791 and became known officially as the University of Pennsylvania. Little momentum was achieved in the first half of the 19th c., but the university experienced great growth in the second half. It was during that period, that most of its graduate schools were

formed, including the Towne Scientific School (1875) and the Wharton School of Business (1881). In 1980, the school had about 18,500 students.

PENNSYLVANIA AND OHIO CANAL. Opened in 1840, it ran from the Ohio R near Pittsburgh to Akron, where it connected with the Ohio and Erie Canal. By the 1850s, it was being replaced by the railroads.

PENNSYLVANIA CANAL SYSTEM. In 1826, a state-sponsored Main Line canal was begun that would connect Philadelphia and Pittsburgh. A railroad was built from Philadelphia to Columbia, where the canal began. Various subsidiary canals branched off the Main Line; they generally followed the Delaware, Lehigh, Ohio, and Monongahela rivers. By 1840, there were 606 miles of canal and 118 miles of railroad in the system. When Pennsylvania defaulted in the payment of interest on its bonds; the legislature halted all work. Some of the canals were sold off. Railroad companies built lines along some canal rights of way. Competition from railroads closed most of the canals, but the canals on the Delaware and Lehigh rivers continued to operate until 1931.

PENNSYLVANIA-CONNECTICUT BOUNDARY DISPUTE. Originated in the overlapping territorial jurisdictions of the charters granted by Charles II to Connecticut (1662) and William Penn (1681); the claim was centered in the Wyoming Valley in what is now NE Pennsylvania. In 1782, an interstate commission under authority of the Articles of Confederation unanimously awarded jurisdiction to Pennsylvania. It was the only such dispute settled by the Articles of Confederation.

PENNSYLVANIA DUTCH. German settlers who first came to Pennsylvania ca. 1727. At the time of the Revolution, they composed about a third of the province's population. Still predominant in the counties of Northampton, Lehigh, Berks, Lancaster, Lebanon, and York. Called Dutch from the German *Deutsch*.

PENNSYLVANIA-MARYLAND BOUNDARY DISPUTE. Grew out of the ambiguous terms of territorial grants made by the crown to William Penn (1681) and to Lord Baltimore (1632). The Privy Council created a boundary in 1685, but invasions from Maryland into Pennsylvania continued, and Pennsylvania settlers were brought before Maryland courts and their property destroyed. Not until 1767 was the northern line of Maryland settled, by two British surveyors, Charles Mason and Jeremiah Dixon, who located it at 39°44'. (See MASON-DIXON LINE.)

PENNSYLVANIA RAILROAD. See RAILROADS, SKETCHES OF PRINCIPAL LINES: PENN CENTRAL.

PENNSYLVANIA-VIRGINIA BOUNDARY DISPUTE. Originated in the ambiguous terms of the grant of 1681 to William Penn and the claim of Virginia to extend over any territory not covered by royal grants. At issue was most of what is now SW Pennsylvania. The MASON-DIXON LINE (1763–67) made it clear that Pennsylvania extended some distance W of the mountains. In 1774, Virginia took possession of Fort Pitt and set up a court there. In 1779, the two states agreed to settle the dispute by extending the Mason-Dixon Line westward.

PENOBSCOT. Maine peninsula that was the center of French and English struggle for control of Maine. The French founded Fort Pentegoet ca. 1625, and Plymouth Plantation established a trading post ca. 1626 that was repeatedly sacked by the French. After 1670, Penobscot was held by the French until Quebec fell to the British in 1759.

PENOBSCOT EXPEDITION (1779). An attempt by Massachusetts to dislodge the British from their stronghold on Penobscot peninsula, Maine. A large naval force and about 900 militia landed from Penobscot Bay, but British naval reinforcments arrived and the patriot attempt ended in disaster.

PENSACOLA. City in the Florida Panhandle, on the Gulf of Mexico. First settled by Spain in 1559, it was long fought over by Spain and France. In 1763, Great Britain obtained Florida and made Pensacola the seat of West Florida. Captured by the Spanish during the American Revolution and restored to Spain in 1783. The British attempted to use it as a base during the War of 1812, but Gen. Andrew Jackson seized it in 1814. Restored to Spain in 1818, but in 1821 it came to the US. The

Confederacy controlled its fort and navy yard early in the Civil War, but Union troops retook the city in 1862. Today, it is an important fishing port and the site of a US naval air station. Pop.: 57,619 (1980).

PENSIONS, MILITARY. Since the Revolution, the US has granted pensions to veterans of its wars, and to members of the regular army and navy in peacetime. Widows of veterans have also often been entitled to pensions. Since World War II, veterans as such (i.e., non-disabled) have not been granted pensions, although numerous other benefits have been available to them.

PENTAGON. Headquarters for the US Defense Department, located in Arlington, Va., on the outskirts of Washington, D.C. When this five-sided structure (hence its name) was opened in 1943, it was the largest office building in the world.

PENTAGON PAPERS. A forty-seven-volume study of US involvement in the Vietnam War, compiled by the Defense Department and including internal working papers from 1945 to 1968. Classified as top secret, the report contained evidence of bad judgment, attempts to cover up mistakes by top officials, and misleading public statements concerning US policy. In 1971, copies of the report were made available to the New York *Times* by Daniel Ellsberg and Anthony J. Russo. After several installments appeared, the government obtained an injunction barring further publication. However, the Supreme Court ruled that the government failed to justify prior restraint and had therefore infringed on the First Amendment's freedom of the press. Subsequently, the Nixon administration indicted Ellsberg and Russo for theft of the papers; but in 1973, the courts threw out the caes on the grounds of gross misconduct by the government.

PENTECOSTAL CHURCHES. Fundamentalist Christian bodies that base their teachings on inspiration of the Bible, the necessity of an emotional conversion, speaking in tongues, and healing by the spirit. Pentacostalism grew out of 19th-c. Methodism, and its largest group is the Assemblies of God. In 1981, there were fifteen Pentecostal denominations in the US., with a membership of more than 2 million.

PENTEGOET, FORT. French post in what is now Castine, Me. Erected ca. 1625, it was seized by the English a year later. Recaptured in 1633, it was one of the French strongholds during the French and Indian War.

PEONAGE. Involuntary servitude under which a debtor is forced to make payment to a master by his labor. Peonage developed especially in the South after the abolition of slavery. Fines imposed for petty crime were paid by an employer who then exacted work from the sentenced person. In 1910, the Supreme Court declared it, in *Bailey v. Alabama*, to be in violation of the Thirteenth and Fourteenth amendments.

PEOPLE'S PARTY. See POPULIST PARTY.

PEORIA. City in Illinois and the site of the first permanent French settlement in the Illinois Country. Fort St. Louis, later known as Fort Pimitoui, was erected in 1680; it probably survived until the transfer of Illinois to the British in 1763. In 1778, a new village was founded nearby, and it came to be called Fort Clark. American settlement began in 1819, and the name was changed to Peoria in 1825. The city became an important corn trading center and manufacturer of agricultural and earthmoving equipment in the late 19th c. Pop.: 124,160 (1980).

PEQUOT TRAIL. An Indian route from New London, Conn., to Providence, R.I. White settlers used the road and by 1691 it was a part of the New York-Boston Post Road.

PEQUOT WAR (1636–37). Connecticut white settlers, aided by Mohegan Indians under Uncas, attacked and burned Pequot forts near present-day Mystic, Conn. Survivors were absorbed into other tribes, and the Pequot ceased to exist as a separate tribe.

PERDICARIS AFFAIR (1905). In 1904, Ion Perdicaris, a US citizen, was abducted near Tangier by a Riffian bandit named Raisuli. The United States demanded Perdicaris's return, and dispatched a warship to Tangier to exert pressure on the sultan of Morocco. The State Department sent its famous dispatch "Perdi-

caris alive or Raisuli dead" just as Perdicaris was being released. That dispatch was wildly applauded by the American public.

PERDIDO. A river flowing through SW Alabama into the Gulf of Mexico. The boundary between French Louisiana and Spanish Florida, since 1783 has been the limit of East Florida, now the state of Florida.

PERMANENT COURT OF ARBITRATION. Also known as the Hague Court of Arbitration; dates from the First Hague Peace Conference of 1899. Between 1899 and 1932, only twenty-one minor matters were referred to it. Although in existence, it has not been used since 1932. Since 1921, the Permanent Court of International Justice has in effect replaced it. In 1980, 74 countries belonged.

PERRY-ELLIOTT CONTROVERSY. At the Battle of Lake Erie (Sept. 10, 1813), J.D. Elliott, commander of the *Niagara*, did not come to the aid of the *Lawrence*, commanded by O.H. Perry, until it was too late. Elliott challenged Perry to a duel in 1818, and Perry brought charges against Elliott for his conduct during the battle. The controversy lasted long after Perry's death, with both men having their champions. Today, most naval historians tend to criticise Elliott for inaction.

PERRY'S EXPEDITION TO JAPAN. In 1852, President Fillmore sent a naval expedition, commanded by Commodore Matthew C. Perry, to Japan to arrange for the protection of US seamen and property shipwrecked off the Japanese coast; to obtain permission for US vessels to secure provisions, water, and fuel; and, most important, to induce Japan to open up its ports for trade. A considerable squadron steamed into Tokyo Bay in July 1853. Perry delivered his messages and announced that he would return the next year for an answer. In February 1854, the Japanese agreed to the American terms and signed the Treaty of Kanagawa.

PERRYVILLE, BATTLE OF (Oct. 8, 1862). A bloody battle near Louisville, Ky. The Confederates achieved a tactical success and remained in possession of the battlefield but retreated to Knoxville, Tenn.

PERSONAL LIBERTY LAWS. State laws aimed at impeding the return of fugitive slaves. Most were adopted after 1842, when a Supreme Court decision declared that state officials could not be forced to enforce the Fugitive Slave Act of 1793 (which demanded the return of fugitive slaves to their owners). After the second Fugitive Slave Act was passed in 1850, the personal liberty laws became highly complex: rigorous requirements for identification and proof of ownership had to be met, perjury and illegal seizures were heavily penalized, and the use of the jury was in effect a promise that the runaway and those who assisted him would have full measure of "liberty" while the pursuer would encounter equal measure of obstruction.

PERTH AMBOY. City in New Jersey, settled 1683–86; it was the capital and port of entry for East Jersey. In the 19th c., it became a resort area; it began to attract heavy industry in the late 19th c. Today, it is an important shipbuilding and oil-refining center and a major port. Pop.: 38.951 (1980).

PET BANKS. When in 1833, President Jackson was determined to remove governmental deposits from the Bank of the United States, certain state banks, called pet banks, were selected to receive future deposits. By 1836, there were 89 such banks.

PETERSBURG, SIEGE OF (1864–65). Union Gen. U.S. Grant decided to approach Richmond from the south through Petersburg. He attacked the city on June 21 but was driven back by R.E. Lee's army. Grant made several further attacks on the city and succeeded in capturing some territory. On October 27, he was again repulsed by Lee and field operations virtually ceased for the winter. In March 1865, Lee attacked Grant's right, but the attack failed. On April 2, Lee was forced to evacuate both Petersburg and Richmond and retreat westward.

PETITION, RIGHT OF. The US Constitution and most state constitutions permit citizens the right to petition the government for a redress of grievances. The right has been extended to encompass anything within the jurisdiction of government.

PETROCHEMICAL INDUSTRY. In the 1850s, petroleum fractions, notably kerosene, were recognized as having important uses. The following half-century saw the rise of the petroleum industry, particularly after the development of the internal combustion engine. With the emphasis on the production of gasoline, little attention was given to other possible uses. The most volatile fractions were allowed to escape into the atmosphere; the gasoline and kerosene fractions were collected; and the heavier residue was extracted for greases or tar or was discarded. In 1928, the industry began to bottle for sale the formerly wasted gases propane and butane and to seek uses for its greases and tars. But not until the 1940s did the industry adopt the practice of producing pure chemical compounds and their conversion into a wide range of commercial products. After World War II, the chemical potentialities of petroleum came to be fully exploited, and because of its convenience, it replaced other natural raw materials. Rubber, refrigerants, plastics, paints, fibers, detergents, and many other products came to be derived from petroleum.

PETROGRAPHY. The systematic description of rocks burgeoned chiefly in Germany in the late 19th c. American geologists went there for their introduction to the science. After 1876, the US Geological Survey and some state surveys published valuable lithographed plates of distinctive rock types as seen in thin sections.The Geophysical Laboratory of the Carnegie Institution was established in 1905; and in the decades that followed, important works on sedimentary and metamorphic rocks were published. The study of sedimentary rocks for the most part did not begin until after the 1920s.

PETROLEUM INDUSTRY. Oil floating on streams was reported in the 17th c.; by the 1830s, druggists sold petroleum as a liniment and a patent medicine. Only in the 1850s was it discovered that, with proper distillation, petroleum could become a luminant. In 1859, E.L. Drake dug a well at Titusville, Pa; by 1861, prospectors in the area were producing more than 2 million barrels annually. Producers of coal oil switched to petroleum as a raw material and produced kerosene. In 1870, John D. Rockefeller established the Standard Oil Co., and by 1880 he controlled about 90 percent of the market. Standard Oil could not control the new oil fields being discovered in Kansas, Ohio, Indiana, Oklahoma,

California, and Texas; and its market share dropped to 65 percent. Nevertheless, in 1911, the Supreme Court ordered the company dissolved. By that time, the industry's major focus had changed from illuminants to gasoline to fuel the new internal combustion engine. From 1919 to 1980, 40–45 percent of the industry's output consisted of automotive gasoline. The 1920s and 1930s saw great improvements in refining techniques, especially in the cracking process whereby long hydrocarbon molecules are broken down under heat and pressure. Octane ratings were increased by the addition of chemical catalysts to the cracking process.

From 1945 to 1980, domestic demand for crude oil nearly quadrupled, causing the US to become for the first time a net importer of oil. This brought on the great oil crises of the 1970s, resulting in enormous increases in costs. Despite efforts to make the US again self-sufficient in the production of crude oil, by the 1980s, the petroleum industry was still importing a large percentage of its crude oil.

PEYOTE CULT. A religious movement that spread among the Plains Indians in the late 19th c. Long used by Mexican Indians for the hallucinational visions it produces, peyote was introduced into the US in 1870 by the Mescalero Apache. It quickly spread to other tribes. Peyote eating was combined with hymn singing and testimonials, with a fusion of Christian elements and native beliefs. Today, most peyotists are members of the Native American Church.

PHARMACEUTICAL INDUSTRY. Botanical extracts and mineral substances were often compounded and distributed by colonial physicians and even by keepers of general stores. During the early 19th c., the first specialized drug houses appeared in Philadelphia; and there was founded in 1821 the College of Apothecaries (later renamed the College of Pharmacy); and there was published the *United States Pharmacopoeia*, an official compendium of medicinal materials. Late in the 19th c., the character of production of pharmaceutical preparations changed substantially. Large-scale, specialized, and even mechanized production gradually diminished the importance of compounding in local pharmacies. In addition, many new substances were being added to the pharmacopoeia. The introduction of aspirin in 1899 indicated the medical and commercial significance of chemical research; gradually chemists isolated the specific therapeutic agents in many of the traditional botanical materials. Tablets or capsules containing specific agents gradually replaced the old elixirs. The general character of the pharmacopoeia was changed by new therapeutic approaches that emerged during the first third of the 20th c., including the development of chemicals that specifically attack disease-causing agents without harming the human host; the identification of essential dietary substances; and the identification of hormones. Antibiotics were the result of British research, but were developed with government urging during World War II by American drug firms. After the war, the companies invested heavily in antibiotics, putting the American industry in the position of international leadership. The 1960s and 1970s saw the wide development of mood-altering and mind-altering drugs, which revolutionized the treatment of the mentally and emotionally ill.

PHARMACY. In the 18th c., many physicians compounded and dispensed their own medicines; at the same time, the professional pharmacist not only compounded and dispensed drugs but also diagnosed and prescribed as well. By the 19th c., many patent and proprietary medicines were sold in general stores and pharmacies. Pharmaceutical education began with the founding of the Philadelphia College of Pharmacy in 1821; in general, other colleges did not follow suit until the late 19th c. At first a two-year curriculum was followed, but by 1900 most schools were requiring four years' study. State boards of pharmacy were established to examine candidates and issue licenses.

PHELPS-GORHAM PURCHASE. A land acquisition made in 1788 in W New York running along the border with Pennsylvania. Oliver Phelps and Nathaniel Gorham bought the land from Massachusetts, and when they were unable to make the payments as agreed, Massachusetts sought to restore its control over the area. In the meantime, the Indians were refusing to give up their rights to part of the land and part of it had been sold to Robert Morris. The matter was not settled for years.

PHI BETA KAPPA SOCIETY. Founded 1776 at William and Mary College, Williamsburg, Va., it became an honor society with members selected on the basis of class standing. In 1980, there were 228 chapters and about 355,000 members.

PHILADELPHIA. Swedes planted the first permanent white settlements within the present city boundaries in the 1640s, but the history of Philadelphia begins with William Penn's Pennsylvania charter of 1681. It became the principal town of that province. By the eve of the American Revolution, some 28,400 people made Philadelphia the largest city in British America. It became the logical site for intercolonial meetings, and despite much conservatism in the city, the first Continental Congress in 1774 and the second Continental Congress from 1775 through most of the war made Philadelphia the hub of the Revolution. Although Congress departed in 1783, the Constitutional Convention met in 1787; and the city was the capital of the US from 1790 to 1800.

The federal period became Philadelphia's golden age: commercial, social, and cultural primacy among American cities as well as political leadership rested there. The establishment of the first Bank of the US in 1791 assured it a financial preeminence it was to hold until the 1830s. New York had always had a better harbor, and the Erie Canal gave New York a great route to the West, ensuring it commercial superiority. Nevertheless, Philadelphia's population continued to surge. There was great industrial development, and the port of Philadelphia remained second only to New York. It was the largest petroleum port, and Philadelphia was the largest petroleum refining center on the East Coast. Major freight yards and rail junctions maintained the city's preeminence as a rail center. In 1980, it was the fourth largest city in the nation with a population of 1,688,210.

PHILADELPHIA, CAPTURE OF THE. During the Barbary Wars, on Oct. 31, 1803, the frigate *Philadelphia*, blockading Tripoli, sailed too close to shore and struck a reef. The ship and its crew of 315 were captured. After prolonged negotiations failed, on the night of Feb. 16, 1804, Stephen Decatur, with some eighty men from the *Intrepid*, cleared the *Philadelphia* of the enemy and burned it.

PHILADELPHIA CORDWAINERS' CASE (1805). Eight union leaders of a strike of Philadelphia journeymen cordwainers were arrested and charged with criminal conspiracy. The mayor's court accepted the prosecution's argument (since refuted) that "a conspiracy of workmen to raise their wages" was criminal at common law. The defendants were found guilty, the strike was broken, and a precedent was set for the criminal prosecution of union activities.

PHILADELPHIA GAS RING. Republican bosses of Philadelphia in the 1860s who gained control of the city's gas department and used it for personal gain. Broken by reformers in the 1880s.

PHILADELPHIA RIOTS (May 6–8, and July 5–8, 1844). Protestant attacks on Irish Catholics. Churches were burned, and immigrants' houses were sacked. A score of persons were killed and nearly 100 injured.

PHILANTHROPIST. The name of several antislavery newspapers. The first was published at Mt. Pleasant, Ohio, from 1817. Another was begun at New Richmond, Ohio, in 1836 and moved to Cincinnati in 1837.

PHILANTHROPY AND BENEVOLENCE. Puritan leaders enjoined their followers to "do good," and philanthropy was an imperative of Quakerism. John Harvard, Benjamin Franklin, and Stephen Girard were examples of early philanthropists who founded schools, libraries, hospitals, and learned societies. The New York Association for Improving the Condition of the Poor (1841) and the Children's Aid Society (1853) were early examples of like organizations founded in virtually every city in the nation. Beginning in the 1840s, much philanthropy was aimed at abolition and efforts to improve the handicapped and mentally ill. The Civil War created the US Sanitary Commission, a precursor of the American Red Cross, and the Freedmen's Bureau for the benefit of former slaves, the first federal welfare program.

In the Gilded Age Andrew Carnegie and John D. Rockefeller emerged as major philanthropic forces. Jane Addams in Chicago and Lillian Wald in New York City pointed toward social work as a profession. The 20th c. saw a proliferation of charitable agencies, such as the Community Chest, the United Jewish Appeal, and the United Way. It also saw the proliferation of the great endowed foundations. The foundations set up by Carnegie and Rockefeller were followed by those of virtually every rich family in the US. The Ford Foundation was the largest. Since the New Deal programs of the 1930s, the federal government has funded many programs that traditionally had been handled by private and religious charities.

PHILIPPI, SKIRMISH AT (June 3, 1861). Probably the first field action of the Civil War. A Confederate force was surprised and routed at Philippi, W.Va. The casualties were few.

PHILIPPINE INSURRECTION (1899–1902). Also known as the Filipino-American War. Although Spain ceded the Philippines to the US at the end of the Spanish-American War, the islands were held by Filipino revolutionaries. Their desire for independence clashed with America's imperialistic intentions. The US force there dispersed the rebel army, which fled into the mountains. Guerrilla warfare under Emilio Aguinaldo continued. A civilian commission headed by William Howard Taft and a military force headed by Gen. Arthur MacArthur attempted to pacify the island. Aquinaldo was captured in March 1901, and US progress continued. In 1902, after two more insurgent generals surrendered, the Americans declared the pacification complete; but sporadic fighting continued throughout American rule.

PHILIPPINE ISLANDS. A Pacific archipelago consisting of more than 7,000 islands and reefs, the population is confined to eleven islands, the largest of which are Luzon and Mindanao. Predominantly Malay in stock, the population is Christian, a result of Spanish conquest in the 16th c. The Philippines came to the US as a result of the Spanish-American War, but only after a long and costly PHILIPPINE INSURRECTION was put down. The US victory over the Filipino nationalists did not put an end to the movement, and in 1934 an act of the US Congress provided for the eventual independence of the islands. In 1935, the Philippines was declared a commonwealth with Manuel Quezon as its president. During World War II, the archipelago was under Japanese control. In 1945, US forces under Gen. Douglas MacArthur retook the Philippines; its former government, which had been in exile in Washington, was restored to power. The Republic of the Philippines came into being on schedule in 1946, with Manuel Roxas as president. Various treaties and agreements tied it closely to the US, including one that gave US armed forces a ninety-nine-year lease on twenty-three bases on the islands. The Philippines remained in diplomatic alignment with the US, but many Filipino politicians urged a more independent stand. In 1972, President Ferdinand Marcos disbanded the Philippine assembly and began to rule by martial law. In 1981, he lifted martial law and was elected to a new term. His autocratic rule continued, however, and political opposition was ruthlessly put down. A measure of political freedom began to be restored in the mid-1980s, but Marcos ruled under a cloud, his position being made even more tenuous by the murder of his chief political rival as he arrived from US exile.

PHILIPPINE SEA, BATTLE OF THE (June 19–20, 1944). Climactic sea battle of World War II. The Japanese and US fleets met off Saipan. Much of the battle was in the air; the Japanese lost 300 planes; the US but 30. The two-day battle cost the Japanese control of the Marianas and the central Pacific.

PHILIPSE'S PATENT. An enormous tract in Putnam County, N.Y., obtained by Adolphe Philipse in 1697.

PHILOSOPHY. Except for the 17th-c. Calvinist apologist Jonathan Edwards, America produced no philosophy of note until the 19th c. The New England transcendentalists, especially Ralph Waldo Emerson, were students of German idealism. Josiah Royce was another idealist. Charles S. Peirce and William James were early exponents of pragmatism and empiricism. They were followed by John Dewey, who expanded their methodological insights into a system he called instrumentalism. Dewey was, with George Santayana and Alfred North Whitehead, the last of the giants. American philosophy of the late 20th c. took several directions: logical positivism, neo-Thomism, and neo-Marxism. Although American philosophy continued to flourish, it lacked the earlier breadth of interest and impact on the larger society.

PHOENIX. The capital and largest city of Arizona; founded 1887 on the Salt R, although an ancient Indian village may have occupied the site. Surrounding farmlands are among the most productive in the nation, and Phoenix acts as a processing and trading center for them. The city also has electronics and aluminum factories. One of America's fastest growing cities, its population in 1980 was 764,911.

PHOENIX. The first entirely American-built steamship, launched 1808. Designed by John Stevens, it was the first steamship to venture upon the open sea.

PHONOGRAPH. First built and patented by Thomas A. Edison in 1877. Improvements were made by C.A. Bell, C.S. Tainter, and Emile Berliner. At the turn of the century, both J.W. Jones and E.R. Johnson, devised methods for cutting the original record in wax and electroplating it for subsequent copying. In 1901, Johnson formed the Victor Talking Machine Co., which later became a part of the Radio Corporation of America (RCA). The advent of the vacuum tube made amplification easy. By the 1930s, all reproduction from records was electronic, and after World War II the long-playing record was introduced and became the industry standard. Stereophonic sound was introduced in the 1950s, and digital recordings made their appearance in the 1970s. Each new advance has increased the fidelity of recorded sound to live sound.

PHOTOGRAPHIC INDUSTRY. Photography began in the 1830s, but the industry as such began in the 1880s, when George Eastman and his associates developed a roll-film system. In 1888, Eastman designed a simple-to-operate, highly portable roll-film camera, the Kodak, that revolutionized the art of photography. The Eastman Kodak Co. maintained a tight patent control over its technical advances and was thus able to hold an almost exclusive position in the market. Early in the 20th c., a cinematographic industry began to grow up, chiefly around the motion picture industry. Here, too, Eastman Kodak dominated the field. In the late 1920s, Ansco became the US outlet for the highly proficient German photographic industry and the main competitor to Kodak. In 1948, the Polaroid Corp. introduced a system that produced finished prints directly from a camera. Kodak, in response to the Polaroid challenge, introduced a series of Instamatic cameras that further simplified negative-positive picture taking, as well as their own instant-print system. In 1982, Kodak introduced the film disk cartridge.

PHYSICS. The archetypical American physicist was Benjamin Franklin, celebrated for his practical lightning rod as well as for his qualitatively speculative and experimental contributions to electrical science. Franklin's great-grandson, A.D. Bache was head of the US Coast Survey, and enlarged the scope of the agency to include studies in geodesy and geophysics. In the 1850s, the survey was the largest US employer of physicists. A.A. Michelson became the first American physicist to win the Nobel Prize (1907), for his measurement of the speed of light and for his invention of the Michelson interferometer. H.A. Rowland also won international attention, for his invention of the Rowland spectral grating and for his determinations of the value of the ohm and of the mechanical equivalent of heat. After 1900, a rise in electrical engineering enrollments created an increased demand for teachers of physics. Employment opportunities for physicists also rose in private industry, especially at General Electric and American Telephone and Telegraph. The federal government established the National Bureau of Standards, which entered a wide area of physical research.

In the early 20th c., the quantum theory of radiation and the theory of relativity attracted such young scientists as R.A. Millikan, Richard Tolman, and G.N. Lewis. By World War I, the profession was focusing increasingly on the physics of the quantized atom. By the end of the 1920s, the US had more than 2,300 physicists, including a number of distinguished Europeans teaching in American universities. The profession was further enriched in the 1930s by such refugees from Nazi Europe as Albert Einstein, Hans Bethe, Felix Bloch, Enrico Fermi, Emilio Segrè, and Edward Teller. By the end of the decade, American physics led the world both in theoretical and experimental research.

During World War II, physicists contributed decisively to the development of microwave radar, the proximity fuze, and solid-fuel rockets. They also worked on the atomic bomb in various laboratories of the Manhattan Project, which was directed by J.R. Oppenheimer. After the war, physicists were recognized as vital to the national defense and welfare; they received massive governmental support, notably from the National Science Foundation, the Atomic Energy Commission (now the Nuclear Regulatory Commission), and the Office of Naval Research. Thus, the profession expanded rapidly, totaling more than 30,000 in the mid-1970s. Working with highly energetic particle accelerators, American physicists were among the world's leaders in uncovering experimental data about elementary particles. Other important fields include plasma and low-temperature physics and astrophysics and relativity.

PHYSIOLOGY. Early physiological accomplishments in the US were few: John Young's digestion experiments (1803), William Beaumont's study of the digestive system (1833), W.J.G. Morton's introduction of ether anesthesia (1846), and S.W. Mitchell's study of snake venom (1860). The transition to a field of study of major importance took place in the 1870s, when scientists trained in the German and British methods were engaged. H.N. Martin organized a laboratory-oriented department of biology at Johns Hopkins in 1876. At Harvard, H.P. Bowditch established the first physiological laboratory in the US for student use in 1871; ultimately, he integrated physiology into the medical program. By the 1920s, virtually all candidates for the M.D. degree were being subjected to an intensive study of physiology. Contemporary physiology is a powerful discipline in its own right, no longer under the aegis of the medical profession.

PICKAWILLANEE. An Indian village near present-day Piqua, Ohio. Founded 1747 by the Miami to trade with the British rather than the French. After two French attempts to destroy the village, the Miami signed a treaty with them and abandoned Pickawillanee.

PICKENS, FORT. On Santa Rosa Island, in Pensacola Bay, Fla. Unused at the time of Florida's secession in 1861, it was quickly occupied by Union soldiers. Remained an important Union stronghold throughout the war.

PICKETING. A tactic used by striking workers, the picket is aimed at impeding deliveries and services; to cause employees to refuse to cross the line to work; to muster consumer sympathy to withhold patronage; and to be a rallying symbol for the strikers. Picketing has also been used to promote other interests, particularly in protests against racial discrimination.

PICKETT'S CHARGE (July 3, 1865). The culminating event of the Battle of Gettysburg. Having failed on July 1 and 2 to rout Union forces, Confederate Gen. R.E. Lee decided to assault their center, using G.E. Pickett's division (augmented with other troops for a total of forty-seven regiments, 15,000 men). The assault failed when the Union forces closed in from three sides; the Rebels lost about 6,000 men.

PIECES OF EIGHT. Spanish silver coins of eight reals (eight bits), also known as pesos or Spanish dollars. They were widely used in the American colonies, and Congress, in 1786, adoped the Spanish milled dollar as the basis of the US coinage system.

PIEDMONT. The area of the eastern US lying at the foot of the easternmost ranges of the Appalachian mountain system; historically, "up-country" and "back-country" are other terms used to designate the Piedmont region. The Piedmont was settled primarily by small farmers; socially and economically democratic, Piedmonters were generally at odds with the Tidewater population.

PIEGAN WAR (1869–70). Invasion of the hunting grounds of the Blackfoot confederacy north of th Missouri R in Montana by miners and ranchers caused the Piegan (one of the bands of the Blackfoot) to retaliate. On Jan. 23, 1870, a US cavalry raid killed 173 Piegan, including Chief Red Horn and many women and children. The attack drew censure from Congress.

PIERRE. Capital city of South Dakota, located near the point where the Bad R joins the Missouri. An important spot for fur traders and the site of Fort Pierre. Pop.: 11,973 (1980).

PIERRE, FORT. Established as a small trading post at the junction of the Bad and Missouri rivers in 1817. The Columbia Fur Co. took it over in 1822 and named it Fort Tecumseh. In 1832, John Jacob Astor built a new post and named it Fort Pierre Chouteau, quickly shortened to Fort Pierre.

PIERRE'S HOLE, BATTLE OF (July 18, 1832). Confrontation between the Gros Ventre Indians and American fur traders at Pierre's Hole, a trading post located in E Idaho.

PIETISM. Religious movement of the late 17th and early 18th c., primarily a reaction to the growing formalism in the German Lutheran church. It emphasized prayer and Bible study and urged lay people to take a larger part. In the US, pietistic influence was chiefly in the Lutheran and Moravian churches.

PIKES PEAK. Mountain discovered 1806 by Zebulon M. Pike. It is located in the Rocky Mountains in El Paso County, Colo. Its altitude is 14,110 feet.

PIKES PEAK GOLD RUSH (1858–59). Meager amounts of gold were discovered in Cherry Creek and other tributaries of the South Platte R in Colorado, July 1858, but exaggerated stories of the finds circulated in the nation's press and set off a gold rush involving some 100,000 persons to Pikes Peak Gold Country, as it became known. (Pikes Peak was seventy-five miles away.) Large amounts of gold were found near Central City in May 1859.

PIKE'S SOUTHWESTERN EXPEDITON (1806–07). Lt. Zebulon M. Pike and a small band of US soldiers explored the Arkansas and Red rivers, to collect information about the newly acquired (by the Louisiana Purchase) territory. The party visited the Pawnee towns in Kansas, reached Colorado, and crossed the Sangre de Cristo Range in midwinter to reach the Canejos R, a tributary of the Rio Grande in New Mexico. After building a fort there, Pike and his party were escorted out of Spanish territory by Spanish troops, who deposited them in Natchitoches, La. Pike's account of his explorations, published 1810, afforded his countrymen their first description of the great Southwest.

PIKE'S UPPER MISSISSIPPI EXPEDITION (1805–06). Lt. Zebulon M. Pike left St. Louis with a small detachment of troops to explore the Mississippi R to its source, to assert the authority of the US over the area, to conciliate the Indians there, and to scout sites for military posts. Pike traveled by sled and toboggan in midwinter, ascended what he thought were the upper reaches of the Mississippi, and falsely named Leech Lake as the source of the river. He met with British traders and Indians, urging them to obey US laws, and made geographical observations.

PILGRIMS. Thirty-five members of an English Separatist church living in the Netherlands, who, with sixty-six English sectarians and servants, sailed from Plymouth, England, on Sept. 16, 1620, on the *Mayflower* and founded Plymouth Colony in New England in December.

PILLOW, FORT (April 12, 1864). After Confederate troops had taken Fort Pillow, Tenn., Union defenders were driven out of the fort, and according to Union sources, several hundred were massacred, supposedly at the order of Gen. Nathan B. Forrest.

PILOT KNOB, BATTLE OF (Sept. 27, 1864). A federal force at Fort Davidson, Pilot Knob, Mo., was the only impediment to Confederate Gen. Sterling Price's march toward St. Louis. Price's troops were bloodily repulsed, but the Union forces retreated.

PIMA. Indian group inhabiting the Salt and Gila river valleys in S Arizona. They spoke a branch of the Uto-Aztecan language and used farming methods that suggest backgrounds in the prehistoric Hohokam culture. When first located by Spanish Jesuits in 1681, there were an estimated 4,000 Pima and 6,000 Papago, to whom the Pima were closely related. Both groups built round, flat-topped, single-family houses in small autonomous villages, led by an elected chief. Both tribes had harvest festivals in four-year cycles, involving masked figures. The Pima had a summer rain festivals, involving licensed public drunkenness, a custom suggesting the Aztec in Mexico. Their wine made from the saguaro cactus was the sole appearance of an aboriginal alcoholic drink N of Mexico.

PIMA REVOLT (1751). The Upper Pima in N Mexico and S Arizona, under the would-be chief Louis Oacpicagigua. In an attempt to oust the Spaniards from the area, about 100 Spaniards were killed, including a number of missionaries. Oacpicagigua was forced to surrender and was jailed.

PIMITOUI, FORT. Built 1692 on the Illinois R near modern Peoria. Nucleus of the first permanent French settlement in Illinois Country.

PINCKNEY PLAN. A detailed plan of government, containing more than thirty provisions later incorporated in the Constitution, introduced by Charles Pinckney at an early session of the Constitutional Convention of 1787. The original plan has not survived; its general scope and contents have been deduced from the convention debates.

PINCKNEY'S TREATY (1795). Negotiated by Thomas Pinckney with Spain. Accepted the boundary claims of the US at the thirty-first parallel, established commercial relations with Spain, stipulated that Spain would not incite the Indians on its frontier to attack Americans, and provided for the free navigation of the Mississippi R by American citizens and Spanish subjects, with a three-year right of deposit at New Orleans.

PINE BARREN SPECULATIONS. Perpetrated principally in Montgomery, Washington, and Franklin counties, Ga., 1793 and 1794. County officials issued warrants to a small group of speculators calling for more than 17 million acres of land, ten times the area actually in those counties.

PINE TREE FLAG. A colonial flag of Massachusetts used as early as 1700. The pine tree became one of the earliest symbols of the union of the thirteen colonies. During the American Revolution, the pine tree was sometimes combined with the rattlesnake flag of the southern colonies with the motto, "Don't Tread on Me."

PINE TREE SHILLING. In 1653, a Massachusetts mint issued a crude silver coin. On the obverse was MASATHVSETS IN. and, within a circle, a pine tree. On the reverse was NEW-ENGLAND, AN. DOM. and 1652, XII (the Roman numerals indicating the number of pence in a shilling).

PIONEER STAGE LINE. Began operating in 1851 between Sacramento and Placerville, Calif. It expanded and in 1861 became a link in the Overland Mail route. A well-graded, 100-mile macadamized road was built from Carson City, Nev., to Placerville. In 1865, it became part of Wells Fargo.

PIOUS FUND CONTROVERSY. A fund was established in the 17th c. to support Jesuit missions in California, and they were taken over by the Mexican government in the 19th c. Payments to the missions ceased when the US assumed control of California, and in 1875 California bishops sued in the Permanent Court of Arbitration at the Hague. Eventually the missions received almost $1.5 million in annuities.

PIPE, INDIAN. Pipe-smoking rituals were stressed by the Plains and Woodlands Indians, and tobacco and items associated with it were sacred almost everywhere. The Plains pipe frequently featured a carved bowl of catlinite, along with the stem, or calumet, which was carved, incised, and decorated and was the more important element of the pipe. The calumet was often carried by ambassadors between federated tribes to symbolize states of war and peace, but it might also be employed as an appeal to spiritual beings. The passing of the pipe, solemnly ritualized as it was, became a social adjunct to its intertribal symbolic use.

PIPELINES, EARLY. In 1862, a 4-inch wooden pipe was laid at Oil Creek, Pa., for a distance of about 1,000 feet. In 1865, a 2-inch wrought-iron oil pipe was laid from Pithole, Pa., to the Oil Creek RR, a distance of over five miles. Despite vandalism from teamsters, who recognized the pipeline as a threat to their occupation, it was a great success and marked the beginning of this method of transporting oil.

PIRACY. Although Massachusettes made piracy punishable by death in 1653, other colonial governors tolerated, even encouraged, "privateering." Colonial merchants and settlers bought pirates' stolen goods, and thus obtained necessary commodities at a cheap price; the practice became widespread after the Navigation Acts halted all foreign ships from trading in the American colonies. English men-of-war ended the reign of terror of pirates along the New England coast in 1721–25. After the American Revolution, piratical attacks on US shipping by French "privateers" brought on the undeclared war between France and the US. Piratical operations of English men-of-war on US coasts and on the high seas, including the impressment of American seamen, led to the War of 1812.

Beginning in 1805, the US navy was engaged in warring on pirates on the Gulf Coast, long haunted by pirates. The Barataria pirates were driven out in 1814, as well as the Aury-Lafitte pirates from Galveston, Tex., in 1817. After 1816, the US faced the problem of dealing with the privateers of the new Latin American republics; but by 1827, the navy had ended all piracy along US coasts.

PITHOLE. Pennsylvania boom town founded in 1864 after a gusher was discovered on Pithole Creek, near the Titusville and Oil City fields. By September 1865, the population had reached 15,000 as daily oil production reached 6,000 barrels. Within six months, the wells failed, and Pithole became a ghost town.

PITT, FORT. Begun 1758 by the British at the confluence of the Monongahela and Allegheny rivers, at the site of the abandoned Fort Duquesne and the present Pittsburgh. In 1774, it was renamed Fort Dunmore and remained in patriot hands through the American Revolution, where it became the base of operations for western campaigns.

PITTMAN ACT (April 23, 1918). It provided for the issuance of Federal Reserve bank notes and the withdrawal of silver dollars and silver certificates. The export of silver was authorized as a way of improving US balance of payments.

PITTSBURGH. City in SW Pennsylvania, situated where the Allegheny and Monongahela rivers form the Ohio, regarded from the earliest days as the gateway to the West. The French built Fort Duquesne there, the British Fort Pitt, and it was the base of operations for the patriot forces' western campaigns in the American Revolution. The small trading post established there had become a city by 1816; with the opening of the Mississippi R, Pittsburgh had begun its development as a commercial city. The War of 1812 gave impetus to its development as an industrial center; the abundance of necessary raw materials made the iron and glass industries of Pittsburgh of national importance. The transition from iron to steel was neither long nor difficult, and the city became the largest steel-producing area in the nation. During World War II, it produced one third of US steel. Afterward the city began an extensive renovation of the Golden Triangle, the city's business district, and introduced comprehensive smoke-control laws. Pop.: 423,938 (1980).

PITTSBURGH, INDIAN TREATY AT (1775). Commissioners from Virginia negotiated with the Indian tribes of the Ohio country. The Delaware, Shawnee, Mingo, Seneca, Wyandot, and Ottawa agreed not to aid the British in the Revolutionary War; in return, the colonists agreed not to settle in Ohio.

PITTSBURGH GAZETTE. First published in 1786 and subsequently published under various names, it is regarded as the first newspaper west of the Allegheny Mountains.

PITTSBURGH RESOLUTIONS (1775). Upon hearing of the battles of Lexington and Concord, settlers in the Pittsburgh area passed resolutions expressing their approval of the conduct of the Minutemen of Massachusetts and friendship for the Indians.

PLACER MINING. A process to separate gold from sand in a stream bed or similar alluvial deposit. It was placer gold that began the California, Pikes Peak, and Klondike gold rushes. It is contrasted with lode mining.

PLAIN, FORT. Built in colonial times near the Mohawk R to protect the farmers of Canajoharie, N.Y., from the Iroquois. Used during the Revolution but its importance ceased after 1781.

PLANK ROADS. Introduced into New York from Canada ca. 1837, they were widely adapted elsewhere.

PLANTATIONS. Settlements in the New World, established under authority of the crown. Selected leaders received the land for the new settlements in trust; they arranged the business details of the planting, distributed the land, and organized local government.

PLANTATION SYSTEM. When Virginia passed to the crown in 1624, it became a commonwealth of independent farms and private plantations. The demand for labor was filled by African slaves brought by Dutch traders. As finally evolved, the system employed large laboring forces (1,000 acres with 100 slaves was considered a highly productive unit), a division of labor, and a routine under the direction of a central authority. Tobacco, rice, sugarcane, and, especially, cotton were the crops. The plantations were self-sustained communities. The slaves were usually worked in gangs, although the skilled slaves were employed in special capacities. In larger establishments, operations were under the control of an overseer. The system was destroyed by the Civil War; although some plantations operated thereafter on a crop-sharing basis. Most broke up into small farms, operated by the individual owner, tenant, or sharecropper.

PLATFORM, PARTY. Some historians have argued that the VIRGINIA AND KENTUCKY RESOLUTIONS of 1798–99 constituted the first party platforms, but the platform in its modern sense did not appear until the 1830s. The platform is the responsibility of a committee of the national convention, and even though it is adopted by the convention as a whole, it tends to be ignored by the party's presidential candidate once he is selected. Although parties and the public have long since ceased to attach great importance to platforms adopted at national conventions, they frequently constitute important sources of evidence of popular thought and legislative action.

PLATT AMENDMENT. The basis for Cuban-American relations from 1901 to 1914, named for Sen. O.H. Platt, chairman of the Senate committee on Cuban relations. The Cuban government accepted its terms, which in effect turned Cuba into a dependency of the US. Repealed in 1934.

PLATTE BRIDGE FIGHT (July 26, 1865). Effort by Sioux, Cheyenne, and Arapaho warriors to destroy a bridge over the North Platte R in Colorado, an important link to the West. Twenty-four US troops were killed and a wagon train was destroyed.

PLATTE PURCHASE. A tract of almost 2 million acres that extended Missouri's boundary to the Platte R. The government bought it from the Indians in 1836 for $7,500 cash and specified amounts of merchandise.

PLATTE RIVER TRAIL. Route to the West through South Pass of the Wind River Range in SW Wyoming. First traversed in 1813. Also known as the California Trail, Mormon Trail, and Overland Trail. The completion of the Union Pacific RR (1869) ended its importance.

PLATTSBURGH, BATTLE OF (Sept. 11, 1814). A land and water engagement at Lake Champlain, N. Y., during the War of 1812. An invasion by British forces from Canada was stopped, and the British were denied control of the Great Lakes.

PLEASANT HILL, BATTLE OF (April 9, 1864). Skirmish near the Red R in Louisiana. The Rebels retreated in disorder toward Shreveport.

PLEDGE OF ALLEGIANCE. Taken from the magazine *Youth's Companion*, one of whose editors, Francis Bellamy, claimed authorship. First recited by school children in 1892. The wording has changed over the years; since 1954, it has been: "I pledge allegiance to the flag of the United States of America and to the Republic for which it stands, one Nation, under God, indivisible, with liberty and justice for all."

PLESSY V. FERGUSON, 163 US 537 (1896). Upheld the validity of an 1890 Louisiana statute that required railroads operating in that state to provide "equal but separate accommodations for the white and colored races." For nearly sixty years thereafter the separate-but-equal doctrine enabled states to legislate segregation of races in almost all areas of public activity, including public schools. The decision was effectively overturned by the Supreme Court in 1954 in *Brown v. Board of Education of Topeka, Kansas.*

PLOESTI OIL FIELDS, AIR RAIDS ON
(1941–44). Oil refineries located around
Ploesti, Rumania, supplied one-third of the
entire oil supply of the Axis during World
War II and were a primary target of Allied air
attacks. An ineffective attempt was made in
1942, but in mid-1943 half of the refinery
production was destroyed. Intensive bombing from April to August effectively destroyed
the area's oil-producing capacity.

PLOWDEN'S NEW ALBION. Colonizing
grant issued 1634 to Sir Edmund Plowden,
the first for what is now New Jersey. The charter copied that of Maryland, and evidently
Plowden, a Roman Catholic, planned New Albion to be a Catholic settlement. He made
four unsuccessful efforts to settle his province. In 1664, the grant was transferred to the
duke of York.

PLUMMER GANG. Fifty outlaws under Henry
Plummer, sheriff of Bannack District (now
Montana), organized in 1863. Called the In-
nocents, 102 robberies and murders were
charged against them until a vigilante committee caught and hanged most of them.

PLYMOUTH, VIRGINIA COMPANY OF
(1606–20). In 1606, two charters were issued for colonizing the New World. The Virginia Co. of London was authorized to plant a
colony in the south and the Virginia Co. of
Plymouth to plant one in the north, with a
one-hundred-mile neutral zone in between.
The Plymouth Co. sent its first expedition in
1606, but they were captured and taken prisoner by the Spanish near Puerto Rico. A second vessel reached Maine and returned with
such glowing accounts that the company sent
two ships in May 1607. The plantation they
established near the mouth of the Kennebec
R was the unfortunate POPHAM COLONY. In
1620, a new company, the Council for New
England was formed.

PLYMOUTH PLANTATION. See NEW PLYM-
OUTH COLONY.

PLYMOUTH ROCK. Traditionally, the spot
where the Pilgrims disembarked on Dec. 16,
1620, at Plymouth, Mass. It was moved
(1920) from its original location in order to
protect and display it.

PLYMOUTH TRADING POST. Established
1633 in the Connecticut Valley, near the
present Windsor, Conn., by Edward Winslow
of Plymouth Colony. Within a few years,
other Massachusetts trading posts were established, leading to the RIVER TOWNS OF
CONNECTICUT.

POCKET VETO. Stratagem by which the president negates legislation without actually ve-
toing it and without giving Congress the opportunity of overriding his veto. The
Constitution (Article I, Section 7) provides
that measures presented by Congress to the
president within ten days of adjournment and
not returned by him before adjournment fail
to become law. First employed by President
Madison.

POINTE COUPEE. An early French settlement in Louisiana on the Mississippi R just
below the mouth of the Red R. It was an important French post until 1762. Many Acadians settled there during the Spanish regime,
and its population remained predominantly
French.

POINT FOUR. US program during the Truman administration that sought to help pov-
erty-stricken peoples through the provision
of technological knowledge and skills and
through capital investment. In 1950, $35
million was appropriated; by 1954, the sum
was $400 million. The program was widened
in the Eisenhower administration; offers of
technical facilities and capital loans and
grants to poor countries became weapons in
the cold war.

POINT PLEASANT, BATTLE OF (Oct. 10,
1774). Confrontation of DUNMORE'S WAR. Lord
Dunmore's Virginia troops were attacked on
the Ohio R by a large force of Shawnee, led
by Chief Cornstalk.

POLAR EXPEDITIONS. In 1753, the *Argo*
left Philadelphia to map the coast of Labrador
to the entrance into Hudson Bay. An antarctic
continent was postulated in 1829, and in
1838–42, a US exploring expedition mapped
the edge of that continent. Systematic US exploration of the polar regions began in the
1840s. Three successive expeditions (1850–
51, 1853–55, and 1860–61) got progressively further northward. Meanwhile, the

navy (1853–56) dispatched an expedition to the North Pacific Ocean and into the Arctic Ocean to Wrangel Island. Two ill-fated expeditions followed the Civil War: the *Polaris* under Charles Hall (1871–73) and the steamer *Jeannette*, which perished in 1881.

From 1885 to 1920, the dominant effort was to reach the North Pole. Most important were the seven successive explorations of Ellesmere Island, N Greenland, and the Arctic Ocean by R.E. Peary (1886–1909) that resulted in his reaching the North Pole on April 6, 1909. Numerous other expeditions in the early 20th c. explored virtually all parts of the arctic regions. After ca. 1919, the airplane changed the character and extent of polar expeditions. These included notable flights to Antarctica. R.E. Byrd flew from Little America to the South Pole in November 1929. During World War II, the US established transarctic air routes; set up air bases and meteorological and other scientific stations; and developed logistic support forces, especially in Alaska, N Canada, Greenland, and Iceland. Following the war, the US carried out an accelerated program of polar exploration and scientific investigation. In Antarctica, the government launched an all-out program of exploration. In 1958, the nuclear submariine *Nautilus* sailed under the Arctic icecap. In Antarctica, a remarkably high degree of international cooperation and participation resulted from the Antarctic Treaty of 1961, signed by twelve governments.

POLICE. The decentralized, local nature of American police agencies reflects their Anglo-Saxon origins. Before the 19th c., England and its colonies relied on constables or sheriffs to maintain order. The problems of lawlessness and disorder associated with urbanization highlighted the inadequacies of these prior systems. The first municipal police force in America was established in New York in 1844; early departments were characterized by political influence, corruption, and inefficiency. Rural areas continued to be served by sheriffs. The Texas Rangers (which actually antedated Texas statehood) was the first state police force, but most state police forces were not established until the 20th c., partly in response to problems caused by the automobile. Although there is no federal police force as such, the Federal Bureau of In-

vestigation performs many of the functions of a national force.

POLICE POWERS. The powers encompassed in the general power to govern, often phrased in terms of the power to legislate for the "public health, safety, welfare, and morals." In US constitutional theory, the police power is usually conceived as a power of the state (as distinct from the powers of the national government). Theoretically, the powers of the federal government of the US are enumerated in Article I, Section 8, of the Constitution, and the Tenth Amendment provides that "the powers not delegated to the US by the Constitution, nor prohibitied by it to the States, are reserved to the States respectively, or to the people." While the Tenth Amendment is the constitutional basis for the state police power as a reserved power, Article I, Section 10, of the Constitution is an explicit list of limits of state power. The Fourteenth Amendment has generally been construed as further limiting the police powers of both the states and the federal government.

POLIOMYELITIS. Also called infantile paralysis. A viral infection that can result in paralysis or death. The first large polio epidemic in the US occurred in 1916 and they occurred regularly thereafter until vaccines developed by Jonas Salk and Albert Sabin were perfected in the 1950s. Since 1965, paralytic polio has become a rare disease, but this status can be maintained only by a continued vaccination program.

POLITICAL ACTION COMMITTEE (PAC). Committees set up by special interest groups, such as labor unions, to lobby for certain causes and to support favored political candidates. Critics have charged that PACs are simply a device to avoid accurate reporting of campaign contributions and a way of circumventing federal spending laws.

POLITICAL ASSESSMENTS. A means of getting funds for political party operations by collecting money from public officeholders. Such assessments of federal employees are illegal under the Hatch Act, but the practice continues to exist to some degree at the state and local level, although a number of states have also outlawed it. More common is the practice of pressuring state and local officeholders to make so-called voluntary contributions to the party in power.

POLITICAL CAMPAIGNS. See CAMPAIGNS, POLITICAL; CAMPAIGNS, PRESIDENTIAL.

POLITICAL PARTIES. The origin and development of the American political parties stand entirely apart from the US Constitution. The framers of that document had hoped that the US government could avoid the "factionalism" brought on by political parties. It was not to be, however; from the initial dualism of the Federalists and the Jeffersonians (Democratic-Republicans), the parties realigned in the 1820s into the Whigs, successors to the Federalists, and the Democrats, led by Andrew Jackson. From 1860 to the present, the Democrats and the Republicans have dominated the American party system.

The organization of both parties takes the form of a pyramid of party committees, beginning at the bottom with local precinct, city, and county committees, and building to a single national committee at the top. In both parties, the national party convention is the highest authority; it defines the powers and the composition of the national committee. Authority within the parties has always been decentralized. In some states, the effective locus of power is the state committee; in others power is further decentralized into autonomous city and county organizations. The national committees of the two parties have never achieved any supremacy in the party organization. The president has customarily subordinated the national committee of his party to his own leadership; in the opposition party, the congressional leadership most frequently provides the voice of the national party.

The American parties have found their major role as the nominators and electors of candidates for public office; once they have elected an official, they have virtually no formal control over him or her. Unlike European political parties, which expect their members to support official party programs, US parties have no mechanism for forcing elected party officials to vote in a particular way.

POLK DOCTRINE (Dec. 2, 1845). President James K. Polk reaffirmed the Monroe Doctrine by announcing US determination "that no future European colony or dominion shall, with our consent, be planted or established on any part of the North American continent." Applied in 1848 to discourage Yucatán from voluntarily ceding itself to some European power, it was looked upon by Latin-American nations as a limitation upon their sovereignty.

POLLOCK'S AID TO THE REVOLUTION. Oliver Pollock acted as mediator between Gov. Patrick Henry of Virginia and the Spanish governor of New Orleans to provide the colonists with large supplies of gunpowder, arms, blankets, sugar, coffee, and other hard-to-acquire supplies. He also supplied similar cargoes for George Rogers Clark in his battle to hold the Illinois Country. By the end of the war, Pollock had advanced for the American cause his entire property amounting to $100,000 and an additional $200,000 he had borrowed; no other person contributed such an amount.

POLLOCK V. FARMERS LOAN AND TRUST COMPANY, 157 US 429 (1895). Supreme Court ruled the 1894 income tax unconstitutional. The decision was unpopular and led ultimately to the passage of the Sixteenth Amendment (1913).

POLL TAX. A tax levied on each person within a particular class (for example, adult male) rather than on his or her property or income. Poll taxes were common in all the colonies and continued to be levied into the 20th c. Many states used the tax as a means of preventing blacks from voting. In 1964, the Twenty-fourth Amendment nullified all state laws requiring payment of a poll tax as a condition for voting in federal elections. In 1966, the Supreme Court ruled that even in state elections the poll tax violates the Fourteenth Amendment.

POMEROY CIRCULAR (1864). Sen. S.C. Pomeroy, a leader of the Radical Republicans, circulated a pronouncement advocating the nomination of Salmon P. Chase for the presidency over the Republican incumbent, Abraham Lincoln. The petition was apparently circulated without the knowledge of Chase, and the movement collapsed quickly after the Ohio Unionists declared themselves for Lincoln.

PONCE DE LEÓN'S DISCOVERY OF FLORIDA (1513). Searching for the island of Bimini, where he expected to find the fountain of youth, de León landed (April 2) on the mainland just N of present St. Augustine and named the land Florida in honor of the Easter season. Back in Spain in 1514, he received a grant to colonize Florida and Bimini. In 1521, he undertook a second expedition from Puerto Rico to Florida. He and his party were attacked by Indians, and in the ensuing battle he was severely wounded. The expedition returned to Cuba, where Ponce de León died.

PONTCHARTRAIN, LAKE. In SE Louisiana, five miles N of New Orleans. It is about 40 miles long and covers about 600 square miles. The lake was used by the British (1763–83) to form a link in the inside passage to the Mississippi. It was connected to New Orleans by canal in 1795 and by railroad in 1831. The lake is crossed by two causeways.

PONTCHARTRAIN DU DÉTROIT, FORT. Established by Antoin de la Mothe Cadillac in 1701. Around it grew up the city of Detroit. The fort, under various names, survived for 125 years.

PONTIAC'S WAR (1763–64). An uprising of Indians after the French and Indian War, in opposition to British expansion in the Great Lakes area. The leader was the Ottawa Chief Pontiac, a long-time enemy of the British. Following the teachings of the Delaware Prophet, Pontiac was able to forge a unity among the Delaware, Shawnee, Chippewa, Miami, Potawatomi, Seneca, Kickapoo, and others. Most had been allies of the French. In May 1763 they captured eight out of the ten British forts. Fort Pitt and Detroit were successfully defended. Pontiac himself led the attack against Detroit, whose commander had been warned of the attack and had closed the gate. Pontiac laid siege to the fort, a tactic unheard of in Indian military history. He was finally forced to retreat up the Maumee R when reinforcements arrived. A formal peace was concluded on July 24, 1764. Later Pontiac tried again to arouse the Indians along the Mississippi R, but he was killed (1769) by an Illinois Indian.

PONTOTOC, TREATY OF (Oct. 20, 1832). Between the US and the Chippewa in what is now Pontotoc County, Miss. The Indians gave up more than 6 million acres and agreed to move W of the Mississippi R, thereby extinguishing the last Indian titles to land in the state.

PONY EXPRESS. In 1860 a contract was granted to the freighting firm of Russell, Majors and Waddell for a fast overland mail service to California over a central route and making use of riders on horseback. Stations were built at intervals of about fifteen miles. Starting a St. Joseph, Mo., the route followed the Oregon-California Trail by way of Fort Kearny and Scottsbluff (Nebraska), Fort Laramie, South Pass, and Fort Bridger (Wyoming), and Salt Lake City. From there the trail went around the southern end of Great Salt Lake, by way of Fort Churchill, Carson City (both in Nevada), and Placerville (California) to Sacramento. The journey took eight days. The express was a giant relay, in which about seventy-five ponies participated in each direction. At each station, the riders quickly transferred the saddlebags to fresh ponies and continued. The service was weekly at first and later semiweekly. Within eighteen months after the service was inaugurated, telegraph lines were joined and all need for the pony express was eliminated. The venture virtually ruined its owners.

POOR PEOPLE'S CAMPAIGN (1968). A march on Washington, D.C., sponsored by the Rev. Martin Luther King, Jr., to dramatize the plight of 30 million Americans living below the poverty line. Marchers began to arrive in May and set up camp in what was named Resurrection City. Divided in leadership with the death of King, the marchers dispersed in June.

POOR RICHARD'S ALMANAC (1732–96). Published in Philadelphia by Benjamin Franklin, it contained, in addition to the usual almanac information, maxims, saws, and pithy sayings written by Franklin. Eventually, 10,000 copies of each edition were printed, making it, after the Bible, the most popular book in the colonies. Franklin sold his interest in the publication in 1758.

POOR WHITES. Before the Civil War, most writers and political commentators were interested only in the aristocracy and their slaves and tended to dismiss almost all the others as "poor whites." After the war, their economic competition with the newly freed blacks was exploited by politicians to create the segregated society that persisted until the 1960s.

POPHAM COLONY. The first attempt by England to colonize the New England coast. On May 31, 1607, the PLYMOUTH COMPANY OF VIRGINIA sent about 120 colonists, sponsored by George Popham, to settle on the Maine coast at the mouth of the Kennebec R. They built Fort George, a storehouse, fifty houses, and a church. They made friends with the Indians and traded with them, and explored up Maine's rivers. But quarrels arose, and all but forty-five men were shipped back to England. In September 1698 the remaining settlers returned home.

POPULAR SOVEREIGNTY. Also known as squatter sovereignty, in US history it has been applied to the theory holding that the settlers in a federal territory had the right to decide whether or not slavery was to be legal in the territory. The KANSAS-NEBRASKA ACT was a triumph for the popular sovereignty theory.

POPULATION, GROWTH, AND MOVEMENTS OF. From 52,000 inhabitants in 1650 to over 226 million in 1980, the population of the area now encompassing the US has grown on an average annual growth of 2.5 percent. Most of this growth came from the excess of births over deaths. It is estimated that in the 1820s there were about 55 births a year per 1,000 population. By 1935–39, the number had fallen below 19; but in the baby boom of the post-World War II years, the number went up to 25. By 1980, the rate had fallen to 16.2 per 1,000. Nothing very precise can be said about the death rate in early years. The death registration was not started until 1900; and the death rate for the total population dropped from 16.2 per 1,000 during 1900–1905 to 8.9 in 1980. Immigration is the other factor in the rising population. In the decade 1840–50, net immigration passed the 1 million mark, mounting to its maximum of 6.3 million from 1900 to 1910. Thereafter, the number dropped significantly.

The most dramatic change in the pattern of settlement has been in the shift from the country to the city. At the first US census in 1790, about 95 percent of the population lived in rural areas. By 1980, this proportion was down to 26.5 percent, and many of those worked in the city. In the early days of the Republic, it probably took about 75 percent of the labor force to produce the nation's food and fiber. In 1980, only 2.7 percent of the total was engaged in agriculture.

POPULISM. Grew out of the agrarian movement of protest of the 1890s against some of the consequences of industrialization. The movement reached its greatest intensity in the depression crisis following the panic of 1893, and it lost its driving force just when success seemed imminent, during the presidential election of 1896. The Republican William McKinley's convincing triumph over William Jennings Bryan removed whatever consolation the Populists might have salvaged from the election. Farm organizations gained considerable political influence in the 20th c., but the hope of building a national party on agrarian principles had disappeared.

POPULIST PARTY. Organized 1892, it grew out of a number of farmers' groups, including the Farmers' Alliance, the Grangers, and the remnants of the Greenback party. Low farm prices and a deflated currency caused many farm families to face the loss of their farms through mortgage foreclosure. Furthermore, farmers generally believed that the railroads were cheating them by overcharging. In 1892, the Populist party nominated James B. Weaver, who won in Colorado, Idaho, Kansas, and Nevada; he also won one electoral vote each in North Dakota and Oregon. They showed strength in Alabama, Georgia, North Carolina, Texas, South Carolina, and Nebraska, even though the Democrats carried those states. In 1896, the Democratic candidate, William Jennings Bryan, adopted a number of the Populist ideas, including the free coinage of silver. As a result, the Populists endorsed him for the presidency (but nominated their own vice-presidential candidate). The Republican victory that year in effect ended the Populist party.

PORK BARREL. In US politics, a derogatory term generally applied to local projects and improvements for which appropriations are obtained by legislators for the benefit of their constituents.

PORTAGES AND WATER ROUTES. In colonial days, travel by water was subject to interruption, either by rapids, shallows, or falls, or at points where the transit from one river to another had to be made. At such places, boat and cargo had to be carried around the obstruction or across the intervening land. At places where the volume of travel was considerable, entrepreneurs frequently maintained horses or oxen at these portages for hauling boats across the land. Eventually, canals and then railroads made these portages unnecessary. Niagara, Erie, Fort Wayne, and Chicago all grew up around portages.

PORT AUTHORITIES. Quasi-public, tax-free organizations that generally derive income from tolls, largely from bridges and tunnels and rentals from airports, heliports, and marine and bus terminals. They generally receive their capital from the floating of bonds, which are to varying degrees guaranteed by state or city governments.

PORT AUTHORITY OF NEW YORK AND NEW JERSEY. Created 1921 by the two states with a view to solving the problems caused by the artificial New York-New Jersey boundary line down the middle of the Hudson R. Its sphere of jurisdiction extends over a twenty-five mile radius from New York Bay. Among the facilities operated by the Port Authority are the Goethels Bridge, the George Washington Bridge, the Lincoln Tunnel, the Port Authority Bus Terminal (in New York City), the Port Authority Trans-Hudson (PATH) System (a subway connecting New York City and New Jersey cities), the areas major airports (Kennedy, LaGuardia, and Newark), and the World Trade Center (New York City).

PORTER CASE. In 1862, Union Gen. Fitz-John Porter was court-martialed for disobeying the orders of Gen. John Pope during the second Battle of Bull Run. In 1863, he was found guilty, but controversy continued to surround the case. In 1886, Congress in effect overturned the court-martial. It has been charged that Porter was used as a scapegoat by the Radical Republicans, who wanted to get at Porter's friend, Gen. G.B. McClellan.

PORT HUDSON, SIEGE OF (March–July 1863). Confederate troops under Gen. J.C. Breckenridge occupied the high bluff of Port Hudson, twenty-five miles N of Baton Rouge, with the purpose of protecting Confederate supplies coming down the Red R. Only after the fall of Vicksburg rendered the stronghold useless did the Confederacy surrender this last stronghold on the Mississippi R.

PORTLAND (Maine). The largest city in Maine, located on a narrow peninsula that juts into Casco Bay. The closest US seaport to Europe, it is an important port of entry for oil and other products. The area was settled as early as 1623, and by 1675 there was a town called Falmouth on the site. It was wiped out in an Indian raid and was resettled in 1716. At the start of the American Revolution, the city was destroyed by the British. It was rebuilt and renamed Portland in 1786. It became a shipbuilding center and later a railroad center. During the 20th c., the city has been an important center for the export of Canadian products. Pop.: 61,572 (1980).

PORTLAND (Oregon). The largest city in Oregon, located on both banks of the Willamette R where it joins the Columbia R. It is an important seaport although it is located 90 miles inland. The site was settled in 1845 by New Englanders, who named it after Portland, Me. In the late 19th c., the city became an important wheat, lumber, and fruit marketing center. The development of hydroelectric power in the area made it a manufacturing center. Aluminum is an important product. Pop: 366,383 (1980).

PORT ROYAL (Nova Scotia). At the site of the present Annapolis Royal, it was an important French outpost against colonial New England. First settled in 1605, by 1684 it was the seat of government for Acadia and was the center from which the French attacked New England shipping and the scene of much illicit trade with New Englanders. It was taken several times by the English and finally ceded to them in 1710. It lost its importance after the English moved the seat of government to Halifax in 1749.

PORT ROYAL (South Carolina). In 1562 the French settled about thirty mostly Huguenots on Parris Island, where they constructed a fort named Charlesfort. They named the harbor Port Royal. The settlement did not survive, and the Spanish built Fort San Marcos near the spot in 1577. After the English settled South Carolina, it continued to be fought over by the English and the Spanish. A center of a major cotton-growing region in the 19th c. Pop.: 2,977 (1980).

PORTSMOUTH. City in Virginia, part of the Norfolk-Portsmouth-Virginia Beach metropolitan area. Founded 1664 on the site of an Indian village and has been the site of a navy yard (the Norfolk Navy Yard, despite its name, is in Portsmouth) since before the American Revolution. It was the scene of much action during the War of 1812 and the Civil War. Pop.: 104,577 (1980).

PORTSMOUTH, TREATY OF (Sept. 5, 1905). Brought to a close the Russo-Japanese War. President Theodore Roosevelt brought the two opponents to the negotiating table at Portsmouth, N. H. He won the Nobel Peace Prize in 1906 for his efforts.

POSTAL SERVICE, UNITED STATES. Local and intercolonial postal services were established in the 17th c. In 1737, Benjamin Franklin was appointed deputy postmaster; he and William Hunter, as joint postmasters for the colonies, effected many improvements. Franklin surveyed new routes and inaugurated overnight service between New York and Philadelphia. In 1775, the Continental Congress appointed a committee headed by Franklin to set up a postal service independent of the crown; Franklin became its postmaster general. The Constitution called for the establishment of post offices and post roads, and the post office was established (1789, 1794) as a permanent part of the federal government. In 1799, government-owned coach service was instituted between New York and Philadelphia; in 1813, all steamship lines were declared post routes. In 1838, the railroads were also declared post routes, and an 1845 law created the system whereby private, or star route, contractors were hired to carry the mail between post offices. Postage stamps made their appearance in 1847 (prior to that, the recipient paid the postage upon delivery). During the second half of the 19th c., the post office system expanded greatly, and covered virtually the en-

tire nation. After 1829, the postmaster general was a member of the president's cabinet, and the postal system became the chief patronage-dispensing agency of the political party in power (almost all postmasters were political appointees). Despite the abuses, the postal system developed into a highly efficient government department. In 1970, the Postal Reorganization Act created an independent government agency, the US Postal Service; it removed the postmaster general from the president's cabinet and effectively eliminated politics from the management of postal affairs. The expectation has been that the Postal Service would become self-supporting.

POST ROADS. The earliest colonial mail carrying, between New York and Boston, and later between New York and Albany, in the late 17th c., traced routes that became what are still called post roads. Many new post roads were created by the Continental Congress. By 1787, post roads had reached as far S as Augusta, Ga., and as far W as Pittsburgh. By 1829, there were 114,780 miles of post roads. The coming of steamships and then the railroad put an end to the importance of the post roads as such, although they remained important highways.

POTASH (potassium carbonate). Long used for bleaching textiles and making glass and soap, potash achieved a new importance with the advent of gunpowder. As early as 1608, Virginia settlers were burning timber to create potash and shipping it to England, and after 1750 Parliament paid a bounty for the production of potash in America. After the Revolution, potash-making became a major US industry; in 1792, Thomas Jefferson listed it as the nation's sixth most important export. Production shifted from Virginia to New England, and after 1840 Ohio was the chief source. By 1850, potash was also widely used as a fertilizer, while forests available for indiscriminate burning were becoming increasingly rare. Germany became the chief source of potash; when World War I cut off this source, a frantic search began for a substitute, and large deposits of potash salts were found near Carlsbad, N.M., which furnish about 90 percent of the nation's supply.

POTATOES. The so-called Irish potato, a native of the Andes, was introduced to England in the 16th c. It was brought into the American colonies in the early 17th c. By the early 18th c., it had become a major crop in Maine, where the production of potato starch became a major industry. Sweet potatoes (botanically unrelated to the Irish potato) were being cultivated by the American Indians when the first settlers arrived. They grow best in the South, where they produce an enormous yield (200 to 400 bushels) per acre. By 1980, annual US production of Irish potatoes had reached 301 million hundredweight; production of sweet potatoes totals over 14 million hundredweight.

POTOMAC, ARMY OF. Created by the Union army in 1861 with Gen. G.B. McClellan as commander; its immediate purpose was to guard the approaches to the Potomac R and thus to protect Washington. The army participated in the PENINSULAR CAMPAIGN, the SEVEN DAYS' BATTLE, and at Antietam and Gettysburg. McClellan was succeeded as commander by A.E. Burnside, Joseph Hooker, G.C. Meade, and, finally, by U.S. Grant.

POTOMAC COMPANY. Organized 1785 to create a waterway connection between the Potomac and Ohio rivers. George Washington was one of its proprietors. Work was begun on several short canals, but the organization was never financially successful. In 1828, it surrendered its charters and rights to the Chesapeake and Ohio Canal Co.

POTOMAC RIVER. Drains the W slopes of the Allegheny Mountains of West Virginia into the Chesapeake Bay. Two main streams, the North Branch and the South Branch, and several minor streams unite to form the upper Potomac. Spaniards probably explored the Potomac estuary before 1570, and it was an important waterway to the early Virginia and Maryland settlers. The falls at Washington, D.C., kept the upper Potomac from becoming a route to the sea, but it developed into an important pathway to the Ohio Valley.

POTSDAM CONFERENCE (1945). The last meeting during World War II of the three allied chiefs of state: Harry S. Truman, Winston Churchill (who was replaced during the conference by the new prime minister, Clement Atlee), and Joseph Stalin. Germany had surrendered, and the conference dealt with the occupation of Germany and reparations to be paid. It also called for the preparation of peace treaties with Germany's former allies and for the Japanese to surrender.

POTTAWATOMIE MASSACRE. The murder of five proslavery settlers at Pottawatomie Creek, Franklin County, Kans., in May 1856. John Brown, four of his sons, and three other free-state men were accused of the crime and warrants for their arrest were issued. But the case never came to trial.

POTTERY. Pottery was made in the colonies by the very earliest settlers; and small potteries in the 17th and 18th c. furnished the local market with lead-glazed red earthenware. The arrival of German potters in the 18th c. changed the character of American pottery from the Atlantic states to the South. Stoneware, fired at a much higher temperature than the redware, was manufactured throughout the Northeast and into the Midwest after the Revolution. An influx of British potters ca. 1825 made New Jersey the principal pottery center, with the Trenton area still the focus of the industry.

POULTRY CASE. See SCHECHTER POULTRY CORPORATION V. UNITED STATES.

POULTRY INDUSTRY. Chickens represent 95 percent of the poultry raised in the US (with turkeys, ducks, geese, and guinea fowl making up the rest). Most poultry today is raised in large farm complexes. California, Georgia, Arkansas, Pennsylvania, and Indiana are the leading producers of chickens. Egg production in 1980 accounted for about $3.3 billion in sales.

POVERTY AND PAUPERISM. Colonial poor laws followed English precedents in assigning responsibility to local authorities, a situation that did not change after independence. Almshouses were created in the early 19th c.; for the most part, they were only custodial institutions for the aged, infant, infirm and handicapped poor. In the 1870s and 1880s, there was a proliferation of private charity organizations, the forerunners of family service agencies. The Homestead Act of 1862 had created and supported public educational institutions for the deaf, blind, and mentally retarded; otherwise, the federal government played no appreciable role in aid to the poor.

The economic upheavals of the Great Depression taxed state, local, and private charitable efforts far beyond their capabilities; and even before Franklin D. Roosevelt took office in 1933, the federal government was already lending states and cities funds that provided 80 percent of all aid to the unemployed. The New Deal policies put into effect by the Roosevelt administration supplied direct federal aid to the poor in a number of ways, including the Works Progress Administration. The Social Security Act of 1935 sought to provide a long-term answer to problems of economic insecurity. Among its more important provisions was a federal payroll tax to finance unemployment insurance and old-age pensions. Grants-in-aid were created for states for federally approved but state-operated programs for maternal and child health; aid to the blind; aid to the aged not eligible for social security; and aid to dependent children. Since then, the federal government has more and more assumed the financial responsibility for aid to the poor. This was especially evident in the 1960s, when President Lyndon B. Johnson launched his war on poverty. His Great Society programs incorporated aid to disadvantaged youth and efforts to improve entire communities. Much of the Johnson poverty program was dismantled by the Nixon administration; and after 1981, the Reagan administration severely cut the amount of federal aid to the poor.

POVERTY POINT. A site in Louisiana containing a wealth of Archaic (between 1300 and 200 BC) artifacts and impressive earthworks and mounds.

POWELL'S EXPLORATIONS (1869, 1871–72). In his first exploration, J.W. Powell, a geologist, explored the length of the Green and Colorado rivers to the mouth of the Virgin R in SE Nevada, a journey of 900 miles. The second exploration, funded by Congress, included a number of other eminent scientists. They explored adjacent rivers and territories and did much to formulate the basic principles of structural geology. Powell published accounts of his explorations in 1875 and 1876.

POWELL'S VALLEY. A long narrow valley in SW Virginia and NE Tennessee leading directly to Cumberland Gap. In 1750, Ambrose Powell, a member of an exploration team, cut his name into a tree; hence the valley's name.

POWERS, SEPARATION OF. A fundamental US constitutional principle, under which governmental powers are vested in three different branches of the government: executive, legislative, and judicial. Its most influential advocate was the 18th.-c. French philosopher Montesquieu, whose writings were well known to the Founding Fathers.

POWHATAN CONFEDERACY. A 17th.-c. chiefdom among the Algonkin-speaking Indians of Virginia. Chief Powhatan inherited dominion over seven local groups and expanded his sway to more than thirty tributary groups, having an estimated population of 9,000. The English settlers, who had need of Indian foodstuffs, treated Powhatan as minor royalty. The marriage of his daughter Pocahontas to John Rolfe was instrumental in concluding peace between the Indians and the English. He died in 1618 and was succeeded by Opechancanough. In 1622, the latter made sudden war against the colonists. The war continued for two decades but finally ended in an Indian defeat in 1644. Thereafter, the colonists incorporated the chiefdom in subordinate status.

POWHATAN INCIDENT (April 1861). When the Civil War broke out, the warship *Powhatan* was ordered by the secretary of state to defend Fort Pickens, Fla. The secretary of the navy, with President Lincoln's consent, ordered the vessel to the defense of Fort Sumter, S.C., instead. A telegram was sent to D.D. Porter, commander of the *Powhatan*, but he believed that only his original orders had the approval of the president and refused to change his course. The Pickens expedition was successful, but without the *Powhatan*'s firepower, the relief of Sumter failed.

POWNALL, FORT. Built by the English in 1759 on the Penobscot R in Maine, it was one of the most defensible strongholds occupied by the British during the French and Indian War.

POWWOW. In the Algonkin language, originally a magical ritual. By 1812, the term was being used in English to designate any gathering of American Indians, whether social or ceremonial.

PRAGMATISM. A worldwide philosophic movement of the late 19th and early 20th c.; it was especially important in the US, where its leading proponents were C.S. Peirce, William James, Josiah Royce, and John Dewey. The pragmatists argued that the truth of an idea lay primarily in its ability to "work." It was a notable attempt to wed science and philosophy.

PRAIRIE. A geographical region of the US, a vast grassland extending through parts of Minnesota, Wisconsin, Illinois, Missouri, Oklahoma, and Texas. Its western boundary merges into the Great Plains.

PRAIRIE DU CHIEN. City in Wisconsin, originally a French settlement, on the Mississippi R near the confluence of the Wisconsin R. Long an important fur-trading center, it fell to the British in 1763, who during the American Revolution, burned the fort. Passed to the US by the Treaty of Ghent (1814). Fort Crawford was built there in 1816, and the city became a steamboat port in the 19th c. Today, it manufactures fertilizer, cement, woolens, and building fixtures. Pop.: 5,859 (1980).

PRAIRIE DU CHIEN, INDIAN TREATY AT (1825). Under the auspices of the federal government, more than 1,000 Sioux, Chippewa, Sauk and Fox, Potawatomi, Winnebago, and Iowa chiefs met and agreed on tribal boundaries.

PRAIRIE GROVE, BATTLE AT (Dec. 7, 1862). Also known as the Battle of Fayetteville or Battle of Illinois Creek. After the Confederate defeat at Corinth, Miss., the Rebel forces were defeated again at Prairie Grove, Ark.

PRAIRIE SCHOONER. A large wagon used for long-distance travel and freight transport in the 19th c., a descendant of the old Conestoga wagon. It was first brought into common use in the Santa Fe trade ca. 1821 and was later used by settlers. It was usually drawn by three to six yoke of oxen or by four to six mules.

PREEMPTION. The right of squatters to first chance at public land being offered for sale. The squatters early pressured Congress to grant them the right of preempting their claims in advance of the land sale, so the settlers would not be obliged to bid against speculators. Congress made several specific preemption grants and in 1841 passed a general law, which gave the preemption right for up to 160 acres.

PRESBYTERIANISM. The Presbytery of Philadelphia was organized in 1701, and by 1716 the church was large enough in America to form itself into a synod representing four presbyteries and thirty ministers. From the beginning, doctrinal and organizational conflicts arose, and various compromises were effected; where reconciliation could not be effected, separate churches were founded. Eventually, two major branches developed: the New Side, with headquarters at New York, and the Old Side, at Philadelphia. The high standards set by the Presbyterians for their ministers led to the founding of numerous colleges across the country, particularly in the West. Schism remained a problem, with the sides later becoming known as the Old School and New School. Both sides were further factionalized by the question of slavery. After the Civil War, Old School and New School factions in both the North and South were reunited, but the Presbyterian churches have continued to be troubled by theological controversies. Two of the largest factions combined in the 1960s, forming the United Presbyterian Church in the USA; with a membership of over 2.5 million, it is by far the largest of the Presbyterian groups in the country.

PRESERVATION MOVEMENT. The Antiquities Act of 1906 authorized the president to declare as national monuments historic landmarks, historic and prehistoric structures, and other objects of historic or scientific value on lands owned by the government. Thus the federal government entered a movement that had begun in the late 19th c. at the state and local level. Since then, the National Trust for Historic Preservation has been created to acquire and maintain national monuments, and the National Park Service is also responsible for preserving landmarks. The federal government also gives financial assistance to states in their efforts to preserve historic monuments.

PRESIDENT. American frigate active in the War of 1812, under the command of Stephen Decatur. Surrendered to the British in 1815 and taken to Spithead, England.

PRESIDENT. The Constitution vests executive power in the president and charges him to take care that the laws are faithfully executed. He is also commander in chief of the armed forces. The presidency has been an evolving, rather than a static, institution; it now differs significantly from what was envisioned for it by the founders. Among the factors that have influenced its development are the following: (1) democratization of the means of nominating and electing the chief executive, lending substance to the claim that he is the only official elected by all the people; (2) ambiguity in the constitutional phrases defining presidential power and duties; (3) expansion in the role of the government, and the consequent creation of a vast bureaucracy under the president; (4) recurring periods of emergency and peril, during which the executive power seems to thrive and expand; and (5) the rise of the US as a major world power and the preoccupation with foreign policy in the political arena. The office is also subject to the influence of personality. Throughout history, a number of broad presidential types have emerged. One is a literalist president, who functions in close obedience to the letter of the Constitution and the traditional separation of powers. More common are presidents near the other end of the continuum: those who view the powers of the office with a maximum liberality, establishing new precedents and breaking old ones. Most modern commentators suggest that national demands and expectations push a president more and more to adopt a strong role.

PRESIDENT, WAR POWERS OF. See WAR POWERS OF THE PRESIDENT.

PRESIDENTIAL DISABILITY. The Constitution (Article II, Section 1) provides that if the president is unable to discharge the powers and duties of his office, they shall devolve on the vice-president. A number of presidents have been disabled for periods of time (James A. Garfield, Woodrow Wilson, Dwight D. Eisenhower). There were no prescribed procedures for establishing such inability or for determining when it had ceased; without such procedures a vice-president might be reluctant to take action for fear that he would be viewed as a usurper and provoke a constitutional crisis. In 1967, the TWENTY-FIFTH AMENDMENT was adopted to deal with this problem.

PRESIDENTIAL ELECTIONS. See CAMPAIGNS, PRESIDENTIAL; ELECTION OF THE PRESIDENT; ELECTORAL COLLEGE.

PRESIDENTIAL EXEMPTION FROM SUBPOENA. In 1807, Chief Justice John Marshall declared that the president could be subpoenaed, but President Jefferson flatly refused to appear. There was no way of forcing his appearance, and a precedent was established to the effect that the president could not be subpoenaed against his will. In 1974, however, the Supreme Court ruled (in *United States v. Nixon*) that tape recordings made by the president could be subpoenaed for a criminal trial. That decision was one of the chain of events leading to the resignation of President Nixon. (See also NIXON, RESIGNATION OF; WATERGATE.)

PRESIDENTIAL MESSAGES. The Constitution (Article II, Section 3) charges the president to give Congress information on the state of the Union. Tradition has dictated that he do so annually. Modern presidents also give an annual economic report and an annual budget message to Congress.

PRESIDENTIAL SUCCESSION. The Constitution (Article II, Section 1) provides for the succession of the vice-president to the presidency in case of death or resignation of the president or his removal from office. The TWENTY-FIFTH AMENDMENT, adopted 1967, defines the constitutional line of succession if the vice-president should succeed to the presidency and then die or be removed from office.

PRESIDENTIAL TITLE. The title by which the new chief executive of the US should be known was the subject of some controversy at the Constitutional Convention of 1787 and immediately thereafter. The Senate of the First Congress decided that the ambassadorial "his excellency" was too paltry for the ruler of a young republic, and urged that the chief executive be addressed as "His Highness, the

President of the United States of America and Protector of their Liberties"; it is stated that this was the title George Washington preferred. The more republican House of Representatives objected and it was agreed that "the present address be 'To the President of the United States,' without addition of title."

PRESIDIO. Spanish institution established primarily to hold the frontiers of Spain's territory in the Southwest. Presidios were forts or posts where soldiers lived with their families, cultivating the surrounding land.

PRESQUE ISLE, FORT. Built 1753 on Lake Erie at the site of present Erie, Pennsylvania, by the French. Taken over by the British in 1759; burned by the Indians during Pontiac's War. A US fort was built nearby in 1795.

PRESS, FREEDOM OF THE. See FREEDOM OF THE PRESS.

PRESS GANG. Armed details sent by the British government to scour English waterfronts or board merchantmen with the purpose of conscripting, or impressing, men into the British navy. Their use in colonial ports was a minor cause of the American Revolution and a major cause of the War of 1812.

PRIBILOF ISLANDS. Islands in the Bering Sea ceded to the US by Russia in 1867. As a major breeding ground for seals, they have been the scene of repeated controversies over the sealing rights of various nations. Eventually, in 1911, a multinational treaty settled the dispute.

PRICE CONTROLS. Except for gold and silver, the federal government traditionally has not taken action in setting prices for any commodities. In the two world wars, however, mechanisms were set up to control inflation and shortages by controlling prices. Milder controls were set during the Korean War; during the Johnson and Nixon administrations, "guidelines" for both wages and prices were issued by the federal government as an antiinflation device.

PRICE IN MISSOURI (1861–64). In 1861, Sterling Price became head of the secessionists in Missouri. After defeating a Union force in August 1861 at Wilson's Creek, and cap-

turing Lexington on September 20, Price and his force of 5,000 officially joined the Confederacy (March 1862). After fighting in Arkansas, he led a large force back into Missouri, but he was unable to capture Jefferson City, the capital. His army was nearly destroyed by a strong Union force at Westport, now Kansas City; he escaped into Arkansas with 6,000 men.

PRICES. Historically, price trends reflect the relative rates of growth in commodity output and money supply. Upward trends favor debtors (including governments) at the expense of creditors, and conversely. Those with fixed incomes suffer when prices rise and benefit when they fall. American prices show four long-range trends: downward in 1607–1720, upward in 1721–1814, downward in 1814–96, and upward after 1896. The decline before 1720 ran counter to the European price level and was probably caused by increasing production of colonial staple crops (tobacco, fish, and Indian corn and other grains). Prices reached their low ca. 1720; after that an expanding money supply helped them to rise. Virtually all the colonies began expanding note issues ca. 1750. The American Revolution brought on inflation as wartime prices rose at various rates. The long-drawn-out Napoleonic Wars turned markets sharply upward, reaching their peak in 1814, a high point in price history. A postwar boom then took place in commodities and western lands, culminating in panics, depression, and a deflation centering in 1821. The 19th c. was characterized by heavy production and unusually cheap foods and farm products. After the Civil War, US and world prices receded remarkably, reaching a record low in 1896. A definitely upward trend characterized 1896–1914, commonly attributed to important gold discoveries in Alaska and South Africa.

The US suffered much less from inflation than Europe during World War I, but a postwar boom raised prices; during the 1920s, prices were an average of 40 percent above what they had been in 1913. Agricultural prices were much below others; securities underwent a boom culminating in the crash of the New York stock market in October 1929. The Great Depression developed in stages. Agricultural products and raw materials dropped most because heavy output faced severe competition in world markets.

Manufacturers' prices were slower to respond, but eventually they were cut also. Federal and state governments tried various approaches to "reflate" prices, some involving radical departures from past policies. Prices rose during World War II, but federally imposed price and wage freezes kept inflation down. When those restraints were removed at the end of the war, the nation went into an inflationary period that has, for the most part, kept on the rise into the 1980s.

PRIGG V. COMMONWEALTH OF PENNSYLVANIA, 16 Peters 539 (1842). Supreme Court ruled that the Fugitive Slave Act of 1793 superseded all state laws on the subject, including a Pennsylvania statute that prohibited the seizure of fugitive slaves.

PRIMARY, DIRECT. System of nominating candidates of a political party for elective office whereby members of the party vote directly from a slate of candidates listed on a ballot. The winners of a direct primary appear on the ballot of the general election, opposite the names of the winners of primaries conducted by the other parties. Today, the direct primary is the most widely used system of candidate selection, replacing the caucuses that formerly were used to select party nominees. Most direct primaries are closed; that is, only registered members of the party may participate. In some states, a runoff primary may be held if none of the candidates for an office receives a majority of the votes.

PRIMARY, WHITE. One of several means used in the first half of the 20th c. to keep southern blacks from voting. In most southern jurisdictions, selection in the Democratic primary was tantamount to election; therefore, blacks, by being barred from voting in the primaries, were effectively disenfranchised. By ca. 1950, the white primary had been legally abolished in all states.

PRIMOGENITURE. Right of the eldest son to inherit the estate of a parent to the exclusion of all other heirs; a holdover from the English common law. Existed in all thirteen colonies. Stimulated by the democratic ideals of the American Revolution, all the states had abolished it by 1798.

PRINCETON, BATTLE OF (Jan. 3, 1777). Major Revolutionary engagement between British forces under Gen. Charles Cornwallis and patriot forces under Gen. George Washington. Attacking from the rear, the patriot forces, with deadly rifle fire, drove the enemy from the field and village and infused new life and hope into a cause that appeared all but lost.

PRINCETON UNIVERSITY. Founded 1746 as the College of New Jersey at Elizabeth, New Jersey; later moved to Newark and, in 1756, to Princeton. Its great period of growth was in the 19th c.; its name was changed to Princeton University in 1896. In 1902, Woodrow Wilson became its president. Achieved another great period of growth in the years after World War II. In 1981, the university had about 6,000 students.

PRINTING. Apparently, the first printing in North America took place at Cambridge, Massachusetts, in 1639; the first press was built at New Haven in 1769. Adam Ramage began building presses in Philadelphia ca. 1800. By mid-century the cylinder press had been perfected; it became the standard for a century. The first successful American typefoundry began operations in Philadelphia in 1796, and the first half of the 19th c. saw great improvements in typefounding. In the second half of the century, Ottmer Mergenthaler perfected the Linotype; another system, the Monotype, also met with great success. Before the middle of the 20th c., other means of achieving similar purposes much more speedily and cheaply were developing. They were often based on seemingly unrelated experiments in the fields of lithography and offset printing, photography and color processes, and the techniques of automation and electronics. Computerized typesetting and printing were widely used after the 1970s.

PRINTMAKING. Woodcuts were printed in Boston as early as 1670; Peter Pelham, a London mezzotint engraver, was the most important printmaker operating in the colonies in the early 18th c. Philadelphia and New York became printmaking centers. Philadelphia produced Alexander Wilson's *American Ornithology* in 1804–14, and forty years later John James Audubon's *Viviparous Quadrupeds of North America*. The New York firm of Currier and Ives, beginning in the 1840s, produced on a vast scale, lithographed, hand-tinted scenes for a mass audience.

PRISON CAMPS, CONFEDERATE. See ANDERSONVILLE; CASTLE THUNDER; CONFEDERATE PRISONS.

PRISON CAMPS, UNION. A fort on Johnson's Island in Lake Erie was converted to a prisoner-of-war camp, and after it was filled, Confederate prisoners were kept at Alton, Ill., and Camp Chase, Ohio. Later in the war, as the number of prisoners increased, prisons were established at Fort Delaware, Del.; Rock Island, Ill.; Point Lookout, Md.; and Elmira, N.Y. In February 1865, the federal government held over 65,000 inmates.

PRISONS AND PRISON REFORM. Prisons were rarely used before the 19th c.; the Walnut Street jail in Philadelphia, opened 1790, was the first such institution in the US. In the early 19th c., two competing models of prisons developed: the Quaker method was designed to save the offender through reflection and penitence; the Auburn system (named for a prison built at Auburn, N.Y.), aimed at producing obedient citizens, housed prisoners under conditions of stern discipline and employed in a system of congregate labor. The Auburn system was to become predominant. By the 1870s, industrial prisons had been established in many states; but both businesses and labor protested the competition of prisonmade goods. Prisons became overcrowded; many pointed out that the function of the prison, reform, had been forgotten. Despite such urgings, prisons changed little until the 1930s. During this period recognition took hold that all prisoners did not require confinement in maximum security cages and that institutions of lesser custody could serve. During the 1950s, there was considerable experimentation with such schemes as work release, study release, and community treatment centers (halfway houses). Efforts were also made to separate the chronic "hard-core" criminals from the young, first-time offenders. However, general dissatisfaction with the prison system remained in the 1980s; evidence that prisons were succeeding in reforming inmates was scarce; and critics charged the prisons were hardly more than overcrowded "warehouses" for society's misfits.

PRISON SHIPS. Used by both the Americans and the British during the Revolution for confining naval prisoners. The former maintained such ships at Boston and New London, Connecticut; and the latter kept them at Halifax, Nova Scotia, Antigua, West Indies, and in Brooklyn. It has been estimated that some 11,500 men died on these ships.

PRIVATEERS AND PRIVATEERING. In King George's War (1744–48), privateering assumed the proportions of a major maritime business; it is said that during the French and Indian War (1754–63), some 11,000 Americans were engaged in such operations. During the American Revolution, most colonies issued letters of marque and reprisal, and the Continental Congress sanctioned privateering: 1,151 American privateers captured about 600 British vessels. By the late 18th c., most European nations were trying to abolish privateering, which often was hardly more than piracy. Its use was widely revived in the Napoleonic Wars, however, and again in the War of 1812. By the time of the Mexican War (1846–48), the US navy was strong enough to not require help from privateers; nevertheless, the US declined to accede to the Declaration of Paris (1860), which outlawed privateering among the principal world powers. But when the Confederacy issued letters of marque, President Lincoln endeavored to treat Rebel privateers as pirates. After the Civil War, no further efforts at privateering were attempted. (See also PRIZE MONEY.)

PRIVILEGES AND IMMUNITIES OF CITIZENS. The Constitution (Article IV, Section 2) guarantees that citizens of each state shall be entitled to all privileges and immunities of citizens in the several states. The Supreme Court (in *Corfield v. Coryell*, 1823) identified them as those "which are, in their nature, fundamental; which belong, of right, to the citizens of all free governments." The Fourteenth Amendment forbids states to make or enforce any law abridging the privileges and immunities of the US. It was aimed at protecting the rights of newly freed blacks, but it was not limited to blacks.

PRIVY COUNCIL. Body of advisers to the English crown. In the 17th c., the council filled a place roughly corresponding to that now occupied by the cabinet. The council contained all the ministers of state. New colonies fell under its special care. It heard appeals from colonial courts; colonial laws were referred to it for approval or veto.

PRIZE COURTS. Courts which pass on the validity and disposition of prizes, a term referring to the seizure of a ship or its cargo by the maritime forces of a belligerent. In the US, jurisdiction in prize matters belongs to the federal district courts, with the right of appeal to the circuit court of appeals and ultimately to the Supreme Court. In modern times, it is generally held that the seizure of aircraft may also fall under the jurisdiction of prize courts.

PRIZEFIGHTING. Introduced into the US by British sailors in the early 19th c. John L. Sullivan did much to make the sport popular in the last part of the century. Other early heroes of the prize ring were James J. Corbett, James J. Jeffries, and Jack Johnson. Jack Dempsey and Gene Tunney were the great champions of the 1920s; Joe Louis dominated the sport in the 1930s and 1940s. Rocky Marciano became champion in 1952 and retired undefeated in 1955. Muhammad Ali (born Cassius Clay) dominated the sport in the 1960s and 1970s.

PRIZE MONEY. The Continental Congress adopted the common practice of splitting with captains and crews of the US navy the proceeds from captured enemy vessels sold by prize courts. Privateers, which were privately owned, received all the proceeds from a sale. In raiding British commerce during the Revolution, privateers took about 600 prizes for the then great total of $18 million. During the Naval War with France, forty-nine men-of-war of the new US navy made ninety-five captures of French vessels. In the War of 1812, 492 American privateers took 1,344 prizes. US naval vessels, while nowhere near as successful, made some spectacular captures. Blockading during the Civil War was profitable for the Union navy. It was already apparent, however, that the use of prize money to pay naval personnel was out-of-date and inefficient. Therefore, in 1898, Congress abolished the prize law and adjusted navy pay scales to what was considered a reasonable rate.

PROCLAMATION OF 1763. Document issued by the British government regulating the settlement of land in North America. Part of it organized the territory in America acquired from France and Spain into the provinces of Quebec, East Florida, West Florida, and Grenada. The second part was aimed at conciliating the Indians. Settlement on Indian land was prohibited, and strict regulations were published for trading with the Indians and buying land from them. Settlers, however, disregarded the proclamations and swarmed over the mountains into Indian country. PONTIAC'S WAR was partly caused by those encroachments.

PROGRESSIVE MOVEMENT. Reform effort of the first two decades of the 20th c.; had supporters in both major political parties, and its goals ranged from prohibition and woman's suffrage to antitrust legislation, industrial regulation, tax reform, and workmen's compensation. The PROGRESSIVE PARTY (1912–16) was a manifestation of the movement.

PROGRESSIVE PARTY (1912–16). Also known as the Bull Moose Party. Instrument by which Theodore Roosevelt ran for president in 1912 after he had been denied the nomination by the Republican party (who nominated the incumbent president, William Howard Taft). The Progressive platform condemned "the unholy alliance between corrupt business and corrupt politics." It called for the adoption of primary elections; the short ballot; initiative, recall, and referendum measures; direct election of US senators; and woman suffrage. It called for minimun wages for women; the eight hour day; industrial safety and health standards; and unemployment insurance. It favored public ownership of natural resources and the graduated income and inheritance tax. Roosevelt won 4.1 million popular votes and 88 electoral votes; but the Democratic candidate, Woodrow Wilson, was elected president. The party went downhill after 1912, and Roosevelt refused to run on its ticket in 1916. Most members reverted to their original party; its remnants formed the PROHIBITION PARTY in 1917.

PROGRESSIVE PARTY (1947–52). Instrument by which Henry A. Wallace ran for the presidency in 1948 against the Democratic incumbent Harry S. Truman. Wallace, who had been vice-president during Franklin D. Roosevelt's third term and a member of Truman's cabinet, looked upon himself as the true heir of the New Deal. He opposed Truman's cold war policies and urged an accommodation with the Soviet Union. The party, which was damaged by charges of being pro-communist, won only a little more than 1 million votes, or 2.4 percent of the popular votes. It ran a candidate in 1952 but only won 140,000 votes.

PROHIBITION. The campaign against the manufacture and sale of alcoholic beverages had three periods of ascendancy. Between 1846 and 1855, thirteen states passed prohibition laws; within a decade nine had been rescinded or declared unconstitutional. In 1880, Kansas wrote prohibition into its constitution, bringing on a revival of the temperance movement, as reflected by the Prohibition party, the Women's Christian Temperance Union, and the Anti-Saloon League. Again results were impermanent; by 1905, only Kansas, Maine, Nebraska, and North Dakota were prohibition states. A new movement began, and by the time the US entered World War I, there were prohibition laws in twenty-six states. In 1917, Congress approved a resolution calling for a constitutional amendment prohibiting the "manufacture, sale or transportation" of intoxicating beverages. Within thirteen months, ratification had been secured and a year later the EIGHTEENTH AMENDMENT went into effect.

Opponents soon directed their attacks against the efforts of government agents to enforce the law. They insisted that corruption was rampant in federal and state enforcement units, and that disrespect for all law was becoming a characteristic of those who flouted the liquor laws with impunity. Popular opposition rose, and in 1932, the Democratic party platform called for repeal of the Eighteenth Amendment. The Democratic landslide that November persuaded Congress to act. In 1933, a resolution was approved, and in less than a year the TWENTY-FIRST AMENDMENT was ratified; it was the end of what its proponents had called the "noble experiment."

PROHIBITION PARTY. Oldest of the third parties in the US, organized 1869. Nominated James Black in 1872 for president; and has run candidates in every presidential election since. The peak of the party's popular support was reached in 1892, when its candidate received 271,000 votes.

PROMONTORY POINT. Site in Utah of the completion, on May 10, 1869, of the first transcontinental railroad. Leland Stanford, president of the Central Pacific RR, using a silver sledgehammer, drove the last golden spike into a polished California laurel tie.

PROPAGANDA. Controlled communication for the purpose of influencing the opinions, emotions, attitudes, or behavior, of an intended audience. America employed propaganda at least as early as the American Revolution; news-sheets and pamphlets carried the speeches and writings of leaders who sought to build a willingness to go to war. The Declaration of Independence, used to unify the colonists, stands as an example of highly effective propaganda. Increased communications capabilities effected by the time of the Civil War made it possible for each side to attempt to strengthen its cause and weaken the opponent. The Emancipation Proclamation (1863) was a masterful propaganda stroke, for once the war became characterized as a crusade against slavery, it became very difficult for any European government to support the Confederacy.

The experiences gained during World War II caused the US to establish (in 1953) the United States Information Agency (USIA) to help achieve foreign policy objectives by influencing public attitudes in other nations, and to advise other nations on the implications of foreign opinion about US policies and objectives.

PROPERTY QUALIFICATIONS. Almost all nations, including Great Britain, had property requirements for voting at the time of the American Revolution, the rationale being that only property owners had "stock" in the state. The original thirteen states followed the tradition; but in the early 19th c., the newly admitted western states had few property requirements for voting. The eastern states tended to reduce their requirements as well. By the time of the Civil War, virtually all property requirements for voting had been eliminated. Today, only in "special districts" (e.g., water and sewage districts, independent school districts) are property requirements legal as a condition of voting.

PROPHET DANCE. Cult movement that arose among Indian tribes of the Pacific Northwest in the 18th c.; emphasized beliefs in the impending destruction of the world and its subsequent renewal.

PROPORTIONAL REPRESENTATION. Electoral device, the intent of which is to make a representative body a faithful image of its electorate. Ideally, the system gives legislative voting strength proportionate to the electoral strength of every shade of societal opinion. In the US, it has been tried at the municipal level but has never been successful.

PROPRIETARY AGENT. Business representative of the proprietor of an American colony. Agents handled the survey and sale of lands, the collection of revenue, and the management of estates.

PROPRIETARY PROVINCES. Historically, the proprietorship succeeded the trading company as a colonizing device. The proprietor was virtually a feudal lord exercising sovereign powers. He could appoint all officials; create courts, hear appeals, and pardon offenders; make laws and issue decrees; raise and command a militia; and establish churches, ports, and towns. The charters of Maryland (Lord Baltimore, proprietor) and Pennsylvania (William Penn, proprietor), however, permitted the proprietor to make laws only with the consent of the freemen. Other proprietorary provinces included Maine (Sir Ferdinando Gorges, proprietor) and New York, New Jersey, and Delaware (the duke of York, proprietor). In 1729, virtually all the proprietary provinces came under the direct control of the king and became crown colonies.

PROSPECTORS. Persons who explore for minerals, especially gold. In the West and Alaska, the prospectors of the 19th c. helped accelerate settlement. Today, prospecting is mostly done by giant corporations making use of sophisticated detection equipment.

PROSTITUTION. Legally, prostitution was for the most part ignored in the US until large urban centers began developing in the late 19th c.; even then, brothels were by general agreement tolerated in segregated "red-light" districts. In the early 20th c., attitudes changed; the federal MANN ACT (1910) made it illegal to transport women across a state line for immoral purposes, and the various states passed anti-brothel legislation. By the 1920s, legally tolerated districts had mostly disappeared. Instead, prostitutes came to rely on the street and the telephone as ways of meeting their clients. By the 1980s, only in Nevada is prostitution legally tolerated (and there on a county-option basis).

PROTECTION. See TARIFF.

PROTECTORATE. Arrangement by which a major power assumes the "protection" (i.e., governance) of another area of the world. The League of Nations and the United Nations made small dependencies protectorates of the major powers until they were deemed prepared for full international activity. The Trust Territory of the Pacific is in effect a US protectorate.

PROVIDENCE. Capital and largest city of Rhode Island; founded on Narragansett Bay in 1636 by Roger Williams (see PROVIDENCE PLANTATIONS). An important port city in the slave trade, with rum manufactured there an important element of that trade. Its ships were later important in the China and India trade. Rubber, plastics, and jewelry are important modern manufactures. Pop.: 156,804 (1980).

PROVIDENCE PLANTATIONS. Original name for the first settlement in Rhode Island, made by Roger Williams in 1636 after he fled Massachusetts to escape religious persecution. He bought a large tract of land from the Narragansett Indians and drew up a covenant for majority rule "only in civill things," thus permitting religious liberty. In 1644, Providence was joined with Newport, Portsmouth, and (in 1647) Warwick in forming what eventually became the colony of Rhode Island and Providence Plantations (which is still the official name for the state of Rhode Island).

PROVINCIAL CONGRESSES. The extralegal, or revolutionary, assemblies that sprang up in most of the colonies in the early stages of the American Revolution grew out of the COMMITTEES OF CORRESPONDENCE and COMMITTEES OF SAFETY that flourished everywhere. The earliest congresses were called to choose delegates to the proposed Continental Congresses of 1774 and 1775. In 1776, the Second Continental Congress urged all provincial congresses to set up their own governments. By then, the congresses had in effect taken over all functions of government. It remained only for each colony to formally set up its own system of government.

PRUDHOMME BLUFFS. Also known as the Third Chickasaw Bluffs, a strategic point on the Mississippi R about 150 miles below the mouth of the Ohio R. It was the site of a fort built by the sieur de La Salle in 1682 and of a new Spanish fort built ca. 1795.

PSYCHOLOGY. During the early 19th c., most US teachers followed the Scottish school of commonsense philosophers, who held that in addition to sensations, inherent moral sense informed a person's mind. Faculty psychology later added the idea that a human mind has the faculties of intellection, feeling, and willing. Later in the century, association psychologists, such as John Stuart Mill and Herbert Spencer, and the neurosphysiologists were influential. The "new psychology," a German import, took over in the 1870s; it presented a trained subject with a sensory stimulus and then recorded what the subject reported was going on in his or her own mind. By 1874, William James had introduced a few instruments for classroom purposes; but the first formal experimental laboratory in the US was created at Johns Hopkins in 1883. The American Psychological Association was founded in 1892, and by the turn of the century, in most universities, the psychology department had separated itself from the philosophy department. James published an enormously influential textbook in 1890 that included neurosphysiological, experimental, and philosophical works. He also discussed the general biological setting and such areas as emotion, instinct, and hypnotism that were not strictly experimental. He introduced the concept of the stream of consciousness and emphasized an adaptive, action-oriented view of humans.

In 1913, J.B. Watson of Johns Hopkins introduced behaviorism, an emphasis on performance rather than conscious thought, and experiments under scientifically controlled conditions. Thus he made animal studies, which had been introduced in 1898 by E.L. Thorndyke, the model for human psychology. World War I saw the introduction of intelligence tests; these were widely applied and studied during the 1920s. The 1930s saw an influx of psychologists from Europe, especially psychoanalysts; learning theory, mental tests, and personality theory were major preoccupations. By the 1980s, neobehaviorism and learning theory were supplemented as central fields by a renewed interest in cognitive processes, while genetic, abnormal, and social psychology all flourished.

"PUBLIC BE DAMNED." Reply by W.H. Vanderbilt, president of the New York Central RR, to a question about the "public benefit." The phrase became symbolic of the attitudes of the "robber barons" of the period.

PUBLIC CREDIT ACT (1790). Federal law sponsored by Secretary of the Treasury Alexander Hamilton. Provided for the payment of the government's obligations at par with interest (except for Continental currency, which was to be redeemed at 100 to 1 in specie); assumption of state debts for services or supplies during the Revolution; and authorization of loans to meet those obligations.

PUBLIC DEBTS. See DEBTS, PUBLIC.

PUBLIC DOMAIN. Land owned by the federal government and distinguished from national domain and acquired land. National domain arises from political jurisdiction; acquired land is either bought or received as gifts. The first portion of the public domain or public land was from cessions to the federal government by seven of the original thirteen states of their western claims. Between 1802 and 1898, huge additions to both the national domain and the public domain were made through the Louisiana Purchase, the Florida Purchase, the lands annexed as the result of the Mexican War, the purchase of Alaska, and the annexation of Hawaii. The disposition of the public domain was a major controversy throughout the 19th c. Land companies were formed to buy the land from the government and sell it to settlers; squatters settled on lands on which they had no legal claims; and there was considerable agitation for the disposal, at reasonable cost, of the land to homesteaders. The Distribution-Preemption Act (1841) was a major victory for the squatters, and the Homestead Act (1862) opened much of the public land free to settlers who would live on and improve the land. Conservationists were determined that a portion of the public land be retained in public ownership; laws were enacted permitting the withdrawal from sale of vast sections of such land. In 1916, the National Park Service was created to administer areas of superlative natural beauty that were being set aside from the public lands as permanent reserves, including Yosemite, Yellowstone, Hot Springs, Glacier, Sequoia, Mount Rainier, Grand Canyon, and Crater Lake. In 1920, the Mineral Leasing Act provided some control over the exploitation of public lands. By the 1980s, there were 186 million acres in the national forests, 26 million acres of which were acquired land bought for watershed protection and other conservation objectives. Best known of the public lands are the 66 million acres in the national parks and national monuments. Of the original 1.23 billion acres in the fifty states, the public domain comprised 762 million acres in 1981.

PUBLIC HEALTH. American colonies as early as the 17th c. took community action in efforts to control disease, prevent famine, and take care of sanitary problems. Port cities established quarantine stations, and pesthouses were built to isolate infected persons. The growth of large urban areas in the 19th c. created new problems. Before midcentury, cities had to expand water and sewer systems; provide for garbage removal; inspect slum housing, factories, and schools; build public dispensaries and hospitals; inaugurate vaccination programs; and foster health education. Primarily a local or state problem, public health was not an active federal concern prior to the turn of the century, when the US Public Health Service came into being. In the early 20th c., many health officials believed that new knowledge and methods would soon eradicate infectious disease. While many diseases (smallpox, diphtheria, typhoid, scarlet fever) were in fact either eliminated completely or greatly diminished, other events,

such as influenza epidemics, pointed up the great difficulties that remained.

PUBLIC LAND COMMISSIONS. Special bodies created from time to time to review federal land policies and to make recommendations for improving it. The first was authorized by Congress in 1879; it recommended far-reaching reforms to protect the public interest but almost none were enacted. In 1903, President Theodore Roosevelt appointed the second. It recommended many of the same reforms as the first, but again Congress was not receptive. The third commission, appointed by President Hoover, recommended that the public lands, minus mineral rights, be turned over to the states. No action was taken. In 1964, a fourth commission was named. It recommended giving more emphasis to the commercial development of the public lands. Conservationists strongly opposed its findings, and no action was taken.

PUBLIC LANDS. See PUBLIC DOMAIN.

PUBLIC LANDS, FENCING OF. The range cattle industry was based on the use of the public domain for grazing purposes. After the invention of barbed wire in the 1870s, and the movement of many settlers to such areas, land companies in the West began illegally enclosing public lands in an effort to control the ranges. Numerous complaints were made to the General Land Office; in 1885 a presidential proclamation and a federal statute ordered the removal of the fences. Eventually, the illegal fencing was removed.

PUBLIC LAND SALES. In the early 19th c., it was government practice to hold public auctions for public land that had been divided into townships. The minimum price was $2.00 per acre until 1820 and $1.25 thereafter. Sales reached their peak in 1836, when 25 million acres were sold; receipts constituted nearly half the government's revenue. Much of the land ended up in the hands of land companies, and anxiety about their claims led squatters to organize in order to protect their squatters' rights before claims could be registered. Opposition to public auctions led the government in the 1850s to slow down sales. After 1862, the HOMESTEAD

ACT made "lands for the landless" government policy.

PUBLIC OPINION. Commonly associated with concepts integral to democracy, public opinion receives very close attention. Majority rule, consent of the governed, and representative government can hardly be discussed without reference to it. Public opinion research has burgeoned in modern times. The poll originated by George Gallup in the 1930s has been the prototype of numerous such organizations. Today, virtually every politician, political party, and special interest organization in the country maintains its own polling mechanism.

PUBLIC OWNERSHIP. During the 19th c., federal ownership was limited principally to the two Banks of the United States, the mint, the post office, and post roads. In 1904, the federal government purchased the Panama Railroad Co., and in 1916, the government was authorized to form corporations to purchase, construct, equip, maintain, and operate merchant vessels. Beginning in the 1920s, both federal and state governments have become the owners of public utilities, especially electricity-producing, facilities. There has also been a great expansion of the lending operations of the federal government. In 1916, twelve farm banks were set up, and since then various other federally financed banks and funds have come into being. As public transportation became unprofitable for private investors, more and more mass-transit systems came into public ownership. Most city bus systems today are municipally owned; and Amtrak, a quasi-public corporation, was established by the federal government to take over the increasingly unprofitable passenger-train business.

PUBLIC REVENUE. See REVENUE, PUBLIC.

PUBLIC UTILITIES. Those industries that supply a vital public need; often they are given a monopoly in their area and in return are expected to supply all segments of the public with their service at a fair price. Commonest are companies supplying electricity, gas, telephone, water, and sewerage. Public transportation companies (airlines, railways, bus companies) are also regarded as public utilities. Early corporations were chartered by special legislative acts; along with each grant of special privilege went the understanding that the corporation so chartered was to serve the public interest; and what the state gave, the state could take away in the event of unsatisfactory performance. Later in the 19th c., the practice of regulating by charter fell into disfavor, and the distinction between public utilities and other industries narrowed. Government regulation of public utilities instead gravitated to the regulatory commissions, beginning with the Interstate Commerce Commission, created 1877. It regulated the railroads, and as other public utilities developed, they were placed under the jurisdiction of specialized federal commissions, such as the Federal Communications Commission, the Federal Power Commission, and the Civil Aeronautics Board.

PUBLIC WORKS ADMINISTRATION (PWA). New Deal agency created 1933 ; provided work for the unemployed by carrying on such public works projects as slum clearance, land conservation, highway and airport construction, and public-buildings construction.

PUEBLO. Indian tribe of Arizona and New Mexico; an essentially uniform culture, but with four distinct languages. Archaeologists trace the Pueblo to the so-called Basket Maker horizon, a desert focus of incipient desert agriculture two millenia old. Their great period, from AD 1000 to AD 1300, was marked by population concentration in Mesa Verde, Chaco Canyon, and other prehistoric monuments. These were marked by multistoried buildings of coursed stone and adobe. The great sites were abandoned because of drought. Spanish knowledge of the Pueblo dates from 1539, and Spanish military pressures instigated the PUEBLO REVOLT of 1680. Although nominally christianized by the Spanish, they retained their aboriginal theocratic organization and managed a syncretism of aboriginal modes and Roman Catholic modes. Some differences in societal structure appear between the western and eastern Pueblo. Hopi and Zuni in the west strongly stress matrilineal kinship; in the east, there is paternal development with dual divisions of village society, the so-called moiety organizations.

PUEBLO INCIDENT (Jan. 23, 1968). North Korean patrol boats captured, without resistance, the USS *Pueblo*, a US navy spy ship. The US claimed it was in international waters; the North Koreans claimed it was in their territory. The US government gained release of the crew eleven months later by signing an apology, which it simultaneously repudiated. The ship remained in North Korea.

PUERTO RICO. Most easterly of the Greater Antilles islands; discovered by Columbus on his second voyage in 1493. Conquered and colonized in 1508 by Juan Ponce de León. The native Arawak Indians were slain, and African slaves were introduced. The Spanish retained the island principally as a key defense outpost. After the Spanish-American War, it became a colony of the US. US companies made large investments in sugar-cane plantations. The islanders, largely of Spanish stock with African and Indian admixtures, became US citizens in 1917. After 1947, they elected their own governor; in 1952 the island became the Commonwealth of Puerto Rico. Since then, several elections have verified the islanders' satisfaction with that status as opposed to statehood or independence. Sugar, pineapples, coffee, and tobacco are the main crops; and since 1957, there has been a highly successful campaign to bring US industries to the island. Pop.: 3,196,520 (1980).

PUGET SOUND. An arm of the Pacific Ocean located in NW Washington. The British explored it 1792. Seattle and Tacoma are important cities on the sound.

PUJO COMMITTEE (1912). The Committee on Banking and Currency of the House of Representatives issued a report, after prolonged hearings, that money and credit were in the hands of a comparatively few men and that a "vast and growing concentration" of control was exerted by them. This disclosure led to the FEDERAL RESERVE ACT (1913) and the CLAYTON ANTITRUST ACT (1914).

PULASKI, FORT. Completed 1847 on Cockspur Island in Savannah harbor. Georgia seized it at the beginning of the Civil War, but Union forces regained it in April 1862 and held it for the remainder of the war.

PULLMANS. Railroad sleeping cars perfected by G.M. Pullman ca. 1858. In 1867, he founded the Pullman Palace Car Co., which set worldwide standards for comfort and luxury in railway travel.

PULLMAN STRIKE (1894). In 1893, the Pullman Co. lowered the wages of its employees by about 25 percent. As a result, about 4,000 employees joined Eugene V. Debs's union in 1894. The company refused to bargain with the union; the local strike soon developed into a general railroad strike. The strikers ignored a federal injunction prohibiting all interference with the trains, and violence resulted. President Cleveland ordered federal troops to Chicago on July 4. Much mob violence and destruction of company property resulted, but by July 13 the strike was broken.

PUMP-PRIMING. Government spending during a recessionary period, in an attempt to stimulate private spending and the expansion of business and industry. Begun 1932 by President Hoover with the Reconstruction Finance Corporation; much expanded under the various NEW DEAL programs of Franklin D. Roosevelt. Today, cutting taxes, thereby creating more disposable income for the public, is an important part of the pump-priming strategies of the government.

PUNISHMENT, CRUEL AND UNUSUAL. The Eighth Amendment to the Constitution prohibits cruel and unusual punishment; it was included in the state constitutions of a number of the original thirteen states. Although efforts have been made to declare the death penalty cruel and unusual, the Supreme Court has resisted such an interpretation.

PUNISHMENTS, COLONIAL. Punishments in colonial America were generally harsh in New York and the South; in New England and the Quaker colonies of Pennsylvania and New Jersey they were more humane. In all the colonies, murder and treason were capital offenses, hanging being the commonest method. Burning and quartering were applied less often. Corporal punishment (whipping, branding, mutilations, ducking) were commonly applied. Imprisonment was rarely used as punishment.

PURE FOOD AND DRUG MOVEMENT. Although colonial and state governments enacted laws to fight adulteration of bread, butter, milk, meat, and other susceptible foods, they were generally ineffective. Beginning 1848, more than 100 pure food and drug laws passed the US Congress; they covered specific products, and only in 1906 did a federal law, the Pure Food and Drug Act, forbid interstate commerce in adulterated and misbranded foods and drugs in general. The courts were generally lenient, however, and light fines and almost no imprisonments resulted from the law. In 1933, the FOOD AND DRUG ADMINISTRATION (FDA) was created; it was greatly strengthened by the Food, Drug, and Cosmetic Act of 1938. The FDA was empowered to set standards that had the force of law. False labeling was extended to include not only erroneous positive statements but also the failure to include adequate warnings. Since then, Congress has on numerous occasions expanded its duties and powers. Meat inspection is under the Department of Agriculture; in 1972 the Consumer Product Safety Commission was given regulatory authority over consumer products not traditionally within the FDA's purview. Illegal drugs are under the jurisdiction of the Drug Enforcement Administration.

PURITANS AND PURITANISM. Religious sect that had its origins in 16th-c. England with persons who wished to "purify" the Church of England of what it considered remnants of Roman Catholicism. They took literally the doctrines of original sin and salvation by faith and set great store by divine revelation. They split into faction, and it was a small congregation of more extreme Puritans who fled to America and established Plymouth colony in 1620; a more mainstream Puritan group established the Massachusetts Bay colony in 1630. Within the next decade, some 20,000 persons came to Massachusetts and Connecticut and built a society and church in strict accordance with Puritan ideals. Ruled by vigorous leaders, these colonies were able to perpetuate Puritanism in America long after the English movement had died out.

QUAKERS. Members of the Society of Friends, founded in England ca. 1650 by George Fox. Fox preached that the Inner Light illuminates the heart of every man and woman, hence there is no place for priest or presbyter. Quaker missionaries were repulsed from Massachusetts, but a few settled in the more tolerant Rhode Island. Continuing persecution in England resulted in William Penn's "Holy Experiment," which were colonies in Pennsylvania and West Jersey. Later meetings were established in Maryland, New York, and North Carolina. But Pennsylvania, especially Philadelphia, remained the center of American Quakers. Quietism and pacifism became central to the sect. Faction resulted in the Great Separation of 1827–28, producing the Orthodox and Hicksite groups. The former evangelical and the latter more Unitarian in tendency. Further factionalism fragmented the religion for the remainder of the 19th c. but diminished in the 20th c. In addition to pacifism, Quakers have been in the forefront of advocating such social reforms as abolitionism, Indian relations, prison reform, education, woman's rights, temperance, and the care of the insane. The American Friends Service Committee was organized to substitute noncombatant relief work for military service. Today, there are about 131,000 Quakers in the US.

QUANTRILL'S RAID (Aug. 21, 1863). W.C. Quantrill, leading a band of Confederate guerrillas, raided Lawrence, Kans., killing, burning, and plundering indiscriminately. More than 150 townspeople were killed. Quickly withdrawing before Union troops could arrive, Quantrill's Raiders withdrew into Missouri with few losses. (See also BORDER WAR.)

QUARTERING. See BILLETING.

QUARTERING ACTS. Series of British laws (1765, 1766, 1775) requiring the colonies to provide barracks for British troops. Widely resented by the colonists and one of the causes of the American Revolution (see also BILLETING).

QUASI-WAR. See NAVAL WAR WITH FRANCE.

QUEBEC, CAPTURE OF (1759). British Gen. James Wolfe, sailing from Louisburg and operating from the Île d'Orléans below Quebec, made many abortive attempts against the city, which was being protected by a French force under Marquis Louis Joseph de Montcalm. Finally, on September 13, a crucial battle took place on the Plains of Abraham, on Quebec's outskirts. Wolfe was killed and Montcalm was mortally wounded. Wolfe's successor closed in on Quebec, and on September 18, it fell to the British, thereby making inevitable British hegemony in Canada.

QUEBEC, PHIPS'S ATTACK ON (1690). Unsuccessful attempt to capture French Canada, staged by Sir William Phips, leading a large land and naval force from New England and New York. Phips was unable to take the strong garrison at Quebec and sailed for home.

QUEBEC ACT (1774). One of the INTOLERABLE ACTS, it extended the boundaries of Quebec to the Ohio and to the Mississippi rivers, thereby closing the interior to the American colonists.

QUEBEC CONFERENCES (1943, 1944). Two World War II conferences between President Franklin D. Roosevelt and Prime Minister Winston Churchill. The first one approved the plans for the Normandy invasion; the second dealt with postwar settlements with Germany and Japan.

QUEEN ANNE'S WAR (1702–13). American counterpoint to the War of the Spanish Succession, fought in the West Indies and on the Carolina and New England frontiers between France and England. Concluded by the Treaty of Utrecht (see UTRECHT, TREATY OF).

QUEENSTON HEIGHTS, BATTLE OF (Oct. 13, 1812). Unsuccessful effort by US forces to invade Canada in the War of 1812. The British commander, Gen. Isaac Brock, was killed.

QUITRENTS. Feudal dues payable by freeholders to the proprietors to whom the land had been granted; later a crown revenue. Ended by the American Revolution.

QUIVIRA. See CORONADO'S EXPEDITION; GRAN QUIVIRA.

QUOTA SYSTEM. The Immigration Act of 1924 allocated quotas for each country outside the Western Hemisphere based on the "national origin" of the US population. This had the effect of giving preference to would-be immigrants from northern and western Europe. The 1965 and 1976 legislation restructured the percentages, aimed at correcting the imbalance, but did not do away with the quota system. (See also IMMIGRATION RESTRICTION.)

RACE RELATIONS. The first Europeans in America labeled the diverse indigenous ethnic groups Indians, and when groups forcibly brought from Africa became Negroes, or blacks, the Europeans conceived themselves as white. Between 1660 and 1770, black chattel slavery was institutionalized into a legal system; at the same time, whites were infiltrating Indian territories, and despite treaties, Indians were being driven from their land and being pushed westward or annihilated, either by war or smallpox. In the early 19th c., the policy toward Indians was their removal to unwanted territories W of the Mississippi R. The Indians resisted, but with the defeat of the Apache in 1886, the Indian wars came to an end. The Indian population had been reduced from about 1 million to about 200,000 and was forced into impoverishment on reservations.

By 1804, the northern states had either eliminated slavery or passed laws calling for its gradual abolition. But in the South, slavery had become even more profitable as cotton became the main crop. By 1860, the number of slaves in the South had reached almost 4 million. The Civil War ended slavery; but, despite the efforts of Reconstruction, did little to improve the economic, political, or social status of southern blacks. With white conservatives fully in political control after ca. 1876, numerous state and local ordinances disenfranchised the blacks and segregated them in virtually all public areas. In the North, blacks could vote and segregation was never formalized into the legal code; but *de facto* segregation existed. In all areas of the country, virtually all blacks were relegated to the lowest menial occupations with little chance for individual improvement.

After the Mexican War, the new Southwest territories contained about 150,000 Mexicans; they quickly became a minority as Americans inundated the territories. By 1900, most had been reduced to landless menial labor. Despite this, more than 700,000 Mexican immigrants came in from rural Mexico between 1900 and 1930. During the same period, Asians (chiefly Chinese and Japanese) were arriving on the West Coast. The Chinese in particular were brought in as cheap, unskilled labor and were subjected to discrimination and acts of violence by native laborers. Opposition to Asian laborers became politically effective, and the immigration laws of 1902 and 1924 virtually terminated all Asian immigration.

By the 20th c., almost all nonwhites were in the lowest occupation and income categories in the US and were attempting to accommodate themselves to this status within segregated areas: barrios, ghettoes, reservations. Although some progress was made in the first half of the century, most progress was forced to wait until the end of World War II. The beginning of that war, in fact, had seen a major racist action by the federal government: the internment of 110,000 persons of Japanese descent living on the West Coast. After the war, a number of nonwhite organizations sought change in American race relations; and the government and the courts, largely reacting to these groups, ended the legality of segregation and discrimination in schools, public accommodations, the armed forces, housing, employment practices, and marriage and voting laws. Therefore, most overt forms of discrimination had been eliminated by the mid-1970s. Changes in dominance and social distance were accompanied by white resistance (known as the white backlash) at the local level, leading to considerable racial strife. The major developments in the 1970s were the increased efforts by the federal government to enforce civil rights laws by implementation of affirmative action and forced integration of schools. The increased number of blacks and Mexican-Americans in elective office was a clear manifestation of their growing political clout. The status of the American Indian was slower to change. (See also AFRO-AMERICANS; CIVIL RIGHTS MOVEMENT; IMMIGRATION RESTRICTION; INDIAN POLICY, NATIONAL; INTEGRATION; JAPANESE EXCLUSION ACTS.)

RACE RIOTS. The most serious early race riots were between the Irish and other whites in Boston in 1837, between blacks and whites in Philadelphia in 1838, between Chinese and whites in San Francisco in 1877, and between Italian and other whites in New Orleans in 1891. In the early 20th c., riots between whites and blacks took place in East St. Louis in 1917, Chicago in 1919, and Detroit and New York City (Harlem) in 1943.

The great civil rights upheavals of the 1960s resulted in a number of serious race riots; more than 250 disturbances occurred, about 50 of which are considered full-fledged riots. They arose chiefly from blacks striking out against racial oppression. Major riots of the period occurred in Birmingham (1963), New York City (1964), Watts, Los Angeles (1965), and Chicago (1966). In 1967, Tampa, Cincinnati, Atlanta, Newark, and Detroit all experienced riots. The assassination of Martin Luther King, Jr., in 1968 set off violence in 125 cities, most especially in Washington, D.C. A commission created by President Lyndon B. Johnson in 1967 reviewed the history of the riots and identified white racism as the main cause.

RADAR. Although Great Britain made the greatest contribution in the development of radar, US research began in the 1930s at the Naval Research Laboratory. By the time the US entered World War II, radar had been installed on several capital warships and in a number of critical shore installations. British and US radar developments were combined, and the resulting equipment was largely interchangeable between the two forces.

RADICAL REPUBLICANS. Extremist wing of the Republican party before, during, and especially after the Civil War. Their original focus was on the immediate abolition of slavery; during the war they pressured President Lincoln for immediate emancipation. Holding a working majority in Congress, they insisted on a stringent plan of reconstruction; and they strongly denounced the more moderate plans of Lincoln and his successor, Andrew Johnson. RECONSTRUCTION, as it finally manifested itself in the former states of the Confederacy, was largely the work of the Radical Republicans, as was the IMPEACHMENT TRIAL OF ANDREW JOHNSON. Lasting accomplishments include passage of the THIRTEENTH AMENDMENT; FOURTEENTH AMENDMENT; and FIFTEENTH AMENDMENT. By the end of the 1870s, they were in decline.

RADICAL RIGHT. Sociopolitical movements and parties that generally constitute a conservative backlash from rapid social and economic change. In the 19th c., this kind of movement was typified by the various nativist, anti-Catholic parties, most especially the Know-Nothings (see AMERICAN PARTY). In the South after the Civil War, the KU KLUX KLAN was an especially virulent form of the radical right. The 1930s witnessed many extremist movements. The most potent on the right was that led by a Catholic priest, Charles E. Coughlin, which was anti-Semitic and increasingly pro-Fascist. After World War II, the threat of communism and the cold war brought forth a wide variety of anticommunist movements, led by Sen. Joseph R. McCarthy (see MCCARTHY-ARMY HEARINGS). In the South, the White Citizens' Councils and a revitalized Klan reacted against the civil rights movement. In the late 1970s and 1980s, a number of movements grew up in reaction to what was considered a "permissive" society; they included the Moral Majority, the Right to Life (antiabortion) movement, and various antifeminist organizations.

RADICALS AND RADICALISM. Radicalism in politics in the late 19th and early 20th c. was centrally associated wtih proposals to alter fundamentally the capitalist economic and social system and replace it with some kind of socialism or, extremely, by anarchy. Radicals demanded far-reaching changes in property relations, distribution of wealth and income, or the status of labor. The Knights of Labor were thought of as a radical group, as were the Greenback Labor party, the Free Silver men, the Single-Taxers, and many leaders of the so-called Populist revolt (see POPULIST PARTY). More orthodox, European-style socialist organizations included the SOCIALIST LABOR PARTY and the American Socialist party. Emma Goldman and Alexander Barkman were the leading anarchists, and the INDUSTRIAL WORKERS OF THE WORLD respresented the syndicalist point of view. After World War I, most radical thought came to be associated with Marxist communism (see COMMUNIST PARTY UNITED STATES OF AMERICA), although it took several forms, particularly during the Great Depression of the 1930s. During the 1960s, radicalism was again prevalent, this time associated with either the antiwar movement or the CIVIL RIGHTS MOVEMENT.

RADIO. In 1906, Reginald Fessenden developed the high frequency alternator, and thus became the person most responsible for a viable system of radiotelephony. Lee De Forest and Edwin H. Armstrong made outstanding improvements in radio technology, and the period 1915–25 saw a rapid increase in experimentation by radiotelephone enthusiasts. In 1919 the Radio Corporation of America (RCA) was formed by absorbing the Marconi Wireless Telegraph Co. and by entering into manufacturing agreements with Westinghouse and General Electric. In 1920, station KDKA, Pittsburgh, initiated radio broadcasting on a regular basis; by 1927, there were 700-odd radio stations broadcasting in the US. In 1934, the Federal Communications Commission (FCC) was created to regulate the industry. Nationwide networks developed, and advertising revenues during the 1930s and 1940s were enormous. Armstrong developed (1925–33) frequency modulation (FM), freer of static and higher in audio fidelity than the previously used amplitude modulation (AM) system. After 1960, it became commercially feasible, and by 1979 was listened to by more people than listened to AM. In the early 1950s, television replaced radio as the premier home entertainment medium; but radio remained an important part of the mass media.

RADIOCARBON DATING. Measurement of the age of dead matter by comparing the radiocarbon content with that in living matter. First discovered in the 1940s, in 1960 Willard F. Libby was awarded the Nobel Prize in Chemistry for his development of the process. Widely used in archaeology to date artifacts.

RADISSON'S VOYAGES (1669). Journals of the French explorer Pierre Esprit Radisson, supposedly recounting his adventures in French Canada. Some of the exploits were probably in fact those of his brother-in-law, the sieur de Groseilliers, who traveled around Lake Huron and Lake Michigan. The book's chief value lies in its descriptions of Indians before they were influenced by white men. His enthusiasm for the fur trade there was one of the causes for the formation of the Hudson's Bay Co.

RAILROAD ADMINISTRATION, US. Established by President Wilson in 1917 to run US railroads for the duration of World War I. In general, personnel and administrative machinery were retained, but under the direct charge of a federal manager. Unified terminals were organized, locomotives and freight cars were standardized, and the purchasing of equipment and supplies was centralized. In 1920, the railroads were returned to private management.

RAILROAD BROTHERHOODS. Trade unions representing about 87 percent of American railroad workers. The five major brotherhoods, all dating from the 19th c., are those comprising locomotive engineers, firemen and enginemen, railroad conductors, trainmen, and switchmen.

RAILROAD LAND GRANTS. See LAND GRANTS FOR RAILWAYS.

RAILROAD MEDIATION ACTS. Various federal laws, the earliest dating from 1898, aimed at preventing railroad strikes by creating mediation procedures. The Railway Labor Act of 1926, amended 1934, remains the basic legislation in the field.

RAILROAD RATE LAW. Attempts to regulate railroad rates by law began in the 1870s at the state level, as farmers in particular suspected the companies of rate-gouging. In 1887 Congress created the Interstate Commerce Commission, which was given jurisdiction over rates. The ICC and Congress continued to wrestle with the problem; by the 1930s, overcharges by the railroads had become less of a problem as competition from trucks increased. The Railroad Revitalization and Regulatory Act of 1976 reversed government policy by calling for less regulation of railroad rates.

RAILROAD RATE WARS. Railroad competition became particularly competitive after 1869 when both the Pennsylvania RR and the New York Central reached the large cities of the Middle West. Recurrent rate wars caused freight rates and passenger fares to fall to absurdly low prices. In 1874, the Baltimore and Ohio RR reached Chicago, thus setting off disastrous rate wars. This ruthless competition led to a traffic-sharing arrangement in 1877, but competition remained unabated in other areas. These rate wars led to the demand for federal legislation. Congress in 1887 created the INTERSTATE COMMERCE COMMISSION, which was given rate-setting powers.

RAILROAD REBATES. See REBATES, RAILROAD.

RAILROAD RETIREMENT ACTS. A 1934 railroad retirement act was declared unconstitutional in 1935, and new legislation was passed. The Railroad Retirement Act of 1937 provided for an industry-wide system of payments into a pension fund by both employers and employees.

RAILROADS. The first chartered railway in America was a three-mile line built in Massachusetts in 1826; it used horses to pull granite stones. The Baltimore and Ohio RR was chartered in 1827 for the purpose of carrying both freight and passengers. The first passengers were carried 1830 in single cars drawn by horses. That same year the B & O experimented with a tiny steam engine, the *Tom Thumb*, built by Peter Cooper. Also in 1830, the South Carolina Canal and RR Co. (later part of the Southern Railway system) inaugurated a six-mile, steam-locomotive passenger service out of Charleston. By 1840, 2,800 miles of railroad had been built, reaching to the Middle West. Virtually the entire East Coast was covered and major cities connected by railroads. In the 1850s, mileage more than trebled, as ambitious efforts to reach the West were fulfilled. Chicago was reached 1852, and the Chicago and Rock Island reached the Mississippi R in 1854. Railroad building had already begun from the west bank of the Mississippi. The first railroad bridge over the Mississippi was opened in 1856, and the Missouri R was reached by the end of the decade. During those years, federal land grants were made to aid in the building of railroads; some 131 million acres of public land were transferred to private ownership. In return, the railroads carried government freight, mail, and troops at reduced rates.

The superior railroad service in the North proved to be a decisive advantage to the Union in the Civil War and proved for the first time the strategic importance of an effective rail system to a nation at war. At the end of the war, the nation witnessed the most dramatic event in railroad history: the completion of transcontinental rail service. It occurred at Promontory, Utah, on May 10, 1869, when construction crews met and joined tracks. A second transcontinental connection was supplied in 1881, and the Pacific Northwest was reached in 1883. The 1880s saw the greatest growth in railway lines, with an average of more than 7,000 miles of new tracks built each year. In 1886, the Supreme Court ruled that Congress had exclusive jurisdiction over interstate commerce and that a state could not regulate even the intrastate portion of an interstate movement. This led to the creation (1887) of the Interstate Commerce Commission (ICC).

Railroads continued to grow in the 20th c.; by 1930, mileage had reached its peak of 430,000 miles. By that time, wooden cars had virtually disappeared, the diesel locomotive had been introduced, and in 1931 air-conditioned passenger cars made their appearance. The 1930s saw the introduction of streamlining; passenger train speeds were increased, and overnight freight service for distances of more than 400 miles was introduced. Central traffic control and train operation by signal indication multiplied the capacity of single-track lines and even made it possible to take up unneeded trackage. The railroads were able to meet all the transportation needs of World War II.

In the immediate postwar years, the railroads carried forward a program of capital improvements, particularly the displacement of the steam locomotive by the diesel-electric. But the great days of the railroad were coming to an end. Trucks were cutting into much of the freight business, and the airplane and the private automobile were making serious inroads into the passenger business. The trend toward merger and consolidation did not prove to be the answer to the railroads' economic problems, as evidenced by the 1970 bankruptcy of the Penn Central. Congress came to the decision that some degree of nationalization was necessary. Amtrak was created 1971; it took over virtually all the passenger service in the nation. In 1976, in an effort to avoid outright nationalizaiton, Congress created the private, but federally financed Consolidated Rail Corporation (Conrail), which took over six bankrupt railroads in the Northeast and Midwest. In 1980 Congress passed a law aimed at deregulating the industry; it was an effort to save the economic future of those railroad companies that were still operating profitably.

RAILROADS, SKETCHES OF PRINCIPAL LINES.

Atchison, Topeka and Santa Fe. Chartered 1869 to connect Atchison and Topeka, Kans., it expanded rapidly. A pioneer in the use of diesel engines, its 13,000 miles of tracks made it first in mileage in the middle decades of the 20th c. Known as the Santa Fe.

Atlantic and Pacific. Land grant railroad chartered 1866 to run from Springfield, Mo., to Needles, Calif. In 1876, the company was reorganized as part of the St. Louis and San Francisco. In 1880, the Santa Fe bought a half interest.

Boston and Maine. Created 1835 out of a number of local lines; serves Massachusetts, New Hampshire, Maine, Vermont, and New York.

Burlington Northern. Formed 1970 and 1980 by the merger of the following lines: *Chicago, Burlington and Quincy.* Its first unit, the Aurora Branch RR was chartered 1849. Expanded rapidly into a system that eventually extended from Chicago and St. Louis to Minneapolis-St. Paul and thence westward to Montana, Wyoming, and Colorado, and southward to the Texas Gulf Coast. The Burlington pioneered in the development of streamline passenger equipment, introducing the Zephyr in 1934. *Great Northern.* The original line, started 1862, was the Saint Paul and Pacific; it built northward and westward. The transcontinental line was opened 1893. Eventually it reached from Minneapolis-St. Paul and the head of the Great Lakes to Vancouver, British Columbia; and Seattle and Portland, Oreg. *Northern Pacific.* The first of the northern-route transcontinental lines, chartered 1864 to connect Great Lakes area and Portland, Oreg. Reached Portland in 1883. By the 1970s, the line operated 6,700 miles of line, extending from Minneapolis-St. Paul and Duluth-Superior, to Seattle and Tacoma, Wash., and Portland. *Saint-Louis-San Francisco.* Begun 1866, it was planned to run from Springfield, Ill., to the Pacific coast; but its origin was changed to St. Louis, and it never reached the coast. It developed 4,800 miles, from St. Louis and Kansas City, Mo., to Oklahoma and N Texas, in the Southwest, and to Florida in the Southeast. Known as the Frisco.

Central of Georgia. Chartered 1833 to connect Savannah and Macon. Operated 2,000 miles in Georgia, Alabama, and Tennessee in the early 1980s.

Chesapeake and Ohio. Began as the 22-mile Louisa RR in Virginia in 1837, grew into a 4,800-mile system extending from Hampton Roads, Va., and Washington, D.C., to Louisville and Chicago. In the early 1960s, it took over the larger Baltimore and Ohio. *Baltimore and Ohio.* Chartered 1827, the B & O, as it was commonly known, was built to Wheeling on the Ohio R by 1852. Later it expanded to Philadelphia and New York City and to Chicago and St. Louis.

Chicago and North Western. Chartered 1848, the first railroad to serve Chicago. In 1867, it was the first line to reach the Missouri R at Omaha, where it connected with the Union Pacific. Acquired the Chicago Great Western in 1968, thus extending its system to 10,700 miles (reduced to 8,786 in 1980).

Chicago, Milwaukee, Saint Paul and Pacific. Chartered 1847 to build a line across Wisconsin to the Mississippi R. By 1900, it operated between the Great Lakes and the Missouri R and later expanded to the West Coast. The Milwaukee, as it is known, operated about 6,800 miles in 1980.

Chicago, Rock Island and Pacific. Incorporated 1847 to build from Rock Island to LaSalle, Ill., but built from Chicago under an amended charter. First railroad to bridge the Mississippi, in 1856. By the 1970s, its lines extended from Chicago, St. Louis, and Memphis on the east, to Minneapolis-St. Paul on the north, Colorado and New Mexico on the west, and the Texas and Louisiana Gulf Coast on the south. Known as the Rock Island, it filed for bankruptcy in the late 1970s.

Delaware and Hudson. Chartered 1823 as a canal company, built a canal and a railroad to bring coal from Carbondale, Pa., to Rondout, N.Y., on the Hudson R. On this line, in 1829, the first steam locomotive on an American railroad made its first (and only) run. The canal was abandoned 1898. The system extends through upstate New York to Montreal.

Denver and Rio Grande Western. Charted 1870 as a narrow-gauge line to run out of Denver to other parts of Colorado and to Salt Lake City. By 1890, its main lines had been converted to standard gauge. By the 1980s, the road operated some 1,850 miles, some still narrow gauge.

Erie Lackawanna. A 2,900-mile road formed 1960 out of the Delaware, Lackawanna and Western and the Erie. In 1976, the company in bankruptcy, became part of Conrail. *Delaware, Lackawanna and Western.* Charted 1851 to build an outlet for the coal of the Lackawanna Valley, it was extended west to Buffalo, north to Lake Ontario, and east to New York via Hoboken, N.J. *Erie.* Chartered as the New York and Erie in 1832 to build from Piermont, N.Y., on the Hudson R, to Dunkirk, N.Y., on Lake Erie. Before merging in 1960, the Erie operated 2,300 miles, extending from New York City to Buffalo, Cleveland, and Chicago.

Florida East Coast. Acquired by Henry M. Flagler in 1885, he steadily pushed it southward from St. Augustine. Reached Miami in 1896 and Key West in 1912. Hurricane damage in 1935 caused abandonment of the Key West extension. In 1980, it operated 870 miles.

Grand Trunk Western. Subsidiary of the Canadian National Railways, it was built from Port Huron and Detroit across Michigan, Indiana, and Illinois, reaching Chicago in 1881. In 1980, it operated 929 miles.

Hannibal and Saint Joseph. A Missouri railway line, completed 1859. St. Joseph was the starting point for the Pony Express and the nearest railroad terminus during the Pikes Peak gold rush, for which the railroad carried the mails.

Illinois Central Gulf. An 8,366-mile line, the result of the 1972 merger of the Gulf, Mobile and Ohio and the Illinois Central. *Gulf, Mobile and Ohio.* In 1940, the Gulf, Mobile and Northern was consolidated with the Mobile and Ohio. The latter operated a line from Mobile to St. Louis. In 1947, the firm absorbed the Alton, which dated from 1847. At the time of its merger, it had a 2,700-mile system extending from Chicago and Kansas City, Mo., to Mobile and New Orleans. *Illinois Central.* Incorporated 1851, it received the first railroad land grant provided by the federal government. After the Civil War, a southern line to the Gulf was acquired. At the time of the 1972 merger, the Illinois Central operated a 6,700-mile system in fourteen states, extending from Chicago west to the Missouri R and south to New Orleans La., and Birmingham, Ala.

Lehigh Valley. Originally chartered as a coal-carrying line, it acquired its present name in 1853 through various mergers. The line extended 925 miles, reaching the Niagara frontier on the west and New York City on the east. It went bankrupt; in 1976 became a part of Conrail.

Louisville and Nashville. Chartered 1850, by 1980 it had created a 6,570-mile line from Chicago, Cincinnati, and St. Louis to Memphis, Atlanta, and New Orleans.

Missouri, Kansas and Texas. Known as the Katy, it was made up of several shorter lines in 1870. A line from Junction City, Kans., was built to Texas by 1872. Expansion created a system of 2,175 miles (1980) from St. Louis and Kansas City, Mo., to San Antonio and Houston.

Missouri Pacific. First chartered 1851 to build a line of 5.5-foot gauge from St. Louis to the West Coast. The first locomotive west of the Mississippi ran on this road in 1852. In 1978, the company acquired the Texas and Pacific. The road expanded from St. Louis, Memphis, and New Orleans to Omaha; Pueblo, Colo.; Laredo, Tex.; and the Gulf Coast. In 1980, it had 11,500 miles. *Texas and Pacific.* Chartered 1871, it took over several earlier short lines. From NE Texas, at Marshall and Texarkana, lines were built westward toward El Paso and eastward to New Orleans. In 1882, at Sierra Blanca, Tex., it met the crews of the Galveston, Harrisburg, and San Antonio, building the Southern Pacific line eastward. The line was completed to New Orleans in 1882. In the early 1970s, the company operated 2,100 miles of line.

Norfolk and Western. A 9-mile line between Petersburg, Va., and the James R, chartered 1836, is the oldest part of the line. Eventually stretched across Virginia from tidewater to Tennessee with extensions westward in to the coal fields. Grew to 2,700 miles with the addition of the Virginian in 1959. In 1964, two other roads, the Nickel Plate and the Wabash, were added, creating a system of 7,558 miles by 1980. *New York, Chicago and Saint Louis.* The Nickel Plate Road, as it was called, opened between Buffalo and Chicago in 1882. Other lines were consolidated into the system and by the early 1970s, the system operated 2,200 miles, extending from Buffalo and Wheeling to Chicago and Peoria, Ill., and St. Louis. *Wabash.* The Northern Cross, 12 miles long, built in 1838, the first railroad in Illinois and the earliest part of the Wabash. Became a system of nearly 3,000 miles, stretching from Buffalo to

Toledo to St. Louis, Kansas City, Mo., Omaha, and Des Moines.

Penn Central. Created 1968 out of the New York Central, the Pennsylvania, and the New York, New Haven and Hartford railroads. The problems facing the Penn Central system forced it into bankruptcy 1970. Congress provided some indirect financial aid, but in 1976 the system became part of Conrail. *New York Central.* The Mohawk and Hudson, oldest of the many companies that made up the New York Central, ran its first train in 1831. The system, through numerous consolidations, grew to more than 10,000 miles, extending from Montreal, Boston, and New York to the Straits of Mackinac, Chicago, and St. Louis. *New York, New Haven and Hartford.* The earliest of its components, the Boston and Providence, began operation 1834. All-rail service between Boston and New York via Springfield was begun in 1848. The New Haven, as the line was known, came to operate 1,800 miles. Between 1907 and 1914, the railroad installed the first railroad electrification. *Pennsylvania.* Chartered 1846 to build a line between Harrisburg and Pittsburgh. The line was expanded to a system of some 10,000 miles, eastward to Philadelphia, New York, Washington, and Norfolk and westward to Chicago and St. Louis. The oldest section of the system, the Camden and Amboy, was completed in 1834.

Pullman Company. George M. Pullman built his first sleeping cars (rebuilt day coaches) in 1858 and his first completely Pullman-built car in 1864. By the end of the century, the name Pullman was synonymous with the sleeping-car business even though the company also manufactured passenger and freight cars. An antitrust suit required the company to divest itself either of its car-manufacturing or car-operating business; therefore, in 1947, the latter was taken over by fifty-seven railroads.

Reading. Successor to the Philadelphia and Reading, the Reading operated 1,200 miles of line in the early 1970s in New York, Pennsylvania, and Delaware. *Old Ironsides,* the first locomotive built by Matthias Baldwin, ran on one of its tracks in 1832. The line, which owned a majority of the stock of the Jersey Central Lines, went bankrupt in the 1970s and became a part of Conrail.

Saint Louis-Southwestern. Known as the Cotton Belt, it started at the Tyler Tap RR in

1871 to connect Tyler, Tex., to a mainline railroad. It expanded to 1,500 miles, connecting St. Louis and Memphis with Fort Worth, Dallas, and Waco, Tex.

Seaboard Coast Line. In 1967 the Atlantic Coast Line and the Seaboard Air Line merged to form the Seaboard Coast Line. Mileage in 1980 was 8,771. *Atlantic Coast Line.* The Richmond and Petersburg was chartered 1836 to connect those two Virginia cities. That and dozens of other small lines in Virginia, the Carolinas, Georgia, Alabama, and Florida became the Atlantic Coast Line in 1900. In the 1970s, the railroad operated 5,600 miles of line and had considerable interest in other railroads. *Seaboard Air Line.* The name was first applied in 1889 to a loose operating association of connecting railroads in Virginia and the Carolinas. The oldest was the Portsmouth and Roanoke, which opened service between Portsmouth, Va., and Weldon, N.C., in 1832. The system grew into a line extending from Norfolk and Richmond to both coasts of Florida.

Soo Line (Minneapolis, Saint Paul and Sault Sainte Marie). Chartered 1873 to connect Minneapolis with Canada at Sault Ste. Marie. It also extended westward, connecting with the Canadian Pacific RR at Portal, N.D. Also operated the Wisconsin Central, giving it entrance to Chicago. The 4,450-mile system (1980) is a separately operated subsidiary of the Canadian Pacific.

Southern Pacific. Chartered 1850 to build from New Orleans westward as the New Orleans, Opelousas and Great Western, it eventually merged with lines in Texas and California. The Southern Pacific, incorporated in California in 1865, undertook the task of building a second transcontinental route and operated in close linkage with the Central Pacific RR. In 1980, the Southern Pacific Co. operated more than 13,000 miles of line.

Southern Railway. Formed 1894 out of several small lines, including the pioneer South Carolina RR. The system came to include the separately operated Cincinnati, New Orleans and Texas Pacific; Alabama Great Southern; New Orleans and Northeastern; Georgia, Southern and Florida; and Carolina and Northwestern railroads. A total mileage of over 10,000 in 1980 extended from Washington, D.C., to Cincinnati and St. Louis to New Orleans, Mobile, and Florida.

Union Pacific. Incorporated 1862 to build westward from the Missouri R to meet the Central Pacific of California building eastward. To that main line, the railroad added numerous short lines by consolidating with smaller companies. In 1980, it operated 9,266 miles of line from Council Bluffs, Iowa, Omaha, Nebr., St. Joseph, Mo., and Kansas City, Mo., to Portland, Oreg., Seattle and Spokane, Wash., and Los Angeles.

Western Pacific. Last of the transcontinental connections was the Western Pacific, which opened in 1909 between Salt Lake City and Oakland-San Francisco. A branch line connecting with the Great Northern opened 1931. Total mileage in 1980 was 1,435.

RAILROADS IN THE CIVIL WAR. Of a total mileage of 31,256 in the US in 1861, less than 30 percent (or about 9,000 miles) was in the Confederate states, soon reduced by northern captures to about 6,000 miles. In general, the northern railroads were better built, equipped, and run. That superiority was in no small measure responsible for the final collapse of the Confederacy.

RAILROAD STRIKE OF 1877. After a 10 percent wage reduction, trainmen on the Baltimore and Ohio halted freight cars. President Hayes sent federal soldiers to break the strike, causing sympathetic strikes in other cities.

RAILROAD STRIKES OF 1886. When the Texas and Pacific RR office at Marshall, Tex., discharged a foreman, 900 men struck, tying up 5,000 miles of railway in the central states. Jay Gould, determined to break the railway workers' union, the KNIGHTS OF LABOR, refused to arbitrate or to reinstate discharged strikers. The strike collapsed, discrediting industrial unionism in general and the Knights of Labor in particular.

RAILROAD SURVEYS, GOVERNMENT. In 1853, Congress appropriated money for a survey of feasible routes for a railroad to the Pacific Coast. Five routes were surveyed, but the surveys did not bring agreement as to a route. When the Pacific Railroad Bill was adopted in 1862, the central route from the western border of Iowa to the California-Nevada line was chosen.

RAILS. The earliest railroads used wooden rails with flat strips of iron secured to the upper surface. The rolling of heavy iron rails was begun in the US in 1844. Steel rails, with greater uniformity, strength, and hardness, were manufactured after ca. 1867. The use of rail welded into strips of one-half mile in length became common in the 1950s.

RAILWAY LABOR ACTS. See RAILROAD MEDIATION ACTS.

RAILWAYS, ELECTRIC. First developed in Great Britain, electric street railways were built in Providence and Kansas City in 1884. By 1890, there were 1,200 miles of such railways in the nation and by 1895, over 10,000 miles. Chicago's elevated lines began to be electrically operated in 1896, followed by those in New York and Boston in 1901. The Chicago, Milwaukee and St. Paul's 645-mile electrification through the Western Mountains, completed 1918, was an epochal achievement. (See also INTERURBAN ELECTRIC LINES; SUBWAYS.)

RAISIN RIVER MASSACRE (Jan. 22, 1813). Battle at Maumee Rapids, above Toledo, on the Raisin R during the War of 1812. An American force was badly defeated by a combined British-Indian attack, at a loss of 900 men killed or taken prisoner.

RALEIGH. City in North Carolina, constructed 1792 as the state capital. A manufacturing and commercial center for electronic, metal, and lumber products, and food-processing. Also an important research center. Pop.: 149,771 (1980).

RALEIGH LETTER (Apr. 17, 1844). Written by Henry Clay, Whig presidential candidate, to explain his opposition to the proposed annexation of Texas; it displeased many southern voters and contributed to his defeat.

RALEIGH'S LOST COLONY. Colonists left Plymouth, England, on May 8, 1587, and reached Roanoke Island, in the Albemarle region of North Carolina (then Virginia) on July 22. On August 18, Virginia Dare was born, the first English child born in America. Her father, John White, on August 27 sailed to England for supplies; he was not able to return until August 1590. He discovered no trace of the colony except the letters "C R O" carved on a tree and the word "CROATOAN"

cut on the doorpost of the palisade. Their fate has never been known.

RALEIGH'S PATENT AND FIRST COLONY. In 1584, Sir Walter Raleigh and his half-brother, Sir Humphrey Gilbert, co-patentees, sent out an expedition that entered Albemarle Sound in July and a few days later landed at Roanoke Island. After two months' exploring and trading with the Indians, they returned to England. In April 1585, Raleigh sent out a colony of 108 men to what had been named Virginia, in honor of Queen Elizabeth. They established their settlement at Roanoke Island with Ralph Lane as governor. War with the Indians broke out in 1586, but the colonists won an easy victory. Unrest and distress increased, however, and all but fifteen returned to England. When RALEIGH'S LOST COLONY arrived on Roanoke in 1587, they found only the bones of one of the men; the fort and the houses were in ruin.

RALEIGH'S TAVERN. Site in Williamsburg, Va., of two (1769, 1774) rebellious sessions of the Virginia house of burgesses.

RAMS, CONFEDERATE. Vessels with massively constructed bows. The novelty of their construction was the armor-plated casemate constructed amidship to house the artillery, with sides sloped to cause the enemy's cannonballs and projectiles to ricochet. The *Virginia*, first and foremost of the type, was constructed on the salvaged hull of the US frigate *Merrimack*.

RANCH. Land on which cattle, sheep, or horses are raised. In the US, most ranching is carried out W of the Mississippi R. The King Ranch in Texas is the largest in the country, comprising about 1 million acres.

RANDOLPH'S COMMISSION. Royal commission established 1676 with Edmund Randolph as head. It was to carry to Massachusetts the crown's decision on the boundary disputes between the Massachusetts Bay Company and the heirs of Sir Ferdinando Gorges in Maine. Randolph made a comprehensive report, adverse as far as Massachusetts was concerned; most serious were the flagrant breaches of the Navigation Acts and the colony's denial of parliamentary authority over the colony. The report was largely responsible for the reopening of the question of the status of the Massachusetts Bay Co., which ended in the annulment of the charter in 1684.

RANGER-DRAKE ENGAGEMENT (April 24, 1778). The American sloop *Ranger*, commanded by John Paul Jones, was victorious over the British ship *Drake* at Carrickfergus, Ireland.

RANGERS. Specially trained small groups of infantry capable of making rapid attacks into enemy territory and withdrawing quickly before the enemy can retaliate. Rangers predate the American Revolution and have been active in most wars, World War I being a notable exception. In the Civil War, Mosby's Rangers and the Texas Rangers are the best known. Six ranger battalions saw action in World War II in Africa, Europe, and the Pacific. Sixteen ranger companies served in Korea. In 1951, ranger-trained personnel were spread among standard infantry units.

RAPPAHANNOCK STATION, BATTLE AT (Nov. 7, 1863). Union victory on the Rappahannock R in Virginia. Gen. G.G. Meade was the Union commander; R.E. Lee the Rebel commander.

RATON PASS. Through the Raton Mountains, on the Colorado-New Mexico border. During the 18th and 19th c., an important gateway between the upper Arkansas basin and E New Mexico.

RATTLESNAKE FLAG. A yellow field bearing a coiled rattlesnake and the motto "Don't Tread on Me," used during the French and Indian War as a colonial symbol. Used unofficially during the Revolutionary War.

RAYSTOWN PATH. Led from near Carlisle, Pennsylvania, in the Susquehanna Valley to present Pittsburgh and to Logstown, eighteen miles below Pittsburgh. Much of it today parallels the Lincoln Highway.

RAZORBACK HOGS. Half-wild mongrel descendants of domestic hogs, once common throughout the South. Derived from European importation, many were as fierce as wild boars.

READING RAILROAD. See RAILROADS, SKETCHES OF PRINCIPLE LINES.

READJUSTER MOVEMENT. Political effort (1871–82) in Virginia aimed at adjusting the state's massive debt so that it would not ruin the state's farmers or result in neglect of public schools. The Readjuster party won the legislature in 1879 and the governorship, in the person of W.E. Cameron, in 1881. In 1882, the legislature passed laws in the economic and social interest of the masses.

REAPER. See AGRICULTURAL MACHINERY; McCORMICK REAPER.

REAPPORTIONMENT, CONGRESSIONAL. See APPORTIONMENT.

REBATES, RAILROADS. In the 1850s, the railroads developed the practice of charging lower rates, offered in the form of a rebate, to favored customers, the Standard Oil Co. being the most outstanding recipient of special treatment. The Interstate Commerce Act (1887) prohibited such rebates, making both the receiver and the giver of the rebate subject to imprisonment and a high fine.

REBELLION, RIGHT OF. According to John Locke, government powers are fiduciary, and the right to revolution exists when a government abuses its authority or oppresses its people. It was largely on this basis that the American patriots justified their rebellion against Great Britain. (See also LOCKE'S POLITICAL PHILOSOPHY.)

RECALL. Electoral process for determining whether voters wish to retain a public official in office before his or her term comes to an end. Can be invoked through a special election upon the filing of a petition signed by a stipulated number of qualified electors. The US Constitution provides no recourse to recall at the federal level; but in 1980, fourteen states had some form of recall mechanism in effect.

RECIPROCAL TRADE AGREEMENTS. In 1934 Congress delegated to the president the power to make foreign-trade agreements with other nations on the basis of a mutual reduction of duties. Between 1934 and 1947, the US made separate trade agreements with twenty-nine countries. After World War II, the various bilateral understandings were combined to form the GENERAL AGREEMENT ON TARIFFS AND TRADE (GATT); nevertheless, the president retained the power to negotiate tariff-reducing arrangements with individual nations or groups of nations.

RECIPROCITY. See RECIPROCAL TRADE AGREEMENTS; TARIFF.

RECLAMATION. In 1902, Congress authorized the secretary of the interior to construct irrigation works in the sixteen western states and to pay for them from a revolving reclamation fund accumulated from the sales of public lands in those states. Within one year, the Reclamation Service (later renamed the Bureau of Reclamation) had authorized three projects: the Newlands in Nevada, the Salt R in Arizona, and the Uncompahgre in Colorado. By 1978, the bureau had built 309 storage dams and dikes, which provided water for over 9 million acres, producing over $4 billion worth of crops a year, and had constructed forty-nine hydroelectric power plants.

RECOGNITION, POLICY OF. Although it is not so specified in the Constitution, the executive has always been discharged to the responsibility of recognizing (or denying recognition to) foreign governments. In 1792, Thomas Jefferson, as secretary of state, established the criteria for recognition. If a new government possessed the machinery of state, if it governed with the assent of a majority of the people, and if it met with no substantial resistance, US recognition followed. Recognition was not a moral act and did not imply approval. Later, an additional criterion was added: the new state's or new government's capacity or willingness to carry out its international obligations. It was on that criterion that the US delayed recognition of the Soviet Union until 1933 and the People's Republic of China until 1978.

RECONSTRUCTION (1865–77). Post-Civil War US policy toward the states of the former Confederacy. In 1863, President Lincoln had offered a plan for the readmittance of the southern states to the Union once the war was over; it was denounced as far too lenient. His successor, Andrew Johnson, likewise was accused of being too lenient on the South, and the RADICAL REPUBLICANS in Congress imposed their own plan. Through a series of RECONSTRUCTION ACTS, they established military law throughout the South as assurance that black rights (including the right to vote) would be protected and called for stringent procedures for the readmittance of the secessionist states. The Thirteenth, Fourteenth, and Fifteenth amendments were passed (see THIRTEENTH AMENDMENT; FOURTEENTH AMENDMENT; FIFTEENTH AMENDMENT). The president's power to act was shackled by the Tenure of Office Act, which led to the impeachment proceeding against Johnson (see IMPEACHMENT TRIAL OF ANDREW JOHNSON). Eventually, all the states were readmitted to the Union, and civil government was reinstituted. By 1876, Republican administrations survived only in Florida, Louisiana, and South Carolina. For a time, blacks continued to vote, although in decreasing numbers. By the turn of the century, they had almost been eliminated from southern politics and conservative white Democrats were firmly in control.

RECONSTRUCTION ACTS. Laws designed to carry out the congressional program of RECONSTRUCTION. The southern states (except Tennessee) were divided into five military districts, under the command of a general officer. Conventions chosen by universal male (i.e., including blacks) suffrage were to frame constitutions, which would have to be accepted by the electorate; then, after ratifying the FOURTEENTH AMENDMENT, the southern states would be readmitted to the Union. After the states refused to call such conventions, the commanding generals were given the power to initiate the voting process, and state governments were specifically made subordinate to the military commanders.

RECONSTRUCTION FINANCE CORPORATION (RFC). Created 1932 under the sponsorship of President Hoover and greatly expanded under the New Deal. Made loans to banks, insurance companies, and industrial corporations as a way of restoring credit during the Great Depression. Toward the end of the decade, it made loans to defense-related industries. Officially dissolved in 1953.

RECRUITMENT. The US armed forces, except during major wars, have depended overwhelmingly on voluntary enlistment. During the Civil War, Union recruitment involved monetary payments for enlistees. In recent years, all the services have emphasized the vocational training available to enlistees.

RED CLOUD'S WAR. See SIOUX WARS.

RED CROSS, AMERICAN. Affiliate of the International Red Cross, founded 1881 by Clara Barton to provide care to ill and wounded soldiers in wartime. Later, disaster relief became a major program of the Red Cross. During World War I, it set up and staffed fifty-eight base hospitals and forty-seven ambulance companies overseas. Extensive war relief for civilians was also carried on. In World War II, it carried on civilian relief operations in sixty countries, recruited nurses for the military services, and established welfare and recreational programs for US troops. In 1948, the Red Cross established a program for providing blood to civilians without charge.

REDEMPTIONERS. White immigrants who, in return for their passage to America from Europe, sold their services for two to seven years. Upon arrival in port, captains of vessels having redemptioners aboard advertised in newspapers the sale of their services to persons who should advance the cost of their passage.

RED LEGS. Members of a secret military society organized in Kansas in 1862, so-called because of their red leggings. Served as federal scouts in border conflicts.

RED LINE MAP. In 1782, Benjamin Franklin marked the boundary of the US for the reference of the French foreign minister in a "strong red line" on a copy of John Mitchell's *Map of British and French Dominions in North America*. The original was lost, but in 1932 a transcript of the map, red line and all, was discovered in the Spanish archives.

RED RIVER BOUNDARY DISPUTE. See GREER COUNTY DISPUTE.

RED RIVER CAMPAIGN (1864). Efforts by the Union army to take the great cotton-growing sections of Louisiana, Arkansas, and Texas. Much of the fighting was in the Shreve-

port area; finally the Union forces were forced to give up the effort.

RED RIVER CART TRAFFIC. The Red River cart was a two-wheeled vehicle with wheels made of sections of tree trunks. It carried a maximum load of 1,000 pounds and was drawn by an ox or pony. The traffic began in 1822: A train of carts a mile long was not at all infrequent. They were loaded at Fort Garry (Winnipeg) or Pembina, North Dakota, with buffalo robes, pemmican, and furs. They followed a trail that went SE along the E bank of the Red R to Fort Snelling. Later the trails crossed the Mississippi R at Sauk Rapids and reached St. Paul.

RED RIVER INDIAN WAR (1874–75). More than fourteen pitched battles fought in the successful effort of the US army to force return several bands of Indians to their reservations. The Indians were encamped along the Red R, its tributaries, and the canyons of the Llano Estacado in W Texas and SE New Mexico.

RED RIVER OF THE NORTH. Forms the border between Minnesota and North Dakota and flows through Manitoba into Lake Winipeg. Discovered by the sieur de La Vérendrye in 1733; became the center of a profitable fur trade. During the late 19th c., thousands of settlers, mostly from northern Europe, poured into the Red R valley. By the beginning of the 20th c., the Red R country was the premier wheat-producing region of the nation.

RED RIVER POST. Fort built 1685 by the Spanish to thwart French encroachments into Texas, on the Red R in NW Louisiana.

RED RIVER RAFT. Logs and other debris that completely blocked the Red R for 180 miles above Coushatta Bayou. Between 1833–39, working under a congressional appropriation, Capt. H.M. Shreve removed it, leaving the river navigable for more than 1,000 miles. Shreveport, named in Shreve's honor, arose as a commercial center of the region as a result.

RED SHIRTS. Bands of armed horsemen who overthrew the RADICAL REPUBLICAN rule in South Carolina in 1877. There were 290 companies composed of 14,350 men. They supported Wade Hampton for governor, and by terrorizing Republicans and blacks, were able to force the flight of the Republicans after federal troops were withdrawn from the state.

REDSTONE OLD FORT. Pioneer name for a Mound Builder entrenchment at the confluence of Dunlap's Creek with the Monongahela R in SW Pennsylvania. Fort Burd was erected there in 1759; in 1785 the site was renamed Brownsville.

REED RULES. Procedural rules adopted by the House of Representatives in 1890 at the behest of Speaker of the House Thomas B. Reed. Although ostensibly aimed at streamlining the procedures of the body, in effect they greatly increased the power of the speaker.

REED TREATY (1858). After the defeat of China in the Anglo-French War (1857–58), the European powers imposed on China the Treaties of Tientsin, which opened up eleven additional treaty ports and in general improved the climate for western commerce there. The US minister, William B. Reed, negotiated a separate US treaty securing equality of treatment extended to other nations.

REFERENDUM. Electoral procedure whereby a public-policy issue is submitted directly to the electorate instead of being decided by representatives. The US Constitution makes no allowance for referendum votes in the national government, but about half the states permit referendums to some extent.

REFORESTATION. Artificial regeneration of forests by tree planting dates back to the colonial period, but as a systematic procedure it is primarily a 20th-c. phenomenon. In 1905, the Forest Service began a program of reforesting national forests; the program continued to grow until, by 1973, the annual reforestation covered nearly 2 million acres of land.

REFORMATORIES. In 1876, the first reformatory for young men was established at Elmira, N.Y. Its program included elementary education for illiterates, designated library hours, lectures by college instructors, and vocational training. The Elmira plan was widely and enthusiastically adopted, but it did not

produce the results expected. Today, various experiments are being tried, including smaller, more open facilities, which are believed to provide a better climate for correctional services. Half-way houses and work-release programs are also experiments.

REFORMED CHURCHES. The American representatives of Dutch Calvinism, they date from the founding of Collegiate Church in New York City in 1628. The Reformed churches have been particularly prone to faction. Today, the leading branches are the Christian Reformed Church, and the Reformed Church in America.

REFRIGERATION. Mechanisms using ammonia and water, heated, cooled, and evaporated, creating a refrigerating effect were developed in France ca. 1858. One variation, the Crosley Icyball was manufactured in the US in the 1930s. Such machines were ultimately replaced by vapor compression machines. In 1930, Thomas Midgley, Jr., created the compound dichlorodifluoromethane. Under the trade name Freon 12, it became the most widely used refrigerant.

REFUGEE TRACT. Narrow strip of about 100,000 acres extending forty-two miles E from the Scioto R at Columbus, Ohio. Set aside in 1801 for Canadian refugees who had aided the American Revolution.

REGICIDES. Three of the men condemned as regicides at the time of the Restoration escaped to New England: Edward Whalley, a cousin of Oliver Cromwell; William Goffe, Whalley's son-in-law; and John Dixwell.

REGISTRATION OF VOTERS. The first voter registration law was enacted in Massachusetts in 1800. Since 1900, reform legislation has made registration laws more effective. In 1970, Congress passed a voting rights act that replaced the confusing pattern of state residency requirements with a universal national law for presidential elections. Nationwide, about 75 percent of those eligible to vote are registered.

REGULATORS. Vigilante groups common in the South after the Civil War. Variously known as the Black-Horse Cavalry and Jayhawkers, they generally rode at night, in disguise, employing arson, murder, and mutilation to terrorize blacks and prevent the exercise of their rights. (See also KU KLUX KLAN.)

REGULATORS (NORTH CAROLINA). Settlers in the backcountry of North Carolina in the 18th c. who opposed the policies of the royal government, particularly what they regarded as oppressive administration by corrupt officials and excessive fees charged them. The governor, William Tryon, in 1768 used the militia at Hillsboro to suppress the Regulators and the movement subsided until 1769, when Regulators drove justices from the bench and threatened violence. They were finally defeated at the Battle of Alamance (May 16, 1771).

REGULATORS (SOUTH CAROLINA). Settlers in the backcountry of South Carolina who organized in 1767–69 to break up bands of horse thieves who had established a reign of terror. The movement died out with the creation of official courts in the area.

RELIEF. From colonial times, local governments provided such relief for the needy as was not provided by churches and neighbors. The Great Depression had a tremendous impact on the philosophy and practice of providing public assistance. With state capabilities totally used up, President Hoover established various emergency relief organizations sponsored and funded by the federal government. Later, the New Deal policies of the Roosevelt administration took for granted a large federal role in the care of the needy. That philosophy has persisted, despite the efforts of conservatives to return much of the welfare programs to the state and local authorities.

RELIGION. Anglicans in the New World envisioned a replication of the English parish system; but almost as soon as Virginia was founded, the settlers began devising their own pattern of church life. The vestry system allowed far more lay control of church affairs than the parish system did. In New England, the Puritan theocracies were independent congregations that owed cooperation, but nothing more, to each other. From the beginning, religious diversity and dissension were problems in New England. Only in Rhode Is-

land did the various sects exist in harmony. The Middle Colonies accepted diversity more easily. In New York, in particular, the Anglicans and Dutch Reformeds coexisted amicably. In Pennsylvania, also, the prevailing Quakers tolerated the establishment of a number of other denominations. During the early 18th c., Anglicanism was widely established in the South, including Maryland, Virginia, North Carolina, and South Carolina. The state churches were all disestablished after the Revolution (although Massachusetts maintained the vestiges of established Congregationalism until 1833). The Constitution specifically prohibits the federal government from favoring one church over another.

The crisis of the Revolution led American religion to reorganize itself along denominational lines. Evangelism and revivalism generated a wide following, particularly in the newly settled West. Western New York, for example, produced two influential movements: the Latter Day Saints (Mormons) and Adventism. Further south, Presbyterianism, Methodism, Baptists, and the Christian Churches (or Disciples of Christ) were especially strong. By 1850, immigration had made the Roman Catholic church the largest single religious body in the US. Immigration also changed the direction of American Lutheranism: many immigrants formed their own synods, causing that denomination to be even more factionalized than the other Protestant sects. The late 19th and early 20th c. saw an increase in the number of Jews in the US (see JUDAISM).

The most significant religious movement of the 20th c. has been the quest for Christian unity. The Federal Council of Churches of Christ was founded in 1908; it was succeeded in 1950 by the National Council of Churches. Many denominations have merged. The Lutherans in particular have shown a tendency to regroup. The Methodists ended their North-South rift (existing since before the Civil War) in 1939. In 1957, the Congregational Christian and the Evangelical and Reformed churches, both the product of earlier mergers, joined to form the United Church of Christ.

RELIGIOUS LIBERTY. At the time of the establishment of the American colonies, unity of religion was generally accepted as essential to the well-being of the state. The American colonies became the first place in the world where complete religious liberty was actually tried in a political state. When Roger Williams established Rhode Island, the principle was there put into operation. Although religious liberty was not practiced in individual colonies (e.g., the Puritan theocracies of New England), persecuted religious groups from almost every country in western Europe were able to establish their own colonies in the New World. By the end of the colonial period, a great majority of the population were unchurched; and unchurched people generally are opposed to granting special privileges to any one religious body. The political leaders who led in the movement to separate church and state, most notably James Madison and Thomas Jefferson, were nonchurch members. All this created a climate in the post-Revolutionary political scene that encouraged state and federal constitutions guaranteeing religious liberty.

REMAGEN. Site of a railroad bridge across the Rhine in Germany captured (Mar. 7–9, 1945) by American troops in World War II.

"REMEMBER THE ALAMO." Battle cry of the Texas Revolution. It referred to the massacre of the Texan force at the ALAMO, a mission in San Antonio (Mar. 6, 1836).

"REMEMBER THE MAINE." Battle cry of the Spanish-American War. It referred to the sinking of the battleship *Maine* in Havana harbor on Feb. 15, 1898.

REMOVAL, EXECUTIVE POWER OF. The power of the president to remove from office executive appointments. The First Congress gave recognition to the proposition that the president's power of removal is inherent in the general grant of executive power. The only serious challenge occurred in 1867 with the TENURE OF OFFICE ACT. President Andrew Johnson's refusal to abide by it led to his impeachment. The law was repealed in 1887. Since then court decisions have overwhelmingly supported the principle.

REMOVAL ACT OF 1830. Legislation authorizing the president to divide territory W of the Mississippi into districts suitable for exchange with Indians living within the US. It also authorized the president to make such exchanges with the Indians.

RENO. Resort city in Nevada, long noted for its very active divorce court. Pop.: 100,756 (1980).

RENO, FORT (Okla.). A post established 1874 in Indian Territory, near the present town of El Reno. It was garrisoned until 1908.

RENO, FORT. A post on the Powder R established 1865 in Wyoming as Fort Connor.

REORGANIZED CHURCH OF JESUS CHRIST OF LATTER-DAY SAINTS. Claims to be the successor of the church organized by Joseph Smith, Jr., in 1830. It broke away from the main Mormon body in 1852 under the leadership of Smith's eldest son.

REPARATION COMMISSION (1920–30). Body set up after World War I to supervise the reparation payments of Germany to the former Allies. It came up with a number of plans, the best known being the YOUNG PLAN. Only a small percentage of the agreed-upon reparations was ever actually paid.

REPRESENTATIVES, HOUSE OF. See CONGRESS, UNITED STATES.

REPUBLICAN PARTY. Founded 1854 in opposition to slavery, coupled with support for railroads, free homesteads, and the opening of the West by free labor. Support for the protective tariff was added as an appeal to the manufacturing interest. In 1856, the party nominated John C. Frémont for the presidency. He was defeated, but in 1860, their candidate, Abraham Lincoln, won every free state but could not deter the southern secessionists and the Civil War. After Lincoln's assassination, the party was run by the Radical Republicans in Congress. Capitalizing on a Democratic party in disarray, Republicans occupied the White House for all but eight of the thirty-two years following the Civil War. During that period, the party ceased championing the rights of the freed blacks and became the protector of northern industrialism and banking and Midwestern agriculture. The party had a brief period of progressivism, conservation, and reform during the administration of Theodore Roosevelt but quickly reverted to conservatism with the administration of William Howard Taft. That tradition was maintained by the series of Republican presidents (Harding, Coolidge, and Hoover) of the 1920s. The party went into a long decline after the election of Franklin D. Roosevelt in 1932. Only a World War II hero, Dwight D. Eisenhower, won the White House for the party (in 1952). The next Republican president was Richard Nixon, whose administration ended in disgrace. He was succeeded by Gerald R. Ford, a traditional Midwestern Republican. He was defeated by Jimmy Carter in 1976, but the Republicans scored a major election victory four years later when the conservative Ronald Reagan became president, and the Senate came to be dominated by Republicans for the first time since the early 1950s.

REPUBLICANS, JEFFERSONIAN. Also known as the Democratic-Republicans, the first opposition party under the new national government. In the first two congresses, the Federalist party aroused the hostility of members who opposed that party's championing of the banking and financial segment of the economy. They also opposed the Federalist liking for aristocratic forms and ceremonies. Federalist horror of the French Revolution tended to make the opposition the party of the common man and gave it its title of "Republican." Thomas Jefferson supplied the necessary leadership and philosophy. Organization spread throughout the country, and Jefferson was elected president in 1800. He was succeeded by James Madison, and there ensued twenty years when the Democratic-Republican party was in reality a collection of sectional and personal factions. There was a gradual increase in suffrage; and with the election of Andrew Jackson in 1928, the party was realigned. The more conservative wing evolved into what became the Whig party, and the Jacksonians became the Democratic party.

RESERVATIONS, INDIAN. See INDIAN RESERVATIONS.

RESERVATION SYSTEM, TERMINATION OF. In 1953, the federal government inaugurated a program calling for a speedy end to federal supervision of Indians of five states

and seven other tribes. Despite intense opposition by the Indians, termination laws were put into effect. The program proved to be disastrous and in 1961 President Kennedy halted further terminations.

RESERVED POWERS OF THE STATES. The Tenth Amendment states, "The powers not delegated to the United States ... are reserved to the States respectively, or to the people." The Supreme Court is the final arbiter in case of conflict between a state and the national government over the right to exercise a governmental power. On occasion, as in the Child Labor Cases, the court has declared acts of Congress invalid because they invaded the reserve powers of the states.

RESERVED POWERS OF THE PEOPLE. The Tenth Amendment reserves all powers not granted to the US by the Constitution, nor prohibited by it, to the states, to the states respectively or to the people. Bills of rights to protect the people from government are found in every state constitution, as well as the US Constitution. In many states, the people have reserved to themselves power to propose new laws through the initiative or to require the submission to popular vote of laws passed by the legislature through the referendum.

RESERVE OFFICERS' TRAINING CORPS (ROTC). Created 1916 by the army and 1925 by the navy as a program to train college students to become officers for active duty in wartime. In 1945 the air force created a program. The primary objective of college military training changed from reserve to active duty service; the bulk of military graduates after 1953 were required to serve two years or more of active duty. The unpopularity of the Vietnam War led to widespread and sometimes violent opposition to military training on civilian campuses. Some colleges abandoned military activity altogether, and most of them discontinued compulsory training. In the 1980s, ROTC began a revival and enrollment was 257,000.

RESETTLEMENT ADMINISTRATION. Created 1933 to resettle farmers from badly eroded and submarginal lands. The program was later made part of the Department of Agriculture.

RESIDENCY REQUIREMENTS FOR VOTING. Until 1970, it was typical to require that a person in order to qualify for voting have one year of residence in the state, six months in the county, and thirty days in the precinct. Such requirements had the effect of disenfranchising millions of voters in a highly mobile society. Congress responded in 1970 with legislation that fixed thirty days as the maximum durational residence requirement for voting in presidential elections. In 1972, the Supreme Court ruled that a thirty-day requirement for voting in state and local elections was adequate.

RESORTS AND SPAS. An interest in mineral springs began in the 18th c., both because of their therapeutic promise and because they became a "fashionable indulgence." Early examples were Stafford Springs, Conn., Berkeley Warm Springs, Va., and especially Saratoga Springs, N.Y. Seaside resorts became popular along the Atlantic coast; Long Branch and Cape May, N.J., catered to the gentry from New York, Philadelphia, and the South; and Newport, R.I., the most fashionable of them all. Mountain resorts included those in the Adirondacks, Berkshires, the Catskills, and the southern Appalachians. As the West was settled, hotels and sanitariums played a significant role in the growth of such cities as Denver and Colorado Springs, San Diego, Pasadena, and Los Angeles, Tucson and Phoenix, and El Paso and San Antonio. Florida also became a major resort area; its buildup as a winter resort was the work of entrepreneurs who mixed railroading and the hotel business. Winter sports became popular in the 1930s, and such ski resorts as Lake Placid, N.Y., and Sun Valley, Idaho, became fashionable winter resorts. Vermont, New Hampshire, and Colorado later became popular ski resorts.

RESTRAINT OF TRADE. The Sherman Antitrust Act of 1890 declared every contract, combination, or conspiracy in restraint of trade or commerce to be illegal. Subsequent legislation dealt more specifically with abuses in restraint of trade. The Clayton Antitrust Act (1914) declared price discrimination illegal when it undermined competition, and outlawed such other restraints as tying and exclusive dealing arrangements. The Federal Trade Commission was created in 1914 to maintain fair competition, and the Robinson-Patman Act of 1936 expanded the area of illegal price actions.

RESUMPTION ACT (Jan. 14, 1875). Legislation calling for the reduction in the greenback total and for their replacement by silver coin. The act was opposed by inflationists.

REUNION. A colony founded 1855 near Dallas, Tex., by French socialists. The population reached 300 but was not successful and disbanded in 1867.

REVENUE, PUBLIC. Before 1913, customs duties and proceeds from the sale of public land constituted the major part of the revenue of the federal government; thereafter, taxes on the income of individuals and corporations became the main source. Excise taxes on the sales of such selected commodities as alcohol and tobacco provide an important but lesser source of revenue. State governments have generally depended most heavily on sales taxes, although most have adopted income taxes. Local governments raise the bulk of their revenue from property taxes.

REVENUE SHARING. System whereby the federal government returns to the states a certain percentage of tax money collected.

REVERE'S RIDE (Apr. 18, 1775). Paul Revere, a Boston silversmith, had arranged to signal a warning to patriots in Charlestown when the British began their march toward Concord. He signaled by two lanterns hung from the tower of the Old North Church in Boston. Borrowing a horse in Charlestown, he started for Concord via Medford, alarming the country as he went. He was arrested but released by a patrol of British troops. He returned to Lexington, and witnessed the first shot fired on the green.

REVOLUTIONARY COMMITTEES. Local groups formed immediately before the Revolutionary War by those eager to promote the spirit of independence from Britain. They were the chief agencies responsible for calling the First Continental Congress in 1774.

REVOLUTIONARY WAR (1775–83). War by which the thirteen American colonies won their independence from Great Britain. Its causes were both economic and political, and between 1770 and 1773, incidents in the colonies escalated the mutual suspicions already generated. Most colonists continued to disclaim independence and only reluctantly accepted the idea of separation from the British Empire. John Locke's familiar compact theory of government provided the theoretical justification for independence as a last resort, an important consideration for a people who were essentially conservative politically.

In 1774, a congress of the colonies met at Philadelphia and debated the issue of the rights of colonies in respect to their responsibilities to the mother country. By the time the Second Continental Congress met, on May 5, 1775, hostilities had already begun. Blood had been shed at Lexington and Concord and colonial militias were being organized and armed. On June 15, George Washington was named commander of the American army, the Revolution had begun, but its objectives were still unresolved. Conservatives still hoped for conciliation, but relations with Britain deteriorated. On July 4, 1776, the Congress adopted a DECLARATION OF INDEPENDENCE, thereby setting the course of the Revolution. Within the colonies, however, there remained a substantial number of LOYALISTS who refused to countenance separation from Britain. Early clashes with the British were not encouraging to the patriots, but the American victory at Saratoga in 1777 can be regarded as a turning point. It led to the Franco-American alliance that was to prove crucial to the American victory. The American army withstood the ordeal of the New Jersey campaign and Valley Forge, and its fortunes improved when the focus shifted to the South. The YORKTOWN CAMPAIGN of 1781 resulted in the defeat of the British and the subsequent Definitive Treaty of Peace, negotiated in Paris in 1783.

Revolutionary War, American Army in. The Revolutionary army stemmed from the various local minutemen, alarm companies, and volunteers who had sprung to arms to meet the British expedition against Lexington and Concord. In June 1775, the Continental Congress authorized the raising of ten companies of riflemen in Virginia, Maryland, and Pennsylvania as the nucleus of a national army and appointed George Washington commander in chief. In July, Washington took command in Massachusetts; he was joined there by the rifle companies and he formed a Continental Army composed of twenty-six regiments or battalions of infantry with a strength of 728 men each, one regiment of riflemen, and one of artillery, for a total of 20,372 men. The army was to be augmented by volunteers; but by the following March fewer than 10,000 men had volunteered. Washington was forced to rely on local militia units to obtain an adequate operating force, and almost all major actions and campaigns were fought with a mixture of these troops.

Revolutionary War, British Army in. In 1775, the British army numbered only about 32,000 men, of whom almost 7,000 were in America. By 1782, there were about 46,000 troops in the colonies, including German mercenaries and American provincials.

Revolutionary War, American Navy in. The American navy at its height consisted of twenty-seven men-of-war, converted from merchant vessels. Other naval vessels were used as bearers of American products to French and Dutch ports in the West Indies, where they were exchanged for war supplies. The colonial navy even took the war to the British coast: The *Reprisal* took or sank eighteen British vessels in Irish waters in 1776. The capture of Philadelphia by the British in 1777 cost the patriots their main naval base; most of the sizable Pennsylvania navy was also wiped out. (Only Delaware and New Jersey lacked a state navy.) The open advent of France into the war probably averted the extinction of the Continental navy. In July 1778, when the Brest fleet sailed for New York, British ships-of-the-line had to concentrate to offer formal battle. French regularization of supplies abated the securing of munitions via the West Indies, and the navy could concentrate on offensives.

Revolutionary War, Foreign Volunteers in. The ideals of the American Revolution found response in a number of Europeans. About thirty volunteers, under Pierrre Augustin Caron de Beaumarchais, landed at Portsmouth, Va., in April 1777. They were followed by the marquis de Lafayette and his eleven officers in July. Only two remained for service, however: the baron de Kalb and Paul Dubuisson. Other prominent foreigners serving the patriot cause were the marquis de la Rouërie; Pierre Charles l'Enfant, who later designed Washington, D.C.; the Poles Thaddeus Kosciusko, who designed the fortifications at West Point, and Count

Casimir Pulaski; and Baron Friedrich von Steuben, a German.

Revolutionary War, Loyalist Troops in. At times, especially 1780–82, Loyalist troops serving in the British army exceeded patriot troops. New York and New England provided scores of British officers ; and New York alone furnished between 6,000 and 16,000 troops. Between 10,000 and 20,000 royal militiamen enrolled and chose their own officers during British occupations in Georgia, the Carolinas, New York, and Maine. Those in the South experienced the bitterest fighting. Elsewhere, notably in Pennsylvania, Loyalist guerrillas seriously annoyed the patriots, although they were not of major help to the British.

REVOLUTION OF 1800. So-called because the election that year of Thomas Jefferson as president marked the end of Federalist party powers and the beginning of a much more democratic approach to government.

REVOLUTION OF 1828. So-called because the election that year of Andrew Jackson brought a more popular type of democracy than had been previously practiced. (See JACK-SONIAN DEMOCRACY.)

RHODE ISLAND. Founded 1636 by colonists who followed Roger Williams to Providence after his banishment from Massachusetts. The exiles agreed that their government applied "only to civill things"; thus they set a precedent for the separation of church and state and for religious freedom. Other exiles from Massachusetts settled at Portsmouth (1638), Newport (1639), and Warwick (1643). Each of the plantations purchased their land from the Indians. The union of these settlements began in 1644, and the first legislature met in 1647. In 1663, a royal charter was obtained; it gave the colony virtual autonomy. In the 18th c., farming was the principal industry, but sailing, especially the slave trade, was vital to the colonial economy. In the 19th c., the area around Providence became highly industrialized, with textile mills being the most important. The state also became a leader in the silver and costume jewelry business. Since World War II, with the decline in the textile business, Rhode Island industry has diversified. Electronics and tourism are major industries. Pop.: 947,154 (1980).

RHODE ISLAND, COLONIAL CHARTERS OF. Roger Williams secured the first charter in 1644 from the earl of Warwick. It provided for an elected president, assistants, and general court; it guaranteed liberty of conscience. The restoration of Charles II in 1660 made necessary a royal charter, which was secured in 1663. It provided for an elected governor, deputy governor, assistants, and general assembly. Separation of church and state was retained, and suffrage was left to colonial control.

RHODES SCHOLARSHIPS. Established by the will of Cecil Rhodes, South African financier, to provide appointments for study at Oxford University to students drawn from eighteen countries. Thirty-two students from the US are selected annually. Appointments are for two years.

RIBBON FARMS. Narrow riverfront farms of French feudal origin in the Detroit area. A typical farm might be one or more arpents (192.24 English feet) wide and either 40 or 80 arpents (1.5 to 3 miles) deep.

RICE, FORT. Post established 1864 in North Dakota on the W bank of the Missouri R, ten miles N of the mouth of the Cannonball R as protection against the Dakota Indians. In 1878 the garrison was transferred to Fort Lincoln.

RICE CULTURE AND TRADE. The Carolina coast, especially in the Charleston area, was the scene of the earliest attempts at rice culture in the late 17th c.; by the 18th c., it was a major export. By the late 19th c., the bulk of rice growing had shifted to Texas, Arkansas, and Louisiana.

RICHELIEU RIVER. Canadian river flowing N from Lake Champlain into the St. Lawrence R; discovered by Samuel de Champlain in 1609 and called by the French the Rivière des Iroquois. It became a major thoroughfare for trade between New England and New France. It remains an important shipping route between Montreal and New York City.

RICHMOND. Capital of Virginia, incorporated 1742. The town's strategic location at the head of navigation made it a commercial center. For strategic reasons, the state capital was moved there from Williamsburg during the American Revolution, and it soon became the political, cultural, and economic hub of the state. In the 19th c., it became an important railroad terminus and an industrial city. In May 1861, the capital of the Confederacy was moved from Montgomery, Ala., to Richmond. It was beleagured in 1862 but relieved by Gen. R.E. Lee in the Seven Days' Battle. Two years later, Union forces under Gen. U.S. Grant began a long siege that ended with the fall of Richmond on Apr. 2, 1865. Postwar recovery was relatively rapid, thanks largely to the prosperous tobacco industry, which was also to soften the effects of the Great Depression. Pop.: 219,214 (1980).

RICHMOND, BATTLE OF (Aug. 29–31, 1862). Defeat of Union forces under Gen. Edmund Kirby-Smith at Richmond, Ky., on their drive to take Lexington.

RICHMOND, CAMPAIGN AGAINST (1864–65). In May 1864, Gen. U.S. Grant and his Union army crossed the Rapidan R and entered the Wilderness, a dense forest in Orange and Spotsylvania counties. Gen. R.E. Lee's much smaller army contested the Union army for eleven months. Furious confrontations took place, including the battles of the Wilderness, Spotsylvania Court House, North Anna River, and Cold Harbor. Grant crossed the James R in June 1864 and attempted to take Richmond via Petersburg. Failures reduced his operations to a nine-months siege of Petersburg. By the following spring, it was necessary for Lee's army to evacuate Petersburg and abandon further defense of Richmond, Apr. 2, 1865. Lee's troops were surrounded at Appomattox and compelled to surrender. Thus ended the Civil War and the Confederacy.

RICHMOND JUNTO. A group headed by Thomas Ritchie that controlled Virginia Democratic politics for more than twenty-five years in the first half of the 19th c. Strongly states' rights in tone, the junto played a large part in defeating Martin Van Buren for the Democratic presidential nomination in 1844.

RICH MOUNTAIN, BATTLE OF (July 11, 1861). Confederate defeat in western Virginia.

RIDGELY, FORT. Established 1853 on the N bank of the Minnesota R to guard Sioux on nearby reservations. It was successfully defended in the 1867 SIOUX UPRISING IN MINNESOTA.

RIFLE. German gunsmiths working in Pennsylvania in the late 18th c. developed from a German model the uniquely American long rifle, also known as the Kentucky rifle. In 1803, the US army first used the rifle, although the unrifled musket continued to dominate the battlefield until the introduction of the rifle-musket, Model 1855, which fired the lead Minié bullet. During the Civil War, many types of breech-loading rifles and carbines were used. Later Model 1873 became the simple and dependable single-shot weapon long standard in the army. A five-shot, bolt-action rifle, Model 1892, replaced it. Model 1892 in turn was replaced by Model 1903, which was the army standard until World War II. It was replaced by the semiautomatic M1 Garand. The M14, which replaced it in 1957, was based on the M1 but was fitted with a twenty-round detachable magazine and a selector switch for fully automatic firing. In 1967, Rifle M16 A1 was adopted.

RIFLE, RECOILLESS. A lightweight, air-cooled, manually operated, breech-loading, single-shot weapon used primarily against tanks and secondarily against fortifications and personnel. It was first developed by the Germans in World War II. The rifle remains motionless when fired.

RIGHT OF SEARCH. See VISIT AND SEARCH.

RIGHT-TO-WORK LAWS. Laws providing that no worker may be required to join a union as a condition of employment. Many such laws were passed during the 1940s and 1950s.

RILEY, FORT. Built 1853 on the N bank of the Kansas R in Kansas; it became important in frontier defense. By 1981, it occupied 56,000 acres.

RINGGOLD-RODGERS EXPLORING EXPEDITION. Naval expedition under the command of Commander Cadwalader Ringgold. It sailed from Norfolk, Va., in 1853 and explored the W Pacific from Tasmania N to Herald Island in the Arctic Ocean. Later it surveyed the Hawaiian and Society islands and the coast of Japan. In 1854, Ringgold fell ill, and Commander John Rodgers assumed command. The survey ended in 1859.

RIO DE JANEIRO CONFERENCE (1947). A meeting of the American republics, resulting in a mutual defense pact known as the Pact of Rio.

RIO GRANDE. River forming the boundary separating the US and Mexico for a distance of 1,300 miles. Known in Mexico as the Rio Bravo del Norte, it is 1,885 miles long but is navigable only for a short distance from its mouth. Its waters have been important for irrigation in the arid Southwest from prehistoric times.

RIO GRANDE, ENGLISH COLONY ON THE. Settlement founded 1834 on the Rio Grande by a colony of English under the sponsorship of John Charles Beales. When Gen. Santa Anna crossed the Rio Grande in 1836 to fight the Texas revolutionaries, the colonists fled to Matamoros. All but two women and three children were massacred by Comanche. The women eventually were ransomed but the children died.

RIO GRANDE, SIBLEY'S OPERATION ON THE (1861–62). Unsuccessful attempt by Confederate forces, under Gen. H.H. Sibley to drive Union soldiers from New Mexico. Despite initial successes, Sibley eventually was forced to retreat into Texas; he had lost over 500 men.

RIO, PACT OF. See RIO DE JANEIRO CONFERENCE.

RIPLEY, FORT. Established 1849 on the W bank of the Mississippi R near the Crow Wing R in what is now Minnesota. Built to control the Winnebago reservation. Abandoned 1877.

RIPPER LEGISLATION. Acts of state legislatures whereby local officials of one party are turned out of office and replaced by political opponents. Civil service protection is sometimes sidestepped by cutting an agency's budget and forcing layoff of staff. Forced early retirement is another such tool.

RIVER AND HARBOR IMPROVEMENTS. The First Congress enacted legislation for the "establishment and support of the Light-houses, Beacons, Buoys, and Public Piers," and since that time such improvements have been the primary responsibility of the federal government. The US Military Academy, established 1802, regularly turned out personnel for the US Army Corps of Engineers, which became the primary agency for roads, canals, dams, and other flood-control projects. In addition, Congress created such special organizations as the Mississippi River Commission, the Missouri River Commission, and the California Debris Commission. By the beginning of the 20th c., a trend toward comprehensive planning and multiple-purpose projects was discernible. The Intracoastal Waterway, authorized in 1909, was to connect all ports from Boston to the Rio Grande. In 1917, flood-control work on the Mississippi was formally recognized as a national responsibility. In 1927, the army undertook a comprehensive survey of the multiple-use potentialities of the nation's rivers, and in 1936 nationwide flood-control activities became a function of the corps. Numerous dams, reservoirs, and canalizations, often against great opposition from environmentalists, resulted.

RIVERMEN OF THE OHIO. Operators of flatboats and keelboats who transported the immigrants headed for the Ohio Valley. Mike Fink was the legendary one.

RIVER NAVIGATION. Early river travel by the Indians was by bullboats (coracles), bark canoes, and pirogues; to these whites added bateaux, keelboats, and barges. Even sailboats were employed. Flatboats (arks or Kentucky boats) were built at the headwaters for the downstream transportation of produce, coal, cattle, and immigrants. Regular packet boats were rare in the western waters, but in the East they existed on the Hudson and Delaware rivers. Both the Spanish and the Americans in turn maintained gunboats on the Mississippi. Robert Fulton's *Clermont* was launched on the Hudson in 1807, but it was not until Henry Shreve's *Washington* was launched in 1816, with its boilers on the deck, that a craft was found suitable for western river navigation. By 1850, railroads had begun to sap the trade from the steamboats and canals. However, barges came into general use for carrying heavy goods and were towed by steamboats.

RIVER TOWNS OF CONNECTICUT. Windsor, Hartford, and Wethersfield, together with Springfield until it was discovered that it lay in Massachusetts. They were settled 1635–36 by groups from the Massachusetts Bay Colony. English proprietors, headed by the earl of Warwick, attempted to establish control over the area. John Winthrop was sent (1635) as governor, and a fort was built at Saybrook. The settlers rejected efforts to govern them from London, and a federation was formed. It evolved into the commonwealth of Connecticut.

RIVINGTON'S GAZETTE. Published in New York City from 1773–83, it became one of the more important colonial newspapers. Strongly Tory, it was useful to the British during their occupation of the city; it did not survive the American victory.

ROADS. As early as 1639, the Massachusetts Bay Colony ordered that roads be laid out. The 18th c. saw the inauguration of stagecoach passenger and mail service over public roads, and the movement to the West depended on reliable roads, the WILDERNESS ROAD being an early example. The new US government in 1802 provided for the building of an East-West road that was eventually to become the National (or Cumberland) Road. In 1792–94, a sixty-six-mile macadamized toll road was built between Philadelphia and Lancaster, the first of a number of toll roads. Shortly after settlers arrived on the Pacific coast, they began to clamor for a safe and practical overland route to serve until a railroad could be built. In 1857, the postmaster general was authorized to provide funds for what became the Butterfield, or Southern Overland, route. In 1860, it was extended N from San Francisco to Portland. The advent of the automobile created new demands for reliable roads, from local farm to market roads to transcontinental highways. Between 1912 and 1930, the LINCOLN HIGHWAY was constructed across the nation. By that time, a nationwide system of roads was in place. The HIGHWAY ACT of 1956 created the Highway Trust Fund for the construction of an interstate highway system and to aid local governments in road building.

ROANOKE, SETTLEMENT AT. See RALEIGH'S PATENT AND FIRST COLONY; RALEIGH'S LOST COLONY.

ROBBER BARONS. Widely used to describe big businessmen of the late 19th c., characterized by a ruthless and unscrupulous drive for monopoly and economic power.

ROBINSON, FORT. Built 1874 on the White R at the Red Cloud agency in Nebraska; used to maintain order among the Sioux warriors recently settled there.

ROBINSON-PATMAN ACT (1936). Passed to protect independent merchants against the preferential wholesale prices of chain stores. It permitted manufacturers to establish a list, or fair, price for items below which they could not be sold.

ROCHESTER. City in New York situated on both sides of the Genesee R near Lake Ontario. A small French fort occupied the site in the 18th c., and the town burgeoned after the opening of the Erie Canal. The city is noted for its tailoring companies and for Eastman-Kodak, which makes it the nation's photographic capital. Pop.: 241,741 (1980).

ROCKEFELLER FOUNDATION. Created by John D. Rockefeller in 1913; by 1981 it had paid out close to $1.54 billion in aid to public health and the medical sciences and to the natural sciences, the social sciences, and the arts and humanities.

ROCKEFELLER UNIVERSITY. Founded 1901 by John D. Rockefeller as the Rockefeller Institute for Medical Research. Simon Flexner, its first director, regarded the investigation of disease as the institute's central purpose; its efforts toward eliminating disease have been on a worldwide scale. It was created a university in 1965, offering only degrees at the doctoral level.

ROCKETS. The prototype of the hand-held bazooka, an antitank rocket widely used in World War II, was created in 1926. The German V-2 liquid-fuel ballistic rocket was a major innovation of that war; and after Germany's defeat, its engineers wre transferred to the US. Both the US and the Soviet Union began intensive rocket development in the 1950s, and both developed intercontinental ballistics missiles (ICBMs) capable of carrying nuclear warheads. In the 1960s, silo-sited and nuclear-submarine-based missiles became a reality; and after 1958, rocket carriers were developed for space missions. Rockets carried men into space, landed men on the moon, and launched planetary probes.

ROCKY MOUNTAIN FUR COMPANY. In business from 1822 to 1834, it was the first to depend primarily on directly trapping beaver rather than by trading with Indians.

ROCKY MOUNTAINS. Vast system that extends from N Mexico to NW Alaska, for 3,000 miles, and forms the continental divide. Spanish pioneers first saw the Rockies in 1540. The presence of precious metals induced the earliest explorations, and trappers and fur traders were the real trailblazers; their pack trains and wagons broke the practicable trails into and over the mountains. Meriwether Lewis and William Clark explored them in 1804–06, as did Zebulon Pike (1806–07). Gold discoveries during the 1850s led to permanent settlements in the Rockies.

RODEOS. Cattle roundups in the American West. During the 1870s and 1880s, as many as 300 riders would gather to collect cattle from the open ranges to be driven to market. Calves would be branded, and strays returned to their proper ranges. Eventually these roundups became festivals of a sort, with various competitions. Out of this grew the professional rodeo; today they draw millions of viewers to watch steer and bronco riding, wild-cow milking, bulldogging, and calf-roping.

RODNEY'S RIDE. In 1776, Caesar Rodney, a Delaware delegate to the Continental Congress, made an eighty-mile dash on horseback from Delaware to Philadelphia in order to cast his vote for independence.

RODRÍGUEZ-CHAMUSCADO EXPEDITION (1580–81). Exploration by Spanish Franciscans across the Rio Grande into New Mexico. They visited Indian towns, and several members, left behind to found missions, were murdered by hostile Indians.

ROGERENES. A nonconformist sect founded ca. 1775 by John Rogers in Connecticut. They believed in separation of church and state and a literal interpretation of the New Testament. They were persecuted by the Connecticut au-

thorities. The sect died out in the first quarter of the 19th c.

ROGERS' RANGERS. Corps of the British-American army during the French and Indian War, commanded by Maj. Robert Rogers. The 600 frontiersmen conducted scores of raids and escaped extermination by a superior French force near Ticonderoga.

ROMAN CATHOLIC CHURCH. See CATHOLICISM.

ROOSEVELT COROLLARY. Set forth by President Theodore Roosevelt in 1904 declaring US right to intervene in Latin American affairs in order to forestall European intervention. It was allegedly a responsibility flowing out of the MONROE DOCTRINE. Presidents Taft and Wilson used it to justify financial controls and interventions.

ROOT ARBITRATION TREATIES (1908–09). Twenty-five bilateral nonaggression pacts negotiated by Secretary of State Elihu Root.

"ROOT, HOG OR DIE." An expression originating in the 19th c., based on the hog's habit of digging for food. It means "Work or starve."

ROOT-TAKAHIRA AGREEMENT (1908). US-Japanese agreement calling for a continuation of the Open Door policy and the independence and integrity of China.

ROSALIE, FORT. Erected 1716 by the French at the site of present Natchez, Miss. It became the headquarters of the Natchez military district in 1722. Destroyed by the Indians and rebuilt, it remained an important French fort until 1763. The British renamed it Fort Panmure.

ROSEBUD INDIAN RESERVATION. Established 1890 in SW South Dakota as home of the Brulé Sioux.

ROSENBERG CASE. In 1951 Julius Rosenberg and his wife Ethel were sentenced to death for furnishing vital information on the atomic bomb to Soviet agents. Evidence was supplied by Ethel Rosenberg's brother, David Greenglass, who was himself sentenced to fifteen years' imprisonment. Despite worldwide appeals to President Eisenhower for leniency, the Rosenbergs were executed at Sing Sing Prison on June 19, 1953. Controversy continues over the case.

ROSS, FORT. A Russian trading post established 1812 on the Pacific Coast, about fifty miles N of San Francisco. It was never successful and was sold in 1841 to John Sutter.

ROUGH RIDERS. Popular name for the cavalry volunteers recruited by Leonard Wood and Theodore Roosevelt for service in the Spanish-American War. Won great public acclaim with their storming of San Juan Hill, in Cuba.

ROUNDUP. See RODEOS.

ROUSE'S POINT BOUNDARY CONTROVERSY. US-British dispute over the New York-Canadian boundary, eventually settled by the WEBSTER-ASHBURTON TREATY of 1842.

ROYAL COLONIES. Except for Connecticut and Rhode Island, the thirteen colonies began as chartered, or proprietary, provinces; but beginning with Virginia in 1624, most of the charters were surrendered to the crown and they became royal colonies. At the time of the Revolution, only Connecticut, Maryland, Pennsylvania, and Rhode Island retained their earlier forms of government. In royal colonies, the king was represented by a royal governor, but each colony also had an elected assembly. That opened the way for popular government, and by 1764 the colonies were essentially self-governing.

ROYAL DISALLOWANCE. Despite the autonomy of the ROYAL COLONIES, the Privy Council had the power to approve or disallow colonial legislation (except in Connecticut and Rhode Island). Few laws were disallowed.

RUBBER INDUSTRY. The practical beginning of the industry was the discovery in 1839 of the vulcanization process by Charles Goodyear. Between 1849 and 1900, the industry's output of manufactured goods (chiefly footwear, mechanicals for use with machinery, proofed and elastic goods, surgical goods, bicycle tires, and toys) increased from $3 million to $53 million. Rubber proved indispensable to the automobile industry, and by World War I the industry was dominated by the big four: Goodyear, Goodrich, Firestone, and US Tire and Rubber. General Tire and Rubber, founded 1915, became the fifth giant in the industry. Akron, Ohio, became the center of rubber manufacture. During World War II, US production of synthetic rubber increased a hundredfold, and about three-fifths of America's needs were being met by synthetics. After the war, the use of synthetics continued to rise.

RUBÍ'S TOUR. In 1766–68, the marqués de Rubí inspected the northern border of New Spain from Texas to Sonora. He made a number of proposals (most later put into effect) for better protection against Indian attacks.

RULES OF THE HOUSE. The set of rules, adopted anew by each Congress, by which the House of Representatives conducts its business. Extensive changes were made in 1970: television coverage was allowed at committee hearings, roll-call votes were made public, and the rights of the minority party were strengthened. Later, live TV coverage of House sessions was permitted. The complete compilation of House rules and precedents fill eleven volumes.

"RUM, ROMANISM AND REBELLION." See BURCHARD INCIDENT.

RUMSEY'S STEAMBOAT. In 1787 James Rumsey designed a boat propelled by water forced out through the stern by a pump operated by a steam engine. A prototype was built in England, but Rumsey died before its successful trial on the Thames R.

RUM TRADE. Began in the New England colonies in the 17th c. Lumber and fishing industry traders sold their products in the West Indies, being paid in molasses. The manufacture of rum from that molasses became one of the earliest New England industries. It became one part of the triangular trade: molasses to New England, rum to Africa, slaves to the West Indies. The Molasses Act of 1733 attempted to limit this trade, and smuggling reached enormous proportions. More stringent efforts to control the rum trade were made in 1763, and those efforts are recognized as one of the principal causes of the American Revolution.

RURAL FREE DELIVERY (RFD). Service initiated in 1898 to bring mail directly to rural people. Within a decade, virtually every part of the nation was receiving mail delivery.

RURAL POST ROADS ACT (1916). Passed to provide aid to the states by the federal government in the construction of rural post roads.

RUSSELL, MAJORS, AND WADDELL. Firm founded 1854 to carry government supplies from Fort Leavenworth, Kans., to the Plains and mountain army posts. The firm expanded quickly, and absorbed other stage lines. In 1860–61, operated the Pony Express, which bankrupted the firm.

RUSSELL SAGE FOUNDATION. One of America's oldest general-purpose foundations, formed 1907 by the wife of Russell Sage, for the improvement of social and living conditions. Its original endowment, later added to, was $10 million.

RUSSIA, US RELATIONS WITH. Russia was a British ally during the American Revolution and did not formally recognize the US until 1809. In 1824, the US and Russia signed a treaty that specified trading rights in the North Pacific. Russia refused to meddle in the US Civil War. Hints of a willingness to sell Alaska were eagerly accepted, and the agreement was signed in 1867. After the Boxer Rebellion in China, Russia continued to occupy Manchuria. In the ensuing war, the US sided with Japan. At the Portsmouth Conference (1905), Theodore Roosevelt hammered out an agreement unfavorable to Russia. With the fall of the Romanov dynasty in 1917, the US recognized the provisional government that replaced the czarist regime. The subsequent takeover by the Bolsheviks, who took Russia out of World War I, resulted in US nonrecognition. In 1933, the US established normal relations with the Soviet Union; but the 1939 Soviet agreement with Nazi Germany, the attack on Finland, and the seizure of the Baltic states again strained relations. When Germany invaded Russia in 1941, the US gave support on a cash-and-carry basis. By the end of World War II, $9.5 billion in US aid had been furnished. The US and the Soviet Union were wary allies; seeds of distrust were laid and they have remained to this day.

The end of World War II saw the disintegration of US-Soviet harmony and the beginning of the COLD WAR. The next decade saw the failure of the Soviet attempt to blockade Berlin (1948), the creation of the North Atlantic Treaty Organization (NATO, 1949), and the belated countercoalition, the Warsaw Pact (1955). In 1950, the attack on South Korea led the US into armed conflict with Soviet-supported powers, Even so, it was Soviet initiatives that helped bring about an armistice in 1953. Joseph Stalin's death in 1953 led to a lessening of tensions resulting in the visit of Nikita Khrushchev to the US and the "spirit of Camp David" summit with President Eisenhower in 1959. Relations worsened in 1960, when the Soviets shot down an American spy plane over Russia, and a 1961 meeting between Khrushchev and President Kennedy failed to produce any agreement on Berlin. In retaliation, the East Germans built the wall sealing off East Berlin from the West. The most serious confrontation since the Berlin blockade occurred in 1962 with the CUBAN MISSILE CRISIS. War was averted, and shortly thereafter relations again improved. A nuclear test ban treaty was signed in 1963, the Strategic Arms Limitation Treaty (1972), the Helsinki agreement on European security and cooperation (1975), all in the spirit of détente. But shortly thereafter, relations again worsened. The Soviet invasion of Afghanistan (which led to US withdrawal from the 1980 Moscow Olympics), its continuing harsh treatment of dissidents and Jews in its own country, and its indirect involvement in Africa, Central America, and the Middle East, all contributed to the bad relations with the US. The conservative administration of Ronald Reagan was less disposed to negotiate with the Soviet Union. Each side denounced the other with increasing vehemence, and each side, more importantly began massive arms buildups. Virtually all arms treaty negotiations were ended, and the relations between the two superpowers were worse than they had been at any time since the cold war. Moscow announced that Soviet athletes would not compete in the 1984 Los Angeles Olympics.

RUSSIAN CLAIMS. The creation of the Russian-American Co. in 1799 was the basis of subsequent Russian claims in North America. They extended from Alaska down the coast to California, where a Russian colony in present

Marin County was established in 1809. Russian colonization of North America was never successful; and in 1867, with the sale of Alaska to the US, Russia gave up all American claims.

RUSTLER WAR (1892). Confrontation in Johnson County, Wyo., between cattlemen and men they claimed were cattle thieves. Hiring professional gunmen, the cattlemen confronted the alleged thieves but soon were besieged on a ranch by a force of 200 men. They were relieved by a cavalry force. The cattlemen were delivered over to civil authorities but all were acquitted.

RUTGERS UNIVERSITY. Founded 1771 as Queens College in New Brunswick, N.J. It was affiliated with the Dutch Reformed church for more than a century. In 1864, it became New Jersey's land-grant college, and in 1945 it officially became the state university. It also maintains campuses at Newark and Camden.

RYSWICK, PEACE OF (1697). Treaty that ended King William's War between the English and French and the Iroquois and French.

SABINE CROSSROADS, BATTLE AT (Apr. 8, 1864). Confederate victory about forty miles S of Shreveport, La.

SACCO-VANZETTI CASE. Two alien anarchists, Nicola Sacco and Bartolomeo Vanzetti, were convicted of a payroll holdup and murder in South Braintree, Mass., in 1920. The case achieved great notoriety, and the court was widely accused of not giving the men a fair trial. After numerous appeals failed, both men were executed in 1927. Today, the guilt of the men is still unestablished, but scholarly legal opinion overwhelmingly holds that the case was not fairly administered.

SACHEM. Inherited chiefdom (through the female line) among the Iroquois. The Onondago had fourteen sachems; the Mohawk and Oneida, nine each; the Cayuga, ten; and the Seneca, eight. A great council of sachems deliberated on all external affairs affecting the tribes.

SACKVILLE-WEST INCIDENT. During the presidential campaign of 1888, Lionel Sack-ville-West, British minister at Washington, expressed in a letter his preference for the incumbent, President Cleveland, over his Republican opponent, Benjamin Harrison. Sackville-West was recalled.

SACO BAY, SETTLEMENT OF. In 1631, a settlement was planted on the Saco R in SW Maine, followed by several others in the area. All were abandoned during King Philip's War in 1675.

SACRAMENTO. Capital of California, located at the confluence of the American and Sacramento rivers. John Sutter established a post there in 1839, and it burgeoned after gold was discovered. The city is connected to San Francisco Bay by a deepwater canal; its industries include meat-packing and fruit processing. Pop.: 275,741 (1980).

SACRAMENTO, BATTLE OF (Feb. 28, 1847). American victory over superior Mexican forces during the Mexican War.

SAFETY FIRST MOVEMENT. Efforts in the late 19th c. to improve safety in US factories. The movement resulted in the various state workmen's compensation laws and in the formation of the National Safety Council in 1913.

SAFETY FUND SYSTEM. Plan initiated in 1829 to protect the financial stability of New York state banks. Each bank contributed a set amount to a fund that would forestall bank failures.

SAGADAHOC. Ancient Indian name for the Kennebec region and river in Maine.

SAG HARBOR. Port on Long Island, New York, used by the British as a military store during the Revolutionary War until destroyed by patriot forces from Connecticut in May 1777. Became great whaling center in the 19th c. Today, a fashionable summer resort.

SAGINAW, FORT. Built in 1822 on the W bank of the Saginaw R in Michigan. Abandoned the next year after a fever epidemic. The present city of Saginaw is on the site.

SAGINAW'S GIG, CRUISE OF THE (1870). After the USS *Saginaw* was wrecked on a reef in the mid-Pacific, five of its men navigated the ship's gig to Honolulu to secure relief. Only one man survived, but rescue operations to the *Saginaw* were successfully carried out.

SAGINAW TREATY (1819). The Chippewa ceded a large tract of land, mostly in Michigan Territory.

SAILOR'S CREEK, BATTLES AT (Apr. 6, 1865). After Confederate forces abandoned Petersburg and Richmond and retreated toward Appomattox, two of their forces were confronted and defeated by Union forces at Sailor's Creek.

SAILORS' SNUG HARBOR. A home for retired seamen established 1801 by the estate of R.R. Randall, a New York City merchant who left a large parcel of Manhattan real estate as endowment. For more than a century, the home was maintained on Staten Island, N.Y.; but in 1976, it moved to new quarters at Sea Level, N.C.

ST. ALBANS RAID (Oct. 19, 1864). A raid into Vermont from Canada by Confederate rangers. Three banks were looted and an unsuccessful attempt was made to burn the town. The rangers escaped back into Canada.

ST. ANTHONY, FALLS OF. A waterfall on the Mississippi R in Minneapolis. Attracted by their water power, settlements grew up there beginning in 1837, and lumber and flour industries developed.

ST. ANTOINE, FORT. French post built 1686 on Lake Pepin (upper Mississippi R). Abandoned 1690.

ST. AUGUSTINE. The oldest settlement in North America, founded 1565 by the Spanish on the Atlantic coast of Florida. When Florida was ceded to the British in 1763, St. Augustine became the capital of East Florida and remained so after the restoration to Spain in 1783. In the early 19th c., it became Florida's leading winter resort. Early center of citrus industry. Today it is a popular resort area. Pop.: 11,985 (1980).

ST. CHARLES, FORT. Established 1732 by the French at Lake of the Woods, Minnesota.

For two decades, it served as a base for explorations of the Northwest.

ST. CLAIR, FORT. Built 1792 between Fort Washington (Cincinnati) and the Lake Erie region as protection against the Indians.

SAINT CLAIR'S DEFEAT (Nov. 4, 1791). Arthur Saint Clair, governor of the Northwest Territory, commanded a large force of American troops to subdue the Indians on the Ohio frontier. Suffered an ignominious rout.

ST. CROIX. River forming part of the border between Maine and New Brunswick. In the 18th c., the precise location of the river was unknown, which led to border disputes between the US and Great Britain. A mixed commission settled the dispute in 1798.

ST. CROIX SETTLEMENT. Colony founded 1604 in Acadia (Nova Scotia) by Samuel de Champlain. In 1605, after scurvy had killed thirty-five of the 100 settlers, the colony was moved to Port Royal (now Annapolis Royal). Later they returned to France, and in 1613 their buildings were destroyed by an English expedition from Virginia.

SAINT-DENIS'S EXPEDITION. In 1714 Louis Juchereau de Saint-Denis led a French expedition from the present Natchitoches, La., into Spanish Texas, thereby establishing a profitable trade.

STE. GENEVIEVE LEAD MINING DISTRICT. Developed in E Missouri ca. 1735 by the English financier John Law. Lead was mined and shipped to Kaskaskia, Ill., and then moved down the Mississippi R.

ST. FRANCIS, ROGERS'S EXPEDITION AGAINST (1759). Campaign of the French and Indian War, led by Maj. Robert Rogers, which wiped out the Abnaki Indians at St. Francis mission village, Quebec. Of the 142 men who attacked St. Francis, 93 returned.

ST. IGNACE MISSION. Built 1671 by the French Jesuits on Mackinac Island; Father Jacques Marquette was in charge. Moved several times and survived until 1765.

ST. JOHN, FORT. Built by the French on Lake Pontchartrain to protect New Orleans from the rear. It was garrisoned at various times by the Spanish, the Americans, and the Confederates. Abandoned after the Civil War.

ST. JOHNS, SIEGE OF (1775). The newly fortified position of St. Johns, on the Richelieu R in Quebec, was the first important obstacle encountered in the American invasion of Canada in 1775. After about two months of siege, the fort capitulated, thus opening the way to Montreal and Quebec.

ST. JOSEPH. City in Missouri, founded 1826 on the Missouri R; original name was Blacksnake Hills. It became an important outfitting stage for the Oregon and California immigrants. It later became a grain and cattle mart; meat-packing, flour milling, and cereal manufacture are important industries. Pop.: 76,691 (1980).

ST. JOSEPH, FORT. Built before 1689 by the French near the present Niles, Mich. The British took it over in 1760. The Spanish held it for twenty-four hours in 1781.

ST. LAWRENCE RIVER. The largest river in North America, explored by Jacques Cartier in 1535 as far as Montreal. With its tributary, the Ottawa R, and with the Great Lakes, it formed the main water thoroughfare from the sea to the interior of the continent. (See also ST. LAWRENCE SEAWAY.)

ST. LAWRENCE SEAWAY. Opened 1959, it stretches 2,342 miles from Lake Superior to the Atlantic and opens the industrial and agricultural heart of North America to deep-draft ocean vessels via three series of locks. The seaway was a cooperative venture between the US and Canada.

ST. LÔ. Town in France, the site of the Battle of the Hedgerows, the opening event of American army activity in Normandy during World War II. The town was captured on July 25, 1944, thereby breaking German defenses in Normandy.

ST. LOUIS. City in Missouri, founded 1763 on the W bank of the Mississippi R by the French. It came to the US with the Louisiana Purchase, and grew rapidly. The steamboat made it an important river port, and iron, lead, and zinc from nearby mines were shipped from the city. Its position as the great river capital of the West was strengthened by the advent of the railroad; by the 1850s, it had become the second largest railroad center in the nation. Today its major industries include aircraft, chemicals, electrical equipment, and iron and steel products. Pop.: 453,085 (1980).

ST. LOUIS, BRITISH ATTACK ON (May 26, 1780). Badly planned attempt to reduce the Spanish and Illinois forces at St. Louis. The collapse of the expedition ended the British menace from the West.

ST. LOUIS, FORT. Built ca. 1682 by the French at Starved Rock, Ill. Later abandoned in favor of Fort Pimitoui (present Peoria).

ST. LOUIS, FORT. Built 1685 on Matagorda Bay on the Texas coast by the sieur de La Salle to house his colony of 180 persons. It was later moved upriver (La Vaca R, probably Garcitas Creek), but sickness, accidents, and desertions plagued the colony. Those few who survived were massacred by Indians in 1689.

SAINT LOUIS MISSOURI FUR COMPANY. Established 1809 to launch hunting and trading expeditons on the upper Missouri R and its tributaries. Although it accomplished a profitable trading and hunting campaign in its early days, it was later badly served by attacks on its forts by the Blackfoot. The company was reorganized, and an 1812 expedition proved profitable. The company was dissolved in 1814. It was succeeded by the Missouri Fur Co.

SAINT LOUIS-SAN FRANCISCO. See RAILROADS, SKETCHES OF PRINCIPAL LINES.

SAINT LOUIS-SOUTHWESTERN. See RAILROADS, SKETCHES OF PRINCIPAL LINES.

ST. MARKS, FORT. Built by the English on Apalachee Bay, Florida, early in the 18th c. By the Definitive Treaty of Peace (1783), it passed to Spain, although a British trading company was allowed to remain. It was used as a blockade-running and saltmaking center by the Confederates during the Civil War. The Union navy launched several attacks against it.

ST. MARTIN'S STOMACH. Alexis St. Martin, a young French-Canadian, was wounded accidentally by a gunshot on Mackinac Island in 1822. He was cared for by William Beaumont, the post surgeon. The patient recovered, but the hole in his stomach did not close; a fold formed a kind of lid that could be pushed aside by a finger. In 1825, Beaumont began testing the time required to digest particular foods by introducing pieces tied to threads into the stomach and withdrawing at intervals. He published his conclusions in 1833, which were important contributions to the knowledge of gastric digestion. St. Martin lived until 1880.

ST. MARYS. The first settlement in Maryland; founded 1634 on the N bank of the Potomac R near its mouth. It was the capital of Maryland until 1694 but declined in the 18th c. until little remained of it.

ST. MARY'S, TREATY OF (1820). The Chippewa ceded to the US a four-mile-square tract at present Sault-Ste. Marie on which Fort Brady was erected.

ST.-MIHIEL, OPERATIONS AT (Sept. 12–16, 1918). The first great American battle in World War I. Obliterated the German salient.

ST. PAUL. Capital of Minnesota, one of the Twin Cities (the other being Minneapolis), situated on the Mississippi R just downstream from its junction with the Minnesota R. Fort Snelling was built in the area in the 1820s, and a settlement known as St. Paul's Landing was founded in 1841. In the 20th c., St. Paul has remained an important commercial and shipping center and is home to the Minnesota Mining and Manufacturing Co. (3-M). Pop.: 270,230 (1980).

ST. PETERSBURG. City on the W shore of Tampa Bay in Florida. It became a railroad terminus in 1888 and is today a resort and retirement center. Pop.: 236,893 (1980).

ST. STEPHENS. Fort built in 1789 by the Spanish at the head of navigation of the Tombigbee R in Florida. It came to the US in 1799.

SAIPAN. Northernmost of the southern Mariana Islands. Heavily fortified by the Japanese,

it was invaded by US marines on June 15, 1944. It took until July 9 to subdue the Japanese. More than 14,000 Americans were killed, and almost the entire Japanese garrison of 30,000 died. Its capture meant that the inner defense line of the Japanese empire had been cracked, and American bombers were within range of the Japanese homeland. The entire Japanese war cabinet resigned forthwith.

SALEM. Town in Massachusetts, first settled in 1626; most famous as the site in 1692 of a wave of witchcraft hysteria, which had spread from Europe. Nineteen persons accused of witchcraft were hanged. By the 19th c., Salem had lost much of its shipping to the larger ports of Boston and New York. Since then, the economy has been based on such diverse industries as shoe and leather goods manufacture and tourism. Pop.: 38,230 (1980).

SALEM. Capital of Oregon; situated on the Willamette R. The first settlement on the site was founded 1840, and the town was laid out in 1854. It is an important food packing and processing center. Pop.: 89,233 (1980).

SALERNO. Seaport in Italy and landing site for Anglo-American forces on Sept. 9, 1943. A strong German counterattack almost succeeded in splitting the Allies. On Sep. 20, German forces started withdrawing to the north, and on Oct. 1, Allied troops entered Naples.

SALES TAXES. They consist of two types: excise taxes and the general sales tax. The excise tax is placed on specified commodities (e.g., alcohol, tobacco). The general sales tax is most often collected at the retail level and is applied to all merchandise; certain items, like food for human consumption, may be excluded. West Virginia first exacted a general sales tax in 1921, and today it is one of the principal sources of revenue of state and local governments.

SALK VACCINE. See POLIOMYELITIS.

SALMON FALLS, ATTACK ON (Mar. 18, 1690). Attack by a force from New France (Canada) on the English settlement at Salmon

Falls, New Hampshire. Buildings and farms were burned, at least thirty persons were killed, and fifty-four persons taken prisoner.

SALMON FISHERIES. Although the Hudson's Bay Co. did a modest salmon business in the 1820s, extensive development of the West Coast industry came in the 1860s. The Columbia R became the center for the industry but eventually salmon fisheries were farmed in all the coastal rivers. By 1890, Alaska had become the dominant producer. In 1930, a US-Canadian fishing agreement was signed, but after World War II, high-seas salmon fishing by the Japanese led to new frictions; in 1953, Japan, Canada, and the US signed an agreement but many issues were left unresolved.

SALT. The American colonies made sea salt at Jamestown and Plymouth, but mostly they imported it from England and the West Indies. Interior America proved to have many brine springs, known as licks (because wild animals gathered there to lick the salt). Salt production began in Scioto County, Ohio, prior to 1800, and ca. 1808 salt was being produced near Charleston, W. Va. New York state produced rock salt. The artificial soda (sodium carbonate) industry came to the US in 1882, and by 1900 accounted for 80 percent of US consumption. About 80 percent of salt produced in the US is still used for industrial purposes. In 1979, US production was 45.8 million short tons.

SALT LAKE CITY. Capital and largest city of Utah, located on the Jordan R thirteen miles E of Great Salt Lake. Founded by Brigham Young and his Mormon followers in 1847. It has been the headquarters of the Mormon church since its founding. Industries include oil refining, food processing, and the manufacture of textiles and electronic equipment. Pop.: 163,033 (1980).

SALT SPRINGS TRACT. A tract of 24,000 acres in the Western Reserve, near Niles, Ohio, granted (1788) to Gen. S.H. Parsons. After his death, the Connecticut Land Co. ignored his heirs, but eventually part of the tract was settled on them.

SALT WAR (1877). A disturbance in El Paso County, Tex., over the free use of the salt

lakes in the area. It developed into a conflict between the Mexican and the American population, in which three men were killed by a mob.

SALVATION ARMY. The US branch of the Salvation Army was founded in 1880 by Evangeline Cory Booth, daughter of the founder in England, William Booth. Membership in 1980 was 414,659.

SALZBURGERS IN GEORGIA. In 1734, seventy-eight Protestants were driven out of Salzburg, Austria, by the bishop. They were settled by James Oglethorpe in Georgia; their settlement on the Savannah R was known as Ebenezer.

SAM HOUSTON, FORT. Army post in San Antonio, Tex. It can be traced back to the Spanish mission San Antonio de Valero, known as the Alamo, which was secularized in 1794. From 1848, it has been used as a US garrison.

SAMOA, AMERICAN. In 1899, the US, Germany, and England agreed to divide the Samoan islands. The six eastern islands came to the US; in 1925 a seventh was added. The governor is named by the US secretary of the interior; the lower house of the legislature is popularly elected; the upper house is composed largely of Samoan chiefs. Tourism and fishing are the main industries. Pop.: 32,000 (1980).

SAMPSON-SCHLEY CONTROVERSY. Public dispute over whether Adm. W.T. Sampson or Commodore W.S. Schley should receive credit for the victory at Santiago (during the Spanish-American War). Eventually, Sampson was declared in charge.

SAN ANTONIO. City in Texas, founded 1718 as a mission and presidio by the Spanish. It was the civil and military capital of Texas during the Spanish-Mexican regime. It was the scene of the assault on the Alamo (1836) during the Texas Revolution. After Texas was annexed, it became the chief military post in a line of forts guarding the southern and western frontiers. Pop.: 785,410 (1980).

SAN ANTONIO MISSIONS. Five mission churches built in the San Antonio vicinity by the Spanish 1718–31; the oldest is San Antonio de Valero (the Alamo).

SAND CREEK MASSACRE (Nov. 29, 1864). Chief Black Kettle of the Cheyenne, having been guaranteed safe conduct by the governor of Colorado Territory, brought his band of 500 to Sand Creek. He was attacked by the militia and about 170 Indians were killed, mostly women and children. The massacre caused further warfare in the Plains.

SAN DIEGO. City in California, a seaport located about twelve miles from the Mexican border. The Spanish founded a presidio there in 1769, but the town that grew up around it was practically extinct when California became a state in 1850. The present metropolis was founded in 1867, and its population boomed after the railroad came in 1884. Today, it is an important aerospace, electronics, and shipbuilding center. It also has important military installations. Pop.: 875,504 (1980).

SANDUSKY. City in Ohio, also the name of the river, bay, and Indian villages in N Ohio. The English erected a post on the bay in 1745 but were replaced by the French in 1751. Both Lower Sandusky (Fremont) and Upper Sandusky were important Indian centers in the American Revolution. The present city of Sandusky (Pop: 31,360 in 1980) was founded in 1817.

SANDWICH ISLANDS. See HAWAII.

SAN FRANCISCO. City in California, founded as the mission San Francisco de Asís by the Spanish in 1776. The trading settlement Yerba Buena (changed to San Francisco in 1848) grew up on the beach, beginning in 1835. New England whalers used the port and for a short period it was under the control of the Hudson's Bay Co. US control resulted from the Mexican War. After gold was discovered, San Francisco boomed, and by 1849 it had a population of 10,000. The city was destroyed by an earthquake and fire in 1906 but was quickly rebuilt. In the 20th c., it became the financial capital of the West and is an important center for corporate headquarters. Pop.: 678,974 (1980).

SAN FRANCISCO DE LOS TEJAS. The first Spanish mission built in Texas; founded 1690

W of the Neches R, near the present Weches. It was abandoned in 1693 but refounded farther inland (near the present Alto) in 1716. In 1730, it was moved to the San Antonio area.

SAN FRANCISCO EARTHQUAKE (April 1906). The first and heaviest shocks came on Apr. 18 and were followed by smaller tremors for the next three days. Serious damage was recorded over a wide area; in San Francisco, buildings crumbled, streets buckled, and gas and water mains ruptured. Fire raged through the central business and residential districts for three days. Some 497 city blocks were razed, or about one-third of the city. There were about 700 deaths, and some 250,000 left homeless.

SAN GABRIEL, BATTLE OF (Jan. 8–9, 1847). Confrontation in the Mexican War at the San Gabriel R near Whittier, Calif. It ended in an American victory. The US troops quickly reoccupied Los Angeles, and three days later the remnants of the Mexican forces surrendered.

SANGRE DE CRISTO GRANT. Vast tract (more than 1 million acres) of land granted in 1844 by the Mexican government to Narcisco Beaubien and S.L. Lee. It was in New Mexico and Colorado and extended from the Rio Grande to the Sangre de Cristo mountains. In 1860, the US Congress confirmed the charter, and it was sold by the heirs.

SAN ILDEFONSO, TREATY OF (1802). Secret treaty whereby Spain retroceded Louisiana to France. Rumors of the transfer led President Jefferson to press for the LOUISIANA PURCHASE.

SANITARY COMMISSION, US. Created during the Civil War for the care of wounded and sick soldiers.

SANITATION. In 1703 a "Common Sewer" was constructed along Broad Street in New York City. In the succeeding years, New York and other towns gradually built more of these sewers. By the 1790s, Boston, Philadephia, and New York were developing elementary water systems. Wooden pipes and primitive steam engines supplied water to the homes of the well-to-do, and occasional hydrants appeared in poorer neighborhoods. The water sources were often polluted, and the frequent loss of pressure combined with bad connections led to contamination. During the 19th c., urbanization crowded the working poor into squalid warrens and created an ideal environment for cholera and other enteric disorders. Health boards emerged, and they occasionally initiated massive sanitary programs that involved removing garbage and dead animals from the streets, emptying privies and cesspools, and draining the many stagnant pools. But the sheer size of the garbage and human waste problems made the fight for a cleaner environment a losing battle. During the later years of the 19th c., water systems were improved and extended, sewer systems began replacing the haphazard construction of individual conduits, and street paving improved drainage and facilitated the collection of garbage. By the advent of the 20th c., the old fears of miasmas and sewer gas were replaced by equally grave apprehensions about germs. Environmental sanitation benefited from the rising standard of living that brought higher standards of personal and public hygiene. Technology solved the problem of safe water supplies through the introduction of rapid sand filtration and chlorination and made possible effective sewer systems in major cities; it facilitated garbage collection and street cleaning and brought profound changes in the food-processing industry.

SAN JACINTO, BATTLE OF (Apr. 21, 1836). Decisive engagement of the Texas Revolution; the Texas army under the command of Gen. Sam Houston surprised the Mexican army under Gen. Santa Anna and defeated it, taking Santa Anna captive. He signed armistice terms under which the other divisions of the Mexican army would immediately evacuate Texas.

SAN JOSE. City in California, established 1777 by the Spanish. It is the commercial and manufacturing center for a rich fruit-growing region; in recent years, factories for making electronic equipment, assembling automobiles, and making farm machinery have been added. Pop.: 636,550 (1980).

SAN JUAN. Capital and largest city of Puerto Rico; first settled in 1521 by the Spanish. It is located on an excellent natural harbor, which was used as a naval base by the Spanish navy. During its colonial period, it was often the scene of battle. Pop.: 535,000 (1980).

SAN JUAN HILL AND EL CANEY, BATTLES OF (July 1, 1898). US victories in the Spanish-American War. Troops under Gen. William Shafter took El Caney, and Col. Theodore Roosevelt's dismounted Rough Riders captured San Juan Hill, which placed the US army in control of high ground overlooking Santiago de Cuba and in position to isolate the city, which surrendered on July 17.

SAN JUAN ISLAND, SEIZURE OF (July 1859). Located midway in the Juan de Fuca Strait, the island was claimed by both the Americans and the Hudson's Bay Co. A contingent of 500 US soldiers invaded the island under the menacing guns of British warships. The American and British governments temporarily settled the dispute in 1860 by arranging for joint occupation. In 1872 William I of Germany arbitrated the matter and settled the boundary line in such a way that the island became US territory.

SAN PASQUAL, BATTLE OF (Dec. 6, 1846). Unsuccessful attempt by eighty mounted Mexicans to stop the advance of US forces under Gen. Stephen Kearney to reach San Diego.

SANTA FE. City and capital of New Mexico founded 1609 by the Spanish as their capital. It suffered severely during the Pueblo revolt of 1680 and was abandoned by the Spanish. Under the Mexicans, it became a trading center. Tourism is its major industry. Pop.: 48,899 (1980).

SANTA FE RAILROAD. See RAILROADS, SKETCHES OF PRINCIPAL LINES: ATCHISON, TOPEKA AND SANTA FE.

SANTA FE TRAIL. An important commerce route from 1821 to 1880. The greater extent of its 780 miles from the Missouri R to Santa Fe, N. Mex., lay across the Plains and avoided the rivers, so that wagons could easily traverse it; it was later extended S from Santa Fe to the Mexican towns of Chihuahua and Durango. The advent of the railroad ended the importance of the trail.

SANTA MARIA. The flagship of Christopher Columbus' fleet of three vessels that reached the New World on Oct. 12, 1492. Two months' late it ran aground and was dismantled.

SANTA ROSA ISLAND, BATTLE ON (Oct. 8–9, 1861). Confederate attack on a Union stronghold on Santa Rosa Island, which was effecting a blockade on Rebel-held Pensacola, Fla. The attack was indecisive and both sides claimed victory.

SANTEE CANAL. Built 1792–1800, it connected the Cooper and Santee rivers in South Carolina. It was never a financial success and was abandoned ca. 1858.

SANTIAGO, BLOCKADE AND BATTLE OF (May–July 1898). A crucial operation of the Spanish-American War. The US navy blockaded Santiago harbor, bottling in and later destroying the Spanish fleet. Meanwhile, land forces won the heights overlooking the city, forcing its surrender (July 17).

SARATOGA (N.Y.), SURRENDER AT (Oct. 17, 1777). Major American victory and turning point in the Revolutionary War. Caused France to enter the war on the side of the patriots. Gen. John Burgoyne's British army had suffered defeat at the second Battle of Freeman's Farm (Oct. 7). Before he could decide his next move, Burgoyne's forces were surrounded by patriot troops under Gen. Horatio Gates. Burgoyne surrendered with the proviso that the British troops be returned to England and take no further part in the war.

SARATOGA SPRINGS. City in EC New York, with more than 100 natural mineral springs. Gideon Putnam founded the town in 1789 and began building the Grand Union Hotel in 1802. Other hotels were built, and the town was a favorite resort throughout the 19th c. Race tracks were opened in the 1860s, and Saratoga Springs became the most famous American spa. Pop.: 23,906 (1980).

SAUGUS FURNACE. Erected near Lynn, Mass., in 1646 to smelt local bog ores. The furnace cast cannon and hollow ware directly from the ore and pig iron. Although never very profitable, it operated intermittently for more than 100 years.

SAULT STE. MARIE. Town on the S bank of the St. Marys R, at the falls (see SAULT STE. MARIE

CANALS). First settled by Father Jacques Marquette in 1668. An important railway and shipping center, and site of numerous industries. Connected by bridge to Sault Ste. Marie, Canada. Pop.: 14,448 (1980).

SAULT STE. MARIE CANALS. Two US canals and one Canadian canal connecting Lake Superior with Lake Huron, also known as the Soo Canals. The first was built in 1855.

SAULT STE. MARIE MISSION AND TRADING POST. Opened 1668 by Father Jacques Marquette; it began early to decline, owing partly to the enterprise of the Hudson's Bay Co. to the north.

SAVANNAH. City in Georgia, located on a plateau overlooking the Savannah R, eighteen miles from the Atlantic Ocean. Settled 1733 by James E. Oglethorpe as the first community in the Georgia colony. It was the capital until 1786. The royal governor fled in 1776 but later restored British authority, and the city remained in British possession until 1783. In 1864, Savannah fell to Union Gen. W.T. Sherman (see SAVANNAH, SIEGE OF). The years 1880-1900 saw economic recovery and some growth. It developed into one of the world's largest cotton and naval stores markets. By the late 20th c., those activities had declined but manufactures included sugar, lumber, fertilizer, paint, roofing, steel products, and gypsum materials. Pop.: 141,634 (1980).

SAVANNAH. The first ship to cross the Atlantic propelled or aided by steam. Built in New York, it sailed from Savannah, Ga., to Liverpool on May 24, 1819, arriving on June 20.

SAVANNAH, SIEGE OF (Dec. 1864). On Dec. 10, Gen. W.T. Sherman began his siege, but the Confederates managed to keep the railroad open to Charleston. Fort McAllister, eighteen miles SW and commanding the southern water approach was captured and connection was established with the Union supply fleet. Greatly outnumbered, the Rebels, on the night of Dec. 20, withdrew into South Carolina.

SAVINGS AND LOAN ASSOCIATIONS. Also known as building and loan associations, cooperative banks (in New England), and homestead associations (in Louisiana), they are mutual organizations. Lenders and borrowers are voting members, and persons placing savings with them are shareholders. A federal law in 1933 provided for nationally chartered federal savings and loan associations; the Federal Savings and Loan Insurance Corporation insures the savings accounts in them; state member associations are not obliged to belong to it, although most large ones do. Associations normally invest about 80 to 85 percent of their funds in mortgages. In the 1970s, they increased their banking services; most, for example, now offer checking accounts and certificates of deposit.

SAVINGS BONDS. Bonds in small denominations were sold to the public during World War I; but sales were then halted until 1935, when "baby bonds" in denominations of $25 to $1,000 were offered to the public. During World War II, defense bonds, later called war bonds, were sold. Savings stamps were offered in denominations of from 10 cents to $5; they bore no interest but could be exchanged for bonds. The stamp program was discontinued in 1970, but the sale of savings bonds continues.

SAWMILLS. By 1634 a sawmill was in operation on the Piscataqua R (between Maine and New Hampshire), and by 1706 there were seventy. Wood-burning steam engines began to be installed ca. 1810, making it possible to manufacture lumber where waterpower was not available. Circular saws, introduced ca. 1850, greatly increased mill capacity. Giant sawmills developed for the most part in the great forest regions W of the Appalachians: in the white-pine belt of the Great Lakes Basin, in the yellow pine area of the South, and in the fir and redwood forests of the Pacific Northwest.

SAYBROOK. Also known as Old Saybrook; town in Connecticut, located on Long Island Sound on the W bank of the Connecticut R. Originally claimed by the Dutch, it was settled in 1635 by immigrants from Massachusetts, who built a fort there as protection for the RIVER TOWNS OF CONNECTICUT. Pop.: 9,287 (1980).

SAYBROOK PLATFORM (1708). Reorganization of the Congregational church; it took away the autonomy of the individual churches and invested it in county associations. They in turn were answerable to an assembly representing the whole colony, thus in effect turning Congregationalism into a form of Presbyterianism.

SCAB. Term of opprobrium for one who takes the job of a union worker during a strike; first used in 1806.

SCALAWAG. Term of opprobrium applied to southerners who joined with the Republican politicians, or carpetbaggers, in the Reconstruction era.

SCALPING. All Indian tribes of the Plains, Great Lakes, Eastern Woodlands, and Gulf cut or tore off part of an enemy's scalp as a trophy of warfare. Natives of California, the Plateau, and the Northwest had practiced scalping, although the practice had begun to fade by the time of the European arrival. Rituals associated with the maintaining of the scalps varied from band to band.

SCHECHTER POULTRY CORPORATION V. UNITED STATES, 295 US 495 (1935). A unanimous Supreme Court decision declaring the National Industrial Recovery Act (NIRA) unconstitutional.

SCHENCK V. UNITED STATES, 249 US 47 (1919). A unanimous Supreme Court decision that upheld the Espionage Act of 1917. In his opinion, Justic Oliver Wendell Holmes made his famous statement that absolute freedom of speech may be curtailed if "the words used ... create a clear and present danger."

SCHENECTADY. City in E New York, founded 1661 on the Mohawk R by the Dutch. The French burned it in 1690, but it was rebuilt. It was an important point on the Erie Canal, and in the 19th c. became known as the Gateway to the West. In the second half of the 19th c., it became famous for its locomotive works and for the General Electric plant. Pop.: 67,972 (1980).

SCHOENBRUNN. Moravian mission for the Delaware Indians, established 1772 near the present New Philadelphia, Ohio. It was destroyed in 1782 during bloody struggles between Indians and white settlers.

SCHOOL, DISTRICT. A small country school organized to serve a particular neighborhood rather than a whole township. It was through the district school that public education was brought to most of the rural population of the nation. By the end of the 19th c., good roads made possible the consolidated school, which has gradually replaced the one-room, ungraded district school.

SCHOOLBOOKS, EARLY. In colonial America, catechisms and the Bible were the most commonly used schoolbooks, although a few small texts and hornbooks of English origins were imported. *The New-England Primer* was in wide use among Calvinists and Lutherans from 1690 until 1800. Noah Webster's speller (1783), grammar (1784), reader (1785), and dictionaries (1806, 1828) long dominated public education. The first text on English composition was published in 1851. History texts tended to stress political and military events and extol American representative democracy. Two especially popular books of reading selections were the *Peter Parley* series and W.H. McGuffey's *Eclectic Reader*, first published in 1836.

SCHOOL LANDS. Congress early made provisions for some of the public lands to be granted to state and local authorities for educational use. Ohio was the first state in which the land grant policy was put into practice (1803). Some states held the lands and proceeds from them as trustees for the townships, while others turned them over to the townships. It was common procedure to require that school funds derived from the sale of such lands be invested in state bonds. Important in making elementary schools possible in communities with a low tax base.

SCHOOLS, PRIVATE. Private instruction was available in Boston by 1630, and in other major cities by the end of the century. During the 18th c., private schools pioneered in teaching modern and practical subjects. Religious schools were opened by the Quakers, Episcopalians, and Lutherans. Jews opened a school in New York City in 1731, and Roman Catholic schools were under way later in the 18th c. The 19th c. saw the spread of the Catholic parochial school system in particular; but in most of the country, an overwhelming percentage of pupils attended public schools. By 1980, slightly over 5 million pupils were in nonpublic schools out of a total school population of almost 47 million. The largest group (about 3 million) attended Catholic schools.

SCHOOLS, PUBLIC. See EDUCATION.

SCHOOL TEACHERS. Teachers were rare in early colonial days; the rudiments were taught at home. Preachers often conducted parish or grammar schools; young college graduates taught school while preparing for professional careers; indentured servants earned their freedom by teaching; and other men and women devoted their lives to education. Girls were generally excluded from colonial public schools; but private schools made progress in educating women. With the founding of normal schools, open to women and chiefly concerned with the training of elementary-school teachers, women replaced men as teachers in the lower schools. It is a tradition that has persisted to modern times.

SCHOONER. A sailing vessel that originated in Gloucester, Mass., ca. 1713. A fore-and-aft-rigged craft with two masts, it was designed for coastwise trade. By the 1880s, it had developed into a much larger vessel, with as many as six masts. Their use declined after ca. 1850, with the advent of steam.

SCIENTIFIC EDUCATION. In the early 19th c., mechanics' institutes, academies, and military schools brought the rudiments of science and engineering to a wide range of scholars. Natural philosophy was supplemented in some of the newer colleges with applied science courses. The US Military Academy at West Point (after 1816) and the Rensselaer Polytechnic Institute (founded 1824) began producing a small but important cadre of professional engineers. Scientific schools, still primarily engineering, were established at Harvard in 1847 and Yale in 1860. Congress aided in the expansion of scientific education with the passage of the Morrill Act (1862), which established the land-grant colleges and the beginning of graduate education. The graduate school, heralded by Johns Hopkins (founded 1876) began the transformation of the American university into a research institution. The phenomenal growth of scientific education in the 20th c. resulted from the increasing demands of a technological society. Beginning in the 1950s, the federal government greatly increased its support of scientific education. Federal support is channeled through the National Science Foundation, the Department of Defense, the Nuclear Regulatory Commission, the National Institutes of Health, and the National Aeronautics and Space Administration.

SCIENTIFIC RESEARCH. See INDUSTRIAL RESEARCH.

SCIENTIFIC SOCIETIES. A broad understanding of the natural sciences was one of the objects of the early learned societies formed in colonial America: the Boston Philosophical Society (1683) and the American Philosophical Society (1743). Numerous groups were founded after the Revolution, and in the first half of the 19th c., they began to become more specialized. The Association of American Geologists and Naturalists (AAGN, 1840) was first, followed by societies of physicists, biologists, amd mathematicians. In 1848, the AAGN became the umbrella group, the American Association for the Advancement of Science (AAAS). Its leadership resulted in the founding of numerous specialized groups. The National Academy of Sciences was founded in 1863; it in turn founded (1916) the National Research Council, which supervised manpower and fund allocation during World War I. The council continued to offer recommendations and attempted to balance support for basic research and applied projects. The American Council of Learned Societies (1916) and the Social Science Research Council (1923) similarly coordinate diverse but parallel professional groups.

SCIOTO COMPANY. A land-buying syndicate established 1787 to buy land in the Ohio Valley. Secured option on the great tract of land N and W of the Ohio Co.'s proposed purchase. The company was active in France; and when the 1792 panic caused the company to default 500 or more Frenchmen were left with worthless options. Congress made good the deeds and awarded them land elsewhere in Ohio.

SCIOTO GAZETTE. Newspaper established in Chillicothe, Ohio, in 1800. It was published continuously until 1939; in 1940, it became the *Chillicothe Gazette*.

SCIOTO TRAIL. Frontier route that followed the Sandusky and Scioto valleys almost due south from Sandusky Bay to the Ohio R through Kentucky to Cumberland Gap. A branch ran SE from the Scioto R along the divide W of the Hocking R to the mouth of the the Great Kanawha R, which it followed into Virginia.

SCOPES TRIAL. In 1925, a high school teacher, John Scopes, was tried for violating a Tennessee law that forbade the teaching of the theory of evolution. The ensuing so-called Monkey Trial aroused worldwide attention. William Jennings Bryan, political leader and fundamentalist, served as a volunteer lawyer for the prosecution. Scopes had as defenders several eminent attorneys, including Clarence S. Darrow. They claimed the law was unconstitutional on a number of grounds. The jury found Scopes guilty, but the Tennessee supreme court later set aside the verdict on technical grounds.

SCOTCH-IRISH. Scottish Protestants who were transplanted to Ulster, Northern Ireland. The migrations from Scotland to Ulster began in 1607 under the sponsorship of James I. By the end of the 17th c., political and religious disabilities caused thousands of these people to immigrate to America. The great influx was greatly accelerated after 1717, when as many as 10,000 arrived in Pennsylvania alone in one year. On their arrival, they tended to penetrate to the frontiers. While they may now be found in every state in the Union (and in Canada), they settled in the greatest numbers in Tennessee, Kentucky, Missouri, Ohio, Indiana, and Illinois.

SCOTT, FORT. Built 1842 on the Marmaton R in Bourbon County, Kans., as an intermediate post between Fort Leavenworth, Kans., and Fort Gibson, Okla. In 1855, the government sold the fort's buildings to settlers, thereby laying the groundwork for the present city of Fort Scott. It is the center for an agricultural and dairy farming area. Pop.: 8,893 (1980).

SCOTT-PILLOW QUARREL. Controversy over whether Gen. Winfield Scott or Gen. G.J.

Pillow should receive credit for the American victories at Chapultepec and Contreras in the Mexican War. After publishing an anonymous and vainglorious account of his military prowess, Pillow was arrested for insubordination and disrespect. He was exonerated but discredited.

SCOTTSBORO CASE. In Scottsboro, Ala., in 1931, eight black teenagers were sentenced to death for allegedly raping two white women and a ninth was sentenced to life imprisonment. The case became an international cause célèbre as various groups, including the Communist party, spearheaded efforts to free the "Scottsboro boys." Finally, in 1937, four of the nine were released, and the other five were given sentences ranging from twenty years to life. Four of them were later paroled and the fifth escaped. In 1966 confidential information came to light that conclusively proved the innocence of the nine defendants.

SCOUTS. White fur trappers and hunters and friendly Indians performed an indispensable service as guides for military campaigns and civilian wagon trains in the West. Among the famous scouts were Kit Carson, Jim Bridger, Bill Williams, Charlie Reynolds, and Buffalo Bill Cody. In the Southwest, friendly Apache scouts actually bore the brunt of many campaigns against hostile Apache, notably in the Geronimo wars of the 1880s.

SCRANTON. City in NE Pennsylvania, located in the Lackawanna Valley, near largest known US deposit of anthracite coal. In the 1980s, Scranton turned out products ranging from plastic appliances to television parts. Pop.: 88,117 (1980).

SCRIPPS INSTITUTION OF OCEANOGRA-PHY. Research organization at La Jolla, Calif., a part of the University of California. It was founded in the 1890s to conduct a systematic biological survey of the Pacific Ocean adjacent to the California coast. Among its fields of research have been physical oceanography, research cruises, and a deep-sea drilling project.

SCULPTURE. Gravestones of 17th-c. New England are the earliest examples of American sculpture. The 18th c. saw the develop-ment of fine wood carving, made use of in furniture making and ship figureheads. After the Revolutionary War, Americans turned to foreign sculptors to produce marble images of their great men. But by the middle of the 19th c., a cadre of native sculptors had developed, including Horatio Greenough, Hiram Powers, and Thomas Crawford. All studied and worked in Italy, as did Henry Kirke Brown, who returned and worked in America. Clark Mills, Erastus Dow, and John Rogers were other talented sculptors of the mid-19th c. With the rise of Augustus Saint-Gaudens and Daniel Chester French, the aesthetics of naturalism was revitalized; France, rather than Italy, became the inspiration of American sculpture. They were the leaders of what became known as the golden age of American sculpture. In the early years of the 20th c., conservatives, represented by the academic tradition, dominated US sculpture. The 1920s and 1930s saw the rise of the Art Deco movement, as represented by Paul Manship. After World War II, American sculpture moved dramatically toward abstract, nonobjective forms. Alexander Calder, David Smith, and Louise Nevelson were prime examples. The 1970s and 1980s saw a wide diversity of styles and media. Found objects, neon tubing, "earthworks," and kinetic machinery were only a few examples.

SCURVY. A disease brought on by the absence of vitamin C, it was diagnosed as early as the 17th c. Seamen were especially vulnerable until lemons and limes were carried aboard ships.

SEABOARD AIR LINE RAILROAD. See RAIL-ROADS, SKETCHES OF PRINCIPAL LINES.

SEALING. Hunting of the small hair seal became important commercially in the late 18th c. American sealing interests have centered largely in islands in the Bering Sea, where at the time of purchase of Alaska herds numbered about 3 million. The rapid rise in the 1880s of pelagic (deep-sea) sealing, which was almost impossible to monitor, threatened the herds. Pelagic sealing was outlawed in 1911 by a treaty signed by Great Britain, Russia, Japan, and the US. Further exploitation steadily reduced the herds and in the 1970s efforts to restrict the killing began.

Twelve nations agreed to give complete protection to some varieties and to restrict the killing of others.

SEAL OF THE CONFEDERATE STATES OF AMERICA. The official emblem of the Confederacy depicted an equestrian statue of George Washington, the date Feb. 22, 1862 (Jefferson Davis's inauguration day), and the motto *Deo Vindice*. Set in silver, it was lost but later recovered and is now displayed in the Museum of the Confederacy in Richmond.

SEAL OF THE UNITED STATES. Also known as the Great Seal, the official emblem of the US government depicts the American eagle, a pyramid, and the Eternal Eye of God, symbols of the Freemasons. The Great Seal is pictured on the US dollar bill. Its design was adopted by Congress in 1782. The seal is kept by the secretary of state and is affixed to important government documents.

SEA OTTER TRADE. The sea otter trade began in the late 18th c. in the Pacific Northwest from the Aleutians to California. The great fur rush was caused by published accounts of Capt. James Cook's last Pacific voyage, 1775–79. The trade came to an end in the 19th c. when ruthless hunting, intensified by firearms, nearly exterminated the animal. An international treaty in 1910 banned the hunting of the sea otter, and the animal had made a comeback by the 1970s.

SEA POWER. For a full century after 1815, a small US fleet supported worldwide ocean trade and fisheries. By 1914, the US was the preeminent non-European sea power. Adm. Alfred Thayer Mahan's theory that naval power and control of the seas are decisive in international politics was widely accepted throughout the world. Since World War I, no nation has adhered consistently to the classic uses of sea power. As a Pacific power, the US followed the classic rules of sea power during World War II. Operating from close-supporting mobile sea bases, elements from all US armed forces advanced amphibiously along the island approaches to Japan. Yet when the US intervened in Vietnam, it foresook transpacific sea-based operations and relied almost totally on land-based forces.

SEARCH AND SEIZURE, UNREASONABLE. The American colonists' hostility to general warrants and writs of assistance is reflected in the Fourth Amendment to the Constitution, which prohibits "unreasonable searches and seizures" and requires that warrants be issued upon "probable cause." This means, in effect, that except for very special circumstances, an officer must obtain a search warrant, which is a written authorization from a judicial official. A person may be arrested without a warrant and may be searched "incident to the arrest" in order to protect the officer from hidden weapons or to prevent destruction of evidence. The Supreme Court has generally approved stop-and-frisk laws that permit an officer to detain briefly a person in a public place and conduct a carefully limited search for weapons. In 1961 (in *Mapp v. Ohio*), the court ruled that the Fourth Amendment is enforceable against the states as well as the federal government and requires the exclusion of evidence that has been illegally secured. By the 1980s, however, this "exclusionary rule" had been severely limited as the court in a series of opinions gave arresting officers more latitude.

SEATTLE. Largest city in Washington, located on the E shore of Puget Sound, on Elliot Bay. Its east side faces Lake Washington. Settled in 1851, its importance as a seaport for lumber grew rapidly after the Civil War. When overland rail connections with the east were completed in the 1890s, Seattle's importance as a shipping and transportation center was established. An aerospace center, in particular the Boeing Corporation, the city also has important fishing, lumbering, metalworking, banking and insurance activities. Pop.: 493,846 (1980).

SECESSION, ORDINANCE OF. The enactment in legal form by which eleven southern states withdrew from the Union in 1860–61. According to the seceding states, they had entered the union by ratifying the Constitution; secession, therefore, was achieved by a repeal of that act of ratification. This was accomplished in each state by a convention.

SECESSION, RIGHT OF. A fundamental principle of the American Revolution was the right of a people to establish, alter, or abolish their government and to institute a new one. Therefore, the southern states were advancing no new theory when they exercised their right to secede in 1860–61. The northern states maintained that the ratification of the Constitution had created a new, sovereign, nonviolable nation. The issue was settled by the Civil War.

SECESSION OF THE SOUTHERN STATES. The election of Abraham Lincoln as president in 1860 created the immediate cause for acts of secession in several of the southern states. Ordinances were passed in Mississippi, Florida, Alabama, Georgia, Louisiana, and Texas. The outgoing president, James Buchanan, believing secession unconstitutional, nevertheless considered himself powerless to act; furthermore he was determined not to risk war by an overt act in protecting federal property in the seceding states or in sustaining the operation of federal laws there. He looked to Congress for compromise; but in the meantime, a crisis evolved at Fort Sumter, in the harbor of Charleston, S.C.: the commandant there refused to give it up to the Confederacy and Buchanan reluctantly sent the *Star of the West* to reinforce the fort. Representatives of the seceded states met at Montgomery, Ala., on Feb. 4, 1861, and organized a new nation. Peaceful secession seemed remote after Lincoln's fateful decision to relieve Fort Sumter, the firing on the fort on Apr. 12, and Lincoln's call for volunteers three days later. This practical state of war compelled the states of the upper South to make a reluctant choice between the Confederacy and the Union. By May 20, Virginia, Arkansas, Tennessee, and North Carolina had also seceded. Opposition to secession in Virginia had led to the separate state of West Virginia. The border states of Kentucky, Maryland, Delaware, and Missouri did not secede.

SECRET SERVICE, UNITED STATES. Created 1865 as part of the Department of the Treasury to suppress counterfeiting. Later, the agency's responsibilities were expanded to the suppression of mail fraud, bank and train robberies, and illicit traffic in whiskey. After the assassination of President McKinley in 1901, it was assigned to protect the president. That role has been expanded to include the protection of presidential candidates, members of the president's family, and former presidents and their families.

SECRET SOCIETIES. Freemasonry, introduced into the colonies from England ca. 1730, has proved the organization that has influenced many similar organizations. Organized for the moral and social welfare of their members, most also perform charitable and educational work. Others include the Oddfellows, the Knights of Pythias, the Elks, the Knights of Columbus, and the Moose. College fraternities and sororities represent another category of the secret society. Today, most of these organizations put more emphasis on their fraternal functions than on their secret rituals. The subversive and revolutionary secret society, so common in Europe, has had an unfruitful field in America, although the prerevolutionary Sons of Liberty, the Knights of the Golden Circle during the Civil War, and the Molly Maguires in the post-Civil War period are somewhat analogous. Antiforeign and anti-Catholic prejudice produced the Know-Nothing party in the 1850s; the Ku Klux Klan resulted from prejudices against blacks, Catholics, and Jews.

SECTIONALISM. The Constitutional Convention bogged down over the question of the economic interests of the South, and manifestations of sectionalism have been present in US political life ever since. In the early 19th c., there were three large and rather ill-defined regions: the North, the South, and the West. Northerners and southerners generally believed that the western lands should be sold to the highest bidder, gaining revenue for the US Treasury. Westerners favored charging settlers only a minimum amount. A profitable trade soon developed between the North and the West, and its expansion depended on a constantly improving system of national roads, canals, and railroads. The North and West demanded that the national government bear the cost; the South objected. The North began demanding a tariff to protect its new industry; the South, trading cotton and tobacco in the world markets, saw such a tariff as a threat to that trade. The tariff issue came to a crisis in 1832 when South Carolina nullifed a tariff law passed by Congress; a compromise resolved the argument. The next great sectional dispute was over the extension of slavery into the western territories; it was settled by the Civil War. After that war, the tariff once again became the most pressing sectional issue. It has become less of a sectional issue today, as industries have become part of every section. Today, the allocation of federal monies and defense contracts are leading issues; the older industrial states in what has become known as the Frost Belt claim that the Sun Belt states of the South and Southwest are receiving an undue proportion of such federal monies.

SECURITIES AND EXCHANGE COMMISSION. Created 1934 to protect the public and investors against malpractices in the securities markets. Those who offer securities for sale must disclose pertinent information before their offering can be registered with the commission as required by law. The commission also supervises national exchanges, brokers, and other investment dealers.

SEDGWICK, FORT. Built 1864 in NE Colorado at the junction of Lodge Pole Creek and the South Platte R to maintain control over the Sioux, Cheyenne, and Arapaho. Abandoned 1871.

SEDITION ACTS. Passed by the Federalist-controlled Congress of 1798, the first such act was intended to halt Democratic-Republican (Jeffersonian) attacks on the government and to ferret out pro-French sympathizers in case of war with France. It was one of the ALIEN AND SEDITION LAWS that helped bring about the defeat of the Federalists in 1800. The law expired in 1801, and during President Jefferson's tenure, all persons convicted under the act were pardoned. Congress voted to repay all fines. The act was generally regarded as unconstitutional; and in 1964 the Supreme Court flatly declared it inconsistent with the First Amendment.

The Sedition Act of 1918 made it a felony to insult the government or to interfere with the war effort. The war hysteria had subsided by 1921, and Congress repealed the law. Similar state laws were generally found to violate the First Amendment. The Smith Act of 1940, while not specifically a sedition act, does prohibit advocacy of forceful overthrow of the government.

SEGREGATION. During the colonial era and early years of the US, white Americans generally kept themselves apart from the Indians. Segregation of the white and black races was a recognized element in the pre-Civil War slave system; and after slavery was abolished, white southerners were determined to continue racial segregation. Laws were passed in the southern states, and in some of the border states, segregating virtually all public conveyances and places. Dual public school systems were established, and neighborhoods and churches were totally segregated. Even in the North, where there were no segregation laws, de facto segregation existed in neighborhoods and certain areas of employment. In 1896, the Supreme Court upheld the state segregation laws in *Plessy v. Ferguson*, which upheld the separate-but-equal concept. Segregation in the North actually increased as more blacks moved there during World War I. Segregation began breaking down in the 1930s, but it was not until the 1950s that real progress toward INTEGRATION began taking place.

SELDEN PATENT. In 1879 George B. Selden made application for a patent for a vehicle propelled by an internal combustion engine; it was finally issued in 1895 and came into the possession of the Electric Vehicle Co. Ten automobile manufacturers agreed, in response to a lawsuit, to pay a royalty. Henry Ford declined, and the courts ruled in his favor.

SELECTIVE SERVICE ACT. See DRAFT.

SELECTMEN. Executive officers chosen by town meetings in all New England states except Rhode Island. Usually there are three in each town, and the office goes back to earliest time. Their functions vary.

SEMICONDUCTORS. See COMPUTERS.

SEMINOLE. One of the Five Civilized Tribes; of Muskhogean stock, they originally spoke Muskogee or Hitchiti. In the early 18th c., they lived along the Chattahoochee R in Georgia, but they began to move into Florida ca. 1700. Their numbers were later augmented by Upper Creek and fugitive black slaves. Although they were town dwellers, they derived their living from farming, supplemented by fishing and hunting. They developed a complex social organizaiton in which military prowess played a major role. The end of the American Revolution brought the Seminole into conflict with Georgia, especially during the War of 1812, when they raided the Georgia border. This led to the first of a long series of SEMINOLE WARS, which culminated in most of them being moved from Florida to a new reservation, the present Seminole County, Okla. In 1901, the Seminole became US citizens. Large oil deposits were found on their land in the 1920s, and in 1964 they received compensation when the Indian Claims Commission ruled that they had been illegally deprived of their lands in Florida. In 1980, there were about 4,000 Seminole in Florida and Oklahoma.

SEMINOLE WARS. Long series (1817–58) of confrontations between the Seminole of Florida and the US. In the first Seminole War (1817–18), Americans under Gen. Andrew Jackson, stationed at Fort Scott, followed the Indians eastward into the Suwannee R area and destroyed all Indian resistance west of the river. In 1821, Florida was transferred from Spain to the US. In 1830 Congress passed the Indian Removal Act, which called for the removal of all Indians to reservations west of the Mississippi. The Seminole, under Osceola, massacred several army companies and devastated NE Florida. This brought on the second Seminole War (1835–42). Gen. T.S. Jesup, commanding US forces, abandoned "civilized" war and seized Osceola under a flag of truce in 1837. By the time he was relieved of duty, almost 3,000 Seminole had been captured and about 100 killed. By 1842, with no more than 300 Seminole left in Florida, the government gave up its efforts to force them to leave. When Florida became a state in 1845, it attempted to expel the Seminole completely. Military patrols vandalized property deep in Indian territory; the foremost Seminole leader, Billy Bowlegs, fought back, thus beginning the third Seminole War (1855–58). In 1858, Bowlegs and 165 of his people surrendered and were shipped west. Later, 75 more migrated, leaving roughly 125 Florida Seminole.

SENATE. See CONGRESS, UNITED STATES.

SENATORS, ELECTION OF. Until 1866, when Congress prescribed a uniform procedure, state legislatures determined their own procedure for electing US senators. Demand for popular election was growing steadily; by the use of the direct primary for nominating senatorial candidates and exaction of pledges from state legislators to support the popular choice, the old system of election was being rapidly nullified when, in 1913, it was formally transferred to the electorate by the Seventeenth Amendment.

SENECA. See IROQUOIS.

SENECA FALLS CONVENTION (1848). The first modern woman's right convention, called by Lucretia Mott and Elizabeth Cady Stanton at Seneca Falls, N.Y. Stanton read a list of many discriminations existing against women, and the convention adopted eleven resolutions, one of them calling for woman suffrage. This convention launched the organized woman's right movement.

SENIORITY SYSTEM. In the US House of Representatives and Senate, members of the majority party with the longest service tend to get the chairmanship of important committees regardless of their ability. The Senate's seniority system dates from 1847, but under the leadership of Lyndon B. Johnson, it was revised in the 1950s to give more choice posts to newer members. The House seniority system dates from 1910.

SEPARATION OF CHURCH AND STATE. The first clause of the First Amendment is devoted to the separation of church and state: "Congress shall make no law respecting an establishment of religion, or prohibiting the free exercise thereof." Most state constitutions have similar restrictions. In many legal cases "establishment" has been the key issue. The Supreme Court has usually followed complete separation, as in decisions forbidding such practices as prayer in public schools.

SEPARATION OF POWERS. See POWERS, SEPARATION OF.

SEPARATIST MOVEMENT. See WESTERN SEPARATION.

SEPARATISTS. Also known as Independents. Radical Puritans in the late 16th c. who advocated thoroughgoing reform within the Church of England; they proposed a congregational, or independent, form of church polity. Each church would be autonomous, independent of bishops and the crown. Several of the early North American colonies were founded by Separatists, including those at Boston, Salem, and Plymouth. Later the term came to be a vague designation of those opposed to Presbyterianism.

SEQUOIA. Genus of coniferous tree found along the Pacific Coast, from California to Oregon. Comprises two species: *Sequoia sempervirens* (the redwood) and *Sequoia gigantea* (the big tree). Their great girth and height make them the largest forest trees in America.

SEQUOIA NATIONAL PARK. Created 1890 in the Sierra Nevadas of E California to protect the giant Sequoia trees, which are among the largest and oldest of living things. Its area encompasses 385,000 acres.

SEQUOYAH, PROPOSED STATE OF. Consideration in the early 20th c. of a state to include the lands of the Indian Territory. Eventually, instead, the Indian Territory and the (white) Oklahoma territories were admitted as a single state, named Oklahoma.

SEQUOYA'S SYLLABARY. The Cherokee alphabet, developed in the 19th c. by Sequoya (George Gist), who was half white and half Cherokee. Using symbols adapted from English, Greek, and Hebrew letters, the syllabary consists of eighty-six characters. It was officially adopted by the Cherokee nation in 1821.

SEVEN CITIES OF CIBOLA. See CIBOLA.

SEVEN DAYS' BATTLES (June 25–July 1, 1862). Succession of battles in which Gen. R.E. Lee's Confederate army forced that under Union Gen. G.B. McClellan to abandon its threatening position E of Richmond and retreat to the James R. Casualties were heavy.

SEVENTEENTH AMENDMENT. Ratified 1913, it called for the popular election of US senators. Previously, they had been chosen by the state legislatures.

SEVENTH-DAY ADVENTISTS. See ADVENTIST CHURCHES.

SEVEN YEARS' WAR. See FRENCH AND INDIAN WAR.

SEVERN, BATTLE OF THE (Mar. 25, 1655). Engagement between the Puritan settlers of Providence (now Annapolis), Maryland, and the colony's Protestant governor, William Stone. Stone was taken prisoner, and for three years the Puritans practically controlled the colony.

SEWARD'S FOLLY. See ALASKA.

SEWING MACHINE. Elias Howe was granted a patent in 1846 for the two-thread, locking stitch sewing machine that became the standard of the industry. Other versions, including the one by Isaac M. Singer, quickly followed. In 1856, the major patents were pooled, and four companies controlled the market until 1877, when the patents expired. The sewing machine was the first widely advertised consumer appliance and revolutionized both home sewing and the clothing industry.

SEYBERT, FORT, MASSACRE AT (Apr. 28, 1758). Attack, during the French and Indian War, on an army post in Pendleton County, West Virginia, by a force of Delaware under Kilbuck (also known as Gelelemend). Seventeen of its occupants were murdered and others carried into captivity.

SHACKAMAXON, TREATY OF. Agreement between William Penn and the Delaware Indians, who met in 1682 at Shackamaxon (now Kensington), the chief village of the Delaware. In 1683, several agreements were made granting Penn and his heirs land in SE Pennsylvania (present-day Bucks County).

SHADES OF DEATH. The densely wooded northern part of the Great Swamp lying some twelve miles SE of Wilkes-Barre, Pa. In 1778, it was the refuge of many survivors fleeing the WYOMING MASSACRE.

SHADRACH FUGITIVE SLAVE CASE. While being held in Boston as a fugitive slave, Shadrach was allowed to walk out of the court and escape to Canada. The incident created new tensions between antislavery and proslavery forces.

SHAKER RELIGION, INDIAN. A nativistic cult started by John Slocum, a Squaxin Indian of Puget Sound, in 1881. He claimed to have died and been resurrected twice. The religion, containing elements of Roman Catholicism, Presbyterianism, and old Indian religions, spread throughout the Northwest and California and is still extant.

SHAKERS. Religious cult founded by Ann Lee Standerin, or Stanley, in 1774. Establishing their first commune at Watervliet, N.Y., in 1776, the Shakers practiced celibacy and performed a ritual dance that often became quite frenzied (hence their name). Spiritualism was an important part of their beliefs. Their membership never exceeded 6,000. Today, they are remembered chiefly for their classically simple furniture and handicrafts.

SHALAM, LAND OF. A communistic agrarian colony established in 1885 in New Mexico. Composed mainly of orphan children, it was a financial failure and broke up in 1901.

SHARECROPPER. Farm tenant who pays rent with a portion (usually half) of the crop he raises. It was once prevalent in the South. A product of Reconstruction, it replaced the prewar slave labor. Working under close supervision, the sharecropper often lacked title to his crop. At harvest, the landlord established the crop's worth, subtracted what was owed him, and remitted the remainder (if any) to the tenant.

SHARE-THE-WEALTH MOVEMENTS. Various mass organizations calling for redistribution of wealth that sprang up during the Great Depression. These included the Townsend plan, Louisiana Sen. Huey P. Long's Share-Our-Wealth Clubs, the National Union for Social Justice party, and Upton Sinclair's End Poverty in California. Mingling utopianism with religious zeal, they adopted such new techniques as national radio hookups and huge conventions characterized by frenzied emotionalism.

SHARPSBURG. See ANTIETAM, BATTLE OF.

SHARPSHOOTER. Member of special volunteer regiments of skilled marksmen in the Union army during the Civil War.

SHARPS RIFLE. Early breechloader, invented by Christian Sharps ca. 1848. First attracted attention in Kansas Border War (1855–56). Widely used by the Union in Civil War.

SHAWMUT. Indian name for the peninsula on which Boston is situated.

SHAWNEE. A tribe of the Algonquin from Tennessee and South Carolina, which ca. 1677–1707 migrated to the Ohio, Susquehanna, and Delaware valleys. Supported by the French and later by the English, the Shawnee led resistance to advancing settlement in the frontier warfare of 1755–95. The Treaty of Greenville (1795) moved them to Indiana; loss of British support as a result of the War of 1812 hastened their rapid dispersion. Today, their main body (about 1,000) is incorporated with the Cherokee in Oklahoma.

SHAWNEE PROPHET. Tenskwatawa, the brother of Tecumseh, founded a nativistic religion strongly influential among the Great Lakes Indians in the early 19th c. Doctrine, similar to that of the Delaware Prophet, predicted return of aboriginal conditions through supernatural means. Indians were to abandon alcohol, and marriage with whites, and live peacefully with each other. During Tecumseh's absence, the prophet led an unsuccessful attack at Tippecanoe (see TIPPECANOE, BATTLE OF).

SHAWOMET. Indian name for what later became Warwick, R. I. Purchased 1642 from the Indians by Samuel Gorton. Massachusetts Bay contested Gorton's ownership and took over colony in 1643. Gorton's claim was later upheld and he renamed it in honor of his protector, the earl of Warwick.

SHAW'S EXPEDITION. In his memoirs, Col. John Shaw claimed that in 1809 he and two associates had traveled from Missouri to the Colorado mountains. There are inaccuracies in his account, and there is no contemporary evidence to support his contention.

SHAYS'S REBELLION (Aug. 1786–Feb. 1787). Conflict arising out of the discontent of small property owners whose possessions were confiscated for overdue debts and delinquent taxes. Spread from Northampton, Mass., throughout New England. Many protestors lacked the property qualifications for voting and had no legal political recourse, and they called for a lightening of taxes and revision of state constitutions. Daniel Shays emerged as the movement's leader. A confrontation with the state militia was avoided in Nov. 1786; but in Jan. 1787, the Shaysites attacked the arsenal at Springfield, looking for arms and supplies. They were dispersed and the rebellion collapsed soon after. Shays escaped to Vermont and eventually was pardoned, as were most of those captured. Governor James Bowdoin was defeated at the next election and reforms in line with the Shaysites' demands were soon made.

SHEEP RAISING. Sheep were introduced into North America in the early 17th c., where they provided wool for homespun clothing. The first merinos were imported in 1801 from France and Spain. With the passage of the Embargo Act (1807), native mills increased and demand for fine-wool sheep (such as the merino) became insatiable. Originally centered in New England, after 1840 the center of sheep raising shifted westward to the Ohio Valley. After the Civil War, sheep raising continued to expand in the West. By 1935, 60 percent were raised W of the Rockies. Sheep raising reached a peak that year: 51.8 million. By 1980, the number of sheep had declined to 12.7 million, about half of which were raised in the western states.

SHEEP WARS. Range battles in the American West between cattle and sheep ranchers. The main cause was that of the grazing habits of sheep, which destroyed the range, sometimes making the lands unusable to cattle herds for months. Sheep also polluted the watering places. By 1875, clashes between cattlemen and sheepmen were regular occurrences along the Texas-New Mexico boundary. In Colorado, Nevada, Idaho, Wyoming, and Montana many men were killed in the bitter wars. They subsided only when the disputed areas were occupied by landowners and with the fencing of the open range.

SHEFFIELD SCIENTIFIC SCHOOL. Founded 1847 at Yale University as the School of Applied Chemistry. Expanded and renamed the Yale Scientific School in 1854; renamed again in 1861 after Joseph E. Sheffield, its great benefactor.

SHELBY'S MEXICAN EXPEDITION (1865). Force of 1,000 former members of the Confederate army, under the command of Gen. J.O. Shelby, who, rather than surrender, voted to go to Mexico and join the army of Emperor Maximilian. They engaged the guerrillas of Benito Juárez who was fighting Maximilian. The unit dispersed at Monterrey; only a remnant under Shelby reached Mexico City. Fearing US displeasure, Maximilian refused their aid. Empress Carlotta gave them land for a colony, which after the overthrow of Maximilian (1867) broke up.

SHENANDOAH. Confederate cruiser, purchased in England in 1864. Captured nearly forty prizes worth about $1.4 million.

SHENANDOAH CAMPAIGN (1864). Coincident with Gen. U.S. Grant's advance (see WILDERNESS, BATTLES OF THE), Union forces in western Virginia moved to clear the Shenandoah Valley and cut Gen. R.E. Lee's supply lines. The Union forces were united for an advance on Lynchburg. Gen. J.A. Early's corps were sent to stop the Federals, move down the valley into Maryland, and threaten Washington. He was successful but was too weakened to breach the defenses of Washington. He withdrew into the valley; late in July, he again crossed into Maryland, destroyed vast supplies, and then safely withdrew. Alarmed by Early's successes, Grant consolidated all Union forces under Gen. Philip Sheridan. Several confrontations between Sheridan and Early ensued, but Sheridan's superior strength eventually prevailed. By mid-December 1864, both Early and Sheridan had been recalled to Virginia.

SHENANDOAH VALLEY. That part of the great valley between the Allegheny and Blue Ridge mountains extending from the Potomac R at Harpers Ferry S to the watershed of the James R a few miles SW of Lexington, Va. The lower valley was settled by English immigrants from tidewater Virginia; the middle valley was settled by Germans; and the upper valley was the part chosen by the Scotch-Irish immigrants, most of whom came from Pennsylvania.

SHERMAN ANTITRUST ACT (1890). The first federal law directed against industrial combination and monopoly. The key provision of the act was incorporated in its first section: "Every contract, combination in the form of trust or otherwise, or conspiracy, in restraint of trade or commerce among the several states, or with foreign nations, is hereby declared to be illegal." The only successful prosecutions under the Sherman Act were against labor unions. During President Wilson's term, Congress passed the Clayton Antitrust Act and the law creating the Federal Trade Commission (both 1914). It is those instruments under which most government antitrust actions have been taken, and the Sherman Act is noteworthy only historically.

SHERMAN SILVER PURCHASE ACT (1890). Provided for the issuance of paper currency guaranteed by silver bullion; it in effect put the nation on bimetal policy. The act increased the circulation of redeemable paper currency in the form of Treasury notes by $156 million; and it accentuated the drain on the government gold reserves by requiring the Treasury notes to be redeemed in gold as long as the Treasury had gold in its possession. The law was repealed in 1893.

SHERMAN'S MARCH THROUGH THE CAROLINAS. In Feb. 1865, Gen. W.T. Sherman left Savannah and proceeded north "to make South Carolina feel the severities of war" and to join with Gen. U.S. Grant in Virginia. By Feb. 17 the army was in Columbia, S. C., which was burned, and by Mar. 10 in Fayetteville, N. C. Opposition increased as the federal troops advanced but they covered 500 miles in eight weeks.

SHERMAN'S MARCH TO THE SEA. Against the judgment of Gen. U.S. Grant, Gen. W.T. Sherman conceived the plan of marching across Georgia from Atlanta to Savannah in order to destroy the food supplies on which the Confederate army largely depended and to break the will of the people to continue the war. On Nov. 15, 1864, he burned Atlanta, preparatory to setting out on his march the next day. With 62,000 men spread out sufficiently to cover a course sixty miles wide, Sherman pointed his course toward the sea. Cutting all communications, Sherman lived off the land through which he marched. His raiding parties ranged widely. By December, he had reached the sea, forcing the Rebel army to flee into South Carolina. On Dec. 21, Sherman took Savannah. Sherman estimated that he had inflicted damages amounting to

$100 million; four-fifths of it was "simple waste and destruction."

SHILOH, BATTLE OF (Apr. 6–7, 1862). One of the bloodiest battles of the Civil War, with losses of more than 10,000 on each side. On Apr. 6, a Confederate army of 60,000 surprised the Union forces at Shiloh Church (or Pittsburg Landing), Tenn., forcing them to retreat across the Tennessee R. The Union army counterattacked the next day, disrupting and confusing the Rebels, who were swept south toward Corinth, Miss. The Confederate general, A.S. Johnston, was killed.

SHIMONOSEKI EXPEDITION (1864). The opening of Japan in 1858 to western trade aroused the opposition of the more conservative Japanese. The lord of the Choshiu clan fired on French, Dutch, and American ships in the Shimonoseki Strait. The USS *Wyoming* sailed to the site and sank two of the Choshiu craft. A $3 million indemnity was extracted from Japan, but the US returned its share.

SHIPBUILDING. One of the leading industries before the American Revolution, especially in New England. Ships could be built in America for about 30 percent less than in England; about a third of ships under British registry were American built. The Golden Age of American shipbuilding (the 1840s and 1850s) saw packets and clippers built on New York's East River and Boston harbor. Bath, Casco Bay, and the central coast of Maine specialized in cargo carriers. After the Civil War, US ships were generally squeezed out of the market, as cheaper coal and iron were available to foreign shipbuilders. Government subsidies in World War I allowed American shipbuilders to overcome these handicaps, but slack demand for new tonnage after the war sent the American shipyards into decline. In World War II, the navy spent $19 billion, building everything from landing craft up to superdreadnoughts and carriers; the Maritime Commission spent $13 billion on 5,777 ships. The end of the war brought another shipbuilding slump. The postwar years produced some distinctive new types of ships: the liner *United States* established a new speed record. The use of nuclear power was initiated by the submarine *Nautilus*; nuclear reactors also powered the giant carrier *Enterprise* and the passenger liner *Savan-*

nab. Foreign shipbuilders took over the major share of new construction, but in the 1980s renewed interest in a strong navy led to increased outlays in ship construction and somewhat revived the industry.

SHIPPING, OCEAN. From early colonial times to ca. 1870, there was little change in the ordinary cargo ships. The conventional major carrier was the three-masted square-rigged ship, or bark. Smaller vessels were also used: two-masted square-rigged brigs for runs to the Mediterranean or the West Indies and still smaller fore- and aft-rigged schooners or sloops for coastal and other short runs. In 1818, the American Black Ball Line began regular sailings from Liverpool to New York, carrying passengers, mail, and fine freight.

In 1838, regular transatlantic service by steam-driven ships began, but ordinary cargoes still continued to go by square-riggers, now somewhat larger. A quiet revolution occurred ca. 1870, with the compound engine, which could profitably carry such heavy cargoes as grain, coal, and sugar. These new freighters gradually drove the square-riggers from their older runs.

By the 1920s, the oil tanker was a prominent part of ocean shipping, and the older type of freighters became known as dry cargo ships. Many tankers were owned by the major oil companies, and many were registered in the merchant marines of Panama and Liberia (to avoid paying high US salaries). Containerization was introduced in the 1960s; shippers assembled the cargo beforehand and sent it aboard the vessel in a single container. By so doing, they saved enormously in wages paid to longshoremen for loading the cargo piece by piece. The most dramatic innovation of the 1960s was the vastly increased tonnage of tankers and bulk carriers. So large were the vessels that offshore loading and unloading became necessary in most ports. Coastal communities, moreover, were concerned with the danger of oil spills, especially after a series of accidents had shown that extensive damage could result.

SHIPS OF THE LINE. Also known as line-of-battle ships, they were the 18th- and 19th- c. counterparts of modern first-class battleships. US ships of the line were about 190 feet long, of about 2,600 tons displacement, and mounted at least 74 guns on three decks. The

America was launched in 1782; in 1813, Congress authorized four more. In 1816, Congress authorized nine, but two were never built. None was ever engaged in battle. The introduction of steam, explosive shells, and armor plate rendered them obsolete.

SHIVAREE. Derived from the French *charivari,* meaning mock music played on pots and pans, it was the custom in rural America, especially in the South, to thus serenade newly wed couples. In New England, the custom was called a serenade or callathump.

SHOE MANUFACTURING. See BOOT AND SHOE MANUFACTURING.

"SHOT HEARD ROUND THE WORLD." A line from R.W. Emerson's *Concord Hymn.* Refers to the opening shot of the American Revolution.

SHOWBOATS. Showboats appeared on the Mississippi and Ohio rivers before the Civil War, and to a lesser extent on the Erie and Pennsylvania canals. Entire circuses were sometimes carried by showboat. In 1925 there were fourteen showboats on the midwestern rivers and one touring Chesapeake Bay and the North Carolina sounds. The last showboat to tour on a regular basis was the *Golden Rod* in 1943.

SHREVEPORT. City in Louisiana, situated on the Red R. It was named for Maj. H.M. Shreve, who invented steam-powered rams to tear a channel through the RED RIVER RAFT, an enormous mass of driftwood that had blocked the Red R to all transportation for many years before 1833. The city was the capital of the Confederate state of Louisiana and the last state capital to surrender to Union forces. Today, it is the center of a major petroleum and gas-producing area and has furniture and paper-making factories. Pop.: 205,815 (1980).

SHREVEPORT RATE CASE (*Houston, E. and W.T.R. Company v. United States*), 234 US 342 (1914). The Supreme Court ruled that the Interstate Commerce Commission may override intrastate rates if interstate commerce is affected.

SIBERIAN EXPEDITION (1918–20). Invasion and occupation of E Siberia by Allied forces during World War I to keep the area out of German hands. Immediate purpose was to rescue the Czechoslovak Legion, which had been attached to the Russian army and found itself isolated after the collapse of the czarist government. British and Japanese troops landed at Vladivostok on Apr. 9, 1918, over the objections of President Wilson. However, he reluctantly allowed US troops to join in after the Allied troops became bogged down in battle with the Bolshevik forces. The Czechs, meantime, complicated the issue by joining forces with the White Army forces against the Bolsheviks. After the Czechs were permitted to evacuate, the last US forces sailed home.

SICILIAN CAMPAIGN. British and American forces invaded Sicily on July 10, 1943, and conquered the island in thirty-eight days. The success of the operation was partly due to the Germans' decision to withdraw to avoid being trapped on the island.

SIC SEMPER TYRANNIS ("Thus always to tyrants"). The motto of Virginia since 1776. When John Wilkes Booth shot President Lincoln on Apr. 14, 1865, he shouted, "Sic semper tyrannis! The South is avenged!"

SIGNAL CORPS, US ARMY. Created 1860, the corps first used A.J. Myer's wigwag system of visual signaling, but in 1862 it introduced the Beardslee magnetoelectric telegraph machine. Later, the corps became responsible for army photography; established a pigeon service; and adapted to its uses the conventional electric telegraph, heliograph, and telephone, as well as radio, radar, and the communications satellite. From 1870 to 1891 was responsible for the weather service.

SIGN LANGUAGE. A method of gesture communication in general use among Indians of the Great Plains, developed because of nomadic existence.

SILK CULTURE AND MANUFACTURE. Efforts at silkworm raising were made in Georgia in the 18th c. and Connecticut in the early 19th c.; but the craze collapsed after ca. 1830. Small silk mills appeared in New England in the early 19th c. Silk throwing (yarn making) reached the factory stage by the 1840s, centered in Philadelphia, New York City, and the Connecticut R valley. After the Civil War, New Jersey, particularly Paterson, became the center of silk manufacturing. Since World War II, the production of synthetic fabrics has shrunk the silk industry. Annual raw-silk consumption fell from a peak of 81 million pounds in 1930 to 1 million pounds in 1980.

SILL, FORT. Military reservation in Oklahoma, established as Camp Wichita in 1869. During the Indian Wars, it was a center of negotiations with the tribes involved and the base for numerous campaigns. Site of army artillery and guided missile centers.

SILVER DEMOCRATS. After 1878, those members of the Democratic party who were active advocates of free coinage of silver at a 16 to 1 ratio to gold. They were victorious at the 1896 national convention. The 1904 Democratic platform also had a free silver plank, but the 1904 Democratic candidate, Alton B. Parker, repudiated free coinage.

SILVER GRAYS. Followers of Millard Fillmore at the 1850 New York state Democratic convention. They opposed the radical antislavery attitude of the majority and later bolted the party.

SILVER LEAGUE. A term applied to any of several pro-silver propaganda organizations of the late 19th c.; the most prominent was the American Bimetallic League.

SILVER LEGISLATION. Early US efforts to establish a bimetallic monetary system were a failure, since the free-market value of silver was higher than its monetary value. Legislation in 1853 left the silver dollar as a standard coin, although the value of silver continued to make its coinage impossible. In a revision of the statutes in 1873, the silver dollar was dropped. That same year, for the first time, the value of silver dropped below the 16 to 1 ratio for the first time; and silver interests backed by agrarian and proinflation elements promoted a return to bimetallism. In the 1870s, 1890s, and 1930s, the efforts of this pressure group almost achieved bimetallism and succeeded in extracting legislation giving a cash subsidy to producers of silver (see BLAND-ALLISON ACT; SHERMAN SILVER PURCHASE ACT). The Silver Purchase Act of 1934 followed an unprecedented drop in the price of silver and provided for the nationalization of domestic stocks of silver until the price should reach a specified level. The sudden rise in the price of silver ruined the currency systems of China and Mexico. Further legislation was required during World War II when a silver shortage developed. Another shortage, caused by industrial demands, came about in the 1960s, and silver was virtually eliminated from the US monetary system. Legislation of 1965 and 1968 provided for coins to be made of other metals and decreed that US Treasury certificates could no longer be redeemed in silver.

SILVER PROSPECTING AND MINING. Large-scale silver mining dates from 1859, when prospectors who were looking for gold found the Comstock, or Ophir, lode in Nevada. Within two decades more than $300 million in silver had been taken from the Comstock. The greatest of the Colorado silver mines, at Leadville, was discovered in 1877. The fortunes of the silver-mining industry was closely tied up with federal monetary policies; with the repeal of the Sherman Silver Purchase Act of 1893, the price of silver fell so low that many mines suspended operation. The industry recovered somewhat in the first decades of the 20th c.; but after 1918 low prices and high production costs limited activity in mining. In 1980, the United States produced 38.1 million fine ounces of silver; most came from mines in Idaho, Arizona, Montana, and Colorado.

SILVER REPUBLICANS. Faction that bolted the Republican party in 1896 and endorsed the Democratic candidate, William Jennings Bryan, who was running on a platform more acceptable to silver interests.

SINGLE TAX. A levy proposed by Henry George in *Progress and Poverty* (1879). In place of all other taxes, George advocated a single tax that would appropriate for government use all the economic rent on land. Similar plan advocated by tax reformers in the 1980s would replace all taxes with a single flat tax.

SINGLETON PEACE PLAN. At the time of Lincoln's death in 1865, J.W. Singleton, a Virginian, was the go-between for peace messages between Lincoln and the Confederates. Nothing came of the mission.

SINKING FUND, NATIONAL. Created by Congress in 1790, it became the instrument by which the federal government regulated the economy by using surplus funds and borrowed money to issue and buy back bonds. It grew during the 19th c., but modern deficit spending has rendered it an obsolete method of controlling the money supply.

SIOUX. See DAKOTA.

SIOUX-CHIPPEWA WAR. From the 17th c., the Sioux and Chippewa battled for control of hunting grounds in Wisconsin and Minnesota. In the mid-18th c., with support from the French, the Chippewa (in alliance with the Fox) drove the Sioux to S Missouri; the consequence was a series of retaliatory raids. Despite US efforts to establish a boundary between the two groups, the conflict worsened in the early 19th c., and the Sioux began moving to the Plains in great numbers leaving the Chippewa in control of the area.

SIOUX CLAIMS COMMISSION. After the Sioux uprising in Minnesota in 1863, Congress abrogated all Sioux treaties and declared their land forfeited. A commission was established to consider white claims against the tribe. $1.3 million in claims was paid out of funds realized from the land forfeiture.

SIOUX COUNCIL (1889). Indian agent James McLaughlin, in secret conference with various Sioux leaders, persuaded them to relinquish for white settlement a large portion of the Great Sioux Reservation. About $7 million was paid to the Indians in compensation.

SIOUX TREATIES. Series of agreement from 1805–89 between the US and various Sioux tribes by which the sovereignty of the US was established over vast Sioux territories in Minnesota and surrounding areas.

SIOUX UPRISING IN MINNESOTA (1862). Following their cession of nearly 1 million acres, the Sioux were crowded into a reservation with no hunting grounds. An uprising began when government payments to the starving Sioux did not arrive on time. Five white settlers were murdered and the Sioux rose in full force and attacked the Indian agency at Redwood, killing twenty more whites. For two weeks, Sioux raiding bands swept through SW Minnesota, killing twenty-four soldiers and more than 300 settlers. After the uprising was put down, thirty-eight Sioux were executed.

SIOUX WARS. There were serious clashes 1854–55 between the Sioux and US troops near Fort Laramie, Wyo.; and the SIOUX UPRISING in 1862 resulted in the dispersement of many of the tribe into Canada, with others joining the Teton Sioux in South Dakota. In 1865, the Tetons joined with the Arapaho and Cheyenne in attacking emigrants on the Bozeman Trail to the Montana goldfields. In 1865, the Teton under Chief Red Cloud defeated an army unit at the Upper Platte Bridge. At the end of the Civil War, additional US troops were sent to the area at an attempt at pacification; but the Sioux were again aroused by the building of additional forts along the Bozeman Trail. Red Cloud's War (1866–67) followed. In 1868, the government agreed to abandon the trail and forts and Red Cloud signed a peace treaty. It guaranteed the Indians possession in perpetuity of the Black Hills, but the discovery of gold there in 1874 brought in prospectors and settlers, which led to the Black Hills War (1876), in which Gen. G.A. Custer and his troops were killed at the Battle of Little Bighorn. The Sioux separated after the battle: American Horse's band was defeated at Slim Buttes; Sitting Bull was pursued into Canada; Crazy Horse and his Oglala fought until hunger forced them to surrender. Relative peace then prevailed until the final Sioux uprising, sometimes called the Messiah War, which attended the religious excitement of the GHOST DANCE in 1890. On Dec. 15, Sitting Bull was killed by police who had been sent to arrest him, and pacification of the Sioux was completed on Dec. 29 with the massacre of some 300 Sioux at the Battle of Wounded Knee.

SIT-INS. During the 1960s, civil rights groups used the sit-in tactic to dramatize their protests or positions on public questions. Government offices, schools, and places of business would be occupied forcing confrontations and often leading to arrests.

SIX NATIONS. See IROQUOIS.

SIXTEENTH AMENDMENT. Ratified in 1913, it authorized Congress to impose the income tax.

SKIING. Although skiing clubs were organized as early as 1867, as a sport skiing did not become popular until the 1930s, with the development of the ski lift. The 1932 Winter Olympics at Lake Placid, N.Y., created enormous interest; by the end of the decade, a collegiate sport had been transformed almost into a mass movement. Technical improvements in skiing equipment in the 1950s further popularized the sport, and snow-making machinery opened new areas to skiers. The Winter Olympics were held in 1960 at Squaw Valley, Calif., and the events were televised to American audiences for the first time. Cross-country skiing (as opposed to Alpine, or downhill, skiing) achieved a new popularity in the 1970s.

SLAUGHTERHOUSE CASES, 16 Wallace 36 (1873). In a case arising out of the granting of a monopoly to a slaughterhouse company by a Louisiana state agency, the Supreme Court ruled that the Fourteenth Amendment's due process clause did not apply; the "one pervading purpose" of the amendment was the protection of the newly freed blacks and was not meant to transfer state power to the federal government.

SLAVE INSURRECTIONS. In 1526, in a Spanish settlement in present South Carolina, several slaves rebelled and fled to live with the Indians; it was the first recorded slave insurrection in what is now the US. In 1712 a slave conspiracy in New York City resulted in the death of nine whites and the execution of twenty-one slaves and the suicide of six others. In 1739, in Cato's Revolt, near Charleston, blacks seized guns and fought the militia before being defeated. About twenty-five whites and fifty blacks were killed. In 1741 a conspiracy among slaves and white servants in New York City led to the execution of thirty-one blacks and four whites. The successful slave revolt in Haiti during the French Revolution led to a series of plots in the South. Others followed up to the Civil War (see GABRIELS'S INSURRECTION; NAT TURNER'S REBELLION; VESEY REBELLION). Each uprising brought a new crop of repressive laws.

SLAVERY. In the early 17th c., the blacks sold in the American colonies by the Dutch were possibly classified as indentured servants, but by the end of the century they were being held in perpetual bondage; by the 1660s, for example, Virginia had enacted laws giving statutory recognition to the institution of slavery. Slavery existed in all the colonies and was so recognized by law. Each region passed in the course of the 18th c. elaborate slave codes to regulate slave activity and to protect white society against black uprisings: Slaves were denied the right to marry, own property, bear arms, or defend themselves against assault. Conversion to Christianity was ruled to have no effect on their status. The slave population grew from 20,000 in 1700 to 500,000 by the American Revolution. In South Carolina, the slave population was 90,000 out of a total population of 130,000.

A serious abolitionist movement by the Quakers began at about the time of the Revolution. The marginal importance of slavery to the North's economy produced a series of laws gradually abolishing slavery in New England and the Middle Atlantic states. Slavery was a divisive issue at the Constitutional Convention of 1787. Several compromises resulted in a provision by which, for purposes of congressional apportionment, a slave was to be counted as three-fifths of a person. The slave trade was permitted until 1808, and the return of fugitive slaves was assured. In 1787 Congress passed the Northwest Ordinance; it prevented the expansion of slavery into the West. But the development of the cotton gin and the subsequent dependence of the South on cotton as the basis of its economy, created a new demand for slavery. After the slave trade was legally abolished in 1808, the domestic trading of slaves became an important activity in the states of the upper South (Virginia and Maryland, in particular), where there was an excess of slaves. During the four decades preceding the Civil War, this trade accounted for the transfer of about 200,000 slaves to the Black Belt area, where great cotton plantations were being established. Despite the ban on the importation of new slaves after 1808, the slave population grew from 750,000 in 1790 to over 4 million in 1860. Of these, only about 500,000 were employed in nonagricultural occupations.

After ca. 1830, virtually all abolitionist sentiment in the South disappeared, but it was increasing steadily in other parts of the country. Thousands of slaves tried to secure their freedom by fleeing from the South via the UN-DERGROUND RAILROAD ; others resisted by SLAVE IN-SURRECTIONS, work slowdowns, and feigning of illness and incompetence. Southern politicians, led by John C. Calhoun of South Carolina, sought to maintain a balance between the free and slave states. The COMPROMISE OF 1850 temporarily settled the dispute and succeeded in preventing the threatened secession of the South from the Union. But tempers were inflamed by the passage of the stringent FUGITIVE SLAVE ACT (1850), Harriet Beecher Stowe's novel *Uncle Tom's Cabin* (1852), the KANSAS-NEBRASKA ACT and conflict of 1854, and the DRED SCOTT CASE of 1857. The nation was brought to the brink of war. A new political coalition, the Republican party, was formed mostly on the issue of abolition of slavery. The election of its candidate, Abraham Lincoln, as president in 1860 convinced most southern whites that the only way to preserve their way of life was to secede from the Union (see SECESSION OF SOUTHERN STATES; CIVIL WAR). Initially, Lincoln made no effort to free the slaves, maintaining that the only purpose of the war was to force the Rebels to return to the Union. Military expediency and growing moral concern soon transformed the conflict into a crusade to free the slaves. Abolitionists and Radical Republicans gradually convinced Congress of the need to abolish slavery. In early 1862, Lincoln signed laws freeing the slaves in the District of Columbia, those who had escaped from the South, and banning slavery in the territories. A preliminary emancipation proclamation was announced in September 1862; it stipulated that all slaves in states still in rebellion on Jan. 1, 1863, would be freed. The southern states remained in rebellion; thus, on Jan. 1, 1863, the formal Emancipation Proclamation was issued. It freed slaves in the Confederacy but left those in the border states (some 800,000) still in bondage. They were not freed until the adoption in December 1865 of the Thirteenth Amendment, which formally brought to an end nearly 250 years of black slavery in America.

SLAVERY, INDIAN. Evidence indicates that few Indian tribes within the present US kept slaves. Several tribes of the Pacific Northwest were exceptions. In general, prisoners of war were taken into the tribe as members. After the white settlers introduced slavery, some Indian tribes maintained black slaves, notably the Five Civilized Tribes, who took their slaves with them when they were removed to Oklahoma. During the Civil War, those tribes allied themselves with the Confederacy.

SLAVE SHIPS. The first definitely authenticated American ship to carry slaves was the *Desire*, sailing out of Salem, Mass., in 1638. Many such vessels were heavily armed both for self-defense and for highjacking other slavers. The vessels were equipped with air scuttles, ports, and open gratings and with a shelf in the middle of the hold known as the slave deck. It extended 6 feet from each side to hold additional slaves; sometimes a second slave deck was added, leaving only 20 inches of headroom, which meant that the slaves were unable to sit upright during the entire voyage. When the slave trade was abolished in 1808, traders turned to fast ships to outrun the British frigates guarding the African coast. Every consideration was sacrificed to speed, and the slave quarters were made even smaller. The last American slaver was probably the *Huntress* of New York, which landed a cargo of slaves in Cuba in 1864.

SLAVE STATES. In 1776, all the states sanctioned slavery. Under the influence of the American Revolution (and the diminishing economic importance of slaves), slavery disappeared N of Delaware and Maryland: Pennsylvania abolished it in 1780; Massachusetts in 1783; Connecticut and Rhode Island in 1784; New York in 1799; and New Jersey in 1804. The Northwest Ordinance (1787) prohibited slavery in that territory. However, the Compromise of 1820 was worked out to define the territory from which slave states might be admitted to the Union. On the eve of the Civil War, the slave states were Alabama, Arkansas, Delaware, Florida, Georgia, Kentucky, Louisiana, Maryland, Mississippi, Missouri, North Carolina, South Carolina, Tennessee, Texas, and Virginia.

SLAVE TRADE. African slaves were brought to the New World (to Haiti) as early as 1501, but the slave trade proper began in 1517, when Charles V issued the Asiento, a policy giving the holder a monopoly on importing slaves to the Spanish dominions. For the next two centuries, the Asiento was a much coveted prize. Portugal's hegemony over the W coast of Africa, valuable for slave trading, was challenged by virtually every other European naval power; but Portugal managed to retain control of much of the area, particularly the area S of the Bight of Benin that became known as the Slave Coast. Slavery was widely practiced within Africa itself. Prisoners of war were routinely kept as slaves; local kings sold their surplus slaves, as well as criminals and debtors to European traders. In times of famine, parents often sold their children. These sources, however, did not meet the constantly growing demand, and soon slave-catching raids were organized by the coastal tribes and such warlike inland tribes as the Ashanti and Dahomey. The trade expanded rapidly after 1650. In 1713, the Treaty of Utrecht gave England the Asiento and a virtual monopoly of the trade N of the equator. The American colonies developed a triangular trade in the mid-18th c.: a captain would load up with trade goods and rum and sail to Africa, where the goods would be exchanged for slaves; he would then land his slaves in the West Indies and take on a cargo of molasses, which he would then transport to New England to be made into rum. As the demand for slaves grew, the traders packed as many slaves as possible onto each ship. With good winds, the voyage could be made with little loss of life in two months; but with contrary winds, most of the slaves could die on the voyage. By the end of the 18th c., strong moral opposition to slave trading had developed. Great Britain abolished the trade in 1807 and the US outlawed it in 1808; the other European powers and South America gradually followed suit. However, the demand for slaves continued to rise, and illegal trafficking in slaves continued. Slavers were declared pirates, and naval ships were authorized to seize any they caught. Slave trading virtually ceased with the US Civil War, although some cargoes of slaves were probably taken to Brazil in the 1870s. During the 300 years of the slave trade, some 15 million blacks were exported from Africa.

SLEEPY HOLLOW. Valley through which flows the Pocantico R near Tarrytown, N.Y.

Made famous by Washington Irving's "The Legend of Sleepy Hollow," published 1819.

SLIDELL'S MISSION TO MEXICO (1845). President Polk sent Congressman John Slidell to Mexico to negotiate boundary disputes. The Mexicans refused to receive him officially and rejected all his proposals. The failure of his mission presaged the MEXICAN WAR.

SLIM BUTTES, BATTLE OF (Sept. 9, 1876). After their defeat at the Battle of Little Bighorn, the US cavalry attacked the Sioux village at Slim Buttes in the Black Hills. The Sioux chief American Horse, mortally wounded, surrendered; Crazy Horse, arriving too late with a large force, attacked but was repulsed.

SLUMS. It was not until the 1832 cholera epidemic that the cities of New York, Philadelphia, and Boston recognized the existence of wretched slums within their midsts. Little was done to alleviate conditions, which worsened in the 1840s with the rapid influx of Irish and German immigrants. Many substantial older houses were rapidly converted into multiple residences with minimal sanitary facilities, and flimsy annexes were added. New York's early building codes endeavored to preserve some open space, but had minimal effect. Solid rows of new five- and six-story tenements extended over wide districts and attracted only the poorest residents. Each fresh invasion of immigrants deteriorated the housing stock. The sudden drop of immigrants during World War I was offset to a large extent by the large movement of southern blacks into the northern and eastern urban centers. The settlement of these blacks in the old immigrant districts spurred migration of former residents to the outskirts and suburbs, creating inner-city black ghettos that added the new dimension of racial prejudice to the problems of the slums. The pattern was to repeat itself in larger dimensions in World War II and after. In addition to the black ghettos, many large cities also had hispanic and oriental slum districts.

The pressure for federal action began in the 1930s, and after World War II, vast slum areas were razed and replaced by public housing projects that were mostly federally financed. Often the result was a concentration of low-cost units in high-rise blocks that exceeded the worst densities of the old slums and a continuation of the social problems resulting from them. During the administration of Lyndon B. Johnson, efforts were made, notably through the model-city projects, to redevelop the blighted areas by refurbishing old buildings, thus preserving the good qualities of the neighborhood. Funds were never sufficient to make an appreciable dent in the cities' slums, however; and the succeeding Nixon administration for the most part terminated the program and merged federal subsidies into the block-grant system that turned responsibility for the fate of the slums back to the cities.

SMALLPOX. Brought to the New World by explorers and settlers, smallpox destroyed many Indian tribes and became epidemic several times in the British colonies in the 17th and 18th c. Elaborate quarantine procedures were instituted early in the 18th c., as was innoculation. The latter was tried first in Boston in 1721, setting off a great public controversy. Fearing that innoculation might set off an epidemic, several colonies passed laws limiting it to periods of epidemic or in isolated hospitals. Vaccination by the innoculation of cowpox was introduced at the end of the 18th c., thereby effectively ending all danger of spreading the disease through innoculation. Despite this advance, vaccination was not universal in the 19th c., largely due to the problems of transporting the vaccine and keeping it uncontaminated. After the pandemic of 1870–75, however, city health departments began making vaccination mandatory; but opposition to the vaccine continued, and the US record of smallpox incidence was one of the world's worst. Use of vaccination increased substantially during the 1930s and World War II; incidence of the disease decreased dramatically. By 1980, thanks greatly to the program of the World Health Organization, the world was considered free of smallpox for the first time in history and vaccination was discontinued.

SMITH, FORT. Army post established 1817 at the confluence of the Arkansas and Poteau rivers on what is now the Arkansas-Oklahoma border. Founded to protect frontier settlements from Indian attacks; by the 1840s an important stopover point for pioneers headed for Santa Fe. In 1865 it was the site of a peace conference between the US and the Five Civilized Tribes, who had allied themselves with the Confederacy.

SMITH ACT (1940). Law declaring it illegal to advocate or teach the forceful overthrow of the government or to belong to any organization advocating such a course of action. Widely criticized as interfering with the right of free speech. In 1951, the Supreme Court upheld its constitutionality; but in 1957, the court held that the teaching or advocacy of the overthrow of the government that was not accompanied by any subversive action was constitutionally protected free speech.

SMITH EXPLORATIONS (1822–31). Several expeditions into the Rocky Mountain area by Jedediah Strong Smith. In 1826, his group was the first to reach the Spanish settlements in California by an overland route. In 1828, after traveling up the Pacific coast, he opened up a new route to Fort Vancouver. In 1831, he was killed by the Comanche while on his way to Santa Fe.

SMITHSONIAN INSTITUTION. Chartered by Congress in 1846 pursuant to the will of the Englishman James Smithson (1765–1829), who bequeathed about a half million dollars for it. Today, the Smithsonian derives its support from both the federal government and private endowments and is considered an independent establishment in the role of a ward of the US government, its trustee. It is the repository of more than 78 million items of scientific, cultural, and historic interest and is the umbrella organization for a large number of component museums, laboratories, and observatories. Included among them are the National Portrait Gallery, the Hirschhorn Museum and Sculpture Garden, the National Air and Space Museum, the Freer Gallery of Art, and the Cooper-Hewitt Museum (New York City).

SMOKY HILL TRAIL. Route from the Missouri Valley to Denver that was widely traveled in the late 1850s. Stage service was instituted 1865 but was displaced by completion of the Kansas Pacific RR in 1870.

SMUGGLING, COLONIAL. Although some violations of the Navigation Acts occurred, the major part of smuggling in the colonies took place after passage of the MOLASSES ACT

(1733). Illicit trade with the non-British West Indies became an economic necessity as an unfavorable balance of trade resulted from the act. The British regarded trade with the French West Indies during the French and Indian War (1754–63) as treasonable and passed the Sugar Act of 1764. The TOWNSHEND ACTS (1767) imposed new duties on trade with England further motivating the colonies toward illegal trade. The Tea Act of 1773 threatened the profits of the tea smugglers, as well as those of law-abiding tea merchants. Smuggling was thus a part of the ferment leading to the American Revolution.

SNAKE RIVER. Stream that rises in Shoshone Lake in Yellowstone National Park; it loops about SW Idaho, forms part of the Idaho-Oregon and Idaho-Washington boundaries, and cuts across SE Washington to empty into the Columbia R. Total length is 1,038 miles. The Lewis and Clark expedition explored the river in 1805; long an important waterway for the fur traders.

SNELLING, FORT. Established 1819 in Minnesota at the junction of the Mississippi and Minnesota R. Headquarters for the Indian agency and protected the headquarters of the American Fur Co. Abandoned 1858 but reoccupied 1861.

SOAP AND DETERGENT INDUSTRY. Soapmaking, using alkali (lye) and animal fats (tallow), began in the early colonies. By the American Revolution, a minor export market to the West Indies had developed. In the 1840s, as soapmaking firms expanded, Cincinnati became the leading soapmaking city. Soap was made in large slabs and these were sold to grocers. Candlemaking was a subsidiary industry for most of the soapmakers until ca. 1900. By that time, soapmakers had begun to brand their products and advertise them. By the 1920s, three firms dominated the field: Colgate-Palmolive-Peet, Lever Brothers, and Proctor and Gamble. Synthetic detergents made their appearance in the 1930s and revolutionized the industry; these were not soaps but chemical syntheses that substituted fatty acids for animal fats. By the 1980s, detergents had almost eliminated soap from the laundry market, but toilet soap remained unchallenged by detergents.

SOCIAL DEMOCRATIC PARTY. Organized 1897 by trade unions, socialist groups, and religious organizations. They elected some local officials and in 1900 nominated Eugene V. Debs for president. He polled 87,814 votes. In 1901 the party merged with other socialist groups to form the SOCIALIST PARTY OF AMERICA.

SOCIAL GOSPEL. Protestant reform movement of the late 19th and early 20th centuries attempting to apply the principles of Christianity to social and economic problems. Aims included abolition of child labor, a shorter work week, improved factory conditins, prison reform, and a living wage for all workers. Many of their suggested reforms were eventually adopted.

SOCIALIST LABOR PARTY. Founded 1877 by the merger of several smaller groups. Advocated industrial unionism as against craft unions; its ideology was thoroughly Marxist. Never achieved political importance, although it nominated a candidate for president in every election from 1892 to 1968.

SOCIALIST MOVEMENT. Socialism manifested itself first in the US with Brook Farm (1841) and the Oneida Colony (1848), but only after the Civil War did Marxist socialism begin to be felt in the country. In 1877, the SOCIALIST LABOR PARTY was formed, and the Populist movement held some ideas in common with the socialists. The SOCIALIST PARTY OF AMERICA was formed 1901 and remained thereafter the major socialist group in the country.

SOCIALIST PARTY OF AMERICA. Formed 1901 by a union of the Social Democratic party and elements of other left-wing movements, including remnants of western populism. Its high point was 1912, when its candidate, Eugene V. Debs, received 6 percent of the vote for president; some 1,200 Socialists were elected to public office that year, including seventy-nine mayors. Refused to support US involvement in World War I, and Debs and many others went to prison. The Bolshevik Revolution in Russia (1917) was the party's turning point. American party leaders were unwilling to reconstitute the party along Leninist lines, and the orthodox communists split away to form their own party. By 1928, the party was less than 10 per-

cent of its 1919 strength and thereafter was an essentially reformist movement whose appeal was largely to the urban middle class. After 1956, the party ceased to nominate candidates for president. In 1972, the party changed its name to Social Democrats USA.

SOCIAL LEGISLATION. In the 19th c., various states built workhouses and almshouses; in 1863 Massachusetts created a unified state board of charities, and other states followed suit. Prison reform, housing and tenement laws, protection of child labor, and health laws were all subjects for state attention. Laws aiding the blind and the deaf, and orphaned or abandoned children were also widely enacted. The federal government did little for social welfare, the general welfare clause of the Constitution being narrowly interpreted to mean that the states had total jurisdiction in the area. All that changed in the NEW DEAL of the Roosevelt administration in the 1930s. The Social Security Act of 1935 is the keystone of modern American social legislation (see SOCIAL SECURITY). It has been amended many times, and its scope and coverage broadened. Federal measures since 1935 have included MEDICARE, the Coal Mines and Safety Act of 1969, the Occupational Safety and Health Act of 1970, various housing acts that financed low-income housing, and the GREAT SOCIETY program's War on Poverty. The federal government made a significant entry into the field of education in 1958 with the National Defense Education Act and in 1965 with the Elementary and Secondary Education Act. Headstart, another Great Society program, encouraged school boards to begin training preschool children, especially those from disadvantaged backgrounds. As the federal involvement in social programs increased, considerable opposition to their costs developed. The Nixon administration dismantled or reduced a number of the Great Society programs and attempted to shift the responsibility back to the state and local governments. In 1980 President Reagan came to office committed to reducing federal social programs. His 1981 budget cut a number of such programs as Aid to Families with Dependent Children, food stamps, school lunches, day care funding, and subsidized housing.

SOCIAL SECURITY. The Social Security Act of 1935, part of the NEW DEAL program of President Franklin D. Roosevelt, provided for a compulsory government system of insurance that provides benefits related to wage loss. The basic law has been amended many times and its coverage greatly increased; by the 1980s, virtually all the gainfully employed were covered, both for retirement pensions and for disability payments. Other parts of the Social Security Act provided for federal grants to the states to help finance public assistance for the needy aged, families with dependent children, and the handicapped. The Social Security Administration, a part of the Department of Health and Human Services, is responsible for carrying out the provisions of the act (except for unemployment insurance, which is part of the Labor Department).

SOCIAL SETTLEMENTS. Neighborhood social-service centers established to aid urban dwellers. Most were formed in the late 19th c.; famous examples are Hull House in Chicago and the Henry Street Settlement in New York City. The number of settlement houses decreased in the 20th c., as more and more of their work was taken over by government social agencies.

SOCIAL WORK. The profession of social work developed early in the 20th c. among volunteers employed in local and charitable organizations, including settlement houses. By World War I, paid workers were displacing wealthy volunteers and professional organizations were being formed. Social work education began ca. 1900; by 1930 two-year graduate programs were becoming standard. In 1980, eighty-seven universities offered masters degrees and twenty-one offered doctoral degrees in social work.

SOCIETY FOR THE PREVENTION OF CRUELTY TO ANIMALS. See ANIMAL PROTECTIVE SOCIETIES.

SOCIETY FOR THE PREVENTION OF CRUELTY TO CHILDREN. Established 1875 as a local New York City organization; by 1900, 150 similar organizations had been founded. Upon receipt of a complaint alleging child neglect or abuse, the agency investigates and offers indicated services to correct unwholesome home conditions and, where appropriate, secures protection of the child by legal proceedings.

SOCIETY FOR THE PROPAGATION OF THE GOSPEL IN FOREIGN PARTS. Also known as the Venerable Society. Formed 1701 to conduct foreign mission work for the Anglican church. During the colonial period, it sent out 309 ordained missionaries and distributed many thousands of Bibles and other religious works. In many colonies, the first schools and the first libraries were founded by the society. Still engaged in missionary activity in various parts of the world.

SOCIETY OF CINCINNATI. See CINCINNATI, SOCIETY OF THE.

SOCIETY OF COLONIAL DAMES. Established 1892 to perpetuate the memory of colonial history. Membership (4,250 in 1980) is open to lineal descendants of men who assisted in the establishment, defense, and preservation of the American colonies.

SOD HOUSE. Dwelling made of dirt, constructed by settlers in the Great Plains in the 19th c. in areas where timber and stone were unavailable. The Plains Indians had long made their permanent winter homes of sod. Some were built half underground as protection against the weather.

SOFT DRINK INDUSTRY. Carbonated soda water, long prized in Europe for its medicinal properties, was introduced to the US in the early 19th c. During the 1830s, soda was eliminated, the result being a drink taken for refreshment rather than for medicinal purposes. The demand for carbonated water (which retained the name "soda water") was intensified a few years later by the introduction of flavorings, sometimes blended with cream, to the drinks dispensed by drug stores. Sale of flavored carbonated drinks in bottles developed soon after; it was a thriving industry by 1899, when 39 million cases (12 bottles per capita) were sold. Introduction of the bottle conveyor belt in the 1920s was the final step toward complete automation of the bottling industry. Local companies such as Coca-Cola, Pepsi-Cola, Hires, and Dr. Pepper began franchising bottlers throughout the country to produce and distribute the finished drinks. Growing competition at the national (and international) level led these companies to adopt vigorous advertising and marketing programs.

SOFT MONEY. The opposite of hard money, which is based on specie (gold or silver). The term originated ca. 1876, when the Greenback party was founded by debtor farmers and others who sought to raise agricultural prices by means of an inflated currency; they thought that the currency should be a government paper one, not redeemable in specie, but convertible on demand into federal interest-bearing notes that would serve as legal tender for the payment of debts and taxes. (See also GREENBACK MOVEMENT.)

SOLDIERS' HOMES. The US Naval Home, for disabled veterans, was opened 1831 in Philadelphia, the first of its kind. Many were created after the Civil War, when Congress created a special agency to administer them. Today, they are under the auspices of the Veterans Administration.

SOLID SOUTH. Term used to refer to the domination of the Democratic party in the southern states during most of the 20th c. A one-party system developed when Republicans became associated in the minds of white voters with the Reconstruction imposed on them after the Civil War. Only in the 1950s did Republicans make political inroads in the South. By the 1980s, there were viable Republican parties in most of the southern states, though the Democratic party remained far stronger. A new element, the black voter, tended to be Democratic, thus helping to maintain the dominance of that party.

SOMERS' VOYAGE TO VIRGINIA (1609). Sir George Somers, representing the Virginia Co., sailed from Plymouth, England, on June 2 with about 800 prospective settlers. One of the ships, with Somers aboard, was separated and foundered off Bermuda, but all passengers were saved. They eventually managed to reach Jamestown, where they joined the other settlers. The settlement of Bermuda by a group of Virginia adventurers in 1612 was a direct outgrowth of Somers' experiences there.

SONS OF LIBERTY. Radical organizations formed in the American Colonies after Parliament's passage of the Stamp Act in 1765. New York and Boston had the most active chapters. Members circulated petitions, intimidated British officials, and in general fomented revolution. During the Civil War, another Sons of Liberty organization was founded among Copperheads, or northerners opposing the Civil War. It is alleged to have had 300,000 members.

SONS OF THE AMERICAN REVOLUTION. Organized in San Francisco in 1875; later merged with other groups. Membership is restricted to lineal descendants of those who saw actual military or naval service during the Revolutionary War. In 1980, it had 21,477 members.

SONS OF THE REVOLUTION. Patriotic organization founded 1876; its membership (6,600 in 1980) consists of male lineal descendants of those who actively participated in procuring American independence during the American Revolution.

SONS OF THE SOUTH. Secret society formed 1854 and devoted to making Kansas a slave state.

SOO CANAL. See SAULT STE. MARIE CANALS.

SOO LINE. See RAILROADS, SKETCHES OF PRINCIPAL LINES.

SOONERS. Nickname for Oklahomans; original persons who illegally entered lands in the Indian Territory prior to the date set by the US government for the opening of the lands to settlement.

SORGHUM. Imported from Liberia in the 1840s as a substitute for sugar cane, sorghum yielded only uncrystallizable glucose syrup. Sorghum syrup was widely used in frontier areas as a substitute for sugar.

SOUTH, ANTEBELLUM. Modified English traditions and institutions dominated southern society from the founding of Jamestown in 1607. The tobacco plantation became the most important economic institution of the English colonies in Virginia and Maryland. Rice, indigo, and naval supplies were important in the Carolinas. Following the invention of the cotton gin in 1793 and the surge in demand for raw cotton in England incident to the Industrial Revolution, it was the cotton planters who mobilized the tremendous energy necessary to cross southern state boundaries; by 1860 they had carried the institution of the plantation all the way to East Texas. In addition, the plantation became a political institution, a little state or subdivision of the state, within which a monopoly of power was exercised by the planter. By virtue of his authority, he pursued a sort of military agriculture, employing a hierarchically ordered, regimented labor, imported and distributed as a utility. The concept of race was elaborated into a set of symbols and dogmas to set the races apart and keep both the mixed and the unmixed portions of the nonwhite population within the ranks of the laboring castes. The southern plantation was highly isolated, and the resultant culture a product of such isolation. Its literature emphasized manners and chivalry and was generally romantic. On the eve of the Civil War, the South was still overwhelmingly rural; its towns and small cities were gracious plantation capitals. There was little place for free public schools until near the end of the pre-Civil War period, but academies were fairly numerous, as were state and denominational colleges. These institutions, as well as military schools, functioned within the plantation system to indoctrinate and to support it. The county developed as the primary social, as well as governmental, unit, with the plantation often functioning as an informal subdivision. The states, too, came under control of planter oligarchies. All lived under the laws sponsored by plantation interests.

SOUTH AMERICA, US RELATIONS WITH. See LATIN AMERICA, US RELATIONS WITH.

SOUTHAMPTON. Resort area on Long Island, N.Y., the oldest English town in New York, founded 1640. Its earliest connections were with Connecticut, but after the English conquest of New Amsterdam, it took its place in the vast proprietary colony of the duke of York.

SOUTH CAROLINA. Explored by the Spanish in 1526; French Huguenots tried to plant a colony at Port Royal in 1562. The English, under charters issued in 1663 and 1665, began continuous settlement at Albemarle Point on the Ashley R in 1670. The Church of England was established 1706. Rice, produced by the labor of black slaves, became the first great staple. The proprietary govern-

ment was overthrown in 1719, and royal government replaced it. Indigo became an important crop. Fear of the Indians was removed by the victory at the Battle of Etchohih (1761); fear of the Spanish was removed when Florida fell to the British in 1763. Merchants and planters engineered revolutionary activity in South Carolina. The patriots drew up a temporary constitution in 1776 and a more permanent one in 1778. After the British took Charleston in 1780, the backcountry held the British at bay until the Continental army could drive the British army back upon its last base at Charleston. In 1790 a new constitution was approved; the state capital was moved from Charleston to Columbia. With the sudden expansion of cotton production after 1793, slavery spread with cotton rapidly into the backcountry. The slave trade ended in 1808, and President Jefferson's EMBARGO ACT struck mortal blows at South Carolina's foreign commerce. With this economic disruption, the merchant class quickly declined in influence. By 1830, virtually all opposition to slavery had ended, and South Carolina, particularly in the person of John C. Calhoun, led the rest of the South in its fiery defense of states' rights.

The Civil War began at Charleston, with the firing on Fort Sumter. It ended disastrously with the burning of Columbia. The state signaled its contrition by ratifying the THIRTEENTH AMENDMENT but balked at accepting the FOURTEENTH AMENDMENT until 1868. The new constitution of 1868 provided for more democratic forms of government, black suffrage, and free public education; but the 1895 constitution drove blacks from the polls. From 1902, when the last black left his seat in the state legislature, until 1970, when blacks reappeared in that body, a segregated society existed.

South Carolina's economy took on new life only with the advent of World War II. The new prosperity rested on the presence of military installations; rapid industrialization of the state; and redevelopment of the port of Charleston. The textile industry remained the major industry, while good water supplies and untapped labor reserves induced many companies to open plants in the state. Pop.: 3,119,208 (1980).

SOUTH CAROLINA, PROPOSED NOBILITY IN. The Fundamental Constitutions of Carolina (1669) called for a hereditary nobility, whose estates were to be inalienable and indivisible. Some proprietors of the colony established estates; twenty-six landgraves and thirteen caciques also acquired estates and seats in the governor's council. These efforts to transfer English feudal law to America produced a half-century of conflict, until South Carolina overthrew the proprietorship and became a royal colony in 1719.

SOUTH CAROLINA, SPANISH EXPEDITIONS AGAINST. From the beginning of the English settlement at Port Royal in 1670, the colonists were harassed by Spanish vessels appearing in Charleston harbor. In 1686, the Spanish, angered by English trading with Florida Indians, destroyed Stuart's Town, near Port Royal, and raided to the north. In 1702, an attack by Spanish Indians was crushed by South Carolina traders and Indians. In 1706, a Franco-Spanish naval attack on Charleston failed disastrously. Forces from St. Augustine, seeking to avenge a Georgia-South Carolina attack on Florida in 1740, were defeated in 1742 at Bloody Marsh, Ga. The Spanish then ended their planned attack on South Carolina.

SOUTH CAROLINA RAILROAD. One of the nation's earliest railways; begun in 1827 and by 1833 was completed to Hamburg, across the river from Augusta, Ga., a distance of 136 miles. Later merged with other lines and eventually (in 1899) became part of the Southern Railway Co.

SOUTH DAKOTA. Southern half of what was the Dakota Territory; admitted as a state 1889. Received its name from the Dakota Sioux who inhabited all sections of it by the mid-18th c.; their descendants are located on nine reservations. All the state W of the Missouri R was part of the great Sioux reservation created by the Treaty of 1868, later broken up by cessions in 1877 and 1889 and by the heavy influx of white settlers, particularly after the discovery of gold in the Black Hills. The state is predominently agricultural; the gold and lead mines have diminished in importance. Numerous ethnic groups make up the population: Norwegians, Germans, Russians, Czechs, Irish, Finns, and French. Pop.: 690,178 (1980).

SOUTHEAST ASIA TREATY ORGANIZATION (SEATO). Formed 1954 by the US, Great Britain, France, Australia, New Zealand, the Philippines, Pakistan, and Thailand for the purpose of mutual protection against outside aggression. Never effective, SEATO was dissolved 1977.

SOUTHERN CHRISTIAN LEADERSHIP CONFERENCE (SCLC). Black civil rights organization founded 1957 on the principle of "nonviolent direct mass action." An umbrella of loosely affiliated organizations, held together mainly by the prestige of its leader, Martin Luther King, Jr.

SOUTHERN CULT. Also known as the Southeastern ceremonial complex, associated with the Mississippian cultures of the Eastern Woodlands between ca. AD 900 and the historic period. The series of rituals, objects, and iconographic elements integrated into the ceremonial complex was a blend of indigenous and Middle American religious themes connected with harvest and renewal. Major cult centers were at Moundville (Alabama), Etowah (Georgia), and Spiro (Oklahoma). Seems certain that human sacrifice was an integral part of the cult activities.

SOUTHERN LITERARY MESSENGER. Magazine published at Richmond, Va., from 1834–64, most famous for one of its editors, Edgar Allan Poe.

SOUTHERN OVERLAND MAIL. Also known as the Butterfield Overland Mail. First land mail route from the East to California. Chartered by Congress in 1857, it began at St. Louis and Memphis and ended at San Francisco. Fort Smith, Ark., El Paso, Tex., and Tucson, Ariz., were important stops. Service began 1858 and included passengers on its route. At the outbreak of the Civil War, the line was moved to a more northerly route.

SOUTHERN PACIFIC RAILROAD. See RAILROADS, SKETCHES OF PRINCIPAL LINES.

SOUTHERN RAILWAY. See RAILROADS, SKETCHES OF PRINCIPAL LINES.

SOUTHERN UNIONISTS. Of the fifteen slave states at the time of the Civil War, the border states of Missouri, Kentucky, Virginia, Maryland, and Delaware were the greatest strongholds of unionism; if war came, they saw themselves as the battlefield. All except Virginia remained in the Union, and that part of Virginia joining free territory broke away and formed the state of West Virginia. There was union sentiment in the Confederacy itself, mostly in the mountains or other less fertile regions where the small farm rather than the plantation was the rule.

SOUTHOLD. Colony on Long Island, N.Y., purchased and settled by migrants from the New Haven colony in 1640. Became a part of Connecticut in 1662; in 1665 it was included in the duke of York's vast holdings.

SOUTH PASS. Route through the Rocky Mountains in Wyoming. Discovered 1824; through it ran the great emigrant trail to Oregon and California.

SOUTH PLATTE ROUTE. Branch of the Oregon, or Overland, Trail; leaves the main trail at Julesburg, Colo., and follows the South Platte R to Denver. Attacked by the Cheyenne in 1865, use of it was suspended for several years.

SOUTHWEST. Roughly the SW quarter of the US, including the states of Oklahoma, Texas, New Mexico, Arizona, and the southern parts of California, Kansas, and Colorado. Most of the area belonged to Spain and then Mexico.

SOUTHWEST, OLD. First applied to the region of present Tennessee and Kentucky but later extended to include Alabama and Mississippi and sometimes even Louisiana and Arkansas. Originally, it came within the limits of Virginia, the Carolinas, and Georgia. Settlement began before the American Revolution. After the war, the states claiming the area ceded their claims and in 1790 the US organized them as Southwest Territory.

SOUTHWEST FUR COMPANY. Organized 1811 by John Jacob Astor; later merged into the AMERICAN FUR COMPANY.

SOUTHWEST POINT. Promontory where the Clinch and Holston rivers form the Tennessee R, in Kingston, Tenn.

SOUTHWEST TERRITORY. See SOUTHWEST, OLD.

SOVEREIGNTY. Legal concept that attempts to explain the final location and source of political authority. Although the states of the US are often termed sovereign, most political scientists agree that sovereignty rests with the US government and finally with the people of the US, who created a national government and delegated to it certain sovereign powers.

SPACE EXPLORATION. The "space race" began in 1957 after the Soviet Union launched *Sputnik*, the first artificial satellite to orbit the earth. Full-scale US effort to develop satellites and spacecraft was begun immediately. Project Mercury began 1961 with a rocket shot of an individual astronaut (Alan B. Shepard, Jr.). The first American to fly a Mercury capsule in orbit was John Glenn in 1962. Project Gemini was the next step; its flights employed two pilots each. In 1965, Edward H. White took a space walk. Project Apollo missions were designed to place a man on the moon. After four preliminary flights, an Apollo crew landed on the moon in July 1969. Neil A. Armstrong and Edwin E. Aldrin made the landing, while Michael Collins operated the command module in orbit around the moon. Millions on earth viewed the operation on live television. Five subsequent landings took place by 1973; the last Apollo mission was a rendezvous with the Soviet Soyuz in 1975. Skylab Project (1973–74) placed a flying laboratory in orbit around the earth at an altitude of 270 miles. Development of a space shuttle, a reusable spacecraft, was beset with initial troubles, but finally in 1981 *Columbia* took off and landed safely in the California desert two days later.

Unmanned satellites have been launched for a myriad of purposes: weather forecasting; scientific fact-gathering, particularly as it relates to the atmosphere and the solar system; communications (including worldwide television transmission); and military intelligence. The fear that the military use of spacecraft might result in war in outer space led to a 1967 treaty in which the US, the Soviet Union, and a number of other powers agreed not to use outer space as a setting for nuclear weaponry.

SPANISH-AMERICAN RELATIONS. Although Spain was at odds with Great Britain at the time, it did not immmediately recognize the independence of the thirteen colonies. It did, however, grant loans and subsidies to the rebels. Its foremost purpose was the recovery of Florida from England. In 1797, Spain and the US signed PINCKNEY'S TREATY, which established the border between the US and Spanish Florida and gave US citizens free navigation of the Mississippi R. In 1800 Spain retroceded Louisiana to France, which promptly sold it to the US. New border disputes arose, concerning Texas to the west and West Florida to the east. In the early 19th c., Spanish civil war at home severely weakened its hold on New World colonies. Florida was ceded to the US; most of Latin American colonies declared their independence from Spain. The US promptly recognized the new republics and imposed the MONROE DOCTRINE over the area, which announced its intention of replacing Spain as the dominant power in the hemisphere. Cuba was next. There had long been a faction in the US, chiefly in the slave states, that had called for the annexation of Cuba. When revolution broke out in Cuba in 1895, the US embarked on an adventurous policy. Public agitation for US intervention, egged on by the Hearst and Pulitzer newspapers, reached fever pitch after the sinking of the *Maine* in Havana harbor. The resulting SPANISH-AMERICAN WAR lasted only three months and brought to the US Puerto Rico, the Philippines, Guam, and a protectorate over Cuba. The US maintained neutrality during the Spanish Civil War of the 1930s but recognized (1939) its winner, Gen. Francisco Franco, and was successful in keeping his regime neutral in World War II, despite his close ties with Nazi Germany. Since World War II, relations between the two nations have steadily improved. The US, in a series of treaties, was granted the right to build military facilities in Spain in return for economic and military aid. The death of Franco (1975) and the restoration of the monarchy and democracy did not significantly alter relations.

SPANISH-AMERICAN WAR (1898). Rebellion broke out in Cuba in 1895; and despite a more conciliatory attitude by Spain, US public opinion, whipped up by the sensationalistic Hearst and Pulitzer newspapers, was stongly in favor of full independence for Cuba. The battleship *Maine*, which had been sent to Cuba as protection for US citizens there, was sunk in Havana harbor on Feb. 15. President McKinley asked Congress for the

authority to intervene; Congress replied by passing a resolution declaring Cuba independent and directing that US armed force be used to put its resolution into effect. A formal declaration of war was voted on Apr. 25. Initial US strategy was to blockade Cuba while the insurgents continued the fight against the Spanish. In the Pacific, Commodore George Dewey sailed from Hong Kong on Apr. 27 and entered Manila Bay on May 2; Manila was easily taken on Aug. 13. Meanwhile, in the Atlantic, the blockade continued as US mobilization was speeded up. American troops landed and took Santiago de Cuba (June 22); they captured the San Juan heights (see SAN JUAN HILL AND EL CANEY, BATTLES OF). On July 3, the Spanish squadron was annihilated; on July 16, the Spaniards signed terms of unconditional surrender. On July 25, Puerto Rico was invaded and fell with virtually no opposition. The peace treaty established Cuba as an independent nation but a protectorate of the US, and ceded Guam, Puerto Rico, and the Philippines to the US.

SPANISH CAPTURE OF BRITISH POSTS (1779–81). On June 21, 1779, after secret support for the American colonists, Spain officially joined France in hostilities against Great Britain. Military operations were concentrated on the Mississippi R and the Gulf of Mexico. The posts at Fort Manchac, Baton Rouge, and Natchez were taken from the British in 1779; Fort Charlotte (Mobile) and Fort George (Pensacola) were taken in 1780. Thus Spain restored its control over East and West Florida.

SPANISH CONSPIRACY. Attempts by Spain in the late 18th c. to defend its interests in Florida and Louisiana by promoting the secession of the West from the US. The Spanish employed bribery, manipulated commerce on the Mississippi R, and exploited sectional rivalry between East and West. The central figure in the Spanish intrigues was James Wilkinson; the focal point was Kentucky and Spain's efforts to have it become an independent nation. Wilkinson took an oath of allegiance to the Spanish crown and became Spain's principal agent; he was on the Spanish payroll for many years, even after becoming (1791) an officer in the US army and US governor of Louisiana. His role was long suspected, but he was never indicted, despite involvement in the BURR CONSPIRACY.

SPANISH DOLLAR. First coined 1728 to replace the piece of eight; widely circulated in the American colonies as a reliable medium of exchange. Congress accepted it 1786 as the basis of the US coinage system.

SPANISH-MISSOURI FUR COMPANY. Organized 1794 and given exclusive trading rights by the Spanish government along the upper Mississippi R. It was not successful, and Clamorgan, Loisel and Co. apparently took over the business.

SPANISH SUCCESSION, WAR OF THE. See QUEEN ANNE'S WAR.

SPANISH TRAIL. Overland trail dating from 1775 connecting Santa Fe and Los Angeles; later an important immigrant route.

SPEAKER OF THE HOUSE OF REPRESENTATIVES. Although the Constitution does not stipulate that the speaker be a member of the House (or even a US citizen), he has always been chosen from membership in the House. The speakership has come to be regarded as second only in power and importance to the presidency, standing behind the vice-president in succession to the presidency. He presides over the House, maintains order, issues rulings, and refers bills and resolutions to the appropriate committees. Until the early 20th c., the speakership was a highly partisan office, used by the majority party to work its will. Until 1910, when an internal revolt sharply curtailed his powers, the speaker for years had named all committee chairmen and appointed all committee members for both majority and minority parties. Today, the role of the speaker is largely dependent on his personal standing within his own party; a strong speaker can come close to controlling the bills that come out of the House, whereas a weak speaker exercises far less influence over his fellow House members. Among the strongest speakers of the 20th c. have been John Nance Garner and Sam Rayburn, both Democrats.

SPECIE. See BIMETALLISM; GOLD STANDARD.

SPECIFIC DUTIES. See DUTIES, AD VALOREM AND SPECIFIC.

SPENCER RIFLE. Self-loading, repeating weapon patented 1860 and adopted by the US army during the Civil War.

SPERMACETI TRUST. Monopoly of New England candlemakers formed in the 1760s, based on the secret process for making candles from the spermaceti and oil from the sperm whale; after the knowledge of the process became widespread, the power of the trust was broken.

SPIRIT LAKE MASSACRE (1857). A small band of Sioux attacked a white settlement at Spirit Lake, Iowa, killing thirty-two persons and taking four women prisoner. Two of them were killed and eventually the other two released.

SPIRIT OF ST. LOUIS. Monoplane used on LINDBERGH'S ATLANTIC FLIGHT.

SPOILS SYSTEM. Arrangement in which loyalty and service to a political party is the primary criterion for appointment to public office. Has always, to some degree, been a part of political life, but in the US President Andrew Jackson is generally credited with legitimizing, articulating, and establishing it in the American political context. Abraham Lincoln removed 75 percent of the incumbent officeholders inherited from his predecessor. The system was especially rampant in state and local governments and was in particular the basis of the strength of the big city political machines. There it was extended to all the contractors and suppliers used by the city government. Pressure to reform the system intensified after President Garfield was killed in 1883 by a demented officeseeker who blamed the president for his not getting a job. In 1883, Congress passed the PENDLETON ACT, which set up the Civil Service Commission and a merit system for appointments to lower federal offices. Since then, successive presidents have extended the Civil Service classification list; today more than 90 percent of all nonelective federal positions are included and are filled by competitive examination. Percentages vary in state and local jurisdiction, but in general are lower than in the federal government.

SPOKANE. City in E Washington, founded 1810 as a British trading house known as Spokane House, on Spokane Falls at the center of the Columbia, Kootenay, and Flathead rivers fur trade. In 1812, John Jacob Astor's Pacific Fur Co. opened a trading post there. Industries include an important aluminum plant, operating with electric power generated from the Spokane R. Pop.: 171,300 (1980).

SPOLIATION CLAIMS. See FRENCH SPOLIATION CLAIMS.

SPOTSWOOD'S IRON FURNACES. The first was built 1716 by Gov. Alexander Spotswood at Germanna, Va., as a charcoal-fired smelting furnace producing sow (or pig) iron from rock ores. Later built at Massaponax and Fredericksville; operated until after the American Revolution.

SPOTSYLVANIA COURTHOUSE, BATTLE OF (May 8–21, 1864). The Union army under Gen. U.S. Grant was on its march from the Wilderness in Virginia when it was stopped by Gen. R.E. Lee's Confederate army at Spotsylvania Courthouse. Grant gradually withdrew his force after fierce hand-to-hand combat. His losses were 17,000; Lee's, 8,000.

SPRINGBOK ADMIRALTY CASE. The English cargo vessel *Springbok* was captured by a Union cruiser in 1862. Although the ship was headed for Nassau, a neutral port, the US claimed that its cargo was eventually headed for the Confederacy through the Union blockade. The courts held that the vessel should be released but the cargo confiscated. The British accepted the decision; and the principle, that of continuous voyage, was often invoked against the US prior to its entry into World War I.

SPRINGER V. UNITED STATES, 102 US 586 (1881). Supreme Court upheld the validity of the federal income tax that had been imposed during the Civil War. In 1894, Congress passed another income tax, but this time the Supreme Court ruled it invalid, thereby making necessary the SIXTEENTH AMENDMENT, ratified 1913.

SPRINGFIELD. Capital city of Illinois, founded 1818 and made the capital in 1837 because of its central location. Pop.: 99,637 (1980).

SPRINGFIELD. City in Massachusetts, founded 1636 on the Connecticut R. Destroyed 1675 during King Philip's War but soon rebuilt. Its arsenal was the major objective of the rebels during SHAYS'S REBELLION (1786). Became an important mill town, using the waterpower of the river; today a major industrial city. Pop.: 152,319 (1980).

SPRINGFIELD. City in SW Missouri, in a dairy farming area. Settled 1829; a stopover in the Butterfield Stage line for emigrants headed toward Texas or California. An important crossroads during the Civil War, controlled by the Confederates until February 1862; after that, by the Union. Pop.: 133,116 (1980).

SPRINGFIELD, BATTLE OF (June 23, 1780). Attempting to take advantage of a rumored mutiny among Gen. George Washington's officers at his headquarters at Morristown, N.J., the British commander, Sir Henry Clinton, invaded New Jersey with 5,000 troops. He was stopped at Springfield and forced to return to Staten Island.

SQUARE DEAL. Name given by Theodore Roosevelt for the platform he espoused as Progressive, or Bull Moose, candidate for president in 1912.

SQUATTER SOVEREIGNTY. See POPULAR SOVEREIGNTY.

SQUIER TREATY (1849). Nicaragua gave the US exclusive rights to a transisthmian canal route through Nicaragua. Discarded 1850 in favor of the CLAYTON-BULWER TREATY with England.

STAFFORD V. WALLACE, 258 US 495 (1922). Supreme Court ruled that the interstate commerce clause of the Constitution gave Congress the authority to regulate the operations of livestock dealers and commission men.

STAGECOACH TRAVEL. Stage lines ran from Boston, New York, and Philadelphia before the American Revolution. In 1785, they were helped financially when Congress subsidized them for carrying the mail. Rapid development of stagecoach facilities W of the Alleghenies did not take place until the Jacksonian era when the Post Office subsidies increased greatly; the mileage of stage lines tripled between 1828 and 1838. Most operations ceased with the coming of the railroads.

STAKED PLAIN. Also called the Llano Estacado; the high level part of NW Texas and E New Mexico. Explored in the 1540s by Coronado; inhabited by the Comanche until 1880. Thereafter it became cattle country, and later a dry farming and oil and natural-gas producing region.

STAMP ACT (1765). Efforts to increase levies from the American colonies by Parliament. Use of stamps was required on all legal and commercial papers, pamphlets, newspapers, almanacs, cards, and dice. News of the Act caused great resentment, and violent colonial opposition finally nullified the act in 1766.

STAMP ACT CONGRESS (1765). As a result of the Stamp Act, Massachusetts' house of representatives issued a call to all colonies to send delegates to New York City. Nine responded and sent representatives, who met from Oct. 7 to Oct. 25. They framed resolutions of colonial rights and grievances and petitioned king and Parliament to repeal the objectionable legislation.

STANDARD OIL COMPANY. Formed 1870 by John D. Rockefeller and his associates in Cleveland; it grew rapidly and by 1879 controlled from 90 to 95 percent of the nation's refining capacity and immense pipeline and storage-tank systems. Became the nucleus of an almost nationwide industrial organization, the richest and most powerful in the country. In 1882, it was organized into a trust with a virtual monopoly in the US. In 1892, Ohio courts ordered the trust dissolved, and twenty constitutent companies were organized. These were gathered in 1899 into the Standard Oil Company (New Jersey). In 1911, a decree of the US Supreme Court forced a more complete dissolution.

STANDARD OIL COMPANY OF NEW JERSEY V. UNITED STATES, 221 US 1 (1911). Supreme Court ruled that the oil company was acting in restraint of trade as defined by the SHERMAN ANTITRUST ACT of 1890 and ordered it to give up control of thirty-seven subsidiary companies.

STANDARDS, NATIONAL BUREAU OF. See NATIONAL BUREAU OF STANDARDS.

STANDARDS OF LIVING. Most often measured by per capita national income. Between 1840 and 1980, per capita income, after allowances for price changes, increased almost ninefold. Standards of living vary from region to region. They have tended to be lower in the Midwest and South than in the Northeast and Far West. But regional differences have narrowed dramatically in recent years. The distribution of income by size has been roughly the same as in most Western European nations for which data are available. Just before the Civil War, the richest 5 percent of US families probably had about eight times as much income as the remaining 95 percent . After the 1920s, the degree of inequality diminished somewhat, the rich losing and the poor gaining. By the 1950s, the richest 5 percent had about five times the income per family of the remaining 95 percent. From then until the mid-1970s, the distribution was rather stable, those in the middle-income groups gaining slightly at the expense of both rich and poor. In the late 1970s and early 1980s, the higher income families became more numerous, mainly because of a large increase in women's employment.

STANDPATTERS. Republicans who stayed with the party's nominee, William Howard Taft, in 1912, when many in the party deserted it for Theodore Roosevelt's PROGRESSIVE PARTY.

STANSBURY EXPLORATION (1849–50). Army expedition, led by Capt. Howard Stansbury, that explored Great Salt Lake, the Mormon colony there, and looked for a new route through the mountains.

STANTON, FORT. Established 1856 in Lincoln County, N. Mex., to hold the Apache in check; abandoned 1896.

STANWIX, FORT. Built 1758 at the Oneida, New York, carrying place, to replace the old fort there. Its strategic location between the upper Mohawk R and Wood Creek made it an important point of defense and a center of Indian trade. Known during the American Revolution as Fort Schuyler; but in 1781, after a flood, it was rebuilt as Fort Stanwix. The present city of Rome was built on its site.

STANWIX, FORT, TREATY OF (1768). The Iroquois and other Indians ceded a large spread of land W of the Appalachians to the English; included was Indiana, ceded to land speculators.

STANWIX, FORT, TREATY OF (1784). The Iroquois ceded land in W New York and about one-fourth of present Pennsylvania to the US. They also relinquished claim to land W of the Ohio R.

STAR OF THE WEST. Unarmed merchant vessel dispatched by President Buchanan in 1861 to reinforce Fort Sumter, S.C. Upon reaching Charleston harbor, it was fired upon and later captured by Confederate forces.

STAR ROUTE FRAUDS. The Post Office was defrauded of more than $4 million by private contractors who carried the mail over roads, designated as star routes. Trials in 1882–83 revealed frauds on ninety-four routes, but no convictions resulted.

STARS, FALLING OF THE (Nov. 12–13, 1833). A meteor shower, visible over a large portion of the US, occurs every November but peaks every 133 years. The 1833 meteors were as thick as snowflakes and alarmed residents across the country, many interpreting it as the end of the world. The meteor shower in 1966 occurred at dawn and was visible only in the West.

STARS AND BARS. See CONFEDERATE FLAG.

STARS AND STRIPES. See FLAG OF THE UNITED STATES.

"STAR-SPANGLED BANNER." The words to the US national anthem, with melody based on an English drinking song, were written by Francis Scott Key in 1812 and inspired by the English attack on Fort McHenry, which he witnessed from a ship in the Baltimore harbor. Long regarded as the national anthem, it was not officially decreed so until 1931.

STARVED ROCK. Rises abruptly 140 feet on the S bank of the Illinois R nearly opposite Utica, Ill. A landmark to the French explorers of the 17th c., who called it *le rocher*. So called because a band of Illinois Indians are supposed to have been besieged on its summit and starved into submission.

STATE, DEPARTMENT OF. Under the Articles of Confederation, Congress created a department of foreign affairs, headed by a secretary, in 1781. Under the Constitution, in 1789, the department became the Department of Foreign Affairs, then gave it responsibility for the direction of "home affairs" and changed its name to the Department of State. Until creation of the Department of the Interior in 1849, the secretary of state handled both foreign affairs and home affairs, including the Patent Office and the census. By the 1980s, the secretary of state administered a large department of the government, acted as principal adviser to the president on foreign affairs, and handled many on-site diplomatic negotiations personally. The secretary of state is the senior member of the president's cabinet.

Thomas Jefferson, the first secretary of state, had a staff of five clerks; two US diplomatic agents were stationed abroad. Only four foreign governments had representatives in the US. In 1981, the State Department employed 23,439 people. As the Department of State grew in size, the problem of coordination within it (and with other federal agencies with overseas responsibilities) also grew. In 1870 the department had only sixteen separate units; by 1948, 113; and the problem has continued to grow. Coordination between the State Department and the NATIONAL SECURITY COUNCIL (NSC) has been a problem since the founding of the latter body. It has become traditional for the secretary of state and the president's assistant for national security affairs (who chairs the NSC) to compete for the position of principal adviser to the president on foreign affairs. In addition to sending emissaries to more than 150 nations, the State Department sends special missions to the United Nations, Organization of American States, North Atlantic Treaty Organization, Organization for Economic Cooperation and Development, International Atomic Energy Agency, European Office of the United Nations, and European Communities.

STATE BOUNDARY DISPUTES. See BOUNDARY DISPUTES BETWEEN THE STATES.

STATE CONSTITUTIONS. Under the US federal system, each state operates under its own constitution. Only nineteen states, as of the early 1980s, still operate under their original constitutions, that of Massachusetts (adopted 1780, but extensively revised) being the oldest. Two other states have constitutions going back to the 18th c.: New Hampshire (1784) and Vermont (1793). As in the US Constitution, in each of the state constitutions, the legislative, executive, and judicial powers are vested in separate and distinct departments. Unlike the federal Constitution, however, the state constitutions tend to be so detailed and rigid as to require frequent change. In every state, amendments or revisions may be proposed either by the legislature or by an elective convention called for that purpose. Specific amendments are usually proposed by the legislature or the voters; more thoroughgoing revision, by constitutional conventions or commissions.

STATE DEBTS. See DEBTS, STATE.

STATE GOVERNMENT. The Second Continental Congress asked each of the thirteen former colonies to prepare a new state constitution; Connecticut and Rhode Island simply erased provisions about their allegiance to the king from their colonial charters and used them as state constitutions. The other eleven states adopted new constitutions that made few obvious changes in the lives of their people. Where necessary, they democratized the electoral process and established permanent legislatures. Many states gave those legislatures power to select both governors and judges, a reaction against the primary role of royal governors in the colonial era. The strong legislature–weak governor tradition lasted well into the 19th c.; it was not until early in the 20th c. that a movement began to strengthen the executive powers of the governors. The situation has since become reversed; today, executive power is generally greater than that of the legislature. Adoption of civil service to staff state administrations transferred much power from patronage to professionalism, or, detractors would say, to bureaucracy.

STATE GOVERNMENTS, COUNCIL OF THE. See COUNCIL FOR NEW ENGLAND.

STATE LAWS, UNIFORM. In the 18th and 19th c., the exercise of state sovereignty resulted in the development of separate and often conflicting state legal systems. A movement to create uniform state laws took hold in the 1890s; a commission has met every year since 1892 drafting uniform acts (more than 150 by 1981), some of which were not adopted by any states. Most successful has been the Uniform Commercial Code, adopted by every state except Louisiana and forming the framework for most business dealings in the US.

STATE-MAKING PROCESS. The US Constitution does not specify how new states are to be added to the Union; various methods have been used. The first states added were Vermont (1791), Kentucky (1792), and Tennessee (1796); they were authorized by acts of Congress. Texas, an independent republic, was annexed by joint resolution of Congress in 1845. Hawaii, also at one time an independent nation, was before becoming a state an incorporated territory. Maine separated from Massachusetts in 1820 and West Virginia from Virginia in 1863. The remainder of the states were carved out of the public lands that had come to the US as the result of various cessions and annexations. The Northwest Ordinance of 1787 was the basis upon which all public lands and foreign possessions of the US were administered for the next century. By its provisions, as soon as an organized territory had maintained self-government and had grown in population enough to justify its becoming a state, Congress passed a specific act under which the residents of the territory could form a constitutional convention. It in turn would submit a constitution to the people; after its acceptance by them, it would be formally presented to Congress for the territory to be admitted to full status in the Union. Each new state, once accepted by Congress, acquired complete equality with all the other states. The Northwest Ordinance forever prohibited slavery within territories soon to be organized. Congress refused to admit Utah until its constitution prohibited polygamy, then practiced by the Mormon majority in that area. Utah complied and was admitted in 1896. Alaska was also admitted under special circumstances, largely because of its large Eskimo and Indian populations and because of its large undeveloped land areas. Puerto Rico, with commonwealth status, has been given the option of requesting statehood. So far, in every election, voters have overwhelmingly opted to maintain the island's commonwealth status. (See also ORDINANCES OF 1784, 1785 AND 1787.)

STATEN ISLAND PEACE CONFERENCE (Sept. 11, 1776). After the Battle of Long Island, crown representatives sent Congress a proposal that an informal peace conference be held. The meeting took place on Staten Island, New York. Benjamin Franklin, John Adams, and Edmund Rutledge represented the Americans; Gen. William Howe and Adm. Richard Howe represented the British. The conference proved fruitless after the British demanded revocation of the Declaration of Independence.

STATES, RELATIONS BETWEEN THE. The US Constitution provides the basic principles governing relations between the states: "Full Faith and Credit shall be given in each State to the public Acts, Records, and judicial proceedings of every other State" and provides for citizens to be entitled to "all Privileges and Immunities of Citizens in the several States." States are prohibited from entering into any "Agreement or Compact with another State" without consent of Congress. Despite this, states have often entered into regional compacts and agreements, especially as concerns water disposition from rivers that flow through a number of states. Congress has rarely imposed its will over such agreements.

STATE SOVEREIGNTY. Under the Articles of Confederation, the states regarded themselves as sovereign in the full meaning of the term. The question of how much sovereignty would be retained by the individual states was a crucial issue of the Constitutional Convention of 1787. It remained unresolved even after the ratification of the document. It was generally assumed that the sovereignty had been divided between the states and the national government without the destruction of its life principle. John C. Calhoun, in promulgating the theory of STATES' RIGHTS, maintained that sovereignty is indivisible and that such sovereignty as is exerted by the federal government was voluntarily given it by the states, who finally retained that sovereignty. Thus the states could renounce the Union if they choose, and resume their independence. The issue was settled in favor of the national government by the Civil War.

STATES' RIGHTS. At the Constitutional Convention of 1787, states' rights proponents pressed to include their ideas in the Constitution, but there was also the desire for a strong national government, with minimal power residing with the states. In 1791, the Tenth Amendment was added, which spelled out the states' right doctrine: "The powers not delegated to the United States by the Constitution, nor prohibited by it to the States, are reserved to the States respectively, or to the people." The Kentucky and Virginia Resolutions (1798), which protested acts passed by the national Congress, were manifestations of states' rights, as was the Hartford Convention of 1814, called by the New Englanders who disagreed with President Madison's wartime policies. The South is the region most often associated with the doctrine. In the first half of the 19th c., when disputes arose over tariffs, public land policies, and the like, southern leaders used arguments based on states' rights in their attempts to protect their regional economic interests. Overriding all other disputes was the question of the extension of slavery into the territories. The Civil War established the supremacy of the national government and relegated the states to lesser political and economic positions. In the first half of the 20th c., southern politicians continued to speak about states' rights, generally in defense of the southern states' resistance to racial integration. The momentous Supreme Court decisions beginning in the 1950s and the various civil rights acts of the 1960s, which together imposed integration over all the country, effectively nullified such arguments.

STATES' RIGHTS DEMOCRATS. Also known as Dixiecrats; those Democrats who bolted the national party in 1948 and ran their own candidate for president. J. Strom Thurmond won the electoral votes of Alabama, Louisiana, Mississippi, and South Carolina, plus one electoral vote in Tennessee. Harry S. Truman won the election, and the party dissolved.

STATUE OF LIBERTY. Located on Liberty (formerly Bedloe's) Island in New York Harbor; conceived by the French sculptor Frédéric August Bartholdi as a gift from the people of France to the people of the US. The colossal copper figure was shipped in sections and unveiled 1886.

STATUTES AT LARGE, UNITED STATES. A chronological publication of the laws enacted at each session of Congress since 1789.

STAY AND VALUATION LAWS. Enacted by the states of Illinois, Missouri, Kentucky, and Tennessee as a result of the PANIC OF 1819. The stay law provided for a moratorium or extension of time for meeting a debt obligation. The valuation laws provided for a local board to set a fair value on property offered in satisfaction of a debt. The state courts declared both varieties unconstitutional.

STEAMBOATING ON WESTERN WATERS. Inaugurated by the *New Orleans* in 1811; steamboats first navigated the Missouri in 1819, the Tennessee in 1821, the upper Mississippi in 1823, and the Illinois in 1828. Before the Civil War, more than forty tributaries of the Mississippi had been navigated. Pittsburgh, Cincinnati, and Louisville were great Ohio ports, while New Orleans dominated the lower Mississippi.

STEAMBOAT MONOPOLIES. In 1807 Robert Fulton secured a twenty-year monopoly on steamboat operations on the Hudson R. Such monopolies were granted by states on a number of rivers, but led to disputes. In 1824, the Supreme Court (in *Gibbons v. Ogden*) destroyed all such monopolistic agreements.

STEAMBOATS. Successful commercial steamboat navigation began with Robert Fulton's *Clermont* in 1807. Within five years, steamboats were successfully plying the western rivers, and became technically more efficient, larger, and more luxurious. They boasted ornate cabins, bars, barber shops, bands and orchestras, and steam whistles and calliopes. Coal gradually replaced wood as fuel. Cargo vessels became enormous; the *J.M. White*, built at Louisville in 1878, was 325 feet long and could carry 8,500 bales of cotton.

STEAM POWER AND ENGINES. In 1755 the first steam engine began operation in the American colonies, at a copper mine in New Jersey. Such engines were large, expensive, and cumbersome, and were only economically feasible for draining valuable mines or providing water for large cities. After improvements made by James Watt in 1764, uses of steam power greatly expanded. In 1802, Oliver Evans of Philadelphia became the first American to make steam engines for the general market; Philadelphia soon became the building center. Demand increased with the widespread use of steamboats on the western rivers, the demand for engines on southern sugar plantations, and the growing coal-mining activities. By 1838, steam power was widely accepted all over the country. Its many uses in manufacturing created the nation's great industrial centers; and the harnessing of steam engines to railroad locomotives created a nationwide transportation system for the first time. In the 20th c., steam power has remained of primary importance only in the generation of electricity in power plants.

STEEL. See IRON AND STEEL INDUSTRY.

STEEL STRIKES. Strikes in the steel industry, beginning with the HOMESTEAD STRIKE in 1892 and usually accompanied by violence, were aimed at gaining union recognition. In 1919, the US Steel Corp. defeated a massive organizing attempt by twenty-four unions led by the AMERICAN FEDERATION OF LABOR (AFL). With this victory, US Steel and the smaller companies (known collectively as Little Steel) were able to maintain an open-shop policy until 1937. After the passage of the National Labor Relations Act in 1935, unions were able at last to force the steel companies to accept unionism. The CONGRESS OF INDUSTRIAL ORGANIZATIONS (CIO) was recognized as the workers' bargaining agent; after US Steel, or Big Steel, capitulated, Little Steel fell in behind. Free collective bargaining between the Steelworkers Union and the industry essentially began in 1946; from that year until 1959, the union struck five times, the longest (in 1959) lasting three months. Unlike earlier strikes, these were peaceful; the companies made no attempt to operate the mills when the union struck. After the 1959 strike, the steel industry entered a long period of relatively peaceful relations with the union. Beginning in the 1970s, the precarious economic condition of the US steel industry, severely curtailed by imported steel, discouraged the workers from making demands that might lead to a strike.

STEERING COMMITTEES. Partisan committees in the Congress whose purpose is to establish party policy. In the Senate, such steering committees date from the 19th c.; they first appeared in the House of Representatives in the 20th c. Today, they are sometimes known as policy committees.

STEPHENSON, FORT, DEFENSE OF (Aug. 1–2, 1813). During the War of 1812, a small US force successfully defended Fort Stephenson (now Fremont, Ohio) against a large, well-organized attack by British and Indian forces. After that defeat, the British made no further effort to invade Ohio.

STERLING IRON WORKS. Built 1738 in the Ramapo Mountains at Sterlington, New York, they are among the oldest iron and steel producing plants in the US. The high-quality iron made there was of invaluable use to the Americans in the Revolutionary War.

STEUBEN, FORT. Built 1786 on the site of present Steubenville, Ohio; apparently burned in 1790.

STEVENS' INDIAN TREATIES. In 1854–55, Gov. I.I. Stevens of Washington Territory, who was also Indian agent there, negotiated a number of treaties with the Indians of the area. The treaties generally concentrated the Indians on reservations.

STOCKS. Punishment apparatus consisting of a frame in which the culprit's hands, or hands and feet, were confined while he or she was kept in a sitting position. Widely used in colonial New England.

STOCKTON. City in California, located in the San Joaquin Valley; prospered after construction of a deep-water channel connecting it to San Francisco, 88 miles away. Industries include food packing and freezing, wine-making, and the shipping of agricultural products. Pop.: 149,779 (1980).

STOCKTON-KEARNY QUARREL (1846–47). Commodore R.F. Stockton was acting as military governor of newly conquered Cali-

fornia when Gen. S.W. Kearney arrived to set up a temporary civil government. Stockton was unwilling to relinquish authority. The issue was only settled when Gen. J.C. Frémont arrived to take over from Kearney. (See also BEAR FLAG REVOLT.)

STOCKYARDS. By the 1860s, livestock had become one of the chief freight items of the western railroads, and at various western termini the early stockyards were either private or owned and operated by the railroads. The great Union Stock Yards of Chicago were opened in 1865, with the railroads operating out of Chicago the principal owners. As the cattle trade moved westward, stockyards were opened in Kansas City (1871), St. Louis (1872), Cincinnati (1874), and St. Paul and Denver (1886).

STODDERT, FORT. Built 1799 near the junction of the Alabama and Tombigbee rivers in Alabama, about 50 miles above Mobile. Became an important settlement and military post and revenue headquarters of the district of Mobile. After Mobile itself was taken from the Spanish in the War of 1812, it lost importance and was abandoned.

STONE FLEETS. During the Civil War, the Union navy sank small sailing vessels, loaded with stone, in the harbors of Southern port cities in the hope of closing those ports to blockade runners. The scheme did not work.

STONINGTON, BOMBARDMENT OF (Aug. 9–12, 1814). During the War of 1812, four British vessels bombarded Stonington, Conn., for three days, probably in anticipation of an attack on nearby New London. Little damage was done.

STONY POINT, CAPTURE OF (July 16, 1779). The British occupied Stony Point, on the W bank of the Hudson R, and Verplancks Point on the E bank; they were a link in the two main roads between New England and Philadelphia. Colonial troops mounted a campaign to retake Stony Point; Gen. Anthony Wayne attacked and took over 500 British prisoners. Although the points were later abandoned, it was an important morale victory for the patriot forces.

STORE BOATS. Flatboats selling groceries, liquors, dry goods, and hardware descended the Ohio and Tennessee rivers in the early 19th c. They tied up at small settlements and plantations to sell their wares.

STORES, GENERAL. Storekeepers in newly settled communities sold and bartered great varieties of merchandise to customers, marketed crops taken in trade, operated local post offices, and provided credit and elementary banking services. From colonial times through much of the 19th c., they constituted the typical retail unit.

STOURBRIDGE LION. First steam locomotive to run on a track in America. Built in England, it made one trip (Aug. 8, 1829) between Carbondale and Honesdale, Pa. It was too heavy for any bridge and had to be discarded.

STRANGITE KINGDOM. J.J. Strang was one of the Mormon prophets vying for leadership after the death of Joseph Smith in 1844. He founded settlements in Wisconsin and on Beaver Islands in Lake Michigan. There he established the Kingdom of God on Earth. In 1856, he was murdered by disgruntled conspirators; and his followers were driven into exile by a frontier mob. Only a few retained the Strangite faith.

STRATEGIC ARMS LIMITATION TALKS (SALT). Begun 1969 between the US and the Soviet Union. The first agreement, SALT I, was reached in 1972; it limited each side to two ABM sites, outlawed mobile land missiles, prohibited interference with spy satellites, and restricted the number of strategic missiles each country could have. A tentative SALT II agreement was made during the Ford administration, and negotiatons were continued under President Carter. In 1979 Carter and Soviet Leader Leonid Brezhnev signed the agreement; they agreed to restrict their arsenals to 2,400 strategic missiles each, 1,320 of which could have multiple warheads. It was denounced by conservatives in Congress; debate continued until January 1980, when Carter asked Congress to delay consideration of the treaty in consequence of the Soviet invasion of Afghanistan. Virtually no effort was made to revive the talks during the early years of the Reagan administration.

STRAUDER V. WEST VIRGINIA, 100 US 303 (1880). Supreme Court upheld parts of the Civil Rights Act of 1866 and declared a West Virginia law restricting jury service to whites to be in violation of the FOURTEENTH AMENDMENT.

STRAWBERRY BANK. Settlement founded ca. 1630 on the Piscataqua R; the present Portsmouth, N.H.

STREET RAILWAYS. The first such car line was constructed in New York City in 1832; it was not a financial success; in 1836 another line was constructed in Boston. In 1856, the modern type of streetcar rail was designed for a Philadelphia line, and by 1860 thirty new lines had been built. By 1890, there were 769 such railways. The early steam cars were highly objectionable, and cable cars next became the most popular form of rapid transit. Electric cars, introduced in the 1880s, soon superseded all other systems (see RAILWAYS, ELECTRIC). Beginning in the 1920s, most street railways began losing money and were gradually replaced by motor buses.

STRICT CONSTRUCTION. Those who favor strict construction believe that no government agency should extend the meaning of any part of the Constitution beyond its literal meaning. Argument over interpretation of the Constitution led to the development of the first political parties; the Federalists, who believed that the federal government ought to be able to interpret its powers loosely (see FEDERALIST PARTY), opposed the Jeffersonian Republicans, who wanted strict limits set on the powers of the federal government (see REPUBLICANS, JEFFERSONIAN). It has remained a source of contention among constitutional scholars.

STRIKES. Most early strikes in the US did not involve a labor organization. The workers merely got together on a temporary basis to present their demands or to take joint action to protect their interests. Early court rulings declared such strikes to be illegal. In 1842, however, the courts ruled that striking per se was not illegal, depending on the means used. In general, labor unions were not yet free to strike; INJUNCTIONS were used against them. In 1932, the Norris-La Guardia Act forbade the use of injunctions in labor disputes and repudiated antiunion (yellow-dog) contracts as a basis for equal and equitable rights. The NATIONAL LABOR RELATIONS ACT of 1935 affirmed labor's right to organize and bargain collectively and, consequently, to strike when necessary. In 1936, a federal law made it illegal to transport a strikebreaker across state lines. Later, the TAFT-HARTLEY ACT (1947) and the Landrum-Griffin Act (1959) limited somewhat labor's right to strike.

STRIP MINING. Technique for extracting minerals from the surface of the earth, used extensively for coal, copper ore, and iron ore. Soil and other material lying above the mineral is first stripped away; power shovels or similar equipment are then used to scoop up the mineral. Strip mining is much less expensive than most other types of mining, and far less dangerous for miners. However, it usually leaves lasting scars on the earth's surface.

STUDENT NONVIOLENT COORDINATING COMMITTEE (SNCC). Founded 1960 to coordinate the southern black college-student nonviolent direct-action protests against segregation. Played an important role in the early 1960s, but ca. 1965 it embraced black separatism and revolutionary violence and quickly declined in influence.

STUDENTS FOR A DEMOCRATIC SOCIETY (SDS). Main organizational expression of the campus-based radical movement known as the New Left in the 1960s. One of the early organizations opposed to the war in Vietnam. By the end of the 1960s, SDS at the national level was an avowedly revolutionary organization. At many schools, notably at Columbia University in 1968, SDS chapters led disruptive protests against university ties with the military and other issues. The radical wing of the movement broke away ca. 1970 and formed the Weather Underground, which placed its emphasis on support for the Third World and black revolutionaries. On most campuses, the SDS chapters soon dissolved.

SUBLETTE'S CUTOFF. Dry branch of the Oregon Trail between South Pass and Bear R, Wyo., fifty-three miles shorter than the better-watered Fort Bridger route. Part of the cutoff was used in 1832 for pack mules by W.L. Sublette, a fur trader.

SUBMARINES. In the Civil War, the Confederacy employed the only real submarine in combat; the *Hunley* was a hand-propelled ironclad vessel with a spar explosive attached to its bow. It attacked a Union corvette in Charleston harbor in 1864; both vessels sank. Modern undersea craft in America evolved from the pioneering work of J.P. Holland and Simon Lake. Holland's most famous craft, named after himself, was built at his own expense and launched in 1897; it became the US Navy's first submarine, in 1900. Lake's company built twenty-seven submarines for the US, the first completed 1911. At the outset of World War I, there were submarines in the fleets of all the major navies; standard length was about 200 feet long. In World War II, two developments, radar and the snorkel, had a major impact on submarine combat. The world's first nuclear-powered submarine, the USS *Nautilus*, was launched 1954. It was 320 feet long and cruised 60,000 miles on its initial fuel; traversed the Arctic Ocean under the ice cap (1958). The majority of US nuclear submarines are primarily intended to destroy enemy submarines; the remainder are the ballistic-missile submarines armed with Polaris or Poseidon missiles for use against cities and other fixed, land targets. In the early 1980s, the US had about eighty attack submarines and forty ballistic-missile submarines.

SUBSIDIES. Throughout US history, state and privately owned transportation improvements have been freely subsidized. In the 19th c., Congress subsidized canals and railroads with both funds and land grants. Mail subsidies to the merchant marine were generously granted during the later 19th c.; and after World War I, large mail subsidies were granted to air transport companies. The Great Depression of the 1930s marked a new era in government subsidies. Not only were loans made to banks, railroads, and industrial corporations at low rates, but outright grants were offered to state and local governments for improvements. Tariffs and cheap postage rates, although not strictly subsidies, have the same effect; they artificially increase the income of producers of the goods involved.

SUBSTITUTES, CIVIL WAR. In the North during the Civil War, a man could avoid military service by hiring a substitute to take his place. Originally the cost was $300 but the price rose sharply as the war progressed.

SUBTREASURIES. After President Jackson had the government's deposits removed from the second Bank of the United States, they were placed in the so-called pet banks (see PANIC OF 1837). This did not prove satisfactory, and an act in 1840 set up an INDEPENDENT TREASURY SYSTEM. Subtreasuries were established in major cities. After 1913, Federal Reserve banks acted as fiscal agents for the government and the subtreasuries were gradually eliminated (see FEDERAL RESERVE SYSTEM).

SUBVERSION. Subversive activities of totalitarian inspiration aroused congressional and public concern in the 1930s; this led to the formation of the HOUSE COMMITTEE ON UN-AMERICAN ACTIVITIES. Concern over subversive activities reached a peak in the years of the cold war following World War II. The existence of a widespread Soviet espionage network in the US became known through the arrest of Igor Gouzenko in Canada in 1946. The subsequent trials of Alger Hiss and Julius and Ethel Rosenberg convinced many that stringent countermeasures were necessary. Sen. Joseph R. McCarthy became chairman of the Senate Committee on Government Operations; he made sensational charges concerning subversive activities both in government and in private industry. The carelessness of his charges brought congressional probes of subversion into a disrepute from which they never fully recovered (see MCCARTHY-ARMY HEARINGS).

SUBWAYS. By the late 19th c., elevated railroads in America's major cities had become unsatisfactory because of noise, unsightliness, and depreciation of adjacent property values. Between 1895 and 1900, Boston replaced 1.7 miles of trolley-car tracks with an underground railroad. New York opened its first subway in 1904 and rapidly expanded its system. Philadelphia opened its subway in 1907. Later Newark, St. Louis, Los Angeles, and Chicago built limited subway lines. In the 1970s, San Francisco and Washington, D.C., opened new subway lines.

SUEZ CRISIS (1956). In July 1956, the US and Great Britain, reacting to an Egyptian trade deal with the Soviet Union, withdrew an offer to aid in the construction of the Aswan High Dam on the Nile R. Egypt retaliated by nationalizing the Suez Canal. Britain and France, part owners of the canal and long dependent on oil supplies brought through it, joined with Israel in military attacks on Egypt. On Oct. 29, Israel invaded the Gaza Strip and the Sinai peninsula, inflicting a stinging defeat on the Egyptian army. Two days later, Britain and France attacked Egypt. The US, backed by the Soviet Union, arranged for a United Nations call for a ceasefire (Nov. 2). An international peace force was dispatched to the area, where it remained until 1967.

SUFFOLK RESOLVES (1774). Passed by a meeting in Massachusetts called to protest the COERCION ACTS, they called for the colonies to refuse to obey the acts; urged weekly militia musters; called for the nonpayment of taxes; and urged nonintercourse with Great Britain. The resolves were endorsed by the Continental Congress.

SUFFRAGE. See FRANCHISE; VOTING; WOMAN'S RIGHTS MOVEMENT.

SUFFRAGE, BLACK. In some of the state constitutions passed after the Revolutionary War, free blacks were permitted to vote; in others they were not. After the Civil War, ratification of the THIRTEENTH AMENDMENT and the FOURTEENTH AMENDMENT made all blacks citizens of both the US and the states in which they lived. Each state was required to provide equal protection of the law for all, a requirement specifically set forth in the FIFTEENTH AMENDMENT. Blacks voted in numbers throughout the South during Reconstruction and in the years immediately following. Soon, however, the states by various official and unofficial ways, were successful in denying the vote to virtually every black. In the 20th c., these laws and customs were gradually declared unconstitutional by the Supreme Court (see GRANDFATHER CLAUSE; POLL TAX; WHITE PRIMARY), and blacks began registering to vote. Subtle and not-so-suble methods were still employed to discourage blacks from voting; and Congress passed the VOTING RIGHTS ACT OF 1965, which suspended literacy tests and other devices still in use to prevent blacks from registering. It also authorized sending federal registrars to areas where local officials refused to obey the law. So successful was the law that by the 1980s there were virtually no roadblocks to black registration and voting.

SUFFRAGE, COLONIAL. Voting qualifications were fixed by each colony; in many the requirements followed the English concept that only those with a "stake in society" (e.g., owned property) should vote. Limitations of race, sex, age, and residence were more often the result of custom than law. Generally, Jews and Roman Catholics were barred, again based on English custom. Women were excluded by statute only in four colonies, but there is rare evidence that any ever voted anywhere. The age qualification was almost universally twenty-one. Pennsylvania's two-year residence requirement was the most stringent. Slaves and indentured servants were denied the franchise; in the Carolinas, Georgia, and Virginia, free blacks as well. Indians did vote at times in Massachusetts.

SUFFRAGE, EXCLUSION FROM THE. It is generally estimated that because of state property and taxpaying qualifications, fewer than one-fourth of all white adult males were eligible to vote in 1787–89. States had largely abandoned property qualifications for voting by 1850. Blacks were enfranchised by the amendments passed after the Civil War, although in actual practice many were excluded until after the passage of the Voting Rights Act of 1965 (see SUFFRAGE, BLACK). The NINETEENTH AMENDMENT (1920) gave women the right to vote; and the TWENTY-SIXTH AMENDMENT (1971) lowered the voting age to 18. Unequal voting power resulting from malapportionment was held unconstitutional in Supreme Court decisions beginning 1962. Thus by the 1980s, every citizen (except certain classes of convicted felons) over eighteen, of whatever sex, color, or race, was legally entitled to vote.

SUFFRAGE, WOMAN. See WOMAN'S SUFFRAGE.

SUGAR ACTS. Regulations imposed on the American colonies by Great Britain in 1764 aimed at ending the smuggling trade in foreign molasses and imposing new duties on wine imported from Madeira. Its major purpose was to give British sugar planters in the West Indies an effective monopoly of the American sugar market. Although it was violently opposed at first, its accompanying bounty-paying arrangements proved to be profitable to the colonies.

SUGARCANE. Brought to the New World by Christopher Columbus and first cultivated successfully in the US (in Louisiana) in the mid-18th c. New cold-resistant varieties along with advances (chiefly steam power) in refining techniques made plantations in Louisiana and Texas especially profitable in the late 19th c. Sugar production ended in Texas in the 1920s, but successfully developed in Florida. Puerto Rico and Hawaii are also important producers of sugar cane.

SUGAR HOUSE PRISONS. There were several sugar refineries in New York City when the American Revolution began. The British used them as prisons; shocking narratives were prevalent of cruelty and privations in these prisons.

SUGAR INDUSTRY. In colonial America, sugar was made from maple sap for household use and local trading. Sugar manufacturing was revolutionized in the 1820s by the advent of the steam engine (for crushing the cane) and in the 1840s by the invention of a multiple-effect system for evaporating cane juice, which replaced open kettle boilers. Prior to 1861, most Louisiana and Texas cane sugar was shipped to the Mississippi Valley. Refiners on the East Coast imported much of their sugar from the West Indies. In the late 19th and early 20th c., the cultivation of sugar beets spread from the Great Lakes to California. By the 1980s, both cane and beet processing was done in large expensive central mills owned by large corporations.

SUGAR ISLANDS. Popular name in colonial times for the sugar-producing islands of the West Indies.

SUGAR TRUST. Generally applied to the American Sugar Refining Co., organized 1891, which maintained a practical monopoly in both refining and selling sugar. Efforts to prosecute the company under the Sherman Antitrust Act were not successful.

SULFUR INDUSTRY. See CHEMICAL INDUSTRY.

SULLIVAN-CLINTON CAMPAIGN (1779). Planned by Gen. George Washington in an effort to curb attacks of the Indians and Tories on the frontiers of New York and Pennsylvania. Command was given to Gen. John Sullivan; the New York wing, charged with keeping the Iroquois in check, was put under the command of Gen. James Clinton. Sullivan and Clinton swept the area of the enemy, and at Newtown, near the present Elmira, N.Y., the Cayuga, Seneca, and Tories made their only stand. They were driven from the field; the patriots pushed forward, burning forty Indian villages and destroying 160,000 bushels of corn. Sullivan then returned to Easton, Pa.

SULLIVAN IN RHODE ISLAND (1778). Gen. John Sullivan, expecting support from the French fleet, planned an attack on the British at Newport. A storm severely damaged the French squadron, which had to retreat to Boston for repairs. Lacking support, Sullivan retreated but was pursued by the British. On Aug. 29, a spirited battle took place at Quaker Hill. The British attacks were repelled; Sullivan retreated to Tiverton before British reinforcements could arrive.

SULLY, FORT. Built 1863 at Pierre, S. Dak., as protection against the Sioux. In 1866, it was moved twenty-eight miles N of Pierre. Abandoned 1891.

SUMNER, FORT. Military post built 1862 on the Pecos R in EC New Mexico; located near Bosque Redondo, a reservation containing 8,000 Navaho and 400 Mescalero Apache prisoners of war. They had been placed there after breaking out of their reservations and making war along the Rio Grande. In 1868, most were placed on a new reservation in their homeland in NE New Mexico and Fort Sumner was abandoned.

SUMNER'S EXPEDITION (1857). Depredations by the Cheyenne in Kansas and Nebraska caused Col. E.V. Sumner to march against them from Fort Leavenworth with six companies of cavalry and three of infantry. On July 29, the cavalry encountered 400 warriors on Solomon Fork of the Kansas R. A pitched battle ensued; Sumner fruitlessly pursued the Indians. Marching 1,000 miles, the soldiers returned to Fort Kearny in August, many barefooted or destitute of clothing.

SUMPTUARY LAWS AND TAXES, COLONIAL. There were sumptuary laws in all the colonies aimed at regulating the consumption of food and clothing, morals, amusements, church attendance, and Sabbath observance. Laws against wearing gold decorations, lace, silk, and similar materials when one's station in life did not warrant such luxuries were confined mostly to the 17th c. and were not peculiar to the New World. Laws against sexual immorality were common in all the colonies but were especially strict in Puritan New England.

SUMTER, FORT. Situated in the mouth of Charleston harbor; after South Carolina passed the Ordinance of Secession in Dec. 1860, Union forces in Charleston removed themselves to Fort Sumter, where they were in effect under siege. After his inauguration, President Lincoln dispatched a fleet to relieve the garrison there. As the US fleet neared, Confederate Gen. P.G.T. Beauregard offered the garrison a final chance to surrender. When the offer was refused, the Rebels opened fire on the fort (Apr. 12, 1861). On Apr. 13, the fort surrendered; the Civil War had begun.

On Apr. 7, 1863, Fort Sumter, garrisoned by Confederates, was attacked by a Union fleet of nine ironclads. This engagement was one of the greatest defeats in US naval history, and it inaugurated the era of the modern steel navy. In August 1863, the great siege of Fort Sumter began and lasted for 567 days. The fort was never surrendered by the Rebels. On Feb. 17, 1865, when the approach of Gen. W.T. Sherman's army of 70,000 made the evacuation of the whole Charleston sector inevitable, the fort was closed and abandoned.

SUN DANCE. One of the great communal rituals of the Plains Indians. Among the major features were a central dance pole, a characteristic lodge, elements of self-torture, the lowering of sexual restrictions, altars, priestly figures, and vows of revenge against enemies. At the dance, held in series of four-day cycles, dancers might skewer the flesh of their back to cords and allow themselves to be suspended from the central pole.

SUNDAY SCHOOLS. The first Sunday school in America was probably in Hanover County, Va., in 1786, organized by the great Methodist proselytizer Francis Asbury. It was later adopted by other Protestant denominations as a way of giving religious instruction.

SUPERIOR, LAKE. Largest of the Great Lakes and the largest body of fresh water in the world; discovered by the French in the early 17th c., when explorers began investigating its various shores and inlets. Forts and missions were established. In 1737, the first sailing ship was built on Lake Superior, commissioned to search for copper mines. In the 19th and 20th c., the center of an important mining region (copper, nickel, iron). To provide access to the lower Great Lakes, a ship canal was built (1855) along the St. Marys R. A number of industrial, manufacturing, and port cities were established on the lake, including Duluth, Minn., Superior, Wisc., and Sault Ste. Marie, Ont.

SUPPLY, CAMP. Post established 1868 on the Canadian R in present NW Oklahoma. Important in the Indian war of 1874–75; abandoned ca. 1895.

SUPREME COURT, UNITED STATES. Created by the JUDICIARY ACT OF 1789; originally consisted of a chief justice and five associate justices. Congress has varied the size of the court, but since 1869, it has comprised a chief justice and eight associate justices. All are appointed by the president with the consent of the Senate and serve for life; they can be removed from office only by impeachment (no justice has ever been impeached). President Lyndon B. Johnson named the first black, Thurgood Marshall, to the court in 1967; Ronald Reagan named the first woman, Sandra Day O'Connor, in 1981.

The court disposes of a large number of cases each year. For example, in the 1980 term, 5,144 cases were filed, 4,357 were disposed of, oral argument was heard in 154 cases, and 123 opinions were written. The regular term begins on the first Monday in October and generally ends the following June. The main business is to review appeals from lower federal courts and state courts in cases arising under the federal Constitution, an act of Congress, or a treaty of the US. Having the power of judicial review, the court may declare federal and state statutes to be unenforceable if found to be in conflict with the Constitution. Since the great power-limiting clauses in the Constitution, such as the due process and equal protection guaranties, are phrased in very broad language, the court has much room to maneuver. It has also had the responsibility of drawing the lines between individual liberties and permissible social controls.

SUPREME COURT PACKING BILLS. Congressional measures designed to alter the composition of the Supreme Court to correct alleged judicial errors or to secure desired decisions. They characteristically have taken the form of enlarging the number of justices, although in 1866 Congress reduced the size of the court from ten to seven in order to prevent President Andrew Johnson from appointing justices who might overrule the Radical Republican program over which Congress and the president were at loggerheads. (In 1869, the number was increased to nine.) The most important court-packing bill was rejected by Congress: Angered by a series of decisions that had emasculated the New Deal, President Franklin D. Roosevelt submitted a plan in 1937 that would have authorized the president to appoint an additional justice for each one who, having reached the age of seventy, failed to retire; the total was not to exceed fifteen. After some five months of intensive congressional and public debate, the Senate rejected the president's proposal.

SURGERY. See MEDICINE AND SURGERY.

SUSAN CONSTANT. Flagship of the three vessels conveying the first English settlement in the New World; along with the *Godspeed* and *Discovery*, it landed at Cape Henry on Chesapeake Bay on Apr. 26, 1607. After surveying the area, the colonists settled at Jamestown in May.

SUSQUEHANNA COMPANY. Organized by a group of Connecticut farmers in 1753 for the purpose of settling on lands in Wyoming Valley, Pennsylvania. Purchased land from the Six Nations and planted a settlement in 1762, which was wiped out by the Indians in 1763. After the Treaty of Stanwix (1768), they founded the town of Wilkes-Barre.

SUTLER MERCHANT. Civilian trader who was given a contract to supply goods for an army post. Sutlers were widely employed in western forts.

SUTTER'S FORT. Built 1841 on the site of what is now Sacramento, Calif. Gold was discovered nearby in 1848, thereby setting off the California gold rush.

SWAMP ANGEL. An 8-inch gun used by Union soldiers in the siege of Charleston in 1863. Mounted on a battery constructed on piles driven into the swamp, it burst after firing thirty-six shots.

SWAMP FIGHT. See GREAT SWAMP FIGHT.

SWAMPLANDS. The public land states contained great areas of swamp and overflowed lands that were neglected by the early settlers, who could not drain them. In 1850, 70 million acres passed into the possession of the states.

SWEATSHOP. Factory characterized by unhealthy working conditions, low wages, and long hours. Historically, the garment trades and cigar manufacturing in the late 19th c. provide the most notorious examples.

SWEDENBORGIANISM. See NEW JERUSALEM, CHURCHES OF THE.

SWEEPING RESOLUTION. Passed by the Ohio legislature in 1810, it declared vacant all judgeships and other state offices filled prior to statehood. Its purpose was to fill the offices with men more amenable to the will of the legislature.

SYCAMORE SHOALS, TREATY OF. In (1775) the Cherokee ceded about 17 million acres to the Transylvania Co. of North Carolina. The land lay between the Kentucky R and the south watershed of the Cumberland R.

SYNDICALISM. In the US, revolutionary industrial unionism, or syndicalism, is mostly identified with the INDUSTRIAL WORKERS OF THE WORLD (IWW), founded 1905 and active until World War I. The aim of syndicalists was the establishment of a producers' cooperative commonwealth, in which industries would be socially owned, and managed by *syndicats*, or labor unions. The syndicalists emphasized the class struggle, were opposed to militarism, imperialism, and patriotism, and advocated direct action, mainly sabotage and the general strike. The IWW never represented an appreciable percentage of US workers; the movement waned after World War I.

SYRACUSE. City in New York, occupying a site long used by Onondaga Indians. Built over salt deposits that provided the Iroquois with the means of preserving their meat. An industrial center. Pop.: 170,105 (1980).

TABERNACLE, MORMON. Large turtle-shaped auditorium in Salt Lake City, completed 1867. Seats 8,000; noted for its acoustic properties.

TACNA-ARICA CONTROVERSY. Two provinces whose ownership was long contested by Peru and Chile. In 1929, the US mediated a solution: Peru got Tacna and Chile got Arica.

TACOMA. City in Washington, an important port on Puget Sound. Industries include paper mills and electric parts factories. Pop.: 158,501 (1980).

TAFIA. Low-grade rum that served as a staple of trade and a medium of exchange between the Indians and the French and Spanish in the Mississippi Valley and the Floridas.

TAFT COMMISSION. Beginning 1900, it supervised the transfer from military to civil government in the Philippines. William Howard Taft was president of the commission and also civil governor after 1901. In 1907, its authority passed to the Philippine legislature.

TAFT-HARTLEY ACT (1947). Passed by Congress over the veto of President Truman; amended the NATIONAL LABOR RELATIONS ACT of 1935 by making illegal a wide range of union activities.

TAFT-ROOSEVELT SPLIT. Differences between the progressive wing of the Republican party, led by former President Theodore Roosevelt, and the more conservative Taft administration began soon after Taft's inauguration in 1909. Matters worsened, and in 1912 Roosevelt opposed Taft for reelection by running on the Progressive, or Bull Moose, ticket (see PROGRESSIVE PARTY). The Republican split resulted in the election of the Democratic candidate, Woodrow Wilson.

TALLAHASSEE. Capital city of Florida and an important shipping and marketing center for a large region of pine forests and farms. Successfully defended during the Civil War against Union attacks. Pop.: 82,548 (1980).

TAMMANY HALL. Founded in New York City in 1789 as a fraternal society, the Society of Saint Tammany soon became a political organization associated with Thomas Jefferson's Democratic-Republican party and, in particular, the Aaron Burr faction in New York state. By the 1850s, Tammany controlled franchises, contracts, and patronage of the city government. With the election of Fernando Wood as mayor in 1854, city hall became a Tammany fiefdom, and was the prototype of the corrupt political machine. With elevation of William Marcy Tweed to grand sachem in 1863, Tammany's corruption became all pervasive (see TWEED RING). It remained firmly in control of New York City, despite its differences with the state Democratic party under Franklin D. Roosevelt, until the election of Fiorello La Guardia as mayor in 1933. Carmine De Sapio briefly revived Tammany Hall in the 1950s but lost control of his district to reformers in 1961. Shortly thereafter, the New York County Democratic committee dropped the name Tammany.

TAMPA. City located on Tampa Bay in W Florida. Tampa Bay was the landing area of Hernando De Soto in 1539, although the Spanish were unable to establish a town on the site because of Indian opposition. The US army established Fort Brooke on the bay in 1824; the city grew up around the fort. Tampa Bay was an important Confederate naval base in the Civil War; the city served as the chief supply base for US forces during the Spanish-American War. Today it is an important industrial and commercial center; the area is a major source of phosphate. Long renowned as a cigar-making center. Pop.: 271,523 (1980).

TAOS. Resort town in New Mexico, on the Rio Grande about seventy miles from Santa Fe. Within three miles of each other stand Taos Pueblo, one of the oldest existing pueblos in the US, and Ranchos de Taos, a Spanish town built before 1680. The pueblo was discovered by the Spaniards in 1540; a mission was established there early in the 17th c. Taos was headquarters for the Indian uprising against the Spanish in 1680 (see PUEBLO RE-

VOLT). The town became a fur center in the 19th c. and an art colony in the 20th. Pop.: 3,369 (1980).

TAOS TRAIL. Ran roughly from Taos, crossed the Sangre de Cristo Range at La Veta Pass, and followed the Huerfano R to the Arkansas R. Served as a road for Spaniards and later for American trappers.

TAPPAN PATENT. Tract of land at Tappan, New York, on the W bank of the Hudson R, bought 1682 from the Indians by a group of Dutch farmers from Manhattan Island. Originally considered part of New Jersey, it later was included in New York state.

TAR. Important product of the American colonies, highly useful to the British navy during the era of wooden ships. In 1705, Parliament established bounties on the production of tar and other naval stores; annual shipments to Britain reached 82,000 barrels. North Carolina was the major producer. In modern times, most tar produced is distilled to yield carbolic acid, naphtha, and other crude products.

TAR AND FEATHERS. Pouring tar over the body and covering it with feathers was an official punishment in England as early as the 12th c. It was never legal in the US but was always a mob demonstration. A number of Loyalists were tarred and feathered at the beginning of the Revolutionary War.

TARAWA (Nov. 20–23, 1943). Tarawa, one of the Gilbert Islands, had been occupied by the Japanese early in World War II. As the opening blow in the American offensive through the central Pacific, US marines made plans to retake the island. Despite heavy preassault bombardment, the marines landing on the island were met with stubbornly strong defenses. Of the first 5,000 Americans who landed, 1,500 were killed or wounded. A Japanese counterattack was defeated on the night of Nov. 22–23; the last defenders were eliminated the next day.

TARIFF. A duty levied on goods coming into the ports of a nation from foreign sources. A policy of absolutely unhampered economic intercourse is described as FREE TRADE. As a practice and as a policy of the national government, levying import duties was born with the Constitution, while the stipulation was clearly made that exports should not be subject to duties. Controversy over tariff for revenue only and tariff for protection of domestic industry began with the First Congress. A bill of 1789, presented by James Madison as a simple means of raising money, emerged as a partially protective measure. In 1791, Secretary of the Treasury Alexander Hamilton pled for further protection but was ignored. A bill passed in 1816 marks the beginning of tariff for protection. Cotton and woolen goods and pig iron and hammered and rolled bars were especially favored. The South was becoming a bitter enemy of a tariff system that seemed to benefit only manufacturers. In 1824, the midwestern states joined the middle Atlantic states, over southern objections, to impose a new tariff considerably higher than the 1816 one. In addition, it placed a tariff on such previously untaxed products as lead, glass, hemp, silk, linens, and cutlery. Pleasing nobody, it became known as the tariff of abominations; even New Englanders objected to the tax on raw wool, molasses, and sailcloth. In 1832, Henry Clay pushed through Congress a bill that removed most of the objections and lowered general duties below those of 1824. But South Carolina declared the act null and void. President Jackson asked Congress for a force act authorizing the use of military power to enforce the act; but a compromise was worked out, thereby avoiding a constitutional crisis. New laws in 1846 and 1857 continued the trend toward lower tariffs; but the panic of 1857 created new demands of protection for American industry. Succeeding acts in 1862 and 1865 raised rates to undreamed-of heights. Revenue was not completely forgotten, but the need to assuage US manufacturers upon whose products heavy internal revenue taxes had been levied was far more important. The end of the Civil War and a growing Treasury surplus soon brought repeal of most internal revenue levies. The tariffs, however, remained basically undisturbed until 1890, when they were again raised. In 1888, the Republicans elected William McKinley president, a confirmed high-tariff advocate. Taxes on tobacco and alcohol were reduced, but other tariffs were raised appreciably. Bounties were given sugar growers; for the first time a reciprocity provision was added. Tariffs were raised even higher in 1897; and by 1898, pressure for reduction had become so great that even the Republicans seemed to promise downward revision. Regardless of these pressures, the tariff remained at astronomical heights until 1913, when the Democrats, under the leadership of President Wilson, provided the first real and consistent reductions since the mid-19th c. Unfortunately, the low duties never had a chance to prove themselves because of World War I.

High protectionists were back in power after the war; in 1921, the Fordney-McCumber Tariff Act called for duties that were the highest in history and sought to withdraw the nation from the economic world. Conditions did not improve materially, and the only answer was more protection. The Smoot-Hawley Act of 1930 set a new record in restrictive legislation. European nations passed retaliatory laws. The depression grew worse, war-debt payments from Europe ceased, and world economy ground to a standstill. The Reciprocal Trade Agreements Act of 1934, passed by the New Deal administration of Franklin D. Roosevelt, inaugurated a series of executive agreements with foreign nations by which the president in part freed trade not only for the US but, also, by applying the most-favored-nation clause principle, for other nations as well. But World War II intervened before results could be measured. At the end of the war, it became obvious that Europe, the major prewar market of the US, must be restored. Thus the MARSHALL PLAN, the Point Four program, and serious other restorative measures were instituted. The General Agreement on Tariffs and Trade (GATT), was formulated by many nations in 1947 and devoted in large part to the reduction of tariffs (see RECIPROCAL TRADE AGREEMENTS). The abolition of trade discrimination was firmly established. Significant reductions in US duties were made in the immediate postwar years. In 1962, the Trade Expansion Act was passed; under it, the president was given permission to make across-the-board tariff cuts on a most-favored-nation basis, to include agricultural items, and to reduce tariff levies up to 100 percent on some items. The general meeting of GATT, called the Kennedy Round, convened in Geneva in 1964. For nearly four years, the GATT delegates argued over reducing international tariff barriers equally. The achievements were substantial. By 1970, however, the protectionist movement had reached its greatest intensity since the days of the Great Depression. Congress passed the Burke-Hartke Act, which provided that the nation should, in effect, return to the tariff rates of the Smoot-Hawley Act of 1930. Foreign reaction was quick and uncompromising. Some European countries placed immediate restrictions on American goods; by 1971, there was pressure to repeal the act and Congress complied. The administrations of the late 1970s and the 1980s generally advocated a free trade policy, despite calls from American manufacturers for import restrictions. They were joined by the labor movement, who called for the protection of American jobs by keeping down imports. Steel and Japanese automobiles were especially regarded as imports that were working to the detriment of the US economy.

TARPLEY LETTER (1849). Hoping to prevent submission or secession of the South, Sen. John C. Calhoun wrote C.S. Tarpley, urging that Mississippi call all those who desired to save the Union and southern institutions to meet and issue an address on southern grievances. The NASHVILLE CONVENTION resulted.

TASK FORCE 58 (1944–45). During World War II, the fast carriers of both the Third and Fifth (or Central Pacific Force) fleets were organized into Task Force 58, whose purpose was to seek out and destroy the Japanese fleet and naval air forces. The task force participated in all the Pacific battles. The system, enabling easy transfer of ship command, worked so well that it became the basis of postwar naval organization.

TAXATION. Taxes in the colonial period were relatively simple and limited. New England favored the poll (capitation or head) tax; the southern colonies depended on import and export duties; and the middle Atlantic colonies evolved a mixed system of import duties, excises on beverages, and property taxes. Until the French and Indian War (1763), England never attempted to collect much revenue from the colonies and engendered much resentment with passage of the SUGAR ACT (1764) and STAMP ACT (1765). The colonists objected to "taxation without representation," laying the basis for the American Revolution a decade later. In 1767,

Parliament imposed import duties through the TOWNSHEND ACTS, but the resulting colonial boycotting of British imports caused Parliament to repeal most of these duties (except on tea).

The Continental Congress, charged by the individual colonies to raise an army and navy for war against England, was not given the authority for raising the heavy war taxes needed to pay for those forces. Instead, it depended for its revenue mainly on the issuance of paper money and on domestic and foreign loans. The newly independent states had the power to levy taxes but were reluctant to do so. The ARTICLES OF CONFEDERATION (1781) continued the policy of not allowing the national government the right of taxation. The costs of running the government were to be proportioned among the various states; however, the states proved indifferent. The framers of the new constitution of 1787 strengthened the national government by empowering Congress "To lay and collect Taxes, Duties, Imposts and Excises, to pay the Debts and provide for the common Defense and general Welfare of the United States" (Article I, Section 8). Congress passed a tariff act in 1789, but when its revenues proved inadequate, an internal revenue system was established. Various excise taxes were imposed, including levies on distilled spirits (leading to the WHISKEY REBELLION of 1794), carriages, snuff, and sugar. In 1798, a direct tax was imposed on dwelling houses, lands, and slaves. Those taxes were extremely unpopular and were reduced by the Jefferson administration. The War of 1812 forced Congress to adopt new taxes, but they were repealed in 1817 in response to public pressure. During the Civil War, Congress again was forced to impose new taxes, including for the first time a progressive income tax. It was repealed in 1872; but in 1894 Congress passed a 2 percent tax on all personal and corporate income over $4,000. The Supreme Court later ruled it a direct tax and therefore unconstitutional. The PROGRESSIVE MOVEMENT had as a major objective the passage of a federal income tax law. Conservative Republicans, in an effort to prevent such a law, put through a 1 percent corporate income tax that was ruled constitutional by the courts. Nevertheless, in 1913 the SIXTEENTH AMENDMENT was ratified; it sanctioned a federal income tax. Since then, progressive corporate and personal income tax has provided an increasingly higher percentage of federal revenue. The formulae by which these taxes are imposed have been constantly revised, and today the tax policy of the federal government is recognized universally as one of the prime motivators of the national economy.

TAXATION, STATE AND MUNICIPAL. In 1789, the states gave up use of import duties to the new federal government; and for most of the 19th c., they relied on the general property tax for most of their revenue. Various other taxes were introduced, including bank taxes, insurance company taxes, general corporation taxes, and inheritance taxes. But in 1902, the general property tax still furnished 52 percent of the revenue of the states. Corporation and personal income taxes became increasingly important; after 1920 gasoline taxes became another leading source of revenue. By 1940, property taxes supplied only one-sixteenth of the total revenue. Since the 1930s, the chief state taxes have been the general sales tax, the gasoline tax, and the payroll tax for unemployment insurance. Revenue has also been produced by specific taxes on the retail sale of tobacco and alcoholic beverages and by inheritance taxes.

By 1900 the general property tax used by counties, municipalities, and other local governing authorities as their principal source of revenue had become a selective tax on real estate and business equipment and inventory. Increasingly after World War II, local governments began imposing payroll, income, sales, gasoline, and automobile taxes; nevertheless, the property tax in the 1970s accounted for most of all local revenue.

TAXATION WITHOUT REPRESENTATION. Became an issue in the American colonies after passage of the TOWNSHEND ACTS 1767. The colonists maintained that in the matter of internal taxation, they were free from parliamentary control. Considering themselves to be totally unrepresented in Parliament, they denied that body's right to impose taxes on them.

TAX COURT OF THE UNITED STATES. Created 1924 as an agency of the executive branch of the government, with power to hear appeals from rulings under the Revenue Act of 1924. In 1969 it was removed to the judicial branch of the federal government. Has power to settle cases concerning deficiencies or overpayment in income, excess profits, estate, gift, and holding company taxes. Its decisions can be appealed to higher courts.

TEA, DUTY ON. Tea coming to colonial America was subject to British import and excise or inland duties. These duties were varied from time to time; in 1773 the East India Co. was permitted to export tea directly to the colonies, thereby bypassing the British duties. This had the effect of creating a monopoly, precipitating agitation in America. (See BOSTON TEA PARTY; TEA PARTIES).

TEACHERS' LOYALTY OATH. Since 1863, nearly two-thirds of the state legislatures have enacted compulsory loyalty oaths for teachers. Most require an affirmation to uphold the federal and state constitutions; but in the cold war period after World War II, many asked for sweeping disclaimers of past beliefs and associations, especially communist or leftwing. In 1925 the Supreme Court ruled that a state could require a teacher to be "of patriotic disposition." Subsequently, the court struck down some loyalty oaths for being so all-encompassing as to infringe on First Amendment rights.

TEA PARTIES. Several prerevolutionary episodes protesting the British taxation on tea. The first, and most famous was the BOSTON TEA PARTY of 1773. Previously, citizens of New York had persuaded consignees to refuse to receive any tea, and the first cargo at that port (April 1774) was turned back; a consignment discovered on board another vessel was thrown into the river. At Portsmouth, N.H., and Philadelphia tea ships were turned away. At Annapolis, Md., citizens forced the owner of an offending vessel to put it to the torch. Edenton, N.C., held the Ladies' Tea Party, at which the women of the town passed resolutions against the use of tea.

TEAPOT DOME SCANDAL. In 1921, President Harding transferred control of the naval oil reserves at Elk Hills, Calif., and Teapot Dome, Wyo., to the Department of the Interior. In 1922, Albert B. Fall, secretary of the interior, without competitive bidding, leased the Teapot Dome fields to Harry F. Sinclair of the Mammoth Oil Co., and Elk Hills to Edward L. Doheny, a personal friend. A congressional investigation revealed that Doheny had lent Fall $100,000 without interest; and that later Sinclair had lent Fall $25,000. Fall was convicted of accepting bribes, but the other two were acquitted.

TECUMSEH, CRUSADE OF (ca. 1806–13). Effort by the Shawnee chief, Tecumseh, and his brother, SHAWNEE PROPHET, to rescue their people from the depredations brought upon them by white encroachments, beginning with the Treaty of Greenville (see GREENVILLE, TREATY OF). Sweeping social and religious reforms were instituted, including abstinence from alcohol, community of property, and adherence to the native way of life. Tecumseh attempted to organize a tribal confederacy and to establish the principle that the land was common property of all tribes, to be alienated only with their common consent.

TEHERAN CONFERENCE (Nov. 28–Dec. 1, 1943). First war conference attended by President Franklin D. Roosevelt, Prime Minister Winston Churchill, and Marshal Joseph Stalin. The leaders made important military decisions regarding a second front in Europe and discussed the boundaries of Poland and the future of Germany. Stalin also renewed his pledge to declare war on Japan.

TELEGRAPH. Samuel Morse and two associates, Leonard D. Gale and Alfred Vail, made their important technical contributions to the telegraph in the 1830s, including the formulation of the Morse Code, a bisignal code that has since evolved into the pulse code system used in digital computers and space telemetry systems. Morse and his associates conducted a public demonstration of their new communications system in 1838; their first intercity line (a forty-mile line between Washington and Baltimore) was not completed until 1844. In 1845, they organized the Magnetic Telegraphic Co.; many small competing telegraph companies were also organized. By 1852, the US had about 15,000 miles of telegraph lines. The Western Union Co., which eventually established an effective national monopoly, was organized 1856; the first transcontinental line was completed 1861. The first successful transatlantic cable became operational in 1866.

TELEPHONE. Several inventors in the 1870s recognized the feasibility of an electromagnetic telephone, the most famous being Alexander Graham Bell; his patent led to the organization of the largest industrial corporation in the world. In 1876, Bell demonstrated the first successful transmission of articulate speech at the Philadelphia Centennial Exposition. The Bell Telephone Co., later the American Telephone and Telegraph Co., was organized 1877. An experimental line between Boston and New York City was completed in 1884 using hard-drawn copper wire. Introduction of loading coils during the first decade of the 20th c. made feasible a 2,000-mile circuit without amplifiers. The Bell Co. maintained an effective monopoly of the industry in the US until the expiration of Bell's patents in the 1890s; most smaller companies were finally absorbed or went out of business. The introduction of electronic vacuum-tube amplifiers made possible the first transcontinental conversation by wire in 1915. The advent of radio-electronic methods enabled the completion of a worldwide telephone system in the 1920s; automatic dialing also was introduced in large cities in the 1920s. Important technical advancements came about at the end of World War II; they included solid-state amplifiers, switching circuits, microwave links, and later the first international communication satellite, Telstar (1962). By the 1980s, the telephone had become an inseparable part of American life; 96 percent of households had a telephone (1980), as compared with 62 percent in 1950.

TELEVISION. Experiments in converting photographic images into an electrical impulse equivalent began as early as 1873, but practical work on television cameras and receivers did not begin until the 1920s, much of it done in the laboratories of the Radio Corp. of America (RCA); the most important innovations were developed by Philo Taylor Farnsworth and Vladimir K. Zworykin. By 1939, the National Broadcasting Co. (a subsidiary of RCA) provided extensive programming over station W2XBS New York. Full commercial program service was authorized for 1941 by the FEDERAL COMMUNICATIONS COMMIS-

SION, but the commercial development of television was to wait until the end of World War II. The television industry expanded spectacularly from six television stations in 1946 to 1,031 in 1981. Color television was introduced in 1953 but did not become commercially feasible for a decade. In the 1970s, the fastest growing segment was cable television; in the 1980s, the popularity of video cassette recorders (VCRs) was phenomenal. With almost 80 million TV sets in the country and an average viewing time of thirty hours per week, television represents a major, if not the major, influence on contemporary Americans.

TELLER AMENDMENT (1898). Disclaimer on the part of the US of any intention to "exercise sovereignty, jurisdiction or control" over Cuba when it should be freed from Spanish rule.

TEMPERANCE MOVEMENT. Lyman Beecher, a Presbyterian minister, began preaching against the evils of alcohol ca. 1810; in 1813, he was one of the founders of the Connecticut Society for the Reformation of Morals, the first temperance society. At about the same time, other such groups were being formed in Massachusetts and New York state. In 1826, the American Society for the Promotion of Temperance was founded; by 1834, it had auxiliaries in every state, approximately 5,000 locals, and 1 million pledge signers. Beneath the surface the temperance movement had been slowly converted into a campaign for prohibition. A few leaders had long been eager to direct the force of law against the liquor traffic and had denounced the licensing of retail liquor dealers. (See PROHIBITION; PROHIBITION PARTY). The Twenty-first Amendment (1933) repealed prohibition. Thereafter, the temperance movement waned; local option was put into effect in a number of states, but by 1966 no statewide prohibition law existed in the US.

TENEMENTS. Legally, all apartment houses; but in common usage, the term defines only substandard housing. In the 19th c., such housing was quickly erected in what soon became the SLUMS of large cities to accommodate the great influx of immigrants. New York City in 1867 established minimum standards for room size, ventilation, and sanitation; in 1879, the city decreed that any new tenement could occupy no more than 60 percent of the lot. This led to the notorious "dumbbell" tenement, so called because of its shape, which was eventually outlawed. Tenements still provide housing for many thousands of families in older cities.

TENNESSEE. First explored by the Spanish Hernando de Soto in 1540, the present Tennessee was claimed by the French in 1673; in the same year, the British laid the foundation for their claim in East Tennessee as fur traders established a profitable business with the Cherokee and Creek. Meanwhile, the French, exploring eastward from the Mississippi R, waged war against the Chickasaw of West Tennessee and attempted to entice the Cherokee of East Tennessee away from their English allies. The area remained in contention until the 18th c. The first permanent settlement was built near the Watauga R in 1768, and in 1772 settlers there formed a government called the Watauga Association. In 1776, they petitioned North Carolina to extend its jurisdiction to them; in 1777, North Carolina created Washington County out of an area that included all of present Tennessee. Despite Indian troubles, white settlement burgeoned. In 1789, following an unsuccessful attempt by the East Tennesseans to form the state of FRANKLIN, North Carolina ceded its rights to the federal government. Congress then organized the Territory South of the Ohio R, and in 1796 made Tennessee the sixteenth state. Primarily agricultural, Tennessee produced mostly corn, cotton, and tobacco. It was divided over leaving the Union; on June 8, 1861, it became the last state to join the Confederacy. It had more battles fought on its soil during the Civil War than any state except Virginia. After the Civil War, the state began to industrialize; coal, iron, and copper were successfully mined; and distilleries, grist and woolen mills, and furniture factories sprang up. In the 1930s, the network of dams for hydroelectric power provided by the Tennessee Valley Authority did much to improve the economy of the state. TVA power was also responsible for the location of the Atomic Power Laboratories at Oak Ridge. Pop.: 3,835,078 (1980).

TENNESSEE. A Confederate ram used as a flagship by Adm. Franklin Buchanan. Captured in the Battle of Mobile Bay in 1864.

TENNESSEE RIVER. Formed by the confluence near Knoxville, Tenn., of the Holston R and the French Broad R. Once known as the Cherokee R, it was extensively used by the Indians. Its valley played an important part in the Anglo-French rivalry for control of the Old Southwest; and the river was an important route for migration. In the 20th c., emphasis has shifted to power production and flood control. The construction during World War I of Wilson Dam and nitrate plants at the Muscle Shoals foresaw the great dams and hydroelectric plants of the TENNESSEE VALLEY AUTHORITY of the 1930s. A canal designed to connect the Tennessee R with the Gulf of Mexico via the Tombigbee R was planned for completion in the 1980s.

TENNESSEE VALLEY AUTHORITY (TVA). In 1933, prodded by President Franklin D. Roosevelt, Congress authorized TVA as a publicly owned, nationally financed, corporation whose purpose was to harness the floods and draw electric power from the torrents of the Tennessee R, which drains a seven-state area of 40,000 square miles. The TVA was also to be a regional planning authority, with a wide mandate for such undertakings as economic development, recreation, reforestation, and production of fertilizer. Private utilities fought TVA power policies in the courts, but by 1941 the authority was operating eleven dams with six more under construction and was selling low-cost electric power to half a million consumers in six states. During World War II, 70 percent of TVA power went to defense industries, chief among them the Oak Ridge atomic project. By 1981, about 2.8 million residential, commercial, and industrial consumers used TVA power.

TENNIS. Properly called lawn tennis; based on the ancient game of court tennis. The modern game was introduced in Great Britain and brought to the US (to Staten Island, N.Y.) in 1874. Within two decades it had spread throughout the country; by 1908, there were 115 tennis clubs in the US, and championships were held in all but three states. The first Davis Cup matches, between the US and Great Britain, were held in 1900. In 1968, efforts to separate the amateurs from the professionals ceased, and the US joined Great Britain in allowing open tournaments, where amateurs could compete against professionals.

TENNIS CABINET. Nickname for the group of friends with whom Theodore Roosevelt rode, walked, and played tennis during his presidency (1901–09). Roosevelt acknowledged asking them for informal advice; they included Gen. Leonard Wood, Gen. T.H. Barry, Robert Bacon, James Garfield, and Gifford Pinchot.

TENURE OF OFFICE ACT (1867). Passed over the veto of President Andrew Johnson; designed to restrict the president's appointing and removing power. By the law, the Senate's consent was required for removals in all cases in which its consent was necessary for appointment. When Johnson attempted to remove Secretary of War Edwin M. Stanton, the Radical Republicans in Congress proceeded with their long-laid plans to impeach the president. Johnson was not convicted, and the act was repealed finally in 1887. In 1926, the Supreme Court indicated that the act had been unconstitutional. (See also IMPEACHMENT TRIAL OF ANDREW JOHNSON.)

TERRITORIAL GOVERNMENTS. The ORDINANCES OF 1784, 1785, AND 1787 became the general model for the handling of all territories that ultimately achieved statehood. A three-stage development was provided for. In the initial stage, the president appointed a territorial governor, a secretary, and three judges. The second stage began when the territory, or any division of it, attained an adult male population of 5,000, the inhabitants then were entitled to set up a legislature. The governor could convene or dissolve the legislature and had an absolute veto over its enactments. Finally, when the total population reached 60,000, the territory could petition Congress for admission to the Union (see STATE-MAKING PROCESS).

With the acquisition of Hawaii (1898) and the possessions resulting from the Spanish-American War, the question arose whether the natives of these overseas possessions were entitled to all of the rights and privileges guaranteed by the Constitution. Eventually, the Supreme Court ruled that incorporated territories were entitled to full constitutional guarantees; in unincorporated territories, Congress was bound to observe only the "fundamental" guarantees embodied in the Constitution. Today, there are no incorporated US territories; the Virgin Islands, Guam, and American Samoa are all unincorporated. Puerto Rico was designated a commonwealth in 1952; the term describes a high degree of local autonomy, under a constitution drafted and adopted by the residents.

TERRITORIAL WATERS. A belt of coastal waters subject to territorial jurisdiction of littoral states but open to passage of foreign ships. Traditionally, many nations claimed a limit of one marine league (three miles) from the coast; today there is no internationally accepted limit. The US claims its territorial waters extend three nautical miles (3.6 statute miles).

TERRITORIES OF THE UNITED STATES. The NORTHWEST ORDINANCE (1787) set the precedent that territorial status was a step on the path to statehood. Alaska and Hawaii, admitted in 1959, were the last territories to become states. Other US possessions include Puerto Rico, a commonwealth since 1952; and the unincorporated territories of Guam, American Samoa, the Trust Territory of the Pacific, and the Virgin Islands.

TERRY'S TEXAS RANGERS. A unit of volunteer cavalry in the Confederate army. B.F. Terry was the organizer and commanding officer; many of his men were former TEXAS RANGERS. In November 1861, the unit joined Gen. A.S. Johnston at Bowling Green, Ky. Terry was killed in the unit's first engagement, at Woodstock, Ky., but his name clung to the organization. It rendered valuable service at Shiloh, around Murfreesboro, Chattanooga, Atlanta, and Knoxville, and in their last engagement at Bentonville, N.C., in 1865.

TEST LAWS. After the Civil War, the US Congress passed a test-oath act that required every federal officeholder to swear that he had "never voluntarily borne arms against the United States" or given aid to those so doing. The act was later to extended to Congress itself and to all lawyers practicing in federal courts. Its purpose was to bar former Confederate leaders from positions of influence. Some states required even more comprehensive oaths; Missouri, for example, required a loyalty oath from all clergymen, teachers,

candidates, and voters. Various constitutional challenges were raised to the oaths; in some cases the Supreme Court ruled that they were bills of attainder or ex post facto. In 1884, Congress repealed the test-oath statutes.

TEXAN EMIGRATION AND LAND COMPANY. Also known as Peters' Colony Co.; introduced over 2,000 families to NC Texas between 1841–48. Originally operating on a contract with the Republic of Texas, it distributed free land (640 acres per settler) in exchange for sections of land for its own purposes. After annexation, the state government was forced to intervene and settle various conflicting claims. Most settlers were allowed to remain on their homestead; the company was compensated with a tract of land in W Texas.

TEXAN PUBLIC LANDS. By the treaty of annexation (1845) between the Republic of Texas and the US, Texas retained ownership of its 167 million acres of public land. Much of this land was ceded to the state university system.

TEXAN-SANTA FE EXPEDITIONS. Under both Spanish and Mexican colonial rule, efforts were made to combine New Mexico and Texas. After independence, the Republic of Texas made one final effort. President Mirabeau Lamar sent a military expedition to Santa Fe in 1841; after harassment by the Kiowa, it was captured by New Mexican troops. The prisoners were taken to Mexico City and became the subject of heated diplomatic controversy. Most were released in 1842.

TEXAS. Spanish interest in Texas dates from 1519; much of W Texas was explored in the 16th c. Spanish claims were contested in 1684, when French colonists and soldiers under the sieur de La Salle erected Fort Louis in the vicinity of Matagorda Bay. In retaliation, Spain established missions and forts in E Texas (bordering on French Louisiana). Spain founded San Antonio in 1718 as its principal military garrison. After Mexico's independence in 1810, Texas became a battleground for a number of filibustering expeditions launched from New Orleans. American colonization of Texas began in 1821 under Moses Austin (carried out by his son Stephen). From the beginning, Americans clashed with the

Mexican authorities; and an independence movement, led by Sam Houston, sought complete autonomy and eventual annexation by the US. A military conflict became inevitable, and the first clash of the Texas Revolution took place at Gonzales on Oct. 2, 1835. The Texans triumphed and quickly took Goliad and then San Antonio. In February 1836, the main Mexican army reached San Antonio, where the Texas defenders were encamped in the Alamo (see ALAMO, SIEGE OF THE). The fall of the Alamo and then Goliad (see GOLIAD, MASSACRE AT), placed the Texan forces in jeopardy. But Gen. Sam Houston fought and won the decisive victory at San Jacinto on Apr. 21, 1836. The Mexican dictator and commander of the army, Gen. Santa Anna, was decisively defeated and captured. In return for his life, Santa Anna recognized the independence of Texas. (See SAN JACINTO, BATTLE OF.)

The Republic of Texas was declared, and Sam Houston was elected president in September 1836. The US and various European nations recognized the new republic, and annexation talks with the US were begun. Mexico never recognized Santa Anna's agreement with the Texans, however, and a new invasion from that country seemed inevitable. Thus US annexation became necessary. Antislavery forces in the US Congress delayed annexation, however, until Dec. 29, 1845, when the Republic of Texas officially joined the Union.

In order to maintain the new state, the US was forced to fight the MEXICAN WAR; the US victory not only clarified Texas's status but brought to the US New Mexico, Arizona, and California. Slavery in Texas continued to be a divisive issue. In the 1850s, loyalty to the Union or secession became the dominant issue. Sam Houston, the chief Unionist, was outvoted and in 1861 Texas seceded and joined the Confederacy. Little fighting took place in the state, but it was an important conduit for supplies for the Confederacy from Mexico. Reconstruction lasted until 1874, when Texas politics passed back to local management. The coming of the railroad brought an economic boom; Texas became the leading cotton-growing state, and its cattle industry boomed. Lumber in East Texas and citrus fruits in the Rio Grande Valley became increasingly important. The oil field that was discovered at Spindletop, near Beaumont, in 1901 revolutionized the state and the national economy. The state has maintained its tremendous economic and population growth in the 20th c. Houston became the petrochemical center of the nation, and Dallas became a leader in finance, marketing, and insurance. By the 1980s, Texas was the third most populous state in the nation. Pop.: 14,228,383 (1980).

TEXAS AND PACIFIC RAILWAY. See RAILROADS, SKETCHES OF PRINCIPAL LINES.

TEXAS NAVY. The Republic of Texas maintained a navy consisting of an eleven-gun steamer, a twenty-two-gun flagship, and five men-of-war. It fought in several battles with the Mexican navy. After annexation, the fleet passed to the US navy.

TEXAS RANGERS. As early as 1826, Texas colonists had a ranger service as protection against Indians. A definite corps of Texas Rangers was organized ca. 1840; it ranged mostly out of San Antonio against both Indians and Mexicans and made the six-shooter the weapon of the West. During the Mexican War, the rangers achieved fame. In the 1870s, they brought law and order to the Rio Grande border. In 1935, the Texas Rangers were merged with the state highway patrol.

TEXTILES. Between the American Revolution and the War of 1812, the immigration of British artisans and the promotion of the American interests in textile manufacturing brought the new British industrial techniques of manufacturing textiles to the US. In defiance of British prohibitory laws, the essential components of the new cotton processing system crossed the Atlantic. This period also saw the invention by Americans of the cotton gin, the rotary cloth shear, and card clothing machines. Backed by Rhode Island mercantile capital, Samuel Slater organized in southern New England a number of small, power-driven spinning factories. They were followed by a number of large and very profitable factories in Massachusetts and other New England states. Thus cotton textile manufacturing was the first American industry to make the transition from a handicraft to the factory system and to develop the automated technology necessary for large-volume production. By 1900, the textile industry was probably the nation's largest single employer of industrial labor and producer of machine-made goods. After the Civil War, the industry began moving South; the trend continued in the 20th c., until many of the old New England mill towns became industrial ghost towns. Beginning in the 1930s, the textile industry was revolutionized by the invention of synthetic yarns,

THAMES, BATTLE OF THE (Oct. 5, 1813). American naval victory on the Thames R near Chatham, Ont., during the War of 1812. Helped restore American dominance in the Northwest.

THANKSGIVING DAY. American holiday initiated by the Plymouth, Mass., colonists after their first harvest in 1621. The custom spread and was given official status by various presidential and state proclamations. In 1941 Congress set the fourth Thursday in November as Thanksgiving.

THEATER. Amateur theatricals began in the American colonies in the late 17th c.; and between 1700 and 1750, strolling players were performing at Williamsburg, New York City, Philadelphia, and other major towns. An English troupe, run by Lewis Hallam and later by David Douglass, toured America from 1752 until 1775, when the Continental Congress banned all "exhibitions of shews, plays, and other expensive diversions and entertainments." The Douglass troupe returned after the war and competed with numerous other companies, chiefly English, that toured the nation's major cities. By ca. 1800, local companies and playwrights were developing. West of the Alleghenies, troupes toured by flatboat and wagon, setting up wherever there was a potential audience. By the 1830s, showboats were plying the Ohio and Mississippi. Edwin Forrest, the first American actor to achieve an international reputation, popularized an "American" style of acting. Much of his success was achieved in plays built around native American themes and characters. Immensely popular at mid-century was the minstrel show featuring white performers in blackface. Burlesques of well-known plays, novels, events, and personalities in light musical productions were also much in demand and became the foundation of the American musical comedy. The western boom towns, brought on by the great mining bonanzas, were a lure to traveling acting troupes, and the completion of the railroad across the con-

tinent opened the entire nation to touring companies.

The 19th-c. theater witnessed a growth of interest in both realism and spectacle. Elaborate scenery was devised to handle increasingly complex and detailed stagecraft. At the same time, a cadre of professional playwrights was developing. Among the most notable were William Clyde Fitch, the actor-playwright William Gillette, and the farceurs, Charles H. Hoyt and Edward Harrigan. Vaudeville became a vital force and remained so until the 1930s. The Yiddish theater in New York began a period of great creativity.

The 20th c. saw the work of European playwrights again popular, including the works of George Bernard Shaw and Henrik Ibsen. The native George M. Cohan made prolific contributions to the stage. After World War I, the US began producing playwrights of international reputation: Maxwell Anderson, Sidney Howard, Robert E. Sherwood, Philip Barry, Elmer Rice, Clifford Odets, S.N. Behrman, Thornton Wilder, Lillian Hellman, and Eugene O'Neill. The years after World War II witnessed the development of a number of new playwrights, notably Tennessee Williams, Arthur Miller, and Edward Albee. The musical theater, which had gone through a great period in the 1920s and 1930s with such composers as Jerome Kern, Cole Porter, Richard Rodgers, George Gershwin, and Irving Berlin, continued to thrive. Among its newer composers were Frederick Loewe, Leonard Bernstein, Jules Styne, Harold Arlen, and Stephen Sondheim. There was a great flowering of avant-garde, experimental theater in the 1960s and 1970s, and a number of important new playwrights came out of the numerous regional and off-Broadway theaters that thrived during that era. David Mamet, Sam Shepard, David Rabe, Lanford Wilson, John Guare, Marsha Norman, and Beth Henley were playwrights to come out of that movement.

THEOCRACY IN NEW ENGLAND. Political regime set up by the founders of the Massachusetts Bay and New Haven colonies. They set out to found a "Bible Commonwealth," in which the fundamental law would be the revealed Word of God. Consequently, the political theory assumed that the colonies were based on the Bible and that all specific laws must be required to show biblical warrant.

THEOSOPHY. The Theosophical Society, based on the movement founded abroad by Helena Blavatsky, was founded in New York City in 1875. Claiming to be a religion-philosophy-science, theosophy aimed at a universal brotherhood of humanity. It studied the ancient scriptures, such as those of Buddhism and Zoroastrianism and put great significance in the psychic and spiritual powers latent in humans. Thesosophy accepts the miracles of Jesus but denies their supernatural character. In the 1980s, there were about 6,000 theosophists in the US.

THIRD PARTIES. See entries for individual parties.

THIRTEENTH AMENDMENT (1865). One of the post-Civil War amendments, it abolished slavery. Ratification by the former seceded states was required as part of President Andrew Johnson's Reconstruction program; and eight of those states were counted officially in the three-fourths of the states necessary to ratify.

THOMAS AMENDMENT (1933). Title III of the Agricultural Adjustment Act of 1933. Gave the president authority to inflate the currency by allowing the Federal Reserve to buy up to $3 billion in government securities, by issuing $3 billion in US notes, and by devaluing the dollar up to 50 percent. (See also AGRICULTURAL ADJUSTMENT ADMINISTRATION.)

THREE-MILE ISLAND. On March 28, 1979, a reactor at the nuclear power plant at Three Mile Island, Pa., was shut down due to a series of mishaps, which could possibly have caused a core meltdown or a hydrogen explosion. It created panic in the nearby population, with many fleeing the area. Although a nuclear accident was avoided, it was a severe blow to advocates of nuclear power who had consistently emphasized the safety of nuclear power.

THREE-MILE LIMIT. See TERRITORIAL WATERS.

THREE NOTCH ROAD. Pioneer road in Mississippi connecting Natchez and St. Stephens, on the lower Tombigbee R. So called from the manner of marking the trees along its course; first marked after the Choctaw cession of 1805 and formed the N boundary of that cession.

THREE RIVERS, BATTLE OF (June 8, 1776). Unsuccessful attempt to capture a British garrison at Three Rivers, Quebec.

THREE SAINTS BAY. Site of the first permanent European settlement in Alaska on the S shore of Kodiak Island. Russian fur traders established a post there in 1784.

TICONDEROGA, CAPTURE OF (1775). Early in the American Revolution, a patriot force co-commanded by Ethan Allen and Benedict Arnold surprised the British garrison at Fort Ticonderoga in NE New York. The fort was subdued without bloodshed.

TICONDEROGA, FORT. Built as Fort Carillon in 1755 by the French; commanded the route between lakes Champlain and George. Renamed Ticonderoga by the British.

TICONDEROGA, OPERATIONS AT (1758–59). The French under Gen. Montcalm built a strong abatis at Fort Ticonderoga, New York, and repulsed an ill-advised attack against it by British troops under Gen. James Abercromby. The British lost almost 2,000 men in the attack. The next summer Sir Jeffrey Amherst conducted a better organized attack on the fort. The French, realizing that sure defeat faced them, blew up the fort and retreated.

TICONDEROGA, TAKING OF (1777). The British retook Fort Ticonderoga after having lost it to the Americans in 1775. Gen. Arthur Saint Clair managed to escape with his patriot force, leaving the fort to the British.

TIDELANDS. Lands lying under the sea beyond the low-water limit of the tide but considered within the territorial waters of a nation. Traditionally, the states proceeded as if they were the owners; but value of the tidelands was heightened when oil was discovered off the Gulf Coast. In 1947, the Supreme Court ruled that the tidelands belonged to the federal government, and the issue became important in the 1952 presidential campaign. Dwight D. Eisenhower, the winner, was pledged to restore the lands to the states. Several laws were passed to accomplish that end, but they led to numerous lawsuits. The issue was finally decided by the Supreme Court in 1960; it ruled that Mississippi, Alabama, and Louisiana owned the rights to the offshore lands for 3.5 miles; and Texas and Florida rights were ruled as extending 3 leagues, or approximately 10.5 miles.

TIDEWATER. That part of the Atlantic coastal plain lying E of the points in rivers reached by oceanic tides. These areas, particularly in Virginia and North Carolina, were the first to be settled; the inhabitants secured control of the government at the expense of the small farmers who had moved beyond into the piedmont, or back country, region. Political animosity between the two groups was especially strong in the late 18th and early 19th c.

"TIMES THAT TRY MEN'S SOULS." Short title of the first of twelve essays published during the American Revolution by Thomas Paine. The first was written in 1776. Collected under the title *The Crisis*, they were intended to bolster the morale of the colonists.

TIN PAN ALLEY. Fictional street in New York City in the early 1900s where popular song publishers were located, initially the area around Twenty-eighth Street and Sixth Avenue. The term suggests the tinny quality of the pianos in the publishers' offices and came to refer to the popular song industry in general.

TINTYPE. Originally introduced as the melainotype and the ferrotype, a distinctly American style of early photograph made by the wet process on black japanned metal; patented 1856.

TIPPECANOE, BATTLE OF (Nov. 7, 1811). Gen. William Henry Harrison, governor of the Indiana Territory, made a preemptive attack on Tecumseh, the Shawnee chief, at Tippecanoe Creek, 150 miles N of Vincennes. The Indian warriors, stirred to a frenzy by Tecumseh's brother, the SHAWNEE PROPHET, attacked the American forces during the night. The battle raged until daybreak, when a series of charges drove the Indians from the field. Harrison razed the Indian town and began his retreat.

"TIPPECANOE AND TYLER TOO!" The campaign slogan of the Whigs in 1840, when William Henry Harrison, the hero of the Battle of Tippecanoe, and John Tyler were their candidates for president and vice-president.

TITHES, SOUTHERN AGRICULTURAL. Because of depreciated currency, the Confederacy resorted to taxing southern farmers in kind; that is, one-tenth of their crops were levied as taxes. It was an important factor in the survival of the Rebel army.

TITHINGMEN. Town officers of colonial New England charged with promoting church attendance and maintaining decorous conduct on the Sabbath.

TITLES OF NOBILITY. See NOBILITY, TITLES OF.

TLINGIT. See HAIDA.

TOBACCO. Christopher Columbus's crew observed the natives of Hispaniola smoking cigars; by 1559 Portugal and Spain imported tobacco leaves for their alleged medical properties. Soon both were raised and smoked in Europe and Asia. The distribution of tobacco use in the New World varied. Tropical South America and the Antilles had the cigar, Mexican Indians smoked corn-husk cigarettes, and the pipe appeared all over. Its association with peace deliberations gave rise to the "peace pipe" concept.

The early southern colonists quickly discovered the potentialities of tobacco as a money crop. John Rolfe's experiments in 1612 to develop a tobacco to replace the indigenous variety soon produced a major exportable staple for Virginia, Maryland, and North Carolina. By the time of the Revolutionary War, 100 million pounds were being exported annually to England. The industry recovered quickly from the war, and by 1790 about 78 percent of the crop was again exported. Tobacco raising expanded westward into the piedmont region of North Carolina and Virginia and into Kentucky, Tennessee, South Carolina, and Georgia. During the 19th c., hybridization and the development of three distinct curing methods (flue, darkfired, and air) resulted in regional differences in the kind of tobacco raised. Cigar tobacco, for example, was raised in the Connecticut R valley. By ca. 1920, however, the cigarette had become the chief means of consuming tobacco and made the bright tobacco of the southern states the world's leading tobacco crop. In 1980, cigarettes accounted for 86 percent of the tobacco consumed in the US.

TOBACCO AS MONEY. In 1619, the Virginia legislature rated tobacco at "three shillings the best and the second sort at 18d. in the pound," and a statute of 1642 made tobacco a legal tender. Maryland and North Carolina also used tobacco as money until the American Revolution. Overproduction and the substitution of poor quality tobacco eventually led to its being phased out as currency.

TOLEDO. Industrial and port city in NW Ohio; located on Lake Erie at the mouth of the Maumee R, the largest river emptying into the Great Lakes and a major water route since Indian days. The Toledo War of 1835–36 was between Michigan and Ohio over the area on which Toledo is situated. The US government settled the argument by awarding Michigan the Upper Peninsula in place of its claim to Toledo. Growth began with the construction of the Wabash and Erie Canal in 1843. Today the port handles soft coal, petroleum, iron ore, cement, and food products. Among Toledo's manufactures, glass ranks high. Pop.: 354,635 (1980).

TOLEDO WAR. See TOLEDO.

TOLERATION ACTS. Various laws in the American colonies assuring freedom of religion. In Virginia and Maryland, dissenters were granted the benefits of the English Toleration Act of 1689. Maryland passed its own Toleration Act in 1649, and Connecticut passed one in 1708.

TOLL BRIDGES AND ROADS, PRIVATE. Privately-owned toll bridges were in operation between New York and Boston as early as 1704, but the first large wave of toll bridge construction began after 1730; turnpike construction began ca. 1800. In some cases, private toll road companies took over publicly built roads and charged tolls established by the state. By 1850, most roads had become free and public; but toll bridges continued in private ownership. By the late 19th c., how-

ever, most toll bridges were built and financed by local or state governments.

TOMAHAWK. Small ax, made by the English and French; quickly adopted as the preferred hand weapon by Algonkin- and Iroquois-speaking Indians.

TOMAHAWK CLAIMS. By blazing, or marking, trees that encompassed the lands they desired, frontiersmen often asserted irregular claims before these lands were surveyed. Colonial land laws often admitted these claims; the national land system gave them no legal recognition.

TOMBIGBEE VALLEY. The NE counties of Mississippi and most of W Alabama drain through the Tombigbee Valley, which played an important part in the history of the Old Southwest. The French built Fort Tombecbee there in 1735 for expeditions against the Chickasaw; it was explored by the British in 1771 to promote commerce with the Choctaw. After the American Revolution, settlers came down the valley; by 1821, steamboats were plying the river.

TOMB OF THE UNKNOWN. See UNKNOWNS, TOMB OF THE.

TOMBSTONE. Former silver-mining town located in the San Pedro R valley in Arizona. Silver was discovered in 1878; during the next two decades the district yield about $40 million in silver and $3 million in gold. A notorious boomtown, attracting prospectors, gunmen, gamblers, and outlaws. The mines were abandoned by ca. 1910 and the town declined rapidly. Pop.: 1,632 (1980).

TOM THUMB. Locomotive built by Peter Cooper in 1830 for the Baltimore and Ohio RR. Prior to it, the B&O had used horse-drawn trains. (See also LOCOMOTIVES.)

TONDEE TAVERN. Built in Savannah a few years before the American Revolution; became known as Georgia's Cradle of Liberty. Early meetings against the crown were held there, and it was used as the legislative meeting chamber for the revolutionary state government.

TONKIN GULF RESOLUTION (Aug. 7, 1964). After two attacks by North Vietnamese torpedo boats on US destroyers in the Gulf of Tonkin, the US Congress passed a resolution giving President Lyndon B. Johnson authority to "take all necessary measures to repel any armed attack against the forces of the United States." Passed almost unanimously, the resolution was so broad as to be a virtual declaration of war. National disillusionment with the VIETNAM WAR, and indications that the administration had been less than forthright about the original attacks, led to the repeal of the resolution in 1971.

TONQUIN. A ship of the expedition that established Astoria, Ore., in 1811. After landing its cargo, it proceeded on a northern trading voyage. Attacked by Indians, who killed most of the crew, it was destroyed by an explosion of gunpowder in the hold.

TONTINE PLAN. A combined lottery and life insurance plan popular in the late 18th c. in America (and in Europe). A group of persons would hold real estate with the idea that it would ultimately be divided among certain surviving members (or a single survivor). The tontine principle became extensively applied to life insurance policies in the 19th c.

TOPEKA. Capital city of Kansas, located at the site of a very old Indian village on the Kansas R. The modern city was founded in 1854 as the terminal for the Atchison, Topeka and Santa Fe RR. An important marketing town and a center for warehouses and grain elevators. Pop.: 115,266 (1980).

TOPEKA MOVEMENT AND CONSTITUTION. Movement for statehood launched by free-state Kansans in opposition to the pro-slavery territorial government that was inaugurated in 1855. The free-staters met in convention and adopted a constitution banning slavery in the proposed state (see KANSAS FREE-STATE PARTY). The US House of Representatives in 1856 voted to admit Kansas as a state under the Topeka constitution, but the Senate rejected it.

TORDESILLAS, TREATY OF (1494). Pope Alexander VI settled the dispute between Spain and Portugal over their New World territories by awarding Spain exclusive dominion over all new lands W and S of a line to be drawn from the North Pole to the South Pole,

100 leagues W of the Azores and Cape Verde Islands. All lands to the E and S of the line were to go to Portugal. The kings of Portugal and Spain accepted the treaty with certain adjustments.

TORIES. See LOYALISTS.

TORONTO. See YORK, CAPTURE AND DESTRUCTION OF.

TORPEDO WARFARE. Developed in the 1860s, by the time of World War I the torpedo had an effective range of 7,000 yards and a speed of 40 knots. The 21-inch torpedo, then the largest, had a bursting charge of 700 pounds of explosive. Until ca. 1900, the principal carrier was the torpedo boat; but after that, the destroyer became the principal US carrier. However it was the submarine that would become the most effective user of the weapon. During World War I, the German U-boat came close to winning the war for the Central Powers. In World War II, the submarine proved even more formidable; tonnage losses to German U-boats rose into the millions before the Allies won the Battle of the Atlantic. In the Pacific, US submarines devastated the Japanese merchant marine and accounted for 28 percent of all Japanese shipping sunk in the war.

TORREYS' TRADING POST. Established 1843 near present Waco, Tex. Site of Republic of Texas councils with Indians.

TOULOUSE, FORT. Established 1714 by the sieur de Bienville on the Coose R near Wetumpka, Ala. Abandoned after English possession. Revived and rechristened Fort Jackson during the Creek Wars, and Andrew Jackson signed treaty with the Creek there Aug. 9, 1814.

TOWBOATING. In 1920 Congress authorized increased outlays for water transportation, which spawned the Inland Waterways Corporation and the Federal Barge Line. The 9-foot channel of the Ohio R in 1929 was followed by improvements on the Mississippi and its tributaries and the Gulf Intra-Coastal Canals. The size and power of the towboats, or tugboats, increased greatly. Of about 350 million tons of cargo transported by some 3,000 towboats in the mid-1970s, almost a third was coal and lignite for generating plants. Petroleum, grain, and sand and gravel were other important commodities.

TOWN GOVERNMENT. A form of local government unique to New England, characterized by its devotion to direct democracy. Traditionallly, the legislative body is the town meeting, which consists of all qualified voters, who meet to choose officials and set basic policy. It also levies taxes and incurs indebtedness. Traditionally, a board of selectmen has been designated as the principal administrative agency of the government. The burdens of day-to-day administration generally falls to the town clerk.

TOWNSEND PLAN. An old-age revolving pension plan proposed in the 1930s by Francis E. Townsend. The plan provided that every person sixty years of age or over should receive from the US Treasury an annuity "not exceeding $200 per month." A stipulation called for the money to be spent in its entirety within the month. The $20 billion a year needed to finance the plan was to be raised by a "duty of 2 per centum upon the gross dollar value of each transaction done within the United States." Townsend's plan speedily enrolled millions of supporters, but Congress repeatedly rejected bills putting the plan into effect, mainly because of opposition of economists. By the end of the decade, the movement had died out.

TOWNSHEND ACTS (1767). Four acts imposed on the American colonies by Parliament. The first act suspended the New York assembly for not complying with the Quartering Act of 1765, which required colonies to supply British troops with shelter and supplies. The second was the Revenue Act, which levied import duties on various products, including tea. The revenue was to go to paying for judges, governors, and other crown employees in the colonies. The third act created a board of customs to collect the taxes. The fourth act repealed the inland duties on tea in England and permitted it to be exported to the colonies free of all British taxes. This would have the effect of creating a British monopoly on the tea trade. The acts were a leading cause of the American Revolution.

TOWSON, FORT. A frontier military post established ca. 1823 on the Red R, in SW Oklahoma. Abandoned ca. 1845.

TRACE. See BUFFALO TRAILS.

TRADE, DOMESTIC. Commerce among the American colonies was extremely limited, partly by design of the mother country and partly because of the difficulties of land transportation and hostility between the colonies. The American Revolution intensified the domestic disputes. Since national power was lacking under the ARTICLES OF CONFEDERATION, the states set up tax barriers against incoming goods or sought to monopolize waterways. No other action in the history of domestic trade has equaled in significance the stipulations in the Constitution that the exchange of goods and services among the states must be open and free. The revolution in transportation, following soon after, gave impetus to interstate trade. The steamboat brought to maturity the expanding market along the southward-flowing rivers W of the Appalachians. Wagons laden with merchandise had long rolled over the mountains to the headwaters of the Ohio. From Pittsburgh and the tributaries of the Ohio hundreds of boats, gathering products and sometimes distributing goods, flowed southward to New Orleans. Goods moved to eastern coastal cities or to foreign markets. The completion of the Erie Canal in 1825 opened the Great Lakes to eastern trade. But the railroads were the greatest single impetus. Beginning in Baltimore in 1828, they spread rapidly north and south and inland to the mountains. Many ports lost business but cities such as Chicago rose to commercial grandeur. The first transcontinental railroad (1869) and others beyond the Mississippi were soon bringing copper, lead, and other metals from the West. Ice-cooled cars began to carry fruits and vegetables from the Pacific coast to eastern cities. Refrigerated cars carried meat from the packing houses of Chicago across the nation. By 1900 goods for personal consumption had begun a steady gain in domestic commerce, and the appearance of the truck and automobile after World War I caused a new revolution in the transportation of goods, as did the use of air express beginning in the 1960s.

TRADE, FOREIGN. Although the US has been relatively self-sufficient, foreign trade has been a dominant factor in the growth of the nation. In the colonial era, foreign trade was primarily involved in outgoing raw materials and incoming manufactured goods. Tobacco, fish, furs, grain, and meat were exchanged for British manufactures. Even limited exports from colonies upset British domestic industries, and the search for new markets was intensified. Thus began the triangular trade: New England Rum was exchanged in Africa for slaves, and the slaves in turn were sold in the West Indies for specie and molasses for the New England rum distillers.

The American Revolution caused the colonies to lose their preferred position in the British trade system. The ports of the West Indies were closed to the ships of the new nation, and other markets became imperative. Beginning ca. 1785, the China trade became increasingly important; furthermore, means were found to evade the restrictions in the West Indies. The Napoleonic Wars, despite the depredations on US shipping, created new demands for American products and trade prospered. The prosperity was short-lived. The EMBARGO ACT and the War of 1812 dealt severe blows to both the domestic economy and foreign trade.

Foreign trade between 1815 and 1860 moved generally upward. Agricultural products, especially cotton, made up most exports. Trade in the Western Hemisphere took large amounts of grain and flour, and English demands increased steadily after repeal of the corn laws in 1846. Tobacco, rice, meat, lumber, naval stores, and barrels and kegs moved out in large quantities. Cottons, woolens, silks, iron, cutlery, and china made up the bulk of the incoming cargoes. As the nation became increasingly industrialized after the Civil War, domestic production and domestic trade were its basic concerns, and the importance of foreign trade decreased greatly. Cotton, wheat, flour, and other farm products continued to move out, and the return flow was made up of tropical foods and materials, coffee, sugar, wool, rubber, silk, paper and a growing amount of raw materials. World War I and the immediate years thereafter saw a great rise in American foreign trade; but the economic structure fell apart in 1929. Prices declined sharply everywhere; world credit and world finance broke down. Foreign exchange transactions were curtailed or taken over completely by governments in many places; and the principal powers sought to maintain themselves by hiding behind high tariffs, trade licenses, and fixed quotas. Toward the end of the 1930s, some progress had been made in easing international trade restrictions, mainly by reciprocity agreements; but it was World War II that was responsible for the dramatic increase in foreign trade. In the war years 1941–45 more than $50 billion in goods went out of American ports ($17 billion came in). But more than half of the exports were lend-lease war materials for the Allies for which no payment was expected. The international economic structure was undergoing a revolution. After the war, the US was the world's leading economic power. The Marshall Plan provided $12 billion in aid for the economic recovery of Europe, and the economy of Japan was systematically rebuilt. The 1950s saw the free trade movement making remarkable headway, as represented by such instruments as the Common Market, the European Free Trade Association, and the Atlantic Community.

But not all was harmony in the new economic community. The foreign trade of the US had undergone profound changes. The great surpluses that had marked US world commerce from the 1870s began in the 1950s to decline. The antiquated steel and automobile industries were crumbling in the face of foreign competition. Textiles, clothing, and footwear poured into the country from such Asian countries as Hong Kong, Taiwan, and Korea. Perhaps most dramatically, the US became for the first time a net importer of petroleum, a condition that was to dominate both commerce and politics in the 1970s. The cost of imported oil was a large factor in the continuing rise in the trade deficit. As that deficit rose, and as more and more US industries succumbed to foreign competition, demands for protectionist measures increased, particularly in so-called buy America movements and calls for legislation requiring manufactured products to contain a certain percentage of American-made parts.

TRADE, FREE. See FREE TRADE.

TRADE ACTS. See NAVIGATION ACTS.

TRADE AGREEMENTS. See RECIPROCAL TRADE AGREEMENTS.

TRADE DOLLAR. Coin specially created in 1873 ostensibly to encourage trade with China, but more probably to provide a market for domestic silver. At least 6 million of the 36 million coins went into US circulation. Redeemed in 1887. (See also CRIME OF 1873.)

TRADEMARKS. As early as 1791, a Boston manufacturer petitioned Congress for the right to register his trademark and have it protected against imitation. First federal act passed in 1870.

TRADE UNIONS. See LABOR.

TRADING COMPANIES. Six incorporated British trading companies played an important part in the early settlement of America: the Virginia Co. (1606), the London and Bristol Co. (1610), the Council for New England (1620), the Bermuda Co. (1622), the Massachusetts Bay Co. (1629), and the Old Providence Co. (1630). The Dutch used a similar organization to settle New York and New Jersey. The Hudson's Bay Co. was a trading company but not a colonizing company. The joint-stock company, similar to the modern corporation, sold shares and the stockholder's liability was limited to his investment. The charter gave the company title to a specific territory and gave it extensive governmental powers over colonies planted in that territory. Associate companies were more similar to the modern limited partnership. Colonies were settled by groups of men called associates who, in return for a title in a specified tract of land, agreed to transport a certain number of settlers in a given area and establish them within a limited time.

TRADING POSTS, FRONTIER. From the beginning, traders and trading posts were important to American colonists. Indians would exchange furs for guns, ammunition, hatchets, knives, kettles, and blankets. During the colonial rivalries, Spain and France also had their strategic trading posts up and down the frontier and along the western rivers. After independence, the federal government authorized (1796) setting up government factories and trading posts; every border fort became a trade center. After the purchase of Louisiana, trading posts were established throughout the trans-Mississippi West with St. Louis and New Orleans the supply centers.

TRAIL DRIVERS. Cowboys who moved cattle from a home range to a distant market. The typical outfit driving 2,500 head of cattle consisted of a boss and from ten to fifteen hands. The men drove and grazed the cattle most of the day, herding them up by night. Ten or twelve miles was considered a good day's drive.

TRAIL OF TEARS. Name given by the Cherokee to the forced journey in 1838 from their lands in the Southeast to Oklahoma. The winter journey was made mostly on foot, and some 4,000 perished.

TRAIN ROBBERIES. The first recorded train robbery was on the New York, New Haven and Hartford RR in 1866; it netted the robbers $700,000. Soon robberies were plaguing western railroads. Notorious among the robbers were the Reno brothers, the Farringtons, Jack Davis, the Jesse and Frank James gang, the Dalton boys, and Sam Bass. After ca. 1900, holdups declined conspicuously.

TRANS-APPALACHIA. That part of North America lying W of the Appalachian Mountains. Used mainly in reference to late colonial and early national history, it refers particularly to the region drained by the Ohio R.

TRANSCENDENTALISM. The liberal social and cultural renaissance in New England (1830–45). Received its chief expression in Ralph Waldo Emerson's individualistic doctrine of self-reliance. Experiments in "plain living and high thinking" like Brook Farm and Fruitlands attracted the exponents of a new self-culture; and social utopians, from vegetarian enthusiasts to abolitionists, found a congenial atmosphere in the movement.

TRANSPORTATION, DEPARTMENT OF. Created by Congress in 1966 out of the Federal Aviation Administration, Bureau of Public Roads, Coast Guard, and various other public bodies with responsibilites in public transportation. The new cabinet-level department was given responsible for developing and monitoring national transportation policy.

TRANSPORTATION AND TRAVEL. Most early American colonists settled near rivers, inlets, and bays adjoining the Atlantic, and water provided their means of travel and transportation, chiefly by numerous types of sailing vessels. Farmers living above seaports moved their produce in flatboats and rafts. At first all land travel was done on foot or horseback. Vehicles were scarce, as were roads to accommodate them. In the cities, carts and chaises appeared in the 17th c., followed by the curricle, chariot, and coach. By the close of the colonial period, a network of dirt and corduroy roads existed throughout the northern and central colonies, and regular stage lines carried passengers and small freight from city to city. The Conestoga wagon partly solved the problem of overland freight. Western settlement was largely made possible by the construction of the National, or Cumberland, Road; state and privately owned turnpikes; a network of canals; and development of trails from the Middle West to New Mexico, Utah, California, and the Northwest. The Erie Canal brought thousands of emigrants into the northern portions of the Old Northwest and provided a direct commercial artery to New York City.

By 1820 steamboat companies were operating on practically all navigable rivers and lakes. During the 1850s, there were over 1,000 on the Mississippi. Railroads began to replace them, and by World War I, steamboats had almost disappeared from the rivers. A revival of river traffic began in the 1920s with barge transport.

By the outbreak of the Civil War, there were 30,000 miles of railroads. The transcontinental railroad was completed in 1869. At the same time, city travel was being revolutionized by railed travel: trolleys, elevated railways, and subways. Interurban electric railways connected the cities with neighboring towns.

The internal combustion engine paved the way for automobile, bus, truck, and airplane transportation and conversion of railroads from steam to diesel power. Motor vehicles served primarily as a feeder to the railroad system; but long distance trucks offered serious competition to railroad freight operations. Motor transportation was greatly aided by the huge public investment in highways and farm-to-market roads, which were eventually to create a national system of all-weather roads. Railroads lost virtually all passenger traffic to the motor bus, airplane, and private automobile; rail freight traffic continued to grow, but modestly.

TRANSYLVANIA COMPANY. Organized 1774 to plant settlements in the western parts of North Carolina and Virginia. A colony was attempted at Boonesborough in 1775, but the governors of the two states invalidated it. In 1778, Virginia awarded the company 200,000 acres in Kentucky; and in 1783, North Carolina awarded it an equal amount in E Tennessee.

TRAPPERS' RENDEZVOUS. Annual gatherings of itinerant fur trappers and Indians to trade their furs for equipment, supplies, money, trade goods, and liquor. The first was held on the Sweetwater R in Wyoming. The Rocky Mountain Fur Co., in particular, made use of the trappers' rendezvous until the 1840s.

TRAPPING. Until the mid-19th c., trapping was a prime factor in the westward movement. Trappers both developed a source of wealth for a growing nation and, more importantly, explored rivers, blazed trails, brought hostile Indians under control, made known the agricultural values of the wilderness, and extended US holdings to the Pacific.

TRAVEL. See TRANSPORTATION AND TRAVEL.

TRAVERSE DE SIOUX, TREATY OF (1851). The Upper Sioux ceded to the US a large portion of their lands in Iowa and Minnesota. Sioux dissatisfaction with the treaty helped bring on the Sioux War of 1862.

TREASON. The US Constitution restrictively defines treason and denies Congress authority to enlarge that definition: "Treason against the United States shall consist only in levying war against them, or in adhering to their enemies, giving them aid and comfort." (Article III, Section 3). The Constitution also provides that conviction for treason be based on the "testimony of two witnesses ... or on confession in open court." Only about fifty treason trials (both federal and state) have been held. In four instances, treason trials bore a political tinge: (1) convictions in the Whiskey Rebellion of 1795 and Fries's Rebellion of 1800; (2) prosecution of Aaron Burr in 1807 for levying war to separate the West from the US; (3) conviction by Rhode Island of Thomas Wilson Dorr in 1844 for an armed effort to install an extralegal government; and (4) conviction by Virginia in 1859 of John Brown for armed insurrection "to free slaves." The Burr treason trial was conducted by Chief Justice John Marshall, who laid down extremely rigorous demands of proof; that precedent has made subsequent convictions difficult; the only significant treason prosecutions have been for aiding enemy spies.

TREASURY, UNITED STATES. Created by Congress in 1789 with Alexander Hamilton as the first secretary. Prime agency for promoting the economic development of the country. The four basic responsibilities are (1) to frame and recommend financial, tax, and fiscal measures; (2) to serve as financial agent for the US government; (3) to enforce certain laws; and (4) to manufacture coins and currency.

TREAT MISSION (1839). James Treat, confidential agent of the Republic of Texas, sought Recognition of Texas independence and of the Rio Grande boundary. The Mexican government refused to negotiate with him.

TREATIES. The US Constitution states that the president "shall have Power, by and with the Advice and Consent of the Senate, to make Treaties. ...." However, treaty-making has become almost completely an executive department function, with the Senate being asked to ratify the finished agreement. The senate role has also been diminished by the increasing use of the executive agreement. Treaty-making under the Constitution was concerned mainly with avoiding entanglement in the Napoleonic Wars. Thereafter attention turned to the westward movement. Treaties were negotiated with European powers (and Mexico) and Indian groups, which ceded land to the US. Russia ceded Alaska to the US in 1867. A treaty with Panama in 1903 ceded the Canal Zone, but a 1978 treaty returned the zone to Panama.

Beginning with the Red Cross Convention of 1854, the US has been party to numerous multilateral treaties; these include the agreements setting up world courts and other instruments of international law. After World War I, the US Senate refused to ratify the treaty that would have made the US a member of the League of Nations. But a number of multilateral treaties went into effect at the end of World War II, including US membership in the United Nations. A number of defensive treaties followed, including membership in the North Atlantic Treaty Organization (1947) and the Southeast Asia Treaty Organization (1954). In the 1970s, efforts to slow down the nuclear arms race led to the Strategic Arms Limitations Treaties with the Soviet Union (1972 and 1979; the latter treaty was not ratified).

TREATIES, COMMERCIAL. Bilateral or multilateral international agreements dealing with matters of trade, navigation, taxation, exchange controls, and the treatment of business persons or corporations of one country in the territory of the treaty partners. They are instruments of foreign economic policy; their major objective is to enhance the economic position of states and their nationals in the world and thereby strengthen power in international affairs. Such agreements may take the form of a formal treaty demanding approval by the Senate or an executive agreement, which does not. The first US commercial treaty was the Treaty of Amity and Commerce with France in 1778.

TREATIES, MOST-FAVORED-NATION. See MOST-FAVORED-NATION PRINCIPLE.

TREDEGAR IRON WORKS. Built in 1836 in Richmond, Va., it was the Confederate government's only source of cannon during the Civil War.

TRELAWNEY PLANTATION. Founded 1631 on Richmond's Island, Me., as a fishing and trading post. Title was based on a grant given Robert Trelawney and Moses Goodyear, merchants of Plymouth, England.

TRENT AFFAIR. Involved the disputed doctrine of the freedom of the seas during the Civil War. Two Confederate diplomats were taken from the British ship *Trent* by Union naval personnel in international waters. The British demanded the release of the diplomats and an apology from the US. After the British minister was instructed to come home if the apology was not forthcoming and British troops were dispatched to Canada, President

Lincoln promptly released the diplomats and apologized.

TRENTON. Capital city of New Jersey, established at the "head of navigation" of the Delaware R. Scene of one of the great battles of the Revolutionary War (see TRENTON, BATTLE OF). Now an industrial center, with specialized manufacturing plants producing steel wire and cable, machinery, chemical products, pottery, and chinaware. Pop.: 92,124 (1980).

TRENTON, BATTLE OF (Dec. 26, 1776). On Christmas night, Gen. George Washington crossed the Delaware R eight miles above Trenton, reaching that town at 8 AM. As he expected, he surprised the Hessian mercenaries, who had been celebrating Christmas the night before. In the forty-minute battle, the Patriots killed 30 Hessians and took 1,000 prisoner.

TRENTON DECREE (1782). A New Jersey court of commissions found in favor of Pennsylvania in a long-time territorial dispute with Connecticut over parts of Pennsylvania.

TREVETT V. WEEDEN (1786). A Rhode Island case in which the doctrine of judicial review is believed to have been first employed. The court ruled unconstitutional an act of the Rhode Island legislature.

TREVILIAN STATION, BATTLE AT (June 11–12, 1864). A Confederate force under Gen. Wade Hampton successfully stopped a drive by Union Gen. P.H. Sheridan to destroy the Virginia Central RR and join a Union force at Charlottesville, Va.

TRIANGLE FIRE (Mar. 25, 1911). The Triangle Shirtwaist Co., occupying part of a loft building in New York City, suffered a disastrous fire that killed 147 workers, mostly women and girls. It was found that little protection against fire had been provided and that virtually no escape routes existed. The disaster led to sweeping reforms in building and factory laws.

TRIANGULAR TRADE. New England colonies were forbidden by English law to manufacture their needs locally. They were forced to balance their trade by engaging in complex trading enterprises, to dispose of diversified surpluses in non-English markets in order to provide purchasing power in England. Preeminent was the triangular, or roundabout, trade. The three corners were, in sequence, a port in the northern colonies, the Gold Coast of Africa, and a port in the West Indies. New England rum was carried to Africa, where it was traded for slaves. They were sold in the West Indies for gold and molasses. The molasses, finally, was brought back to New England to be converted into rum.

TRIBUTE. The piratical Barbary governments of Morocco, Algiers, Tunis, and Tripoli demanded a fixed annuity from the naval powers in order to assure their ships safe transit through the Mediterranean. The eventual refusal to continue such tribute payments led to the BARBARY WARS.

TRIPARTITE AGREEMENT (1936). Currency-stabilizing agreement entered into by France, England, and the US following suspension of the gold standard by the latter two countries.

TRIPOLI, WAR WITH. See BARBARY WARS.

TRIST MISSION. Initial US effort to end the Mexican War. N.P. Trist was recalled when the US decided on harsher terms. He later negotiated the 1848 treaty ending the war.

TRUMAN ASSASSINATION ATTEMPT (Nov. 1, 1950). Two Puerto Rican nationalists attempted to assassinate President Harry S. Truman at Blair House in Washington. Confederates meanwhile attacked the House of Representatives. One assailant was killed; the other was sentenced to death for the killing of a guard (commuted by Truman to life imprisonment).

TRUMAN DOCTRINE. In 1947, President Truman extended military and economic aid to Greece and Turkey in order to avert a communist takeover.

TRUSTS. National monopolies first became apparent in American industry after the Civil War as cheaper transportation widened markets. The first trust was the Standard Oil Co., founded in 1879 and renamed the Standard Oil Trust in 1882. To form it, numerous refining, pipeline, and other companies assigned their stock to a board of trustees at a stipulated price and received trust certificates; the trustees had legal and voting rights in the stocks, and the stockholders received the profits. It was quickly followed by trusts in cotton, linseed oil, cattle feeders, and whiskey. The power of these trusts to set prices in a national market and to freeze out competition led to great public agitation. Attempts at the state level to control them were ineffective, and even the federal SHERMAN ANTITRUST ACT proved unable to stop the formation of what soon became known as holding companies. In 1901 the billion-dollar US Steel Corp. was founded; and by 1904, there were 318 trusts that controlled 20 percent of the manufacturing capital of the country. In that same year, the trust-busting activities of the Theodore Roosevelt administration began to succeed; the successful government prosecution of the Northern Securities Co., a railroad trust, set the stage for forty-four suits brought against trusts, holding companies, and combinations. In 1914 the CLAYTON ANTITRUST ACT and the act creating the FEDERAL TRADE COMMISSION (FTC) gave additional weapons to the federal government. Since then, the antitrust division of the Justice Department and the FTC have been the government agencies chiefly responsible for controlling trusts (and their modern equivalents, the conglomerate corporation).

TRUST TERRITORY OF THE PACIFIC. A group of about 2,000 islands in the Mariana, Caroline, and Marshall groups administered by the US under mandate of the United Nations. The seat of government is Saipan, in the Marianas. The high commissioner is appointed by the president. The bicameral, popularly elected legislature has broad lawmaking powers. Judges are appointed by the US secretary of the interior. The people, Micronesians, number about 130,000. They speak nine mutually unintelligible languages.

TRUTH-IN-LENDING ACT (1968). This act requires that money lenders disclose information about credit transactions in terms of the annual rate calculated under specified procedures.

TRYON'S LINE. Boundary between North Carolina and Indian country established by William Tryon, royal governor, in 1767. Ran from the Reedy R, where the North Carolina-South Carolina line terminated, to the top of Tryon Mountain, from where it followed a straight course to Chiswell's Mines (present Austinville, Va.) on the New R.

TSIMSHIAN. See HAIDA.

TUBAC. The first Spanish settlement in Arizona, founded ca. 1750 about twenty miles N of the Mexican border, on the Santa Cruz R. A presidio was founded there in 1752 but was moved to Tucson in 1776. Small garrison maintained there until the Mexican War.

TUBERCULOSIS. Formerly known as consumption and the white plague, it was one of the great killer diseases in American history. Its incidence began rising in the 18th c. and reached a peak in the mid-19th c. Early treatment consisted of shutting the patient in a closed room away from drafts (and fresh air), or else moving the patient to a warmer climate. In 1882, the tubercle bacillus was discovered and it became evident that substandard living conditions added greatly to its incidence. In 1889, a New York City Health Department report stated that the disease was communicable and clearly preventable. After 1897, the city required the reporting of cases and supervised the treatment of patients. Other state and city health departments soon established similar programs. This large-scale attack brought a sharp reduction in the national tubercular death rate. Today, antibiotics are employed in the treatment.

TUCSON. City in Arizona, founded in 1776 as a presidio to defend Spanish settlers from the Apache. Surrendered to US during Mexican War. Capital of Arizona Territory 1867–77. Cattle industry centers on Tucson and is an important resort and retirement center. Pop. 330,537 (1980).

TULE LAKE, BATTLES OF (1873). Sieges during the Modoc War, in the lava beds S of Tule Lake on the California-Oregon boundary. Attacks by US cavalry lasted from January to April.

TULLAHOMA CAMPAIGN (June-August 1863). Successful efforts by Union Gen. William Rosecrans to maneuver Confederate

Gen. Braxton Bragg out of Tennessee and to occupy Chattanooga.

TULSA. A center of the Oklahoma oil industry. The city grew rapidly after oil was discovered in 1901. Company headquarters, banks, pipeline terminals, and refineries were established to serve the industry. Aircraft building and repair are other major industries. Pop. 360,919 (1980).

TUNIS. See BARBARY WARS.

TUNNELS. In 1821, a tunnel was completed through a hill at Pottsville, Pa., to carry the Schuylkill Canal. The first US railway tunnel was probably that of the New York and Harlem RR at Ninety-first Street in New York City (1837). Hammer drilling was used until ca. 1865, when the pneumatic drill and nitroglycerin began to be used to shatter the rock. The safest and most economical method of tunneling, the trench method, was first used in the early 20th c.: Cylindrical concreted sections were poured on land, sealed at both ends, towed to position, and sunk into a trench previously dredged in the riverbed, and then covered with gravel. The longest tunnel built by this method is the Chesapeake Bay Tunnel (1960–64).

TURNER'S REBELLION. See NAT TURNER'S REBELLION.

TUSCARORA WAR (1711–13). White encroachments in E North Carolina and vicious practices of white traders led to an uprising of the Tuscarora (September 1711) that almost wiped out the white settlement. A three-day engagement, near present Snow Hill, N.C., ended with the Tuscarora's defeat. Most of them trekked northward to join the Five Nations, which thereafter was known as the Six Nations.

TUSKEGEE INSTITUTE. Founded 1881 at Tuskegee, Ala., as a coeducational college for black youths. Booker T. Washington was chosen to head the school, which received its charter from the Alabama legislature. George Washington Carver conducted his famous experiments there. Today, Tuskegee has university status.

TVA. See TENNESSEE VALLEY AUTHORITY.

TWEED RING. Political machine in New York City in the 1860s and 1870s, led by William Marcy Tweed. As head of TAMMANY HALL, the Democratic organization, Tweed was sovereign; he controlled the police, district attorney, courts, and most of the newspapers. It has been estimated that the Tweed ring frauds robbed the city treasury of $200 million. He was eventually exposed and convicted; he died in jail.

TWELFTH AMENDMENT (1803). Provided for presidential electors to cast separate ballots for president and vice-president. Passed after the acute situation that developed in 1800 when both Thomas Jefferson and Aaron Burr received the same number of votes, thereby forcing the election into the House of Representatives. The original Constitution had called for the person with the greatest number of electoral votes to become president, and the person with the second largest number to be elected vice-president.

TWENTIETH AMENDMENT. See LAME-DUCK AMENDMENT.

TWENTY-FIRST AMENDMENT (1933). Provided for repeal of the Eighteenth Amendment, which had imposed PROHIBITION on the nation.

TWENTY-SECOND AMENDMENT (1951). Provides that "No person shall be elected to the office of President more than twice." It resulted from Republican agitation over Franklin D. Roosevelt's running for four terms of office, thereby breaking the tradition of a president only serving two terms.

TWENTY-THIRD AMENDMENT (1961). Gives residents of the District of Columbia the right to vote in presidential elections.

TWENTY-FOURTH AMENDMENT (1964). Eliminated the use of the POLL TAX in federal elections.

TWENTY-FIFTH AMENDMENT (1967). Provided new rules for presidential and vice-presidential succession. It creates a procedure for the vice-president to become acting president in case the president is unable to discharge his duties as president. It also calls for the naming of a new vice-president whenever the former vice-president succeeds to the presidency.

TWENTY-SIXTH AMENDMENT (1971). Lowered the voting age from twenty-one to eighteen in federal and state elections.

TWIN CITIES. Minneapolis and St. Paul, Minn., situated at the head of navigation of the Mississippi R.

"TWISTING THE BRITISH LION'S TAIL." A phrase that became popular in the 19th c., particularly in districts with a large Irish constituency. Orators boasted that the US had whipped England twice and could and would do it again on any provocation.

TWO-THIRDS RULE. From 1832 until 1936, the Democratic party required a two-thirds majority to gain the nomination for president. The difficulty of achieving such a majority tended to create situations where party leaders could bargain among themselves for the nomination.

TYDINGS-MCDUFFIE ACT (1934). Provided for the independence of the Philippine Islands in 1946. It was ratified by the Philippine legislature.

U-BOATS. See SUBMARINES.

U-2 INCIDENT (1960). On May 5, the Soviet Union announced that a US U-2 spy plane had been shot down over the Soviet Union. The US denied the account, but on May 7, the Soviets produced the captured pilot, Francis Gary Powers, who confessed to being a spy for the Central Intelligence Agency. On May 16, the Paris summit conference opened and Soviet Premier Nikita Khrushchev demanded that all such activities be renounced. President Dwight Eisenhower refused and the conference broke up. Powers was sentenced to life imprisonment by the Soviets but was released in 1962 in exchange for a Soviet spy.

UNCLE SAM. Nickname for the US government. First used during the War of 1812, its source was long in question. But in 1961 Congress officially recognized Samuel Wilson (1766–1854), a meat supplier to the government, as the original Uncle Sam.

UNCLE TOM'S CABIN. A novel by Harriet Beecher Stowe, published in 1852. Three hundred thousand copies were sold the first year and more than one million by 1860. The most potent and influential of the accounts of slavery, it fed the Abolitionist cause.

UNDERGROUND RAILROAD. The informal network of sympathetic northerners who helped guide fugitive slaves through the free states to Canada in the years before the Civil War.

UNEMPLOYMENT. The US has suffered throughout its history from a wide variety of causes of unemployment as it moved from a predominantly agricultural to an industrial society. Federal concern with unemployment dates from the Great Depression and New Deal efforts to ameliorate its consequences. Despite all efforts, unemployment remained a problem until World War II, when virtual full employment was the rule. In 1946, the Full Employment Act made full employment a matter of public policy. Since then, the unemployment rate has been one of the major indicators of the state of the economy. The unemployment of persons under age twenty-five is generally at a higher rate than for others, because they have not had the opportunity to acquire skills. Blacks and other ethnic minorities also suffer a disproportionately high rate of unemployment. High unemployment during the 1970s was attributed to a number of causes: Persons born during the postwar baby boom were reaching the working age, more women were entering the job market, automation was reducing the demand for unskilled workers, and a number of labor-intensive industries (e.g., garment manufacturing) were fleeing to countries with cheaper labor. Unemployment was more than 10 percent in 1982, the highest rate since the Great Depression.

UNEMPLOYMENT INSURANCE. Monetary benefits paid by the states to unemployed workers established under the authority of the Social Security Act of 1935. The unemployment insurance program is administered by the individual states.

UNICAMERAL LEGISLATURES. All the original colonies except New Hampshire and South Carolina were governed by unicameral assemblies. When the states were formed, only Pennsylvania and Georgia opted for the unicameral system. Both later switched to a bicameral system. Renewed interest in the unicameral system was shown in the 1920s, although only Nebraska adopted a one-house legislature (in 1934).

UNIFICATION CHURCH. A Christian religious group founded in 1954 by Sun Myung Moon in Korea. It became especially strong in the US in the 1970s, particularly among young people, who sometimes were called Moonies. Its founder was convicted of tax evasion in 1982.

UNIFORM CODE OF MILITARY JUSTICE. The basic federal statute governing the military justice system. Traditionally, members of the US army were governed by the Articles of War, and navy personnel came under the Articles for the Government of the Navy. Following World War II, there was a pervasive opinion in Congress that the basic laws governing all the US armed forces should be the same. In 1950, the uniform code was passed and became effective in 1951. It has been revised several times.

UNION, FORT. Established 1851 N of present Watrous, N. Mex., to protect settlers from the Apache and Ute. One of the most important forts of the Southwest, it often served as headquarters of the Department of New Mexico. Abandoned 1891.

UNION, FORT. Established 1832 on the N bank of the Missouri R, just above the mouth of the Yellowstone R in North Dakota by the American Fur Co. Its purpose was trade with the Assiniboine and as a central depot to the company's scattered outposts. In existence until 1867.

UNION CANAL. A canal connecting the Schuykill and Susquehanna rivers in Pennsylvania, completed 1828. Abandoned 1885.

UNION COLONY. Founded 1869 at Greeley, Colo., by New Yorkers who characterized themselves as being of high moral character and as abstainers from alcohol. The success of this semicooperative venture stimulated similar undertakings.

UNION DEMOCRATS. A coalition of conservatives during the Civil War who supported the war aims of the conservative Republicans to preserve the Union and not interfere with slavery. In 1864, a Union Democrat, Andrew Johnson, was chosen as Abraham Lincoln's running mate.

UNION LABOR PARTY. Organized 1887 in an attempt to unite the remnants of the Greenback Labor party with wage earners. Nominated Alson J. Streeter for president in 1888; but he received only 147,000 votes.

UNION NAVY. The Union navy, with some 700 active ships at the height of the Civil War, gave the North overwhelming advantages in mobility and flexibility. It allowed the Union to maintain a blockade of more than 3,000 miles of Confederate coastline from Virginia to Texas, an economic and military disaster for the Confederacy. On western waters, particularly the Mississippi R, Union gunboats divided the South.

UNION PACIFIC RAILROAD. See RAILROADS, SKETCHES OF PRINCIPAL LINES.

UNION PARTY. A coalition of Republicans and Union, or War, Democrats; it won most of the important state elections in 1861.

UNION SHOP. A place of business requiring all employees to belong to the labor union representing the workers. New employees are required to join the union within a fixed period.

UNIONS, LABOR. See LABOR.

UNITED COLONIES OF NEW ENGLAND. Also known as the New England Confederation, it was established in 1643 as the governing body of the four colonies of Massachusetts, Plymouth, Connecticut, and New Haven. Rhode Island and Maine were excluded because of their political and religious uncongeniality. It was ruled by a board of two commissioners from each colony. It lost influence after Connecticut absorbed New Haven in 1662 but continued to exist until the annulment of the Massachusetts charter in 1684.

UNITED EMPIRE LOYALISTS. The name applied to inhabitants of the thirteen colonies who remained loyal to the crown at the time of the Revolution, particularly to those who migrated to Canada (see also LOYALISTS).

UNITED MINE WORKERS (UMW). An industrial union representing coal miners, founded 1890. Under the presidency of John L. Lewis (1920–60), it developed into one of the nation's strongest unions. Both its membership and influence waned in the 1970s.

UNITED NATIONS (UN). Established 1945 with a mission to keep peace among nations and to improve living conditions in the world. The name "United Nations" began to be used during World War II to designate the countries that were at war against the Axis. After preliminary meetings, the UN was established and a charter adopted at San Francisco between April 25 and June 26, 1945. Its headquarters are in New York City, and in mid-1983 there were 157 members. The UN's major components are the General Assembly, to which every UN member has one delegate with one vote. The Security Council originally had eleven members, expanded to fifteen in 1965. Its five permanent members (the major powers at the end of World War II) are the United States, the Soviet Union, China, Great Britain, and France. The other seats on the council are elected from the member nations for two-year terms. The five permanent members have veto power over any actions of the council. The Economic and Social Council has jurisdiction over the numerous specialized agencies under the UN umbrella, including the World Health Organization, the International Labor Organization, the International Bank for Reconstruction and Development, UNESCO (the United Nations Educational, Scientific, and Cultural Organization), and UNICEF. The Trusteeship Council supervises the trust territories with an eye toward bringing them to full independence. The International Court of Justice is the judicial branch of the UN and sits in the Hague. It continues the work done by the predecessor World Court. The Secretariat is the administrative section of the UN and is composed mostly of civil servants and headed by the secretary-general.

UNITED PRESS INTERNATIONAL (UPI). A worldwide news gathering and distributing agency created 1958 by the merger of the United Press (founded in the 1880s as competition to the ASSOCIATED PRESS) and the International News Service (founded 1909). The agency has about 2,400 newspaper clients (half in the US) and about 3,600 radio and television station clients.

UNITED SERVICE ORGANIZATION (USO). Organized in 1940 to provide entertainment and other services to military personnel.

UNITED STATES. A 44-gun frigate launched in 1797; it was the first vessel of the US navy. It took seven prizes in the Naval War with France, and it performed well in the War of 1812. In 1861, it was burned at the Norfolk Navy Yard to prevent its falling into the hands of the Rebels.

UNITED STATES, BANK OF THE. See BANK OF THE UNITED STATES.

UNITED STATES CODE. See CODE, UNITED STATES.

UNITED STATES OF AMERICA. First used officially as a name for the thirteen colonies in the Declaration of Independence. It was then taken over by the Articles of Confederation and the Constitution. For a brief period in 1778, the nation was styled the United States of North America; but Congress decreed that the word "North" be dropped.

UNITED STATES STEEL CORPORATION. Formed 1901 by combining ten corporations. The largest owners of the prior companies were Andrew Carnegie, Henry Clay Frick, and Elbert Gary. J. Pierpont Morgan was the banker who financed the merger. One of the world's largest steel companies, it is sometimes known as "Big Steel."

"UNITED WE STAND, DIVIDED WE FALL." A favorite toast, in varying forms, of political orators of the late 18th and 19th c.

UNIT RULE. A practice formerly observed by the Democrats at national conventions; the entire vote of a state delegation must be cast as a unit for the candidate preferred by a majority of the delegation. The rule was officially sanctioned but optional with the various state delegations. In 1968, the party voted to release all delegates from the unit rule constraint.

UNIVERSITIES, STATE. The University of North Carolina began instruction in 1795, the first state university to open. Franklin College (Georgia) opened in 1801. The Northwest Ordinance of 1787 encouraged the founding of universities in the West; and Ohio University opened in 1804 and Miami University opened in 1809. By 1861, there were twenty-one state universities. The Morrill Act (1862) provided land grants to the states for the establishment of colleges; the second Morrill Act (1890) furnished funds to the land-grant institutions; and the Hatch Experiment Station Act (1887) provided money for agricultural and scientific research. After World War II, a number of states (especially California and New York) expanded and unified their universities.

UNKNOWNS, TOMB OF THE. In Arlington National Cemetery, Va., near Washington, D.C.; dedicated in 1921 as the Tomb of the Unknown Soldier as a memorial to all US soldiers and sailors who lost their lives in World War I. In 1958, two other nameless service men, representing members killed in World War II and Korea, were buried in the tomb; and the name was changed. In 1984 a fourth unknown serviceman, from the Vietnam War, was interred.

UNREASONABLE SEARCH AND SEIZURE. See SEARCH AND SEIZURE, UNREASONABLE.

UPPER PENINSULA OF MICHIGAN. A geographically distinct region added to Michigan in 1837 as compensation for the so-called Toledo Strip ceded by Michigan to Ohio as part of the settlement of their long-standing boundary dispute. (See OHIO-MICHIGAN BOUNDARY DISPUTE.)

URBAN RENEWAL. During the 1930s, the federal government sponsored public housing projects to clear slums and replace them with housing for low-income families. The first comprehensive piece of national housing legislation was passed in 1949; the federal government offered loans to local governments to enable them to plan for, acquire, and clear slum areas for urban renewal. By the early 1970s, that legislation had resulted in the relocation of more than a half million persons, the provision of new homes for over 600,000 persons, and the rehabilitation of about 150,000 structures containing about 300,000 housing units. The Housing Act of 1975 refocused federal urban renewal efforts; all federal aids for community development were lumped into a block grant composition in which every city shares. By the 1980s, private renewal efforts were far outstripping federally financed projects.

UTAH. The first recorded European visit to what is now Utah was in 1776, although Spaniards from Santa Fe probably visited much earlier. Between 1811-40, mountain men hunted there, and after 1841 government explorers and emigrants crossed Utah. Permanent settlements were begun by the Mormons, after they had been expelled from Nauvoo, Ill., in 1846. The Mormon vanguard, led by Brigham Young, entered Salt Lake Valley in 1847; by 1868, about 68,000 immigrants had followed the Mormon Trail into Utah. Indians were moved to reservations in the 1860s, resulting in the Black Hawk War (1865-68). Mormon efforts to establish the state of Deseret were denied by Congress, and the Territory of Utah, with Brigham Young as governor, was created in 1850. Relations between Mormons and non-Mormons worsened, and Utah was occupied by federal troops (1857-61). The federal crusade against the Mormons took the form of judicial actions against Mormon polygamists; test cases taken before the Supreme Court proved fruitless for the Mormons. In 1890 the Mormon church officially foreswore polygamy, and in 1896 Utah became a state. Utah's pioneer character persisted until the 1930s, modified by the gradual coming of electricity and the automobile. Major changes during and after World War II included rapid increases in population and expansion in business, industry, and education. About 68 percent of Utah's population (1,461,037 in 1980) remains Mormon.

UTE. Indian tribe occupying C and W Colorado and all of E Utah in 1845. Theirs was a traditional Basin-type gathering culture until the late 18th c., when they began to obtain horses and adapted to the Plains culture.

UTRECHT, TREATY OF (1713). Concluded Queen Anne's War; France restored to Great Britain the Hudson Strait and Bay within boundaries to be decided later. France also ceded to Britain the island of Saint Christopher, Acadia, and Newfoundland. France acknowledged British sovereignty over the Five Nations of the Iroquois, and each party agreed not to interfere with Indians under the other's influence. Spain agreed that no part of Spanish America would ever be transferred to any foreign power.

VALCOUR ISLAND, BATTLE OF (Oct. 11, 1776). Unsuccessful attempt by patriot forces under Gen. Benedict Arnold to take control of Lake Champlain from the British. Despite the defeat of Arnold's forces, his resistance delayed British invasion for a year.

VALLANDIGHAM INCIDENT. Clement L. Vallandigham, an Ohio Copperhead leader, was convicted in 1863 of treason by courtmartial and imprisoned. President Lincoln commuted his sentence to banishment to the Confederacy. Vallandigham instead settled in Canada. He later returned to Ohio and ran for governor. To avoid a backlash from his supporters, he was not reimprisoned.

VALLEY FORGE. After serious defeats and the British occupation of Philadelphia (the national capital), Gen. George Washington led his 11,000 regular troops twenty-five miles away to Valley Forge to take up winter quarters (1777–78). The winter was unusually severe. Soldiers deserted, fever, probably typhus, and smallpox were epidemic, and medical supplies were lacking. About 2,500 men died.

VALVERDE, BATTLE OF (Feb. 21, 1862). A Confederate force under Gen. H.H. Sibley invaded New Mexico at Valverde. A stronger Union force was unable to stop them, but the Confederates were later defeated and forced to retreat.

VANCOUVER, FORT. Situated on the N bank of the Columbia R about 100 miles from its mouth and the site of present Vancouver, Wash., it was the headquarters of the Hudson's Bay Co. 1825–45.

VANCOUVER'S EXPLORATION. In 1791 Capt. George Vancouver was sent by Great Britain to survey the American Pacific shoreline. Arriving off the coast of California in April 1792, he skirted the N California and S Oregon coasts. Explored the mouth of the Co-

lumbia R, Juan de Fuca Strait, and Puget Sound.

VANDALIA COLONY. A project, never realized, to plant a settlement on the Ohio R in the early 1770s. It was strongly opposed by influential Virginians who held claims over the same territory. The Revolution ended the scheme.

VAN ZANDT, FREE STATE OF. A NE Texas county created in 1848. Named for Isaac Van Zandt, a prominent Republic of Texas diplomat.

VAUDEVILLE. Live variety shows, extremely popular in the United States in the late 19th and early 20th c. Originally known as variety, the French term *vaudeville* came to be universally used to describe the programs, which consisted of comedy acts, singing, dancing, acrobatics, and animal acts. Between 1910–30, motion pictures gradually supplanted vaudeville.

VENANGO. Site at the junction of French Creek and the Allegheny R in NW Pennsylvania, long occupied by Indians. Later, it became important in the fur-trading business and was fought over by the French and English. The French built Fort Machault there in 1754; it fell to the British, who built Fort Venango in 1760. The latter was burned by Indians in 1763. After the Revolutionary War, the Americans built Fort Franklin on the site.

VENEZUELA BOUNDARY CONTROVERSY. Conflict over the dividing line between British Guiana and Venezuela. The controversy dragged on from 1814 until 1885, when Britain suddenly extended its claims to include a region where gold was being reported. The US began pressuring the two sides for a settlement by arbitration. Finally, in 1895, US Secretary of State Richard Olney demanded a settlement, invoking the Monroe Doctrine. After initially refusing the US role, Britain agreed to let Olney arbitrate. In 1899, Olney's decision awarded the land "grabbed" by Britain in 1885 to Venezuela; the rest of the boundary followed the old British claim.

VERACRUZ INCIDENT (1914). Under orders from President Wilson, US troops captured the city of Veracruz, Mexico. It resulted from a US quarrel with the revolutionary president of Mexico, Victoriano Huerto, who had arrested some US marines at Tampico. In July, Huerta was forced to resign the presidency.

VERMONT. During the colonial period, both New York and New Hampshire had claims on what is now Vermont. New York's claims collapsed with the coming of the Revolutionary War, and Vermont declared itself (1777) an independent republic, an interim measure until statehood could be bestowed. In 1791, upon a cash payment to settle New York's claims, it was admitted to the Union, the first to be admitted after the original thirteen. Although migration from southern New England swelled its population by about 200,000 by the time of the War of 1812, Vermont remained one of the nation's smallest states. Manufacturing, dairy farming, timber and pulpwood, and tourism are its main industries. Pop.: 511,456 (1980).

VERRAZZANO-NARROWS BRIDGE. Crosses the Narrows of New York harbor connecting Staten Island and Brooklyn. Opened in 1964, it reaches a height of 228 feet (making it high enough to clear the tallest ships likely to enter the harbor) and is 4,260 feet in length, making it the longest suspension bridge in the world.

VERSAILLES, TREATY OF (1919). The peace treaty ending World War I, it was signed by the US, Great Britain, France, Italy, Japan, and twenty-three other Allied powers and Germany. It contained provisions for the establishment of the LEAGUE OF NATIONS, for the redrawing of Germany's borders, and for harsh reparations to be paid by Germany. The US never ratified the treaty because of opposition to the League of Nations. The war between Germany and the US was formally ended in 1921 by the Treaty of Berlin.

VESEY REBELLION. In 1821 Denmark Vesey, a slave, led a plot to annihilate the white population of Charleston, S.C. The plot supposedly involved as many as 3,000 slaves. He and the principal conspirators were executed.

VETERANS ADMINISTRATION. The US government agency that handles matters of disability, compensation, pension, home and educational loan benefits, medical care, and housing for American veterans. It was established as an independent agency in 1930, taking over the functions of the Veterans Bureau, the Bureau of Pensions, and the National Home for Volunteer Soldiers.

VETERANS DAY. A federal legal holiday, observed on November 11, the day World War I ended. Until 1954, the holiday had been observed as ARMISTICE DAY.

VETERANS' ORGANIZATIONS. The first veterans' association in the US was the Society of the Cincinnati, founded in 1783. Veterans of the Union army founded the Grand Army of the Republic in 1866; it went out of existence when the last Civil War veteran died in 1956. The American Legion, founded 1919, remains the largest of veterans' groups with a membership of 2.6 million. Other such groups include the Veterans of Foreign Wars (founded 1899), the Disabled American Veterans (1919), and the American Veterans of World War II, Korea, and Vietnam (AMVETS, originally founded 1944).

VETERINARY MEDICINE. The first American work that included a discussion of animal disease, *Husband-man's Guide*, was published in Boston in 1710; America's first veterinary surgeon opened a practice in New York in 1803. The short-lived Boston Veterinary Institute opened in 1855, and the first successful school, the New York College of Veterinary Surgeons was opened in 1857. The most prestigious was the American Veterinary College, which opened in New York in 1875. Other successful schools were opened in Chicago and Kansas City. The first of the university schools was established at Iowa State University in 1879, followed by the University of Pennsylvania in 1884.

Large-scale animal disease began to be a problem ca. 1860. The Morrill Land Grant Act of 1862 accelerated the establishment of agricultural colleges, most of which offered instruction in veterinary science. After World War II, employment opportunities for veterinarians broadened greatly; and many graduates specialized in such areas as public health, laboratory animal medicine, zoo animal practice, medical research, and equine practice.

VETO POWER, PRESIDENTIAL. The framers of the Constitution apparently conceived of the presidential veto as one of the checks and balances designed to prevent legislative encroachments on the executive branch. Within ten days of its submission to him, the president may either sign a legislative act into law or veto it; or he can do nothing, in which case it becomes law without his signature. The item veto is not permitted; either the president vetoes the entire bill or no part of it. Congress may repass a vetoed bill, but a two-thirds majority in each house is required. If Congress adjourns within ten days after submitting the bill to the president, his failure to act kills the bill (the pocket veto). The veto was used sparingly by the first seven presidents. Andrew Jackson used it frequently to impose his policy views on Congress; since that time, presidents have never hesitated to use it.

VIAL'S ROAD. Traced by Pedro Vial from Santa Fe to St. Louis in 1792 at great personal danger. It was planned as a route to use in trading with the French, but it was never realized.

VICE-PRESIDENCY. The office of vice-president was established by the Constitution to provide a successor if the president should die in office, resign, or become incapable of carrying out his duties. The vice-president was also made the presiding officer of the Senate and could cast the deciding vote there in case of a tie. Any other duties are at the discretion of the president. Eight vice-presidents have succeeded directly to the presidency; and five others have been elected in their own right. One of them, Gerald R. Ford, was appointed vice-president when the incumbent (Spiro T. Agnew) resigned; then he succeeded to the presidency when Richard Nixon resigned. Ford had been named under the provisions of the TWENTY-FIFTH AMENDMENT.

VICKSBURG. A city on the high E bank of the Mississippi R in Mississippi, just below the mouth of the Yazoo R. The French built Fort St. Pierre on the site in 1719; later (1791) the Spanish established Fort Nogales there. The British changed the name to Fort McHenry, and river traders called it Walnut Hill. Permanent settlement began in 1814, when Newitt Vick, a Methodist missionary, established a mission there. A town was laid out and incorporated in 1825. After the removal of the Choctaw, Vicksburg prospered and competed with Natchez as Mississippi's center of wealth and political power. It was strategically important during the Civil War (see VICKSBURG IN THE CIVIL WAR). The decline of steamboating reduced the city's importance as a river port, but in the 20th c., harbor improvements and a bridge across the river again made Vicksburg a major transport center. Pop: 25,434 (1980).

VICKSBURG IN THE CIVIL WAR. With the fall of New Orleans to Union forces in April 1862, Vicksburg's importance as an obstacle to Union control of the Mississippi R was evident to the Confederacy. Fortifications of the city began, and so did Union Gen. U.S. Grant's campaign against the city. After several unsuccessful attempts, Grant moved down the W bank of the river, recrossed below Vicksburg, and attacked the city from the east. The city was put under siege, aided by bombardment from the Union fleet. Each Union attack was repulsed with heavy losses. Dwindling food and ammunition supplies finally forced the Rebels to surrender (on July 4, 1863).

VICKSBURG RIOTS (1874). White citizens of Vicksburg, opposing the policies and actions of the Reconstruction state government created disturbances in which two whites and twenty-nine blacks were killed.

VIETNAM WAR (1957–75). Began as a communist insurgency supported by North Vietnam, and later involved direct North Vietnamese intervention. The US fought in conjunction with South Vietnam. There were 45,943 US battle deaths, the fourth most costly American war in terms of loss of life. The Vietnam War followed the Indochina War of 1946–54, in which France sought to reestablish its colonial control over the area. The Geneva Accords that ended that war in effect created two nations: North Vietnam (under communist control) and South Vietnam (under noncommunist control). The US became a protector of South Vietnam, which soon became the object of communist guerrillas, or Vietcong. By 1963, President Kennedy had increased US advisers to 23,000. The assassination of President Ngo Dinh Diem (purportedly with US acquiescence) resulted in a series of unstable governments. In August 1964, two US destroyers were attacked in the Gulf of Tonkin. President Lyndon B. Johnson asked for and got from Congress a resolution that in effect gave him carte blanche to escalate the war at will. Escalation took place gradually, and by the end of 1969, US forces reached a peak of 543,400. As the war dragged on and as optimistic forecasts by the US military again and again turned out to be unfulfilled, opposition to the war became a divisive issue in the US. President Nixon entered office committed to bringing the war to a close, but deescalation proved to be slow and difficult. In 1973, a cease-fire was finally effected, and US troops were withdrawn. Through 1973–74, the North Vietnamese violated the cease-fire by massing more men and supplies within South Vietnam. In January 1975, they launched a major attack that ended with the complete collapse of the South Vietnamese government. The communists gained control over all of Vietnam and also neighboring Cambodia and Laos. It was the longest American war and also the only unalloyed military defeat in US history.

VIGILANTES. Members of citizens' committees set up in western communities to maintain order before law courts were organized and peace officers were elected. In some instances, action was little more than that of a mob.

VILLA RAID AT COLUMBUS. (Mar. 9, 1916). A raid against US nationals at Columbus, N. Mex., led by Pancho Villa. The cavalry stationed there drove the Mexicans back across the border. The raid was directly responsible for the US punitive expedition into Mexico.

VILLASUR EXPEDITION (1720). Don Pedro de Villasur left Santa Fe with a party of about 100 for a reconnaissance of the French position to the east. The party was attacked by the Pawnee, allies of the French, near present North Platte, Nebr. Forty-four members of the party were killed, including Villasur.

VILLERE'S PLANTATION, BATTLE AT (Dec. 23, 1814). Gen. Andrew Jackson defeated the British in an engagement a few miles S of New Orleans. The British retired until they were decisively defeated at the Battle of New Orleans Jan. 8, 1815.

VINCENNES. French fort and settlement on the Wabash R in Indiana, located on the site of an Indian village. Fur traders made the site their headquarters as early as 1700, and by mid-century the fort was surrounded by 5,000 acres farmed by French settlers. The British took Vincennes in 1777, and Americans under George Rogers Clark captured the post in 1779. It was the first capital (1800–13) of the Indiana Territory. Pop.: 20,857 (1980).

VINCENNES, TREATY OF (1803). Nine Indian tribes (Shawnee, Potawatomi, Miami, Wea, Eel River, Delaware, Piankashaw, Kaskaskia, and Kickapoo) ceded large tracts of their land in Indiana Territory to the US.

VINLAND. The name used by medieval Scandinavian historians and saga writers for that part of North America visited by Norse mariners ca. AD 1000. Newfoundland has generally been designated as the site of Vinland.

VIRGINIA. The first permanent English settlement was established in 1607 at Jamestown, on a peninsula on the James R. The London Co., the original proprietor, went into bankruptcy in 1624 and thereafter the colony was ruled directly by the crown; after 1619, there was a house of burgesses. Tobacco, raised by black slaves from Africa, became the most important crop. In 1669, Williamsburg became the capital and Richmond, laid out in 1737, became capital in 1779. During the 18th c., the population of Virginia grew from an estimated 72,000 to over 807,000 (slaves constituted 42 percent). The state was a major scene of battle during the latter stages of the Revolutionary War; final surrender of British forces was at Yorktown Oct. 19, 1781. Virginians dominated the presidency until 1824. Agriculture remained the chief occupation, with tobacco raising being joined by wheat and other grains being grown in the tidewater and lower piedmont. Cattle raising and orchard cultivation became important in the Shenandoah Valley and Blue Ridge foothills. In the early 19th c., the population center shifted to the west but political control remained with the old tidewater aristocracy. Western agitation for a more equitable constitution was partially realized in 1829, but full white male suffrage was still denied. The state was the scene of almost continuous warfare between 1861 and 1865. Extensive areas of the state and major cities were largely destroyed. In 1863, the fifty western counties reconstituted themselves as the new state of West Virginia; thus the state lost nearly 35 percent of its land area and 25 percent of its population. At the end of the war, a half million Virginia slaves were emancipated, and the state had to accept a harsh Reconstruction government. In 1870, Virginia reentered the Union with a new constitution guaranteeing universal suffrage, a free public school system, and a system of local democracy. Despite some boom-and-bust problems, the state recovered economically in the latter 19th c. The economy in the 20th c. has been based more on industry than on traditional agriculture. Coal exporting, textiles, and furniture making are important industries. There are numerous federal facilities in the state, and the government is the second largest source of employment. Tourism is also important. Pop.: 5,346,279 (1980).

VIRGINIA. The first steamboat to navigate the upper Mississippi R above the Des Moines Rapids; it was built in Wheeling in 1819 and reached Fort Snelling, Minn., in 1823. It hit a snag and sank later that year.

VIRGINIA, UNIVERSITY OF. Founded 1819 by Thomas Jefferson, who was architect of its original buildings. The university's specific contributions to American education have been the secularization of scientific thought and the establishment of the elective system of study.

VIRGINIA AND KENTUCKY RESOLUTIONS (1798-99). The Virginia resolutions were written by James Madison and the Kentucky ones by Thomas Jefferson. Their immediate purpose was to protest the ALIEN AND SEDITION LAWS, passed in 1798 by the Federalist administration. Both maintained that the federal government had overstepped its authority and that state sovereignty was being impinged upon. The resolutions passed in the two states for which they are named; other states received them coolly. They were later used by states' rights advocates to advance their claims.

VIRGINIA CAPES, BATTLE OF (Sept. 5-9, 1781). Naval engagement of the American Revolution. The French navy, under the command of Adm. de Grasse, sealed up the British forces of Gen. Cornwallis at Yorktown, Va., leading to the surrender that established American independence.

VIRGINIA CITY. The largest and most famous of Nevada's early mining towns; established in 1859, by the 1870s it had a population of 30,000. It quickly declined as the ores of the Comstock mining region ran out. It became a ghost town; but in the 20th c., many of its buildings were restored and it became a popular tourist center.

VIRGINIA COMPANY OF LONDON. The commercial enterprise that was chartered in 1606 to plant colonies in the New World. It was chartered to found "the first colony" in Virginia and "the second colony" (see PLYMOUTH, VIRGINIA COMPANY OF). Jamestown was the first colony planted in Virginia. It did not prosper, and even the profitable tobacco raising did not turn around the finances of the company. It was finally dissolved in 1624 and Virginia became a crown colony.

VIRGINIA DECLARATION OF RIGHTS (1776). Formulated by George Mason and adopted by the Virginia Convention even before it voted for independence, the declaration became the model for other state bills of rights and for the federal Bill of Rights.

VIRGINIA EXILES. Prominent Philadelphia Quakers who were exiled to Winchester, Va., in 1777-78 for their British sympathies. Probably most were merely pacifists.

VIRGINIA INDIAN COMPANY. Established 1714 by the royal governor of Virginia and given exclusive control over trade with the Indians. It reopened trade with the Catawba and Cherokee and opened a pass through the Blue Ridge Mountains. The Privy Council dissolved the company in 1717 on the ground that it was a monopoly.

VIRGINIA MILITARY RESERVE IN OHIO. When Virginia ceded its claims to the Ohio country, it reserved a large tract between the Little Miami and Scioto rivers as bounty land to be given veterans of the Revolutionary

War. Many war veterans assigned their land to speculators, who came to control large tracts. In 1852, the Virginia legislature released all further claims on the lands. Total grants on military bounties had totaled more than 4 million acres; almost 76 million acres were turned over to Ohio.

VIRGINIA OF SAGADAHOCK. Built in 1607 in Maine, it was the first ship built by Englishmen in the New World.

VIRGINIA PATH. The route taken by Indians through Virginia from the Potomac R to the Carolinas.

VIRGINIA PLAN. A strongly nationalistic plan for the new government, proposed to the Constitutional Convention of 1787 by Edmund Randolph of Virginia. It called for a bicameral legislature, with the upper house being chosen out of the lower house. Congress would elect the executive and judiciary and would have the authority to disallow any state laws it deemed contravening federal law.

VIRGINIA RESOLUTIONS (1847). The first of the state resolutions imploring the national government to keep a hands-off policy toward slavery.

VIRGINIA RESOLVES (1769). The first American protest against the TOWNSHEND ACTS and against the treatment of Massachusetts for resenting those acts. Adoption of the resolves, which were sponsored by George Mason and George Washington, led to similar adoptions by other colonial assemblies.

VIRGIN ISLANDS. Sixty-eight islands in the Caribbean Sea, of which St. Croix, St. Thomas, and St. John are the largest. They were bought from Denmark in 1917. They are governed by a popularly elected territorial governor and a unicameral legislature. Tourism is the principal industry. Pop.: 95,000 (1980).

VIRGINIUS AFFAIR (1873). The Spanish captured a ship of US registry, the *Virginius*, which was carrying arms to Cuban rebels, and executed as pirates its captain and fifty-three crew members and passengers. The US drafted a virtual ultimatum to Spain, even though the ship's registration papers had been fraudulently obtained and it was actually owned by a Cuban revolutionary committee. Spain accepted the US demands. The ship was returned but sank en route. The survivors were surrendered and an indemnity paid.

VISIBLE ADMIXTURE LAW (1859). Ohio law declaring that all persons having a "distinct and visible admixture of African blood" should be denied the vote. Declared unconstitutional in 1860 by state supreme court.

VISIT AND SEARCH. A procedure whereby a naval vessel of a belligerent stops a foreign vessel on the high seas on the suspicion of assisting the enemy through the transport of contraband goods. It has long been a permissible act in international law.

VISTA. See VOLUNTEERS IN SERVICE TO AMERICA.

VITAL STATISTICS. Even before the Constitution decreed that a decenniel federal census be taken, New York and Rhode Island carried out relatively frequent population enumerations; Massachusetts and Virginia took censuses less often. The federal census, launched in 1790, broadened the scope of its demographic inquiries several times during the 19th c. In addition, by 1800 several large eastern cities were regularly recording deaths, and sometimes births, for public health purposes; this reporting was frequently expanded during epidemics. By the 1860s, vital statistics were being published regularly and widely in medical journals, but also in the reports of hospitals, asylums, health departments and registration offices of many older cities and states. The American Statistical Association was established in 1839; texts on vital statistics were available by 1890, and around this time instruction in the subject began to be offered in medical schools. Mechanization of vital statistics processing began in the 1880s with the use of the Hollerith tabulating machine to handle census data, and spread rapidly. At about the same time, a significant improvement was effected by the creation of the national death registration area (followed by birth and marriage registration areas); this device brought about uniform registration procedures and standards for the entire country.

VOICE OF AMERICA. A broadcasting service that came into being during World War II to combat enemy propaganda and explain to the world America's wartime goals. It was continued after the war as an integral part of an information program of the US and its policies. It is part of the US Information Agency.

VOLSTEAD ACT (1919). Also called the National Prohibition Act, it created the legal mechanism to enforce the EIGHTEENTH AMENDMENT.

VOLUNTEERS IN SERVICE TO AMERICA (VISTA). Established as a domestic Peace Corps in 1965, it is an organization of volunteers who work among poor Americans in areas where there are few public services. It was combined in 1971 with ACTION, an agency supervising and coordinating foreign and domestic aid programs.

VOTING RIGHTS ACT OF 1965. Federal legislation the purpose of which was to remove the last barriers to voting by all qualified persons, especially blacks. Passed during the administration of Lyndon B. Johnson, it and the Civil Rights Act of 1964 ended virtually all forms of legal racial discrimination. The Voting Rights Act made the literacy test (long used in the South to keep blacks off the voting rolls) illegal; prohibited all use of the poll tax; called for criminal penalties against any official who denied any qualified voter the right to vote; and called for federal examiners in areas where there was evidence of a pattern of discrimination.

VOYAGEURS. Fur traders, especially Frenchmen, who plied American rivers of the Great Lakes and Northwest from the 17th c. onward.

WABASH AND ERIE CANAL. Waterway begun in 1829 to follow the Maumee and Wabash rivers in connecting Lake Erie and the Ohio R. When it was finally completed in 1856, its 452 miles connecting Toledo and Evansville made it the longest canal in the US. Abandoned in 1875.

WABASH RAILROAD. See RAILROADS, SKETCHES OF PRINCIPAL LINES: NORFOLK AND WESTERN.

WABASH TOWNS, EXPEDITIONS AGAINST (May and Aug. 1791). Indians op-erating from their towns on the Wabash and Eel rivers in N Indiana constantly raided across the Ohio R into Kentucky. Two US army expeditions were mounted against them, and many of their villages and crops were burned. The Indians retaliated, defeating Gen. Arthur St. Clair on November 4 near the present Fort Wayne.

WAGE AND PRICE CONTROLS. Federal rent controls were imposed during World War I; and in World War II, the Office of Price Administration (OPA) was created to set maximum prices for goods. It also provided for the rationing of scarce civilian goods to the public. At the same time, wages were stabilized by a Wage Stabilization Board. Rents were also controlled. Most controls ended at the end of the war but many were reimposed during the Korean War. In their efforts to control inflation, Presidents Kennedy, Johnson, Nixon, and Carter all used various "guidelines" that were aimed at keeping both wages and prices under control. Only under the Nixon plan, inaugurated in 1971, was there an enforcement mechanism.

WAGES AND HOURS OF LABOR, REGULATION OF. At the beginning of the 19th c., the number of work hours ranged upward from twelve hours a day, six days a week. Public agitation in the 1820s led to the ten-hour day, sixty-hour week. After the Civil War, the eight-hour day became the focus of a national movement, and recurring efforts were made to pass federal and state laws mandating it. Employers vigorously resisted these efforts, and during the 19th c. the courts struck down many such laws on the grounds that they abridged freedom-to-contract rights. The first enforceable law limiting hours of work for women and children was passed in Massachusetts in 1879. The courts proved more adamant where male workers were concerned. In 1916, Congress passed a law calling for the eight-hour day for railroad employees; and in 1917, the Supreme Court upheld an Oregon law establishing ten hours for most men in industry. Thus the precedent for government action was established. In 1935, the Supreme Court invalidated the National Industrial Recovery Act; but Congress repassed the Fair Labor Standards Act in 1938, which established a minimum wage and regulated hours of labor. In 1941 the Supreme Court upheld the national minimum wage law as a valid exercise of the federal power to regulate interstate commerce.

WAGES AND HOURS ACT. See FAIR LABOR STANDARDS ACT.

WAGNER ACT. See NATIONAL LABOR RELATIONS ACT.

WAGON BOX FIGHT (Aug. 2, 1867). Sioux under Red Cloud attacked a woodcutting detail near Fort Phil Kearny, Wyo. Thirty-two men retreated to a corral built of wagon boxes, from which they repulsed the Sioux. Seven soldiers and an estimated 180 Sioux were killed.

WAGON MANUFACTURERS. In the 19th c., wagons were built by local craftsmen who worked in small shops, often with blacksmiths making and attaching the iron components and wheels coming from wheelsmiths. By the early 1900s, mechanization and specialization had reduced prices of wagons and were carried over into the automobile industry.

WAGON TRAIN CHARGE (Nov. 8, 1874). Leading a cavalry detachment, Lt. F.D. Baldwin routed Grey Beard's camp at McClellan's Creek on the Llano Estacado of Texas, recapturing two children.

WAGON TRAINS. For protection and efficiency, traders and emigrants to the West before 1880 often gathered their wagons into trains, the earliest being ca. 1832 and reached their peak in the 1840s. In 1849, 5,516 wagons passed Fort Kearney on the Platte R, bound for California or the Columbia Valley. Some wagon trains were five miles long. With the completion of the transcontinental railroad in 1869, the use of wagon trains quickly declined.

WAKARUSA WAR (1862). Between proslavery and antislavery Missourians at Franklin on the Wakarusa R. After a week, the territorial governor was able to effect a treaty.

WAKE, DEFENSE OF (Dec. 8–23, 1941). Wake, an atoll flanking the Japanese islands of Marshall and Mariana, was garrisoned by US marines; they withstood several fierce Japanese onslaughts. Eight of their twelve fighter planes were destroyed, and the marines were finally forced to surrender. Eighty-one marines were killed or wounded.

WAKEFIELD. Plantation birthplace of George Washington, on the Potomac R in Westmoreland County, Va. The house had been built by the Washington family in 1718; it burned in 1779.

WALDEN. A pond near Concord, Mass. In 1814, Henry David Thoreau described his solitary life in a cabin on the shore of the pond in *Walden: or Life in the Woods*. The essays are notable for their philosophical individualism and their observations of nature.

WALDENSES. Heretical Protestant sect originating in France. In 1893 they established a colony at Valdese, N.C. Originally operated as a commune, the community operated a wine press, hosiery mills, cotton mills, lumber mills, a bakery, and a macaroni factory.

WALDO PATENT. Included in the grant of James I to the Council of New England in 1620, it embraced land from Muscongus Bay to the Penobscot R in Maine. In 1731 Gen. Samuel Waldo claimed the patent and settled the land. He increased his holdings to a half million acres, which fell to his children. After the American Revolution, much of the patent was purchased by Gen. Henry Knox. Eventually, much of it was divided among his creditors.

WALKER EXPEDITION. The first American trapping expedition to cross the Sierra Nevada into California. Joseph R. Walker led his expedition down the Humboldt R to the Carson Sink and Walker Lake in W Nevada, then over the Sierra Nevada to the present Yosemite. He discovered the California Sequoia. Descending to the San Joaquin Valley, Walker continued to the coast.

WALKER'S FILIBUSTERING EXPEDITIONS (1853–60). William Walker, with a small force, landed in Baja California, which he proclaimed an independent republic, naming himself as president. Shortly thereafter, he also claimed Sonora; but US pressure soon brought his venture to an end. In 1855, he accepted the invitation of a revolutionary faction in Nicaragua to bring an armed force into the country. He invaded and captured Granada and became commander in chief of the army. The US recognized the government in 1856, and Walker had himself chosen president. However, he came into competition with US business interests and surrendered to the US navy. He made two further attempts to conquer Nicaragua. On the second, in 1860, he was captured, condemned by a court-martial, and executed.

WALK-IN-THE-WATER. The first steamboat, launched 1818, to navigate the upper Great Lakes. It was built near Buffalo, N.Y., and named after an Indian chief. Wrecked in 1821.

WALLACE, FORT. Built 1865 at the junction of Pond Creek and Smoky Hill R, S of the present Wallace, Kans. Important during the building of the Union Pacific RR and the Cheyenne raids. Abandoned in 1882.

WALLA WALLA SETTLEMENTS. Communiities established in the first half of the 19th c. on the Columbia R near its junction with the Walla Walla R in Washington state. Fort Nez Percé, built 1818, protected them; they included settlements on the sites of the present Wallula and Walla Walla.

WALLOONS. French-speaking Protestants from NE France (modern Belgium). They were the first colonizers of New Netherland.

WALL STREET. Street in Manhattan, synonymous with US financial interests. Named because of a stockade built across lower Manhattan in 1653. It was the site of New York's principal merchants in the late 18th c., and Federal Hall, the nation's first capitol, was on the street. The New York Stock Exchange was established there in 1817; other exchanges, banks, insurance companies, shipping agencies, and corporations also congregated in the area.

WAMPUM. Strings of beads and shells, used to recount events, messages, treaties, or rituals. Among the Algonkin tribes, wampum was the badge of chiefly rank. The Iroquois borrowed the idea. In New Netherland it was used as a medium of exchange.

WANGHIA, TREATY OF (1844). First treaty between the US and China. It ensured extraterritorial rights for US citizens in China, opened five Chinese ports to US traders, and gave the US most-favored-nation status.

WAPPINGER CONFEDERACY. A 17th-c. confederation of nine Algonkin-speaking tribes on the E bank of the Hudson R from Poughkeepsie to New York City and extending into the Connecticut R valley. They were finally merged with the Delaware.

WAR, ARTICLES OF. See UNIFORM CODE OF MILITARY JUSTICE.

WAR, DECLARATION OF. The Constitution places the power to declare war on Congress. This seems to be in conflict with the president's status as commander in chief of the armed forces, which gives him the power to move troops wherever he chooses. Neither the Korean War nor the Vietnam War were ever officially declared as wars by Congress. (See also WAR POWERS OF THE PRESIDENT.)

WAR AND ORDNANCE, BOARD OF. An agency created by the Continental Congress in 1776 to assume administrative control of the army. Originally composed of five members of Congress, the board's size and composition changed several times. In 1781, a department of war was authorized and the board of war theoretically ceased to exist.

WAR BONNET CREEK, FIGHT ON (July 17, 1876). The US cavalry encountered a band of Cheyenne at the present Hat Creek at Montrose, Nebr., who had escaped from a reservation to join Sitting Bull. The Indians were driven back to the reservation, and Buffalo Bill Cody killed Yellow Hand (or Yellow Hair) in the battle.

WAR CRIMES TRIAL (1945–46). At Nuremberg, Germany, surviving Nazi leaders were tried before an international tribunal as war criminals charged with violating international law, waging aggressive warfare, and committing "crimes against humanity." Nineteen of twenty-two high officials were found guilty. Twelve were sentenced to death, and eight were actually hanged. Comparable trials of Japanese leaders held at Tokyo in 1946–48 had similar results.

WAR DEMOCRATS. The Democratic wing in the North that supported the Union during the Civil War.

WAR DEPARTMENT. Created 1789 as a civilian agency under the president to administer the army. The secretary of war was a member of the president's cabinet (along with the secretary of the navy) until 1947, when the War Department became the Department of Defense and the cabinet officer became the secretary of the defense.

WARD LEADERS. A ward, precinct, or assembly district official elected or appointed to maximize voter turnout in support of his or her party's candidates. Nonelectoral functions include maintaining the party cadre betwen elections and aiding citizens seeking governmental action.

WAR HAWKS. Term applied to members of Congress who advocated the War of 1812. Among the strongest of the war hawks were the Northwesterners, who held the British responsible for their Indian troubles and hoped to drive the British out of Canada, and southerners, who planned to wrest Florida from Spain, England's ally.

WAR OF 1812. Provoked by Great Britain's maritime policy in its war with Napoleon and by its overfriendly relations with the Indian tribes of the Northwest. The war was facilitated by the desire in the West and South to secure possession of Canada and Florida. British impressment of US sailors and the confiscation of US ships began ca. 1807; and neither the Embargo Act nor the Nonintercourse Act corrected the situation. Western WAR HAWKS resented British support for the Shawnee chief Tecumseh, who strongly opposed white encroachment on Indian lands. In the South, the United States claimed a portion of Spanish West Florida and had begun to absorb it piecemeal. Spain's alliance with Britain offered an excuse for seizing both East Florida and West Florida. Congress was fired up by the War Hawks, and on June 4, 1812, war was declared. Early encounters with the British were disastrous; Detroit fell, the NIAGARA CAMPAIGNS were a failure, as was the effort on Lake Champlain. The next year saw some improvement; Detroit was retaken, and there was a British defeat on the Thames. But 1813 also saw the burning of Buffalo, an unsuccessful attempt by the Americans to take Montreal, and the British capture of Fort Niagara. By mid-1814, the British were present in such force that US troops could hope only to hold their own. The British burned Washington, D.C., but failed to take Baltimore. Troops advancing from Montreal reached Plattsburgh, N.Y., but were forced to retreat in the face of the American fleet in Lake Champlain. In general, the small US navy fared better against the British than did the army; although the British clamped a tight blockade against southern ports. The war ruined farmers, merchants, and bankers, particularly in New England, where there was great opposition to the war. US and British negotiators met at Ghent in the summer of 1814. A treaty was signed on Dec. 24, 1814; both sides accepted the peace *status quo ante bellum* as to territory. At New Orleans (two weeks after the signing of peace treaty), Gen. Andrew Jackson inflicted on the British the most crushing defeat of the war.

WAR ON POVERTY. Begun in 1964 as a key to President Lyndon B. Johnson's Great Society program. It aimed at reducing poverty through a wide variety of government aid programs. Much of the program was terminated by the succeeding administration of Richard Nixon.

WAR POWERS OF THE PRESIDENT. The president can initiate and wage wars on the authority of his constitutional designation as commander in chief. Although Congress is empowered to declare war, the presidents have often committed the armed forces to conflict; only five of eleven wars have been declared by Congress: the War of 1812, the Mexican War, the Spanish-American War, and the two world wars. The power to wage war gives the president many choices, particularly in the modern age when the president alone decides when to use nuclear and thermonuclear weapons. The president can initiate a blockade, as President Kennedy did in the 1962 Cuban missile crisis; he can direct military campaigns, as President Lincoln did during the Civil War; he can send US troops to "advise" friendly governments, as Presidents Eisenhower, Kennedy, Johnson, and Nixon did before and during the Vietnam War; he can order the secret bombing of a neutral nation, as President Nixon did in Cambodia during the Vietnam War; and the president can mine the harbor of a neutral nation, as the Central Intelligence Agency did in 1984 in Nicaragua on the orders of President Reagan. The Vietnam War led to the War Powers Act of 1973; it requires the president to report emergency military action to Congress within 48 hours. Combat action must end in 60 days unless Congress authorizes the action. Congress can order immediate removal of the forces by adopting a resolution not subject to presidential veto.

WARREN, FORT FRANCIS E. Established 1867 at Cheyenne, Wyo., to protect the Union Pacific RR against attacks from the Cheyenne, Nez Percé, and Sioux. Originally called Fort Russell, its name was changed in 1929.

WARREN COMMISSION. Appointed on Nov. 29, 1963, by President Lyndon B. Johnson to report on the assassination of President Kennedy. Chief Justice Earl Warren headed it. The commission and its staff reviewed reports by various government agencies, particularly the Federal Bureau of Investigation (FBI), and it heard and weighed the testimony of witnesses. Its report, issued on Sept. 24, 1964, concluded that Lee Harvey Oswald acted alone in killing the president and that no conspiracy was involved. It criticized the FBI and Secret Service for inadequately protecting the president and poorly coordinating their information. The report aroused controversy, and a large literature has been created by its critics.

WARREN'S TRADING POSTS. Abel Warren established at least three trading posts on the Red R between Texas and Oklahoma. The first, established in 1836, was in Fannin County, Texas; the second, maintained from 1837–48, was in Love County, Okla.; and the third, built in 1848, was in Cotton County, Okla.

WARRIORS PATH, GREAT. The war road between the Shawnee and Wyandot of the Ohio country and the Catawba and Cherokee in W North Carolina. It ran along the upper Licking R in E Kentucky and the Red R branch of the Kentucky R to the Cumberland Gap. It passed down Powell Valley and crossed the Clinch and Holston rivers. There it divided, going E to the Catawba towns, and W across the Nolichuckey and the French Broad rivers to the Overhill Cherokee towns.

WARS AND CAMPAIGNS, INDIAN. Indian wars and campaigns before the Civil War cannot be grouped conveniently. After the war, they fall into three classifications: wars of the Great Plains, the Southwest, and the Northwest. Important wars and campaigns are as follows: 1790–95 Northwestern Indian War (Ohio), 1811–13 Northwestern Indian War (Indiana), 1812 Seminole War (Florida), 1813 Peoria War (Illinois), 1813–14 Creek War (Georgia, Alabama, Mississippi, Tennessee), 1817–18 Seminole War (Florida, Georgia), 1823 Arikara and Blackfoot War (Missouri R region, Dakota Territory), 1832 Black Hawk War (Illinois, Wisconsin), 1835–42 Seminole War (Florida, Georgia, Alabama), 1836–37 Creek War (Georgia, Alabama), 1836–37 Sabine, or Southwestern, War (Louisiana), 1847–50 Cayuse War (Oregon), 1849–61 Campaigns against the Navaho, Comanche, Cheyenne, Lipan, and Kickapoo (Texas, New Mexico), 1850–53 Utah Indian War, 1851–52 California Indian War, 1851–56 Rogue R War against the Yakima, Klikitat, Klamath, and Salmon R tribes (Oregon, Washington), 1855–56 Campaign against the Sioux, Cheyenne, and Arapaho, 1855–58 Seminole War (Florida), 1857 Campaign against the Sioux (Minnesota, Iowa), 1858 Campaign against the Northern Indians (Washington Territory), 1858 Campaign against the Spokane, Coeur d'Alene, and Paloo (Washington Territory), 1858 Campaign against the Navaho (New Mexico), 1858–59 Campaign against the Wichita (Indian Territory), 1861–90 Apache wars, including campaigns against Victorio and Geronimo, 1862–67 Sioux War (Minnesota, Dakota Territory), 1863–70 Campaigns against the Cheyenne, Arapaho, Kiowa, and Comanche (Kansas, Colorado, Indian Territory), 1865–68 Northwestern Indian War (Oregon, Idaho, California, Nevada), 1867–81 Campaigns against the Lipan, Kiowa, Kickapoo, and Comanche, 1872–73 Modoc War (Oregon), 1874–75 Campaigns against the Cheyenne, Arapaho, Kiowa, Comanche, and Sioux (Kansas, Colorado, Texas, New Mexico, Indian Territory), 1874–79 Campaigns against the Sioux and Cheyenne (Wyoming,

Nebraska, Dakotas, Nevada, Montana, Indian Territory), 1877 Nez Percé War (Utah), 1878 Bannock War against the Bannock, Paiute, Shoshone (Idaho, Washington, and Wyoming territories), 1878 Campaign against the Ute (Colorado), 1879 Campaign against the Sheepeater (Idaho), 1879–80 Campaigns against the Ute (Colorado, Utah), 1890–91 Sioux Campaign (South Dakota), 1895 Campaign against the Bannock, 1898 Campaign against the Chippewa (Leech Lake, Minnesota).

WARSHIPS. In 1775, the Continental Congress had two merchantmen converted to warships. Frigates, brigs, sloops, and schooners were also constructed or bought, giving the navy a total of 340. After independence, the US sold them all. In the next decade, Barbary pirates and the Quasi-War with France caused the building of a navy. The small US navy acquitted itself well during the War of 1812. In 1817, the navy listed 110 sailing ships and one steamer. In 1845, when the Mexican War began, there were 67 sailing ships and 9 steamers. By the end of the Civil War, only 109 of 681 ships were sail. By the 1870s, the era of sailing warships was over.

The first steam warship, the *Demologos*, was designed by Robert Fulton in the War of 1812; then came the frigate *Fulton*, launched in 1817. Naval experts were skeptical about steamers, particularly the vulnerability of the large paddle wheels. In the 1840s, the screw propeller replaced the paddles, and by the Civil War the US navy had 20 wooden, screw-propelled men-of-war. The battle between the ironclads CSS *Virginia* (better known by its previous name *Merrimack*) and the USS *Monitor* at Hampton Roads in 1862 was the first between armored ships and between two powered only by steam. During 1890–1900, armor improved in quality, guns increased in power, mines became more reliable, and the self-propelled torpedo was perfected. After 1865, the US navy consisted of old wooden cruisers and obsolete monitors. In 1883, Congress appropriated money for new steel cruisers *Atlanta, Boston,* and *Chicago*; and a new dispatch boat, the *Dolphin*, formed the nucleus of what became known as the New Navy. By the Spanish-American War, the US had four battleships, three other armored ships, and over 20 cruisers, gunboats, and torpedo boats. Twelve new battleships were added, but they were all made obsolete by the

new British *Dreadnought*, which was faster, larger, and carried guns of the largest caliber. The first equivalent US ships were completed in 1910. Other ships were the heavy cruiser, the light cruiser, and the destroyer. Between the two world wars came the aircraft carrier; its chief weapons were the bombers that took off and landed from its deck. In World War II, aircraft carriers facilitated battles between fleets hundreds of miles apart. The first nuclear submarine was the *Nautilus*, built in 1954. Nuclear power made warships faster, more reliable, and free of their bases. Aircraft carriers, destroyers, and cruisers were equipped with nuclear power. Missiles replaced guns on large ships; a typical warship of the 1980s carried antisubmarine and antiaircraft missiles in addition to, or instead of, guns.

WARWICK COMMISSION. Established 1643 to control colonial affairs after the Puritan Revolution in England. Despite its extensive powers, it interfered little in the colonies. It granted Rhode Island a charter in 1644. In 1649, its powers were revoked.

WASHAKIE, FORT. An army post (1869–1909) maintained near Lander, Wyo., for the protection of the Shoshone on the Wold River reservation.

WASHINGTON, D.C. Capital city of the US since 1800; located on a peninsula formed by the Potomac and Anacostia rivers and is coexistent with the District of Columbia, situated between Maryland and Virginia. George Washington chose the site for what was to be called Federal City; and Pierre Charles L'Enfant designed the broad avenues radiating from public buildings and monuments (although his plans were imperfectly followed). The Capitol and the White House were the first two major projects.

The Constitution empowered Congress to "exercise exclusive Legislation" over the District of Columbia; its citizens had no vote in federal elections, and only intermittently were they permitted a say in local affairs. In 1973, Congress allowed citizens to elect their own mayor, a 13-member council, and neighborhood councils. Congress kept control of the budget and veto power of the councils. The Twenty-third Amendment to the Constitution (1961) gave residents of the District of Columbia the right to vote in presidential elections. In addition to the operations of the federal government, tourism is an important Washington industry. Pop.: 637,651 (1980).

WASHINGTON, D.C., BURNING OF (Aug. 24–25, 1814). During the War of 1812, British regulars invaded Washington, burned the Capitol, the White House, and the Treasury, reducing to ruins the departments of state and war, private dwellings, and various other establishments.

WASHINGTON, FORT. Built during the American Revolution at the upper end of Manhattan Island to guard the Hudson R (Fort Lee was across the river in New Jersey). On Nov. 16, 1776, it was surrendered to the British.

WASHINGTON, FORT. Built in 1789 at Cincinnati, Ohio, to protect settlements. After Gen. Anthony Wayne defeated the Indians at the Battle of Fallen Timbers (1794), its importance declined. It was abandoned in 1804.

WASHINGTON, STATE OF. Spanish explorers were in the area as early as 1774, and in 1778 Capt. James Cook reached Nootka Sound. In 1792, Robert Gray discovered the Columbia R and George Vancouver mapped Puget Sound and surrounding waters. Lewis and Clark in 1803–06 went from St. Louis to the Columbia R and back. Various fur companies established trading posts in the area, and after 1821 the Hudson's Bay Co. dominated trade in the area. Britain and the US both claimed the area, known as the Oregon Country. Permanent settlement began in the 1840s, and the US and Britain finally settled their border disputes in the 1850s. In 1848, Congress created the Oregon Territory; and in 1853, the Washington Territory was created. Sawmills were built around Puget Sound for lumber, piling, and ship timber. Mining rushes increased the population, but development was slowed by Indian troubles in the late 1850s. The area grew rapidly for the rest of the 19th c. The Northern Pacific RR was completed in 1883; and in 1889 Washington was admitted to the Union by the Omnibus Bill, which also admitted North Dakota, South Dakota, and Montana. Timber and fishing remain major industries; extensive shipbuild-

ing began in World War I, and extensive dam building and its resultant hydroelectric power has led to much industrializaiton. Pop.: 4,130,163 (1980).

WASHINGTON, TREATY OF (1871). The amicable settlement of the Alabama Claims and other differences between the US and Great Britain.

WASHINGTON AND LEE UNIVERSITY. Founded 1749 at Lexington, Va., as Augusta Academy. In 1798 it became Washington Academy, later Washington College. Robert E. Lee became president in 1865, and one year after his death in 1870, it became Washington and Lee University.

WASHINGTON DISTRICT. In 1775, the settlers in the Tennessee country on the Watauga and Nolichuckey rivers assumed for their region the name of Washington District, the first territorial division in America to be named for George Washington.

WASHINGTON ELM. The tree under which George Washington took command of the US army on July 3, 1775, on Cambridge Common in Massachusetts. It fell in 1924.

WASHINGTON MONUMENT. Erected in Washington, D.C., to honor George Washington; completed in 1884, it was the highest masonry structure in the world (555 feet, 5 1/8 inches).

WASHINGTON NAVAL CONFERENCE (1921–22). Called to deal with the arms race and security in the Pacific. In the Big Four Treaty, the United States, Great Britain, France, and Japan promised to respect each others' possessions in the Pacific. In other treaties, the nations called for the Open Door to China and provided for a ten-year holiday in the construction of warships.

WASHINGTON'S FAREWELL ADDRESS. Published in 1796, it set forth President Washington's reasons for not running for a third term as president. It also presents his belief in a strong union; states the principles of domestic contentment and foreign respect; and justifies his neutrality toward France and England.

WATAUGA SETTLEMENT AND ASSOCIATION. In 1769 two settlements were established on the Watauga R in Tennessee country. In 1762, these communities, along with settlements in between the two, formed Watauga Association, which was later joined by settlers on the Nolichuckey R.

WATERBURY. A city on the Naugatuck R in Connecticut. It was established as Mattatuck plantation in 1677. In the 18th c., it was noted for its clock manufacture. Since the early 19th c., it has been an important center for brass manufacture. Pop.: 103,266 (1980).

WATERGATE. The scandals of Richard M. Nixon's presidency, resulting from a break-in at the Democratic campaign headquarters at the Watergate office building in Washington, D.C., on June 17, 1972. The burglars were arrested, and two of them had on their persons the White House telephone number of E. Howard Hunt. A cover-up began immediately; on August 29, Nixon declared that his counsel John W. Dean III had concluded that "no one in the White House" was "involved." The five burglars and two associates, Hunt and J. Gordon Liddy, were convicted. In March, federal judge John J. Sirica released a letter stating that higher-ups were involved. Nixon professed ignorance but his claims were challenged by his own conduct, investigations by the Senate Watergate committee (chaired by Sen. Sam Ervin), studies by the House Judiciary Committee, and tapes of White House conversations. In April, Nixon accepted "responsibility" but denied any prior knowledge of a cover-up. White House aides, including John Mitchell, Dean, H.R. Haldeman, and John D. Erlichman, were indicted, convicted, and imprisoned. Nixon was named as an unindicted coconspirator. Nixon fired Special Prosecutor Archibald Cox for his probing; Cox's successor, Leon Jaworski, was denied requests for evidence. Impeachment charges asserted that Nixon had obstructed justice and failed to uphold the law. On Aug. 9, 1974, before the House could vote on the impeachment charges, Nixon resigned. His successor, Gerald R. Ford, pardoned Nixon for any crimes he might have committed while president.

WATER LAW. Old English law gave the owner of the banks of a river unrestricted used of the water passing through his property. That concept was altered in the West, where irrigation necessary for crops sometimes caused the entire stream to be diverted.

WATERPOWER. A traditional method of generating waterpower was a paddlewheel near a waterfall. The water was diverted into a ditch and conveyed to the waterwheel located beside the mill. Such waterpower was brought increasingly into use from ca. 1820 to meet the needs of an emerging industrialism. By 1840, there were well over 50,000 gristmills and sawmills in the US. The largest complexes were found on the Merrimack and Connecticut rivers in New England and provided the power base of some of the country's largest industrial centers. The turbine was introduced into the US ca. 1850; but the cost advantages of waterpower were soon being matched by the steam engine. Large-scale waterpower entered a new age with the Niagara hydroelectric power project in the 1890s. After 1900, HYDROELECTRIC POWER was produced in plants of enormous capacity and distributed over long distances by high-tension power lines.

WATER POWER ACT (1920). Established a Federal Power Commission empowered to issue licenses for the construction of power facilities on US water reserves on public lands and navigable streams. It also was authorized to regulate rates and security issues of licensees.

WATER SUPPLY AND CONSERVATION. Until the 1790s, most cities depended on water drawn from public pumps, wells, and rainwater. Those sources proved insufficient, and New York and Baltimore turned its problems over to private water companies; Philadelphia's city government built its own water works. A steam-driven pumping system proved insufficient, and in 1822 the Fairmount Water Works relied on a dam across the Schuykill R and on waterwheels that pumped the water into a reservoir, from which the water ran by gravity to the city streets. It became the prototype for other city systems. As the cities grew into the suburbs, the problem of contaminating the reservoirs became a serious problem; Chicago, Cleveland, and Newark all experienced typhoid epidemics after untreated sewage had found its way into the city water supply. The water needs of the arid Southwest, particularly Los Angeles, challenged engineering. Eventually, water was brought 392 miles (along the Colorado River Aqueduct) to supply the city. Maintaining the purity of water supplies continued to be a problem; the Safe Drinking Water Act of 1974 authorized the Environmental Protection Agency to establish national standards for drinking water.

WATERWAYS, INLAND. The US system of inland waterways of 27,000 miles of navigable rivers and canals bears approximately 15 percent of the total intercity freight movement. In the colonial period, ships sailed the coastal and tidewater streams. Waterways also provided routes for pioneers. After the invention of the steamship, the western waters proved especially useful in the movement of both people and freight. The War of 1812 demonstrated the need for improved transportation, and many canals were built. The most ambitious was the Erie Canal, opened in 1825. By 1850, there were about 4,000 miles of canals in the US. The coming of the railroad caused many of the canals to fall into disuse. A reemergence of the waterways occurred early in the 20th c., the result of government development of waterways for flood control, irrigation, power production, recreation, and navigation. The Inland Waterways Commission was established to improve the nation's commercial waterways. The diesel-powered tugboat, special barges and tankers, and all-weather, 24-hour navigational systems led to greatly increased traffic on the waterways. Modern projects include the Atlantic Intracoastal and Gulf Intracoastal waterways; protected channels; the recanalization of the Ohio R; and the development of both the Columbia R and the Saint Lawrence Seaway (opened 1959).

WAUHATCHIE, BATTLE OF (Oct. 28–29, 1863). Fought at the foot of Lookout Mountain during Union Gen. U.S. Grant's advance on Chattanooga. Despite a strong attack from the Rebels, the Union forces saved their supply line from Nashville.

WAYNE, FORT. Built 1794 by Gen. Anthony Wayne at the junction of the St. Joseph and St. Marys rivers, in present Indiana. The Treaty of Fort Wayne was negotiated there between William Henry Harrison, governor of the Indiana Territory, and the Delaware, Potawatomi, Miami, and Eel River tribes. The Indians ceded much of their land. The treaty was a major reason for their support of the British during the War of 1812, during which the fort was besieged by the British and the Indians, but Harrison relieved it. Abandoned 1819.

WAYNE CAMPAIGN (1792–95). After the Revolutionary War, the Indians of the Ohio country, who had been allies of the British, continued to oppose US activities in the area. In 1793, Gen. Anthony Wayne advanced to Fort Washington (Cincinnati), then to Greenville, and sent a detachment to build Fort Defiance. He pursued the Indians down the Maumee R and defeated them decisively at Fallen Timbers. That victory assured US predominance in the area and forced the British to accept Jay's Treaty. The Treaty of Greenville (1795) gave S and E Ohio to the US.

WAYS AND MEANS, COMMITTEE ON. Established in the House of Representatives in 1795, it has jurisdiction over all revenue measures and has been at the center of struggles over reciprocal trade, social security, Medicare, and tax policies in general.

WEATHER SERVICE, NATIONAL. Established 1870 as part of the army; removed to the Department of Agriculture in 1891, to the Department of Commerce in 1940, and to the National Oceanographic and Atmospheric Administration in 1970. It reports the weather of the US and its possessions and provides forecasts to the general public, issues warnings against such destructive natural events as hurricanes, tornadoes, floods, and provides special services in support of aviation, marine activities, agriculture, forestry, urban air-quality control, and other weather-sensitive activities.

WEBSTER-ASHBURTON TREATY (1842). Settled dispute over the boundary between Maine and New Brunswick between the US and Great Britain. The present-day boundaries are the result of the treaty.

WEBSTER-FAIRBANK TRIALS (1844–45). Delia A. Webster and Calvin Fairbank abducted a family of slaves from Lexington, Ky., through the Underground Railroad. Both were tried, convicted, and served prison sentences.

WEBSTER-HAYNE DEBATE (January 1830). Between two US senators: Robert Y. Hayne of South Carolina and Daniel Webster of Massachusetts. At issue was the question of slavery, particularly as it applied to the sale of the public lands of the West. Hayne denounced the East, claiming that the federal government threatened the states' independence. Webster argued that twenty-four separate states could not individually interpret the Constitution.

WEBSTER'S BLUE-BACKED SPELLER. Popular name for Noah Webster's *Elementary Spelling Book*, published first in 1783. Nearly 100 million copies were printed (under a variety of names).

WEEHAWKEN. Township in NE New Jersey, on the Hudson R opposite New York City. Site of dueling ground where Alexander Hamilton was killed by Aaron Burr on July 11, 1801.

"WE HAVE MET THE ENEMY, AND THEY ARE OURS." Message dispatched by Oliver Hazard Perry, commander of the US fleet, after defeating the British in the Battle of Lake Erie on Sept. 10, 1813.

WELLS, FARGO AND COMPANY. Organized 1852 to furnish ocean service between New York and San Francisco via Panama. Within a decade, it was operating throughout the West as a letter carrier and transporter of gold, silver and bullion. It later expanded throughout the Pacific and Central America. It merged with the American Express Co. in 1918 but continued for thirty years to operate railroads in Mexico and Cuba. As a subsidiary of American Express, it became an armored-car service.

WEST, AMERICAN. The acquisition of the West began in 1763 after the French and Indian War when France ceded Canada and the Old Northwest to Great Britain. After the American Revolution, the size of the nation was almost doubled by the Louisiana Purchase. The annexation of Texas and the resulting Mexican War brought Texas, New Mexico, Arizona, and California into the US. The Oregon controversy between the US and Great Britain was settled in 1846, and the Northwest was settled by thousands of emigrants, most of whom arrived by way of the Oregon Trail. The final connection between East and West was made after the Civil War when transcontinental railroads were completed.

WESTERN, FORT. Built 1754 on the Kennebec R at the site of present Augusta, Me., to protect traders and promote trade with the Indians.

WESTERN BOUNDARIES (1783–98). The Definitive Treaty of Peace with Great Britain laid down the N boundary (later rectified and dilineated) as far as the Lake of the Woods in Minnesota. From the Lake of the Woods it continued W to the Mississippi R; then went down to 31° N latitude, E to the Chattahoochee R; followed it to the Flint R, on what is now the SW border of Georgia; then to the St. Marys R, which forms part of the SE border of Georgia; and down the Atlantic. England at first refused to evacuate its strategic frontier posts (e.g., Detroit, Niagara, Oswego), because of the importance of the fur trade in the vicinity. In the Southwest, Spain kept posts along the Mississippi (e.g., Memphis, Vicksburg, Natchez). Within a decade, however, the US was able to redeem its territories with Jay's Treaty (1794) with England and Pinckney's Treaty (1795) with Spain.

WESTERN DESIGN. Plan of the English Protector Oliver Cromwell, to usurp Spain in the Caribbean. In 1655, he sent a military force to the area; it was repulsed from Santa Domingo but took Jamaica.

WESTERN ENGINEER. The first steamboat to ascend the Missouri R to Council Bluffs, in 1820.

WESTERN EXPLORATION. In 1804, President Jefferson sent Meriwether Lewis and William Clark up the Missouri R to seek a water route to the Pacific; to council with the Indians; and to observe the land and its resources. They left from St. Louis, wintered with the Mandan in Dakota, and crossed the Rockies to the mouth of the Columbia R. Zebulon M. Pike in 1805–06 examined the Upper Mississippi and in 1806–07 explored the Red and Arkansas rivers area. He crossed the Rio Grande and was detained by the Spanish. During the next three decades, there were studies of the Ouachita and lower Red rivers, and the Arkansas and Canadian rivers. Naturalists were also researching the West. The fur trade greatly expanded knowledge of the West; by the second decade of the 19th c., traders had got as far as the Pacific. The Department of War authorized studies by topographers, botanists, geologists, and zoologists that resulted in *Pacific Railroad Reports* (1855–60); the purpose of the study was to recommend continental rail routes. The US Geological Survey of 1879 marked the end of the age of exploration.

WESTERN FEDERATION OF MINERS. Labor union of miners and smelters in the Rocky Mountain states; originally part of the AFL, it broke away and joined the more radical Industrial Workers of the World in 1905. Between 1894 and 1897, it led strikes in Leadville, Cripple Creek, and Coeur d'Alene. It rejoined the AFL in 1911.

WESTERN PACIFIC. See RAILROADS, SKETCHES OF PRINCIPAL LINES.

WESTERN RESERVE. Part of NE Ohio along the S shore of Lake Erie, once belonging to Connecticut. The charter that Connecticut obtained from King Charles II in 1662 extended westward to the Pacific; but in 1786 Connecticut ceded all its western lands except for the Western Reserve. In 1792, a half million acres there were assigned to Connecticut towns for losses they suffered in the American Revolution; and in 1795, the rest of the Reserve was sold to thirty-five Connecticut landowners. Moses Cleaveland in 1796 supervised a survey for settlement. In 1800, Connecticut and the US arranged for the Western Reserve to become part of the Ohio Territory.

WESTERN SEA, SEARCH FOR THE. Attempts to find a way across the continent to the Pacific Ocean led to the exploration of many lakes and rivers. French explorers went from Lake Superior to the Lake of the Woods, Minnesota, and from there to Lake Winnipeg and the Saskatchewan R. Beginning in the late 18th c., both branches of the Saskatchewan were ascended to their sources in the Cana-

dian Rockies. The Pacific was reached via this route in 1793. Lewis and Clark ascended the Missouri R in 1804 and reached the Columbia R in 1805. Simon Fraser descended the river that bears his name to the sea in 1808.

WESTERN SEPARATISM. Settlers in Kentucky and Tennessee grew resentful of Spanish control of navigation on the western rivers. News of John Jay's proposed compromise treaty with Spain in 1786 nearly led to insurrection. Intrigue and negotiation with Spain (see SPANISH CONSPIRACY), with France, and with England leading to possible separation, followed in the Kentucky and Tennessee districts. Calmer judgment prevailed and both entered the Union. With Jay's Treaty (1794) and Pinckney's Treaty (1795) western discontent ended.

WESTERN UNION TELEGRAPH COMPANY. Organized 1856 out of several small companies to use the recently invented printed telegraph. By 1860, it had reached from the Atlantic to the Mississippi R and from the Great Lakes to the Ohio R. In 1861, it became the first transcontinental telegraph line; and by 1900, it had a million miles of telegraph lines and two international cables. By the 1980s, Western Union was involved in satellite communications and computer systems.

WEST FLORIDA. See FLORIDA.

WEST FLORIDA, ANNEXATION OF (1810–11). In 1810, inhabitants of West Florida near the Mississippi R revolted against Spain and requested annexation with the US (see MOBILE PACT). President Madison asserted the right to West Florida by virtue of the Louisiana Purchase (1803) and ordered the territorial governor of Orleans to extend authority over the district.

WEST FLORIDA CONTROVERSY. The area from the Mississippi R to the Perdido R on the Gulf of Mexico was included in Spain's claims from 1492 on, but from 1699 to 1763 France occupied it as part of Louisiana. Great Britain held it from 1763 until the the end of the American Revolution, when it reverted to Spain. The US claimed it as part of the Louisiana Purchase; Spain refuted the claim but could not defend it. US frontiersmen rebelled against Spain in 1810 and President Madison ordered the territorial governor of Orleans to extend authority over the district. Spain relinquished all claims in 1819.

WEST INDIA TRADE. Colonial commerce with the West Indies was known as the triangular trade. Colonial ships with soap, candles, buttons, provisions, sheep and hogs, lumber, horses, and rum sailed to the coast of Africa for slaves; in the West Indies, the slaves were traded for sugar and molasses, distilled in New England into rum, which was sold in New York and Philadelphia.

WEST JERSEY. By the Quintipartite Deed (1676), a line running from Little Egg Harbor to the Delaware R at the forty-first parallel divided the province of New Jersey. Sir George Carteret received East Jersey, and Quakers West Jersey. In 1675, colonies were founded at Salem and Burlington, which became the chief port and capital. In 1702, the province was surrendered to the crown.

WEST JERSEY CONCESSIONS. Provisions for the colonization and governemnt of West Jersey, drawn up by William Penn and approved by the proprietors in 1677. Government rested on a bill of rights, absolute religious freedom, public trial by jury, right of petition, freedom from arbitrary arrest or imprisonment for debt, and equal taxation. The province was governed by the concessions until it was taken over by the crown in 1702.

WESTMINSTER, TREATY OF (1674). Between England and the Netherlands, it provided for the return of the colony of New Netherland to England.

WEST VIRGINIA. Entered the Union as a state in 1863 due to opposition of its inhabitants to seceding and joining the Confederacy along with the rest of Virginia. The area was settled beginning ca. 1731 by chiefly English, Scotch-Irish, and German stock. Early in the 19th c., significant differences arose between eastern and western Virginia. In 1861, when Virginia adopted its ordinance of secession, counties in the NW part of the state set up the Restored Government, which remained loyal to the Union. The next year, the Restored Government consented to the formation of the state of West Virginia; and in 1863 it en-

tered the Union. With abundunt resources, West Virginia made striking industrial advances during its first half-century of statehood. The state's economic lifeblood was the coal industry; World War I provided the impetus for giant chemical industries in the Kanawha and Ohio valleys and for the steel industry in the northern panhandle. After World War II, the state suffered severe population losses, partly the result of technological unemployment caused by the mechanization of the coal mines and an increase in surface mining. Pop.: 1,949,644 (1980).

WESTWARD MOVEMENT. The movement from the Eastern Seaboard of the US to the rest of the continent. Westward movement began in 1635, when a group of Massachusetts Bay colonists moved into the Connecticut Valley. Struggles between the English and French, and Indian raids, temporarily halted the movement; but by 1754, the New England frontier had been extended well into Vermont, New Hampshire, and Maine. The settlement of interior New York was long delayed because of the unenlightened policy of the colony; however, German immigrants began settlement ca. 1710. In Pennsylvania, settlement by 1750 extended along the foot of the mountains from Easton SW to the Maryland line. In the South, there were two streams of settlers: those who pushed westward from the tidewater and those who moved southward from Pennsylvania. By 1700, Virginia was well occupied as far W as the fall line. During the first quarter of the 18th c., the country between the fall line and the Blue Ridge Mountains was settled. The Shenandoah Valley received most of its settlers from Pennsylvania. The occupation of the piedmont and mountain regions of the Carolinas came a little later, again with most of the settlers coming from the North.

The westward advance was halted by the French and Indian War; but no sooner was peace restored (1763), than the movement recommenced. Settlers from Virginia moved inland as far as the Forks of the Ohio. In Virginia, the Carolinas, and Georgia cabins appeared farther up the westward-flowing streams. Settlers moved into Tennessee ca. 1769, and before the beginning of the Revolutionary War, settlements were made in West Florida. By this time, settlements had been established in C Kentucky. The close of the Revolutionary War was followed by a great outpouring of people, principally from Virginia and North Carolina, into Kentucky and Tennessee. Across the Ohio R, there also appeared the vanguard of the stream of emigrants who soon transformed that region into a land of homes, farms, and towns. The decade following the War of 1812 saw the entire frontier move westward. So many settlers poured into the Old Southwest that Mississippi and Alabama were admitted into the Union before the end of the decade. The movement into the Old Northwest resulted in the creation of the states of Indiana and Illinois. Across the Mississippi, the influx of settlers set the stage for the admission of Missouri. By 1830 settlers were moving into the territories of Michigan and Arkansas, and there were probably 20,000 Americans in Texas, which still belonged to Mexico. During the 1830s, Michigan and Arkansas were admitted to the Union, and the territories of Wisconsin and Iowa were created. The 1840s were notable years in the westward movement. Settlements appeared on the Pacific coast, as pioneers began moving over the Oregon Trail to the Pacific Northwest. The Mormons made their trek to Utah, and at the close of the decade came the rush to the gold field of California. During the 1850s, migration to Oregon, California, and Texas continued unabated. New Mexico, Kansas, Colorado, Nevada, Idaho, and Montana drew large migrations. It was during the 1870s and 1880s that the Great Plains, the last American frontier, received the greatest number of westward-moving settlers. By 1890, Kansas and Nebraska were populous states, and the newly admitted states of North Dakota and South Dakota had substantial populations. There was a dramatic rush of settlers to Oklahoma. With the closing decade of the 19th c., the story of the westward movement in America came to a close. The farmers' frontier had advanced into some part of every region and secton, and the pioneer phase of the occupation of the land within the continental borders of the United States, excluding Alaska, was finished.

WETHERSFIELD. See RIVER TOWNS OF CONNECTICUT.

WHALING. In the 18th and 19th c., the whaling industry provided oil for lamps and sper-

maceti for candles. Whaling was pursued by some of the earliest settlers of Massachusetts and Long Island. Nantucket and New Bedford became the great whaling centers of the world; their ships hunted whales over virtually the entire world. In the 19th c., Pacific whaling was almost an American monopoly; after the advent of steam whalers ca. 1879, San Francisco became a major whaling port. Whaling ended in the first decade of the 20th c. because of the discovery of petroleum, the development of electricity, and the scarcity of whales.

WHEAT. Introduced by the early colonists, wheat quickly became the major cash crop. In the mid-18th c., it expanded from the middle colonies to Maryland and Virginia and across the Appalachians. By 1840, Ohio was the premier wheat-producing state, but by 1860 Illinois took the lead. Minnesota became the leading producer ca. 1890 and then moved onto the Great Plains. Numerous varieties were introduced and developed in order to accommodate the wide climatic and soil conditions.

Until the early national period, wheat was sown by broadcasting and reaped by sickles and threshed by flails. In rapid succession in the 19th c., sowing with drills replaced broadcasting, cradles took the place of sickles, and the cradles in turn were replaced by reapers and binders. Steam-powered threshing machines superseded flails. In the 1930s, the small combine combined reaping and threshing into one operation. The marketing of wheat went through parallel changes. After the Civil War, wheat began to flow first to the country elevators and from there to terminal elevators, from which it was sold through grain exchanges.

Since colonial times, wheat growers have produced a surplus for export; and in modern times, this surplus has often proved to be unmarketable. However, since the early 1970s, the Soviet Union has been a major buyer of surplus US wheat.

WHEELER-HOWARD ACT (1934). The act gave Indians on reservatons the right to local self-government; it also gave Indians preference for employment in the Indian Office, as well as created special funds for the education of Indian youths. It made provisions for the enlargement of Indian lands by alloting to the tribes surplus lands previously available for public sale.

WHEELING. City in West Virginia, situated on the Ohio R. The site was settled in 1769 and later Fort Fincastle (renamed Fort Henry) was built there. Wheeling grew rapidly after the advent of steamboats on the Ohio and with the completion of the Cumberland Road from the East. In 1853, the Baltimore and Ohio RR reached Wheeling. Wheeling was the capital of the new state of West Virginia from its formation during the Civil War until 1870. An industrial center, Wheeling is a center for the tobacco, glass, tableware, packing, and brewing industries. Pop.: 43,070 (1980).

WHIG PARTY. A major US political party organized in the 1830s by opponents of Andrew Jackson's Democratic party. The party's leaders were mainly representatives of the vested property interests, and Jackson's war on the Bank of the US was the galvanizing issue. William Henry Harrison's successful campaign for the presidency in 1840 gave the party important strength in the backcountry and made it temporarily the nation's dominant party. Henry Clay promptly laid down a nationalistic program to which the majority of the party rallied. John Tyler, who succeeded Harrison as president, was read out of the party; and in 1844 Clay ran for president against the victorious James Polk. The issues of the annexation of Texas and the extension of slavery proved a menace to the party's solidarity, and by 1852 the party had begun to disintegrate.

WHIP, PARTY. Party leader in both the Senate and the House of Representatives. In the House, the party whip ranks immediately below the speaker and majority leader (if in the minority party, he is second behind the minority leader); in the Senate, the whip is second in the party hierarchy behind the majority (or minority) leader. The whip's duties are to secure the necessary party votes on crucial issues.

WHISKEY. Pennsylvania and Maryland were the chief (rye) whiskey producers of the colonial era. Kentuckians discovered that whiskey could be produced from Indian corn, and this eventually became America's leading spirituous product, replacing the rye whiskey

and New England rum. Bourbon County, producing the whiskey of that name, became the center of corn whiskey production. Tennessee and Illinois also produced whiskey. The Prohibition era (1919–33) destroyed many long-established distilleries. Production resumed after repeal, but American taste for Bourbon whiskey has declined in the years since: In 1935, Kentucky produced 197 million gallons, and by 1972 the total had fallen to 126 million gallons.

WHISKEY REBELLION (1794). The excise tax of 1791 taxed whiskey, which was the chief transportable and barterable product of the westerners. It furnished a convenient peg on which those settlers hung a wide variety of grievances against the federal government. In July 1794, a federal marshal was attacked in Allegheny County, Pa., and several hundred men attacked the regional inspector of the excise. Pittsburgh was another scene of disorder. On August 7, President Washington ordered the disaffected westerners to their homes and called up the militia. Unable to achieve a settlement, Washington ordered militia to occupy the western counties (the occupation continued until November). More than a score of prisoners were sent to Philadelphia for trial, but all were released.

WHISKEY RING. A group of western distillers and Internal Revenue Service officials who formed a conspiracy to evade the whiskey tax. In 1875, more than 230 were indicted and 110 were convicted. During the trials, it was strongly intimated that some of the money involved became funds of the Republican party and that not only President Grant's private secretary, but also the president himself, was involved.

WHISKEY TOWNS. Grew up around saloons established just outside the borders of Indian lands where the sale of liquor was prohibited.

WHISTLE STOPS. Small towns where passenger trains would not regularly make a stop. If someone wanted to board the train at such a place, a special signal would be shown and the engineer would acknowledge it by blowing his whistle. The term entered presidential politics, when, to reach the people of small towns and country districts, a candidate would have the train halted at whistle stops.

WHITE CITIZENS COUNCILS. Organized in the South in the late 1950s to obstruct racial integration. Originating in Mississippi, the council advocated white supremacy and racial separation and resorted to economic pressure against local advocates of desegregation.

WHITEHALL, TREATY OF (1686). Provided for the end of hostilities in America between England and France; a board of commissioners was to adjust Anglo-French disputes in the New World, but it never accomplished its ends because of the English Revolution of 1688.

WHITE HOUSE. The residence, in Washington, D.C., of every president since John Adams became its first occupant in 1800. Originally known as the Executive Mansion, it was designed by James Hoban, an Irish-American architect. Benjamin Latrobe contributed to the design. The West Wing, built in 1902, contains the offices of the president and his staff, including the Oval Office.

WHITE HOUSE OF THE CONFEDERACY. A Greek Revival mansion in Richmond, designed by Robert Mills and built in 1818. In 1861, it became the residence of Confederate President Jefferson Davis. It is today the home of the Museum of the Confederacy.

WHITE LEAGUE. Organized in Louisiana in 1874, it consisted of loosely connected political clubs aimed at restoring white political control over the state by eliminating the Reconstruction Republicans. Having attained its aims, it disappeared ca. 1877.

WHITEMARSH. A township in Pennsylvania near Philadelphia, site of Gen. George Washington's encampment in November and December 1777.

WHITE PLAINS, BATTLE OF (Oct. 28, 1776). Gen. George Washington's troops had taken a strong position across the roads leading up to the Hudson R from New England. The British, under Gen. William Howe, attempted to gain a hill near White Plains, which would be used to attack the patriot force. But the colonials occupied the hill first and the British were forced to retreat.

WHITE WOMAN OF THE GENESEE. Name applied to Mary Jemison, who at the age of fourteen had been captured (in 1758) by the Iroquois. She married a Delaware, and they and their eight children settled on the Genesee R in New York state. They maintained a large herd of cattle on a tribal grant of land that was confirmed (1817) by New York state.

WHITMAN MASSACRE (Nov. 29, 1847). Marcus Whitman was a missionary doctor to the Cayuse near present Walla Walla, Wash. An attack by the Indians resulted in the massacre of Whitman, his wife, and twelve others. Fifty-three women and children were taken prisoner by the Indians and had to be ransomed by the Hudson's Bay Co.

WICHITA. City in Kansas on the Arkansas R, started as a trading post in 1864. In 1872, Wichita became the railhead of the Texas cattle drive. Today, aircraft construction and oil recovery and refining are important industries. Pop.: 279,272 (1980).

WICKERSHAM COMMISSION. Appointed by President Hoover in 1929, it dealt with prohibition, juvenile delinquency, and law enforcement problems. Its findings were published in 1931 and are remembered chiefly for the statement that most US criminals were foreign born.

WIDE-AWAKES. An antiforeign, anti-Catholic organization that flourished ca. 1850. The name was later also used for Republican marching clubs.

WIGWAM. In New England, a dome-shaped structure or a similar elongated form, covered with bark, mats, or thatch. An Algonkin word, the term later was used for structures more correctly termed tepees.

WILDCAT BANKS. State-chartered banks in the 1830s and 1840s, so-called because of their remote locations. They tended to print banknotes (known as wildcat money) in great quantities, and many of them went out of business in the various panics of that era.

WILDERNESS, BATTLES OF THE (May 5–7, 1864). Confederate Gen. R.E. Lee attacked the Union army under Gen. U.S. Grant in the heavily wooded and tangled region known as the Wilderness in Virginia; Lee expected the terrain to neutralize somewhat Grant's two-to-one superiority in numbers and artillery. After two days of fighting, Grant withdrew to Spotsylvania Courthouse.

WILDERNESS ROAD. A road from eastern Virginia through the Cumberland Gap to the interior of Kentucky and thence to the Ohio and beyond. A rudimentary route was blazed by Daniel Boone and a party of about thirty woodsmen in 1775. Its total length was 300 miles, and for more than fifty years it was a principal avenue for the movement of immigrants to the West. Today it is part of US Route 25.

WILDLIFE CONSERVATION. Local game laws were passed as early as 1639; they regulated the taking of game, fish, and birds, and provided typically for a closed season and a fine for offenders. Centralized state regulations began in the late 19th c. A North Dakota law (1895) requiring a hunting license was widely adopted by other states. By 1904 most states had some kind of fish and game agency. The federal government took an important step in 1900 with the passage of a law making it illegal to ship game killed in violation of state law across state lines. The concept of refuges began with the creation of Yellowstone National Park in 1872, and an act of 1913 placed migratory and insectivorous birds under federal authority. The National Park Service and the Fish and Wildlife Service became the major federal agencies for wildlife conservation. Various private groups have also been important in the formulation of a national wildlife policy; they include the Sierra Club, the Audubon societies, the North American Wildlife Conference, and the American Ornithological Union.

WILD RICE (*Zizania aquatica*). Native to North America (and not a true rice), it conditioned to a great degree the life of certain Indian tribes in Wisconsin and Minnesota, including the Chippewa, eastern Sioux, and Menomini.

WILD WEST SHOW. An entertainment featuring exhibitions typical of the life of cowboy, Indian, and soldier. The most famous was that of Buffalo Bill (William F. Cody), which first performed in 1883 and existed in one form or other for thirty years. The decline of wild west shows was blamed on the new motion picture.

WILKES EXPLORING EXPEDITION (1838–42). Authorized originally by Congress to investigate the great holes that were believed to lay at the poles of the earth. A fleet of six ships, under the command of Lt. Charles Wilkes, sailed from Hampton Roads, Va., in August 1838. In the course of four years, the expedition cruised most of the Pacific; charted and surveyed upward of 200 islands, the Northwest coast, and San Francisco Bay; and coasted the Antarctic continent for 1,500 miles. It returned with collections in natural history unprecedented in magnitude.

WILKES FUND DISPUTE. A fund of £17,000 was raised to pay the debts of and defend John Wilkes, British political writer, charged with libeling King George III in 1763; in 1769, the South Carolina House of Commons voted £1,500 to that fund. The crown denied its right to do this, the commons defended it, and the controversy continued until the beginning of the Revolution.

WILKINSON, FORT. Built ca. 1767 on the Oconee R near Milledgeville, Ga. Troops were withdrawn after a treaty with the Creek was negotiated in 1802.

WILLAMETTE VALLEY SETTLEMENTS. Colonies in the French Prairie, the region within the great bend of the Willamette R below Salem, Oreg.; first settled by French-Canadians ca. 1830, followed by nine Methodist missionaries' settlements in 1834–41. A government was formed in 1843 and included officials of the Hudson's Bay Co., which was active in the area. By 1845, the population had reached about 6,000.

WILLIAM AND MARY, COLLEGE OF. Founded 1693 at Williamsburg, Va. Many early students were leaders in the Revolution, including Thomas Jefferson, James Monroe, Edmund Randolph, and Benjamin Harrison. Schools of medicine, law, and modern languages were established in 1779. It is state supported, coeducational, and has university status.

WILLIAM HENRY, FORT, MASSACRE AT (Aug. 10, 1757). A large French contingent besieged the British fort, at the head of Lake George, N.Y. The French commander, the marquis de Montcalm, agreed to a safe-conduct for the garrison soldiers, but the Algonkin allies of the French began a general massacre. Although some accounts put the number massacred as high as 1,500, the best evidence is that about 50 were killed.

WILLIAMSBURG. City in SE Virginia, located on the peninsula formed by the York and James R. Founded 1633; succeeded Jamestown as the most important town in early Virginia. Became the capital in 1699 and remained the economic, educational, religious, and social center of the colony. It was occupied by the British toward the end of the Revolution. In 1779 the state capital was moved to Richmond, a more central location. Union troops occupied the town in 1862 and remained there for the rest of the Civil War. Beginning in 1926, under grants from John D. Rockefeller, the town was extensively restored and has become a major tourist attraction.

WILLIAMSBURG, BATTLE OF (May 5, 1862). Clash between the retreating Confederate army of J.E. Johnston and the Union army under Gen. G.B. McClellan. Both sides lost over 2,000 men.

WILLIAMS V. MISSISSIPPI, 170 US 213 (1898). Supreme Court ruled that the state's literacy test did not deny blacks equal protection of the law.

WILLING EXPEDITION (1778–79). James Willing led a party of about thirty men, whose purpose was to despoil British property and trade on the lower Mississippi R. They were joined by a contingent from New Orleans and harassed residents of British Florida, especially around Natchez.

WILMINGTON. Largest city in Delaware; founded 1638 as Fort Christina, a Swedish trading post on the Delaware R. The area later came under the proprietorship of William Penn. The E.I. DuPont de Nemours Co. was founded there in 1802; the city's development has been closely tied to the chemical company and the DuPont family. Vulcanized rubber manufacturing, auto assembly, paper production, and iron and steel are other important industries. Pop.: 70,193 (1980).

WILMOT PROVISO (1846). An antislavery amendment offered to the bill appropriating money for peace negotiations to end the Mexican War. Sponsored by David Wilmot, a representative from Pennsylvania, it stipulated that "neither slavery nor involuntary servitude shall ever exist in any part of said territory"; that is, territory ceded by Mexico to the US. Never approved by the Senate.

WINDMILLS. The occupation of western lands after the Civil War that lay beyond the belt of regular rains, springs, streams, and hand-dug wells made windmills a necessity. Well-drilling machinery and practical mills made them a possiblity. Popularized in the 1870s (and again in the 1970s, as an energy conserving source of power), they came to dot the prairie states.

WINDSOR. See RIVER TOWNS OF CONNECTICUT.

WINE AND WINEMAKING. In 1619 the Virginia Co. sent experienced French winemakers to Virginia to grow grapes and start manufacturing wine; the experiment failed. Later wine was produced for home consumption throughout the colonies; the first commercial wineries in the US were established in Ohio in the 1850s. Within a decade, however, California became the leading wine-producing state. Hundreds of European grape varieties were introduced there; but an infestation of phylloxera, a devastating genus of plant lice, hit the industry in the 1870s, destroying virtually all the vines. National prohibition, beginning in 1919, dealt California vintners an even more shattering blow. Only after World War II did the California winemaking industry begin to recuperate. By the 1980s, in both quality and quantity, California had become one of the world's premier winemaking areas. Winemaking is also an important industry in upstate New York.

WINNEBAGO. Tribe of Indians, originally located in EC Wisconsin. Nearly destroyed in a war with the Illinois; by 1671 only about

3,800 remained. Pushed west by governmental decree, they settled in Iowa and Minnesota. During the Civil War, most were moved again, this time to the Dakota Territory.

WINNEBAGO, FORT. Built 1827 in Wisconsin after the Winnebago War. A supply center during the Blackhawk War of 1832; abandoned 1845.

WINNEBAGO WAR (1827). Winnebago resentment of the coming of settlers to SW Wisconsin led to the uprising. Vigorous measures of the US army snuffed out the war before it was much begun.

WINSTON-SALEM. City in NC North Carolina formed in 1913 by the combination of two much older towns. Salem was established in 1753 by Moravian settlers. Winston was established in 1849 and became an industrial center. Winston-Salem is one of the largest tobacco processing and cigarette manufacturing centers in the world. Pop.: 131,885 (1980).

WISCONSIN. The French first explored the area in the 17th c. Green Bay was the strategic entrance to the Fox-Wisconsin rivers waterway that connected with the Mississippi R and was vital to French fur traders until the War of 1812. The Indians of Wisconsin were an important military resource of the French in the long wars with the British. After the eventual British triumph in 1763, the Indians transferred their allegiance and were British allies in the American Revolution. At the end of that war, Wisconsin became American in name, although it was some time before British influence could be removed from the area. After 1787 it became successively part of the Northwest Territory, Indiana Territory (1800), Illinois Territory (1809), and Michigan Territory (1818). Wisconsin Territory was created in 1836; statehood was achieved in 1848. By that time, pacification of the Indians had been achieved; much of the Black Hawk War (1832) was fought in Wisconsin, and with the suppression of the Indians, white settlement followed quickly. By 1850, the population had grown to 305,000. A mining rush to the Galena district brought settlers in large numbers to that area, but most settlers were farmers. Wheat, dairy products, and livestock were the chief cash crops. Flour milling and lumbering were the principal industries. Later, paper, heavy machinery, machine tools, electrical machinery, agricultural implements, beer, cars and trucks, aluminum wire, and gasoline engines were produced. Pop.: 4,705,335 (1980).

WITCHCRAFT. The belief in witchcraft came to America with the colonists. In the 17th c., witches were executed all through New England. In 1692 in Salem Village (now Danvers), a group of young women and girls, who had been amusing themselves listening to the lurid tales of Tituba, an old slave, showed signs of hysteria. They presently began to accuse people of bewitching them. A powerful and inflammatory sermon was preached at the village church against the machinations of the devil; civil magistrates entered the case. A special court was created by the governor, and between May and September several hundred persons were arrested; nineteen were hanged and many imprisoned. Despite scattered outbreaks in the South and Rhode Island, these trials practically ended prosecutions for witchcraft.

WITCH-HUNT. Term of opprobrium used to characterize the post-World War II obsession with communist conspiracies. In 1947, President Truman, reacting to conservative pressures, set up a federal loyalty review program. The dangers posed by the threat of the Soviet Union in the early days of the cold war and the goading of Republicans who accused Truman and the Democrats of being "soft on communism" led to the sensational trial of the Communist party leadership. Deeming the Smith Act of 1940 inadequate, Congress passed the Internal Security Act of 1950, usually known as the McCarren Act. Of more immediate impact were Sen. Joseph R. McCarthy's attempts to take over the loyalty program at all levels. Beginning in 1950, McCarthy claimed to have a long list of communists who were working in the State Department. Naming names and figures without producing much substantial evidence, McCarthy accused a large number of persons, both in and out of the government, of being either communists or sympathizers (see MCCARTHY-ARMY HEARINGS). The most publicized cases of the 1950s were the confrontation between Alger Hiss and Whittaker Chambers and the trial of Julius and Ethel Rosenberg.

WITHLACOOCHEE RIVER, BATTLES AT (Dec. 31, 1835; Feb. 27–March 6, 1836). Confrontations in C Florida between the Seminole under Osceola and Alligator and the US army during the SEMINOLE WARS.

"WITH MALICE TOWARD NONE, WITH CHARITY FOR ALL." Opening phrases of the last sentence of President Lincoln's second inaugural address.

WOLFF PACKING COMPANY V. COURT OF INDUSTRIAL RELATIONS, 262 US 522 (1923). Supreme Court ruled that the Kansas legislature's fixing of wages in a packing plant was a deprivation of property and a denial of freedom of contract guaranteed by the FOURTEENTH AMENDMENT.

WOMAN'S CHRISTIAN TEMPERANCE UNION (WCTU). Established 1873; held its first national convention 1874. The WCTU soon had chapters in every state fighting for the prohibition of alcoholic beverages; national PROHIBITION, effective in 1919, represented the WCTU's greatest triumph.

WOMAN'S PARTY, NATIONAL. Founded 1914, to put pressure on the Democratic party to secure the right of women to vote. Their peaceful demonstrations at times turned into riots as mobs attacked the women and destroyed their banners. Many women were jailed and drew attention to their campaign through hunger strikes. The passage of the NINETEENTH AMENDMENT in 1920 represented the party's triumph.

WOMAN'S RIGHTS MOVEMENT. The real beginning was in Seneca Falls, N.Y., in 1848, when a group of women active in the antislavery cause convened to discuss the status of women. At that convention, Elizabeth Cady Stanton, Lucretia Mott, and others laid the groundwork for a series of meetings and new associations. After the Civil War, the movement split. One group attacked organized religion openly and worked with immigrant groups who were organizing unions in industry. Another group nominated Victoria Woodhull, an advocate of free love and socialism, for president of the US in 1872. After the turn of the century, various women's groups, including the WOMEN'S CHRISTIAN TEMPERANCE UNION and the Women's Christian Association, joined in a federation to secure the vote for women; and their more radical sisters joined with them in national organization toward that end. Women secured the vote only after a long struggle and after another split in the movement occurred between women who wanted to work legally state by state and women who organized ongoing militant actions in the nation's capital (see WOMAN'S PARTY, NATIONAL).

After securing the vote through ratification of the Nineteenth Amendment in 1920, gaining improved working conditions in factories, and bettering the legal status of women in marriage and divorce, women retired temporarily from organized activity pertaining to women's rights. The movement began a new burst of activity in the 1960s. Groups such as the National Organization of Women (NOW) were formed, and their focus was on passage of the EQUAL RIGHTS AMENDMENT to the Constitution. The amendment was defeated in 1982, but many states passed individual equal rights amendments.

WOMAN'S SUFFRAGE. Under English rule a few colonies, notably New York, permitted women of property to "vote their estates"; but with independence such suffrage was taken away. Woman suffrage was included in the program adopted at the Seneca Falls, N.Y., convention of 1848, and became a central issue of the woman's rights movement. Efforts to secure the rights of women to vote along with the enfranchisement of blacks by the Fourteenth and Fifteenth amendments failed. Two organizations developed in the 1870s: the American Woman Suffrage Association, led by Lucy Stone and Julia Ward Howe, and the National Woman Suffrage Association, championed by Elizabeth Cady Stanton and Susan B. Anthony. They later united as the National American Woman Suffrage Association. Gradually, some states gave women limited suffrage, usually for municipal elections. Wyoming Territory gave women the right to vote when it came into existence in 1869; and the right was retained when it became a state in 1890. Other states followed: Colorado (1893), Utah and Idaho (1896), Washington (1910), California (1911), Arizona, Kansas, and Oregon (1912), Illinois and Alaska Territory (1913), Nevada and Montana (1914), and New York (1917). In 1913, radical suffragists began to pressure President Wilson's administration to secure passage of a proposed amendment to the US Constitution by using militant methods, which the mainstream women's movement disapproved. Consequently, the radicals organized the National Woman's party. In January 1918, Wilson came out for the amendment, which passed Congress the next year and was ratified in time for the national election of 1920.

WOMEN IN THE MILITARY SERVICES. The Army Nurse Corps was organized 1901 and the Navy Nurse Corps in 1908. During World War I, both the navy and the marines enlisted some women to do clerical work, but such employment ended with the war and only the nurse corps survived. Following a precedent set by the British in World War II, the US army in 1942 established the Women's Army Auxiliary Corps (WAAC), forerunner of the Women's Army Corps (WAC) formed in 1943. The navy followed suit with the Women Accepted for Voluntary Emergency Service (WAVE); the marines with Women Marines (WM); the coast guard with the SPARS (taking the name from the coast guard motto "Semper Paratus; Always Ready"); and the army air forces, which became the US air force in 1947, with the WASPs (Women Airforce Service Pilots), who ferried aircraft and performed other non-combat flying duties (its members wore uniforms but were actually civilians under contract). Later, air force women became known as WAFs (Women in the Air Force). All of the women's services were made permanent after World War II; over time, their duties became more integrated with the men's, and eventually all the service academies opened their ranks to women.

WOODEN INDIAN. All through the 19th c., the gaudily painted effigy of an Indian carved from wood was a familiar figure beside the doors of tobacco shops in America. The first small images of this sort were seen in England in the 17th c.

WOOD LAKE, BATTLE OF (Sept. 23, 1862). Foragers from the army encampment at Wood Lake, Minn., stumbled on Little Crow's warriors. Quickly reinforced, the army decisively defeated the Sioux.

WOODLAND TRADITION. Advanced Archaic and Formative cultures of North America that made fabric-marked pottery, constructed burial mounds and earthworks, and cultivated some domesticated plants. The Woodland Tradition originated in the Great Lakes area by ca. 1000 BC and climaxed during the Early and Middle (300 BC–AD 700) and Late (AD 700–1700) periods in the Adena and Hopewell cultures. After AD 700, emergence of Mississippian cultures with new ceramic and artifact traditions greatly decreased the areal extent of Woodland Tradition cultures.

WOODSTOCK MUSIC FESTIVAL (Aug 16, 1969). A rock concert attended by 300,000 fans near Bethel, N.Y. Despite rain, traffic jams, and water shortages, the good nature of the mostly youthful fans created a myth that gained national attention, and the festival's name was used to describe an entire generation: the Woodstock Generation.

WOOL GROWING AND MANUFACTURE. Sheep were brought to North America by the earliest colonists, and the household manufacture of wool was widespread. Wool manufacture in the colonies was discouraged by England, although itinerant weavers and weaving shops were common. The Revolution spurred efforts to expand both wool growing and manufacturing. The introduction early in the 19th c. of many Spanish merinos enabled growers to provide a fine wool suitable to the needs of an expanding market. By the mid-19th c., wool production moved westward, particularly to Ohio. Manufacture continued to be chiefly done in New England and in the middle Atlantic states. The Civil War brought unprecedented prosperity to the industry; with cotton in short supply in the North, demand for woolens increased. At war's end, farms and factories had enlarged their productive capacities, and a huge surplus of wool resulted. Since that time, the importance of wool growing in the US has been steadily diminishing. In 1884 stock sheep numbered 51 million; by 1973 that number had diminished to only 15 million. South Dakota, Texas, and the Far West are the major producers. Wool manufacturing has also decreased in economic importance, largely because of the growing dependence of the textile industry on synthetic fibers.

WORCESTER. City in Massachusetts; first settled 1682 but abandoned in 1702 due to Indian attacks. Permanently settled 1713. Grew rapidly after 1828, when the Blackstone Canal connected it with Providence, R.I., and the sea, providing an outlet for the city's textile mills. Today, Worcester has a mixed industrial output, including a number of different machine and metal products. Pop.: 161,799 (1980).

WORCESTER V. GEORGIA, 6 Peters 515 (1832). In an opinion written by Chief Justice John Marshall, the US Supreme Court ruled that the Cherokee were a nation under the protection of the US and free from the jurisdiction of Georgia.

WORKINGMEN'S PARTY. Political organization formed 1828 that campaigned against the competition of prison contract labor and for free education. Active primarily in Philadelphia and New York City, the movement spread rapidly in New York state. In 1830 it broke into factions and soon disappeared.

WORKS PROGRESS ADMINISTRATION (WPA). Created as part of the NEW DEAL in 1935; its purpose was to organize "light" public works projects, as opposed to the "heavy" projects sponsored by the PUBLIC WORKS ADMINISTRATION (PWA) and the Tennessee Valley Authority (TVA). As it turned out, the WPA (later renamed the Works Projects Administration) became the government's major public works effort under the direction of Harry Hopkins (1935–39). The WPA approved an impressive range of projects, including the Federal Theatre Project, the Federal Arts Project, the Federal Writers Project, programs for a wide variety of unemployed professionals, including dentists, taxidermists, and biologists. But its main objective was toward offering employment to semiskilled and unskilled workers. By 1941 the agency had spent $11.3 billion to provide work for 8 million. The WPA had built 1,634 new schools, 105 airports, 3,000 tennis courts, 3,300 storage dams, 103 golf courses, and 5,800 mobile libraries. In 1943, with wartime production absorbing virtually all the unemployed, the WPA was disbanded.

WORLD BANK. Popular name for the International Bank for Renconstruction and Devel-

opment, a UN agency. It offers economic aid and technical advice to UN member states, particularly the developing nations.

WORLD COURT. See INTERNATIONAL COURT OF JUSTICE.

WORLD WAR I (1914–18). When the European powers were propelled into World War I in 1914, President Wilson urged Americans to remain "impartial in thought as well as action." That became increasingly difficult as German submarine action in the North Atlantic began to result in American deaths, particularly after the sinking of the *Lusitania* in 1915. German Kaiser Wilhelm II was persuaded that France and Britain could be crushed by unrestricted submarine action before the US could make its weight felt. Therefore, on Jan. 31, 1917, Germany informed all neutrals that its U-boats would sink all vessels without warning. Wilson broke diplomatic relations but still hoped to avoid war. Within a few weeks, U-boats sank four US ships at a cost of fifteen lives. Wilson asked Congress for a declaration of war on April 2; it was granted on April 6.

Allied fortunes were at their lowest point. Russia was riven by revolution and beginning to collapse. Mutiny spread through the French army, and the Battle of Passchendaele resulted in almost a quarter million British casualties. The Italians lost 300,000 men at the Battle of Caporetto. The U-boat threat was at its worst. Only the US navy, through its convoy system, was able to reduce losses sharply and thus ended the crisis. An advance contingent of the American Expeditionary Forces (AEF), under Gen. J.J. Pershing arrived in Paris on July 4. US army strength was only about 300,000 men; Congress therefore passed the Selective Service Act, eventually drafting 1.8 million men out of a total of 4 million total strength. The railroads were nationalized, and the National War Labor Board was organized to coordinate the war effort. Pershing recommended sending 1 million men to France by the end of 1918. He resisted Allied pressure to integrate the US troops into Allied divisions as replacements. By the end of May, US forces were participating actively in the fighting. The first American action was in Lorraine. On May 27, two US divisions threw back a German assault at Château Thierry, and on June 6, one of the divisions counterattacked at Belleau Wood. It was a costly debut (almost 10,000 casualties), but the moral effect was good. In August and September, the US attacked a salient near Saint-Mihiel and along the W bank of the Meuse R through the Argonne Forest in the direction of Sedan. It was the greatest battle fought by the AEF to that time (1.25 million participated, incurring 120,000 casualties). The overall German position was becoming desperate, and in October peace negotiations began. The kaiser began to listen to the voices of a disillusioned people and sent representatives to Paris to discuss armistice terms. On November 9 he abdicated and fled into exile. The fighting ended at 11 AM, Nov. 11, 1918. More than 8.5 million men died in the war among total casualties of 37.5 million. American casualties were 320,710.

WORLD WAR I, RELIEF IN. The American Red Cross spent some $200 million altogether in Europe during 1914–23. The American Relief Administration (ARA) was created in 1919 to administer a congressional appropriation of $100 million for European aid. Herbert Hoover was appointed director-general. The ARA instituted child feeding, transported or allocated food for private agencies, and transmitted $6 million in privately raised funds to Europe. The American Friends Service Committee (Quakers) concentrated on child feeding in Germany, 1919–22, where they distributed $9 million worth of relief. By the end of 1926, the Jewish Joint Distribution Committee had spent $69 million abroad, sending a vast number of food packages and bulk sales to Poland, Austria, and Russia. Near East Relief distributed some $28 million in supplies. The Young Men's Christian Association and Young Women's Christian Association, the Federal Council of Churches, Knights of Columbus, National Catholic Welfare Council, and the Rockefeller Foundation all made large gifts to ARA.

WORLD WAR I PEACE CONFERENCE (Jan. 18, 1919–June 28, 1919). Peace negotiations had begun in October 1918, when Germany proposed to President Wilson a peace conference based on his FOURTEEN POINTS. Wilson had little difficulty in accepting the German offer, but Great Britain protested against the doctrine of freedom of the seas and France wanted an "elucidation" that Germany would pay war damages. Nevertheless, with these two specific exceptions, the Fourteen Points became the framework within which the negotiators arrived at the Treaty of Versailles (see VERSAILLES, TREATY OF). It was followed by treaties with Austria, Bulgaria, Hungary, and Turkey, all similar to the treaty with Germany.

WORLD WAR I WAR DEBTS. During and immediately after World War I, America's allies (not including czarist Russia) borrowed more than $10 billion from the US Treasury. In 1922 Congress created a commission to make arrangements for the repayment of the debt, with interest. The commission managed to reach agreement with thirteen European debtor nations. The settlements all provided for repayment over a sixty-two-year period. The governments of four principal debtor nations (Great Britain, France, Italy, and Belgium) believed that the debts should have been canceled altogether. They settled most unwillingly. The US in 1931 declared a moratorium on repayments because of the international banking crisis brought on by the Great Depression. After the moratorium expired, only Finland resumed payments.

WORLD WAR II. By 1939 the National Socialist (Nazi) government in Germany had rearmed the nation, reentered the Rhineland (1936), forced a union with Austria (1938), seized Czechoslovakia (1938), made a nonaggression pact with Russia to protect its eastern frontier (Aug. 23, 1939), and then overran Poland (Sept. 1–Oct. 6, 1939). That last action brought Great Britain and France into the war. In May 1940, a power thrust swept German troops forward through France, driving British troops back across the Channel, and forcing France to surrender (June 22). An attack on England failed in the air and did not materialize on land. Open breach of the nonaggression pact was followed by a German invasion of Russia in June 1941. Meanwhile, Japan had been fortifying Pacific islands and encroaching on China, starting open war at Peking in 1937.

The US opposed Japanese expansion but calculated that the issues of the Orient would have to be largely decided in Europe. While maintaining a formal neutrality, the US embarked on an ambitious lend-lease arrangement with Britain. At the same time, rearmament at home began and a peacetime conscription program was put into effect. In August 1941, President Franklin D. Roosevelt and Prime Minister Winston Churchill met in Newfoundland to formulate war plans; out of that meeting came the ATLANTIC CHARTER. On Dec. 7, 1941, a sneak attack by Japanese planes severely crippled the US fleet at PEARL HARBOR, dooming US troops in the Philippines. The next day Congress declared war on Japan and on December 11 war was declared on Italy and Germany. Full mobilization of the nation then began in earnest. Roosevelt and Churchill met again to determine the Allies' grand war strategy, which was to defeat Germany first while containing Japan.

Campaign in the Pacific. After Pearl Harbor, the Japanese quickly overran the Philippines, Guam, and Wake; seized Attu and Kiska in the Aleutians; and were making inroads in New Guinea. Gen. Douglas MacArthur was ordered from the Philippines to Australia, from where he was to command the Pacific operations. By 1943, US troops were able to show some gains. Guadalcanal was taken (February) and Bougainville (November). By February 1944, many Japanese stations in the Solomons were isolated, and MacArthur then leapfrogged ground units along the N coast of New Guinea and W to Morotai by September 1944. Previously, and almost concurrently, the navy and marine and army troops were successfully hitting the Marshall Islands at Eniwetok and Kwajalein, the Gilberts at Makin and Tarawa, and the Marianas at Guam and Saipan. The Palau Islands were gained in October 1944, thereby assuring American control of the approaches to the Philippines. Two years earlier, in the Coral Sea and at Midway, the US navy had severely crippled the Japanese fleet. Air and submarine attacks on the Philippines had a weakening effect. In October 1944, MacArthur's forces, supported by the Third Fleet under Adm. W.F. Halsey, returned to the Philippines by landing on Leyte. A major, final Japanese naval effort near Leyte was met by the US navy, and the Japanese fleet was largely wiped out. Army progress thereafter was faster; Manila and Corregidor fell in February 1945, and Mindanao in March.

It had been initially expected that the US would need the China mainland as a base for the invasion of Japan. However, efforts to reinforce the Chinese against the Japanese had not been successful. Japanese thrusts against Gen. J.W. Stilwell, operating in the China-Burma-India theater, had forced Allied troops into a disastrous retreat. Furthermore, the sea and land successes by spring 1945 made it possible to think of an actual invasion of Japan without using China.

Campaigns in Africa and Italy. Pressures, notably from the Soviet Union, early began building for an invasion of the European mainland. To accomplish this aim, Allied troops invaded NW Africa from Casablanca to Oran and Algiers on Nov. 8, 1942. The forces pushed eastward, ending in a great German surrender at Tunis, Bizerte, and Cape Bon in May 1943. The next step was an Anglo-American invasion of Sicily; it began in July 1943, and by September the Italian mainland was invaded. Italy surrendered, but the Germans occupied Rome and took control of the Italian government. After a long check midway up the Italian boot on a line through Cassino, a dangerous landing was made at Anzio in January 1944. Fierce German counterattacks were stopped; the Allies rushed to Rome, which fell on June 4. The rest of Italy was pacified, and Allied troops could be diverted to support the Normandy invasion by a landing in S France.

Campaigns in France, Germany, and the Low Countries. Operation Overlord, the principal invasion of the continent, was finally set for June 6, 1944: D-Day. US Gen. D.D. Eisenhower was the supreme commander and British Gen. B.L. Montgomery was in command of all ground forces. It turned out to be the greatest amphibious invasion in history; 5,300 ships and and landing craft were involved, and some 12,000 paratroopers were involved. In all, more than 600,000 Allied troops were put ashore in France. The invasion took place on the Normandy coast, from the Cherbourg peninsula to the mouth of the Orne R. The Germans had reinforced their positions, despite aerial bombardments of road and rail lines and convoys in motion. Allied progress for the first month was slow, but in late July, the US infantry and tanks pierced the enemy line near Saint-Lô and swung rapidly to the southwest, capturing outflanked German troops. Despite heavy German defenses, resistance in N France crumbled and Allied forces raced toward Paris. It fell on Aug. 25 with scarcely a battle. But the German withdrawal was mostly successful.

A landing was made in S France in August 1944 by a Franco-American force. It swept up the Rhone Valley, and by September the German army in SW France had surrendered. Also by September, the general US eastward advance was checked, largely because the forces had run ahead too fast for their supplies. German units halted the major Allied offensive (Sept.17–25) to capture the Rhine bridges at Arnhem. But France was almost completely liberated. The strategy was to make the final major Allied effort over the Rhine R north of Cologne and through the open country N of the Ruhr. Aachen fell in October. Applying pressure on their left, the Americans thinned their center. There the Germans struck hard on Dec. 16 in the wooded Ardennes, in a final bid with a newly trained and reorganized force. The Americans swung into SE Belgium, receiving reserves from the British. Allied losses were high, but they were able to replace all lost equipment through an efficient supply pipeline. Thus the Battle of the Bulge was the Germans' final effort (SEE BULGE, BATTLE OF THE). In the end, they could not match the weight of US industrial support. In February 1945, US armies struck out into the Palatinate and pushed the German forces back across the Rhine. On March 7, US forces dashed over the railway bridge at Remagen; and the northern crossing of the Rhine was effected on March 22. Germany had now practically collapsed. The British raced toward Hamburg and the Baltic. The US army pressed through to Leipzig, and met the Russians at Torgau on the Elbe R on Apr. 25, 1945. A southern flank swung southward toward Austria at Linz and toward Italy at the Brenner Pass. There they met up with another US army coming out of Italy, where German resistance had likewise collapsed. On May 7, 1945, Germany signed a surrender at Allied headquarters at Rheims.

Surrender of Japan. Progress in the Pacific theater by this time had been substantial. US ships and planes dominated the sea and air close to Japan. American planes were bombing Tokyo regularly; a single attack, on Mar. 9, 1945, devastated 16 square miles and killed 80,000 people. But the Japanese were still unwilling to surrender. Approved by Roosevelt, scientists had devised a bomb based on atomic fission. A demand was made upon Japan on July 26 for surrender, threatening with repeated warnings the destruction of eleven Japanese cities. The Japanese rulers scorned the threats. President Truman gave his consent for the use of the bomb. On Aug. 6, Hiroshima was hit, with 75,000 killed. There were more warnings, but still no surrender. On Aug. 9, Nagasaki was bombed and 39,000 people killed. Five days later, on Aug. 14, the Japanese agreed to surrender. The official instrument of surrender was signed on Sept. 2, 1945, on board the battleship *Missouri* in Tokyo Bay.

WORMLEY CONFERENCE (1877). In a meeting held at Wormley's Hotel in Washington, D.C., the Democrats agreed to a counting of the electoral votes that would make the Republican candidate, Rutherford B. Hayes, president. In return, the Republicans would withdraw federal troops from the southern states, thus consenting to the overthrow of the carpetbag governments in those states.

WOUNDED KNEE, BATTLE OF (Dec. 29, 1890). Culmination of the Messiah War, an outgrowth of the GHOST DANCE excitement among the Sioux Indians; last major clash of Indians with US troops, at Wounded Knee, S.Dak., and a massacre, rather than a battle. Chief Sitting Bull had been killed resisting Indian police sent to arrest him. Some of his followers fled to join Chief Big Foot, a leader of the Ghost Dance religion. His band numbered 120 men and 230 women and children. On Dec. 29, when the Indians were being disarmed, a shot (by an unknown person) was fired. The cavalrymen opened fire on the Indians, killing about 300. The casualties of the soldiers were 29 dead and 33 wounded. Wounded Knee ended the resistance of the Indians on the western plains to white settlement.

WRITS OF ASSISTANCE. Search warrants issued to customs officers by the courts of the various colonies. Seem to have excited little controversy until the 1760s, when the TOWNSHEND ACTS (1767) authorized them. There were initial delays in issuing them, and eventually the courts of Connecticut, Rhode Island, New York, New Jersey, Pennsylvania, Maryland, Virginia, and North Carolina directly refused to issue them, stating in some cases that the forms presented to the judges were unconstitutional. Finally, in 1772 the customs officers reported that they had secured writs in East Florida, West Florida, South Carolina, Bahama, Bermuda, New Hampshire, Nova Scotia, and Quebec. It was the raising of the issue that made writs a common grievance as stated in the Declaration of Independence.

WYANDOTTE CONSTITUTION (1859). Constitution under which Kansas became a state; drafted at Wyandotte (now Kansas City, Kans.). Prohibited slavery and reduced Kansas to its present boundaries.

WYOMING. Before 1865, occupancy of the area had been limited to Indians (Oglala and Brulé Sioux, Arapaho, Cheyenne, Crow, and Shoshone), some mountain men, and some soldiers. Congress created Wyoming Territory (out of parts taken from Dakota, Idaho, and Utah territories) in 1868 and admitted it to the Union in 1890. Several communities sprang up along the Union Pacific RR line: Cheyenne, Laramie, Rawlins, Rock Springs, Green River, and Evanston. After ca. 1880, the open-range cattle industry provided the chief economic activity. Today, cattle and sheep raising is still important, and it is ranked as one of the five leading oil states. Tourism is another important industry. Pop.: 470,816 (1980).

WYOMING VALLEY, SETTLEMENT OF. In 1753, the Susquehanna Co. was formed to settle Connecticut pioneers in the Wyoming Valley in the Susquehanna Valley in present Pennsylvania; according to Connecticut's charter of 1662, the area lay within CONNECT- ICUT'S WESTERN LANDS. In 1754, the company bought a large tract from the Six Nations; but the first settlers did not go out until 1762. The Indians drove them out, and no further attempt was made to settle until 1769, when more than 100 settlers arrived. There followed many years of strife, called the YANKEE- PENNAMITE WARS. In 1775, the Pennsylvania proprietary government made an unsuccessful invasion of the valley. The Wyoming settlers supplied so many men for the Continental army during the Revolutionary War that the settlements were depleted of able-bodied men to defend themselves against Indians and Tories. Over 200 settlers were killed in the Wyoming Massacre of 1778. Eventually it was

decided that the settlements were under the jurisdiction of Pennsylvania; but a compromise was reached, and the titles of the Connecticut settlers were confirmed.

XYZ AFFAIR (1797–98). American ministers in France were approached by three representatives (identified in dispatches as X, Y, and Z) of Foreign Minister Talleyrand offering to complete a treaty if a $250,000 gratuity were offered Talleyrand. News of the offer leaked out, causing much anger in the US. Congress abrogated the treaties of 1778, suspended commercial relations with France, and authorized the seizure of French vessels. Talleyrand, thoroughly alarmed at the threat of war, embarked on serious negotiations with the Americans.

YADKIN RIVER SETTLEMENTS. The Yadkin R valley of North Carolina was settled after 1740. A few Germans settled along the river ca. 1750, and in 1753 Moravians from Pennsylvania planted the Wachovia Colony and founded three towns: Betharaba, Bethania, and Salem. From that date to the outbreak of the American Revolution, thousands of Scotch-Irish and Germans moved to the valley.

YAKIMA INDIAN WARS (1855–58). In August 1855, parties of prospectors passing through Yakima country in Washington were attacked by the Yakima and Klikitat. When the Indian agent went to confer with Kamaiakan, chief of the Yakima, he was killed. US army regulars were called in and swept the Indians from the country. At the same time, Indians were driven from the Walla Walla Valley and forced across the Snake R. Indian uprisings resulted in a wide area, and the army stepped up its activities. By fall 1858, the Indians' power had been broken and they were forced into submission.

YALE UNIVERSITY. Founded 1701 at Killingworth, now Clinton, Conn.; the school moved to Saybrook in 1707 and to New Haven in 1716. In 1718, Eli Yale gave it a stock of East India goods, which were sold for £562; in gratitude, the school was named for him. Greatest period of growth was in the 19th c.

YALTA CONFERENCE (Feb. 4–11, 1945). World War II conference attended by President Franklin D. Roosevelt, Prime Minister Winston Churchill, and Premier Joseph Stalin. Occurring at the end of the European conflict, its purpose was to make plans for the administering of the defeated Axis after the war. Among the agreements: (1) Germany was to be jointly occupied by the US, the Soviet Union, Great Britain, and France; (2) a United Nations conference was to be called to establish the world body; (3) Poland's eastern border was determined, and Poland was guaranteed a democratic government; (4) democratically elected governments were guaranteed for other liberated European nation; (5) Russia was to enter the war against Japan as soon as the war in Europe was over; and (6) Soviet interest in Manchuria and other Asian centers would be respected.

YAMASEE WAR (1715–16). Confrontation between the British colony of South Carolina and an Indian federation led by the Yamasee and supported by Spain. South Carolina gradually gained the upper hand; the Indians mostly migrated westward, seeking protection from the French at Mobile.

"YANKEE DOODLE." Popular American song of the 18th c. Its origins are unknown, but it may have been introduced by the English Grenadier Guards ca. 1750. Its words probably originated after 1764.

YANKEE NOTIONS. A large number of small items (brooms, pots, pans, tongs, roasting ovens, clocks, spinning wheels, wooden bowls, and plates) made in New England from the early 18th c. They were made in the winter when farming was impossible and sold in the spring and summer by peddlers who traveled to the South or the western frontiers.

YANKEE-PENNAMITE WARS (1769–72, 1775, and 1784). Series of conflicts in Pennsylvania brought on by conflicting claims of the colonies of Connecticut (Yankees) and Pennsylvania (Pennamites) for a large part of what is now Pennsylvania. By 1772, Connecticut settlers had established control over the WYOMING VALLEY, the center of the controversy. Later, however, Pennsylvania was able to establish its control over the entire area, although in some cases those holding Connecticut titles were allowed to remain on the land.

YAZOO-CHATTAHOOCHEE LINE. Running between the rivers named was the N limit of British West Florida by Order in Council of 1764. Important as a factor in Spain's boundary dispute with the US, 1783–93, which was settled by PINCKNEY'S TREATY; became the first northern boundary of the Mississippi Territory in 1798.

YAZOO FRAUD (1795). The Georgia legislature, nearly all of whose members had been bribed by four land companies, sold 35 million acres, comprising the present states of Alabama and Mississippi, to the four companies for half a million dollars. It became a public scandal and a new legislature repealed the law in 1796.

YELLOW DOG CONTRACT. Agreement signed by a worker in which he promises not to join a union while working for the company. Widely used during the labor strife of the 1870s; by the 1890s, fifteen states had passed laws outlawing the yellow dog contract. Early in the 20th c., the Supreme Court generally voided such state laws, and use of the yellow dog contract increased. The New Deal labor legislation of the 1930s resulted in a finding of the National Labor Relations Board in 1935 that an employer was engaging in an unfair labor practice if he demanded that workers sign such an agreement.

YELLOW FEVER. Yellow fever, then known as Barbados distemper, is cited as a problem in New England as early as 1647. An epidemic broke out in Boston in 1694, and subsequently, despite its endemic focus on the African coast, yellow fever emerged as a peculiarly American disease (the American plague). It spread throughout the continent with the worst epidemic occurring in 1793 in Philadelphia. In 1900 the US Army Yellow Fever Commission, headed by Walter Reed, was sent to track the pestilence to Cuba. The group proved that the infection is transmitted by the bite of the female *Aëdes aegypti* mosquito. W.C. Gorgas, chief sanitary officer of the Panama Canal Commission from 1904–13 eliminated the mosquito in the region of the canal and made possible the building of the canal. The last epidemic of yellow fever in the US occurred in New Orleans in 1905. Vaccines against the disease were developed in the 1940s and are required of anyone traveling to a hazardous area.

YELLOW JOURNALISM. Term applied to sensationalism in news presentation, first used in the 1880s. After his purchase of the *New York World*, Joseph Pulitzer used high-pressure methods to boost circulation. One innovation was an early comic strip known as the "Yellow Kid." From this character, the name "yellow journalism" evolved.

YELLOW PERIL. A racial epithet widely employed in Europe and America in the late 19th and early 20th c. to describe Asians, or the yellow races. In the US, fear of the "barbarian hordes of Asia" resulted in the Chinese Exclusion Acts passed between 1880 and 1904 and the immigration legislation of 1924 that excluded all Asian aliens from US citizenship (see IMMIGRATION RESTRICTION).

YELLOWSTONE. First steamboat to navigate the upper Missouri R, between Omaha and Fort Union, Mont.; built at Louisville for the American Fur Co. and made its first trip in 1831.

YELLOWSTONE NATIONAL PARK. The world's first national park; created by Congress in 1872, it comprises 2.2 million acres of scenic grandeur in Wyoming, Montana, and Idaho.

YELLOWSTONE RIVER EXPEDITIONS (1819–25). Attempts by the US army to explore the upper Missouri R as far as its confluence with the Yellowstone R. The first expedition, traveling on unsuitable steamboats, only managed to reach Council Bluffs. In 1825, a second expedition was sent, this time to pacify Indians in the area. Gen. Henry Atkinson led a party in keelboats and arrived at the Yellowstone and returned the same season. This show of force resulted in treaties with fifteen tribes.

YORK. City in SE Pennsylvania; capital of the US from Sept. 30, 1777, to June 27, 1778, when Philadelphia was captured by the British.

YORK, ATTACK ON (1692). Led by Madokawando, 150 Abnaki attacked the frontier town of York, Maine, killing about 50 out of a population of 500.

YORK, CAPTURE AND DESTRUCTION OF (1813). Early in the War of 1812, an American force was sent to attack York (now Toronto), Ontario. The main body of troops, under Gen. Zebulon Pike, forced the British to retreat. The Americans captured one battery, but a powder magazine exploded, killing about 100 Americans and 40 British; Pike was mortally wounded. Despite this setback, the Americans defeated the defenders, and destroyed many military stores. They then evacuated the post on May 8 and it was reoccupied by the British. The American forces recaptured it without opposition on July 30.

YORK'S, DUKE OF, PROPRIETARY. After the British captured New Netherland from the Dutch, King Charles II bestowed it on his brother James Stuart, duke of York (and the future King James II). The duke's proprietary stretched from the Connecticut R to the Delaware R and Delaware Bay and included Martha's Vineyard, Nantucket, Long Island, and parts of Maine. All legislative, executive, and judicial power was vested in the duke; he delegated authority to governors, but was closely involved in policy. The lands were ruled by a code known as the Duke's Laws. The duke's possessions west of the Delaware were given to William Penn in 1682, and to the east there was considerable overlap with Connecticut claims. The duke of York ascended the throne in 1685 and was forced to abdicate in 1688, leaving considerable legal uncertainties in his proprietary.

YORKTOWN. Port town on the York R in Virginia, established ca. 1691; the first customhouse in America was built there in 1706. Yorktown's prosperity was destroyed by the Revolutionary War, although its historical place in history was assured because it was the site of Gen. Charles Cornwallis's surrender in October ending the war. Also the scene of fighting during the Civil War.

YORKTOWN CAMPAIGN (Aug. 30–Oct. 19, 1781). The decisive fighting that won independence for the thirteen colonies at Yorktown, Va. Unsuccessful in his Carolina campaign, British Gen. Charles Cornwallis retreated into Virginia, fortified Yorktown, and awaited reinforcements from Gen. Henry Clinton in New York. The British force was carefully watched by the forces under the command of the marquis de Lafayette. Clinton delayed sending the reinforcements, however, and the French fleet laid a blockade on the coast. Gen. George Washington's army, augmented by a force under French Gen. Jean Baptiste de Rochambeau, hurried to the scene. Early in September, Adm. de Grasse and the French fleet won a decisive victory in the Battle of the Virginia Capes. Unmenaced by the British fleet, Washington and Rochambeau were able to lay siege on Yorktown carefully and deliberately. Thinking himself abandoned, Cornwallis formally surrendered his troops.

YOSEMITE NATIONAL PARK. Created 1890 in the California High Sierra country; consists of 760,917 acres, in which is located the Yosemite Valley and the Mariposa grove of giant sequoia trees.

"YOUNG AMERICA." A phrase generic to the period 1840–52, designating anything that exhibited the youthful spirit of energy and enterprise characteristic of the times. Historically, it was a concept related to ideas of capitalistic progress, rampant nationalism, and romantic individualism.

YOUNG MEN'S AND YOUNG WOMEN'S HEBREW ASSOCIATIONS (YM-YWHA). The first YMHA was organized 1854, an outgrowth of Jewish literary societies; the first YWHA was formed 1888. The organizations were especially active in teaching citizenship and English to the unprecedented numbers of Jewish immigrants who came to America between 1881 and 1910. Today, the YM-YWHAs operate chiefly as Jewish community centers; there are about 400 of them.

YOUNG MEN'S CHRISTIAN ASSOCIATION (YMCA). Movement begun in England in 1844; the first American YMCA was founded at Boston in 1851; within three years, forty more units were established in the US. The YMCA went through another rapid growth after the Civil War. Their buildings served both as residential hotels and religious, cultural, and recreational centers, a pattern that still exists.

YOUNG PLAN. Post-World War I German reparation schedule, named for its devisor, Owen D. Young. It set forth a schedule of annuity payments by Germany that, it was thought, would be within the capacity of that country to pay. The plan went into effect in 1929, but in 1932 over 90 percent of the reparations that were to have been paid under the plan were canceled.

YOUNGSTOWN. Industrial city in Ohio on the banks of the Mahoning R. Founded 1797, the city was part of the Western Reserve; started producing iron ca. 1820 and became a major steel producer in the 1890s. Grew rapidly in the early 20th c., but was severely hurt by the diminishing prosperity of the steel industry beginning in the 1950s. Pop.: 115,436 (1980).

YOUNG WOMEN'S CHRISTIAN ASSOCIATION (YWCA). First established in England in 1855, the YWCA reached the US in 1858. The YWCAs provide residential hotels for women, classes, athletic programs, recreational facilities, and lectures and forums.

YOUTH ADMINISTRATION, NATIONAL (NYA). Established 1935 as part of the WORKS PROGRESS ADMINISTRATION (WPA), it was one of the New Deal programs of President Franklin D. Roosevelt. Devised to create useful work for some of the 2.8 million young people who were on relief in 1935. Dissolved 1943, during World War II.

YOUTH MOVEMENTS. See articles on individual organizations and movements.

YUCATÁN. In 1848 a revolutionary movement in Yucatán appealed to the US for help against the central government in Mexico City. President Polk asked Congress for authority to send help, stating that the US could not risk seeing the territory fall to Spain or Great Britain. Neither of those nations showed interest in annexing Yucatán, however, and the revolt there was eventually suppressed.

YUKON. River that rises in British Columbia, flows N through Yukon Territory, and then across Alaska. First explored by the Russians in 1842 and by representatives of the Hudson's Bay Co. in 1850. Became an important transportation route after gold was discovered in the Yukon in the 1870s.

YUMA, FORT. Located at the confluence of the Colorado and Gila rivers on the Arizona-California border. Began as a crude ferry service operated by the Yuma in the late 18th c. for travelers between Santa Fe and California and Sonora. The US army first camped there in 1848, and they built a fort there in 1850, which flourished as a station on early stagecoach lines; in 1884 it was turned into an Indian school.

YUROK. A native American culture in NW California and coastal Oregon; included were such tribal groups as the Yurok, Wiyot, Karok, Hupa, and Tolowa. These groups, of varying language families, lived as small population enclaves along the beaches and in the valleys near the coast. Modified plank houses and acorn and salmon dependence characterized the culture.

ZANE'S TRACE AND GRANTS. In 1796 Congress authorized Ebenezer Zane to build a trace through Ohio. This was first a bridle path from the Ohio R at Wheeling to Limestone (later Maysville), Ky. The path E of Zanesville later was developed into the NATIONAL ROAD. As payment for building the trace, Congress gave Zane three sections of land. The first of these was at the Muskingum R, the second at the Hocking R, and the third at the Scioto R.

ZARAH, FORT. Built 1864 on Walnut Creek, about four miles E of present Great Bend, Kans. Its purpose was to furnish the army with a base against the Kiowa and Comanche. Abandoned 1869.

ZENGER TRIAL (1735). Peter Zenger, printer of the *New York Weekly Journal*, was arrested and charged with seditious libel by the colonial governor of New York. His lawyer Alexander Hamilton admitted the publication, but denied that it was libel unless false and sought to prove the truth of the statements; the court held that the fact of publication was sufficient to convict and excluded the truth from the evidence. Hamilton appealed to the jury to judge both the law and the fact; Zenger was found not guilty, thereby setting an important precedent for American freedom of the press.

ZIMMERMAN TELEGRAM (1917). During World War I, the British intercepted a telegram from German Foreign Secretary Arthur Zimmerman to the German minister in Mexico. It directed the minister to arrange an alliance with Mexico; if Mexico would attack the US on its southwestern border, Germany would agree to Mexico's recovery of Texas, New Mexico, and Arizona. Publication of the note was an important factor in the US declaration of war against Germany.

ZINC. See NONFERROUS METALS.

ZION NATIONAL PARK. Established 1919 in SW Utah; its central feature is Zion Canyon. Also notable for unusual rock formations, some of which are brilliantly colored.

ZOAR SOCIETY. German Separatist movement that founded Zoar, in Tuscarawas County, Ohio, in 1817. All property was communally owned. The society attained its greatest prosperity in the 1850s but was dissolved in 1898.

ZONING ORDINANCES. Local regulations that specify the uses to which property may be put, the height and bulk of structures, the area of a lot that may be occupied, and the density of population on the lot. The first comprehensive zoning ordinance was adopted in New York City in 1916, and the practice spread rapidly in the 1920s.

ZOOLOGICAL PARKS. The Philadelphia Zoo, opened 1874, is regarded as America's first. Chicago and Cincinnati opened zoos the next year. Early zoos displayed their animals in barred cages, but in 1921, using a system developed in Germany, St. Louis opened a new zoo in which animals lived in spacious enclosures and were confined by hidden moats. Since then, most zoos have attempted to house their animals in environments as near the natural ones as can be duplicated.

ZUNI. A tribe of village-dwelling Indians of New Mexico. They were discovered 1539 by Spaniards in search of the seven cities of Cibola, which were supposed to be rich in gold. The Zuni turned back the Spanish; but in

1540 Francisco Vasquez de Coronado led an army into the country and easily captured their towns. The Zuni, like the Hopi, are a strongly matrilineal society, the individual acquiring clan membership through his mother. They stress the element of the secret society, initiated by males acting as priests to carry on the ceremonies to bring rain.

ZWAANENDAEL COLONY. Also known as Swaanendael ("valley of the swans"); founded on the W shore of Delaware Bay near present Lewes, Del., in 1631 under the auspices of the Dutch West India Co. A palisaded building called Fort Optlandt was erected, but in 1632 the entire settlement was massacred by Indians.

Appendix

DECLARATION OF INDEPENDENCE

In Congress, July 4, 1776
The Unanimous Declaration of the
Thirteen United States of America

WHEN in the course of human events, it becomes necessary for one people to dissolve the political bands which have connected them with another, and to assume among the powers of the earth, the separate and equal station to which the laws of nature and of nature's God entitle them, a decent respect to the opinions of mankind requires that they should declare the causes which impel them to the separation.

We hold these truths to be self-evident: that all men are created equal; that they are endowed by their Creator with certain unalienable rights; that among these are life, liberty, and the pursuit of happiness; that, to secure these rights, governments are instituted among men, deriving their just powers from the consent of the governed; that whenever any form of government becomes destructive of these ends, it is the right of the people to alter or to abolish it, and to institute new government, laying its foundation on such principles, and organizing its powers in such form, as to them shall seem most likely to effect their safety and happiness. Prudence, indeed, will dictate that governments long established should not be changed for light and transient causes; and accordingly all experience hath shewn that mankind are more disposed to suffer, while evils are sufferable, than to right themselves by abolishing the forms to which they are accustomed. But when a long train of abuses and usurpations, pursuing invariably the same object, evinces a design to reduce them under absolute despotism, it is their right, it is their duty, to throw off such government, and to provide new guards for their future security. Such has been the patient sufferance of these colonies; and such is now the necessity which constrains them to alter their former systems of government. The history of the present King of Great Britain is a history of repeated injuries and usurpations, all having in direct object the establishment of an absolute tyranny over these states. To prove this, let facts be submitted to a candid world.

He has refused his assent to laws, the most wholesome and necessary for the public good.

He has forbidden his governors to pass laws of immediate and pressing importance, unless suspended in their operation till his assent should be obtained; and, when so suspended, he has utterly neglected to attend to them.

He has refused to pass other laws for the accommodation of large districts of people, unless those people would relinquish the right of representation in the legislature, a right inestimable to them, and formidable to tyrants only.

He has called together legislative bodies at places unusual, uncomfortable, and distant from the depository of their public records, for the sole purpose of fatiguing them into compliance with his measures.

He has dissolved representative houses repeatedly, for opposing, with manly firmness, his invasions on the rights of the people.

He has refused for a long time, after such dissolutions, to cause others to be elected; whereby the legislative powers, incapable of annihilation, have returned to the people at large for their exercise; the state remaining, in the mean time, exposed to all the dangers of invasion from without and convulsions within.

He has endeavored to prevent the population of these states; for that purpose obstructing the laws for naturalization of foreigners; refusing to pass others to encourage their migrations hither, and raising the conditions of new appropriations of lands.

He has obstructed the administration of justice, by refusing his assent to laws for establishing judiciary powers.

He has made judges dependent on his will alone, for the tenure of their offices, and the amount and payment of their salaries.

He has erected a multitude of new offices, and sent hither swarms of officers to harass our people and eat out their substance.

He has kept among us, in times of peace, standing armies, without the consent of our legislatures.

He has affected to render the military independent of, and superior to, the civil power.

He has combined with others to subject us to a jurisdiction foreign to our constitution and unacknowledged by our laws, giving his assent to their acts of pretended legislation:

For quartering large bodies of armed troops among us;

For protecting them, by a mock trial, from punishment for any murders which they should commit on the inhabitants of these states;

For cutting off our trade with all parts of the world;

For imposing taxes on us without our consent;

For depriving us, in many cases, of the benefits of trial by jury;

For transporting us beyond seas, to be tried for pretended offenses;

For abolishing the free system of English laws in a neighboring province, establishing therein an arbitrary government, and enlarging its boundaries, so as to render it at once an example and fit instrument for introducing the same absolute rule into these colonies;

For taking away our charters, abolishing our most valuable laws, and altering fundamentally the forms of our governments;

For suspending our own legislatures, and declaring themselves invested with power to legislate for us in all cases whatsoever.

He has abdicated government here, by declaring us out of his protection and waging war against us.

He has plundered our seas, ravaged our coasts, burnt our towns, and destroyed the lives of our people.

He is at this time transporting large armies of foreign mercenaries to complete the works of death, desolation, and tyranny already begun with circumstances of cruelty and perfidy scarcely paralleled in the most barbarous ages, and totally unworthy the head of a civilized nation.

He has constrained our fellow-citizens, taken captive on the high seas, to bear arms against their country, to become the executioners of their friends and brethren, or to fall themselves by their hands.

He has excited domestic insurrections among us, and has endeavored to bring on the inhabitants of our frontiers the merciless Indian savages, whose known rule of warfare is an undistinguished destruction of all ages, sexes, and conditions.

In every stage of these oppressions we have petitioned for redress in the most humble terms; our repeated petitions have been answered only by repeated injury. A prince, whose character is thus marked by every act which may define a tyrant, is unfit to be the ruler of a free people.

Nor have we been wanting in our attentions to our British brethren. We have warned them, from time to time, of attempts by their legislature to extend an unwarrantable jurisdiction over us. We have reminded them of the circumstances of our emigration and settlement here. We have appealed to their native justice and magnanimity; and we have conjured them, by the ties of our common kindred, to disavow these usurpations, which would inevitably interrupt our connections and correspondence. They, too, have been deaf to the voice of justice and of consanguinity. We must, therefore, acquiesce in the necessity which denounces our separation, and hold them, as we hold the rest of mankind, enemies in war, in peace friends.

We, therefore, the representatives of the United States of America, in General Congress assembled, appealing to the Supreme Judge of the world for the rectitude of our intentions, do, in the name and by the authority of the good people of these colonies, solemnly publish and declare, that these United Colonies are, and of right ought to be, FREE AND INDEPENDENT STATES; that they are absolved from all allegiance to the British crown, and that all political connection between them and the state of Great Britain is, and ought to be, totally dissolved; and that, as free and independent states, they have full power to levy war, conclude peace, contract alliances, establish commerce, and to do all other acts and things which independent states may of right do. And for the support of this declaration, with a firm reliance on the protection of Divine Providence, we mutually pledge to each other our lives, our fortunes, and our sacred honor.

CONSTITUTION
OF
THE UNITED STATES

PREAMBLE

WE THE PEOPLE of the United States, in Order to form a more perfect Union, establish Justice, insure domestic Tranquility, provide for the common defence, promote the general Welfare, and secure the Blessings of Liberty to ourselves and our Posterity, do ordain and establish this Constitution for the United States of America.

ARTICLE I

Section 1. All legislative Powers herein granted shall be vested in a Congress of the United States, which shall consist of a Senate and House of Representatives.

Section 2. The House of Representatives shall be composed of Members chosen every second Year by the People of the several States, and the Electors in each State shall have the Qualifications requisite for Electors of the most numerous Branch of the State Legislature.

No Person shall be a Representative who shall not have attained to the age of twenty five Years, and been seven Years a Citizen of the United States, and who shall not, when elected, be an Inhabitant of that State in which he shall be chosen.

Representatives and direct Taxes shall be apportioned among the several States which may be included within this Union, according to their respective Numbers, which shall be determined by adding to the whole Number of free Persons, including those bound to Service for a Term of Years, and excluding Indians not taxed, three fifths of all other Persons. The actual Enumeration shall be made within three Years after the first Meeting of the Congress of the United States, and within every subsequent Term of ten Years, in such Manner as they shall by Law direct. The Number of Representatives shall not exceed one for every thirty Thousand, but each State shall have at Least one Representative; and until such enumeration shall be made, the State of New Hampshire shall be entitled to chuse three, Massachusetts eight, Rhode-Island and Providence Plantations one, Connecticut five, New-York six, New Jersey four, Pennsylvania eight, Delaware one, Maryland six, Virginia ten, North Carolina five, South Carolina five, and Georgia three.

When vacancies happen in the Representation from any State, the Executive Authority thereof shall issue Writs of Election to fill such Vacancies.

The House of Representatives shall chuse their Speaker and other Officers; and shall have the sole Power of Impeachment.

Section 3. The Senate of the United States shall be composed of two Senators from each State, chosen by the Legislature thereof, for six Years; and each Senator shall have one Vote.

Immediately after they shall be assembled in Consequence of the first Election, they shall be divided as equally as may be into three Classes. The Seats of the Senators of the first Class shall be vacated at the Expiration of the second Year, of the second Class at the Expiration of the fourth Year, and of the third Class at the Expiration of the sixth Year, so that one third may be chosen every second Year; and if Vacancies happen by Resignation, or otherwise, during the Recess of the Legislature of any State, the Executive thereof may make temporary Appointments until the next Meeting of the Legislature, which shall then fill such Vacancies.

No Person shall be a Senator who shall not have attained to the Age of thirty Years, and been nine Years a Citizen of the United States, and who shall not, when elected, be an Inhabitant of that State for which he shall be chosen.

The Vice-President of the United States shall be President of the Senate, but shall have no Vote, unless they be equally divided.

The Senate shall chuse their other Officers, and also a President pro tempore, in the Absence of the Vice-President, or when he shall exercise the Office of President of the United States.

The Senate shall have the sole Power to try all Impeachments. When sitting for that Purpose, they shall be on Oath or Affirmation. When the President of the United States is tried the Chief Justice shall preside: And no Person shall be convicted without the Concurrence of two thirds of the Members present.

Judgment in Cases of Impeachment shall not extend further than to removal from Office, and disqualification to hold and enjoy any Office of honor, Trust or Profit under the United States: but the Party convicted shall nevertheless be liable and subject to Indictment, Trial, Judgment and Punishment, according to Law.

Section 4. The Times, Places and Manner of holding Elections for Senators and Representatives, shall be prescribed in each State by the Legislature thereof; but the Congress may at any time by Law make or alter such Regulations, except as to the Places of chusing Senators.

The Congress shall assemble at least once in every Year, and such Meeting shall be on the first Monday in December, unless they shall by Law appoint a different Day.

Section 5. Each House shall be the Judge of the Elections, Returns and Qualifications of its own Members, and a Majority of each shall constitute a Quorum to do Business; but a smaller Number may adjourn from day to day, and may be authorized to compel the Attendance of absent Members, in such Manner, and under such Penalties as each House may provide.

Each House may determine the Rules of its Proceedings, punish its Members for disorderly Behaviour, and, with the Concurrence of two thirds, expel a Member.

Each House shall keep a Journal of its Proceedings, and from time to time publish the same, excepting such Parts as may in their Judgment require Secrecy; and the Yeas and Nays of the Members of either House on any question shall, at the Desire of one fifth of those Present, be entered on the Journal.

Neither House, during the Session of Congress, shall, without the Consent of the other, adjourn for more than three days, nor to any other Place than that in which the two Houses shall be sitting.

Section 6. The Senators and Representatives shall receive a Compensation for their Services, to be ascertained by Law, and paid out of the Treasury of the United States. They shall in all Cases, except Treason, Felony and Breach of the Peace, be privileged from Arrest during their Attendance at the Session of their respective Houses, and in going to and returning from the same; and for any Speech or Debate in either House, they shall not be questioned in any other Place.

No Senator or Representative shall, during the Time for which he was elected, be appointed to any civil Office under the Authority of the United States, which shall have been created, or the Emoluments whereof shall have been encreased during such time; and no Person holding any Office under the United States, shall be a Member of either House during his Continuance in Office.

Section 7. All Bills for raising Revenue shall originate in the House of Representatives; but the Senate may propose or concur with Amendments as on other Bills.

Every Bill which shall have passed the House of Representatives and the Senate, shall, before it become a Law, be presented to the President of the United States; If he approve he shall sign it, but if not he shall return it, with his Objections to that House in which it shall have originated, who shall enter the Objections at large on their Journal, and proceed to reconsider it. If after such Reconsideration two thirds of that House shall agree to pass the Bill, it shall be sent, together with the Objections, to the other House, by which it shall likewise be reconsidered, and if approved by two thirds of that House, it shall become a Law. But in all such Cases the Votes of both Houses shall be determined by yeas and Nays, and the Names of the Persons voting for and against the Bill shall be entered on the Journal of each House respectively. If any Bill shall not be returned by the President within ten Days (Sundays excepted) after it shall have been presented to him, the Same shall be a Law, in like Manner as if he had signed it, unless the Congress by their Adjournment prevent its Return, in which Case it shall not be a Law.

Every Order, Resolution, or Vote to which the Concurrence of the Senate and House of Representatives may be necessary (except on a question of Adjournment) shall be presented to the President of the United States;

and before the Same shall take Effect, shall be approved by him, or being disapproved by him, shall be repassed by two thirds of the Senate and House of Representatives, according to the Rules and Limitations prescribed in the Case of a Bill.

Section 8. The Congress shall have Power To lay and collect Taxes, Duties, Imposts and Excises, to pay the Debts and provide for the common Defence and general Welfare of the United States; but all Duties, Imposts and Excises shall be uniform throughout the United States;

To borrow Money on the credit of the United States;

To regulate Commerce with foreign Nations, and among the several States, and with the Indian Tribes;

To establish an uniform Rule of Naturalization, and uniform Laws on the subject of Bankruptcies throughout the United States;

To coin Money, regulate the Value thereof, and of foreign Coin, and fix the Standard of Weights and Measures;

To provide for the Punishment of counterfeiting the Securities and current Coin of the United States;

To establish Post Offices and post Roads;

To promote the Progress of Science and useful Arts, by securing for limited Times to Authors and Inventors the exclusive Right to their respective Writings and Discoveries;

To constitute Tribunals inferior to the supreme Court;

To define and punish Piracies and Felonies committed on the high Seas, and Offences against the Law of Nations;

To declare War, grant Letters of Marque and Reprisal, and make Rules concerning Captures on Land and Water;

To raise and support Armies, but no Appropriation of Money to that Use shall be for a longer Term than two Years;

To provide and maintain a Navy;

To make Rules for the Government and Regulation of the land and naval Forces;

To provide for calling forth the Militia to execute the Laws of the Union, suppress Insurrections and repel Invasions;

To provide for organizing, arming, and disciplining, the Militia, and for governing such Part of them as may be employed in the Service of the United States, reserving to the States respectively, the Appointment of the Officers, and the Authority of training the Militia according to the discipline prescribed by Congress;

To exercise exclusive Legislation in all Cases whatsoever, over such District (not exceeding ten Miles square) as may, by Cession of Particular States, and the Acceptance of Congress, become the Seat of the Government of the United States, and to exercise like Authority over all Places purchased by the Consent of the Legislature of the State in which the Same shall be, for the Erection of Forts, Magazines, Arsenals, dock-Yards, and other needful Buildings;—And

To make all Laws which shall be necessary and proper for carrying into Execution the foregoing Powers, and all other Powers vested by this Constitution in the Government of the United States, or in any Department or Officer thereof.

Section 9. The Migration or Importation of such Persons as any of the States now existing shall think proper to admit, shall not be prohibited by the Congress prior to the Year one thousand eight hundred and eight, but a Tax or duty may be imposed on such Importation, not exceeding ten dollars for each Person.

The Privilege of the Writ of Habeas Corpus shall not be suspended, unless when in Cases of Rebellion or Invasion the public Safety may require it.

No Bill of Attainder or ex post facto Law shall be passed.

No Capitation, or other direct, Tax shall be laid, unless in Proportion to the Census or Enumeration herein before directed to be taken.

No Tax or Duty shall be laid on Articles exported from any State.

No Preference shall be given by any Regulation of Commerce or Revenue to the Ports of one State over those of another: nor shall Vessels bound to, or from, one State, be obliged to enter, clear or pay Duties in another.

No Money shall be drawn from the Treasury, but in Consequence of Appropriations made by Law; and a regular Statement and Account of the Receipts and Expenditures of all public Money shall be published from time to time.

No Title of Nobility shall be granted by the United States: And no Person holding any Office of Profit or Trust under them, shall, without the Consent of the Congress, accept of any present, Emolument, Office, or Title, of any kind whatever, from any King, Prince, or foreign State.

Section 10. No State shall enter into any Treaty, Alliance, or Confederation; grant Letters of Marque and Reprisal; coin Money; emit Bills of Credit; make any Thing but gold and silver Coin a Tender in Payment of Debts; pass any Bill of Attainder, ex post facto Law, or Law impairing the Obligation of Contracts, or grant any Title of Nobility.

No State shall, without the Consent of the Congress, lay any Imposts or Duties on Imports or Exports, except what may be absolutely necessary for executing its inspection Laws: and the net Produce of all Duties and Imposts, laid by any State on Imports or Exports, shall be for the Use of the Treasury of the United States; and all such Laws shall be subject to the Revision and Controul of the Congress.

No State shall, without the Consent of Congress, lay any Duty of Tonnage, keep Troops, or Ships of War in time of Peace, enter into any Agreement or Compact with another State, or with a foreign Power, or engage in War, unless actually invaded, or in such imminent Danger as will not admit of delay.

ARTICLE II

Section 1. The executive Power shall be vested in a President of the United States of America. He shall hold his Office during the Term of four Years, and, together with the Vice-President, chosen for the same Term, be elected, as follows.

Each State shall appoint, in such Manner as the Legislature thereof may direct, a Number of Electors, equal to the whole Number of Senators and Representatives to which the State may be entitled in the Congress: but no Senator or Representative, or Person holding an Office of Trust or Profit under the United States, shall be appointed an Elector.

The Electors shall meet in their respective States, and vote by Ballot for two Persons, of whom one at least shall not be an Inhabitant of the same State with themselves. And they shall make a List of all the Persons voted for, and of the Number of Votes for each; which List they shall sign and certify, and transmit sealed to the Seat of the Government of the United States, directed to the President of the Senate. The President of the Senate shall, in the Presence of the Senate and House of Representatives, open all the Certificates, and the Votes shall then be counted. The Person having the greatest Number of Votes shall be the President, if such Number be a Majority of the whole Number of Electors appointed; and if there be more than one who have such Majority, and have an equal Number of Votes, then the House of Representatives shall immediately chuse by Ballot one of them for President; and if no Person have a Majority, then from the five highest on the List the said House shall in like Manner chuse the President. But in chusing the President, the Votes shall be taken by States, the Representation from each State having one Vote; A quorum for this Purpose shall consist of a Member or Members from two thirds of the States, and a Majority of all the States shall be necessary to a Choice. In every Case, after the Choice of the President, the Person having the greatest Number of Votes of the Electors shall be the Vice-President. But if there should remain two or more who have equal Votes, the Senate shall chuse from them by Ballot the Vice-President.

The Congress may determine the Time of chusing the Electors, and the Day on which they shall give their Votes; which Day shall be the same throughout the United States.

No Person except a natural born Citizen, or a Citizen of the United States, at the time of the Adoption of this Constitution, shall be eligible to the Office of President; neither shall any person be eligible to that Office who shall not have attained to the Age of thirty five Years, and been fourteen Years a Resident within the United States.

In Case of the Removal of the President from Office, or of his Death, Resignation, or Inability to discharge the Powers and Duties of the said Office, the Same shall devolve on the Vice-President, and the Congress may by Law provide for the Case of Removal, Death, Resignation or Inability, both of the President and Vice-President, declaring what Officer shall then act as President, and such Officer shall act accordingly, until the Disability be removed, or a President shall be elected.

The President shall, at stated Times, receive for his Services, a Compensation, which shall neither be encreased nor diminished during the Period for which he shall have been elected, and he shall not receive within that Period any other Emolument from the United States, or any of them.

Before he enter on the Execution of his Office, he shall take the following Oath or Affirmation:—"I do solemnly swear (or affirm) that I will faithfully execute the Office of President of the United States, and will to the best of my Ability, preserve, protect and defend the Constitution of the United States."

Section 2. The President shall be Commander in Chief of the Army and Navy of the United States, and of the Militia of the several States, when called into the actual Service of the United States; he may require the Opinion, in writing, of the principal Officer in each of the executive Departments, upon any Subject relating to the Duties of their respective Offices, and he shall have Power to grant Reprieves and Pardons for Offences against the United States, except in Cases of Impeachment.

He shall have Power, by and with the Advice and Consent of the Senate, to make Treaties, provided two thirds of the Senators present concur; and he shall nominate, and by and with the Advice and Consent of the Senate, shall appoint Ambassadors, other public Ministers and Consuls, Judges of the supreme Court, and all other Officers of the United States, whose Appointments are not herein otherwise provided for, and which shall be established by Law: but the Congress may by Law vest the Appointment of such inferior Officers, as they think proper, in the President alone, in the Courts of Law, or in the Heads of Departments.

The President shall have Power to fill up all Vacancies that may happen during the Recess of the Senate, by granting Commissions which shall expire at the End of their next Session.

Section 3. He shall from time to time give to the Congress Information of the State of the Union, and recommend to their Consideration such Measures as he shall judge necessary and expedient; he may, on extraordinary Occasions, convene both Houses, or either of them, and in Case of Disagreement between them, with Respect to the Time of Adjournment, he may adjourn them to such Time as he shall think proper; he shall receive Ambassadors and other public Ministers; he shall take Care that the Laws be faithfully executed, and shall Commission all the Officers of the United States.

Section 4. The President, Vice-President and all civil Officers of the United States, shall be removed from Office on Impeachment for, and Conviction of, Treason, Bribery, or other high Crimes and Misdemeanors.

ARTICLE III

Section 1. The judicial Power of the United States, shall be vested in one supreme Court, and in such inferior Courts as the Congress may from time to time ordain and establish. The Judges, both of the supreme and inferior Courts, shall hold their Offices during good Behaviour, and shall, at stated Times, receive for their Services, a Compensation, which shall not be diminished during their Continuance in Office.

Section 2. The judicial Power shall extend to all Cases, in Law and Equity, arising under this Constitution, the Laws of the United States, and Treaties made, or which shall be made, under their Authority;—to all Cases affecting Ambassadors, other public Ministers and Consuls;—to all Cases of admiralty and maritime Jurisdiction;—to Controversies to which the United States shall be a Party;—to Controversies between two or more States;—between a State and Citizens of another State;—between Citizens of different States;—between Citizens of the same State claiming Lands under Grants of different States, and between a State, or the Citizens thereof, and foreign States, Citizens or Subjects.

In all Cases affecting Ambassadors, other public Ministers and Consuls, and those in which a State shall be Party, the supreme Court shall have original Jurisdiction. In all the other Cases before mentioned, the supreme Court shall have appellate Jurisdiction, both as to Law and Fact, with such Exceptions, and under such Regulations as the Congress shall make.

The Trial of all Crimes, except in Cases of Impeachment, shall be by Jury; and such Trial shall be held in the State where the said Crimes shall have been committed; but when not committed within any State, the Trial shall be at such Place or Places as the Congress may by Law have directed.

Section 3. Treason against the United States, shall consist only in levying War against them, or in adhering to their Enemies, giving them Aid and Comfort. No Person shall be convicted of Treason unless on the Testimony of two Witnesses to the same overt Act, or on Confession in open Court.

The Congress shall have Power to declare the Punishment of Treason, but no Attainder of Treason shall work Corruption of Blood, or Forfeiture except during the Life of the Person attainted.

ARTICLE IV

Section 1. Full Faith and Credit shall be given in each State to the public Acts, Records, and judicial Proceedings of every other State. And the Congress may by general Laws prescribe the Manner in which such Acts, Records and Proceedings shall be proved, and the Effect thereof.

Section 2. The Citizens of each State shall be entitled to all Privileges and Immunities of Citizens in the several States.

A person charged in any State with Treason, Felony, or other Crime, who shall flee from Justice, and be found in another State, shall on Demand of the executive Authority of the State from which he fled, be delivered up, to be removed to the State having Jurisdiction of the Crime.

No Person held to Service or Labour in one State, under the Laws thereof, escaping into another, shall, in Consequence of any Law or Regulation therein, be discharged from such Service or Labour, but shall be delivered up on Claim of the Party to whom such Service or Labour may be due.

Section 3. New States may be admitted by the Congress into this Union; but no new States shall be formed or erected within the Jurisdiction of any other State; nor any State be formed by the Junction of two or more States, or Parts of States, without the Consent of the Legislatures of the States concerned as well as of the Congress.

The Congress shall have Power to dispose of and make all needful Rules and Regulations respecting the Territory or other Property belonging to the United States; and nothing in this Constitution shall be so construed as to Prejudice any Claims of the United States, or of any particular State.

Section 4. The United States shall guarantee to every State in this Union a Republican Form of Government, and shall protect each of them against Invasion; and on Application of the Legislature, or of the Executive (when the Legislature cannot be convened) against domestic Violence.

ARTICLE V

The Congress, whenever two thirds of both Houses shall deem it necessary, shall propose Amendments to this Constitution, or, on the Application of the Legislatures of two thirds of the several States, shall call a Convention for proposing Amendments, which, in either Case, shall be valid to all Intents and Purposes, as Part of this Constitution, when ratified by the Legislatures of three fourths of the several States, or by Conventions in three fourths thereof, as the one or the other Mode of Ratification may be proposed by the Congress; Provided that no Amendment which may be made prior to the Year One thousand eight hundred and eight shall in any Manner affect the first and fourth Clauses in the Ninth Section of the first Article; and that no State, without its Consent, shall be deprived of its equal Suffrage in the Senate.

ARTICLE VI

All Debts contracted and Engagements entered into, before the Adoption of this Constitution, shall be as valid against the United States under this Constitution, as under the Confederation.

This Constitution, and the Laws of the United States which shall be made in Pursuance thereof; and all Treaties made, or which shall be made, under the Authority of the United States, shall be the supreme Law of the Land; and the Judges in every State shall be bound thereby, any Thing in the Constitution or Laws of any State to the Contrary notwithstanding.

The Senators and Representatives before mentioned, and the Members of the several State Legislatures, and all executive and judicial Officers, both of the United States and of the several States, shall be bound by Oath or Affirmation, to support this constitution; but no religious Test shall ever be required as a Qualification to any Office or public Trust under the United States.

ARTICLE VII

The Ratification of the Conventions of nine States, shall be sufficient for the Establishment of this Constitution between the States so ratifying the Same.

AMENDMENT I

Congress shall make no law respecting an establishment of religion, or prohibiting the free exercise thereof; or abridging the freedom of speech, or of the press; or the right of the people peaceably to assemble, and to petition the Government for a redress of grievances.

AMENDMENT II

A well regulated Militia, being necessary to the security of a free State, the right of the people to keep and bear Arms, shall not be infringed.

AMENDMENT III

No soldier shall, in time of peace be quartered in any house, without the consent of the Owner, nor in time of war, but in a manner to be prescribed by law.

AMENDMENT IV

The right of the people to be secure in their persons, houses, papers, and effects, against unreasonable searches and seizures, shall not be violated, and no Warrants shall issue, but upon probable cause, supported by Oath or affirmation, and particularly describing the place to be searched, and the persons or things to be seized.

AMENDMENT V

No person shall be held to answer for a capital, or otherwise infamous crime, unless on a presentment or indictment of a Grand Jury, except in cases arising in the land or naval forces, or in the Militia, when in actual service in time of War or public danger; nor shall any person be subject for the same offence to be twice put in jeopardy of life or limb; nor shall be compelled in any criminal case to be a witness against himself, nor be deprived of life, liberty, or property, without due process of law; nor shall private property be taken for public use, without just compensation.

AMENDMENT VI

In all criminal prosecutions, the accused shall enjoy the right to a speedy and public trial, by an impartial jury of the State and district wherein the crime shall have been committed, which district shall have been previously ascertained by law, and to be informed of the nature and cause of the accusation; to be confronted with the witnesses against him; to have compulsory process for obtaining witnesses in his favor, and to have the Assistance of Counsel for his defence.

AMENDMENT VII

In Suits at common law, where the value in controversy shall exceed twenty dollars, the right of trial by jury shall be preserved, and no fact tried by a jury, shall be otherwise reexamined in any Court of the United States, than according to the rules of the common law.

AMENDMENT VIII

Excessive bail shall not be required, nor excessive fines imposed, nor cruel and unusual punishments inflicted.

AMENDMENT IX

The enumeration in the Constitution, of certain rights, shall not be construed to deny or disparage others retained by the people.

AMENDMENT X

The powers not delegated to the United States by the Constitution, nor prohibited by it to the States, are reserved to the States respectively, or to the people.

AMENDMENT XI

The Judicial power of the United States shall not be construed to extend to any suit in law or equity, commenced or prosecuted against one of the United States by Citizens of another State, or by Citizens or Subjects of any Foreign State.

AMENDMENT XII

The Electors shall meet in their respective states and vote by ballot for President and Vice-President, one of whom, at least, shall not be an inhabitant of the same state with themselves; they shall name in their ballots the person voted for as President, and in distinct ballots the person voted for as Vice-President, and they shall make distinct lists of all persons voted for as President, and of all persons voted for as Vice-President, and of the number of votes for each, which lists they shall sign and certify, and transmit sealed to the seat of the government of the United States, directed to the President of the Senate;—The President of the Senate shall, in the presence of the Senate and House of Representatives, open all the certificates and the votes shall then be counted;—The person having the greatest number of votes for President, shall be the President, if such number be a majority of the whole number of Electors appointed; and if no person have such majority, then from the persons having the highest numbers not exceeding three on the list of those voted for as President, the House of Representatives shall choose immediately, by ballot, the President. But in choosing the President, the votes shall be taken by states, the representation from each state having one vote; a quorum for this purpose shall consist of a member or members from two-thirds of the states, and a majority of all the states shall be necessary to a choice. And if the House of Representatives shall not choose a President whenever the right of choice shall devolve upon them, before the fourth day of March next following, then the Vice-President shall act as President, as in the case of the death or other constitutional disability of the President.—The person having the greatest number of votes as Vice-President, shall be the Vice-President, if such number be a majority of the whole number of Electors appointed, and if no person have a majority, then from the two highest numbers on the list, the Senate shall choose the Vice-President; a quorum for the purpose shall consist of two-thirds of the whole number of Senators, and a majority of the whole number shall be necessary to a choice. But no person constitutionally ineligible to the office of President shall be eligible to that of Vice-President of the United States.

AMENDMENT XIII

Section 1. Neither slavery nor involuntary servitude, except as a punishment for crime whereof the party shall have been duly convicted, shall exist within the United States, or any place subject to their jurisdiction.

Section 2. Congress shall have power to enforce this article by appropriate legislation.

AMENDMENT XIV

Section 1. All persons born or naturalized in the United States, and subject to the jurisdiction thereof, are citizens of the United States and of the State wherein they reside. No State shall make or enforce any law which shall abridge the privileges or immunities of citizens of the United States; nor shall any State deprive any person of life, liberty, or property, without due process of law; nor deny to any person within its jurisdiction the equal protection of the laws.

Section 2. Representatives shall be apportioned among the several States according to their respective numbers, counting the whole number of persons in each State, excluding Indians not taxed. But when the right to vote at any election for the choice of electors for President and Vice-President of the United States, Representatives in Congress, the Executive and Judicial officers of a State, or the members of the Legislature thereof, is denied to any of the male inhabitants of such State, being twenty-one years of age, and citizens of the United States, or in any way abridged, except for participation in rebellion, or other crime, the basis of representation therein shall be reduced in the proportion which the number of such male citizens shall bear to the whole number of male citizens twenty-one years of age in such State.

Section 3. No person shall be a Senator or Representative in Congress, or elector of President and Vice-President, or hold any office, civil or military, under the United States, or under any State, who, having previously taken an oath, as a member of Congress, or as an officer of the United States, or as a member of any State legislature, or as an executive or judicial officer of any State, to support the Constitution of the United States, shall have engaged in insurrection or rebellion against the same, or given aid or comfort to the enemies thereof. But Congress may by a vote of two-thirds of each House, remove such disability.

Section 4. The validity of the public debt of the United States, authorized by law, including debts incurred for payment of pensions and bounties for services in suppressing insurrection or rebellion, shall not be questioned. But neither the United States nor any State shall assume or pay any debt or obligation incurred in aid of insurrection or rebellion against the United States, or any claim for the loss or emancipation of any slave; but all such debts, obligations and claims shall be held illegal and void.

Section 5. The Congress shall have power to enforce, by appropriate legislation, the provisions of this article.

AMENDMENT XV

Section 1. The right of citizens of the United States to vote shall not be denied or abridged by the United States or by any State on account of race, color, or previous condition of servitude.

Section 2. Congress shall have power to

enforce this article by appropriate legislation.

AMENDMENT XVI

The Congress shall have power to lay and collect taxes on incomes, from whatever source derived, without apportionment among the several States, and without regard to any census or enumeration.

Section 1. The Senate of the United States shall be composed of two Senators from each State, elected by the people thereof, for six years; and each Senator shall have one vote. The electors in each State shall have the qualifications requisite for electors of the most numerous branch of the State legislatures.

Section 2. When vacancies happen in the representation of any State in the Senate, the executive authority of such State shall issue writs of election to fill such vacancies: Provided, That the legislature of any State may empower the executive thereof to make temporary appointments until the people fill the vacancies by election as the legislature may direct.

Section 3. This amendment shall not be so construed as to affect the election or term of any Senator chosen before it becomes valid as part of the Constitution.

AMENDMENT XVIII

Section 1. After one year from the ratification of this article the manufacture, sale, or transportation of intoxicating liquors within, the importation thereof into, or the exportation thereof from the United States and all territory subject to the jurisdiction thereof for beverage purposes is hereby prohibited.

Section 2. The Congress and the several States shall have concurrent power to enforce this article by appropriate legislation.

Section 3. This article shall be inoperative unless it shall have been ratified as an amendment to the Constitution by the legislatures of the several States, as provided in the Constitution, within seven years from the date of the submission hereof to the States by the Congress.

AMENDMENT XIX

Section 1. The right of citizens of the United States to vote shall not be denied or abridged by the United States or by any State on account of sex.

Section 2. The Congress shall have power

to enforce this article by appropriate legislation.

AMENDMENT XX

Section 1. The terms of the President and Vice-President shall end at noon on the 20th day of January, and the terms of Senators and Representatives at noon on the 3d day of January, of the years in which such terms would have ended if this article had not been ratified; and the terms of their successors shall then begin.

Section 2. The Congress shall assemble at least once in every year, and such meeting shall begin at noon on the 3d day of January, unless they shall by law appoint a different day.

Section 3. If, at the time fixed for the beginning of the term of the President, the President elect shall have died, the Vice-President elect shall become President. If a President shall not have been chosen before the time fixed for the beginning of his term, or if the President elect shall have failed to qualify, then the Vice-President elect shall act as President until a President shall have qualified; and the Congress may by law provide for the case wherein neither a President elect nor a Vice-President elect shall have qualified, declaring who shall then act as President, or the manner in which one who is to act shall be selected, and such person shall act accordingly until a President or Vice-President shall have qualified.

Section 4. The Congress may by law provide for the case of the death of any of the persons from whom the House of Representatives may choose a President whenever the right of choice shall have devolved upon them, and for the case of the death of any of the persons from whom the Senate may choose a Vice-President whenever the right of choice shall have devolved upon them.

Section 5. Sections 1 and 2 shall take effect on the 15th day of October following the ratification of this article.

Section 6. This article shall be inoperative unless it shall have been ratified as an amendment to the Constitution by the legislatures of three-fourths of the several States within seven years from the date of its submission.

AMENDMENT XXI

Section 1. The eighteenth article of amendment to the Constitution of the United States is hereby repealed.

Section 2. The transportation or importation into any State, Territory, or possession of the United States for delivery or use therein of intoxicating liquors, in violation of the laws thereof, is hereby prohibited.

Section 3. This article shall be inoperative unless it shall have been ratified as an amendment to the Constitution by conventions in the several States, as provided in the Constitution, within seven years from the date of the submission hereof to the States by the Congress.

AMENDMENT XXII

Section 1. No person shall be elected to the office of the President more than twice, and no person who has held the office of President, or acted as President, for more than two years of a term to which some other person was elected President shall be elected to the office of the President more than once. But this Article shall not apply to any person holding the office of President when this Article was proposed by the Congress, and shall not prevent any person who may be holding the office of President, or acting as President, during the term within which this Article becomes operative from holding the office of President or acting as President during the remainder of such term.

Section 2. This Article shall be inoperative unless it shall have been ratified as an amendment to the Constitution by the legislatures of three-fourths of the several States within seven years from the date of its submission to the States by the Congress.

AMENDMENT XXIII

Section 1. The District constituting the seat of Government of the United States shall appoint in such manner as the Congress may direct:

A number of electors of President and Vice-President equal to the whole number of Senators and Representatives in Congress to which the District would be entitled if it were a State, but in no event more than the least populous State; they shall be in addition to those appointed by the States, but they shall be considered, for the purposes of the election of President and Vice-President, to be electors appointed by a State; and they shall meet in the District and perform such duties as provided by the twelfth article of amendment.

Section 2. The Congress shall have power to enforce this article by appropriate legislation.

AMENDMENT XXIV

Section 1. The right of citizens of the United States to vote in any primary or other election for President or Vice-President, for electors for President or Vice-President, or for Senator or Representative in Congress, shall not be denied or abridged by the United States or any State by reason of failure to pay any poll tax or other tax.

Section 2. The Congress shall have power to enforce this article by appropriate legislation.

AMENDMENT XXV

Section 1. In case of the removal of the President from office or of his death or resignation, the Vice-President shall become President.

Section 2. Whenever there is a vacancy in the office of the Vice-President, the President shall nominate a Vice-President who shall take office upon confirmation by a majority vote of both Houses of Congress.

Section 3. Whenever the President transmits to the President pro tempore of the Senate and the Speaker of the House of Representatives his written declaration that he is unable to discharge the powers and duties of his office, and until he transmits to them a written declaration to the contrary, such powers and duties shall be discharged by the Vice-President as Acting President.

Section 4. Whenever the Vice-President and a majority of either the principal officers of the executive departments or of such other body as Congress may by law provide, transmit to the President pro tempore of the Senate and the Speaker of the House of Representatives their written declaration that the President is unable to discharge the powers and duties of his office, the Vice-President shall immediately assume the powers and duties of the office as Acting President.

Thereafter, when the President transmits to the President pro tempore of the Senate and the Speaker of the House of Representatives his written declaration that no inability exists, he shall resume the powers and duties of his office unless the Vice-President and a majority of either the principal officers of the executive department or of such other body as Congress may by law provide, transmit within four days to the President pro tempore of the Senate and the Speaker of the House of Representatives their written declaration that the President is unable to discharge the powers and duties of his office. Thereupon Congress shall decide the issue, assembling within forty-eight hours for that purpose if not in session. If the Congress, within twenty-one days after receipt of the latter written declaration, or, if Congress is not in session, within twenty-one days after Congress is required to assemble, determines by two-thirds vote of both Houses that the President is unable to discharge the powers and duties of his office, the Vice-President shall continue to discharge the same as Acting President; otherwise, the President shall resume the powers and duties of his office.

AMENDMENT XXVI

Section 1. The right of citizens of the United States, who are eighteen years of age or older, to vote shall not be denied or abridged by the United States or any State on account of age.

Section 2. The Congress shall have power to enforce this article by appropriate legislation.